THE CONTEMPORARY WORLD
CANADA
UNITED STATES
Alaska (U.S.)
Greenland (Den.)
ICELAND
ATLANTIC OCEAN
PACIFIC OCEAN
Azores (Port.)
PORTUGAL
FRANCE
MOROCCO
Canary Is. (Sp.)
Western Sahara (Mor.)
MAURITANIA
CAPE VERDE
SENEGAL
GAMBIA
GUINEA-BISSAU
GUINEA
BURKINA FASO
SIERRA LEONE
LIBERIA
CÔTE D'IVOIRE
Bermuda (U.K.)
Hawaii (U.S.)
MEXICO
BAHAMAS
DOMINICAN REPUBLIC
HAITI
CUBA
JAMAICA
BELIZE
HONDURAS
GUATEMALA
EL SALVADOR
NICARAGUA
COSTA RICA
PANAMA
Puerto Rico (U.S.)
ST. KITTS AND NEVIS
ANTIGUA AND BARBUDA
Guadeloupe (Fr.)
DOMINICA
Martinique (Fr.)
ST. VINCENT AND THE GRENADINES
ST. LUCIA
BARBADOS
GRENADA
TRINIDAD AND TOBAGO
GUYANA
SURINAME
French Guiana (Fr.)
VENEZUELA
COLOMBIA
ECUADOR
Galápagos Is. (Ec.)
PERU
BRAZIL
BOLIVIA
PARAGUAY
CHILE
URUGUAY
ARGENTINA
Easter I. (Chile)
Falkland Is. (U.K.)
SAMOA
TONGA
Equator
N
E
S
W
0
1,500
3,000 miles
0
1,500
3,000 kilometers
80°N
60°N
40°N
20°N
0°
20°S
40°S
60°S
80°S
160°W
140°W
120°W
100°W
80°W
60°W
40°W
20°W

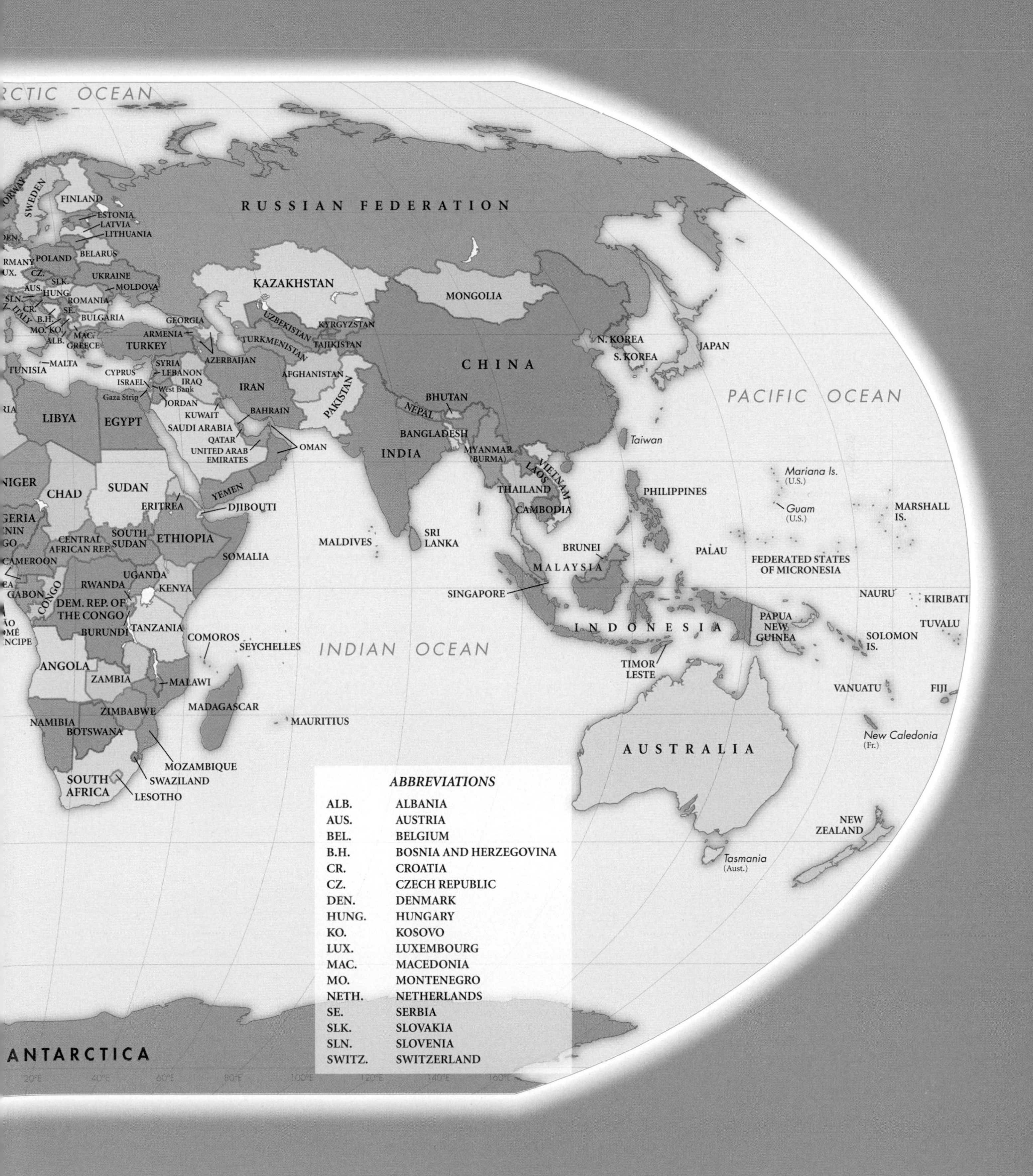

ABBREVIATIONS

ALB.	ALBANIA
AUS.	AUSTRIA
BEL.	BELGIUM
B.H.	BOSNIA AND HERZEGOVINA
CR.	CROATIA
CZ.	CZECH REPUBLIC
DEN.	DENMARK
HUNG.	HUNGARY
KO.	KOSOVO
LUX.	LUXEMBOURG
MAC.	MACEDONIA
MO.	MONTENEGRO
NETH.	NETHERLANDS
SE.	SERBIA
SLK.	SLOVAKIA
SLN.	SLOVENIA
SWITZ.	SWITZERLAND

A HISTORY OF

World Societies

Tenth
EDITION

Volume 1
To 1600

A HISTORY OF World Societies

John P. McKay • *University of Illinois at Urbana-Champaign*

Bennett D. Hill • *Late of Georgetown University*

John Buckler • *Late of University of Illinois at Urbana-Champaign*

Patricia Buckley Ebrey • *University of Washington*

Roger B. Beck • *Eastern Illinois University*

Clare Haru Crowston • *University of Illinois at Urbana-Champaign*

Merry E. Wiesner-Hanks • *University of Wisconsin–Milwaukee*

Jerry Dávila • *University of Illinois at Urbana-Champaign*

Bedford/St. Martin's | BOSTON ◆ NEW YORK

FOR BEDFORD/ST. MARTIN'S

Director of Development for History: Jane Knetzger
Senior Developmental Editor: Sara Wise
Senior Production Editor: Christina M. Horn
Production Supervisor: Samuel Jones
Executive Marketing Manager: Sandra McGuire
Associate Editor: Robin Soule
Editorial Assistant: Arrin Kaplan
Production Assistant: Erica Zhang
Copy Editor: Jennifer Brett Greenstein
Indexer: Leoni Z. McVey
Cartography: Mapping Specialists, Ltd.
Page Layout: Boynton Hue Studio
Photo Researcher: Bruce Carson
Senior Art Director: Anna Palchik
Text Design: Marsha Cohen
Cover Design: Donna Lee Dennison
Cover Art: Portrait of a Man. Werner Forman Archive/ The Bridgeman Art Library.
Composition: Jouve
Printing and Binding: RR Donnelley and Sons

Manufactured in the United States of America.

9 8 7 6 5
f e d c

For information, write: Bedford/St. Martin's, 75 Arlington Street, Boston, MA 02116 (617-399-4000)

ISBN 978-1-4576-5993-5 (Combined Edition)
ISBN 978-1-4576-8544-6 (Loose-leaf Edition)
ISBN 978-1-4576-5994-2 (Volume 1)
ISBN 978-1-4576-8547-7 (Loose-leaf Edition, Volume 1)
ISBN 978-1-4576-5995-9 (Volume 2)
ISBN 978-1-4576-8549-1 (Loose-leaf Edition, Volume 2)
ISBN 978-1-4576-8518-7 (Volume A)
ISBN 978-1-4576-8519-4 (Volume B)
ISBN 978-1-4576-8522-4 (Volume C)
ISBN 978-1-319-05370-3 (Hardcover Edition)

Distributed outside North America by
PALGRAVE MACMILLAN
Houndmills, Basingstoke, Hampshire RG21 6XS
Companies and representatives throughout the world.

ISBN 978-1-137-47316-5 (Combined Edition)
ISBN 978-1-137-47317-2 (Volume 1)
ISBN 978-1-137-47321-9 (Volume 2)

A catalogue record for this book is available from the British Library.

ACKNOWLEDGMENTS
Acknowledgments and copyrights appear on the same page as the text and art selections they cover; these acknowledgments and copyrights constitute an extension of the copyright page. It is a violation of the law to reproduce these selections by any means whatsoever without the written permission of the copyright holder.

Preface

Why This Book This Way

The tenth edition of *A History of World Societies* continues to provide the social and cultural focus, comprehensive regional organization, and global perspective that have long been hallmarks of the book. All three of these qualities have been greatly enhanced by the addition of a new member to the author team, Jerry Dávila from the University of Illinois, who brings expertise in Latin America and the twentieth century. A renowned scholar of Brazil whose work focuses on race and social policy, Jerry offers a fresh perspective to our coverage of Latin America and to the final chapters in the book, which he has completely reconceptualized.

Not only do we thus continue to benefit from a collaborative team of regional experts with deep experience in the world history classroom, but we are also pleased to introduce a suite of digital tools designed to save you time and to help students gain confidence and learn historical thinking skills.

New Tools for the Digital Age

Because we know that your classroom needs are changing rapidly, we are excited to announce that *A History of World Societies* is available with **LaunchPad**. Free when packaged with the book, LaunchPad's course space and interactive e-book are ready to use as is (or can be edited and customized with your own material) and can be assigned right away. Developed with extensive feedback from history instructors and students, LaunchPad includes the complete narrative e-book, as well as abundant primary documents, maps, images, assignments, and activities. The aims of key learning outcomes are addressed via formative and summative assessments, short-answer and essay questions, multiple-choice quizzing, and **LearningCurve**, an adaptive learning tool designed to get students to read before they come to class. Available with training and support, LaunchPad can help you take your teaching into a new era. To learn more about the benefits of LearningCurve and LaunchPad, see "Versions and Supplements" on page xv. In addition, the following sections will show you how specific skills-based features of *A History of World Societies* can be enhanced by the ability to assign and track student work in LaunchPad.

The Story of *A History of World Societies*

In this age of global connections, with their influence on the global economy, global migration patterns, popular culture, and global warming, among other aspects of life, the study of world history is more vital and urgent than ever before. An understanding of the broad sweep of the human past helps us comprehend today's dramatic changes and enduring continuities. People now migrate enormous distances and establish new lives far from their places of birth, yet migration has been a constant in history since the first humans walked out of Africa. Satellites and cell phones now link nearly every inch of the planet, yet the expansion of communication networks is a process that is thousands of years old. Children who speak different languages at home now sit side by side in schools and learn from one another, yet intercultural encounters have long been a source of innovation, transformation, and at times, unfortunately, conflict.

This book is designed for twenty-first-century students who will spend their lives on this small interconnected planet and for whom an understanding of only local or national history will no longer be sufficient. We believe that the study of world history in a broad and comparative context is an exciting, important, and highly practical pursuit. It is our conviction, based on considerable experience in introducing large numbers of students to world history, that a book reflecting current trends in scholarship can excite readers and inspire an enduring interest in the long human experience.

Our strategy has been twofold. First, we have made social and cultural history the core elements of our narrative. We seek to re-create the lives of ordinary people in appealing human terms and also to highlight the interplay between men's and women's lived experiences and the ways they reflect on these to create meaning. Thus, in addition to foundational works of philosophy and literature, we include popular songs and stories. We present objects along with texts as important sources for studying history, and this has allowed us to incorporate the growing emphasis on material culture in the work of many historians. At the same time, we have been mindful of the need to give great economic, political, and intellectual developments the attention they deserve. We want to give individual students and instructors an integrated perspective so that they can pursue—on their own or in the classroom—the themes and questions that they find particularly exciting and significant.

Second, we have made every effort to strike an effective global and regional balance. The whole world interacts today, and to understand the interactions and what they mean for today's citizens, we must study the whole world's history. Thus we have adopted a comprehensive regional organization with a global perspective that is clear and manageable for students. For example, Chapter 7 introduces students in depth to East Asia, and at the same time the chapter highlights the cultural connections that occurred via the Silk Road and the spread of Buddhism. We study all geographical areas, conscious of the separate histories of many parts of the world, particularly in the earliest millennia of human development. We also stress the links among cultures, political units, and economic systems, for these connections have made the world what it is today. We make comparisons and connections across time as well as space, for understanding the unfolding of the human story in time is the central task of history.

Primary Sources for Teaching Critical Thinking and Analysis

A History of World Societies offers an extensive program of primary source assignments to help students master a number of key learning outcomes, among them **critical thinking**, **historical thinking**, **analytical thinking**, and **argumentation**, as well as learning about the **diversity of world cultures**. When assigned in LaunchPad, all primary source features are accompanied by multiple-choice quizzes that help you ensure students come to class prepared.

For the tenth edition, we have augmented our Viewpoints primary source feature to highlight the diversity of the world's people in response to reviewers' enthusiastic endorsement of this feature. The new edition offers in each chapter two sets of paired primary documents on a topic that illuminates the human experience, allowing us to provide more concrete examples of differences in the ways people thought. Anyone teaching world history has to emphasize larger trends and developments, but students sometimes get the wrong impression that everyone in a society thought alike. We hope that teachers can use these passages to get students thinking about diversity within and across societies. The **66 Viewpoints assignments** — two in each chapter — introduce students to working with sources, encourage critical analysis, and extend the narrative while giving voice to the people of the past. Each includes a brief introduction and questions for analysis, and in LaunchPad they are also accompanied by multiple-choice questions. Carefully chosen for accessibility, each pair of documents presents views on a diverse range of topics. **NEW** Viewpoints topics include "Addressing the Gods in Mesopotamia and Egypt"; "The Inglorious Side of War in the *Book of Songs* and the *Patirruppattu*"; "Hellenistic and Chinese Spells"; "Freeing Slaves in Justinian's *Code* and the Qur'an"; early Chinese and Portuguese accounts of Africa; Protestant and Neo-Confucian ideas on behavior; "Jahangir and Louis XIV on Priorities for Monarchs"; "Jean-Jacques Rousseau and Mary Wollstonecraft on Women's Nature and Education"; perspectives on Indian cotton manufacturing in India and Britain; "African Views of the Scramble for Africa"; the abolition of slavery in the Americas; and women activists in Mexico.

Each chapter also continues to include a longer primary source feature titled **Listening to the Past**, chosen to extend and illuminate a major historical issue considered in each chapter. The feature presents a single original source or several voices on the subject to help instructors teach the important skills of **critical thinking** and **analysis**. Each opens with an introduction and closes with questions for analysis that invite students to evaluate the evidence as historians would, and again, in LaunchPad, multiple-choice questions are provided. Selected for their interest and significance and carefully placed within their historical context, these sources, we hope, allow students to "hear the past" and to observe how history has been shaped by individuals. **NEW** topics include "The Teachings of Confucius"; "Gregory of Tours on the Veneration of Relics"; "Courtly Love Poetry"; "Stefan Zweig on Middle-Class Youth and Sexuality" (in early-twentieth-century Europe); "Reyita Castillo Bueno on Slavery and Freedom in Cuba"; "C. L. R. James on Pan-African Liberation"; and lyrics from a Brazilian band on globalization.

In addition to using documents as part of our special feature program, we have quoted extensively from a wide variety of **primary sources within the narrative**, demonstrating in our use of these quotations that they are the "stuff" of history. Thus primary sources appear as an integral part of the narrative as well as in extended form in the Listening to the Past and expanded Viewpoints chapter features.

New assignable **Online Document Projects** in LaunchPad offer students more practice in interpreting primary sources. Each project, based on the Individuals in Society feature described in the next section, prompts students to explore a key question through analysis of multiple sources. Chapter 22's project, for example, asks students to analyze documents on the complexities of the Haitian Revolution and the conditions that made Toussaint L'Ouverture's story possible. Auto-graded multiple-choice questions based on the documents help students analyze the sources.

Finally, we have revised our **primary source documents collection**, *Sources for World Societies*, to add more visual sources and to closely align the readings with the chapter topics and themes of the tenth edition. The documents are now available in a fully assignable and assessable electronic format within each LaunchPad unit, and the accompanying multiple-choice questions measure comprehension and hold students accountable for their reading.

Student Engagement with Biography

In our years of teaching world history, we have often noted that students come alive when they encounter stories about real people in the past. To give students a chance to see the past through ordinary people's lives, each chapter includes one of the popular **Individuals in Society** biographical essays, each of which offers a brief study of an individual or group, informing students about the societies in which the individuals lived. This feature grew out of our long-standing focus on people's lives and the varieties of historical experience, and we believe that readers will empathize with these human beings who themselves were seeking to define their own identities. The spotlighting of individuals, both famous and obscure, perpetuates the book's continued attention to cultural and intellectual developments, highlights human agency, and reflects changing interests within the historical profession as well as the development of "micro-history." As described previously, in LaunchPad, this feature includes an associated Online Document Project. **NEW** features include essays on Sudatta, a lay follower of the Buddha; Cosimo and Lorenzo de' Medici; Malintzin; and Sieng, a Mnong refugee living in the United States.

Connecting History to Real-World Applications

Back again are the popular **Global Trade** features, essays that focus on a particular commodity, exploring the world trade, social and economic impact, and cultural influence of that commodity. Each essay is accompanied by a detailed map showing the trade routes of the commodity. We believe that careful attention to all these essays will enable students to appreciate the complex ways in which trade has connected and influenced various parts of the world. All the Global Trade features are fully assignable and assessable in LaunchPad.

Geographic and Visual Literacy

We recognize students' difficulties with geography and visual analysis, and the new edition retains our **Mapping the Past map activities** and **Picturing the Past visual activities**. Included in each chapter, these activities ask students to analyze a map or visual and make connections to the larger processes discussed in the narrative, giving them valuable practice in reading and interpreting maps and images. In LaunchPad, these activities are assignable and students can submit their work. Throughout the textbook and online in LaunchPad, more than **100 full-size maps** illustrate major developments in the chapters. In addition, **82 spot maps** are embedded in the narrative to show specific areas under discussion.

Chronological Reasoning

To help students make comparisons, understand changes over time, and see relationships among contemporaneous events, each chapter ends with a **chapter chronology** that reviews major developments discussed in the chapter. A **unified timeline** at the end of the text, and available from every page in LaunchPad, allows students to compare developments over the centuries.

Active Reading

With the goal of making this the most student-centered edition yet, we paid renewed attention to the book's reading and study aids:

- **Focus questions** at the start of each main heading help guide students in their reading. These questions are repeated in the chapter review section.
- In LaunchPad, instructors can assign the **NEW Guided Reading Exercise** for each chapter, which prompts students to read actively to collect information that answers a broad analytic question central to the chapter as a whole.
- The chapter-closing **Connections** feature synthesizes main developments and makes connections and comparisons between countries and regions to explain how events relate to larger global processes, such as the influence of the Silk Road, the effects of the transatlantic slave trade, and the ramifications of colonialism.
- A **NEW Chapter Summary** reinforces key chapter events and ideas for students.
- **Review and Explore** at the end of each chapter includes a list of key terms, chapter focus questions, and **NEW Make Connections questions** that prompt students to assess larger developments across chapters.
- **Key terms** are bolded in the text, defined in the margin, and listed in the chapter review to promote clarity and comprehension, and **phonetic spellings** are located directly after terms that readers are likely to find hard to pronounce.

All our changes to the book, large and small, are intended to give students and instructors an integrated perspective so that they can pursue—on their own or in the classroom—the historical questions that they find particularly exciting and significant.

Organizational and Textual Changes

To meet the demands of the evolving course, we have made several major changes in the organization of chapters to reflect the way the course is taught today. The most dramatic changes are the reordering of Chapter 17: The Islamic World Powers, 1300–1800 (formerly Chapter 20) and a complete overhaul of the final section of the book covering the postwar era. This new placement for our coverage of Islam reflects a growing interest among instructors and students in the Islamic world and highlights early Islamic cultural contributions.

To address the concerns of instructors who teach from the second volume of the text, we have added a new section on the Reformation to Chapter 18 so that students whose courses begin with Chapters 15 or 16 will now receive that coverage in Volume 2. The new section includes the Protestant and Catholic Reformations as well as religious violence and witch-hunts.

In its examination of the age of revolution in the Atlantic world, Chapter 22 now incorporates revolutions in Latin America. In order to provide a more global perspective on European politics, culture, and economics in the early modern period, Chapter 23 on the Industrial Revolution considers industrialization more broadly as a global phenomenon with a new section titled "The Global Picture." Together, the enhanced global perspectives of these chapters help connect the different regions of the globe and, in particular, help explain the crucial period when Europe began to dominate the rest of the globe.

The final section of the text, covering the post-1945 period, has also been completely reworked. In addition to updating all the postwar chapters through 2014, Jerry Dávila substantially rewrote the last four chapters and streamlined them into three, creating a more tightly focused and accessible section that now divides the period chronologically as follows: Chapter 31: Decolonization, Revolution, and the Cold War, 1945–1968; Chapter 32: Liberalization, 1968–2000s; Chapter 33: The Contemporary World in Historical Perspective. The last three chapters are now organized around two dominant themes of the postwar world: liberation movements that challenged power structures such as colonialism and racial supremacism; and the spread of liberalization that characterized the end of the Cold War in particular, marking the rise of free markets and liberal political systems. The final chapter examines the significance of social movements in shaping a contemporary world that continues to struggle with historic conflicts and inequalities.

In terms of specific textual changes, we have worked hard to keep the book up-to-date and to strengthen our comprehensive, comparative, and connective approach. Moreover, we revised every chapter with the goal of readability and accessibility. Highlights of the new edition include:

- Chapter 1 includes new information on the recent archaeological find at Göbekli Tepe in present-day Turkey that suggests that cultural factors may have played a role in the development of agriculture.
- Chapter 2 has new coverage on Egyptian society and a discussion of gender distinctions in Sumerian society.
- In Chapter 6, the section on the founding of Rome has been completely rewritten.
- Chapter 8 contains a new section on Christian missionaries and conversion, and it explains the process of the Christianization of barbarian Europe.
- Chapter 11 now centers on the ways in which systems of religious belief shaped ancient societies of the Americas and provided tools people used to understand and adapt to their world. It also looks at the role of sources produced after the European encounter in shaping our understanding of the histories of indigenous American empires.
- An expanded discussion of witchcraft in Chapter 15 now includes practices of indigenous peoples in the New World.
- Chapter 18 has enhanced coverage of Russian imperial expansion as well as a new section called "People Beyond Borders" that includes piracy and gives students a feeling for the ways in which imperial borders were often more real on the map than in real life.
- In Chapter 19, a new section called "The Early Enlightenment" clarifies the mixture of religious, political, and scientific thought that characterized the early period of the Enlightenment.
- Chapter 22 emphasizes the indigenous origins of the Haitian revolution by highlighting the African backgrounds of slaves and the considerable military experience many of them had, which helps explain how they could defeat the French and British.
- Chapter 23 has been heavily revised to reflect new scholarship on industrialization and to provide a broader, more comparative perspective.
- A new section in Chapter 24 on social and economic conflict connects the industrialization of continental Europe with the political coverage of the revolutions of 1848.
- Chapter 27 now focuses on the Americas within the framework of liberalism and examines connections between the experiences of settlement, state formation, and economic integration in the United States and Latin America.
- Chapter 29 contains more detail on the reforms of Amanullah Khan in the section on the modernization of Afghanistan.
- As noted previously, the final three chapters of the book have been entirely rewritten by new author Jerry Dávila.

In sum, we have tried to bring new research and interpretation into our global history because our goal is to keep our book stimulating, accurate, and current for students and instructors.

Acknowledgments

It is a pleasure to thank the many instructors who critiqued the book in preparation for this revision:

Stewart Anderson, *Brigham Young University*
Brian Arendt, *Lindenwood University*
Stephen Auerbach, *Georgia College*
Michael Bardot, *Lincoln University*
Natalie Bayer, *Drake University*
Michael Bazemore, *William Peace University*
Brian Becker, *Delta State University*
Rosemary Bell, *Skyline College*
Chris Benedetto, *Granite State College*
Wesley L. Bishop, *Pitt Community College*
Robert Blackey, *California State University–San Bernardino*
Edward Bond, *Alabama A&M University*
Nathan Brooks, *New Mexico State University*
Jurgen Buchenau, *The University of North Carolina at Charlotte*
Paul Buckingham, *Morrisville State College*
Steven B. Bunker, *University of Alabama*
Kate Burlingham, *California State University, Fullerton*
David Bush, *The College of the Siskiyous*
Laura M. Calkins, *Texas Tech University*
Robert Caputi, *Erie Community College–North Campus*
Lucia Carter, *Mars Hill College*

Lesley Chapel, *Saginaw Valley State University*
Nevin Crouse, *Chesapeake College*
Everett Dague, *Benedictine College*
Jeffrey Demsky, *San Bernardino Valley College*
Peter de Rosa, *Bridgewater State University*
Nicholas Di Liberto, *Newberry College*
Randall Dills, *University of Louisville*
Shawn Dry, *Oakland Community College*
Roxanne Easley, *Central Washington University*
John Fielding, *Mount Wachusett Community College*
Barbara Fuller, *Indian River State College*
Dolores Grapsas, *New River Community College*
Emily Fisher Gray, *Norwich University*
Gayle Greene-Aguirre, *Mississippi Gulf Coast Community College*
Neil Greenwood, *Cleveland State Community College*
Christian Griggs, *Dalton State College*
W. Scott Haine, *Cañada College*
Irwin Halfond, *McKendree University*
Alicia Harding, *Southern Maine Community College*
Jillian Hartley, *Arkansas Northeastern College*
Robert Haug, *University of Cincinnati*
John Hunt, *Utah Valley University*
Fatima Imam, *Lake Forest College*
Rashi Jackman, *De Anza College*
Jackie Jay, *Eastern Kentucky University*
Timothy Jenks, *East Carolina University*
Andrew Kellett, *Harford Community College*
Christine Kern, *Edinboro University*
Christopher Killmer, *St. Johns River State College*
Mark Klobas, *Scottsdale Community College*
Chris Laney, *Berkshire Community College*
Erick D. Langer, *Georgetown University*
Mary Jean Lavery, *Delaware County Community College*
Mark Lentz, *University of Louisiana, Lafayette*
Darin Lenz, *Fresno Pacific University*
Yi Li, *Tacoma Community College*
Jonas Liliequist, *Umeå University*
Ron Lowe, *University of Tennessee at Chattanooga*
Mary Lyons-Carmona, *University of Nebraska at Omaha*
Elizabeth S. Manley, *Xavier University of Louisiana*
Brandon D. Marsh, *Bridgewater College*
Sean F. McEnroe, *Southern Oregon University*
John McLeod, *University of Louisville*
Brendan McManus, *Bemidji State University*
Christina Mehrtens, *University of Massachusetts–Dartmouth*
Charlotte Miller, *Middle Georgia State College*
Robert Montgomery, *Baldwin Wallace University*
Curtis Morgan, *Lord Fairfax Community College*
Richard Moss, *Harrisburg Area Community College*
Larry Myers, *Butler Community College*
Erik Lars Myrup, *University of Kentucky*
April Najjaj, *Mount Olive College*
Katie Nelson, *Weber State University*
Lily Rhodes Novicki, *Virginia Western Community College*
Monica Orozco, *Westmont College*
Neal Palmer, *Christian Brothers University*
Jenifer Parks, *Rocky Mountain College*
Melinda Pash, *Fayetteville Technical Community College*
Tao Peng, *Minnesota State University–Mankato*
Patricia Perry, *St. Edward's University*
William Plants, *University of Rio Grande/Rio Grande Community College*
Joshua Pollock, *Modesto Junior College*
Fabrizio Prado, *College of William & Mary*
Daniel Prosterman, *Salem College*
Tracie Provost, *Middle Georgia College*
Melissa Redd, *Pulaski Technical College*
Charles Reed, *Elizabeth City State University*
Leah Renold, *Texas State University*
Kim Richardson, *Front Range Community College*
David Ruffley, *Colorado Mountain College*
Martina Saltamacchia, *University of Nebraska at Omaha*
Karl Schmidt, *South Dakota State University*
Kimberly Schutte, *SUNY–The College at Brockport*
Eva Seraphin, *Irvine Valley College*
Courtney Shah, *Lower Columbia College*
Jeffrey Shumway, *Brigham Young University*
David Simonelli, *Youngstown State University*
James Smith, *Southwest Baptist University*
Kara D. Smith, *Georgia Perimeter College*
Ilicia Sprey, *Saint Joseph's College*
Rachel Standish, *San Joaquin Delta College*
Kate Staples, *West Virginia University*
Brian Strayer, *Andrews University*
Sonia Chandarana Tandon, *Forsyth Technical Community College*
James Todesca, *Armstrong Atlantic State University*
Elisaveta Todorova, *University of Cincinnati*
Dianne Walker, *Baton Rouge Community College*
Kenneth Wilburn, *East Carolina University*
Carol Woodfin, *Hardin-Simmons University*
Laura Zeeman, *Red Rocks Community College*

It is also a pleasure to thank the many editors who have assisted us over the years, first at Houghton Mifflin and now at Bedford/St. Martin's. At Bedford/St. Martin's, these include senior development editors Sara Wise and Laura Arcari; associate editor Robin Soule; editorial assistant Arrin Kaplan; former executive editor Traci Mueller Crowell; director of development Jane Knetzger; publisher for history Mary Dougherty; photo researcher Bruce Carson; text permissions editor Eve Lehmann; and senior production editor Christina Horn, with the assistance of Erica Zhang and the guidance of Sue Brown, director of editing and design, and managing editor Michael Granger. Other key contributors were page makeup artist Cia Boynton, copy editor Jennifer Brett Greenstein, proofreaders Linda McLatchie and Angela Morrison, indexer Leoni McVey, and cover designer Donna Dennison. We would also like to thank former vice president for editorial humanities Denise Wydra and former president Joan E. Feinberg.

Many of our colleagues at the University of Illinois, the University of Washington, the University of Wisconsin–Milwaukee, and Eastern Illinois University continue to provide information and stimulation, often without even knowing it. We thank them for it. The authors recognize John P. McKay, Bennett D. Hill, and John Buckler, the founding authors of this textbook, whose vision set a new standard for world history textbooks. The authors also thank the many students over the years with whom we have used earlier editions of this book. Their reactions and opinions helped shape our revisions to this edition, and we hope it remains worthy of the ultimate praise they bestowed, that it is "not boring like most textbooks." Merry Wiesner-Hanks would, as always, like to thank her husband, Neil, without whom work on this project would not be possible. Clare Haru Crowston thanks her husband, Ali, and her children, Lili, Reza, and Kian, who are a joyous reminder of the vitality of life that we try to showcase in this book. Roger Beck thanks Ann for supporting him while she was completing her Ph.D. He is also grateful to the World History Association for all past, present, and future contributions to his understanding of world history. Jerry Dávila thanks Liv, Ellen, and Alex, who are reminders of why history matters.

Each of us has benefited from the criticism of his or her coauthors, although each of us assumes responsibility for what he or she has written. Merry Wiesner-Hanks has written and revised Chapters 1, 2, 5, 6, 8, 14, and 15; Patricia Buckley Ebrey has written and revised Chapters 3, 4, 7, 9, 12, 13, 17, 21, and 26; Roger B. Beck has written and revised Chapters 10, 20, 25, and 28–30; Clare Haru Crowston has written and revised Chapters 16, 18, 19, and 22–24; and Jerry Dávila has completely rewritten Chapters 11, 27, and 31–33.

Versions and Supplements

Adopters of *A History of World Societies* and their students have access to abundant print and digital resources and tools, including documents, assessment and presentation materials, the acclaimed Bedford Series in History and Culture volumes, and much more. And for the first time, the full-featured LaunchPad course space provides access to the narrative with all assignment and assessment opportunities at the ready. See below for more information, visit the book's catalog site at **bedfordstmartins.com/mckayworld/catalog**, or contact your local Bedford/St. Martin's sales representative.

Get the Right Version for Your Class

To accommodate different course lengths and course budgets, *A History of World Societies* is available in several different formats, including three-hole-punched loose-leaf Budget Books versions and low-priced PDF e-books, such as the *Bedford e-Book to Go for A History of World Societies* from our Web site and other PDF e-books from other commercial sources. And for the best value of all, package a new print book with LaunchPad at no additional charge to get the best each format offers—a print version for easy portability and reading with a LaunchPad interactive e-book and course space with loads of additional assignment and assessment options.

- **Combined Volume** (Chapters 1–33): available in paperback, loose-leaf, and e-book formats and in LaunchPad
- **Volume 1, To 1600** (Chapters 1–16): available in paperback, loose-leaf, and e-book formats and in LaunchPad
- **Volume 2, Since 1450** (Chapters 16–33): available in paperback, loose-leaf, and e-book formats and in LaunchPad
- **Volume A: To 1500** (Chapters 1–14): available in paperback
- **Volume B: From 800 to 1815** (Chapters 11–22): available in paperback
- **Volume C: From 1775 to the Present** (Chapters 22–33): available in paperback

As noted below, any of these volumes can be packaged with additional titles for a discount. To get ISBNs for discount packages, see the online catalog at **bedfordstmartins.com/mckayworld/catalog** or contact your Bedford/St. Martin's representative.

NEW • Assign LaunchPad—a Content-Rich and Assessment-Ready Interactive e-Book and Course Space

Available for discount purchase on its own or for packaging with new books at no additional charge, LaunchPad is a breakthrough solution for today's courses. Intuitive and easy to use for students and instructors alike, LaunchPad is ready to use as is, and can be edited, customized with your own material, and assigned in seconds. *LaunchPad for A History of World Societies* includes Bedford/St. Martin's high-quality content all in one place, including the full interactive e-book and the *Sources of World Societies* documents collection, plus LearningCurve formative quizzing, guided reading activities designed to help students read actively for key concepts, additional primary sources, images, videos, chapter summative quizzes, and more.

Through a wealth of formative and summative assessments, including short-answer and essay questions, multiple-choice quizzing, and the adaptive learning program of LearningCurve (see the full description ahead), students gain confidence and get into their reading *before* class. Map and visual activities engage students with visual analysis and critical thinking as they work through each unit, while special boxed features become more meaningful through automatically graded multiple-choice exercises and short-answer questions that prompt students to analyze their reading.

LaunchPad easily integrates with course management systems, and with fast ways to build assignments, rearrange chapters, and add new pages, sections, or links, it lets teachers build the courses they want to teach and hold students accountable. For more information, visit **launchpadworks.com** or contact us at **history@bedfordstmartins.com** to arrange a demo.

NEW • Assign LearningCurve So Your Students Come to Class Prepared

Students using LaunchPad receive access to LearningCurve for *A History of World Societies*. Assigning LearningCurve in place of reading quizzes is easy, and the reporting features help you track overall class trends and spot topics that are giving students trouble so you can adjust your lectures and class activities. This online learning tool is popular with students because it was designed to help them rehearse content at their own pace in a nonthreatening, gamelike environment. The feedback for wrong answers provides instructional coaching and sends students back to the book for review. Students answer as many questions as necessary to reach a target score, with repeated chances to revisit material they haven't mastered. When LearningCurve is assigned, students come to class better prepared.

Take Advantage of Instructor Resources

Bedford/St. Martin's has developed a rich array of teaching resources for this book and for this course. They range from lecture and presentation materials and assessment tools to course management options. Most can be found in LaunchPad or can be downloaded or ordered at **bedfordstmartins.com/mckayworld/catalog**.

Instructor's Resource Manual. The instructor's manual offers both experienced and first-time instructors tools for preparing lectures and running discussions. It includes chapter content learning objectives, teaching strategies, and a guide to chapter-specific supplements available for the text, plus suggestions on how to get the most out of LearningCurve and a survival guide for first-time teaching assistants.

Guide to Changing Editions. Designed to facilitate an instructor's transition from the previous edition of *A History of World Societies* to the tenth edition, this guide presents an overview of major changes as well as changes in each chapter.

Computerized Test Bank. The test bank includes a mix of fresh, carefully crafted multiple-choice, short-answer, and essay questions for each chapter. All questions appear in Microsoft Word format and in easy-to-use test bank software that allows instructors to add, edit, re-sequence, and print questions and answers. Instructors can also export questions into a variety of formats, including Blackboard, Desire2Learn, and Moodle.

The Bedford Lecture Kit:* PowerPoint Maps and Images.** Look good and save time with ***The Bedford Lecture Kit. These presentation materials are downloadable individually from the Instructor Resources tab at **bedfordstmartins.com/mckayworld/catalog**. They include all maps, figures, and images from the textbook in JPEG and PowerPoint formats.

Package and Save Your Students Money

For information on free packages and discounts up to 50 percent, visit **bedfordstmartins.com/mckayworld/catalog**, or contact your local Bedford/St. Martin's sales representative. The products that follow all qualify for discount packaging.

The Bedford Series in History and Culture. More than 100 titles in this highly praised series combine first-rate scholarship, historical narrative, and important primary documents for undergraduate courses. Each book is brief, inexpensive, and focused on a specific topic or period. For a complete list of titles, visit **bedfordstmartins.com/history/series**.

Rand McNally Atlas of World History. This collection of almost 70 full-color maps illustrates the eras and civilizations in world history from the emergence of human societies to the present.

The Bedford Glossary for World History. This handy supplement for the survey course gives students historically contextualized definitions for hundreds of terms—from *abolitionism* to *Zoroastrianism*—that they will encounter in lectures, reading, and exams.

World History Matters: A Student Guide to World History Online. Based on the popular "World History Matters" Web site produced by the Center for History and New Media, this unique resource, edited by Kristin Lehner (The Johns Hopkins University), Kelly Schrum (George Mason University), and T. Mills Kelly (George Mason University), combines reviews of 150 of the most useful and reliable world history Web sites with an introduction that guides students in locating, evaluating, and correctly citing online sources.

Trade Books. Titles published by sister companies Hill and Wang; Farrar, Straus and Giroux; Henry Holt and Company; St. Martin's Press; Picador; and Palgrave Macmillan are available at a 50 percent discount when packaged with Bedford/St. Martin's textbooks. For more information, visit **bedfordstmartins.com/tradeup**.

A Pocket Guide to Writing in History. This portable and affordable reference tool by Mary Lynn Rampolla provides reading, writing, and research advice useful to students in all history courses. Concise yet comprehensive advice on approaching typical history assignments, developing critical reading skills, writing effective history papers, conducting research, using and documenting sources, and avoiding plagiarism—enhanced with practical tips and examples throughout—have made this slim reference a bestseller.

A Student's Guide to History. This complete guide to success in any history course provides the practical help students need to be successful. In addition to introducing students to the nature of the discipline, author Jules Benjamin teaches a wide range of skills from preparing for exams to approaching common writing assignments, and explains the research and documentation process with plentiful examples.

Brief Contents

Contents

 Access the interactive content online. See inside the front cover for more information.

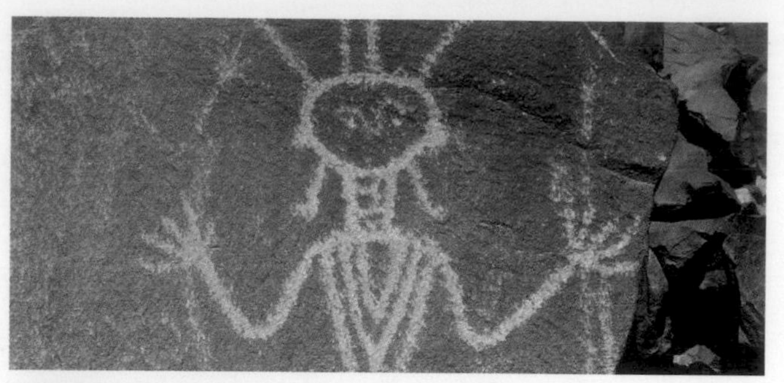

2 The Rise of the State in Southwest Asia and the Nile Valley

3200–500 B.C.E. 31

3 The Foundation of Indian Society

to 300 C.E. 63

8 Continuity and Change in Europe and Western Asia 250–850 207

9 The Islamic World 600–1400 235

10 African Societies and Kingdoms

11 The Americas

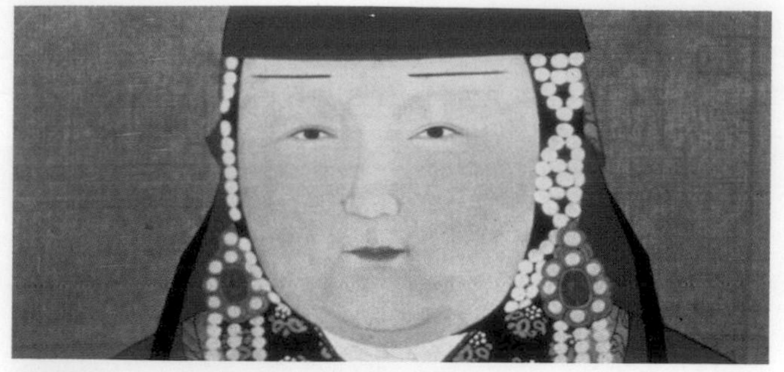

12 Cultural Exchange in Central and Southern Asia 300–1400 329

13 States and Cultures in East Asia 800–1400 363

14 Europe in the Middle Ages 800–1450 391

15 Europe in the Renaissance and Reformation 1350–1600 425

16 The Acceleration of Global Contact 1450–1600 457

Maps, Figures, and Tables

MAPS

Chapter 14

Chapter 15

Chapter 16

FIGURES AND TABLES

Special Features

VIEWPOINTS

LISTENING TO THE PAST

INDIVIDUALS IN SOCIETY

GLOBAL TRADE

The Earliest Human Societies
to 2500 B.C.E.

West African Man

Humans began to portray themselves on the surfaces of places where they lived and traveled as early as 50,000 B.C.E. Most of these paintings have vanished, but some have been redone, as in this rock painting from the region of Niger in Africa, which shows a person, perhaps a shaman, wearing a large headdress. (© David Coulson/Robert Estall photo agency/Alamy)

LearningCurve
After reading the chapter, go online and use LearningCurve to retain what you've read.

Chapter Preview

Evolution and Migration
Paleolithic Society, 250,000–9000 B.C.E.
The Development of Agriculture in the Neolithic Era, ca. 9000 B.C.E.
Neolithic Society

When does history begin? Previous generations of historians generally answered that question with "when writing begins." Thus they started their histories with the earliest known invention of writing, which happened about 3200 B.C.E. in the Tigris and Euphrates River Valleys of Mesopotamia, in what is now Iraq. Anything before that was "prehistory." That focus on only the last five thousand years leaves out most of the human story, however, and today historians no longer see writing as such a sharp dividing line. They explore all eras of the human past through many different types of sources, and some push the beginning of history back to the formation of the universe, when time itself began. This very new conceptualization of "big history" is actually similar in scope to the world's oldest histories, because for thousands and perhaps tens of thousands of years many peoples have narrated histories of their origins that also begin with the creation of the universe.

Exploring the entire human past means beginning in Africa, where millions of years ago humans evolved from a primate ancestor. They migrated out of Africa in several waves, walking along coasts and over land, eventually spreading across much of the earth. Their tools were initially multipurpose sharpened stones and sticks, but gradually they invented more specialized tools that enabled them to obtain food more easily, make clothing, build shelters, and decorate their surroundings. Environmental changes, such as the advance and retreat of the glaciers, shaped life dramatically and may have led to the most significant change in all of human history, the domestication of plants and animals.

Evolution and Migration

☐ How did humans evolve, and where did they migrate?

Studying the earliest era of human history involves methods that seem simple—looking carefully at an object—as well as new high-tech procedures, such as DNA analysis. Through such research, scholars have examined early human evolution, traced the expansion of the human brain, and studied migration out of Africa and across the planet. Combined with spoken language, that larger brain enabled humans to adapt to many different environments and to be flexible in their responses to new challenges.

Understanding the Early Human Past

People throughout the world have developed systems of classification that help them understand things: earth and sky; seen and unseen; animal, vegetable, and mineral; past, present, and future. Among these systems of classification was one invented in eighteenth-century Europe that divided all living things on earth into groups. Each of these divisions—such as that between plants and animals—is further subdivided into smaller and smaller groups, such as class, order, family, and genus. The final important division is the species, which is generally defined as a group of organisms that can interbreed with one another and produce fertile offspring of both sexes.

In their natural state, members of a species resemble one another, but over time they can become increasingly dissimilar. (Think of Chihuahuas and Great Danes, both members of the same species.) Ever since humans began shaping the world around them, this process has often been the result of human action. But in the long era before humans, the increasing dissimilarity resulted, in the opinion of most scientists, from the process of natural selection. Small variations within individuals in one species enabled them to acquire more food and better living conditions and made them more successful in breeding, thus allowing them to pass their genetic material on to the next generation. When a number of individuals within a species became distinct enough that they could no longer interbreed successfully with others, they became a new species. Species also become extinct, particularly during periods of mass extinctions such as the one that killed the dinosaurs about 65 million years ago. Natural processes of species formation and extinction continue, although today changes in the biosphere—the living matter in the world—result far more from human action than from natural selection.

The scientists who developed this system of organizing the world placed humans within it, using the same means of classification that they used for all other living things. Humans were in the animal kingdom, the order of Primates, the family Hominidae, and the genus *Homo*. Like all classifications, this was originally based on externally visible phenomena: humans were placed in the Primates order because, like other primates, they have hands that can grasp, eyes facing forward to allow better depth perception, and relatively large brains; they were placed in the **hominid** family along with chimpanzees, gorillas, and orangutans because they shared even more features with these great apes. Over 98 percent of human DNA is the same as that of chimpanzees, which indicates to most scientists that humans and chimpanzees share a common ancestor. That common ancestor probably lived between 5 million and 7 million years ago.

Genetic analysis is one of many types of technology used by scholars who study early humans. They often use chemical and physical tests to evaluate bones and other body parts left by humans and the animals they ate, and to study the material surrounding these remains. One of the most important of these tests is the analysis of the radioactive isotope of carbon, C-14, which appears in all things that were once alive. C-14 breaks down at a rate that is known, so that measuring the amount of C-14 that remains in an object allows scientists to determine how old the object is.

Archaeologists at a Dig These researchers at a Native American site in the Boise National Forest in Idaho follow careful procedures to remove objects from the soil and note their location. The soil itself may also yield clues, such as seeds or pollen, about what was growing in the area, allowing better understanding of the people who once lived at the site. (David R. Frazier/Science Source)

Physical remains were the earliest type of evidence studied to learn about the distant human past, and scholars used them to develop another system of classification, one that distinguished between periods of time rather than types of living creatures. (Constructing models of time is called "periodization.") They gave labels to eras according to the primary materials out

• **hominids** Members of the family Hominidae that contains humans, chimpanzees, gorillas, and orangutans.

of which tools that survived were made. Thus the earliest human era became the Stone Age, the next era the Bronze Age, and the next the Iron Age. They further divided the Stone Age into the Old Stone Age, or **Paleolithic era**, during which people used stone, bone, and other natural products to make tools and gained food largely by **foraging**—that is, by gathering plant products, trapping or catching small animals and birds, and hunting larger prey. This was followed by the New Stone Age, or **Neolithic era**, which saw the beginning of agricultural and animal domestication. People around the world adopted agriculture at various times, and some never did, but the transition between the Paleolithic and the Neolithic is usually set at about 9000 B.C.E., the point at which agriculture was first developed.*

Geologists refer to the last twelve thousand years as the Holocene (meaning very recent) epoch, a period so short given the 4.5 billion years of the solar system that it often does not show up on geologic timelines. The entire history of the human species fits well within the Holocene and the previous geologic epoch, the Pleistocene (PLIGH-stuh-seen), which began about 2.5 million years ago.

The Pleistocene was marked by repeated advances in glaciers and continental ice sheets. Glaciers tied up huge quantities of the earth's water, leading to lower sea levels, making it possible for animals and eventually humans to walk between places that were separated by oceans during interglacial times. Animals and humans were also prevented from migrating to other places by the ice sheets themselves, however, and the colder climate made large areas unfit to live in. Climate thus dramatically shaped human cultures.

Genetic analysis can indicate many things about the human family, and physical remains can provide some evidence about how people lived in the distant past, but the evidence is often difficult to interpret. By themselves, tools and other objects generally do not reveal who made or used them (though sometimes this can be determined from the location in which they were found), nor do they indicate what the objects meant to their creators or users. Thus, to learn about the early human past, scholars often also study groups of people from more recent times whose technology and way of life offer parallels with those of people in the distant past. They read written reports of conquerors, government officials, and missionaries who encountered groups that lived by foraging, and they directly observe the few remaining groups that maintain a foraging lifestyle today. Such evidence is also problematic, however. Outsiders had their own perspectives, generally regarded those who lived by foraging as inferior, and often misinterpreted what they were seeing. Contemporary foragers are not fully cut off from the modern world, nor is it correct to assume that their way of living has not changed for thousands of years, particularly because adaptability is a key feature of the foraging way of life. Thus evidence from more recent groups must be used carefully, but it can provide valuable clues.

Hominid Evolution

Using many different pieces of evidence from all over the world, archaeologists, paleontologists, and other scholars have developed a view of human evolution whose basic outline is widely shared, though there are disagreements about details. Most primates, including other hominids such as chimpanzees and gorillas, have lived primarily in trees, but at some point a group of hominids in East Africa began to spend more time on the ground, and between 6 and 7 million years ago they began to walk upright at least some of the time. Very recently, scientists have determined that skeletal remains from the genus *Ardipithecus*, which probably date from 4.4 million years ago, indicate a combination of two-limbed movement on land and four-limbed movement in trees. *Ardipithecus* also had smaller canine teeth than do modern chimpanzees, and male and female canine teeth were equal in size, which suggests that there was less male-male combat and perhaps closer male-female relations than among earlier hominids.

Over many generations, the skeletal and muscular structure of some hominids evolved to make upright walking easier, and they gradually became fully bipedal. The earliest fully bipedal hominids, whom paleontologists place in the genus *Australopithecus*, lived in south-

- **Paleolithic era** Period during which humans used tools of stone, bone, and wood and obtained food by gathering and hunting. Roughly 250,000–9000 B.C.E.
- **foraging** A style of life in which people gain food by gathering plant products, trapping or catching small animals and birds, and hunting larger prey.
- **Neolithic era** Period beginning in 9000 B.C.E. during which humans obtained food by raising crops and animals and continued to use tools primarily of stone, bone, and wood.

***A note on dates:** This book generally uses B.C.E. (Before the Common Era) and C.E. (Common Era) when giving dates, a system of chronology based on the Christian calendar and now used widely around the world. Scholars who study the very earliest periods of hominid and human history usually use the phrase "years ago" to date their subjects, as do astrophysicists and geologists; this is often abbreviated as B.P. (Before the Present). Because the scale of time covered in Chapter 1 is so vast, a mere 2,000 years does not make much difference, and so B.C.E. and "years ago" have similar meaning.

ern and eastern Africa between 2.5 and 4 million years ago. Here they left bones, particularly in the Great Rift Valley that stretches from Ethiopia to Tanzania. Walking upright allowed australopithecines to carry and use things, which allowed them to survive better and may have also spurred brain development.

About 3.4 million years ago, some hominids began to use naturally occurring objects as tools, and sometime around 2.5 million years ago, one group of australopithecines in East Africa began to make and use simple tools, evolving into a different type of hominid that later paleontologists judged to be the first in the genus *Homo*. Called *Homo habilis* ("handy human"), they made sharpened stone pieces, which archaeologists call hand axes, and used them for various tasks. This suggests greater intelligence, and the skeletal remains support this, for *Homo habilis* had a larger brain than did the australopithecines.

The Great Rift Valley

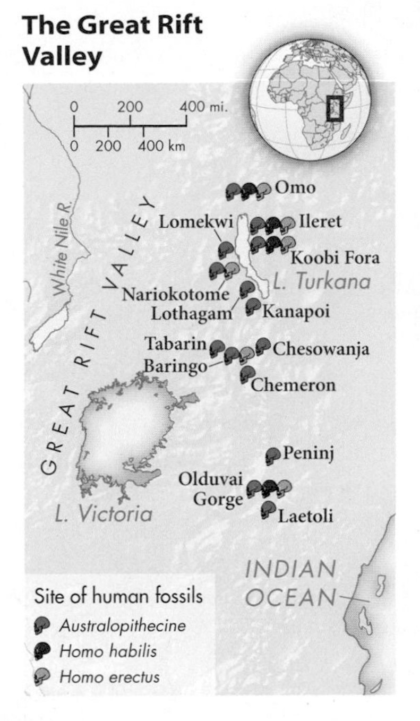

About 2 million years ago, another species, called *Homo erectus* ("upright human"), evolved in East Africa. *Homo erectus* had still larger brains and made tools that were slightly specialized for various tasks, such as handheld axes, cleavers, and scrapers. Archaeological remains indicate that *Homo erectus* lived in larger groups than had earlier hominids and engaged in cooperative gathering, hunting, and food preparation. The location and shape of the larynx suggest that members of this species were able to make a wider range of sounds than were earlier hominids, so they may have relied more on vocal sounds than on gestures to communicate ideas to one another.

One of the activities that *Homo erectus* carried out most successfully was moving (Map 1.1). Gradually small groups migrated out of East Africa onto the open plains of central Africa, and from there into northern Africa. From 1 million to 2 million years ago, the earth's climate was in a warming phase, and these hominids ranged still farther, moving into western Asia by as early as 1.8 million years ago. Bones and other materials from China and the island of Java in Indonesia indicate that *Homo erectus* had reached there by about 1.5 million years ago, migrating over large landmasses as well as along the coasts. (Sea levels were lower than they are today, and Java could be reached by walking.) *Homo erectus* also walked north, reaching what is now Spain by at least 800,000 years ago and what is now Germany by 500,000 years ago. In each of these places, *Homo erectus* adapted gathering and hunting techniques to the local environment, learning how to find new sources of plant food and how to best catch local animals. Although the climate was warmer than it is today, central Europe was not balmy, and these hominids may have used fire to provide light and heat, cook food, and keep away predators. Many lived in the open or in caves, but some built simple shelters, another indication of increasing flexibility and problem solving.

Fossil Footprints from Laetoli in Tanzania About 3.5 million years ago, several australopithecines walked in wet ash from a volcanic eruption. Their footprints, discovered by the archaeologist Mary Leakey, indicate that they walked fully upright and suggest that they were not solitary creatures, for they walked close together. (John Reader/Science Source)

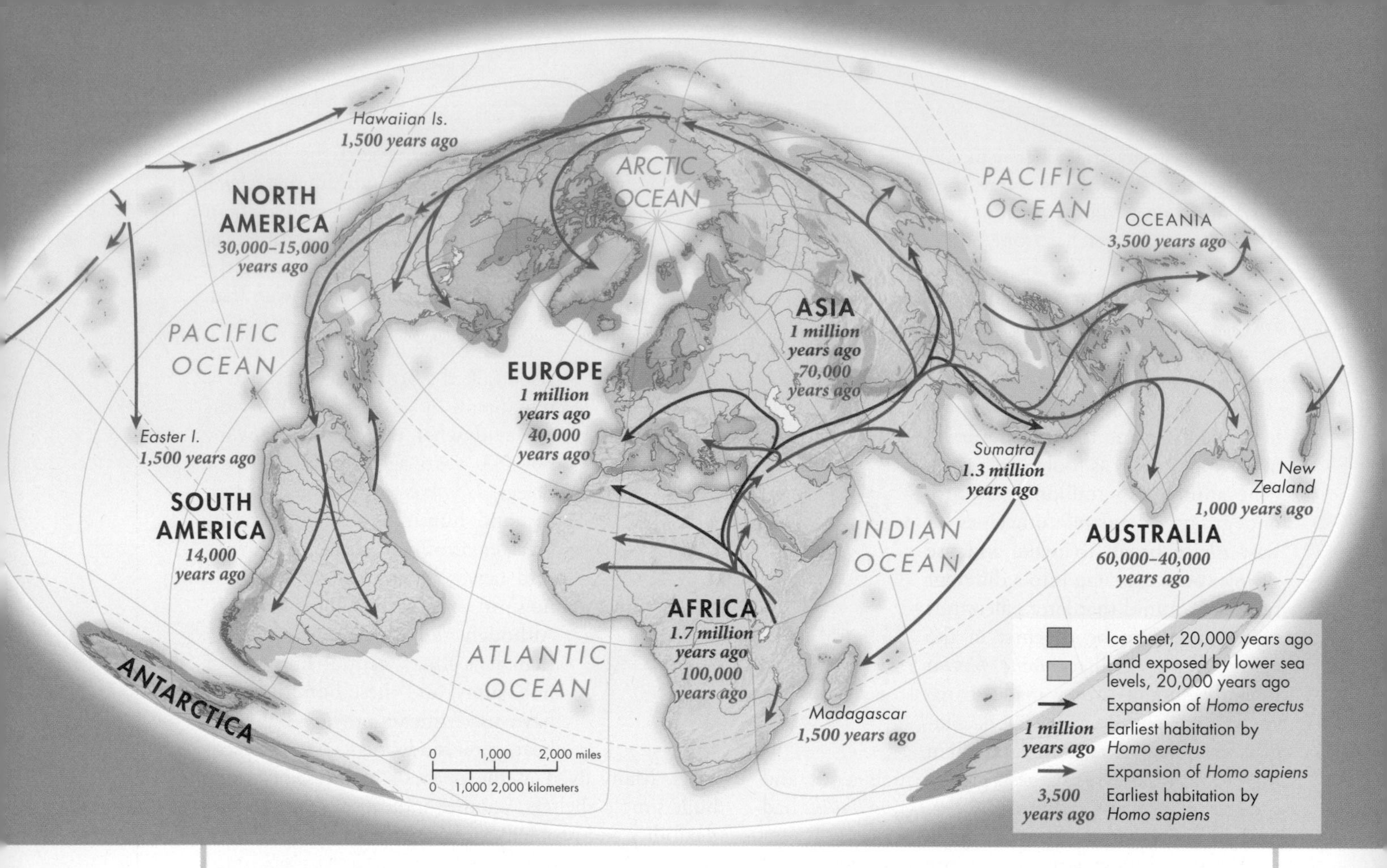

Mapping the Past

MAP 1.1 Human Migration in the Paleolithic and Neolithic Eras

ANALYZING THE MAP What were the major similarities and differences between the migrations of *Homo erectus* and those of *Homo sapiens*? How did environmental factors shape human migration?

CONNECTIONS What types of technology were required for the migration patterns seen here? What do these migration patterns suggest about the social organization of early people?

Homo Sapiens, "Thinking Humans"

Homo erectus was remarkably adaptable, but another hominid proved still more so: *Homo sapiens* ("thinking human"). A few scientists think that *Homo sapiens* evolved from *Homo erectus* in a number of places in Afroeurasia, but the majority think that, like hominid evolution from earlier primates, this occurred only in East Africa. The evidence is partly archaeological, but also genetic. One type of DNA, called mitochondrial DNA, indicates that modern humans are so similar genetically that they cannot have been evolving for the last 1 million or 2 million years. This evidence suggests that the evolution of *Homo sapiens* has instead taken place for only about 250,000 years. Because there is greater human genetic variety today in Africa than in other parts of the world, the evidence also suggests that *Homo sapiens* have lived there the longest, so that Africa is where they first emerged. According to this hypothesis, all modern humans are descended from a relatively small group in East Africa.

Although there is some debate about where and when *Homo sapiens* emerged, there is little debate about what distinguished these humans from earlier hominids: a bigger brain, in particular a bigger forebrain, the site of conscious thought. The ability to think reflectively allowed for the creation of symbolic language, that is, for language that follows certain rules and that can refer to things or states of being that are not necessarily present. Greater intelligence allowed *Homo sapiens* to better understand and manipulate the world around them, and symbolic language allowed this understanding to be communicated within a group and passed from one generation to the next. Through spoken language *Homo sapiens* began to develop collective explanations for the world around them that we would now call religion, science, and philosophy. Spoken language also enabled *Homo sapiens* to organize socially into larger groups, thus further enhancing their ability to affect the natural world.

The advantages of a larger brain seem evident to us, so we may not think to ask why hominids evolved this way. Large brains also bring disadvantages, however. They take more energy to run than other parts of the body, so that large-brained animals have to eat more than small-brained ones. Large brains create particular problems for bipedal mammals, for the narrow pelvic structure that works best for upright walking makes giving birth to a large-headed infant difficult and painful.

The question of why hominids developed ever-larger brains might best be answered by looking at how paleontologists think it happened. As *Homo habilis*, *Homo erectus*, and *Homo sapiens* made and used tools, the individuals whose mental and physical abilities allowed them to do so best were able to obtain more food and were more likely to mate and have children who survived. Thus bigger brains led to better tools, but the challenges of using and inventing better tools also created selective pressure that led to bigger brains.

The same thing may have happened with symbolic language and thought. A slightly bigger brain allowed for more complex thought and better language skills (aided by anatomical changes in the vocal tract and larynx that allowed for a greater range of sounds). These thinking and speaking skills enabled individuals to better attract mates and fend off rivals, which meant a greater likelihood of passing on the enhanced brain to the next generation. As we know from contemporary research on the brain, learning language promotes the development of specific areas of the brain.

The growth in brain size and complexity may also have been linked to social organization. Individuals who had better social skills were more likely to mate than those who did not—this has been observed in chimpanzees and, of course, in modern humans—and thus to pass on their genetic material. Social skills were particularly important for females, because the combination of bipedalism and growing brain size led to selective pressure for hominid infants to be born at an even earlier stage in their development than other primate infants. Thus the period when human infants are dependent on others is very long, and mothers with good social networks to assist them were more likely to have infants who survived. Humans are unique in the duration and complexity of their care for children, and cooperative child rearing, along with the development of social skills and the adaptability this encouraged, may have been an impetus to brain growth.

All these factors operated together in processes that promoted bigger and better brains. In the Paleolithic period, *Homo sapiens'* brains invented highly specialized tools made out of a variety of materials that replaced the more general-purpose stone tools made by *Homo erectus*: barbed fishhooks and harpoons, snares and traps for catching small animals, bone needles for sewing clothing, awls for punching holes in leather, nets for catching fish, sharpened flint pieces bound to wooden or bone handles for hunting or cutting, and slings for carrying infants. By 25,000 years ago, and perhaps earlier, humans in some parts of the world were weaving cloth and baskets, and by 17,000 years ago they were using bows and atlatls (AHT-lah-tuhlz)—notched throwing sticks made of bone, wood, or antler—to launch arrows and barbs with flint points bound to wooden shafts. The archaeological evidence for increasingly sophisticated language and social organization is less direct than that for tool use, but it is hard to imagine how humans could have made the tools they did—or would have chosen to decorate so many of them—without both of these.

Migration and Differentiation

Like *Homo erectus* had earlier, groups of *Homo sapiens* moved. By 200,000 years ago they had begun to spread across Africa, and by 120,000 years ago they had begun to migrate out of Africa to Eurasia (see Map 1.1). They most likely walked along the coasts of India and Southeast Asia, and then migrated inland. At the same time, further small evolutionary changes led to our own subspecies of anatomically modern humans, *Homo sapiens sapiens* (which literally translates as "thinking thinking humans"). *Homo sapiens sapiens* moved into areas where there were already *Homo erectus* populations, eventually replacing them, leaving *Homo sapiens* as the only survivors and the ancestors of all modern humans.

The best-known example of interaction between *Homo erectus* and *Homo sapiens sapiens* is that between Neanderthals (named after the Neander Valley in Germany, where their remains were first discovered) and a group of anatomically modern humans called Cro-Magnons. **Neanderthals** lived throughout Europe and western Asia beginning about 150,000 years ago, had brains as large as those of modern humans, and used tools, including spears and scrapers for animal skins, that enabled them to survive in the cold climate of Ice Age central Europe and Russia. They built freestanding houses, and they decorated objects and themselves with red ochre, a form of colored clay. They sometimes buried their dead carefully with tools, animal bones, and perhaps flowers, which suggests that they understood death to have a symbolic meaning. These characteristics led them to be originally categorized as a branch of *Homo sapiens*, but DNA evidence from Neanderthal

- **Neanderthals** Group of *Homo erectus* with brains as large as those of modern humans that flourished in Europe and western Asia between 150,000 and 30,000 years ago.

bones now indicates that they were a separate branch of highly developed *Homo erectus.*

Cro-Magnon peoples moved into parts of western Asia where Neanderthals lived by about 70,000 years ago, and into Europe by about 45,000 years ago. The two peoples appear to have lived side by side for millennia, hunting the same types of animals and gathering the same types of plants. In 2010 DNA evidence demonstrated that they also had sex with one another, for between 1 and 4 percent of the DNA in modern humans living outside of Africa likely came from Neanderthals. The last evidence of Neanderthals as a separate species comes from about 30,000 years ago, and it is not clear exactly how they died out. They may have been killed by Cro-Magnon peoples, or they simply may have lost the competition for food as the climate worsened around 30,000 years ago and the glaciers expanded.

Until very recently Neanderthals were thought to be the last living hominids that were not *Homo sapiens*, but in 2003 archaeologists on the Indonesian island of Flores discovered bones and tools of three-foot-tall hominids that dated from only about 18,000 years ago. A few scientists view them as very small or malformed *Homo sapiens*, but most see them as a distinct species, probably descended from *Homo erectus* as were Neanderthals. Nicknamed "hobbits," the Flores hominids or their ancestors appear to have lived on the island for more than 800,000 years.

Homo erectus migrated great distances, but *Homo sapiens sapiens* made use of greater intelligence and better toolmaking capabilities to migrate still farther. They used simple rafts to reach Australia by at least 50,000 years ago, and by 35,000 years ago had reached New Guinea. By at least 15,000 years ago, humans had walked across the land bridges then linking Siberia and North America at the Bering Strait and had crossed into the Americas. Because by 14,000 years ago humans were already in southern South America, ten thousand miles from the land bridges, many scholars now think that people came to the Americas much earlier. They think humans came from Asia to the Americas perhaps as early as 20,000 or even 30,000 years ago, walking or using rafts along the coasts. (See Chapter 11 for a longer discussion of this issue.)

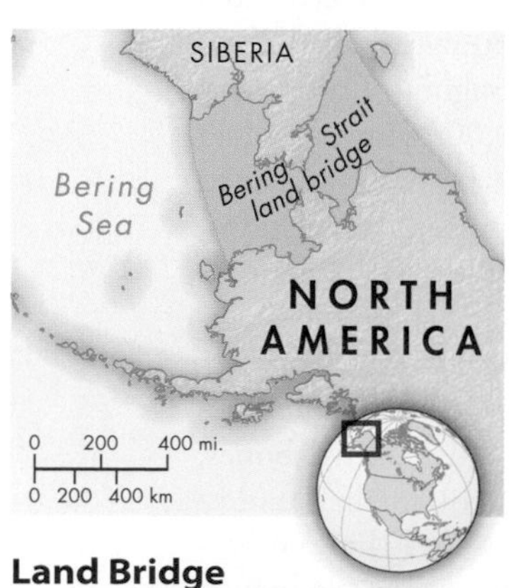

Land Bridge Across the Bering Strait, ca. 15,000 B.C.E.

With the melting of glaciers sea levels rose, and parts of the world that had been linked by land bridges, including North America and Asia as well as many parts of Southeast Asia, became separated by water. This cut off migratory paths but also spurred innovation. Humans designed and built ever more sophisticated boats and learned how to navigate by studying wind and current patterns, bird flights, and the position of the stars. They sailed to increasingly remote islands, including those in the Pacific, the last parts of the globe to be settled. The western Pacific islands were inhabited by about 2000 B.C.E., Hawaii by about 500 C.E., and New Zealand by about 1000 C.E. (For more on the settlement of the Pacific islands, see page 357.)

Polynesian Oceangoing Sailing Canoe This is a Hawaiian replica of the type of large double-hulled canoe in which Polynesians sailed around the Pacific as they settled many different island groups. This canoe, called the Hokule'a, has taken many voyages using traditional Pacific techniques of celestial navigation. The two hulls provided greater stability, and canoes designed like this sailed thousands of miles over the open ocean. (© Monte Costa/PhotoResourceHawaii.com)

Once humans had spread out over much of the globe, groups often became isolated from one another, and people mated only with other members of their own group or those who lived nearby, a practice anthropologists call endogamy. Thus, over thousands of generations, although humans remained one species, *Homo sapiens sapiens* came to develop differences in physical features, including skin and hair color, eye and body shape, and amount of body hair. Language also changed over generations, so that thousands of different languages were eventually spoken. Groups created widely varying cultures and passed them on to their children, further increasing diversity among humans.

Beginning in the eighteenth century, European natural scientists sought to develop a system that would explain human differences at the largest scale. They divided people into very large groups by skin color and other physical characteristics and termed these groups "races," a word that had originally meant lineage. They first differentiated these races by continent of origin—Americanus, Europaeus, Asiaticus, and Africanus—and then by somewhat different geographic areas. The word *Caucasian* was first used by the German anatomist and naturalist Johann Friedrich Blumenbach (1752–1840) to describe light-skinned people of Europe and western Asia because he thought that their original home was most likely the Caucasus Mountains on the border between Russia and Georgia. He thought that they were the first humans and the most attractive. This meaning of *race* has had a long life, though biologists and anthropologists today do not use it, as it has no scientific meaning or explanatory value. All humans are one species with less genetic variety than chimpanzees.

Paleolithic Hand Axes Like most Paleolithic stone tools, these two hand axes from Libya in northern Africa were made by chipping flakes off stone to form a sharpened edge. Although they are traditionally called axes, they were used for a variety of purposes, including skinning, cutting, and chopping. (Robert Harding Images/Masterfile)

Paleolithic Society, 250,000–9000 B.C.E.

☐ What were the key features of Paleolithic society?

Eventually human cultures became widely diverse, but in the Paleolithic period people throughout the world lived in ways that were similar to one another. Archaeological evidence and studies of modern foragers suggest that people lived in small groups of related individuals and moved throughout the landscape in search of food. Most had few material possessions, only what they could carry, although in areas where food resources were especially rich, such as along seacoasts, they built structures and lived more permanently in one place. In the later Paleolithic, people in many parts of the world created art and music and developed religious ideas that linked the natural world to a world beyond.

Foraging for Food

Paleolithic peoples have often been called hunter-gatherers, but recent archaeological and anthropological research indicates that both historical and contemporary hunter-gatherers have depended much more on gathered foods than on hunted meat. Thus it would be more accurate to call them "gatherer-hunters," and most scholars now call them foragers, a term that highlights the flexibility and adaptability in their search for food. Most of what foragers ate were plants, and much of the animal protein in their diet came from foods gathered or scavenged rather than hunted directly: insects, shellfish, small animals caught in traps, fish and other sea creatures caught in weirs and nets, and animals killed by other predators. Gathering and hunting probably varied in importance from year to year depending on environmental factors and the decisions of the group.

Paleolithic peoples did hunt large game. Groups working together forced animals over cliffs, threw spears, and, beginning about 15,000 B.C.E., used bows and atlatls to shoot projectiles so that they could stand farther away from their prey while hunting. The final retreat of the glaciers also occurred between 10,000 and 15,000 years ago, and the warming climate was less favorable to the very large mammals that had roamed the open spaces of many parts of the world. Wooly mammoths, mastodons, and wooly rhinos all died out in Eurasia in this **megafaunal extinction**, as did camels, horses, and sloths in the Americas and giant kangaroos and wombats in Australia. In many places, these extinctions occurred just about the time that modern humans appeared, and increasing numbers of scientists think that they were at least in part caused by human hunting.

• **megafaunal extinction** Die-off of large animals in many parts of the world about 15,000–10,000 B.C.E., caused by climate change and perhaps human hunting.

Most foraging societies that exist today or did so until recently have some type of **division of labor** by sex, and also by age, with children and older people responsible for different tasks than adult men and women. Men are more often responsible for hunting, through which they gained prestige as well as meat, and women for gathering plant and animal products. This has led scholars to assume that in Paleolithic society men were also responsible for hunting, and women for gathering. Such a division of labor is not universal, however: in some of the world's foraging cultures, such as the Agta of the Philippines, women hunt large game, and in many they participate in group hunts. The stone and bone tools that remain from the Paleolithic period give no clear evidence of who used them, and the division of labor may have been somewhat flexible, particularly during periods of scarcity.

Obtaining food was a constant preoccupation, but it was not a constant job. Studies of recent foragers indicate that, other than in times of environmental disasters such as prolonged droughts, people need only about ten to twenty hours a week to gather food and carry out the other tasks needed to survive, such as locating water and building shelters. The diet of foragers is varied and nutritious: low in fat and salt, high in fiber, and rich in vitamins and minerals. The slow pace of life and healthy diet did not mean that Paleolithic life spans approached those of the modern world, however. People avoided such contemporary killers as heart disease and diabetes, but they often died at young ages from injuries, infections, animal attacks, and interpersonal violence. Mothers and infants died in childbirth, and many children died before they reached adulthood.

Total human population thus grew very slowly during the Paleolithic. Scholars can make rough estimates only, but one of them proposes that there were perhaps 500,000 humans in the world about 30,000 years ago. By about 10,000 years ago this number had grown to 5 million—ten times as many people. This was a significant increase, but it took twenty thousand years. (By contrast, the earth's population today is more than 7 billion; it was slightly under 1 billion a mere 300 years ago.) The low population density meant that human impact on the environment was relatively small, although still significant. In addition to contributing to the extinction of some large animals, Paleolithic people may have also shaped their environments by setting fires, which encouraged the growth of new plants and attracted animals that fed on them, making hunting or snaring game easier. This practice was a factor in the spread of plants that thrived best with occasional burning, such as the eucalyptus in Australia.

• **division of labor** Differentiation of tasks by gender, age, training, status, or other social distinction.

Family and Kinship Relationships

Small bands of humans—twenty or thirty people was a standard size for foragers in harsh environments—were scattered across broad areas, but this did not mean that each group lived in isolation. Their travels in search of food brought them into contact with one another, not simply for talking and celebrating, but also for providing opportunities for the exchange of sexual partners, which was essential to group survival. Today we understand that having sexual relations with close relatives is disadvantageous because it creates greater risk of genetic disorders. Earlier societies did not have knowledge of genetics, but most of them developed rules against sexual relations among immediate family members. Mating arrangements varied in their permanence, but many groups seem to have developed a somewhat permanent arrangement whereby a man or woman left his or her original group and joined the group of his or her mate, what would later be termed marriage.

Within each band, and within the larger kin groups, individuals had a variety of identities; they were simultaneously fathers, sons, husbands, and brothers, or mothers, daughters, wives, and sisters. Each of these identities was relational (parent to child, sibling to sibling, spouse to spouse), and some of them, especially parent to child, gave one power over others. In many areas kin groups remained significant power structures for millennia, and in some areas they still have influence over major aspects of life, such as an individual's job or marital partner. Paleolithic people were not differentiated by wealth, for in a foraging society accumulating material goods was not advantageous. But they were differentiated by such factors as age, gender, and position in a family, and no doubt by personal qualities such as intelligence, courage, and charisma.

Stereotypical representations of Paleolithic people often portray a powerful fur-clad man holding a club and dragging off a (usually attractive) fur-clad woman by her hair, or men going off to hunt while women and children crouched around a fire, waiting for the men to bring back great slabs of meat. Studies of the relative importance of gathering to hunting, women's participation in hunting, and gender relations among contemporary foraging peoples have led some analysts to turn these stereotypes on their heads. They see Paleolithic bands as egalitarian groups in which the contributions of men and women to survival were recognized and valued, and in which both men and women had equal access to the limited amount of resources held by the group. Other scholars argue that this is also a stereotype, overly romanticizing Paleolithic society. They note that although social relations among foragers were not as hierarchical as they were in other types of societies, many foraging groups had one person who

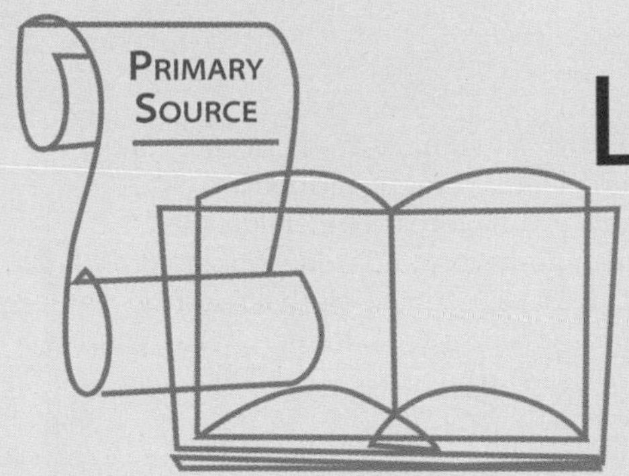

Listening to the Past

Paleolithic Venus Figures

Written sources provide evidence about the human past only after the development of writing, allowing us to listen to the voices of people long dead. For most of human history, however, there were no written sources, so we "listen" to the past through objects. Interpreting written documents is difficult, and interpreting archaeological evidence about the earliest human belief systems is even more difficult and often contentious. For example, small stone statues of women with enlarged breasts and buttocks dating from the later Paleolithic period (roughly 33,000–9000 B.C.E.) have been found in many parts of Europe. These were dubbed "Venus figures" by nineteenth-century archaeologists, who thought they represented Paleolithic standards of female beauty just as the goddess Venus represented classical standards. A reproduction of one of these statues, the six-inch-tall Venus of Lespugue made from a mammoth tusk about 25,000 years ago in southern France, is shown here. Venus figures provoke more questions than answers: Are they fertility goddesses, evidence of people's beliefs in a powerful female deity? Or are they aids to fertility, carried around by women hoping to have children—or perhaps hoping not to have more—and then discarded in the household debris where they have been most commonly found? Or are they sexualized images of women carried around by men, a sort of Paleolithic version of the centerfold in a men's magazine? Might they have represented different things to different people? Like so much Paleolithic evidence, Venus figurines provide tantalizing evidence about early human cultures, but evidence that is not easy to interpret.

The Venus of Lespugue from France, made from tusk ivory around 25,000 years ago (reproduction). (Ronald Sheridan/© Ancient Art & Architecture Collection, Ltd.)

QUESTIONS FOR ANALYSIS

1. As you look at this statue, does it seem to link more closely with fertility or with sexuality? How might your own situation as a twenty-first-century person shape your answer to this question?
2. Some scholars see Venus figures as evidence that Paleolithic society was egalitarian or female dominated, but others point out that images of female deities or holy figures are often found in religions that deny women official authority. Can you think of examples of the latter? Which point of view seems most persuasive to you?

held more power than others, and that person was almost always a man. This debate about gender relations is often part of larger discussions about whether Paleolithic society—and by implication, "human nature"—was primarily peaceful and nurturing or violent and brutal, and whether these qualities are gender related. Like much else about the Paleolithic, sources about gender and about violence are fragmentary and difficult to interpret; there may simply have been a diversity of patterns, as there is among more modern foragers. (See "Listening to the Past: Paleolithic Venus Figures," above.)

Whether peaceful and egalitarian or violent and hierarchical, heterosexual relations produced children, who were cared for as infants by their mothers or other women who had recently given birth. Breast milk was the only food available that infants could easily digest, so mothers nursed their children for several years. Along with providing food for infants, extended nursing brings a side benefit: it suppresses ovulation and thus acts as a contraceptive. Foraging groups needed children to survive, but too many could tax scarce food resources. Many groups may have practiced selective infanticide or abandonment. They may also have exchanged children of different ages with other groups, which further deepened kinship connections between groups. Other than for feeding, children were most likely cared for by other male and female members of the group as well as by their mothers during the long period of human childhood.

Cultural Creations and Spirituality

Early human societies are often described in terms of their tools, but this misses a large part of the story. Beginning in the Paleolithic, human beings have expressed themselves through what we would now term the arts or culture: painting and decorating walls and objects, making music with their voices and a variety of instruments, imagining and telling stories, dancing alone or in groups. Evidence from the Paleolithic, particularly from after about 50,000 years ago, includes flutes, carvings, jewelry, and paintings done on cave walls and rock outcroppings that depict animals, people, and symbols. In many places these paintings show the outline of a human hand—often done by blowing pigment around it—or tracings of the fingers, a simple art form that allowed individuals to say "I was here." (See "Viewpoints 1.1: Paleolithic Hand Markings," at right.)

Some cultural creations appear to have had a larger purpose: they may have been created to honor and praise ancestors or leaders, help people remember events and traditions, or promote good hunting or safe childbirth. Some were easy to do, and everyone in a culture was expected to participate in some way: to dance in order to bring rain or give thanks, to listen when stories were told, to take part in ceremonies. Other creations required particular talents or training and were probably undertaken only by specialists.

At the same time that people marked and depicted the world around them, they also appear to have developed ideas about supernatural forces that controlled some aspects of the natural world and the place of humans in it, what we now term spirituality or religion. The Neanderthals' careful burial of their dead suggests to some scholars that they had ideas about an afterlife or at least something beyond the visible world, and there is no doubt that this was the case for Paleolithic *Homo sapiens*. Paleolithic burials, paintings, and objects suggest that people may have thought of their world as extending beyond the visible. People, animals, plants, natural occurrences, and other things around them had spirits, an idea called **animism**. The only evidence of Paleolithic animism that survives is physical, of course, but more recent animist traditions carry on this understanding of the spiritual nature and interdependence of all things, as in this contemporary Chinook blessing from northwestern North America:

> We call upon the Earth, our planet home, with its beautiful depths and soaring heights, its vitality and abundance of life, and together we ask that it *Teach us, and show us the Way*. . . .
>
> We call upon the creatures of the fields and the forests and the seas, our brothers and sisters the wolves and the deer, the eagle and dove, the great whales and the dolphin, the beautiful orca and salmon who share our Northwest home, and ask them to *Teach Us and show us the Way*.[1]

Death took people from the realm of the living, but for Paleolithic groups people continued to inhabit an unseen world, along with spirits and deities, after death; thus kin groups included deceased as well as living members of a family. The unseen world regularly intervened in the visible world, for good and ill, and the actions of dead ancestors, spirits, and gods could be shaped by living people. Concepts of the supernatural pervaded all aspects of life; hunting, birth, death, and natural occurrences such as eclipses, comets, and rainbows all had religious meaning. Supernatural forces were understood to determine the basic rules for human existence, and upsetting these rules could lead to chaos.

Ordinary people learned about the unseen world through dreams and portents, and messages and revelations were also sent more regularly to **shamans**, spiritually adept men and women who communicated with the unseen world. Shamans created complex rituals through which they sought to ensure the health and prosperity of an individual, family, or group. Many cave paintings show herds of prey animals, and several include a masked human figure usually judged to be a shaman performing some sort of ritual. Objects understood to have special power, such as carvings or

Paleolithic Flute This flute, carved from the wing bone of a griffon vulture, was unearthed in a cave in Germany along with pieces of other flutes made from mammoth ivory and stone tools. Dating from at least 33,000 B.C.E., it is the oldest musical instrument ever found and suggests that music has long been an important part of human culture. (H. Jensen/University of Tübingen)

- **animism** Idea that people, animals, plants, natural occurrences, and other parts of the physical world have spirits.
- **shamans** Spiritually adept men and women who communicated with the unseen world.

Primary Sources

Viewpoints 1.1

Paleolithic Hand Markings

• *Paleolithic finger and hand markings have been found all over the world. They were made in a variety of ways—running fingers over wet or soft stone, dipping a hand in pigment and pressing it onto a surface, or tracing around a hand. The most common pigment was made from red ochre, a naturally occurring mixture of clay and iron oxide that is plentiful and quite permanent. Humans have been using red ochre, which varies in color from yellow to red to brown to purple, for more than a hundred thousand years, burying pieces of it with bodies, sprinkling it on cave floors, and mixing it with liquids such as urine, animal fat, blood, egg whites, or water to make paint. In 2011 scientists in South Africa discovered abalone shells holding paint made from red ochre, charcoal, and liquid, along with specialized stone and bone tools, that date to about 100,000 B.C.E., in what they dubbed the "world's oldest art studio."*

Handprints from Cueva de las Manos (Cave of the Hands) in Argentina, ca. 8000 B.C.E. These handprints, made by blowing paint made from red ochre around the hand through a bone pipe, are from different individuals. All are slightly smaller than adult hands, so they were most likely made by adolescents. Most are left hands, which indicates that even in the Paleolithic, most people were right-handed, since they would have held the pipe for blowing in the hand they normally used for tasks. (© Hubert Stadler/Corbis)

QUESTIONS FOR ANALYSIS

1. Why, in your opinion, was the human hand such a common image in Paleolithic art?
2. Some scholars have suggested that because Paleolithic hand markings were often made by children or adolescents, they were done as part of coming-of-age ceremonies or other spiritual rituals. Others suggest that they were made as part of play or as adolescent rebellion akin to today's graffiti. Which explanation seems most plausible to you?

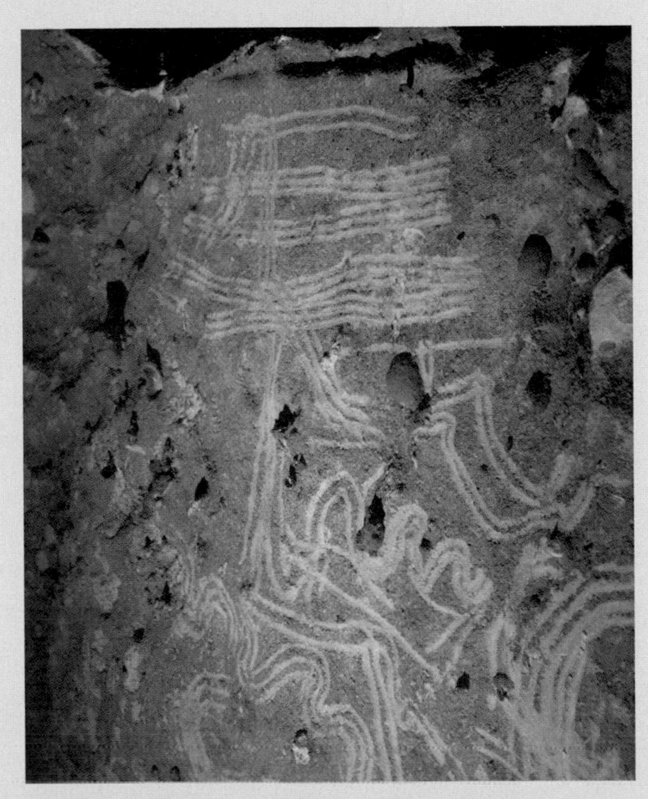

Finger Marks from Rouffignac Cave in France, 18,000–9000 B.C.E. The finger marks of a young child are among those made by a group of adults and children who each left such finger flutings in the wet surfaces of the cave, far from the entrance, indicating that they would have used torches to see as they decorated the walls and ceiling. Through comparing these finger marks with those made by girls' and boys' fingers today, archaeologists judge them to have been made by a girl. She ran the three middle fingers of each hand down the wall of the cave at the same time, which meant someone else was holding the torch for her to see. (© Leslie Van Gelder)

□ Picturing the Past

Cave Paintings of Horses and a Horned Aurochs from Lascaux Cave, Southern France, ca. 15,000 B.C.E. The artist who made these amazing animals in charcoal and red ochre first smoothed the surface, just as a contemporary artist might. This cave includes paintings of hundreds of animals, including predators such as lions, as well as abstract symbols. (JM Labat/Photo Researchers, Inc.)

ANALYZING THE IMAGE The artist painted the animals so close together that they overlap. What might this arrangement have been trying to depict or convey?

CONNECTIONS Why might Paleolithic people have made cave paintings? What do these paintings suggest about Stone Age culture and society?

masks in the form of an animal or person, could give additional protection, as could certain plants or mixtures eaten, sniffed, or rubbed on the skin. Shamans thus also operated as healers, with cures that included what we would term natural medicines and religious healing.

Judging by practices from later periods, the rituals and medicines through which shamans and healers operated were often closely guarded secrets, but they were passed orally from one spiritually adept individual to another, so that gradually a body of knowledge developed around the medicinal properties of local plants and other natural materials. By observing natural phenomena and testing materials for their usable qualities, Paleolithic people began to invent what would later be called science.

The Development of Agriculture in the Neolithic Era, ca. 9000 B.C.E.

□ How did plant and animal domestication develop, and what effects did it have on human society?

Foraging remained the basic way of life for most of human history, and for groups living in extreme environments, such as tundras or deserts, it was the only possible way to survive. In a few especially fertile areas, however, the natural environment provided enough food that people could become more settled. As they remained in one place, they began to plant seeds as

Neolithic Tools from Lakes in Switzerland These highly specialized tools include arrow points, awls, chisels, scrapers, stone ax blades in antler sockets, sickle blades, and round spindle whorls, designed to twist fibers into thread. The people who made and used them lived in wooden houses on stilts over the water, and the mud of the lake bed preserved even the bone and antler. (Courtesy of Peter A. Bostrom)

well as gather wild crops, to raise certain animals instead of hunting them, and to selectively breed both plants and animals to make them more useful to humans. This seemingly small alteration was the most important change in human history; because of its impact it is often termed the **Agricultural Revolution**. Plant and animal domestication marked the transition from the Paleolithic to the Neolithic. It allowed the human population to grow far more quickly than did foraging, but it also required more labor, which became increasingly specialized.

The Development of Horticulture

Areas of the world differed in the food resources available to foragers. In some, acquiring enough food to sustain a group was difficult, and groups had to move constantly. In others, moderate temperatures and abundant rainfall allowed for verdant plant growth; or seas, rivers, and lakes provided substantial amounts of fish and shellfish. Groups in such areas were able to become more settled. About 15,000 years ago, the earth's climate entered a warming phase, and the glaciers began to retreat. As the earth became warmer, the climate became wetter, and more parts of the world were able to support sedentary or semi-sedentary groups of foragers.

In several of these places, foragers began planting seeds in the ground along with gathering wild grains, roots, and other foodstuffs. By observation, they learned the optimum times and places for planting. They removed unwanted plants through weeding and selected the seeds they planted in order to get crops that had favorable characteristics, such as larger edible parts. For grain crops, people chose plants with larger kernels clustered together that ripened all at one time and did not just fall on the ground, qualities that made harvesting more efficient. Through this human intervention, certain crops became **domesticated**, that is, modified by selective breeding so as to serve human needs, in this case to provide a more reliable source of food. Archaeologists trace the development and spread of plant raising by noting when the seeds and other plant parts they discover show evidence of domestication.

This early crop planting was done by individuals using hoes and digging sticks, and it is often termed **horticulture** to distinguish it from the later agriculture using plows. In some places, digging sticks were weighted with stones to make them more effective (earlier archaeologists thought these stones were the killing parts of war clubs). Intentional crop planting developed first in the area archaeologists call the Fertile Crescent, which runs from present-day Lebanon,

- **Agricultural Revolution** Dramatic transformation in human history resulting from the change from foraging to raising crops and animals.
- **domesticated** Plants and animals modified by selective breeding so as to serve human needs; domesticated animals will behave in specific ways and breed in captivity.
- **horticulture** Crop raising done with hand tools and human power.

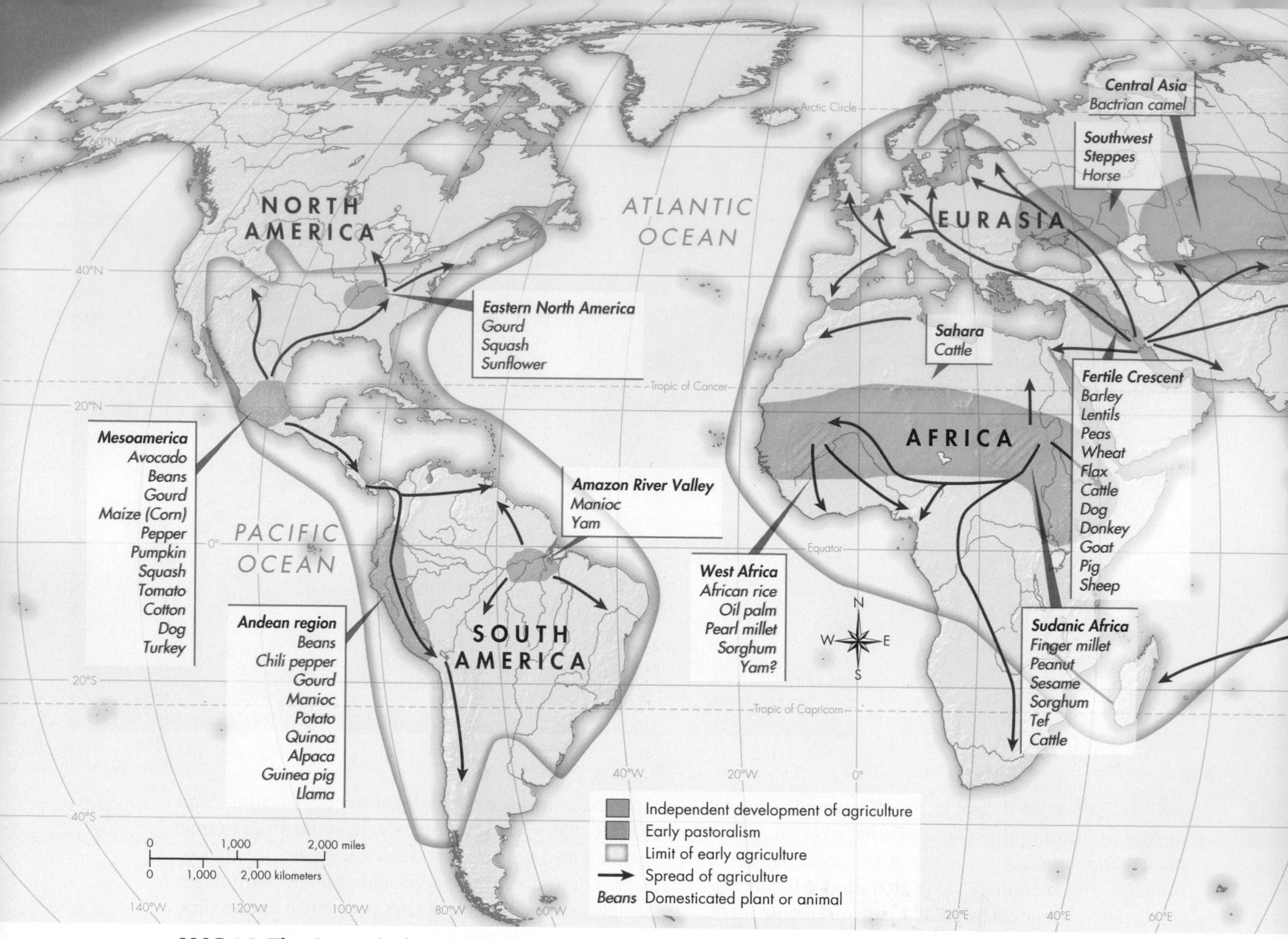

MAP 1.2 The Spread of Agriculture and Pastoralism Local plants and animals were domesticated in many different places. Agriculturalists and pastoralists spread the knowledge of how to raise them, and spread the plants and animals themselves through migration, trade, and conquest.

Israel, and Jordan north to Turkey and then south to the Iran-Iraq border (Map 1.2). About 9000 B.C.E. people there began to plant seeds of the wild wheat and barley they had already been harvesting, along with seeds of legume crops, such as peas and lentils, and of the flax with which they made linen cloth. They then modified these crops through domestication. By about 8000 B.C.E. people were growing sorghum and millet in parts of the Nile River Valley, and perhaps yams in western Africa. By about 7000 B.C.E. they were growing domesticated rice, millet, and legumes in China; yams and taro in Papua New Guinea; and perhaps squash in Mesoamerica. In each of these places, the development of horticulture occurred independently, and it may have happened in other parts of the world as well. Archaeological evidence does not survive well in tropical areas like Southeast Asia and the Amazon Basin, which may have been additional sites of plant domestication.

The Fertile Crescent

Black Sea
ANATOLIA
Çatal Hüyük
MESOPOTAMIA
Tigris R.
Euphrates R.
ARABIAN DESERT
Probable ancient coastline
Fertile Crescent

Nowhere do archaeological remains alone answer the question of who within any group first began to cultivate crops, but the fact that, among foragers, women were primarily responsible for gathering plant products suggests that they may also have been the first to plant seeds in the ground. In many parts of the world, crops continued to be planted with hoes and digging sticks for millennia, and crop raising remained primarily women's work, while men hunted or later raised animals.

Why, after living successfully as foragers for tens of thousands of years, did humans in so many parts of the world all begin raising crops at about the same time? The answer to this question is not clear, but crop rais-

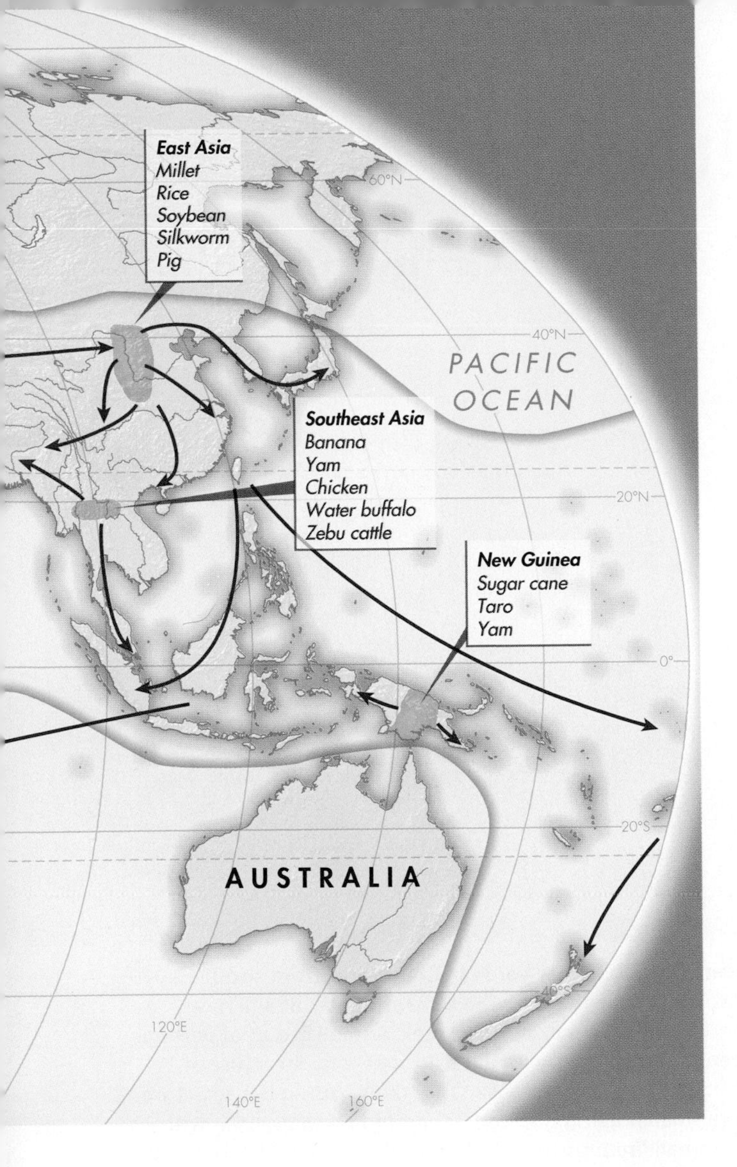

ing may have resulted from population pressures in those parts of the world where the warming climate provided more food. More food meant lower child mortality and longer life spans, which allowed communities to grow. Naturally occurring and then planted foods included cereal crops, which were soft enough for babies to eat, so that women could stop nursing their children at a younger age. Women lost the contraceptive effects of breast-feeding, so children may have been born at more frequent intervals, further speeding up population growth. Thus people had a choice: they could move to a new area—the solution that foragers had relied on when faced with the problem of food scarcity—or they could develop ways to increase the food supply to keep up with population growth, a solution that the warming climate was making possible. They chose the latter and began to plant more intensively, beginning cycles of expanding population and intensification of land use that have continued to today.

A recent archaeological find at Göbekli Tepe in present-day Turkey, at the northern edge of the Fertile Crescent, suggests that cultural factors may have played a role in the development of agriculture. Here, around 9000 B.C.E. hundreds of people came together to build rings of massive, multi-ton, elaborately carved limestone pillars and then covered them with dirt and built more. The people who created this site lived some distance away, where archaeological evidence indicates they first carved the pillars. The evidence also reveals that they ate wild game and plants, not crops. The project may have unintentionally spurred the development of new methods of food production that would allow the many workers to be fed efficiently. Indeed, it is very near here that evidence of the world's oldest domesticated wheat has been discovered. Archaeologists speculate that the symbolic, cultural, or perhaps religious importance of the structure can help explain why the people building it changed from foraging to agriculture.

Whatever the reasons for the move from foraging to crop raising, within several centuries of initial crop planting, people in the Fertile Crescent, parts of China, and the Nile Valley were relying on domesticated food products alone. They built permanent houses near one another in villages surrounded by fields, and they invented new ways of storing foods, such as in pottery made from clay. (See "Viewpoints 1.2: Stone Age Houses in Chile and China," page 18.) Villages were closer together than were the camps of foragers, so population density as well as total population grew.

A field of planted and weeded crops yields ten to one hundred times as much food—measured in calories—as the same area of naturally occurring plants, a benefit that would have been evident to early crop planters. It also requires much more labor, however, which was provided both by the greater number of people in the community and by those people working longer hours. In contrast to the twenty hours a week foragers spent on obtaining food, farming peoples were often in the fields from dawn to dusk, particularly during planting and harvest time, but also during the rest of the growing year because weeding was a constant task. Early farmers were also less healthy than foragers were. Their narrower range of foodstuffs made them more susceptible to disease and nutritional deficiencies such as anemia.

Foragers who lived at the edge of horticultural communities appear to have recognized the negative aspects of crop raising, for they did not immediately adopt this new way of life. Instead farming spread when a village became too large and some residents moved to a new area, cleared land, planted seeds, and built a new village, sometimes intermarrying with the local people. Because the population of farming communities grew so much faster than that of foragers,

Primary Sources

Viewpoints 1.2

Stone Age Houses in Chile and China

• *One of the central issues facing most human groups has been shelter from the elements. People's varying solutions to this issue reflect the environmental challenges and opportunities offered by their particular surroundings. Not only are houses physical structures, however, but they also reflect, communicate, and shape cultural and social values. The photographs on this page show the remains of houses built during the Paleolithic and Neolithic periods in two parts of the world very far from one another.*

Monte Verde Monte Verde in Chile dates from about 12,000 B.C.E. The archaeologists who have studied this site have concluded that here, along a creek, a small group of perhaps twenty to thirty people built a 20-foot-long structure of wooden poles covered by animal skins. Within the structure were smaller living quarters separated by skins, each with its own small fire pit, around which archaeologists have found stone tools, rope made of reeds, and many different types of foraged food, including wild potatoes and seaweed that came from coastal areas far away. (Courtesy of Tom D. Dillehay)

QUESTIONS FOR ANALYSIS

1. From the photographs and the descriptions, what similarities and differences do you see in the two types of houses?
2. Monte Verde was a Paleolithic community of foragers, and Banpo a Neolithic community of agriculturalists. How might the differences between the two houses have been shaped by the technology of food production? What other factors might account for the differences?
3. It is easy to see the vast differences between these houses and those of today, but what similarities do you find? What social and cultural values might lie behind these similarities?

Banpo The village of Banpo near Xi'an in China dates from about 4500 B.C.E. Archaeologists have concluded that a group of several hundred people built fifty or so houses there, along with kilns for making pottery and cellars for storage. They built each house by digging a shallow hole as a foundation, surrounding this with walls made of stakes interwoven with branches and twigs, and plastering this with mud, which dried to become wind and water resistant. They made the roof out of thatch made from millet and rice stalks, grains they raised that formed the main part of their diet. (JTB Photo/SuperStock)

Pillar at Göbekli Tepe The huge limestone pillars arranged in rings at the Paleolithic site Göbekli Tepe are somewhat humanoid in shape, and the carvings are of dangerous animals, including lions, boars, foxes, snakes, vultures, and scorpions. The structure required enormous skill and effort of the people who built it, and clearly had great importance to them. (Vincent J. Musi/National Geographic Creative)

however, horticulture quickly spread into fertile areas. By about 6500 B.C.E. farming had spread northward from the Fertile Crescent into Greece, and by 4000 B.C.E. farther northward all the way to Britain; by 4500 B.C.E. it had spread southward into Ethiopia. At the same time, crop raising spread out from other areas in which it was first developed, and slowly larger and larger parts of China, South and Southeast Asia, and East Africa became home to horticultural villages.

People adapted crops to their local environments, choosing seeds that had qualities that were beneficial, such as drought resistance. They also domesticated new kinds of crops. In the Americas, for example, by about 3000 B.C.E. corn was domesticated in southern Mexico and potatoes and quinoa in the Andes region of South America, and by about 2500 B.C.E. squash and beans in eastern North America. These crops then spread, so that by about 1000 B.C.E. people in much of what is now the western United States were raising corn, beans, and squash. In the Indus Valley of South Asia, people were growing dates, mangoes, sesame seeds, and cotton along with grains and legumes by 4000 B.C.E. Accordingly, crop raising led to dramatic human alteration of the environment.

Certain planted crops eventually came to be grown over huge areas of land, so that some scientists describe the Agricultural Revolution as a revolution of codependent domestication: humans domesticated crops, but crops also "domesticated" humans so that they worked long hours spreading particular crops around the world. Of these, corn has probably been the most successful; more than half a million square miles around the world are now planted in corn.

In some parts of the world horticulture led to a dramatic change in the way of life, but in others it did not. Horticulture can be easily combined with gathering and hunting, as plots of land are usually small; many cultures, including some in Papua New Guinea and North America, remained mixed foragers and horticulturists for thousands of years. Especially in deeply wooded areas, people cleared small plots by chopping and burning the natural vegetation, and planted crops in successive years until the soil eroded or lost its fertility, a method termed "slash and burn." They then moved to another area and began the process again, perhaps returning to the first plot many years later, after the soil had rejuvenated itself. Groups using shifting slash-and-burn cultivation remained small and continued to rely on the surrounding forest for much of their food.

Animal Domestication and the Rise of Pastoralism

At roughly the same time that they domesticated certain plants, people also domesticated animals. The earliest animal to be domesticated was the dog, which separated genetically as a subspecies from wolves at least 15,000 years ago and perhaps earlier. The mechanism of dog domestication is hotly debated: did it result only from human action, as foragers chose and bred animals that would help them with the hunt rather than attack them, or was it also caused by selective pressure resulting from wolf action, as animals less afraid of human contact came around campsites and then bred with one another? However it happened, the relationship benefited both: humans gained dogs' better senses of smell and hearing and their body warmth, and dogs gained new food sources and safer surroundings. Not surprisingly, humans and domestic dogs migrated together, including across the land bridges to the Americas and on boats to Pacific islands.

Sheep Herders in Western China Pastoral economies thrive in many parts of the world today, particularly in areas that are too dry for agriculture, including central Australia, Central Asia, northern and western Africa, and much of the U.S. West. As in early pastoralism, contemporary herders choose and breed their animals for qualities that will allow them to prosper in the local environment. (Yvan Travert/akg-images)

Dogs fit easily into a foraging lifestyle, but humans also domesticated animals that led them to completely alter their way of life. In about 9000 B.C.E., at the same time they began to raise crops, people in the Fertile Crescent domesticated wild goats and sheep, probably using them first for meat, and then for milk, skins, and eventually fleece (see Map 1.2). They learned from observation and experimentation that traits are passed down from generation to generation, and they began to breed the goats and sheep selectively for qualities that they wanted, including larger size, greater strength, better coats, increased milk production, and more even temperaments. Sometimes they trained dogs to assist them in herding, and then selectively bred the dogs for qualities that were advantageous for this task. The book of Genesis in the Bible, written in the Fertile Crescent sometime in the first millennium B.C.E., provides an early example of selective breeding. Jacob makes a deal with his father-in-law to take only those goats and sheep that are spotted, but he secretly increases the number of spotted animals in the flock by placing a spotted stick "before the eyes . . . of the strongest of the flocks . . . whenever they were breeding" so that more and stronger spotted animals were born (Genesis 30:41). This method was based on the idea—accepted for a very long time—that what a pregnant animal or woman saw during pregnancy would influence the outcome; although this notion has been firmly rejected in modern science, the Bible notes that the scheme was successful and that Jacob "grew exceedingly rich, and had large flocks."

Sometime after goats and sheep, pigs were domesticated in both the Fertile Crescent and China, as were chickens in southern Asia. Like domesticated crops, domesticated animals eventually far outnumbered their wild counterparts. For example, in the United States today (excluding Alaska), there are about 77 million dogs, compared to about 6,000 wolves. (Including Alaska would add about 150,000 dogs and 10,000 wolves.) There are more than 1.5 billion cattle, with enormous consequences for the environment. Animal domestication also shaped human evolution; groups that relied on animal milk and milk products for a significant part of their diet tended to develop the ability to digest milk as adults, while those that did not remained lactose intolerant as adults, the normal condition for mammals.

Sheep and goats allow themselves to be herded, and people developed a new form of living, **pastoralism**, based on herding and raising livestock. In areas with sufficient rainfall and fertile soil, pastoralism can be relatively sedentary and thus is easily combined with horticulture; people built pens for animals, or in colder climates constructed special buildings or took them into their houses. They learned that animal manure increases crop yields, so they gathered the manure from enclosures and used it as fertilizer.

- **pastoralism** An economic system based on herding flocks of goats, sheep, cattle, or other animals.

Increased contact with animals and their feces also increased human contact with various sorts of disease-causing pathogens, including minor illnesses such as the common cold and deadly killers such as influenza, bubonic plague, and smallpox. This was particularly the case where humans and animals lived in tight quarters. Thus pastoralists and agriculturalists developed illnesses that had not plagued foragers, and the diseases became endemic, that is, widely found within a region without being deadly. Ultimately people who lived with animals developed resistance to some of these illnesses, but foragers' lack of resistance to many illnesses meant that they died more readily after coming into contact with new endemic diseases, as was the case when Europeans brought smallpox to the Americas in the sixteenth century.

In drier areas, flocks need to travel long distances from season to season to obtain enough food, so some pastoralists became nomadic. Nomadic pastoralists often gather wild plant foods as well, but they tend to rely primarily on their flocks of animals for food. Pastoralism was well suited to areas where the terrain or climate made crop planting difficult, such as mountains, deserts, dry grasslands, and tundras. Eventually other grazing animals, including cattle, camels, horses, yak, and reindeer, also became the basis of pastoral economies in Central and West Asia, many parts of Africa, and far northern Europe.

Plow Agriculture

Horticulture and pastoralism brought significant changes to human ways of life, but the domestication of certain large animals had an even bigger impact. Cattle and water buffalo were domesticated in some parts of Asia and North Africa in which they occurred naturally by at least 7000 B.C.E., and horses, donkeys, and camels by about 4000 B.C.E. All these animals can be trained to carry people or burdens on their backs and to pull loads dragged behind them, two qualities that are rare among the world's animal species. In many parts of the world, including North America and much of South America and sub-Saharan Africa, no naturally occurring large species could be domesticated. In the mountainous regions of South America, llamas and alpacas were domesticated to carry packs, but the steep terrain made it difficult to use them to pull loads. The domestication of large animals dramatically increased the power available to humans to carry out their tasks, which had both an immediate effect in the societies in which this happened and a long-term effect when these societies later encountered societies in which human labor remained the only source of power.

The pulling power of animals came to matter most, because it could be applied to food production. Sometime in the seventh millennium B.C.E., people attached wooden sticks to frames that animals dragged through the soil, thus breaking it up and allowing seeds to sprout more easily. These simple scratch plows were pulled first by cattle and water buffalo, and later by horses. Over millennia, moldboards—angled pieces that turned the soil over, bringing fresh soil to the top—were added, which reduced the time needed to plow and allowed each person to work more land.

Using plows, Neolithic people produced a significant amount of surplus food, which meant that some people in the community could spend their days performing other tasks, increasing the division of labor. Surplus food had to be stored, and some began to specialize in making products for storage, such as pots, baskets, bags, bins, and other kinds of containers. Others specialized in making tools, houses, and other items needed in village life, or for producing specific types of food, including alcoholic beverages made from fermented fruits and grains. Families and households became increasingly interdependent, trading food for other commodities or services. In the same way that foragers had continually improved their tools and methods, people improved the processes through which they made things. Sometime in the fifth millennium B.C.E., pot makers in Mesopotamia invented the potter's wheel, which by a millennium later had been

Neolithic Pot, from China, ca. 2600–2300 B.C.E. This two-handled pot, made of baked ceramics in the Yellow River Valley, is painted in a swirling red and black geometric design. Neolithic agricultural communities produced a wide array of storage containers for keeping food and other commodities from one season to the next. (Museum purchase, Fowler McCormack, Class of 1921. Fund. y1979-94. Photo: Bruce M. White/Princeton University Art Museum/Art Resource, NY)

adapted for use on carts and plows pulled by animals. Wheeled vehicles led to road building, and wheels and roads together made it possible for people and goods to travel long distances more easily, whether for settlement, trade, or conquest.

Stored food was also valuable and could become a source of conflict, as could other issues in villages where people lived close together. Villagers needed more complex rules than did foragers about how food was to be distributed and how different types of work were to be valued. Certain individuals began to specialize in the determination and enforcement of these rules, and informal structures of power gradually became more formalized as elites developed. These elites then distributed resources to their own advantage, often using force to attain and maintain their power.

Neolithic Society

☐ How did growing social and gender hierarchies and expanding networks of trade increase the complexity of human society in the Neolithic period?

The division of labor that plow agriculture allowed led to the creation of **social hierarchies**, the divisions between rich and poor, elites and common people that have been a central feature of human society since the Neolithic era. Plow agriculture also strengthened differentiation based on gender, with men becoming more associated with the world beyond the household and women with the domestic realm. Social hierarchies were reinforced over generations as children inherited goods and status from their parents; even the gods were increasingly understood to be arranged in a hierarchy, and assuring fertility became the most important religious practice. People increasingly communicated ideas within local and regional networks of exchange, just as they traded foodstuffs, tools, and other products.

Social Hierarchies and Slavery

Archaeological finds from Neolithic villages, particularly burials, show signs of growing social differentiation. Some people were buried with significant amounts of jewelry, household goods, weapons, and other objects, while others were buried with very little. How were some people able to attain such power over their neighbors that they could even take valuable commodities with them to the grave? This is one of the key questions in all of human history. Written sources do not provide a clear answer, because social hierarchies were already firmly in place by the time writing was invented, so that scholars have largely relied on archaeological sources.

Within foraging groups, some individuals already had more authority because of their links with the world of gods and spirits, positions as heads of kin groups, or personal characteristics. These three factors gave individuals advantages in agricultural societies, and the advantages became more significant over time as there were more resources to control. Priests and shamans developed more elaborate rituals and became full-time religious specialists, exchanging their services in interceding with the gods for food. In many communities, religious specialists were the first to work out formal rules of conduct that later became oral and written codes of law, generally explaining that these represented the will of the gods. The codes threatened divine punishment for those who broke them, and they often required people to accord deference to priests as the representatives of the gods, so that they became an elite group with special privileges.

Individuals who were the heads of large families or kin groups had control over the labor of others, and this power became more significant when that labor brought material goods that could be stored. Material goods—plows, sheep, cattle, sheds, pots, carts—gave one the ability to amass still more material goods, and the gap between those who had them and those who did not widened. Storage also allowed wealth to be retained over long periods of time and handed down from one family member to another, so that over generations small differences in wealth grew larger. The ability to control the labor of others could also come from physical strength, a charismatic personality, or leadership talents, and such traits may have also led to greater wealth.

Wealth itself could command labor, as individuals or families could buy the services of others to work for them or impose their wishes through force, hiring soldiers to threaten or carry out violence. Eventually some individuals bought others outright. As with social hierarchies in general, slavery predates written records, but it developed in almost all agricultural societies. Like animals, slaves were a source of physical power for their owners, providing them an opportunity to amass still more wealth and influence. In the long era before the invention of fossil fuel technology, the ability to exploit animal and human labor was the most impor-

- **social hierarchies** Divisions between rich and poor, elites and common people that have been a central feature of human society since the Neolithic era.
- **patriarchy** Social system in which men have more power and access to resources than women and some men are dominant over other men.

tant mark of distinction between elites and the rest of the population. As we will see in later chapters, landownership was often what distinguished elites from others, but that land was valuable only if there were people living on it who were required to labor for the owner.

Gender Hierarchies and Inheritance

Along with hierarchies based on wealth and power, the development of agriculture was intertwined with a hierarchy based on gender. The system in which men have more power and access to resources than women and some men are dominant over other men is called **patriarchy**. Every society in the world that has left written records has been patriarchal, but patriarchy came before writing, and searching for its origins involves interpreting many different types of sources. Some scholars see the origins of gender inequality in the hominid past, noting that male chimpanzees form alliances to gain status against other males and engage in cooperative attacks on females, which might have also happened among early hominids. Other scholars see the origins in the Paleolithic, with the higher status of men in lineage groups.

Plow agriculture heightened patriarchy. Although farming with a hoe was often done by women, plow agriculture came to be a male task, perhaps because of men's upper-body strength or because plow agriculture was more difficult to combine with care for infants and small children than was horticulture. The earliest depictions of plowing are on Mesopotamian cylinder seals, and they invariably show men with the cattle and plows. At the same time that cattle began to be raised for pulling plows and carts rather than for meat, sheep began to be raised primarily for wool. Spinning thread and weaving cloth became primarily women's work; the earliest Egyptian hieroglyph for weaving is, in fact, a seated woman with a shuttle, and a Confucian moral saying from ancient China asserts that "men plow and women weave." Spinning and weaving were generally done indoors and involved simpler and cheaper tools than plowing; they could also be taken up and put down easily, and so could be done at the same time as other tasks.

Though in some ways this arrangement seems complementary, with each sex doing some of the necessary labor, plow agriculture increased gender hierarchy. Men's responsibility for plowing and other agricultural tasks took them outside the household more often than women's duties did, enlarging their opportunities for leadership. This role may have led to their being favored as inheritors of family land and the right to farm communally held land, because when inheritance systems were established in later millennia, they often favored sons when handing down land. In some places inheritance was traced through the female line, but in such systems women themselves did not necessarily inherit goods or property; instead a man inherited from his mother's brother rather than from his father. Accordingly, over generations, women's independent access to resources decreased, and it became increasingly difficult for women to survive without male support.

As inherited wealth became more important, men wanted to make sure that their sons were theirs, so they restricted their wives' movements and activities. This was especially the case among elite families. Among foragers and horticulturalists, women needed to be mobile for the group to survive; their labor outdoors was essential. Among agriculturalists, the labor of animals, slaves, and hired workers could substitute for that of women in families that could afford them. Thus in some Neolithic societies, there is evidence that women spent more and more of their time within the household, either indoors or behind walls and barriers that separated the domestic realm from the wider world. Social norms and ideals gradually reinforced this pattern, so that by the time written laws and other records emerged in the second millennium B.C.E., elite women were expected to work at tasks that would not take them beyond the household or away from male supervision. Non-elite women also tended to do work that could be done within or close by the household, such as cooking, cloth production, and the care of children, the elderly, and small animals. A special program set up under the third-century-B.C.E. Indian emperor Ashoka, for example, supported poor women by paying them to spin and weave in their own homes.

Social and gender hierarchies were enhanced over generations as wealth was passed down unequally, and they were also enhanced by rules and norms that shaped sexual relationships, particularly heterosexual ones. However their power originated, elites began to think of themselves as a group set apart from the rest by some element that made them distinctive—such as military prowess, natural superiority, or connections with a deity. They increasingly understood this distinctive quality to be hereditary and developed traditions—later codified as written laws—that stipulated which heterosexual relationships would pass this quality on, along with passing on wealth. Relationships between men and women from elite families were formalized as marriage, through which both status and wealth were generally passed down. Relationships between elite men and non-elite women generally did not function in this way, or did so to a lesser degree; the women were defined as concubines or mistresses, or simply as sexual outlets for powerful men. The 1780 B.C.E. Code of Hammurabi, for example, one of the world's earliest law codes, sets out differences in inheritance for the sons a man had with his wife and those he had with a servant or slave, while not mentioning daughters at all:

> If his wife bear sons to a man, [and] his maid-servant [has] also borne sons, [but] the father while still living . . . did not say to the sons of the maid-servant: "My sons," and then the father dies, then the sons of the maid-servant shall not share with the sons of the wife, but the freedom of the maid and her sons shall be granted.[2]

Relations between an elite woman and a non-elite man generally brought shame and dishonor to the woman's family and sometimes death to the man. (Early rules and laws about sex generally did not pay much attention to same-sex relations because these did not produce children that could threaten systems of inheritance.)

Thus, along with the distinctions among human groups that resulted from migration and were enhanced by endogamy, distinctions developed within groups that were reinforced by social endogamy, what we might think of as the selective breeding of people. Elite men tended to marry elite women, which in some cases resulted in actual physical differences over generations, as elites had more access to food and were able to become taller and stronger. By 1800 C.E., for example, men in the highest level of the English aristocracy were five inches taller than the average height of all English people.

No elite can be completely closed to newcomers, however, because the accidents of life and death, along with the genetic problems caused by repeated close intermarriage, make it difficult for any small group to survive over generations. Thus mechanisms were developed in many cultures to adopt boys into elite families, to legitimate the children of concubines and slave women, or to allow elite girls to marry men lower on the social hierarchy. All systems of inheritance also need some flexibility. The inheritance patterns in some cultures favored male heirs exclusively, but in others close relatives were favored over those more distant, even if this meant allowing daughters to inherit. The drive to keep wealth and property within a family or kin group often resulted in women inheriting, owning, and in some cases managing significant amounts of wealth, a pattern that continues today. Hierarchies of wealth and power thus intersected with hierarchies of gender in complex ways, and in many cultures age and marital status also played roles. In many European and African cultures, for example, widows were largely able to control their own property, while unmarried sons were often under their father's control even if they were adults.

Trade and Cross-Cultural Connections

The increase in food production brought by the development of plow agriculture allowed Neolithic villages to grow ever larger. By 7000 B.C.E. or so, some villages in the Fertile Crescent may have had as many as ten thousand residents. One of the best known of these, Çatal Hüyük in what is now modern Turkey, shows evidence of trade as well as of the specialization of labor. Çatal Hüyük's residents lived in mud-brick houses whose walls were covered in white plaster and whose interiors were kept very clean, for all trash was taken outside the town. The houses were built next to one another with no lanes or paths separating them, and people seem to have entered through holes in the roofs; the rooftops may have also served as a place for people to congregate, for there is no sign of large public buildings. The men and women of the town grew wheat, barley, peas, and almonds and raised sheep and perhaps cattle, though they also seem to have hunted. They made textiles, pots, figurines, baskets, carpets, copper and lead beads, and other goods, and decorated their houses with murals showing animal and human figures. They gathered, sharpened, and polished obsidian, a volcanic rock that could be used for knives, blades, and mirrors, and then traded it with neighboring towns, obtaining seashells and flint. From here the obsidian was exchanged still farther away, for Neolithic societies slowly developed local and then regional networks of exchange and communication.

Among the goods traded in some parts of the world was copper. Pure copper occurs close to the surface in some areas, and people, including those at Çatal Hüyük, hammered it into shapes for jewelry and tools. More often, copper, like most metals, occurs mixed with other materials in a type of rock called ore, and by about 5500 B.C.E. people in the Balkans had learned that copper could be extracted from ore by heating it in a smelting process. Smelted copper was poured into molds and made into spear points, axes, chisels, beads, and other objects. (See "Individuals in Society: The Iceman," at right.) Smelting techniques were discovered independently in many places around the world, including China, Southeast Asia, West Africa, and the Andes region. Pure copper is soft, but through experimentation artisans learned that it would become harder if they mixed it with other metals such as arsenic, zinc, or tin during heating, creating an alloy called bronze.

Because it was stronger than copper, bronze had a far wider range of uses, so much so that later historians decided that its adoption marked a new period in human history, the Bronze Age. Like all new technologies, bronze arrived at different times in different places, so the dates of the Bronze Age vary. It began

Individuals in Society

The Iceman

ON SEPTEMBER 19, 1991, TWO GERMAN VACATIONERS climbing in the Italian Alps came upon a corpse lying facedown and covered in ice. Scientists determined that the Iceman, as the corpse is generally known, died 5,300 years ago. He was between twenty-five and thirty-five years old at the time of his death, and he stood about five feet two inches tall. An autopsy revealed much about the man and his culture. The bluish tinge of his teeth showed a diet of milled grain, which proves that he came from an environment where crops were grown. The Iceman hunted as well as farmed: he was found with a bow and arrows and shoes of straw, and he wore a furry cap and a robe of animal skins that had been stitched together with thread made from grass.

The equipment discovered with the Iceman demonstrates that his people mastered several technologies. He carried a hefty copper ax, made by someone with a knowledge of metallurgy. In his quiver were numerous wooden arrow shafts and two finished arrows. The arrows had sharpened flint heads and feathers attached to the ends of the shafts with resin-like glue. Apparently the people of his culture knew the value of feathers to direct the arrow and thus had mastered the basics of ballistics. His bow was made of yew, a relatively rare wood in central Europe that is among the best for archers.

Yet a mystery still surrounds the Iceman. When his body was first discovered, scholars assumed that he was a hapless traveler overtaken in a fierce snowstorm. But the autopsy found an arrowhead lodged under his left shoulder. The Iceman was not alone on his last day. Someone was with him, and that someone had shot him from below and behind. The Iceman is the victim in the first murder mystery in Europe, and the case will never be solved.

The artifacts found with the body tell scientists much about how the Iceman lived. The Iceman's shoes, made with a twine framework stuffed with straw and covered with skin, indicate that he used all parts of the animals he hunted. (discovery: Courtesy, Roger Teissl; shoes: South Tyrol Museum of Archaeology, http://www.iceman.it)

QUESTIONS FOR ANALYSIS

1. What does the autopsy of the corpse indicate about the society in which the Iceman lived?
2. How do the objects found with the Iceman support the generalizations about Neolithic society in this chapter?

LaunchPad

Online Document Project

What can artifacts tell us about Neolithic society? Examine the objects found with the Iceman, and then complete a quiz and writing assignment based on the evidence and details from this chapter.

See inside the front cover to learn more.

Stone Circle at Nabta Playa, Egypt, ca. 4800 B.C.E. This circle of stones, erected when the Egyptian desert received much more rainfall than it does today, may have been a type of calendar marking the summer solstice. Circular arrangements of stones or ditches were constructed in many places during the Neolithic era, and most no doubt had calendrical, astronomical, and/or religious purposes. (Courtesy of Raymond Betz)

about 3000 B.C.E. in some places, and by about 2500 B.C.E. bronze technology was having an impact in many parts of the world, especially in weaponry. The end of the Bronze Age came with the adoption of iron technology, which also varied in its beginnings from 1200 B.C.E. to 300 B.C.E. (See "Global Trade: Iron," page 50.) All metals were expensive and hard to obtain, however, which meant that stone, wood, and bone remained important materials for tools and weapons long into the Bronze Age.

Objects were not the only things traded over increasingly long distances during the Neolithic period, for people also carried ideas as they traveled on foot or camels, and in boats, wagons, or carts. Knowledge about the seasons and the weather was vitally important for those who depended on crop raising, and agricultural peoples in many parts of the world began to calculate recurring patterns in the world around them, slowly developing calendars. Scholars have demonstrated that people built circular structures of mounded earth or huge upright stones to help them predict the movements of the sun and stars, including Nabta Playa, erected about 4500 B.C.E. in the desert west of the Nile Valley in Egypt, and Stonehenge, erected about 2500 B.C.E. in southern England.

The rhythms of the agricultural cycle and patterns of exchange also shaped religious beliefs and practices. Among foragers, human fertility is a mixed blessing, as too many children can overtax food supplies, but among crop raisers and pastoralists, fertility—of the land, animals, and people—is essential. Shamans and priests developed ever more elaborate rituals designed to assure fertility, in which the gods were often given something from a community's goods in exchange for their favor, such as food offerings, animal sacrifices, or sacred objects. In many places gods came to be associated with patterns of birth, growth, death, and regeneration. They could bring death and destruction, but they also created life. Figurines, carvings, and paintings from the Neolithic include pregnant women and women giving birth, men with erect penises, and creatures that are a combination of a man and a male animal such as a bull or goat. Like humans, the gods came to have a division of labor and a social hierarchy. Thus there were rain gods and sun gods, sky goddesses and moon goddesses, gods that assured the health of cattle or the growth of corn, goddesses of the hearth and home. Powerful father and mother gods sometimes presided, but they were challenged and overthrown by virile young male gods, often in epic battles. Thus, as human society was becoming more complex, so was the unseen world.

Chapter Summary

Through studying the physical remains of the past, sometimes with very new high-tech procedures such as DNA analysis, scholars have determined that human evolution involved a combination of factors, including bipedalism, larger brain size, spoken symbolic language, and longer periods of infancy. Humans invented ever more complex tools, many of which were made of stone, from which later scholars derived the name for this earliest period of human history, the Paleolithic era. These tools allowed Paleolithic peoples to shape the world around them. During this era, humans migrated out of Africa, adapting to many different environments and developing diverse cultures. Early humans lived in small groups of related individuals, moving through the landscape as foragers in the search for food. Social and gender hierarchies were probably much less pronounced than they would become later. Beginning around 50,000 B.C.E. people in many parts of the world began to decorate their surroundings with images that suggest they had developed ideas about supernatural or spiritual forces.

Beginning about 9000 B.C.E. people living in southwest Asia, and then elsewhere, began to plant seeds as well as gather wild crops, raise certain animals, and selectively breed both plants and animals to make them more useful to humans. This domestication of plants and animals was the most important change in human history and marked the beginning of the Neolithic era. Crop raising began as horticulture, in which people—often women—used hand tools to plant and harvest. Animal domestication began with sheep and goats, which were often herded from place to place, a system called pastoralism. The domestication of large animals led to plow agriculture, through which humans could raise much more food, and the world's population grew. Plow agriculture allowed for a greater division of labor, which strengthened social hierarchies based on wealth and gender. Neolithic agricultural communities developed technologies to meet their needs and often traded with one another for products that they could not obtain locally. Religious ideas came to reflect the new agricultural society, with fertility as the most important goal and the gods, like humans, arranged in a hierarchy.

CHRONOLOGY

ca. 4.4 million years ago	*Ardipithecus* evolve in Africa
ca. 2.5–4 million years ago	*Australopithecus* evolve in Africa
ca. 500,000–2 million years ago	*Homo erectus* evolve and spread out of Africa
ca. 250,000–9000 B.C.E.	Paleolithic era
ca. 250,000 years ago	*Homo sapiens* evolve in Africa
ca. 30,000–150,000 years ago	Neanderthals flourish in Europe and western Asia
ca. 120,000 years ago	*Homo sapiens* migrate out of Africa to Eurasia
ca. 50,000 years ago	Human migration to Australia
ca. 20,000–30,000 years ago	Possible human migration from Asia to the Americas
ca. 25,000 B.C.E.	Earliest evidence of woven cloth and baskets
ca. 15,000 B.C.E.	Earliest evidence of bows and atlatls; humans cross the Bering Strait land bridge to the Americas
ca. 15,000–10,000 B.C.E.	Final retreat of glaciers; megafaunal extinctions
ca. 9000 B.C.E.	Beginning of the Neolithic; horticulture; domestication of sheep and goats
ca. 7000 B.C.E.	Domestication of cattle; plow agriculture
ca. 5500 B.C.E.	Smelting of copper
ca. 5000 B.C.E.	Invention of pottery wheel
ca. 3200 B.C.E.	Earliest known invention of writing
ca. 3000 B.C.E.	Development of wheeled transport; beginning of bronze technology
ca. 2500 B.C.E.	Bronze technology becomes common in many areas; beginning of the Bronze Age

NOTES

1. Chinook Blessing Litany, in Wilma Mankiller, ed., *Every Day Is a Good Day: Reflections by Contemporary Indigenous Women* (Golden, Colo.: Fulcrum Publishing, 2004), pp. 170, 171. Copyright © 2004 by Wilma P. Mankiller. Used by permission of Fulcrum Publishing.
2. Code of Hammurabi, article 171, translated by L. W. King (1910), Internet Ancient History Sourcebook, http://www.fordham.edu/halsall/ancient/hamcode.html#text.

CONNECTIONS

The human story is often told as a narrative of unstoppable progress toward greater complexity. The simple stone hand axes of the Paleolithic were replaced by the specialized tools of the Neolithic and then by bronze, iron, steel, plastic, and silicon. The small kin groups of the Paleolithic gave way to Neolithic villages that grew ever larger until they became cities and eventually today's megalopolises. Egalitarian foragers became stratified by divisions of wealth and power that were formalized as aristocracies, castes, and social classes, leading to today's vast divisions between wealth and poverty. Oral rituals of worship, healing, and celebration in which everyone participated grew into a dizzying array of religions, philosophies, and branches of knowledge presided over by specialists including priests, scholars, scientists, doctors, generals, and entertainers. The rest of this book traces this story and explores the changes over time that are the central thread of history.

As you examine what—particularly in world history—can seem to be a staggering number of developments, it is also important to remember that many things were slow to change and that some aspects of human life in the Neolithic, or even the Paleolithic, continued. Foraging, horticulture, pastoralism, and agriculture have been the primary economic activities of most people throughout the entire history of the world. Though today there are only a few foraging groups in very isolated areas, there are significant numbers of horticulturalists and pastoralists, and their numbers were much greater just a century ago. At that point the vast majority of the world's people still made their living directly through agriculture. The social patterns set in early agricultural societies—with most of the population farming the land and a small number of elite who lived off their labor—lasted for millennia. You have no doubt recognized other similarities between the early peoples discussed in this chapter and the people you see around you, and it is important to keep these continuities in mind as you embark on your examination of human history.

Review and Explore

Make It Stick

LearningCurve

Go online and use LearningCurve to retain what you've read.

Identify Key Terms

Identify and explain the significance of each item below.

hominids (p. 3)
Paleolithic era (p. 4)
foraging (p. 4)
Neolithic era (p. 4)
Neanderthals (p. 7)
megafaunal extinction (p. 9)
division of labor (p. 10)
animism (p. 12)
shamans (p. 12)
Agricultural Revolution (p. 15)
domesticated (p. 15)
horticulture (p. 15)
pastoralism (p. 20)
social hierarchies (p. 22)
patriarchy (p. 23)

Review the Main Ideas

Answer the focus questions from each section of the chapter.

1. How did humans evolve, and where did they migrate? (p. 2)
2. What were the key features of Paleolithic society? (p. 9)
3. How did plant and animal domestication develop, and what effects did it have on human society? (p. 14)
4. How did growing social and gender hierarchies and expanding networks of trade increase the complexity of human society in the Neolithic period? (p. 22)

Make Connections

Analyze the larger developments and continuities within and across chapters.

1. Why is the Agricultural Revolution called the most important change in human history?
2. What continuities persisted between the Paleolithic and Neolithic eras?
3. Why and how did social hierarchies develop?

LaunchPad
Online Document Project

The Iceman's World

What can artifacts tell us about Neolithic society?
Examine the objects found with the Iceman, and then complete a quiz and writing assignment based on the evidence and details from this chapter.

See inside the front cover to learn more.

Suggested Reading

Burenhelt, Goren. *People of the Stone Age: Hunter-Gatherers and Early Farmers.* 1994. Short articles and extensive illustrations of the transition to agriculture, presented as part of the American Museum of Natural History's excellent *Illustrated History of Humankind.*

Christian, David. *Maps of Time: An Introduction to Big History.* 2002. An elegant examination of the story of the cosmos, from the Big Bang to today.

Diamond, Jared. *Guns, Germs, and Steel: The Fates of Human Societies*, 2d ed. 2005. Extremely influential and wide-ranging examination of the long-term impact of agriculture, animal domestication, and the environment on differing rates of development around the world.

Ehrlich, Paul R., and Anne H. Ehrlich. *Dominant Animal: Human Evolution and the Environment.* 2009. By two of today's leading biologists; traces the impact of humans on the planet from the Paleolithic to today.

Fagan, Brian M. *People of the Earth: An Introduction to World Prehistory*, 13th ed. 2009. A thorough survey that presents up-to-date scholarship, designed for students.

Gamble, Clive. *Timewalkers: The Prehistory of Global Colonization.* 2006. A lively examination of how and why humans came to be everywhere in the world.

Hawkes, Kristen, and Richard R. Paine. *The Evolution of Human Life History.* 2006. A series of articles that examine the ways in which the distinctions between humans and other animals came to be.

Hrdy, Sarah Blaffer. *Mothers and Others: The Evolutionary Origins of Human Understanding.* 2009. Provides the new, more egalitarian perspective on evolution.

Lewin, Roger. *Human Evolution: An Illustrated Introduction*, 5th ed. 2004. A relatively compact and very readable introduction that includes the newest archaeological and chemical evidence.

Lewis-Williams, David, and David Pearce. *Inside the Neolithic Mind: Consciousness, Cosmos, and the Realm of the Gods.* 2005. An analysis of Neolithic belief systems and the cultural products that resulted from them.

McCarter, Susan Foster. *Neolithic.* 2007. An introductory survey of the development and impact of agriculture, with many illustrations.

Pinker, Steven. *How the Mind Works*, 2d ed. 2009. An insightful examination of how the mind evolved, along with a survey of modern brain science.

Pollan, Michael. *The Omnivore's Dilemma: A Natural History of Four Meals.* 2007. A witty and thoughtful look at the way food is produced today, and how this contrasts with our foraging past.

Tattersall, Ian. *Masters of the Planet: The Search for Our Human Origins.* 2012. An up-to-date survey of how humans evolved, in a lively narrative written for general readers.

The Rise of the State in Southwest Asia and the Nile Valley

3200–500 B.C.E.

2

Persian Archers

In this colorful decorative frieze made of glazed brick, men wearing long Persian robes and laced ankle boots carry spears, bows, and quivers. This reconstruction in the Louvre Museum in Paris was made from material found in the palace of King Darius I of Persia in Susa, built about 510 B.C.E. Enough bricks were found there to suggest that there were originally many archers, perhaps representing Darius's royal guards or symbolizing the entire Persian people. (Louvre, Paris, France/Erich Lessing/Art Resource, NY)

LearningCurve
After reading the chapter, go online and use LearningCurve to retain what you've read.

Chapter Preview

Five thousand years ago, humans were living in most parts of the planet. They had designed technologies to meet the challenges presented by deep forests and jungles, steep mountains, and blistering deserts. As the climate changed, they adapted, building boats to cross channels created by melting glaciers and finding new sources of food when old sources were no longer plentiful. In some places the new sources included domesticated plants and animals, which allowed people to live in much closer proximity to one another than they had as foragers.

That proximity created opportunities, as larger groups of people pooled their knowledge to deal with life's challenges, but it also created problems. Human history from that point on can be seen as a response to these opportunities, challenges, and conflicts. As small villages grew into cities, people continued to develop technologies and systems to handle new issues. To control their more complex structures, people created systems of governance that were not based on the kin group, as well as military forces and taxation systems. In some places they invented writing to record taxes, inventories, and payments, and they later put writing to other uses. The first places where these new technologies and systems were introduced were the Tigris and Euphrates River Valleys of southwest Asia and the Nile Valley of northeast Africa, areas whose histories became linked through trade, military conquests, and migrations.

Writing, Cities, and States

- How does writing shape what we can know about the past, and how did writing develop to meet the needs of cities and states?

The remains of buildings, burial sites, weapons, tools, artwork, and other handmade objects provide our only evidence of how people lived, thought, felt, and died during most of the human past. Beginning about 5,000 years ago, however, people in some parts of the world developed a new technology, writing, the surviving examples of which have provided a much wider range of information. Writing developed to meet the needs of more complex urban societies that are often referred to as "civilizations." In particular, writing met the needs of the state, a new political form that developed during the time covered in this chapter.

Written Sources and the Human Past

Writing is closely tied to the idea of history itself. The term *history* comes from the Greek word *historia*, coined by Herodotus (hi-ROD-duh-tuhs) (ca. 484–ca. 425 B.C.E.) in the fifth century B.C.E. to describe his inquiry into the past. As Herodotus used them, the

Clay Letter Written in Cuneiform and Its Envelope, ca. 1850 B.C.E. In this letter from a city in Anatolia, located on the northern edge of the Fertile Crescent in what is now southern Turkey, a Mesopotamian merchant complains to his brother at home, hundreds of miles away, that life is hard and comments on the trade in silver, gold, tin, and textiles. Correspondents often enclosed letters in clay envelopes and sealed them by rolling a cylinder seal across the clay, leaving the impression of a scene, just as you might use a stamped wax seal today. Here the very faint impression of the sender's seal at the bottom shows a person, probably the owner of the seal, being led in a procession toward a king or god. (© The Trustees of the British Museum/Art Resource, NY)

words *inquiry* and *history* are the same. Herodotus based his *Histories*, at their core a study of the origins of the wars between the Persians and the Greeks that occurred about the time he was born, on the oral testimony of people he had met as he traveled. Many of these people had been participants in the wars, and Herodotus was proud that he could rely so much on the eyewitness accounts of the people involved. Today we call this methodology "oral history," and it remains a vital technique for studying the recent past. Following the standard practice of the time, Herodotus most likely read his *Histories* out loud at some sort of public gathering. Herodotus also wrote down his histories and consulted written documents. From his day until quite recently, this aspect of his methods has defined history and separated it from prehistory: history came to be regarded as the part of the human past for which there are written records. In this view, history began with the invention of writing in the fourth millennium B.C.E. in a few parts of the world.

As noted in Chapter 1, this line between history and prehistory has largely broken down. Historians who study human societies that developed systems of writing continue to use many of the same types of physical evidence as do those who study societies without writing. For some cultures, the writing or record-keeping systems have not yet been deciphered, so our knowledge of these people also depends largely on physical evidence. Scholars can read the writing of a great many societies, however, adding greatly to what we can learn about them.

Much ancient writing survives only because it was copied and recopied, sometimes years after it was first produced. The oldest known copy of Herodotus's *Histories*, for example, dates from about 900 C.E., nearly a millennium and a half after he finished this book. The survival of a work means that someone from a later period—and often a long chain of someones—judged it worthy of the time, effort, and resources needed to produce copies. The copies may not be completely accurate, either because the scribe made an error or because he (or, much less often, she) decided to change something. Historians studying ancient works thus often try to find as many early copies as they can and compare them to arrive at the version they think is closest to the original.

The works considered worthy of copying tend to be those that, like the *Histories*, are about the political and military events involving major powers, those that record religious traditions, or those that come from authors who were later regarded as important. By contrast, written sources dealing with the daily life of ordinary men and women were few to begin with and were rarely saved or copied because they were not considered significant.

Some early written texts survive in their original form because people inscribed them in stone, shells, bone, or other hard materials, intending them to be permanent. Stones with inscriptions were often erected in the open in public places for all to see, so they include text that leaders felt had enduring importance, such as laws, religious proclamations, decrees, and treaties. (The names etched in granite on the Vietnam Veterans Memorial in Washington, D.C., are perhaps the best-known modern example, but inscriptions can be found on nearly every major public building.) Sometimes this permanence was accidental: in ancient Mesopotamia (in the area of modern Iraq), all writing was initially made up of indentations on soft clay tablets, which then hardened. Hundreds of thousands of these tablets have survived, the oldest dating to about 3200 B.C.E., and from them historians have learned about many aspects of everyday life. By contrast, writing in Egypt at the same time was often done in ink on papyrus sheets, made from a plant that grows abundantly in Egypt. Some of these papyrus sheets have survived, but papyrus is much more fragile than hardened clay, so most have disintegrated. In China, the oldest surviving writing is on bones and turtle shells from about 1200 B.C.E., but it is clear that writing was done much earlier on less permanent materials such as silk and bamboo. (For more on the origins of Chinese writing, see page 95.)

However they have survived and however limited they are, written records often become scholars' most important original sources for investigating the past. Thus the discovery of a new piece of written evidence from the ancient past—such as the Dead Sea Scrolls, which contain sections of the Hebrew Bible and were first seen by scholars in 1948—is always a major event. But reconstructing and deciphering what are often crumbling documents can take decades, and disputes about how these records affect our understanding of the past can go on forever.

Cities and the Idea of Civilization

Along with writing, the growth of cities has often been a way that scholars mark the increasing complexity of human societies. In the ancient world, residents of cities generally viewed themselves as more advanced and sophisticated than rural folk—a judgment still made today. They saw themselves as more "civilized," a word that comes from the Latin adjective *civilis*, which refers to a citizen either of a town or of a larger political unit such as an empire.

This depiction of people as either civilized or uncivilized was gradually extended to whole societies. Beginning in the eighteenth century European scholars described those societies in which political, economic, and social organizations operated on a large scale, not primarily through families and kin groups, as "civilizations." Civilizations had cities; laws that governed human relationships; codes of manners and social conduct that regulated how people were to behave; and scientific, philosophical, and theological ideas that explained the larger world. Generally only societies that used writing were judged to be civilizations, for writing allowed more permanent expression of thoughts, ideas, and feelings. Human societies in which people were nomadic or lived in small villages without formal laws, and in which traditions and ideas were passed down orally, were generally not regarded as civilizations.

Until the middle of the twentieth century, historians often referred to the earliest places where writing and cities developed as the "cradles of civilization," proposing a model of development for all humanity patterned on that of an individual person. However, the idea that all human societies developed (or should develop) in a uniform process from a "cradle" to a "mature" civilization has now been largely discredited, and some world historians choose not to use the word *civilization* at all because it could imply that some societies are superior to others. But they have not rejected the idea that about 5,000 years ago a new form of human society appeared.

The Rise of States, Laws, and Social Hierarchies

Cities concentrated people and power, and they required more elaborate mechanisms to make them work than had small agricultural villages and foraging groups. These mechanisms were part of what political scientists call "the state," an organization distinct from a tribe or kinship group in which a small share of the population is able to coerce resources out of everyone else in order to gain and then maintain power. In a state, the interest that gains power might be one particular family, a set of religious leaders, or even a charismatic or talented individual able to handle the problems of dense urban communities.

However they are established, states coerce people through violence, or the threat of violence, and develop permanent armies for this purpose. Using armed force every time they need food or other resources is not very efficient, however, so states also establish bureaucracies and systems of taxation. States also need to keep track of people and goods, so they sometimes develop systems of recording information and accounting, usually through writing, though not always. In the Inca Empire of the Andes, for example, information about money, goods, and people was recorded on collections of colored knotted strings called *khipus* (see page 299). Systems of recording information allow the creation of more elaborate rules of behavior, often written down in the form of law codes, which facilitate further growth in state power, or in the form of religious traditions, which specify what sort of behavior is pleasing to the gods or other supernatural forces.

Written laws and traditions generally create more elaborate social hierarchies, in which divisions between elite groups and common people are established more firmly. They also generally heighten gender hierarchies. Those who gain power in states are most often men, so they tend to establish laws and norms that favor males in marriage, property rights, and other areas.

Whether we choose to call the process "the birth of civilization" or "the growth of the state," in the fourth millennium B.C.E., Neolithic agricultural villages expanded into cities that depended largely on food produced by the surrounding countryside while people living in cities carried out other tasks. The organization of a more complex division of labor was undertaken by an elite group, which enforced its will through laws, taxes, and bureaucracies backed up by armed force or the threat of it. Social and gender hierarchies became more complex and rigid. All this happened first in Mesopotamia, then in Egypt, and then in India and China.

Mesopotamia from Sumer to Babylon

- How did the peoples of Mesopotamia form states and develop new technologies and institutions?

States first developed in Mesopotamia, where sustained agriculture reliant on irrigation from the Euphrates and Tigris Rivers resulted in larger populations, a division of labor, and the growth of cities. Priests and rulers developed ways to control and organize these complex societies, including armies, taxation systems, and written records. Conquerors from the north unified Mesopotamian city-states into larger empires and spread Mesopotamian culture over a large area.

Environmental Challenges, Irrigation, and Religion

Mesopotamia was part of the Fertile Crescent, where settled agriculture first developed (see pages 15–16). The earliest agricultural villages in Mesopotamia were in the northern, hilly parts of the river valleys, where there is abundant rainfall for crops. Farmers had brought techniques of crop raising southward by about 5000 B.C.E., to the southern part of Mesopotamia known as Sumer (SOO-mer). In this arid climate farmers developed large-scale irrigation, which required organized group effort but allowed the population to grow. By about 3800 B.C.E. one of these agricultural villages, Uruk (OO-rook), had expanded significantly, becoming what many historians view as the world's first city, with a population that eventually numbered more than fifty thousand. Over the next thousand years, other cities emerged in Sumer, trading with one another and creating massive hydraulic projects including reservoirs, dams, and dikes to prevent major floods. These cities built defensive walls, marketplaces, and large public buildings; each came to dominate the surrounding countryside, becoming city-states independent from one another, though not very far apart.

The city-states of Sumer relied on irrigation systems that required cooperation and at least some level of social and political cohesion. The

Sumerian Harpist This small clay tablet, carved between 2000 B.C.E. and 1500 B.C.E., shows a seated woman playing a harp. Her fashionable dress and hat suggest that she is playing for wealthy people, perhaps at the royal court. Images of musicians are common in Mesopotamian art, which indicates that music was important in Mesopotamian culture and social life. (Erich Lessing/Art Resource, NY)

authority to run this system was, it seems, initially assumed by Sumerian priests. Encouraged and directed by their religious leaders, people built temples on tall platforms in the center of their cities. Temples grew into elaborate complexes of buildings with storage space for grain and other products and housing for animals. (Much later, by about 2100 B.C.E., some of the major temple complexes were embellished with a huge stepped pyramid, called a ziggurat, with a shrine on the top.) Surrounding the temple and other large buildings were the houses of ordinary citizens, each constructed around a central courtyard.

To Sumerians, and to later peoples in Mesopotamia as well, many different gods and goddesses controlled the world, a religious idea later scholars called **polytheism**. Each deity represented cosmic forces such as the sun, moon, water, and storms. The gods judged good and evil and would punish humans who lied or cheated. Gods themselves suffered for their actions, sometimes for no reason at all, just as humans did. People believed that humans had been created to serve the gods and generally anticipated being well treated by the gods if they served them well. The best way to honor the gods was to make any temple built for them as grand and impressive as possible, because the temple's size demonstrated the strength of the community and the power of its chief deity. Once it was built, the temple itself, along with the shrine on the top of the ziggurat, was often off-limits to ordinary people. Instead the temple was staffed by priests and priestesses who carried out rituals to honor the god or goddess.

Sumerian Politics and Society

Exactly how kings emerged in Sumerian society is not clear. Scholars have suggested that during times of crisis, a chief priest or sometimes a military leader assumed what was supposed to be temporary authority over a city. He established an army, trained it, and led it into battle, making increasing use of bronze weaponry that became more common after 2500 B.C.E. Temporary power gradually became permanent kingship, and kings in some Sumerian city-states began to hand down the kingship to their sons, establishing patriarchal hereditary dynasties in which power was handed down through the male line. This is the point at which written records of kingship begin to appear. The symbol of royal status was the palace, which came to rival the temple in its grandeur.

Kings made alliances with other powerful individuals, often through marriage. Royal family members were responsible for many aspects of government. Kings worked closely with religious authorities and relied on ideas about their connections with the gods, as well as the kings' military might, for their power. Royal children, both sons and daughters, were sometimes priests and priestesses in major temples. Acting together, priests, nobles, and kings in Sumerian cities used force, persuasion, and threats of higher taxes to maintain order, keep the irrigation systems working, and keep food and other goods flowing.

The king and the nobles held extensive tracts of land, as did the temple; these lands were worked by the palace's or the temple's clients—free men and women who were dependent on the palace or the temple. They received crops and other goods in return for their labor. Although this arrangement assured the clients of a livelihood, the land they worked remained the possession of the palace or the temple. Some individuals and families owned land outright and paid their taxes in the form of agricultural products or items they made.

At the bottom rung of society were slaves. Slavery, like many other aspects of society, predates written records, so we are not sure exactly how and when people first began to own other people. Like animals, slaves were a source of physical power for their owners, providing them an opportunity to amass more wealth and influence.

Each of these social categories included both men and women, but their experiences were not the same, for Sumerian society made distinctions based on gender. Most elite landowners were male, but women who held positions as priestesses or as queens ran their own estates independently of their husbands and fathers. Some women owned businesses and took care of their own accounts. They could own property and distribute it to their offspring. Sons and daughters inherited from their parents, although a daughter received her inheritance in the form of a dowry, which technically remained hers but was managed by her husband or husband's family after marriage. The Sumerians established the basic social, economic, and intellectual patterns of Mesopotamia and influenced their neighbors to the north and east.

Writing, Mathematics, and Poetry

The origins of writing probably date back to the ninth millennium B.C.E., when people in southwest Asia used clay tokens as counters for record keeping. By the fourth millennium people had realized that impressing the tokens on soft clay, or drawing pictures of the

- **polytheism** The worship of many gods and goddesses.
- **cuneiform** Sumerian form of writing; the term describes the wedge-shaped marks made by a stylus.
- **epic poem** An oral or written narration of the achievements and sometimes the failures of heroes that embodies people's ideas about themselves.

tokens on clay, was simpler than making tokens. This breakthrough in turn suggested that more information could be conveyed by adding pictures of other objects, and slowly the new technology of writing developed. The result was a complex system of pictographs in which each sign pictured an object, such as "star" (line A of Figure 2.1). These pictographs were the forerunners of the Sumerian form of writing known as **cuneiform** (kyou-NEE-uh-form), from the Latin term for "wedge shaped," used to describe the indentations made by a sharpened stylus in clay.

Scribes could combine pictograms to express meaning. For example, the sign for "woman" (line B) and the sign for "mountain" (line C) were combined, literally, into "mountain woman" (line D), which meant "slave woman" because the Sumerians regularly obtained their slave women from wars against enemies in the mountains. Pictographs were initially limited in that they could not represent abstract ideas, but the development of ideograms—signs that represented ideas—made writing more versatile. Thus the sign for "star" could also be used to indicate "heaven," "sky," or even "god." The real breakthrough came when scribes started using signs to represent sounds. For instance, the symbol for "water" (two parallel wavy lines) could also be used to indicate "in," which sounded the same as the spoken word for "water" in Sumerian.

The development of the Sumerian system of writing was piecemeal, with scribes making changes and additions as they were needed. The system became so complicated that the Sumerians established scribal schools, which by 2500 B.C.E. flourished throughout the region. Students at the schools were all male, and most came from families in the middle range of urban society. Each school had a master, a teacher, and monitors. Discipline was strict, and students were caned for sloppy work and misbehavior. One graduate of a scribal school had few fond memories of the joy of learning:

> My headmaster read my tablet, said:
> "There is something missing," caned me.
> . . .
> The fellow in charge of silence said:
> "Why did you talk without permission," caned me.
> The fellow in charge of the assembly said:
> "Why did you stand at ease without permission,"
> caned me.[1]

Scribal schools were primarily intended to produce individuals who could keep records of the property of temple officials, kings, and nobles. Thus writing first developed as a way to enhance the growing power of elites, not to record speech.

Sumerians wrote numbers as well as words on clay tablets, and some surviving tablets show multiplication and division problems. Mathematics was not just a theoretical matter to the people living in Mesopotamia, because the building of cities, palaces, temples, and canals demanded practical knowledge of geometry and trigonometry. The Sumerians and later Mesopotamians made significant advances in mathematics using a numerical system based on units of sixty, ten, and six, from which we derive our division of hours into sixty minutes and minutes into sixty seconds. They also developed the concept of place value—that the value of a number depends on where it stands in relation to other numbers.

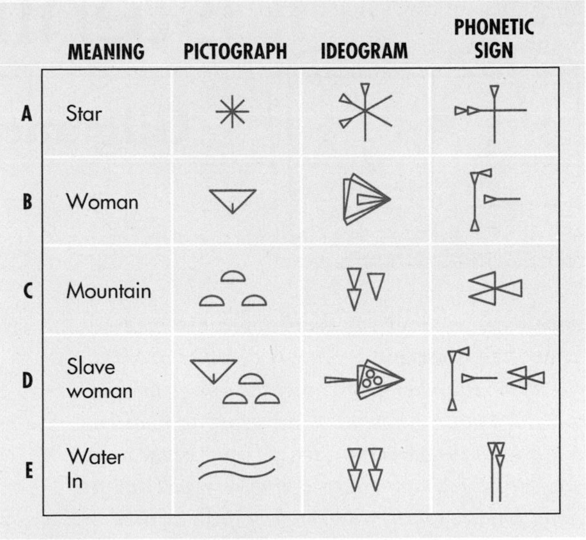

	MEANING	PICTOGRAPH	IDEOGRAM	PHONETIC SIGN
A	Star			
B	Woman			
C	Mountain			
D	Slave woman			
E	Water In			

FIGURE 2.1 Sumerian Writing (Source: S. N. Kramer, *The Sumerians: Their History, Culture, and Character.* Copyright © 1963 by the University of Chicago Press. Reproduced with permission of UNIVERSITY OF CHICAGO PRESS in the format Republish in a book via Copyright Clearance Center.)

Written texts were not an important part of Sumerian religious life, nor were they central to the religious practices of most of the other peoples in this region. Stories about the gods circulated orally and traveled with people when they moved up and down the rivers, so that gods often acquired new names and new characteristics over the centuries. Sumerians also told stories about heroes and kings, many of which were eventually reworked into the world's first **epic poem**, the *Epic of Gilgamesh* (GIL-guh-mesh), which was later written down. An epic poem is a narration of the achievements, labors, and sometimes failures of heroes that embodies people's ideas about themselves. Historians can use epic poems to learn about various aspects of a society, and to that extent epics can be used as historical sources. The epic recounts the wanderings of Gilgamesh—the semihistorical king of Uruk—and his search for eternal life, and it grapples with enduring questions about life and death, friendship, humankind and deity, and immortality. (See "Listening to the Past: Gilgamesh's Quest for Immortality," page 38.)

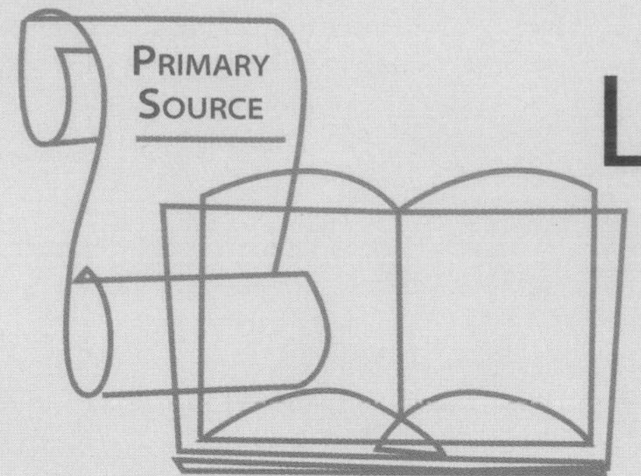

Listening to the Past

Gilgamesh's Quest for Immortality

The human desire to escape the grip of death appears in many cultures. The Epic of Gilgamesh *is perhaps the earliest recorded treatment of this topic. The oldest elements of the epic go back to stories told in the third millennium* B.C.E. *According to tradition, Gilgamesh was a king of the Sumerian city of Uruk. In the story, Gilgamesh is not fulfilling his duties as the king very well and sets out with his friend Enkidu to perform wondrous feats against fearsome agents of the gods. Together they kill several supernatural beings, and the gods decide that Enkidu must die. He foresees his own death in a dream.*

"Listen again, my friend [Gilgamesh]! I had a dream in the night.
The sky called out, the earth replied,
I was standing in between them.
There was a young man, whose face was obscured.
His face was like that of an Anzu-bird.
He had the paws of a lion, he had the claws of an eagle.
He seized me by my locks, using great force against me. . . .
He seized me, drove me down to the dark house, dwelling of Erkalla's god [the underworld], . . .
On the road where travelling is one way only,
To the house where those who stay are deprived of light. . . ."

Enkidu sickens and dies. Gilgamesh is distraught and determined to become immortal. He decides to journey to Ut-napishtim and his wife, the only humans who have eternal life. Everyone he meets along the way asks him about his appearance, and Gilgamesh always answers with the same words:

"How could my cheeks not be wasted, nor my face dejected,
Nor my heart wretched, nor my appearance worn out,
Nor grief in my innermost being,
Nor my face like that of a long-distance traveller,
Nor my face weathered by wind and heat
Nor roaming open country clad only in a lionskin?
My friend was the hunted mule, wild ass of the mountain, leopard of open country,
Enkidu my friend was the hunted mule, wild ass of the mountain, leopard of open country.
We who met, and scaled the mountain,
Seized the Bull of Heaven [the sacred bull of the goddess Ishtar] and slew it,
Demolished Humbaba [the ogre who guards the forest of the gods] who dwelt in the Pine Forest,
Killed lions in the passes of the mountains,
My friend whom I love so much, who experienced every hardship with me,
Enkidu my friend whom I love so much, who experienced every hardship with me—
The fate of mortals conquered him!
For six days and seven nights I wept over him: I did not allow him to be buried
Until a worm fell out of his nose.
I was frightened and
I am afraid of Death, and so I roam open country.
The words of my friend weigh upon me. . . .
I roam open country on long journeys.
How, O how could I stay silent, how, O how could I keep quiet?
My friend whom I love has turned to clay: Enkidu my friend whom I love has turned to clay.
Am I not like him? Must I lie down too,
Never to rise, ever again?"

Gilgamesh finally reaches Ut-napishtim, to whom he tells his story, and who says to him:

"Why do you prolong grief, Gilgamesh?
Since [the gods made you] from the flesh of gods and mankind,
Since [the gods] made you like your father and mother
[Death is inevitable] . . . ,
Nobody sees the face of Death,
Nobody hears the voice of Death.

Empires in Mesopotamia

The wealth of Sumerian cities also attracted conquerors from the north. Around 2300 B.C.E. Sargon, the king of a region to the north of Sumer, conquered a number of Sumerian cities with what was probably the world's first permanent army and created a large state. The symbol of his triumph was a new capital, the city of Akkad (AH-kahd). Sargon also expanded the Akkadian empire westward to northern Syria, which became the breadbasket of the empire. He encouraged trading networks that brought in goods from as far away as the Indus River in South Asia and what is now Turkey (Map 2.1). Sargon spoke a different language than did the Sumerians, one of the many languages that scholars identify as belonging to the Semitic language family,

Savage Death just cuts mankind down.
Sometimes we build a house, sometimes we make a nest,
But then brothers divide it upon inheritance.
Sometimes there is hostility in [the land],
But then the river rises and brings flood-water. . . .
The Anunnaki, the great gods, assembled;
Mammitum [the great mother goddess] who creates fate
decreed destinies with them.
They appointed death and life.
They did not mark out days for death,
But they did so for life. ”

Gilgamesh asks Ut-napishtim how he and his wife can be immortal like the gods, if death is inevitable. Ut-napishtim tells him the story of how they survived a flood sent by the gods and the chief god Enlil blessed them with eternal life. Gilgamesh wants this as well, but fails two opportunities Ut-napishtim provides for him to achieve it. At the end of the epic, he simply returns to Uruk with the boatman Ur-shanabi, to whom he points out the glories of the city:

“Go up on to the wall of Uruk, Ur-shanabi, and walk around,
Inspect the foundation platform and scrutinize the brickwork!
Testify that its bricks are baked bricks,
And that the Seven Counsellors must have laid its foundations!
One square mile is city, one square mile is orchards, one square
mile is claypits, as well as the open ground of Ishtar's
temple.
Three square miles and the open ground comprise Uruk. ”

Source: *Myths from Mesopotamia: Creation, the Flood, Gilgamesh, and Others*, trans. Stephanie Dalley (Oxford: Oxford University Press, 1989), pp. 88–89, 103–104, 107, 108–109, 120. Used by permission of Oxford University Press.

Gilgamesh, from decorative panel of a lyre unearthed at Ur.
(Courtesy of the Penn Museum, Image #150108)

QUESTIONS FOR ANALYSIS

1. What does the *Epic of Gilgamesh* reveal about Sumerian attitudes toward the gods and human beings?
2. What does the epic tell us about Sumerian views of the nature of human life? Where do human beings fit into the cosmic world?
3. At the end of his quest, did Gilgamesh achieve immortality? If so, what was the nature of that immortality?

which includes modern-day Hebrew and Arabic. Akkadians adapted cuneiform writing to their own language, and Akkadian became the diplomatic language used over a wide area.

Sargon tore down the defensive walls of Sumerian cities and appointed his own sons as their rulers to help him cement his power. He also appointed his daughter, Enheduana (2285–2250 B.C.E.), as high priestess in the city of Ur. Here she wrote a number of hymns, especially those in praise of the goddess Inanna, becoming the world's first author to put her name to a literary composition. (See “Viewpoints 2.1: Addressing the Gods in Mesopotamia and Egypt,” page 41.)

Sargon's dynasty appears to have ruled Mesopotamia for about 150 years, and then collapsed, in part because of a period of extended drought. Various city-

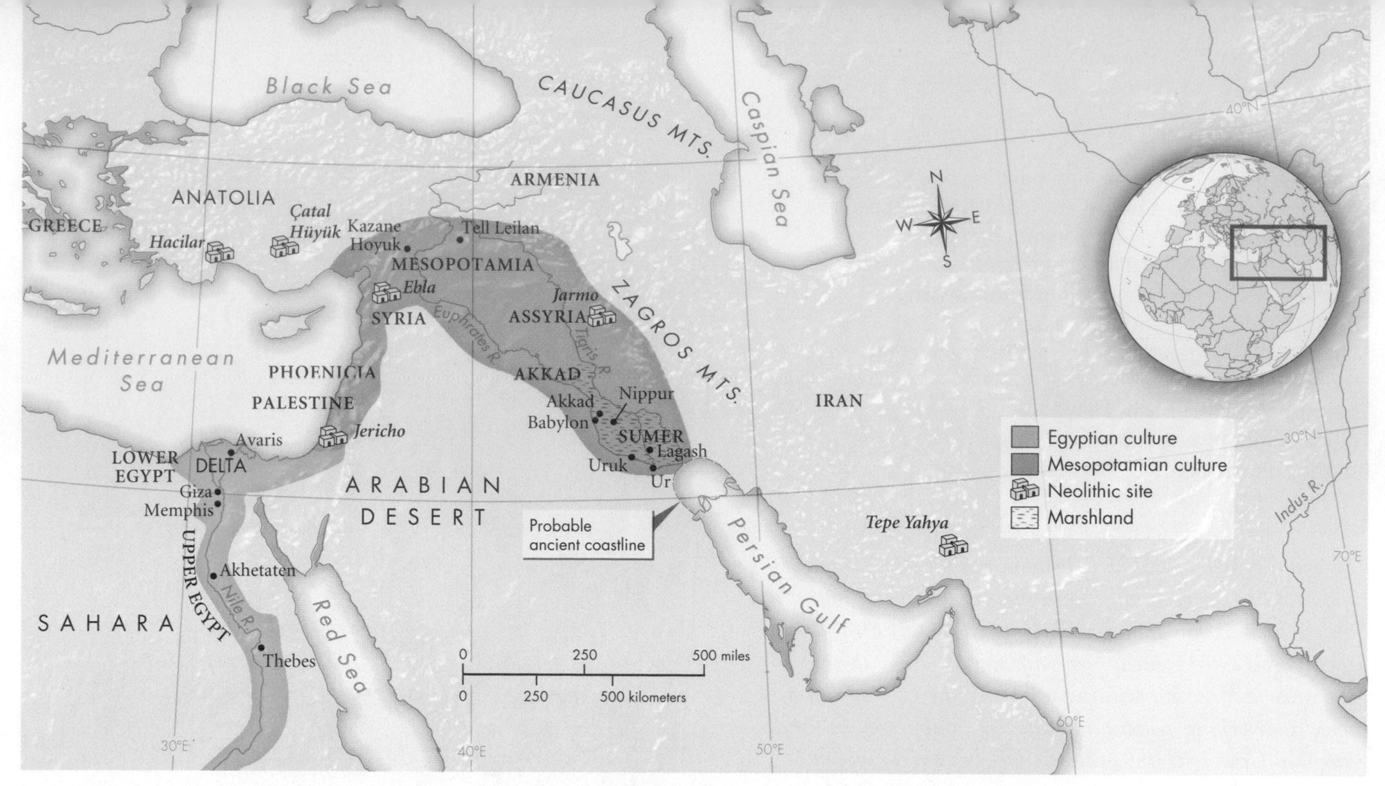

MAP 2.1 Spread of Cultures in Southwest Asia and the Nile Valley, ca. 3000–1640 B.C.E.
This map illustrates the spread of the Mesopotamian and Egyptian cultures through the semicircular stretch of land often called the Fertile Crescent. From this area, the knowledge and use of agriculture spread throughout western Asia, northern Africa, and Europe.

states then rose to power, one of which was centered on the city of Babylon. Babylon was in an excellent position to dominate trade on both the Tigris and Euphrates Rivers, and it was fortunate in having a very able ruler in Hammurabi (hahm-moo-RAH-bee) (r. 1792–1750 B.C.E.). Initially a typical king of his era, he unified Mesopotamia later in his reign by using military force, strategic alliances with the rulers of smaller territories, and religious ideas. As had earlier rulers, Hammurabi linked his success with the will of the gods. He connected himself with the sun-god Shamash, the god of law and justice, and encouraged the spread of myths that explained how Marduk, the primary god of Babylon, had been elected king of the gods by the other deities in Mesopotamia. Marduk later became widely regarded as the chief god of Mesopotamia, absorbing the qualities and powers of other gods. Babylonian ideas and beliefs thus became part of the cultural mixture of Mesopotamia, which spread far beyond the Tigris and Euphrates Valleys to the shores of the Mediterranean Sea and the Harappan cities of the Indus River Valley (see pages 65–68).

Sargon of Akkad
This bronze head, with elaborately worked hair and beard, might portray the great conqueror Sargon of Akkad (though his name does not appear on it). The eyes were originally inlaid with precious jewels, which have since been gouged out. Produced about 2300 B.C.E., this head was found in the Assyrian capital of Nineveh, where it had been taken as loot. (© Interfoto/Alamy)

Life Under Hammurabi

Hammurabi's most memorable accomplishment was the proclamation of an extensive law code, introduced about 1755 B.C.E. Hammurabi's was not the first law code in Mesopotamia; the earliest goes back to about 2100 B.C.E. Like the codes of the earlier lawgivers,

Viewpoints 2.1

Addressing the Gods in Mesopotamia and Egypt

• *Hymns and incantations to the gods are among the earliest written works in Mesopotamia and Egypt. Enheduana, the daughter of Sargon of Akkad, was appointed by her father as high priestess in the Sumerian city of Ur, where she wrote a number of literary and religious works, which were frequently recopied long after her death. The first text below is a part of her best-known work, a hymn to the goddess Inanna. The second text below was inscribed on a wall of the royal burial chambers in the pyramid of the Egyptian king Unas (r. 2375–2345 B.C.E.) at Saqqara, a burial ground near the Nile. It is one of many incantations designed to assist the king's ascent to the heavens and transformation into a god.*

Enheduana's "Exaltation of Inanna"

"Your divinity shines in the pure heavens. . . . Your torch lights up the corners of heaven, turning darkness into light. The men and women form a row for you and each one's daily status hangs down before you. Your numerous people pass before you, as before Utu [the sun-god], for their inspection. No one can lay a hand on your precious divine powers; all your divine powers. . . . You exercise full ladyship over heaven and earth; you hold everything in your hand. Mistress, you are magnificent, no one can walk before you. You dwell with great An [the god of the heavens] in the holy resting-place. Which god is like you in gathering together . . . in heaven and earth? You are magnificent, your name is praised, you alone are magnificent!

I am En-hedu-ana, the high priestess of the moon god. . . . Mercy, compassion, care, lenience and homage are yours, and to cause flood storms, to open hard ground and to turn darkness into light. My lady, let me proclaim your magnificence in all lands, and your glory! Let me praise your ways and greatness! Who rivals you in divinity? Who can compare with your divine rites? . . . An and Enlil [the chief god of Sumer] have determined a great destiny for you throughout the entire universe. They have bestowed upon you ladyship in the assembly chamber. Being fitted for ladyship, you determine the destiny of noble ladies. Mistress, you are magnificent, you are great! Inanna, you are magnificent, you are great! My lady, your magnificence is resplendent. May your heart be restored for my sake! Your great deeds are unparalleled, your magnificence is praised! Young woman, Inanna, your praise is sweet!"

Pyramid Text of King Unas

"Re-Atum [the sun god], this Unas comes to you,
A spirit indestructible
Who lays claim to the place of the four pillars!
Your son comes to you, this Unas comes to you,
May you cross the sky united in the dark,
May you rise in lightland, the place in which you shine!
Osiris, Isis, go proclaim to Lower Egypt's gods
And their spirits:
"This Unas comes, a spirit indestructible,
Like the morning star above Hapy [the god of the flooding of the Nile],
Whom the water-spirits worship;
Whom he wishes to live will live,
Whom he wishes to die will die!"
. . .
Thoth [the god of law and science], go proclaim to the gods of the west
And their spirits:
"This Unas comes, a spirit indestructible,
Decked above the neck as Anubis,
Lord of the western height,
He will count hearts, he will claim hearts,
Whom he wishes to live will live,
Whom he wishes to die will die!""

Sources: Excerpts from J. A. Black et al., *Electronic Text Corpus of Sumerian Literature* (http://etcsl.orinst.ox.ac.uk/), Oxford 1998–2006, http://etcsl.orinst.ox.ac.uk/cgi-bin/etcsl.cgi?text=t.4.07.3#; Miriam Lichtheim, *Ancient Egyptian Literature: A Book of Readings*. Vol. 1: *The Old and Middle Kingdoms*. Reproduced with permission of UNIVERSITY OF CALIFORNIA PRESS in the format Book via Copyright Clearance Center.

QUESTIONS FOR ANALYSIS

1. What powers and qualities of the goddess Inanna does Enheduana praise? What powers does the author of the pyramid text ascribe to the god-king Unas?
2. Enheduana was a member of the ruling dynasty of Akkad, and Unas was the king of Egypt. How did their social position shape their relationship to the gods? What differences do you see in their relationships to the gods in the two works?

Hammurabi's law code proclaimed that he issued his laws on divine authority "to establish law and justice in the language of the land, thereby promoting the welfare of the people." Hammurabi's code set a variety of punishments for breaking the law, including fines and physical punishment such as mutilation, whipping, and burning. It demanded that the punishment fit the crime, calling for "an eye for an eye and a tooth for a tooth," at least among social equals, although higher-ranking people could pay a fine to lower-ranking victims instead of having an arm broken or losing an eye.

Hammurabi's code provides a wealth of information about daily life in Mesopotamia, although, like all law codes, it prescribes what the lawgivers hope will be the situation rather than providing a description of real life. We cannot know if its laws were enforced, but we can use it to see what was significant to people in Hammurabi's society. Because of farming's fundamental importance, the code dealt extensively with agriculture. Tenants faced severe penalties for neglecting the land or not working it at all. Since irrigation was essential to grow crops, tenants had to keep the canals and ditches in good repair. Anyone whose neglect of the canals resulted in damaged crops had to either bear the cost of losses or be sold into slavery. The code also regulated other trades, and artisans had to guarantee the quality of their goods and services to consumers. Hammurabi gave careful attention to marriage and the family. As elsewhere in the area, marriage had aspects of a business agreement. The groom or his father offered the prospective bride's father a gift, and if this was acceptable, the bride's father provided his daughter with a dowry, which technically remained hers. The penalty for adultery, defined as sex between a married woman and a man not her husband, was death, but a husband had the power to spare his wife by obtaining a pardon for her from the king. (Sex between a married man and a woman who was not his wife was not defined as adultery and carried no penalty.) A father could not disinherit a son without just cause, and the code ordered the courts to forgive a son for his first offense. On family matters and other issues, Hammurabi's code influenced other law codes, including those later written down in Hebrew Scripture (see page 53).

Law Code of Hammurabi Hammurabi ordered his code to be inscribed on stone pillars and set up in public throughout the Babylonian empire. At the top of the pillar Hammurabi (left) is depicted receiving the rod and ring of authority from Shamash, the god of law and justice.

The Egyptians

☐ How did the Egyptians create a prosperous and long-lasting society?

At about the same time that Sumerian city-states expanded and fought with one another in the Tigris and Euphrates Valleys, a more cohesive state under a single ruler grew in the valley of the Nile River in North Africa. This was Egypt, which for long stretches of history was prosperous and secure. At various times groups invaded and conquered Egypt or migrated into Egypt seeking better lives. Often these newcomers adopted aspects of Egyptian religion, art, and politics, and Egyptians also carried their traditions with them when they established an empire and engaged in trade.

The Nile and the God-King

The Greek historian and traveler Herodotus called Egypt the "gift of the Nile," and no other single geographical factor had such a fundamental and profound impact on Egyptian life, society, and history as this river (Map 2.2). The Nile flooded once a year for a period of several months, bringing fertile soil and moisture for farming. In contrast to the violent and destructive floods of the Tigris and Euphrates, Nile floods were relatively gentle, and Egyptians praised the Nile primarily as a creative and comforting force:

> Hail to thee, O Nile, that issues from the earth and comes to keep Egypt alive! . . .
> He that waters the meadows which Ra created,
> He that makes to drink the desert . . .
> He who makes barley and brings emmer [wheat] into being . . .
> He who brings grass into being for the cattle . . .
> He who makes every beloved tree to grow . . .
> O Nile, verdant art thou, who makest man and cattle to live.[2]

Through the fertility of the Nile and their own hard work, Egyptians produced an annual agricultural surplus, which in turn sustained a growing and prosperous population. The Nile also unified Egypt, serving as a highway that promoted easy communication.

The political power structures that developed in Egypt came to be linked with the Nile. Somehow the idea developed that a single individual, a king, was responsible for the rise and fall of the Nile. The king came to be viewed as a descendant of the gods and thus a god himself. This belief came about before the development of writing in Egypt, so the precise details of its origins have been lost. Political unification most likely proceeded slowly, but stories told about early kings highlighted one who had united Upper Egypt—the upstream valley in the south—and Lower Egypt—the delta area of the Nile that empties into the Mediterranean Sea—into a single kingdom around 3100 B.C.E. Historians later divided Egyptian history into dynasties, or families, of kings, and more recently into periods with distinctive characteristics (see Thematic Chronology, above). The political unification of Egypt in the Archaic Period (3100–2660 B.C.E.) ushered in the period known as the Old Kingdom (2660–2180 B.C.E.), an era of prosperity, artistic flowering, and the evolution of religious beliefs.

The focal point of religious and political life in the Old Kingdom was the king, who commanded the wealth, resources, and people of Egypt. The king's surroundings had to be worthy of a god, and only a magnificent palace was suitable for his home; in fact, the word **pharaoh**, which during the New Kingdom (1570–1070 B.C.E.) came to be used for the king, originally meant "great house." Just as the kings occupied a great house in life, so they reposed in great pyramids after death. Built during the Old Kingdom, these massive stone tombs contained all the things needed by the king in his afterlife and also symbolized the king's power and his connection with the sun-god.

PERIODS OF EGYPTIAN HISTORY

PERIOD	DATES	SIGNIFICANT EVENTS
Archaic	3100–2660 B.C.E.	Unification of Egypt
Old Kingdom	2660–2180 B.C.E.	Construction of the pyramids
First Intermediate	2180–2080 B.C.E.	Political chaos
Middle Kingdom	2080–1640 B.C.E.	Recovery and political stability
Second Intermediate	1640–1570 B.C.E.	Hyksos migrations; struggles for power
New Kingdom	1570–1070 B.C.E.	Creation of an Egyptian empire; growth in wealth
Third Intermediate	1100–653 B.C.E.	Political fragmentation and conquest by outsiders

Like the Mesopotamians, the Egyptians were polytheistic, worshipping many gods of all types, some mightier than others. They developed complex ideas of their gods that reflected the world around them, and these views changed over the many centuries of Egyptian history as gods took on new attributes and often merged with one another. During the Old Kingdom, Egyptians considered the sun-god Ra the creator of life. Much later, during the New Kingdom (see page 46), the pharaohs of a new dynasty favored the worship of a different sun-god, Amon, whom they described as creating the entire cosmos by his thoughts. As his cult grew, Amon came to be identified with Ra, and eventually the Egyptians combined them into one sun-god, Amon-Ra.

The Egyptians likewise developed views of an afterlife that reflected the world around them and that changed over time. During the later part of the Old Kingdom, the walls of kings' tombs were carved with religious texts that provided spells that would bring the king back to life and help him ascend to heaven. (See "Viewpoints 2.1: Addressing the Gods in Mesopotamia and Egypt," page 41.) Toward the end of the Old

- **Hammurabi's law code** A proclamation issued by Babylonian king Hammurabi to establish laws regulating many aspects of life.
- **pharaoh** The title given to the king of Egypt in the New Kingdom, from a word that meant "great house."

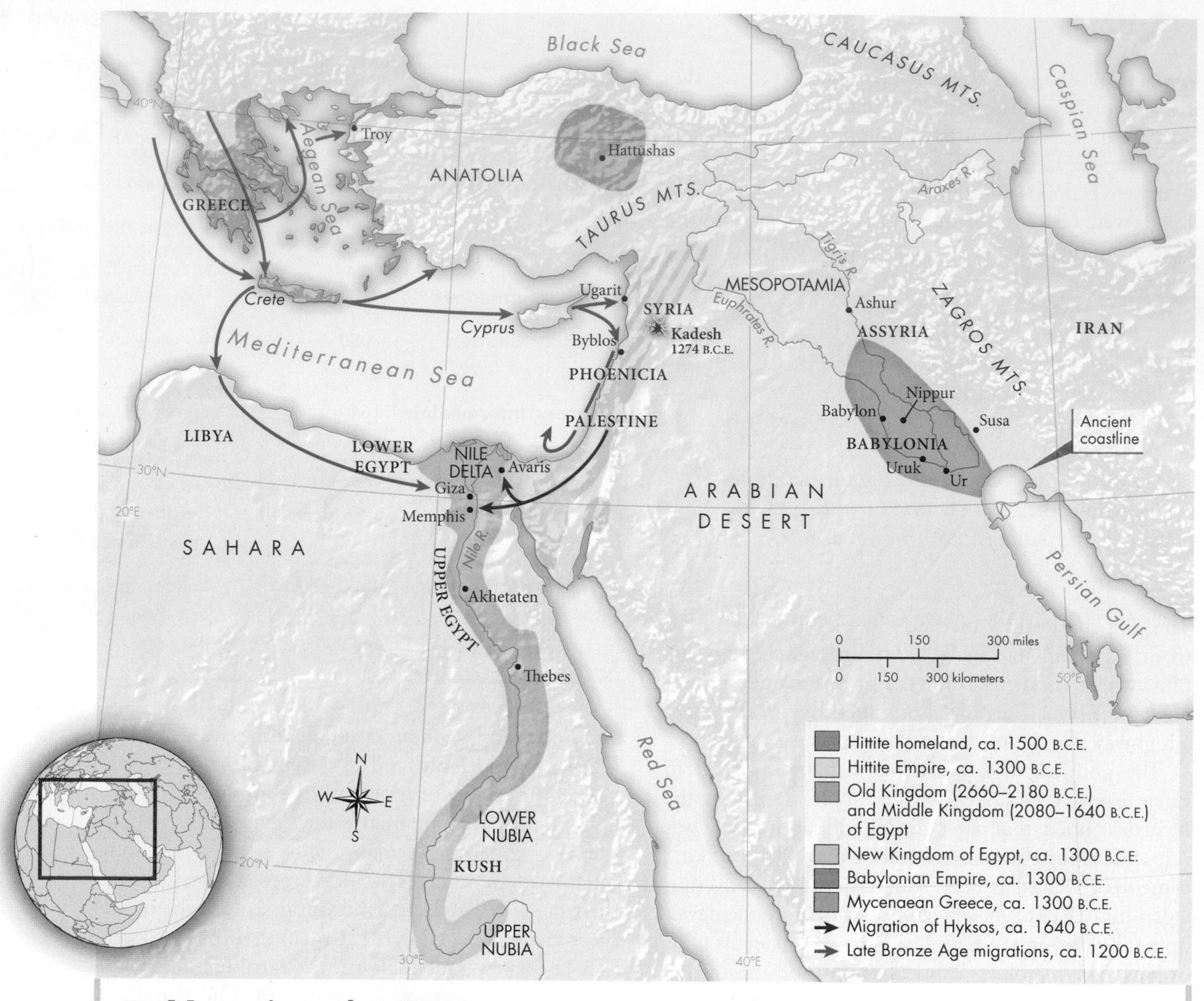

Mapping the Past

MAP 2.2 Empires and Migrations in the Eastern Mediterranean The rise and fall of empires in the eastern Mediterranean were shaped by internal developments, military conflicts, and the migration of peoples to new areas.

ANALYZING THE MAP At what point was the Egyptian Empire at its largest? The Hittite Empire? What were the other major powers in the eastern Mediterranean at this time?

CONNECTIONS What were the major effects of the migrations of the Hyksos? Of the late Bronze Age migrations? What clues does the map provide as to why the late Bronze Age migrations had a more powerful impact than those of the Hyksos?

Kingdom, the tombs of powerful nobles also contained such inscriptions, an indication that more people expected to gain everlasting life. In the Middle Kingdom (2080–1640 B.C.E.), new types of spells appeared on the coffins of even more people, a further expansion in admissions to the afterlife. During the New Kingdom, a time when Egypt came into greater contact with the cultures of the Fertile Crescent, Egyptians developed even more complex ideas about the afterlife, recording these in written funerary manuscripts that have come to be known as the *Book of the Dead*. These texts explained that the soul left the body to become part of the divine after death and told of the god Osiris (oh-SIGH-ruhs), who died each year and was then brought back to life by his wife Isis (IGH-suhs) when the Nile flooded. Osiris eventually became king of the dead, weighing dead humans' hearts to determine whether they had lived justly enough to deserve ever-

Picturing the Past

Egyptian Home Life This grave painting depicts an intimate moment in the life of an aristocratic family, with the father and mother in the center and their children around them. (Giraudon/The Bridgeman Art Library)

ANALYZING THE IMAGE What evidence do you find in the painting that Egyptian artists based the size of figures on people's status in the household?

CONNECTIONS Based on your reading, how might an image of a poor family differ from this depiction?

lasting life. Egyptians also believed that proper funeral rituals, in which the physical body was mummified, were essential for life after death, so Osiris was assisted by Anubis, the jackal-headed god of mummification.

To ancient Egyptians, the king embodied justice and order—harmony among people, nature, and the divine. Kings did not always live up to this ideal, of course. The two parts of Egypt were difficult to hold together, and several times in Egypt's long history there were periods of civil war and political fragmentation, which scholars term the First (2180–2080 B.C.E.) and Second (1640–1570 B.C.E.) Intermediate Periods. Yet the monarchy survived, and in each period a strong warrior-king arose to restore order and expand Egyptian power.

Egyptian Society and Work

Egyptian society reflected the pyramids that it built. At the top stood the pharaoh, who relied on a circle of nobles, officials, and priests to administer his kingdom. All of them were assisted by scribes, who used a writing system perhaps adapted from Mesopotamia or perhaps developed independently. Egyptian scribes actually created two writing systems: one called hieroglyphics for engraving important religious or political texts on stone or writing them on papyrus made from reeds growing in the Nile Delta, and a much simpler system called hieratic that allowed scribes to write more quickly and was used for the documents of daily life. Students learned hieratic first, and only those from well-off families or whose families had high aspirations took the time to learn hieroglyphics. The cities of the Nile Valley were also home to artisans of all types, along with merchants and other tradespeople. A large group of farmers made up the broad base of the social pyramid.

For Egyptians, the Nile formed an essential part of daily life. During the flooding season—from June to October—farmers worked on the pharaoh's building programs and other tasks away from their fields. When the water began to recede, they diverted some of it into ponds for future irrigation and began planting wheat and barley for bread and beer, using plows pulled by oxen or people. From October to February, farmers planted and tended crops, and from February until the next flood, they harvested them. As in Mesopotamia, common people paid their obligations to their superiors in products and in labor. People's labor obligations in the Old Kingdom may have included forced work on the pyramids and canals, although recent research suggests that most people who built the pyramids were paid for their work. Some young men were drafted into the pharaoh's army, which served as both a fighting force and a labor corps.

The lives of all Egyptians centered around the family. Just as in Mesopotamia, marriage was a business arrangement. A couple's parents arranged the marriage, which seems to have taken place at a young age. Once couples were married, having children, especially sons, was a high priority, as indicated by surviving charms to promote fertility and prayers for successful childbirth. Boys continued the family line, and only they could perform the proper burial rites for their father. Most Egyptian men had only one wife, but among the wealthy some had several wives or concubines. Ordinary women were expected to obey their fathers, husbands, and other men, but they possessed considerable economic and legal rights. They could own land in their own names, operate businesses, and testify in court. Literature and art depict a world in which ordinary husbands and wives enjoyed each other's company.

Migrations, Revivals, and Collapse

While Egyptian civilization flourished in the Nile Valley, various groups migrated throughout the Fertile Crescent and then accommodated themselves to local cultures (see Map 2.2). Some settled in the Nile Delta, including a group the Egyptians called Hyksos, meaning "rulers of the uplands." Although they were later portrayed as a conquering horde, the Hyksos were actually migrants looking for good land, and their entry into the delta, which began around 1800 B.C.E., was probably gradual and generally peaceful. The newcomers began to worship Egyptian deities and modeled their political structures on those of the Egyptians.

The Hyksos brought with them methods of making bronze (see Chapter 1) and casting it into weapons that became standard in Egypt. They thereby brought Egypt fully into the Bronze Age culture of the Mediterranean world. The Hyksos also introduced horse-drawn chariots and the composite bow, made of multiple materials for greater strength, which along with bronze weaponry revolutionized Egyptian warfare. The migration of the Hyksos, combined with a series of famines and internal struggles for power, led Egypt to fragment politically in what later came to be known as the Second Intermediate Period.

In about 1570 B.C.E. a new dynasty of pharaohs arose, pushing the Hyksos out of the delta and conquering territory to the south and northeast. These warrior-pharaohs inaugurated what scholars refer to as the New Kingdom, a period characterized not only by enormous wealth and conscious imperialism but also by a greater sense of insecurity because of new contacts and military engagements. By expanding Egyptian power beyond the Nile Valley, the pharaohs created the first Egyptian empire, and they celebrated their triumphs with monuments on a scale unparalleled since the pyramids of the Old Kingdom. Their giant statues and rich tombs might also indicate an expansion of imported slave labor, although some scholars are rethinking the extent of slave labor in the New Kingdom.

The New Kingdom pharaohs include a number of remarkable figures. Among these was Hatshepsut (haht-SHEP-soot) (r. ca. 1479–ca. 1458 B.C.E.), one of the few female pharaohs in Egypt's long history who seized the throne for herself and used her reign to promote building and trade. (See "Individuals in Society: Hatshepsut and Nefertiti," right.) Amenhotep III (ah-men-HOE-tep) (r. ca. 1388–ca. 1350 B.C.E.) corresponded with other powerful kings in Babylonia and other kingdoms in the Fertile Crescent, sending envoys, exchanging gifts, making alliances, and in some cases marrying their daughters. Amenhotep III was succeeded by his son, who took the name Akhenaten (ah-keh-NAH-tuhn) (r. 1351–1334 B.C.E.). He renamed himself as a mark of his changing religious ideas, choosing to worship a new sun-god, Aten, instead of the traditional Amon or Ra. He was not a monotheist—someone who worships only one god—but he did order the erasure of the names of other sun-gods from the walls of buildings, the transfer of taxes from the traditional priesthood of Amon-Ra, and the building of huge new temples to Aten. Akhenaten's wife Nefertiti (nehf-uhr-TEE-tee) supported his religious ideas, but this new religion, imposed from above, failed to find a place among the people, and after his death traditional religious practices returned.

One of the key challenges facing the pharaohs after Akhenaten was the expansion of the kingdom of the

Individuals in Society

Hatshepsut and Nefertiti

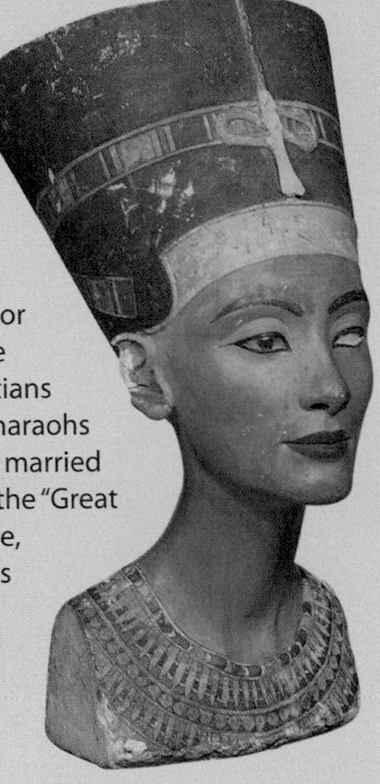

Painted limestone bust of Nefertiti. (bpk, Berlin/Aegyptisches Museum, Staatliche Museen, Berlin, Germany/ Photo: Margarete Buesing/Art Resource, NY)

Granite head of Hatshepsut. (bpk, Berlin/ Aegyptisches Museum, Staatliche Museen, Berlin, Germany/Photo: Margarete Buesing/Art Resource, NY)

EGYPTIANS UNDERSTOOD THE PHARAOH TO be the living embodiment of the god Horus, the source of law and morality, and the mediator between gods and humans. His connection with the divine stretched to members of his family, so his siblings and children were also viewed as in some ways divine. Because of this, a pharaoh often took his sister or half-sister as one of his wives. This concentrated divine blood set the pharaonic family apart from other Egyptians (who did not marry close relatives) and allowed the pharaohs to imitate the gods, who in Egyptian mythology often married their siblings. A pharaoh chose one of his wives to be the "Great Royal Wife," or principal queen. Often this was a relative, though sometimes it was one of the foreign princesses who married pharaohs to establish political alliances.

The familial connection with the divine allowed a handful of women to rule in their own right in Egypt's long history. We know the names of four female pharaohs, of whom the most famous was Hatshepsut. She was the sister and wife of Thutmose II and, after he died, served as regent — as adviser and co-ruler — for her young stepson Thutmose III, who was the son of another woman. Hatshepsut sent trading expeditions and sponsored artists and architects, ushering in a period of artistic creativity and economic prosperity. She built one of the world's great buildings, an elaborate terraced temple at Deir el Bahri, which eventually served as her tomb. Hatshepsut's status as a powerful female ruler was difficult for Egyptians to conceptualize, and she is often depicted in male dress or with a false beard, thus looking more like the male rulers who were the norm. After her death, Thutmose III tried to destroy all evidence that she had ever ruled, smashing statues and scratching her name off inscriptions, perhaps because of personal animosity and perhaps because he wanted to erase the fact that a woman had once been pharaoh. Only within recent decades have historians and archaeologists begun to (literally) piece together her story.

Though female pharaohs were very rare, many royal women had power through their position as Great Royal Wives. The most famous was Nefertiti (ca. 1370–1330 B.C.E.), the wife of Akhenaten. Her name means "the perfect (or beautiful) woman has come," and inscriptions give her many other titles.

Nefertiti used her position to spread the new religion of the sun-god Aten. Together she and Akhenaten built a new palace at Akhetaten, the present-day Amarna, away from the old centers of power. There they developed the cult of Aten to the exclusion of the traditional deities. Nearly the only literary survivor of their religious belief is the "Hymn to Aten," which declares Aten to be the only god. It describes Nefertiti as "the great royal consort whom he, Akhenaten, loves. The mistress of the Two Lands, Upper and Lower Egypt."

Nefertiti is often shown as being the same size as her husband, and in some inscriptions she is performing religious rituals that would normally have been carried out only by the pharaoh. The exact details of her power are hard to determine, however. An older theory held that her husband removed her from power, though there is also speculation that she may have ruled secretly in her own right after his death. Her tomb has long since disappeared, though some scholars believe that an unidentified mummy discovered in 2003 in Egypt's Valley of the Kings may be Nefertiti's.

QUESTIONS FOR ANALYSIS

1. Why might it have been difficult for Egyptians to accept a female ruler?
2. What opportunities do hereditary monarchies such as that of ancient Egypt provide for women? How does this fit with gender hierarchies in which men are understood as superior?

LaunchPad
Online Document Project

Considering Egyptian views of gender roles, what complexities did Egyptian writers and artists face in depicting Hatshepsut? Analyze written and visual representations of Hatshepsut, and then complete a quiz and writing assignment based on the evidence and details from this chapter.

See inside the front cover to learn more.

Hittite Archer in a Chariot In this stylized stone carving made about 1000 B.C.E. in Anatolia (modern-day Turkey), a Hittite archer driven in a chariot shoots toward his foes, while a victim of an earlier shot is trampled beneath the horse's hooves. The arrows might have been tipped with iron, which was becoming a more common material for weapons and tools. (Museum of Anatolian Civilizations, Ankara, Turkey/Gianni Dagli Orti/The Art Archive at Art Resource, NY)

Hittites. At about the same time that the Sumerians were establishing city-states, speakers of **Indo-European languages** migrated into Anatolia, modern-day Turkey. Indo-European is a large family of languages that includes English, most of the languages of modern Europe, ancient Greek, Latin, Persian, Hindi, Bengali, and Sanskrit (for more on Sanskrit, see page 68). It also includes Hittite, the language of one of the peoples who migrated into this area. Information about the Hittites comes from archaeological sources and also from written cuneiform tablets that provide details about politics and economic life. These records indicate that beginning about 1600 B.C.E., Hittite kings began to conquer more territory (see Map 2.2). As the Hittites expanded southward, they came into conflict with the Egyptians, who were establishing their own larger empire. There were a number of battles, but both sides seem to have recognized the impossibility of defeating the other, and in 1258 the Egyptian king Ramesses II (r. ca. 1290–1224 B.C.E.) and the Hittite king Hattusili III (r. ca. 1267–1237 B.C.E.) concluded a peace treaty, which was recorded in both Egyptian hieroglyphics and Hittite cuneiform.

The treaty brought peace between the Egyptians and the Hittites for a time, but this stability did not last. Within several decades of the treaty, groups of seafaring peoples whom the Egyptians called "Sea Peoples" raided, migrated, and marauded in the eastern Mediterranean, disrupting trade and in some cases looting and destroying cities. Just who these people were and where they originated is much debated among scholars, but their raids, combined with the expansion of the Assyrians (see page 55), led to the collapse of the Hittite Empire and the fragmentation of the Egyptian empire in what historians later termed the Third Intermediate Period (1100–653 B.C.E.). There is evidence of drought, and some scholars have suggested that a major volcanic explosion in Iceland cooled the climate for several years, leading to a series of poor harvests. All of these developments are part of a general "Bronze Age Collapse" in the period around 1200 B.C.E. that historians see as a major turning point.

The political and military story of battles, waves of migrations, and the rise and fall of empires can mask striking continuities in the history of Egypt and its neighbors. Disrupted peoples and newcomers shared practical concepts of agriculture and metallurgy with one another, and wheeled vehicles allowed merchants to transact business over long distances. Merchants, migrants, and conquerors carried their gods and goddesses with them, and religious beliefs and practices blended and changed. Cuneiform tablets, wall inscriptions, and paintings testify to commercial exchanges and cultural accommodation, adoption, and adaptation.

The Emergence of New States

The Bronze Age Collapse was a time of massive political and economic disruption, but it was also a period of the spread of new technologies, especially iron. Iron appears to have been smelted in Anatolia as early as 2500 B.C.E., but it was too brittle to be of much use until about 1100 B.C.E., when techniques improved and iron weapons gradually became stronger and cheaper than their bronze counterparts. Thus, in the schema of dividing history into periods according to the main material out of which tools are made (see Chapter 1), the **Iron Age** began in about 1100 B.C.E. Iron weapons became important items of trade around the Mediter-

- **Indo-European languages** A large family of languages that includes English, most of the languages of modern Europe, ancient Greek, Latin, Persian, Hindi, Bengali, and Sanskrit, the sacred tongue of ancient India.
- **Iron Age** Period beginning about 1100 B.C.E. when iron became the most important material for weapons and tools in some parts of the world.
- **Phoenicians** People of the prosperous city-states in what is now Lebanon who traded and founded colonies throughout the Mediterranean and spread the phonetic alphabet.

ranean and throughout the Tigris and Euphrates Valleys, and the technology for making them traveled as well. (See "Global Trade: Iron," page 50.)

The decline of Egypt allowed new powers to emerge. South of Egypt along the Nile was a region called Nubia, which as early as 2000 B.C.E. served as a conduit of trade through which ivory, gold, ebony, and other products flowed north from sub-Saharan Africa. Small kingdoms with large buildings and rich tombs arose in this area. As Egypt expanded during the New Kingdom, it took over northern Nubia, incorporating it into the growing Egyptian empire. The Nubians adopted many features of Egyptian culture, including Egyptian gods, the use of hieroglyphs, and the building of pyramids. Many Nubians became officials in the Egyptian bureaucracy and officers in the army, and there was significant intermarriage between the two groups.

Nubian Cylinder Sheath This small silver sheath made about 520 B.C.E., perhaps for a dagger, shows a winged goddess on one side and the Egyptian god Amon-Ra (not visible in this photograph) on the other. It and others like it were found in the tombs of the king of Kush and suggest ways that Egyptian artistic styles and religious ideas influenced cultures farther up the Nile. (Cylinder sheath of Amani-natake-lebte, Nubian, Napatan Period, reign of King Amani-natake-lebte, 538–519 B.C.E. Findspot: Sudan, Nubia, Nuri, Pyramid 10. Gilded silver, colored paste inclusions. Height by diameter: 12 x 3.1 cm. (4¾ x 1¼ in.). Museum of Fine Arts, Boston. Harvard University–Museum of Fine Arts Expedition, 20.275. Photograph © 2014 Museum of Fine Arts, Boston)

With the contraction of the Egyptian empire, an independent kingdom, Kush, rose to power in Nubia, with its capital at Napata in what is now Sudan. The Kushites conquered southern Egypt, and in 727 B.C.E. the Kushite king Piye (r. ca. 747–716 B.C.E.) swept through the entire Nile Valley to the delta in the north. United once again, Egypt enjoyed a brief period of peace during which the Egyptian culture continued to influence that of its conquerors. In the seventh century B.C.E. invading Assyrians pushed the Kushites out of Egypt, and the Kushite rulers moved their capital farther up the Nile to Meroë, where they built hundreds of pyramids. Meroë became a center of iron production, its iron products the best in the world, smelted using wood from the vast forests in the area. Meroë traded iron goods to much of Africa and across the Red Sea and the Indian Ocean to India. Gold and cotton textiles also provided wealth to the Kushite kingdom, which in the third century B.C.E. developed its own alphabet. It was simpler than the Egyptian alphabet, but Meroitic script has not yet been deciphered.

While Kush expanded in the southern Nile Valley, another group rose to prominence along the Mediterranean coast of modern Lebanon. These people established the prosperous commercial centers of Tyre, Sidon, and Byblos, all cities still thriving today. These peoples were master shipbuilders, and from about 1100 B.C.E. to 700 B.C.E. many of the residents of these cities became the seaborne merchants of the Mediterranean. Their most valued products were purple and blue textiles, from which originated their Greek name, **Phoenicians**, meaning "Purple People." They also worked bronze and iron, which they shipped processed or as ore, and made and traded glass products. Phoenician ships often carried hundreds of jars of wine, and the Phoenicians introduced grape growing to new regions around the Mediterranean, dramatically increasing the amount of wine available for consumption and trade. They imported rare goods and materials, including hunting dogs, gold, and ivory, from Persia in the east and from their neighbors to the south.

The variety and quality of the Phoenicians' trade goods generally made them welcome visitors. They established colonies and trading posts throughout the Mediterranean and as far west as the Atlantic coast of modern-day Portugal. In the ninth

Phoenician Settlements in the Mediterranean

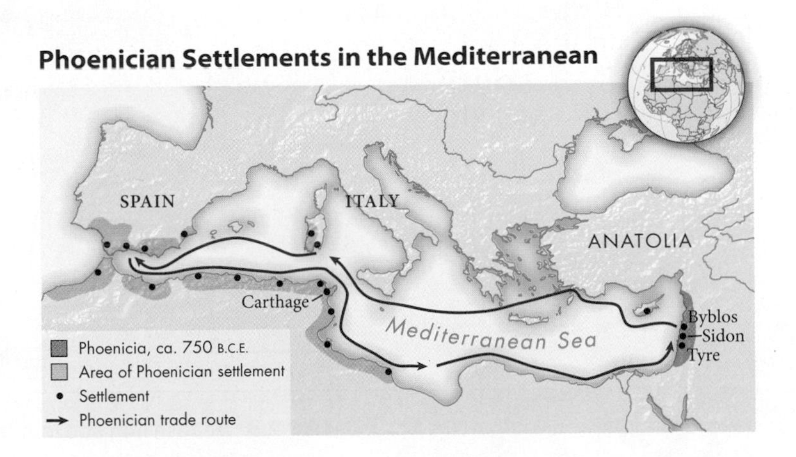

Global Trade

Iron

Iron has shaped world history more than any other metal, even more than gold and silver. In its pure state iron is soft, but adding small amounts of carbon and various minerals, particularly at very high temperatures, transforms it into a material with great structural strength. Tools and weapons made of iron dramatically shaped interactions between peoples in the ancient world, and machines made of iron and steel literally created the modern world.

Human use of iron began during the Paleolithic era, when people living in what is now Egypt used small pieces of hematite, a type of iron oxide, as part of their tools, along with stone, bone, and wood. Beginning around 4000 B.C.E. people in several parts of the world began to pick up iron-nickel meteorites and pound them into shapes. Such meteorites were rare, and the objects produced from them were luxury goods, not things for everyday use. Jewelry, weapons, and occasionally tools from meteoric iron have also been found in China, Africa, and North and South America. These were traded over very long distances, including thousands of miles around the Arctic, where indigenous peoples traded sharpened pieces from a gigantic iron meteorite that fell in Greenland for use as harpoon tips and knife blades.

Iron is the most common element in the earth, but most iron on or near the earth's surface occurs in the form of ore, which must be smelted to extract the metal. This is also true of copper and tin, but these can be smelted at much lower temperatures than iron, so they were the first metals to be produced to any great extent and were usually mixed together to form bronze. As artisans perfected bronze metalworking techniques, they also experimented with iron. They developed a long and difficult process to smelt iron, using burning charcoal and a bellows (which raised the temperature further) to extract the iron from the ore. This was done in an enclosed furnace, and

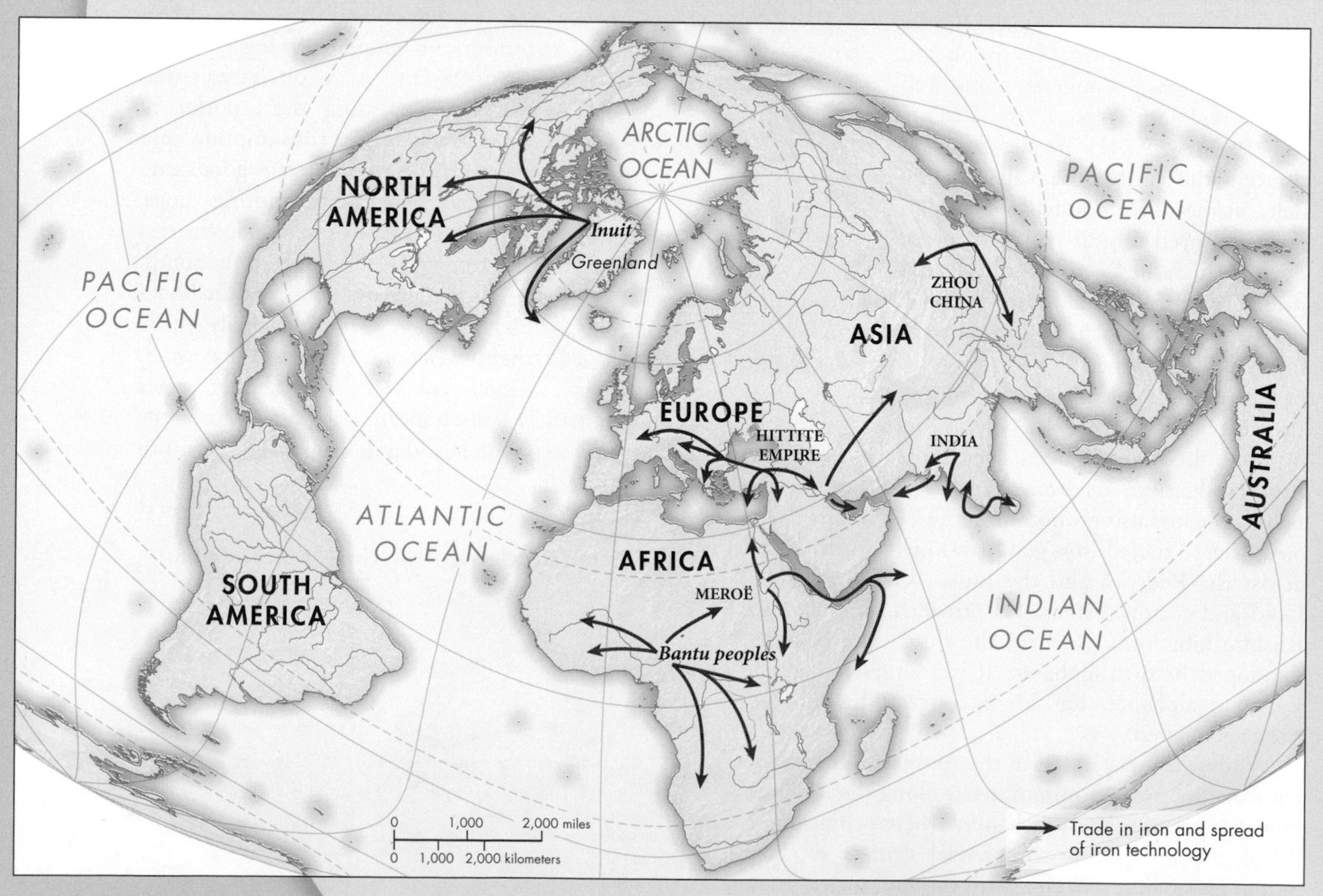

MAP 2.3 Trade in Iron and Iron Technology, to 500 B.C.E.

the process was repeated a number of times as the ore was transformed into wrought iron, which could be formed into shapes.

Exactly where and when the *first* smelted iron was produced is a matter of debate — many places would like to have this honor — but it happened independently in several different places. In Anatolia (modern-day Turkey), the first smelted weapon has been dated to around 2500 B.C.E., but most of the iron produced was too brittle to be of much use until 1100 B.C.E., when techniques improved. Iron weapons gradually became stronger and began to be traded around the Mediterranean. By 1700 B.C.E. artisans in northern India were making and trading iron implements. By 1200 B.C.E. iron was being produced and sold in southern India, though scholars debate whether smelting was discovered independently there or learned through contact with ironmaking cultures to the north. Iron objects were traded from Anatolia north into Greece, central Europe, and western Asia, and by 500 B.C.E. knowledge of smelting had traveled these routes as well.

Smelting was discovered independently in what is now Nigeria in western Africa about 1500 B.C.E. by a group of people who spoke Bantu languages. They carried iron hoes, axes, shovels, and weapons, and the knowledge of how to make them, as they migrated south and east over many centuries, gave them a distinct advantage over foraging peoples. In East Africa, the Kushite people learned the advantages of iron weaponry when the iron-using Assyrians drove them out of Egypt, and they then established a major center of iron production at Meroë and traded down the African coast and across the sea to India.

Ironworkers continued to experiment and improve their products. The Chinese probably learned smelting from Central Asian steppe peoples, but in about 500 B.C.E. artisans in China developed techniques of making cast iron using molds, whereby implements could be made much more efficiently. Somewhere in the Near East ironworkers discovered that if the relatively brittle wrought iron objects were placed on a bed of burning charcoal and then cooled quickly, the outer layer would form into a layer of a much harder material, steel. Goods made of cast iron were usually traded locally because they were heavy, but fine sword and knife blades of steel traveled long distances, and the knowledge of how to make them followed.

century B.C.E. they founded the city of Carthage in modern-day Tunisia, which became the leading city in the western Mediterranean, although it would one day struggle with Rome for domination of the region (see pages 151–153). The Phoenicians' voyages brought them into contact with the Greeks, to whom they introduced many aspects of the older and more urbanized cultures of Mesopotamia and Egypt.

The Phoenicians' overwhelming cultural achievement was the spread of a completely phonetic system of writing — that is, an alphabet (Figure 2.2). Writers of cuneiform and hieroglyphics had developed signs that were used to represent sounds, but these were always used with a much larger number of ideograms. Sometime around 1800 B.C.E., workers in the Sinai Peninsula, which was under Egyptian control, began to use only phonetic signs to write, with each sign designating one sound. This system vastly simplified writing and reading and spread among common people as a practical means of record keeping and communication. Egyptian scribes and officials continued to use hieroglyphics, but the Phoenicians adapted the simpler system for their own language and spread it around the Mediterranean. The Greeks modified this alphabet for their own language, and the Romans later based their alphabet — the script we use to write English today — on Greek. Alphabets based on the Phoenician alphabet were also created in the Persian Empire and formed the basis of Hebrew, Arabic, and various alphabets of South and Central Asia. The system invented by ordinary people and spread by Phoenician merchants is the origin of most of the world's phonetic alphabets in use today.

The Hebrews

☐ How did the Hebrews create an enduring written religious tradition?

The legacy of another people who took advantage of Egypt's collapse to found an independent state may have been even more far-reaching than that of the Phoenicians. For a period of several centuries, the Hebrews controlled first one and then two small states on the western end of the Fertile Crescent. Politically unimportant when compared with the Egyptians or Babylonians, the Hebrews created a new form of religious belief, a monotheism based on the worship of an all-powerful god they called **Yahweh** (YAH-way). Beginning in the late seventh century B.C.E. the Hebrews began to write down their religious ideas, traditions,

- **Yahweh** All-powerful god of the Hebrew people and the basis for the enduring religious traditions of Judaism.

FIGURE 2.2 Origins of the Alphabet List of hieroglyphic, Ugaritic, Phoenician, Greek, and Roman sign forms. (Source: A. B. Knapp, *The History and Culture of Ancient Western Asia and Egypt.* Reproduced with permission of Wadsworth Publishing Company in the format Book via Copyright Clearance Center.)

HIEROGLYPHIC	REPRESENTS	UGARITIC	PHOENICIAN	GREEK	ROMAN
	Throw stick	T		Γ	G
	Man with raised arms			E	E
	Basket with handle			K	K
	Water			M	M
	Snake			N	N
	Eye		O	O	O
	Mouth		?	Π	P
	Head		9	P	R
	Pool with lotus flowers		W	Σ	S
	House		9	B	B
	Ox-head		K	A	A

laws, advice literature, prayers, hymns, history, and prophecies in a series of books. These were gathered together centuries later to form the Hebrew Bible, which Christians later adopted and termed the "Old Testament" to parallel specific Christian writings in the "New Testament." These writings later became the core of the Hebrews' religion, Judaism, named after Judah, the southern of the two Hebrew kingdoms. Jews today revere these texts, as do many Christians, and Muslims respect them, all of which gives them particular importance.

The Hebrew State

Most of the information about the Hebrews comes from the Bible, which, like all ancient documents, must be used with care as a historical source. Archaeological evidence has supported many of its details, and because it records a living religious tradition, extensive textual and physical research into everything it records continues, with enormous controversies among scholars about how to interpret findings.

The Hebrews were nomadic pastoralists who may have migrated into the Nile Delta from the east seeking good land for their herds of sheep and goats. According to the Hebrew Bible, they were enslaved by the Egyptians but were led out of Egypt by a charismatic leader named Moses. The Hebrews settled in the area between the Mediterranean and the Jordan River known as Canaan and were organized into tribes, each tribe consisting of numerous families who thought of themselves as related to one another. They slowly adopted agriculture and, not surprisingly, at times worshipped the agricultural gods of their neighbors, including Baal, an ancient fertility god represented as a golden calf. In this they followed the common historical pattern of newcomers by adapting the culture of an older, well-established people.

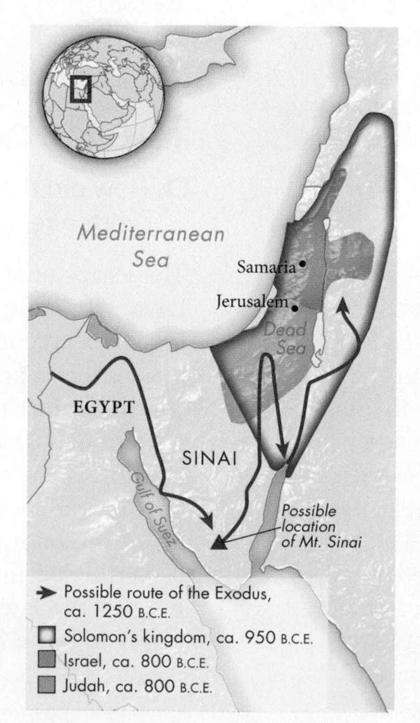

The Hebrew Exodus and State, ca. 1250–800 B.C.E.

The Bible reports that the greatest danger to the Hebrews came from a group known as the Philistines (FIH-luh-steenz), who migrated to and established a kingdom in Canaan. The Philistines' superior technology and military organization at first made them invincible, but the Hebrews found a leader in Saul, who with his men fought the Philistines. Saul subsequently established a monarchy over the Hebrew tribes, an event conventionally dated to about 1025 B.C.E. Saul's work was carried on by

David of Bethlehem, who captured the city of Jerusalem, which he made the religious and political center of the realm. His military successes enlarged the kingdom and his reign was a period of vitality. David's son Solomon (r. ca. 965–925 B.C.E.) launched a building program that the biblical narrative describes as including cities, palaces, fortresses, and roads. The most symbolic of these projects was the Temple of Jerusalem, which became the home of the Ark of the Covenant, the chest that contained the holiest Hebrew religious articles. The Temple of Jerusalem was intended to be the religious heart of the kingdom, a symbol of Hebrew unity and of Yahweh's approval of the Hebrew state.

This state did not last long. At Solomon's death his kingdom broke into political halves. The northern part became Israel, with its capital at Samaria, and the southern half was Judah, with Jerusalem remaining its center. War broke out between the northern and southern halves, and the Assyrians wiped out the northern kingdom in 722 B.C.E. Judah survived numerous invasions until the Babylonians crushed it in 587 B.C.E. The survivors were sent into exile in Babylonia, a period commonly known as the Babylonian Captivity. In 538 B.C.E. the Persian king Cyrus the Great conquered the Babylonians and permitted some forty thousand exiles to return to Jerusalem (see page 56 and "Viewpoints 2.2: Rulers and Divine Favor: Cyrus the Great in the Cyrus Cylinder and Hebrew Scripture," page 54). They rebuilt the temple, although politically the area was simply part of the Persian Empire.

Hebrew Seal Archaeologists found this stone seal in 2012 while unearthing an ancient drainage channel in central Jerusalem. Dating from the seventh or sixth century B.C.E., the tiny seal would have been set in a ring and used for signing letters. The inscription reads, "Belonging to Matanyahu . . . ," a name that is found in Hebrew Scripture and is very close to the name of the current prime minister of Israel, Benjamin Netanyahu. (Bible Land Pictures/akg-images)

The Jewish Religion

During and especially after the Babylonian Captivity, the most important Hebrew texts of history, law, and ethics were edited and brought together in the Torah, the first five books of the Hebrew Bible. Here the exiles redefined their beliefs and practices, establishing what they believed to be the law of Yahweh. Fundamental to an understanding of the Jewish religion is the concept of the Covenant, an agreement that people believed to exist between themselves and Yahweh. According to the Bible, Yahweh appeared to the tribal leader Abraham, promising him that he would be blessed, as would his descendants, if they followed Yahweh. (Because Judaism, Christianity, and Islam all regard this event as foundational, they are referred to as the "Abrahamic religions.") Yahweh next appeared to Moses when he was leading the Hebrews out of Egypt, and Yahweh made a covenant with the Hebrews: if they worshipped Yahweh as their only god, he would consider them his chosen people and protect them from their enemies. Individuals such as Abraham and Moses who acted as intermediaries between Yahweh and the Hebrew people were known as "prophets." Much of the Hebrew Bible consists of writings in the prophets' voices, understood as messages from Yahweh to the Hebrews.

Worship was embodied in a series of rules of behavior, the Ten Commandments, which Yahweh gave to Moses; these required certain kinds of religious observances and forbade the Hebrews to steal, kill, lie, or commit adultery, thus creating a system of ethical absolutes. From the Ten Commandments a complex system of rules of conduct was created and later written down as Hebrew law. Like the followers of other religions, Jews engaged in rituals through which they showed their devotion. They were to please Yahweh by living up to high moral standards and by worshipping him above all other gods. Increasingly this was understood to be a commandment to worship Yahweh alone. The later prophets such as Isaiah created a system of ethical monotheism, in which goodness was understood to come from a single transcendent god, and in which religious obligations included fair and just behavior toward other people as well as rituals.

Like Mesopotamian deities, Yahweh punished people, but the Hebrews also believed he would pro-

Viewpoints 2.2

Rulers and Divine Favor: Cyrus the Great in the Cyrus Cylinder and Hebrew Scripture

• *In Mesopotamia—and elsewhere in the ancient world—individuals who established large empires through conquest often subsequently proclaimed that their triumph was the result of divine favor, and they honored the gods of the regions they conquered. King Cyrus the Great of Persia appears to have followed this tradition. A text written in cuneiform on a sixth-century-B.C.E. Babylonian clay cylinder presents Cyrus describing the way in which the main Babylonian god, Marduk, selected him to conquer Babylon and restore proper government and worship. Cyrus is also portrayed as divinely chosen in the book of Isaiah in Hebrew Scripture, probably written sometime in the late sixth century B.C.E., after Cyrus allowed the Jews to return to Jerusalem. Because Cyrus was not a follower of the Jewish god, however, the issue of divine favor was more complicated.*

The Cyrus Cylinder

"I am Cyrus, king of the universe, the great king, the powerful king, king of Babylon, king of Sumer and Akkad, king of the four quarters of the world. . . .

When I went as harbinger of peace i[nt]o Babylon I founded my sovereign residence within the palace amid celebration and rejoicing. Marduk, the great lord, bestowed on me as my destiny the great magnanimity of one who loves Babylon, and I every day sought him out in awe. My vast troops marched peaceably in Babylon, and the whole of [Sumer] and Akkad had nothing to fear. I sought the welfare of the city of Babylon and all its sanctuaries. As for the population of Babylon, . . . [w]ho as if without div[ine intention] had endured a yoke not decreed for them, I soothed their weariness, I freed them from their bond. . . . Marduk, the great lord, rejoiced at [my good] deeds, and he pronounced a sweet blessing over me, Cyrus, the king who fears him, and over Cambyses, the son [my] issue, [and over] all my troops, that we might proceed further at his exalted command."

The Book of Isaiah, Chapter 45

"Thus said the Lord to Cyrus, His anointed one—whose right hand He has grasped, Treading down nations before him, Ungirding the loins of kings, Opening doors before him, and letting no gate stay shut: I will march before you, and level the hills that loom up; I will shatter doors of bronze and cut down iron bars. I will give you treasures concealed in the dark and secret hoards—So that you may know that it is I the LORD, the God of Israel, who call you by name. For the sake of My servant Jacob, Israel My chosen one, I call you by name, I hail you by title, though you have not known Me. I am the LORD, and there is none else; beside Me, there is no God. I engird you, though you have not known Me. . . .

It was I who roused him [that is, Cyrus] for victory, and who level all roads for him. He shall rebuild My city, and let My exiled people go, without price and without payment—said the LORD of hosts."

Sources: Cylinder inscription translation by Irving Finkel, curator of Cuneiform Collections at the British Museum, www.britishmuseum.org. "The Book of Isaiah" in *Tanakh: A New Translation of The Holy Scriptures According to the Traditional Hebrew Text.*

QUESTIONS FOR ANALYSIS

1. How would you compare the portrayal of Cyrus in the two texts?
2. The Babylonians were polytheistic, and the Hebrews were monotheistic. How does this shape the way divine actions and favor are portrayed in the texts?
3. Both of these texts have been very influential in establishing the largely positive historical view of Cyrus. What limitations might there be in using these as historical sources?

tect them all, not simply kings and powerful priests, and make them prosper if they obeyed his commandments. A hymn recorded in the Hebrew Bible's book of Psalms captures this idea:

> Blessed is every one who fears the Lord, who walks in his ways!
> You shall eat the fruit of the labor of your hands;
> you shall be happy, and it shall be well with you.
> Your wife will be like a fruitful vine without your house;
> your children will be like olive shoots around your table.
> Lo, thus shall the man be blessed who fears the Lord. (Psalms 128:1–4)

The religion of the Hebrews was thus addressed to not only the elites but also the individual. Because kings or other political leaders were not essential to its practice, the rise or fall of a kingdom was not crucial to the religion's continued existence. Religious leaders were important in Judaism, but personally following the instructions of Yahweh was the central task for observant Jews in the ancient world.

Hebrew Society

The Hebrews were originally nomadic, but they adopted settled agriculture in Canaan, and some lived in cities. Over time, communal use of land gave way to family or private ownership, and devotions to the traditions of Judaism replaced tribal identity.

Family relationships reflected evolving circumstances. Marriage and the family were fundamentally important in Jewish life. Celibacy was frowned upon, and almost all major Jewish thinkers and priests were married. As in Mesopotamia and Egypt, marriage was a family matter, too important to be left solely to the whims of young people. Although specific rituals may have been expected to ensure ritual purity in sexual relations, sex itself was viewed as part of Yahweh's creation and the bearing of children was seen in some ways as a religious function. Sons were especially desired because they maintained the family bloodline while keeping ancestral property in the family. A firstborn son became the head of the household upon his father's death. Mothers oversaw the early education of the children, but as boys grew older, their fathers provided more of their education.

The development of urban life among Jews created new economic opportunities, especially in crafts and trade. People specialized in certain occupations, such as milling flour, baking bread, making pottery, weaving, and carpentry. As in most ancient societies, these crafts were family trades.

The Assyrians and Persians

☐ How did the Assyrians and the Persians consolidate their power and control the subjects of their empires?

Small kingdoms like those of the Phoenicians and the Jews could exist only in the absence of a major power. In the ninth century B.C.E. one major power arose in the form of the Assyrians, who starting in northern Mesopotamia created an empire through often-brutal military conquests. And from a base in what is now southern Iran, the Persians established an even larger empire, developing effective institutions of government.

Assyria, the Military Monarchy

Starting from a base in northern Mesopotamia around 900 B.C.E., the Assyrians began a campaign of expansion and domination, conquering, exacting tribute, and building new fortified towns, palaces, and temples. Over the next several centuries, Babylonia, Syria, Phoenicia, Israel, and many other states fell. By means of almost constant warfare, the Assyrians created an empire that stretched from their capital of Nineveh on the Tigris River to central Egypt. Revolt against the Assyrians inevitably promised the rebels bloody battles and cruel sieges followed by surrender, accompanied by systematic torture and slaughter, and sometimes deportations.

Assyrian methods were certainly harsh, but in practical terms Assyria's success was due primarily to the size of its army of infantrymen, archers, and charioteers and to the army's sophisticated and effective military organization. In addition, the Assyrians developed a wide variety of siege machinery and techniques, including excavations to undermine city walls and battering rams to knock down walls and gates. Never before in this area had anyone applied such technical knowledge to warfare. The Assyrians even invented the concept of a corps of engineers who bridged rivers with pontoons or provided soldiers with inflatable skins for swimming. The Assyrians also knew how to coordinate their efforts, both in open battle and in siege warfare. Not only did the Assyrians know how to win battles, but they also knew how to take advantage of their victories. As early as the eighth century B.C.E., the Assyrian kings began to organize their conquered territories into an empire. The lands closest to Assyria became provinces governed directly by Assyrian officials. Kingdoms beyond the provinces were not annexed but became dependent states that followed Assyria's lead and also paid Assyria a hefty tribute.

Assyrian Warriors Attack a City In this Assyrian carving from a royal throne room made about 865 B.C.E., warriors cross a river on inflated skins, which both support them and provide air for breathing underwater. Such innovative techniques, combined with a large army and effective military organization, allowed the Assyrians to establish a large empire. (Werner Forman Archive/British Museum, London. Location: 10. © 2004 Werner Forman/TopFoto/The Image Works)

By the seventh century B.C.E. Assyrian power seemed firmly established. Yet the downfall of Assyria was swift and complete. Babylon won its independence in 626 B.C.E. and joined forces with a new group, the Medes, an Indo-European-speaking people from Persia. Together the Babylonians and the Medes destroyed the Assyrian Empire in 612 B.C.E., paving the way for the rise of the Persians. The Hebrew prophet Nahum spoke for many when he asked: "Nineveh is laid waste: who will bemoan her?" (Nahum 3:7). Their cities destroyed and their power shattered, the Assyrians seemed to disappear from history.

Modern archaeology has brought the Assyrians out of obscurity. In the nineteenth century archaeologists unearthed huge sculpted figures of winged bulls, human-headed lions, and sphinxes, along with cuneiform tablets that recounted everything from military campaigns to business relationships. For the kings' palaces, Assyrian artists carved reliefs that showed scenes of war as a series of episodes that progressed from the time the army marched out until the enemy was conquered. In doing so, they created a visual narrative of events, a form still favored by comic-book artists and the authors of graphic novels.

The Rise and Expansion of the Persian Empire

As we have seen, Assyria rose to power from a base in the Tigris and Euphrates River Valleys of Mesopotamia, which had seen many earlier empires. The Assyrians were defeated by a coalition that included not only a Mesopotamian power—Babylon—but also a people with a base of power in a part of the world that had not been the site of earlier urbanized states: Persia (modern-day Iran), a stark land of towering mountains and harsh deserts with a broad central plateau in the heart of the country (Map 2.4).

Iran's geographical position and topography explain its traditional role as the highway between western and eastern Asia. Nomadic peoples migrating south from the broad steppes of Russia and Central Asia have streamed into Iran throughout much of history. (For an in-depth discussion of these groups, see Chapter 12.) Confronting the uncrossable salt deserts, most have turned either westward or eastward, moving on until they reached the advanced and wealthy urban centers of Mesopotamia and India. Cities did emerge along these routes, however, and Iran became the area where nomads met urban dwellers.

Among these nomads were Indo-European-speaking peoples who migrated into this area about 1000 B.C.E. with their flocks and herds. They were also horse breeders, and the horse gave them a decisive military advantage over those who already lived in the area. One of these groups was the Medes, who settled in northern Iran and built their capital city at Ecbatana, the modern Hamadan. With the rise of the Medes, the balance of power in western Asia shifted east of Mesopotamia for the first time.

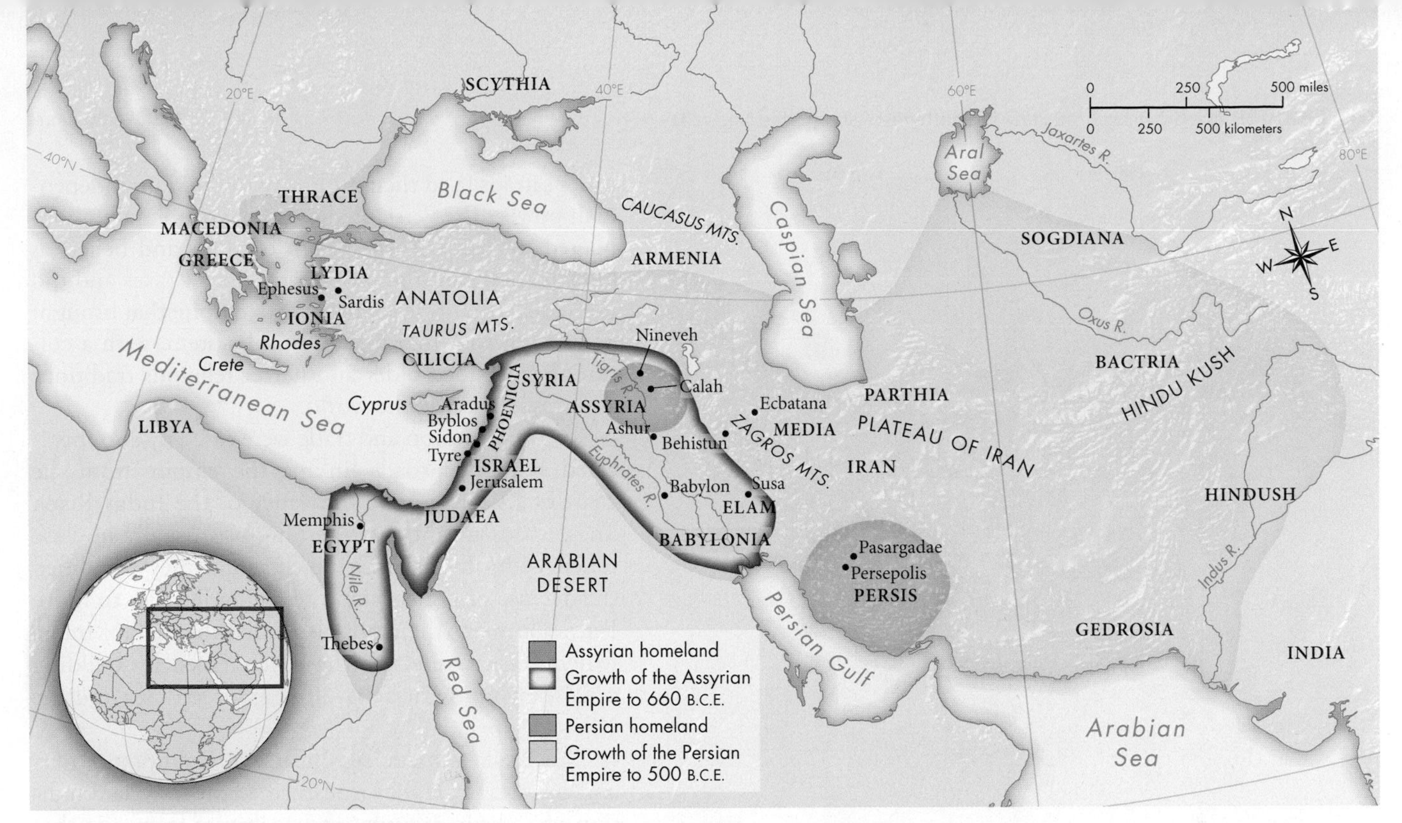

MAP 2.4 The Assyrian and Persian Empires, ca. 1000–500 B.C.E. The Assyrian Empire at its height around 650 B.C.E. included almost all of the old centers of power in the ancient Near East. By 500 B.C.E., however, the Persian Empire was far larger, extending from the Mediterranean Sea to the Indus River.

In 550 B.C.E. Cyrus the Great (r. 559–530 B.C.E.), king of the Persians (another Indo-European-speaking group) and one of the most remarkable statesmen of antiquity, conquered the Medes. Cyrus then set out to win control of the shore of the Mediterranean and thus of the terminal ports of the great trade routes that crossed Iran and Anatolia and to secure eastern Iran from the threats of nomadic invasions. In a series of major campaigns Cyrus achieved both goals. He conquered the various kingdoms of the Tigris and Euphrates Valleys and swept into Anatolia, easily overthrowing the young kingdom of Lydia. His generals subdued the Greek cities along the coast of Anatolia and the Phoenician cities south of these, thus gaining him flourishing ports on the Mediterranean. From Lydia, Cyrus marched to the far eastern corners of Iran and conquered the regions of Parthia and Bactria in Central Asia, though he ultimately died on the battlefield there.

After his victories, Cyrus made sure the Persians were portrayed as liberators, and in some cases he was more benevolent than most conquerors. According to later Greek sources, he spared the life of the conquered king of Lydia, Croesus, who then became his adviser. According to his own account, he freed all the captive peoples, including the Hebrews, who were living in forced exile in Babylon. He returned the Hebrews' sacred objects to them and allowed those who wanted to do so to return to Jerusalem, where he paid for the rebuilding of their temple. (See "Viewpoints 2.2: Rulers and Divine Favor: Cyrus the Great in the Cyrus Cylinder and Hebrew Scripture," page 54.)

Cyrus's successors continued the Persian conquests, creating the largest empire the world had yet seen. Darius (r. 521–486 B.C.E.) conquered Scythia in Central Asia, along with much of Thrace and Macedonia, areas north of the Aegean Sea. Thus, within forty years the Persians had transformed themselves from a subject people to the rulers of a vast empire that included all the oldest kingdoms and peoples of the region (see Map 2.4). Darius began to call himself "King of Kings." Invasions of Greece by Darius and his son Xerxes were unsuccessful, but the Persian Empire lasted another two hundred years, until it became part of the empire of Alexander the Great (see page 131).

The Persians also knew how to preserve the peace they had won on the battlefield. To govern the empire, they created an efficient administrative system based in their newly built capital city of Persepolis, near modern Shiraz, Iran. Under Darius, they divided the empire into districts and appointed either Persian or local nobles as administrators called satraps to head each one. The satrap controlled local government, collected taxes, heard legal cases, and maintained order. He was assisted by a council and also by officials and army leaders sent from Persepolis who made sure that he knew the will of the king and that the king knew what was going on in the provinces. This system decreased opposition to Persian rule by making local elites part of the system of government, although some-

Scythian Saddlecloth This red felt saddlecloth, dating from the fifth century B.C.E., is decorated with appliqués showing a winged griffon vulture with its claws in the back of a horned ibex. It was made by one of the nomadic peoples of western Asia, an area the Greeks called Scythia, some of which was conquered by the Persians. Items of daily use decorated with animals may have been thought to offer protection or assist in a hunt; this cloth was placed in a tomb, where it was preserved through the millennia by being frozen. (Hermitage, St. Petersburg, Russia/Photo © Boltin Picture Library/The Bridgeman Art Library)

• **Zoroastrianism** Religion based on the teachings of Zoroaster that emphasized the individual's responsibility to choose between good and evil.

times satraps used their authority to build up independent power. The Persians allowed the peoples they conquered to maintain their own customs and beliefs as long as they paid the proper amount of taxes and did not rebel. Their rule resulted in an empire that brought people together in a new political system, with a culture that blended older and newer religious traditions and ways of seeing the world.

Communication and trade were eased by a sophisticated system of roads linking the empire from the coast of Asia Minor to the valley of the Indus River. These roads meant that the king was usually in close touch with officials and subjects, and they simplified the defense of the empire by making it easier to move Persian armies. The roads also aided the flow of trade, which Persian rulers further encouraged by building canals, including one that linked the Red Sea and the Nile.

The Persians made significant contributions to art and culture. In art they transformed the Assyrian tradition of realistic monumental sculpture from one that celebrated gory details of slaughter to one that showed both the Persians and their subjects as dignified. Because they depicted both themselves and non-Persians realistically, Persian art is an excellent source of information about the weapons, tools, clothing, and even hairstyles of many peoples of the area.

The Religion of Zoroaster

Persian religion was originally polytheistic and tied to nature, with Ahuramazda (ah-HOOR-uh-MAZ-duh) as the chief god. Around 600 B.C.E. the ideas of Zoroaster (zoh-roh-ASS-tuhr), a thinker and preacher whose dates are uncertain, began to gain prominence. Zoroaster is regarded as the author of key religious texts, which were later gathered together in a collection of sacred texts called the Avesta. He introduced new spiritual concepts, stressing devotion to Ahuramazda alone and emphasizing the individual's responsibility to choose between the forces of creation, truth, and order and those of nothingness, chaos, falsehood, and disorder. Zoroaster taught that people possessed free will and that they must rely on their own consciences to guide them through an active life in which they focused on "good thoughts, good words, and good deeds." Their decisions were crucial, he warned, for there would come a time of reckoning. At the end of time, the forces of order would win, and the victorious Ahuramazda, like the Egyptian god Osiris, would preside over a last judgment to determine each person's eternal fate.

Scholars—and contemporary Zoroastrians—debate whether Zoroaster saw the forces of disorder as a malevolent deity named Angra Mainyu who was co-eternal with and independent from Ahuramazda, or whether he was simply using this term to mean "evil thoughts" or "a destructive spirit." Later forms of **Zoroastrianism** followed each of these lines of understanding. Most Zoroastrians believed that Ahuramazda and Angra Mainyu were locked together in a cosmic battle for the human race, a religious conceptualization that scholars call dualism. Some, however, had a more monotheistic interpretation and saw Ahuramazda as the only uncreated god.

Whenever he actually lived, Zoroaster's writings were communicated by teachers, and King Darius began to use Zoroastrian language and images. Under the protection of the Persian kings, Zoroastrian ideas spread throughout Iran and the rest of the Persian Empire, and then into central China. Zoroastrianism became the official religion of the later Persian Empire ruled by the Sassanid dynasty, and much later Zoroastrians migrated to western India, where they became known as Parsis and still live today. Zoroastrianism survived the fall of the Persian Empire to influence Christianity, Islam, and Buddhism, largely because of its belief in a just life on earth and a happy afterlife. Good behavior in the world, even though unrecognized at the time, would receive ample reward in the hereafter. Evil, no matter how powerful a person had been in life, would be punished after death. In some form or another, Zoroastrian concepts still pervade many modern religions and Zoroastrianism still exists as a religion.

CHRONOLOGY

ca. 3800 B.C.E.	Establishment of first cities in Sumeria
ca. 3200 B.C.E.	Earliest surviving cuneiform writing
2660–2180 B.C.E.	Period of the Old Kingdom in Egypt
2500 B.C.E.	Bronze weaponry becomes common in Mesopotamia
ca. 2300 B.C.E.	Establishment of Akkadian empire
1792–1750 B.C.E.	Hammurabi rules Babylon
ca. 1600 B.C.E.	Hittites begin to expand their empire
ca. 1570–1070 B.C.E.	Period of the New Kingdom in Egypt
ca. 1200 B.C.E.	Bronze Age Collapse; destruction and drought
ca. 1100 B.C.E.	Iron technology improves; beginning of the Iron Age; Phoenicians begin to trade in the Mediterranean
ca. 965–925 B.C.E.	Hebrew kingdom ruled by Solomon
ca. 900–612 B.C.E.	Assyrian Empire
722 B.C.E.	Kingdom of Israel destroyed by the Assyrians
587 B.C.E.	Kingdom of Judah destroyed by the Babylonians
550 B.C.E.	Cyrus the Great consolidates the Persian Empire

Chapter Summary

Beginning about 5,000 years ago, people in some parts of the world invented writing, in large part to meet the needs of the state, a new structure of governance in which leaders gained and maintained power through organized violence, bureaucracies, systems of taxation, social and gender hierarchies, and often written laws. States first developed in the southern part of Mesopotamia known as Sumer, where priests and rulers invented ways to control and organize people who lived in cities reliant on irrigation. Conquerors from the north unified Mesopotamian city-states into larger empires and spread Mesopotamian culture over a large area.

During the third millennium B.C.E. Egypt grew into a cohesive state under a single ruler in the Nile River Valley that provided rich farmland and an avenue of communication. For long stretches of history, Egypt was prosperous and secure in the Nile Valley, although at times various groups migrated into or invaded and conquered this kingdom. During the period known as the New Kingdom, warrior-kings created a large Egyptian empire. Newcomers and Egyptians often adopted aspects of each other's cultures. After the collapse of the New Kingdom, the Nubian rulers of Kush conquered Egypt, and another group, the Phoenicians, came to dominate trade in the Mediterranean, spreading a letter alphabet. Another group, the Hebrews, created a new form of religious belief based on the worship of a single all-powerful god. The Hebrews wrote down their religious laws and traditions in a series of books, which became the core of the Hebrews' religion, Judaism.

In the ninth century B.C.E. the Assyrians used a huge army and sophisticated military tactics to create an empire from a base in northern Mesopotamia. The

Persians established an even larger empire, developing effective institutions of government and building roads. The Persians generally allowed their subjects to continue their own customs, traditions, and religions. Around 600 B.C.E. a new religion grew in Persia based on the teachings of the prophet Zoroaster, who emphasized the individual's responsibility to choose between good and evil.

NOTES

1. *The Sumerians: Their History, Culture, and Character* by Samuel Noah Kramer, p. 238. Reproduced with permission of UNIVERSITY OF CHICAGO PRESS in the format Republish in a book via Copyright Clearance Center.
2. James B. Pritchard, ed., *Ancient Near Eastern Texts Relating to the Old Testament—Third Edition with Supplement.* © 1950, 1955, 1969, renewed 1978 by Princeton University Press. Reprinted by permission of Princeton University Press.

CONNECTIONS

"History is written by the victors" goes a common saying often incorrectly attributed to Winston Churchill. This is not always true; people who have been vanquished in wars or devastated by oppression have certainly made their stories known. But in other ways it is always true, for writing created records and therefore was the origin of what many people understand as history. Writing was invented to serve the needs of people who lived close to one another in cities and states, and almost everyone who could write lived in states. Because most history, including this book, concentrates on areas with states, the next two chapters examine the states that were developing in India and China during the period discussed in this chapter. In Chapter 5 we pick up on developments in the Mediterranean that link to those in Mesopotamia, Egypt, and Persia discussed in this chapter.

It is important to remember that, as was the spread of agriculture, the growth of the state was a slow process. States became the most powerful and most densely populated forms of human society, and today almost everyone on the planet is at least hypothetically a citizen of a state (or sometimes of more than one, if he or she has dual citizenship). Just 300 years ago, however, only about a third of the world was governed by states; in the rest of the world, people lived in bands of foragers, villages led by kin leaders, family groups of pastoralists, chiefdoms, confederations of tribes, or other forms of social organization. In 500 B.C.E. perhaps only a little over 5 percent of the world's population lived in states. In his *Histories*, Herodotus pays primary attention to the Persians and the Greeks, both of whom had writing and states, but he also discusses many peoples who had neither. In their attempts to provide a balanced account of all the world's peoples, historians today are also looking beyond written sources. Those sources invariably present only part of the story, as Winston Churchill—a historian as well as a political leader—noted in something he actually *did* say: "History will bear me out, particularly as I shall write that history myself."

Review and Explore

Make It Stick

LearningCurve
Go online and use LearningCurve to retain what you've read.

Identify Key Terms

Identify and explain the significance of each item below.

polytheism (p. 36)
cuneiform (p. 37)
epic poem (p. 37)
Hammurabi's law code (p. 42)
pharaoh (p. 43)
Indo-European languages (p. 48)
Iron Age (p. 48)
Phoenicians (p. 49)
Yahweh (p. 51)
Zoroastrianism (p. 59)

Review the Main Ideas

Answer the focus questions from each section of the chapter.

1. How does writing shape what we can know about the past, and how did writing develop to meet the needs of cities and states? (p. 32)
2. How did the peoples of Mesopotamia form states and develop new technologies and institutions? (p. 35)
3. How did the Egyptians create a prosperous and long-lasting society? (p. 42)
4. How did the Hebrews create an enduring written religious tradition? (p. 51)
5. How did the Assyrians and the Persians consolidate their power and control the subjects of their empires? (p. 55)

Make Connections

Analyze the larger developments and continuities within and across chapters.

1. What aspects of life in the Neolithic period continued with little change in the states of Mesopotamia and Egypt? What were the most important differences?
2. How were the empires that developed in Mesopotamia, Egypt, and Persia similar to one another? Which of the characteristics you have identified as a similarity do you predict will also be found in later empires, and why?
3. Most peoples in the ancient world gained influence over others and became significant in history through military conquest and the establishment of empires. By contrast, how did the Phoenicians and the Hebrews shape the development of world history?

LaunchPad
Online Document Project

Depicting a Goddess-King

Considering Egyptian views of gender roles, what complexities did Egyptian writers and artists face in depicting Hatshepsut?

Analyze written and visual representations of Hatshepsut, and then complete a quiz and writing assignment based on the evidence and details from this chapter.

See inside the front cover to learn more.

Suggested Reading

Brosius, Maria. *The Persians: An Introduction*. 2006. Covers all of Persian history.

Bryce, Trevor. *The Kingdom of the Hittites*, new ed. 2005. The definitive study of the Hittites.

Edwards, David N. *The Nubian Past*. 2004. Examines the history of Nubia and the Sudan, using archaeological and written sources.

Gates, Charles. *Ancient Cities: The Archaeology of Urban Life in the Ancient Near East and Egypt, Greece, and Rome*. 2003. Provides a survey of ancient life, including society and culture, that relies primarily on archaeological evidence.

Goldenberg, Robert. *The Origins of Judaism: From Canaan to the Rise of Islam*. 2007. Examines the development of Jewish ideas and traditions.

Leick, Gwendolyn. *The Babylonians*. 2002. Introduces all aspects of Babylonian life and culture.

Markoe, Glenn E. *The Phoenicians*. 2000. Presents these seafarers at home and abroad in the Mediterranean.

Meyers, Carol. *Rediscovering Eve: Ancient Israelite Women in Context*. 2012. A brief study designed for general readers that draws on archaeology and ethnography along with biblical texts.

Niditch, Susan. *Ancient Israelite Religion*. 1997. A brief but broad interpretation of Jewish religious developments.

Podany, Amanda. *Brotherhood of Kings: How International Relations Shaped the Ancient Near East*. 2010. Examines a thousand years of diplomacy among rulers.

Robinson, Andrew. *The Story of Writing: Alphabets, Hieroglyphs, and Pictograms*. 2007. A brief account of the scripts used in the major civilizations of the ancient world and of the major scripts we use today, with many illustrations.

Van de Mieroop, Marc. *A History of the Ancient Near East, 3000–332 B.C.E.* 2010. A concise history from Sumerian cities to Alexander the Great.

Visicato, Giuseppe. *The Power and the Writing: The Early Scribes of Mesopotamia*. 2000. Studies the practical importance of early Mesopotamian scribes.

Vivante, Bella. *Daughters of Gaia: Women of the Ancient World*. 2008. Explores the political, religious, and economic activities of actual women, and also examines ideas about gender.

The Foundation of Indian Society to 300 C.E.

Female Spirit from an Indian Stupa
Royal patronage aided the spread of Buddhism in India, especially the patronage of King Ashoka, who sponsored the construction of numerous Buddhist monuments. This head of a female spirit (called a *yakshini*) is from the stupa that Ashoka had built at Bharhut in central India. (Sudarsana Yakshini, relief from Stupa of Bharhut, Madhya Pradesh, India/De Agostini Picture Library/G. Nimatallah/The Bridgeman Art Library)

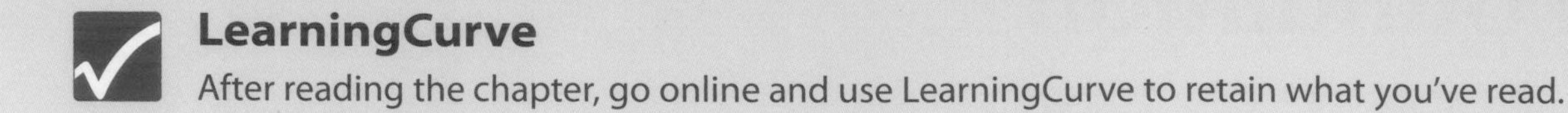

LearningCurve
After reading the chapter, go online and use LearningCurve to retain what you've read.

Chapter Preview

During the centuries when the peoples of ancient Mesopotamia and Egypt were developing urban civilizations, people in India were wrestling with the same challenges—food production, building of cities, political administration, and questions about human life and the cosmos. Like the civilizations of the Nile River Valley and southwestern Asia, the earliest Indian civilization centered on a great river, the Indus. From about 2800 B.C.E. to 1800 B.C.E., the Indus Valley, or Harappan, culture thrived and expanded over a huge area.

A very different Indian society emerged after the decline of this civilization. It was dominated by the Aryans, warriors who spoke an early version of Sanskrit. The Indian caste system and the Hindu religion, key features of Indian society that continued into modern times, had their origins in early Aryan society. By the middle of the first millennium B.C.E., the Aryans had set up numerous small kingdoms throughout north India. This was the great age of Indian religious creativity, when Buddhism and Jainism were founded and the early Brahmanic religion of the Aryans developed into Hinduism.

The first major Indian empire, the Mauryan Dynasty, emerged in the wake of the Greek invasion of north India in 326 B.C.E. This dynasty reached its peak under King Ashoka, who actively promoted Buddhism both within his realm and beyond it. Not long after his reign, however, the empire broke up, and for several centuries India was politically divided. Although India never had a single language and only periodically had a centralized government, cultural elements dating back to the ancient period—the core ideas of Brahmanism, the caste system, and the early epics—spread through trade and other contact, even when the subcontinent was divided into competing kingdoms.

The Land and Its First Settlers, ca. 3000–1500 B.C.E.

☐ What does archaeology tell us about the Harappan civilization in India?

The subcontinent of India, a landmass as large as western Europe, juts southward into the warm waters of the Indian Ocean. Today this region is divided into the separate countries of Pakistan, Nepal, India, Bangladesh, and Sri Lanka, but these divisions are recent, and for this discussion of premodern history, the entire subcontinent will be called India.

In India, as elsewhere, the possibilities for both agriculture and communication have always been shaped by geography. Some regions of the subcontinent are among the wettest on earth; others are arid deserts and scrubland. Most areas in India are warm all year, with high temperatures over 100°F; average temperatures range from 79°F in the north to 85°F in the south. Monsoon rains sweep northward from the Indian Ocean each summer. The lower reaches of the Himalaya Mountains in the northeast are covered by dense forests that are sustained by heavy rainfall. Immediately to the south are the fertile valleys of the Indus and Ganges Rivers. These lowland plains, which stretch all the way across the subcontinent, were tamed for agriculture over time, and India's great empires were centered there. To their west are the deserts of Rajasthan and southeastern Pakistan, historically important in part because their flat terrain enabled invaders to sweep into India from the northwest. South of the great river valleys rise the jungle-clad Vindhya Mountains and the dry, hilly Deccan Plateau. Only along the western coast of this part of India do the hills give way to narrow plains where crop agriculture flourished (see Map 3.2, page 81). India's long coastlines and predictable winds fostered maritime trade with other countries bordering the Indian Ocean.

Neolithic settlement of the Indian subcontinent occurred somewhat later than in the Nile River Valley and southwestern Asia, but agriculture followed a similar pattern of development and was well established by about 7000 B.C.E. Wheat and barley were the early crops, probably having spread in their domesticated form from what is today the Middle East. Farmers also domesticated cattle, sheep, and goats and learned to make pottery.

The story of the first civilization in India is one of the most dramatic in the ancient world. From the Bible, people knew about ancient Egypt and Sumer for centuries, but it was not until 1921 that archaeologists found astonishing evidence of a thriving and sophisticated Bronze Age urban culture dating to about 2500 B.C.E. at Mohenjo-daro in what is now Pakistan.

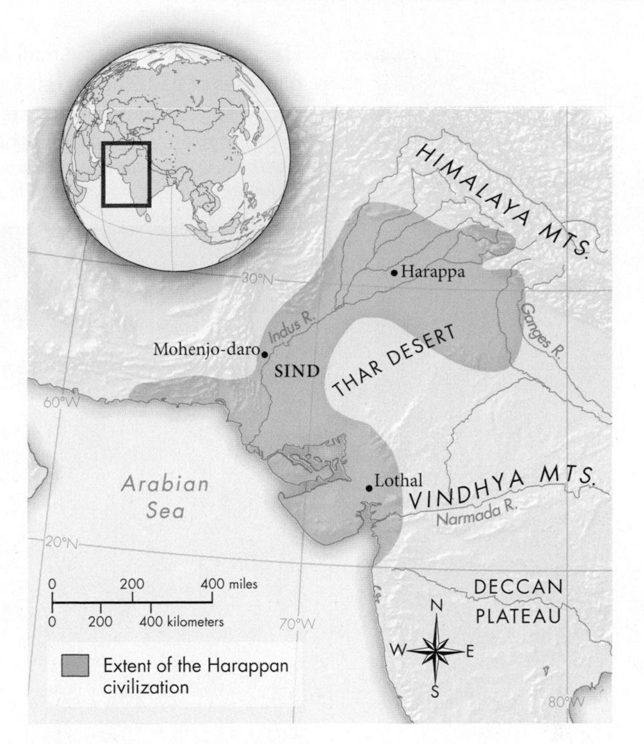

MAP 3.1 Harappan Civilization, ca. 2500 B.C.E. The earliest civilization in India developed in the Indus River Valley in the west of the subcontinent.

This civilization is known today as the Indus Valley or the **Harappan** (huh-RAH-puhn) civilization, from the modern names of the river and city near where the first ruins were discovered. Archaeologists have discovered some three hundred Harappan cities and many more towns and villages in both Pakistan and India, making it possible to see both the vast regional extent of the Harappan civilization and its evolution over a period of nearly a millennium (Map 3.1). It was a literate civilization, like those of Egypt and Mesopotamia, but no one has been able to decipher the more than four hundred symbols inscribed on stone seals and copper tablets. It is even possible that these symbols are not words but rather names or even nonlinguistic symbols. The civilization flourished most from 2500 B.C.E. to 2000 B.C.E.

The Harappan civilization extended over nearly five hundred thousand square miles in the Indus Valley, making it more than twice as large as ancient Egypt or Sumer. Yet Harappan civilization was marked by striking uniformity. Throughout the region, for instance, even in small villages, bricks were made to the same

• **Harappan** The first Indian civilization; also known as the Indus Valley civilization.

Harappan Artifacts Small objects like seals and jewelry found at Harappan sites provide glimpses of early Indian religious imagination and daily life. The molded tablet shown (left) depicts a female deity standing above an elephant battling two tigers. The jewelry found at these sites, such as the pieces below, makes much use of gold and precious stones. (both photos: © M. Kenoyer/Harappa.com. Courtesy, Department of Archeology and Museums, Government of Pakistan)

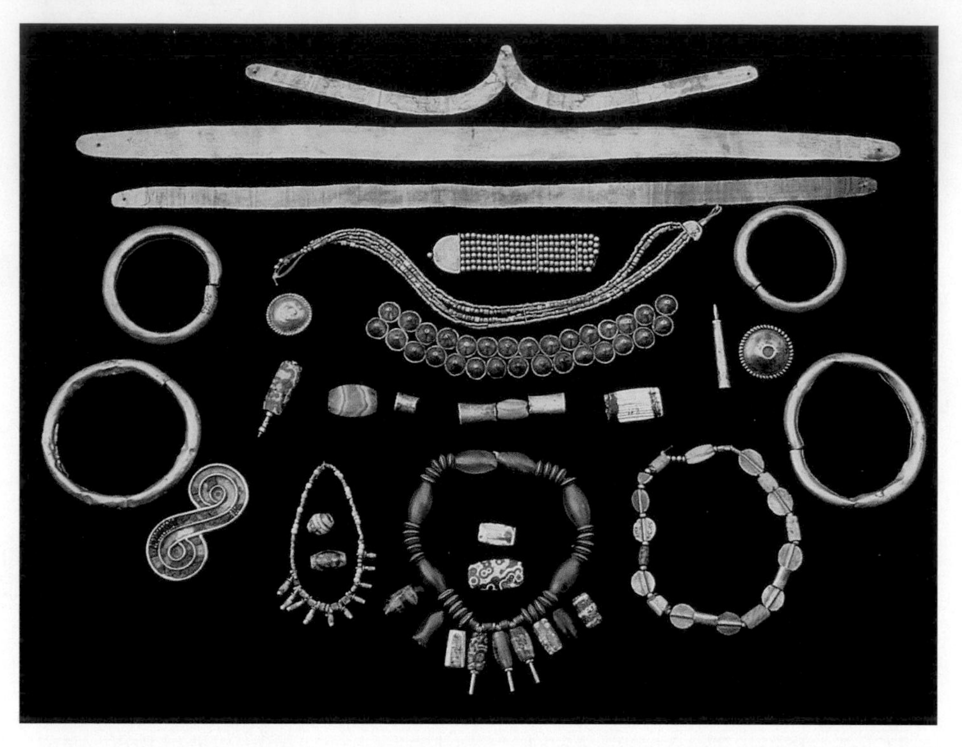

standard proportion (4:2:1). Figurines of pregnant women have been found throughout the area, suggesting common religious ideas and practices.

Like Mesopotamian cities, Harappan cities were centers for crafts and trade and were surrounded by extensive farmland. Craftsmen produced ceramics decorated with geometric designs. The Harappans were the earliest known manufacturers of cotton cloth, and this cloth was so abundant that goods were wrapped in it for shipment. Trade was extensive. As early as the reign of Sargon of Akkad in the third millennium B.C.E. (see page 38), trade between India and Mesopotamia carried goods and ideas between the two cultures, probably by way of the Persian Gulf. The Harappan port of Lothal had a stone dock 700 feet long, next to which were massive granaries and bead-making factories. Hundreds of seals were found there, some of Persian Gulf origin, indicating that Lothal was a major port of exit and entry.

The cities of Mohenjo-daro in southern Pakistan, and Harappa, some 400 miles to the north, were huge for this period, more than 3 miles in circumference, with populations estimated at 35,000 to 40,000. Both were defended by great citadels that towered 40 to 50 feet above the surrounding plain. The cities had obviously been planned and built before being settled—they were not the outcomes of villages that grew and sprawled haphazardly. Large granaries stored food. Streets were straight and varied from 9 to 34 feet in width. The houses were substantial, many two stories tall, some perhaps three. The focal point of a house was a central courtyard onto which the rooms opened, much like many houses today in both rural and urban India.

Perhaps the most surprising aspect of the elaborate planning of these cities was their complex system of drainage, which at Mohenjo-daro is well preserved. Each house had a bathroom with a drain connected to brick-lined sewers located under the major streets. Openings allowed the refuse to be collected, probably to be used as fertilizer on nearby fields. No other ancient city had such an advanced sanitation system.

Both Mohenjo-daro and Harappa also contained numerous large structures, which archaeologists think were public buildings. One of the most important was the large ventilated storehouse for the community's grain. Mohenjo-daro also had a marketplace or place of assembly, a palace, and a huge pool some 39 feet long by 23 feet wide by 8 feet deep. Like the later Roman baths, it had spacious dressing rooms for the bathers. Because the Great Bath at Mohenjo-daro resembles the ritual purification pools of later India, some scholars have speculated that power was in the hands of a priest-

Mohenjo-daro Mohenjo-daro was a planned city built of fired mud brick. Its streets were straight, and covered drainpipes were installed to carry away waste. From sites like this, we know that the early Indian political elite had the power and technical expertise to organize large, coordinated building projects. Found in Mohenjo-daro, this small ceramic figurine (right) shows a woman adorned with necklaces and an elaborate headdress. (site: © M. Kenoyer/Harrapa.com. Courtesy, Department of Archeology and Museums, Government of Pakistan; figurine: © Angelo Hornak/Alamy)

king and that the Great Bath played a role in the religious rituals of the city. In contrast to ancient Egypt and Mesopotamia, no great tombs have been discovered in Harappa, making it more difficult to envision the life of the elite.

The prosperity of the Indus civilization depended on constant and intensive cultivation of the rich river valley. Although rainfall seems to have been greater than in recent times, the Indus, like the Nile, flowed through a relatively dry region made fertile by annual floods and irrigation. And as in Egypt, agriculture was aided by a long, hot growing season and near-constant sunshine.

Because no one has yet deciphered the written language of the Harappan people, their political, intellectual, and religious life is largely unknown. There clearly was a political structure with the authority to organize city planning and facilitate trade, but we do not even know whether there were hereditary kings. There are clear similarities between Harappan and Sumerian civilization, but the differences are just as clear. For instance, the Harappan script, like the Sumerian, was incised on clay tablets and seals, but it has no connection to Sumerian cuneiform, and the artistic style of the Harappan seals is distinct.

Soon after 2000 B.C.E., the Harappan civilization mysteriously declined. The port of Lothal was abandoned by about 1900 B.C.E., and other major centers came to house only a fraction of their earlier populations. Scholars have proposed many explanations for the mystery of the abandonment of these cities. The decline cannot be attributed to the arrival of powerful invaders, as was once thought. Rather it was internally generated. Environmental theories include an earthquake that led to a shift in the course of the river, or a severe drought. Perhaps the long-term practice of irrigation led to the buildup of salt and alkaline in the soil until they reached levels toxic to plants, forcing the Harappan people to move in search of arable land. Some scholars speculate that long-distance commerce collapsed, leading to an economic depression. Others theorize that the population fell prey to diseases, such as malaria, that caused people to flee the cities.

Even though the Harappan people apparently lived on after scattering to villages, the large urban centers were abandoned, and key features of their high culture were lost. For the next thousand years, India had no large cities, no kiln-fired bricks, and no written language. There are, however, many signs of continuity with later Indian civilization, ranging from the sorts of pottery ovens used to some of the images of gods.

Some scholars speculate that the people of Harappa were the ancestors of the Tamils and other Dravidian-speaking peoples of modern south India.

The Aryans During the Vedic Age, ca. 1500–500 B.C.E.

☐ What kind of society and culture did the Indo-European Aryans create?

After the decline of the Harappan civilization, a people who called themselves **Aryans** became dominant in north India. They were speakers of an early form of Sanskrit, an Indo-European language closely related to ancient Persian and more distantly related to Latin, Greek, Celtic, and their modern descendants, such as English. For example, the Sanskrit *nava*, "ship," is related to the English word *naval*; *deva*, "god," to *divine*; and *raja*, "ruler," to *regal*. The word *Aryan* itself comes from *Arya*, "noble" or "pure" in Sanskrit, and has the same linguistic root as *Iran* and *Ireland*. The Aryans flourished during the Vedic Age (ca. 1500–500 B.C.E.). Named for the Vedas, a large and significant body of ancient sacred works written in Sanskrit, this period witnessed the Indo-Aryan development of the caste system and the Brahmanic religion and the writing of the great epics that represent the earliest form of Indian literature.

Aryan Dominance in North India

Until relatively recently, the dominant theory was that the Aryans came into India from outside, perhaps as part of the same movements of people that led to the Hittites occupying parts of Anatolia, the Achaeans entering Greece, and the Kassites conquering Sumer—all in the period from about 1900 B.C.E. to 1750 B.C.E. Some scholars, however, have proposed that the Indo-European languages spread to this area much earlier; to them it seems possible that the Harappan people were speakers of an early Indo-European language. If that was the case, the Aryans would be one of the groups descended from this early population.

Modern politics complicates analysis of the appearance of the Aryans and their role in India's history. Europeans in the eighteenth and nineteenth centuries developed the concept of Indo-European languages, and they did so in an age both highly conscious of race and in the habit of identifying races with languages. The racist potential of the concept was exploited by the Nazis, who glorified the Aryans as a superior race. Even in less politicized contexts, the notion of a group of people who entered India from outside and made themselves its rulers is troubling to many. Does it mean that the non-Aryans are the true Indians? Does it add legitimacy to those who in later times conquered India from outside? Does it justify or undermine the caste system? One of the difficulties faced by scholars who wish to take a dispassionate view of these issues is that the evidence for the earlier Harappan culture is entirely archaeological, while the evidence for the Aryans is almost entirely based on linguistic analysis of modern languages and orally transmitted texts of uncertain date.

The central source of information on the early Aryans is the ***Rig Veda***, the earliest of the Vedas, originally an oral collection of hymns, ritual texts, and philosophical treatises composed in Sanskrit between 1500 B.C.E. and 500 B.C.E. Like Homer's epics in Greece, written in this same period (see page 119), these texts were transmitted orally and are in verse. The *Rig Veda* portrays the Aryans as warrior tribes who glorified military skill and heroism; loved to drink, hunt, race, and dance; and counted their wealth in cattle. The Aryans did not sweep across India in a quick campaign, nor were they a disciplined army led by one conqueror. Rather they were a collection of tribes that frequently fought with each other and only over the course of several centuries came to dominate north India. (See "Viewpoints 3.1: Divine Martial Prowess from the *Rig Veda* and the *Epic of Gilgamesh*," page 70.)

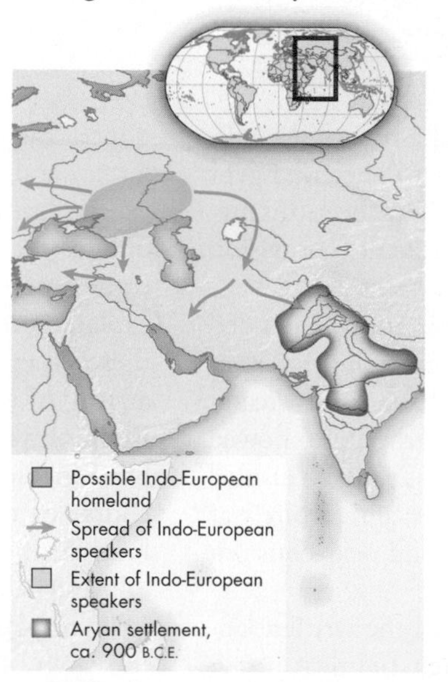

Indo-European Migrations and the Vedic Age

The key to the Aryans' success probably lay in their superior military technology. Those they fought often lived in fortified towns and put up a strong defense against them, but Aryan warriors had superior technology, including two-wheeled chariots, horses, and bronze swords and spears. Their epics present the struggle for north India in religious terms, describing their chiefs as godlike heroes and their opponents as irreligious savages who did not perform the proper sacrifices. In time, however, the Aryans clearly absorbed much from those they conquered, such as agricultural techniques and foods.

At the head of each Aryan tribe was a chief, or raja (RAH-juh), who led his followers in battle and ruled

Bronze Sword This bronze sword, with a rib in the middle of the blade for strength, is a striking example of the quality of Aryan arms. Superior weapons gave the Aryans military advantage. (© The Trustees of the British Museum/Art Resource, NY)

them in peacetime. The warriors in the tribe elected the chief for his military skills. Next in importance to the chief was the priest. In time, priests evolved into a distinct class possessing precise knowledge of the complex rituals and of the invocations and formulas that accompanied them, rather like the priest classes in ancient Egypt, Mesopotamia, and Persia. Below them in the pecking order was a warrior nobility who rode into battle in chariots and perhaps on horseback. The warrior class met at assemblies to reach decisions and advise the raja. The common tribesmen tended herds and worked the land. To the conquered non-Aryans fell the drudgery of menial tasks. It is difficult to define precisely their social status. Though probably not slaves, they were certainly subordinate to the Aryans and worked for them in return for protection.

Over the course of several centuries, the Aryans pushed farther east into the valley of the Ganges River, at that time a land of thick jungle populated by aboriginal forest peoples. The tremendous challenge of clearing the jungle was made somewhat easier by the introduction of iron around 1000 B.C.E., probably by diffusion from Mesopotamia. (See "Global Trade: Iron," page 50.) Iron made it possible to produce strong axes and knives relatively cheaply.

The Aryans did not gain dominance over the entire Indian subcontinent. South of the Vindhya range, people speaking Dravidian languages maintained their control. In the great Aryan epics the *Ramayana* and *Mahabharata*, the people of the south and Sri Lanka are spoken of as dark-skinned savages and demons who resisted the Aryans' conquests. Nevertheless, these epics would become part of the common cultural heritage of all of India.

As Aryan rulers came to dominate large settled populations, the style of political organization changed from tribal chieftainship to territorial kingship. In other words, the ruler now controlled an area with people living in permanent settlements, not a nomadic tribe that moved as a group. Moreover, kings no longer needed to be elected by the tribe; it was enough to be invested by priests and to perform the splendid royal ceremonies they designed. The priests, or **Brahmins**, supported the growth of royal power in return for royal confirmation of their own power and status. The Brahmins also served as advisers to the kings. In the face of this royal-priestly alliance, the old tribal assemblies of warriors withered away. By the time Persian armies reached the Indus around 513 B.C.E., there were sixteen major Aryan kingdoms in north India.

Life in Early India

Caste was central to the social life of these north Indian kingdoms. Early Aryan society had distinguished among the warrior elite, the priests, ordinary tribesmen, and conquered subjects. These distinctions gradually evolved into the **caste system**, which divided society into strictly defined hereditary groups. Society was conceived of as four hierarchical strata whose members did not eat with or marry each other. These strata, or varnas, were Brahmin (priests), Kshatriya (warriors and officials), Vaishya (merchants), and Shudra (peasants and laborers). The Shudra stratum, which encompassed most of the conquered people, was the largest. By contrast, the three upper varnas probably accounted for no more than 30 percent of the population. The caste system thus allowed the numerically outnumbered Aryans to maintain dominance over their subjects and not be culturally absorbed by them.

Social and religious attitudes supported the caste system. Aryans considered the work of artisans impure. They left all such work to the local people, who were probably superior to them in these arts anyway. Trade, by contrast, was not viewed as demeaning. Brahmanic texts of the period refer to trade as equal in value to farming, serving the king, or being a priest.

- **Aryans** The dominant people in north India after the decline of the Indus Valley civilization; they spoke an early form of Sanskrit.
- ***Rig Veda*** The earliest collection of Indian hymns, ritual texts, and philosophical treatises, it is the central source of information on early Aryans.
- **Brahmins** Priests of the Aryans; they supported the growth of royal power in return for royal confirmation of their own religious rights, power, and status.
- **caste system** The Indian system of dividing society into hereditary groups whose members interacted primarily within the group, and especially married within the group.

Viewpoints 3.1

Divine Martial Prowess from the *Rig Veda* and the *Epic of Gilgamesh*

• *Depictions of heroic military leaders and their interactions with their closest followers are found in the literature of many early societies. Sometimes the closest followers had once been opponents but were won over after recognizing the victor's strength and courage. Not uncommonly, the martial heroes are depicted as gods who resemble men in many ways. In India, one of the documents recounting such heroes is the* Rig Veda, *a collection of hymns that is the best source of information about the early Aryans. In the excerpt that follows, Indra, the king of the gods, boasts of his might to a band of fighters. It can be compared to the second document, from the Sumerian* Epic of Gilgamesh, *which describes how Enkidu became a follower of Gilgamesh after being defeated by him in hand-to-hand combat.*

"Indra and the Maruts" from the *Rig Veda*

" [*Maruts:*] "Indra, where are you coming from, all alone though you are so mighty? What is your intention, true lord? Will you make a pact with us, now that you have met us in our finery? Master of bay horses, tell us what your purpose is for us." . . .

[*Indra:*] "Where was that independent spirit of yours, Maruts, when you left me all alone in the fight with the dragon? *I* was the one, fierce and strong and mighty, who bent aside the lethal weapons of every enemy with my own weapons."

[*Maruts:*] "You did much with us as allies, with our many powers yoked in common, O bull. For we will do much, most valiant Indra, if we set our minds and will to do it, O Maruts."

[*Indra:*] "*I* killed Vrtra, O Maruts, by my Indra-power, having grown strong through my own glorious rage. With the thunderbolt on my arm I made these all-luminous waters move well for man."

[*Maruts:*] "No one can overcome your power, generous Indra; no one your equal is known to exist among the gods; no one being born now or already born could get such power. Do the things you will do, as you have grown strong."

[*Indra:*] "Even when I am alone, my formidable power must be vast; whatever I boldly set out to do, I do. For I am known as terrible, O Maruts; whatever I set in motion, Indra himself is master of that. Your praise has made me rejoice, lordly Maruts, the sacred chant worthy of hearing that you made here for me — for Indra the bull, the good fighter — that you my friends made in person for me, your friend, in person." "

"Enkidu and Gilgamesh" from the *Epic of Gilgamesh*

" [Enkidu said,] "I will go to the place where Gilgamesh lords it over the people, I will challenge him boldly, and I will cry aloud in Uruk, 'I have come to change the old order, for I am the strongest here.'"

Now Enkidu strode in front and the woman followed behind. He entered Uruk, that great market, and all the folk thronged round him where he stood in the street in strong-walled Uruk. The people jostled; speaking of him they said, "He is the spit of Gilgamesh." "He is shorter." "He is bigger of bone." "This is the one who was reared on the milk of wild beasts. His is the greatest strength." The men rejoiced: "Now Gilgamesh has met his match. This great one, this hero whose beauty is like a god, he is a match even for Gilgamesh."

In Uruk the bridal bed was made, fit for the goddess of love. The bride waited for the bridegroom, but in the night Gilgamesh got up and came to the house. Then Enkidu stepped out, he stood in the street and blocked the way. Mighty Gilgamesh came on and Enkidu met him at the gate. He put out his foot and prevented Gilgamesh from entering the house, so they grappled, holding each other like bulls. They broke the doorposts and the walls shook, they snorted like bulls locked together. They shattered the doorposts and the walls shook. Gilgamesh bent his knee with his foot planted on the ground and with a turn Enkidu was thrown. Then immediately his fury died. When Enkidu was thrown he said to Gilgamesh, "There is not another like you in the world. Ninsun, who is as strong as a wild ox in the byre, she was the mother who bore you, and now you are raised above all men, and [the god] Enlil has given you the kingship, for your strength surpasses the strength of men." So Enkidu and Gilgamesh embraced and their friendship was sealed. "

Sources: *The Rig Veda: An Anthology of the One Hundred and Eight Hymns*, selected, translated, and annotated by Wendy Doniger O'Flaherty (London: Penguin Classics, 1981). Copyright © Wendy Doniger O'Flaherty, 1981. Reproduced by permission of Penguin Books Ltd.; *The Epic of Gilgamesh*, translated with an introduction by N. K. Sandars (London: Penguin Classics, 1960, Third Edition 1972). Copyright © N. K. Sandars, 1960, 1964, 1972. Reproduced by permission of Penguin Books Ltd.

QUESTIONS FOR ANALYSIS

1. In what ways do Indra and Gilgamesh resemble each other?
2. As works of literature, what do these two selections have in common?

In the *Rig Veda*, the caste system is attributed to the gods:

> When they divided [the primeval man], into how many different portions did they arrange him? What became of his mouth, what of his two arms? What were his two thighs and his two feet called?
>
> His mouth became the brahman, his two arms was made into the [kshatriya]; his two thighs became the vaishyas, of his two feet the shudra was born.[1]

As priests, the Brahmins were expected to memorize every syllable and tone of the Vedas so that their rituals would please the gods. They not only conducted the traditional ceremonies but also developed new ones for new circumstances. As agriculture became more important to the Aryans, for example, Brahmins acted as agents of Agni, the god of fire, to purify the land for crops. The Brahmins also knew the formulas and spells that were effective against diseases and calamities.

Those without places in the four varnas—that is, newly conquered peoples and those who had lost their caste status through violations of ritual—were outcastes. That simply meant that they belonged to no caste. In time, some of them became "untouchables" because they were "impure." They were scorned because they earned their living by performing such "polluting" jobs as slaughtering animals and dressing skins.

Slavery was a feature of early social life in India, as it was in Egypt, Mesopotamia, and elsewhere in antiquity. People captured in battle often became slaves, but captives could also be ransomed by their families. Later, slavery was less connected with warfare and became more of an economic and social institution. A free man might sell himself and his family into slavery because he could not pay his debts. At the same time, he could, if clever, hard-working, or fortunate, buy his and his family's way out of slavery. At birth, slave children automatically became the slaves of their parents' masters. Indian slaves could be bought, used as collateral, or given away.

Women's lives in early India varied according to their social status, much as men's did. Like most nomadic tribes, the Aryans were patrilineal and patriarchal (tracing descent through males and placing power in the senior men of the family). Thus the roles of women in Aryan society probably were more subordinate than were the roles of women in local Dravidian groups, many of which were matrilineal (tracing descent through females). But even in Aryan society women were treated somewhat more favorably than in later Indian society. They were not yet given in child-marriage, and widows had the right to remarry. In epics such as the *Ramayana*, women are often portrayed as forceful personalities, able to achieve their goals both by using feminine ploys to cajole men and by direct action. (See "Listening to the Past: Conversations Between Rama and Sita from the *Ramayana*," page 72.)

Brahmanism

The Aryans recognized a multitude of gods who shared some features with the gods of other early Indo-European societies such as the Persians and Greeks. Some of them were great brawling figures, such as Agni, the god of fire, a particularly important god; Indra, wielder of the thunderbolt and god of war, who each year slew a dragon to release the monsoon rains; and Rudra, the divine archer who spread disaster and disease by firing his arrows at people. Others were shadowy figures, such as Dyaus, the father of the gods, related to the Greek Zeus. Varuna, the god of order in the universe, was a hard god, quick to punish those who sinned and thus upset the balance of nature. Ushas, the goddess of dawn, was a gentle deity who welcomed the birds, gave delight to human beings, and warded off evil spirits.

Ordinary people dealt with these gods through priests who made animal sacrifices to them. By giving valued things to the gods, people strengthened both the power of the gods and their own relationships with them. Gradually, under the priestly monopoly of the Brahmins, correct sacrifice and proper ritual became so important that most Brahmins believed that a properly performed ritual would force a god to grant a worshipper's wish. Ordinary people could watch a ceremony, such as a fire ritual, which was often held outdoors, but could not perform the key steps in the ritual.

The *Upanishads* (oo-PAH-nih-shadz), composed between 750 B.C.E. and 500 B.C.E., record speculations about the mystical meaning of sacrificial rites and about cosmological questions of man's relationship to the universe. They document a gradual shift from the mythical worldview of the early Vedic Age to a deeply philosophical one. Associated with this shift was a movement toward asceticism (uh-SEH-tuh-sihz-uhm)—severe self-discipline and self-denial. In search of wisdom, some men (but not women) retreated to the forests. These ascetics concluded that disciplined meditation on the ritual sacrifice could produce the same results as the physical ritual itself. Thus they reinterpreted ritual sacrifices as symbolic gestures with mystical meanings.

Ancient Indian cosmology (theories of the universe) focused not on a creator who made the universe out of nothing, but rather on endlessly repeating cycles. Key ideas were **samsara**, the reincarnation of souls by

• **samsara** The transmigration of souls by a continual process of rebirth.

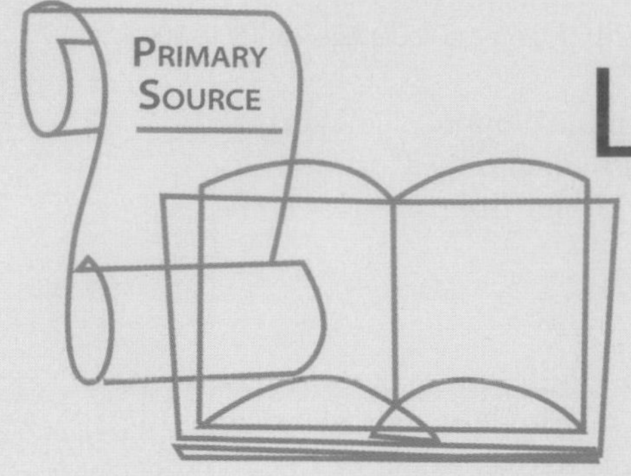

Listening to the Past

Conversations Between Rama and Sita from the *Ramayana*

The Ramayana, *an epic poem of about fifty thousand verses, is attributed to the third-century-*B.C.E. *poet Valmiki. Its main character, Rama, the oldest son of a king, is an incarnation of the great god Vishnu. As a young man, he wins the princess Sita as his wife when he alone among her suitors proves strong enough to bend a huge bow. Rama and Sita love each other deeply, but court intrigue disturbs their happy life. After the king announces that he will retire and consecrate Rama as his heir, the king's beautiful junior wife, wishing to advance her own son, reminds the king that he has promised her a favor of her choice. She then asks to have him appoint her son heir and to have Rama sent into the wilderness for fourteen years. The king is forced to consent, and Rama obeys his father.*

The passage below gives the conversations between Rama and Sita after Rama learns he must leave. In subsequent parts of the very long epic, the lovers undergo many other tribulations, including Sita's abduction by the lord of the demons, the ten-headed Ravana, and her eventual recovery by Rama with the aid of monkeys.

The Ramayana *eventually appeared in numerous versions in all the major languages of India. Hearing it recited was said to bring religious merit. Sita, passionate in her devotion to her husband, has remained the favorite Indian heroine. Rama, Sita, and the monkey Hanuman are cult figures in Hinduism, with temples devoted to their worship.*

"For fourteen years I must live in Dandaka, while my father will appoint Bharata prince regent. I have come to see you before I leave for the desolate forest. You are never to boast of me in the presence of Bharata. Men in power cannot bear to hear others praised, and so you must never boast of my virtues in front of Bharata. . . . When I have gone to the forest where sages make their home, my precious, blameless wife, you must earnestly undertake vows and fasts. You must rise early and worship the gods according to custom and then pay homage to my father Dasaratha, lord of men. And my aged mother Kausalya, who is tormented by misery, deserves your respect as well, for she has subordinated all to righteousness. The rest of my mothers, too, must always receive your homage. . . . My beloved, I am going to the great forest, and you must stay here. You must do as I tell you, my lovely, and not give offense to anyone."

So Rama spoke, and Sita, who always spoke kindly to her husband and deserved kindness from him, grew angry just because she loved him, and said, "My lord, a man's father, his mother, brother, son, or daughter-in-law all experience the effects of their own past deeds and suffer an individual fate. But a wife, and she alone, bull among men, must share her husband's fate. Therefore I, too, have been ordered to live in the forest. It is not her father or mother, not her son or friends or herself, but her husband, and he alone, who gives a woman permanent refuge in this world and after death. If you must leave this very day for the trackless forest, Rama, I will go in front of you, softening the thorns and sharp *kusa* grass. Cast out your anger and resentment, like so much water left after drinking one's fill. Do not be reluctant to take me, my mighty husband. There is no evil in me. The shadow of a husband's feet in any circumstances surpasses the finest mansions, an aerial chariot, or even flying through the sky. . . . O Rama, bestower of honor, you have the power to protect any other person in the forest. Why then not me? . . .

"If I were to be offered a place to live in heaven itself, Rama, tiger among men, I would refuse it if you were not there. I will go to the trackless forest teeming with deer, monkeys, and elephants, and live there as in my father's house, clinging to your feet alone, in strict self-discipline. I love no one else; my heart is so attached to you that were we to be parted I am resolved to die. Take me, oh please grant my request. I shall not be a burden to you." . . .

a continual process of rebirth, and **karma**, the tally of good and bad deeds that determined the status of an individual's next life. Good deeds led to better future lives, evil deeds to worse future lives—even to reincarnation as an animal. The wheel of life included human beings, animals, and gods. Reward and punishment worked automatically; there was no all-knowing god who judged people and could be petitioned to forgive a sin, and each individual was responsible for his or her own destiny in a just and impartial world.

To most people, especially those on the low end of the economic and social scale, these ideas were attractive. By living righteously and doing good deeds, people could improve their lot in the next life. Yet there was another side to these ideas: the wheel of life could be seen as a treadmill, giving rise to a yearning for release from the relentless cycle of birth and death. One solution offered in the *Upanishads* was moksha, or release from the wheel of life. Brahmanic mystics claimed that life in the world was actually an illusion and that the

When Sita finished speaking, the righteous prince, who knew what was right and cherished it, attempted to dissuade her. . . .

"Sita, give up this notion of living in the forest. The name 'forest' is given only to wild regions where hardships abound. . . . There are lions that live in mountain caves; their roars are redoubled by mountain torrents and are a painful thing to hear — the forest is a place of pain. At night worn with fatigue, one must sleep upon the ground on a bed of leaves, broken off of themselves — the forest is a place of utter pain. And one has to fast, Sita, to the limit of one's endurance, wear clothes of barkcloth and bear the burden of matted hair. . . . There are many creeping creatures, of every size and shape, my lovely, ranging aggressively over the ground. . . . Moths, scorpions, worms, gnats, and flies continually harass one, my frail Sita — the forest is wholly a place of pain. . . ."

Sita was overcome with sorrow when she heard what Rama said. With tears trickling down her face, she answered him in a faint voice. . . . "If from feelings of love I follow you, my pure-hearted husband, I shall have no sin to answer for, because my husband is my deity. My union with you is sacred and shall last even beyond death. . . . If you refuse to take me to the forest despite the sorrow that I feel, I shall have no recourse but to end my life by poison, fire, or water."

Though she pleaded with him in this and every other way to be allowed to go, great-armed Rama would not consent to taking her to the desolate forest. And when he told her as much, Sita fell to brooding, and drenched the ground, it seemed, with the hot tears that fell from her eyes. . . . She was nearly insensible with sorrow when Rama took her in his arms and comforted her. . . . "Without knowing your true feelings, my lovely, I could not consent to your living in the wilderness, though I am perfectly capable of protecting you. Since you are determined to live with me in the forest, Sita, I could no sooner abandon you than a self-respecting man his reputation. . . . My father keeps to the path of righteousness and truth, and I wish to act just as he instructs me. That is the eternal way of righteousness. Follow me, my timid one, be my companion in righteousness. Go now and bestow precious objects on the brahmins, give food to the mendicants and all who ask for it. Hurry, there is no time to waste."

Finding that her husband had acquiesced in her going, the lady was elated and set out at once to make the donations. ”

Source: *The Ramayana of Valmiki: An Epic of India*. Vol. 2: *Ayodhyakanda*, trans. Sheldon I. Pollock, ed. Robert P. Goldman (Princeton, N.J.: Princeton University Press, 1986), pp. 134–142, modified slightly.

Rama and Sita in the forest, from an eighteenth-century miniature painting. (Indian miniature, Kangra School, Moghul era, ca. 1780–85/Bhuri-Singh-Museum/R. and S. Michaud/akg-images)

QUESTIONS FOR ANALYSIS

1. What can you infer about early Indian family life and social relations from this story?
2. What do Sita's words and actions indicate about women's roles in Indian society of the time?
3. What do you think accounts for the continuing popularity of the story of Rama throughout Indian history?

only way to escape the wheel of life was to realize that ultimate reality was unchanging.

The unchanging ultimate reality was called **brahman**. This important concept has been translated many ways. Scholars have offered both brief phrases — "the cosmic principle," "the principle of religious reality," "absolute reality," "eternal truth," and "universal soul" — and somewhat longer descriptions: "holy or sacred power that is the source and sustainer of the universe," "the ultimate unchanging reality, composed of pure being and consciousness," and "eternal, unchanging, infinite, and transcendent reality that is the divine ground of everything in this universe." Brahman was contrasted to the multitude of fleeting phenomena that people consider important in their daily lives. The

- **karma** The tally of good and bad deeds that determines the status of an individual's next life.
- **brahman** The unchanging ultimate reality, according to the *Upanishads*.

individual soul or self was ultimately the same substance as the universal brahman, in the same way that each spark is in substance the same as a large fire.

The *Upanishads* gave the Brahmins a high status to which the poor and lowly could aspire in a future life. Consequently, the Brahmins greeted the concepts presented in these works and those who taught them with tolerance and understanding and made a place for them in traditional religious practice. The rulers of Indian society also encouraged the new trends, since the doctrines of samsara and karma encouraged the poor and oppressed to labor peacefully and dutifully. Thus, although the new doctrines were intellectually revolutionary, in social and political terms they supported the existing power structure.

India's Great Religions

- What ideas and practices were taught by the founders of Jainism, Buddhism, and Hinduism?

By the sixth and fifth centuries B.C.E., cities had reappeared in India, and merchants and trade were thriving. Bricks were again baked in kilns and used to build ramparts around cities. One particular kingdom, Magadha, had become much more powerful than any of the other states in the Ganges plain, defeating its enemies by using war elephants and catapults for hurling stones. Written language had also reappeared.

This was a period of intellectual ferment throughout Eurasia—the period of the early Greek philosophers, the Hebrew prophets, Zoroaster in Persia, and Confucius and the early Daoists in China. In India it led to numerous sects that rejected various elements of Brahmanic teachings. The two most influential were Jainism and Buddhism. Their founders were contemporaries living in the Ganges plain. Hinduism emerged in response to these new religions but at the same time was the most direct descendant of the old Brahmanic religion.

Jainism

The key figure of Jainism, Vardhamana Mahavira (fl. ca. 520 B.C.E.), was the son of the chief of a small state and a member of the warrior class. Like many ascetics of the period, he left home to become a wandering holy man. For twelve years, from ages thirty to forty-two, he traveled through the Ganges Valley until he found enlightenment and became a "completed soul." Mahavira taught his doctrines for about thirty years, founding a disciplined order of monks and gaining the support of many lay followers, male and female.

Mahavira accepted the Brahmanic doctrines of karma and rebirth but developed these ideas in new directions, founding the religion referred to as **Jainism**. He asserted that human beings, animals, plants, and even inanimate objects all have living souls enmeshed in matter, accumulated through the workings of karma. Even a rock has a soul locked inside it, enchained by matter but capable of suffering if someone kicks it. The souls conceived by the Jains have finite dimensions. They float or sink depending on the amount of matter with which they are enmeshed. The ascetic, who willingly undertakes suffering, can dissipate some of the accumulated karma and make progress toward liberation. If a soul at last escapes from all the matter weighing it down, it becomes lighter than ordinary objects and floats to the top of the universe, where it remains forever in bliss.

Jain Ascetic The most extreme Jain ascetics not only endured the elements without the help of clothes, but also were generally indifferent to bodily comfort. The Jain saint depicted in this eighth-century-C.E. cave temple has maintained his posture for so long that vines have grown up around him. (Courtesy, Robert Fisher)

Mahavira's followers pursued such liberation by living ascetic lives and avoiding evil thoughts and actions. The Jains considered all life sacred and tried to live without destroying other life. Some early Jains went to the extreme of starving themselves to death, since it is impossible to eat without destroying at least plants, but most took the less extreme step of distinguishing between different levels of life. The most sacred lifeforms were human beings, followed by animals, plants, and inanimate objects. A Jain who wished to avoid violence to life became a vegetarian and took pains not to kill any creature, even tiny insects in the air and soil. Farming was impossible for Jains, who tended instead to take up trade. Among the most conservative Jains, priests practiced nudity, for clinging to clothes, even a loincloth, was a form of attachment. Lay Jains could pursue Jain teachings by practicing nonviolence and not eating meat. The Jains' radical nonviolence was motivated by a desire to escape the karmic consequences of causing harm to a life. In other words, violence had to be avoided above all because it harms the person who commits it.

For the first century after Mahavira's death, the Jains were a comparatively small and unimportant sect. Jainism began to flourish under the Mauryan Dynasty (ca. 322–185 B.C.E.; see pages 81–83), and Jain tradition claims the Mauryan Empire's founder, Chandragupta, as a major patron. About 300 B.C.E. the Jain scriptures were recorded, and the religion split into two sects, one maintaining the tradition of total nudity, the other choosing to wear white robes on the grounds that clothes were an insignificant external sign, unrelated to true liberation. Over the next few centuries, Jain monks were particularly important in spreading northern culture into the Deccan and Tamil regions of south India.

Although Jainism never took hold as widely as Hinduism and Buddhism (discussed below), it has been an influential strand in Indian thought and has several million adherents in India today. Fasting and nonviolence as spiritual practices in India owe much to Jain teachings. In the twentieth century Mohandas Gandhi, leader of the Indian independence movement, was influenced by these ideas through his mother, and the American civil rights leader Dr. Martin Luther King, Jr., was influenced by Gandhi.

Siddhartha Gautama and Buddhism

Siddhartha Gautama (fl. ca. 500 B.C.E.), also called Shakyamuni ("sage of the Shakya tribe"), is best known as the Buddha ("enlightened one"). He was a contemporary of Mahavira and came from the same warrior social class. He was born the son of a chief of one of the tribes in the Himalayan foothills in what is now Nepal. At age twenty-nine, unsatisfied with his life of comfort and troubled by the suffering he saw around him, he left home to become a wandering ascetic. He traveled south to the kingdom of Magadha, where he studied with yoga masters, but later took up extreme asceticism. According to tradition, while meditating under a bo tree at Bodh Gaya, he reached enlightenment—that is, perfect insight into the processes of the universe. After several weeks of meditation, he preached his first sermon, urging a "middle way" between asceticism and worldly life. For the next forty-five years, the Buddha traveled through the Ganges Valley, propounding his ideas, refuting his adversaries, and attracting followers. To reach as wide an audience as possible, the Buddha preached in the local language, Magadhi, rather than in Sanskrit, which was already becoming a priestly language. Probably because he refused to recognize the divine authority of the Vedas and dismissed sacrifices, he attracted followers mostly from among merchants, artisans, and farmers, rather than Brahmins.

In his first sermon the Buddha outlined his main message, summed up in the **Four Noble Truths** and the **Eightfold Path**. The Four Noble Truths are as follows: (1) pain and suffering, frustration, and anxiety are ugly but inescapable parts of human life; (2) suffering and anxiety are caused by human desires and attachments; (3) people can understand these weaknesses and triumph over them; and (4) this triumph is made possible by following a simple code of conduct, the Eightfold Path. The basic insight of Buddhism is thus psychological. The deepest human longings can never be satisfied, and even those things that seem to give pleasure cause anxiety because we are afraid of losing them. Attachment to people and things causes sorrow at their loss.

The Buddha offered an optimistic message in that all people can set out on the Eightfold Path toward liberation. All they have to do is take a series of steps, beginning with recognizing the universality of suffering ("right knowledge"), deciding to free themselves from it ("right purpose"), and then choosing "right conduct" (including abstaining from taking life), "right speech," "right livelihood," and "right endeavor." The seventh step is "right awareness," constant contemplation of one's deeds and words, giving full

- **Jainism** Indian religion whose followers consider all life sacred and avoid destroying other life.
- **Four Noble Truths** The Buddha's message that pain and suffering are inescapable parts of life; suffering and anxiety are caused by human desires and attachments; people can understand and triumph over these weaknesses; and this triumph is made possible by following a simple code of conduct.
- **Eightfold Path** The code of conduct set forth by the Buddha in his first sermon, beginning with "right conduct" and ending with "right contemplation."

Picturing the Past

Gandharan Frieze Depicting the Buddha This carved stone from ca. 200 C.E. is one in a series portraying scenes from the life of the Buddha. From the Gandharan kingdom (located in modern Pakistan), this frieze depicts the Buddha seated below the bo tree, where he was first enlightened. (Scenes from the life of the Buddha, Kushan Dynasty [stone]/Freer Gallery, Smithsonian Institution, Washington, D.C., U.S.A./The Bridgeman Art Library)

ANALYZING THE IMAGE What are the people around the Buddha doing? What animals are portrayed?

CONNECTIONS Does this frieze effectively convey any Buddhist principles? If so, which ones?

thought to their importance and whether they lead to enlightenment. "Right contemplation," the last step, entails deep meditation on the impermanence of everything in the world. Those who achieve liberation are freed from the cycle of birth and death and enter the state called nirvana, a kind of blissful nothingness and freedom from reincarnation.

Buddhism differed from Brahmanism and later Hinduism in that it ignored the caste system. Everyone, noble and peasant, educated and ignorant, male and female, could follow the Eightfold Path. Moreover, the Buddha was extraordinarily nondogmatic. Convinced that each person must achieve enlightenment on his or her own, he emphasized that the path was important only because it led the traveler to enlightenment, not for its own sake. He compared it to a raft, essential to cross a river but useless once the traveler reaches the far shore. There was no harm in honoring local gods or observing traditional ceremonies, as long as one remembered the goal of enlightenment and did not let sacrifices become snares or attachments. The willingness of Buddhists to tolerate a wide variety of practices aided the spread of the religion.

Like Mahavira, the Buddha formed a circle of disciples, primarily men but including some women as well. He continually reminded them that each person must reach ultimate fulfillment by individual effort, but he also recognized the value of a group of people striving together for the same goal.

The Buddha's followers transmitted his teachings orally until they were written down in the second or first century B.C.E. These scriptures are called sutras.

The form of monasticism that developed among the Buddhists was less strict than that of the Jains. Buddhist monks moved about for eight months of the year (except the rainy season), begging for their one meal a day, but they could bathe and wear clothes. Within a few centuries Buddhist monks began to overlook the rule that they should travel. They set up permanent monasteries, generally on land donated by kings or other patrons. Orders of nuns also appeared, giving women the opportunity to seek truth in ways men had traditionally used. The main ritual that monks and nuns performed in their monastic establishments was the communal recitation of the sutras. Lay Buddhists could aid the spread of the Buddhist teachings by providing food for monks and support for their monasteries, and they could pursue their own spiritual progress by adopting practices such as abstaining from meat and alcohol. (See "Individuals in Society: Sudatta, Lay Follower of the Buddha," page 78.)

Because Buddhism had no central ecclesiastical authority like the Christian papacy, early Buddhist communities developed several divergent traditions and came to stress different sutras. One of the most important of these, associated with the monk-philosopher Nagarjuna (fl. ca. 100 C.E.), is called **Mahayana**, or "Great Vehicle," because it was a more inclusive form of the religion. It drew on a set of discourses allegedly given by the Buddha and kept hidden by his followers for centuries. One branch of Mahayana taught that reality is empty (that is, nothing exists independently of itself). Another branch held that ultimate reality is consciousness, that everything is produced by the mind.

Just as important as the metaphysical literature of Mahayana Buddhism was its devotional side, influenced by the religions then prevalent in Central Asia, such as Zoroastrianism (see page 58). The Buddha became deified and was placed at the head of an expanding pantheon of other Buddhas and **bodhisattvas** (boh-dih-SUHT-vuhz). Bodhisattvas were Buddhas-to-be who had stayed in the world after enlightenment to help others on the path to salvation. The Buddhas and bodhisattvas became objects of veneration, especially the Buddha of Infinite Light, Amitabha, and the bodhisattva of infinite compassion and mercy, Avalokitesvara (uh-vuh-lohk-ih-TAYSH-veh-ruh). With the growth of Mahayana, Buddhism attracted more and more laypeople.

Buddhism remained an important religion in India until about 1200 C.E. By that time it had spread widely through East, Central, and Southeast Asia. After 1200 C.E. Buddhism declined in India, losing out to both Hinduism and Islam, and the number of Buddhists in India today is small. Buddhism never lost its hold in Nepal and Sri Lanka, however, and today it is also a major religion in Southeast Asia, Tibet, China, Korea, and Japan.

Hinduism

Both Buddhism and Jainism were direct challenges to the old Brahmanic religion. Both rejected animal sacrifice, which by then was a central element in the rituals performed by Brahmin priests. Even more important, both religions tacitly rejected the caste system, accepting people of any caste into their ranks. Over the next several centuries (ca. 400 B.C.E.–200 C.E.), in response to this challenge, the Brahmanic religion evolved in a more devotional direction, developing into the religion commonly called Hinduism. In Hinduism Brahmins retained their high social status, but it became possible for individual worshippers to have more direct contact with the gods, showing their devotion without using priests as intermediaries.

The bedrock of Hinduism is the belief that the Vedas are sacred revelations and that a specific caste system is implicitly prescribed in them. Hinduism is a guide to life, the goal of which is to reach union with brahman, the unchanging ultimate reality. There are four steps in this search, progressing from study of the Vedas in youth to complete asceticism in old age. In their quest for brahman, people are to observe **dharma** (DAHR-muh), the moral law. Dharma stipulates the legitimate pursuits of Hindus: material gain, as long as it is honestly and honorably achieved; pleasure and love for the perpetuation of the family; and moksha, release from the wheel of life and unity with brahman. Because it recognizes the need for material gain and pleasure, Hinduism allows a joyful embracing of life. This certainly was part of its appeal.

Hinduism assumes that there are innumerable legitimate ways of worshipping brahman, including devotion to personal gods. After the third century B.C.E. Hinduism began to emphasize the roles and personalities of thousands of powerful gods. Brahma, the creator; Shiva, the cosmic dancer who both creates and destroys; and Vishnu, the preserver and sustainer of creation, were three of the main male deities. Important female deities included Lakshmi, goddess of wealth, and Saraswati, goddess of learning and music. These gods were usually represented by images, either small ones in homes or larger ones in temples. People could show devotion to their personal gods by reciting hymns or scriptures and by making offerings of food or flowers before these images. A worshipper's devotion to one god did not entail denial of other deities; ultimately all

- **Mahayana** The "Great Vehicle," a tradition of Buddhism that aspires to be more inclusive.
- **bodhisattvas** Buddhas-to-be who stayed in the world after enlightenment to help others on the path to salvation.
- **dharma** The Sanskrit word for moral law, central to both Buddhist and Hindu teachings.

Individuals in Society

Sudatta, Lay Follower of the Buddha

DURING THE DECADES WHEN THE BUDDHA TRAVELED around north India spreading his teachings, he attracted both disciples and lay followers. Stories of the Buddha's interactions with them were passed down orally for centuries, and undoubtedly were elaborated over time. Still, these accounts give us a sense of what life was like in early India. The wealthy banker or merchant Sudatta is a good example of an ardent lay follower. He was so generous to others that he is normally referred to by his epithet, Anathapindada, which means "benefactor of the needy."

The people depicted here are performing the Buddhist ritual of circumambulating a stupa (a mound containing the ashes or other relics of a monk). (British Museum, London/Erich Lessing/Art Resource, NY)

Sudatta met the Buddha in the first year after his enlightenment. In one early conversation with him, Sudatta asks if he must leave the world to attain nirvana:

> Now, I have heard thy disciples praise the bliss of the hermit and denounce the unrest of the world. "The Holy One," they say, "has given up his kingdom and his inheritance, and has found the path of righteousness, thus setting an example to all the world how to attain Nirvana." My heart yearns to do what is right and to be a blessing unto my fellows. Let me then ask you, Must I give up my wealth, my home, and my business enterprises, and, like you, go into homelessness in order to attain the bliss of a religious life?

The Buddha replied that the crucial issue was the way an individual looked on wealth. Anyone who cleaves to wealth needs to cast it aside, but anyone who "possessing riches, uses them rightly, will be a blessing unto his fellows." It is cleaving to wealth and power that enslaves people, not the mere possession of wealth. Artisans, merchants, or officers of the king who stay in the world should concentrate on performing their duties well. "If they live in the world not a life of self but a life of truth, then surely joy, peace, and bliss will dwell in their minds."*

Sudatta purchased a large park to provide a place where the Buddha and his disciples could live during the rainy season and had many buildings built there. The Buddha returned to this Jetavana Monastery many times and frequently gave sermons there. Sudatta also provided food for monks and gave generously to the poor and needy. As a result of his generosity, Sudatta was gradually reduced to poverty himself. Then, through divine intervention, those who owed him money returned it, making him wealthy once again.

Stories recounted that Sudatta's family, including his three daughters, became pious followers. Although Sudatta's son initially resisted the Buddha, he eventually became a generous patron himself. The Buddha himself helped convert Sudatta's unpleasant daughter-in-law. Once when the Buddha was preaching at Sudatta's home, he was disrupted by the sounds of Sudatta's son's wife scolding the servants. The Buddha asked to have her brought to him, and he instructed her on the proper conduct of wives. There were three types of bad wives, he told her: the destructive wife, who is pitiless, fond of other men, and contemptuous of her husband; the thievish wife, who squanders the family wealth; and the mistress wife, who is rude, lazy, and domineering. These he contrasted with the four kinds of good wives: the motherly wife, who cares for her husband as a mother for her son; the sisterly wife, who defers to her husband in the same affectionate way that a younger sister defers to her older brother; the friend wife, who loves her husband as if he were her best friend; and the handmaiden wife, who is calm, patient, and obedient. Deeply moved by these teachings, the daughter-in-law determined to be a handmaiden wife.

Sudatta died before the Buddha. A sutra that survives purports to be the sermon that two of the Buddha's chief disciples preached to him on his deathbed. They counseled Sudatta on how to face his situation by training himself to decide not to cling to what is seen, heard, sensed, thought, attained, sought after, or pondered by the intellect.

QUESTIONS FOR ANALYSIS

1. What can you infer about the circumstances of the early followers of the Buddha from the life of Sudatta?
2. What insights does the life of Sudatta provide into the ways faith in Buddhism was spread?

LaunchPad
Online Document Project

What made Buddhism accessible to everyone? Read a selection of Buddhist parables, and then complete a quiz and writing assignment based on the evidence and details from this chapter.

See inside the front cover to learn more.

*Paul Carus, *The Gospel of Buddha* (Chicago: Open Court, 1894/1915), pp. 61–63, slightly modified.

were manifestations of brahman, the ultimate reality. Hinduism's embrace of a large pantheon of gods enabled it to incorporate new sects, doctrines, beliefs, rites, and deities.

A central ethical text of Hinduism is the *Bhagavad Gita* (BAH-guh-vahd GEE-tuh), a part of the world's longest ancient epic, the *Mahabharata*. The *Bhagavad Gita* offers guidance on the most serious problem facing a Hindu—how to live in the world and yet honor dharma and thus achieve release from the wheel of life. The heart of the *Bhagavad Gita* is the spiritual conflict confronting Arjuna, a human hero about to ride into battle against his kinsmen. As he surveys the battlefield, struggling with the grim notion of killing his relatives, Arjuna voices his doubts to his charioteer, none other than the god Krishna. When at last Arjuna refuses to spill his family's blood, Krishna instructs him on the true meaning of Hinduism:

> You grieve for those beyond grief,
> and you speak words of insight;
> but learned men do not grieve
> for the dead or the living.
> Never have I not existed,
> nor you, nor these kings;
> and never in the future
> shall we cease to exist.
> Just as the embodied self
> enters childhood, youth, and old age,
> so does it enter another body;
> this does not confound a steadfast man.
> Contacts with matter make us feel
> heat and cold, pleasure and pain.
> Arjuna, you must learn to endure
> fleeting things—they come and go!
> When these cannot torment a man,
> when suffering and joy are equal
> for him and he has courage,
> he is fit for immortality.
> Nothing of nonbeing comes to be,
> nor does being cease to exist;
> the boundary between these two
> is seen by men who see reality.
> Indestructible is the presence
> that pervades all this;
> no one can destroy
> this unchanging reality.
> Our bodies are known to end,
> but the embodied self is enduring,
> indestructible, and immeasurable;
> therefore, Arjuna, fight the battle!
> He who thinks this self a killer
> and he who thinks it killed,
> both fail to understand;
> it does not kill, nor is it killed.
> It is not born,
> it does not die;
> having been,
> it will never not be;
> unborn, enduring,
> constant, and primordial,
> it is not killed
> when the body is killed.[2]

The God Vishnu Vishnu is depicted here coming to the rescue of an elephant in the clutches of a crocodile. It comes from the fifth-century-C.E. Dasavatara Temple in Uttar Pradesh. (© akg-images/Jean-Louis Nou/The Image Works)

Krishna then clarifies the relationship between human reality and the eternal spirit. He explains compassionately to Arjuna the duty to act—to live in the world and carry out his duties as a warrior. Indeed, the *Bhagavad Gita* emphasizes the necessity of action, which is essential for the welfare of the world. For Arjuna the warrior's duty is to wage war in compliance with his dharma. Only those who live within the divine law without complaint will be released from rebirth. One person's dharma may be different from another's, but both individuals must follow their own dharmas.

Hinduism provided a complex and sophisticated philosophy of life and a religion of enormous emotional appeal that was attractive to ordinary Indians. Over time it grew to be the most common religion in India. Hinduism validated the caste system, adding to the stability of everyday village life, since people all knew where they stood in society. Hinduism also inspired the preservation of literary masterpieces in Sanskrit and the major regional languages of India. Among these are the *Puranas*, which are stories of the gods and great warrior clans, and the *Mahabharata* and *Ramayana*, which are verse epics of India's early kings.

Western Contact and the Mauryan Unification of North India, ca. 513–185 B.C.E.

- What was the result of Indian contact with the Persians and Greeks, and what were the consequences of unification under the Mauryan Empire?

In the late sixth century B.C.E., with the creation of the Persian Empire that stretched from the west coast of Anatolia to the Indus River (see pages 56–58), west India was swept up in events that were changing the face of the ancient Near East. A couple of centuries later, by 322 B.C.E., the Greeks had supplanted the Persians in northwest India. Chandragupta saw this as an opportunity to expand his territories, and he successfully unified all of north India. The Mauryan (MAWR-ee-uhn) Empire that he founded flourished under the reign of his grandson, Ashoka, but after Ashoka's death the empire declined.

Encounters with the West

India became involved in the turmoil of the sixth century B.C.E. when the Persian emperor Darius conquered the Indus Valley and Kashmir about 513 B.C.E. Persian control did not reach eastward beyond the Punjab, but even so it fostered increased contact between India and the Near East and led to the introduction of new ideas, techniques, and materials into India. From Persian administrators Indians learned more about how to rule large tracts of land and huge numbers of people. They also learned the technique of minting silver coins, and they adopted the Persian monetary standard to facilitate trade with other parts of the empire. Even states in the Ganges Valley, which were never part of the Persian Empire, adopted the use of coinage.

Another result of contact with Persia was introduction of the Aramaic script, used to write the official language of the Persian Empire. To keep records and publish proclamations just as the Persians did, Indians in northwest India adapted the Aramaic script for writing several local languages (elsewhere, Indians developed the Brahmi script, the ancestor of the script used for modern Hindi). In time the sacred texts of the Buddhists and the Jains, as well as epics and other literary works, came to be recorded using Aramaic script to write down Indian languages.

The Persian Empire in turn succumbed to Alexander the Great, and in 326 B.C.E. Alexander led his Macedonian and Greek troops through the Khyber Pass into the Indus Valley (discussed in Chapter 5 on page 131). The India that Alexander encountered was composed of many rival states. He defeated some of these states in the northwest and heard reports of others. Porus, king of west Punjab, fought Alexander with a battalion of two thousand war elephants. After being defeated, he agreed to become a subordinate king under Alexander.

The Greeks were intrigued by the Indian culture they encountered. Alexander had heard of the sophistication of Indian philosophers and summoned some to instruct him or debate with him. The Greeks were also impressed with Indian cities, most notably Taxila, a major center of trade in the Punjab. The Greeks described it as "a city great and prosperous, the biggest of those between the Indus River and the Hydaspes [the modern Jhelum River]—a region not inferior to Egypt in size, with especially good pastures and rich in fine fruits."[3]

Hellenistic Influences in Gandharan Art Because Alexander the Great's army had reached Gandhara and Hellenistic states subsequently controlled it for more than a century, the art of this region was strongly influenced by Greek artistic styles. This stucco figure was excavated from a site in eastern Afghanistan where some twenty-three thousand Greco-Buddhist sculptures were found. Hellenistic influence, as evidenced by the drape of the clothing and the modeling of the head, is particularly easy to recognize in this piece. (Erich Lessing/Art Resource, NY)

From Taxila, Alexander followed the Indus River south, hoping to find the end of the world. His men, however, mutinied and refused to continue. When Alexander turned back, he left his general Seleucus (suh-LOO-kuhs) in charge of his easternmost region.

Chandragupta and the Founding of the Mauryan Empire

The one to benefit most from Alexander's invasion was Chandragupta, the ruler of a growing state in the Ganges Valley. He took advantage of the crisis caused by Alexander's invasion to expand his territories, and by 322 B.C.E. he had made himself sole master of north India (Map 3.2). In 304 B.C.E. he defeated the forces of Seleucus.

With stunning effectiveness, Chandragupta applied the lessons learned from Persian rule. He adopted the Persian practice of dividing the area into provinces. Each province was assigned a governor, usually drawn from Chandragupta's own family. He established a complex bureaucracy to see to the operation of the state and a bureaucratic taxation system that financed public services through taxes on agriculture. He also built a regular army, complete with departments for everything from naval matters to the collection of supplies.

For the first time in Indian history, one man governed most of the subcontinent, exercising control through delegated power. From his capital at Pataliputra in the Ganges Valley, Chandragupta sent agents to the provinces to oversee the workings of government and to keep him informed of conditions in his realm. In designing his bureaucratic system, Chandragupta enjoyed the able assistance of his great minister Kautilya, who wrote a treatise called the *Arthashastra* on how a king should seize, hold, and manipulate power, rather like the Legalist treatises produced in China later that century (discussed in Chapter 4 on page 109). Kautilya urged the king to use propaganda to gain support, for instance, to disguise secret agents to look like gods so that people would be awed when they saw him in their company. He stressed the importance of seeking the enemies of his enemies, who would make good allies. When a neighboring prince was in trouble, that was the perfect time to attack him. Interstate relations were likened to the law of the fish: the large swallow the small. (See "Viewpoints 3.2: On Enemies, from the *Code of Manu* and the *Arthashastra*," page 82.)

Megasthenes, a Greek ambassador sent by Seleucus, spent fourteen years in Chandragupta's court. He left a lively description of life there. He described the city as square and surrounded by wooden walls, twenty-two miles on each side, with 570 towers and 64 gates. It had a university, a library, and magnificent palaces, temples, gardens, and parks. The king personally presided over court sessions where legal cases were heard and petitions received. The king claimed for the state all mines and forests, and there were large state farms, granaries, shipyards, and spinning and weaving factories. Even prostitution was controlled by the state. Only a portion of the empire was ruled so directly, according to Megasthenes. In outlying areas, local kings were left in place if they pledged loyalty. Megasthenes described Chandragupta's fear of treachery and assassination attempts:

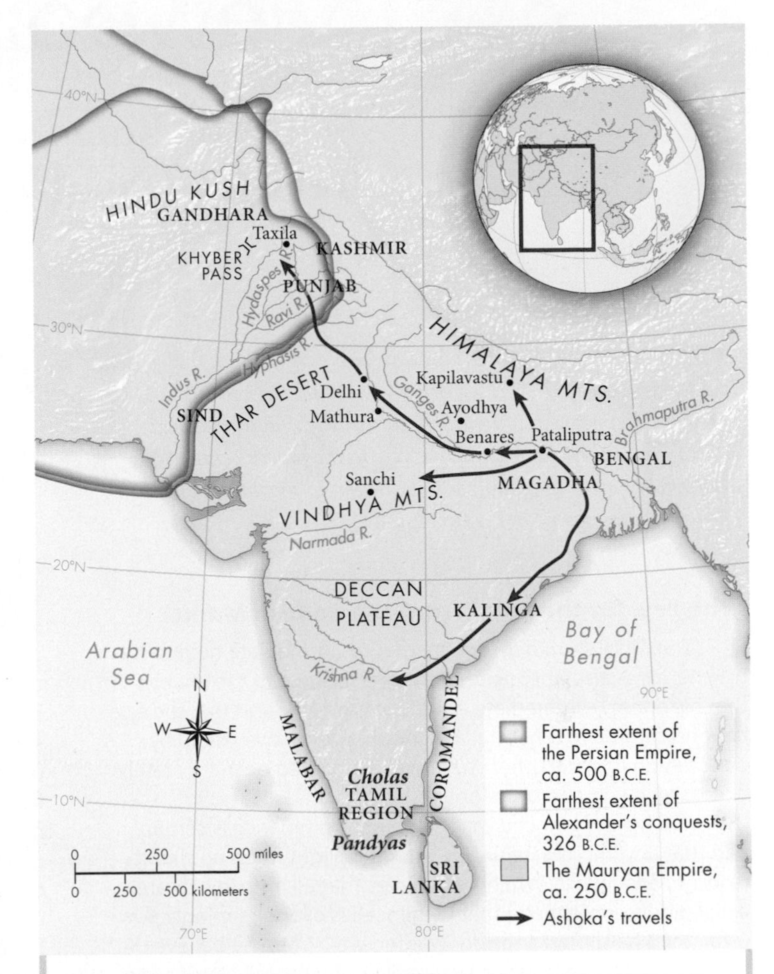

Mapping the Past

MAP 3.2 The Mauryan Empire, ca. 250 B.C.E. The Ganges River Valley was the heart of the Mauryan Empire. Although India is protected from the cold by mountains in the north, mountain passes in the northwest allowed both migration and invasion.

ANALYZING THE MAP Where are the major rivers of India? How close are they to mountains?

CONNECTIONS Can you think of any reasons that the Persian Empire and Alexander's conquests both reached into the same region of northwest India?

Viewpoints 3.2

On Enemies, from the *Code of Manu* and the *Arthashastra*

• *Advice on how to rule is found in two early Indian books, the* Code of Manu, *dating perhaps to the second century* C.E., *and the* Arthashastra, *attributed to Kautilya, with material dating from the fourth century* B.C.E. *to the fourth century* C.E. *Both books cover many topics in addition to the advice on dealing with enemies excerpted below.*

"The Law for the King" from the *Code of Manu*

"[The King] should recognize that his immediate neighbor is his enemy, as also anyone rendering assistance to the enemy; that his enemy's immediate neighbor is an ally; and that the one beyond these two is neutral. He should prevail over them by conciliation and the other strategies, employed both separately and collectively, and by valor and policy. . . .

When he is convinced that his future dominance is certain and that any immediate disadvantage is slight, then he should resort to an alliance. When he believes that all his subjects are exceedingly content and that he himself is overwhelmingly powerful, then he should consider waging war. When he believes in his heart that his own army is in high spirit and prosperous and that the opposite is true of his adversary, then he should march into battle against his enemy. When he is weak in terms of mounted units and infantry, then he should diligently remain stationary, while gradually appeasing the enemy. When the king believes that the enemy is stronger in every respect, then he should divide his army in two and accomplish his objective. When he has become extremely vulnerable to his enemy's forces, then he should quickly seek asylum with a strong and righteous king. Should that king keep both his own subjects and the forces of his enemy in check, he should always serve him like a teacher with all his strength. Even in that case, however, if he notices a liability resulting from his asylum, he should, even in that condition, resort to the good war without hesitation. A politically astute king should employ all the strategies in such a way that his allies, neutrals, or enemies do not prevail over him."

"Capture of the Enemy by Means of Secret Contrivances" from the *Arthashastra*

"Contrivances to kill the enemy may be formed in those places of worship and visit, which the enemy, under the influence of faith, frequents on occasions of worshipping gods and of pilgrimage. A wall or stone, kept by mechanical contrivance, may, by loosening the fastenings, be let to fall on the head of the enemy when he has entered into a temple; stones and weapons may be showered over his head from the topmost story; or a door-panel may be let to fall; or a huge rod kept over a wall or partly attached to a wall may be made to fall over him; or weapons kept inside the body of an idol may be thrown over his head; or the floor of those places where he usually stands, sits, or walks may be besprinkled with poison mixed with cow-dung or with pure water; or, under the plea of giving him flowers, scented powders, or of causing scented smoke, he may be poisoned. . . .

Or on the occasion of feeding the people in honor of gods or of ancestors or in some festival, he may make use of poisoned rice and water, and having conspired with his enemy's traitors, he may strike the enemy with his concealed army; or, when he is surrounded in his fort, he may lie concealed in a hole bored into the body of an idol after eating sacramental food and setting up an altar; . . . and when he is forgotten, he may get out of his concealment through a tunnel, and, entering into the palace, slay his enemy while sleeping, or loosening the fastening of a machine he may let it fall on his enemy; or when his enemy is lying in a chamber which is besmeared with poisonous and explosive substances, or which is made of lac [varnish], he may set fire to it."

Sources: Patrick Olivelle, trans., *Manu's Code of Law* (Oxford: Oxford University Press, 2005), pp. 162–163. © 2004 by the University of Texas Center for Asian Studies. Used by permission of Oxford University Press, USA; Kautilya, *Kautilya's Arthashastra*, trans. R. Shamasastry (Bangalore: Government Press, 1915).

QUESTIONS FOR ANALYSIS

1. What can you infer about interstate relations in the period these texts were written?
2. How alike are these documents in their approach toward dealing with enemies?
3. How do these texts add to your understanding of early Indian religion?

> Nor does the king sleep during the day, and at night he is forced at various hours to change his bed because of those plotting against him. . . . When he leaves to hunt, he is thickly surrounded by a circle of women, and on the outside by spear-carrying bodyguards. The road is fenced off with ropes, and to anyone who passes within the ropes as far as the women death is the penalty.[4]

Those measures apparently worked, as Chandragupta lived a long life. According to Jain tradition, Chandragupta became a Jain ascetic and died a peaceful death in 298 B.C.E. Although he personally adopted a nonviolent philosophy, he left behind a kingdom with the military might to maintain order and defend India from invasion.

The North Gate at Sanchi This is one of four ornately carved gates guarding the stupa at Sanchi in the state of Madhya Pradesh in India. Containing the relics of the Buddha, this Buddhist memorial shrine was originally commissioned by Ashoka, but the gateways were added later. (Jean-Louis Nou/akg-images)

The Reign of Ashoka, ca. 269–232 B.C.E.

Chandragupta's grandson Ashoka proved to be one of India's most remarkable figures. The era of Ashoka was enormously important in the religious history of the world, because Ashoka embraced Buddhism and promoted its spread beyond India.

As a young prince, Ashoka served as governor of two prosperous provinces where Buddhism flourished. At the death of his father about 274 B.C.E., Ashoka rebelled against his older brother, who had succeeded as king, and after four years of fighting won his bid for the throne. Crowned king, Ashoka ruled intelligently and energetically. He was equally serious about his pleasures, especially those of the banquet hall and harem.

In the ninth year of his reign, 261 B.C.E., Ashoka conquered Kalinga, on the east coast of India. In a grim and savage campaign, Ashoka reduced Kalinga by wholesale slaughter. As Ashoka himself admitted, "One hundred and fifty thousand were forcibly abducted from their homes, 100,000 were killed in battle, and many more died later on."[5] Instead of exulting like a conqueror, however, Ashoka was consumed with remorse and revulsion at the horror of war. He embraced Buddhism and used the machinery of his empire to spread Buddhist teachings throughout India. He supported the doctrine of not hurting humans or animals that was then spreading among religious people of all sects in India. He banned animal sacrifices, and in place of hunting expeditions he took pilgrimages. Two years after his conversion, he undertook a 256-day pilgrimage to all the holy sites of Buddhism, and on his return he sent missionaries to all known countries. Ashoka's remarkable crisis of conscience changed the way he ruled. He emphasized compassion, nonviolence, and adherence to dharma. He appointed officials to oversee the moral welfare of the realm and required local officials to govern humanely. He may have perceived dharma as a kind of civic virtue, a universal ethical model capable of uniting the diverse peoples of his extensive empire. Ashoka erected stone pillars, on the Persian model, with inscriptions to inform the people of his policies. He also had long inscriptions carved into large rock surfaces near trade routes. In his last important inscription he spoke of his efforts to encourage his people toward the path of righteousness:

> I have had banyan trees planted on the roads to give shade to man and beast; I have planted mango groves, and I have had ponds dug and shelters erected along the roads at every eight kos. Everywhere I have had wells dug for the benefit of man and beast. But his benefit is but small, for in many ways the kings of olden time have worked for the welfare of the world; but what I have done has been done that men may conform to righteousness.[6]

These inscriptions are the earliest fully dated Indian texts. (Until the script in which they were written was deciphered in 1837, nothing was known of Ashoka's achievements.) The pillars on which they are inscribed are also the first examples of Indian art to survive since the end of the Indus civilization.

Ashoka felt the need to protect his new religion and to keep it pure. He warned Buddhist monks that he would not tolerate schism—divisions based on differences of opinion about doctrine or ritual. According to Buddhist tradition, a great council of Buddhist monks was held at Pataliputra, where the earliest canon of Buddhist texts was codified. At the same time, Ashoka honored India's other religions, even building shrines for Hindu and Jain worshippers. In one edict he banned rowdy popular fairs, allowing only religious gatherings.

Despite his devotion to Buddhism, Ashoka never neglected his duties as emperor. He tightened the central government of the empire and kept a close check on local officials. He built roads and rest spots to improve communication within the realm. These measures also facilitated the march of armies and the armed enforcement of Ashoka's authority. Ashoka described his work: "Whatever good I have done has indeed been accomplished for the progress and welfare of the world. By these shall grow virtues namely: proper support of mother and father, regard for preceptors and elders, proper treatment of Brahmins and ascetics, of the poor and the destitute, slaves and servants."[7]

Ashoka's inscriptions indirectly tell us much about the **Mauryan Empire**. He directly administered the central part of the empire, focusing on Magadha. Beyond it were four large provinces under princes who served as viceroys, each with its own sets of smaller districts and officials. The interior of south India was described as inhabited by undefeated forest tribes. Farther south, along the coasts, were peoples that Ashoka maintained friendly relations with but did not rule, such as the Cholas and Pandyas. Relations with Sri Lanka were especially close under Ashoka, and the king sent a branch of the tree under which the Buddha gained enlightenment to the Sri Lankan king. According to Buddhist legend, Ashoka's son Mahinda traveled to Sri Lanka to convert the people there.

The Kushan Empire, ca. 200 B.C.E.

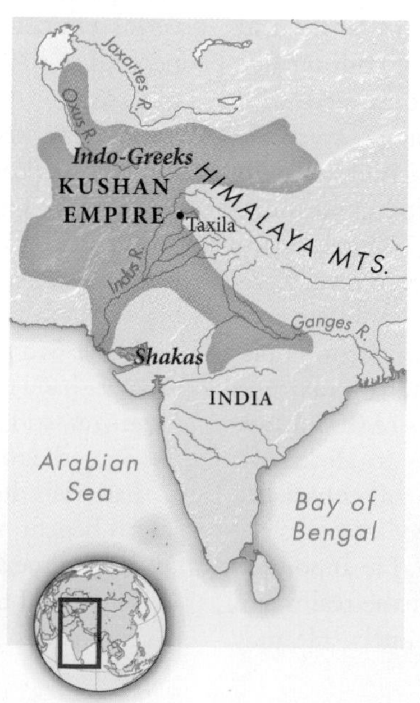

Ashoka ruled for thirty-seven years. After he died in about 232 B.C.E., the Mauryan Dynasty went into decline, and India broke up into smaller units, much like those in existence before Alexander's invasion. Even though Chandragupta had instituted bureaucratic methods of centralized political control and Ashoka had vigorously pursued the political and cultural integration of the empire, the institutions they created were not entrenched enough to survive periods with weaker kings.

Small States and Trading Networks, 185 B.C.E.–300 C.E.

☐ How was India shaped by political disunity and contacts with other cultures during the five centuries from 185 B.C.E. to 300 C.E.?

After the Mauryan Dynasty collapsed in 185 B.C.E., and for much of subsequent Indian history, political unity would be the exception rather than the rule. By this time, however, key elements of Indian culture—the caste system; the religious traditions of Hinduism, Buddhism, and Jainism; and the great epics and legends—had given India a cultural unity strong enough to endure even without political unity.

In the years after the fall of the Mauryan Dynasty, a series of foreign powers dominated the Indus Valley and adjoining regions. The first were hybrid Indo-Greek states ruled by the inheritors of Alexander's defunct empire stationed in what is now Afghanistan. The city of Taxila became a major center of trade, culture, and education, fusing elements of Greek and Indian culture.

The great, slow movement of nomadic peoples out of East Asia that brought the Scythians to the Near East brought the Shakas to northwest India. They controlled the region from about 94 B.C.E. to 20 B.C.E., when they were displaced by a new nomadic invader, the Kushans, who ruled the region of today's Afghanistan, Pakistan, and west India as far south as Gujarat. Buddhist sources refer to their king Kanishka (r. ca. 78–ca. 103 C.E.) as not only a powerful ruler but also a major patron of Buddhism. The famous silk trade from China to Rome (see "Global Trade: Silk," page 186) passed through his territory.

During the Kushan period, Greek culture had a considerable impact on Indian art. Indo-Greek artists and sculptors working in India adorned Buddhist shrines, modeling the earliest representation of the Buddha on Hellenistic statues of Apollo. Another contribution from the Indo-Greek states was coin cast with images of the king, which came to be widely adopted by Indian rulers, aiding commerce and adding evidence of rulers' names and sequence to the historical record. Places where coins are found also show patterns of trade.

Cultural exchange also went in the other direction. Old Indian animal folktales were translated into Syriac and Greek and these translated versions eventually made their way to Europe. South India in this period was also the center of active seaborne trade, with networks reaching all the way to Rome. Indian sailing technology was highly advanced, and much of this trade was in the hands of Indian merchants. Roman traders based in Egypt followed the routes already used by Arab traders, sailing with the monsoon from the Red Sea to the west coast of India in about two weeks, and returning about six months later when the direction of the winds reversed. In the first century C.E. a Greek merchant involved in this trade reported that the traders sold coins, topaz, coral, crude glass, copper, tin, and lead and bought pearls, ivory, silk (probably originally from China), jewels of many sorts (probably many from Southeast Asia), and above all cinnamon and pepper. More Roman gold coins of the first and second centuries C.E. have been found near the southern tip of India than in any other area. The local rulers had slits made across the image of the Roman emperor to show that his sovereignty was not recognized, but they had no objection to the coins' circulating. (By contrast, the Kushan rulers in the north had Roman coins melted down to make coins with their own images on them.)

Even after the fall of Rome, many of the traders on the southwest coast of India remained. These scattered communities of Christians and Jews lived in the coastal cities into modern times. When Vasco da Gama, the Portuguese explorer, reached Calicut in 1498, he found a local Jewish merchant who was able to interpret for him.

During these centuries there were significant advances in science, mathematics, and philosophy. Indian astronomers charted the movements of stars and planets and recognized that the earth was spherical. In the realm of physics, Indian scientists, like their Greek counterparts, conceived of matter in terms of five elements: earth, air, fire, water, and ether. This was also the period when Indian law was codified. The ***Code of Manu***, which lays down family, caste, and commercial law, was compiled in the second or third century C.E., drawing on older texts.

Regional cultures tend to flourish when there is no dominant unifying state, and the Tamils of south India were one of the major beneficiaries of the collapse of the Mauryan Dynasty. The period from 200 B.C.E. to 200 C.E. is considered the classical period of Tamil culture, when many great works of literature were written under the patronage of the regional kings. Some of the poems written then provide evidence of lively commerce, mentioning bulging warehouses, ships from many lands, and complex import-export procedures. From contact of this sort, the south came to absorb many cultural elements from the north, but also retained differences. Castes were present in the south before contact with the Sanskrit north, but took distinct forms, as the Kshatriya (warrior) and Vaishya (merchant) varnas were hardly known in the far south.

CHRONOLOGY

2800–2000 B.C.E.	Height of Harappan civilization
ca. 1500–500 B.C.E.	Vedic Age; flourishing of Aryan civilization; *Rig Veda*
ca. 1000 B.C.E.	Introduction of iron
750–500 B.C.E.	*Upanishads*
ca. 513 B.C.E.	Persians conquer the Indus Valley and Kashmir
ca. 500 B.C.E.	Founding of Buddhism and Jainism
ca. 400 B.C.E.–200 C.E.	Gradual evolution of the Brahmanic religion into Hinduism
326 B.C.E.	Alexander the Great enters Indus Valley
ca. 322–185 B.C.E.	Mauryan Empire
ca. 300 B.C.E.	Jain religion splits into two sects
ca. 269–232 B.C.E.	Reign of Ashoka
ca. 150 B.C.E.–250 C.E.	Classical period of Tamil culture
ca. 100 C.E.	More inclusive Mahayana form of Buddhism emerges
ca. 200 C.E.	*Code of Manu*

- **Mauryan Empire** The first Indian empire founded by Chandragupta.
- ***Code of Manu*** The codification of early Indian law that lays down family, caste, and commercial law.

Chapter Summary

Civilization first emerged in the Indus River Valley of India in the third millennium B.C.E. The large cities of this Harappan civilization were carefully planned, with straight streets and sewers; buildings were of kiln-dried brick. Harappan cities were largely abandoned by 1800 B.C.E. for unknown reasons.

A few centuries later, the Aryans, speakers of an early form of the Indo-European language Sanskrit, rose to prominence in north India, marking the beginning of the Vedic Age. Aryan warrior tribes fought using chariots and bronze swords and spears, gradually expanding into the Ganges River Valley. The first stages of the Indian caste system date to this period, when warriors and priests were ranked above merchants, artisans, and farmers. The Vedas document the religious ideas of this age, such as the importance of sacrifice and the notions of karma and rebirth.

Beginning around 500 B.C.E. three of India's major religions emerged. Mahavira, the founder of the Jain religion, taught his followers to live ascetic lives, avoid harming any living thing, and renounce evil thoughts and actions. The founder of Buddhism, Siddhartha Gautama, or the Buddha, similarly taught his followers a path to liberation that involved freeing themselves from desires, avoiding violence, and gaining insight. Hinduism developed in response to the popularity of Jainism and Buddhism, both of which rejected animal sacrifice and ignored the caste system. Hindu traditions validated sacrifice and caste and developed devotional practice, giving individuals a more personal relationship with the gods they worshipped.

From contact with the Persians and Greeks in the sixth century B.C.E. and fourth century B.C.E., respectively, new political techniques, ideas, and art styles and the use of money entered the Indian repertoire. Shortly after the arrival of the Greeks, much of north India was politically unified by the Mauryan Empire under Chandragupta. His grandson Ashoka converted to Buddhism, promoted its spread inside and outside of India, and had stone monuments inscribed with his proclamations.

After the decline of the Mauryan Empire, India was politically fragmented for several centuries. Indian cultural identity remained strong, however, because of shared literature and religious ideas. In the northwest, new nomadic groups, the Shakas and the Kushans, emerged. Cultural interchange was facilitated through trade both overland and by sea.

NOTES

1. *Rig Veda 10.90*, in *Sources of Indian Tradition* by Ainslie Thomas Embree, Stephen N. Hay, and William Theodore. Reproduced with permission of COLUMBIA UNIVERSITY PRESS in the format Book via Copyright Clearance Center.
2. Excerpt from Barbara Miller, *The Bhagavad-Gita* (New York: Columbia University Press), pp. 31–32, translation copyright © 1986 by Barbara Stoler Miller. Used by permission of Bantam Books, an imprint of Random House, a division of Random House LLC. All rights reserved. Any third-party use of this material, outside of this publication, is prohibited. Interested parties must apply directly to Random House LLC for permission.
3. Arrian, *Anabasis* 5.8.2; Plutarch, *Alexander* 59.1; trans. John Buckler.
4. *Strabo* 15.1.55, trans. John Buckler.
5. Quoted in H. Kulke and D. Rothermund, *A History of India*, 3d ed. (London: Routledge, 1998), p. 62.
6. Embree et al., *Sources of Indian Tradition*, p. 148. Reproduced with permission of COLUMBIA UNIVERSITY PRESS in the format Book via Copyright Clearance Center.
7. Quoted in B. G. Gokhale, *Asoka Maurya* (New York: Twayne Publishers, 1966), p. 169.

CONNECTIONS

India was a very different place in the third century C.E. than it had been in the early phase of Harappan civilization more than two thousand years earlier. The region was still divided into many different polities, but people living there in 300 shared much more in the way of ideas and traditions. The great epics such as the *Mahabharata* and the *Ramayana* provided a cultural vocabulary for groups that spoke different languages and had rival rulers. New religions had emerged, notably Buddhism and Jainism, and Hinduism was much more a devotional religion. Contact with ancient Mesopotamia, Persia, Greece, and Rome had brought new ideas, practices, and products.

During this same time period, civilization in China underwent similar expansion and diversification. China was farther away than India from other Eurasian centers of civilization, and its developments were consequently not as closely linked. Logographic writing appeared with the Bronze Age Shang civilization and was preserved into modern times, in striking contrast to India and lands to its west, which developed alphabetical writing systems. Still, some developments affected both India and China, such as the appearance of chariots and horseback riding. The next chapter takes up the story of these developments in early China. In Chapter 12, after considering early developments in Europe, Asia, Africa, and the Americas, we return to the story of India.

Review and Explore

Make It Stick

LearningCurve
Go online and use LearningCurve to retain what you've read.

Identify Key Terms

Identify and explain the significance of each item below.

Harappan (p. 65)
Aryans (p. 68)
Rig Veda (p. 68)
Brahmins (p. 69)
caste system (p. 69)
samsara (p. 71)
karma (p. 72)
brahman (p. 73)
Jainism (p. 74)
Four Noble Truths (p. 75)
Eightfold Path (p. 75)
Mahayana (p. 77)
bodhisattvas (p. 77)
dharma (p. 77)
Mauryan Empire (p. 84)
Code of Manu (p. 85)

Review the Main Ideas

Answer the focus questions from each section of the chapter.

1. What does archaeology tell us about the Harappan civilization in India? (p. 65)
2. What kind of society and culture did the Indo-European Aryans create? (p. 68)
3. What ideas and practices were taught by the founders of Jainism, Buddhism, and Hinduism? (p. 74)
4. What was the result of Indian contact with the Persians and Greeks, and what were the consequences of unification under the Mauryan Empire? (p. 80)
5. How was India shaped by political disunity and contacts with other cultures during the five centuries from 185 B.C.E. to 300 C.E.? (p. 84)

Make Connections

Analyze the larger developments and continuities within and across chapters.

1. In what ways did ancient India follow patterns of development similar to those seen elsewhere?
2. What are the similarities and differences between the religious ideas and practices of early India and those that emerged in the Nile River Valley and southwest Asia?
3. How was the development of India's material culture affected by developments elsewhere?

LaunchPad
Online Document Project

Accessible Enlightenment

What made Buddhism accessible to everyone?

Read a selection of Buddhist parables, and then complete a quiz and writing assignment based on the evidence and details from this chapter.

See inside the front cover to learn more.

Suggested Reading

Basham, A. L. *The Wonder That Was India*, 3d rev. ed. 1968. Classic appreciative account of early Indian civilization by a scholar deeply immersed in Indian literature.

Dehejia, Vidya. *Indian Art.* 1997. Well-illustrated introduction to the visual feast of Indian art.

Embree, Ainslee, ed. *Sources of Indian Tradition*, 2d ed. 1988. An excellent introduction to Indian religion, philosophy, and intellectual history through translations of major sources.

Koller, John M. *The Indian Way*, 2d ed. 2004. An accessible introduction to the variety of Indian religions and philosophies.

Kulke, Hermann, and Dietmar Rothermund. *A History of India*, 3d ed. 1998. A good balanced introduction to Indian history.

Lopez, Donald S., Jr. *The Story of the Buddha: A Concise Guide to Its History and Teachings*. 2001. Emphasizes Buddhist practice, drawing examples from many different countries and time periods.

Miller, Barbara, trans. *The Bhagavad-Gita: Krishna's Counsel in Time of War*. 1986. One of several excellent translations of India's classical literature.

Possehl, Gregory L. *The Indus Civilization*. 2002. Overview of Harappan civilization, by one of the on-site researchers.

Renfew, Colin. *Archaeology and Language: The Puzzle of Indo-European Origins*. 1987. In-depth analysis of the question of the origins of the Aryans.

Scharff, Harmut. *The State in Indian Tradition*. 1989. Scholarly analysis of the period from the Aryans to the Muslims.

Thapar, Romilia. *Early India to 1300*. 2002. Overview by a leading Indian historian.

Wright, Rita P. *The Ancient Indus: Urbanism, Economy, and Society*. 2010. Broad-ranging overview that brings in Mesopotamian sources.

China's Classical Age

to 221 B.C.E.

4

Bronze Head from China
Archaeological discoveries continue to expand our knowledge of the cultures and civilizations of early China. This large bronze mask was found among a large set of sacrificial offerings in the modern province of Sichuan. These unusual objects, which were found only there, suggest a distinct culture. (Sanxingdui Three Star Mound Museum, Guanghan Chengdu Sichuan, China/© William Perry/Alamy)

LearningCurve
After reading the chapter, go online and use LearningCurve to retain what you've read.

Chapter Preview

The Emergence of Civilization in China
The Shang Dynasty, ca. 1500–1050 B.C.E.
The Early Zhou Dynasty, ca. 1050–400 B.C.E.
The Warring States Period, 403–221 B.C.E.
Confucius and His Followers
Daoism, Legalism, and Other Schools of Thought

In comparison to India and Mesopotamia, China developed in relative isolation. Communication with West and South Asia was very difficult, impeded by high mountains and vast deserts. Though there was some trade, the distances were so great that they did not allow the kind of cross-fertilization that occurred in western Eurasia. Moreover, there were no cultural breaks comparable to the rise of the Aryans in India or the Assyrians in Mesopotamia to introduce new peoples and languages. The impact of early China's relative isolation is found in many distinctive features of its culture. Perhaps the most important is its writing system; unlike the other major societies of Eurasia, China retained a logographic writing system with a symbol for each word. This writing system shaped not only Chinese literature and thought but also key social and political processes, such as the nature of the ruling class and interactions with non-Chinese peoples.

Chinese history is commonly discussed in terms of a succession of dynasties. The Shang Dynasty (ca. 1500–1050 B.C.E.) was the first to have writing, metalworking, cities, and chariots. The Shang kings played priestly roles, serving as intermediaries with both their royal ancestors and the high god Di. The Shang were overthrown by one of their vassal states, which founded the Zhou Dynasty (ca. 1050–256 B.C.E.). The Zhou rulers set up a decentralized feudal governmental structure that evolved over centuries into a multistate system. As warfare between the states intensified in the sixth century B.C.E., social and cultural change quickened. Aristocratic privileges declined, and China entered one of its most creative periods, when the philosophies of Confucianism, Daoism, and Legalism were developed.

The Emergence of Civilization in China

☐ What was the impact of China's geography on the development of Chinese societies?

The term *China*, like the term *India*, does not refer to the same geographical entity at all points in history. The historical China, also called China proper, was smaller than present-day China, not larger like the historical India. The contemporary People's Republic of China includes Tibet, Inner Mongolia, Turkestan, Manchuria, and other territories that in premodern times were neither inhabited by Chinese nor ruled directly by Chinese states.

The Impact of Geography

As in most areas of the world, the geography of the region has had an impact on the development of Chinese civilization from ancient times to the present. China proper, about a thousand miles north to south and east to west, occupies much of the temperate zone of East Asia (Map 4.1). The northern part, drained by the Yellow River, is colder, flatter, and more arid than the south. Rainfall in many areas is less than twenty inches a year, making the land well suited to crops like wheat and millet. The dominant soil is **loess**—fine wind-driven earth that is fertile and easy to work even with simple tools. The soil gives the Yellow River its characteristic color, and because so much of the loess ends up as silt in the river, the riverbed rises and easily floods unless diked. Drought is another perennial problem for farmers in the north. The Yangzi (YANG-zuh) River is the dominant feature of the warmer, wetter, and more lush south, a region well suited to rice cultivation. Farmers in recent centuries have been able to get two rice crops a year from the land around the Yangzi River and farther south. The Yangzi and its many tributaries are navigable, so boats were traditionally the preferred means of transportation in the south.

Mountains, deserts, and grasslands separated China proper from other early civilizations. Between China and India lay Tibet, with its vast mountain ranges and high plateaus. North of Tibet are great expanses of desert where nothing grows except in rare oases, and north of the desert, grasslands stretch from Ukraine to eastern Siberia. Chinese civilization did not spread into any of these Inner Asian regions, above all because they were not suited to growing crops. Inner Asia, where raising animals is a more productive use of land than planting crops, became the heartland of China's traditional enemies, such as the nomadic tribes of the Xiongnu (SHUHNG-noo) and Mongols.

Neolithic Jade Plaque This small plaque (2½ inches by 3¼ inches), dating from about 2000 B.C.E., is similar to others of the Liangzhu area near modern Shanghai. It is incised to depict a human figure that merges into a monster mask. The lower part could be interpreted as his arms and legs but at the same time resembles a monster mask with bulging eyes, prominent nostrils, and a large mouth. (Zhejiang Provincial Institute of Cultural Relics and Archeology/Uniphoto Press, Japan/Ancient Art & Architecture Collection, Ltd.)

Early Agricultural Societies of the Neolithic Age

From about 10,000 B.C.E. agriculture was practiced in China. It apparently originated independently of somewhat earlier developments in Egypt and Mesopotamia but was perhaps influenced by developments in Southeast Asia, where rice was also cultivated very early. By 5000 B.C.E. there were Neolithic village settlements in several regions of China. The primary Neolithic crops were drought-resistant millet, grown in the loess soils of the north, and rice, grown in the wetlands of the lower reaches of the Yangzi River, where inhabitants supplemented their diet with fish. In both areas pigs, dogs, and cattle were domesticated, and by 3000 B.C.E. sheep had become important in the north and water buffalo in the south. Silk production can also be traced back to this period.

Over the course of the fifth to third millennia B.C.E., many distinct regional Neolithic cultures emerged. One such culture emerged in the northwest during the fourth and third millennia B.C.E. These people are known for their fine red pottery vessels decorated in

• **loess** Soil deposited by wind; it is fertile and easy to work.

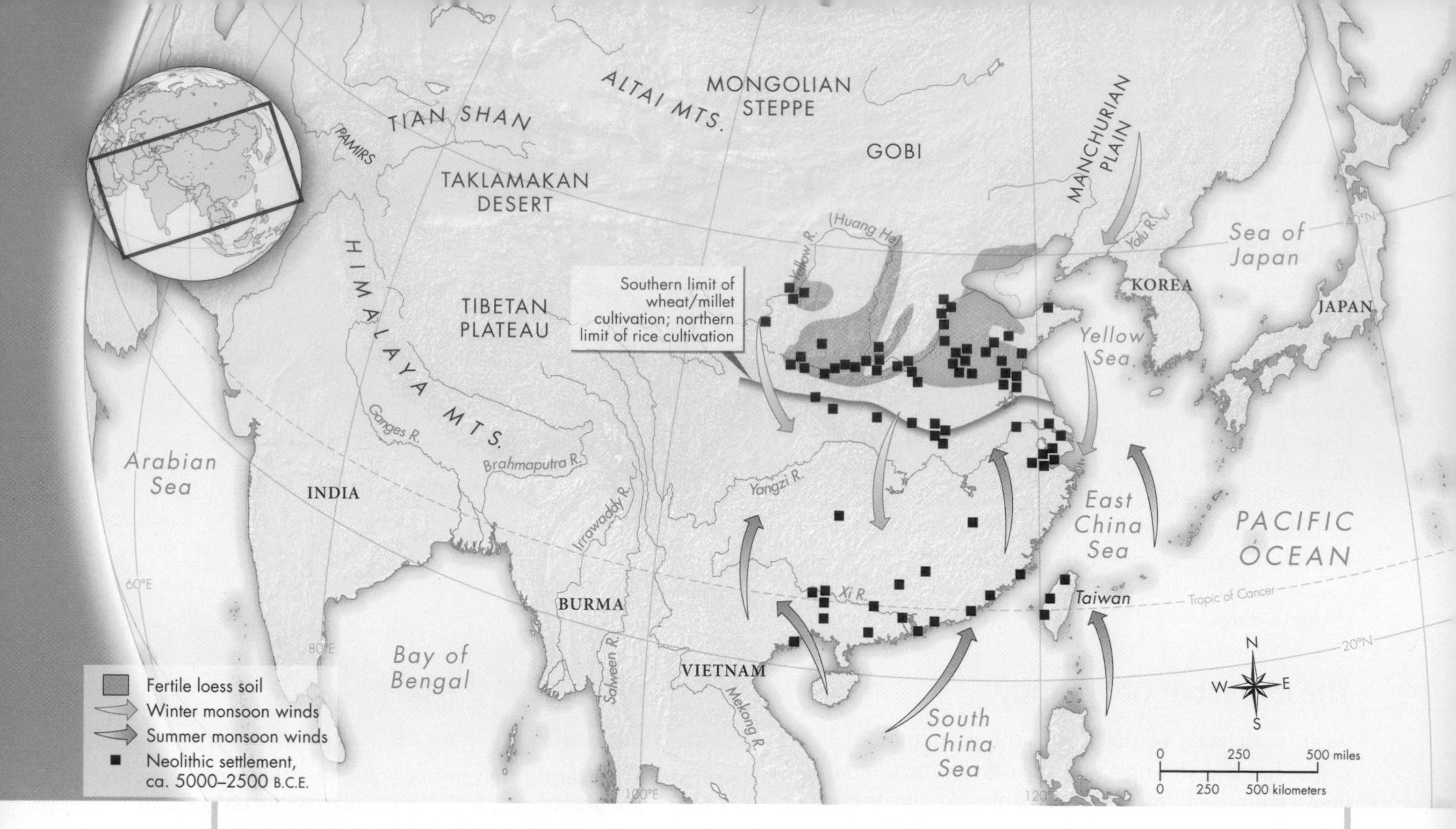

Mapping the Past

MAP 4.1 The Geography of Historical China Chinese civilization developed in the temperate regions drained by the Yellow and Yangzi Rivers.

ANALYZING THE MAP Trace the routes of the Yellow and Yangzi Rivers. Where are the areas of loess soil? Where are the Neolithic sites concentrated?

CONNECTIONS Does China's geography explain much about its history? (See also Map 4.2.) What geographical features had the greatest impact in the Neolithic Age? How might the fact that the Yellow and Yangzi Rivers flow west to east, rather than north to south, have influenced the development of Chinese society?

black pigment with bold designs, including spirals, sawtooth lines, and zoomorphic stick figures. At the same time in the east, a different culture made pottery that was rarely painted but had distinctive shapes, including three-legged, deep-bodied tripods. Jade ornaments, blades, and ritual objects, sometimes of extraordinary craftsmanship, have been found in several eastern sites but are rare in western ones.

These Neolithic societies left no written records, but we know from the material record that over time they came to share more social and cultural practices. Many practices related to the treatment of the dead spread to other groups from their original area, including use of coffins, large numbers of grave goods, and divination aimed at communicating with ancestors or gods based on interpreting cracks in cattle bones. Fortified walls made of rammed earth were built around settlements in many places, suggesting not only increased contact between Neolithic societies but also increased conflict. (For more on life in Neolithic societies, see Chapter 1.)

The Shang Dynasty, ca. 1500–1050 B.C.E.

- What was life like during the Shang Dynasty, and what effect did writing have on Chinese culture and government?

Archaeological evidence indicates that after 2000 B.C.E. a Bronze Age civilization appeared in north China that shared traits with Bronze Age civilizations elsewhere in Eurasia, such as Mesopotamia, Egypt, and Greece. These traits included writing, metalworking, domestication of the horse, class stratification, and cult centers. The archaeological findings are linked to the Shang Dynasty, long known from early texts.

Shang Society

Shang civilization was not as densely urban as that of Mesopotamia, but Shang kings ruled from large settlements (Map 4.2). The best excavated is **Anyang**, from which the Shang kings ruled for more than two centuries. At the center of Anyang were large palaces, temples, and altars. These buildings were constructed on rammed-earth foundations (a feature of Chinese building practice that would last for centuries). Outside the central core were industrial areas where bronzeworkers, potters, stone carvers, and other artisans lived and worked. Many homes were built partly below ground level, probably as a way to conserve heat. Beyond these urban settlements were farming areas and large forests. Deer, bears, tigers, wild boars, elephants, and rhinoceros were still plentiful in north China in this era.

Texts found in the Shang royal tombs at Anyang show that Shang kings were military chieftains. The king regularly sent out armies of three thousand to five thousand men on campaigns, and when not at war they would go on hunts lasting for months. They fought rebellious vassals and foreign tribes, but the situation constantly changed as vassals became enemies and enemies accepted offers of alliance. War booty was an important source of the king's revenue, especially the war captives who could be made into slaves. Captives not needed as slaves might end up as sacrificial victims—or perhaps the demands of the gods and ancestors for sacrifices were a motive for going to war.

Bronze-tipped spears and battle axes were widely used by Shang warriors, giving them an advantage over less technologically advanced groups. Bronze was also used for the fittings of the chariots that came into use around 1200 B.C.E. Chariot technology apparently spread by diffusion across Asia, passing from one society to the next. The chariot provided commanders with mobile stations from which they could supervise their troops; it also gave archers and soldiers armed with long battle axes increased mobility.

Shang power did not rest solely on military supremacy. The Shang king was also the high priest, the one best qualified to offer sacrifices to the royal ancestors and the high god Di. Royal ancestors were viewed as able to intervene with Di, send curses, produce dreams, assist the king in battle, and so on. The king divined his ancestors' wishes by interpreting the cracks made in heated cattle bones or tortoise shells prepared for him by professional diviners.

The Shang royal family and aristocracy lived in large houses built on huge platforms of rammed earth similar to those used in the Neolithic period. Shang palaces were undoubtedly splendid but were constructed of perishable material like wood, and nothing of them remains today, giving China none of the ancient stone buildings and monuments so characteristic of the West. What has survived are the lavish underground tombs built for Shang kings and their consorts.

MAP 4.2 The Shang and Early Zhou Dynasties, ca. 1500–400 B.C.E. The early Zhou government controlled larger areas than the Shang did, but the independent states of the Warring States Period were more aggressive about pushing out their frontiers, greatly extending the geographical boundaries of Chinese civilization.

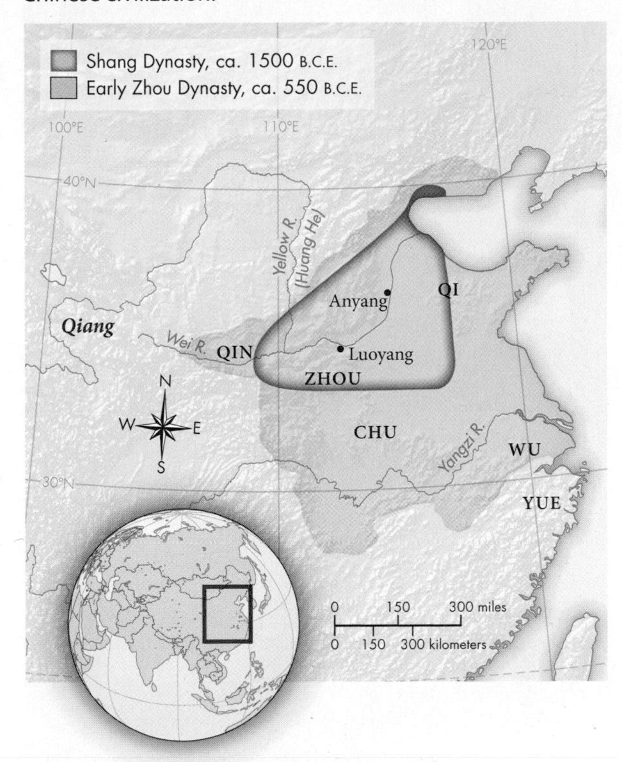

The one royal tomb not robbed before it was excavated was for Lady Hao, one of the many wives of the king Wu Ding (ca. 1200 B.C.E.). The tomb was filled with almost 500 bronze vessels and weapons, over 700 jade and ivory ornaments, and 16 people who would tend to Lady Hao in the afterlife. Human sacrifice did not occur only at funerals. Inscribed bones report sacrifices of war captives in the dozens and hundreds. Some of those buried with kings were not sacrificial victims but followers or servants. The bodies of people who voluntarily followed their ruler to the grave were generally buried with their own ornaments and grave goods such as weapons.

Shang society was marked by sharp status distinctions. The king and other noble families had family and clan names transmitted along patrilineal lines, from father to son. Kingship similarly passed along patrilineal lines, from elder to younger brother and from father to son, but never to or through sisters or daughters. The kings and the aristocrats owned slaves, many

• **Anyang** One of the Shang Dynasty capitals from which the Shang kings ruled for more than two centuries.

Royal Burials at Anyang Eleven large tombs and more than a thousand small graves have been excavated at the royal burial ground at Anyang. In 2005 seven pits were discovered in which horses and chariots had been buried to accompany a king in the afterlife. (© CHINA NEWSPHOTO/Reuters/Corbis)

of whom had been captured in war. In the urban centers there were substantial numbers of craftsmen who worked in stone, bone, and bronze.

Shang farmers were obligated to work for their lords (making them essentially serfs). Their lives were not that different from the lives of their Neolithic ancestors, and they worked the fields with similar stone tools. They usually lived in small, compact villages surrounded by fields. Some new crops became common in Shang times, most notably wheat, which had spread from western Asia. Farmers probably also raised silkworms, from whose cocoons fine silk garments could be made for the ruling elite.

- **taotie** A stylized animal face commonly seen in Chinese bronzes.
- **logographic** A system of writing in which each word is represented by a single symbol, such as the Chinese script.

Bronze Metalworking

As in Egypt, Mesopotamia, and India, the development of more complex forms of social organization in Shang China coincided with the mastery of metalworking, specifically bronze. The bronze industry required the coordination of a large labor force and skilled artisans. Bronze was used more for ritual than for war in Shang times. Most surviving Shang bronze objects are vessels such as cups, goblets, steamers, and cauldrons that would have originally been used during sacrificial ceremonies. They were beautifully formed in a great variety of shapes and sizes.

The decoration on Shang bronzes seems to say something interesting about Shang culture, but scholars do not agree about what that is. In the art of ancient Egypt, Assyria, and Babylonia, representations of agriculture (domesticated plants and animals) and of social hierarchy (kings, priests, scribes, and slaves) are very common, matching our understandings of the social, political, and economic development of those societies. In Shang China, by contrast, images of wild animals predominate. Some animal images readily suggest possible meanings. Jade cicadas were sometimes found in the mouths of the dead, and images of cicadas on bronzes are easy to interpret as images evocative of rebirth in the realm of ancestral spirits, as cicadas spend years underground before emerging. Birds, similarly, suggest to many the idea of messengers that can communicate with other realms, especially realms in the sky. More problematic is the most common image, the stylized animal face called the **taotie** (taow-tyeh). To some it is a monster—a fearsome image that would scare away evil forces. Others imagine a dragon—an animal whose vast powers had more positive associations. Some hypothesize that it reflects masks used in rituals. Others associate it with animal sacrifices, totemism, or shamanism. Still others see these images as hardly more than designs. Without new evidence, scholars can only speculate.

Bronze technology spread beyond Shang territories into areas the Shang would have considered enemy lands. In 1986, in the western province of Sichuan, discovery was made of a bronze-producing culture contemporaneous with the late Shang but very different from it. Two sacrificial pits contained the burned remains of elephant tusks and a wide range of gold, bronze, jade, and stone objects. Among them were life-size statues and many life-size bronze heads, all with angular facial features and enormous eyes. No human sacrifices were found, leading some scholars to speculate that the masks were used to top wood or clay statues buried in place of humans in a sacrificial ceremony. Archaeologists are continuing to excavate in this region, and new discoveries are gradually providing fuller understanding of the religion of the people who lived there.

The Development of Writing

The survival of divination texts inscribed on bones from Shang tombs demonstrates that writing was already a major element in Chinese culture by 1200 B.C.E. Writing must have been developed earlier, but the early stages cannot be traced, probably because writing was done on wood, bamboo, silk, or other perishable materials.

The invention of writing had profound effects on China's culture and government. A written language made possible a bureaucracy capable of keeping records and corresponding with commanders and governors far from the palace. Hence literacy became the ally of royal rule, facilitating control over a wide realm. Literacy also preserved the learning, lore, and experience of early Chinese society and facilitated the development of abstract thought.

Like ancient Egyptian and Sumerian scripts, the Chinese script was **logographic**: each word was represented by a single symbol. In the Chinese case, some of the symbols were pictures, but for the names of abstract concepts other methods were adopted. Sometimes the symbol for a different word was borrowed because the two words were pronounced alike. Sometimes two different symbols were combined; for instance, to represent different types of trees, the symbol for "tree" could be combined with another symbol borrowed for its pronunciation (Figure 4.1).

In western Eurasia logographic scripts were eventually modified or replaced by phonetic scripts, but that never happened in China (although, because of changes in the spoken language, today many words are represented by two or three characters rather than a single one). Because China retained its logographic writing

Bronze Vessels The Shang Dynasty bronze vessel on the top, dating to the twelfth century B.C.E. and about 10 inches tall, is covered with symmetrical animal imagery, including stylized taotie masks. The early Zhou Dynasty inscribed bronze pan (bottom), dating to before 900 B.C.E., was one of 103 vessels discovered in 1975 by farmers clearing a field. The inscription tells the story of the first six Zhou kings and of the family of scribes who served them. (pan: Shanxi Zhou Yuan Museum/Uniphoto Press, Japan/Ancient Art & Archeology Collection, Ltd.; taotie vessel: Ritual Wine Container with Cover (Fangyi). China, Shang Dynasty (ca. 1600–1046 B.C.E.), 12th century B.C.E. Bronze. Purchase, Arthur M. Sackler Gift, 1974 [1974.268.2a, b]/The Metropolitan Museum of Art, New York, NY, USA/ Image copyright © The Metropolitan Museum of Art/Image source: Art Resource, NY)

WORD	ox	goat, sheep	tree	moon	earth	water	to show, declare	then (men and bowl)	heaven	to pray
SHANG SYMBOL										
MODERN CHARACTER	牛	羊	木	月	土	水	示	就	天	祝

FIGURE 4.1 The Origins of Chinese Writing The modern Chinese writing system (bottom row) evolved from the script employed by diviners in the Shang period (top row). (Source: Adapted from Patricia Buckley Ebrey, *The Cambridge Illustrated History of China* [Cambridge: Cambridge University Press, 1996], p. 26. Reprinted by permission of Cambridge University Press.)

system, many years were required to gain full mastery of reading and writing, which added to the prestige of education.

Why did China retain a logographic writing system even after encounters with phonetic ones? Although phonetic systems have many real advantages, especially with respect to ease of learning to read, there are some costs to dropping a logographic system. Since characters did not change when the pronunciation changed, educated Chinese could read texts written centuries earlier without the need for translation. Moreover, as the Chinese language developed regional variants, readers of Chinese could read books and letters by contemporaries whose oral language they could not comprehend. Thus the Chinese script played a large role in holding China together and fostering a sense of connection with the past. In addition, many of China's neighbors (Japan, Korea, and Vietnam, in particular) adopted the Chinese script, allowing communication through writing between people whose languages were totally unrelated. In this regard, Chinese characters were like Arabic numerals, which have the same meaning however they are pronounced (Table 4.1).

• TABLE 4.1 Pronouncing Chinese Words

Phonetic equivalents for the vowels and especially perplexing consonants are given here.

Letter	Phonetic Equivalent in Chinese
a	ah
e	uh
i	ee; except after *z*, *c*, and *ch*, when the sound is closer to *i* in *it*
u	oo; as in English *food*
c	ts (*ch*, however, is like English *ch*)
q	ch
z	dz
zh	j
x	sh

- ***Book of Documents*** One of the earliest Chinese books, containing documents, speeches, and historical accounts about early Zhou rule.
- **Mandate of Heaven** The theory that Heaven gives the king a mandate to rule only as long as he rules in the interests of the people.
- **shi** The lower ranks of Chinese aristocracy; these men could serve in either military or civil capacities.
- ***Book of Songs*** The earliest collection of Chinese poetry; it provides glimpses of what life was like in the early Zhou Dynasty.

The Early Zhou Dynasty, ca. 1050–400 B.C.E.

☐ How was China governed, and what was life like during the Zhou Dynasty?

The Shang campaigned constantly against enemies in all directions. To the west of the Shang were the fierce Qiang (chyang), considered barbarian tribesmen by the Shang and perhaps speaking an early form of Tibetan. Between the Shang capital and the Qiang were the Zhou (joe), who seem to have both inherited cultural traditions from the Neolithic cultures of the northwest and absorbed most of the material culture of the Shang. In about 1050 B.C.E. the Zhou rose against the Shang and defeated them in battle. Their successors maintained the cultural and political advances that the Shang rulers had introduced.

Zhou Politics

The early Zhou period is the first one for which transmitted texts exist in some abundance. The ***Book of Documents*** (ca. 900 B.C.E.) describes the Zhou conquest of the Shang as the victory of just and noble warriors over decadent courtiers led by an irresponsible and sadistic king. These documents also show that the Zhou recognized the Shang as occupying the center of the known world, were eager to succeed them in that role, and saw history as a major way to legitimate power.

Like the Shang kings, the Zhou kings sacrificed to their ancestors, but they also sacrificed to Heaven. The *Book of Documents* assumes a close relationship between Heaven and the king, who was called the Son of Heaven. According to the documents, Heaven gives the king a mandate to rule only as long as he rules in the interests of the people. Because the last king of the Shang had been decadent and cruel, Heaven took the mandate away from him and entrusted it to the virtuous Zhou kings. Because this theory of the **Mandate of Heaven** does not seem to have had any place in Shang cosmology, it may have been developed by the early Zhou rulers as a kind of propaganda to win over the former subjects of the Shang. Whatever its origins, it remained a central feature of Chinese political ideology from the early Zhou period on.

Rather than attempt to rule all their territories directly, the early Zhou rulers set up a decentralized feudal system. They sent relatives and trusted subordinates with troops to establish walled garrisons in the conquered territories. Such a vassal was generally able to pass his position on to a son, so that in time the domains became hereditary. By 800 B.C.E. there were about two hundred lords with domains large and small. Each lord appointed officers to serve him in ritual, administrative, or military capacities. These posts and their associated titles tended to become hereditary as well.

The decentralized rule of the early Zhou period carried within it the danger that the regional lords would become so powerful that they would no longer obey the commands of the king. As generations passed and ties of loyalty and kinship grew more distant, this happened. In 771 B.C.E. the Zhou king was killed by an alliance of non-Chinese tribesmen and Zhou vassals. One of his sons was put on the throne, and then for safety's sake the capital was moved east out of the Wei River Valley to modern Luoyang, just south of the Yellow River in the heart of the central plains (see Map 4.2, page 93).

The revived Zhou Dynasty never fully regained control over its vassals, and China entered a prolonged period without a strong central authority. For a few centuries a code of chivalrous or sportsmanlike conduct still regulated warfare between the states: one state would not attack another that was in mourning for its ruler; during battles one side would not attack before the other side had time to line up; ruling houses were not wiped out, so that successors could continue to sacrifice to their ancestors; and so on. Thereafter, however, such niceties were abandoned, and China entered a period of nearly constant conflict.

Winged Immortal Less than 8 inches tall, this bronze candelabra is in the shape of an immortal. Those who mastered the secrets of not dying were thought to be able to fly through the heavens. (Werner Forman/akg-images)

Life During the Zhou Dynasty

During the early Zhou period, aristocratic attitudes and privileges were strong. Inherited ranks placed people in a hierarchy ranging downward from the king to the rulers of states with titles like duke and marquis, to the hereditary great officials of the states, to the lower ranks of the aristocracy — men who could serve in either military or civil capacities, known as **shi** — and finally to the ordinary people (farmers, craftsmen, and traders). Patrilineal family ties were very important in this society, and at the upper reaches, at least, sacrifices to ancestors were one of the key rituals used to forge social ties.

Glimpses of what life was like at various social levels in the early Zhou Dynasty can be found in the ***Book of Songs*** (ca. 900 B.C.E.), which contains the earliest Chinese poetry. Some of the songs are hymns used in court religious ceremonies, such as offerings to ancestors. Others clearly had their origins in folk songs. The seasons set the pace for rural life, and the songs contain many references to seasonal changes, such as the appearance of insects like grasshoppers and crickets. Some of these songs depict farmers clearing fields, plowing and planting, gathering mulberry leaves for silkworms, and spinning and weaving. Farming life involved not merely cultivating crops like millet, hemp (for cloth), beans, and vegetables but also hunting small animals and collecting grasses and rushes to make rope and baskets. (See "Viewpoints 4.1: The Inglorious Side of War in the *Book of Songs* and the *Patirruppattu*," page 98.)

Many of the folk songs are love songs that depict a more informal pattern of courtship than the one that prevailed in later China. One stanza reads:

> Please, Zhongzi,
> Do not leap over our wall,
> Do not break our mulberry trees.
> It's not that I begrudge the mulberries,
> But I fear my brothers.
> You I would embrace,
> But my brothers' words — those I dread.[1]

Viewpoints 4.1

The Inglorious Side of War in the *Book of Songs* and the *Patirruppattu*

• *The* Book of Songs, *the earliest collection of Chinese poetry, dating back to around 800 B.C.E., includes not only poems that glorify the valiant military victor, but also ones that look at war from the side of ordinary soldiers forced to march and fight. These poems can be compared to others written by poets at court in south India, which were preserved in* Patirruppattu, *an anthology from the classical period of Tamil literature, about 150 B.C.E.–250 C.E.*

Soldiers' Complaints in the *Book of Songs*

Minister of War,
We are the king's claws and fangs.
Why should you roll us on from misery to misery,
Giving us no place to stop in or take rest?

Minister of War,
We are the king's claws and teeth.
Why should you roll us from misery to misery,
Giving us no place to come to and stay?

Minister of War,
Truly you are not wise.
Why should you roll us on from misery to misery?
We have mothers who lack food.

. . .

What plant is not faded?
What day do we not march?
What man is not taken
To defend the four bounds?

What plant is not wilting?
What man is not taken from his wife?
Alas for us soldiers,
Treated as though we are not fellow-men!

Are we buffaloes, are we tigers,
That our home should be these desolate wilds?
Alas for us soldiers,
Neither by day nor night can we rest!

The fox bumps and drags
Through the tall, thick grass.
Inch by inch move our barrows
As we push them along the track.

The Waste of War from *Patirruppattu*

HARVEST OF WAR

Great king
you shield your men from ruin,
so your victories, your greatness
are bywords.

Loose chariot wheels
lie about the battleground
with the long white tusks
of bull-elephants.

Flocks of male eagles
eat carrion
with their mates.

Headless bodies
dance about
before they fall
to the ground.

Blood glows,
like the sky before nightfall,
in the red center
of the battlefield.

Demons dance there.
And your kingdom
is an unfailing harvest
of victorious wars.

BATTLE SCENE

You might ask,
"This Porai, so fierce in war,
how big
are his armies, really?"
Listen,
new travelers on the road!

As the enemy mob scampers and flees
and kings die on the field,

I've no body count
of those who kill as they fall,
and falling,
dance the victory dance
with lifted hands.

I've no count of the well-made chariots
that run all over them,
wheel-rims hardly worn,

nor of the horses, the men,
numberless,
I've not counted them.

And those elephants of his,
they cannot be pegged down,
they twist goads out of shape,

they stamp even on the moving shadows
of circling eagles,
and stampede like the cattle
of the Konkars
with pickax troops on a wasteland of pebbles, they really move, those elephants in his army:
I can see them but I cannot count them.

QUESTIONS FOR ANALYSIS

1. Who is speaking in these poems?
2. What can you infer about warfare of the periods from these pieces?
3. How significant do you think it is that the Chinese poems were composed seven centuries or more before the Indian ones?

Sources: Excerpt from "The Minister of War" in *The Book of Songs*, translated from the Chinese by Arthur Waley. Published by George Allen & Unwin, 1937; reprint Grove Press, 1960. Used by permission of The Arthur Waley Estate; A. K. Ramanujan, ed. and trans., *Poems of Love and War: From the Eight Anthologies and the Ten Long Poems of Classical Tamil* (New York: Columbia University Press, 1985), pp. 115–117. Copyright 1985 by Columbia University Press. Reproduced by permission of Columbia University Press in the format Textbook via Copyright Clearance Center.

There were also songs of complaint, such as this one in which the ancestors are rebuked for failing to aid their descendants:

> The drought has become so severe
> That it cannot be stopped.
> Glowing and burning,
> We have no place.
> The great mandate is about at an end.
> Nothing to look forward to or back upon.
> The host of dukes and past rulers
> Does not help us.
> As for father and mother and the ancestors,
> How can they bear to treat us so?[2]

Other songs in this collection are court odes that reveal attitudes of the aristocrats. One such ode expresses a deep distrust of women's involvement in politics:

> Clever men build cities,
> Clever women topple them.
> Beautiful, these clever women may be
> But they are owls and kites.
> Women have long tongues
> That lead to ruin.
> Disorder does not come down from heaven;
> It is produced by women.[3]

Part of the reason for distrust of women in politics was the practice of concubinage. Rulers regularly demonstrated their power and wealth by accumulating large numbers of concubines (legal spouses who ranked lower than the wife) and by having children by several women. In theory, succession went to the eldest son of the wife, then to younger sons by her, and only in their absence to sons of concubines; but in actual practice, the ruler of a state or the head of a powerful ministerial family could select a son of a concubine to be his heir if he wished. This led to much scheming for favor among the various sons and their mothers and the common perception that women were incapable of taking a disinterested view of the larger good.

Social and economic change quickened after 500 B.C.E. Cities began appearing all over north China. Thick earthen walls were built around the palaces and ancestral temples of the ruler and other aristocrats, and often an outer wall was added to protect the artisans, merchants, and farmers who lived outside the inner wall. Accounts of sieges launched against these walled citadels, with scenes of the scaling of walls and the storming of gates, are central to descriptions of military confrontations in this period.

The development of iron technology in the early Zhou Dynasty promoted economic expansion and

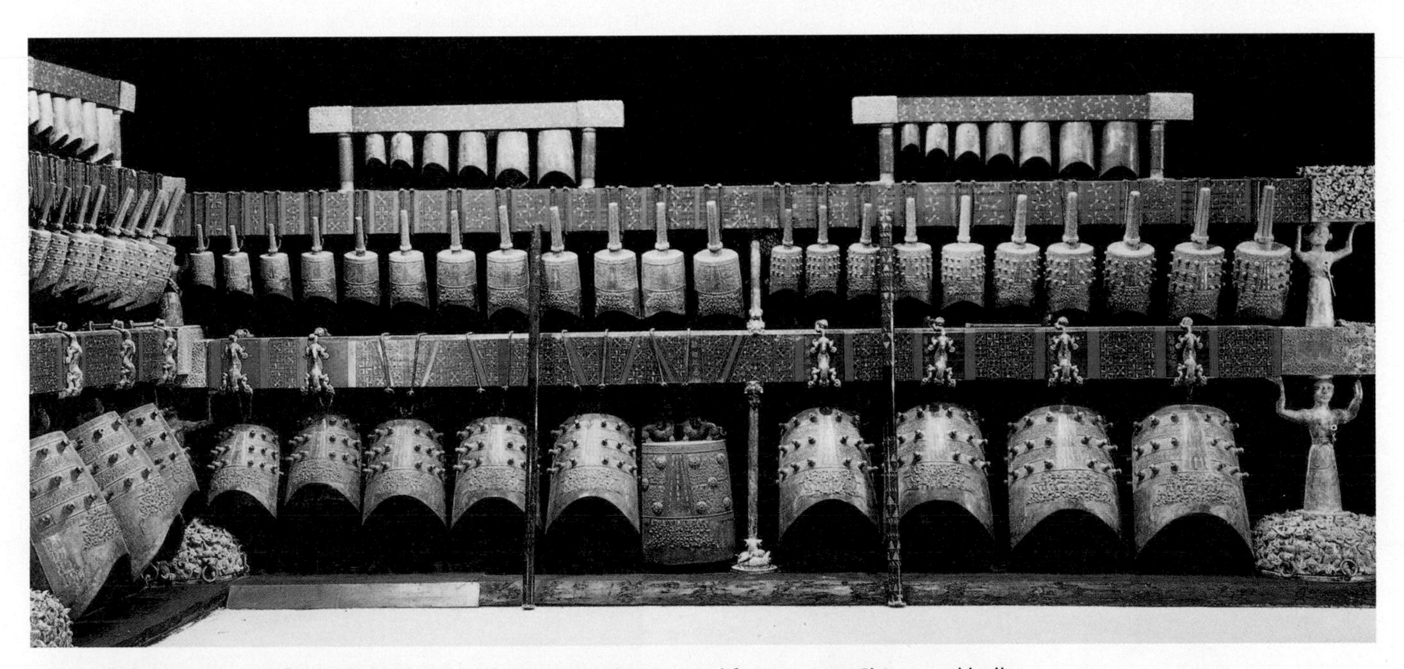

Bells of the Marquis of Zeng Music played a central role in court life in ancient China, and bells are among the most impressive bronze objects of the period. The tomb of a minor ruler who died about 400 B.C.E. contained 124 musical instruments, including drums, flutes, mouth organs, pan pipes, zithers, a set of 32 chime stones, and this 64-piece bell set. The bells bear inscriptions that name the two tones each bell could make, depending on where it was struck. Five men, using poles and mallets and standing on either side of the set of bells, would have played the bells by hitting them from outside. (Hubei Provincial Museum/Uniphoto Press, Japan/Ancient Art & Architecture Collection, Ltd.)

Individuals in Society

Lord Mengchang

DURING THE WARRING STATES PERIOD, MEN COULD RISE to high rank on the basis of talent. Lord Mengchang rose on the basis of his people skills: he treated his retainers so well that he attracted thousands of talented men to his service, enabling him to rise to prime minister of his native state of Qi (chee) in the early third century B.C.E.

Lord Mengchang's beginnings were not promising. His father, a member of the Qi royal family, already had more than forty sons when Mengchang was born, and he ordered the mother, one of his many concubines, to leave the baby to die. She, however, secretly reared him, and while still a child he was able to win his father's approval through his cleverness.

At his father's death Mengchang succeeded him. Because Mengchang would provide room and board to men who sought to serve him, he soon attracted a few thousand retainers, many of humble background, some fleeing justice. Every night, we are told, he ate with them all in his hall, treating them equally no matter what their social origins.

Most of the stories about Mengchang revolve around retainers who solved his problems in clever ways. Once, when Mengchang had been sent as an envoy to Qin, the king of Qin was persuaded not to let so talented a minister return to help Qi. Under house arrest, Mengchang was able to ask one of the king's consorts to help him, but in exchange she wanted a fur coat kept in the king's treasury. A former thief among Mengchang's retainers stole it for him, and Mengchang was soon on his way. By the time he reached the barrier gate, Qin soldiers were pursuing him, and he knew that he had to get through quickly. One of his retainers imitated the crowing of a cock, which got the other cocks to crow, making the guards think it was dawn, so they opened the gates and let his party through.

When Mengchang served as prime minister of Qi, his retainers came up with many clever stratagems that convinced the nearby states of Wei and Han to join Qi in resisting Qin. Several times, one of his retainers of modest origins, Feng Xuan (schwan), helped Mengchang withstand the political vicissitudes of the day. When sent to collect debts owed to Mengchang in his fief of Xue, Feng Xuan instead forgave all the debts of those too poor to repay their loans. Later, when Lord Mengchang lost his post at court and returned to his fief, most of his retainers deserted him, but he found himself well loved by the local residents, all because of Feng Xuan's generosity in his name. After Mengchang reattained his court post and was traveling back to Qi, he complained to Feng Xuan about those who had deserted him. Feng Xuan, we are told, got down from the carriage and bowed to Lord Mengchang, and when pressed said that the lord should accept the retainers' departures as part of the natural order of things:

> Wealth and honor attract while poverty and lowliness repel; such is the nature of things. Think of it like the market. In the morning it is crowded and in the evening it is deserted. This is not because people prefer the morning to the evening, but rather because what they want can not be found there [in the evening]. Do not let the fact that your retainers left when you lost your position lead you to bar them from returning. I hope that you will treat them just the way you did before.*

Mengchang promoted trade by issuing bronze coins. Some Zhou coins, like the one shown here with the mold used to cast it, were shaped like miniature knives. (© The Trustees of the British Museum/Art Resource, NY)

QUESTIONS FOR ANALYSIS

1. How did Mengchang attract his many retainers, and how did their service benefit him?
2. Who in this story benefited from hereditary privilege, and who advanced because of ability? What does this suggest about social mobility during the Warring States Period?
3. Many of the stories about Mengchang are included in *Intrigues of the Warring States*, a book that Confucians disapproved of. What do you think they found objectionable?

LaunchPad
Online Document Project

How did rulers and their subordinates interact during the Warring States Period? Read a selection of stories from the Warring States Period, and then complete a quiz and writing assignment based on the evidence and details from this chapter.

See inside the front cover to learn more.

**Shi ji* 75.2362. Translated by Patricia Ebrey.

allowed some people to become very rich. By the fifth century B.C.E. iron was being widely used for both farm tools and weapons. In the early Zhou, inherited status and political favor had been the main reasons some people had more power than others. Beginning in the fifth century wealth alone was also an important basis for social inequality. Late Zhou texts frequently mention trade across state borders in goods such as furs, copper, dyes, hemp, salt, and horses. People who grew wealthy from trade or industry began to rival rulers for influence. Rulers who wanted trade to bring prosperity to their states welcomed traders and began making coins to facilitate trade.

Social mobility increased over the course of the Zhou period. Rulers often sent out their own officials rather than delegate authority to hereditary lesser lords. This trend toward centralized bureaucratic control created opportunities for social advancement for the shi on the lower end of the old aristocracy. Competition among such men guaranteed rulers a ready supply of able and willing subordinates, and competition among rulers for talent meant that ambitious men could be selective in deciding where to offer their services. (See "Individuals in Society: Lord Mengchang," at left.)

The Warring States, 403–221 B.C.E.

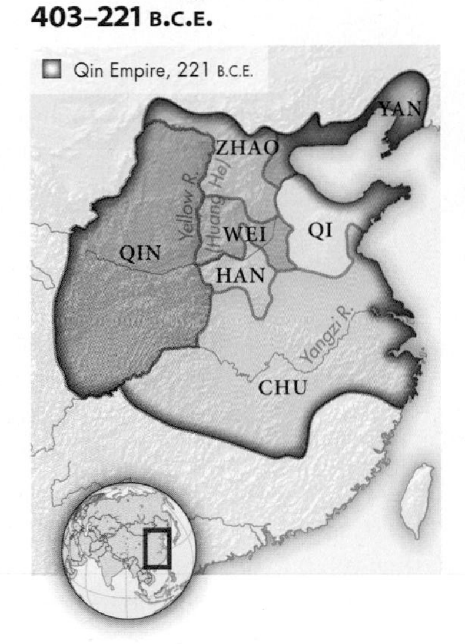

Religion in Zhou times was not simply a continuation of Shang practices. The practice of burying the living with the dead—so prominent in the royal tombs of the Shang—steadily declined in the middle Zhou period. Still, a ruler who died in 433 B.C.E. had his female musicians buried with him, evidence that some rulers still had their servants accompany them in death. The musicians and their instruments also testify to the role that music played in court entertainment. New deities and cults also appeared, especially in the southern state of Chu, where areas that had earlier been considered barbarian were being incorporated into the cultural sphere of the Central States, as the core region of China was called. The state of Chu expanded rapidly in the Yangzi Valley, defeating and absorbing fifty or more small states as it extended its reach north to the heartland of Zhou and east to absorb the old states of Wu and Yue. By the late Zhou period, Chu was on the forefront of cultural innovation and produced the greatest literary masterpiece of the era, the *Songs of Chu*, a collection of fantastical poems full of images of elusive deities and shamans who can fly through the spirit world. Images found in Chu tombs, painted on coffins or pieces of silk, show both fearsome deities and spirit journeys.

The Warring States Period, 403–221 B.C.E.

☐ How did advances in military technology contribute to the rise of independent states?

By 400 B.C.E. advances in military technology were undermining the old aristocratic social structure of the Zhou. Large, well-drilled infantry armies able to withstand and defeat chariot-led forces became potent military forces in the **Warring States Period**, which lasted from 403 B.C.E. to 221 B.C.E. Fueled by the development of new weaponry and war tactics, the Chinese states destroyed each other one by one until only one state was left standing—the state of Qin (chin). In response to the human and economic costs of war, rulers sought ways to increase population and expand trade even while they destroyed one another.

New Technologies for War

By 300 B.C.E. states were sending out armies of a few hundred thousand drafted foot soldiers, usually accompanied by horsemen. Adding to their effectiveness was the development of the **crossbow** around 350 B.C.E. The intricate bronze trigger of the crossbow allowed a foot soldier to shoot farther than could a horseman carrying a light bow. One text of the period reports that a skilled soldier with a powerful crossbow and a sharp sword was the match of a hundred ordinary men. To defend against crossbows, soldiers began wearing armor and helmets. Most of the armor was made of leather strips tied with cords. Helmets were sometimes made of iron. (See "Global Trade: Iron," page 50.)

The introduction of cavalry in this period further reduced the need for a chariot-riding aristocracy. Shooting bows and arrows from horseback was first perfected by non-Chinese peoples to the north of China proper, who at that time were making the transition to a nomadic pastoral economy. The northern state of Jin developed its own cavalry to defend itself

- **Warring States Period** The period of Chinese history between 403 B.C.E. and 221 B.C.E. when states fought each other and one state after another was destroyed.
- **crossbow** A powerful mechanical bow developed during the Warring States Period.

Mounted Swordsman This depiction of a warrior fighting a leopard decorates a bronze mirror inlaid with gold and silver dating from the Warring States Period. (From *Gugong wenwu yuekan*, 91 [1990])

from the attacks of these horsemen. Once it started using cavalry against other Chinese states, they too had to master the new technology. From this time on, acquiring and pasturing horses was a key component of military preparedness.

Because of these developments, rulers wanted to increase their populations, to have more commoners to serve as foot soldiers and more craftsmen to supply more weapons. To increase agricultural output, they brought new land into cultivation, drained marshes, and dug irrigation channels. Rulers began surveying their land and taxing farmers. They wanted to undermine the power of lords over their subjects in order to get direct access to the peasants' labor power. Serfdom thus gradually declined. Registering populations led to the extension of family names to commoners at an earlier date than anywhere else in the world.

The development of infantry armies also created the need for a new type of general, and rulers became less willing to let men lead troops merely because of aristocratic birth. In *The Art of War* (453–403 B.C.E.), Sun Wu described the ideal general as a master of maneuver, illusion, and deception. He argued that heroism is a useless virtue that leads to needless deaths. Discipline, however, is essential, and he insisted that the entire army had to be trained to follow the orders of its commanders without questioning them. He also explicitly called for use of deceit:

> War is the Way of deceit. Thus one who is competent pretends to be incompetent; one who uses [his army] pretends not to use it; one who draws near pretends to be distant; one who is distant pretends to draw near. If [the enemy desires] some advantage, entice him [with it]. If he is in disorder, seize him. If he is substantial, be prepared for him. If he is strong, evade him. If he is enraged, irritate him [further]. If he is humble, make him haughty. If he is rested, make him toil. If he is intimate [with his ranks], separate them. Attack where he does not expect it and go where he has not imagined. This is how military experts are victorious.[4]

The Victorious States

During the Warring States Period, states on the periphery of the Zhou realm had more room to expand than states in the center. With access to more resources, they were able to pick off their neighbors, one after the other. Still, for two centuries the final outcome was far from clear, as alliances among states were regularly made and nearly as regularly broken.

By the third century B.C.E. there were only seven important states remaining. These states were much more centralized than their early Zhou predecessors. Their kings had eliminated indirect control through vassals and in their place dispatched royal officials to remote cities, controlling them from a distance through the transmission of documents and dismissing them at will. Before the end of the third century B.C.E. one state, Qin, conquered all of the others, a development discussed in Chapter 7.

Confucius and His Followers

- What ideas did Confucius teach, and how were they spread after his death?

The Warring States Period was the golden age of Chinese philosophy, the era when the "Hundred Schools of Thought" contended. During the same period in which Indian sages and mystics were developing religious speculation about karma, souls, and ultimate reality (see Chapter 3), Chinese thinkers were arguing about the ideal forms of social and political organization and man's connections to nature.

Confucius

Confucius (traditional dates: 551–479 B.C.E.) was one of the first men of ideas. As a young man, he had served in the court of his home state of Lu without gaining much influence. After leaving Lu, he set out with a small band of students and wandered through neighboring states in search of a ruler who would take his advice. We know what he taught from the *Analects*, a collection of his sayings put together by his followers after his death. (See "Listening to the Past: The Teachings of Confucius," page 104.)

The thrust of Confucius's thought was ethical rather than theoretical or metaphysical. He talked repeatedly of an ideal age in the early Zhou Dynasty when everyone was devoted to fulfilling his or her role: superiors looked after those dependent on them; inferiors devoted themselves to the service of their superiors; parents and children, husbands and wives all wholeheartedly embraced what was expected of them. Confucius saw five relationships as the basis of society: between ruler and subject; between father and son; between husband and wife; between elder brother and younger brother; and between friend and friend. Mutual obligations of a hierarchical sort underlay the first four of these relationships — the senior leads and protects; the junior supports and obeys. The exception was the relationship between friends, which was conceived in terms of mutual obligations between equals.

A man of moderation, Confucius was an earnest advocate of gentlemanly conduct. He redefined the term *gentleman* (*junzi*) to mean a man of moral cultivation rather than a man of noble birth. He repeatedly urged his followers to aspire to be gentlemen rather than petty men intent on personal gain. Confucius did not advocate social equality, but his teachings minimized the importance of class distinctions and opened the way for intelligent and talented people to rise in the social scale. The Confucian gentleman found his calling in service to the ruler. Loyal advisers should encourage their rulers to govern through ritual, virtue, and concern for the welfare of their subjects, and much of the *Analects* concerns the way to govern well. To Confucius the ultimate virtue was **ren** (humanity). A person of humanity cares about others and acts accordingly:

> [The disciple] Zhonggong asked about humanity. Confucius said, "When you go out, treat everyone as if you were welcoming a great guest. Employ people as though you were conducting a great sacrifice. Do not do unto others what you would not have them do unto you. Then neither in your country nor in your family will there be complaints against you."[5]

In the Confucian tradition, studying texts came to be valued over speculation, meditation, and mystical identification with deities. Confucius encouraged the men who came to study with him to master the poetry, rituals, and historical traditions that we know today as Confucian classics.

The Spread of Confucian Ideas

The eventual success of Confucian ideas owes much to Confucius's followers in the three centuries following his death. The most important of them were Mencius (ca. 370–300 B.C.E.) and Xunzi (ca. 310–215 B.C.E.).

Mencius, like Confucius, traveled around offering advice to rulers of various states. Over and over he tried to convert them to the view that the ruler able to win over the people through benevolent government would succeed in unifying "all under Heaven." Mencius proposed concrete political and financial measures to ease tax burdens and otherwise improve the people's lot. Men willing to serve an unworthy ruler earned his contempt, especially when they worked hard to fill the ruler's coffers or expand his territory. In one conversation, the king of Qi asked if it was true that the founder of the Zhou Dynasty had taken up arms against his lord, the last king of Shang. Mencius replied that that was what the histories said. The king then asked, "Then is it permissible for a subject to assassinate his lord?" Mencius replied:

> Someone who does violence to the good we call a villain; someone who does violence to the right we call a criminal. A person who is both a villain and a criminal we call a scoundrel. I have heard that the scoundrel Zhou [the last Shang king] was killed, but have not heard that a lord was killed.[6]

With his disciples and fellow philosophers, Mencius also discussed other issues in moral philosophy, arguing strongly, for instance, that human nature is fundamentally good, as everyone is born with the capacity to recognize what is right and act on it. Anyone who saw a baby about to fall into a well would immediately come to its rescue. This would not be "because he wanted to improve his relations with the child's parents, nor because he wanted a good reputation among his friends and neighbors, nor because he disliked hearing the child cry."[7] Rather it would be because he has an inborn feeling of commiseration from which other virtues can grow.

Xunzi, a half century later, took the opposite view of human nature, arguing that people are born selfish and that only through education and ritual do they learn to put moral principle above their own interest. Much of what is desirable is not inborn but must be taught:

> When a son yields to his father, or a younger brother yields to his elder brother, or when a son takes on the work for his father or a younger brother for his elder

• **ren** The ultimate Confucian virtue; it is translated as perfect goodness, benevolence, humanity, human-heartedness, and nobility.

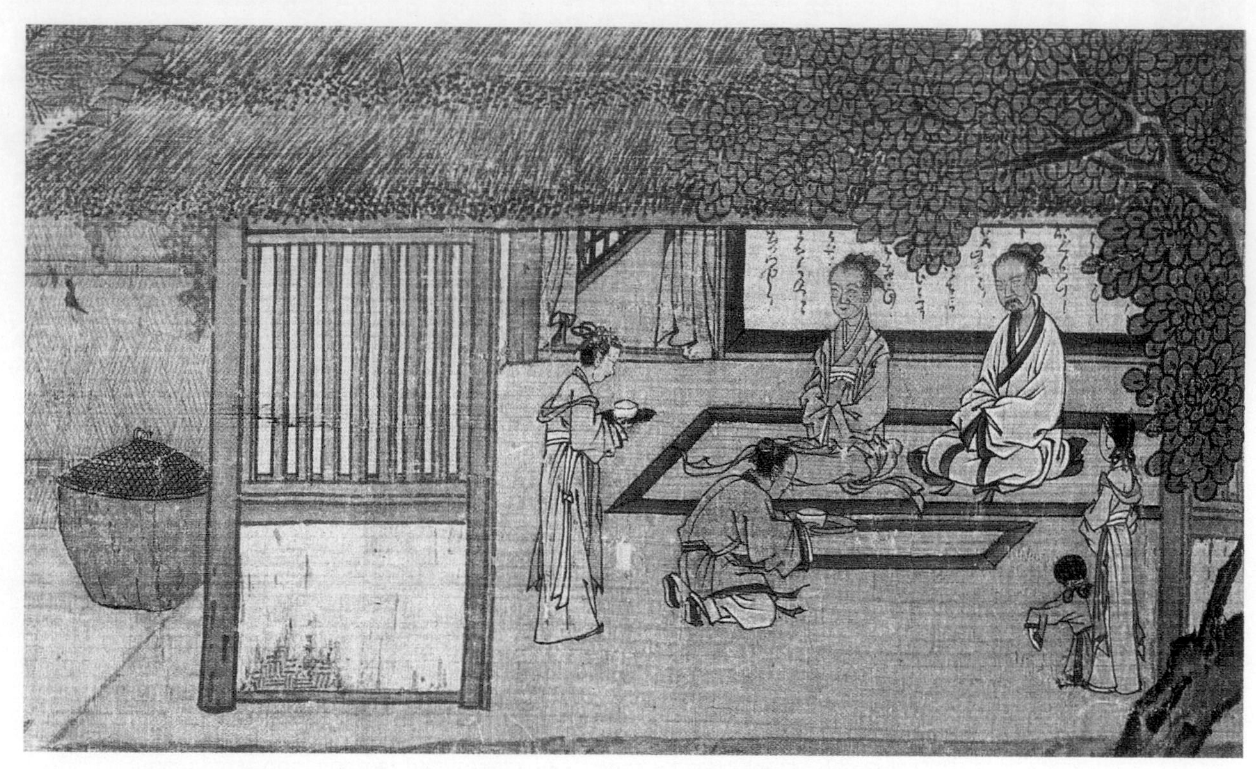

Serving Parents with Filial Piety This twelfth-century-C.E. illustration of a passage in the *Classic of Filial Piety* shows how commoners should serve their parents: by working hard at productive jobs such as farming and tending to their parents' daily needs. The married son and daughter-in-law offer food or drink to the older couple as their own children look on, thus learning how they should treat their own parents after they become aged. (National Palace Museum, Taiwan/The Art Archive at Art Resource, NY)

sustain the social hierarchy. Xunzi compared and contrasted ritual and music: music shapes people's emotions and creates feelings of solidarity, while ritual shapes people's sense of duty and creates social differentiation.

The Confucian vision of personal ethics and public service found a small but ardent following during the Warring States Period. In later centuries rulers came to see men educated in Confucian virtues as ideal advisers and officials. Neither revolutionaries nor flatterers, Confucian scholar-officials opposed bad government and upheld the best ideals of statecraft. Confucian political ideals shaped Chinese society into the twentieth century.

The Confucian vision also provided a moral basis for the Chinese family that continues into modern times. Repaying parents and ancestors came to be seen as a sacred duty. Because people owe their very existence to their parents, they should reciprocate by respecting their parents, making efforts to please them, honoring their memories, and placing the interests of the family line above personal preferences, all of which were aspects of **filial piety**. Since the family line is a patrilineal line from father to son to grandson, placing great importance on it has had the effect of devaluing women.

• **filial piety** Reverent attitude of children to their parents extolled by Confucius.

Daoism, Legalism, and Other Schools of Thought

☐ How did the teachings of Daoism, Legalism, and other schools of thought differ from Confucianism?

During the Warring States Period, rulers took advantage of the destruction of states to recruit newly unemployed men to serve as their advisers and court assistants. Lively debate often resulted as these strategists proposed policies and refuted opponents. Followers took to recording their teachers' ideas, and the circulation of these "books" (rolls of silk, or strips of wood or bamboo tied together) served to stimulate further debate.

Many of these schools of thought directly opposed the ideas of Confucius and his followers. Most notable

Viewpoints 4.2

Mozi and Xunzi on Divine Response

• *In early China, people had diverse understandings of the nature of gods, ghosts, ancestors, and the deity Heaven. Confucius strongly supported the practice of ritual, especially sacrifices to ancestors, but he avoided talk about gods or ghosts, preferring to focus on the human world. Mozi, in the next century, was concerned that skepticism about the gods would lead people to act in undesirable ways because they would not fear divine punishment. Xunzi, later still, approved of rituals for their social effects and drew a distinction between what the educated and the uneducated thought about the spirit world.*

Mozi, from *The Mozi*

"Long ago, in the time of Lord Zhuang of Qi [794–731 B.C.E.], there were two ministers named Wangli Guo and Zhongli Jiao. These two men had been engaged in a lawsuit for three years, but no judgment had been handed down. Lord Zhuang thought of executing them both, but he was afraid of killing an innocent man. He also thought of acquitting them both, but he was afraid of setting free one who was guilty. He therefore ordered the two men to bring a lamb and take an oath on the Qi altar of the soil. The two men agreed to take the oath of blood. The throat of the lamb was cut, its blood sprinkled on the altar, and Wangli Guo's version of the case read through to the end. Zhongli Jiao's version was read, but before it had been read half through, the lamb rose up, butted Zhongli Jiao, broke his leg, and then struck him down on the altar. At that time there were none of the attendants of Qi who did not see what happened, and no one in distant regions who did not hear about it. It was recorded in the spring and autumn annals of Qi, and the feudal lords handed down the story, saying, "All those who take oaths in insincerity will incur the punishment of the ghosts and spirits with just such rapidity!" If we examine what is written in the book, how can we doubt that ghosts and spirits exist?

Therefore Mozi said: Even in the deep valleys, the broad forests, the dark and distant places where no one lives, you must not fail to act with sincerity, for the ghosts and spirits will see you even there!"

Xunzi, from *The Xunzi*

"You pray for rain and it rains. Why? For no particular reason, I say. It is just as though you had not prayed for rain and it rained anyway. The sun and moon undergo an eclipse and you try to save them; a drought occurs and you pray for rain; you consult the arts of divination before making a decision on some important matter. But it is not as though you could hope to accomplish anything by such ceremonies. They are done merely for ornament. Hence the gentleman regards them as ornaments, but the common people regard them as supernatural. He who considers them ornaments is fortunate; he who considers them supernatural is unfortunate."

Source: Burton Watson, trans., *The Basic Writings of Mo Tzu, Hsün Tzu, and Han Fei Tzu* (New York: Columbia University Press, 1967), pp. 98–99, 85.

QUESTIONS FOR ANALYSIS

1. What can you infer about ordinary people's ideas about religion from these passages? How complete a view of the religious attitudes of the time do you think these passages give us?
2. Which of these thinkers do you find more persuasive, and why? How would people of the time have read these arguments?

were the Daoists, who believed that the act of striving to improve society only made it worse, and the Legalists, who argued that a strong government depended not so much on moral leadership as on effective laws and procedures.

Daoism

Confucius and his followers believed in moral action. They thought men of virtue should devote themselves to making the government work to the benefit of the people. Those who came to be labeled Daoists disagreed. They thought striving to make things better generally made them worse. Daoists defended private life and wanted the rulers to leave the people alone. They sought to go beyond everyday concerns and to let their minds wander freely. Rather than making human beings and human actions the center of concern, they focused on the larger scheme of things, the whole natural order identified as the Way, or **Dao**.

Early Daoist teachings are known from two surviving books, the *Laozi* and the *Zhuangzi*, both dating to the third century B.C.E. Laozi, the putative author of the *Laozi*, may not be a historical figure, but the text ascribed to him has been of enduring importance. A recurrent theme in this brief, aphoristic text is the mystical superiority of yielding over assertion and silence over words: "The Way that can be discussed is not the constant Way."[9] The highest good is like water: "Water benefits all creatures but does not compete. It occupies the places people disdain and thus comes near to the Way."[10]

Because purposeful action is counterproductive, the ruler should let people return to a natural state of ignorance and contentment:

> Do not honor the worthy,
> And the people will not compete.
> Do not value rare treasures,
> And the people will not steal.
> Do not display what others want,
> And the people will not have their hearts confused.
> A sage governs this way:
> He empties people's minds and fills their bellies.
> He weakens their wills and strengthens their bones.
> Keep the people always without knowledge and without desires,
> For then the clever will not dare act.
> Engage in no action and order will prevail.[11]

- **Dao** The Way, a term used by Daoists to refer to the natural order and by Confucians to refer to the moral order.
- **Legalists** Political theorists who emphasized the need for rigorous laws and laid the basis for China's later bureaucratic government.

In the philosophy of the *Laozi*, the people would be better off if they knew less, gave up tools, renounced writing, stopped envying their neighbors, and lost their desire to travel or engage in war.

Zhuangzi (369–286 B.C.E.), the author of the book of the same name, shared many of the central ideas of the *Laozi*. He was proud of his disinterest in politics. In one of his many anecdotes, he reported that the king of Chu once sent an envoy to invite him to take over the government of his realm. In response Zhuangzi asked the envoy whether a tortoise that had been held as sacred for three thousand years would prefer to be dead with its bones venerated or alive with its tail dragging in the mud. When the envoy agreed that life was preferable, Zhuangzi told the envoy to leave. He preferred to drag his tail in the mud.

The *Zhuangzi* is filled with parables, flights of fancy, and fictional encounters between historical figures, including Confucius and his disciples. A more serious strain of Zhuangzi's thought concerned death. He questioned whether we can be sure life is better than death. People fear what they do not know, the same way a captive girl will be terrified when she learns she is to become the king's concubine. Perhaps people will discover that death has as many delights as life in the palace.

When a friend expressed shock that Zhuangzi was not weeping at his wife's death but rather singing, Zhuangzi explained:

> When she first died, how could I have escaped feeling the loss? Then I looked back to the beginning before she had life. Not only before she had life, but before she had form. Not only before she had form, but before she had vital energy. In this confused amorphous realm, something changed and vital energy appeared; when the vital energy was changed, form appeared; with changes in form, life began. Now there is another change bringing death. This is like the progression of the four seasons of spring and fall, winter and summer. Here she was lying down to sleep in a huge room and I followed her, sobbing and wailing. When I realized my actions showed I hadn't understood destiny, I stopped.[12]

Zhuangzi was similarly iconoclastic in his political philosophy. In one parable a wheelwright insolently tells a duke that books are useless because all they contain are the dregs of men long dead. The duke, offended, threatens execution unless the wheelwright can explain his remark. The wheelwright replies:

> I see things in terms of my own work. When I chisel at a wheel, if I go slow, the chisel slides and does not stay put; if I hurry, it jams and doesn't move properly. When it is neither too slow nor too fast, I can feel it

in my hand and respond to it from my heart. My mouth cannot describe it in words, but there is something there. I cannot teach it to my son, and my son cannot learn it from me. So I have gone on for seventy years, growing old chiseling wheels. The men of old died in possession of what they could not transmit. So it follows that what you are reading are their dregs.[13]

To put this another way, truly skilled craftsmen respond to situations spontaneously; they do not analyze or reason or even keep in mind the rules they have mastered. This strain of Daoist thought denies the validity of verbal reasoning and the sorts of knowledge conveyed through words.

Daoism can be seen as a response to Confucianism, a rejection of many of its basic premises. Nevertheless, over the course of Chinese history, many people felt the pull of both Confucian and Daoist ideas and studied the writings of both schools. Even Confucian scholars who had devoted much of their lives to public service might find that the teachings of the *Laozi* or *Zhuangzi* helped to put their frustrations in perspective. Whereas Confucianism often seems sternly masculine, Daoism is more accepting of feminine principles and even celebrates passivity and yielding. Those drawn to the arts were also often drawn to Daoism, with its validation of spontaneity and freedom. Rulers, too, were drawn to the Daoist notion of the ruler who can have great power simply by being himself without instituting anything.

Legalism

Over the course of the fourth and third centuries B.C.E., one small state after another was conquered, and the number of surviving states dwindled. Rulers fearful that their states might be next were ready to listen to political theorists who claimed expertise in the accumulation of power. These theorists, labeled **Legalists** because of their emphasis on the need for rigorous laws, argued that strong government depended not on the moral qualities of the ruler and his officials, as Confucians claimed, but on establishing effective laws and procedures. Legalism, though eventually discredited, laid the basis for China's later bureaucratic government.

In the fourth century B.C.E. the state of Qin radically reformed itself along Legalist lines. The king of Qin abolished the aristocracy. Social distinctions were to be based on military ranks determined by the objective criterion of the number of enemy heads cut off in battle. In place of the old fiefs, the Qin king created counties and appointed officials to govern them according to the laws he decreed at court. To increase the population, Qin recruited migrants from other states with offers of land and houses. To encourage farmers to work hard and improve their land, they were allowed to buy and sell it. Ordinary farmers were thus freed from serf-like obligations to the local nobility, but direct control by the state could be even more onerous. Taxes and labor service obligations were heavy. Travel required a permit, and vagrants could be forced into

Picturing the Past

Inscribed Bamboo Slips In 1993 Chinese archaeologists discovered a late-fourth-century-B.C.E. tomb in Hubei province that contained 804 bamboo slips bearing some 12,000 Chinese characters. Scholars have been able to reconstruct more than a dozen books from them, many of them previously unknown. (Private Collection/Archives Charmet/The Bridgeman Art Library)

ANALYZING THE IMAGE Can you spot any repeated characters? Can you see any very simple characters?

CONNECTIONS What were the consequences of recording texts on bamboo or wooden strips? How might doing so have shaped reading and writing in Zhou times? For modern archaeologists who discover these texts in tombs, would the medium used pose any challenges?

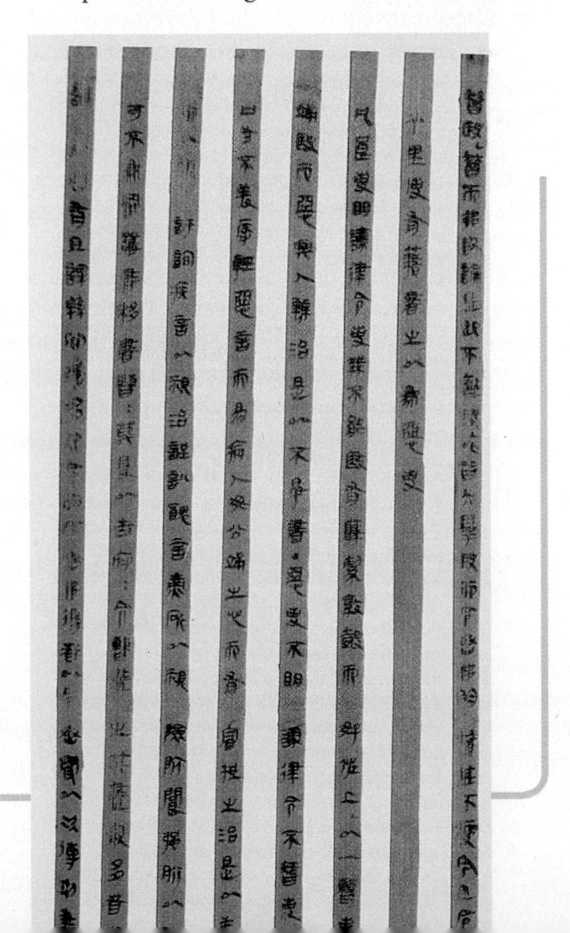

Phoenix and Tigers Divine animals, such as dragons and phoenixes, are often portrayed in the art of the Warring States Period, especially in the south, where the art of lacquered wood was perfected. (Werner Forman/akg-images)

penal labor service. All families were grouped into mutual responsibility groups of five and ten families; whenever anyone in the group committed a crime, all the others were equally liable unless they reported it.

Legalism found its greatest exponent in Han Feizi (ca. 280–233 B.C.E.), who had studied with the Confucian master Xunzi but had little interest in Confucian values of goodness or ritual. In his writings he warned rulers of the political pitfalls awaiting them. They had to be careful where they placed their trust, for "when the ruler trusts someone, he falls under that person's control."[14] This is true even of wives and concubines, who think of the interests of their sons. Given subordinates' propensities to pursue their own selfish interests, the ruler should keep them ignorant of his intentions and control them by manipulating competition among them. Warmth, affection, or candor should have no place in his relationships with others.

Han Feizi saw the Confucian notion that government could be based on virtue as naive. Even parents, he argued, treat their sons and daughters differently based on their assessment of long-term advantage. That is, they celebrate when a son is born, because he will be able to continue the family, but are dejected when a daughter is born, since she will eventually leave. In Han Feizi's view, it is unrealistic to expect people with no close kinship tie to treat each other more altruistically than parents treat their children. If rulers would make the laws and prohibitions clear and the rewards and punishments automatic, then the officials and common people would be easy to govern. Uniform laws get people to do things they would not otherwise be inclined to do, such as work hard and fight wars; such laws are thus essential to the goal of establishing hegemony over all the other states.

The laws of the Legalists were designed as much to constrain officials as to regulate the common people. The third-century-B.C.E. tomb of a Qin official has yielded statutes detailing the rules for keeping accounts, supervising subordinates, managing penal labor, conducting investigations, and many other responsibilities of officials. Infractions were generally punishable through the imposition of fines.

Legalism saw no value in intellectual debate or private opinion. Divergent views of right and wrong lead to weakness and disorder. The ruler should not allow others to undermine his laws by questioning them. In Legalism, there were no laws above or independent of the wishes of the rulers, no laws that might set limits on rulers' actions in the way that natural or divine laws did in Greek thought (see Chapter 5).

Rulers of several states adopted some Legalist ideas, but only the state of Qin systematically followed them. The extraordinary but brief success Qin had with these policies is discussed in Chapter 7.

Yin and Yang

Confucians, Daoists, and Legalists had the greatest long-term impact on Chinese civilization, but the Hundred Schools of Thought also included everyone from logicians, hedonists, and utopians to natural philosophers who analyzed the workings of nature.

A key idea developed by the natural philosophers was the concept of **yin and yang**, first described in the divination manual called the *Book of Changes* (ca. 900 B.C.E.), and developed into much more elaborate theories by late Zhou theorists. Yin is the feminine, dark,

- **yin and yang** A concept of complementary poles, one of which represents the feminine, dark, and receptive, and the other the masculine, bright, and assertive.

receptive, yielding, negative, and weak; yang is the masculine, bright, assertive, creative, positive, and strong. Yin and yang are complementary poles rather than distinct entities or opposing forces. The movement of yin and yang accounts for the transition from day to night and from summer to winter. These models based on observation of nature were extended to explain not only phenomena we might classify as natural, such as illness, storms, and earthquakes, but also social phenomena, such as the rise and fall of states and conflict in families. In all these realms, unwanted things happen when the balance between yin and yang gets disturbed.

In recent decades archaeologists have further complicated our understanding of early Chinese thought by unearthing records of the popular religion of the time—astrological manuals, handbooks of lucky and unlucky days, medical prescriptions, exercises, and ghost stories. The tomb of an official who died in 316 B.C.E., for example, has records of divinations showing that illness was seen as the result of unsatisfied spirits or malevolent demons, best dealt with through performing exorcisms or offering sacrifices to the astral god Taiyi (Grand One).

CHRONOLOGY

ca. 5000 B.C.E.	Emergence of regional Neolithic settlements
ca. 1500–1050 B.C.E.	Shang Dynasty
ca. 1200 B.C.E.	Evidence of writing found in royal tombs; chariots come into use
ca. 1050–256 B.C.E.	Zhou Dynasty
ca. 900 B.C.E.	*Book of Songs, Book of Changes, Book of Documents*
551–479 B.C.E.	Confucius
ca. 500 B.C.E.	Iron technology in wide use; cities spread across the central Zhou states
500–200 B.C.E.	Golden age of Chinese philosophy
453–403 B.C.E.	*The Art of War*
403–221 B.C.E.	Warring States Period; decline of the Zhou Dynasty
ca. 370–300 B.C.E.	Mencius
ca. 350 B.C.E.	Infantry armed with crossbows
ca. 310–215 B.C.E.	Xunzi
ca. 300–200 B.C.E.	Early Daoist teachings outlined in the *Laozi* and the *Zhuangzi*

Chapter Summary

After several thousand years of Neolithic cultures, beginning after 2000 B.C.E., Bronze Age civilization developed in China, with cities, writing, and sharp social distinctions. Shang kings led armies and presided at sacrifices to the high god Di and the imperial ancestors. The Shang armies' bronze-tipped weapons and chariots gave them technological superiority over their neighbors. War booty, including slaves who were often sacrificed to the gods, provided the Shang king with revenue.

The Zhou Dynasty, which overthrew the Shang in about 1050 B.C.E., parceled out its territory to hereditary lords. The earliest Chinese books date to this period. The *Book of Documents* provides evidence of the belief in the Mandate of Heaven, which justified Zhou rule. Because the last Shang king had not ruled in the interests of the people, Heaven took the mandate away from him and conferred it on a worthier person. The *Book of Songs* offers glimpses into what life was like for elites and ordinary people alike in the early Zhou.

By the Warring States Period, which began in 403 B.C.E., the old domains had become independent states. As states destroyed each other, military technology made many advances, including the introduction of cavalry, infantry armies, and the crossbow. Despite its name, the Warring States Period was the golden age of Chinese philosophy. Confucius and his followers promoted the virtues of sincerity, loyalty, benevolence, filial piety, and duty. Mencius urged rulers to rule through goodness and argued that human nature is good. Xunzi stressed the power of ritual and argued that human nature is selfish and must be curbed through education. Daoists and Legalists rejected all these ideas. The Daoists Laozi and Zhuangzi looked beyond the human realm to the entire cosmos and spoke of the relativity of concepts such as good and bad and life and death. Legalists heaped ridicule on the Confucian idea that a ruler could get his people to be good by being good himself and proposed instead rigorous laws with strict rewards and punishments. Natural philosophers explained the changes of seasons and health and illness in terms of the complementary forces of yin and yang.

NOTES

1. Reprinted with the permission of Simon & Schuster Publishing Group from the Free Press edition of *Chinese Civilization: A Sourcebook*, 2nd Edition, by Patricia Buckley Ebrey, p. 11. Copyright © 1993 by Patricia Buckley Ebrey. All rights reserved.
2. Edward Shaughnessy, "Western Zhou History," in *The Cambridge History of Ancient China*, ed. M. Loewe and E. Shaughnessy (New York: Cambridge University Press, 1999), p. 336. Reprinted with the permission of Cambridge University Press.
3. Patricia Buckley Ebrey, *Cambridge Illustrated History of China* (Cambridge: Cambridge University Press, 1996), p. 34.
4. Victor H. Mair, Nancy S. Steinhardt, and Paul Goldin, ed., *Hawai'i Reader in Traditional Chinese Culture* (Honolulu: University of Hawai'i Press, 2005), p. 117.
5. Reprinted with the permission of Simon & Schuster Publishing Group from Ebrey, *Chinese Civilization*, p. 19.
6. Reprinted with the permission of Simon & Schuster Publishing Group from ibid., p. 23.
7. Reprinted with the permission of Simon & Schuster Publishing Group from ibid.
8. Reprinted with the permission of Simon & Schuster Publishing Group from ibid., p. 26.
9. Reprinted with the permission of Simon & Schuster Publishing Group from ibid., p. 27.
10. Reprinted with the permission of Simon & Schuster Publishing Group from ibid., p. 28, modified.
11. Reprinted with the permission of Simon & Schuster Publishing Group from ibid., p. 28.
12. Reprinted with the permission of Simon & Schuster Publishing Group from ibid., p. 31.
13. Reprinted with the permission of Simon & Schuster Publishing Group from ibid.
14. Reprinted with the permission of Simon & Schuster Publishing Group from ibid, p. 33.

CONNECTIONS

China's transition from Neolithic farming villages to a much more advanced civilization with writing, metalworking, iron coinage, crossbows, philosophical speculation, and competing states occurred centuries later than in Mesopotamia or India, but by the Warring States Period China was at much the same stage of development as other advanced societies in Eurasia. Although many elements of China's civilization were clearly invented in China—such as its writing system, its method of casting bronze, and its Confucian philosophy—it also adopted elements that diffused across Asia, such as the cultivation of wheat, the horse-driven chariot, and riding horseback.

Greece, the subject of the next chapter, is located very close to the ancient Near Eastern civilizations, so its trajectory was quite different from China's. It was also much smaller than China, yet in time had enormous impact on the wider world. With India and China in mind, the originality of the political forms and ideas of early Greece will stand out more clearly. We return to China's history in Chapter 7, after looking at Greece and Rome.

Review and Explore

Make It Stick

LearningCurve
Go online and use LearningCurve to retain what you've read.

Identify Key Terms

Identify and explain the significance of each item below.

loess (p. 91)
Anyang (p. 93)
taotie (p. 94)
logographic (p. 95)
Book of Documents (p. 96)
Mandate of Heaven (p. 96)
shi (p. 97)
Book of Songs (p. 97)
Warring States Period (p. 101)
crossbow (p. 101)
ren (p. 103)
filial piety (p. 106)
Dao (p. 108)
Legalists (p. 109)
yin and yang (p. 110)

Review the Main Ideas

Answer the focus questions from each section of the chapter.

1. What was the impact of China's geography on the development of Chinese societies? (p. 91)
2. What was life like during the Shang Dynasty, and what effect did writing have on Chinese culture and government? (p. 92)
3. How was China governed, and what was life like during the Zhou Dynasty? (p. 96)
4. How did advances in military technology contribute to the rise of independent states? (p. 101)
5. What ideas did Confucius teach, and how were they spread after his death? (p. 102)
6. How did the teachings of Daoism, Legalism, and other schools of thought differ from Confucianism? (p. 106)

Make Connections

Analyze the larger developments and continuities within and across chapters.

1. Which features of early China's history seem closest to developments in other early civilizations, such as Mesopotamia, Egypt, and India?
2. Why do we refer to the ideas developed in India in the second half of the first millennium B.C.E. as religion and those developed in China as philosophy? Is this a useful distinction? Why or why not?
3. How does the political history of China from 500 B.C.E. to 250 B.C.E. help us understand the emergence of philosophies as different as Confucianism, Daoism, and Legalism?

LaunchPad
Online Document Project

The Limits of Loyalty

How did rulers and their subordinates interact during the Warring States Period?

Read a selection of stories from the Warring States Period, and then complete a quiz and writing assignment based on the evidence and details from this chapter.

See inside the front cover to learn more.

Suggested Reading

Blunden, Caroline, and Mark Elvin. *Cultural Atlas of China*. 1983. Valuable for both its historical maps and its well-illustrated topical essays.

Chang, Kwang-chih, and Xu Pingfang. *The Formation of Chinese Civilization: An Archaeological Perspective*. 2005. Essays by leading archaeologists in China.

de Bary, William Theodore, and Irene Bloom. *Sources of Chinese Tradition*. 1999. Large collection of primary sources for Chinese intellectual history, with lengthy introductions.

Ebrey, Patricia Buckley. *Cambridge Illustrated History of China*, 2d ed. 2010. Well-illustrated brief overview of Chinese history.

Graham, A. C. *Disputers of the Tao: Philosophical Argument in Ancient China*. 1989. A philosophically rich overview of the intellectual flowering of the Warring States Period.

Ledderose, Lothar. *Ten Thousand Things: Module and Mass Production in Chinese Art*. 2000. A new interpretation of Chinese culture in terms of modules; offers fresh perspectives on the Chinese script and the production of bronzes.

Lewis, Mark. *Writing and Authority in Early China*. 1999. An examination of early Chinese thought in terms of the ways that texts create authority.

Loewe, Michael, and Edward Shaughnessy, eds. *The Cambridge History of Ancient China: From the Origins of Civilization to 221 B.C.* 1999. An authoritative collection of chapters, half by historians, half by archaeologists.

Mote, F. W. *Intellectual Foundations of China*. 1989. Brief but stimulating introduction to early Chinese thought.

Puett, Michael. *To Become a God: Cosmology, Sacrifice, and Self-Divinization in Early China*. 2004. Brings an anthropological perspective to the development of early Chinese thought.

Shankman, Steven, and Stephen W. Durrant. *Early China / Ancient Greece: Thinking Through Comparisons*. 2002. A collection of articles that encourage cross-cultural comparisons.

Sterckx, Roel, ed. *Of Tripod and Palate: Food, Politics, and Religion in Traditional China*. 2005. Provides a fresh look at many elements in early Chinese culture.

Thorp, Robert. *China in the Early Bronze Age: Shang Civilization*. 2005. Clear synthesis based on recent research.

Thorp, Robert, and Richard Vinograd. *Chinese Art and Culture*. 2001. Broad coverage of all of China's visual arts.

Yang, Xin, ed. *The Golden Age of Chinese Archaeology*. 1999. The well-illustrated catalogue of a major show of Chinese archaeological finds.

The Greek Experience

3500–30 B.C.E.

5

Greek Boy with Goose

In the Hellenistic culture that developed across a huge area after Alexander the Great's conquests, wealthy urban residents wanted art that showed real people rather than gods. This statue of a little boy wrestling a goose, originally carved about 200 B.C.E., no doubt found an eager buyer. (© Vanni Archive/Art Resource, NY)

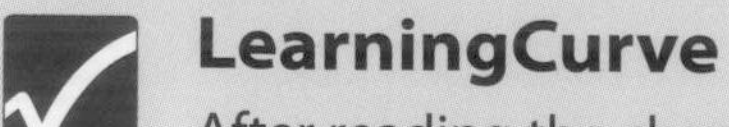

LearningCurve

After reading the chapter, go online and use LearningCurve to retain what you've read.

Chapter Preview

Greece in the Bronze Age, ca. 3000–800 B.C.E.

The Development of the Polis in the Archaic Age, ca. 800–500 B.C.E.

Turmoil and Culture in the Classical Period, 500–338 B.C.E.

Hellenistic Society, 323–30 B.C.E.

Hellenistic Religion, Philosophy, and Science

Humans came into Greece over many thousands of years, in waves of migrants whose place of origin and cultural characteristics have been the source of much scholarly debate. The people of ancient Greece built on the traditions and ideas of earlier societies to develop a culture that fundamentally shaped the civilization of the western part of Eurasia much as the Chinese culture shaped the civilization of the eastern part. The Greeks were the first in the Mediterranean and neighboring areas to explore many of the questions about the world around them and the place of humans in it that continue to concern thinkers today. Drawing on their day-to-day experiences as well as logic and empirical observation, they developed ways of understanding and explaining the world around them, which grew into modern philosophy and science. They also created new political forms and new types of literature and art.

Historians, archaeologists, and classicists divide the history of the Greeks into three broad periods: the Helladic period, which covered the Bronze Age, roughly 3000 B.C.E. to 1200 B.C.E.; the Hellenic period, from the Bronze Age Collapse to the conquest of Greece by Macedonia in 338 B.C.E.; and the Hellenistic period, stretching from the death of Alexander the Great, the ruler of Macedonia, in 323 B.C.E. to the Roman conquest in 30 B.C.E. of the kingdom established in Egypt by Alexander's successors. During the Hellenic period, Greeks developed a distinctive form of city-state known as the polis and made lasting cultural and intellectual achievements. During the Hellenistic period, Macedonian and Greek armies defeated the Persian Empire and built new cities and kingdoms, spreading Greek ideas as far as India (see Chapter 3). During their conquests they blended their ideas and traditions with those of the societies they encountered, creating a vibrant culture.

Greece in the Bronze Age, ca. 3000–800 B.C.E.

☐ How did the geography of Greece shape its earliest history?

Hellas, as the Greeks call their land, encompasses the Greek peninsula with its southern peninsular extension, known as the Peloponnesus (peh-luh-puh-NEE-suhs), and the islands surrounding it, an area known as the Aegean (ah-JEE-uhn) basin (Map 5.1). In ancient times this basin included the Greek settlements in Ionia, the western coast of the area known as Anatolia in modern western Turkey. During the Bronze Age, which for Greek history is called the "Helladic period," early settlers in Greece began establishing small communities contoured by the mountains and small plains that shaped the land. The geographical fragmentation of Greece encouraged political fragmentation. Early in Greek history several kingdoms did emerge—the Minoan on the island of Crete and the Mycenaean on the mainland—but the rugged terrain prohibited the growth of a great empire like those of Mesopotamia and Egypt. The Minoan and Mycenaean societies flourished for centuries until the Bronze Age Collapse, when Greece entered a period of decline known as the Dark Age (ca. 1100–800 B.C.E.).

The Minoans and Mycenaeans

On the large island of Crete, Bronze Age farmers and fishermen began to trade their surpluses with their neighbors, and cities grew, housing artisans and merchants. Beginning about 2000 B.C.E. Cretans voyaged throughout the eastern Mediterranean and the Aegean, carrying the copper and tin needed to make bronze as well as many other goods. Social hierarchies developed, and in many cities certain individuals came to hold power, although exactly how this happened is not

MAP 5.1 Classical Greece, ca. 450 B.C.E. In antiquity the home of the Greeks included the islands of the Aegean and the western shore of Turkey as well as the Greek peninsula itself. Crete, the home of Minoan civilization, is the large island at the bottom of the map. The Peloponnesian peninsula, where Sparta is located, is connected to the rest of mainland Greece by a very narrow isthmus at Corinth.

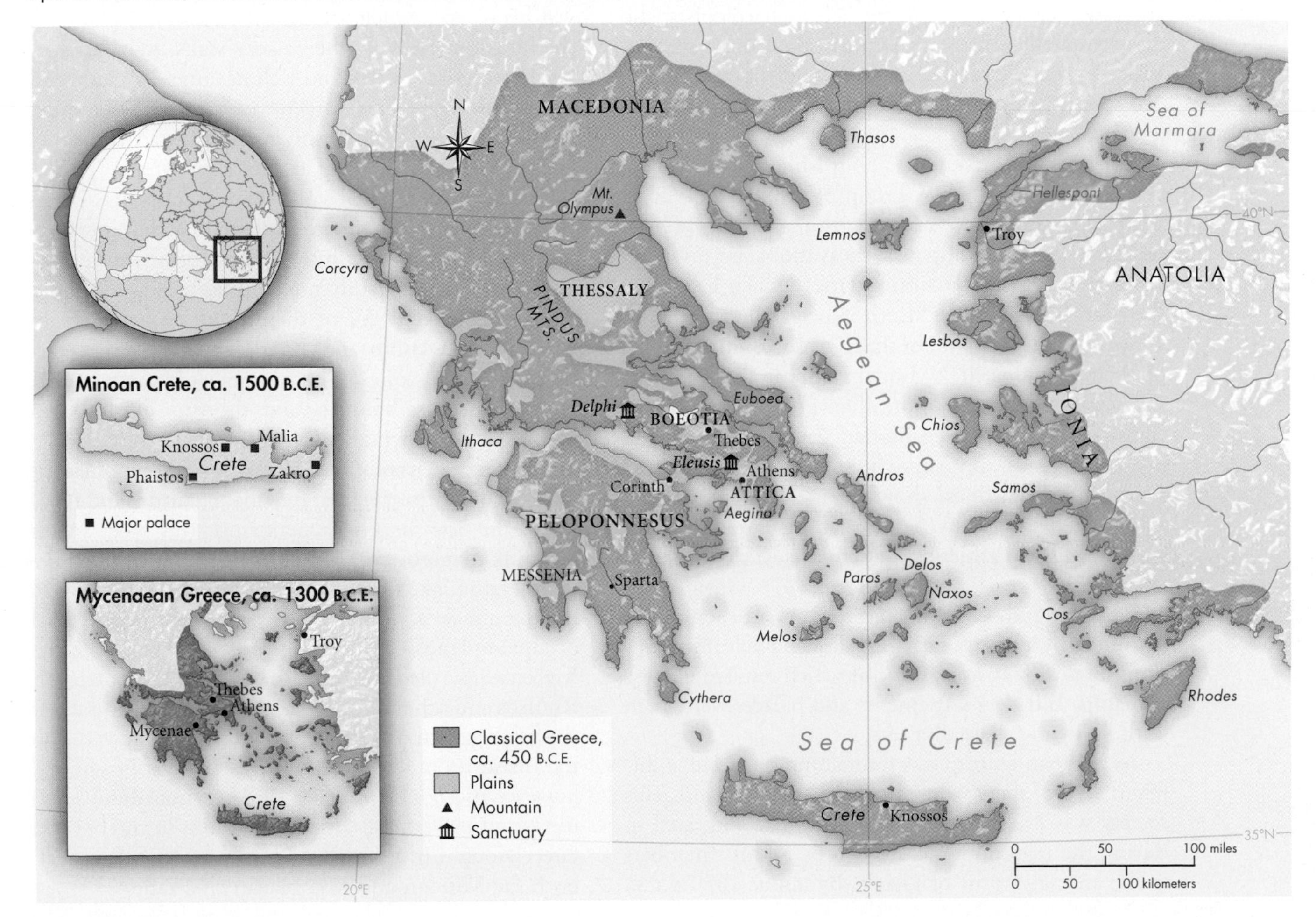

Mycenaean Dagger Blade This scene in gold and silver on the blade of an iron dagger depicts hunters armed with spears and protected by shields defending themselves against charging lions. The Mycenaeans were a robust, warlike people who enjoyed the thrill and the danger of hunting. (From the Royal Tomb IV, Mycenae, found by H. Schliemann. National Archeological Museum, Athens, Greece/Ancient Art & Architecture Collection, Ltd./The Bridgeman Art Library)

clear. The Cretans began to use writing about 1900 B.C.E., in a form later scholars called Linear A, but this script has not been deciphered. What we can know about the culture of Crete thus depends on archaeological and artistic evidence, and of this there is a great deal. At about the same time that writing began, rulers in several cities of Crete began to build large structures with hundreds of interconnected rooms. The largest of these, at Knossos (NOH-suhs), has over a thousand rooms along with pipes for bringing in drinking water and sewers to get rid of waste. The archaeologists who discovered these huge structures called them palaces, and they named the flourishing and vibrant culture of this era Minoan, after the mythical king of Crete, Minos.

Few specifics are known about Minoan political life except that a king and a group of nobles stood at its head. Minoan society was long thought to have been relatively peaceful, but new excavations are revealing more and more walls around cities, which has called the peaceful nature of Minoan society into question, although there is no doubt that it was wealthy. In terms of their religious life, Minoans appear to have worshipped goddesses far more than gods. Whether this translated into more egalitarian gender roles for real people is unclear, but surviving Minoan art, including frescoes and figurines, shows women as well as men leading religious activities, watching entertainment, and engaging in athletic competitions, such as leaping over bulls.

Beginning about 1700 B.C.E. Minoan society was disrupted by a series of earthquakes and volcanic eruptions on nearby islands, some of which resulted in large tsunamis. But new settlements and palaces were often built following these disasters.

As Minoan culture was flourishing on Crete, a different type of society developed on the mainland. This society was founded by groups who had migrated in during the period after 2000 B.C.E., and its members spoke an early form of Greek. By about 1650 B.C.E. one group of these immigrants had raised palaces and established cities at Thebes, Athens, Mycenae (migh-SEE-nee), and elsewhere. These palace-centers ruled by local kings formed a loose hegemony under the authority of the king of Mycenae, and the archaeologists who first discovered traces of this culture called it the Mycenaean (migh-see-NEE-ahn).

As in Crete, the political unit was the kingdom, and the king and his warrior aristocracy stood at the top of society. The seat and symbol of the king's power was his palace, which was also the economic center of the kingdom. Within the palace's walls, royal artisans fashioned gold jewelry and rich ornaments, made and decorated fine pottery, forged weapons, prepared hides and wool for clothing, and manufactured the other goods needed by the king and his supporters.

Palace scribes kept records with a script known as Linear B, which has been deciphered, so that information on Mycenaean culture comes from inscriptions and other forms of written records as well as buildings and other objects. All of these point to a society in which war was common. Mycenaean cities were all fortified by thick stone walls, and graves contain spears, javelins, swords, helmets, and the first examples of metal armor known in the world.

Contacts between the Minoans and Mycenaeans were originally peaceful, and Minoan culture and trade goods flooded the Greek mainland. But most scholars think that around 1450 B.C.E., possibly in the wake of an earthquake that left Crete vulnerable, the Mycenaeans attacked Crete, destroying many towns and occupying Knossos. For about the next fifty years, the Mycenaeans ruled much of the island. The palaces at Knossos and other cities of the Aegean became grander as wealth gained through trade and tribute flowed into the treasuries of various Mycenaean kings. Prosperity, however, did not bring peace, and between about 1300 B.C.E. and 1000 B.C.E. various kingdoms in and beyond Greece fought in a savage series of wars that destroyed both the Minoan and Mycenaean civilizations.

The fall of the Minoans and Mycenaeans was part of what some scholars see as a general collapse of Bronze Age civilizations in the eastern Mediterranean, including the end of the Egyptian New Kingdom and the fall of the Hittite Empire (see Chapter 2). This collapse appears to have had a number of causes: internal economic and social problems, including perhaps slave revolts; invasions and migrations by outsiders, who destroyed cities and disrupted trade and production; changes in warfare and weaponry, particularly the adoption of iron weapons, which made foot soldiers the most important factor in battles and reduced the power of kings and wealthy nobles fighting from chariots; and natural disasters such as volcanic eruptions, earthquakes, and droughts, which reduced the amount of food and contributed to famines.

The "Dark Age"

In Greece these invasions, migrations, disasters, and social problems worked together to usher in a period of poverty and disruption that historians have traditionally called the "Dark Age" of Greece (ca. 1100–800 B.C.E.). Cities were destroyed, population declined, villages were abandoned, and trade decreased. Pottery became simpler, and jewelry and other grave goods became less ornate. Even writing, which was not widespread before this period, was a casualty of the chaos.

The Bronze Age Collapse led to the widespread and prolonged movement of Greek peoples, both within Greece itself and beyond. They dispersed beyond mainland Greece farther south to the islands of the Aegean Sea and in greater strength across the Aegean to the shores of Anatolia (see Map 5.1), arriving at a time when traditional states and empires had collapsed. By the conclusion of the Dark Age, the Greeks had spread their culture throughout the Aegean basin, and like many other cultures around the Mediterranean and the Near East, they had adopted iron.

Archaeological sources from the Dark Age are less rich than those from the periods that came after, so they are often used in conjunction with literary sources written in later centuries to give us a more complete picture of the era. These included tales of the heroic deeds of legendary heroes similar to the epic poems of Mesopotamia and the *Ramayana* in India. Sometime in the eighth or seventh century B.C.E. many of these were gathered together in two long epic poems: the *Iliad*, which tells the story of the Trojan War, a war similar to those fought by Mycenaean kings, and the *Odyssey*, which records the adventures of one of the heroes of that war. These poems were recited orally, and once writing was reintroduced to Greece, they were written down and attributed to a poet named Homer, though scholars debate whether Homer was an actual historical individual. The two poems present human and divine characters who are larger than life but also petty, vindictive, pouting, and deceitful, flaws that drive the action forward, usually with tragic results. The heart of the *Iliad* concerns the quarrel between the Mycenaean king, Agamemnon, and the stormy hero of the poem, Achilles (uh-KIHL-eez), and how this brought suffering to the Mycenaeans, whom Homer calls Achaeans. The first lines of the *Iliad* capture both the anger and the anguish:

> Sing, O goddess, the anger of Achilles son of Peleus, that brought countless ills upon the Achaeans. Many a brave soul did it send hurrying down to Hades [Hell], and many a hero did it yield as prey to dogs and vultures.[1]

The Development of the Polis in the Archaic Age, ca. 800–500 B.C.E.

☐ What was the role of the polis in Greek society?

Homer lived in the era after the Dark Age, which later historians have termed the Archaic age (800–500 B.C.E.). The most important political change in this period was the development of the **polis** (PAH-luhs; plural *poleis*), a word generally translated as "city-state." With the polis, the Greeks established a new type of political structure. During the Archaic period, poleis established colonies throughout much of the Mediterranean, spreading Greek culture, and two particular poleis, each with a distinctive system of government, rose to prominence on the Greek mainland: Sparta and Athens.

Organization of the Polis

The Greek polis was not the first form of city-state to emerge. The earliest states in Sumer were also city-states, as were many of the small Mycenaean kingdoms. What differentiated the new Greek model from older city-states was that the polis was more than a political institution—it was a community of citizens with their own customs and laws. With one exception, the poleis that emerged after 800 B.C.E. did not have kings but instead were self-governing. The physical, religious, and political forms of the polis varied from place to place, but everywhere it was relatively small, reflecting the fragmented geography of Greece. The very smallness of the polis enabled Greeks to see how they fit individually into the overall system, and thus how the

• **polis** Generally translated as "city-state," it was the basic political and institutional unit of ancient Greece.

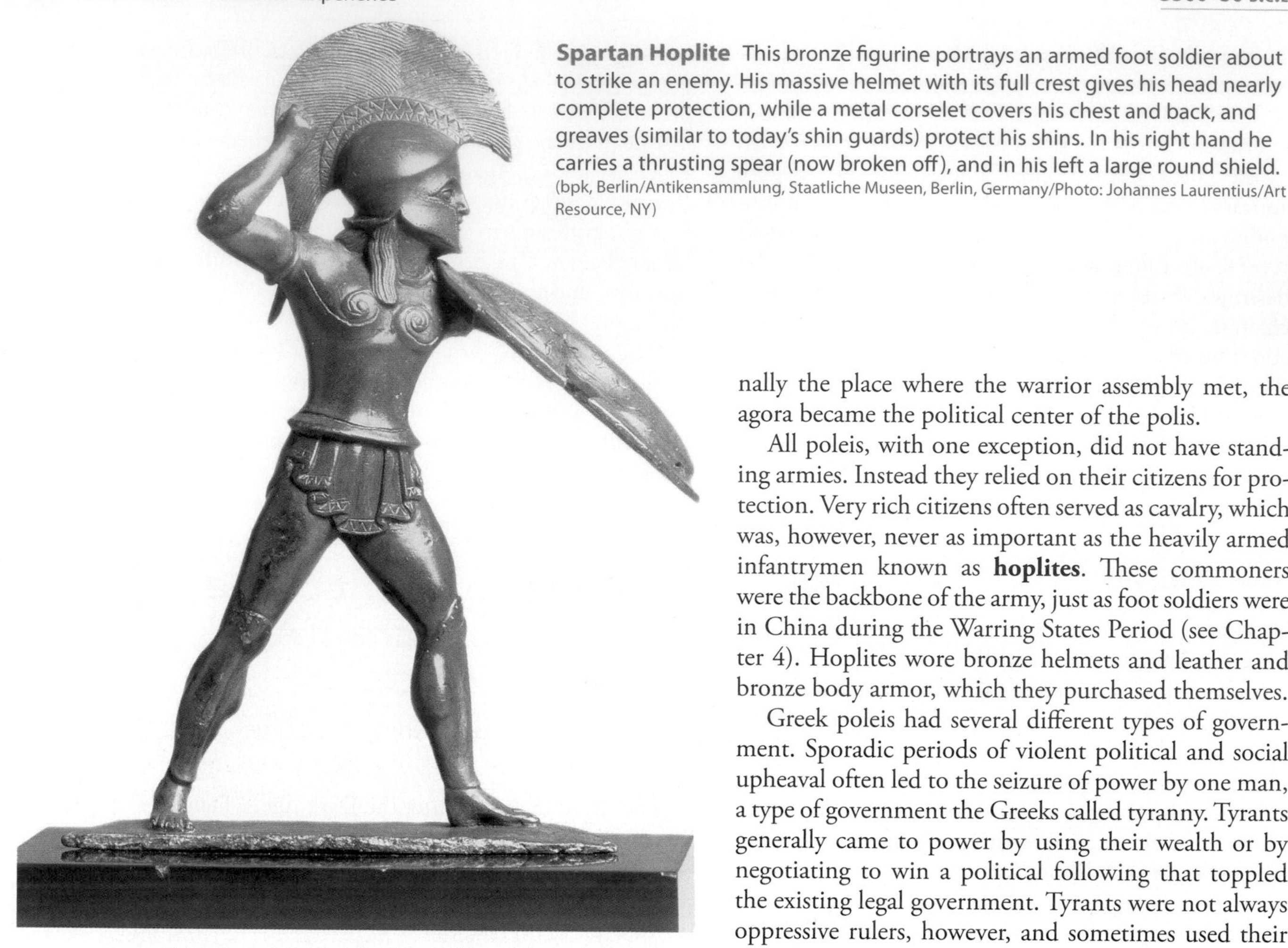

Spartan Hoplite This bronze figurine portrays an armed foot soldier about to strike an enemy. His massive helmet with its full crest gives his head nearly complete protection, while a metal corselet covers his chest and back, and greaves (similar to today's shin guards) protect his shins. In his right hand he carries a thrusting spear (now broken off), and in his left a large round shield. (bpk, Berlin/Antikensammlung, Staatliche Museen, Berlin, Germany/Photo: Johannes Laurentius/Art Resource, NY)

individual parts made up the social whole. This notion of community was fundamental to the polis and was the very badge of Greekness.

The polis included a city and its surrounding countryside. The countryside was essential to the economy of the polis and provided food to sustain the entire population. The people of the polis typically lived in a compact group of houses within the city, which by the fifth century B.C.E. was generally surrounded by a wall. Many left the city each morning to work their fields or tend their flocks of sheep and goats, and they returned at night. Another feature was a usually elevated area called the acropolis, where the people erected temples, altars, public monuments, and various dedications to the gods of the polis. The polis also contained a public square or marketplace, the agora, where there were porticoes, shops, public buildings, and courts. Originally the place where the warrior assembly met, the agora became the political center of the polis.

All poleis, with one exception, did not have standing armies. Instead they relied on their citizens for protection. Very rich citizens often served as cavalry, which was, however, never as important as the heavily armed infantrymen known as **hoplites**. These commoners were the backbone of the army, just as foot soldiers were in China during the Warring States Period (see Chapter 4). Hoplites wore bronze helmets and leather and bronze body armor, which they purchased themselves.

Greek poleis had several different types of government. Sporadic periods of violent political and social upheaval often led to the seizure of power by one man, a type of government the Greeks called tyranny. Tyrants generally came to power by using their wealth or by negotiating to win a political following that toppled the existing legal government. Tyrants were not always oppressive rulers, however, and sometimes used their power to benefit average citizens.

Democracy translates as "the power of the people" but was actually rule by citizens, not the people as a whole. Almost all Greek cities defined a citizen as an adult man with at least one citizen parent (or at some times and places, two citizen parents). Thus citizens shared ancestry as well as a place of residence. Women were citizens for religious and reproductive purposes, but their citizenship did not give them the right to participate in government. Free men who were not children of a citizen, known as resident foreigners, and slaves were not citizens and had no political voice. Thus ancient Greek democracy did not reflect the modern concept that all people are created equal, but it did permit male citizens to share equally in determining the diplomatic and military policies of the polis without respect to wealth.

Oligarchy, which literally means "the rule of the few," was government by a small group of wealthy citizens. Many Greeks preferred oligarchy because it provided more political stability than did democracy. Although oligarchy was the government of the prosperous, it left the door open for political and social advancement. If members of the polis could meet property or money qualifications, they could enter the governing circle.

- **hoplites** Heavily armed citizens who served as infantrymen and fought to defend the polis.
- **democracy** A type of Greek government in which all citizens administered the workings of government.
- **oligarchy** A type of Greek government in which citizens who owned a certain amount of property ruled.

Overseas Expansion

The development of the polis coincided with the growth of the Greek world in both wealth and numbers, bringing new problems. The increase in population created more demand for food than the land could supply. The resulting social and political tensions drove many people to seek new homes outside of Greece (Map 5.2).

Greeks traveled throughout the Mediterranean, sailing in great numbers to Sicily and southern Italy, where there was ample space for expansion. Here they established prosperous cities and often intermarried with local people. Some adventurous Greeks sailed farther west to Sardinia, France, Spain, and perhaps even the Canary Islands. In Sardinia they first established trading stations, and then permanent towns. From these new outposts Greek influence extended to southern France.

In contrast to earlier military invasions and migrations of peoples, these were very often intentional colonizing ventures, organized and planned by a specific polis seeking new land for its residents, or by the losers in a political conflict within a polis who were forced to leave. Colonization changed the entire Greek world, both at home and abroad. In economic terms the expansion of the Greeks created a much larger market for agricultural and manufactured goods.

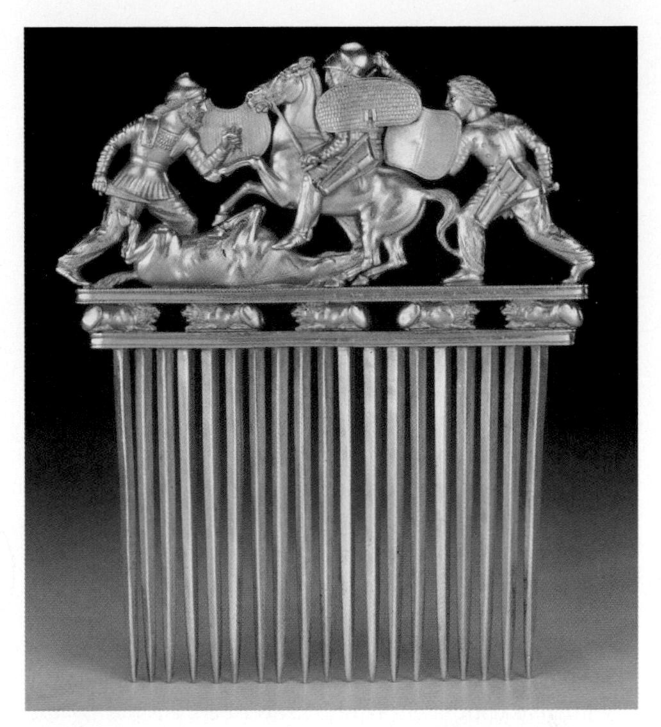

Golden Comb This golden comb, made about 400 B.C.E. in Scythia (now part of Ukraine), shows a battle between three warriors, perhaps the three brothers who are the legendary founders of Scythia. Their dress shows a combination of Greek and Eastern details; the mounted horseman is clothed with largely Greek armor, while the warriors on foot are wearing Eastern dress. The comb may have been made by a Greek craftsman who had migrated to the Black Sea area, as the Greeks established colonies there, but it was buried in a Scythian burial mound. (From Solokha burial mound, 4th century B.C./Hermitage, St. Petersburg, Russia/Photo © Boltin Picture Library/The Bridgeman Art Library)

The Growth of Sparta

Many different poleis developed during the Archaic period, but Sparta became the leading military power in Greece. To expand their polis, the Spartans did not

MAP 5.2 Greek Colonization, ca. 750–550 B.C.E. The Greeks established colonies along the shores of the Mediterranean and Black Seas, spreading Greek culture and creating a large trading network.

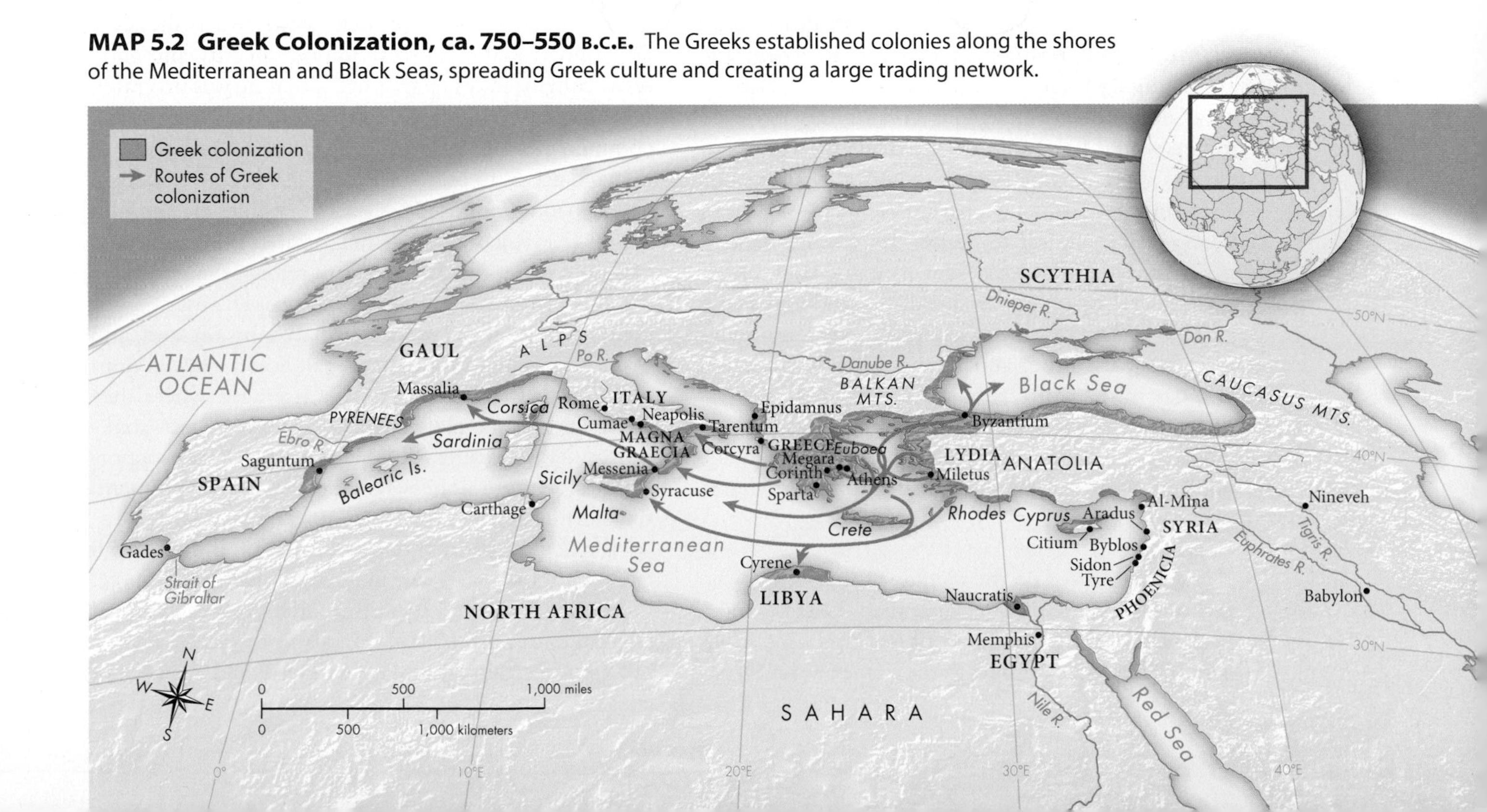

establish colonies but instead conquered Messenia (muh-SEE-nee-uh), a rich, fertile region in the southwestern Peloponnesus. They turned the Messenians into helots (HEH-luhts), unfree residents forced to work state lands. The helots soon rose in a revolt that took the Spartans thirty years to crush. Afterward, non-nobles who had shared in the fighting as foot soldiers appear to have demanded rights equal to those of the nobility and a voice in the government. (In more recent history, similar demands in the United States during the Vietnam War led to a lowering of the voting age to eighteen, to match the age at which soldiers were drafted.) Under intense pressure the aristocrats agreed to remodel the state into a new system.

The plan for the new system in Sparta was attributed to the lawgiver Lycurgus (ligh-KUHR-guhs), who may or may not have been an actual person. According to later Greek sources, political distinctions among Spartan men were eliminated, and all citizens became legally equal. Two kings, who were primarily military leaders, and a council of nobles shared executive power with five ephors (EH-fuhrs), overseers elected by the citizens. Helots worked the land, while Spartan citizens devoted their time to military training, and Sparta became extremely powerful.

In the system attributed to Lycurgus, every citizen owed primary allegiance to Sparta. Suppression of the individual along with an emphasis on military prowess led to a barracks state. Even family life was sacrificed to the polis. After long, hard military training that began at age seven, citizens became lifelong soldiers, the best in Greece. In battle Spartans were supposed to stand and die rather than retreat. Because men often did not see their wives or other women for long periods, not only in times of war but also in times of peace, their most meaningful relations were same-sex ones. The Spartan military leaders may have viewed such relationships as militarily advantageous because they believed that men would fight even more fiercely for lovers and comrades. An anecdote frequently repeated about one Spartan mother sums up Spartan military values. As her son was setting off to battle, the mother handed him his shield and advised him to come back either victorious and carrying the shield, or dead and being carried on it. Spartan men were expected to train vigorously, do with little, and like it, qualities reflected even today in the word *spartan*.

Spartans expected women in citizen families to be good wives and strict mothers of future soldiers. Xenophon, a later Athenian admirer of the Spartans, commented:

> [Lycurgus] insisted on the training of the body as incumbent no less on the female than the male; and in pursuit of the same idea instituted rival contests in running and feats of strength for women as for men. His belief was that where both parents were strong their progeny would be found to be more vigorous.[2]

With men in military service much of their lives, women in citizen families ran the estates and owned land in their own right, and they were not physically restricted or secluded.

The Evolution of Athens

Like Sparta, Athens faced pressing social and economic problems during the Archaic period, but the Athenian response was far different from that of the Spartans. Instead of creating a state devoted to the military, the Athenians created a state that became a democracy. For Athens, the late seventh century B.C.E. was a time of turmoil, the causes of which are unclear. In 621 B.C.E. Draco (DRAY-koh), an Athenian aristocrat, under pressure from small landholders and with the consent of the nobles, published the first law code of the Athenian polis. His code was harsh—and for this reason was the origin of the word *draconian*—but it embodied the ideal that the law belonged to all citizens. Yet the aristocracy still governed Athens oppressively, and the social and economic situation remained dire. Despite Draco's code, noble landholders continued to force small farmers and artisans into economic dependence. Many families were sold into slavery as settlement for debts, while others were exiled and their land mortgaged to the rich.

One person who recognized these problems was Solon (SOH-luhn), an aristocrat and a poet. Reciting his poems in the Athenian agora, where anyone could hear his call for justice and fairness, Solon condemned his fellow aristocrats for their greed and dishonesty. According to later sources, Solon's sincerity and good sense convinced other aristocrats that he was no crazed revolutionary. Moreover, he gained the trust of the common people, whose problems provoked them to demand access to political life, much as commoners in Sparta had. Around 594 B.C.E. the nobles elected him *archon* (AHR-kahn), chief magistrate of the polis, and gave him extraordinary power to reform the state.

Solon immediately freed all people enslaved for debt, recalled all exiles, canceled all debts on land, and made enslavement for debt illegal. Solon allowed non-nobles into the old aristocratic assembly, where they could vote in the election of magistrates. Later sixth-century-B.C.E. leaders further broadened the opportunities for commoners to take part in government, transforming Athens into a democracy.

The democracy functioned on the ideal that all full citizens should play a role in government. In 487 B.C.E. the election of the city's nine archons was replaced by reappointment by lot, which meant that any citizen with a certain amount of property had a chance of becoming an archon. This system gave citizens prestige, although the power of the archons gradually dwindled as military leaders called *strategoi* became increasingly important. Making laws was the responsibility of two bodies, the *boule* (BOO-lee), or council, composed of five hundred members, and the *ecclesia* (ee-KLEE-zhee-uh), the assembly of all citizens. By supervising the various committees of government and proposing bills and treaties to the ecclesia, the boule guided Athenian political life. Nonetheless, the ecclesia, open to all male citizens over eighteen years of age, had the final word through its votes.

Turmoil and Culture in the Classical Period, 500–338 B.C.E.

☐ In the classical period, how did war influence Greece, and how did the arts, religion, and philosophy develop?

From the time of the Mycenaeans, violent conflict was common in Greek society, and this did not change in the fifth century B.C.E., the beginning of what scholars later called the classical period of Greek history, which they date from about 500 B.C.E. to the conquest of Greece by Philip of Macedon in 338 B.C.E. First, the Greeks beat back the armies of the Persian Empire. Then, turning their spears against one another, they destroyed their own political system in a century of warfare that began with the Peloponnesian War. Some thoughtful Greek historians recorded these momentous events. Despite the violence or to some degree because of it, playwrights and thinkers pondered the meaning of the universe and the role of humans in it, and artists and architects created new styles to celebrate Greek achievements. Thus, although warfare was one of the hallmarks of the classical period, intellectual and artistic accomplishments were as well.

The Deadly Conflicts, 499–404 B.C.E.

In 499 B.C.E. the Greeks who lived in Ionia unsuccessfully rebelled against the Persian Empire, which had ruled the area for fifty years (see Chapter 2). The Athenians provided halfhearted help to the Ionians, and in retaliation the Persians struck at Athens, only to be surprisingly defeated by the Athenian hoplites at the Battle of Marathon. (According to legend, a Greek runner carried the news of the victory to Athens. When the modern Olympics began in 1896, they included a long-distance running race between Marathon and Athens, a distance of about twenty-five miles, designed to honor the ancient Greeks.) In 480 B.C.E. the Persian king Xerxes (ZUHRK-seez) personally led a massive invasion of Greece. Under the leadership of Sparta, many Greek poleis, though not all, united to fight the Persians, and they engaged in major battles at the pass of Thermopylae and in the waters off Artemisium. The larger Persian army was victorious and occupied Athens, but only a month or so later the Greeks defeated the Persian navy in the decisive Battle of Salamis, an island across from Athens, and in 479 B.C.E. they overwhelmed the Persian army at Plataea.

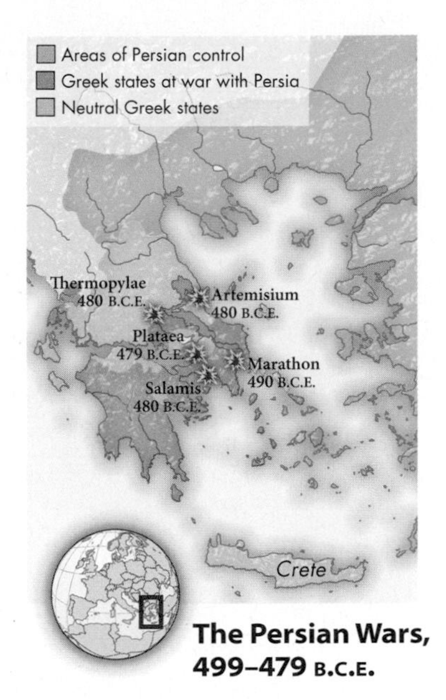

The Persian Wars, 499–479 B.C.E.

The victorious Athenians and their allies then formed the Delian League, a military alliance intended to liberate Ionia from Persian rule and keep the Persians out of Greece. While driving the Persians out of Asia Minor, the Athenians also turned the league into an Athenian empire. They reduced their allies to the status of subjects, often collecting tribute by force and taking control of their economic resources. Athenian ideas of freedom and democracy did not extend to the citizens of other cities, and cities that objected to or revolted over Athenian actions were put down. (See "Viewpoints 5.1: Two Opinions About Athenian Democracy," page 124.)

The Delian League, ca. 478–431 B.C.E.

Delian League
Allied with Delian League, 446 B.C.E.
• Athenian military settlement
Thasos
Corcyra
PERSIAN EMPIRE
BEOETIA
Megara
Athens
Delos
Corinth
Sparta

Under their great leader Pericles (PEHR-uh-kleez) (ca. 494–429 B.C.E.), the Athenians grew so powerful and aggressive that they alarmed Sparta and its allies. In 431 B.C.E. Athenian imperialism finally drove Sparta into the conflict known as the Peloponnesian War. The Peloponnesian War lasted a generation (431–404 B.C.E.) and brought in its wake disease, widespread civil wars, destruction, famine, and huge loss of life. With thousands of soldiers, Athens launched an attack on the island of Sicily, which ended in disaster. The Spartans encouraged revolts in cities that were subject to Athens and defeated the once-mighty Athenian fleet in naval battles. In 404 B.C.E. the Athenians finally surrendered, and Sparta stripped it of its empire. Conflicts among the states of Greece continued, however.

Viewpoints 5.1

Two Opinions About Athenian Democracy

• *Modern scholars often debate the extent and character of Athenian democracy, but such debates actually started in ancient Athens itself. Pericles, the leader of Athens, portrayed Athenian democracy very positively in a public funeral speech given, according to the historian Thucydides, in 430 B.C.E. to honor those who had died in the first year of the Peloponnesian War against Sparta. By contrast, five years later an unknown author highlighted a more negative view of Athenian democracy.*

Pericles's Funeral Speech

" Our constitution does not copy the laws of neighbouring states; we are rather a pattern to others than imitators ourselves. Its administration favours the many instead of the few; this is why it is called a democracy. If we look to the laws, they afford equal justice to all in their private differences; if no social standing, advancement in public life falls to reputation for capacity, class considerations not being allowed to interfere with merit; nor again does poverty bar the way, if a man is able to serve the state, he is not hindered by the obscurity of his condition. . . .

The magnitude of our city draws the produce of the world into our harbour, so that to the Athenian the fruits of other countries are as familiar a luxury as those of his own. . . .

Nor are these the only points in which our city is worthy of admiration. We cultivate refinement without extravagance and knowledge without effeminacy; wealth we employ more for use than for show, and place the real disgrace of poverty not in owning to the fact but in declining the struggle against it. Our public men have, besides politics, their private affairs to attend to, and our ordinary citizens, though occupied with the pursuits of industry, are still fair judges of public matters. . . .

In short, I say that as a city we are the school of Hellas, while I doubt if the world can produce a man who, where he has only himself to depend upon, is equal to so many emergencies, and graced by so happy a versatility, as the Athenian. "

Unknown Author on the Athenian Constitution

" As for the constitution of the Athenians, their choice of this type of constitution I do not approve, for in choosing thus they choose that thieves should fare better than the elite. . . . I shall say that at Athens the poor and the commons seem justly to have the advantage over the well-born and the wealthy; for it is the poor which mans the fleet and has brought the state her power. . . . [However] in those offices which bring security to the whole people if they are in the hands of good citizens, but, if not, ruin, the poor desires to have no share. . . . All those offices, however, whose end is pay and family benefits the poor do seek to hold. . . .

Secondly, some people are surprised that everywhere they give the advantage to thieves, the poor, and the radical elements rather than to the elite. This is just where they will be seen to be preserving democracy. For if the poor and the common people and the worse elements are treated well, the growth of these classes will exalt the democracy; whereas if the rich and the elite are treated well the democrats strengthen their own opponents. In every land the elite are opposed to democracy. Among the elite there is very little license and injustice, very great discrimination as to what is worthy, while among the poor there is very great ignorance, disorderliness, and thievery. . . .

Of such mainland states as are subject to Athenian rule the large are in subjection because of fear, the small simply because of need; there is not a city which does not require both import and export trade, and it will not have that unless it is subject to Athens — the rulers of the seas. . . . The Athenians alone possess the wealth of the Hellenes and the foreigners. "

Sources: Thucydides, *History of the Peloponnesian War*, trans. Richard Crawley (New York: Modern Library, 1951), pp. 103–106; unknown author in Fred Fling, ed., *A Source Book of Greek History* (Boston: D. C. Heath, 1907), pp. 155–158.

QUESTIONS FOR ANALYSIS

1. What differences do you see between the views of Pericles and the unknown author about whether democracy promotes merit and good government, and about whether the poor should have a voice in government?
2. How do the two authors differ about the reasons that Athens dominated trade?

Writers at the time described and analyzed these wars, seeking to understand their causes and consequences. Herodotus (ca. 484–425 B.C.E.) traveled the Greek world to piece together the course of the Persian wars. Although he consulted documents when he could find them, he relied largely on the memories of the participants, and he presented all sides if there were conflicting views. Thucydides (ca. 460–ca. 399 B.C.E.) was an Athenian general in the Peloponnesian War but was banished early in the conflict because of a defeat; after this he traveled throughout Greece seeking information about the war from all sides. His account of the war saw human greed and desire for power as the root of the conflict, and he viewed the war itself as a disaster. As he told it, at the outbreak a Spartan ambassador warned the Athenians: "This day will be the beginning of great evils for the Greeks."[3] Thucydides agreed.

Athenian Arts in the Age of Pericles

In the midst of the warfare of the fifth century B.C.E., Pericles turned Athens into the showplace of Greece. He appropriated Delian League money to pay for a huge building program to rebuild the city that had been destroyed during the Persian occupation in 480 B.C.E. and to display to all Greeks the glory of the Athenian polis. Workers erected temples and other buildings as patriotic memorials housing statues and carvings, often painted in bright colors, showing the gods in human form and celebrating the Athenian victory over the Persians. (The paint later washed away, leaving the generally white sculpture that we think of as "classical.") The Acropolis in the center of the city was crowned by the Parthenon, a temple that celebrated the greatness of Athens and its patron goddess, Athena, who was represented by a huge statue.

□ Picturing the Past

The Acropolis of Athens The natural rock formation of the Acropolis probably had a palace on top as early as the Mycenaean period, when it was also surrounded by a defensive wall. Temples were constructed beginning in the sixth century B.C.E., and after the Persian wars Pericles ordered the reconstruction and expansion of many of these, as well as the building of new and more magnificent temples and an extension of the defensive walls. The largest building is the Parthenon, a temple dedicated to the goddess Athena, which originally housed a 40-foot-tall statue of Athena made of ivory and gold sheets attached to a wooden frame. Much of the Parthenon was damaged when it was shelled during a war between Venice and the Ottoman Empire in the seventeenth century, and air pollution continues to eat away at the marble. (Marie Mauzy/Art Resource, NY)

ANALYZING THE IMAGE Imagine yourself as an Athenian walking up the hill toward the Parthenon. What impression would the setting and the building itself convey?

CONNECTIONS What were the various functions of the Acropolis?

Other aspects of Athenian culture were also rooted in the life of the polis. The development of drama was tied to the religious festivals of the city, especially those to the god of wine, Dionysus. The polis sponsored plays as part of the city's religious festivals and required wealthy citizens to pay the expenses of their production. Many plays were highly controversial, with overt political and social commentary, but they were neither suppressed nor censored. Not surprisingly, given the incessant warfare, conflict was a constant element in Athenian drama, and playwrights used their art in attempts to portray, understand, and resolve life's basic conflicts.

Aeschylus (EHS-kuh-luhs) (525–456 B.C.E.) was the first dramatist to explore such basic questions as the rights of the individual, the conflict between the individual and society, and the nature of good and evil. In his trilogy of plays, *The Oresteia*, he treats the themes of betrayal, murder, and reconciliation, urging the use of reason and justice to reconcile fundamental conflicts. The final play concludes with a prayer that civil dissension never be allowed to destroy Athens.

The plays of Sophocles (SAH-fuh-kleez) (496–406 B.C.E.) also deal with matters personal, political, and divine. In *Antigone*—which tells of how a king's mistakes in judgment lead to the suicides of his son, his son's fiancée, and his wife—Sophocles emphasizes the precedence of divine law over political law and family custom. In the closing lines he writes:

> Good sense is by far the chief part of happiness; and we must not be impious towards the gods. The great words of boasters are always punished with great blows, and as they grow old teach them wisdom.[4]

In *Oedipus the King*, Sophocles tells the story of a good man doomed by the gods to kill his father and marry his mother. When Oedipus fails to avoid his fate, he blinds himself in despair and flees into exile. In *Oedipus at Colonus*, Sophocles treats the last days of the broken man, whose patient suffering and uncomplaining piety ultimately win the blessings and honor of the gods.

Euripides (yoo-RIH-puh-deez) (ca. 480–406 B.C.E.) likewise explored the theme of personal conflict within the polis and sounded the depths of the individual. With Euripides drama entered a new and more personal phase. To him the gods mattered far less than people.

Aeschylus, Sophocles, and Euripides are considered writers of tragedies: the stories of flawed people who bring disaster on themselves because their passions overwhelm reason. Athens also produced writers of comedies, who used humor as political commentary in an effort to suggest and support the best policies for the polis. Although comedies treated the affairs of the polis bawdily and often coarsely, they too were performed at religious festivals. Best known of the comedians is Aristophanes (eh-ruh-STAH-fuh-neez) (ca. 445–386 B.C.E.), a merciless critic of cranks, quacks, and fools. He used his art of sarcasm to dramatize his ideas on the right conduct of citizens and their leaders for the good of the polis.

Families and Sexual Relations

The Athenians, like other Greeks, lived with comparatively few material possessions in houses that were rather simple. A typical Athenian house consisted of a series of rooms opening onto a central courtyard that contained a well, an altar, and a washbasin. Larger houses often had a front room where the men of the family ate and entertained guests, as well as women's quarters at the back. Meals consisted primarily of various grains, especially wheat and barley, as well as lentils, olives, figs, grapes, fish, and a little meat, foods that are now part of the highly touted "Mediterranean diet."

In the city a man might support himself as a craftsman, potter, bronze-smith, or tanner, or he could contract with the polis to work on public buildings. Certain crafts, including spinning and weaving, were generally done by women. Men and women without skills worked as paid laborers. Slavery was commonplace in Greece, as it was throughout the ancient world. Slaves, who were paid for their work, were usually foreigners and often "barbarians," people whose native language was not Greek.

The social conditions of Athenian women have been the subject of much debate, in part because the sources are fragmentary. The available sources suggest that women rarely played notable roles in public affairs, and we know the names of no female poets, artists, or philosophers from classical Athens. The status of a free woman was strictly protected by law. Only her sons could be citizens. Only she was in charge of the household and the family's possessions, yet the law gave her these rights primarily to protect her husband's interests. Women in Athens and elsewhere in Greece, like those in Mesopotamia, brought dowries to their husbands upon marriage, which went back to their fathers in cases of divorce.

In ancient Athens the main function of women from citizen families was to bear and raise children. The ideal for Athenian citizen women was a secluded life in which the only men they usually saw were relatives and tradesmen. How far this ideal was actually a reality is impossible to know, but women in citizen families probably spent most of their time at home, leaving the house only to attend religious festivals, and perhaps occasionally plays, although this is debated. In their quarters of the house they oversaw domestic slaves and hired labor, and together with servants and friends worked wool into cloth. Women from nonciti-

Hetaera and Young Man In this scene painted on the inside of a drinking cup, a hetaera holds the head of a young man who has clearly had too much to drink. Sexual and comic scenes were common on Greek pottery, particularly on objects that would have been used at a private dinner party hosted by a citizen, known as a symposium. Wives did not attend symposia, but hetaerae and entertainers were often hired to perform for the male guests. (© Martin Von Wagner Museum der Universitat Wurzburg. Foto: P. Neckermann, courtesy of E. Oehrlein)

zen families lived freer lives, although they worked harder and had fewer material comforts. They performed manual labor in the fields or sold goods and services in the agora, going about their affairs much as men did. Among the services women and men sold was sex. Women who sold sexual services ranged from poor streetwalkers to sophisticated courtesans known as hetaerae, who added intellectual accomplishments to physical beauty. Hetaerae accompanied men in public settings where their wives would not have been welcome, serving men as social as well as sexual partners.

Same-sex relations were generally accepted in all of ancient Greece, not simply in Sparta. In classical Athens part of a male adolescent citizen's training might entail a hierarchical sexual and tutorial relationship with an older man, who most likely was married and may have had female sexual partners as well. These relationships between young men and older men were often celebrated in literature and art, in part because Athenians regarded perfection as possible only in the male. Women were generally seen as inferior to men, dominated by their bodies rather than their minds.

How often actual sexual relations between men or between men and women approached the ideal in Athens is very difficult to say, as most of our sources are prescriptive, idealized, or fictional. A small number of sources refer to female-female sexual desire, the most famous of which are a few of the poems of Sappho (SA-foh), a female poet of the sixth century B.C.E. The Greeks praised her skills as a lyric poet, but over the last century she has become better known for her sexuality than for her writing. Today the English word *lesbian* is derived from Sappho's home island of Lesbos in the northern Aegean Sea.

Same-sex relations did not mean that people did not marry, for Athenians saw the continuation of the family line as essential. Sappho, for example, appears to have been married and had a daughter. Sexual desire and procreation were both important aspects of life, but ancient Greeks did not necessarily link them.

Public and Personal Religion

Like most peoples of the ancient world, the Greeks were polytheists, worshipping a variety of gods and goddesses who were immortal but otherwise acted just like people. As elsewhere, Greek religion was primarily a matter of ritual, with rituals designed to appease the divinities believed to control the forces of the natural world. Processions, festivals, and sacrifices offered to the gods were frequently occasions for people to meet together socially, times of cheer or even drunken excess. Migration, invasion, and colonization brought the Greeks into contact with other peoples and caused their religious beliefs to evolve.

By the classical era, the primary gods were understood to live metaphorically on Mount Olympus, the highest mountain in Greece. Zeus was the king of the gods and the most powerful of them, and he was married to Hera, who was also his sister (just as, in Egypt, Isis was Osiris's wife and sister; see Chapter 2). Zeus and Hera had several children, including Ares, the god of war, and Zeus's children with other women included gods such as Apollo and Athena and heroes such as Hercules and Perseus. Apollo represented the epitome of youth, beauty, and athletic skill, and he served as the patron god of music and poetry. His half-sister Athena was a warrior-goddess who had been born from the head of Zeus.

Besides these Olympian gods, each polis had its own minor deities, each with his or her own local group of worshippers. The polis administered the cults and religious festivals, and everyone was expected to participate in these civic rituals, which were similar to today's patriotic parades or ceremonies. In contrast to Mesopotamia, Egypt, and Vedic India, priests held little power in Greece; their purpose was to care for temples and sacred property and to conduct the proper rituals, but not to make religious or political rules or doctrines, much less to enforce them. Much religion was local and domestic, and individual families honored various deities privately in their homes. Many people also believed that magic rituals and spells were effective and sought the assistance of individuals reputed to have special knowledge or powers to cure disease, drive away ghosts, bring good weather, or influence the actions of others. (See "Viewpoints 5.2: Hellenistic and Chinese Spells," at right.)

Along with public and family forms of honoring the gods, some Greeks also participated in what later historians have termed **mystery religions**, in which participants underwent an initiation ritual and gained secret knowledge that they were forbidden to reveal to the uninitiated. One of these was the religion of Dionysus (digh-uh-NIGH-suhs), the god of wine and powerful emotions. He was killed and then reborn and became the center of a mystery religion offering rebirth. As the god of wine, Dionysus also represented freedom from the normal constraints of society, and his worshippers were reported to have danced ecstatically.

The Greeks also shared some Pan-Hellenic festivals, the chief of which were held at Olympia to honor Zeus and at Delphi to honor Apollo. The festivities at Olympia included athletic contests that inspired the modern Olympic games. Held every four years after they started in 776 B.C.E., the contests attracted visitors from all over the Greek world and lasted until the fourth century C.E., when they were banned by a Christian emperor because they were pagan. The Pythian games at Delphi were also held every four years, and these contests included musical and literary competitions.

The Flowering of Philosophy

Just as the Greeks developed rituals to honor gods, they spun myths and epics to explain the origins of the universe. Over time, however, as Greeks encountered other peoples with different beliefs, some of them began to question their old gods and myths, and they sought rational rather than supernatural explanations for natural phenomena. These Greek thinkers, based in Ionia, are called the Pre-Socratics because their rational efforts preceded those of the better-known Socrates. Taking individual facts, they wove them into general theories that led them to conclude that, despite appearances, the universe is actually simple and subject to natural laws. Although they had little impact on the average Greek, the Pre-Socratics began an intellectual revolution with their idea that nature was predictable, creating what we now call philosophy and science.

Drawing on their observations, the Pre-Socratics speculated about the basic building blocks of the universe, and most decided that all things were made of four simple substances: fire, air, earth, and water. Democritus (dih-MAW-kruh-tuhs) (ca. 460 B.C.E.) broke this down further and created the atomic theory that the universe is made up of invisible, indestructible particles. The stream of thought started by the Pre-Socratics branched into several directions. Hippocrates (hih-PAW-kruh-teez) (ca. 470–400 B.C.E.) became the most prominent physician and teacher of medicine of his time. He sought natural explanations for diseases and natural means to treat them. Illness was caused not by evil spirits, he asserted, but by physical problems in the body, particularly by imbalances in what he saw as four basic bodily fluids: blood, phlegm, black bile, and yellow bile. In a healthy body these fluids, called humors, were in perfect balance, and medical treatment of the ill sought to help the body bring them back into balance. Hippocrates seems to have advocated letting nature take its course and not intervening too much, though later medicine based on the humoral theory would be much more interventionist, with bloodletting emerging as the central treatment for many illnesses.

The Sophists (SOFF-ihsts), a group of thinkers in fifth-century-B.C.E. Athens, applied philosophical speculation to politics and language, questioning the beliefs and laws of the polis to understand their origin. They believed that excellence in both politics and language could be taught, and they provided lessons for the young men of Athens who wished to learn how to persuade others in the often-tumultuous Athenian democracy. Their later opponents criticized them for charging fees and also accused them of using rhetoric to deceive people instead of presenting the truth. (Today the word *sophist* is usually used in this sense, describing someone who deceives people with clever-sounding but false arguments.)

Socrates (SOK-ruh-teez) (ca. 470–399 B.C.E.), whose ideas are known only through the works of others, also applied philosophy to politics and to people. He seemed to many Athenians to be a Sophist because he also questioned Athenian traditions, although he never charged fees. His approach when exploring ethical issues and defining concepts was to start with a general topic or problem and to narrow the matter to its essentials. He did so by continuously questioning participants in a discussion or argument rather than lecturing, a process known as the Socratic method. Because he posed questions rather than giving answers, it is difficult to say exactly what Socrates thought about many things, although he does seem to have felt

• **mystery religions** Belief systems that were characterized by secret doctrines, rituals of initiation, and sometimes the promise of rebirth or an afterlife.

Viewpoints 5.2

Hellenistic and Chinese Spells

• *Throughout the ancient world, people carried out rituals and ceremonies to attract good spirits and drive away bad ones, and in many places they also sought to use the spirits and gods to accomplish tasks for them. Most of these rituals were oral, but sometimes they were written down. The first text is from a Hellenistic spell inscribed on a lead tablet, directed toward Anubis, the dog-headed Egyptian god of the underworld, through which a woman named Sophia seeks to attract a woman named Gorgonia. With the religious mixing common in the Hellenistic world, the text mentions a number of Egyptian and Greek deities of the underworld and was most likely written by a professional spell caster. The second text is from a Chinese manuscript from the third century B.C.E., written on bamboo slips (for an example of these, see Chapter 4, page 109) and discovered in a tomb. It provides a series of spells designed to identify demons and instruct people in how to lessen the demons' power.*

Hellenistic Spell of Attraction

"Fundament of the gloomy darkness, jagged-toothed dog, covered with coiling snakes, turning three heads, traveler in the recesses of the underworld, come, spirit-driver, with the Erinyes [or Furies, Greek goddesses of vengeance, often shown with snake hair and whips], savage with their stinging whips; holy serpents, maenads [frenzied female followers of Dionysus], frightful maidens, come to my wroth incantations. Before I persuade by force this one and you, render him immediately a fire-breathing daemon. Listen and do everything quickly, in no way opposing me in the performance of this action; for you are the governors of the earth." . . . By means of this corpse-daemon inflame the heart, the liver [which people also saw as a location of emotions], the spirit of Gorgonia, whom Nilogenia bore, with love and affection for Sophia, whom Isara bore. . . . Drive Gorgonia, whom Nilogenia bore, drive her, torment her body night and day, force her to rush forth from every place and every house, loving Sophia, whom Isara bore, she, surrendered like a slave, giving herself and all her possessions to her, because this is the will and command of the great god. . . . "Blessed lord of the immortals, holding the scepters of Tartaros and of terrible, fearful Styx (?) and of life-robbing Lethe, the hair of Kerberos trembles in fear of you, you crack the loud whips of the Erinyes; the couch of Persephone delights you, when you go to the longed bed, whether you be the immortal Sarapis, whom the universe fears, whether you be Osiris, star of the land of Egypt; your messenger is the all-wise boy; yours is Anubis, the pious herald of the dead. Come hither, fulfill my wishes, because I summon you by these secret symbols."

Chinese Spells to Repel Demons

Spellbinding to inflict odium on demons. The Wang-hang [demons who live underground] who injure people treat people unpropitiously. Let the way for how to spellbind them be declared, to enable the people to not encounter the baleful and calamitous. What demons detest are namely reclining in a crouch, sitting like a winnowing basket, interlinked motion [with the legs apart and extended], and the leaning stand [all postures thought to make the body resistant to demons]. . . .

The dwelling places of the great spirits cannot be passed through. They like to injure people. Make pellets from dog excrement and carry them when passing through. Throw them at the spirit when it appears, and it will not injure people. . . .

If human or birds or beasts as well as the six domestic animals constantly roam through a person's domicile, these are spirits from above who like to descend and take pleasure in entering. Have boys and girls who have never entered the domicile beat drums, ring bells with clappers, and screech at them, and they will not come.

Sources: Bernadette J. Brooten, *Love Between Women: Early Christian Responses to Female Homoeroticism* (Chicago: University of Chicago Press, 1996), pp. 83–87. Reproduced with permission of UNIVERSITY OF CHICAGO PRESS in the format Republish in a book via Copyright Clearance Center; Donald Harper, "A Chinese Demonography of the Third Century B.C.," *Harvard Journal of Asiatic Studies*, 45, no. 2 (December 1985): 480, 495, 496.

QUESTIONS FOR ANALYSIS

1. In the Hellenistic spell, what feelings does Sophia direct Anubis and the other spirits mentioned to create in Gorgonia, and what behavior is the expected result of these feelings?
2. In the Chinese spell, what actions are people to take to drive away demons?
3. Belief in the power of spirits is sometimes viewed as making people feel helpless and fatalistic. Do these sources provide evidence of this? Why or why not?

Religious Procession in Hellenic Greece This painted wooden slab from about 540 B.C.E., found in a cave near Corinth, shows adults and children about to sacrifice a sheep to the deities worshipped in this area. The participants are dressed in their finest clothes and crowned with garlands. Music adds to the festivities. Rituals such as this were a common part of religious life throughout Greece. The boys are shown with tanned skin and women with white, reflecting the ideal that men's lives took place largely outside in the sun-filled public squares, and women's in the shaded interiors of homes. The woman at the front of the procession has her hair up, indicating her married status, while the women at the rear have the long uncovered hair of unmarried women. (Pitsa/National Archeological Museum, Athens, Greece/Gianni Dagli Orti/De Agostini Picture Library/The Bridgeman Art Library)

that through knowledge people could approach the supreme good and thus find happiness. He clearly thought that Athenian leaders were motivated more by greed and opportunism than by a desire for justice in the war with Sparta, and he criticized Athenian democracy openly. Many Athenians viewed Socrates with suspicion because he challenged the traditional beliefs and values of Athens. His views brought him into conflict with the government. The leaders of Athens tried him for corrupting the youth of the city, and for impiety, that is, for not believing in the gods honored in the city. In 399 B.C.E. they executed him.

Most of what we know about Socrates comes from his student Plato (427–347 B.C.E.), who wrote dialogues in which Socrates asks questions and who also founded the Academy, a school dedicated to philosophy. Plato developed the theory that there are two worlds: the impermanent, changing world that we know through our senses, and the eternal, unchanging realm of "forms" that constitute the essence of true reality. According to Plato, true knowledge and the possibility of living a virtuous life come from contemplating ideal forms—what later came to be called **Platonic ideals**—not from observing the visible world. Thus, if you want to understand justice, asserted Plato, you should think about what would make perfect justice instead of studying the imperfect examples of justice around you. Plato believed that the ideal polis could exist only when its leaders were well educated.

Plato's student Aristotle (384–322 B.C.E.) also thought that true knowledge was possible, but he believed that such knowledge came from observation of the world, analysis of natural phenomena, and logical reasoning, not contemplation. Aristotle thought that everything had a purpose, so that to know something, one also had to know its function. (See "Listening to the Past: Aristotle on the Family and Slavery, from *The Politics*," page 132.) The range of Aristotle's thought is staggering. His interests embraced logic, ethics, natural science, physics, politics, poetry, and art. He studied the heavens as well as earth and judged the earth to be the center of the universe, with the stars and planets revolving around it.

Plato's idealism profoundly shaped Western philosophy, but Aristotle came to have an even wider influence. For many centuries in Europe, the authority of his ideas was second only to the Bible's, and his ideas had a great impact in the Muslim world as well. His works—which are actually a combination of his lecture notes and those of his students, copied and recopied many times—were used as the ultimate proof that something was true, even if closer observation of the phenomenon indicated that it was not. Thus, ironically, Aristotle's authority was sometimes invoked in a way that contradicted his own ideas. Despite these limitations, the broader examination of the universe and the place of humans in it that Socrates, Plato, and Aristotle engaged in is widely regarded as Greece's most important intellectual legacy.

The philosophers of ancient Athens lived at roughly the same time as major thinkers in religious and philosophical movements in other parts of the world, including Mahavira (the founder of Jainism), the Buddha, Confucius, and several prophets in Hebrew Scripture. All of these individuals thought deeply about how to live a moral life, and all had tremendous influence on later intellectual, religious, and social developments. There is no evidence that they had any contact with one another, but the parallels among them are strong enough that some historians describe the period from about 800 B.C.E. to 200 B.C.E. as the "Axial Age," by which they mean that this was a pivotal period of intellectual and spiritual transformation.

Hellenistic Society, 323–30 B.C.E.

□ How did Alexander the Great's conquests shape society in the Hellenistic period?

The Greek city-states wore themselves out fighting one another, and Philip II, the ruler of Macedonia, a kingdom in the north of Greece, gradually conquered one after another and took over their lands. He then turned against the Persian Empire but was killed by an assassin. His son Alexander continued the fight. A brilliant military leader, Alexander conquered the entire Persian Empire from Libya in the west to Bactria in the east (see Map 5.3, page 134). He also founded new cities in which Greek and local populations mixed, although he died while planning his next campaign. Alexander left behind an empire that quickly broke into smaller kingdoms, but more importantly, his death in 323 B.C.E. ushered in an era, the **Hellenistic**, in which Greek culture, the Greek language, and Greek thought spread as far as India, blending with local traditions. The end of the Hellenistic period is generally set at 30 B.C.E., the Roman conquest of the Hellenistic kingdom of Egypt, but many aspects of Hellenistic culture continued to flourish under Roman governance.

From Polis to Monarchy, 404–200 B.C.E.

Immediately after the Peloponnesian War, Sparta began striving for empire over all of the Greeks but could not maintain its hold. In 371 B.C.E. an army from the polis of Thebes destroyed the Spartan army, but the Thebans were unable to bring peace to Greece. Philip II, ruler of the kingdom of Macedonia on the northern border of Greece (r. 359–336 B.C.E.), turned the situation to his advantage. By clever use of his wealth and superb army, Philip won control of the northern Aegean, and in 338 B.C.E. he defeated a combined Theban-Athenian army, conquering Greece. Because the Greek city-states could not put aside their quarrels with one another, they fell to an invader, an event that historians see as marking the end of the classical period.

After his victory, Philip united the Greek states with his Macedonian kingdom and got the states to cooperate in a crusade to liberate the Ionian Greeks from Persian rule. Before he could launch his crusade, Philip fell to an assassin's dagger in 336 B.C.E. His young son Alexander, who had been tutored by Aristotle, vowed to carry on Philip's mission and led an army of Macedonians and Greeks into western Asia. He won major battles against the Persians and seized Egypt from them without a fight. After honoring the priestly class, Alexander was proclaimed pharaoh, the legitimate ruler of Egypt. He ordered the building of a new city where the Nile meets the Mediterranean, a city that would soon be called Alexandria and that within a century would grow into an enormous city, rivaling Chang-an in China and Pataliputra in the Mauryan Empire of India. He also took the principal Persian capital of Persepolis and performed a symbolic act of retribution by burning the buildings of Xerxes, the invader of Greece during the Persian wars 150 years earlier.

By 330 B.C.E. the Persian Empire had fallen, but Alexander had no intention of stopping, and he set out to conquer much of the rest of Asia. He plunged eastward into lands completely unknown to the Greek world. After four years of fighting his soldiers crossed the Indus River (in the area that is now Pakistan), and finally, at the Hyphasis River, the troops refused to go farther. Alexander was enraged by the mutiny, but the army stood firm. Still eager to explore the limits of the world, Alexander turned south to the Arabian Sea and then back west (Map 5.3).

He never saw Macedonia again, however, as he died in Babylon in 323 B.C.E. from fever, wounds, and excessive drinking. He was only thirty-two, but in just thirteen years he had created an empire that stretched from his homeland of Macedonia to India, gaining the title "the Great" along the way. Alexander was instrumental in changing the face of politics in the eastern

- **Platonic ideals** In Plato's thought, the eternal unchanging ideal forms that are the essence of true reality.
- **Hellenistic** Literally means "like the Greek"; describes the period from the death of Alexander the Great in 323 B.C.E. to the Roman conquest of Egypt in 30 B.C.E., when Greek culture spread.

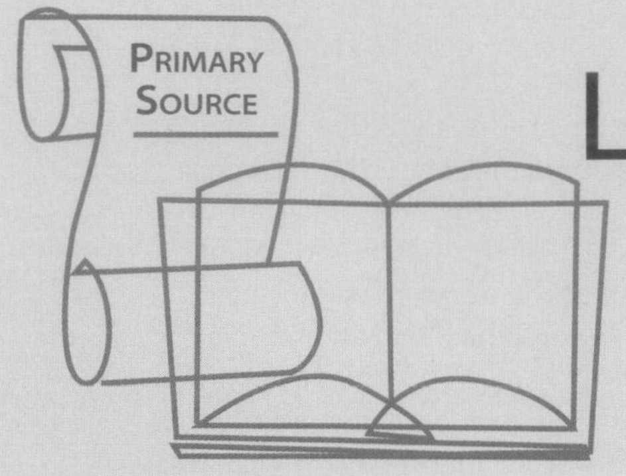

Listening to the Past

Aristotle on the Family and Slavery, from *The Politics*

The Athenian philosopher Aristotle sought to understand everything in the world around him, including human society as well as the physical world. In The Politics*, one of his most important works, he examines the development of government, which he sees as originating in the family. Thus, before discussing power relations within the city, he discusses them within the household, which requires him to confront the issue of slavery and the very unequal relations between men and women.*

"The city belongs among the things that exist by nature, and man is by nature a political animal. . . .

He who thus considers things in their first growth and origin, whether a state or anything else, will obtain the clearest view of them. . . . Out of these two relationships between man and woman, master and slave, the first thing to arise is the family, and Hesiod is right when he says,

First house and wife and an ox for the plough,

for the ox is the poor man's slave. The family is the association established by nature for the supply of men's everyday wants.

Seeing then that the state is made up of households, before speaking of the state we must speak of the management of the household. The parts of household management correspond to the persons who compose the household, and a complete household consists of slaves and freemen. . . .

Property is a part of the household, and the art of acquiring property is a part of the art of managing the household; for no man can live well, or indeed live at all, unless he be provided with necessaries. And as in the arts which have a definite sphere the workers must have their own proper instruments for the accomplishment of their work, so it is in the management of a household. Now instruments are of various sorts; some are living, others lifeless; in the rudder, the pilot of a ship has a lifeless, in the look-out man, a living instrument; for in the arts the servant is a kind of instrument. Thus, too, a possession is an instrument for maintaining life. And so, in the arrangement of the family, a slave is a living possession. . . .

It is clear that the rule of the soul over the body, and of the mind and the rational element over the passionate, is natural and expedient; whereas the equality of the two or the rule of the inferior is always hurtful. The same holds good of animals in relation to men; for tame animals have a better nature than wild, and all tame animals are better off when they are ruled by man; for then they are preserved. Again, the male is by nature superior, and the female inferior; and the one rules, and the other is ruled; this principle, of necessity, extends to all mankind.

Where then there is such a difference as that between soul and body, or between men and animals (as in the case of those whose business is to use their body, and who can do nothing better), the lower sort are by nature slaves, and it is better for them as for all inferiors that they should be under the rule of a master. For he who can be, and therefore is, another's and he who participates in the rational principle enough to apprehend, but not to have, such a principle, is a slave by nature. Whereas the lower animals cannot even apprehend a principle; they obey their instincts. And indeed the use made of slaves and of tame animals is not very different; for both with their bodies minister to the needs of life. . . .

A question may indeed be raised, whether there is any excellence at all in a slave beyond and higher than merely instrumental and ministerial qualities — whether he can have the virtues of temperance, courage, justice, and the like; or whether slaves possess only bodily and ministerial qualities. And, whichever way we answer the question, a difficulty arises; for, if they have virtue, in what will they differ from freemen? On the other hand, since they are men and share in rational principle, it seems absurd to say that they have no virtue. A similar question may be raised about women and children, whether they too have virtues: ought a woman to be temperate and brave and just, and is a child to be called temperate, and

Mediterranean. His campaign swept away the Persian Empire, and in its place he established a Macedonian monarchy, although this fell apart with his death. Several of the chief Macedonian generals aspired to become sole ruler, which led to a civil war that lasted for decades and tore Alexander's empire apart. By the end of this conflict, the most successful generals had carved out their own smaller monarchies, although these continued to be threatened by internal splits and external attacks.

Ptolemy (TAH-luh-mee) seized Egypt, and his descendants, the Ptolemies, ruled Egypt for nearly three hundred years, until the death of the last Ptolemaic ruler, Cleopatra VII, in 30 B.C.E. Antigonus and his descendants, the Antigonids (an-TIH-guh-nuhds), gained control of the Macedonian kingdom in Europe, which they held until they were overthrown by the Romans in 168 B.C.E. (see Chapter 6). Seleucus won the bulk of Alexander's empire, his monarchy extending from western Asia to India (see page 134), but this

In this painting from the side of a vase made in the fifth century B.C.E., a well-to-do young woman sits on an elegant chair inside a house, spinning and weaving. The bed piled high with coverlets on the left was a symbol of marriage in Greek art. The young woman's body language and facial expression suggest that she was not particularly happy with her situation. (Erich Lessing/Art Resource, NY)

intemperate, or not. . . . Here the very constitution of the soul has shown us the way; in it one part naturally rules, and the other is subject, and the virtue of the ruler we maintain to be different from that of the subject; the one being the virtue of the rational, and the other of the irrational part. Now, it is obvious that the same principle applies generally, and therefore almost all things rule and are ruled according to nature. But the kind of rule differs; the freeman rules over the slave after another manner from that in which the male rules over the female, or the man over the child; although the parts of the soul are present in any of them, they are present in different degrees. For the slave has no deliberative faculty at all; the woman has, but it is without authority, and the child has, but it is immature. So it must necessarily be supposed to be with the moral virtues also; all should partake of them, but only in such manner and degree as is required by each for the fulfillment of his duty. . . . Clearly, then, moral virtue belongs to all of them; but the temperance of a man and of a woman, or the courage and justice of a man and of a woman, are not, as Socrates maintained, the same; the courage of a man is shown in commanding, of a woman in obeying. . . .

All classes must be deemed to have their special attributes; as the poet says of women,

Silence is a woman's glory,

but this is not equally the glory of man. The child is imperfect, and therefore obviously his virtue is not relative to himself alone, but to the perfect man and to his teacher, and in like manner the virtue of the slave is relative to a master. Now we determined that a slave is useful for the wants of life, and therefore he will obviously require only so much virtue as will prevent him from failing in his duty through cowardice or lack of self-control. ”

Source: Aristotle, *Politics*, Book 1, trans. Benjamin Jowett, http://classics.mit.edu/Aristotle/politics.1.one.html.

QUESTIONS FOR ANALYSIS

1. What does Aristotle see as the purpose of the family, and why does he begin his discussion of politics with relations within the family?
2. How does Aristotle explain and justify slavery? Given what you have read about Athenian slavery, does this argument make sense to you?
3. How does Aristotle explain and justify the differences between men and women?

Seleucid (SUH-loo-suhd) kingdom gradually broke into smaller states. In terms of political stability and peace, these monarchies were no improvement on the Greek polis.

To encourage obedience, Hellenistic kings often created ruler cults that linked the king's authority with that of the gods, or they adopted ruler cults that already existed, as Alexander did in Egypt. This created a symbol of unity within kingdoms ruling different peoples who at first had little in common; however, these kingdoms never won the deep emotional loyalty that Greeks had once felt for the polis. Kings sometimes gave the cities in their territory all the external trappings of a polis, such as a council or an assembly of citizens, but these had no power. The city was not autonomous, as the polis had been, but had to follow royal orders. Hellenistic rulers generally relied on paid professionals to staff their bureaucracies and on trained, paid, full-time soldiers rather than citizen hoplites to fight their wars.

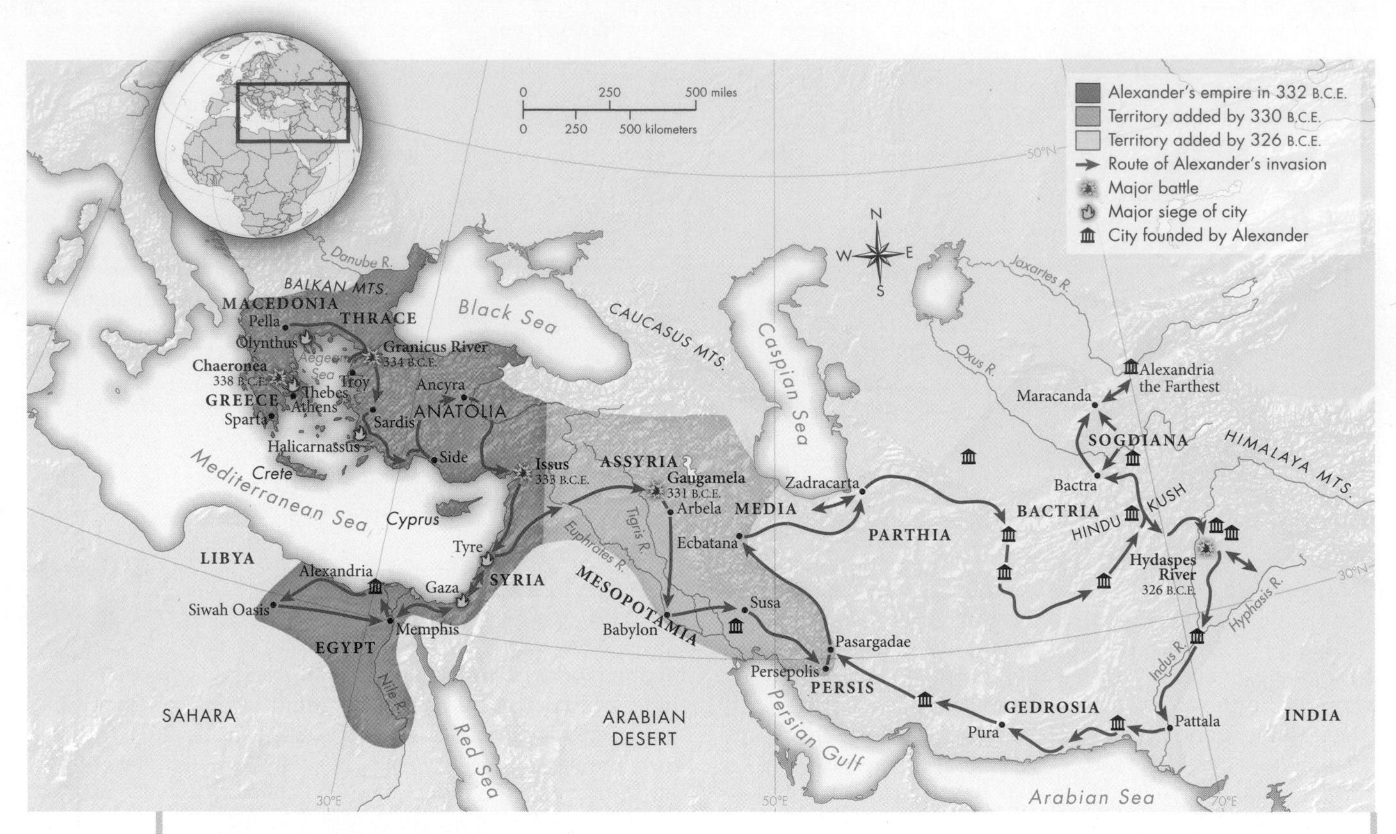

Mapping the Past

MAP 5.3 Alexander's Conquests, 336–324 B.C.E. Alexander's campaign of conquest was extensive and speedy. More important than the great success of his military campaigns was his founding of Hellenistic cities.

ANALYZING THE MAP Where are most of the cities founded by Alexander located in relation to Greece? What does this suggest about his aims?

CONNECTIONS Compare this map with Map 5.2, which shows Greek colonization in the Hellenic period (page 121). What are the major differences between the two processes of expansion?

Building a Hellenized Society

Alexander's most important legacy was clearly not political unity. Instead it was the spread of Greek ideas and traditions across a wide area, a process scholars later called **Hellenization**. To maintain contact with the Greek world as he moved farther eastward, Alexander founded new cities and military colonies and settled Greek and Macedonian troops and veterans in them. This practice continued after his death, with more than 250 new cities founded in North Africa, West and Central Asia, and southeastern Europe. These cities and colonies became powerful instruments in the spread of Hellenism and in the blending of Greek and other cultures. Wherever it was established, the Hellenistic city resembled a modern city. It was a cultural center with theaters, temples, and libraries—a seat of learning and a place for amusement. The Hellenistic city was also an economic center—a marketplace and a scene of trade and manufacturing.

The ruling dynasties of the Hellenistic world were Macedonian in origin, and Greeks and Macedonians initially filled all important political, military, and diplomatic positions. The prevailing institutions and laws were Greek, and Greek became the common spoken language of the entire eastern Mediterranean. Instead of the different dialects spoken in Greece itself, a new Greek dialect called the koine (kaw-NAY), which means common, became the spoken language of traders, the royal court, the bureaucracy, and the army across the Hellenistic world. Everyone, Greek or easterner, who wanted to find an official position or compete in business had to learn it. Those who did gained an avenue of social mobility, and as early as the third century B.C.E. local people in some Greek cities began to rise in power and prominence. Cities granted citizenship to Hellenized natives, although there were fewer political benefits of citizenship than there had been in the classical period because real power was held

- **Hellenization** The spread of Greek ideas, culture, and traditions to non-Greek groups across a wide area.

by monarchs, not citizens. Cultural influences in the other direction occurred less frequently because they brought fewer advantages. Few Greeks learned a non-Greek language unless they were required to because of their official position. Greeks did begin to worship local deities, but often these were somewhat Hellenized and their qualities blended with those of an existing Greek god or goddess.

In the booming city of Alexandria, the Ptolemies generally promoted Greek culture over that of the local Egyptians. This favoritism eventually led to civil unrest, but it also led the Ptolemies to support anything that enhanced Greek learning or traditions. Ptolemaic kings established what became the largest library in the ancient world, where scholars copied works loaned from many places onto papyrus scrolls, translating them into Greek if they were in other languages. They also studied the newest discoveries in science and mathematics. Alexandria was home to the largest Jewish community in the ancient world, and here Jewish scholars translated the Hebrew Bible into Greek for the first time.

The kings of Bactria and Parthia spread Greek culture far to the east, and their kingdoms became outposts of Hellenism, from which the rulers of China and India learned of sophisticated societies other than their own. Some Bactrian and Parthian rulers converted to Buddhism, and the Buddhist ruler of the Mauryan Empire in northern India, Ashoka, may have ordered translations of his laws into Greek for the Greek-speaking residents of Bactria and Parthia. In the second century B.C.E., after the collapse of the Mauryan Empire, Bactrian armies conquered part of northern India, establishing several small Indo-Greek states where the mixing of religious and artistic traditions was particularly pronounced (see Chapter 3).

The Bactrian city of Ay Khanoum on the Oxus River, on the border of modern Afghanistan, is a good example of a brand-new city where cultures met. It had Greek temples and administration buildings, and on a public square was a long inscription carved in stone in Greek verse relating Greek ideals:

> In childhood, learn good manners
> In youth, control your passions
> In middle age, practice justice
> In old age, be of good counsel
> In death, have no regrets.[5]

The city also had temples to local deities and artwork that blended Greek and local styles (for an example, see page 80).

Yet the spread of Greek culture was wider than it was deep, as it generally did not extend far beyond the reaches of the cities. Many urban residents adopted the aspects of Hellenism that they found useful, but people in the countryside generally did not embrace it, nor were they encouraged to.

The Growth of Trade and Commerce

Not only did Alexander's conquests change the political face of the ancient world, but the spread of Greeks eastward also created new markets, causing trade to flourish. The economic connections of the Hellenistic world later proved valuable to the Romans, allowing them to trade products and ideas more easily over a broad area.

When Alexander conquered the Persian Empire, he found the royal treasury filled with vast sums of gold and silver and other valuables. The victors used this wealth to finance the building of roads, the development of harbors, and especially, as noted earlier, the founding of new cities. These cities opened whole new markets to merchants who eagerly took advantage of the unforeseen opportunities. Whenever possible, merchants sent their goods by water, but overland trade also became more prominent in the Hellenistic era. Overland trade with India was organized by Asian merchants and conducted by camel caravans through the harsh terrain of western Asia. Once goods reached the Hellenistic monarchies, Greek merchants took a hand in the trade. Commerce from the east arrived at

Metal Plate from Ay Khanoum This spectacular metal plate, made in the Bactrian city of Ay Khanoum in the second century B.C.E., probably depicts the goddess Cybele being pulled in a chariot by lions with the sun-god above. Worship of Cybele, an earth-mother goddess, spread into Greece from Turkey and was then spread by her Greek followers as they traveled and migrated. (Photo by Thierry Olivier/Musée Guimet/Getty Images)

Egypt and the harbors of Palestine, Phoenicia, and Syria. From these ports goods flowed to Greece, Italy, and Spain. This period also saw the development of standardized business customs, so that merchants of different nationalities, aided especially by the koine, communicated in a way understandable to them all. Trade was further facilitated by the coining of money, which provided merchants with a standard way to value goods as well as a convenient method of payment.

The increased volume of trade helped create prosperity that made luxury goods affordable to more people. As a result, overland traders brought easily transportable luxuries such as gold, silver, and precious stones to market. They extended their networks into China, from which the most prominent good in terms of volume was silk. The trade in silk later gave the major east-west route its name: the Great Silk Road. (See "Global Trade: Silk," page 186.) In return the peoples of the eastern Mediterranean sent east manufactured or extracted goods, especially metal weapons, cloth, wine, and olive oil. (For more on the Silk Road in East Asia, see Chapter 7.)

More economically important than trade in exotic goods were commercial dealings in essential commodities like raw materials and grain and industrial products such as pottery. The Hellenistic monarchies usually raised enough grain for their own needs as well as a surplus for export. For the cities of Greece and the Aegean the trade in grain was essential, because many of them could not grow enough in their mountainous terrain. Fortunately for them, abundant wheat supplies were available nearby in Egypt and in the area north of the Black Sea.

The Greek cities often paid for their grain by exporting olive oil, wine, honey, dried fruit, nuts, and vegetables. Another significant commodity supplied by the Greeks was fish, which for export was salted, pickled, or dried. This trade was doubly important because fish provided poor people with protein, an essential element of their diet.

Slaves were a staple of Hellenistic trade, traveling in all directions on both land and sea routes. Ancient authors cautioned against having too many slaves from one area together, as this might encourage them to revolt. War provided prisoners for the slave market; to a lesser extent, so did kidnapping and capture by pirates, although the origin of most slaves is unknown. Both old Greek states and new Hellenistic kingdoms were ready slave markets, and throughout the Mediterranean world slaves were almost always in demand for work in shops, fields, farms, mines, and the homes of wealthier people.

Most trade in bulk commodities like grain and wood was seaborne, and Hellenistic merchant ships

Harbor and Marketplace at Delos During the Hellenistic period, the tiny island of Delos in the Aegean became a thriving trading center, with a paved marketplace filled with shops and stands, as well as temples paid for by merchants and ship captains. From Delos cargoes were shipped to virtually every part of the Mediterranean. Liquids such as wine and oil were generally shipped in amphoras (inset) made of baked clay. Amphoras were easy and cheap to make and surprisingly durable. (harbor: age fotostock/SuperStock; amphora: Alexis Rosenfeld/Photo Researchers, Inc.)

were the workhorses of the day. A merchant ship had a broad beam, which made it more stable and allowed large cargoes, and it relied on sails for propulsion. Such ships were far more seaworthy than Hellenistic warships, which were long, narrow, and built for speed. A small crew of experienced sailors easily handled the merchant vessels. Aside from providing work for sailors, maritime trade presented opportunities for shipbuilders, dockworkers, teamsters, and pirates. Piracy was a constant factor in the Hellenistic world and remained so until Rome cleared it from the seas.

Despite the increase in trade, the Hellenistic period did not see widespread improvements in the way most people lived and worked. Cities flourished, but many people who lived in rural areas were actually worse off than they had been before, because of higher levels of rents and taxes. Technology was applied to military needs, but not to the production of food or other goods. Manual labor, not machinery, continued to turn out the agricultural produce, raw materials, and manufactured goods the Hellenistic world used. The Greek historian Diodorus gives a picture of this hard labor, commenting on life in the gold mines owned by the Ptolemy rulers of Egypt:

> The kings of Egypt condemn [to the mines] those found guilty of wrong-doing and those taken prisoner in war, those who were victims of false accusations and were put into jail because of royal anger. . . . The condemned—and they are very many—all of them are put in chains, and they work persistently and continually, both by day and throughout the night, getting no rest and carefully cut off from escape.[6]

The Ptolemies even condemned women and children to work in the mines. Besides gold and silver, used primarily for coins and jewelry, bronze continued to be used for shields, and iron for weapons and tools.

Hellenistic Religion, Philosophy, and Science

□ How did religion, philosophy, and science develop in the Hellenistic world?

The mixing of peoples in the Hellenistic era influenced religion, philosophy, and science. The Hellenistic kings built temples to the old Olympian gods and promoted rituals and ceremonies like those in earlier Greek cities, but new deities also gained prominence. More people turned to mystery religions that blended Greek and non-Greek elements. Others turned to practical philosophies that provided advice on how to live a good life. In the scholarly realm, Hellenistic thinkers made advances in mathematics, astronomy, and mechanical design. Additionally, physicians used observation and dissection to better understand the way the human body works.

Religion in the Hellenistic World

When Hellenistic kings founded cities, they also built temples—staffed by priests and supported by taxes—for the old Olympian gods. In this way they spread Greek religious beliefs throughout the Hellenistic world. The transplanted religions, like those in Greece itself, sponsored literary, musical, and athletic contests, which were staged in beautiful surroundings among splendid Greek-style buildings. Greeks and non-Greeks in the Hellenistic world also honored and worshipped deities that had not been important in the Hellenic period or that were a blend of imported Greek and indigenous gods and goddesses. Tyche (TIGH-kee), for example, was a new deity, the goddess and personification of luck, fate, chance, and fortune. Temples to her were built in major cities of the eastern Mediterranean, including Antioch and Alexandria, and her image was depicted on coins and bas-reliefs. Contemporaries commented that when no other cause could be found for an event, Tyche was responsible.

Increasingly, many people were attracted to mystery religions, which in the Hellenic period had been linked to specific gods in particular places, so that people who wished to become members had to travel. But new mystery religions, like Hellenistic culture in general, were not tied to a particular place; instead they were spread throughout the Hellenistic world, and temples of the new deities sprang up wherever Greeks lived.

Mystery religions incorporated aspects of both Greek and non-Greek religions and claimed to save their adherents from the worst that fate could do. Most taught that by the rites of initiation, in which the secrets of the religion were shared, devotees became united with a deity who had also died and risen from the dead. The sacrifice of the god and his victory over death saved the devotee from eternal death. Similarly, mystery religions demanded a period of preparation in which the converts strove to become pure and holy, that is, to live by the religion's precepts. Once aspirants had prepared themselves, they went through the initiation, usually a ritual of great emotional intensity symbolizing the entry into a new life.

Among the mystery religions the Egyptian cult of Isis took the Hellenistic world by storm. In Egyptian mythology Isis brought her husband, Osiris, back to life (see page 44), and during the Hellenistic era this power came to be understood by her followers as extending to them as well. She promised to save any mortal who came to her, and her priests asserted that she had

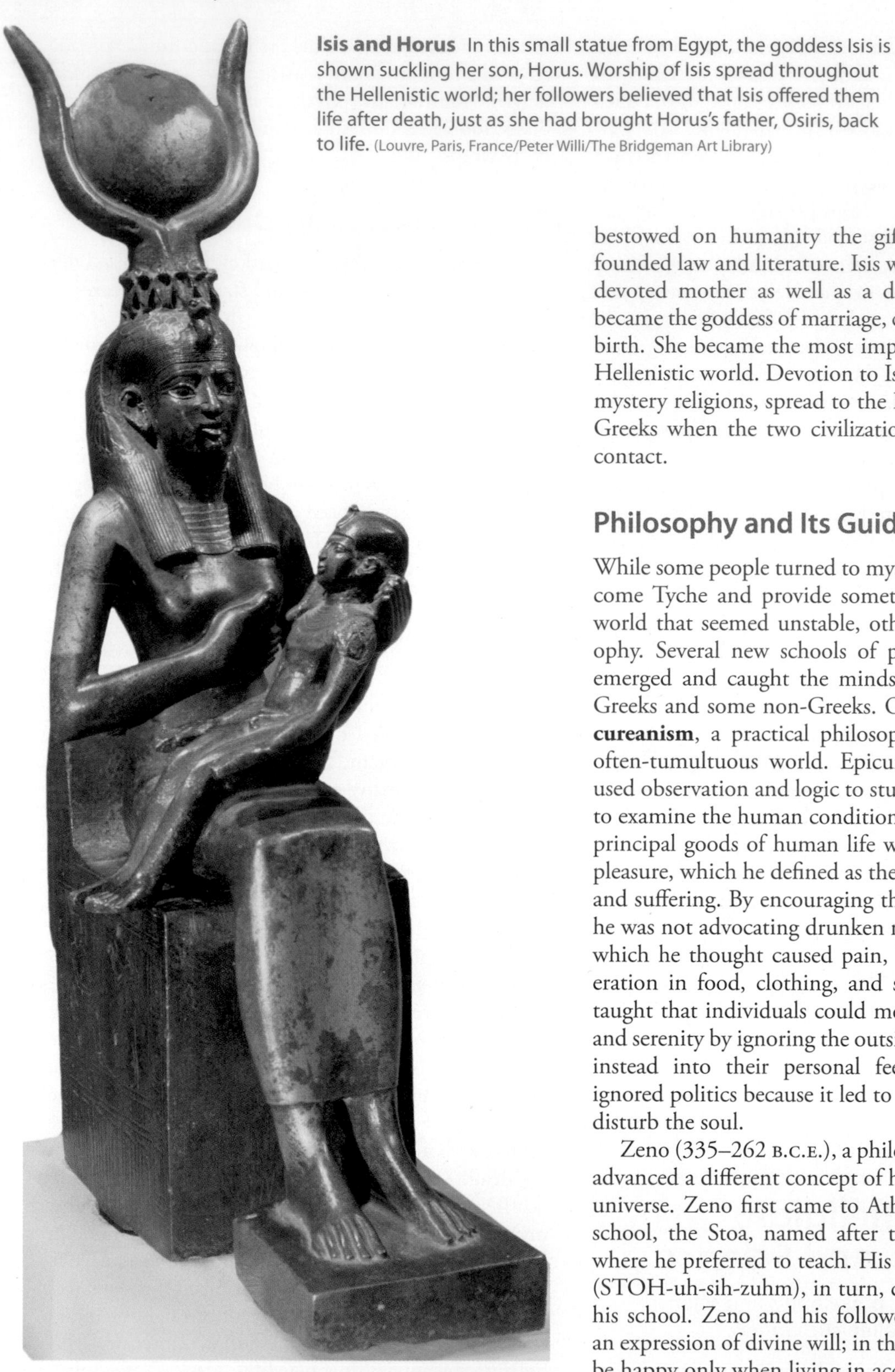

Isis and Horus In this small statue from Egypt, the goddess Isis is shown suckling her son, Horus. Worship of Isis spread throughout the Hellenistic world; her followers believed that Isis offered them life after death, just as she had brought Horus's father, Osiris, back to life. (Louvre, Paris, France/Peter Willi/The Bridgeman Art Library)

bestowed on humanity the gift of civilization and founded law and literature. Isis was understood to be a devoted mother as well as a devoted wife, and she became the goddess of marriage, conception, and childbirth. She became the most important goddess of the Hellenistic world. Devotion to Isis, and to many other mystery religions, spread to the Romans as well as the Greeks when the two civilizations came into greater contact.

Philosophy and Its Guidance for Life

While some people turned to mystery religions to overcome Tyche and provide something permanent in a world that seemed unstable, others turned to philosophy. Several new schools of philosophical thought emerged and caught the minds and hearts of many Greeks and some non-Greeks. One of these was **Epicureanism**, a practical philosophy of serenity in an often-tumultuous world. Epicurus (340–270 B.C.E.) used observation and logic to study the world and also to examine the human condition. He decided that the principal goods of human life were contentment and pleasure, which he defined as the absence of pain, fear, and suffering. By encouraging the pursuit of pleasure, he was not advocating drunken revels or sexual excess, which he thought caused pain, but promoting moderation in food, clothing, and shelter. Epicurus also taught that individuals could most easily attain peace and serenity by ignoring the outside world and looking instead into their personal feelings. His followers ignored politics because it led to tumult, which would disturb the soul.

Zeno (335–262 B.C.E.), a philosopher from Cyprus, advanced a different concept of human beings and the universe. Zeno first came to Athens to form his own school, the Stoa, named after the covered walkways where he preferred to teach. His philosophy, **Stoicism** (STOH-uh-sih-zuhm), in turn, came to be named for his school. Zeno and his followers considered nature an expression of divine will; in their view, people could be happy only when living in accordance with nature. They stressed the unity of humans and the universe, stating that all people were obliged to help one another.

The Stoics' most lasting practical achievement was the creation of the concept of natural law. They concluded that as all people were kindred, partook of divine reason, and were in harmony with the universe, one natural law governed them all.

- **Epicureanism** A system of philosophy based on the teachings of Epicurus, who viewed a life of contentment, free from fear and suffering, as the greatest good.
- **Stoicism** A philosophy, based on the ideas of Zeno, that held that people could only be happy when living in accordance with nature and accepting whatever happened.

Hellenistic Married Life This small terra-cotta figurine from Myrina in what is now Turkey, made in the second century B.C.E., shows a newly married couple sitting on a bridal bed. The groom is drawing back the bride's veil, and she is exhibiting the modesty that was a desired quality in young women. Figurines representing every stage of life became popular in the Hellenistic period and were used for religious offerings in temples and sacred places. This one was found in a tomb. (Louvre, Paris, France/Erich Lessing/Art Resource, NY)

Hellenistic Science and Medicine

In the scholarly realm, Hellenistic thinkers made advances in mathematics, astronomy, and mechanical design. The most notable of the Hellenistic astronomers was Aristarchus of Samos (ca. 310–230 B.C.E.). Aristarchus rightly concluded that the sun is far larger than the earth and that the stars are enormously distant from the earth. He also argued against Aristotle's view that the earth is the center of the universe, instead propounding the heliocentric theory—that the earth and planets revolve around the sun. His theory was discussed for several centuries, then forgotten, and was resurrected in the sixteenth century C.E. by the brilliant Polish astronomer Nicolaus Copernicus.

In geometry Euclid (YOO-kluhd) (fl. ca. 300 B.C.E.), a mathematician living in Alexandria, compiled a valuable textbook of existing knowledge. His *The Elements of Geometry* became the standard introduction to the subject. Generations of students from antiquity to the present have learned the essentials of geometry from it.

The greatest thinker of the Hellenistic period was Archimedes (ahr-kuh-MEE-deez) (ca. 287–212 B.C.E.). A clever inventor, he devised new artillery for military purposes. In peacetime he created the water screw to draw water from a lower to a higher level. (See "Individuals in Society: Archimedes, Scientist and Inventor," page 140.) He also invented the compound pulley to lift heavy weights. His chief interest, however, lay in pure mathematics. He founded the science of hydrostatics (the study of fluids at rest) and discovered the principle that the weight of a solid floating in a liquid is equal to the weight of the liquid displaced by the solid.

Archimedes willingly shared his work with others, among them Eratosthenes (ehr-uh-TOSS-thuh-neez) (285–ca. 204 B.C.E.), who was the librarian of the vast Ptolemaic royal library in Alexandria. Eratosthenes used mathematics to further the geographical studies for which he is most famous. He concluded that the earth is a spherical globe and calculated the circumference of the earth geometrically, estimating it at about 24,675 miles. He was not wrong by much: the earth is actually 24,860 miles in circumference.

As the new artillery devised by Archimedes indicates, Hellenistic science was used for purposes of war as well as peace. Theories of mechanics were applied to build military machines. Fully realizing the practical possibilities of the first effective artillery in Western history, Philip of Macedonia had introduced the machines to the broader world in the middle of the fourth century B.C.E. The catapult became the most widely used

Individuals in Society

Archimedes, Scientist and Inventor

ARCHIMEDES WAS BORN IN THE GREEK CITY OF SYRACUSE in Sicily, an intellectual center in which he pursued scientific interests. He was the most original thinker of his time and a practical inventor. In his book *On Plane Equilibriums*, he dealt for the first time with the basic principles of mathematics, including the principle of the lever. He once said that if he were given a lever and a suitable place to stand, he could move the world. He also demonstrated how easily his compound pulley could move huge weights with little effort:

> A three-masted merchant ship of the royal fleet had been hauled on land by hard work and many hands. Archimedes put aboard her many men and the usual freight. He sat far away from her; and without haste, but gently working a compound pulley with his hand, he drew her towards him smoothly and without faltering, just as though she were running on the surface.*

He likewise invented the Archimedian screw, a pump to bring subterranean water up to irrigate fields, which quickly came into common use. In his treatise *On Floating Bodies*, Archimedes founded the science of hydrostatics. He concluded that an object will float if it weighs less than the water it displaces, and that whenever a solid floats in a liquid, the weight of the solid equals the weight of the liquid displaced. This discovery and his reaction to it have become famous:

> When he was devoting his attention to this problem, he happened to go to a public bath. When he climbed down into the bathtub there, he noticed that water in the tub equal to the bulk of his body flowed out. Thus, when he observed this method of solving the problem, he did not wait. Instead, moved with joy, he sprang out of the tub, and rushing home naked he kept indicating in a loud voice that he had indeed discovered what he was seeking. For while running he was shouting repeatedly in Greek, "Eureka, eureka" ("I have found it, I have found it").†

War between Rome and Syracuse unfortunately interrupted Archimedes's scientific life. In 213 B.C.E., during the Second Punic War, the Romans besieged the city. Hiero, its king and Archimedes's friend, asked the scientist for help in repulsing Roman attacks. Archimedes began to build remarkable devices that served as artillery. One weapon shot missiles to break up infantry attacks. Others threw huge masses of stones that fell on the enemy with incredible speed and noise. They tore gaping holes in the Roman lines and broke up attacks. For use against Roman warships he is said to have designed a machine with beams from which large claws dropped onto the hulls of enemy warships, hoisted them into the air, and dropped them back into the sea. Later Greek authors reported that he destroyed Roman ships with a series of polished mirrors that focused sunlight and caused the ships to catch fire. Modern experiments re-creating Archimedes's weapons have found that the claw may have been workable, but the mirrors probably were not, as they required a ship to remain stationary for the fire to ignite. It is not certain whether his war machines were actually effective, but later people recounted tales that the Romans became so fearful that whenever they saw a bit of rope or a stick of timber projecting over one of the walls protecting Syracuse, they shouted, "There it is. Archimedes is trying some engine on us," and fled. After many months the Roman siege was successful, however, and Archimedes was killed by a Roman soldier.

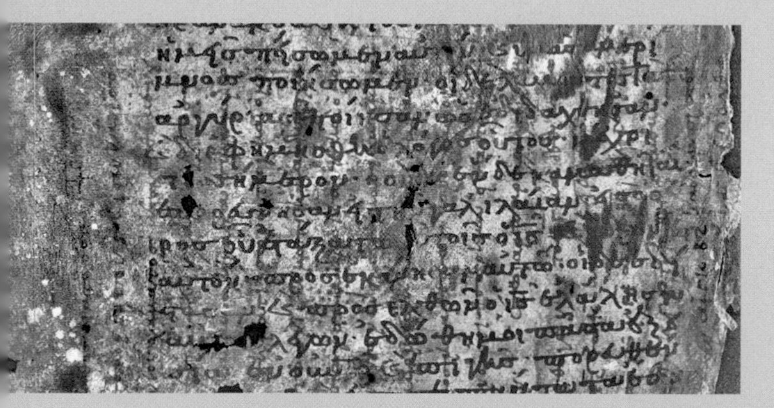

Several of Archimedes's treatises were found on a palimpsest, a manuscript that has been scraped and washed so that another text can be written over it, thus reusing the expensive parchment. Reusing parchment was a common practice in the Middle Ages, but the original text can sometimes be reconstructed. Using digital processing with several types of light and X-rays to study this thirteenth-century-C.E. prayer book, scientists were slowly able to decipher the texts by Archimedes that were underneath, including one that had been completely lost. (Image by the Rochester Institute of Technology. Copyright resides with the owner of the Archimedes Palimpsest, but digital images of the entire manuscript can be found at www.archimedespalimpsest.org.)

QUESTIONS FOR ANALYSIS

1. How did Archimedes combine theoretical mathematics and practical issues in his work?
2. What applications do you see in the world around you of the devices Archimedes improved or invented, such as the lever, the pulley, and artillery?

LaunchPad
Online Document Project

What advances in technological warfare occurred during the Hellenistic period? Read accounts of the siege of Syracuse, and then complete a quiz and writing assignment based on the evidence and details from this chapter.

See inside the front cover to learn more.

*Plutarch, *Life of Marcellus*. †Vitruvius, *On Architecture*, 9 Preface, 10.

artillery piece. As the Assyrians had earlier, engineers built siege towers, large wooden structures that served as artillery platforms, and put them on wheels so that soldiers could roll them up to a town's walls. Generals added battering rams to bring down large portions of walls. If these new engines made warfare more efficient, they also added to the misery of the people, as war often directly involved the populations of cities. War and illness fed the need for medical advances, and doctors as well as scientists combined observation with theory during the Hellenistic period. Herophilus, who lived in the first half of the third century B.C.E., worked in Alexandria and studied the writings attributed to Hippocrates. He approached the study of medicine in a systematic, scientific fashion: he dissected dead bodies and measured what he observed. He was the first to accurately describe the nervous system and studied the liver, lungs, uterus, and brain, which he considered the center of intelligence. His students carried on his work, searching for the causes and nature of illness and pain.

Medical study did not lead to effective cures for the infectious diseases that were the leading cause of death for most people, however, and people used a variety of ways to attempt to combat illness. Medicines prescribed by physicians or prepared at home often included natural products blended with materials understood to work magically. People in the Hellenistic world may have thought that fate determined what would happen, but they also actively sought to make their lives longer and healthier.

CHRONOLOGY

ca. 3000–1200 B.C.E.	Helladic period
ca. 2000–1100 B.C.E.	Minoan and Mycenaean civilizations
ca. 1200–323 B.C.E.	Hellenic period
ca. 1100–800 B.C.E.	Greece's Dark Age; population declines, trade decreases, writing disappears
ca. 800–500 B.C.E.	Archaic age; rise of the polis; Greek colonization of the Mediterranean
ca. 700–500 B.C.E.	Sparta and Athens develop distinctive political institutions
ca. 500–338 B.C.E.	Classical period; development of drama, philosophy, and major building projects in Athens
499–404 B.C.E.	Persian and Peloponnesian wars
336–324 B.C.E.	Alexander the Great's military campaigns
323–30 B.C.E.	Hellenistic period
323–ca. 300 B.C.E.	Civil wars lead to the establishment of the Ptolemaic, Antigonid, and Seleucid dynasties
168 B.C.E.	Roman overthrow of the Antigonid dynasty
30 B.C.E.	Roman conquest of Egypt; Ptolemaic dynasty ends

Chapter Summary

Greece's mountainous terrain encouraged the development of small, independent communities and political fragmentation. Sometime after 2000 B.C.E. two kingdoms—the Minoan on Crete and the Mycenaean on the mainland—did emerge, but these remained smaller than the great empires of Mesopotamia, India, and China. The fall of these kingdoms led to a period of disruption and decline known as the Greek Dark Age (ca. 1100–800 B.C.E.). However, Greek culture survived, and Greeks developed the independent city-state, known as the polis. Greeks also established colonies and traveled and traded as far east as the Black Sea and as far west as the Atlantic Ocean. Two poleis became especially powerful: Sparta, which created a military state in which men remained in the army most of their lives, and Athens, which created a democracy in which male citizens had a direct voice. In the classical period, between 500 B.C.E. and 338 B.C.E., Greeks engaged in war with the Persians and with one another, but they also created drama, philosophy, and magnificent art and architecture.

In the middle of the fourth century B.C.E. the Greek city-states were conquered by the Macedonians under King Philip II and his son Alexander. A brilliant military leader, Alexander conquered the entire Persian Empire and founded new cities in which Greek and local populations mixed. His successors continued to build cities and colonies, which were centers of trade and spread Greek culture over a broad area, extending as far east as India. The mixing of peoples in the Hellenistic era influenced religion, philosophy, and science. New deities gained prominence, and many people turned to mystery religions that blended Greek and non-Greek elements as they offered followers secret knowledge and eternal life. Others turned to practical philosophies that provided advice on how to live a good life. Advances were made in technology, mathematics, science, and medicine, but these were applied primarily to military purposes, not to improving the way ordinary people lived and worked.

NOTES

1. Homer, *Iliad*, trans. Samuel Butler, Book 1, lines 1–5.
2. *The Works of Xenophon*, trans. Henry G. Dakyns (London: Macmillan and Co., 1892), p. 296.
3. Thucydides 2.12, trans. J. Buckler.
4. Sophocles, *Antigone*, ed. and trans. Hugh Lloyd-Jones (Cambridge, Mass.: Harvard University Press, 1994), p. 127.
5. Ahmad Hasan Dani et al., *History of Civilizations of Central Asia* (Paris: UNESCO, 1992), p. 107.
6. Diodoros 3.12.2–3, trans. J. Buckler.

CONNECTIONS

The ancient Greeks built on the achievements of earlier societies in the eastern Mediterranean, but they also added new elements, including history, drama, philosophy, science, and realistic art. The Greek world was largely conquered by the Romans, as you will learn in the following chapter, and the various Hellenistic monarchies became part of the Roman Empire. In cultural terms the lines of conquest were reversed: the Romans derived their alphabet from the Greek alphabet, though they changed the letters somewhat. Roman statuary was modeled on Greek and was often, in fact, made by Greek sculptors, who found ready customers among wealthy Romans. Furthermore, the major Roman gods and goddesses were largely the same as Greek ones, though they had different names. Although the Romans did not seem to have been particularly interested in the speculative philosophy of Socrates and Plato, they were drawn to the more practical philosophies of the Epicureans and Stoics. And like the Hellenistic Greeks, many Romans turned to mystery religions that offered secret knowledge and promised eternal life.

The influence of the ancient Greeks was not limited to the Romans, of course. As discussed in Chapter 3, art and thought in northern India was shaped by the blending of Greek and Buddhist traditions. And as you will see in Chapter 15, European thinkers and writers made conscious attempts to return to classical ideals in art, literature, and philosophy during the Renaissance. In America political leaders from the Revolutionary era on decided that important government buildings should be modeled on the Parthenon or other temples, complete with marble statuary of their own heroes. In some ways, capitol buildings in the United States are good symbols of the legacy of Greece—gleaming ideals of harmony, freedom, democracy, and beauty that (as with all ideals) do not always correspond with realities.

Review and Explore

Make It Stick

LearningCurve

Go online and use LearningCurve to retain what you've read.

Identify Key Terms

Identify and explain the significance of each item below.

polis (p. 119)
hoplites (p. 120)
democracy (p. 120)
oligarchy (p. 120)
mystery religions (p. 128)
Platonic ideals (p. 130)
Hellenistic (p. 131)
Hellenization (p. 134)
Epicureanism (p. 138)
Stoicism (p. 138)

Review the Main Ideas

Answer the focus questions from each section of the chapter.

1. How did the geography of Greece shape its earliest history? (p. 117)
2. What was the role of the polis in Greek society? (p. 119)
3. In the classical period, how did war influence Greece, and how did the arts, religion, and philosophy develop? (p. 123)
4. How did Alexander the Great's conquests shape society in the Hellenistic period? (p. 131)
5. How did religion, philosophy, and science develop in the Hellenistic world? (p. 137)

Make Connections

Analyze the larger developments and continuities within and across chapters.

1. Philosophers and religious thinkers in ancient India, China, and Greece, such as Mahavira and the Buddha (Chapter 3), Confucius and Zhuangzi (Chapter 4), and Socrates and Zeno (this chapter), all developed ideas about the ultimate aim of human life. What similarities and differences do you see among them?
2. The Persian Empire (Chapter 2) first brought India and the Mediterranean in contact with one another, and these contacts increased with the conquests of Alexander (Chapter 3 and this chapter). What were the major results of these contacts in terms of politics, culture, and economics?
3. Looking at your own town or city, what evidence do you find of the cultural legacy of ancient Greece?

LaunchPad
Online Document Project

Technological Warfare

What advances in technological warfare occurred during the Hellenistic period?

Read accounts of the siege of Syracuse, and then complete a quiz and writing assignment based on the evidence and details from this chapter.

See inside the front cover to learn more.

Suggested Reading

Beard, Mary. *The Parthenon*. 2010. A cultural history of Athens's most famous building, including the many controversies that surround it.

Bowden, Hugh. *Mystery Cults of the Ancient World*. 2010. Examines the main mystery religions of the ancient Mediterranean, using artistic and literary evidence.

Burkert, Walter. *Greek Religion*. 1987. The authoritative study of ancient religious beliefs, with much material from the sources.

Cartledge, Paul. *The Spartans: The World of the Warrior Heroes of Ancient Greece*. 2002. A readable general book on the history and legacy of Sparta.

Davidson, James. *Courtesans and Fishcakes: The Consuming Passions of Classical Athens*. 1999. A witty examination of sex, wine, food, and other objects of desire, based on plays, poems, speeches, and philosophical treatises.

Errington, R. Malcolm. *A History of the Hellenistic World, 323–30 B.C.* 2008. Easily the best coverage of the period: full, scholarly, and readable.

Freeman, Philip. *Alexander the Great*. 2010. Designed for general readers, this excellent biography portrays Alexander as both ruthless and cultured.

Hansen, Mogens Herman. *Polis: An Introduction to the Ancient Greek City-State*. 2006. The authoritative study of the polis.

Holland, Tom. *Persian Fire: The First World Empire and the Battle for the West*. 2007. Designed for general audiences, a dramatic retelling of conflict between the Greeks and the Persians.

Kagan, Donald. *Pericles of Athens and the Birth of Democracy*. 1991. A readable account of political changes in the era of Pericles.

Manning, J. G. *The Last Pharaohs: Egypt Under the Ptolemies, 305–30 B.C.* 2009. Examines the impact of the Ptolemies on Egyptian society and the way their state blended Greek and Egyptian elements.

Osborne, Robin. *Greece in the Making, 1200–479 B.C.* 2003. Traces the evolution of Greek communities from villages to cities and the development of their civic institutions.

Patterson, Cynthia B. *The Family in Greek History*. 2001. Treats public and private family relations.

Roochnik, David. *Retrieving the Ancients: An Introduction to Greek Philosophy*. 2004. A sophisticated and well-written narrative of ancient Greek thought designed for students.

The World of Rome

ca. 1000 B.C.E.–400 C.E.

6

Woman from Pompeii

This brightly painted fresco from a villa in Pompeii shows a young woman carrying a tray in a religious ritual. Pompeii was completely buried in ash in a volcanic explosion in 79 C.E., and excavations have revealed life in what was a vacation spot for wealthy Romans. (Detail of the Initiate, from the Catechism Scene, North Wall fresco/Villa dei Misteri, Pompeii/The Bridgeman Art Library)

LearningCurve

After reading the chapter, go online and use LearningCurve to retain what you've read.

Chapter Preview

Like the Persians under Cyrus, the Mauryans under Chandragupta, and the Macedonians under Alexander, the Romans conquered vast territories. With a republican government under the leadership of the Senate, a political assembly whose members were primarily wealthy landowners, the Romans conquered all of Italy, then the western Mediterranean basin, and then areas in the East that had been part of Alexander the Great's empire. As they did, they learned about and incorporated Greek art, literature, philosophy, and religion, but the wars of conquest also led to serious problems that the Senate proved unable to handle. After a grim period of civil war that ended in 31 B.C.E., the emperor Augustus restored peace and expanded Roman power and law as far east as the Euphrates River, creating the institution that the modern world calls the "Roman Empire." Later emperors extended Roman authority farther still, so that at its largest the Roman Empire stretched from England to Egypt and from Portugal to Persia.

Roman history is generally divided into three periods: the monarchical period, traditionally dated from 753 B.C.E. to 509 B.C.E., in which the city of Rome was ruled by kings; the republic, traditionally dated from 509 B.C.E. to 27 B.C.E., in which it was ruled by the Senate; and the empire, from 27 B.C.E. to 476 C.E., in which Roman territories were ruled by an emperor.

The Romans in Italy

☐ How did the Romans come to dominate Italy, and what political institutions did they create?

The colonies established by Greek poleis (city-states) in the Hellenic era included a number along the coast of southern Italy and Sicily, an area already populated by a variety of different groups that farmed, fished, and traded. So many Greek settlers came to this area that it later became known as Magna Graecia—Greater Greece. Although Alexander the Great created an empire that stretched from his homeland of Macedonia to India, his conquests did not reach as far as southern Italy and Sicily. Thus the Greek colonies there remained independent, and they transmitted much of their culture to people who lived farther north in the Italian peninsula. These included the Etruscans (ih-TRUHS-kuhns), who built the first cities north of Magna Graecia, and then the Romans, who eventually came to dominate the peninsula. In addition to allying with conquered peoples and granting them citizenship, the Romans established a republic ruled by a Senate. However, social conflicts over the rights to power eventually erupted and had to be resolved.

The Etruscans

The culture that is now called Etruscan developed in north-central Italy about 800 B.C.E. Recent studies of DNA evidence have indicated that the Etruscans most likely originated in Turkey or elsewhere in southwest Asia, although when they migrated to Italy is not clear. The Etruscans spoke a language that was very different from Greek and Latin, but they adopted the Greek alphabet to write their language. We know they wrote letters, records, and literary works, but once the Romans conquered them, knowledge of how to read and write Etruscan died out. Also, the writings themselves largely disappeared, other than inscriptions on stone or engravings in metal. Modern scholars have learned to read Etruscan again to some degree, but most of what we know about their civilization comes from archaeological evidence and from the writings of other peoples who lived around them at the same time.

The Etruscans, ca. 500 B.C.E.

The Etruscans established permanent settlements that evolved into cities resembling the Greek city-states (see page 119) and thereby built a rich cultural life, full of art and music, that became the foundation of civilization in much of Italy. They spread their influence over the surrounding countryside, which they farmed and mined for its rich mineral resources. From an early period the Etruscans began to trade natural products, especially iron, with their Greek neighbors to the south and with other peoples throughout the Mediterranean in exchange for luxury goods. Etruscan cities appear to have been organized in leagues, and beginning about 750 B.C.E. the Etruscans expanded southward into central Italy through military actions on land and sea and through the establishment of colony cities. In the process they encountered a small collection of villages subsequently called Rome.

The Founding of Rome

Archaeological evidence indicates that the ancestors of the Romans began to settle on the hills east of the Tiber during the early Iron Age, around 1000 B.C.E. to 800 B.C.E. Archaeological sources provide the most important information about this earliest period of Roman history, but later Romans told a number of stories about the founding of Rome. These mix legend and history, but they illustrate the traditional ethics, morals, and ideals of Rome.

The Romans' foundation myths were told in a number of different versions. In the most common of these, Romulus and Remus founded the city of Rome, an event later Roman authors dated precisely to 753 B.C.E. These twin brothers were the sons of the war god Mars, and their mother, Rhea Silvia, was a descendant of Aeneas, a brave and pious Trojan who left Troy after it was destroyed by the Greeks in the Trojan War. The brothers, who were left to die by a jealous uncle, were raised by a female wolf. When they were grown they decided to build a city in the hills that became part of Rome, but they quarreled over which hill should be

Sarcophagus of Seianti Hanunia Tlesnasa The woman portrayed on this lavish sarcophagus is the wealthy Etruscan Seianti Hanunia Tlesnasa. Although she is portrayed as a lovely young woman, analysis of the teeth on the body indicates that she was about fifty when she died. The influence of Hellenistic Greek art on Etruscan art is apparent in almost every feature of the sarcophagus. (© The Trustees of the British Museum/Art Resource, NY)

the site of the city; Romulus killed Remus and named the city after himself. He also established a council of advisers later called the **Senate**, which means "council of old men." He and his mostly male followers expanded their power over neighboring peoples, in part by abducting and marrying their women. The women then arranged a peace by throwing themselves between their brothers and their husbands, convincing them that killing kin would make the men cursed. The Romans, favored by the gods, continued their rise to power. Despite its tales of murder and kidnapping, this founding myth ascribes positive traits to the Romans: they are descended from gods and heroes, can thrive in wild and tough settings, will defend their boundaries at all costs, and mix with other peoples rather than simply conquering them. Also, the story portrays women who were ancestors of Rome as virtuous and brave.

Later Roman historians continued the story by describing a series of kings after Romulus—the traditional number is seven—each elected by the Senate. According to tradition, the last three kings were Etruscan, and another tale about female virtue was told to explain why the Etruscan kings were overthrown. In this story, of which there are several versions, the son of King Tarquin, the Etruscan king who ruled Rome,

MAP 6.1 Roman Italy and the City of Rome, ca. 218 B.C.E. As Rome expanded, it built roads linking major cities and offered various degrees of citizenship to the territories it conquered or with which it made alliances. The territories outlined in green that are separate from the Italian peninsula were added by 218 B.C.E., largely as a result of the Punic Wars.

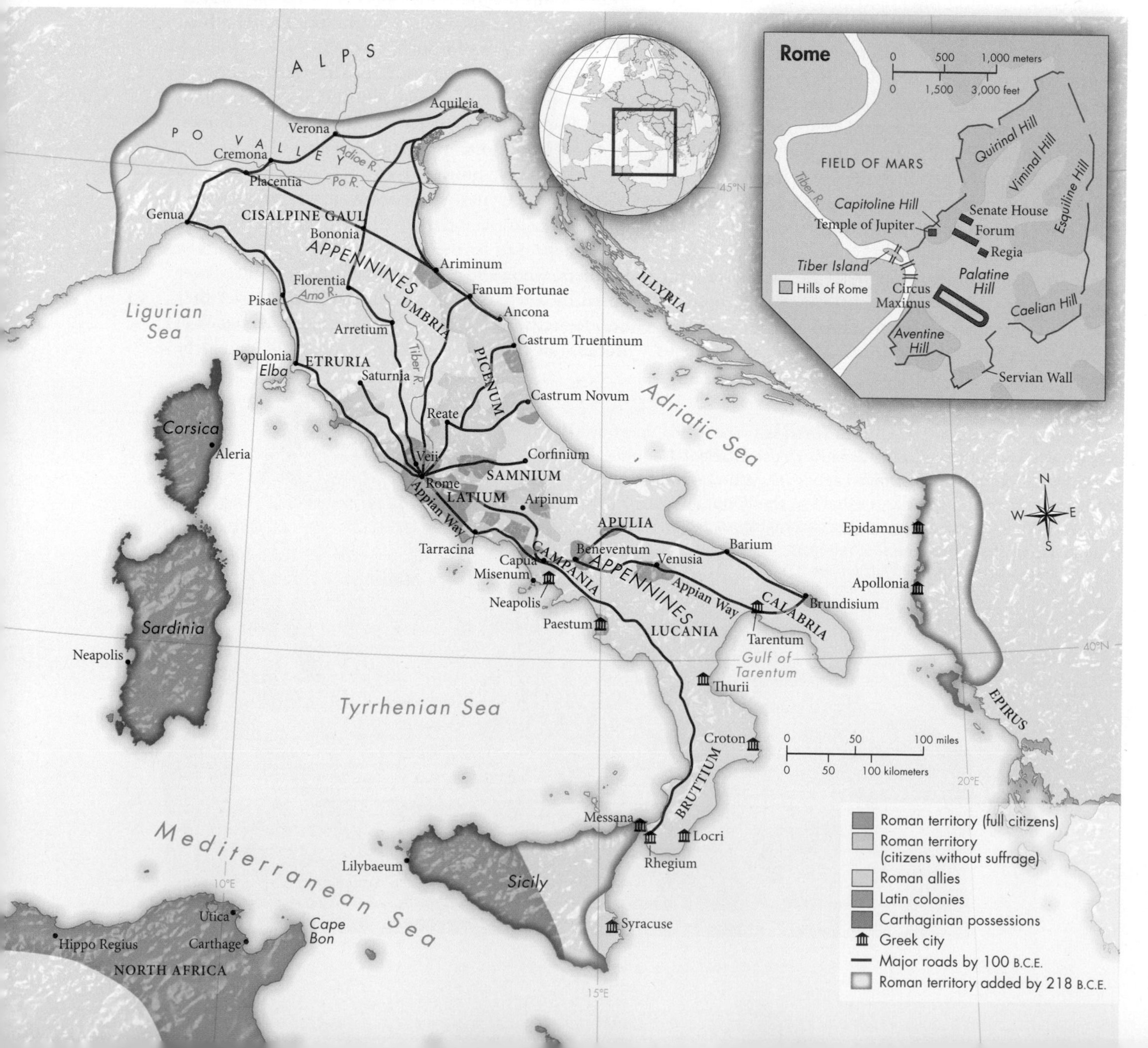

raped Lucretia, a virtuous Roman wife, in her own home. She demanded that her husband and father seek vengeance and then committed suicide in front of them. Her father and husband and the other Roman nobles swore on the bloody knife to avenge Lucretia's death by throwing out the Etruscan kings, and they did. Whether any of this story was true can never be known, but Romans generally accepted it as history and dated the expulsion of the Etruscan kings to 509 B.C.E. They thus saw this year as marking the end of the monarchical period and the dawn of the republic, which had come about because of a wronged woman and her demands.

Most historians today view the idea that Etruscan kings ruled the city of Rome as legendary, but they stress the influence of the Etruscans on Rome. The Etruscans transformed Rome into a real city with walls, temples, a drainage system, and other urban structures. The Romans adopted the Etruscan alphabet, which the Etruscans themselves had adopted from the Greeks. Even the toga, the white woolen robe worn by citizens, came from the Etruscans, as did gladiatorial combat honoring the dead. In engineering and architecture the Romans adopted some design elements and the basic plan of their temples, along with paved roads, from the Etruscans.

In this early period the city of Rome does appear to have been ruled by kings, as were most territories in the ancient world. A hereditary aristocracy also developed—again, an almost universal phenomenon—which advised the kings and may have played a role in choosing them. And sometime in the sixth century B.C.E. a group of aristocrats revolted against these kings and established a government in which the main institution of power would be the Senate, an assembly of aristocrats, rather than a single monarch. Executive power was in the hands of leaders called **consuls**, but there were always two of them and they were elected for one-year terms only, not for life. Rome thereby became a republic, not a monarchy. Thus at the core of the myths is a bit of history.

The Roman Conquest of Italy

In the years following the establishment of the republic, the Romans fought numerous wars with their neighbors on the Italian peninsula. The Roman army was made up primarily of citizens of Rome, who were organized for military campaigns into legions; those who could afford it bought their own weapons and armor. War also involved diplomacy, at which the Romans became masters. At an early date they learned the value of alliances, which became a distinguishing feature of Roman expansion in Italy.

In 387 B.C.E. the Romans suffered a major setback when the Celts—or Gauls, as the Romans called them—invaded the Italian peninsula from the north, swept aside a Roman army, and sacked the city of Rome. More intent on loot than land, the Celts agreed to abandon Rome in return for a thousand pounds of gold. In the century that followed, the Romans rebuilt their city and recouped their losses. They brought Latium and their Latin allies fully under their control and conquered Etruria. In a series of bitter wars the Romans also subdued southern Italy, including much of Magna Graecia, and then turned north. Their superior military institutions, organization, and manpower allowed them to conquer or bring under their influence most of Italy by about 265 B.C.E. (Map 6.1).

As they expanded their territory, the Romans spread their religious traditions throughout Italy, blending them with local beliefs and practices. Religion for the Romans was largely a matter of honoring the state and the family. The main goal of religion was to secure the peace of the gods, what was termed *pax deorum*, and to harness divine power for public and private enterprises. Religious rituals were an important way of expressing common values, which for Romans meant those evident in their foundation myths: bravery, morality, seriousness, family, and home. In the city of Rome the shrine of Vesta, the goddess of hearth and home, was tended by six "vestal virgins" chosen from patrician families. Roman military losses were sometimes blamed on inattention by the vestal virgins, another link between female honor and the Roman state. Victorious generals made sure to honor the gods of people they had conquered and by doing so transformed them into gods they could also call on for assistance in their future campaigns. As the Romans conquered the cities of Magna Graecia, the Greek deities were absorbed into the Roman pantheon.

Once they had conquered an area, the Romans did what the Persians had earlier done to help cement their new territory: they built roads. Roman roads facilitated the flow of communication, trade, and armies from the capital to outlying areas. They were the tangible sinews of unity, and many were marvels of engineering, as were the stone bridges the Romans built over Italy's many rivers.

In politics the Romans shared full Roman citizenship with many of their oldest allies, particularly the inhabitants of the cities of Latium. In other instances they granted citizenship without the franchise, that is, without the right to vote or hold Roman office. These allies were subject to Roman taxes and calls for military service but ran their own local affairs.

- **Senate** The assembly that was the main institution of power in the Roman Republic, originally composed only of aristocrats.
- **consuls** Primary executives in the Roman Republic, elected for one-year terms, who commanded the army in battle, administered state business, and supervised financial affairs.

Coin Showing a Voter This coin from 63 B.C.E. shows a citizen dropping a tablet into a voting urn, the Roman equivalent of today's ballot box. The *V* on the tablet means a yes vote, and an inscription on the coin identifies the moneyer, the official who controlled coin production and decided what would be shown on them. This moneyer, Lucius Cassius Longinus, depicted a vote held fifty years earlier about whether an ancestor of his should be named prosecutor in a trial charging three vestal virgins with unchastity. As was common among moneyers, Longinus chose this image as a way to advance his political career, in this case by suggesting his family's long history of public office. (Bibliothèque Nationale, Paris, France/Snark/Art Resource, NY)

The Roman State

Along with citizenship, the republican government was another important institution of Roman political life. The Romans summed up their political existence in a single phrase: *senatus populusque Romanus*, "the Senate and the Roman people," which they abbreviated "SPQR." This sentiment reflects the republican ideal of shared government rather than power concentrated in a monarchy. It stands for the beliefs, customs, and laws of the republic—its unwritten constitution that evolved over two centuries to meet the demands of the governed.

In the early republic, social divisions determined the shape of politics. Political power was in the hands of a hereditary aristocracy—the **patricians**, whose privileged legal status was determined by their birth as members of certain families. Patrician men dominated the affairs of state, provided military leadership in time of war, and monopolized knowledge of law and legal procedure. The common people of Rome, the **plebeians** (plih-BEE-uhns), were free citizens with a voice in politics, but they had few of the patricians' political and social advantages. While some plebeian merchants rivaled the patricians in wealth, most plebeians were poor artisans, small farmers, and landless urban dwellers.

The Romans created several assemblies through which men elected high officials and passed ordinances. The most important of these was the Senate, a political assembly that by tradition was established by Romulus and in reality most likely originated in the monarchical period as a council of the heads of powerful families who advised the king. During the republic, the Senate advised the consuls and other officials about military and political matters and handled government finances. Because the Senate sat year after year with the same members, while the consuls changed annually, it provided stability, and its advice came to have the force of law. Another responsibility of the Senate was to handle relations between Rome and other powers, as Polybius, a Greek politician and historian writing in the middle of the second century B.C.E., reported:

> If it is necessary to send an embassy to reconcile warring communities, or to remind them of their duty, or sometimes to impose requisitions upon them, or to receive their submission, or finally to proclaim war against them—this too is the business of the Senate.[1]

The highest officials of the republic were the two consuls, positions initially open only to patrician men. The consuls commanded the army in battle, administered state business, and supervised financial affairs. When the consuls were away from Rome, praetors (PREE-tuhrz) could act in their place; they could also command armies, interpret law, and administer justice. After the age of overseas conquests (see below), the Romans divided their lands in the Mediterranean into provinces governed by ex-consuls and ex-praetors. Because of these officials' experience in Roman politics, they were suited to administer the affairs of the provinces and to adapt Roman law and customs to new contexts. Other officials worked with the Senate to oversee the public treasury, register citizens, and supervise the city of Rome.

A lasting achievement of the Romans was their development of law. Roman civil law, the *ius civile*, consisted of statutes, customs, and forms of procedure that regulated the lives of citizens. As the Romans came into more frequent contact with foreigners, the praetors applied a broader *ius gentium*, the "law of the peoples," to such matters as peace treaties, the treatment of prisoners of war, and the exchange of diplomats. In the ius gentium, all sides were to be treated the same regardless of their nationality. By the late republic, Roman jurists had widened this still further into the concept of *ius naturale*, "natural law" based in part on Stoic beliefs (see page 138). Natural law, according to these thinkers, is made up of rules that govern

- **patricians** The Roman hereditary aristocracy, who held most of the political power in the republic.
- **plebeians** The common people of Rome, who were free but had few of the patricians' advantages.

human behavior that come from applying reason rather than customs or traditions, and so apply to all societies. In reality, Roman officials generally interpreted the law to the advantage of Rome, of course, at least to the extent that the strength of Roman armies allowed them to enforce it. But Roman law came to be seen as one of Rome's most important legacies.

Social Conflict in Rome

Inequality between plebeians and patricians led to a conflict known as the Struggle of the Orders. In this conflict the plebeians sought to increase their power by taking advantage of the fact that Rome's survival depended on its army, which needed plebeians to fill the ranks of the infantry. According to tradition, in 494 B.C.E. the plebeians literally walked out of Rome and refused to serve in the army. Their general strike worked, and the patricians made important concessions. They allowed the plebeians to elect their own officials, the tribunes, who could bring plebeian grievances to the Senate for resolution and could also veto the decisions of the consuls. Thus, as in Archaic age Greece (see page 120), political rights were broadened because of military needs for foot soldiers.

The law itself was the plebeians' primary target. As noted above, only the patricians knew what the law was, and only they could argue cases in court. All too often they used the law for their own benefit. The plebeians wanted the law codified and published. After much struggle, in 449 B.C.E. the patricians surrendered their legal monopoly and codified and published the Laws of the Twelve Tables, so called because they were inscribed on twelve bronze plaques. The Laws of the Twelve Tables covered many legal issues, including property ownership, guardianship, inheritance, and punishments for various crimes. The patricians also made legal procedures public so that plebeians could argue cases in court. Several years later the patricians passed a law that for the first time allowed patricians and plebeians to marry one another.

After a ten-year battle, the Licinian-Sextian laws passed in 367 B.C.E. gave wealthy plebeians access to all the offices of Rome, including the right to hold one of the two consulships. Once plebeians could hold the consulship, they could also sit in the Senate and advise on policy. Though decisive, this victory did not automatically end the Struggle of the Orders. That happened only in 287 B.C.E. with the passage of the *lex Hortensia*, which gave the resolutions of the *concilium plebis*, the plebeian assembly, the force of law for patricians and plebeians alike. This compromise established a new elite of wealthy plebeians and patricians. Yet the Struggle of the Orders had made all citizens equal before the law, resulting in a Rome stronger and more united than before.

Roman Expansion and Its Repercussions

☐ How did Rome expand its power beyond Italy, and what were the effects of this expansion?

As the republican government was developing, Roman territory continued to expand. In a series of wars the Romans conquered lands all around the Mediterranean, creating an overseas empire that brought them unheard-of power and wealth. As a result, many Romans became more cosmopolitan and comfortable, and they were especially influenced by the culture of one conquered land: Greece. Yet social unrest also came in the wake of the wars, opening unprecedented opportunities for ambitious generals who wanted to rule Rome like an empire. Civil war ensued, which was quelled briefly by the great politician and general Julius Caesar. His grandnephew Octavian, better known to history as Augustus, finally restored peace and order to Rome.

Overseas Conquests and the Punic Wars, 264–133 B.C.E.

The Romans did not map out grandiose strategies to conquer the world, as had Alexander the Great. Rather they responded to situations as they arose. This meant that they sought to eliminate any state they saw as a military threat.

Their presence in southern Italy brought the Romans to the island of Sicily, where they confronted another great power in the western Mediterranean, Carthage (CAHR-thij). The city of Carthage had been founded by Phoenicians as a trading colony in the eighth century B.C.E. (see page 48). It commanded one of the best harbors on the northern African coast and was supported by a fertile inland. By the fourth century B.C.E. the Carthaginians began to expand their holdings, and they engaged in war with the Etruscans and

The Carthaginian Empire and the Roman Republic, 264 B.C.E.

Two Triremes Race In this fresco painting from the temple of Isis in Pompeii, two triremes — narrow warships powered by several banks of long oars — race in what was most likely a festival celebrating the goddess. Greeks, Carthaginians, and Romans all used triremes, which had bronze front pieces designed to smash into enemy ships. The one hundred to two hundred oarsmen had to row in time to achieve the necessary speed, which took long practice, so this religious celebration also served a military purpose.

Greeks. At the end of a long string of wars, the Carthaginians had created and defended a mercantile empire that stretched from western Sicily to beyond Gibraltar.

The conflicting ambitions of the Romans and Carthaginians led to the first of the three **Punic Wars**. During the course of the first war, which lasted from 264 B.C.E. to 241 B.C.E., Rome built a navy and defeated Carthage in a series of sea battles. Sicily became Rome's first province, but despite a peace treaty, the conflict was not over.

Carthaginian armies moved into Spain, where Rome was also claiming territory. The brilliant Carthaginian general Hannibal (ca. 247–183 B.C.E.) marched an army of tens of thousands of troops — and, more famously, several dozen war elephants — from Spain across what is now France and over the Alps into Italy, beginning the Second Punic (PYOO-nik) War (218–201 B.C.E.). Hannibal won three major victories, including a devastating blow at Cannae in southeastern Italy in 216 B.C.E. There he inflicted perhaps fifty thousand casualties on the Romans. He then spread devastation throughout Italy, and a number of cities in central and southern Italy rebelled against Rome because it appeared to them that Hannibal would be victorious. Yet Hannibal was not able to win areas near Rome in central Italy. His allies, who included Philip V, the Antigonid king of Macedonia (see page 131), did not supply him with enough food and supplies to sustain his troops, and Rome fought back.

The Roman general Scipio Africanus (ca. 236–ca. 183 B.C.E.) copied Hannibal's methods of mobile warfare and guerrilla tactics and made more extensive use of cavalry than had earlier Roman commanders. He took Spain from the Carthaginians and then struck directly at Carthage itself, prompting the Carthaginians to recall Hannibal from Italy to defend the homeland. In 202 B.C.E., near the town of Zama, Scipio defeated Hannibal in one of the world's truly decisive battles. Scipio's victory meant that the world of the western Mediterranean would henceforth be Roman. Roman language, law, and culture, fertilized by Greek influences, would in time permeate this entire region.

The Second Punic War contained the seeds of still other wars. Unabated fear of Carthage led to the Third Punic War (149–146 B.C.E.), a needless, unjust, and savage conflict that ended when Scipio Aemilianus, a grandson by adoption of Scipio Africanus, destroyed the hated rival and burned Carthage to the ground.

After the Second Punic War, the Romans turned east. The Roman legions were victorious over Macedonian troops, and the Romans made Antigonid Macedonia into a Roman province. Then they moved farther east and defeated the Seleucid monarchy. In 133 B.C.E. the king of Pergamum in Asia Minor willed his kingdom to Rome when he died. The Ptolemies of Egypt retained formal control of their kingdom, but they obeyed Roman wishes in terms of trade policy.

- **Punic Wars** A series of three wars between Rome and Carthage in which Rome emerged the victor.
- **paterfamilias** The oldest dominant male of the family, who held great power over the lives of family members.

Declaring the Mediterranean *mare nostrum*, "our sea," the Romans began to create a political and administrative machinery to hold the Mediterranean together under a mutually shared cultural and political system of provinces ruled by governors sent from Rome.

Not all Romans were joyful over Rome's conquest of the Mediterranean world; some considered that victory a misfortune. The historian Sallust (86–34 B.C.E.), writing from hindsight, complained that the acquisition of an empire was the beginning of Rome's troubles:

> But when through labor and justice our Republic grew powerful . . . then fortune began to be harsh and to throw everything into confusion. The Romans had easily borne labor, danger, and hardship. To them leisure, riches—otherwise desirable—proved to be burdens and torments. So at first money, then desire for power, grew great. These things were a sort of cause of all evils.[2]

New Influences and Old Values in Roman Culture

With the conquest of the Mediterranean world, Rome became a great city. The spoils of war went to build theaters, stadiums, and other places of amusement, and Romans and Italian townspeople began to spend more of their time in leisure pursuits. This new urban culture reflected Hellenistic influences. Romans developed a liking for Greek literature, and it became common for an educated Roman to speak both Latin and Greek. Furthermore, the Roman conquest of the Hellenistic East resulted in wholesale confiscation of Greek paintings and sculpture to grace Roman temples, public buildings, and private homes.

The Greek custom of bathing also gained popularity in the Roman world. Increasingly, Romans built large public buildings containing pools supplied by intricate systems of aqueducts, which by the early empire became essential parts of the Roman city. These structures were more than just places to bathe. Baths included gymnasia where men exercised, snack bars and halls where people chatted and read, and even libraries and lecture halls. Women had opportunities to bathe, generally in separate facilities or at separate times, and both women and men went to the baths to see and be seen. Conservative commentators objected to these new pastimes as a corruption of traditional Roman values, but most Romans saw them as a normal part of urban life.

New customs did not change the core Roman social structures. The male head of the household was called the **paterfamilias**, and he had great power over his children. Initially this seems to have included power over life and death, but by the second century B.C.E. his authority had been limited by law and custom. Fathers continued to have the power to decide how family resources should be spent, however, and sons did

Roman Bath This Roman bath in Bath, England (a city to which it gave its name), was built around a natural hot spring beginning in the first century C.E. The Romans spread the custom of bathing, which they had adopted from the Greeks, to the outer reaches of their empire. In addition to hot water, bathers used oil for massage and metal scrapers to clean and exfoliate their skin. Many Roman artifacts have been unearthed at Bath, including a number of curse tablets, small tablets made of lead calling on the gods to harm someone, which were common in the Greco-Roman world. Not surprisingly, many of the curse tablets found at Bath relate to the theft of clothing while people were bathing. (Walter Zerta/© Cuboimages srl/ Alamy)

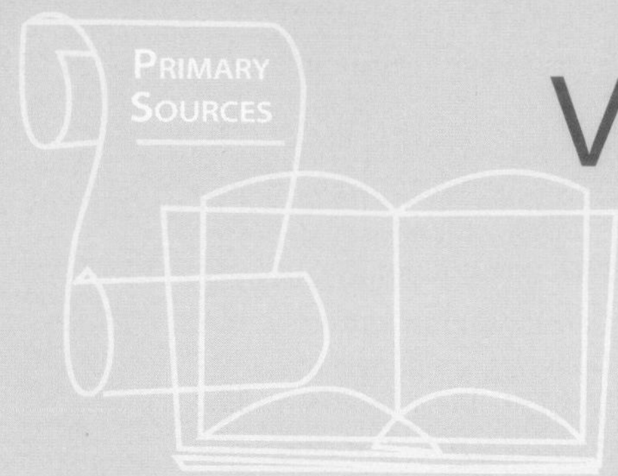

Viewpoints 6.1

On Roman Wives, from a Tombstone Inscription and Juvenal's Sixth Satire

• *Most Romans married, and a great variety of sources portray husbands and wives visually and in words. These include idealizations, such as those found on tombstones, and biting critiques, including those by satirists such as the poet Juvenal.*

Epitaph on a Roman Tombstone from Around 130 B.C.E.

"Stranger, my message is short. Stand by and read it through. Here is the unlovely tomb of a lovely woman. Her parents called her Claudia by name. She loved her husband with all her heart. She bore two sons; of these she leaves one on earth; under the earth she has placed the other. She was charming in converse, yet gentle in bearing. She kept house, she made wool. That's my last word. Go your way."

Juvenal's Sixth Satire, Written Sometime in the Early Second Century C.E.

"[Y]ou are preparing for a covenant, a marriage-contract and a betrothal; you are by now getting your hair combed by a master barber; you have also perhaps given a pledge to her finger. What! Postumus, are you, you who once had your wits, taking to yourself a wife? Tell me . . . what snakes are driving you mad? Can you submit to a she-tyrant when there is so much rope to be had, so many dizzy heights of windows standing open? . . . If you are honestly uxorious, and devoted to one woman, then bow your head and submit your neck ready to bear the yoke. Never will you find a woman who spares the man who loves her; for though she be herself aflame, she delights to torment and plunder him. So the better the man, the more desirable he be as a husband, the less good by far will he get out of his wife. No present will you ever make if your wife forbids; nothing will you ever sell if she objects; nothing will you buy without her consent. She will arrange your friendships for you; she will turn your now-aged friend from the door which saw the beginnings of his beard. . . . Give up all hope of peace so long as your mother-in-law is alive. It is she that teaches her daughter to revel in stripping and despoiling her husband; it is she that teaches her to reply to a seducer's love-letters in no unskilled and innocent fashion; she eludes or bribes your guards. . . . The bed that holds a wife is never free from wrangling and mutual bickerings; no sleep is to be got there! It is there that she sets upon her husband, more savage than a tigress that has lost her cubs; conscious of her own secret slips, she affects a grievance, abusing his boys, or weeping over some imagined mistress. She has an abundant supply of tears always ready in their place, awaiting her command in which fashion they should flow. . . . But whence come these monstrosities? you ask; from what fountain do they flow? In days of old, the wives of Latium were kept chaste by their humble fortunes. It was toil and brief slumbers that kept vice from polluting their modest homes; hands chafed and hardened by Tuscan fleeces, Hannibal nearing the city, and husbands standing to arms. . . . We are now suffering the calamities of long peace. Luxury, more deadly than any foe, has laid her hand upon us, and avenges a conquered world."

Sources: Tombstone: Naphtali Lewis and Meyer Reinhold, *Roman Civilization*, vol. 1 (New York: Columbia University Press, 1990), p. 524; Juvenal: *Juvenal*, trans. G. G. Ramsay, Loeb Classical Library (Cambridge, Mass.: Harvard University Press, 1918), pp. 85, 99, 101, 103, 105, 107.

QUESTIONS FOR ANALYSIS

1. How does the wife in Juvenal's satire compare to the wife in the epitaph?
2. How does the type of sources that these are — one a tombstone inscription and one a satire — shape their portrayals of Roman wives?
3. Juvenal wrote more than two centuries after the tombstone was erected. In his opinion, how had Roman history in the intervening centuries shaped the behavior of Roman wives?

not inherit until after their fathers had died. Women could inherit and own property, though they generally received a smaller portion of any family inheritance than their brothers. The Romans praised women, like Lucretia of old, who were virtuous and loyal to their husbands and devoted to their children. (See "Viewpoints 6.1: On Roman Wives, from a Tombstone Inscription and Juvenal's Sixth Satire," above.) Very young children were under their mother's care, and most children learned the skills they needed from their own parents. For children from wealthier urban families, opportunities for formal education increased in the late republic. Boys and girls might be educated in their homes by tutors, who were often Greek slaves, and boys also might go to a school, paid for by their parents.

Most Romans continued to work long days, but an influx of slaves from Rome's conquests provided labor for the fields, mines, and cities. To the Romans slavery was a misfortune that befell some people, but it did not entail any racial theories. For loyal slaves the Romans always held out the possibility of freedom, and manumission—the freeing of individual slaves by their masters—became common. Nonetheless, slaves rebelled from time to time in large-scale revolts put down by Roman armies.

Membership in a family did not end with death, as the spirits of the family's ancestors were understood to remain with the family. They and other gods regarded as protectors of the household—collectively these were called the *lares* and *penates*—were represented by small statues that stood in a special cupboard, were honored at family celebrations, and were taken with the family when they moved.

The Late Republic and the Rise of Augustus, 133–27 B.C.E.

The wars of conquest eventually created serious political problems for the Romans. When the soldiers returned home, they found their farms practically in ruins. Many were forced to sell their land to ready buyers who had grown rich from the wars. These wealthy men created huge estates called latifundia. Now landless, veterans moved to the cities, especially Rome, but could not find work. These developments not only created unrest in the city but also threatened Rome's army by reducing its ranks. The Romans had always believed that only landowners should serve in the army, for only they had something to fight for. Landless men, even if they were Romans and lived in Rome, were forbidden to serve. The landless veterans were willing to follow any leader who promised help. The leader who answered their call was Tiberius Gracchus (163–133 B.C.E.), an aristocrat who was appalled by the situation. Elected tribune in 133 B.C.E., he proposed dividing public land among the poor. But a group of wealthy senators murdered him, launching a long era of political violence that would destroy the republic. Still, Tiberius's brother Gaius Gracchus (153–121 B.C.E.) passed a law providing the urban poor with cheap grain and urged practical reforms. Once again senators tried to stem the tide of reform by murdering him.

The next reformer, Gaius Marius (ca. 157–86 B.C.E.), recruited landless men into the army to put down a rebel king in Africa. He promised them land for their service. But after his victory, the Senate refused to honor his promise. From then on, Roman soldiers looked to their commanders, not to the Senate or the state, to protect their interests. Rome was also dividing into two political factions, both of which wanted political power. Both factions named individuals as supreme military commander, and each led Roman troops against an external enemy but also against each other. One of these generals, Sulla, gained power in Rome, and in 81 B.C.E. the Senate made him dictator, an official office in the Roman Republic given to a man who was granted absolute power temporarily to handle emergencies such as war. Dictators were supposed to step down after six months—and more than eighty dictators had done so in Roman history—but Sulla held this position for nine years, and after that it was too late to restore the republican constitution. Sulla's abuse of political office became the blueprint for later leaders.

The history of the late republic is the story of power struggles among many famous Roman figures against a background of unrest at home and military campaigns abroad. Pompey (PAHM-pee), who had been one of Sulla's officers, used military victories in Spain to force the Senate to allow him to run for consul. In 59 B.C.E. he was joined in a political alliance called the First Triumvirate by Crassus, another ambitious politician and the wealthiest man in Rome, and by Julius Caesar (100–44 B.C.E.). Born of a noble family, Caesar, an able general, was also a brilliant politician with unbridled ambition and a superb orator with immense literary ability. Recognizing that military success led to power, he led his troops to victory in Spain and Gaul, modern France. The First Triumvirate fell apart after Crassus was killed in battle in 53 B.C.E. while trying to conquer Parthia, leaving Caesar and Pompey in competition with each other for power. The result was civil war. The Ptolemaic rulers of Egypt became mixed up in this war, particularly Cleopatra VII, who allied herself with Caesar and had a son by him. (See "Individuals in Society: Queen Cleopatra," page 156.) Although the Senate backed Pompey, Caesar was victorious. The Senate then began appointing Caesar to various offices, including that of consul, dictator, and imperator (ihm-puh-RAH-tuhr), a title given to victorious commanders. Caesar began to make a number of legal and economic reforms, acting on his own authority, though often with the approval of the Senate, which he packed with his supporters. He issued laws about debt, the collection of taxes, and the distribution of grain and land. Roman allies in Italy were to have full citizenship. He founded new colonies, which were to be populated by veterans and the poor.

Caesar was wildly popular with most people in Rome, but some senators opposed his rise to what was becoming absolute power. In 44 B.C.E. a group of conspirators assassinated him and set off another round of civil war. (See "Listening to the Past: Cicero and the Plot to Kill Caesar," page 158.) His grandnephew and heir, the eighteen-year-old Octavian (63 B.C.E.–14 C.E.), joined with two of Caesar's followers, Marc Antony and Lepidus, in the Second Triumvirate. After defeating Caesar's murderers, they had a falling-out. Octavian forced Lepidus out of office and waged war against Antony, who had now also become allied with Cleopatra. In 31 B.C.E., with the might of Rome at his back, Octavian defeated the combined forces of Antony and Cleopatra at the Battle of Actium in

Individuals in Society

Queen Cleopatra

CLEOPATRA VII (69–30 B.C.E.) WAS A PTOLEMY, A MEMBER of the dynasty of Hellenistic rulers of Egypt who had established power in the third century B.C.E. Although she was a Greek, she was passionately devoted to her Egyptian subjects and was the first in her dynasty who could speak Egyptian as well as Greek. Just as ancient pharaohs had linked themselves with the gods, she had herself portrayed as the goddess Isis and may have seen herself as a reincarnation of Isis (see page 44).

At the same time that civil war was raging in the late Roman Republic, Cleopatra and her brother Ptolemy XIII were in a dispute over who would be supreme ruler in Egypt. Julius Caesar captured the Egyptian capital of Alexandria, Cleopatra arranged to meet him, and the two became lovers, although Cleopatra was much younger and Caesar was married. The two apparently had a son, Caesarion, and Caesar's army defeated Ptolemy's army, ending the power struggle. In 46 B.C.E. Cleopatra arrived in Rome, where Caesar put up a statue of her as Isis in one of the city's temples. The Romans hated her because they saw her as a decadent Eastern queen and a threat to what were considered traditional Roman values.

After Caesar's assassination, Cleopatra returned to Alexandria. There she became involved in the continuing Roman civil war that now pitted Octavian, Caesar's heir, against Marc Antony, who commanded the Roman army in the East. When Antony visited Alexandria in 41 B.C.E. he met Cleopatra, and though he was already married to Octavian's sister, he became her lover. He abandoned (and later divorced) his Roman wife, married Cleopatra in 37 B.C.E., and changed his will to favor his children by Cleopatra. Antony's wedding present to Cleopatra was a huge grant of territory, much of it Roman, that greatly increased her power and that of all her children, including Caesarion. Antony also declared Caesarion to be Julius Caesar's rightful heir.

Octavian used the wedding gift as the reason to declare Antony a traitor. He and other Roman leaders described Antony as a romantic fool captivated by the seductive Cleopatra. Roman troops turned against Antony and joined with Octavian, and at the Battle of Actium in 31 B.C.E. Octavian defeated the army and navy of Antony and Cleopatra. Antony committed suicide, as did Cleopatra shortly afterward. Octavian ordered the teenage Caesarion killed, but the young children of Antony and Cleopatra were allowed to go back to Rome, where they were raised by Antony's widow. In another consequence of Octavian's victory, Egypt became a Roman province.

Roman sources are viciously hostile to Cleopatra, and she became the model of the alluring woman whose sexual attraction led men to their doom. Stories about her beauty, sophistication, lavish spending, desire for power, and ruthlessness abounded and were retold for centuries. The most dramatic story was that she committed suicide through the bite of a poisonous snake, which may have been true and which has been the subject of countless paintings. Her tumultuous relationships with Caesar and Antony have been portrayed in plays, novels, movies, and television programs.

The only portraits of Cleopatra that date from her own lifetime are on the coins that she issued. This one, made at the mint of Alexandria, shows her as quite plain, reinforcing the point made by Cicero that her attractiveness was based more on intelligence and wit than on physical beauty. The reverse of the coin shows an eagle, a symbol of rule. (© The Trustees of the British Museum/Art Resource, NY)

QUESTIONS FOR ANALYSIS

1. How did Cleopatra benefit from her relationships with Caesar and Antony? How did they benefit from their relationships with her?
2. How did ideas about gender and Roman suspicion of the more sophisticated Greek culture combine to shape Cleopatra's fate and the way she is remembered?
3. "Individuals in Society: Hatshepsut and Nefertiti" in Chapter 2 (see page 47) also focuses on leading female figures in Egypt, but these two women lived more than a thousand years before Cleopatra. How would you compare their situation with hers?

LaunchPad Online Document Project

What do Roman depictions of Cleopatra reveal about the attitudes and values of her time? Explore Roman accounts of Cleopatra to see what light they shed on political, social, and cultural values in the late republic and early empire, and then complete a quiz and writing assignment based on the evidence and details from this chapter.

See inside the front cover to learn more.

Greece. His victory ended the age of civil war. For his success, in 27 B.C.E. the Senate gave Octavian the name Augustus, meaning "revered one." Although the Senate did not mean this to be a decisive break, that date is generally used to mark the end of the Roman Republic and the start of the Roman Empire.

The Successes of Augustus

After Augustus ended the civil wars, he faced the monumental problems of reconstruction. He had to rebuild effective government, pay his army for its services, care for the welfare of the provinces, and address the danger of various groups on Rome's frontiers. Augustus was highly successful in meeting these challenges.

Augustus claimed that he was restoring the republic, but he was actually transforming the government into one in which all power was held by a single ruler. Augustus fit his own position into the republican constitution not by creating a new office for himself but by gradually taking over many of the offices that traditionally had been held by separate people.

The Senate named him often as both consul and tribune. He was also named imperator and held control of the army, which he made a permanent standing organization. Furthermore, recognizing the importance of religion, he had himself named *pontifex maximus*, or chief priest. The Senate also gave him the honorary title *princeps civitatis*, "first citizen of the state." That title had no official powers attached to it and had been used for centuries. Only later would *princeps civitatis* become the basis of the word *prince*, meaning "sovereign ruler," although "prince" quite accurately describes what Augustus actually was.

Considering what had happened to Julius Caesar, Augustus wisely wielded all this power in the background, and his period of rule is officially called the "principate." The Senate continued to exist as a court of law and deliberative body. Without specifically saying so, however, Augustus created the office of emperor. The English word *emperor* is derived from the Latin word *imperator*, an origin that reflects the fact that Augustus's command of the army was the main source of his power. In other reforms, Augustus made provincial administration more orderly and improved its functioning. He further professionalized the army and awarded grants of land in the frontier provinces to veterans who had finished their twenty-year service. He encouraged local self-government and the development of cities. As a spiritual bond between the provinces and Rome, Augustus encouraged the cult of *Roma et Augustus* (Rome and Augustus) as the guardian of the state. The cult spread rapidly and became a symbol of Roman unity. Augustus had himself portrayed on coins standing alongside the goddess Victory and on celebratory stone arches built to commemorate military victories. In addition, he had temples, stadiums, marketplaces, and public buildings constructed in Rome and other cities.

Augustus as Imperator In this marble statue, found in the villa of Augustus's widow, Augustus is dressed in a military uniform and in a pose usually used to show leaders addressing their troops. This emphasizes his role as imperator, the head of the army. The figures on his breastplate show various peoples the Romans had defeated or with whom they had made treaties, along with assorted deities. Although Augustus did not declare himself a god — as later Roman emperors would — this statue shows him barefoot, just as gods and heroes were in classical Greek statuary, and accompanied by Cupid riding a dolphin, both symbols of the goddess Venus, whom he claimed as an ancestor. (Vatican Museums and Galleries, Vatican City/The Bridgeman Art Library)

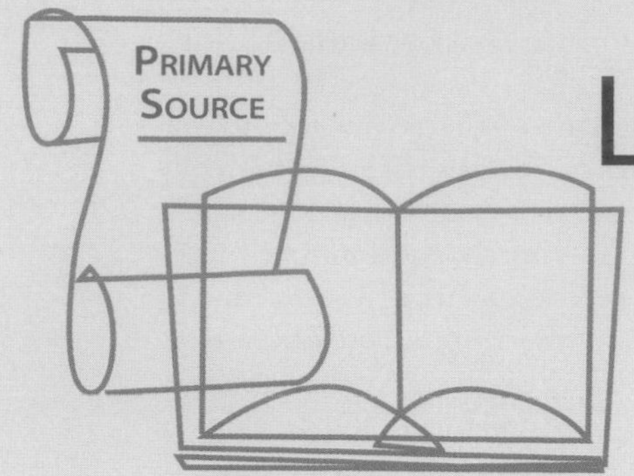

Listening to the Past

Cicero and the Plot to Kill Caesar

Marcus Tullius Cicero was born in January 106 B.C.E. After an excellent education, he settled in Rome to practice law. His meteoric career took him to the consulship in 63 B.C.E. By the time of Caesar's return to Rome in 49 B.C.E., Cicero was a senior statesman with great importance as a lawyer and thinker and with powerful influence through his oratorical skills. Caesar wrote Cicero a flattering letter telling him that "your approval of my actions elates me beyond words. . . . As for yourself, I hope I shall see you at Rome so that I can avail myself as usual of your advice and resources in all things." Cicero tended to favor Pompey, however, thinking that Caesar was a greater danger to traditional republican institutions. He was not involved in the plot to assassinate Caesar, perhaps because the conspirators did not trust him to keep the matter quiet. He was involved in the jockeying for power that followed, however, as evidenced by the following letters and speeches.*

Trebonius, one of the assassins, wrote to Cicero describing the murder, and on February 2, 43 B.C.E., Cicero gave this frank opinion of the events:

"Would to heaven you had invited me to that noble feast that you made on the Ides of March: no remnants, most assuredly, should have been left behind. Whereas the part you unluckily spared gives us so much perplexity that we find something to regret, even in the godlike service that you and your illustrious associates have lately rendered to the republic. To say the truth, when I reflect that it was owing to the favor of so worthy a man as yourself that Antony now lives to be our general bane, I am sometimes inclined to be a little angry with you for taking him aside when Caesar fell as by this means you have occasioned more trouble to myself in particular than to all the rest of the whole community.† "

By the "part [of the feast] you unluckily spared," Cicero meant Marc Antony, Caesar's firm supporter and a fierce enemy of the assassins, whom Cicero feared. Still undecided about what to do after the assassination, Cassius, one of the leaders of the plot, wrote to Cicero asking for advice. Cicero responded, again emphasizing that the conspirators should have killed Antony as well, and clearly miffed that he had not been consulted:

"Where to advise you to begin to restore order I must acknowledge myself at a loss. To say the truth, it is the tyrant alone, and not the tyranny, from which we seem to be delivered: for although the man [Caesar] is destroyed, we still servilely maintain all his despotic ordinances. We do more: and under the pretence of carrying his designs into execution, we approve of measures which even he himself would never have pursued. . . . This outrageous man [Antony] represents me as the principal advisor and promoter of your glorious efforts. Would to heaven the charge were true! For had I been a party in your councils, I should have put it out of his power thus to bother and embarrass our plans. But this was a point that depended on yourselves to decide; and since the opportunity is now over, I can only wish that I were capable of giving you any effective advice. But the truth is that I am utterly at a loss in how to act myself. For what is the purpose of resisting where one cannot oppose force by force?‡ "

At this stage the young Octavian, Caesar's designated heir, sought Cicero's advice. In a series of letters to his close friend Atticus, Cicero discussed the situation, upset that Decimus Brutus, a general who was one of the conspirators, was not taking charge of the situation:

"On the second or third of November 44 B.C.E. a letter arrived from Octavian. He has great schemes afoot. He has won the veterans at Casilinum and Calatia over to his views, and no wonder since he gives them 500 denarii apiece. He plans to make a round of the other colonies. His object is plain: war with Antony and himself as commander-in-chief. So it looks to me as though in a few days' time we shall be in arms. But whom are we to follow? Consider his name; consider his age. . . . In short, he proffers himself as our leader and expects me to back him up. For my part I have recommended him to go to Rome. I imagine he will have the city rabble behind him, and the honest men too if he convinces them of his sincerity. Ah Brutus, where are you? What a golden opportunity you are losing! I could not foretell *this*, but I thought something of the kind would happen.§ "

In the social realm, Augustus promoted marriage and childbearing through legal changes that released free women and freedwomen (female slaves who had been freed) from male guardianship if they had given birth to a certain number of children. Men and women who were unmarried or had no children were restricted in the inheritance of property. Moralists denounced any sexual relationship in which men squandered money or became subservient to those of lower social status, but no laws banned prostitution or same-sex relationships.

Aside from addressing legal issues and matters of state, Augustus actively encouraged poets and writers. For this reason the period of his rule is known as the "golden age" of Latin literature. Roman poets and prose writers celebrated human accomplishments in works

Bust of Cicero. (Galleria degli Uffizi, Florence, Italy/The Bridgeman Art Library)

Four days later Cicero records news of the following developments:

"Two letters for me from Octavian in one day! Now he wants me to return to Rome at once, says he wants to work through the senate. . . . In short, he presses and I play for time. I don't trust his age and I don't know what he's after. . . . I'm nervous of Antony's power and don't want to leave the coast. But I'm afraid of some star performance during my absence. Varro [an enemy of Antony] doesn't think much of the boy's [Octavian's, who was only eighteen] plan; I take a different view. He has a strong force at his back and *can* have Brutus. And he's going to work quite openly, forming companies at Capua and paying out bounties. War is evidently coming any minute now.** "

Even though he contemptuously called him a "boy," Cicero decided to openly side with Octavian. On April 21, 43 B.C.E., he denounced Antony in a speech to the Senate. He reminded his fellow senators how they had earlier opposed Antony:

"Do you not remember, in the name of the immortal gods, what resolutions you have made against these men [Antony and his supporters]? You have repealed the acts of Antony. You have taken down his law. You have voted that they were carried by violence and with a disregard of the auspices. You have called out the troops throughout all Italy. You have pronounced that colleague and ally of all wickedness a public enemy. What peace can there be with this man? Even if he were a foreign enemy, still, after such actions as have taken place, it would be scarcely possible by any means whatever to have peace. Though seas and mountains and vast regions lay between you, still you would hate such a man without seeing him. But these men will stick to your eyes, and when they can to your very throats; for what fences will be strong enough for us to restrain savage beasts? Oh, but the result of war is uncertain. It is at all events in the power of brave men such as you ought to be to display your valor, for certainly brave men can do that, and not to fear the caprice of fortune.†† "

Antony and Octavian briefly reconciled and formed the Third Triumvirate. An ill and aging Cicero was declared an enemy of the state and sought to leave Italy, but was intercepted by Antony's men. When Cicero stretched his head out of the window of the litter in which he was being carried, indicating he would surrender, a centurion slit his throat. His head and hands were cut off on Antony's orders and displayed in the Roman Forum. Octavian's opinion about all this as it happened is disputed, but years later he said of Cicero: "A learned man, learned and a lover of his country."‡‡

QUESTIONS FOR ANALYSIS

1. What can you infer from these letters about how well prepared the conspirators and other leaders in the Senate such as Cicero were to take control of the government after Caesar's death?
2. What do these sources suggest about Cicero's importance and the role of his speeches in the Senate?

**To Atticus* 9.16.2 in D. R. Shackleton-Bailey, *Cicero's Letters to Atticus*, vol. IV (Cambridge, U.K.: Cambridge University Press, 1968), pp. 203–205.

†*To Trebonius* in T. de Quincy, *Cicero: Offices, Essays, and Letters* (New York: E. P. Dutton, 1942), pp. 328–329.

‡*To Cassius*, ibid., pp. 324–325.

§*To Atticus* 16.8.1–2 in D. R. Shackleton-Bailey, *Cicero's Letters to Atticus*, vol. VI (Cambridge, U.K.: Cambridge University Press, 1967), pp. 185–187.

***To Atticus* 16.9, ibid., p. 189.

††*The Fourteenth Phillipic* in C. D. Yonge, *Cicero, Select Orations* (New York: Harper and Brothers, 1889), p. 499.

‡‡Plutarch, *Cicero* 49.15.

that were highly polished, elegant in style, and intellectual in conception.

Rome's greatest poet was Virgil (70–19 B.C.E.), whose masterpiece is the *Aeneid* (uh-NEE-id), an epic poem that is the Latin equivalent of the Greek *Iliad* and *Odyssey* (see page 119) or the Indian *Ramayana* (see page 72). Virgil's account of the founding of Rome and the early years of the city gave final form to the legend of Aeneas, the Trojan hero (and ancestor of Romulus and Remus; see page 147) who escaped to Italy at the fall of Troy:

> Arms and the man I sing, who first made way,
> predestined exile, from the Trojan shore
> to Italy, the blest Lavinian strand.
> Smitten of storms he was on land and sea

Picturing the Past

Ara Pacis In the middle years of Augustus's reign, the Roman Senate ordered a huge altar, the Ara Pacis, built to honor him and the peace he had brought to the empire. This was decorated with life-size reliefs of Augustus and members of his family, prominent Romans, and other people and deities. One side, shown here, depicts a goddess figure, most likely the goddess Peace herself, with twin babies on her lap, flanked by nymphs representing land and sea, and surrounded by plants and animals. (De Agostini Picture Library/Gianni Dagli Orti/The Bridgeman Art Library)

ANALYZING THE IMAGE What do the elements depicted here most likely symbolize?

CONNECTIONS The Ara Pacis was a work of public art designed to commemorate the deeds of Augustus. Why might the Senate have commissioned such a work? Can you think of contemporary parallels?

by violence of Heaven, to satisfy
stern Juno's sleepless wrath; and much in war
he suffered, seeking at the last to found
the city, and bring o'er his fathers' gods
to safe abode in Latium; whence arose
the Latin race, old Alba's reverend lords,
and from her hills wide-walled, imperial Rome.[3]

As Virgil told it, Aeneas became the lover of Dido (DIGH-doh), the widowed queen of Carthage, but left her because his destiny called him to found Rome. Swearing the destruction of Rome, Dido committed suicide, and, according to Virgil, her enmity helped cause the Punic Wars. In leaving Dido, an "Eastern" queen, Aeneas put the good of the state ahead of marriage or pleasure. The parallels between this story and the real events involving Antony and Cleopatra were not lost on Virgil's audience. Making the public aware of these parallels, and of Virgil's description of Aeneas as an ancestor of Julius Caesar, fit well with Augustus's aims. Therefore, he encouraged Virgil to write the *Aeneid* and made sure it was circulated widely immediately after Virgil died.

One of the most significant aspects of Augustus's reign was Roman expansion into northern and western Europe (Map 6.2). Augustus completed the conquest of Spain, founded twelve new towns in Gaul, and saw that the Roman road system linked new settlements with one another and with Italy. After hard fighting, he made the Rhine River the Roman frontier in Germania (Germany). Meanwhile, generals conquered areas as far as the Danube River, and Roman

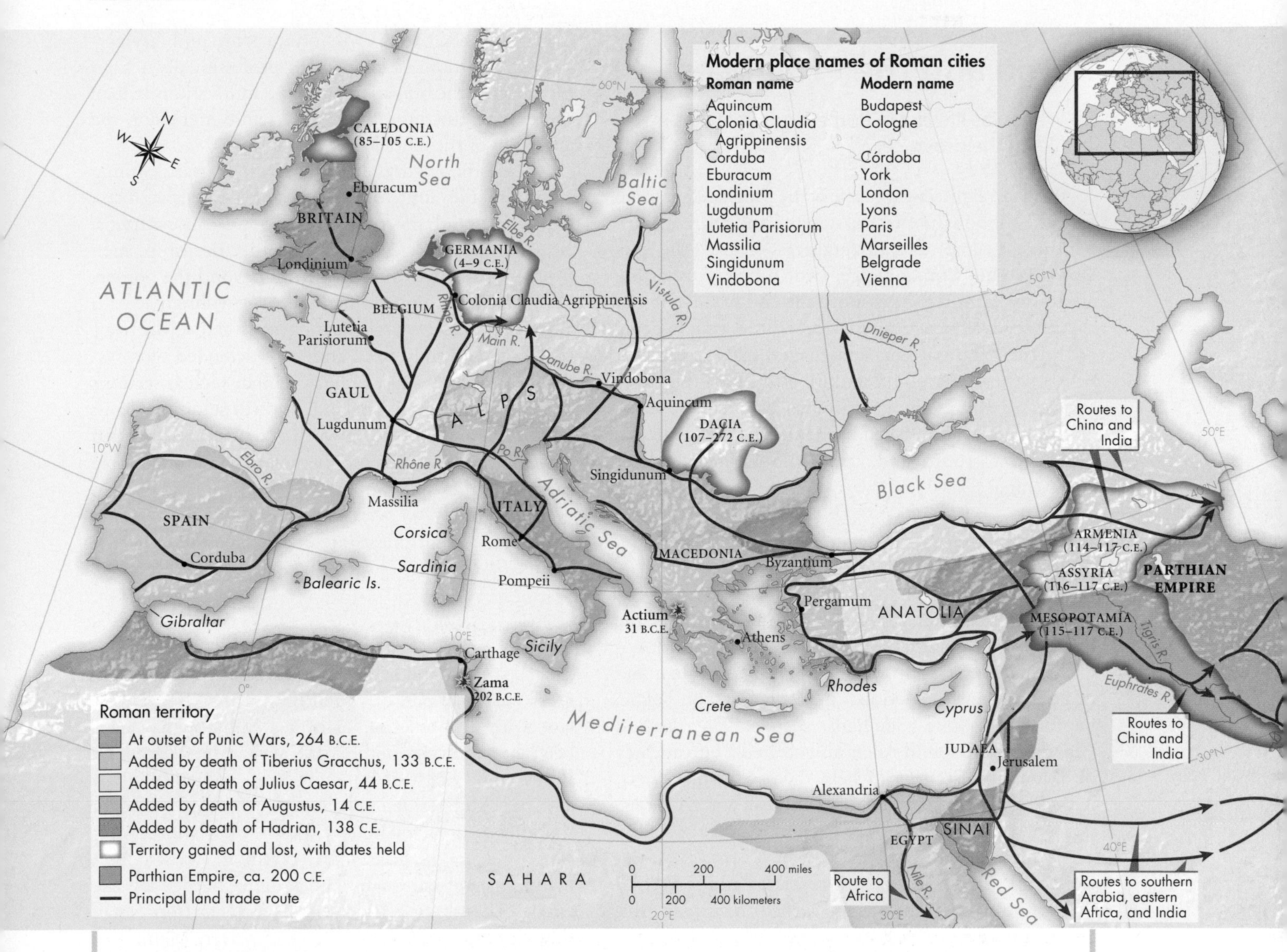

Mapping the Past

MAP 6.2 Roman Expansion, 262 B.C.E.–180 C.E. Rome expanded in all directions, eventually controlling every shore of the Mediterranean and vast amounts of land.

ANALYZING THE MAP How would you summarize the pattern of Roman expansion—that is, which areas were conquered first and which later? How long was Rome able to hold on to territories at the outermost boundaries of its empire?

CONNECTIONS Many of today's major cities in these areas were founded as Roman colonies. Why do you think so many of these cities were founded along the northern border of Roman territory?

legions penetrated the areas of modern Austria, southern Bavaria, and western Hungary. The regions of modern Serbia, Bulgaria, and Romania also fell. Within this area the legionaries built fortified camps. Roads linked these camps with one another, and settlements grew up around the camps, eventually becoming towns. Traders began to frequent the frontier and to do business with the people who lived there; as a result, for the first time, central and northern Europe came into direct and continuous contact with Mediterranean culture.

Romans did not force their culture on native people in Roman territories. However, just as earlier ambitious people in the Hellenistic world knew that the surest path to political and social advancement lay in embracing Greek culture and learning to speak Greek (see page 134), those determined to get ahead now learned Latin and adopted aspects of Roman culture.

Rome and the Provinces

☐ What was life like in Rome, and what was it like in the provinces?

In the late eighteenth century the English historian Edward Gibbon dubbed the stability and relative peace within the empire that Augustus created the **pax Romana**, the "Roman peace," which he saw as lasting about two hundred years, until the end of the reign of the emperor Marcus Aurelius in 180 C.E. People being conquered by the Romans might not have agreed that things were so peaceful, but during this time the growing city of Rome saw great improvements, and trade and production flourished in the provinces. Rome also expanded eastward and came into indirect contact with China.

Political and Military Changes in the Empire

For fifty years after Augustus's death in 14 C.E. the dynasty that he established—known as the Julio-Claudians because all were members of the Julian and Claudian clans—provided the emperors of Rome. Some of the Julio-Claudians, such as Tiberius and Claudius, were sound rulers and created a bureaucracy of able administrators to help them govern. Others, including Caligula and Nero, were weak and frivolous.

In 68 C.E. Nero's inept rule led to military rebellion and widespread disruption. Yet only two years later Vespasian (r. 69–79 C.E.), who established the Flavian dynasty, restored order. He also turned Augustus's principate into a hereditary monarchy and expanded the emperor's powers. The Flavians (69–96 C.E.) restored discipline in the army and carried on Augustus's work in Italy and on the frontiers. During the brief reign of Vespasian's son Titus, Mount Vesuvius in southern Italy erupted, destroying Pompeii and other cities and killing thousands of people. (See "Viewpoints 6.2: Roman and Chinese Officials in Times of Disaster," at right.) The Flavians paved the way for the Antonines (96–192 C.E.), a dynasty of emperors under whose leadership the Roman Empire experienced a long period of prosperity and the height of the pax Romana. Wars generally ended victoriously and were confined to the frontiers. Second-century emperors made further changes in government. Hadrian (HAY-dree-uhn), who became emperor in 117 C.E., made the imperial bureaucracy created by Claudius more organized. He established imperial administrative departments and separated civil service from military service. In addition, he demanded professionalism from members of the bureaucracy. These innovations helped the empire run more efficiently while increasing the authority of the emperor.

The Roman army also saw changes, transforming from a mobile unit to a much larger defensive force, with more and more troops who were noncitizens. Because army service could lead to citizenship, men from the provinces and even from beyond the borders of the Roman Empire joined the army willingly to gain citizenship, receive a salary, and learn a trade. The frontiers became firmly fixed and were defended by a system of forts and walls, some of which, such as sections of Hadrian's Wall in England, are still standing today. Behind these walls, the network of roads was expanded and improved, both to supply the forts and to reinforce them in times of trouble. The Roman road system eventually grew to over fifty thousand miles, longer than the current interstate highway system in the United States; some of those roads are still usable today.

Life in Imperial Rome

The expansion and stabilization of the empire created great wealth, much of which flowed into Rome. The city, with a population of over a million, may have been the largest city in the world at that time. Although Rome could boast of stately palaces, noble buildings, and beautiful residential areas, most people lived in shoddily constructed houses. They took whatever work was available, making food, clothing, construction materials, and the many other items needed by the city's residents, or selling these products from small shops or at the city's many marketplaces. Many residents of the city of Rome were slaves, who ranged from highly educated household tutors or government officials or widely sought sculptors to workers who engaged in hard physical tasks.

Fire and crime were perennial problems even in Augustus's day, and sanitation was poor. In the second century urban planning and new construction greatly improved the situation. For example, engineers built an elaborate system that collected sewage from public baths, the ground floors of buildings, and public latrines. They also built hundreds of miles of aqueducts, most of them underground, to bring fresh water into the city from the surrounding hills. The aqueducts, powered entirely by gravity, were a sophisticated system that required regular maintenance. Building aqueducts required thousands and sometimes tens of thousands of workers, who were generally paid out of the imperial treasury.

Rome grew so large that it became ever more difficult to feed its residents. Emperors solved the problem

• **pax Romana** The "Roman peace," a period during the first and second centuries C.E. of political stability and relative peace.

Viewpoints 6.2

Roman and Chinese Officials in Times of Disaster

• *Government officials in ancient empires were often confronted with natural disasters, and their response to them was seen as a mark of their character and capabilities, just as it is today. In the first text below, the Roman author Pliny the Younger describes the actions of his uncle Pliny the Elder during the eruption of Mount Vesuvius in 79 C.E. In the second text, the Chinese historian Sima Qian (145–ca. 85 B.C.E.; see page 182) describes the actions of the official Ji An during a famine.*

Pliny the Younger on Pliny the Elder

" My uncle was stationed at Misenum, in active command of the fleet. On 24 August, in the early afternoon, my mother drew his attention to a cloud of unusual size and appearance. . . . My uncle's scholarly acumen saw at once that it was important enough for a closer inspection, and he ordered a boat to be made ready, . . . [but] what he had begun in a spirit of inquiry he completed as a hero. He gave orders for the warships to be launched and went on board himself with the intention of bringing help to many more people. . . . He hurried to the place which everyone else was hastily leaving, steering his course straight for the danger zone. He was entirely fearless, describing each new movement and phase of the portent to be noted down exactly as he observed them. Ashes were already falling, hotter and thicker as the ships drew near, followed by bits of pumice and blackened stones, charred and cracked by the flames. . . . He was able to bring his ship in. . . .

Meanwhile on Mount Vesuvius broad sheets of fire and leaping flames blazed at several points, their bright glare emphasized by the darkness of night. . . . The buildings were now shaking with violent shocks, and seemed to be swaying to and fro as if they were torn from their foundations. . . . My uncle decided to go down to the shore and investigate on the spot the possibility of any escape by sea, but he found the waves still wild and dangerous. . . . He stood leaning on two slaves and then suddenly collapsed, I imagine because the dense fumes choked his breathing. . . . His body was found intact and uninjured, still fully clothed and looking more like sleep than death. "

Sima Qian on Ji An

" During the reign of Emperor Jing, Ji An, on the recommendation of his father, was appointed as a mounted guard to the heir apparent. . . . When a great fire broke out in Henei and destroyed over 1,000 houses, the emperor . . . sent Ji An to observe the situation. On his return he reported, "The roofs of the houses were so close together that the fire spread from one to another; that is why so many homes were burned. It is nothing to worry about. As I passed through Henan on my way, however, I noted that the inhabitants were very poor, and over 10,000 families had suffered so greatly from floods and droughts that fathers and sons were reduced to eating each other. I therefore took it upon myself to use the imperial seals to open the granaries of Henan and relieve the distress of the people. I herewith return the seals and await punishment for overstepping my authority in this fashion."

The emperor, impressed with the wisdom he had shown, overlooked the irregularity of his action and transferred him to the post of governor. . . . Ji An studied the doctrines of the Yellow Emperor and Lao Zi. . . . He was sick a great deal of the time, confined to his bed and unable to go out, and yet after only a year or so as governor of Donghai he had succeeded in setting the affairs of the province in perfect order and winning the acclaim of the people. "

Sources: *The Letters of Pliny the Younger*, translated with an introduction by Betty Radice (London: Penguin Classics, 1963, reprinted 1969). Copyright © Betty Radice, 1963, 1969. Reproduced by permission of Penguin Books Ltd.; *Records of the Grand Historian: Han Dynasty II*, by SIMA QIAN. Reproduced with permission of COLUMBIA UNIVERSITY PRESS in the format Book via Copyright Clearance Center.

QUESTIONS FOR ANALYSIS

1. How do the two officials respond to the disasters, and how do the authors of these works judge their responses?
2. What cultural ideals do the authors convey in their descriptions of these officials?

by providing citizens with free oil, wine, and grain for bread. By doing so, they also stayed in favor with the people. They and other sponsors also entertained the people with gladiatorial contests in which participants fought using swords and other weapons. Games were advertised on billboards, and spectators were given a program with the names and sometimes the fighting statistics of the pairs, so that they could bet more easily. Some gladiators were criminals or prisoners of war, but by the imperial period increasing numbers were volunteers, often poor immigrants who saw gladiatorial combat as a way to support themselves. All gladiators were trained in gladiatorial schools and were legally slaves, although they could keep their winnings and a few became quite wealthy. The Hollywood portrayal of gladiatorial combat has men fighting to their death, but this was increasingly rare, as the owners of especially skilled fighters wanted them to continue to compete. The Romans were even more addicted to chariot racing than to gladiatorial shows. Winning charioteers were idolized just as sports stars are today.

Prosperity in the Roman Provinces

As the empire grew and stabilized, many Roman provinces grew prosperous through the growth of agriculture, trade, and industry, among other factors. Peace and security opened Britain, Gaul, and the lands of the Danube to settlers from other parts of the Roman Empire. Veterans were given small parcels of land in the provinces, becoming tenant farmers. The garrison towns that grew up around provincial military camps became the centers of organized political life, and some grew into major cities.

The rural population throughout the empire left few records, but the inscriptions that remain point to a melding of cultures. One sphere where this occurred was language. People used Latin for legal and state religious purposes, but gradually Latin blended with the original language of an area and with languages spoken by those who came into the area later. Slowly what would become the Romance languages of Spanish, Italian, French, Portuguese, and Romanian evolved. Religion was another site of cultural exchange and mixture. Romans moving into an area learned about and began to venerate local gods, and local people learned about Roman ones. Gradually hybrid deities and rituals developed. The process of cultural exchange was at first more urban than rural, but the importance of cities and towns to the life of the wider countryside ensured that its effects spread far afield.

The Romans were the first to build cities in northern Europe, but in the eastern Mediterranean they ruled cities that had existed before Rome itself was even a village. Here there was much continuity in urban life from the Hellenistic period. There was less construction than in the Roman cities of northern and western Europe because existing buildings could simply be put to new uses.

The expansion of trade during the pax Romana made the Roman Empire an economic as well as a political force. Britain and Belgium became prime grain producers, with much of their harvests going to the armies of the Rhine, and Britain's wool industry probably got its start under the Romans. Italy and southern Gaul produced huge quantities of wine, which was shipped in large pottery jugs wherever merchant vessels could carry it. Roman colonists introduced the olive to southern Spain and northern Africa, which soon produced most of the oil consumed in the western part of the empire. In the East the olive oil production of Syrian farmers reached an all-time high, and Egypt produced tons of wheat that fed the Roman populace.

The growth of industry in the provinces was another striking development of this period. Cities in Gaul and Germany eclipsed the old Mediterranean manufacturing centers, and in the second century C.E. Gaul and Germany took over the pottery market. (See "Global Trade: Pottery," page 166.) Lyons in Gaul and later Cologne in Germany became the new centers of the glassmaking industry, and the cities of Gaul were nearly unrivaled in the manufacture of bronze and brass. Aided by all this growth in trade and industry, Europe and western Asia were linked in ways they had not been before.

Eastward Expansion and Contacts Between Rome and China

As the Romans drove farther eastward, they encountered the Parthians, who had established a kingdom in what is now Afghanistan and Iran in the Hellenistic period (see page 135). In the second century the Romans tried unsuccessfully to drive out the Parthians, who came to act as a link between Roman and Chinese merchants. Chinese merchants sold their wares to the Parthians, who then carried the goods overland to Mesopotamia or Egypt, from which they were shipped throughout the Roman Empire. In 226 C.E. the Parthians were defeated by the Sassanids, a new dynasty in the area (see page 209). When the Romans continued their attacks against this new enemy, the Sassanid king Shapur conquered the Roman legions of the emperor Valerian, whom he took prisoner. Shapur employed the captured Roman soldiers and engineers to build roads, bridges, dams, and canals, and their designs and methods were later used throughout the Sassanid empire.

Although warfare disrupted parts of western Asia, it did not stop trade that had prospered from Hellenistic times (see page 135). Silk was still a major commodity

Roman Architecture These three structures demonstrate the beauty and utility of Roman architecture. The Coliseum in Rome (below), a sports arena that could seat fifty thousand spectators, built between 70 C.E. and 80 C.E., was the site of gladiatorial games, animal spectacles, and executions. The Pantheon in Rome (right), a temple dedicated to all the gods, was built in its present form about 130 C.E., after earlier temples on the site had burned down. Its dome, 140 feet in diameter, remains the largest unreinforced concrete dome in the world. Romans also used concrete for more everyday purposes. The Pont du Gard at Nîmes in France (above) is a bridge over a river that carried an aqueduct supplying millions of gallons of water per day to the Roman city of Nîmes in Gaul; the water flowed in a channel at the very top. Although this bridge was built largely without mortar or concrete, many Roman aqueducts and bridges relied on concrete and sometimes iron rods for their strength.

(Pont du Gard: De Agostini Picture Library/O. Geddo/ The Bridgeman Art Library; Pantheon: Gianni Dagli Orti/The Art Archive at Art Resource, NY; Coliseum: The Bridgeman Art Library)

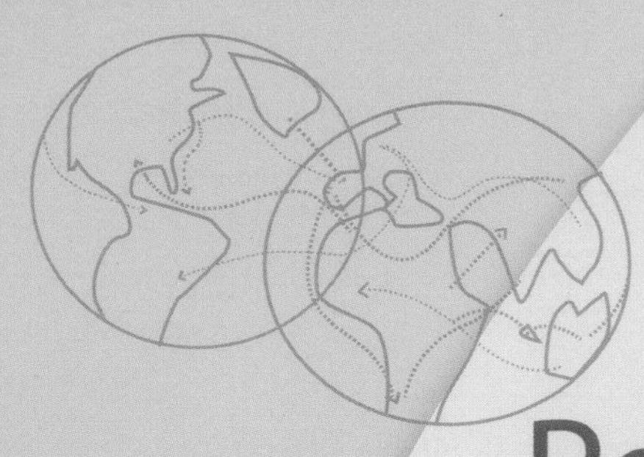

Global Trade

Pottery is used primarily for dishes today, but it served a surprisingly large number of purposes in the ancient world. Families used earthen pottery for cooking and tableware, for storing grains and liquids, and for lamps. On a larger scale, pottery was used for the transportation and protection of goods traded overseas, much as today's metal storage containers are used.

The creation of pottery dates back to the Neolithic period. Few resources were required to make it, only abundant sources of good clay and wheels upon which potters could throw their vessels. Once made, the pots were baked in specially constructed kilns. Although the whole process was relatively simple, skilled potters formed groups that made utensils for entire communities. Later innovations occurred when the artisans learned to glaze their pots by applying a varnish before baking them in a kiln.

The earliest potters focused on coarse ware: plain plates, cups, and cooking pots that remained virtually unchanged throughout antiquity. Increasingly, however, potters began to decorate these pieces with simple designs. In this way pottery became both functional and decorative. One of the most popular pieces was the amphora, a large two-handled jar with a wide mouth, a round belly, and a base. It became the workhorse of maritime shipping because it protected contents from water and rodents, was easy and cheap to produce, and could be reused (see page 136). Amphoras contained goods as varied as wine and oil, spices and unguents, dried fish and pitch. The amphora's dependability and versatility kept it in use from the fourth century B.C.E. to the beginning of the Middle Ages.

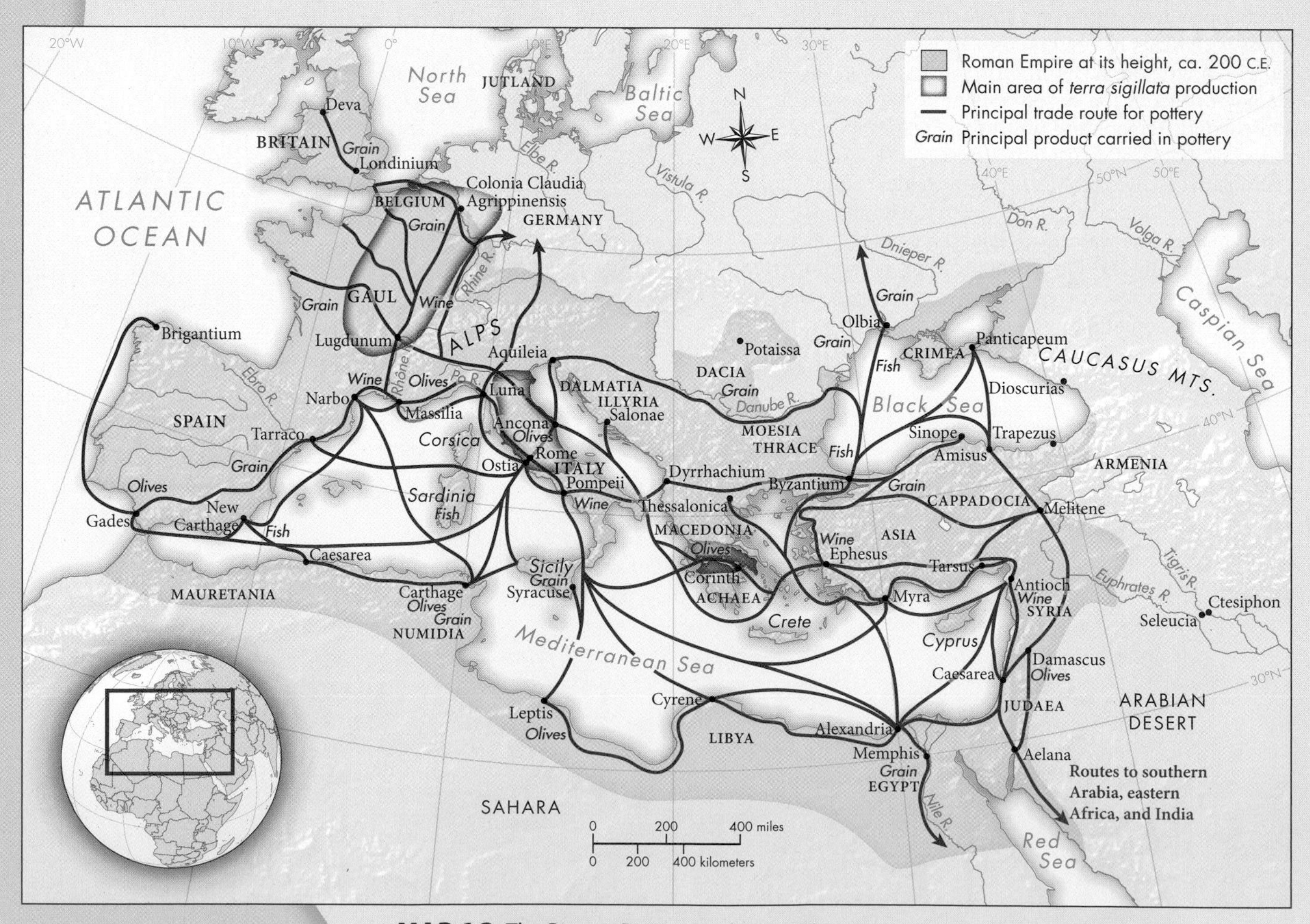

MAP 6.3 The Roman Pottery Trade, ca. 200 C.E.

In the Hellenistic and Roman periods, amphoras became common throughout the Mediterranean and carried goods eastward to the Black Sea, Persian Gulf, and Red Sea. The Ptolemies of Egypt sent amphoras and their contents even farther, to Arabia, eastern Africa, and India. Thus merchants and mariners who had never seen the Mediterranean depended on these containers.

Other pots proved as useful as the amphora, and all became a medium of decorative art. By the eighth century B.C.E. Greek potters and artists had begun to decorate their wares by painting them with patterns and scenes from mythology, legend, and daily life. They portrayed episodes such as famous chariot races or battles from the *Iliad*. Some portrayed the gods, such as Dionysus at sea. These images widely spread knowledge of Greek religion and culture. In the West, especially, the Etruscans in Italy and the Carthaginians in North Africa eagerly welcomed the pots, their decoration, and their ideas. The Hellenistic kings shipped these pots as far east as China. Pottery thus served as a means of cultural exchange among people scattered across huge portions of the globe.

The Romans took the manufacture of pottery to an advanced stage by introducing a wider range of vessels and by making some in industrial-scale kilns that were large enough to fire tens of thousands of pots at once. The most prized pottery was *terra sigillata*, reddish decorated tableware with a glossy surface. Methods for making terra sigillata spread from Italy northward into Europe, often brought by soldiers in the Roman army who had been trained in pottery-making in Italy. They set up facilities to make roof tiles, amphoras, and dishes for their units, and local potters began to copy their styles and methods of manufacturing. Terra sigillata often portrayed Greco-Roman gods and heroes, and so the pottery spread Mediterranean myths and stories. Local artisans added their own distinctive flourishes and sometimes stamped their names on the pots; these individual touches have allowed archaeologists to trace the pottery trade throughout the Roman Empire in great detail.

from east to west, along with other luxury goods. In return the Romans traded glassware, precious gems, and slaves. The Parthians added exotic fruits, rare birds, rugs, and other products.

The pax Romana was also an era of maritime trade, and Roman ships sailed from Egyptian ports to the mouth of the Indus River, where they purchased local merchandise and wares imported by the Parthians. Merchants who made the voyage contended with wind, shoal waters, and pirates. Despite the dangers and discomforts, some hardy mariners pushed down the African coast and into the Indian Ocean, where they traded with equally hardy local sailors. Roman coins have been found in Sri Lanka and Vietnam, clear evidence of trade connections, although most likely no merchant traveled the entire distance.

The period of this contact coincided with the era of Han greatness in China (see pages 180–181). The Han emperor Wu encouraged trade by sea as well as by land, and during the reign of the Roman emperor Nerva (r. 96–98 C.E.), a later Han emperor sent an ambassador, Gan Ying, to make contact with the Roman Empire. Gan Ying made it as far as the Persian Gulf ports, where he heard about the Romans from Parthian sailors and reported back to his emperor that the Romans were wealthy, tall, and strikingly similar to the Chinese. His report became part of a group of accounts about the Romans and other "western" peoples that circulated widely among scholars and officials in Han China. Educated Romans did not have a corresponding interest in China. For them, China remained more of a mythical than a real place, and they never bothered to learn more about it.

The Coming of Christianity

☐ What was Christianity, and how did it affect life in the Roman Empire?

During the reign of the emperor Tiberius (r. 14–37 C.E.), in the Roman province of Judaea, which had been created out of the Jewish kingdom of Judah, a Jewish man named Jesus of Nazareth preached, attracted a following, and was executed on the order of the Roman prefect Pontius Pilate. At the time this was a minor event, but Christianity, the religion created by Jesus's followers, came to have an enormous impact first in the Roman Empire and later throughout the world.

Factors Behind the Rise of Christianity

The civil wars that destroyed the Roman Republic left their mark on Judaea, where Jewish leaders had taken sides in the conflict. The turmoil created a climate of violence throughout the area, and among the Jews movements in opposition to the Romans spread. Some of these groups, such as the Zealots, encouraged armed rebellion against Roman rule. Many Jews came to believe that a final struggle was near and that it would lead to the coming of a savior, or **Messiah**, a descendant of King David who would destroy the Roman legions and inaugurate a period of happiness and plenty for Jews. This apocalyptic belief was an old one among Jews, but by the first century C.E. it had become more widespread than ever.

The pagan world also played its part in the story of early Christianity. The term **pagan**, which originally referred to those who lived in the countryside, came to refer to those who practiced religions other than Judaism or Christianity. This included religions devoted to the traditional Roman gods of the hearth, home, and countryside. Known as syncretistic religions, these religions blended Roman and indigenous deities. The cult of the emperor spread through the erection of statues, temples, and monuments, and mystery religions offered the promise of life after death (see Chapter 5). Many people in the Roman Empire practiced all of these religions, combining them in whatever way seemed most beneficial or satisfying to them.

The Life and Teachings of Jesus

Into this climate of Messianic hope and Roman religious blending came Jesus of Nazareth (ca. 3 B.C.E.–29 C.E.). According to Christian Scripture, he was born to deeply religious Jewish parents and raised in Galilee, stronghold of the Zealots and a trading center where Greeks and Romans interacted with Jews. His ministry began when he was about thirty, and he taught by preaching and telling stories.

Like Socrates and the Buddha, Jesus left no writings. Accounts of his sayings and teachings first circulated orally among his followers and were later written down. The principal evidence for his life and deeds are the four Gospels of the Bible (Matthew, Mark, Luke, and John), books that are part of what Christians later termed the New Testament. These Gospels—the name means "good news"—are records of Jesus's teachings, written sometime in the late first century to build a community of faith. The Gospels include certain details of Jesus's life, but they were not meant to be biographies. Their authors had probably heard many different people talk about what Jesus said and did, and there are discrepancies among the four accounts. These differences indicate that early followers had a diversity of beliefs about Jesus's nature and purpose. This diversity of beliefs about Jesus continues today. Some see him as a moral teacher, some as a prophet, and many as the son of God who rose from the dead and is himself divine.

Depiction of Jesus This mural, from a Roman camp at Dura-Europos on the Euphrates River, may be the earliest known depiction of Jesus. Dating to 235 C.E., it depicts Jesus healing a paralytic man, an incident described in the New Testament. Early Christians used art to spread their message. (Yale University Art Gallery, Dura-Europos Collection)

However, almost all the early sources agree on certain aspects of Jesus's teachings: he preached of a heavenly kingdom of eternal happiness in a life after death and of the importance of devotion to God and love of others. His teachings were based on Hebrew Scripture and reflected a conception of God and morality that came from Jewish tradition. Jesus's orthodoxy enabled him to preach in the synagogue and the temple, but he deviated from orthodoxy in insisting that he taught in

- **Messiah** In Jewish belief, a savior who would bring a period of peace and happiness for Jews; many Christians came to believe that Jesus was that Messiah.
- **pagan** Originally referring to those who lived in the countryside, the term came to mean those who practiced religions other than Judaism or Christianity.

his own name, not in the name of Yahweh (the Hebrew name for God). The Greek translation of the Hebrew word *Messiah* is *Christus*, the origin of the English word *Christ*. Was Jesus the Messiah, the Christ? A small band of followers thought so, and Jesus claimed that he was. Yet Jesus had his own conception of the Messiah. He would establish a spiritual kingdom, not an earthly one. As recounted in one of the Gospels, he commented:

> Do not lay up for yourselves treasures on earth, where moth and rust consume and where thieves break in and steal, but lay up for yourselves treasures in heaven, where neither moth nor rust consumes and where thieves do not break in and steal. For where your treasure is, there will your heart be also. (Matthew 6:19–21)

The Roman official Pontius Pilate knew little about Jesus's teachings. He was concerned with maintaining peace and order. According to the New Testament, crowds followed Jesus into Jerusalem at the time of Passover, a highly emotional point in the Jewish year that marked the Jewish people's departure from Egypt under the leadership of Moses (see page 52). The prospect that these crowds would spark violence alarmed Pilate. Some Jews believed that Jesus was the long-awaited Messiah. Others hated and feared him because they thought him religiously dangerous. To avert riot and bloodshed, Pilate condemned Jesus to death, and his soldiers carried out the sentence. On the third day after Jesus's crucifixion, some of his followers claimed that he had risen from the dead. For his earliest followers and for generations to come, the resurrection of Jesus became a central element of faith.

The Spread of Christianity

The memory of Jesus and his teachings survived and flourished. Believers in his divinity met in small assemblies or congregations, often in one another's homes, to discuss the meaning of Jesus's message and to celebrate a ritual (later called the Eucharist or Lord's Supper) commemorating his last meal with his disciples before his arrest. Because they expected Jesus to return to the world very soon, they regarded earthly life and institutions as unimportant. Only later did these congregations evolve into what came to be called the religion of Christianity, with a formal organization and set of beliefs.

The catalyst in the spread of Jesus's teachings and the formation of the Christian Church was Paul of Tarsus, a well-educated Hellenized Jew who was comfortable in both the Roman and the Jewish worlds. The New Testament reports that at first Paul persecuted members of the new sect, but on the road to the city of Damascus in Syria he was converted to belief in Jesus and became a vigorous promoter of Jesus's ideas. Paul traveled all over the Roman Empire and wrote letters of advice to many groups. These letters were copied and widely circulated, transforming Jesus's ideas into more specific moral teachings. As a result of his efforts, Paul became the most important figure in changing Christianity from a Jewish sect into a separate religion, and many of his letters became part of Christian Scripture.

The breadth of the Roman Empire was another factor behind the spread of Christianity. If all roads led to Rome, they also led outward to the provinces. This enabled early Christians to spread their faith easily throughout the world known to them, as Jesus had told his followers to do in the Gospels, thus making his teachings universal. The Romans also considered their empire universal, and the early Christians combined the two concepts of universalism.

Though most of the earliest converts seem to have been Jews, or Greeks and Romans who were already interested in Jewish moral teachings, Paul urged that Gentiles, or non-Jews, be accepted on an equal basis. The earliest Christian converts included people from all social classes. These people were reached by missionaries and others who spread the Christian

Christian Oil Lamp When Christianity spread in the Roman Empire, many believers purchased household goods with Christian symbols. This pottery lamp for an ordinary home, dating from the fourth century C.E., is marked with a common symbol for Jesus, the letters *XP* (chi rho), the first two letters in Greek for *Christos*, "Christ." (photo by Z. Radovan, Jerusalem/Bible Land Pictures/akg-images)

message through family contacts, friendships, and business networks. Many women were active in spreading Christianity. Paul greeted male and female converts by name in his letters and noted that women often provided financial support for his activities. The growing Christian communities differed over the extent to which women should participate in the workings of the religion; some favored giving women a larger role in church affairs, while others were more restrictive.

People were attracted to Christian teachings for a variety of reasons. It was in many ways a mystery religion, offering its adherents special teachings that would give them immortality. But in contrast to traditional mystery religions, Christianity promised this immortality widely, not only to a select few. Christianity also offered the possibility of forgiveness, for believers accepted that human nature is weak and that even the best Christians could fall into sin. But Jesus loved sinners and forgave those who repented. Christianity was also attractive to many because it gave the Roman world a cause. Instead of passivity, Christians stressed the ideal of striving for a goal. By spreading the word of Christ, Christians played their part in God's plan for the triumph of Christianity on earth. They were not discouraged by temporary setbacks, believing Christianity to be invincible. Christianity likewise gave its devotees a sense of identity and community, which was very welcome in the often highly mobile world of the Roman Empire. To stress the spiritual kinship of this new type of community, Christians often called one another brother and sister. Also, many Christians took Jesus's commandment to love one another as a guide and provided support for widows, orphans, and the poor, just as they would for family members.

The Growing Acceptance and Evolution of Christianity

At first, most Roman officials largely ignored the followers of Jesus, viewing them simply as one of the many splinter groups within Judaism, but slowly some came to oppose Christian practices and beliefs. They considered Christians to be subversive dissidents because they stopped practicing traditional rituals and they objected—often publicly or in writing—to the cult of the emperor. Some Romans thought that Christianity was one of the worst of the mystery cults, with immoral and indecent rituals. Pagans also feared that the Greco-Roman gods would withdraw their favor from the Roman Empire because of the Christian insistence that the pagan gods either did not exist or were evil spirits. And many worried that Christians were trying to destroy the Roman family with their insistence on a new type of kinship and pointed to Jesus's words in the Gospels saying that salvation was far more important than family relationships.

Persecutions of Christians, including torture and executions, were organized by governors of Roman provinces and sometimes by the emperor, beginning with Nero. Most persecutions were local and sporadic in nature, however, and some of the gory stories about the martyrs are later inventions, designed to strengthen believers with accounts of earlier heroes. Responses to Christianity on the part of Roman emperors varied. Some left Christians in peace, while others ordered them to sacrifice to the emperor and the Roman gods or risk death.

By the second century Christianity was changing. The belief that Jesus was soon coming again gradually waned, and as the number of converts increased, permanent institutions were established instead of simple house churches. These included buildings and a hierarchy of officials often modeled on those of the Roman Empire. **Bishops**, officials with jurisdiction over a certain area, became especially important. They began to assert that they had the right to determine the correct interpretation of Christian teachings and to choose their successors.

Christianity also began to attract more highly educated individuals who developed complex theological interpretations of issues that were not clear in scripture. Often drawing on Greek philosophy and Roman legal traditions, they worked out understandings of such issues as how Jesus could be both divine and human and how God could be both a father and a son (and later a spirit as well, a Christian doctrine known as the Trinity). Bishops and theologians often modified teachings that seemed upsetting to Romans, such as Jesus's harsh words about wealth and family ties. Given all these changes, Christianity became more formal in the second century, with power more centralized.

Turmoil and Reform

- How did the emperors respond to political, economic, and religious issues in the third and fourth centuries?

The prosperity and stability of the second century gave way to a period of domestic upheaval and foreign invasion in the Roman Empire that historians have termed the "crisis of the third century." Trying to repair the damage was the major work of the emperors Diocletian (r. 284–305) and Constantine (r. 306–337), both of whom rose to leadership through the ranks of the mili-

- **bishop** A Christian Church official with jurisdiction over a certain area and the power to determine the correct interpretation of Christian teachings.

tary. They enacted political and religious reforms that dramatically changed the empire.

Political Measures

During the crisis of the third century the Roman Empire was stunned by civil war, as different individuals, generally military commanders from the border provinces, claimed rights to leadership of the empire. Beginning in 235, emperors often ruled for only a few years or even months. Army leaders in the provinces declared their loyalty to one faction or another, or they broke from the empire entirely, thus ceasing to supply troops or taxes. Non-Roman groups on the frontiers took advantage of the chaos to invade Roman-held territory along the Rhine and Danube, occasionally even crossing the Alps to maraud in Italy. In the East, Sassanid armies advanced all the way to the Mediterranean. By the time peace was restored, the empire's economy was shattered, cities had shrunk in size, and many farmers had left their lands.

Diocletian, who had risen through the ranks of the military to become emperor in 284, ended the period of chaos. Under Diocletian the princeps became *dominus*, "lord," reflecting the emperor's claim that he was "the elect of god," ruling because of divine favor. To underscore the emperor's exalted position, Diocletian and his successor, Constantine, adopted the court ceremonies and trappings of the Persian Empire.

Diocletian recognized that the empire had become too large for one man to handle and so in 293 divided it into a western and an eastern half. He assumed direct control of the eastern part, giving a colleague the rule of the western part along with the title *augustus*, which had become synonymous with *emperor*. Diocletian and his fellow augustus further delegated power by appointing two men to assist them. Each man was given the title *caesar* to indicate his exalted rank. Although this system is known as the tetrarchy (TEH-trahr-kee), meaning "rule of four," Diocletian was clearly the senior partner and final source of authority.

The Division of the Roman World, 293 C.E.

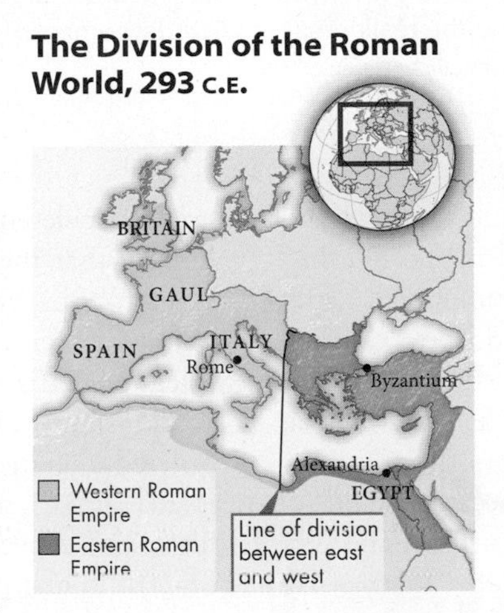

Although the tetrarchy soon failed, Diocletian's division of the empire into two parts became permanent. After a brief civil war following Diocletian's death, Constantine eventually gained authority over the entire empire but ruled from the East. Here he established a new capital for the empire at Byzantium, an old Greek city on the Bosporus, a strait on the boundary between Europe and Asia. He named it "New Rome," though it was soon called Constantinople. In his new capital Constantine built palaces, warehouses, public buildings, and even a hippodrome for horse racing, modeling them on Roman buildings. In addition, he built defensive works along the borders of the empire, trying hard to keep it together, as did his successors. Despite their efforts, however, the eastern and the western halves drifted apart.

The emperors ruling from Constantinople could not provide enough military assistance to repel invaders in the western half of the Roman Empire, and Roman authority there slowly disintegrated. In 476 a Germanic chieftain, Odoacer, deposed the Roman emperor in the West and did not take on the title of emperor, calling himself instead the king of Italy. This date thus marks the official end of the Roman Empire in the West, although the Roman Empire in the East, later called the Byzantine Empire, would last for nearly another thousand years.

Economic Issues

Along with political challenges, major economic problems also confronted Diocletian and Constantine, including inflation and declining tax revenues. Their attempts to solve them illustrate the methods and limitations of absolute monarchy. In an attempt to curb inflation, Diocletian took a step unprecedented in Roman history: he issued an edict that fixed maximum prices and wages throughout the empire. He and his successors dealt with the tax system just as strictly and inflexibly. Taxes became payable in kind, that is, in goods and services instead of money. All those involved in the growing, preparation, and transportation of food and other essentials were locked into their professions, as the emperors tried to assure a steady supply of these goods. A baker, for example, could not go into any other business, and his son was required to take up the trade at his death. In this period of severe depression, many localities could not pay their taxes. In such cases local tax collectors, who were themselves locked into service, had to make up the difference from their own funds. This system soon wiped out a whole class of moderately wealthy people and set the stage for the lack of social mobility that was a key characteristic of European society for many centuries to follow.

The emperors' measures did not really address Rome's central economic problems. During the turmoil of the third and fourth centuries, many free farmers

Gladiator Mosaic Made in the first half of the fourth century C.E., this mosaic from an estate outside Rome includes the name of each gladiator next to the figure. At the top a gladiator stands in a victory pose, while the fallen gladiator at the bottom is marked with the symbol Ø, indicating that he has died in combat. Many of the gladiators in this mosaic, such as those at the left, appear less fit and fearsome than the gladiators depicted in movies, more closely reflecting the reality that gladiatorial combat was a job undertaken by a variety of people. (Galleria Borghese, Rome, Italy/Scala/Art Resource, NY)

and their families were killed by invaders or renegade soldiers, or abandoned farms ravaged in the fighting. Consequently, large tracts of land lay untended. Landlords with ample resources began at once to claim as much of this land as they could, often hiring back the free farmers who had previously worked the land as paid labor or tenants. The huge estates that resulted, called villas, were self-sufficient and became islands of stability in an unsettled world. In return for the protection and security landlords could offer, many small landholders gave over their lands and their freedom. To guarantee a supply of labor, landlords denied them the freedom to move elsewhere. Henceforth they and their families worked their patrons' land, not their own. Free men and women were becoming tenant farmers bound to the land, what would later be called serfs.

The Acceptance of Christianity

The crisis of the third century seemed to some emperors, including Diocletian, to be the punishment of the gods. Diocletian increased persecution of Christians, hoping that the gods would restore their blessing on Rome. Yet his persecutions were never very widespread or long-lived, and by the late third century most Romans tolerated Christianity, even if they did not practice it.

Constantine reversed Diocletian's policy and instead ordered toleration of all religions in the Edict of Milan, issued in 313. He supported the church throughout his reign, expecting in return the support of church officials in maintaining order, and late in his life he was baptized as a Christian. Constantine also freed the clergy from imperial taxation and endowed the building of Christian churches. He allowed others to make gifts to the church as well, decreeing in 321: "Every man, when dying, shall have the right to bequeath as much of his property as he desires to the holy and venerable Catholic Church. And such wills are not to be broken."[4] Constantine also declared Sunday a public holiday, choosing it over the Jewish holy day of Saturday because it fit with his own worship of the sun-god, a practice shared by many Romans. Christians henceforth altered their practices to follow the emperor's decrees.

Helped in part by its favored position in the empire, Christianity slowly became the leading religion, and emperors after Constantine continued to promote it. In 380 the emperor Theodosius (r. 379–395) made Christianity the official religion of the empire. He allowed the church to establish its own courts and to use its own body of law, called "canon law." With this he laid the foundation for later growth in church power (see Chapter 8).

Chapter Summary

The Italian peninsula was settled by many different groups, including Greeks in the south and Etruscans in the north. The Etruscans built cities and expanded southward into central Italy, where they influenced the culture of the small town that was growing into the city of Rome. Rome prospered and expanded its own territories, establishing a republican government led by the Senate and broadening the base of power to address social conflicts. In a series of wars (most significantly, the Punic Wars) the Romans conquered the Mediterranean, creating an overseas empire that brought them unheard-of power and wealth, but also social unrest and civil war. The meteoric rise to power of the politician and general Julius Caesar in the first century B.C.E. led to his assassination, but his grandnephew Augustus finally restored peace and order to Rome. He assumed many of the traditional republican offices, but in actuality he turned the republic into an empire.

Augustus and his successors further expanded Roman territories, and by the second century C.E. the Roman Empire extended from Scotland in the northwest to Persia in the east and Egypt in the south. The city of Rome became the magnificent capital of the empire, increasingly adorned with beautiful buildings and improved urban housing. The Roman provinces and frontiers also saw extensive prosperity through the growth of agriculture, industry, and trade connections that extended to India and China. Christianity, a religion created by the followers of Jesus of Nazareth, spread across the empire, beginning in the first century C.E. Initially some Roman officials and emperors persecuted Christians, but gradually hostility decreased, particularly as Christianity modified its teachings to make them more acceptable to wealthy and educated Romans and developed institutions modeled on those of the Roman Empire. Emperors in the fourth century first allowed Christianity and then made it the official religion of the empire, one of many measures through which they attempted to

CHRONOLOGY

753 B.C.E.	Traditional founding of the city of Rome
509 B.C.E.	Traditional date of the establishment of the Roman Republic
451–449 B.C.E.	Laws of the Twelve Tables written and issued
ca. 265 B.C.E.	Romans control most of Italy
264–241 B.C.E.; 218–201 B.C.E.; 149–146 B.C.E.	Punic Wars
53–31 B.C.E.	Civil wars among rival claimants to power
44 B.C.E.	Assassination of Julius Caesar
31 B.C.E.	Octavian (Augustus) defeats Antony and Cleopatra
27 B.C.E.	Senate grants Octavian the title "Augustus"; date marks the beginning of the Roman Empire
27 B.C.E.–68 C.E.	Julio-Claudian emperors; expansion into northern and western Europe
ca. 3 B.C.E.–29 C.E.	Life of Jesus
69–96 C.E.	Flavian emperors; restoration of order after civil wars
96–192 C.E.	Antonine emperors; prosperity and the height of the pax Romana
235–284 C.E.	Third-century crisis; civil war; invasions; economic decline
284–337 C.E.	Diocletian and Constantine attempt to reconstruct the empire
313 C.E.	Emperor Constantine issues Edict of Milan, allowing practice of all religions in the Roman Empire
380 C.E.	Emperor Theodosius makes Christianity the official religion of the empire
476 C.E.	Odoacer deposes the last Roman emperor in the West

solve the problems created by invasions and political turmoil. Their measures were successful in the East, where the Roman Empire lasted for another thousand years, but not in the West, where the Roman Empire ended in the fifth century.

NOTES

1. Polybius, *Histories*, vol. 1, trans. Evelyn Shuckburgh (New York: Macmillan and Co., 1889), p. 469.
2. Sallust, *War with Cataline* 10.1–3, trans. John Buckler.
3. Virgil, *Aeneid*, trans. Theodore C. Williams (Boston: Houghton Mifflin, 1910).
4. Maude Aline Huttman, ed. and trans., *The Establishment of Christianity and the Proscription of Paganism* (New York: AMS Press, 1967), p. 164.
5. Tacitus, *Agricola*, trans. A. R. Birley (Oxford: Oxford University Press, 1999), p. 22.

CONNECTIONS

The Roman Empire, with its powerful—and sometimes bizarre—leaders, magnificent buildings, luxurious clothing, and bloody amusements, has long fascinated people. Politicians and historians have closely studied the reasons for its successes and have even more closely analyzed the weaknesses that led to its eventual collapse. Despite the efforts of emperors and other leaders, the Western Roman Empire slowly broke apart and by the fifth century C.E. no longer existed. By the fourteenth century European scholars were beginning to see the fall of the Roman Empire as one of the great turning points in Western history, the end of the classical era. That began the practice of dividing Western history into different periods—eventually, the ancient, medieval, and modern eras. Those categories still shape the way that Western history is taught and learned.

This three-part conceptualization also shapes the periodization of world history. As you saw in Chapter 4 and will see in Chapter 7, China is also understood to have had a classical age, and, as you will read in Chapter 11, the Maya of Mesoamerica did as well. The dates of these ages are different from those of the classical period in the Mediterranean, but there are striking similarities among all three places: successful large-scale administrative bureaucracies were established, trade flourished, cities grew, roads were built, and new cultural forms developed. In all three places—and in other countries described as having a classical era—this period was followed by an era of less prosperity and more warfare and destruction.

No large-scale story of rise and fall captures the experience of everyone, of course. For many people in the Roman world, neither the change from republic to empire nor the end of the empire altered their lives very much. They farmed or worked in cities, and hoped for the best for their families. They took in new ideas but blended them with old traditions. And for some, the judgment of later scholars that there was a pax Romana would have seemed a cruel joke. These people might have agreed with the statement the Roman historian Tacitus put in the mouth of Calgacus, a leader of the Britons, right before a battle with Roman invaders of his homeland: "They make a desert and call it 'peace.'"[5]

Review and Explore

Make It Stick

LearningCurve
Go online and use LearningCurve to retain what you've read.

Identify Key Terms

Identify and explain the significance of each item below.

Senate (p. 148)
consuls (p. 149)
patricians (p. 150)
plebeians (p. 150)
Punic Wars (p. 152)
paterfamilias (p. 153)
pax Romana (p. 162)
Messiah (p. 168)
pagan (p. 168)
bishop (p. 170)

Review the Main Ideas

Answer the focus questions from each section of the chapter.

1. How did the Romans come to dominate Italy, and what political institutions did they create? (p. 146)
2. How did Rome expand its power beyond Italy, and what were the effects of this expansion? (p. 151)
3. What was life like in Rome, and what was it like in the provinces? (p. 162)
4. What was Christianity, and how did it affect life in the Roman Empire? (p. 167)
5. How did the emperors respond to political, economic, and religious issues in the third and fourth centuries? (p. 170)

Make Connections

Analyze the larger developments and continuities within and across chapters.

1. What allowed large empires in the ancient world, including the Persian (Chapter 2), the Mauryan (Chapter 3), and the Roman, to govern vast territories and many different peoples successfully?
2. Looking over the long history of Rome, do interactions with non-Romans or conflicts among Romans themselves appear to be the most significant drivers of change? Why?
3. No classical Chinese thinker knew about Roman political developments, but the issues they considered, such as how to achieve order and what made government strong, could also be applied to Rome. How do you think Confucians, Daoists, and Legalists (Chapter 4) would have assessed the Roman Republic? The Roman Empire?

LaunchPad
Online Document Project

Queen Cleopatra

What do Roman depictions of Cleopatra reveal about the attitudes and values of her time?

Explore Roman accounts of Cleopatra to see what light they shed on political, social, and cultural values in the late republic and early empire, and then complete a quiz and writing assignment based on the evidence and details from this chapter.

See the inside front cover to learn more.

Suggested Reading

Aldrete, Gregory S. *Daily Life in the Roman City*. 2004. Reveals the significance of ordinary Roman life in the city of Rome, its port Ostia, and Pompeii.

Canfora, Luciano. *Julius Caesar: The Life and Times of the People's Dictator*. 2007. Provides a new interpretation of Caesar that puts him fully in the context of his times.

Clark, Gillian. *Christianity and Roman Society*. 2004. Surveys the evolution of Christian life among Christians and with their pagan neighbors.

Evans, J. K. *War, Women, and Children in Ancient Rome*. 2000. Provides a concise survey of how war affected the home front in wartime.

Everitt, Anthony. *Augustus: The Life of Rome's First Emperor*. 2007. A lively biography that traces Augustus's rise to power.

Forsythe, Gary A. *A Critical History of Early Rome from Prehistory to the First Punic War*. 2005. Uses archaeological findings as well as written sources to examine the political, social, and religious developments of early Rome.

Freeman, Charles. *A New History of Early Christianity*. 2010. A survey of the first four centuries of Christianity, written for a general audience.

Goldsworthy, Adrian. *Roman Warfare*. 2000. A concise treatment of warfare from republican to imperial times.

Haynes, Sybille. *Etruscan Civilization: A Cultural History*. 2005. Deals with cultural history, with special emphasis on Etruscan women.

Holland, Tom. *Rubicon, the Triumph and Tragedy of the Roman Republic*. 2003. Gives a lively account of the disintegration of the republic from the Gracchi to Caesar's death.

Joshel, Sandra R. *Slavery in the Roman World*. 2010. An overview of Roman slavery, designed for students.

Knapp, Robert. *Invisible Romans*. 2011. A view of Roman life that focuses on ordinary men and women: soldiers, slaves, laborers, housewives, gladiators, and outlaws.

Kyle, Donald G. *Sport and Spectacle in the Ancient World*. 2007. Deals in grim detail with the ritualized violence of the gladiatorial games.

Warrior, Valerie. *Roman Religion*. 2006. A relatively brief study that examines the actual practices of Roman religion in their social contexts.

East Asia and the Spread of Buddhism

221 B.C.E.–800 C.E.

7

Palace Maid

Ceramic models of attractive young women were often placed in Chinese tombs, reflecting hopes for the afterlife. (© Panorama/The Image Works)

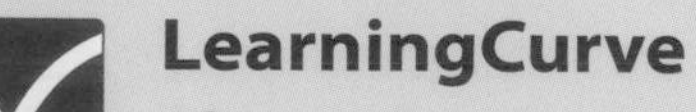

LearningCurve
After reading the chapter, go online and use LearningCurve to retain what you've read.

Chapter Preview

East Asia was transformed over the millennium from 221 B.C.E. to 800 C.E. At the beginning of this era, China had just been unified into a single state upon the Qin defeat of all the rival states of the Warring States Period, but it still faced major military challenges with the confederation of the nomadic Xiongnu to its north. At the time China was the only place in East Asia with writing, large cities, and complex state organizations. Over the next several centuries, East Asia changed dramatically as new states emerged. To protect an emerging trade in silk and other valuables, Han China sent armies far into Central Asia. War, trade, diplomacy, missionary activity, and the pursuit of learning led the Chinese to travel to distant lands and people from distant lands to go to China. Among the results were the spread of Buddhism from India and Central Asia to China and the adaptation of many elements of Chinese culture by near neighbors, especially Korea and Japan. Buddhism came to provide a common set of ideas and visual images to all the cultures of East Asia, much the way Christianity linked societies in Europe.

Increased communication stimulated state formation among China's neighbors: Tibet, Korea, Manchuria, Vietnam, and Japan. Written Chinese was increasingly used as an international language by the ruling elites of these countries, and the new states usually adopted political models from China as well. By 800 C.E. each of these regions was well on its way to developing a distinct political and cultural identity.

The Age of Empire in China: The Qin and Han Dynasties

☐ What were the social, cultural, and political consequences of the unification of China under the strong centralized governments of the Qin and Han empires?

In much the same period in which Rome created a huge empire, the Qin and Han rulers in China created an empire on a similar scale. Like the Roman Empire (see Chapter 6), the Chinese empire was put together through force of arms and held in place by sophisticated centralized administrative machinery. The governments created by the Qin and Han Dynasties affected many facets of Chinese social, cultural, and intellectual life.

The Qin Unification, 221–206 B.C.E.

In 221 B.C.E., after decades of constant warfare, Qin (chin), the state that had adopted Legalist policies during the Warring States Period (see page 109), succeeded in defeating the last of its rivals, and China was unified for the first time in many centuries. Deciding that the title "king" was not grand enough, the king of Qin invented the title "emperor" (*huangdi*). He called himself the First Emperor (*Shihuangdi*) in anticipation of a long line of successors. His state, however, did not long outlast him.

Once he ruled all of China, the First Emperor and his shrewd Legalist minister Li Si embarked on a sweeping program of centralization that touched the lives of nearly everyone in China. To cripple the nobility of the defunct states, who could have posed serious threats, the First Emperor ordered the nobles to leave their lands and move to the capital. The private possession of arms was outlawed to make it more difficult for subjects to rebel. The First Emperor dispatched officials to administer the territory that had been conquered and controlled the officials through a long list of regulations, reporting requirements, and penalties for inadequate performance. These officials owed their power and positions entirely to the favor of the emperor and had no hereditary rights to their offices.

To harness the enormous human resources of his people, the First Emperor ordered a census of the population. Census information helped the imperial bureaucracy to plan its activities: to estimate the cost of public works, the tax revenues needed to pay for them, and the labor force available for military service and building projects. To make it easier to administer all regions uniformly, the Chinese script was standardized, outlawing regional variations in the ways words were written. The First Emperor also standardized weights, measures, coinage, and even the axle lengths of carts (important because roads became deeply rutted from carts' wheels). To make it easier for Qin armies to move rapidly, thousands of miles of roads were built. Good roads indirectly facilitated trade. Most of the labor on the projects came from drafted farmers or convicts working out their sentences.

Some modern Chinese historians have glorified the First Emperor as a bold conqueror who let no obstacle stop him, but the traditional evaluation was almost entirely negative. For centuries Chinese historians castigated him as a cruel, arbitrary, impetuous, suspicious, and superstitious megalomaniac. Hundreds of thousands of subjects were drafted to build the **Great Wall** (ca. 230–208 B.C.E.), a rammed-earth fortification along the northern border between the Qin realm and the land controlled by the nomadic Xiongnu. After Li Si complained that scholars (especially Confucians) used records of the past to denigrate the emperor's achievements and undermine popular support, the emperor had all writings other than useful manuals on topics such as agriculture, medicine, and divination collected and burned. As a result of this massive book burning, many ancient texts were lost.

Assassins tried to kill the First Emperor three times, and perhaps as a consequence he became obsessed with discovering the secrets of immortality. He spent lavishly on a tomb designed to protect him in the afterlife. Although the central chambers have not yet been excavated, in nearby pits archaeologists have unearthed thousands of life-size terra-cotta figures of armed soldiers and horses lined up to protect him.

Army of the First Emperor The thousands of life-size ceramic soldiers buried in pits about a half mile from the First Emperor's tomb help us imagine the Qin military machine. It was the Qin emperor's concern with the afterlife that led him to construct such a lifelike guard. The soldiers were originally painted in bright colors, and they held real bronze weapons. (Robert Harding World Imagery)

Like Ashoka in India a few decades earlier (see page 83), the First Emperor erected many stone inscriptions to inform his subjects of his goals and accomplishments. He had none of Ashoka's modesty, however. On one stone he described the conquest of the other states this way:

> The six states, insatiable and perverse, would not make an end of slaughter, until, pitying the people, the emperor sent troops to punish the wicked and display his might. His penalties were just, his actions true, his power spread far, all submitted to his rule. He wiped out tyrants, rescued the common people, brought peace to the four corners of the earth. His enlightened laws spread far and wide as examples to All Under Heaven until the end of time. Great is he indeed! The whole universe obeys his sagacious will; his subjects praise his achievements and have asked to inscribe them on stone for posterity.[1]

• **Great Wall** A rammed-earth fortification built along the northern border of China during the reign of the First Emperor.

After the First Emperor died in 210 B.C.E., the Qin state unraveled. The Legalist institutions designed to concentrate power in the hands of the ruler made the stability of the government dependent on his strength and character, and his heir proved ineffective. The heir was murdered by his younger brother, and uprisings soon followed.

The Han Dynasty, 206 B.C.E.–220 C.E.

The eventual victor in the struggle for power that ensued in the wake of the collapse of the Qin Dynasty was Liu Bang, known in history as Emperor Gaozu (r. 202–195 B.C.E.). The First Emperor of Qin was from the Zhou aristocracy. Gaozu was, by contrast, from a modest family of commoners, so his elevation to emperor is evidence of how thoroughly the Qin Dynasty had destroyed the old order.

Gaozu did not disband the centralized government created by the Qin, but he did remove its most unpopular features. Harsh laws were canceled, taxes were sharply reduced, and a policy of noninterference was adopted in an effort to promote economic recovery. With policies of this sort, relative peace, and the extension of China's frontiers, the Chinese population grew rapidly (Map 7.1). The census of 2 C.E. recorded a population of 58 million, the earliest indication of China's large population. Few other societies kept such good

MAP 7.1 The Han Empire, 206 B.C.E.–220 C.E. The Han Dynasty asserted sovereignty over vast regions from Korea in the east to Central Asia in the west and Vietnam in the south. Once garrisons were established, traders were quick to follow, leading to considerable spread of Chinese material culture in East Asia. Chinese goods, especially silk, were in demand far beyond East Asia, promoting long-distance trade across Eurasia.

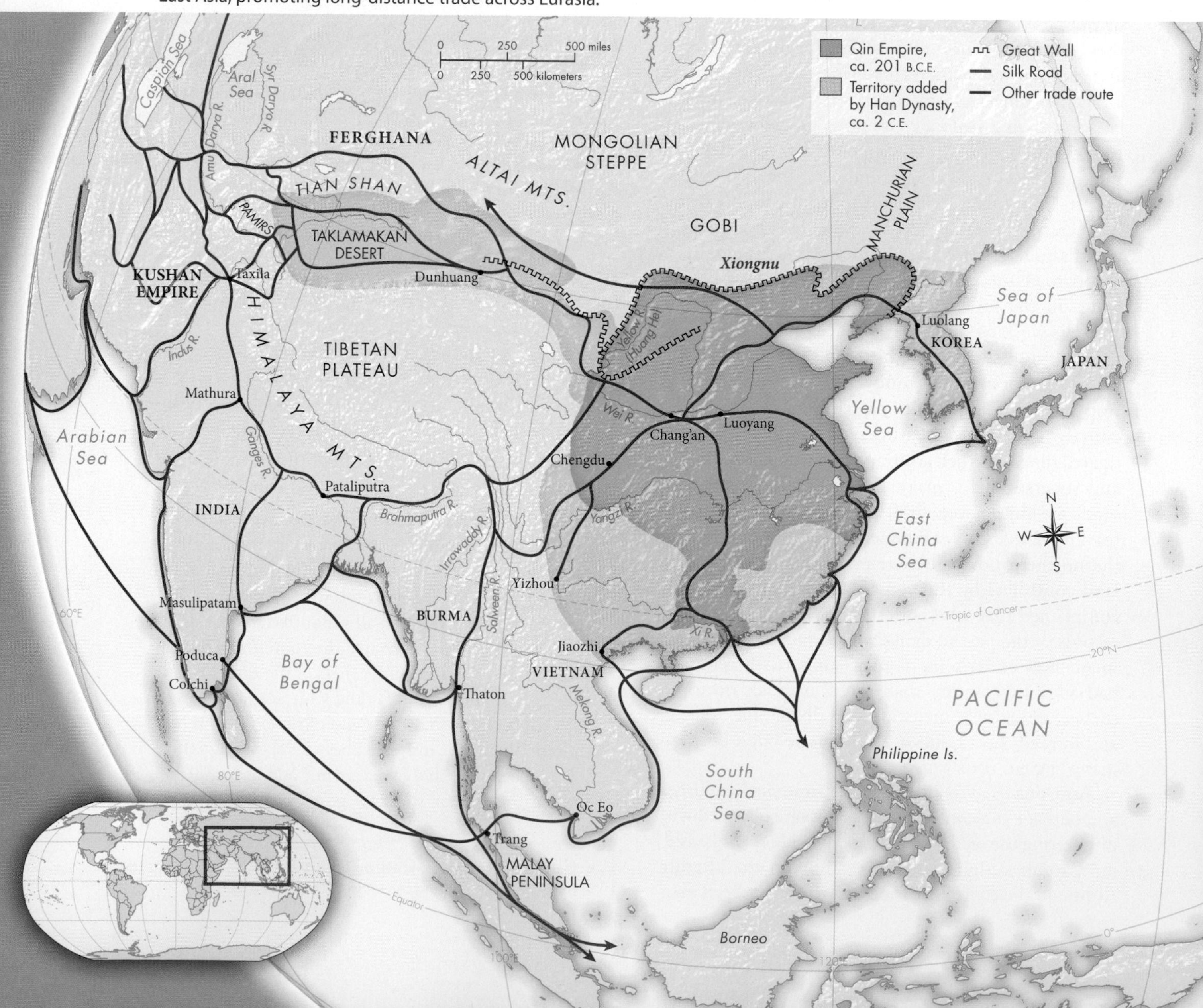

records, making comparisons difficult, but high-end estimates for the Roman Empire are in a similar range (50–70 million).

The Han government was largely supported by the taxes and forced labor demanded of farmers, but this revenue regularly fell short of the government's needs. To pay for his military campaigns, Emperor Wu, the "Martial Emperor" (r. 141–87 B.C.E.), took over the minting of coins, confiscated the land of nobles, sold offices and titles, and increased taxes on private businesses. A widespread suspicion of commerce as an unproductive exploitation of the true producers made it easy to levy especially heavy assessments on merchants. The worst blow to businessmen, however, was the government's decision to enter into market competition with them by selling the commodities that had been collected as taxes. In 119 B.C.E. government monopolies were established in the production of iron, salt, and liquor. These enterprises had previously been sources of great profit for private entrepreneurs. Large-scale grain dealing also had been a profitable business, and the government now took that over as well. Grain was to be bought where it was plentiful and its price low and to be either stored in granaries or transported to areas of scarcity. This procedure was supposed to eliminate speculation in grain, provide more constant prices, and bring profit to the government.

Bronze Mirror The backs of bronze mirrors were frequently decorated with images of deities and animals and with auspicious words. As viewers turned the mirrors, they saw different scenes. This Han mirror features an outer border with semicircles decorated with cloud patterns and squares with words written on them. In the center are deities. (Mirror Featuring Deities and Kings in Three Sections Surrounded by Rings of Squares and Semicircles [bronze]. Eastern Han Dynasty [25–220]/Cleveland Museum of Art, Ohio, U.S.A./Gift of Drs. Thomas and Martha Carter in Honor of Sherman E. Lee/The Bridgeman Art Library)

Han Intellectual and Cultural Life

In contrast to the Qin Dynasty, which favored Legalism, the Han came to promote Confucianism and recruit officials on the basis of their Confucian learning or Confucian moral qualities. The Han government's efforts to recruit men trained in the Confucian classics marked the beginning of the Confucian scholar-official system, one of the most distinctive features of imperial China.

However, the Confucianism that made a comeback during the Han Dynasty was a changed Confucianism. Although Confucian texts had fed the First Emperor's bonfires, some dedicated scholars had hidden their books, and others had memorized whole works: one ninety-year-old man was able to recite two long books almost in their entirety. The ancient books recovered in this way—called the **Confucian classics**—were revered as repositories of the wisdom of the past. Confucian scholars treated these classics with piety and attempted to make them more useful as sources of moral guidance by writing commentaries on them. Many Confucian scholars specialized in a single classic, and teachers passed on to their disciples their understanding of each sentence in the work. Other Han Confucians went to the opposite extreme, developing comprehensive cosmological theories that explained the world in terms of cyclical flows of yin and yang (see page 110) and the five phases (fire, water, earth, metal, and wood). Some used these theories to elevate the role of the emperor, who alone had the capacity to link the realms of Heaven, earth, and man. Natural disasters such as floods or earthquakes were viewed as portents that the emperor had failed in his role of maintaining the proper balance among the forces of Heaven and earth.

Han art and literature reveal a fascination with omens, portents, spirits, immortals, and occult forces. Emperor Wu tried to make contact with the world of gods and immortals through elaborate sacrificial offerings of food and wine, and he welcomed astrologers, alchemists, seers, and shamans to his court. He marveled at stories of deities such as the Queen Mother of

• **Confucian classics** The ancient texts recovered during the Han Dynasty that Confucian scholars treated as sacred scriptures.

the West and the Yellow Emperor, who took his entire court with him when he ascended to the realm of the immortals. Much of this interest in immortality and communicating with the spirit world was absorbed into the emerging religion of Daoism, which also drew on the philosophical ideas of Laozi and Zhuangzi (see page 108).

A major intellectual accomplishment of the Han Dynasty was history writing. Sima Qian (145–ca. 85 B.C.E.) wrote a comprehensive history of China from the time of the mythical sage-kings of high antiquity to his own day, dividing his account into a chronology recounting political events, biographies of key individuals, and treatises on subjects such as geography, taxation, and court rituals. As an official of the emperor, he had access to important people and documents and to the imperial library. Like the Greek historians Herodotus and Thucydides (see page 125), Sima Qian believed fervently in visiting the sites where history was made, examining artifacts, and questioning people about events. He was also interested in China's geography and local history. The result of his research, ten years or more in the making, was ***Records of the Grand Historian***, a massive work of literary and historical genius. In the chapter devoted to moneymakers, he described how the Ping family made its fortune:

> Lu people are customarily cautious and miserly, but the Ping family of Cao were particularly so. They started out by smelting iron and in time accumulated a fortune of a hundred million cash. All the members of the family from the father and elder brothers down to the sons and grandsons, however, made a promise that they would "Never look down without picking up something useful; never look up without grabbing something of value." They traveled about to all the provinces and kingdoms, selling goods on credit, lending money and trading. It was because of their influence that so many people in Zou and Lu abandoned scholarship and turned to the pursuit of profit.[2]

From examples like these, Sima Qian concluded that wealth has no permanent master: "It finds its way to the man of ability like the spokes of a wheel converging upon the hub, and from the hands of the worthless it falls like shattered tiles."[3] For centuries to come, Sima Qian's work set the standard for Chinese historical writing, although most of the histories modeled after it covered only a single dynasty. The first of these was the work of three members of the Ban family in the first century C.E. (See "Individuals in Society: The Ban Family," at right.)

• ***Records of the Grand Historian*** A comprehensive history of China written by Sima Qian.

The circulation of books like Sima Qian's was made easier by the invention of paper, which the Chinese traditionally date to 105 C.E. Scribes had previously written on strips of bamboo and wood or rolls of silk. Cai Lun, to whom the Chinese attribute the invention of paper, worked the fibers of rags, hemp, bark, and other scraps into sheets of paper. Paper, thus, was somewhat similar to the papyrus made from pounded reeds in ancient Egypt. Though much less durable than wood, paper was far cheaper than silk and became a convenient means of conveying the written word. Compared to papyrus, it depended less on a specific source of plant fiber and so could be produced in many areas.

Inner Asia and the Silk Road

The difficulty of defending against the nomadic pastoral peoples to the north in the region known as Inner Asia is a major reason China came to favor a centralized bureaucratic form of government. Resources from the entire subcontinent were needed to maintain control of the northern border.

Chinese civilization did not spread easily to the grasslands north of China proper, because those lands were too dry and cold to make good farmland. Herding sheep, horses, camels, and other animals made better economic use of those lands. By the third century B.C.E. several different peoples practicing nomadic pastoralism lived in those regions, moving with their herds north in summer and south in winter. Families lived in tents that could be taken down and moved to the next camp. Herds were tended on horseback, and everyone learned to ride from a young age. Especially impressive from the Chinese perspective was the ability of nomad horsemen to shoot arrows while riding horseback. Chinese farmers and Inner Asian herders had such different modes of life that it is not surprising that they had little respect for each other. For most of the imperial period, Chinese farmers looked on the northern non-Chinese horsemen as gangs of bullies who thought robbing was easier than working for a living. The nomads identified glory with military might and viewed farmers as contemptible weaklings.

In the late third century B.C.E. the Xiongnu (possibly the same group that was known in the West as the Huns) formed the first great confederation of nomadic tribes (see Map 7.1). The Qin's Great Wall was built to defend against the Xiongnu, and the Qin sent out huge armies in pursuit of them. The early Han emperors tried to make peace with them, offering generous gifts of silk, rice, cash, and even imperial princesses as brides. But these policies were controversial, since critics thought they merely strengthened the enemy. Xiongnu power did not wane, and in 166 B.C.E. 140,000 Xiongnu raided to within a hundred miles of the Chinese capital.

Individuals in Society

The Ban Family

BAN BIAO (3–54 C.E.), A SUCCESSFUL OFFICIAL FROM A family with an envied library, had three highly accomplished children: his twin sons, the general Ban Chao (32–102) and the historian Ban Gu (32–92); and his daughter, Ban Zhao (ca. 45–120). After distinguishing himself as a junior officer in campaigns against the Xiongnu, Ban Chao was sent in 73 C.E. to the western regions to see about the possibility of restoring Chinese overlordship there, which had been lost several decades earlier. Ban Chao spent most of the next three decades in Central Asia. Through patient diplomacy and a show of force, he re-established Chinese control over the oasis cities of Central Asia, and in 92 he was appointed protector general of the area.

His twin brother, Ban Gu, was one of the most accomplished writers of his age, excelling in a distinctive literary form known as the rhapsody (*fu*). His "Rhapsody on the Two Capitals" is in the form of a dialogue between a guest from Chang'an and his host in Luoyang. It describes the palaces, spectacles, scenic spots, local products, and customs of the two great cities. Emperor Zhang (r. 76–88) was fond of literature and often had Ban Gu accompany him on hunts or travels. He also had him edit a record of the court debates he held on issues concerning the Confucian classics.

Ban Biao was working on the *History of the Former Han Dynasty* when he died in 54. Ban Gu took over this project, modeling it on Sima Qian's *Records of the Grand Historian*. He added treatises on law, geography, and bibliography, the last a classified list of books in the imperial library.

Because of his connection to a general out of favor, Ban Gu was sent to prison in 92, where he soon died. At that time the *History of the Former Han Dynasty* was still incomplete. The emperor called on Ban Gu's widowed sister, Ban Zhao, to finish it. She came to the palace, where she not only worked on the history but also became a teacher of the women of the palace. According to the *History of the Later Han*, she taught them the classics, history, astronomy, and mathematics. In 106 an infant succeeded to the throne, and the widow of an earlier emperor became regent. This empress frequently turned to Ban Zhao for advice on government policies.

Ban Zhao credited her own education to her learned father and cultured mother and became an advocate of the education of girls. In her *Admonitions for Women*, Ban Zhao objected that many families taught their sons to read but not their daughters. She did not claim girls should have the same education as boys; after all, "just as yin and yang differ, men and women have different characteristics." Women, she wrote, will do well if they cultivate womanly virtues such as humility. "Humility means yielding and acting respectful, putting others first and oneself last, never mentioning one's own good deeds or denying one's own faults, enduring insults and bearing with mistreatment, all with due trepidation."* In subsequent centuries Ban Zhao's *Admonitions* became one of the most commonly used texts for the education of Chinese girls.

Ban Zhao, Han Dynasty historian. (© Fotoe/Uniphoto Press, Japan/Ancient Art & Architecture Collection, Ltd.)

QUESTIONS FOR ANALYSIS

1. What inferences can you draw from the fact that a leading general had a brother who was a literary man?
2. What does Ban Zhao's life tell us about women in her society? How do you reconcile her personal accomplishments with the advice she gave for women's education?

*Patricia Buckley Ebrey, ed., *Chinese Civilization: A Sourcebook*, 2d ed., revised and expanded (New York: Free Press, 1993), p. 75.

LaunchPad
Online Document Project

What do Ban Zhao's writings reveal about attitudes toward women during her time? Read sources by and about Ban Zhao, and then complete a quiz and writing assignment based on the evidence and details from this chapter.

See inside the front cover to learn more.

Xiongnu Metalwork The metal ornaments of the Xiongnu provide convincing evidence that they were in contact with nomadic pastoralists farther west in Asia, such as the Scythians, who also fashioned metal plaques and buckles in animal designs. This buckle or ornament is made of gold and is about 3 inches tall. (Belt buckle with paired felines attacking ibexes. 3rd–2nd B.C.E. Central Asia, Mongolia or southern Siberia. Gold. Gift of J. Pierpont Morgan, 1917 [17.190.1672]. The Metropolitan Museum of Art, New York, NY, USA/Image copyright © The Metropolitan Museum of Art/Image source: Art Resource, NY)

Emperor Wu then decided that China had to push the Xiongnu back. He sent several armies of 100,000 to 300,000 troops deep into Xiongnu territory. These costly campaigns were of limited value because the Xiongnu were a moving target: fighting nomads was not like attacking walled cities. If the Xiongnu did not want to fight the Chinese troops, they simply moved their camps. To try to find allies and horses, Emperor Wu turned his attention west, toward Central Asia. From an envoy he sent into Bactria, Parthia, and Ferghana in 139 B.C.E., the Chinese learned for the first time of other civilized states comparable to China. The envoy described Ferghana as an urban society 10,000 *li* (about 3,000 miles) west of China, where grapes were grown for wine and the horses were particularly fine. In Parthia he was impressed by the use of silver coins stamped with the image of the king's face. These regions, he reported, were familiar with Chinese products, especially silk, and did a brisk trade in them.

In 114 B.C.E. Emperor Wu sent an army into Ferghana and gained recognition of Chinese overlordship in the area, thus obtaining control over the trade routes across Central Asia commonly called the **Silk Road** (see Map 7.1). The city-states along this route could carry out the trade on which they depended more conveniently with Chinese garrisons to protect them.

At the same time, Emperor Wu sent troops into northern Korea to establish military districts that would flank the Xiongnu on their eastern border. By 111 B.C.E. the Han government also had extended its rule south into Nam Viet, which extended from south China into what is now northern Vietnam. Thus, during Emperor Wu's reign, the territorial reach of the Han state was vastly extended.

During the Han Dynasty, China developed a **tributary system** to regulate contact with foreign powers. States and tribes beyond its borders sent envoys bearing gifts and received gifts in return. Over the course of the dynasty, the Han government's outlay on these gifts was huge, perhaps as much as 10 percent of state revenue. In 25 B.C.E., for instance, the government gave tributary states twenty thousand rolls of silk cloth and about twenty thousand pounds of silk floss. Although the tributary system was a financial burden to the Chinese, it reduced the cost of defense and offered China confirmation that it was the center of the civilized world.

The silk given to the Xiongnu and other northern tributaries often entered the trading networks of Persian, Parthian, and Indian merchants, who carried it by caravans across Asia. There was a market both for skeins of silk thread and for silk cloth woven in Chinese or Syrian workshops. Caravans returning to China carried gold, horses, and occasionally handicrafts of West Asian origin, such as glass beads and cups. Through the trade along the Silk Road, the Chinese learned of new foodstuffs, including walnuts, pomegranates, sesame, and coriander, all of which came to be grown in China. This trade was largely carried by the two-humped Bactrian camel, which had been bred in Central Asia since the first century B.C.E. With a heavy coat of hair to withstand the bitter cold of winter, each camel could carry about five hundred pounds of cargo. (See "Global Trade: Silk," page 186.)

Maintaining a military presence so far from the center of China was expensive. To cut costs, the government set up self-supporting military colonies, recruited Xiongnu tribes to serve as auxiliary forces, and established vast government horse farms. Still, military expenses threatened to bankrupt the Han government.

- **Silk Road** The trade routes across Central Asia linking China to western Eurasia.
- **tributary system** A system first established during the Han Dynasty to regulate contact with foreign powers. States and tribes beyond its borders sent envoys bearing gifts and received gifts in return.

Life in Han China

How were ordinary people's lives affected by the creation of a huge Han bureaucratic empire? The lucky ones who lived in Chang'an or Luoyang, the great cities of the empire, got to enjoy the material benefits of increased long-distance trade and a boom in the production of luxury goods.

The government did not promote trade per se. The Confucian elite, like ancient Hebrew wise men, considered trade necessary but lowly. Agriculture and crafts were more honorable because they produced something, but merchants merely took advantage of others' shortages to make profits as middlemen. In a debate conducted in 81 B.C.E., the Confucian scholars argued: "If a country possesses a wealth of fertile land and yet its people are underfed, the reason is that merchants and workers have prospered while agriculture has been neglected."[4] This attitude justified the government's takeover of the grain, iron, and salt businesses. Still, the government indirectly promoted commerce by building roads and defending cities.

Markets were the liveliest places in the cities. Besides stalls selling goods of all kinds, markets offered fortune-tellers and entertainers. People flocked to puppet shows and performances of jugglers and acrobats. The markets were also used for the execution of criminals, to serve as a warning to onlookers.

Government patronage helped maintain the quality of craftsmanship in the cities. By the beginning of the first century C.E. China also had about fifty state-run ironworking factories. Chinese metalworking was the most advanced in the world at the time. In contrast to Roman blacksmiths, who hammered heated iron to make wrought iron tools, the Chinese knew how to liquefy iron and pour it into molds, producing tools with a higher carbon content that were harder and more durable. Han workmen turned out iron plowshares, agricultural tools with wooden handles, and weapons and armor.

Iron was replacing bronze in tools, but bronze-workers still turned out a host of goods. Bronze was prized for jewelry, mirrors, and dishes. Bronze was also used for minting coins and for precision tools such as carpenters' rules and adjustable wrenches. Surviving bronze gear-and-cog wheels bear eloquent testimony to the sophistication of Han machinery. Han metal-smiths were mass-producing superb crossbows long before the crossbow was dreamed of in Europe.

The bulk of the population in Han times and even into the twentieth century consisted of peasants living in villages of a few hundred households. Because the Han empire, much like the contemporaneous Roman Empire, drew its strength from a large population of free peasants who contributed both taxes and labor services to the state, the government had to try to keep peasants independent and productive. The economic insecurity of smallholders was described by one official in 178 B.C.E. in terms that could well have been repeated in most later dynasties:

> They labour at plowing in the spring and hoeing in the summer, harvesting in the autumn and storing foodstuff in winter, cutting wood, performing labour service for the local government, all the while exposed to the dust of spring, the heat of summer, the storms of autumn, and the chill of winter. Through all four seasons they never get a day off. They need funds to cover such obligations as entertaining guests, burying the dead, visiting the sick, caring for orphans, and bringing up the young. No matter how hard they work they can be ruined by floods or droughts, or cruel and arbitrary officials who impose taxes at the wrong times or keep changing their orders. When taxes fall due, those with produce have to sell it at half price [to raise the needed cash], and those without [anything to sell] have to borrow [at such high rates] they will have to pay back twice what they

Ceramic Model of a Pigsty Chinese farmers regularly raised pigs, keeping them in walled-off pens and feeding them scraps. This Han Dynasty model of such a pigsty was placed in a tomb to represent the material goods one hoped the deceased would enjoy in the afterlife. (Funerary model of a pigsty [earthenware], Western Han Dynasty [206 B.C.–A.D. 24]/Minneapolis Institute of Arts, Minnesota, U.S.A./Gift of Alan and Dena Naylor in memory of Thomas E. Leary/The Bridgeman Art Library)

Global Trade

Silk

Silk was one of the earliest commodities to stimulate international trade. By 2500 B.C.E. Chinese farmers had domesticated *Bombyx mori*, the Chinese silkworm, and by 1000 B.C.E. they were making fine fabrics with complex designs. Sericulture (silkmaking) is labor-intensive. In order for silkworms to spin their cocoons, they have to be fed chopped leaves from mulberry trees every few hours, day and night, during the month between hatching and spinning. The cocoons consist of a single filament several thousand feet long but a minuscule 0.025 millimeter thick. More than two thousand cocoons are needed to make a pound of silk. After the cocoons are boiled to loosen the natural gum that binds the filament, several strands of filament are twisted together to make yarns.

What made silk the most valued of all textiles was its beauty and versatility. It could be made into sheer gauzes, shiny satins, multicolored brocades, and plush velvets. Fine Han silks have been found in Xiongnu tombs in northern Mongolia. Korea and Japan not only imported silk but also began silk production themselves, and silk came to be used in both places in much the way it was used in China — for the clothes of the elite, for temple banners, and as a surface for writing and painting. Central Asia, Persia, India, and Southeast Asia also became producers of silk in distinctive local styles. Lacking suitable climates to produce silk, Mongolia and Tibet remained major importers of Chinese silks into modern times.

What makes the silk trade famous, however, is not the trade within Asia but the trade across Asia to Europe. In Roman times silk carried by caravans across Asia or by ships across the Indian Ocean became a high-status luxury item, said to cost its weight in gold. To satisfy Roman taste, imported silk fabrics were unraveled and rewoven in

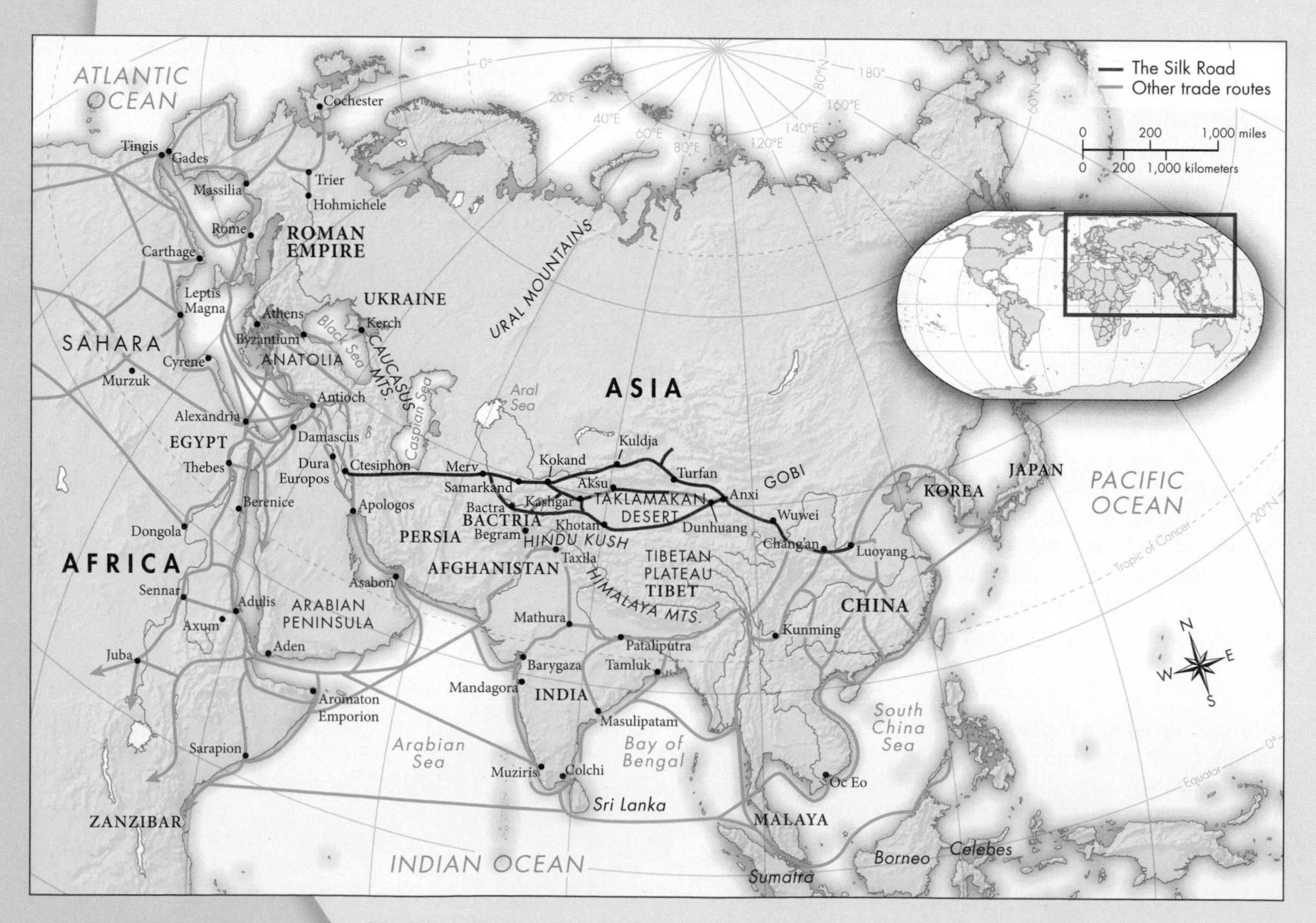

MAP 7.2 The Silk Trade in the Seventh Century C.E.

Syrian workshops. Although the techniques of sericulture gradually spread through Asia, they remained a mystery in the West until the Byzantine emperor Justinian in the sixth century C.E. had two monks bring back silkworms from China along with knowledge of how to care for them and process their cocoons.

In medieval times most of the silk imported into Europe came from Persia, the Byzantine Empire, or the Arab world. Venetian merchants handled much of the trade. Some of this fabric still survives in ancient churches, where it was used for vestments and altar clothes and to wrap relics. In the eleventh century Roger I, king of Sicily, captured groups of silk-workers from Athens and Corinth and moved them to Sicily, initiating the production of silk in western Europe. Over the next couple of centuries, Italy became a major silk producer, joined by France in the fifteenth century.

When the Venetian merchant Marco Polo traveled across Asia in the late thirteenth century, he found local silk for sale in Baghdad, Georgia, Persia, and elsewhere, but China remained the largest producer. He claimed that more than a thousand cartloads of silk were brought into the capital of China every day.

With the development of the sea route between western Europe and China from the sixteenth century on, Europe began importing large quantities of Chinese silk, much of it as silk floss — raw silk — to supply Italian, French, and English silk weavers. In 1750 almost 77.2 tons of raw silk and nearly 20,000 bolts of silk cloth were carried from China to Europe. By this period the aristocracy of Europe regularly wore silk clothes, including silk stockings.

Mechanization of silkmaking began in Europe in the seventeenth century. The Italians developed machines to "throw" the silk — doubling and twisting raw silk into threads suitable for weaving. In the early nineteenth century the introduction of Jacquard looms using punched cards made complex patterns easier to weave.

In the 1920s the silk industry was hit hard by the introduction of synthetic fibers, especially rayon and nylon. In the 1940s women in the United States and Europe switched from silk stockings to the much less expensive nylon stockings. European production of silk almost entirely collapsed. After China re-entered world trade in the early 1980s, China rapidly expanded its silk production for export. By 2003 there were more than two thousand silk enterprises in China, employing a million workers and supplying 80 percent of the total world trade in silk.

> borrowed. Some as a consequence sell their lands and houses, even their children and grandchildren.[5]

To fight peasant poverty, the government kept land taxes low (one-thirtieth of the harvest), provided relief in time of famine, and promoted up-to-date agricultural methods. Still, many hard-pressed peasants were left to choose between migration to areas where new lands could be opened and quasi-servile status as the dependents of a magnate. Throughout the Han period, Chinese farmers in search of land to till pushed into frontier areas, expanding Chinese domination at the expense of other ethnic groups, especially in central and south China.

The Chinese family in Han times was much like Roman (see page 153) and Indian (see page 71) families. In all three societies senior males had great authority, parents arranged their children's marriages, and brides normally joined their husbands' families. Other practices were more distinctive to China, such as the universality of patrilineal family names, the practice of dividing land equally among the sons in a family, and the great emphasis placed on the virtue of filial piety. The brief *Classic of Filial Piety*, which claimed that filial piety was the root of all virtue, gained wide circulation in Han times. The virtues of loyal wives and devoted mothers were extolled in the *Biographies of Exemplary Women*, which told the stories of women from China's past who were notable for giving their husbands good advice, knowing how to educate their sons, and sacrificing themselves when forced to choose between their fathers and husbands. The book also contained a few cautionary tales of scheming, jealous, manipulative women who brought destruction to all around them. One of the most commonly used texts for the education of women is Ban Zhao's *Admonitions for Women*, in which she extols the feminine virtues, such as humility. (See "Individuals in Society: The Ban Family," page 183.)

China and Rome

The empires of China and Rome (discussed in Chapter 6) were large, complex states governed by monarchs, bureaucracies, and standing armies. Both reached the people directly through taxation and conscription policies, and both invested in infrastructure such as roads and waterworks. The empires faced the similar challenge of having to work hard to keep land from becoming too concentrated in the hands of hard-to-tax wealthy magnates. In both empires people in neighboring areas that came under political domination were attracted to the conquerors' material goods, productive techniques, and other cultural products, resulting in gradual cultural assimilation. China and Rome also had similar frontier problems and tried similar solutions, such as recruiting "barbarian" soldiers and settling soldier-colonists.

Nevertheless, the differences between Rome and Han China are worth as much notice as the similarities. The Roman Empire was linguistically and culturally more diverse than China. In China there was only one written language; people in the Roman Empire still wrote in Greek and several other languages, and people in the eastern Mediterranean could claim more ancient civilizations. China did not have comparable cultural rivals. Politically the dynastic principle was stronger in China than in Rome. Han emperors were never chosen by the army or by any institution comparable to the Roman Senate, nor were there republican ideals in China. In contrast to the graduated forms of citizenship in Rome, Han China drew no distinctions between original and added territories. The social and economic structures also differed in the two empires. Slavery was much more important in Rome than in China, and merchants were more favored. Over time these differences put Chinese and Roman social and political development on different trajectories.

The Fall of the Han and the Age of Division

In the second century C.E. the Han government suffered a series of blows. A succession of child emperors required regents to rule in their place until they reached maturity, allowing the families of empresses to dominate the court. Emperors, once grown, turned to **eunuchs** (castrated palace servants) for help in ousting the empresses' families, only to find that the eunuchs were just as difficult to control. In 166 and 169 scholars who had denounced the eunuchs were arrested, killed, or banished from the capital and official life. Then in 184 a millenarian religious sect rose in massive revolt. The armies raised to suppress the rebels soon took to fighting among themselves. In 189 one general slaughtered two thousand eunuchs in the palace and took the Han emperor captive. After years of fighting, a stalemate was reached, with three warlords each controlling distinct territories in the north, the southeast, and the southwest. In 220 one of them forced the last of the Han emperors to abdicate, formally ending the Han Dynasty.

The period after the fall of the Han Dynasty is often referred to as the **Age of Division** (220–589). A brief reunification from 280 to 316 came to an end when non-Chinese who had been settling in north China since Han times seized the opportunity afforded by the political turmoil to take power. For the next two and a half centuries, north China was ruled by one or more non-Chinese dynasties (the Northern Dynasties), and the south was ruled by a sequence of four short-lived Chinese dynasties (the Southern Dynasties) centered in the area of the present-day city of Nanjing.

In the south a hereditary aristocracy entrenched itself in the higher reaches of officialdom. These families intermarried only with families of equivalent pedigree and compiled lists and genealogies of the most eminent families. They saw themselves as maintaining the high culture of the Han and looked on the emperors of the successive dynasties as upstarts—as military men rather than men of culture. In this aristocratic culture the arts of poetry and calligraphy flourished, and people began collecting writings by famous calligraphers.

Establishing the capital at Nanjing, south of the Yangzi River, had a beneficial effect on the economic development of the south. To pay for an army and to support the imperial court and aristocracy in a style that matched their pretensions, the government had to expand the area of taxable agricultural land, whether by settling migrants or converting the local inhabitants into taxpayers. The south, with its temperate climate and ample supply of water, offered nearly unlimited possibilities for such development.

The Northern Dynasties are interesting as the first case of alien rule in China. Ethnic tensions flared from time to time. In the late fifth century the Northern Wei (way) Dynasty (386–534) moved the capital from near the Great Wall to the ancient city of Luoyang, adopted Chinese-style clothing, and made Chinese the official language. But the armies remained in the hands of the non-Chinese Xianbei tribesmen. Soldiers who saw themselves as marginalized by the pro-Chinese reforms rebelled in 524. For the next fifty years north China was torn apart by struggles for power. It had long been the custom of the northern pastoral tribes to enslave those they captured; sometimes the residents of entire cities were enslaved. In 554, when the city of Jiangling was taken, a hundred thousand civilians were enslaved and distributed to generals and officials.

The Spread of Buddhism Out of India

☐ How did Buddhism find its way into East Asia, and what was its appeal and impact?

In much the same period that Christianity was spreading out of its original home in ancient Israel, Buddhism was spreading beyond India. Buddhism came to Central, East, and Southeast Asia with merchants and missionaries along the overland Silk Road, by sea from

- **eunuchs** Castrated males who played an important role as palace servants.
- **Age of Division** The period after the fall of the Han Dynasty, when China was politically divided.

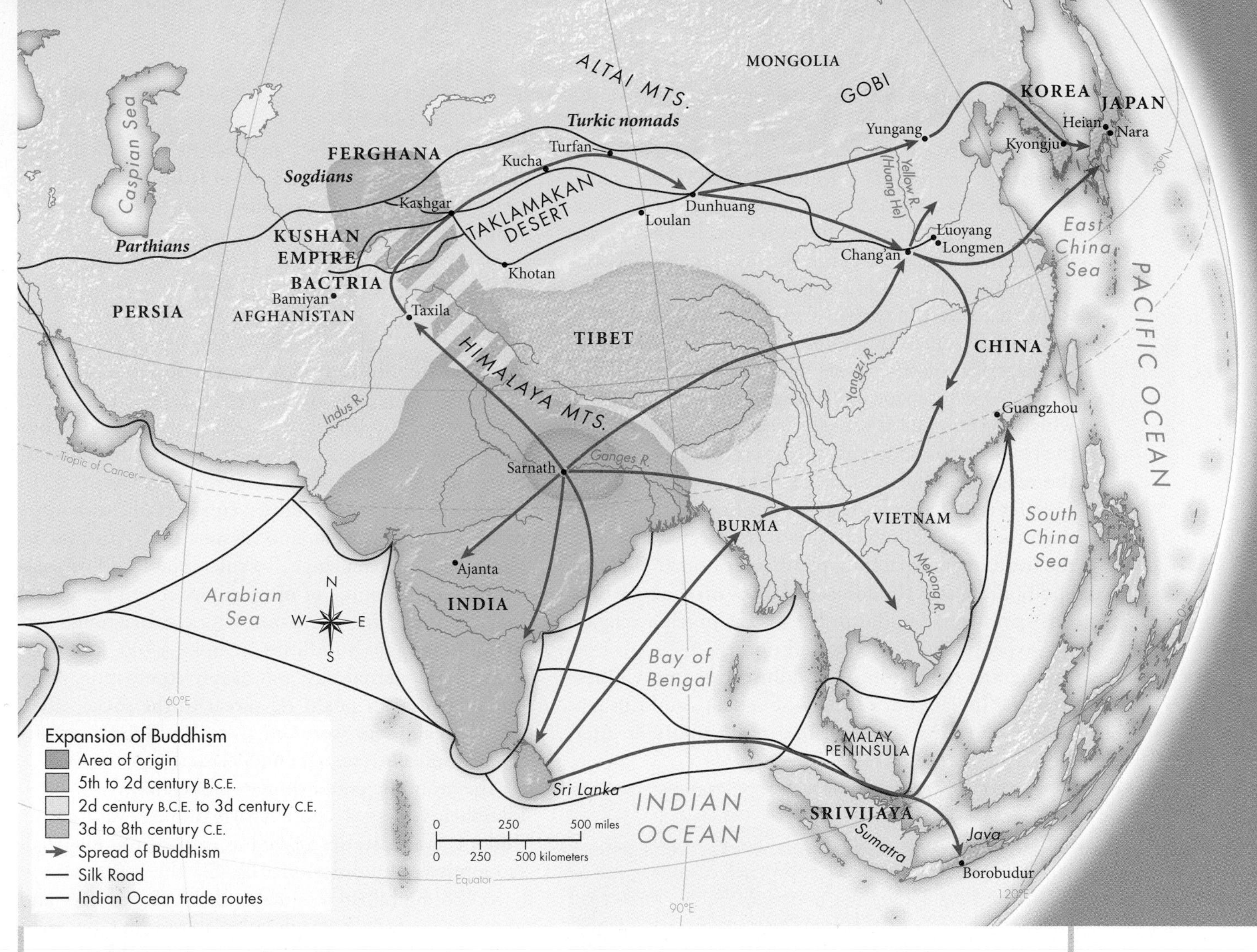

Mapping the Past

MAP 7.3 The Spread of Buddhism, ca. 500 B.C.E.–800 C.E. Buddhism spread throughout India in Ashoka's time and beyond India in later centuries. The different forms of Buddhism found in Asia today reflect this history. The Mahayana Buddhism of Japan came via Central Asia, China, and Korea, with a secondary later route through Tibet. The Theravada Buddhism of Southeast Asia came directly from India and indirectly through Sri Lanka.

ANALYZING THE MAP Trace the routes of the spread of Buddhism by time period. How fast did Buddhism spread?

CONNECTIONS Why do you think Buddhism spread more to the east of India than to the west?

India and Sri Lanka, and also through Tibet. Like Christianity, Buddhism was shaped by its contact with cultures in the different areas into which it spread, leading to several distinct forms.

Buddhism's Path Through Central Asia

Central Asia is a loose term used to refer to the vast area between the ancient civilizations of Persia, India, and China. Modern political borders are a product of competition for empire among the British, Russians, and Chinese in the mid-nineteenth century and have relatively little to do with the earlier history of the region. Through most of recorded history, the region was ethnically and culturally diverse; it was home to urban centers, especially at the oases along the Silk Road, and to animal herders in the mountains and grasslands.

Under Ashoka in India (see pages 83–85), Buddhism began to spread to Central Asia. This continued under the Kushan empire (ca. 50–250 C.E.), especially under the greatest Kushan king, Kanishka I (ca. 100 C.E.). In this region, where the influence of Greek art was strong, artists began to depict the Buddha in human form. Over the next several centuries most of the city-states of Central Asia became centers of Buddhism, from Bamiyan northwest of Kabul, to Kucha, Khotan, Loulan, Turfan, and Dunhuang (Map 7.3). Because the remarkable Buddhist civilization of Central Asia was later supplanted by Islam, it was not until early in the twentieth century that European archaeologists discovered its traces. The main sites yielded not only numerous Buddhist paintings but also thousands of texts in a variety of languages. In Khotan, for instance, an Indian language was used for administrative purposes long after the fall of the Kushan empire. Other texts were in various Persian languages, showing the cultural mix of the region.

The form of Buddhism that spread from Central Asia to China, Japan, and Korea was called Mahayana, which means "Great Vehicle" (see page 77), reflecting the claims of its adherents to a more inclusive form of the religion. Influenced by the Iranian religions then prevalent in Central Asia, Buddhism became more devotional. The Buddha came to be treated as a god, the head of an expanding pantheon of other Buddhas and bodhisattvas (Buddhas-to-be). With the growth of this pantheon, Buddhism became as much a religion for laypeople as for monks and nuns.

The first translators of Buddhist texts into Chinese were not Indians but Parthians, Sogdians, and Kushans from Central Asia. One of the most important interpreters of Buddhism in China was the eminent Central Asian monk Kumarajiva (350–413) from Kucha, who settled in Chang'an and directed several thousand monks in the translation of Buddhist texts.

Meditating Monk This monk, wearing the traditional patchwork robe, sits in the crossed-legged meditation position. His small niche is to the left of the main image of the Buddha in cave 285 at Dunhuang, a cave completed in 539 C.E. under the patronage of a prince of the Northern Wei imperial house who was then the local governor. (Photo: Lois Conner. Courtesy, Dunhuang Academy)

The Appeal and Impact of Buddhism in China

Why did Buddhism find so many adherents in China during the three centuries after the fall of the Han Dynasty in 220? There were no forced conversions, but still the religion spread rapidly. In the unstable political environment, many people were open to new ideas. To Chinese scholars the Buddhist concepts of the reincarnation of souls, karma, and nirvana posed a stimulating intellectual challenge. To rulers the Buddhist religion offered a source of magical power and a political tool to unite Chinese and non-Chinese. In a rough and tumultuous age Buddhism's emphasis on kindness, charity, and eternal bliss was deeply comforting. As in India, Buddhism posed no threat to the social order, and the elite who were drawn to Buddhism encouraged its spread to people of all classes.

The monastic establishment grew rapidly in China. Like their Christian counterparts in medieval Europe, Buddhist monasteries played an active role in social, economic, and political life. By 477 there were said to be 6,478 Buddhist temples and 77,258 monks and nuns in the north. Some decades later south China had 2,846 temples and 82,700 clerics. Given the importance of family lines in China, becoming a monk was a major decision, since a man had to give up his surname and take a vow of celibacy, thus cutting himself off from the ancestral cult. Those not ready to become monks or nuns could pursue Buddhist goals as pious laypeople by performing devotional acts and making contributions to monasteries. Among the most generous patrons were rulers in both the north and south.

In China women turned to Buddhism as readily as men. Although birth as a female was considered lower than birth as a male, it was also viewed as temporary, and women were encouraged to pursue salvation on terms nearly equal to those of men. Joining a nunnery became an alternative for a woman who did not want to marry or did not want to stay with her husband's family in widowhood. (See "Listening to the Past: Sixth-Century Biographies of Buddhist Nuns," page 192.) Later, the only woman ruler of China, Empress Wu, invoked Buddhist principles to justify her role (see page 193), further evidence of how Buddhism brought new understandings of gender.

Buddhism had an enormous impact on the visual arts in China, especially sculpture and painting. Before Buddhism, Chinese had not set up statues of gods in temples, but now they decorated temples with a profusion of images. Inspired by the cave temples of India and Central Asia, Buddhists in China, too, carved caves into rock faces to make temples.

Not everyone was won over by Buddhist teachings. Critics of Buddhism labeled it immoral, unsuited to China, and a threat to the state since monastery land was not taxed and monks did not perform labor service. Twice in the north orders were issued to close monasteries and force monks and nuns to return to lay life, but these suppressions did not last long. No attempt was made to suppress belief in Buddhism, and the religion continued to thrive in the subsequent Sui and Tang periods.

The Chinese Empire Re-created: Sui (581–618) and Tang (618–907)

☐ What were the lasting accomplishments of the Sui and Tang Dynasties?

Political division was finally overcome when the Sui Dynasty conquered its rivals to reunify China in 581. Although the dynasty lasted only thirty-seven years, it left a lasting legacy in the form of political reform, the construction of roads and canals, and the institution of written merit-based exams for the appointment of officials. The Tang Dynasty that followed would last for centuries and would build upon the Sui's accomplishments to create an era of impressive cultural creativity and political power.

The Sui Dynasty, 581–618

In the 570s and 580s the long period of division in China was brought to an end under the leadership of the Sui (sway) Dynasty. Yang Jian, who both founded the Sui Dynasty and oversaw the reunification of China, was from a Chinese family that had intermarried with the non-Chinese elite of the north. His conquest of the south involved naval as well as land battles, with thousands of ships on both sides contending for control of the Yangzi River. The Sui reasserted Chinese control over northern Vietnam and campaigned into Korea and against the new force on the steppe, the Turks. The Sui strengthened central control of the government by curtailing the power of local officials to appoint their own subordinates and by instituting in 605 C.E. competitive written examinations for the selection of officials. Preparing for such exams would come to dominate the lives of educated men in later centuries.

The crowning achievement of the Sui Dynasty was the construction of the **Grand Canal**, which connected the Yellow and Yangzi River regions. The canal facilitated the shipping of tax grain (that is, grain paid as tax) from the prosperous Yangzi Valley to the centers of political and military power in north China. Henceforth the rice-growing Yangzi Valley and south China played an ever more influential role in the country's economic and political life, strengthening China's internal cohesion and facilitating maritime trade with Southeast Asia, India, and areas farther west.

Despite these accomplishments, the Sui Dynasty lasted for only two reigns. The ambitious projects of the two Sui emperors led to exhaustion and unrest, and in the ensuing warfare Li Yuan, a Chinese from the same northwest aristocratic circles as the founder of the Sui, seized the throne.

The Tang Dynasty, 618–907

The dynasty founded by Li Yuan, the Tang, was one of the high points of traditional Chinese civilization. Especially during this dynasty's first century, its capital, Chang'an, was the cultural center of East Asia, drawing in merchants, pilgrims, missionaries, and students to a degree never matched before or after. This position of strength gave the Chinese the confidence to be open to learning from the outside world, leading to a more cosmopolitan culture than in any other period before the twentieth century.

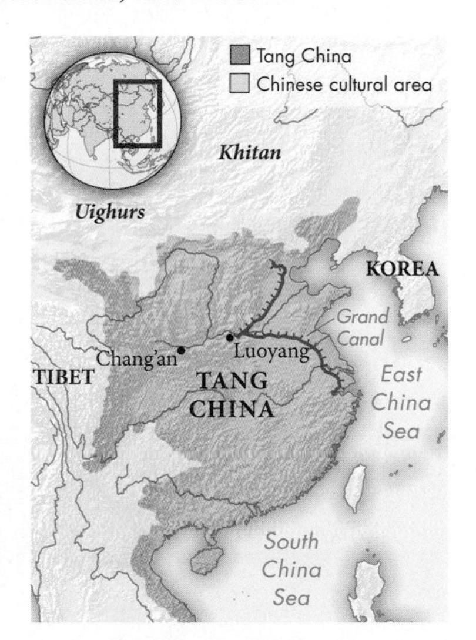

Tang China, ca. 750 C.E.

The first two Tang rulers, Gaozu (Li Yuan, r. 618–626) and Taizong (r. 626–649), were able monarchs. Adding to their armies auxiliary troops composed of Turks, Tanguts, Khitans, and other non-Chinese led by their own chieftains, they campaigned into Korea, Vietnam, and Central Asia. In 630 the Chinese turned against their former allies, the Turks, gaining territory from them and winning for Taizong the title of Great Khan, so that

• **Grand Canal** A canal, built during the Sui Dynasty, that connected the Yellow and Yangzi Rivers, notable for strengthening China's internal cohesion and economic development.

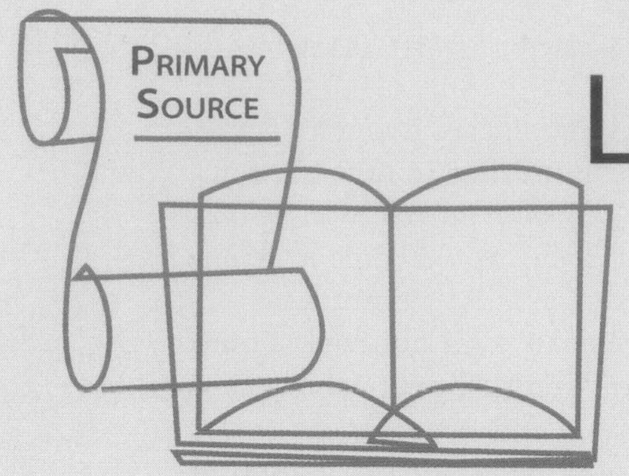

Listening to the Past

Sixth-Century Biographies of Buddhist Nuns

Women drawn to Buddhism could leave secular life to become nuns. Most nuns lived with other nuns in convents, but they could also work to spread Buddhist teachings outside the cloister. The first collection of biographies of eminent nuns in China was written in 516. Among the sixty-five nuns whose lives it recounted are these three.

Kang Minggan

"Minggan's secular surname was Zhu, and her family was from Kaoping. For generations the family had venerated the [Buddhist] teachings known as the Great Vehicle.

A bandit who wanted to make her his wife abducted her, but, even though she suffered increasing torment, she vowed not to give in to him. She was forced to serve as a shepherdess far from her native home. Ten years went by and her longing for her home and family grew more and more intense, but there seemed to be no way back. During all this she kept her mind fixed on the Three Treasures, and she herself wished to become a nun.

One day she happened to meet a Buddhist monk, and she asked him to bestow on her the five fundamental precepts [of a Buddhist householder]. He granted her request and also presented her with a copy of the Bodhisattva Guanshiyin Scripture, which she then practiced chanting day and night without pause.

Deciding to return home to build a five-story pagoda, she fled to the east in great anxiety and distress. At first she did not know the road but kept traveling both day and night. When crossing over a mountain she saw a tiger lying only a few steps away from her. After momentary terror she composed her mind, and her hopes were more than met, for the tiger led the way for her, and, after the days had grown into weeks, she finally arrived in her home territory of Qing Province. As she was about to enter the village, the tiger disappeared, but at that moment, having arrived in the province, Minggan was again abducted, this time by Ming Bolian. When word reached her family, her husband and son ransomed her, but the family did not let her carry out her wishes [to enter the life of a Buddhist nun]. Only after three years of cultivating stringent religious practices was she able to follow her intention. As a nun, she especially concentrated on the cultivation of meditation, and she kept all the regulations of a monastic life without any transgressions. If she happened to commit a minor fault, she would confess it several mornings in a row, ceasing only after she received a sign or a good omen. Sometimes as a good omen she saw flowers rain down from the sky or she heard a voice in the sky or she saw a Buddha image or she had auspicious dreams.

As Minggan approached old age, her moral cultivation was even more strict and lofty. All the men and women north of the Yangtze River honored her as their spiritual teacher in whom they could take refuge.

In the spring of 348 of the Jin dynasty, she, together with Huichan and others — ten in all — traveled south, crossed the Yangtze River, and went to see the minister of public works, He Chong, in the capital of the Eastern Jin dynasty. As soon as he met them, he showed them great respect. Because at that time there were no convents in the capital region He Chong converted one of his private residences into a convent for them.

He asked Minggan, "What should the convent be named?"

She replied, "In the great realm of the Jin dynasty all the four Buddhist assemblies of monks, nuns, and male and female householders are now established for the first time. Furthermore, that which you as donor have established will bestow blessings and merit. Therefore, let us call the convent 'Establishing Blessings Convent.'" He Chong agreed to her suggestion. Not long afterward Minggan took sick and died."

Daoqiong

"Daoqiong's secular surname was Jiang. Her family was from Danyang. When she was a little more than ten years old, she was already well educated in the classics and history, and after her full admission to the monastic assembly she became learned in the Buddhist writings as well and also diligently cultivated a life of asceticism. In the Taiyuan reign period [376–396] of the

for a short period he was simultaneously head of both the Chinese and the Turkish empires.

In the civil sphere Tang accomplishments far outstripped anything known in Europe until the growth of national states in the seventeenth century. Tang emperors subdivided the administration of the empire into departments, much like the numerous agencies of modern governments. They built on the Sui precedent of using written examinations to select officials. Although only about thirty men were recruited this way each year, the prestige of passing the examinations became so great that more and more men attempted them. Candidates had to master the Confucian classics and the rules of poetry, and they had to be able to analyze practical administrative and political matters. Government schools were founded to prepare the

Eastern Jin dynasty, the empress admired her exalted conduct, and, whenever she wished to gain merit by giving gifts or by listening to religious exhortations, she most often depended on the convent where Daoqiong lived for such opportunities. Ladies of noble family vied with one another to associate with Daoqiong.

In 431 she had many Buddhist images made and placed them everywhere: in Pengcheng Monastery, two gold Buddha images with a curtained dais and all accessories; in Pottery Office Monastery, a processional image of Maitreya, the future Buddha, with a jeweled umbrella and pendants; in Southern Establishing Joy Monastery, two gold images with various articles, banners, and canopies. In Establishing Blessings Convent, she had an image of the reclining Buddha made, as well as a hall to house it. She also had a processional image of the bodhisattva, Puxian [or Samantabhadra], made. Of all these items, there was none that was not extremely beautiful. Again, in 438, Daoqiong commissioned a gold Amitayus [or Infinite Life] Buddha, and in the fourth month and tenth day of that same year a golden light shone forth from the mark between the eyebrows of the image and filled the entire convent. The news of this event spread among religious and worldly alike, and all came to pay honor, and, gazing at the unearthly brilliance, there was none who was not filled with great happiness. Further, using the materials bequeathed to her by the Yuan empress consort, she extended the convent to the south to build another meditation hall. ❞

In 910 a Buddhist nun of the Universal Light convent named Yanhui commissioned a painting of Guanyin and had her own portrait painted in the corner to show her devotion to the bodhisattva. Like other nuns, she had had her head shaved. (© The Trustees of the British Museum/Art Resource, NY)

Daozong

❝ Daozong, whose family origins are unknown, lived in Three-Story Convent in Jiangling. As a child she had no intention of setting herself apart; as an adult she did not consider associating with others a defilement. She merely followed a course along the boundary between the wise and the foolish, and, although outwardly she seemed muddled, yet within she traversed hidden profundities.

On the full-moon night of the fifteenth day of the third month, in 463 . . . , Daozong, as an offering to the Buddha, purified herself in a fire fed by oil. Even though she was engulfed by flames up to her forehead, and her eyes and ears were nearly consumed, her chanting of the scriptures did not falter. Monastics and householders sighed in wonder; the demonic and upright were alike startled. When the country heard this news, everyone aspired to attain enlightenment. The appointed court scholar . . . , Liu Qiu, especially revered her and composed a Buddhist-style poetic verse to praise her. ❞

Source: Kathryn Ann Tsai, trans., *Lives of the Nuns: Biographies of Chinese Buddhist Nuns from the Fourth to Sixth Centuries*.

QUESTIONS FOR ANALYSIS

1. Why were the lives of these three particular nuns considered worth recording? What was admirable or inspiring about their examples?
2. What do the nuns' spiritual journeys reveal about the virtues associated with Buddhist monastic life?
3. Do you see a gender element in these accounts? Were the traits that made a nun admirable also appropriate for monks?

sons of officials and other young men for service as officials.

The mid-Tang Dynasty saw two women — Empress Wu and Consort Yang Guifei — rise to positions of great political power. Empress Wu was the consort of the weak and sickly Emperor Gaozong. After Gaozong suffered a stroke in 660, she took full charge. She continued to rule after Gaozong's death, summarily deposing her own two sons and dealing harshly with all opponents. In 690 she proclaimed herself emperor, the only woman who took that title in Chinese history. To gain support, she circulated a Buddhist sutra that predicted the imminent reincarnation of the Buddha Maitreya as a female monarch, during whose reign the world would be free of illness, worry, and disaster. Although despised by later Chinese historians as an

Figurine of a Woman Notions of what makes women attractive have changed over the course of Chinese history. Figurines found in Tang tombs, like this one, show that full-figured women with plump faces were admired in the mid- and late Tang. Emperor Xuanzong's favorite, Yang Guifei, was said to be a plump woman, and the fashion is thought to have spread from the court. (Werner Forman/Art Resource, NY)

evil usurper, Empress Wu was an effective leader. It was not until she was over eighty that members of the court were able to force her out in favor of her son.

Her grandson, the emperor Xuanzong (r. 713–756), presided over a brilliant court and patronized leading poets, painters, and calligraphers in his early years. In his later years, however, after he became enamored of his consort Yang Guifei, he did not want to be bothered by the details of government. In this period ample and rounded proportions were much admired in women, and Yang was said to be such a full-figured beauty. The emperor allowed her to place friends and relatives in important positions in the government. One of her favorites was the general An Lushan, who, after getting into a quarrel with Yang's brother over control of the government, rebelled in 755. Xuanzong had to flee the capital, and the troops that accompanied him forced him to have Yang Guifei executed.

The rebellion of An Lushan was devastating to the Tang Dynasty. Peace was restored only by calling on the Uighurs (WEE-gurz), a Turkish people allied with the Tang, who looted the capital after taking it from the rebels. After the rebellion was finally suppressed in 763, the central government had to keep meeting the extortionate demands of the Uighurs. Many military governors came to treat their provinces as hereditary kingdoms and withheld tax returns from the central government. In addition, eunuchs gained increasing power at court and were able to prevent both the emperors and the Confucian officials from doing much about them.

Tang Culture

The reunification of north and south led to cultural flowering. The Tang capital cities of Chang'an and Luoyang became great metropolises; Chang'an and its suburbs grew to more than 2 million inhabitants (probably making it the largest city in the world at the time). The cities were laid out in rectangular grids and contained a hundred-odd walled "blocks" inside their walls. Like the gates of the city, the gates of each block were locked at night.

In these cosmopolitan cities, knowledge of the outside world was stimulated by the presence of envoys, merchants, pilgrims, and students who came from neighboring states in Central Asia, Japan, Korea, Tibet, and Southeast Asia. Because of the presence of foreign merchants, many religions were practiced, including Nestorian Christianity, Manichaeism, Zoroastrianism, Judaism, and Islam, although none of them spread into the Chinese population the way Buddhism had a few centuries earlier. Foreign fashions in hair and clothing were often copied, and foreign amusements such as the Persian game of polo found followings among the well-to-do. The introduction of new musical instruments and tunes from India, Iran, and Central Asia brought about a major transformation in Chinese music.

The Tang Dynasty was the great age of Chinese poetry. Skill in composing poetry was tested in the civil service examinations, and educated men had to be able to compose poems at social gatherings. The pain of parting, the joys of nature, and the pleasures of wine and friendship were all common poetic topics. One of Li Bo's (701–762) most famous poems describes an evening of drinking with only the moon and his shadow for company:

> A cup of wine, under the flowering trees;
> I drink alone, for no friend is near.
> Raising my cup I beckon the bright moon,
> For he, with my shadow, will make three men.
> The moon, alas, is no drinker of wine;
> Listless, my shadow creeps about at my side.

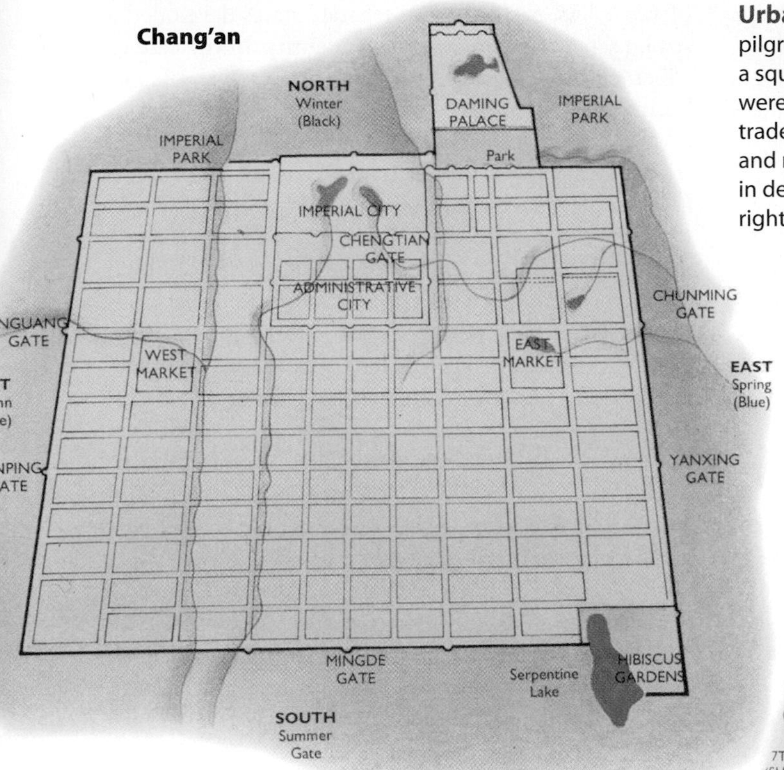

Urban Planning Chang'an in Tang times attracted merchants, pilgrims, and students from all over East Asia. The city was laid out on a square grid (left) and divided into walled wards, the gates to which were closed at night. Temples were found throughout the city, but trade was limited to two government-supervised markets. In the eighth and ninth centuries the Japanese copied the general plan of Chang'an in designing their capitals—first at Nara, then at Heian, shown on the right. (Cradles of Civilization/Visual Connection Archive)

. . .
Now we are drunk, each goes his way.
May we long share our odd, inanimate feast,
And we meet at last on the cloudy River of the sky.[6]

The poet Bo Juyi (772–846) often wrote of more serious subjects. At times he worried about whether he was doing his job justly and well:

From these high walls I look at the town below
Where the natives of Pa cluster like a swarm of flies.
How can I govern these people and lead them aright?
I cannot even understand what they say.
But at least I am glad, now that the taxes are in,
To learn that in my province there is no discontent.[7]

In Tang times Buddhism fully penetrated Chinese daily life. Stories of Buddhist origin became widely known, and Buddhist festivals, such as the festival for feeding hungry ghosts in the summer, became among the most popular holidays. Buddhist monasteries became an important part of everyday life. They ran schools for children. In remote areas they provided lodging for travelers. Merchants entrusted their money and wares to monasteries for safekeeping, in effect transforming the monasteries into banks and warehouses. The wealthy often donated money or land to support temples and monasteries, making monasteries among the largest landlords.

At the intellectual and religious level, Buddhism was developing in distinctly Chinese directions. Two schools that thrived were Pure Land and Chan. **Pure Land** appealed to laypeople because its simple act of calling on the Buddha Amitabha and his chief helper, the compassionate bodhisattva Guanyin, could lead to rebirth in Amitabha's paradise, the Pure Land. Among the educated elite the **Chan** school (known in Japan as Zen) also gained popularity. Chan teachings rejected the authority of the sutras and claimed the superiority of mind-to-mind transmission of Buddhist truths. The "northern" Chan tradition emphasized meditation and monastic discipline. The "southern" tradition was even more iconoclastic, holding that enlightenment could be achieved suddenly through insight into one's own true nature, even without prolonged meditation.

- **Pure Land** A school of Buddhism that taught that by calling on the Buddha Amitabha, one could achieve rebirth in Amitabha's Pure Land paradise.
- **Chan** A school of Buddhism (known in Japan as Zen) that rejected the authority of the sutras and claimed the superiority of mind-to-mind transmission of Buddhist truths.

Five-Stringed Pipa/Biwa This musical instrument, decorated with fine wood marquetry, was probably presented by the Tang court to a Japanese envoy. It was among the objects placed in a Japanese royal storage house (Shōsōin) in 756. (Kyodo News International, Inc.)

Opposition to Buddhism reemerged in the late Tang period. In addition to concerns about the fiscal impact of removing so much land from the tax rolls and so many men from government labor service, there were concerns about Buddhism's foreign origins. As China's international position weakened, xenophobia surfaced. During the persecution of 845, more than 4,600 monasteries and 40,000 temples and shrines were destroyed, and more than 260,000 Buddhist monks and nuns were forced to return to secular life. Although this ban was lifted after a few years, the monastic establishment never fully recovered. Buddhism retained a strong hold among laypeople, and basic Buddhist ideas like karma and reincarnation had become fully incorporated into everyday Chinese thinking. But Buddhism was never again as central to Chinese life.

The East Asian Cultural Sphere

- What elements of Chinese culture were adopted by Koreans, Vietnamese, and Japanese, and how did they adapt them to their own circumstances?

During the millennium from 200 B.C.E. to 800 C.E., China exerted a powerful influence on its immediate neighbors, who began forming states of their own. By Tang times China was surrounded by independent states in Korea, Manchuria, Tibet, the area that is now Yunnan province, Vietnam, and Japan. All of these states were much smaller than China in area and population, making China by far the dominant force politically and culturally until the nineteenth century. Nevertheless, each of these separate states developed a strong sense of its independent identity. In the case of Tibet, cultural borrowing was more often from neighboring India than from China.

The earliest information about each of these countries is found in Chinese sources. Han armies brought Chinese culture to Korea and Vietnam, but even in those cases much cultural borrowing was entirely voluntary as the elite, merchants, and craftsmen adopted the techniques, ideas, and practices they found appealing. In Japan much of the process of absorbing elements of Chinese culture was mediated via Korea. In Korea, Japan, and Vietnam the fine arts—painting, architecture, and ceramics in particular—were all strongly influenced by Chinese models. Tibet, though a thorn in the side of Tang China, was as much in the Indian sphere of influence as in the Chinese and thus followed a somewhat different trajectory. Most significantly, it never adopted Chinese characters as its written language, nor was it as influenced by Chinese artistic styles as were other areas. Moreover, the form of Buddhism that became dominant in Tibet came directly from India, not through Central Asia and China.

In each area Chinese-style culture was at first adopted by elites, but in time many Chinese products and ideas, ranging from written language to chopsticks and soy sauce, became incorporated into everyday life. By the eighth century the written Chinese language was used by educated people throughout East Asia. Educated Vietnamese, Koreans, and Japanese could communicate in writing when they could not understand each other's spoken languages, and envoys to Chang'an could in this way carry out "brush conversations" with each other. The books that educated people read included the Chinese classics, histories, and poetry, as well as Buddhist sutras translated into Chinese. The great appeal of Buddhism known primarily through Chinese translation was a powerful force promoting cultural borrowing.

Vietnam

Vietnam is today classed with the countries to its west as part of Southeast Asia, but its ties are at least as strong to China, and its climate is much like that of southernmost China—subtropical, with abundant rain and rivers. The Vietnamese first appear in Chinese sources as a people of south China called the Yue, who gradually migrated farther south as the Chinese state expanded. The people of the Red River Valley in northern Vietnam had achieved a relatively advanced level of Bronze Age civilization by the first century B.C.E. The bronze heads of their arrows were often dipped in poison to facilitate killing large animals such as elephants, whose tusks were traded to China for iron. Power was held by hereditary tribal chiefs who served as civil, religious, and military leaders, with the king as the most powerful chief.

The collapse of the Qin Dynasty in 206 B.C.E. had an impact on this area because a former Qin general, Zhao Tuo (Trieu Da in Vietnamese), finding himself in the far south, set up his own kingdom of Nam Viet (Nan Yue in Chinese). This kingdom covered much of south China and was ruled by Trieu Da from his capital near the present site of Guangzhou. Its population consisted chiefly of the Viet people. After killing all officials loyal to the Chinese emperor, Trieu Da adopted the customs of the Viet and made himself the ruler of a vast state that extended as far south as modern-day Da Nang.

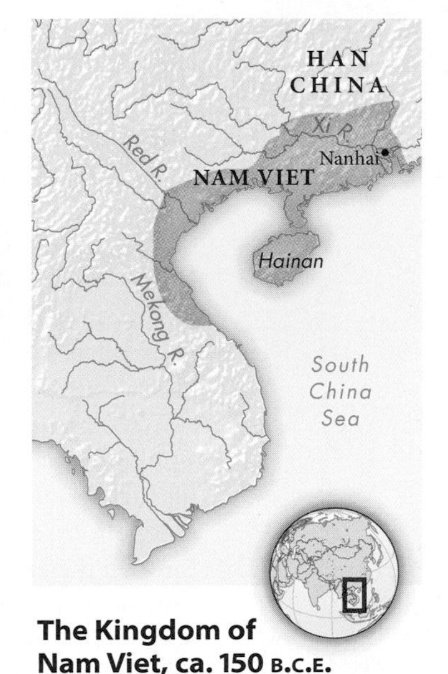

The Kingdom of Nam Viet, ca. 150 B.C.E.

After almost a hundred years of diplomatic and military duels between the Han Dynasty and Trieu Da and his successors, Nam Viet was conquered in 111 B.C.E. by Chinese armies. Chinese administrators were assigned to replace the local nobility. Chinese political institutions were imposed, and Confucianism was treated as the official ideology. The Chinese language was introduced as the medium of official and literary expression, and Chinese characters were adopted as the written form for the Vietnamese spoken language. The Chinese built roads, waterways, and harbors to facilitate communication within the region and to ensure that they maintained administrative and military control over it. Chinese art, architecture, and music had a powerful impact on their Vietnamese counterparts.

Chinese innovations that were beneficial to the Vietnamese were readily integrated into the indigenous culture, but the local elite were not reconciled to Chinese political domination. The most famous early revolt took place in 39 C.E., when two widows of local aristocrats, the Trung sisters, led an uprising against foreign rule. After overwhelming Chinese strongholds, they declared themselves queens of an independent Vietnamese kingdom. Three years later a powerful army sent by the Han emperor re-established Chinese rule.

China retained at least nominal control over northern Vietnam through the Tang Dynasty, and there were no real borders between China proper and Vietnam during this time. The local elite became culturally dual, serving as brokers between the Chinese governors and the native people.

Korea

Korea is a mountainous peninsula some 600 miles long extending south from Manchuria and Siberia. At its tip it is about 120 miles from Japan (Map 7.4). Archaeological, linguistic, and anthropological evidence indicates that the Korean people share a common ethnic origin with other peoples of North Asia, including those of Manchuria, Siberia, and Japan. Linguistically, Korean is not related to Chinese.

Iron Artifacts from Korean Tomb In the third and second centuries B.C.E. iron and bronze were being used in Korea to make mirrors, bells, and practical tools. (National Museum of Gwangju, Korea/EuroCreon/Ancient Art & Architecture Collection, Ltd.)

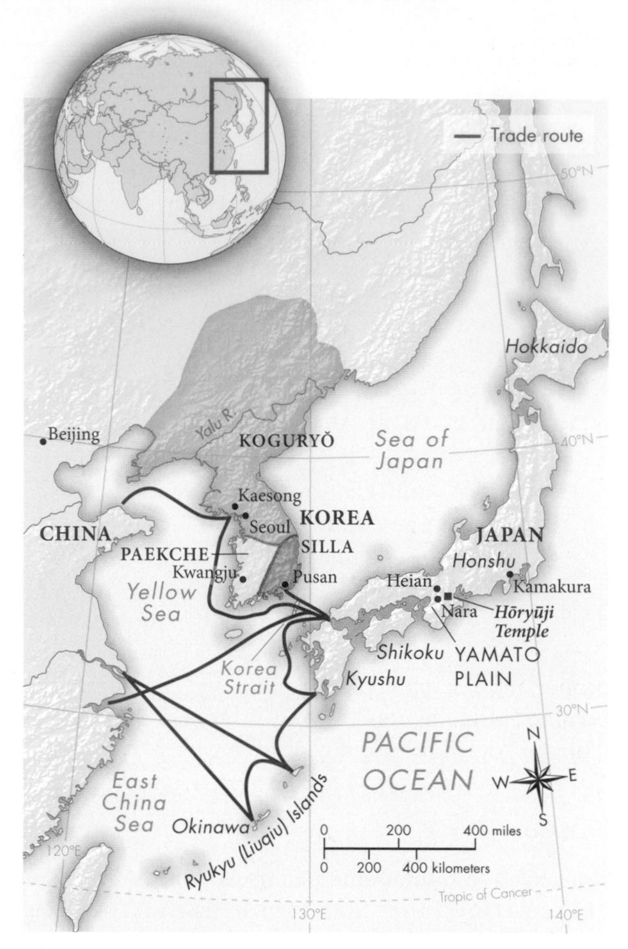

MAP 7.4 Korea and Japan, ca. 600 C.E. Korea and Japan are of similar latitude, but Korea's climate is more continental, with harsher winters. Of Japan's four islands, Kyushu is closest to Korea and mainland Asia.

Korea began adopting elements of technology from China in the first millennium B.C.E., including bronze and iron technology. Chinese-Korean contact expanded during the Warring States Period, when the state of Yan extended into part of Korea. In about 194 B.C.E. Wiman, an unsuccessful rebel against the Han Dynasty, fled to Korea and set up a state called Choson in what is now northwest Korea and southern Manchuria. In 108 B.C.E. this state was overthrown by Han armies. Four prefectures were established there, and Chinese officials were dispatched to govern them.

The impact of the Chinese prefectures in Korea was similar to that of the contemporaneous Roman colonies in Britain in encouraging the spread of culture and political forms. The prefectures survived not only through the Han Dynasty, but also for nearly a century after the fall of the dynasty, until 313 C.E. The Chinese never controlled the entire Korean peninsula, however. The Han commanderies coexisted with the native Korean kingdom of Koguryŏ, founded in the first century B.C.E. Chinese sources describe this kingdom as a society of aristocratic tribal warriors who had under them a mass of serfs and slaves, mostly from conquered tribes. After the Chinese colonies were finally overthrown, the kingdoms of Paekche and Silla emerged farther south on the peninsula in the third and fourth centuries C.E., leading to what is called the Three Kingdoms Period (313–668 C.E.). In all three Korean kingdoms Chinese was used as the language of government and learning. Each of the three kingdoms had hereditary kings, but their power was curbed by the existence of very strong hereditary elites.

Buddhism was officially introduced in Koguryŏ from China in 372 and in the other states not long after. Buddhism connected Korea to societies across Asia. Buddhist monks went back and forth between China and Korea. One even made the journey to India and back, and others traveled on to Japan to aid in the spread of Buddhism there.

When the Sui Dynasty finally reunified China in 589, it tried to establish control of at least a part of Korea. But the Korean kingdoms were much stronger than their predecessors in Han times, and they repeatedly repulsed Chinese attacks. The Tang government then tried allying itself with one state, Silla, to fight the others. Silla and Tang jointly destroyed Paekche in 660 and Koguryŏ in 668. With its new resources Silla was able to repel Tang efforts to make Korea a colony but agreed to vassal status. The unification under Silla marked the first political unification of Korea.

Gold Ornaments for Queen's Crown In the fifth and sixth centuries C.E. royal crowns for Korean kings and queens were regularly embellished with gold that would have glittered as the monarchs walked. (De Agostini Picture Library/The Bridgeman Art Library)

Viewpoints 7.1

Chinese and Japanese Principles of Good Government

• *Confucian principles of government, first developed in the Han Dynasty, in time had considerable influence beyond China's borders, especially in Korea and Japan. The two seventh-century texts below look at good government from different sides. The first comes from an essay written in 648 in China by the Tang emperor Taizong, addressed to the heir apparent to encourage him to aspire to the Confucian understanding of the ideal ruler. The second text, issued by Prince Shōtoku in Japan in 604 is addressed to his officials. In both cases only the first item is included in full, but the titles of the other items are listed.*

Taizong's Plan for an Emperor

1. The Body of the Sovereign: The people are the origin of the state. The state is the foundation of the sovereign. The body of the lord of men should be like the great holy peaks, lofty and towering and unmovable. It should be like sun and moon, constant in their brilliance, and illuminating all alike. He is the one to whom the myriad people look up, to whom the entire empire turns. His will should be broad and magnanimous, sufficient to bind them together. His heart should be impartial and just, sufficient for him to make forceful decisions. Without awesome power, he will have no means to affect the most distant regions: without benign liberality he will have no means to cherish his people. He must comfort the nine grades of his kinsfolk by humanity. He must bind his great ministers to him by the rites. In serving his ancestors, he must bear in mind his filial obligations: in occupying his position [as ruler] he must remember to be reverent. He must repress his own [personal interests] and toil diligently, so as to put into practice virtue and righteousness. Such then is the body of the sovereign.
2. Establishing One's Kinsmen. . . .
3. Seeking Sage-Worthies. . . .
4. Carefully Examine Candidates for Offices. . . .
5. Accepting Remonstrance. . . .
6. Ridding Yourself of Flatterers. . . .
7. Guarding Against Excess. . . .
8. Esteem Frugality. . . .
9. Rewards and Punishments. . . .
10. Giving Due Attention to Agriculture. . . .
11. Reviewing Preparations for War. . . .
12. Honoring Learning. . . .

Sources: Denis Twitchett, "*How to Be an Emperor:* T'ang T'ai-tsung's Vision of His Role," *Asia Major* 3d ser. 9.1–2 (1996): 57–58. Reprinted by permission of the Institute of History and Philology of Academic Sinica, Taipei, Taiwan; Prince Shōtoku adapted from W. G. Aston, *Nihongi: Chronicles of Japan from the Earliest Times to A.D. 697* (London: Kegan Paul, Trench and Trübner, 1896), II, pp. 128–133.

Prince Shōtoku's Seventeen-Article Edict

1. Harmony is to be valued, and contentiousness avoided. All men are inclined to partisanship and few are truly discerning. Hence there are some who disobey their lords and fathers or who maintain feuds with the neighboring villages. But when those above are harmonious and those below are conciliatory and there is concord in the discussion of all matters, the disposition of affairs comes about naturally. Then what is there that cannot be accomplished?
2. Sincerely reverence the Three Treasures [The Buddha, the Law, and the Sangha]. . . .
3. When you receive the imperial commands, fail not scrupulously to obey them. . . .
4. The ministers and functionaries should make ritual decorum their leading principle, for the leading principle in governing the people consists in ritual decorum. . . .
5. Ceasing from gluttony and abandoning covetous desires, deal impartially with the suits which are submitted to you. . . .
6. Chastise that which is evil and encourage that which is good. . . .
7. Let every man have his own charge, and let not the spheres of duty be confused. . . .
8. Let the ministers and functionaries attend the court early in the morning, and retire late. . . .
9. Trustworthiness is the foundation of right. . . .
10. Let us cease from wrath and refrain from angry looks. . . .
11. Give clear appreciation to merit and demerit, and deal out to each its sure reward or punishment. . . .
12. Let not the provincial authorities or the local nobles levy exaction on the people. . . .
13. Let all persons entrusted with office attend equally to their functions. . . .
14. Ye ministers and functionaries! Be not envious. . . .
15. To turn away from that which is private and to set our faces toward that which is public this is the path of a minister. . . .
16. Let the people be called up for labor service only at seasonable times. . . .
17. Matters should not be decided by one person alone. . . .

QUESTIONS FOR ANALYSIS

1. What similarities do you see in these two documents? In what sense can both be considered Confucian?
2. What differences in these documents can you attribute to the differences between China and Japan in the seventh century?

For the next century Silla embarked on a policy of wholesale borrowing of Chinese culture and institutions. Annual embassies were sent to Chang'an, and large numbers of students studied in China. The Silla government was modeled on the Tang, although modifications were made to accommodate Korea's more aristocratic social structure.

Japan

Japan does not touch China as do Korea, Tibet, and Vietnam. The heart of Japan is four mountainous islands off the coast of Korea (see Map 7.4). Since the land is rugged and lacking in navigable waterways, the Inland Sea, like the Aegean in Greece, was the easiest avenue of communication in early times. Hence the land bordering the Inland Sea—Kyushu, Shikoku, and Honshu—developed as the political and cultural center of early Japan. Geography also blessed Japan with a moat—the Korea Strait and the Sea of Japan. Consequently, the Japanese for long periods were free to develop their way of life without external interference.

Japan's early development was closely tied to that of the mainland, especially to Korea. Physical anthropologists have discerned several major waves of immigrants into Japan. People of the Jōmon culture, established by about 10,000 B.C.E., after an influx of people from Southeast Asia, practiced hunting and fishing and fashioned clay pots. New arrivals from northeast Asia brought agriculture and a distinct culture called Yayoi (ca. 300 B.C.E.–300 C.E.). Later Yayoi communities were marked by complex social organization with rulers, soldiers, artisans, and priests. During the Han Dynasty, objects of Chinese and Korean manufacture found their way into Japan, an indication that people were traveling back and forth as well. In the third century C.E. Chinese histories begin to report on the land called Wa made up of mountainous islands. It had numerous communities with markets, granaries, tax collection, and class distinctions. The people ate with their fingers, used body paint, purified themselves by bathing after a funeral, and liked liquor.

One of the most distinctive features of early Japan was its female rulers. A Chinese historian wrote:

> The country formerly had a man as ruler. For some seventy or eighty years after that there were disturbances and warfare. Thereupon the people agreed upon a woman for their ruler. Her name was Pimiko. She occupied herself with magic and sorcery, bewitching the people. Though mature in age, she remained unmarried. She had a younger brother who assisted her in ruling the country. After she became the ruler, there were few who saw her. She had one thousand women as attendants, but only one man. He served her food and drink and acted as a medium of communication. . . .
>
> When Pimiko passed away, a great mound was raised, more than a hundred paces in diameter. Over a hundred male and female attendants followed her to the grave. Then a king was placed on the throne, but the people would not obey him. Assassination and murder followed; more than one thousand were thus slain.
>
> A relative of Pimiko named Iyo, a girl of thirteen, was then made queen and order was restored.[8]

During the fourth through sixth centuries new waves of migrants from Korea brought the language that evolved into Japanese. They also brought sericulture (silkmaking), bronze swords, crossbows, iron plows, and the Chinese written language. In this period a social order similar to Korea's emerged, dominated by a warrior aristocracy organized into clans. Clad in helmet and armor, these warriors wielded swords, battle-axes, and often bows, and some rode into battle on horseback. Those vanquished in battle were made slaves. Each clan had its own chieftain, who marshaled clansmen for battle and served as chief priest. Over time the clans fought with each other, and their numbers were gradually reduced through conquest and alliance. By the fifth century the chief of the clan that claimed descent from the sun-goddess, located in the Yamato plain around modern Osaka, had come to occupy the position of Great King—or Queen, for as the quotation above shows, female rulers were not uncommon in this period.

The Yamato rulers used their religion to subordinate the gods of their rivals, much as Hammurabi had used Marduk in Babylonia (see page 40). They established the chief shrine of the sun-goddess near the seacoast, where she could catch the first rays of the rising sun. Cults to other gods were also supported as long as they were viewed as subordinate to the sun-goddess. This native religion was later termed **Shinto**, the Way of the Gods. Buddhism was formally introduced in 538 C.E. and coexisted with the Shinto reverence for the spirits of ancestors and all living things.

In the sixth century Prince Shōtoku (574–622) undertook a sweeping reform of the state designed to strengthen Yamato rule by adopting Chinese-style bureaucratic practices (though not the recruitment of officials by examination). His Seventeen Principles of 604 drew from both Confucian and Buddhist teachings. (See "Viewpoints 7.1: Chinese and Japanese Principles of Good Government," page 199.) In it he likened the ruler to Heaven and instructed officials to put their duty to the ruler above the interest of their families. He instituted a ladder of official ranks similar

• **Shinto** The Way of the Gods, Japan's native religion.

Viewpoints 7.2

Coping with Epidemics in Japan and Byzantium

• *Major epidemics struck across Eurasia many times, but Japan was far enough from the mainland to escape most of them. The first text below is an order issued by the Japanese central government to the provincial governments in 737 after the arrival of a devastating epidemic, probably smallpox. The second text is an account from the Byzantine historian Procopius of a deadly plague that hit Constantinople in 542.*

Japanese Proclamation of 737

"One: This infection is called "red swellings." When it first begins, it is similar to autumnal fevers. Suffering in bed lasts for three or four days in some cases, five or six in others, before the blotches appear. For three or four days as the swellings appear, the limbs and internal organs become hot as if on fire. . . .

Two: Wrap the victim's abdomen and hips thoroughly in hemp cloth or floss silk. Without fail, keep the patient warm. Never let him become chilled.

Three: When there is no floor, do not lie directly on the earth. Spread a straw mat on the ground and lie down to rest.

Four: We recommend the drinking of rice gruel, either thick or thin, and broth made from boiled rice or millet. But do not eat raw fish or fresh fruits and vegetables. Also do not drink water or suck ice. . . .

Five: In general, people with this illness have no appetite. Force the patient to eat. . . .

Six: For twenty days after the illness passes do not carelessly eat raw fish or fresh fruit or vegetables; do not drink water, take a bath, have sex, force yourself to do anything, or walk in wind and rain. If you overdo it, a relapse will begin immediately. . . .

Seven: In general, if you want to bring this illness under control, do not use pills or powders. If a fever arises, take only a little ginseng boiled in water.

Concerning the above, since the 4th month all in the capital and Kinai have been bedridden with this disease. Many have died. We are also aware that people in the provinces have been afflicted with this distress. So we have written up this set of instructions. Each provincial governor should send it along to his neighbor. When it arrives, make a copy and designate one official at the district office who holds the position of secretary or higher to act as the messenger. The messenger should go quickly to the next place without delaying. The provincial office shall make a tour of its jurisdiction and announce these instructions to the people. If they have no rice for gruel, the province shall make an estimate, grant grain relief from government stores, and report to the Council. When the order arrives, carry it out."

Procopius on the Plague of Justinian

"[542 C.E.] During these times there was a pestilence, by which the whole human race came near to being annihilated. . . . In the second year it reached Byzantium in the middle of spring, where it happened that I was staying at that time. . . .

Those who were attending [the victims] were in a state of constant exhaustion and had a most difficult time of it throughout. . . . [The patients] had also great difficulty in the matter of eating, for they could not easily take food. And many perished through lack of any man to care for them, for they were either overcome by hunger, or threw themselves down from a height. . . . Death came in some cases immediately, in others after many days; and with some the body broke out with black pustules about as large as a lentil and these did not survive even one day, but all succumbed immediately. With many also a vomiting of blood ensued without visible cause and straightway brought death. . . .

And it fell to the lot of the emperor, as was natural, to make provision for the trouble. He therefore detailed soldiers from the palace and distributed money, commanding Theodorus to take charge of this work. . . . Theodorus, by giving out the emperor's money and by making further expenditures from his own purse, kept burying the bodies which were not cared for. And when it came about that all the tombs which had existed previously were filled with the dead, then they dug up all the places about the city one after the other, laid the dead there, each one as he could, and departed; but later on those who were making these trenches, no longer able to keep up with the number of the dying, mounted the towers of the fortifications in Sycae, and tearing off the roofs threw the bodies in there in complete disorder; and they piled them up just as each one happened to fall, and filled practically all the towers with corpses, and then covered them again with their roofs. . . . Indeed in a city which was simply abounding in all good things starvation almost absolute was running riot."

Sources: Reprinted by permission of the Harvard Asia Society from William Farris, *Population and Epidemic Disease in Early Japan, 645–900* (Harvard University Asia Center, 1985), pp. 60–61. Procopius, *History of the Wars*, trans. H. B. Dewing, Loeb Classical Library (Cambridge, Mass.: Harvard University Press, 1914), pp. 451–473.

QUESTIONS FOR ANALYSIS

1. The first document is a decree issued during an epidemic, and the second is a narrative looking back on an epidemic that has already run its course. What differences in these accounts reflect the nature of the documents?
2. What differences in the understanding of disease can you detect in these accounts?
3. What clues do these accounts provide about the identity of the diseases in the epidemics?

part of the Eurasian landmass, Japan had been relatively isolated from many deadly diseases, so when diseases arrived with travelers, people did not have immunity. The great smallpox epidemic of 735–737 is thought to have reduced the population of about 5 million by 30 percent. (See "Viewpoints 7.2: Coping with Epidemics in Japan and Byzantium," page 201.)

The Buddhist monasteries that ringed Nara were both religious centers and wealthy landlords, and the monks were active in the political life of the capital. Copying the policy of the Tang Dynasty in China, the government ordered every province to establish a Buddhist temple with twenty monks and ten nuns to chant sutras and perform other ceremonies on behalf of the emperor and the state. When an emperor abdicated in 749 in favor of his daughter, he became a Buddhist monk, a practice many of his successors would later follow.

Many of the temples built during the Nara period still stand, the wood, clay, and bronze statues in them exceptionally well preserved. The largest of these temples was the Tōdaiji, with its huge bronze statue of the Buddha, which stood fifty-three feet tall and was made from more than a million pounds of metal. When the temple and statue were completed in 752, an Indian monk painted the eyes, and the ten thousand monks present for the celebration had a magnificent vegetarian feast. Objects from the dedication ceremony were placed in a special storehouse, the Shōsōin, and about ten thousand of them are still there, including books, weapons, mirrors, screens, and objects of gold, lacquer, and glass, most made in China but some coming from Central Asia and Persia via the Silk Road.

CHRONOLOGY

ca. 230–208 B.C.E.	Construction of Great Wall
221 B.C.E.	China unified under Qin Dynasty
206 B.C.E.–220 C.E.	Han Dynasty
145–ca. 85 B.C.E.	Sima Qian, Chinese historian
114 B.C.E.	Han government gains control over Silk Road trade routes across Central Asia
111 B.C.E.	Emperor Wu conquers Nam Viet
108 B.C.E.	Han government establishes colonies in Korea
105 C.E.	Chinese invention of paper
ca. 200 C.E.	Buddhism begins rapid growth in China
220–589 C.E.	Age of Division in China
313–668 C.E.	Three Kingdoms Period in Korea
372 C.E.	Buddhism introduced in Korea
538 C.E.	Buddhism introduced in Japan
581–618 C.E.	Sui Dynasty
604 C.E.	Prince Shōtoku introduces Chinese-style government in Japan
605 C.E.	Introduction of merit-based examination system for the selection of officials in China
618–907 C.E.	Tang Dynasty; great age of Chinese poetry
668 C.E.	First political unification of Korea under Silla
690 C.E.	Empress Wu declares herself emperor, becoming the only Chinese woman emperor
710 C.E.	Nara made the capital of Japan
735–737 C.E.	Smallpox epidemic in Japan
845 C.E.	Tang emperor begins persecution of Buddhism

Chapter Summary

After unifying China in 221 B.C.E., the Qin Dynasty created a strongly centralized government that did away with noble privilege. The First Emperor standardized script, coinage, weights, and measures. He also built roads, the Great Wall, and a huge tomb for himself. During the four centuries of the subsequent Han Dynasty, the harsher laws of the Qin were lifted, but the strong centralized government remained. The Han government promoted internal peace by providing relief in cases of floods, droughts, and famines and by keeping land taxes low for the peasantry. The Han government sent huge armies against the nomadic Xiongnu, whose confederation threatened them in the north, but the Xiongnu remained a potent foe. Still, Han armies expanded Chinese territory in many directions. For nearly four centuries after the fall of the Han Dynasty, China was divided among contending states. After 316 the north was in the hands of non-Chinese rulers, while the south had Chinese rulers.

In the first and second centuries C.E. merchants and missionaries brought Buddhism to China. Many elements of Buddhism were new to China — a huge body of scriptures, celibate monks and nuns, traditions of depicting Buddhas and bodhisattvas in statues and paintings, and a strong proselytizing tradition. Rulers became major patrons in both north and south.

Unlike the Roman Empire, China was successfully reunified in 589 C.E. The short Sui Dynasty was followed by the longer Tang Dynasty. Tang China regained overlordship of the Silk Road cities in Central Asia. The Tang period was one of cultural flowering, with achievements in poetry especially notable. Music was enriched with instruments and tunes from Persia. Tang power declined after 755, when a powerful general turned his army against the government. Although the rebellion was suppressed, the government was not able to regain its strong central control. Moreover, powerful states were formed along Tang's borders. At court, eunuchs gained power at the expense of civil officials.

Over the ten centuries covered in Chapter 7, Korea, Japan, and Vietnam developed distinct cultures while adopting elements of China's material, political, and religious culture, including the Chinese writing system. During the Tang era, ambitious Korean and Japanese rulers sought Chinese expertise and Chinese products, including Chinese-style centralized governments and the Chinese written language.

NOTES

1. Li Yuning, ed., *The First Emperor of China* (White Plains, N.Y.: International Arts and Sciences Press, 1975), pp. 275–276, slightly modified.
2. Burton Watson, trans., *Records of the Grand Historian of China*, vol. 2 (New York: Columbia University Press, 1961), p. 496.
3. Ibid., p. 499.
4. Patricia Buckley Ebrey, ed., *Chinese Civilization: A Sourcebook*, 2d ed., revised and expanded (New York: Free Press, 1993), p. 62.
5. Patricia Buckley Ebrey, *Cambridge Illustrated History of China* (Cambridge: Cambridge University Press, 1996), p. 74.
6. Arthur Waley, trans., *More Translations from the Chinese* (New York: Knopf, 1919), p. 27.
7. Ibid., p. 71.
8. *Sources of Japanese Tradition*, by William Theodore de Bary, Donald Keene, George Tanabe, and Paul Varley, eds. Reproduced with permission of COLUMBIA UNIVERSITY PRESS in the format Book via Copyright Clearance Center.

CONNECTIONS

East Asia was transformed in the millennium between the Qin unification in 221 B.C.E. and the end of the eighth century C.E. The Han Dynasty and four centuries later the Tang Dynasty proved that a centralized, bureaucratic monarchy could bring peace and prosperity to populations of 50 million or more spread across China proper. By 800 C.E. neighboring societies along China's borders, from Korea and Japan on the east to the Uighurs and Tibetans to the west, had followed China's lead, forming states and building cities. Buddhism had transformed the lives of all of these societies, bringing new ways of thinking about life and death and new ways of pursuing spiritual goals.

In the same centuries that Buddhism was adapting to and simultaneously transforming the culture of much of eastern Eurasia, comparable processes were at work in western Eurasia, where Christianity continued to spread. The spread of these religions was aided by increased contact between different cultures, facilitated in Eurasia by the merchants traveling the Silk Road or sailing the Indian Ocean. Where contact between cultures wasn't as extensive, as in Africa (discussed in Chapter 10), religious beliefs were more localized. The collapse of the Roman Empire in the West during this period was not unlike the collapse of the Han Dynasty, but in Europe the empire was never put back together at the level that it was in China, where the Tang Dynasty by many measures was more splendid than the Han. The story of these centuries in western Eurasia is taken up in the next two chapters, which trace the rise of Christianity and Islam and the movement of peoples throughout Europe and Asia. Before returning to the story of East Asia after 800 in Chapter 13, we will also examine the empires in Africa (Chapter 10) and the Americas (Chapter 11).

Review and Explore

Make It Stick

LearningCurve
Go online and use LearningCurve to retain what you've read.

Identify Key Terms

Identify and explain the significance of each item below.

Great Wall (p. 179)
Confucian classics (p. 181)
Records of the Grand Historian (p. 182)
Silk Road (p. 184)
tributary system (p. 184)
eunuchs (p. 188)
Age of Division (p. 188)
Grand Canal (p. 191)
Pure Land (p. 195)
Chan (p. 195)
Shinto (p. 200)
Nara (p. 202)

Review the Main Ideas

Answer the focus questions from each section of the chapter.

1. What were the social, cultural, and political consequences of the unification of China under the strong centralized governments of the Qin and Han empires? (p. 178)
2. How did Buddhism find its way into East Asia, and what was its appeal and impact? (p. 188)
3. What were the lasting accomplishments of the Sui and Tang Dynasties? (p. 191)
4. What elements of Chinese culture were adopted by Koreans, Vietnamese, and Japanese, and how did they adapt them to their own circumstances? (p. 196)

Make Connections

Analyze the larger developments and continuities within and across chapters.

1. What philosophies or other cultural elements in pre-imperial China (see Chapter 4) help explain China's development after 221 B.C.E.?
2. How did Buddhism in early India compare to Buddhism in Tang China?
3. How did the influence of Han and Tang China on neighboring regions compare to the influence of Rome on its neighbors?

LaunchPad
Online Document Project

Ban Zhao Offers Advice to Elite Women

What do Ban Zhao's writings reveal about attitudes toward women during her time?

Read sources by and about Ban Zhao, and then complete a quiz and writing assignment based on the evidence and details from this chapter.

See inside the front cover to learn more.

Suggested Reading

Barfield, Thomas. *Perilous Frontier: Nomadic Empires and China, 221 B.C.–A.D. 1757.* 1989. A bold interpretation of the relationship between the rise and fall of dynasties in China and the rise and fall of nomadic confederations that derived resources from them.

Elvin, Mark. *The Pattern of the Chinese Past.* 1973. Analyzes the military dimensions of China's unification.

Farris, Wayne. *Population, Disease, and Land in Early Japan, 645–900.* 1985. Shows the impact of the eighth-century introduction of smallpox to Japan on the government and rural power structure.

Hardy, Grant. *Worlds of Bronze and Bamboo: Sima Qian's Conquest of History.* 1999. An excellent introduction to the methods of China's earliest historian. Although Sima Qian seems to present just the facts, Hardy shows how he brings out different perspectives and interpretations in different chapters.

Holcomb, Charles. *The Genesis of East Asia, 221 B.C.–A.D. 907.* 2001. A thought-provoking analysis of the connections between China and Korea, Japan, and Vietnam that emphasizes the use of the Chinese script.

Lee, Peter H. *Sourcebook of Korean Civilization.* 1993. Excellent collection of primary sources.

Lewis, Mark Edward. *China's Cosmopolitan Empire: The Tang Dynasty.* 2009. This accessible and lively survey complements the author's works on the Han Dynasty (*The Early Chinese Empires*) and the period of division (*China Between Empires*).

Schafer, Edward. *The Golden Peaches of Samarkand.* 1963. Draws on Tang literature to show the place of the western regions in Tang life and imagination.

Scheidel, Walter, ed. *Rome and China: Comparative Perspectives on Ancient World Empires.* 2009. Contributors compare legal and military institutions, trade, money, and charity.

Seth, Michael J. *A Concise History of Korea: From the Neolithic Period Through the Nineteenth Century.* 2006. An up-to-date and well-balanced introduction to Korean history.

Totman, Conrad. *A History of Japan.* 1999. A broad and up-to-date history of Japan.

Varley, H. Paul. *Japanese Culture.* 2000. An accessible introduction to Japanese history and culture.

Waley, Arthur. *The Life and Times of Po Chu-i, 772–846 A.D.* 1949. A lively biography of a Tang official, which draws heavily on his poetry.

Watt, James C. Y. *China: Dawn of a Golden Age 200–750 A.D.* 2004. A well-illustrated catalogue of a major art and archaeological exhibition.

Wright, Arthur. *Buddhism in Chinese History.* 1959. This short book remains a good introduction to China's encounter with Buddhism and the ways Buddhism was adapted to China.

Continuity and Change in Europe and Western Asia
250–850

8

Orthodox Icon of Jesus
In this painted icon, made for the monastery of Saint Catherine in Egypt in the eighth century, Jesus is shown on the cross, with two angels above him. Icons were important objects of veneration in the Eastern Christian, or Orthodox, Church, although they were also a source of controversy, as some church leaders thought that people were not simply using them as an aide to piety, but worshipping the image. (Kharbine-Tapabor/The Art Archive at Art Resource, NY)

LearningCurve
After reading the chapter, go online and use LearningCurve to retain what you've read.

Chapter Preview

From the third century onward the Western Roman Empire slowly disintegrated, and in 476 the Ostrogothic chieftain Odoacer deposed the Roman emperor in the West and did not take on the title of emperor. This date thus marks the official end of the Roman Empire in the West, although much of the empire had come under the rule of various barbarian tribes well before that (see Chapter 6). Scholars have long seen this era as one of the great turning points in Western history, but during the last several decades focus has shifted to continuities as well as changes. What is now usually termed "late antiquity" has been recognized as a period of creativity and adaptation in Europe and western Asia, not simply of decline and fall.

The two main agents of continuity were the Eastern Roman (or Byzantine) Empire and the Christian Church. The Byzantine Empire lasted until 1453, a thousand years longer than the Western Roman Empire, and it preserved and transmitted much of Greco-Roman law and philosophy. Missionaries and church officials spread Christianity within and far beyond the borders of what had been the Roman Empire, carrying Christian ideas and institutions west to Ireland and east to Central and South Asia. The main agent of change in late antiquity was the migration of barbarian groups throughout much of Europe and western Asia. They brought different social, political, and economic structures with them, but as they encountered Roman and Byzantine culture and became Christian, their own ways of doing things were also transformed.

The Byzantine Empire

☐ How did the Byzantine Empire preserve the legacy of Rome?

The Byzantine (or Eastern Roman) Empire (Map 8.1) preserved the forms, institutions, and traditions of the old Roman Empire, and its people even called themselves Romans. Byzantine emperors traced their lines back past Constantine to Augustus, and the Senate in Constantinople carried on the traditions of the old Roman Senate. Most important, however, is how Byzantium protected the intellectual heritage of Greco-Roman civilization and then passed it on.

Sources of Byzantine Strength

While the western parts of the Roman Empire gradually succumbed to barbarian invaders, the Byzantine Empire survived Germanic, Persian, and Arab attacks.

In 540 a force of Xiongnu (whom the Greeks and Romans called Huns) and Bulgars reached the gates of Constantinople. In 583 the Avars, a mounted Mongol people who had swept across Russia and the Balkans, seized Byzantine forts along the Danube and also reached the walls of Constantinople. Between 572 and 630 the Greeks were repeatedly at war with the Sassanid Persians (see page 210). Beginning in 632 Muslim forces pressured the Byzantine Empire (see Chapter 9).

Why didn't one or a combination of these enemies capture Constantinople, as the Ostrogoths had taken Rome? The answer lies in strong military leadership and even more in the city's location and excellent fortifications. During the long reign of the emperor Justinian (r. 527–565), Byzantine generals were able to reconquer much of Italy and North Africa from barbarian groups, making them part of the Eastern Roman Empire. The Byzantines ruled most of Italy from 535 to 572 and the southern part of the peninsula until the eleventh century. They ruled North Africa until it was conquered by Muslim forces in the late seventh century. Under the skillful command of General Priskos (d. 612), Byzantine armies inflicted a severe defeat on the Avars in 601. Massive triple walls, built by the emperors Constantine and Theodosius II (408–450) and kept in good repair by later emperors, protected Constantinople from sea invasion. Within the walls huge cisterns provided water, and vast gardens and grazing areas supplied vegetables and meat so the defending people could hold out far longer than the besieging army. Attacking Constantinople by land posed greater geographical and logistical problems than a seventh- or eighth-century government could solve. The site was not absolutely impregnable—as the Venetians would later demonstrate in 1204 and the Ottoman Turks in 1453—but it was almost so. Because the city survived, the empire, though reduced in territory, endured.

The Sassanid Empire and Conflicts with Byzantium

For several centuries the Sassanid empire of Persia was Byzantium's most regular foe. Ardashir I (r. 224–243), the ruler of a small state and the first of the Sassanid dynasty, conquered the Parthian empire in 226 (see Map 6.2, page 161). Ardashir kept expanding his holdings to the east and northwest. He moved the capital of this new Sassanid empire to Ctesiphon (TEH-suh-fahn), in the fertile Tigris-Euphrates Valley, from where it retained control of much of the Persian Gulf. Like all empires, the Sassanid depended on agriculture for its economic prosperity, but its location also proved well suited for commerce (see Map 8.1). A lucrative caravan trade linked the Sassanid empire to the Silk Road and China (see "Global Trade: Silk," page 186). Persian metalwork, textiles, and glass were exchanged for Chinese silks, and this trade brought about considerable cultural contact between the Sassanids and the Chinese.

MAP 8.1 The Byzantine and Sassanid Empires, ca. 600 Both the Byzantine and Sassanid Empires included territory that had earlier been part of the Roman Empire. The Sassanid Persians fought Roman armies before the founding of the Byzantine Empire. Later Byzantium and the Sassanids engaged in a series of wars that weakened both and brought neither lasting territorial acquisitions.

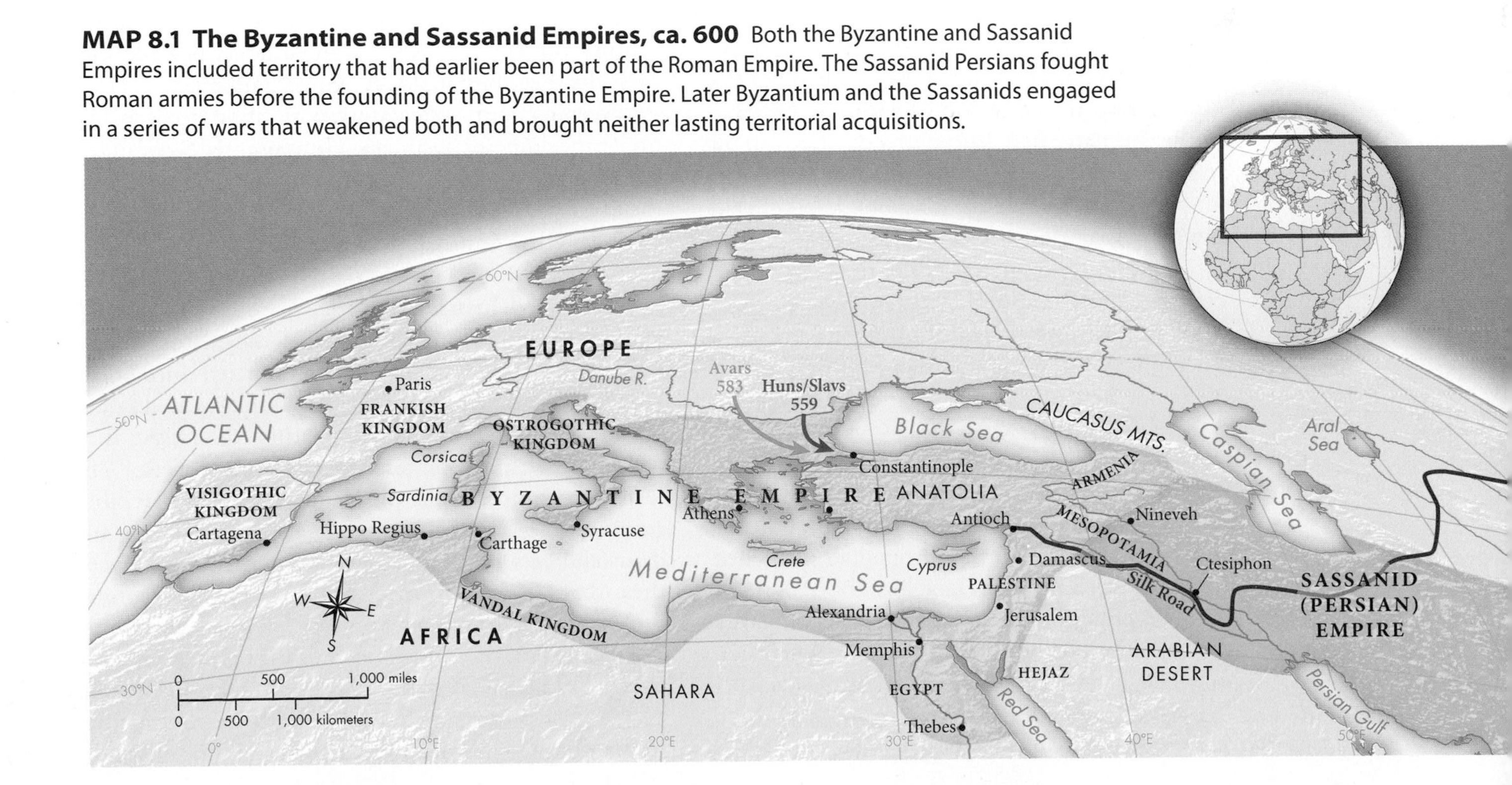

Sassanid Cameo In this cameo—a type of jewelry made by carving into a multicolored piece of rock—the Sassanid king Shapur and the Byzantine emperor Valerian fight on horseback, each identifiable by his distinctive clothing and headgear. This does not record an actual hand-to-hand battle, but uses the well-muscled rulers as symbols of their empires. (Erich Lessing/Art Resource, NY)

Whereas the Parthians had tolerated many religions, the Sassanid Persians made Zoroastrianism the official state religion. Religion and the state were inextricably tied together. The king's power rested on the support of nobles and Zoroastrian priests who monopolized positions in the court and in the imperial bureaucracy. A highly elaborate court ceremonial and ritual exalted the status of the king and emphasized his semidivine pre-eminence over his subjects. (The Byzantine monarchy, the Roman papacy, and the Muslim caliphate subsequently copied aspects of this Persian ceremonial.)

Adherents to religions other than Zoroastrianism, such as Jews and Christians, faced discrimination. The Jewish population in the Sassanid empire was sizable because the Romans had forced many Jews out of Israel and Judaea after a series of revolts against Roman rule, a dispersal later termed the diaspora. Jews suffered intermittent persecution under the Sassanids, as did Christians, whom followers of Zoroastrianism saw as being connected to Rome and Constantinople.

An expansionist foreign policy brought Persia into frequent conflict with Rome and then with Byzantium. Neither side was able to achieve a clear-cut victory until the early seventh century, when the Sassanids advanced all the way to the Mediterranean and even took Egypt in 621. Their victory would be very short-lived, however, as the taxes required to finance the wars and conflicts over the succession to the throne had weakened the Persians. Under Emperor Heraclius I (r. 610–641), the Byzantines crushed the Persians in a series of battles ending with one at Nineveh in 627. Just five years later, the first Arabic forces inspired by Islam entered Persian territories, and by 651 the Sassanid dynasty had collapsed (see page 239).

• **Justinian's *Code*** Multipart collection of laws and legal commentary issued in the sixth century by the emperor Justinian.

Justinian's Code of Law

Byzantine emperors organized and preserved Roman law, making a lasting contribution to the medieval and modern worlds. Roman law had developed from many sources—decisions by judges, edicts of emperors, legislation passed by the Senate, and opinions of jurists expert in the theory and practice of law. By the fourth century Roman law had become a huge, bewildering mass. Its sheer bulk made it almost unusable.

Sweeping and systematic codification took place under the emperor Justinian. He appointed a committee of eminent jurists to sort through and organize the laws. The result was the *Corpus Juris Civilis* (Body of Civil Law), a multipart collection of laws and legal commentary issued from 529 to 534 that is often simply termed **Justinian's *Code***. The first part of this work, the *Codex*, brought together all the existing imperial laws into a coherent whole, eliminated outmoded laws and contradictions, and clarified the law itself. The second part of Justinian's compilation, the *Digest*, is a collection of the opinions of the foremost Roman jurists on complex legal problems. The third part, the *Institutes*, is a handbook of civil law designed for students and beginning jurists. All three parts were given the force of law and formed the backbone of Byzantine jurisprudence from that point on. (See "Viewpoints 8.1: Freeing Slaves in Justinian's *Code* and the Qur'an," at right.) Like so much of classical culture, Justinian's *Code* was lost in western Europe with the end of the Roman Empire, but it was rediscovered in the eleventh

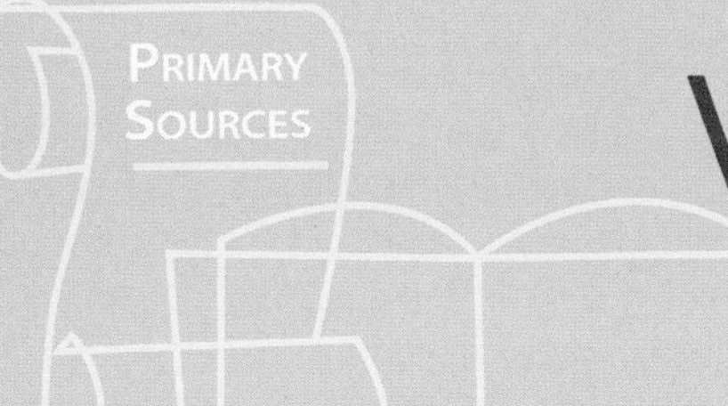

Viewpoints 8.1

Freeing Slaves in Justinian's *Code* and the Qur'an

• *Slavery was a common condition in most agricultural societies in the ancient world, including all of those around the Mediterranean. Both Justinian's* Code *and the Qur'an, the sacred book of Islam (see page 238), contain many provisions regarding slaves. Among these are statements about manumission, the freeing of slaves by their owners.*

Justinian's *Code*

" Freedmen are those who have been manumitted from legal servitude. Manumission is the "giving of liberty." For while any one is in slavery, he is under "the hand" and power of another, but by manumission he is freed from this power. This institution [i.e., slavery] took its rise from the law of nations; for by the law of nature all men were born free; and manumission was not heard of, as slavery was unknown. But when slavery came in by the law of nations, the boon [blessing] of manumission followed. And whereas we all were denominated by the one natural name of "men," the law of nations introduced a division into three kinds of men, namely, freemen, and in opposition to them, slaves; and thirdly, freedmen who had ceased to be slaves.

Manumission is effected in various ways; either in the face of the Church, according to the imperial constitutions, or by *vindicta* [a legal procedure in which a free person touched a slave with a rod and asked a judge for his or her freedom], or in the presence of friends, or by letter, or by testament, or by any other expression of a man's last will. And a slave may also gain his freedom in many other ways, introduced by the constitutions of former emperors, and by our own. [*Institutes*, Book 1, Chapter 5] . . .

We grant permission to the master, during his lifetime, to make use of his female slaves, as well as of their offspring, in any way that he may desire, and to dispose of them by his last will in accordance with his wishes; that is to say, bequeath them as slaves to others, or leave them by name to his heirs to remain in servitude. But if he should pass them over in silence, then, after his death, they shall obtain their freedom, which will date from the death of their master. [*Codex*, Book 7: Title 15, no. 3] "

Qur'an

" Righteousness is not that you turn your faces toward the east or the west, but [true] righteousness is [in] one who believes in Allah, the Last Day, the angels, the Book, and the prophets and gives wealth, in spite of love for it, to relatives, orphans, the needy, the traveler, those who ask [for help], and for freeing slaves; [and who] establishes prayer and gives *zakah* [alms for the poor]; [those who] fulfill their promise when they promise; and [those who] are patient in poverty and hardship and during battle. Those are the ones who have been true, and it is those who are the righteous. [Sura 2:177]

But let them who find not [the means for] marriage abstain [from sexual relations] until Allah enriches them from His bounty. And those who seek a contract [for eventual emancipation] from among whom your right hands possess [that is, those slaves who desire to purchase their freedom from their owners for a price agreed upon by both] — then make a contract with them if you know there is within them goodness and give them from the wealth of Allah which He has given you. [Sura 24:33] "

Sources: *The Institutes of Justinian*, trans. Thomas Collett Sandars (London: Longman, 1962), p. 17; *The Civil Law*, trans. S. P. Scott, vol. 14 (Cincinnati: Central Trust Company, 1932), p. 139; *The Qur'an*, Saheeh International English Translation (Jeddah, Saudi Arabia: Abul-Qasim Publishing House, 1997), pp. 24, 340. Copyright Abul-Qasim Publishing House, 1997.

QUESTIONS FOR ANALYSIS

1. In the sections from Justinian's *Code*, is slavery seen as natural or as a human creation? How could slaves be freed?
2. In the two verses from the Qur'an, how can slaves attain their freedom?
3. How is the act of freeing slaves viewed in these two sources?

century and came to form the foundation of law for nearly every modern European nation.

Byzantine Intellectual Life

Just as they valued the law, the Byzantines prized education. As a result, many masterpieces of ancient Greek literature survived to influence the intellectual life of the modern world. The literature of the Byzantine Empire was predominantly Greek, although politicians, scholars, and lawyers also spoke and wrote Latin. Among members of the large reading public, history was a favorite subject.

The most remarkable Byzantine historian was Procopius (ca. 500–ca. 562), who left a rousing account of Justinian's reconquest of North Africa and Italy, but also wrote the *Secret History*, a vicious and uproarious attack on Justinian and his wife, the empress Theodora. (See "Individuals in Society: Theodora of Constantinople," page 212.)

Individuals in Society

Theodora of Constantinople

THE MOST POWERFUL WOMAN IN BYZANTINE HISTORY was the daughter of a bear trainer for the circus. Theodora (ca. 497–548) grew up in what her contemporaries regarded as an undignified and morally suspect atmosphere, and she worked as a dancer and actress, both dishonorable occupations in the Roman world. Despite her background, she caught the eye of Justinian, who was then a military leader and whose uncle (and adoptive father) Justin had himself risen from obscurity to become the ruler of the Byzantine Empire. Under Justinian's influence, Justin changed the law to allow an actress who had left her disreputable life to marry whom she liked, and Justinian and Theodora married in 525. When Justinian was proclaimed co-emperor with his uncle Justin on April 1, 527, Theodora received the rare title of *augusta*, empress. Thereafter her name was linked with Justinian's in the exercise of imperial power.

A sixth-century mosaic of the empress Theodora, made of thousands of tiny cubes of glass, shows her with a halo — a symbol of power — and surrounded by officials, priests, and court ladies. (Basilica of San Vitale, Italy/Photo © Tarker/The Bridgeman Art Library)

Most of our knowledge of Theodora's early life comes from the *Secret History*, a tell-all description of the vices of Justinian and his court written by Procopius around 550. Procopius was the official court historian and thus spent his days praising those same people. In the *Secret History*, however, he portrays Theodora and Justinian as demonic, greedy, and vicious, killing courtiers to steal their property. In scene after detailed scene, Procopius portrays Theodora as particularly evil, sexually insatiable, and cruel, a temptress who used sorcery to attract men, including the hapless Justinian.

In one of his official histories, *The History of the Wars of Justinian*, Procopius presents a very different Theodora. Riots between the supporters of two teams in chariot races had turned deadly, and Justinian wavered in his handling of the perpetrators. Both sides turned against the emperor, besieging the palace while Justinian was inside it. Shouting "*Nika!*" (Victory), the rioters swept through the city, burning and looting. Justinian's counselors urged flight, but, according to Procopius, Theodora rose and declared:

> For one who has reigned, it is intolerable to be an exile. . . . If you wish, O Emperor, to save yourself, there is no difficulty: we have ample funds and there are the ships. Yet reflect whether, when you have once escaped to a place of security, you will not prefer death to safety. I agree with an old saying that the purple [that is, the color worn only by emperors] is a fair winding sheet [to be buried in].

Justinian rallied, ordered more than thirty thousand men and women executed, and crushed the revolt.

Other sources describe or suggest Theodora's influence on imperial policy. Justinian passed a number of laws that improved the legal status of women, such as allowing women to own property and to be guardians over their own children. He forbade the exposure of unwanted infants, which happened more often to girls than to boys, since boys were valued more highly. Theodora presided at imperial receptions for Arab sheiks, Persian ambassadors, Germanic princesses from the West, and barbarian chieftains from southern Russia. When Justinian fell ill from the bubonic plague in 542, Theodora took over his duties. Justinian is reputed to have consulted her every day about all aspects of state policy, including religious policy regarding the doctrinal disputes that continued throughout his reign.

Theodora's influence over her husband and her power in the Byzantine state continued until she died, perhaps of cancer, twenty years before Justinian. Her influence may have even continued after death, for Justinian continued to pass reforms favoring women and, at the end of his life, accepted an interpretation of Christian doctrine she had favored. Institutions that she established, including hospitals and churches, continued to be reminders of her charity and piety.

Theodora has been viewed as a symbol of the use of beauty and cleverness to attain position and power, and also as a strong and capable co-ruler who held the empire together during riots, revolts, and deadly epidemics. Just as she fascinated Procopius, she continues to intrigue writers today, who make her a character not only in historical works, but also in science fiction and fantasy.

QUESTIONS FOR ANALYSIS

1. How would you assess the complex legacy of Theodora?
2. Since Procopius's public and private views of the empress are so different, should he be trusted at all as a historical source? Why or why not?

LaunchPad Online Document Project

What do Procopius's descriptions of Theodora and Justinian tell us about the problems and challenges his society faced? Examine sources that reveal the connections Procopius saw between Byzantium's rulers and the rapid decline he perceived in Byzantine society, and then complete a quiz and writing assignment based on the evidence and details from this chapter.

See inside the front cover to learn more.

Greek Fire In this illustration from a twelfth-century manuscript, sailors shoot Greek fire toward an attacking ship from a pressurized tube that looks strikingly similar to a modern flamethrower. The exact formula for Greek fire has been lost, but it was probably made from a petroleum product because it continued burning on water. Greek fire was particularly important in Byzantine defenses of Constantinople from Muslim forces in the late seventh century. (Prado, Madrid, Spain/The Bridgeman Art Library)

Although the Byzantines discovered little that was new in mathematics and geometry, they made advances in military applications. For example, they invented an explosive liquid that came to be known as "Greek fire." The liquid was heated and propelled by a pump through a bronze tube, and as the jet left the tube, it was ignited—somewhat like a modern flamethrower. Greek fire saved Constantinople from Arab assault in 678 and was used in both land and sea battles for centuries, although modern military experts still do not know the exact nature of the compound.

The Byzantines devoted a great deal of attention to medicine, and their general level of medical competence was far higher than that of western Europeans. Yet their physicians could not cope with the terrible disease, often called "the Justinian plague," that swept through the Byzantine Empire and parts of western Europe between 542 and 560. (See "Viewpoints 7.2: Coping with Epidemics in Japan and Byzantium," page 201.) Probably originating in northwestern India and carried to the Mediterranean region by ships, the disease was similar to the bubonic plague. Characterized by high fevers, chills, delirium, and enlarged lymph nodes, or by inflammation of the lungs that caused hemorrhages of black blood, the plague killed tens of thousands of people. The epidemic had profound political as well as social consequences. It weakened Justinian's military resources, thus hampering his efforts to restore unity to the Mediterranean world.

Life in Constantinople

By the seventh century Constantinople was the greatest city in the Christian world: a large population center, the seat of the imperial court and administration, and the pivot of a large volume of international trade. Given that the city was a natural geographical connecting point between East and West, its markets offered goods from many parts of the world. Furs and timber flowed across the Black Sea from the Rus (Russia) to the capital, as did slaves across the Mediterranean from northern Europe and the Balkans via Venice. Spices, silks, jewelry, and other luxury goods came to Constantinople from India and China by way of Arabia, the Red Sea, and the Indian Ocean. In return, the city exported glassware, mosaics, gold coins, silk cloth, carpets, and a host of other products, with much foreign trade in the hands of Italian merchants. At the end of the eleventh century Constantinople may have been the world's third-largest city, with only Córdoba in Spain and Kaifeng in China larger.

Although merchants could become fabulously wealthy, the landed aristocracy always held the dominant social position, as in western Europe and China. By contrast, merchants and craftsmen, even when they acquired considerable wealth, never won social prominence. Aristocrats and monasteries usually invested their wealth in real estate, which involved little risk but brought little gain.

Constantinople did not enjoy constant political stability. Between the accession of Emperor Heraclius in 610 and the fall of the city to Western Crusaders in 1204 (see page 404), four separate dynasties ruled at Constantinople. Imperial government involved such intricate court intrigue, assassination plots, and military revolts that the word *byzantine* is sometimes used in English to mean extremely entangled and complicated politics.

What do we know about private life in Constantinople? Research has revealed a fair amount about the Byzantine *oikos* (OI-kohs), or household. The typical household in the city included family members and servants, some of whom were slaves. Artisans lived and worked in their shops, while clerks, civil servants, minor officials, and business people—those who today would be called middle class—commonly dwelled in multistory buildings perhaps comparable to the apartment complexes of modern American cities. Wealthy aristocrats resided in freestanding mansions that frequently included interior courts, galleries, large reception halls, small sleeping rooms, reading and writing rooms, baths, and chapels.

In the homes of the upper classes, the segregation of women seems to have been the first principle of interior design. As in ancient Athens, private houses contained a *gynaeceum* (guy-neh-KEE-uhm), or women's apartment, where women were kept strictly separated from the outside world. The fundamental reason for this segregation was the family's honor. As an eleventh-century Byzantine writer put it, "An unchaste daughter is guilty of harming not only herself but also her parents and relatives. That is why you should keep your daughters under lock and key, as if proven guilty or imprudent, in order to avoid venomous bites."[1]

As it was throughout the world, marriage was part of a family's strategy for social advancement. Both the immediate family and the larger kinship group participated in the selection of a bride or a groom, choosing a spouse who might enhance the family's wealth or prestige.

Sarcophagus of Helena This marble sarcophagus was made for Helena, the mother of Emperor Constantine, at her death. Its detailed carvings show victorious Roman horsemen and barbarian prisoners. Like her son, Helena became a Christian, and she was sent by Constantine on a journey to bring sacred relics from Jerusalem to Constantinople as part of his efforts to promote Christianity in the empire. (© Vanni Archive/Art Resource, NY)

The Growth of the Christian Church

☐ How did the Christian Church become a major force in Europe?

As the Western Roman Empire disintegrated, the Christian Church survived and grew, becoming the most important institution in Europe. The able administrators of the church developed permanent institutions that drew on the Greco-Roman tradition but also expressed Christian values.

The Evolution of Church Leadership and Orthodoxy

Believers in early Christian communities chose their own leaders, but as the centuries passed appointment by existing church leaders or secular rulers became the common practice. During the reign of Diocletian (r. 284–305), the Roman Empire had been divided for administrative purposes into geographical units called **dioceses**, and Christianity adopted this pattern. Each diocese was headed by a bishop, who was responsible for organizing preaching, overseeing the community's goods, maintaining orthodox (established or correct) doctrine, and delegating responsibilities for preaching and teaching. The center of a bishop's authority was his cathedral, a word deriving from the Latin *cathedra*, meaning "chair."

The early Christian Church benefited from the administrative abilities of church leaders. Bishop

Ambrose of Milan (339–397) was typical of the Roman aristocrats who held high public office, converted to Christianity, and subsequently became bishops. Like many bishops, Ambrose had a solid education in classical law and rhetoric, which he used to become an eloquent preacher. He had a strong sense of his authority and even stood up to Emperor Theodosius (r. 379–395), who had ordered Ambrose to hand over his major church—called a basilica—to the emperor:

> At length came the command, "Deliver up the Basilica"; I reply, "It is not lawful for us to deliver it up, nor for your Majesty to receive it. By no law can you violate the house of a private man, and do you think that the house of God may be taken away? . . . But do not burden your conscience with the thought that you have any right as Emperor over sacred things. . . . It is written, God's to God and Caesar's to Caesar. The palace is the Emperor's, the churches are the Bishop's. To you is committed jurisdiction over public, not over sacred buildings."[2]

The emperor relented. Ambrose's assertion that the church was supreme in spiritual matters and the state in secular issues was to serve as the cornerstone of the church's position on church-state relations for centuries. Because of his strong influence, Ambrose came to be regarded as one of the "fathers of the church," that is, early Christian thinkers whose authority was regarded as second only to the Bible in later centuries.

Although conflicts like these between religious and secular leaders were frequent, the church also received support from the emperors. In 380 Theodosius made Christianity the official religion of the empire, and later in his reign he authorized the closure or destruction of temples and holy sites dedicated to the traditional Roman and Greek gods. In return for such support, the emperors expected the Christian Church's assistance in maintaining order and unity.

Christians disagreed with one another about many issues, which led to schisms (SKIH-zuhms), denunciations, and sometimes violence. In the fourth and fifth centuries disputes arose over the nature of Christ. For example, Arianism, developed by Arius (ca. 250–336), a priest of Alexandria, held that Jesus was created by the will of God the Father and thus was not co-eternal with him. Arian Christians reasoned that Jesus the Son must be inferior to God the Father, because the Father was incapable of suffering and did not die. Emperor Constantine, who legalized Christianity in 312, rejected the Arian interpretation and decided that religious disagreement meant civil disorder. In 325 he summoned a council of church leaders to Nicaea in Asia Minor and presided over it personally. The council produced the Nicene (nigh-SEEN) Creed, which defined the position that Christ is "eternally begotten of the Father" and of the same substance as the Father. Arius and those who refused to accept Nicene Christianity were banished. Their interpretation of the nature of Christ was declared a **heresy**, that is, a belief that contradicted the interpretation the church leaders declared was correct, which was termed orthodoxy. These actions did not end Arianism, however. Several later emperors were Arian Christian, and Arian missionaries converted many barbarian tribes who were attracted by the idea that Jesus was God's second-in-command, which fit well with their own warrior hierarchies and was less complicated than the idea of two persons with one substance. The Nicene interpretation eventually became the most widely held understanding of the nature of Christ, however, and is accepted today by the Roman Catholic Church, the Eastern Orthodox Churches, and most Protestant Churches.

The Nicene Creed says little specifically about the Holy Spirit, but in the following centuries the idea that the Father, Son, and Holy Spirit are "one substance in three persons"—the Trinity—became a central doctrine in Christianity, though again there were those who disagreed. Disputes about the nature of Christ also continued, with factions establishing themselves as separate Christian groups. The Nestorians, for example, regarded the divine and human natures in Jesus as distinct from one another, whereas the orthodox opinion was that they were united. The Nestorians split from the rest of the church in the fifth century after their position was outlawed and settled in Persia. Nestorian Christian missionaries later founded churches in Central Asia, India, and China (see Chapter 12).

The Western Church and the Eastern Church

The leader of the church in the West, the bishop of Rome, became more powerful than his counterpart in the Byzantine East for a variety of reasons. Most significantly, bishops of Rome asserted that Rome had a special place in Christian history. According to tradition, Saint Peter, chief of Jesus's disciples, had lived in Rome and been its first bishop. Thus, as successors of Peter, the bishops of Rome—known as **popes**, from the Latin word *papa*, meaning "father"—claimed a privileged position in the church hierarchy, an idea called the Petrine Doctrine. They urged other churches to appeal to Rome for the resolution of disputed issues and sent letters of guidance to other bishops. (The

- **dioceses** Geographic administrative districts of the church, each under the authority of a bishop and centered around a cathedral.
- **heresy** A religious practice or belief judged unacceptable by church officials.
- **popes** Heads of the Roman Catholic Church, who became political as well as religious authorities. The period of a pope's term in office is called a pontificate.

Saint Jerome and Saint Ambrose This wood carving shows Saint Ambrose and Saint Jerome, two of the most important early church fathers, hard at work writing. Divine inspiration appears in the form of an angel and a dove. (Duomo, Modena, Italy/Alinari/Art Resource, NY)

Christian Church headed by the pope in Rome was generally called the Roman Church in this era, and later the Roman Catholic Church. The word *catholic* derives from a Greek word meaning "general," "universal," or "worldwide.")

The popes also expanded the church's secular authority. They made treaties with barbarian leaders, charged taxes, enforced laws, and organized armies. The Western Christian Church headed by the pope in Rome would become the most enduring nongovernmental institution in world history.

By contrast, in the East the emperor's jurisdiction over the church was fully acknowledged, even though the bishops of Antioch, Alexandria, Jerusalem, and Constantinople had more power than other bishops. As in Rome, there was a head of the church in Constantinople, called the patriarch, but he did not develop the same powers that the pope did in the West because there was never a similar power vacuum into which he needed to step. He and other high church officials were appointed by the emperor. The Eastern emperors looked on religion as a branch of the state, and they considered it their duty to protect the faith not only against heathen outsiders but also against heretics within the empire. Following the pattern set by Constantine, the emperors summoned councils of bishops and theologians to settle doctrinal disputes. They and the Eastern bishops did not accept Rome's claim to primacy, and gradually the Byzantine Christian Church, generally called the **Orthodox Church**, and the Roman Church began to diverge. (*Orthodoxy* with a capital *O* refers to the Eastern Church, and *orthodoxy* with a lowercase *o* means correct doctrine as defined by church leaders.) In addition, other branches of Christianity in the East, including the Nestorians, Maronites, and Copts, developed their own distinctive theological ideas and patterns of organization. Some of these later joined with Roman Catholicism and affirmed the primacy of the pope, but many remain independent branches of Christianity today. About 20 percent of the population of Lebanon in 2010, for example, was Maronite Christian, and about 10 percent of the population of Egypt was Coptic Christian.

• **Orthodox Church** Another name for the Eastern Christian Church, over which emperors continued to have power.

Christian Monasticism

Christianity began and spread as a city religion. With time, however, some especially pious Christians started to feel that a life of asceticism (extreme material sacrifice, including fasting and the renunciation of sex) was a better way to show their devotion to Christ's teachings, just as followers of Mahavira or the Buddha had centuries earlier in South Asia (see Chapter 3). Asceticism was—and is—a common part of many religious traditions, either as a temporary practice during especially holy times or as a permanent way of life.

Ascetics often separate themselves from their families and normal social life, and this is what Christian ascetics did. Individuals and small groups withdrew from cities and moved to the Egyptian desert, where they sought God through prayer in caves and shelters in the desert or mountains. These individuals were called hermits (from the Greek word *eremos*, meaning "desert") or monks (from the Greek word *monos*, meaning "alone"). Gradually, large groups of monks emerged in the deserts of Upper Egypt, creating a style of life known as monasticism. Many devout women were also attracted to this eremitical type of monasticism, becoming nuns. Although monks and nuns led isolated lives, ordinary people soon recognized them as holy people and sought them as spiritual guides.

Church leaders did not really approve of eremitical life. Hermits sometimes claimed to have mystical experiences—direct communications with God. If hermits could communicate directly with the Lord, what need had they for priests, bishops, and the institutional church? The church hierarchy instead encouraged those who wanted to live ascetic lives of devotion to do so in communities. Communal living in a monastery, they argued, provided an environment for training the aspirant in the virtues of charity, poverty, and freedom from self-deception. Consequently, in the fourth, fifth, and sixth centuries many different kinds of communal monasticism developed in Gaul, Italy, Spain, Anglo-Saxon England, and Ireland.

In 529 Benedict of Nursia (ca. 480–547), who had experimented with both the eremitical and the communal forms of monastic life, wrote a brief set of regulations for the monks who had gathered around him at Monte Cassino, between Rome and Naples. Benedict's guide for monastic life, known as *The Rule of Saint Benedict*, slowly replaced all others, and it has influenced all forms of organized religious life in the Roman Church. The guide outlined a monastic life of regularity, discipline, and moderation in an atmosphere of silence. Under Benedict's regulations, monks spent part of each day in formal prayer, chanting psalms and other prayers from the Bible. The rest of the day was passed in manual labor, study, and private prayer. The monastic life as conceived by Saint Benedict provided opportunities for men of different abilities and talents—from mechanics to gardeners to literary scholars. The Benedictine form of religious life also appealed to women, because it allowed them to show their devotion and engage in study. Benedict's twin sister, Scholastica (480–543), adapted the *Rule* for use by her community of nuns.

Benedictine monasticism also succeeded partly because it was so materially successful. In the seventh and eighth centuries Benedictine monasteries pushed back forests and wastelands, drained swamps, and experimented with crop rotation, making a significant contribution to the agricultural development of Europe. In the process they sometimes earned immense wealth. Monasteries also conducted schools for local young people. Some learned about prescriptions and herbal remedies and went on to provide medical treatment for their localities. Others copied manuscripts and wrote books. Local and royal governments drew on the services of the literate men and able administrators the monasteries produced.

Because all monasteries followed rules, men who lived a communal monastic life came to be called regular clergy, from the Latin word *regulus* (rule). In contrast, priests and bishops who staffed churches in which people worshipped and who were not cut off from the world were called secular clergy. According to official church doctrine, women were not members of the clergy, but this distinction was not clear to most people.

Monasticism in the Orthodox world differed in fundamental ways from the monasticism that evolved in western Europe. First, while *The Rule of Saint Benedict* gradually became the universal guide for all western European monasteries, each monastic house in the Byzantine world developed its own set of rules for organization and behavior. Second, education never became a central feature of the Orthodox houses. Monks and nuns had to be literate to perform the services of the choir, and children destined for the monastic life were taught to read and write, but no monastery assumed responsibility for the general training of the local young. Since bishops and patriarchs of the Orthodox Church were recruited only from the monasteries, however, these institutions did exercise cultural influence.

Christian Ideas and Practices

- How did Christian thinkers adapt classical ideas to Christian teachings, and what new religious concepts and practices did they develop?

The growth of Christianity was tied not just to institutions such as the papacy and monasteries but also to ideas. Initially, Christians rejected Greco-Roman culture. Gradually, however, Christian leaders and thinkers developed ideas that drew on classical influences, though there were also areas of controversy that differed in the Western and Eastern Churches.

Christianity and Classical Culture

In the first century Christians believed that Christ would soon fulfill his promise to return and that the end of the world was near; therefore, they saw no point in devoting time to learning. By the second century, however, these apocalyptic expectations were diminishing, and church leaders began to incorporate elements of Greek and Roman philosophy and learning into Christian teachings (see page 168). They found support for this incorporation in the written texts that circulated among Christians. In the third and fourth centuries these texts were brought together as the New

Testament of the Bible, with general agreement about most of what should be included but sharp disputes about some books. Although some of Jesus's sermons as recorded in the Gospels (see page 168) urged followers to avoid worldly attachments, other parts of the Bible advocated acceptance of existing social, economic, and political structures. Christian thinkers built on these, adapting Christian teachings to fit with Roman realities and Roman ideas to fit with Christian aims, just as Buddhist thinkers adapted Buddhist teachings when they spread them to Central Asia, China, Korea, and Japan (see Chapter 7).

Saint Jerome (340–419), a distinguished theologian and linguist regarded as a father of the church, translated the Old Testament and New Testament from Hebrew and Greek, respectively, into vernacular Latin. Called the Vulgate, his edition of the Bible served as the official translation until the sixteenth century, and scholars rely on it even today. Familiar with the writings of classical authors such as Cicero and Virgil, Saint Jerome believed that Christians should study the best of ancient thought because it would direct their minds to God. He maintained that the best ancient literature should be interpreted in light of the Christian faith.

Christian attitudes toward gender and sexuality provide a good example of the ways early Christians first challenged and then largely adopted the views of their contemporary world. In his plan of salvation Jesus considered women the equal of men. Women were among the earliest converts to Christianity and took an active role in its spread, preaching, acting as missionaries, being martyred alongside men, and perhaps even baptizing believers. Because early Christians believed that the second coming of Christ was imminent, they devoted their energies to their new spiritual family of co-believers. Also, they often met in people's homes and called one another brother and sister, a metaphorical use of family terms that was new to the Roman Empire. Some women embraced the ideal of virginity and either singly or in monastic communities declared themselves "virgins in the service of Christ." All this initially made Christianity seem dangerous to many Romans, who viewed marriage as the foundation of society and the proper patriarchal order.

Not all Christian teachings about gender were radical, however. In the first century male church leaders began to place restrictions on female believers. Women were forbidden to preach and were gradually excluded from holding official positions in Christianity other than in women's monasteries. In so limiting the activities of female believers, Christianity was following well-established social patterns, just as it modeled its official hierarchy after that of the Roman Empire.

Christian teachings about sexuality also built on and challenged classical models. The rejection of sexual activity involved an affirmation of the importance of a spiritual life, but it also incorporated hostility toward the body found in some Hellenistic philosophies. Just as spirit was superior to matter, the thinking went, the mind was superior to the body. Though Christian teachings affirmed that God had created the material world and sanctioned marriage, most Christian think-

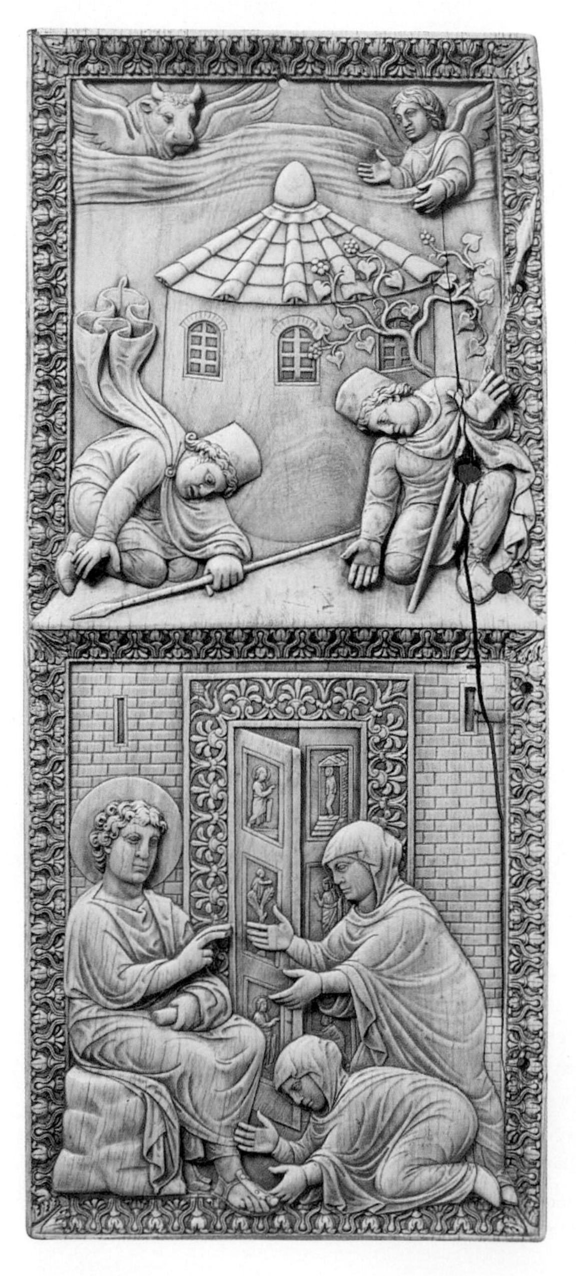

The Marys at Jesus's Tomb This late-fourth-century ivory panel tells the biblical story of Mary Magdalene and another Mary who went to Jesus's tomb to anoint the body (Matthew 28:1–7). At the top guards collapse when an angel descends from Heaven, and at the bottom the Marys listen to the angel telling them that Jesus has risen. Here the artist uses Roman artistic styles to convey Christian subject matter, synthesizing classical form and Christian teaching. (Castello Sforzesco Milan, Italy/Scala/Art Resource, NY)

ers also taught that celibacy was the better life and that anything that distracted one's attention from the spiritual world performed an evil function. For most clerical writers (who were themselves male), this temptation came from women, and in some of their writings women themselves are portrayed as evil, the "devil's gateway." Thus the writings of many church fathers contain a strong streak of misogyny (hatred of women), which was passed down to later Christian thinkers.

Saint Augustine on Sin, Grace, and Redemption

One thinker had an especially strong role in shaping Christian views about sexual activity and many other issues: Saint Augustine of Hippo (354–430), the most influential church father in the West. Augustine was born into an urban family in what is now Algeria in North Africa. His father, a minor civil servant, was a pagan; his mother, Monica, was a devout Christian. He gained an excellent education, fathered a son, and experimented with various religious ideas. In adulthood he converted to his mother's religion, eventually becoming bishop of the city of Hippo Regius. Augustine gained renown as a preacher, a vigorous defender of orthodox Christianity, and the author of more than ninety-three books and treatises.

Augustine's autobiography, *The Confessions*, is a literary masterpiece and one of the most influential books in Western history. Written in the rhetorical style and language of late Roman antiquity, it marks a synthesis of Greco-Roman forms and Christian thought. *The Confessions* describes Augustine's moral struggle, the conflict between his spiritual aspirations and his sensual self. Many Greek and Roman philosophers had taught that knowledge would lead to virtue. Augustine came to reject this idea, claiming that people do not always act on the basis of rational knowledge. Instead the basic or dynamic force in any individual is the will. When Adam ate the fruit forbidden by God in the Garden of Eden (Genesis 3:6), he committed the "original sin" and corrupted the will, wrote Augustine. Adam's sin did not simply remain his own but was passed on to all later humans through sexual intercourse; even infants were tainted. Original sin thus became a common social stain, in Augustine's opinion, transmitted by sexual desire. By viewing sexual desire as the result of Adam and Eve's disobedience to divine instructions, Augustine linked sexuality even more clearly with sin than had earlier church fathers. According to Augustine, because Adam disobeyed God, all human beings have an innate tendency to sin: their will is weak. But Augustine held that God restores the strength of the will through grace, which is transmitted in certain rituals that the church defined as **sacraments**. Augustine's ideas on sin, grace, and redemption became the foundation of all subsequent Western Christian theology, Protestant as well as Catholic.

The Iconoclastic Controversy

Augustine's ideas about original sin did not become important in the Eastern Orthodox Church, where other issues seemed more significant. In the centuries after Constantine, the most serious dispute within the Orthodox Church concerned icons—images or representations of God the Father, Jesus, and the saints in painting, bas-relief, or mosaic. Since the third century the church had allowed people to venerate icons. Although all prayer was to be directed to God the Father, Christian teaching held that icons representing the saints fostered reverence and that Jesus and the saints could most effectively plead a cause to God the Father. (For more about the role of saints, see page 226.) Iconoclasts, those who favored the destruction of icons, argued that people were worshipping the image itself rather than what it signified. This, they claimed, constituted idolatry, a violation of one of the Ten Commandments, the religious and moral code found in Hebrew Scripture that was also sacred to Christians.

The result of this dispute was a terrible theological conflict, the **iconoclastic controversy**, that split the Byzantine world for a century. In 730 the emperor Leo III (r. 717–741) ordered the destruction of icons. The removal of these images from Byzantine churches provoked a violent reaction: entire provinces revolted, and the Byzantine Empire and the Roman papacy severed relations. Since Eastern monasteries were the fiercest defenders of icons, Leo's son Constantine V (r. 741–775), nicknamed Copronymous ("Dung-name") by his enemies, took the war to the monasteries. He seized their property, executed some of the monks, and forced other monks into the army. Theological disputes and civil disorder over the icons continued intermittently until 843, when the icons were restored.

The implications of the iconoclastic controversy extended far beyond strictly theological issues. Iconoclasm raised the question of the right of the emperor to intervene in religious disputes—a central problem in the relations between church and state. Iconoclasm antagonized the pope and served to encourage him in his quest for an alliance with the Frankish monarchy (see page 227). This further divided the two parts of Christendom, and in 1054 a theological disagreement led the pope in Rome and the patriarch of Constantinople to declare each other a heretic. The outcome was

- **sacraments** Certain rituals of the church believed to act as a conduit of God's grace, such as the Eucharist and baptism.
- **iconoclastic controversy** The conflict over the veneration of religious images in the Byzantine Empire.

a continuing schism between the Roman Catholic and the Orthodox Churches.

From a cultural perspective, the ultimate acceptance of icons profoundly influenced subsequent religious art within Christianity. The Greco-Roman tradition of giving divine figures human forms continued in both Eastern and Western Christianity, in contrast to Judaism and Islam, in which images of divine figures were often prohibited. These images became important tools in conversion and in people's devotional lives.

Migrating Peoples

☐ How did the barbarians shape social, economic, and political structures in Europe and western Asia?

Along with *The Confessions*, Augustine's other major work was *The City of God*, a work that develops a Christian view of history and was written in direct response to what many people in Rome thought was a disaster: the capture of the city in 410 by Visigothic forces. The Visigoths were one of the many peoples moving west and south from Central Asia and northern Europe that the Romans—and later historians—labeled "barbarians" (Map 8.2). The word *barbarian* comes from the Greek *barbaros*, meaning someone who did not speak Greek. (To the Greeks, others seemed to be speaking nonsense syllables; *barbar* is the Greek equivalent of "blah-blah" or "yada-yada.") The Greeks used this word to include people such as the Egyptians, whom the Greeks respected. The Romans usually used the Latin version of *barbarian* to mean the peoples who lived beyond the northeastern boundary of Roman territory, whom they regarded as unruly, savage, and primitive. (See "Viewpoints 8.2: Roman and Byzantine Views of Barbarians," page 222.) That value judgment is generally also present when we use *barbarian* in English, but there really is no other word to describe the many different peoples who lived to the north of the Roman Empire. Thus historians of late antiquity use the word *barbarian* to designate these peoples, who spoke a variety of languages but had similarities in their basic social, economic, and political structures. Many of these historians find much to admire in barbarian society.

Barbarians included many different ethnic groups with social and political structures, languages, laws, and beliefs developed in central and northern Europe and western Asia over many centuries. Among the largest barbarian groups were the Celts (whom the Romans called Gauls) and Germans; Germans were further subdivided into various tribes, such as Ostrogoths, Visigoths, Burgundians, and Franks. *Celt* and *German* are often used as ethnic terms, but they are better understood as linguistic terms, a Celt being a person who spoke a Celtic language, an ancestor of the modern Gaelic or Breton languages, and a German one who spoke a Germanic language, an ancestor of modern German, Dutch, Danish, Swedish, and Norwegian. Celts, Germans, and other barbarians brought their customs and traditions with them when they moved south and west, and these gradually combined with classical and Christian customs and beliefs to form new types of societies. From this cultural mix the Franks emerged as an especially strong and influential force, and they built a lasting empire (see page 227).

Social and Economic Structures

Barbarian groups usually resided in small villages, and climate and geography determined the basic patterns of agricultural and pastoral life. Many groups settled on the edges of clearings where they raised barley, wheat, oats, peas, and beans. Men and women tilled their fields with simple scratch plows, which broke the soil with wooden spikes, and harvested their grain with small iron sickles. The kernels of grain were eaten as porridge, ground up for flour, or fermented into strong, thick beer. Most of people's caloric intake came from grain in some form.

Within the villages, there were great differences in wealth and status. Free men and their families constituted the largest class, and the number of cattle these men possessed indicated their wealth and determined their social status. Free men also took part in tribal warfare. Slaves acquired through warfare worked as farm laborers, herdsmen, and household servants. Barbarian society was patriarchal: within each household the father had authority over his wife, children, and slaves. Some wealthy and powerful men had more than one wife, a pattern that continued even after they became Christian, but polygamy was not widespread among ordinary people. Once women were widowed, they sometimes assumed their husbands' rights over family property and took guardianship of their children.

Tribes, Warriors, and Laws

The basic social and political unit among barbarian groups was the tribe or confederation, made up of kin groups whose members believed they were all descended from a common ancestor. Tribes were led by chieftains, recognized by tribe members as the strongest and bravest in battle. Each chief was elected from among the male members of the most powerful family. He led the tribe in war, settled disputes among its members, conducted negotiations with outside powers, and offered sacrifices to the gods. As barbarian groups migrated into and conquered parts of the Western Roman Empire, their chiefs became even more power-

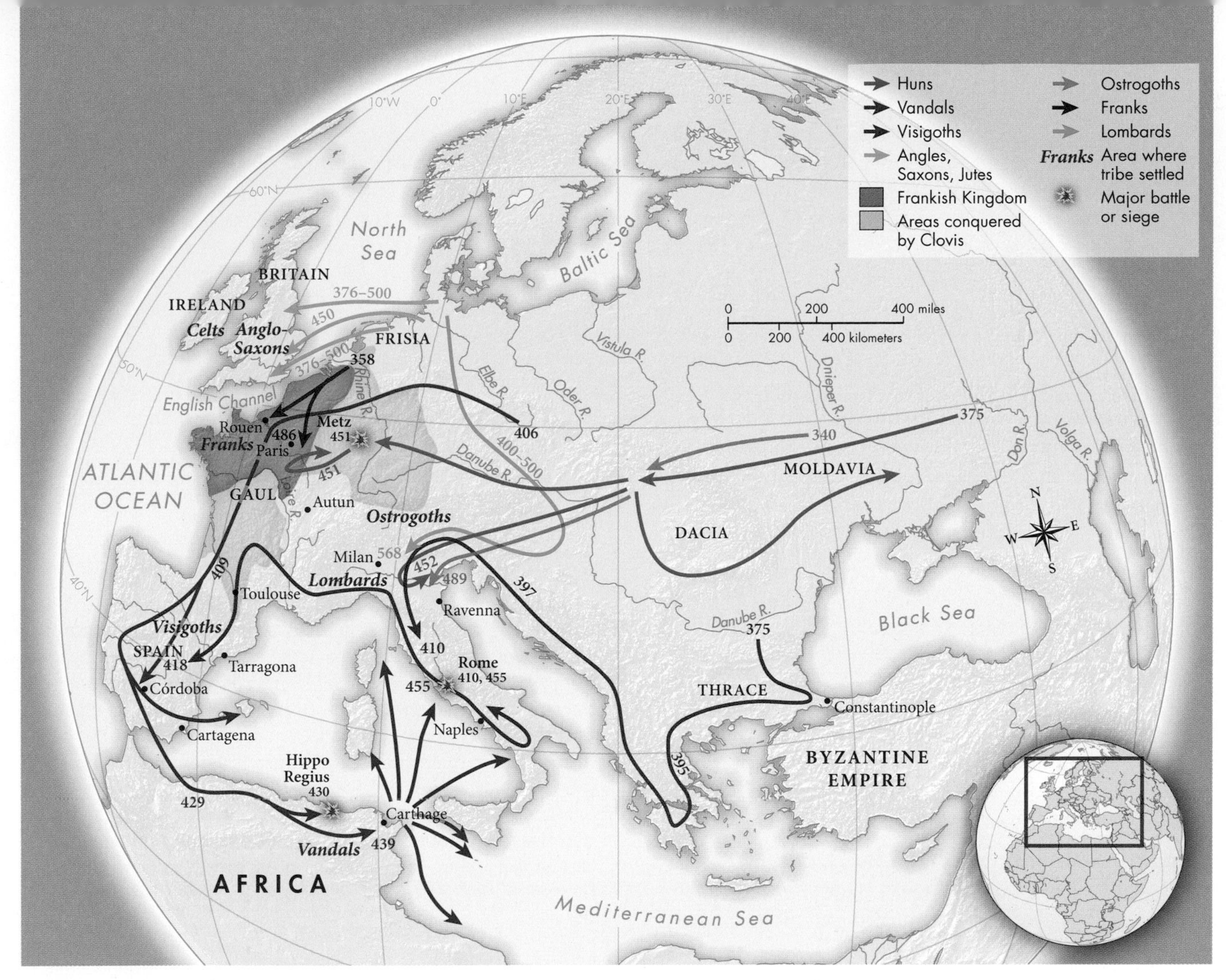

MAP 8.2 The Barbarian Migrations, ca. 340–500 Various barbarian groups migrated throughout Europe and western Asia in late antiquity, pushed and pulled by a number of factors. Many of them formed loosely structured states, of which the Frankish kingdom would become the most significant.

ful. Often chiefs adopted the title of king, though this title implies broader power than they actually had.

Closely associated with the chief in some tribes was the comitatus (kuhm-ee-TAH-tuhs), or war band. The warriors swore loyalty to the chief and fought alongside him in battle. Warriors may originally have been relatively equal to one another, but during the migrations and warfare of the second through the fourth centuries, the war band was transformed into a system of stratified ranks. When tribes settled down, warriors also began to acquire land as both a mark of prestige and a means to power. Social inequalities emerged and gradually grew stronger. These inequalities help explain the origins of the European noble class.

Early barbarian tribes had no written laws. Law was custom, but certain individuals were often given special training in remembering and retelling laws from generation to generation. Beginning in the late fifth century, however, some chieftains began to collect, write, and publish lists of their customs and laws.

Barbarian law codes often included clauses designed to reduce interpersonal violence. Any crime that involved a personal injury, such as assault, rape, and murder, was given a particular monetary value, called the **wergeld** (WEHR-gehld) (literally "man-money" or "money to buy off the spear"), that was to be paid by a person accused of a crime to the victim or the victim's family. If the accused agreed to pay the wergeld and if the victim or his or her family accepted the payment, there was peace. If the accused refused to pay the wergeld or if the victim or family refused to accept it, a blood feud ensued.

The wergeld varied according to the severity of the crime and also the social status and gender of the victim, as shown in these clauses from the law code of the Salian Franks, one of the barbarian tribes.

> If any person strike another on the head so that the brain appears, and the three bones which lie above the brain shall project, he shall be sentenced to 1200 denars, which make 300 shillings. . . .

- **wergeld** Compensatory payment for death or injury set in many barbarian law codes.

Viewpoints 8.2

Roman and Byzantine Views of Barbarians

• *The earliest written records about the barbarian groups that migrated, attacked, and sometimes conquered the more urbanized and densely populated areas of Europe and western Asia all come from the pens of educated Greeks, Romans, and Byzantines. They provide us with important information about barbarians, but always from the perspective of outsiders with a particular point of view. The selections below are typical of such commentary. The first is from the fourth-century Roman general and historian Ammianus Marcellinus, who fought in Roman armies against Germanic tribes, the Huns, and the Persians and later wrote a history of the Roman Empire. The second is from the sixth-century Byzantine historian Agathias, describing recent encounters between the forces of the Byzantine emperor Justinian and various Germanic tribes.*

Ammianus Marcellinus on the Huns, ca. 380

"The people of the Huns, but little known from ancient records, dwelling beyond the Maeotic Sea near the ice-bound ocean, exceed every degree of savagery. . . . They all have compact, strong limbs and thick necks, and are so monstrously ugly and misshapen, that one might take them for two-legged beasts or for the stumps, rough-hewn into images, that are used in putting sides to bridges. But although they have the form of men, however ugly, they are so hardy in their mode of life that they have no need of fire nor of savory food, but eat the roots of wild plants and the half-raw flesh of any kind of animal whatever, which they put between their thighs and the backs of their horses, and thus warm a little. They are never protected by any buildings, but they avoid these like tombs. . . . They are not at all adapted to battles on foot, but they are almost glued to their horses, which are hardy, it is true, but ugly. . . . They fight from a distance with missiles having sharp bone [points], instead of the usual (metal) parts, joined to the shafts with wonderful skill; then they gallop over the intervening spaces and fight hand to hand with swords, regardless of their own lives. . . . No one in their country ever plows a field or touches a plow-handle. They are all without fixed abode, without hearth, or law, or settled mode of life, and keep roaming from place to place, like fugitives, accompanied by wagons in which they live; in wagons their wives weave for them their hideous garments, in wagons they cohabit with their husbands, bear children, and rear them to the age of puberty."

Agathias on the Franks

"The Franks are not nomads, as indeed some barbarian peoples are, but their system of government, administration and laws are modelled more or less on the Roman pattern, apart from which they uphold similar standards with regard to contracts, marriage, and religious observance. They are in fact all Christians and adhere to the strictest orthodoxy. They also have magistrates in their cities and priests and celebrate the feasts in the same way we do, and, for a barbarian people, strike me as extremely well-bred and civilized and as practically the same as ourselves except for their uncouth style of dress and peculiar language. I admire them for their other attributes and especially for the spirit of justice and harmony which prevails amongst them."

Sources: Reprinted by permission of the publishers and the Trustees of the Loeb Classical Library® from *Ammianus Marcellinus: Volume I*, Loeb Classical Library Volume 331, with an English translation by John C. Rolfe (Cambridge, Mass.: Harvard University Press), pp. 383, 385. Copyright © 1939 by the President and Fellows of Harvard College. Loeb Classical Library® is a registered trademark of the President and Fellows of Harvard College; Agathias, *The Histories*, translated by Joseph D. Frendo (Berlin: Walter de Gruyter, 1975), p. 10.

QUESTIONS FOR ANALYSIS

1. What qualities of the Huns does Ammianus Marcellinus find admirable? What does he criticize?
2. What qualities of the Franks does Agathias praise? Why does he find these qualities admirable?
3. How does the fact that both Ammianus Marcellinus and Agathias come from agricultural societies with large cities shape their views of barbarians?

> If any one have killed a free woman after she has begun bearing children, he shall be sentenced to 2400 denars, which make 600 shillings.[3]

In other codes as well, a crime against a woman of childbearing years often carried a wergeld as substantial as that for a man of higher stature, suggesting that barbarians were concerned about maintaining their population levels.

Like most people of the ancient world, barbarians worshipped hundreds of gods and goddesses with specialized functions. They regarded certain natural features as sacred because these were linked to deities. Rituals to honor the gods were held outdoors rather than in temples or churches,

Visigothic Work and Play This page comes from one of the very few manuscripts from the time of the barbarian invasions to have survived, a copy of the first five books of the Old Testament — the Pentateuch — made around 600, perhaps in Visigothic Spain or North Africa. The top shows biblical scenes, while the bottom shows people engaged in everyday activities: building a wall, drawing water from a well, and trading punches. (Bibliothèque Nationale, Paris, France/The Art Archive at Art Resource, NY)

often at certain points in the yearly agricultural cycle. Among the Celts, religious leaders called druids had legal and educational as well as religious functions, orally passing down laws and traditions from generation to generation. Bards singing poems and ballads also passed down myths and stories of heroes and gods, which were written down much later.

Migrations and Political Change

Migrating groups that the Romans labeled barbarians had moved southward and eastward off and on since about 100 C.E. (see page 171). As their movements became more organized in the third and fourth centuries, Roman armies sought to defend the Rhine-Danube border of the Roman Empire, but with troop levels low because Italians were increasingly unwilling to serve in the army, generals were forced to recruit barbarians, some of whom rose to the highest ranks.

Why did the barbarians migrate? In part, they were searching for more regular supplies of food, better farmland, and a warmer climate. Conflicts within and among barbarian groups also led to war and disruption, which motivated groups to move. Franks fought Alemanni (another Germanic tribe) in Gaul, while Visigoths fought Vandals in the Iberian Peninsula and across North Africa. Roman expansion led to further movement of barbarian groups but also to the blending of cultures.

The spread of the Celts presents a good example of both conflict and assimilation. Celtic-speaking peoples had lived in central Europe since at least the fifth century B.C.E. and had spread out from there to the Iberian Peninsula in the west, Hungary in the east, and the British Isles in the north. As Julius Caesar advanced northward into what he termed Gaul (present-day France), he defeated many Celtic tribes (see page 155). Celtic peoples conquered by the Romans often assimilated to Roman ways, adopting the Latin language and many aspects of Roman culture. Also, Celts and Romans intermarried, and many Celtic men became Roman citizens and joined the Roman army. By the fourth century C.E., however, Gaul and Britain were under pressure from Germanic groups moving westward.

Roman troops withdrew from Britain, and Celtic-speaking peoples clashed with Germanic-speaking invaders, of whom the largest tribes were the Angles and the Saxons. Some Celtic-speakers moved farther west, to Brittany (modern northwestern France), Wales, Scotland, and Ireland. Others remained and intermarried with Germanic peoples, their descendants forming a number of small Anglo-Saxon kingdoms.

In eastern Europe, a significant factor in barbarian migration and the merging of various Germanic groups was pressure from nomadic steppe peoples from Central Asia. These included the Alans, Avars, Bulgars, Khazars, and most prominently the Huns, who attacked the Black Sea area and the Eastern Roman Empire beginning in the fourth century. Under the leadership of their warrior-king Attila, the Huns attacked the Byzantine Empire in 447 and then turned westward, allying with some Germanic groups and moving into what is now France. After Attila turned his army southward and crossed the Alps into Italy, a papal delegation, including Pope Leo I himself, asked him not to attack Rome. Though papal diplomacy was later credited with stopping the advance of the Huns, their dwindling food supplies and a plague that spread among their troops were probably much more important factors. The Huns retreated from Italy, and within a year Attila was dead. Later leaders were not as effective, and the Huns never again played a significant role in European history. Their conquests had pushed many Germanic groups together, however, which transformed smaller bands of people into larger, more unified peoples who could more easily pick the Western Roman Empire apart.

After they conquered an area, barbarians generally established states ruled by kings. However, the kingdoms did not have definite geographical borders, and their locations shifted as tribes moved. Eventually, barbarian kingdoms came to include Italy itself. The Western Roman emperors increasingly relied on barbarian commanders and their troops to maintain order, and, as we saw in Chapter 6, in 476 the barbarian chieftain Odoacer deposed Romulus Augustus, the last person to have the title of Roman emperor in the West. Odoacer did not take the title of emperor, calling himself instead the king of Italy, so that this date marks the official end of the Roman Empire in the West. From Constantinople, Eastern Roman emperors such as Justinian (see page 210) worked to reconquer at least some of the West from barbarian tribes. They were occasionally successful but could not hold the empire together for long.

Anglo-Saxon Helmet This ceremonial bronze helmet from seventh-century England was found inside a ship buried at Sutton Hoo. The nearly 100-foot-long ship was dragged overland before being buried completely. It held one body and many grave goods, including swords, gold buckles, and silver bowls made in Byzantium. The unidentified person who was buried here was clearly wealthy and powerful, and so was very likely a chief.

Christian Missionaries and Conversion

☐ How did the church convert barbarian peoples to Christianity?

The Mediterranean served as the highway over which Christianity spread to the cities of the Roman Empire. Christian teachings were initially carried by all types of converts, but they were often spread into the countryside and into areas beyond the borders of the empire by those who had dedicated their lives to the church, such as monks. Such missionaries were often sent by popes specifically to convert certain groups. As they preached to barbarian peoples, the missionaries developed new techniques to convert them.

Missionaries' Actions

Throughout barbarian Europe, religion was not a private or individual matter; it was a social affair, and the religion of the chieftain or king determined the religion of the people. Thus missionaries concentrated their initial efforts not on ordinary people but on kings or tribal chieftains and the members of their families, who then ordered their subjects to convert. Because they had more opportunity to spend time with missionaries, queens and other female members of the royal family were often the first converts in an area, and they influenced their husbands and brothers. Germanic kings sometimes accepted Christianity because they came to believe that the Christian God was more powerful than pagan gods and that the Christian God—in either its Arian or Roman version—would deliver victory in battle. They also appreciated that Christianity taught obedience to kingly as well as divine authority. Christian missionaries were generally literate, and they taught reading and writing to young men who became priests or officials in the royal household, a service that kings appreciated.

Many barbarian groups were converted by Arian missionaries, who also founded dioceses. Bishop Ulfilas (ca. 310–383), for example, an Ostrogoth himself, translated the Bible from Greek into the Gothic language even before Jerome wrote the Latin Vulgate, creating a new Gothic script in order to write it down. Over the next several centuries this text was recopied many times and carried with the Gothic tribes as they migrated throughout southern Europe. In the sixth and seventh centuries most Goths and other Germanic tribes converted to Roman Christianity, sometimes peacefully and sometimes as a result of conquest. Ulfilas's Bible—and the Gothic script he invented—were forgotten and rediscovered only a thousand years later.

Tradition identifies the conversion of Ireland with Saint Patrick (ca. 385–461). After a vision urged him to Christianize Ireland, Patrick studied in Gaul and in 432 was consecrated a bishop. He then returned to Ireland, where he converted the Irish tribe by tribe, first baptizing the king.

The Christianization of the English began in earnest in 597, when Pope Gregory I (pontificate 590–604) sent a delegation of monks to England. The conversion of the English had far-reaching consequences because Britain later served as a base for the Christianization of Germany and other parts of northern Europe (Map 8.3). Between the fifth and tenth centuries the majority of people living on the European continent and the nearby islands accepted the Christian religion—that is, they received baptism, though baptism in itself did not automatically transform people into Christians.

In eastern Europe missionaries traveled far beyond the boundaries of the Byzantine Empire. In 863 the emperor Michael III (r. 842–867) sent the brothers Cyril (826–869) and Methodius (815–885) to preach Christianity in Moravia (an eastern region of the modern Czech Republic). Cyril invented a Slavic alphabet using Greek characters, later called the Cyrillic alphabet in his honor. In the tenth century other missionaries spread Christianity, the Cyrillic alphabet, and Byzantine art and architecture to Russia. The Byzantines were so successful that the Russians would later claim to be the successors of the Byzantine Empire.

The Process of Conversion

When a ruler marched his people to the waters of baptism, the work of Christianization had only begun. Christian kings could order their subjects to be baptized, married, and buried in Christian ceremonies, which ordinary people did increasingly across Europe. Churches could be built, and people could be required to attend services and belong to parishes, but the process of conversion was a gradual one.

How did missionaries and priests get masses of pagan and illiterate peoples to understand Christian ideals and teachings? They did it through preaching, assimilation of pagan customs, the ritual of penance, and veneration of the saints. Those who preached aimed to present the basic teachings of Christianity and strengthen the newly baptized in their faith through stories about the lives of Christ and the saints.

Deeply ingrained pagan customs and practices, however, could not be stamped out by words alone or even by imperial edicts. Thus Christian missionaries often pursued a policy of assimilation, easing the conversion of pagan men and women by stressing similarities between their customs and beliefs and those of Christianity. In the same way that classically trained scholars such as Jerome and Augustine blended Greco-Roman and Christian ideas, missionaries and converts mixed barbarian pagan ideas and practices with Christian ones. For example, bogs and lakes sacred to Germanic gods became associated with saints, as did various aspects of ordinary life, such as traveling, planting crops, and worrying about a sick child. Aspects of existing midwinter celebrations, which often centered on the return of the sun as the days became longer, were assimilated into celebrations of Christmas. Spring rituals involving eggs and rabbits (both symbols of fertility) were added to celebrations of Easter.

The ritual of **penance** was also instrumental in teaching people Christian ideas. Christianity taught that certain actions and thoughts were sins, meaning that they were against God's commands. Only by confessing sins and asking forgiveness could a sinning believer be reconciled with God. Confession was initially a public ritual, but by the fifth century individual confession to a parish priest was more common. During this ritual the individual knelt before the priest, who questioned him or her about sins he or she might have committed. The priest then set a penance such as fasting or saying specific prayers to allow the person to atone for the sin. Penance gave new converts a sense of the behavior expected of Christians, encouraged the private examination of conscience, and offered relief from the burden of sinful deeds.

• **penance** Ritual in which Christians asked a priest for forgiveness for sins and the priest set certain actions to atone for the sins.

Picturing the Past

Hōryūji Temple Japanese Buddhist temples, like those in China and Korea, consisted of several buildings within a walled compound. The buildings of the Hōryūji Temple (built between 670 and 711, after Prince Shōtoku's original temple burned down) include the oldest wooden structures in the world and house some of the best early Buddhist sculpture in Japan. The three main buildings depicted here are the pagoda, housing relics; the main hall, with the temple's principal images; and the lecture hall, for sermons. The five-story pagoda could be seen from far away, much like the steeples of cathedrals in medieval Europe. (Michael Hitoshi/The Image Bank/Getty Images)

ANALYZING THE IMAGE How are the buildings arranged? How large is the compound? What is interesting about the roofs?

CONNECTIONS Was this temple laid out primarily for the convenience of monks who resided there or more for lay believers coming to worship? How would their needs differ?

to China's, admonished the nobility to avoid strife and opposition, and urged adherence to Buddhist precepts. Near his seat of government, Prince Shōtoku built the magnificent Hōryūji Temple and staffed it with monks from Korea. He also opened direct relations with China, sending four missions during the brief Sui Dynasty. State-building efforts continued through the seventh century and culminated in the establishment in 710 of Japan's first long-term true city, the capital at **Nara**, north of modern Osaka. Nara, which was modeled on the Tang capital of Chang'an, gave its name to an era that lasted until 794 and was characterized by the avid importation of Chinese ideas and methods. Seven times missions with five hundred to six hundred men were sent on the dangerous sea crossing and long overland journey to Chang'an. As Buddhism developed a stronghold in Japan, it inspired many trips to China to acquire sources and to study at Chinese monasteries. Chinese and Korean craftsmen were often brought back to Japan, especially to help with the decoration of the many Buddhist temples then under construction. Musical instruments and tunes were imported as well, many originally from Central Asia. Chinese practices were instituted, such as the compilation of histories and law codes, the creation of provinces, and the appointment of governors to collect taxes from them. By 750 some seven thousand men staffed the central government.

Increased contact with the mainland had unwanted effects as well. In contrast to China and Korea, both

- **Nara** Japan's capital and first true city; it was established in 710 and modeled on the Tang capital of Chang'an.

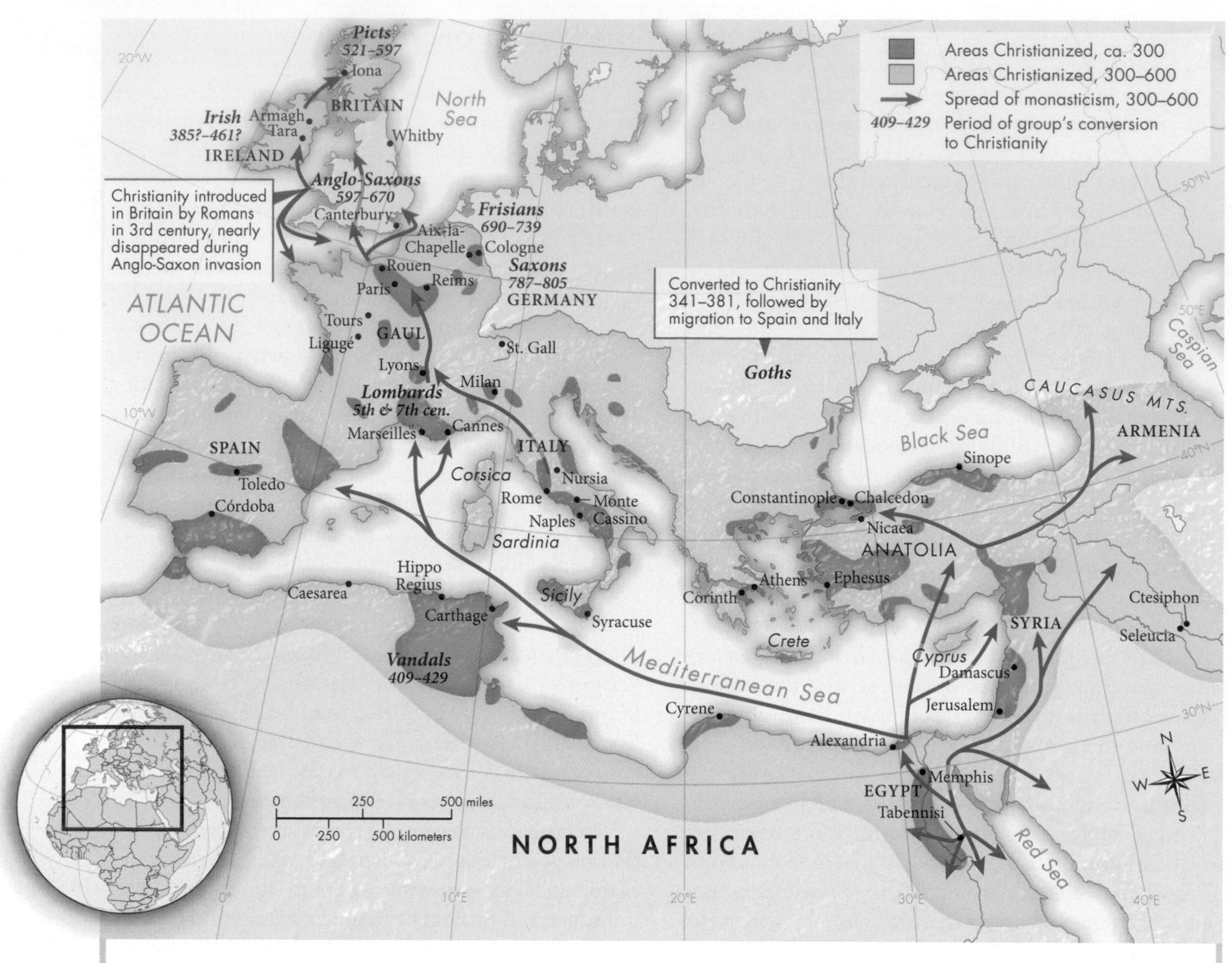

Mapping the Past

MAP 8.3 The Spread of Christianity, ca. 300–800 Originating in the area near Jerusalem, Christianity spread throughout and then beyond the Roman world.

ANALYZING THE MAP Based on the map, how did the roads and sea-lanes of the Roman Empire influence the spread of Christianity?

CONNECTIONS How does the map support the conclusion that Christianity began as an urban religion and then spread into more rural areas?

Although confession became mostly a private affair, most religious observances continued to be community matters, as they had been in the ancient world. People joined with family members, friends, and neighbors to celebrate baptisms and funerals, presided over by a priest.

Veneration of **saints**, people who had lived (or died) in a way that was spiritually heroic or noteworthy, was another way that Christians formed stronger connections with their religion. Saints were understood to provide protection and assistance to worshippers, and parish churches often housed saints' relics, that is, bones, articles of clothing, or other objects associated with them. The relics served as links between the material world and the spiritual, and miracle stories about saints and their relics were an important part of Christian preaching and writing. (See "Listening to the Past: Gregory of Tours on the Veneration of Relics," page 228.)

Christians came to venerate the saints as powerful and holy. They prayed to saints or to the Virgin Mary to intercede with God, or they simply asked the saints to assist and bless them. The entire village participated

• **saints** People who were venerated for having lived or died in a way that was spiritually heroic or noteworthy.

in processions marking saints' days or important points in the agricultural year, often carrying images of saints or their relics around the houses and fields. The decision to adopt Christianity was often made first by an emperor or king, but actual conversion was a local matter, as people came to feel that the parish priest and the saints provided them with benefits in this world and the world to come.

Frankish Rulers and Their Territories

☐ How did the Franks build and govern a European empire?

Most barbarian kingdoms did not last very long, but one that did—and that came to have a decisive role in history—was that of the Franks. The Franks were a confederation of Germanic peoples who came from the marshy lowlands north and east of the northernmost part of the Roman Empire. In the fourth and fifth centuries they settled within the empire and allied with the Romans, some attaining high military and civil positions. Though at that time the Frankish kingdom was simply one barbarian kingdom among many, rulers after the influential Clovis used a variety of tactics to expand their holdings, enhance their authority, and create a stable system. Charles the Great (r. 768–814), generally known by the French version of his name, Charlemagne (SHAHR-luh-mayne), created the largest state in western Europe since the Roman Empire.

The Merovingians and Carolingians

The Franks believed that Merovech, a semi-legendary figure, founded their ruling dynasty, which was thus called Merovingian (mehr-uh-VIHN-jee-uhn). The reign of Clovis (r. ca. 481–511) was decisive in the development of the Franks as a unified people. Through military campaigns, Clovis acquired the central provinces of Roman Gaul and began to conquer southern Gaul from other Germanic tribes. His wife, Clotild, a Roman Christian, pressured him to convert, but he refused. His later biographer Gregory of Tours, a bishop in the Frankish kingdom in the sixth century, attributed his conversion to a battlefield vision, just as Emperor Constantine's biographers had reported about his conversion. Gregory wrote:

> Queen Clotild continued to pray that her husband might recognize the true God and give up his idol-worship. Nothing could persuade him to accept Christianity. Finally war broke out against the Alemanni and in this conflict he was forced by necessity to accept what he had refused of his own free will. It so turned out that when the two armies met on the battlefield there was a great slaughter and the troops of Clovis were rapidly being annihilated. He raised his eyes to heaven when he saw this, felt compunction in his heart and was moved to tears. "Jesus Christ," he said, "you who Clotild maintains to be the Son of the living God, you who deign to give help to those in travail and victory to those who trust in you, in faith I beg the glory of your help. If you will give me victory over my enemies, and if I may have evidence to that miraculous power which the people dedicated to your name say that they have experienced, then I will believe in you and I will be baptized in your name." . . . Even as he said this the Alemanni turned their backs and began to run away. As soon as they saw that their King was killed, they submitted to Clovis. "We beg you," they said, "to put an end to this slaughter. We are prepared to obey you." Clovis stopped the war. He made a speech in which he called for peace. Then he went home. He told the Queen how he had won a victory by calling on the name of Christ.[4]

Most historians today conclude that Clovis's conversion to Roman Christianity was a pragmatic choice: it brought him the crucial support of the bishops of Gaul in his campaigns against tribes that were still pagan or had accepted the Arian version of Christianity. As the defender of Roman Christianity against heretical tribes, Clovis went on to conquer the Visigoths, extending his domain to include much of what is now France and southwestern Germany.

Following Frankish traditions in which property was divided among male heirs, at Clovis's death his kingdom was divided among his four sons. For the next two centuries rulers of the various kingdoms fought one another in civil wars, and other military leaders challenged their authority. So brutal and destructive were these wars that at one time the term "Dark Ages" was used to apply to the entire Merovingian period, although more recently historians have noted that the Merovingians also developed new political institutions, so the era was not uniformly bleak.

Merovingian kings based some aspects of their government on Roman principles. For example, they adopted the Roman concept of the *civitas*—Latin for a city and its surrounding territory. A count presided over the civitas, raising troops, collecting royal revenues, and providing justice. Many counts were not conquerors from outside, but came from families that had been administrators in Gaul when it was ruled by the Romans. Within the royal household, Merovingian politics provided women with opportunities, and some queens not only influenced but occasionally also dominated events. Because the finances of the kingdom were merged with those of the royal family, queens

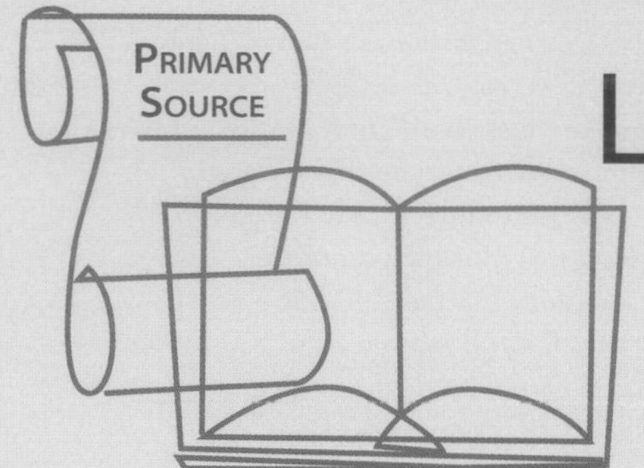

Listening to the Past

Gregory of Tours on the Veneration of Relics

Accounts of the miracles associated with the relics of saints were an important part of Christian preaching and writing, designed to win converts, strengthen their faith, and provide spiritual guidance. Gregory of Tours (ca. 539–594), a bishop in the Frankish kingdom, described events surrounding relics in Glory of the Martyrs. *He begins with a discussion of relics associated with the cross on which Jesus had been crucified, the discovery of which was attributed to Emperor Constantine's mother, Helena, who gathered many relics in and around Jerusalem and brought them back to Constantinople. Pieces of this relic were distributed widely throughout Europe, and elaborately decorated reliquaries were made to hold them. As Gregory notes here, some went to the convent in Poitiers (in west-central France) that had been founded by the Merovingian Frankish queen Radegund shortly before Gregory wrote this.*

" The cross of the Lord that was found by the empress Helena at Jerusalem is venerated on Wednesday and Friday. Queen Radegund, who is comparable to Helena in both merit and faith, requested relics of this cross and piously placed them in a convent at Poitiers that she founded out of her own zeal. She repeatedly sent servants to Jerusalem and throughout the entire region of the East. These servants visited the tombs of holy martyrs and confessors and brought back relics of them all. After placing them in the silver reliquary with the holy cross itself, she thereafter deserved to see many miracles. . . .

A girl named Chrodigildis was punished by the loss of her eyesight while she was living in the territory of Le Mans after the death of her father. Later, however, while the blessed Queen Radegund was still alive, at the command of King Chilperic she entered the rule of the aforementioned convent. With the most blessed Radegund as a guide, she bowed before the holy reliquary and there kept vigils with the other nuns. When morning came and the others left, she remained in the same place prostrate on the ground. In a vision it seemed to her as if someone had opened her eyes. One eye was restored to health; while she was still concerned about the other, suddenly she was awakened by the sound of a door being unlocked and regained the sight of one eye. There is no doubt that this was accomplished by the power of the cross. The possessed, the lame, and also other ill people are often cured at this place. Enough on this topic. . . .

Through their confession [that is, their not being deterred by persecution] the glorious martyrs have earned the unspeakable benefits of gifts that are always salutary. To petitioners they have revealed themselves by this power that the Lord Creator shared with them. I know that this happened just as my deacon recently told me. This deacon received relics of some martyrs and confessors [heroic believers] from pope Pelagius [II] of Rome [pontificate 579–590]. A large chorus of monks who were chanting psalms and a huge crowd of people escorted him to Ostia. After he boarded a ship the sails were unfurled and hoisted over the rigging of a mast that presented the appearance of a cross. As the wind blew, they set out on the high seas. When they were sailing to reach the port of Marseilles, they began to approach a certain place where a mountain of stone rose from the shore of the sea and, sinking a bit, stretched into the sea to the top of the water. As the wind forced them on, the ship was lifted by a mighty blast into danger. When the ship was shaken as if struck by the rock, the sailors recognized their peril and announced their death. The deacon lifted the reliquary with the holy relics. He groaned and in a loud voice began to invoke the names of the individual saints. He prayed that their power might liberate from danger those who were about to die. The ship, as I said, sailed closer and closer to the rock. Suddenly, out of respect for the holy relics, a wind blew from that spot with great force against the other wind. It crushed the waves and repulsed the opposing wind. By recalling the ship to the deep sea, the wind freed everyone from the danger of death. So they circumvented this impending danger, and by the grace of the Lord and the protection of the saints they arrived at the port they had hoped for. . . .

often had control of the royal treasury just as more ordinary women controlled household expenditures.

At the king's court—that is, wherever the king was present—an official called the mayor of the palace supervised legal, financial, and household officials; the mayor of the palace also governed in the king's absence. In the seventh century the position as mayor was held by members of an increasingly powerful family, the **Carolingians** (ka-ruh-LIHN-jee-uhns), who advanced themselves through advantageous marriages, a well-earned reputation for military strength, and the help of the church.

Eventually the Carolingians replaced the Merovingians as rulers of the Frankish kingdom, cementing their authority when the Carolingian Charles Martel defeated Muslim invaders in 732 at the Battle of Poitiers (PWAH-tee-ay) in central France. Muslims and Christians have interpreted the battle differently. Muslims

In this sixth-century ivory carving, two men in a wagon, accompanied by a procession of people holding candles, carry relics of a saint to a Christian church under construction. New churches often received holy items when they were dedicated, and processions were common ways in which people expressed community devotion. (Cathedral Treasury, Trier. Photo: Ann Muenchow)

Because he [Gregory's father] wished himself to be protected by relics of saints, he asked a cleric to grant him something from these relics, so that with their protection he might be kept safe as he set out on this long journey. He put the sacred ashes in a gold medallion and carried it with him. Although he did not even know the names of the blessed men, he was accustomed to recount that he had been rescued from many dangers. He claimed that often, because of the powers of these relics, he had avoided the violence of bandits, the dangers of floods, the threats of turbulent men, and attacks from swords.

I will not be silent about what I witnessed regarding these relics. After the death of my father my mother carried these relics with her. It was the time for harvesting the crops, and huge piles of grain had been collected on the threshing floors. . . . The threshers kindled fires for themselves from the straw. . . . Quickly, fanned by the wind, the fire spread to the piles of grain. The fire became a huge blaze and was accompanied by the shouts of men, the wails of women, and the crying of children. This happened in our field. When my mother, who was wearing these relics around her neck, learned of this, she rushed from the meal and held the sacred relics in front of the balls of flames. In a moment the entire fire so died down that no sparks were found among the piles of burned straw and the seeds. The grain the fire had touched had suffered no harm.

Many years later I received these relics from my mother. While I was travelling from Burgundy to Clermont, a huge storm appeared in my path. The storm frequently flashed with lightning in the sky and rumbled with loud crashes of thunder. Then I took the holy relics from my pocket and raised my hand before the cloud. The cloud immediately divided into two parts and passed by on the right and the left; it threatened neither me nor anyone else. Then, as a presumptuous young man is expected to behave, I began to be inflated by the arrogance of vainglory. I silently thought that this concession had been made especially for me, rather than because of the merits of the saints. I boasted to my travelling companions and insisted that I had deserved that which God had bestowed upon my naïveté. Immediately my horse suddenly slipped beneath me and threw me to the ground. I was so seriously bruised during this accident that I could hardly get up. I understood that this accident had happened because of my pride; and it was sufficient to note that afterwards the urge of vainglory did not bother me. For if it happened that I was worthy to observe some manifestations of the powers of saints, I have proclaimed that they were due to the gift of God through the faith of the saints. ”

Source: Gregory of Tours, *Glory of the Martyrs*, trans. Raymond Van Dam (Liverpool: Liverpool University, 1988) pp. 22, 24, 106–109. Reprinted with permission of Liverpool University Press.

QUESTIONS FOR ANALYSIS

1. According to Gregory, what gives relics their power, and why should they be venerated?
2. The veneration of relics involved both public display for community devotion and personal ownership for private needs. What examples of each do you see in Gregory's text?
3. Gregory was a historian who wrote chronicles of the Frankish kingdom as well as spiritual works such as this one. How does he use the techniques of a historian, such as identifying his sources, in this work? How do these support his assertions about the power of relics?

considered it a minor skirmish and attributed the Frankish victory to Muslim difficulties in maintaining supply lines over long distances and to ethnic conflicts and unrest in Islamic Spain. Charles Martel and later Carolingians used the victory to portray themselves as defenders of Christendom against the Muslims.

The Battle of Poitiers helped the Carolingians acquire more support from the church, perhaps their most important asset. They further strengthened their ties to the church by supporting the work of missionaries who preached Christian principles—including the duty to obey secular authorities—to pagan peoples and by allying themselves with the papacy against other Germanic tribes.

- **Carolingian** A dynasty of rulers that took over the Frankish kingdom from the Merovingians in the seventh century; *Carolingian* derives from the Latin word for "Charles," the name of several members of this dynasty.

Picturing the Past

Charlemagne and His Wife

This illumination from a ninth-century manuscript portrays Charlemagne with one of his wives. Marriage was an important tool of diplomacy for Charlemagne, and he had a number of wives and concubines. (Erich Lessing/Art Resource, NY)

ANALYZING THE IMAGE What does Charlemagne appear to be doing? How would you characterize his wife's reaction?

CONNECTIONS Does this depiction of a Frankish queen match what you've read about female rulers in this era, such as Theodora and Clotild?

The Warrior-Ruler Charlemagne

The most powerful of the Carolingian rulers was Charlemagne, who fought more than fifty campaigns and became the greatest warrior of the early Middle Ages. Through brutal military expeditions that brought wealth — lands, booty, slaves, and tribute — and by peaceful travel, personal appearances, shrewd marital alliances, and the sheer force of his personality, Charlemagne sought to awe newly conquered peoples and rebellious domestic enemies. By around 805 the Frankish kingdom included all of continental Europe except Spain, Scandinavia, southern Italy, and the Slavic fringes of the East.

For administrative purposes, Charlemagne divided his entire kingdom into counties. Each of the approximately six hundred counties was governed by a count, who had full military and judicial power and held his office for life but could be removed by the emperor for misconduct. As a link between local authorities and the central government, Charlemagne appointed officials called *missi dominici*, "agents of the lord king." Each year beginning in 802 two missi, usually a count and a bishop or abbot, visited assigned districts. They checked up on the counts and their districts' judicial, financial, and clerical activities.

Charlemagne's Conquests, ca. 768–814

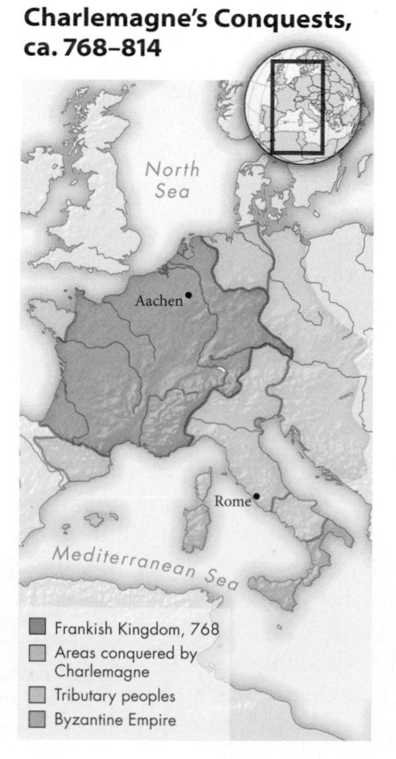

In the autumn of the year 800 Charlemagne visited Rome, where on Christmas Day Pope Leo III crowned him emperor. The event had momentous consequences. In taking as his motto *Renovatio romani imperi* (Revival of the Roman Empire), Charlemagne was deliberately perpetuating old Roman imperial ideas while identifying with the new Rome of the Christian Church. From Baghdad, the Abbasid Empire's caliph, Harun al-Rashid (r. 786–809), congratulated Charlemagne on his coronation with the gift of an elephant. The elephant survived for nearly a decade, though like everyone else at Charlemagne's capital of Aachen (on the western border of modern Germany), it lived in a city that was far less sophisticated, healthy, and beautiful than Abbasid Baghdad. Although the Muslim caliph recognized Charlemagne as a fellow sovereign, the Byzantines regarded his papal coronation as rebellious and Charlemagne as a usurper. His crowning as emperor thus marked a decisive break between Rome and Constantinople and gave church authorities in the West proof that the imperial title could only be granted by the pope.

As he built an empire through conquest and strategic alliances, Charlemagne also set in motion a cultural revival that later historians called the "Carolingian Renaissance."

The Carolingian Renaissance was a rebirth of interest in, study of, and preservation of the language, ideas, and achievements of classical Greece and Rome. Scholars at Aachen copied Greco-Roman and Christian books and manuscripts and created libraries housed in churches and monasteries. Furthermore, Charlemagne urged monasteries to promote Christian learning, and both men's and women's houses produced beautiful illustrated texts, preserving Christian and classical works for subsequent generations.

Charlemagne left his vast empire to his sole surviving son, Louis the Pious (r. 814–840), who attempted to keep the empire intact. This proved to be impossible. Members of the nobility engaged in plots and open warfare against the emperor, often allying themselves with one of Louis's three sons. In 843, shortly after Louis's death, those sons agreed to the **Treaty of Verdun**, which divided the empire into three parts: Charles the Bald received the western part, Lothair the middle and the title of emperor, and Louis the eastern part, from which he acquired the title "the German." Though of course no one knew it at the time, this treaty set the pattern for political boundaries in Europe that have been maintained through today. Other than brief periods under Napoleon and Hitler, Europe would never again see as large a unified state as it had under Charlemagne, which is one reason he has become a symbol of European unity in the twenty-first century.

The weakening of central power was hastened by invasions and migrations from the north, south, and east. Thus Charlemagne's empire ended in much the same way that the Roman Empire had earlier, from a combination of internal weakness and external pressure.

CHRONOLOGY

224–651	Sassanid dynasty
325	Nicene Creed produced
340–419	Life of Saint Jerome
354–430	Life of Saint Augustine
380	Theodosius makes Christianity official religion of Roman Empire
ca. 385–461	Life of Saint Patrick
476	Odoacer deposes the last Roman emperor in the West
ca. 481–511	Reign of Clovis
527–565	Reign of Justinian
529	Writing of *The Rule of Saint Benedict*
535–572	Byzantines reconquer and rule Italy
730–843	Iconoclastic controversy
768–814	Reign of Charlemagne
843	Treaty of Verdun divides Carolingian kingdom

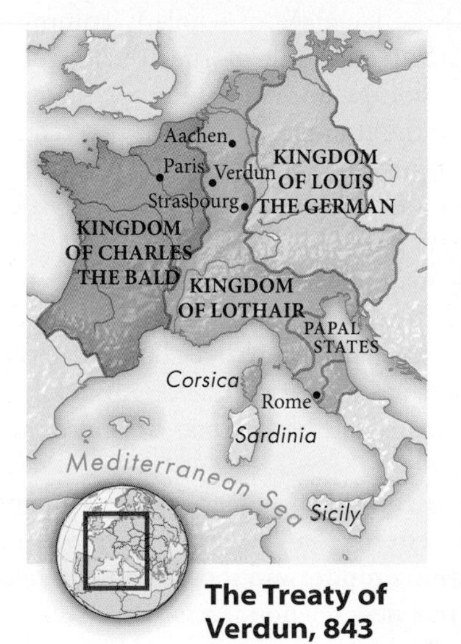

The Treaty of Verdun, 843

Chapter Summary

During the sixth and seventh centuries the Byzantine Empire survived waves of attacks, owing to effective military leadership and to fortifications around Constantinople. Byzantine emperors organized and preserved Roman institutions, and the Byzantine Empire survived until 1453. The emperor Justinian oversaw creation of a new uniform code of Roman law. The Byzantines prized education, and because of them many aspects of ancient Greek thought survived to influence the intellectual life of the Muslim world and eventually that of western Europe.

Christianity gained the support of the fourth-century emperors, and the church gradually adopted the Roman system of hierarchical organization. The church possessed able administrators and leaders. Bishops expanded their activities, and in the fifth century the bishops of Rome, taking the title "pope," began to stress their supremacy over other Christian communities. Monasteries offered opportunities for individuals to develop deeper spiritual devotion and also provided a model of Christian living and places for

• **Treaty of Verdun** A treaty ratified in 843 that divided Charlemagne's territories among his three surviving grandsons; their kingdoms set the pattern for the modern states of Germany, France, and Italy.

education and learning. Christian thinkers reinterpreted the classics in a Christian sense, incorporating elements of Greek and Roman philosophy into Christian teachings.

Barbarian groups migrated throughout Europe and Central Asia beginning in the second century. Among barbarians, the basic social unit was the tribe, made up of kin groups and led by a tribal chieftain. Missionaries and priests persuaded pagan and illiterate peoples to accept Christianity by stressing similarities between pagan customs and beliefs and those of Christianity, and introducing the ritual of penance and the veneration of saints. Most barbarian kingdoms were weak and short-lived, though the kingdom of the Franks was relatively more unified and powerful. Rulers first in the Merovingian dynasty, and then in the Carolingian, used military victories, carefully calculated marriage alliances, and the help of the church to enhance their authority. Carolingian government reached the peak of its power under Charlemagne, who brought much of Europe under his authority through military conquest and strategic alliances.

NOTES

1. Quoted in E. Patlagean, "Byzantium in the Tenth and Eleventh Centuries," in *A History of Private Life*. Vol. 1: *From Pagan Rome to Byzantium*, ed. P. Ariès and G. Duby (Cambridge, Mass.: Harvard University Press, 1987), p. 573.
2. R. C. Petry, ed., *A History of Christianity: Readings in the History of Early and Medieval Christianity* (Englewood Cliffs, N.J.: Prentice-Hall, 1962), p. 70.
3. E. F. Henderson, ed., *Select Historical Documents of the Middle Ages* (London: G. Bell and Sons, 1912), pp. 176, 189.
4. Gregory of Tours, *The History of the Franks*, trans. with an introduction by Lewis Thorpe (London: Penguin Books, 1974), pp. 141–144. Copyright © Lewis Thorpe, 1974, London. Reproduced by permission of Penguin Books Ltd.

CONNECTIONS

For centuries the end of the Roman Empire in the West was seen as a major turning point in history, the fall of the sophisticated and educated classical world to uncouth and illiterate tribes. Over the last several decades, however, many historians have put a greater emphasis on continuities. Barbarian kings relied on officials trained in Roman law, and Latin remained the language of scholarly communication and the Christian Church. Greco-Roman art and architecture still adorned the land, and people continued to use Roman roads, aqueducts, and buildings. In eastern Europe and western Asia, the Byzantine Empire preserved the traditions of the Roman Empire and protected the intellectual heritage of Greco-Roman culture for another millennium.

Very recently, however, some historians and archaeologists have returned to an emphasis on change. They note that people may have traveled on Roman roads after the end of the Roman Empire, but the roads were rarely maintained, and travel itself was much less secure than during the empire. Merchants no longer traded over long distances, so people's access to goods produced outside their local area plummeted. Knowledge about technological processes such as the making of glass and roof tiles declined or disappeared. Although intermarriage and cultural assimilation occurred among Romans and barbarians, violence and great physical destruction also existed, even in Byzantium.

In the middle of the era covered in this chapter, a new force emerged that had a dramatic impact on much of Europe and western Asia—Islam. In the seventh and eighth centuries Sassanid Persia, much of the Byzantine Empire, and the barbarian kingdoms in the Iberian Peninsula fell to Arab forces carrying this new religion. As we have seen in this chapter, a reputation as victors over Islam helped the Franks establish the most powerful state in Europe. As we will see when we pick up the story of Europe again in Chapter 14, Islam continued to shape European culture and politics in subsequent centuries. In terms of world history, the expansion of Islam may have been an even more dramatic turning point than the fall of the Roman Empire. Here, too, however, there were continuities, as the Muslims adopted and adapted Greek, Byzantine, and Persian political and cultural institutions.

Review and Explore

Make It Stick

LearningCurve
Go online and use LearningCurve to retain what you've read.

Identify Key Terms

Identify and explain the significance of each item below.

Justinian's *Code* (p. 210)
dioceses (p. 214)
heresy (p. 215)
popes (p. 215)
Orthodox Church (p. 216)
sacraments (p. 219)
iconoclastic controversy (p. 219)
wergeld (p. 221)
penance (p. 225)
saints (p. 226)
Carolingian (p. 228)
Treaty of Verdun (p. 231)

Review the Main Ideas

Answer the focus questions from each section of the chapter.

1. How did the Byzantine Empire preserve the legacy of Rome? (p. 208)
2. How did the Christian Church become a major force in Europe? (p. 214)
3. How did Christian thinkers adapt classical ideas to Christian teachings, and what new religious concepts and practices did they develop? (p. 217)
4. How did the barbarians shape social, economic, and political structures in Europe and western Asia? (p. 220)
5. How did the church convert barbarian peoples to Christianity? (p. 224)
6. How did the Franks build and govern a European empire? (p. 227)

Make Connections

Analyze the larger developments and continuities within and across chapters.

1. The end of the Roman Empire in the West in 476 has long been viewed as one of the most important turning points in history. Do you agree with this idea? Why or why not?
2. How did the Christian Church adapt to Roman and barbarian society? How was it different in 850 than it had been in 100?
3. In what ways were the spread of Buddhism (Chapter 7) and the spread of Christianity similar? In what ways were they different?

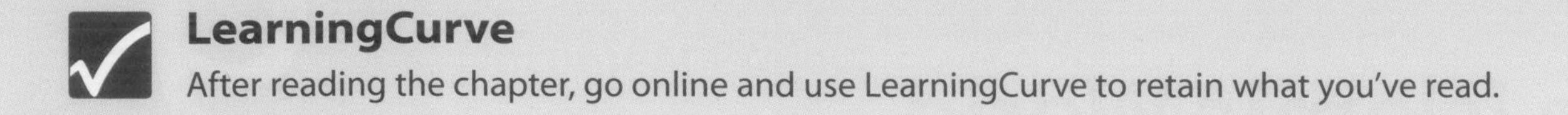

LearningCurve
After reading the chapter, go online and use LearningCurve to retain what you've read.

Chapter Preview

Around 610 in the city of Mecca in what is now Saudi Arabia, a merchant called Muhammad had a religious vision that inspired him to preach God's revelations to the people of Mecca. By the time he died in 632, he had many followers in Arabia, and a century later his followers controlled what is now Syria, Palestine, Egypt, Iraq, Iran, northern Africa, Spain, and southern France. Within another century Muhammad's beliefs had been carried across Central Asia to the borders of China and India. The speed with which Islam spread is one of the most amazing stories in world history, and scholars have pointed to many factors that must have contributed to its success. Military victories were rooted in strong military organization and the practice of establishing garrison cities in newly conquered territories. The religious zeal of new converts certainly played an important role. So too did the political weakness of many of the governments then holding power in the lands where Islam extended, such as the Byzantine government centered in Constantinople. Commerce and trade also spread the faith of Muhammad.

Although its first adherents were nomads, Islam developed and flourished in a mercantile milieu. By land and sea, Muslim merchants transported a rich variety of goods across Eurasia. On the basis of the wealth that trade generated, a gracious, sophisticated, and cosmopolitan culture developed with centers at Baghdad and Córdoba. During the ninth, tenth, and eleventh centuries, the Islamic world witnessed enormous intellectual vitality and creativity. Muslim scholars produced important work in many disciplines, especially mathematics, medicine, and philosophy. This brilliant civilization profoundly influenced the development of both Eastern and Western civilizations.

The Origins of Islam

☐ From what kind of social and economic environment did Muhammad arise, and what did he teach?

The Arabian peninsula, about a third of the size of Europe or the United States, covers about a million square miles, much of it desert. By the seventh century C.E. farming prevailed in the southwestern mountain valleys with their ample rainfall. In other areas scattered throughout the peninsula, oasis towns sustained sizable populations including artisans, merchants, and religious leaders. Outside the towns were Bedouin (BEH-duh-uhn) nomadic tribes who moved from place to place, grazing their sheep, goats, and camels. Though always small in number, Bedouins were the most important political and military force in the region because of their toughness, solidarity, fighting traditions, possession of horses and camels, and ability to control trade and lines of communication. Mecca became the economic and cultural center of western Arabia, in part because pilgrims came to visit the Ka'ba, a temple containing a black stone thought to be a god's dwelling place. Muhammad's roots were in this region.

Arabian Social and Economic Structure

The basic social unit of the Bedouins and other Arabs was the tribe. Consisting of people connected through kinship, tribes provided protection and support and in turn expected members' total loyalty. Like the Germanic peoples in the age of their migrations (see pages 220–224), Arab tribes were not static entities but rather continually evolving groups. A particular tribe might include both nomadic and sedentary members.

As in other nomadic societies, nomads in Arabia depended on agriculturally productive communities for food they could not produce, as well as cloth, metal products, and weapons. Nomads paid for these goods with livestock, milk and milk products, hides, and hair, items in demand in oasis towns. Nomads acquired additional income by serving as desert guides and as guards for caravans, or by creating the need for guards by plundering caravans and extorting protection money.

In northern and central Arabia in the early seventh century, tribal confederations led by their warrior elite were dominant. In the southern parts of the peninsula, however, priestly aristocracies tended to hold political power. Many oasis or market towns had a holy family who served the deity of the town and acted as the guardian of the deity's shrine. At the shrine its priest would try to settle disputes among warring tribes. All Arabs respected the shrines because they served as neutral places for such arbitration.

Page from Arabic Manuscript The aesthetic appeal of Arabic calligraphy is easy to recognize in this page from a fourteenth-century manuscript. (Abraham Destroys the Idols of the Sabians, from *The Chronology of Ancient Nations* by Al-Biruni, 1307/Edinburgh University Library, Scotland/With kind permission of the University of Edinburgh/The Bridgeman Art Library)

The power of the northern warrior class rested on its fighting skills. The southern religious aristocracy, by contrast, depended on its religious and economic power. The political genius of Muhammad was to bind together these different tribal groups into a strong, unified state.

Muhammad's Rise as a Religious Leader

Much like the earliest sources for Jesus and the Buddha, the earliest account of the life of Muhammad (ca. 570–632) comes from oral traditions passed down among followers. According to these traditions, Muhammad was orphaned at the age of six and brought up by his paternal uncle. As a young man, he became a merchant in the caravan trade that crisscrossed the Arabian

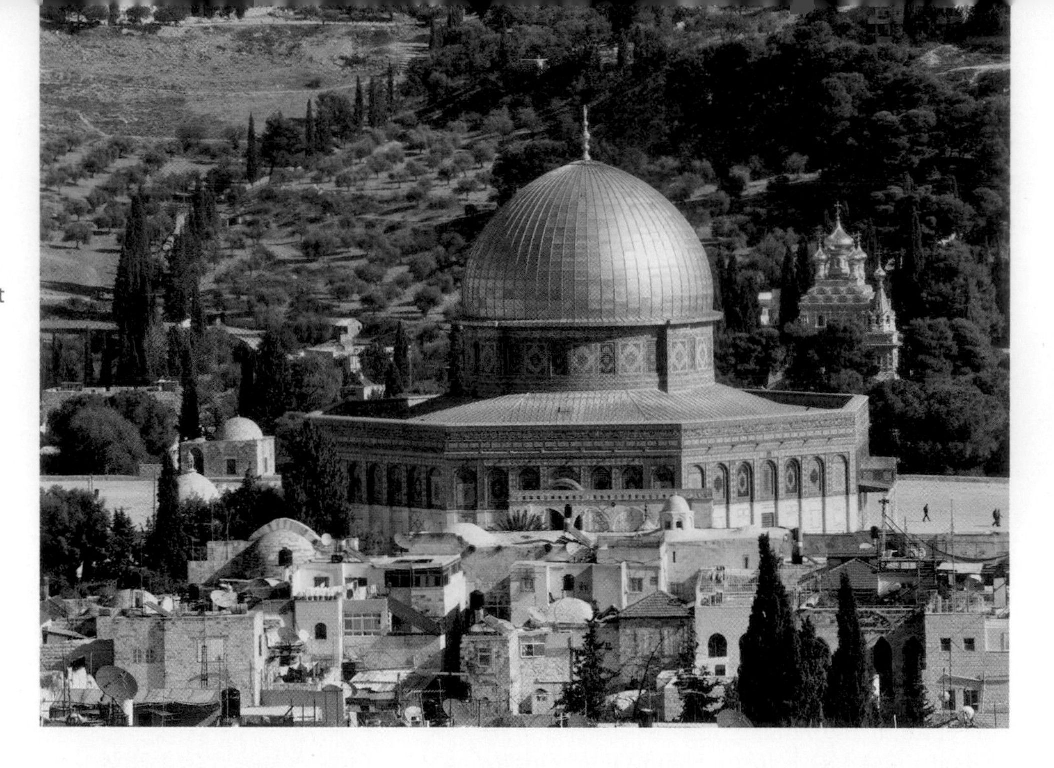

Dome of the Rock, Jerusalem Completed in 691 and revered by Muslims as the site where Muhammad ascended to Heaven, the Dome of the Rock is the oldest surviving Islamic sanctuary and, after Mecca and Medina, the holiest place in Islam. Although influenced by Byzantine and Persian architecture, it also has distinctly Arabic features, such as the 700 feet of carefully selected Qur'anic inscriptions and vegetal motifs that grace the top of the outer walls. (imagebroker.net/SuperStock)

desert. Later he entered the service of a wealthy widow, Khadija, and their subsequent marriage brought him financial security. Muhammad was extremely pious and devoted to contemplation. At about age forty, in a cave in the hills near Mecca where he was accustomed to praying, Muhammad had a vision of an angelic being who commanded him to preach the revelations that God would be sending him. Muhammad began to preach to the people of Mecca, urging them to give up their idols and to submit to the one indivisible God. After his death, scribes organized the revelations jotted down by followers or memorized into chapters. In 651 they published the version of them that Muslims consider authoritative, the **Qur'an** (kuh-RAHN). Muslims revere the Qur'an for its sacred message and for the beauty of its Arabic language.

For the first two or three centuries after the death of Muhammad, there was considerable debate about theological issues, such as the oneness of God, the role of angels, the prophets, the Scriptures, and Judgment Day, as well as about political issues, such as the authority of Muhammad and that of the caliph (KAY-lihf; political ruler, successor to Muhammad). Likewise, religious scholars had to sort out and assess the **hadith** (huh-DEETH), collections of the sayings of or anecdotes about Muhammad. Controversies over the authenticity of particular sayings continued for centuries. Muhammad's example as revealed in the hadith became the legal basis for the conduct of every Muslim. The life of Muhammad provides the "normative example," or **Sunna**, for the Muslim believer. Muhammad's example became central to the Muslim way of life.

- **Qur'an** The sacred book of Islam.
- **hadith** Collections of the sayings of and anecdotes about Muhammad.
- **Sunna** An Arabic term meaning "trodden path." The term refers to the deeds and sayings of Muhammad, which constitute the obligatory example for Muslim life.
- **Five Pillars of Islam** The basic tenets of the Islamic faith; they include reciting a profession of faith in God and in Muhammad as God's prophet, praying five times daily, fasting and praying during the month of Ramadan, making a pilgrimage to Mecca once in one's lifetime, and contributing alms to the poor.
- **umma** A community of people who share a religious faith and commitment rather than a tribal tie.

The Tenets of Islam

Islam, the strict monotheistic faith that is based on the teachings of Muhammad, rests on the principle of the oneness and omnipotence of God (Allah). The word *Islam* means "surrender to God," and *Muslim* means "a person who submits." Muslims believe that Muhammad was the last of the prophets, completing the work begun by Abraham, Moses, and Jesus. According to the Qur'an, the coming of the final prophet was acknowledged by both Jewish and Christian authorities. The Qur'an asserts that the Prophet Muhammad descended from Adam, the first man, and that the Prophet Abraham built the Ka'ba. The Qur'an holds that the holy writings of both Jews and Christians represent divine revelation, but it claims that both Jews and Christians tampered with the books of God.

Muslims believe that they worship the same God as Jews and Christians. Monotheism had flourished in Middle Eastern Semitic and Persian cultures for centuries before Muhammad. Islam appropriates much of the Old and New Testaments of the Bible but often retells the narratives with significant shifts in meaning. Islam recognizes Moses's laws about circumcision, ritual bathing, and restrictions on eating pork and shellfish, and the Qur'an calls Christians "nearest in love" to Muslims. Muhammad insisted that he was not preaching a new message; rather, he was calling people back to the one true God, urging his contemporaries to reform their lives, to return to the faith of Abraham, the first monotheist.

Unlike the Old Testament, much of which is a historical narrative, or the New Testament, which is a collection of essays on the example and teachings of Jesus, the Qur'an is a collection of directives issued in God's name. Its organization is not strictly topical or chronological. To deal with seeming contradictions, later commentators explained the historical circumstances behind each revelation.

The Qur'an prescribes a strict code of moral behavior. A Muslim must recite the profession of faith in God and in Muhammad as his prophet: "There is no God but God, and Muhammad is his Prophet." A believer must also pray five times a day, fast and pray during the sacred month of Ramadan, make a pilgrimage (hajj) to the holy city of Mecca once during his or her lifetime, and give alms to the Muslim poor. These fundamental obligations are known as the **Five Pillars of Islam**.

Islam forbids alcoholic beverages and gambling. It condemns usury in business—that is, lending money and charging the borrower interest—and taking advantage of market demand for products by charging high prices. Muslim jurisprudence condemned licentious behavior by both men and women and specified the same punishments for both. (By contrast, contemporary Frankish law punished prostitutes but not their clients.)

Like the Christian Judgment Day, on the Islamic Judgment Day God will separate the saved and the damned. The Qur'an describes in detail the frightful tortures with which God will punish the damned and the heavenly rewards of the saved and the blessed.

Islamic States and Their Expansion

- What made possible the spread of Islam, and what forms of government were established to rule Muslim lands?

According to Muslim tradition, Muhammad's preaching at first did not appeal to many people—for the first three years he attracted only fourteen believers. In preaching a transformation of the social order and calling for the destruction of the idols in the Ka'ba, Muhammad challenged the power of the local elite and the pilgrimage-based economy. As a result, the townspeople of Mecca turned against him, and he and his followers were forced to flee to Medina. This *hijra* (hih-JIGH-ruh), or emigration, occurred in 622, and Muslims later dated the beginning of their era from it.

At Medina, Muhammad attracted increasing numbers of believers, many of whom were Bedouins who supported themselves by raiding caravans en route to Mecca, setting off a violent conflict between Mecca and Medina. After eight years of strife, Mecca capitulated. In this way, by the time Muhammad died in 632, he had welded together all the Bedouin tribes.

Muhammad displayed genius as both political strategist and religious teacher. He gave Arabs the idea of a unique and unified **umma** (UH-muh), or community, made up of all those whose primary identity and bond was a common religious faith, not a tribal tie. The umma was to be a religious and political community led by Muhammad for the achievement of God's will on earth. In the early seventh century the southern Arab tribal confederations lacked cohesiveness and were constantly warring. The Islamic notion of an absolute higher authority transcended the boundaries of individual tribal units and fostered political consolidation. All authority came from God through Muhammad.

Islam's Spread Beyond Arabia

After the Prophet's death, Islam quickly spread far beyond Arabia. In the sixth century two powerful empires divided the Middle East: the Greek-Byzantine empire centered at Constantinople and the Persian-Sassanid empire concentrated at Ctesiphon (near Baghdad in present-day Iraq). The Byzantine Empire stood for Hellenistic culture and championed Christianity (see Chapter 8). The Sassanid empire espoused Persian cultural traditions and favored the religious faith known as Zoroastrianism (see pages 58–59). Although each empire maintained an official state religion, neither possessed religious unity. Both had sizable Jewish populations, and within Byzantium sects that Orthodox Greeks considered heretical—Monophysites and Nestorians—were politically divisive forces. From the fourth through sixth centuries the Byzantines and Sassanids fought each other fiercely, each trying to expand its territories at the expense of the other and to control and tax the rich trade coming from Arabia and the Indian Ocean region. Many peripheral societies were drawn into the conflict. The resulting disorder facilitated the growth of Muslim states.

The second and third successors of Muhammad, Umar (r. 634–644) and Uthman (r. 644–656), launched a two-pronged attack against the Byzantine and Sassanid Empires. One force moved north from Arabia against the Byzantine provinces of Syria and Palestine (see page 209). From Syria, the Muslims conquered the rich province of Egypt, taking the commercial and intellectual hub of Alexandria in 642. Simultaneously, Arab armies swept into the Sassanid empire. The Muslim defeat of the Persians at Nihawand in 642 signaled the collapse of this empire (Map 9.1).

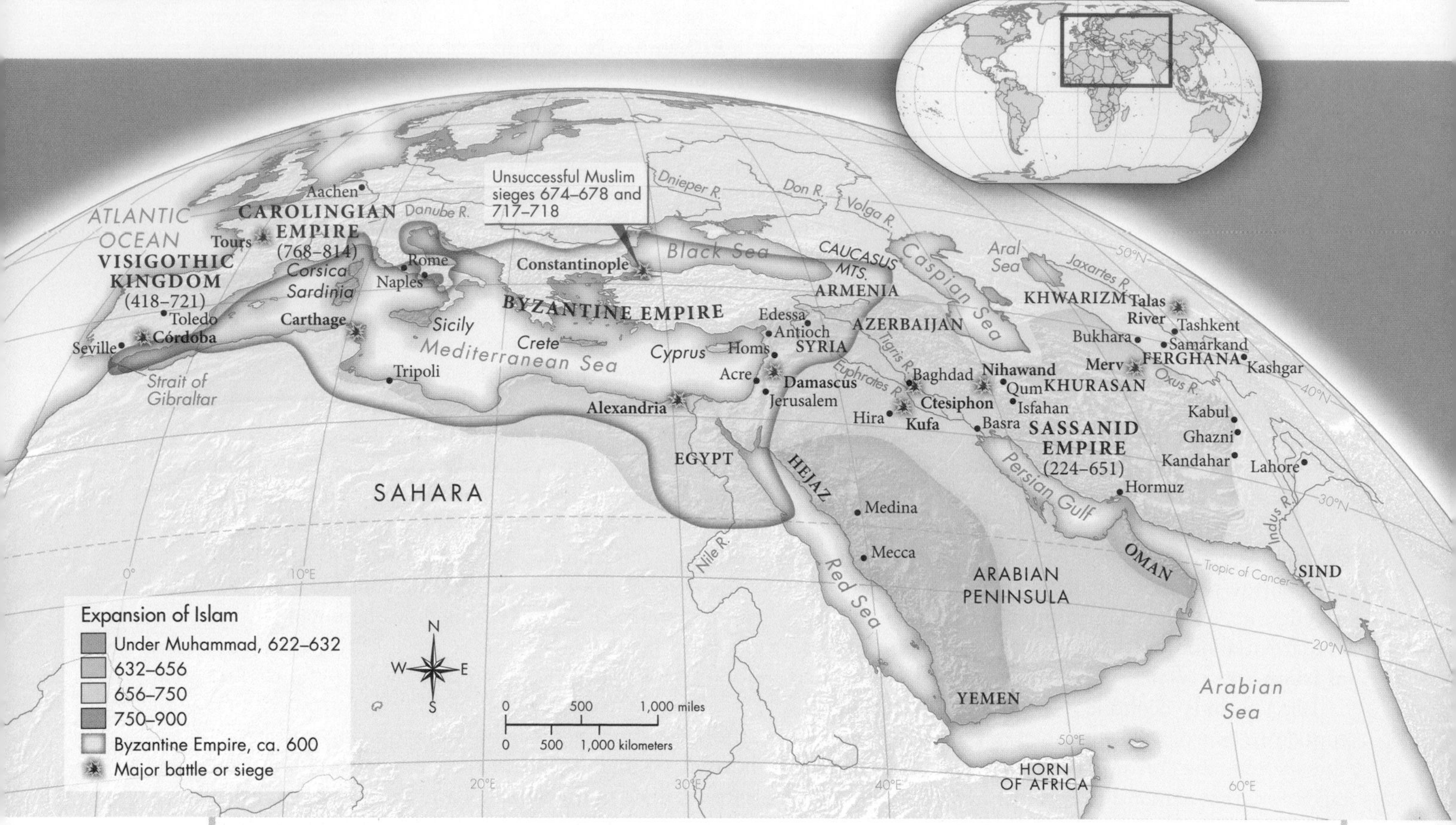

Mapping the Past

MAP 9.1 The Expansion of Islam, 622–900 The rapid expansion of Islam in a relatively short span of time testifies to the Arabs' superior fighting skills, religious zeal, and economic ambition as well as to their enemies' weakness. Plague, famine, and political troubles in Sassanid Persia contributed to Muslim victory there.

ANALYZING THE MAP Trace the routes of the spread of Islam by time period. How fast did it spread? How similar were the climates of the regions that became Muslim?

CONNECTIONS Which were the most powerful and populous of the societies that were absorbed into the Muslim world? What regions or societies were more resistant?

The Muslims continued their drive eastward and in the mid-seventh century occupied the province of Khurasan, where the city of Merv became the center of Muslim control over eastern Persia and the base for campaigns farther east. By 700 the Muslims had crossed the Oxus River and swept toward Kabul, today the capital of Afghanistan. They then penetrated Kazakhstan and seized Tashkent, one of the oldest cities in Central Asia. The clash of Muslim horsemen with a Chinese army at the Talas River in 751 marked the farthest Islamic penetration into Central Asia. From southern Persia, a Muslim force marched into the Indus Valley in northwest India and in 713 founded an Islamic community there. Beginning in the eleventh century Muslim dynasties from Ghazni in Afghanistan carried Islam deeper into the Indian subcontinent (see page 347).

To the west, Arab forces moved across North Africa and crossed the Strait of Gibraltar. In 711 at the Guadalete River they easily defeated the Visigothic kingdom of Spain. A few Christian princes supported by Merovingian rulers held out in the Cantabrian Mountains, but the Muslims controlled most of Spain until the thirteenth century. Advances into France were stopped in 732 when the Franks defeated Arab armies in a battle near the city of Tours, and Muslim occupation of parts of southern France did not last long.

Reasons for the Spread of Islam

By the beginning of the eleventh century the crescent of Islam had flown from the Iberian heartlands to northern India. How can this rapid and remarkable expansion be explained? The internal view of Muslim historians was that God supported the Islamic faith and aided its spread. The external, especially European, view was that the Muslim concept of jihad (JEE-hahd), or struggle, was the key element. The Qur'an does not precisely explain jihad. Some Muslim scholars hold that it signifies the individual struggle against sin and toward perfection on "the straight path" of Islam. Others claim that jihad has a social and communal implication—a militancy as part of a holy war against unbelievers living in territories outside the control of the Muslim community.

Today, few historians emphasize religious zeal alone but rather point to a combination of the Arabs' military advantages and the political weaknesses of their opponents. The Byzantine and Sassanid Empires had just fought a grueling century-long war and had also been weakened by the plague, which hit urban, stationary populations harder than nomadic populations. Equally important are the military strength and tactics of the Arabs. For example, rather than scattering as landlords of peasant farmers over conquered lands, Arab soldiers remained together in garrison cities, where their Arab ethnicity, tribal organization, religion, and military success set them apart. All soldiers were registered in the **diwān** (dih-WAHN), an administrative organ adopted from the Persians or Byzantines. Soldiers received a monthly ration of food for themselves and their families and an annual cash stipend. In return, they had to be available for military service. Fixed salaries, regular pay, and the lure of battlefield booty attracted rugged tribesmen from Arabia.

The Arab commanders recognized the economic benefits of capturing the major cities of the region. Arab caravans frequented the market towns of southern Syria and the rich commercial centers of the north, such as Edessa, Aleppo, and Damascus. Syria's economic prosperity probably attracted the Muslims, and perhaps Muhammad saw the land as a potential means of support for the poor who flooded into Medina. Syria also contained sites important to the faith: Jerusalem, where Jesus and other prophets mentioned in the Qur'an had lived and preached, and Hebron, the traditional burial place of Abraham, the father of monotheism.

The Caliphate and the Split Between Shi'a and Sunni Alliances

When Muhammad died in 632, he left a large Muslim umma, but this community stood in danger of disintegrating into separate tribal groups. How was the vast empire that came into existence within one hundred years of his death to be governed? Neither the Qur'an nor the Sunna offered guidance concerning the succession.

In this crisis, according to tradition, a group of Muhammad's ablest followers elected Abu Bakr (573–634), the Prophet's father-in-law and close supporter, and hailed him as caliph, a term combining the ideas of leader, successor, and deputy (of the Prophet). This election marked the victory of the concept of a universal community of Muslim believers.

Because the law of the Qur'an was meant to guide the community, there had to be an authority to enforce the law, and the caliph assumed this responsibility. Muslim teaching holds that the law is paramount. God is the sole source of the law, and the ruler is bound to obey the law. Government exists not to make law but to enforce it. Religious leaders and institutions act as a check on political leaders who drift too far from religious standards. The creation of Islamic law in an institutional sense took three or four centuries and is one of the great achievements of medieval Islam.

In the two years of his rule (632–634), Abu Bakr governed on the basis of his personal prestige within the Muslim umma. He sent out military expeditions, collected taxes, dealt with tribes on behalf of the entire community, and led the community in prayer. Gradually, under Abu Bakr's first three successors, Umar (r. 634–644), Uthman (r. 644–656), and Ali (r. 656–661), the caliphate emerged as an institution. Umar succeeded in exerting his authority over the Bedouin tribes involved in ongoing conquests. Uthman asserted the right of the caliph to protect the economic interests of the entire umma. Also, Uthman's publication of the definitive text of the Qur'an showed his concern for the unity of the umma. However, Uthman was from a Mecca family that had resisted the Prophet until the capitulation of Mecca in 630, and he aroused resentment when he gave favors to members of his family. Opposition to Uthman coalesced around Ali, and when Uthman was assassinated in 656, Ali was chosen to succeed him.

The issue of responsibility for Uthman's murder raised the question of whether Ali's accession was legitimate. Uthman's cousin Mu'awiya, a member of the Umayyad family who had built a power base as governor of Syria, refused to recognize Ali as caliph. In the ensuing civil war Ali was assassinated, and Mu'awiya (r. 661–680) assumed the caliphate. Mu'awiya founded the Umayyad Dynasty and shifted the capital of the Islamic state from Medina in Arabia to Damascus in Syria. Although electing caliphs remained the Islamic ideal, beginning with Mu'awiya, the office of caliph increasingly became hereditary. Two successive dynasties, the Umayyad (661–750) and the Abbasid (750–1258), held the caliphate.

From its inception the caliphate rested on the theoretical principle that Muslim political and religious

• **diwān** A unit of government.

unity transcended tribalism. Mu'awiya sought to enhance the power of the caliphate by making tribal leaders dependent on him for concessions and special benefits. At the same time, his control of a loyal and well-disciplined army enabled him to take the caliphate in an authoritarian direction. Through intimidation he forced the tribal leaders to accept his son Yazid as his heir, thereby establishing the dynastic principle of succession. By distancing himself from a simple life within the umma and withdrawing into the palace that he built at Damascus, and by surrounding himself with symbols and ceremony, Mu'awiya laid the foundations for an elaborate caliphal court. Many of Mu'awiya's innovations were designed to protect him from assassination. A new official, the *hajib*, or chamberlain, restricted access to the caliph, who received visitors while he was seated on a throne surrounded by bodyguards.

The assassination of Ali and the assumption of the caliphate by Mu'awiya had another profound consequence. It gave rise to a fundamental division in the umma and in Muslim theology. Ali had claimed the caliphate on the basis of family ties—he was Muhammad's cousin and son-in-law. When Ali was murdered, his followers argued that Ali had been the Prophet's designated successor—partly because of the blood tie, partly because Muhammad had designated Ali **imam** (ih-MAHM), or leader in community prayer. These supporters of Ali were called **Shi'a** (SHEE-uh), meaning "supporters" or "partisans" of Ali (Shi'a are also known as Shi'ites). In succeeding generations, opponents of the Umayyad Dynasty emphasized their blood descent from Ali and claimed to possess divine knowledge that Muhammad had given them as his heirs.

Those who accepted Mu'awiya as caliph insisted that the central issue was adhering to the practices and beliefs of the umma based on the precedents of the Prophet. They came to be called **Sunnis** (SOO-neez), which derived from *Sunna* (examples from Muhammad's life). When a situation arose for which the Qur'an offered no solution, Sunni scholars searched for a precedent in the Sunna, which gained an authority comparable to the Qur'an itself.

Both Sunnis and Shi'a maintain that authority within Islam lies first in the Qur'an and then in the Sunna. Who interprets these sources? Shi'a claim that the imam does, for he is invested with divine grace and insight. Sunnis insist that interpretation comes from the consensus of the **ulama**, the group of religious scholars.

Throughout the Umayyad period, the Shi'a constituted a major source of discontent. They condemned the Umayyads as worldly and sensual rulers, in contrast to the pious true successors of Muhammad. A rival Sunni clan, the Abbasid (uh-BA-suhd), exploited the situation, agitating the Shi'a and encouraging dissension among tribal factions. The Abbasids contrasted their own piety with the pleasure-loving style of the Umayyads.

The Abbasid Caliphate

In 747 the Abbasid leader Abu' al-Abbas led a rebellion against the Umayyads, and in 750 he won general recognition as caliph. Damascus had served as the headquarters of Umayyad rule. Abu' al-Abbas's successor, al-Mansur (r. 754–775), founded the city of Baghdad in 762 and made it his capital. Thus the geographical center of the caliphate shifted eastward to former Sassanid territories. The first three Abbasid caliphs crushed their opponents, turned against many of their supporters, and created a new ruling elite drawn from newly converted Persian families that had traditionally served the ruler. The Abbasid revolution established a basis for rule and citizenship more cosmopolitan and Islamic than the narrow, elitist, and Arab basis that had characterized Umayyad government.

The Abbasids worked to identify their rule with Islam. They patronized the ulama, built mosques, and supported the development of Islamic scholarship. Although at first Muslims represented only a small minority of the conquered peoples, Abbasid rule provided the religious-political milieu in which Islam gained, over time, the allegiance of the vast majority of the populations from Spain to Afghanistan.

The Abbasids also borrowed heavily from Persian culture. Following Persian tradition, the Abbasid caliphs claimed to rule by divine right, as reflected in the change of their title from "successor of the Prophet" to "deputy of God." A majestic palace with hundreds of attendants and elaborate court ceremonies deliberately isolated the caliph from the people he ruled. Subjects had to bow before the caliph and kiss the ground, symbolizing his absolute power.

Under the third caliph, Harun al-Rashid (r. 786–809), Baghdad emerged as a flourishing commercial, artistic, and scientific center—the greatest city in Islam

- **imam** The leader in community prayer.
- **Shi'a** Arabic term meaning "supporters of Ali"; they make up one of the two main divisions of Islam.
- **Sunnis** Members of the larger of the two main divisions of Islam; the division between Sunnis and Shi'a began in a dispute about succession to Muhammad, but over time many differences in theology developed.
- **ulama** A group of religious scholars whom Sunnis trust to interpret the Qur'an and the Sunna.
- **emirs** Arab governors who were given overall responsibility for public order, maintenance of the armed forces, and tax collection.
- **shari'a** Muslim law, which covers social, criminal, political, commercial, and religious matters.

Abbasid Wooden Doors These ninth-century wooden doors are thought to come from Samarra, a city about 125 miles upstream from Baghdad, which briefly served as the capital in the ninth century. (Doors, pair, Abbasid Period, 9th century. Carved wood. Fletcher Fund, 1931 [31.119.1.2] [31.119.1, 31.119.2]. Photo: Schecter Lee/The Metropolitan Museum of Art, New York, NY, USA/ Image copyright © The Metropolitan Museum of Art/Image source: Art Resource, NY)

and one of the most cosmopolitan cities in the world. Its population of about a million people—an astoundingly large size for preindustrial times—created a huge demand for goods and services, and Baghdad became an entrepôt (trading center) for textiles, slaves, and foodstuffs coming from Oman, East Africa, and India. The city also became intellectually influential. Harun al-Rashid organized the translation of Greek medical and philosophical texts. As part of this effort the Christian scholar Hunayn Ibn Ishaq (808–873) translated Galen's medical works into Arabic and made Baghdad a center for the study and practice of medicine. Likewise, impetus was given to the study of astronomy, and through a program of astronomical observations, Muslim astronomers sought to correct and complement Ptolemaic astronomy, which held that the earth is a stationary object at the center of the universe. Above all, studies in Qur'anic textual analysis, history, poetry, law, and philosophy—all in Arabic—reflected the development of a distinctly Islamic literary and scientific culture.

An important innovation of the Abbasids was the use of slaves as soldiers. The caliph al-Mu'taşim (r. 833–842) acquired several thousand Turkish slaves who were converted to Islam and employed in military service. Scholars have offered varied explanations for this practice: that the use of slave soldiers was a response to a manpower shortage; that as highly skilled horsemen, the Turks had military skills superior to those of the Arabs and other peoples; and that al-Mu'taşim felt he could trust the Turks more than the Arabs, Persians, Khurasans, and other recruits. In any case, slave soldiers—later including Slavs, Indians, and sub-Saharan blacks—became a standard feature of Muslim armies in the Middle East until the twentieth century.

Administration of the Islamic Territories

The Islamic conquests brought into being a new imperial system. The Muslims adopted the patterns of administration used by the Byzantines in Egypt and Syria and by the Sassanids in Persia. Specifically, Arab **emirs**, or governors, were appointed and given overall responsibility for public order, maintenance of the armed forces, and tax collection. Below them, experienced native officials—Greeks, Syrians, and Copts (Egyptian Christians)—remained in office. Thus there was continuity with previous administrations.

The Umayyad caliphate witnessed the further development of the imperial administration. At the head stood the caliph, who led military campaigns against unbelievers. Theoretically, he had the ultimate responsibility for the interpretation of the sacred law. In practice, however, the ulama interpreted the law as revealed in the Qur'an and the Sunna. In the course of time, the ulama's interpretations constituted a rich body of law, the **shari'a** (shuh-REE-uh), which covered social, criminal, political, commercial, and religious matters. The ulama enjoyed great prestige in the Muslim community and was consulted by the caliph on difficult legal and spiritual matters. The *qadis* (KAH-dees), or judges, who were well versed in the sacred law, carried out the judicial functions of the state. Nevertheless, Muslim law prescribed that all people have access to

Ivory Chest of Pamplona, Spain The court of the Spanish Umayyads prized small, intricately carved ivory chests, often made in a royal workshop and used to store precious perfumes. This exquisite side panel depicts an eleventh-century caliph flanked by two attendants. An inscription on the front translates as "In the Name of God. Blessings from God, goodwill, and happiness." (Museo Navarra, Pamplona, Spain/Institut Amatller d'Art Hispanic)

the caliph, and he set aside special times for hearing petitions and for directly redressing grievances.

The central administrative organ was the diwān, which collected the taxes that paid soldiers' salaries (see page 241) and financed charitable and public works, such as aid to the poor and the construction of mosques, irrigation works, and public baths. Another important undertaking was a relay network established to rapidly convey letters and intelligence reports between the capital and distant outposts. The relay system made it possible for the caliph to respond quickly when news reached him of revolts by emirs and other officials far from the capital.

The early Abbasid period witnessed considerable economic expansion and population growth, complicating the work of government. New and specialized departments emerged, each with a hierarchy of officials. The most important new official was the vizier (vuh-ZEER), a position that the Abbasids adopted from the Persians. The vizier was the caliph's chief assistant, advising the caliph on matters of general policy, supervising the bureaucratic administration, and, under the caliph, overseeing the army, the provincial governors, and relations with foreign governments. Depending on the caliph's personality, viziers could acquire extensive power, and some used their offices for personal gain. Although some viziers' careers ended with their execution, there were always candidates seeking the job.

Fragmentation and Military Challenges, 900–1400

☐ How were the Muslim lands governed from 900 to 1400, and what new challenges did rulers face?

In theory, the caliph and his central administration governed the whole empire, but in practice, the many parts of the empire enjoyed considerable local independence. As long as public order was maintained and taxes were forwarded, the central government rarely interfered. At the same time, the enormous distance between many provinces and the imperial capital made it difficult for the caliph to prevent provinces from breaking away. Local, ethnic, or tribal loyalties, combined with fierce ambition, led to the creation of regional dynasties in much of the Islamic world, including Spain, Persia, Central Asia, northern India, and Egypt. None of these states repudiated Islam, but they did stop sending tax revenues to Baghdad. Moreover, states frequently fought costly wars against their neighbors in their attempts to expand. Sometimes these conflicts were worsened by Sunni-Shi'a antagonisms. All these developments, as well as invasions by Turks and Mongols, posed challenges to central Muslim authority.

Breakaway Territories and Shi'a Gains

One of the first territories to break away from the Baghdad-centered caliphate was Spain. In 755 an Umayyad prince who had escaped death at the hands of the Abbasids and fled to Spain set up an independent regime at Córdoba (see Map 9.1). Other territories soon followed. In 800 the emir in Tunisia in North Africa set himself up as an independent ruler and refused to place the caliph's name on the local coinage. And in 820 Tahir, the son of a slave, was rewarded with the governorship of Khurasan because he had supported the caliphate. Once he took office, Tahir

The Patio of the Lions at Alhambra, Fourteenth Century The fortress that the Moorish rulers of Spain built at Granada is considered one of the masterpieces of Andalusian art, notable for the fine carving of geometrical designs and Arabic calligraphy. (George Holton/Photo Researchers, Inc.)

ruled independently of Baghdad, not even mentioning the caliph's name in the traditional Friday prayers in recognition of caliphal authority.

In 946 a Shi'a Iranian clan overran Iraq and occupied Baghdad. The caliph was forced to recognize the clan's leader as commander in chief and to allow the celebration of Shi'a festivals—though the caliph and most of the people were Sunnis. A year later the caliph was accused of plotting against his new masters, snatched from his throne, dragged through the streets, and blinded. Blinding was a practice adopted from the Byzantines as a way of rendering a ruler incapable of carrying out his duties. This incident marked the practical collapse of the Abbasid caliphate. Abbasid caliphs, however, remained as puppets of a series of military commanders and symbols of Muslim unity until the Mongols killed the last Abbasid caliph in 1258 (see page 246).

In another Shi'a advance, the Fatimids, a Shi'a dynasty that claimed descent from Muhammad's daughter Fatima, conquered North Africa and then expanded into the Abbasid province of Egypt, founding the city of Cairo as their capital in 969. For the next century or so, Shi'a were in ascendancy in much of the western Islamic world.

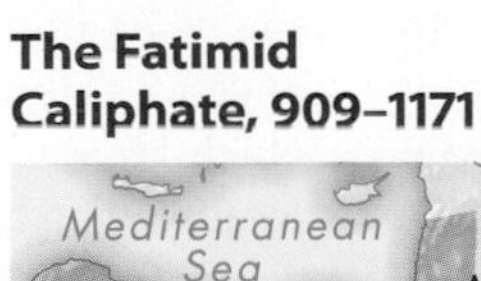

The Fatimid Caliphate, 909–1171

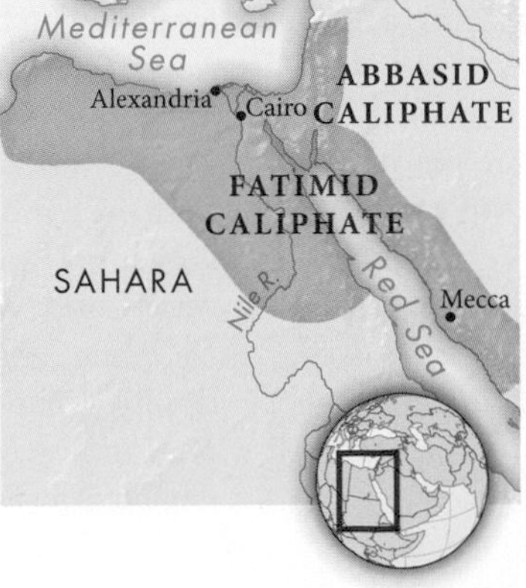

The Ascendancy of the Turks

In the mid-tenth century the Turks began to enter the Islamic world in large numbers. First appearing in Mongolia in the sixth century, groups of Turks, such as the Seljuks, gradually appeared across the grasslands of Eurasia. Skilled horsemen, they became prime targets for Muslim slave raids, as they made good slave soldiers. Once the Turks understood that Muslims could not be captured for slaves, more and more of them converted to Sunni Islam and often became *ghazi*, frontier raiders, who attacked unconverted Turks to capture slaves.

In the 1020s and 1030s Seljuk Turks overran Persia and then pushed into Iraq and Syria. Baghdad fell to them on December 18, 1055, and the caliph became a puppet of the Turkish sultan—literally, "he with authority." The Turkish elite rapidly gave up pastoralism and took up the sedentary lifestyle of the people they governed.

The Turks brought badly needed military strength to the Islamic world. They played a major part in recovering Jerusalem after it was held for nearly a century, from 1099 to 1187, by the European Crusaders (who had fought to take Christian

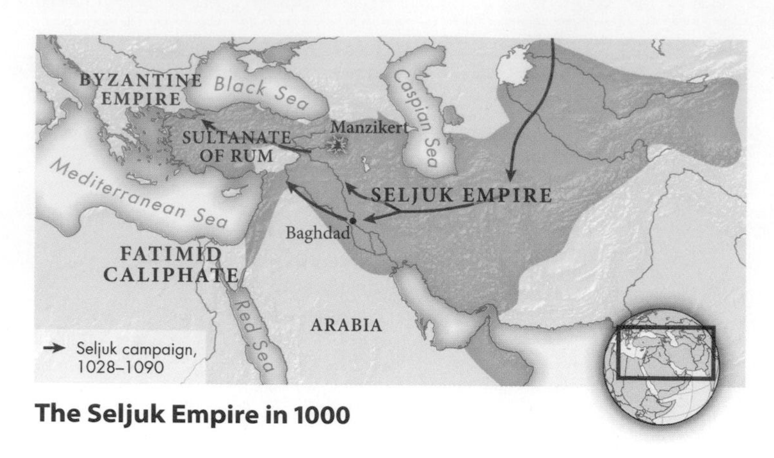

The Seljuk Empire in 1000

holy lands back from the Muslims; see pages 402–404). They also were important in preventing the later Crusades from accomplishing much. Moreover, the Turks became staunch Sunnis and led a campaign against the Shi'a.

The influx of Turks from 950 to 1100 also helped provide a new expansive dynamic. At the Battle of Manzikert in 1071, Seljuk Turks broke through Byzantine border defenses, opening Anatolia to Turkish migration. Over the next couple of centuries, perhaps a million Turks entered the area—including bands of ghazis and dervishes (Sufi brotherhoods; see page 261). Seljuk Turks set up the Sultanate of Rum in Anatolia, which lasted until the Mongols invaded in 1243. With the Turks came many learned men from the Persian-speaking East. Over time, many of the Christians in Anatolia converted to Islam and became fluent in Turkish.

The Mongol Invasions

In the early thirteenth century the Mongols arrived in the Middle East. Originally from the grasslands of Mongolia, in 1206 they proclaimed Chinggis Khan (ca. 1162–1227) as their leader, and he welded Mongol, Tartar, and Turkish tribes into a strong confederation that rapidly subdued neighboring settled societies (see pages 336–342). After conquering much of north China, the Mongols swept westward, leaving a trail of blood and destruction. They used terror as a weapon, and out of fear many cities surrendered without a fight.

In 1219–1221, when the Mongols first reached the Islamic lands, the areas from Persia through the Central Asian cities of Herat and Samarkand were part of the kingdom of Khwarizm. The ruler—the son of a Turkish slave who had risen to governor of a province—was a conqueror himself, having conquered much of Persia. He had the audacity to execute Chinggis's envoy, and Chinggis retaliated with a force of a hundred thousand soldiers that sacked city after city, often slaughtering the residents or enslaving them and sending them to Mongolia. Millions are said to have died. The irrigation systems that were needed for agriculture in this dry region had been neglected for some time, and with the Mongol invasions they suffered a fatal blow.

Not many Mongol forces were left in Persia after the campaign of 1219–1221, and another army, sent in 1237, captured the Persian city of Isfahan. In 1251 the decision was taken to push farther west. Chinggis Khan's grandson Hülegü (1217–1265) led an attack on the Abbasids in Baghdad, sacking and burning the city and killing the last Abbasid caliph in 1258. The fall of Damascus followed in 1260. Mamluk soldiers from Egypt, however, were able to withstand the Mongols and win a major victory at Ayn Jalut in Syria, which has been credited with saving Egypt and the Muslim lands in North Africa and perhaps Spain. At any rate, the desert ecology of the region did not provide suitable support for the Mongol armies, which required five horses for each soldier. Moreover, in 1260 the Great Khan (ruler of Mongolia and China) died, and the top Mongol generals withdrew to Mongolia for the selection of the next Great Khan.

Hülegü and his descendants ruled the central Muslim lands (referred to as the Il-khanate) for eighty years. In 1295 his descendant Ghazan embraced Islam and worked for the revival of Muslim culture. As the Turks had done earlier, the Mongols, once converted, injected new vigor into the faith and spirit of Islam. In the Il-khanate the Mongols governed through Persian viziers and native financial officials.

Muslim Society: The Life of the People

☐ What social distinctions were important in Muslim society?

When the Prophet appeared, Arab society consisted of independent Bedouin tribal groups loosely held together by loyalty to a strong leader and by the belief that all members of a tribe were descended from a common ancestor. Heads of families elected the sheik, or tribal chief. He was usually chosen from among elite warrior families who believed their bloodlines made them superior. According to the Qur'an, however, birth counted for nothing; piety was the only criterion for honor: "O ye folk, verily we have created you male and female. . . . Verily the most honourable of you in the sight of God is the most pious of you."[1] The idea of social equality was a basic Muslim doctrine.

When Muhammad defined social equality, he was thinking about equality among Muslims alone. But even among Muslims, a sense of pride in ancestry could not be destroyed by a stroke of the pen. Claims based

Great Mosque at Isfahan in Persia Begun in the late eighth century and added to over the centuries, the Great Mosque in Isfahan is one of the masterpieces of Islamic architecture. The huge dome and the vaulted niches around the courtyard are covered with blue, turquoise, white, and yellow tile. (© Roger Wood/Corbis)

on birth remained strong among the first Muslims, and after Islam spread outside of Arabia, full-blooded Arab tribesmen regarded themselves as superior to foreign converts.

The Social Hierarchy

In the Umayyad period, Muslim society was distinctly hierarchical. At the top of the hierarchy were the caliph's household and the ruling Arab Muslims. Descended from Bedouin tribespeople and composed of warriors, veterans, governing officials, and townsmen, this class constituted the ruling elite. It was a relatively small group, greatly outnumbered by Muslim villagers and country people.

Converts constituted the second class in Islamic society, one that grew slowly over time. Converts to Islam had to attach themselves to one of the Arab tribes in a subordinate capacity. Many resented having to do this, since they believed they represented a culture superior to that of Arab tribespeople. From the Muslim converts eventually came the members of the commercial and learned professions—merchants, traders, teachers, doctors, artists, and interpreters of the shari'a. Second-class citizenship led some Muslim converts to adopt Shi'ism (see page 242). Even so, over the centuries, Berber, Copt, Persian, Aramaean, and other converts to Islam intermarried with their Muslim conquerors. Gradually, assimilation united peoples of various ethnic backgrounds.

Dhimmis (zih-MEEZ)—including Jews, Christians, and Zoroastrians—formed the third stratum. Considered "protected peoples" because they worshipped only one God, they were allowed to practice their religions, maintain their houses of worship, and conduct their business affairs as long as they gave unequivocal recognition to Muslim political supremacy and paid a small tax. Because many Jews and Christians were well educated, they were often appointed to high positions in provincial capitals as well as in Damascus and Baghdad. Restrictions placed on Christians and Jews were not severe, and outbursts of violence against them were rare. However, their social position deteriorated during the Crusades and the Mongol invasions, when there was a general rise of religious loyalties. At those times, Muslims suspected the dhimmis, often rightly, of collaborating with the enemies of Islam.

How did the experience of Jews under Islam compare with that of Jews living in Christian Europe? Recent scholarship shows that in Europe Jews were first marginalized in the Christian social order and then completely expelled from it. In Islam Jews, though marginalized, participated fully in commercial and professional activities, some attaining economic equality with their Muslim counterparts. (See "Viewpoints 9.1: Jews in Muslim Lands," page 248.) The seven-

• **dhimmis** A term meaning "protected peoples"; they included Jews, Christians, and Zoroastrians.

Separating Men and Women in a Mosque
In this mid-sixteenth-century illustration of the interior of a mosque, a screen separates the women, who are wearing veils and tending children, from the men. The women can hear what is being said, but the men cannot see them.
(Ouseley Add 24 folio 55v/Bodleian Libraries, The University of Oxford, UK/The Bridgeman Art Library)

role in rallying support for the movement opposing Ali, who succeeded Uthman in 656 (see page 241). However, by the Abbasid period the status of women had declined. The practices of the Byzantine and Persian lands that had been conquered, including seclusion of women, were absorbed. The supply of slave women increased substantially. Some scholars speculate that as wealth replaced ancestry as the main criterion of social status, men more and more viewed women as possessions, as a form of wealth.

Men were also seen as dominant in their marriages. The Qur'an states that "men are in charge of women because Allah hath made the one to excel the other, and because they (men) spend of their property (for the support of women). So good women are obedient, guarding in secret that which Allah hath guarded."[2] A thirteenth-century commentator on this passage argued from it that women are incapable of and unfit for any public duties, such as participating in religious rites, giving evidence in the law courts, or being involved in any public political decisions. This view came to be accepted, and later interpreters further categorized the ways in which men were superior to women.

In many present-day Muslim cultures, few issues are more sensitive than the veiling and seclusion of women. These practices have their roots in pre-Islamic times, and they took firm hold in classical Islamic society. As Arab conquerors subjugated various peoples, they adopted some of the vanquished peoples' customs. Veiling was probably of Byzantine or Persian origin. The head veil seems to have been the mark of freeborn urban women; wearing it distinguished them from slave women. Country and desert women did not wear veils because they interfered with work. The veil also indicated respectability and modesty. The Qur'an contains no specific rule about the veil, but its few vague references have been interpreted as sanctioning the practice. An even greater restriction on women than veiling was the practice of seclusion, the harem system. The English word *harem* comes from the Arabic *haram*, meaning "forbidden" or "sacrosanct," which the women's quarters of a house or palace were considered to be. The practice of secluding women also derives from Arabic contacts with Persia and other Eastern cultures. By 800 women in more prosperous households stayed out of sight. The harem became another symbol of male prestige and prosperity, as well as a way to distinguish upper-class from lower-class women.

Marriage, the Family, and Sexuality

The Sunni aphorism "There shall be no monkery in Islam" captures the importance of marriage in Muslim culture and the Muslim belief that a sexually frustrated person is dangerous to the community. Islam had no roles for the celibate. In the Muslim world, as in China, every man and woman is expected to marry unless physically incapable or financially unable. Marriage is seen as a safeguard of virtue, essential to the stability both of the family and of society.

As in medieval Europe and traditional India and China, marriage in Muslim society was considered too important an undertaking to be left to the romantic emotions of the young. Families or guardians, not the prospective bride and groom, identified suitable partners and finalized the contract. The official wedding ceremony consisted of an offer and its acceptance by representatives of the bride's and groom's parents at a meeting before witnesses. A wedding banquet at which men and women feasted separately followed; the quality of the celebration, of the gifts, and of the food depended on the relative wealth of the two families.

Because it was absolutely essential that the bride be a virgin, marriages were arranged shortly after the onset of the girl's menstrual period at age twelve or thirteen. Husbands were commonly ten to fifteen years older. Youthful marriages ensured a long period of fertility.

A wife's responsibilities depended on the wealth and occupation of her husband. A farmer's wife helped in the fields, ground the corn, carried water, prepared food, and did the myriad tasks necessary in rural life. Shopkeepers' wives in the cities sometimes helped in business. In an upper-class household, the wife supervised servants, looked after all domestic arrangements, and did whatever was needed for her husband's comfort.

In every case, children were the wife's special domain. A mother exercised authority over her children and enjoyed their respect. A Muslim tradition asserts that "paradise is at the mother's feet." Thus, as in Chinese culture, the prestige of the young wife depended on the production of children — especially sons — as rapidly as possible. A wife's failure to have children was one of the main reasons for a man to divorce his wife or take a second wife.

Like the Jewish tradition, Muslim law permits divorce. The law prescribes that if a man intends to divorce his wife, he should avoid hasty action and not have intercourse with her for three months; it is hoped that during that time they will reconcile. If the woman turns out to be pregnant, her husband knows that he is the father. Although divorce is allowed, it is not encouraged. One commentator cited the Prophet as saying, "The lawful thing which God hates most is divorce."[3]

In contrast to the traditional Christian view of sexual activity as inherently shameful and only a cure for lust even within marriage, Islam maintains a healthy acceptance of sexual pleasure for both males and females. The Qur'an permits a man to have four wives, provided that all are treated justly. Some modern Muslim commentators link this provision to a surplus of women that resulted from the wars during the Prophet's lifetime. The vast majority of Muslim males were monogamous because only the wealthy could afford to support more than one wife.

Trade and Commerce

☐ Why did trade thrive in Muslim lands?

Unlike the Christian West or the Confucian East, Islam looked favorably on profit-making enterprises. Muhammad had earned his living in business as a representative of the city of Mecca, which carried on a brisk trade from southern Palestine to southwestern Arabia. According to the sayings of the Prophet: "The honest, truthful Muslim merchant will stand with the martyrs on the Day of Judgment. I commend the merchants to you, for they are the couriers of the horizons and God's trusted servants on earth."[4]

The Qur'an, moreover, has no prohibition against trade with Christians or other unbelievers. In fact, non-Muslims, including the Jews of Cairo and the Armenians in the central Islamic lands, were prominent in mercantile networks.

Waterways served as the main commercial routes of the Islamic world (Map 9.2). They included the Mediterranean and Black Seas; the Caspian Sea and the Volga River, which gave access deep into Russia; the Aral Sea, from which caravans departed for China; the Gulf of Aden; and the Arabian Sea and the Indian Ocean, which linked the Persian Gulf region with eastern Africa, the Indian subcontinent, and eventually Indonesia and the Philippines.

Cairo was a major Mediterranean entrepôt for intercontinental trade. Foreign merchants from Central Asia, Persia, Iraq, Europe (especially Venice), the Byzantine Empire, and Spain sailed up the Nile to the Aswan region, traveled east from Aswan by caravan to the Red Sea, and then sailed down the Red Sea to Aden, where they entered the Indian Ocean on their way to India. They exchanged textiles, glass, gold, silver, and copper for Asian spices, dyes, and drugs and for Chinese silks and porcelains. Muslim and Jewish merchants dominated the trade with India, and all spoke and wrote Arabic. Their commercial practices included the *sakk* (the Arabic word is the root of the English *check*), an order to a banker to pay money held on account to a third party; the practice can be traced to Roman Palestine. Muslims also developed other business innovations, such as the bill of exchange, a written order from one person to another to pay a specified sum of money to a designated person or party, and the idea of the joint stock company, an arrangement that lets a group of people invest in a venture and share its profits (and losses) in proportion to the amount each has invested.

Trade also benefited from improvements in technology. The adoption from the Chinese of the magnetic compass, an instrument for determining directions at sea by means of a magnetic needle turning on a pivot, greatly helped navigation of the Arabian Sea and the Indian Ocean. The construction of larger ships led to a shift in long-distance cargoes from luxury goods such as pepper, spices, and drugs to bulk goods such as sugar, rice, and timber. Venetian galleys sailing the Mediterranean came to carry up to 250 tons of cargo, but the Arab and Persian ships plying the Indian Ocean were built to carry up to 400 tons. The teak forests of western India supplied the wood for Arab ships.

In this period Egypt became the center of Muslim trade, benefiting from the decline of Iraq caused by the Mongol capture of Baghdad and the fall of the Abbasid caliphate (see page 246). Beginning in the late twelfth

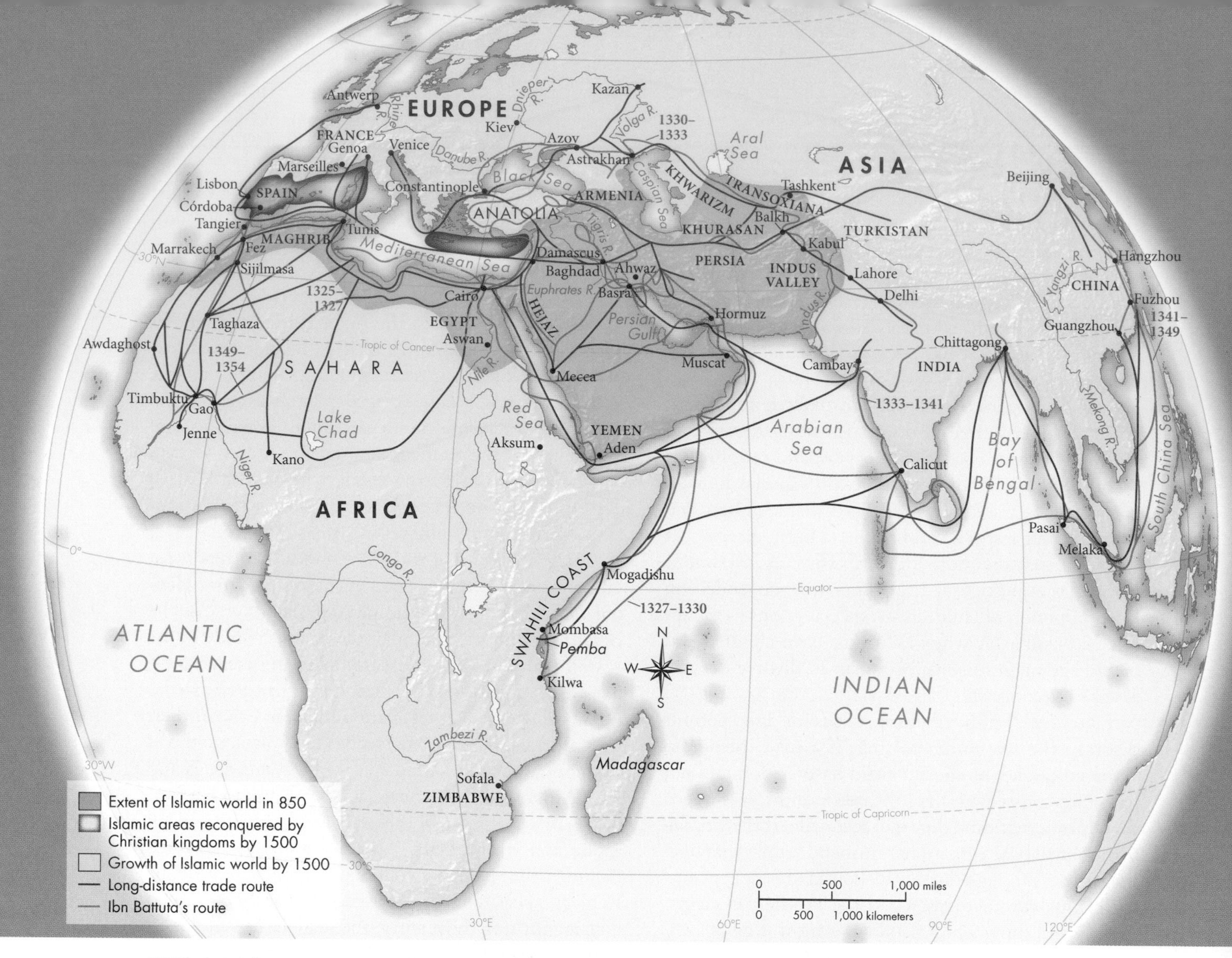

MAP 9.2 The Expansion of Islam and Its Trading Networks in the Thirteenth and Fourteenth Centuries By 1500 Islam had spread extensively in North and East Africa, and into the Balkans, the Caucasus, Central Asia, India, and the islands of Southeast Asia. Muslim merchants played a major role in bringing their religion as they extended their trade networks. They were active in the Indian Ocean long before the arrival of Europeans.

century Persian and Arab seamen sailed down the east coast of Africa and established trading towns between Somalia and Sofala (see pages 285–291). These thirty to fifty urban centers—each merchant-controlled, fortified, and independent—linked Zimbabwe in southern Africa with the Indian Ocean trade and the Middle Eastern trade.

A private ninth-century list mentions a great variety of commodities transported into and through the Islamic world by land and by sea:

> Imported from India: tigers, leopards, elephants, leopard skins, red rubies, white sandal-wood, ebony, and coconuts
> From China: aromatics, silk, porcelain, paper, ink, peacocks, fiery horses, saddles, felts, cinnamon
> From the Byzantines: silver and gold vessels, embroidered cloths, fiery horses, slave girls, rare articles in red copper, strong locks, lyres, water engineers, specialists in plowing and cultivation, marble workers, and eunuchs
> From Egypt: ambling donkeys, fine cloths, papyrus, balsam oil, and, from its mines, high-quality topaz
> From the Khazars [a people living on the northern shore of the Black Sea]: slaves, slave women, armor, helmets, and hoods of mail
> From Ahwaz [a city in southwestern Persia]: sugar, silk brocades, castanet players and dancing girls, kinds of dates, grape molasses, and candy.[5]

Did Muslim economic activity amount to a kind of capitalism? If capitalism is defined as private (not state) ownership of the means of production, the production of goods for sale, profit as the main motive for economic activity, competition, and a money economy, then, unquestionably, the medieval Muslim economy had capitalistic features. Until the sixteenth century much more world trade went through Muslim than European hands.

One byproduct of the extensive trade through Muslim lands was the spread of useful plants. Cotton, sugarcane, and rice spread from India to other places with suitable climates. Citrus fruits made their way to Muslim Spain from Southeast Asia and India. The value of this trade contributed to the prosperity of the Abbasid era.

Cultural Developments

☐ What new ideas and practices emerged in the arts, sciences, education, and religion?

Long-distance trade provided the wealth that made possible a gracious and sophisticated culture in the cities of the Muslim world. (See "Individuals in Society: Ibn Battuta," page 256.) Education helped foster achievements in the arts and sciences, and Sufism brought a new spiritual and intellectual tradition.

The Cultural Centers of Baghdad and Córdoba

Although cities and mercantile centers dotted the entire Islamic world, the cities of Baghdad and Córdoba, at their peak in the tenth century, stand out as the finest examples of cosmopolitan Muslim civilization. On Baghdad's streets thronged a kaleidoscope of races, creeds, costumes, and cultures, an almost infinite variety of peoples: returning travelers, administrative officials, slaves, visitors, and merchants from Asia, Africa, and Europe. Shops and marketplaces offered a dazzling and exotic array of goods from all over the world.

The caliph Harun al-Rashid presided over a glamorous court. He invited writers, dancers, musicians, poets, and artists to live in Baghdad, and he is reputed to have rewarded one singer with 100,000 silver pieces for a single song. This brilliant era provided the background for the tales that appear in *The Thousand and One Nights*.

The central story of this fictional collection concerns the attempt of a new bride, Scheherazade, to keep her husband, Shahyar, legendary king of Samarkand, from killing her out of certainty that she will be unfaithful like his first wife. In efforts to delay her execution, she entertains him with one tale a night for 1,001 nights. In the end, Scheherazade's efforts succeed, and her husband pardons her. Among the tales she tells him are such famous ones as "Aladdin and His Lamp," "Sinbad the Sailor," and "Ali Baba and the Forty Thieves." Though filled with folklore, the *Arabian Nights* (as it is also called) has provided many of the images through which Europeans have understood the Islamic world.

Córdoba in southern Spain competed with Baghdad for the cultural leadership of the Islamic world. In the tenth century no city in Asia or Europe could equal dazzling Córdoba. Its streets were well paved and lighted, and the city had an abundant supply of fresh water. With a population of about 1 million, Córdoba contained 1,600 mosques, 900 public baths, 213,177 houses for ordinary people, and 60,000 mansions for generals, officials, and the wealthy. In its 80,455 shops, 13,000 weavers produced silks, woolens, and brocades that were internationally famous. Córdoba was also a great educational center with 27 free schools and a library containing 400,000 volumes. (By contrast, the renowned Benedictine abbey of Saint-Gall in Switzerland had about 600 books.) Moreover, Córdoba's scholars made contributions in chemistry, medicine and surgery, music, philosophy, and mathematics. It was through Córdoba and Persia that the Indian game of chess entered western Europe. The contemporary Saxon nun Hrosthwita of Gandersheim (d. 1000) described Córdoba as the "ornament of the world."[6]

Education and Intellectual Life

Muslim culture valued learning, especially religious learning, because knowledge provided the guidelines by which men and women should live. Parents thus established elementary schools for the training of their children. After the caliph Uthman (see page 241) ordered the preparation of an approved text of the Qur'an and had copies of it made, the Qur'an became the basic text. From the eighth century onward, formal education for young men involved reading, writing, and the study of the Qur'an, believed essential for its religious message and for its training in proper grammar and syntax.

Islam is a religion of the law, taught at **madrasas** (muh-DRA-suhs), schools for the study of Muslim law and religion. Many madrasas were founded between 1000 and 1350. By 1193 thirty madrasas existed in Damascus, with sixty more established there between 1200 and 1250. Aleppo, Jerusalem, Alexandria, and above all Cairo also witnessed the foundation of madrasas.

Schools were urban phenomena. Wealthy merchants endowed them, providing salaries for teachers, stipends for students, and living accommodations for both. All Islamic higher education rested on a close

• **madrasa** A school for the study of Muslim law and religion.

Mechanical Hand Washer Building on the work of the Greek engineer and inventor Archimedes (see page 140), the Arab scientist Ibn al-Razzaz al-Raziri (fl. ca. 1200) designed practical devices to serve general social needs and illustrated them in a mechanical engineering handbook. In this diagram, a device in the form of a servant pours water with its right hand and offers a towel with its left. The device resembles a modern faucet that releases water when hands are held under it. (Freer Gallery of Art, Smithsonian Institution, USA/The Bridgeman Art Library)

but, because of the basic Islamic principle that "men are the guardians of women, because God has set the one over the other," the law excluded women from participating in the legal, religious, or civic occupations for which the madrasa prepared young men. Moreover, educational theorists insisted that men should study in a sexually isolated environment because feminine allure would distract them. Nevertheless, many young women received substantial educations at home. The daughter of Ali Ibn Muhammad al-Diruti al-Mahalli, for example, memorized the Qur'an, learned to write, and received instruction in several sacred works. According to one biographical dictionary covering the lives of 1,075 women, 411 of them had memorized the Qur'an, studied with a particular teacher, and received a certificate.

In comparing Islamic higher education during the twelfth through fourteenth centuries with that available in Europe or China at the same time (see pages 369, 411), there are some striking similarities and some major differences. In both Europe and the Islamic countries religious authorities ran most schools, while in China the government, local villages, and lineages ran schools, and private tutoring was very common. In the Islamic world, as in China, the personal relationship of teacher and student was seen as key to education. In Europe the reward for satisfactorily completing a course of study was a degree granted by the university. In China, at the very highest levels, the state ran a civil service examination system that rewarded achievement with appointments in the state bureaucracy. In Muslim culture, by contrast, it was not the school or the state but the individual teacher whose evaluation mattered and who granted certificates.

Still, there were also some striking similarities in the practice of education. Students in all three cultures had to master a sacred language (Latin, Arabic, or classical Chinese). In all three cultures education rested heavily on the study of basic religious, legal, or philosophical texts: the Old and New Testaments or the Justinian *Code* in Europe; the Confucian classics and commentaries in China; the Qur'an, hadith, and legal texts deriving from them in the Muslim world. Also, in all three cultures memorization played a large role in the acquisition and transmission of learning. Furthermore, teachers in all three societies lectured on particular passages, and leading teachers might disagree fiercely about the correct interpretations of a particular text, forcing students to question, to think critically, and to choose among divergent opinions. All these similarities in educational practice contributed to cultural cohesion and ties among the educated living in scattered localities.

In the Muslim world the spread of the Arabic language, not only among the educated classes but also among all the people, was the decisive element in the creation of a common culture. Recent scholarship demonstrates that after the establishment of the Islamic empire, the spread of the Arabic language was more important than religion in fostering cultural change. Whereas conversion to Islam was gradual, linguistic conversion went much faster. Arabic became the official language of the state and its bureaucracies in former Byzantine and Sassanid territories, and Muslim conquerors forbade Persian-speaking people to use their native language. Islamic rulers required tribute from monotheistic peoples—the Persians and Greeks—but they did not force them to change their religions. Conquered peoples were, however, compelled to submit to a linguistic conversion—to adopt the Arabic language. In time Arabic produced a cohesive and "inter-

Viewpoints 9.2

Amusing Animal Stories by Bar-Hebraeus and Aesop

• *In thirteenth-century Syria, Gregory Bar-Hebraeus wrote not only on serious subjects such as religion and philosophy but also on more playful subjects, and his works include a large collection of amusing stories. Persian, Hebrew, Indian, and Christian wise men appear in these tales, as do animals, clowns, and thieves. The stories that feature talking animals are reminiscent of Aesop's* Fables, *an older set of stories in which animals have distinct humanlike character traits. Aesop's* Fables *can be traced back to Greek and Latin versions but were added to over time, so all cannot have been written by the Greek storyteller Aesop. Two of his fables are included here for comparison with Bar-Hebraeus's tales.*

Bar-Hebraeus's *Laughable Stories*

"A wolf, a fox, and a lion having banded themselves together snared a goat, a stag, and a hare. And the lion said to the wolf, "Divide these among us." The wolf said, "The goat is for you, the stag is for me, and the hare is for the fox." When the lion heard these words he became furious and leaped upon the wolf and choked him. Then he said to the fox, "You divide them." The fox said to him, "The goat is for your breakfast, the hare for your lunch, and the stag for your supper." The lion then asked him, "Where have you learned to make such an equitable division?" The fox replied, "From this wolf which lies before you, O my lord the king."

A wolf, a fox, and a hare found a lamb, and they said to each other, "He who is the oldest among us shall eat him." The hare said, "I was born before God created the heavens and the earth," and the fox said, "You are right indeed, for I was present when you were born," and the wolf, at the same time seizing the lamb, said, "My stature and capacity are witnesses that I am older than you both," so he ate the lamb."

Aesop's *Fables*

"The Birds waged war with the Beasts, and each were by turns the conquerors. A Bat, fearing the uncertain issues of the fight, always fought on the side which he felt was the strongest. When peace was proclaimed, his deceitful conduct was apparent to both combatants. Therefore being condemned by each for his treachery, he was driven forth from the light of day, and henceforth concealed himself in dark hiding-places, flying always alone and at night.

A Wolf, having stolen a lamb from a fold, was carrying him off to his lair. A Lion met him in the path, and seizing the lamb, took it from him. Standing at a safe distance, the Wolf exclaimed, "You have unrighteously taken that which was mine from me!" To which the Lion jeeringly replied, "It was righteously yours, eh? The gift of a friend?""

Sources: Gregory Bar Hebraeus, *The Laughable Stories*, trans. E. A. W. Budge (London: Luzac, 1897), pp. 90–91, slightly modified; *Aesop's Fables*, trans. G. F. Townsend (London: G. Routledge and Sons, 1882), pp. 45, 73.

QUESTIONS FOR ANALYSIS

1. What makes stories with animal characters interesting?
2. Could Bar-Hebraeus have been inspired by Aesop's *Fables*? What is your evidence?
3. What are the moral messages in each of these stories, and what can you learn about each culture from these messages?

national" culture over a large part of the Eurasian world. Among those who wrote in Arabic was the erudite Gregory Bar-Hebraeus (1226–1286), a bishop of the Syrian Orthodox Church. He wrote widely on philosophy, poetry, language, history, and theology, sometimes in Syriac, sometimes in Arabic (see "Viewpoints 9.2: Amusing Animal Stories by Bar-Hebraeus and Aesop," above).

As a result of Muslim creativity and vitality, modern scholars consider the years from 800 to 1300 to be one of the most brilliant periods in the world's history. Near the beginning of this period the Persian scholar al-Khwarizmi (d. ca. 850) harmonized Greek and Indian findings to produce astronomical tables that formed the basis for later Eastern and Western research. Al-Khwarizmi also studied mathematics, and his textbook on algebra (from the Arabic *al-jabr*) was the first work in which the word *algebra* is used to mean the "transposing of negative terms in an equation to the opposite side."

Muslim medical knowledge far surpassed that of the West. The Baghdad physician al-Razi (865–925), the first physician to make the clinical distinction between measles and smallpox, produced an encyclopedic treatise on medicine that was translated into Latin and circulated widely in the West. In Córdoba the great surgeon al-Zahrawi (d. 1013) produced an important work in which he discussed the cauterization of wounds (searing them with a branding iron) and the crushing of stones in the bladder. Muslim science reached its peak in the work of Ibn Sina of Bukhara (980–1037), known in the West as Avicenna. His *al-Qanun* codified all Greco-Arabic medical thought, described the contagious nature of tuberculosis and the spreading of diseases, and listed 760 drugs.

Muslim scholars also wrote works on geography, jurisprudence, and philosophy. Al-Kindi (d. ca. 870) was the first Muslim thinker to try to harmonize Greek philosophy and the religious precepts of the Qur'an. He sought to integrate Islamic concepts of human beings and their relations to God and the universe with the principles of ethical and social conduct discussed by Plato and Aristotle. Inspired by Plato's *Republic* and Aristotle's *Politics*, the distinguished philosopher al-Farabi (d. 950) wrote a political treatise describing an ideal city whose ruler is morally and intellectually perfect and who has as his goal the citizens' complete happiness. Avicenna maintained that the truths found by human reason cannot conflict with the truths revealed in the Qur'an. Ibn Rushid, or Averroës (1126–1198),

☐ Picturing the Past

Sufi Collective Ritual Collective or group rituals, in which Sufis tried through ecstatic experiences to come closer to God, have always fascinated outsiders, including non-Sufi Muslims. Here the sixteenth-century Persian painter Sultan Muhammad illustrates the writing of the fourteenth-century lyric poet Hafiz. Notice the various musical instruments and the delicate floral patterns so characteristic of Persian art. (Or. Ms. 104, from *The Kulliyyati-I Sa'di* [The Collected Works of Sa'di], 1556, vellum/Edinburgh University Library, Scotland/With kind permission of the University of Edinburgh/The Bridgeman Art Library)

ANALYZING THE IMAGE What sort of architectural space is depicted here? What distinctions do you see among the people in terms of how they dress and what they are doing?

CONNECTIONS How common are music and dance in religion? What do they provide?

of Córdoba, a judge in Seville and later the royal court physician, paraphrased and commented on the works of Aristotle. He insisted on the right to subject all knowledge, except the dogmas of faith, to the test of reason and on the essential harmony of religion and philosophy.

The Mystical Tradition of Sufism

Like the world's other major religions — Buddhism, Hinduism, Judaism, and Christianity — Islam also developed a mystical tradition: Sufism (SOO-fih-zuhm). It arose in the ninth and tenth centuries as a popular reaction to the materialism and worldliness of the later Umayyad regime. Sufis sought a personal union with God — divine love and knowledge through intuition rather than through rational deduction and study of the shari'a. The earliest of the Sufis followed an ascetic routine (denial of physical desires to achieve a spiritual goal), dedicating themselves to fasting, prayer, meditation on the Qur'an, and the avoidance of sin.

The woman mystic Rabi'a (717–801) epitomized this combination of renunciation and devotion. An attractive woman who refused marriage so that nothing would distract her from a total commitment to God, Rabi'a attracted followers, for whom she served as a spiritual guide. One of her poems captures her deep devotion: "O my lord, if I worship thee from fear of hell, and if I worship thee in hope of paradise, exclude me thence, but if I worship thee for thine own sake, then withhold not from me thine eternal beauty."[7]

Between the tenth and the thirteenth centuries groups of Sufis gathered around prominent leaders called *shaykhs*; members of these groups were called *dervishes*. Dervishes entered hypnotic or ecstatic trances, either through the constant repetition of certain prayers or through physical exertions such as whirling or dancing (hence the English phrase "whirling dervish" for one who dances with abandonment).

Some Sufis acquired reputations as charismatic holy men to whom ordinary Muslims came seeking spiritual consolation, healing, charity, or political mediation between tribal and factional rivals. Other Sufis became known for their writings. Probably the most famous medieval Sufi was the Spanish mystic-philosopher Ibn al'Arabi (1165–1240). He traveled widely in Spain, North Africa, and Arabia seeking masters of Sufism. In Mecca he received a "divine commandment" to begin his major work, *The Meccan Revelation*, which evolved into a personal encyclopedia of 560 chapters. Also at Mecca, the wisdom of a beautiful young girl inspired him to write a collection of love poems, *The Interpreter of Desires*, for which he composed a mystical commentary. In 1223, after visits to Egypt, Anatolia, Baghdad, and Aleppo, Ibn al'Arabi concluded his pilgrimage through the Islamic world at Damascus, where he produced *The Bezels [Edges] of Wisdom*, considered one of the greatest works of Sufism.

Muslim-Christian Encounters

☐ How did Muslims and Christians come into contact with each other, and how did they view each other?

During the early centuries of its development, Islam came into contact with the other major religions of Eurasia — Hinduism in India, Buddhism in Central Asia, Zoroastrianism in Persia, and Judaism and Christianity in western Asia and Europe. However, the relationship that did the most to define Muslim identity was the one with Christianity. To put this another way, the most significant "other" to Muslims in the heartland of Islam was Christendom. The close physical proximity and the long history of military encounters undoubtedly contributed to making the Christian-Muslim encounter so important to both sides.

European Christians and Middle Eastern Muslims shared a common Judeo-Christian heritage. In the classical period of Islam, Muslims learned about Christianity from the Christians they met in conquered territories; from the Old and New Testaments; from Jews; and from Jews and Christians who converted to Islam. Before 1400 there was a wide spectrum of Muslim opinion about Jesus and Christians. At the time of the Crusades and the Christian reconquest of Muslim Spain (the *reconquista*, 722–1492), polemical anti-Christian writings appeared. In other periods, Muslim views were more positive.

In the Middle Ages, Christians and Muslims met frequently in business and trade. Commercial contacts, especially when European merchants resided for a long time in the Muslim East, gave Europeans, notably the Venetians, familiarity with Muslim art and architecture. Likewise, when in the fifteenth century Muslim artists in the Ottoman Empire and in Persia became acquainted with Western artists, such as Gentile Bellini, they admired and imitated them. Also, Christians very likely borrowed aspects of their higher education system from Islam.

In the Christian West, Islam had the greatest cultural impact in Andalusia in southern Spain. Between roughly the eighth and twelfth centuries Muslims, Christians, and Jews lived in close proximity in Andalusia, and some scholars believe the period represents a remarkable era of interfaith harmony. Many Christians adopted Arabic patterns of speech and dress, gave up

Playing Chess This page from a thirteenth-century book on chess and other games depicts a Moor and a Christian playing chess together. (Biblioteca Monasterio del Escorial, Madrid, Spain/Index/The Bridgeman Art Library)

the practice of eating pork, and developed a special appreciation for Arabic music and poetry. Some Christian women of elite status chose the Muslim practice of going out in public with their faces veiled. Records describe Muslim and Christian youths joining in celebrations and merrymaking. These assimilated Christians, called **Mozarabs** (moh-ZAR-uhbz), did not attach much importance to the doctrinal differences between the two religions.

However, Mozarabs soon faced the strong criticism of both Muslim scholars and Christian clerics. Muslim teachers feared that close contact between people of the two religions would lead to Muslim contamination and become a threat to the Islamic faith. Christian bishops worried that a knowledge of Islam would lead to confusion about essential Christian doctrines. Both Muslim scholars and Christian theologians argued that assimilation led to moral decline.

Thus, beginning in the late tenth century, Muslim regulations closely defined what Christians and Muslims could do. A Christian, however much assimilated, remained an unbeliever, a word that carried a pejorative connotation. Mozarabs had to live in special sections of cities; could not learn the Qur'an, employ Muslim workers or servants, or build new churches; and had to be buried in their own cemeteries. A Muslim who converted to Christianity was sentenced to death. By about 1250 the Christian reconquest of Muslim Spain had brought most of the Iberian Peninsula under Christian control. With their new authority, Christian kings set up schools that taught both Arabic and Latin to train missionaries.

Beyond Andalusian Spain, mutual animosity limited contact between people of the two religions. The Muslim assault on Christian Europe in the eighth and ninth centuries — with villages burned, monasteries sacked, and Christians sold into slavery — left a legacy of bitter hostility. Christians felt threatened by a faith that acknowledged God as creator of the universe but denied the Trinity and that accepted Jesus as a prophet but denied his divinity. Europeans' perception of Islam as a menace helped inspire the Crusades of the eleventh through thirteenth centuries (see pages 402–405).

Despite the conflicts between the two religions, Muslim scholars often wrote sympathetically about Jesus. For example, the great historian al-Tabari (d. 923), relying on Arabic sources, wrote positively of Jesus's life, focusing on his birth and crucifixion. Also, Ikhwan al-Safa, an eleventh-century Islamic brotherhood, held that in his preaching Jesus deliberately rejected the

• **Mozarabs** Christians who adopted some Arabic customs but did not convert.

harsh punishments reflected in the Jewish Torah and tried to be the healing physician, teaching by parables and trying to touch people's hearts by peace and love. The prominent theologian and qadi (judge) of Teheran, Abd al-Jabbar (d. 1024), though not critical of Jesus, argued that Christians had rejected Jesus's teachings: they failed to observe the ritual purity of prayer, substituting poems by Christian scholars for scriptural prayers; they gave up circumcision, the sign of their covenant with God and Abraham; they moved the Sabbath from Saturday to Sunday; they allowed the eating of pork and shellfish; and they adopted a Greek idea, the Trinity, defending it by quoting Aristotle. Thus, al-Jabbar maintained—and he was followed later by many other Muslim theologians and scholars—that Christians failed to observe the laws of Moses and Jesus and distorted Jesus's message.

In the Christian West, both positive and negative views of Islam appeared in literature. The Bavarian knight Wolfram von Eschenbach's *Parzival* and the Englishman William Langland's *Piers the Plowman*—two medieval poems that survive in scores of manuscripts, suggesting that they circulated widely—reveal broad-mindedness and tolerance toward Muslims. Some travelers in the Middle East were impressed by the kindness and generosity of Muslims and with the strictness and devotion with which Muslims observed their faith. Frequently, however, Christian literature portrayed Muslims as the most dreadful of Europe's enemies, guilty of every kind of crime. In his *Inferno*, for example, the great Florentine poet Dante (1265–1321) placed the Muslim philosophers Avicenna and Averroës with other virtuous "heathens," among them Socrates and Aristotle, in the first circle of Hell, where they endured only moderate punishment. Muhammad, however, Dante consigned to the ninth circle, near Satan himself, where he was condemned as a spreader of discord and scandal and suffered perpetual torture.

Even when they rejected each other most forcefully, the Christian and Muslim worlds had a significant impact on each other. Art styles, technology, and even institutional practices spread in both directions. During the Crusades Muslims adopted Frankish weapons and methods of fortification. Christians in contact with Muslim scholars recovered ancient Greek philosophical texts that survived only in Arabic translation.

CHRONOLOGY

622	Muhammad and his followers emigrate from Mecca to Medina
632	Muhammad dies; Abu Bakr becomes the first caliph
642	Muslim defeat of the Persians marks end of the Sassanid empire
651	Publication of the Qur'an
661	Ali assassinated; split between Shi'a and Sunnis
711	Muslims defeat Visigothic kingdom in Spain
722–1492	Progressive loss of most of Spain to the Christian reconquest (*reconquista*)
750–1258	Abbasid caliphate
762	Baghdad founded by Abbasids
800–1300	Height of Muslim learning and creativity
869–883	Zanj (slave) revolts
950–1100	Entry on a large scale of Turks into the Middle East
1055	Baghdad falls to Seljuk Turks
1099–1187	Christian Crusaders hold Jerusalem
1258	Mongols capture Baghdad and kill the last Abbasid caliph

Chapter Summary

Muhammad, born in the Arabian peninsula, experienced a religious vision, after which he preached to the people to give up their idols and submit to the one indivisible God. He believed in the same God as the Christians and Jews and taught strict monotheism. Islam, the religion based on Muhammad's teachings, appropriated much of the Old and New Testaments of the Bible. After Muhammad's death, his followers gathered his revelations, eventually producing the Qur'an.

Within the span of a century, Muslims carried their faith from the Arabian peninsula through the Middle East, to North Africa and Spain, and to the borders of China and India. Successors to Muhammad established the caliphate, which through two successive dynasties coordinated rule over Muslim lands. A key challenge faced by the caliphate was a fundamental division in Muslim theology between the Sunnis and the Shi'a.

Over time, many parts of the Muslim empire gained considerable local independence. Far-flung territories such as Spain began to break away from the Baghdad-centered caliphate. By the tenth century Turks played a more important role in the armies and came to be the effective rulers in much of the Middle East. They were succeeded by the Mongols, who invaded the Middle East in the thirteenth century and ruled the central Muslim lands for eighty years.

Muslim society was distinctly hierarchical. In addition to a structure that privileged the ruling Arab Muslims over converts to Islam, then over Jews, Christians, and Zoroastrians, there were also a substantial number of slaves, generally war captives. Slaves normally were converted to Islam and might come to hold important positions, especially in the army. Distinctions between men and women in Islamic society were strict. Over time, the seclusion and veiling of women became common practices, especially among the well-to-do.

Islam did not discourage trade and profitmaking. By land and sea Muslim merchants transported a rich variety of goods across Asia, the Middle East, Africa, and western Europe. As trade thrived, innovations such as money orders to bankers, bills of exchange, and joint stock companies aided the conduct of business.

Wealth from trade made possible a gracious and sophisticated culture in the cities of the Muslim world, especially Baghdad and Córdoba. During this period Muslim scholars produced important work in many disciplines, especially mathematics, medicine, and philosophy. A new spiritual and intellectual tradition arose in the mystical practices of Sufism. Muslims, Christians, and Jews interacted in many ways during this period. At the time of the Crusades and of the Christian reconquest of Muslim Spain, polemical anti-Christian writings appeared, but in other periods Muslim views were more positive. Many Christians converted in the early centuries of the spread of Islam. Others such as the Mozarabs assimilated into Muslim culture while retaining their religion.

NOTES

1. Quoted in R. Levy, *The Social Structure of Islam*, 2d ed. (Cambridge: Cambridge University Press, 1957), p. 56.
2. Quoted in B. F. Stowasser, "The Status of Women in Early Islam," in *Muslim Women*, ed. F. Hussain (New York: St. Martin's Press, 1984), p. 25.
3. F. E. Peters, *A Reader on Classical Islam* (Princeton, N.J.: Princeton University Press, 1994), p. 250.
4. Quoted in B. Lewis, ed. and trans., *Islam from the Prophet Muhammad to the Capture of Constantinople*. Vol. 2: *Religion and Society*, 35w from p. 126. © 1974 by Bernard Lewis. Used by permission of Oxford University Press, USA, www.oup.com.
5. Ibid., pp. 154–157.
6. R. Hillenbrand, "Cordoba," in *Dictionary of the Middle Ages*, vol. 3, ed. J. R. Strayer (New York: Scribner's, 1983), pp. 597–601.
7. Margaret Smith, *Readings from the Mystics of Islam* (London: Luzac and Co., 1950), p. 11.

CONNECTIONS

During the five centuries that followed Muhammad's death, his teachings came to be revered in large parts of the world, from Spain to Afghanistan. Although in some ways similar to the earlier spread of Buddhism out of India and Christianity out of Palestine, the spread of Islam occurred largely through military conquests that extended Muslim lands. Still, conversion was never complete; both Christians and Jews maintained substantial communities within Muslim lands. Moreover, cultural contact among Christians, Jews, and Muslims was an important element in the development of each culture.

Muslim civilization in these centuries drew from many sources, including Persia and Byzantium, and in turn had broad impact beyond its borders. Muslim scholars preserved much of early Greek philosophy and science through translation into Arabic. Trade connected the Muslim lands both to Europe and to India and China.

During the first and second centuries after Muhammad, Islam spread along the Mediterranean coast of North Africa, which had been part of the Roman world. The next chapter explores other developments in the enormous and diverse continent of Africa during this time. Many of the written sources that tell us about the African societies of these centuries were written in Arabic by visitors from elsewhere in the Muslim world. Muslim traders traveled through many of the societies in Africa north of the Congo, aiding the spread of Islam to the elites of many of these societies. Ethiopia was an exception, as Christianity spread there from Egypt before the time of Muhammad and retained its hold in subsequent centuries. Africa's history is introduced in the next chapter.

Review and Explore

Make It Stick

LearningCurve
Go online and use LearningCurve to retain what you've read.

Identify Key Terms

Identify and explain the significance of each item below.

Qur'an (p. 238)
hadith (p. 238)
Sunna (p. 238)
Five Pillars of Islam (p. 239)
umma (p. 239)
diwān (p. 241)
imam (p. 242)
Shi'a (p. 242)
Sunnis (p. 242)
ulama (p. 242)
emirs (p. 243)
shari'a (p. 243)
dhimmis (p. 247)
madrasa (p. 255)
Mozarabs (p. 262)

Review the Main Ideas

Answer the focus questions from each section of the chapter.

1. From what kind of social and economic environment did Muhammad arise, and what did he teach? (p. 237)
2. What made possible the spread of Islam, and what forms of government were established to rule Muslim lands? (p. 239)
3. How were the Muslim lands governed from 900 to 1400, and what new challenges did rulers face? (p. 244)
4. What social distinctions were important in Muslim society? (p. 246)
5. Why did trade thrive in Muslim lands? (p. 253)
6. What new ideas and practices emerged in the arts, sciences, education, and religion? (p. 255)
7. How did Muslims and Christians come into contact with each other, and how did they view each other? (p. 261)

Make Connections

Analyze the larger developments and continuities within and across chapters.

1. How does the spread of Islam compare to the spread of earlier universal religions, such as Buddhism and Christianity?
2. In what ways was the development of culture in the Islamic lands shaped by trade and thriving cities?
3. What are the similarities in the role of teachers and holy books in Islamic lands, Europe, and China? What are the differences?

Nok Woman Hundreds of terra-cotta sculptures such as the head of this woman survive from the Nok culture, which originated in the central plateau of northern Nigeria in the first millennium B.C.E. (Werner Forman/Art Resource, NY)

1492 (see page 438); and with sub-Saharan peoples, with whom they traded across the Sahara Desert. The Swahili peoples along the East African coast developed a maritime civilization and had rich commercial contacts with southern Arabia, the Persian Gulf, India, China, and the Malay Archipelago.

The ancient Greeks called the peoples who lived south of the Sahara *Ethiopians*, which means "people with burnt faces." The Berbers also described this region based on its inhabitants, coining the term *Akal-n-Iquinawen*, which survives today as *Guinea*. The Arabs used the term *Bilad al-Sudan*, which survives as *Sudan*. The Berber and Arab terms both mean "land of the blacks." Short-statured peoples, sometimes inaccurately referred to as Pygmies, inhabited the equatorial rain forests. South of those forests, in the continent's southern third, lived the Khoisan (KOI-sahn), people who were primarily hunters but also had domesticated livestock.

Ancient Egypt, at the crossroads of three continents, was a melting pot of different cultures and peoples. Many diverse peoples contributed to the great achievements of Egyptian culture. Many scholars believe that Africans originating in the sub-Sahara resided in ancient Egypt, primarily in Upper Egypt (south of what is now Cairo), but that other ethnic groups constituted the majority of the population.

Early African Societies

- How did agriculture affect life among the early societies in the western Sudan and among the Bantu-speaking societies of central and southern Africa?

New crops introduced from Asia and the establishment of settled agriculture profoundly changed many African societies, although the range of possibilities largely depended on local variations in climate and geography. Bantu-speakers took the knowledge of domesticated livestock and agriculture, along with the ironworking skills that had developed in northern and western Africa, and spread them south across central and southern Africa. The most prominent feature of early West African society was a strong sense of community based on blood relationships and religion. Extended families made up the villages that collectively formed small kingdoms.

Agriculture and Its Impact

Agriculture began very early in Africa. Knowledge of plant cultivation moved west from the Levant (modern Israel and Lebanon), arriving in the Nile Delta in Egypt about the fifth millennium B.C.E. Settled agriculture then traveled down the Nile Valley and moved west across the Sahel to the central and western Sudan. West Africans were living in agricultural communities by the first century B.C.E. From there plant cultivation spread to the equatorial forests. African farmers learned to domesticate plants, including millet, sorghum, and yams. Cereal-growing people probably taught forest people to plant grains on plots of land cleared by a method known as "slash and burn." Gradually most Africans evolved a sedentary way of life: living in villages, clearing fields, relying on root crops, and fishing. Hunting-and-gathering societies survived only in scattered parts of Africa, particularly in the central rain forest region and in southern Africa.

Between 1500 B.C.E. and 1000 B.C.E. agriculture also spread southward from Ethiopia along the Great Rift Valley of present-day Kenya and Tanzania. Archaeological evidence reveals that the peoples of East Africa grew cereals, raised cattle, and used wooden and stone tools. Cattle raising spread more quickly than did planting, the herds prospering on the open savannas that are free of tsetse (SEHT-see) flies, which are devastating to cattle. Early East African peoples prized cattle highly. Many trading agreements, marriage alliances, political compacts, and treaties were negotiated in terms of cattle.

Cereals such as millet and sorghum are indigenous to Africa. Scholars speculate that traders brought

Rock Painting at Tassili, Algeria This scene of cattle grazing while a man stands guard over them was found on a rock face in Tassili n'Ajjer, a mountainous region in the Sahara where over fifteen thousand of these paintings have been catalogued. The oldest date back 9,000–12,000 years. Behind the man are perhaps his two children at play and his two wives working together in the compound. A cow stands in the enclosure to the right. (George Holton/Photo Researchers, Inc. Colorization by Robin Treadwell)

bananas, taros (a type of yam), sugarcane, and coconut palms to Africa from Southeast Asia. Because tropical forest conditions were ideal for banana plants, their cultivation spread rapidly. Throughout sub-Saharan Africa native peoples also domesticated donkeys, pigs, chickens, geese, and ducks, although all these came from outside Africa. The guinea fowl appears to be the only animal native to Africa that was domesticated, despite the wide varieties of animal species in Africa. All the other large animals—elephants, hippopotamuses, giraffes, rhinoceros, and zebras—were simply too temperamental to domesticate.

The evolution from a hunter-gatherer life to a settled life had profound effects. In contrast to nomadic societies, settled societies made shared or common needs more apparent, and those needs strengthened ties among extended families. Agricultural and pastoral populations also increased, though scholars speculate that this increase did not remain steady, but rather fluctuated over time. Nor is it clear that population growth was accompanied by a commensurate increase in agricultural output.

Early African societies were similarly influenced by the spread of ironworking, though scholars dispute the route by which this technology spread to sub-Saharan Africa. Some believe the Phoenicians brought the iron-smelting technique to northwestern Africa, from which it spread southward. Others insist it spread westward from the Meroë (MEHR-oh-ee) region of the Nile. Most of West Africa had acquired ironworking by 250 B.C.E., however, and archaeologists believe Meroë achieved pre-eminence as an iron-smelting center only in the first century B.C.E. Thus a stronger case can probably be made for the Phoenicians. The great trans-Saharan trade routes (see page 273) may have carried ironworking south from the Mediterranean coast. In any case, ancient iron tools found at the village of Nok on the Jos Plateau in present-day Nigeria seem to prove that ironworking industries existed in West Africa by at least 700 B.C.E. The Nok culture, which enjoys enduring fame for its fine terra-cotta sculptures, flourished from about 800 B.C.E. to 200 C.E.

Bantu Migrations

The spread of ironworking is linked to the migrations of Bantu-speaking peoples. Today the overwhelming majority of the 70 million people living south of the Congo River speak a **Bantu** language. Because Muslims or Europeans rarely penetrated into the interior, and Bantu-speakers (except the Swahili, for example) seldom had written languages, very few written sources for the early history of central and southern Africa survive. Lacking written sources, modern scholars have tried to reconstruct the history of Bantu-speakers on the basis of linguistics, oral traditions (rarely reliable beyond three hundred years back), archaeology, and anthropology. Botanists and zoologists have played particularly critical roles in providing information about early diets and environments.

The word *Bantu* is a linguistic classification, and linguistics (the study of the nature, structure, and modification of human speech) has helped scholars explain

- **Bantu** Speakers of a Bantu language living south and east of the Congo River.

the migratory patterns of African peoples east and south of the equatorial forest. There are hundreds of Bantu languages, including Zulu, Sotho, and Xhosa, which are part of the southern African linguistic and cultural mix, and Swahili, which is spoken in eastern, and to a limited extent central, Africa.

Bantu-speaking peoples originated in the Benue region, the borderlands of modern Cameroon and Nigeria. In the second millennium B.C.E. they began to spread south and east into the equatorial forest zone. Historians still debate why they began this movement. Some hold that rapid population growth sent people in search of land. Others believe that the evolution of centralized kingdoms allowed rulers to expand their authority, while causing newly subjugated peoples to flee in the hope of regaining their independence.

Since the early Bantu-speakers had words for fishing, fishhooks, fish traps, dugout canoes, paddles, yams, and goats, linguists assume that they were fishermen and that they cultivated root crops. Because initially they lacked words for grains and cattle herding, they probably were not involved in grain cultivation or livestock domestication. During the next fifteen hundred years, however, Bantu-speakers migrated throughout the savanna, adopted mixed agriculture, and learned ironworking. Mixed agriculture (cultivating cereals and raising livestock) and ironworking were practiced in western East Africa (the region of modern Burundi) in the first century B.C.E. In the first millennium C.E. Bantu-speakers migrated into eastern and southern Africa. Here the Bantu-speakers, with their iron weapons, either killed, drove off, or assimilated the hunting-gathering peoples they met. Some of the assimilated inhabitants gradually adopted a Bantu language, contributing to the spread of Bantu culture.

The settled cultivation of cereals, the keeping of livestock, and the introduction of new crops such as the banana—together with Bantu-speakers' intermarriage with indigenous peoples—led over a long period to considerable population increases and the need to migrate farther. However, the so-called Bantu migrations should not be seen as a single movement sweeping across Africa from west to east to south and displacing all peoples in its path. Rather, those migrations were an extended series of group interactions between Bantu-speakers and pre-existing peoples in which bits of culture, languages, economies, and technologies were shared and exchanged to produce a wide range of cultural variation across central and southern Africa.[1]

Bantu Migrations, ca. 1000 B.C.E.–1500 C.E.

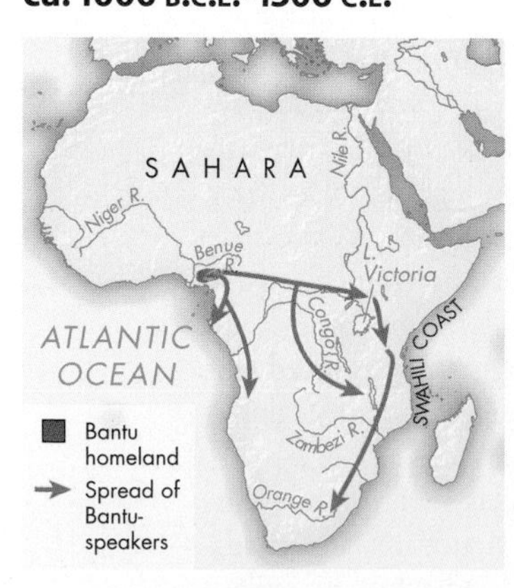

The Bantu-speakers' expansion and subsequent land settlement that dominated eastern and southern African history in the first fifteen hundred years of the Common Era were uneven. Significant environmental differences determined settlement patterns. Some regions had plenty of water, while others were very arid. These differences resulted in very uneven population distribution. The greatest population density seems to have been in the region bounded on the west by the Congo River and on the north, south, and east by Lakes Edward and Victoria and Mount Kilimanjaro, constituting parts of modern Uganda, Rwanda, and Tanzania. There the agricultural system rested on sorghum and yam cultivation. Between 900 C.E. and 1100 C.E. bananas and plantains (a starchy form of the banana) arrived from Asia. Because cultivation required little effort and the yield was much higher than for yams, bananas soon became the Bantu people's staple crop. The rapid growth of the Bantu-speaking population led to further migration southward and eastward. By the eighth century the Bantu-speaking people had crossed the Zambezi River and had begun settling in the region of present-day Zimbabwe. By the fifteenth century they had reached Africa's southeastern coast.

Life in the Kingdoms of the Western Sudan, ca. 1000 B.C.E.–800 C.E.

The **Sudan** is the region bounded by the Sahara to the north, the Gulf of Guinea to the south, the Atlantic Ocean to the west, and the mountains of Ethiopia to the east (see Map 10.1). In the western Sudan savanna—where the Bantu migrations originated—a series of dynamic kingdoms emerged in the millennium before European intrusion began in the 1400s and 1500s.

Between 1000 B.C.E. and 200 C.E. the peoples of the western Sudan made the momentous shift from nomadic hunting to settled agriculture. The rich savanna proved ideally suited to cereal production, especially rice, millet, and sorghum. People situated near the Senegal River and Lake Chad supplemented their diet with fish. Food supply affects population, and the region's inhabitants—known as the Mande-speakers and the Chadic-speakers, or Sao (sowl)—increased dramatically in number. By 400 C.E. the entire savanna, particularly around Lake Chad, the Niger River bend, and present-day central Nigeria, had a large population.

Families and clans affiliated by blood kinship lived together in villages or small city-states. The extended family formed the basic social unit. A chief, in consultation with a council of elders, governed a village.

Some villages seem to have formed kingdoms. In this case, village chiefs were responsible to regional heads, who answered to provincial governors, who in turn were responsible to a king. The kings and their families formed an aristocracy.

Kingship in the Sudan may have emerged from the priesthood, whose members were believed to make rain and to have contact with spirit powers. African kings always had religious sanction or support for their authority and were often considered divine. In this respect, early African kingship bears a strong resemblance to Germanic kingship of the same period (discussed in Chapter 14). The king's authority rested in part on his ability to negotiate with outside powers, such as the gods.

Although the Mende in modern Sierra Leone was one of the few African societies to be led by female rulers, women exercised significant power and autonomy in many African societies. Among the Asante in modern-day Ghana, one of the most prominent West African peoples, the king was considered divine but shared some royal power with the Queen Mother. She was a full member of the governing council and enjoyed full voting power in various matters of state. The Queen Mother initially chose the future king from eligible royal candidates. He then had to be approved by both his elders and the commoners. Among the Yoruba in modern Nigeria, the Queen Mother held the royal insignia and could refuse it if the future king did not please her. She also placed the royal beaded crown on the king's head. The institutions of female chiefs, known as *iyalode* among the Yoruba and *omu* among the Igbo in modern Nigeria, were established to represent women in the political process. The *omu* was even considered a female co-ruler with the male chief.

Western Sudanese religious practices, like African religions elsewhere, were animistic and polytheistic. Most people believed that a supreme being had created the universe and was the source of all life. Most African religions also recognized ancestral spirits, which might seek God's blessings for families' and communities' prosperity and security as long as these groups behaved appropriately. If not, the ancestral spirits might not protect them from harm, and illness and misfortune could result. Some African religions believed as well that nature spirits lived in such things as the sky, forests, rocks, and rivers. These spirits controlled natural forces and had to be appeased. During the annual agricultural cycle, for example, all the spirits had to be propitiated from the time of clearing the land through sowing the seed to the final harvest. Because special ceremonies were necessary to satisfy the spirits, special priests with the knowledge and power to communicate with them through sacred rituals were needed. Family and village heads were often priests. Each family head was responsible for ceremonies honoring the family's dead and living members.[2]

In some West African societies, oracles who spoke for the gods were particularly important. Some of the most famous were the Ibo oracles in modern Nigeria. These were female priestesses who were connected with a particular local deity that resided in a sacred cave or other site. Inhabitants of surrounding villages would come to the priestess to seek advice about such matters as crops and harvests, war, marriage, legal issues, and religion. Clearly, these priestesses held much power and authority, even over the local male rulers.

Kinship patterns and shared religious practices helped to bind together the early western Sudan kingdoms. Islam's spread across the Sahara by at least the ninth century C.E., however, created a north-south religious and cultural divide in the western Sudan. Islam advanced across the Sahel into modern Mauritania, Mali, Burkina Faso, Niger, northern Nigeria, and Chad but halted when it reached the West African savanna and forest zones. Societies in these southern zones maintained their traditional animistic religious practices. Muslim empires along the Niger River's great northern bend evolved into formidable powers ruling over sizable territory as they seized control of the southern termini of the trans-Saharan trade. What made this long-distance trade possible was the "ship of the desert," the camel.

The Trans-Saharan Trade

☐ What characterized trans-Saharan trade, and how did it affect West African society?

"Trans-Saharan trade" refers to the north-south trade across the Sahara (Map 10.2). The camel had an impact on this trade comparable to the very important impact of horses and oxen on European agriculture. Although scholars dispute exactly when the camel was introduced from Central Asia—first into North Africa, then into the Sahara and the Sudan—they agree that it was before 200 C.E. Camels can carry about five hundred pounds as far as twenty-five miles a day and can go for days without drinking, living on the water stored in their stomachs. Temperamental and difficult to work with, camels had to be loaded on a daily, sometimes twice-daily, basis, and much of the cargo for a

• **Sudan** The African region surrounded by the Sahara, the Gulf of Guinea, the Atlantic Ocean, and the mountains of Ethiopia.

linked the entire world, exclusive of the Western Hemisphere.

Second, trade in gold and other goods created a desire for slaves. Slaves were West Africa's second-most valuable export (after gold). Slaves worked the gold and salt mines, and in Muslim North Africa, southern Europe, and southwestern Asia there was a high demand for household slaves among the elite. African slaves, like their early European and Asian counterparts, seem to have been peoples captured in war. Recent research suggests, moreover, that large numbers of black slaves were also recruited for Muslim military service through the trans-Saharan trade. Manumission (the freeing of individual slaves), high death rates from disease, and the assimilation of some blacks into Muslim society meant that the demand for slaves remained high for centuries. Table 10.1 shows the scope of the trans-Saharan slave trade. The total number of blacks enslaved over an 850-year period may be tentatively estimated at more than 4 million.[3]

Slavery in Muslim societies, as in European and Asian countries before the fifteenth century, was not based on skin color. Muslims also enslaved Caucasians who had been purchased, seized in war, or kidnapped from Europe. Wealthy Muslim households in Córdoba, Alexandria, and Tunis often included slaves of a number of races, all of whom had been completely cut off from their cultural roots. Likewise, West African kings who sold blacks to northern traders also bought a few white slaves — Slavic, British, and Turkish — for their own domestic needs. Race had little to do with the phenomenon of slavery.

The third important effect of trans-Saharan trade on West African society was its role in stimulating the development of urban centers. Scholars date the growth of African cities from around the early ninth century. Families that had profited from trade tended to congregate in the border zones between the savanna and the Sahara. They acted as middlemen between the miners to the south and the Muslim merchants from the north. By the early thirteenth century these families had become powerful merchant dynasties. Muslim traders from the Mediterranean settled permanently in the trading depots, from which they organized the trans-Saharan caravans. The concentration of people stimulated agriculture and the craft industries. Gradually cities of sizable population emerged. Jenne, Gao, and Timbuktu, which enjoyed commanding positions on the Niger River bend, became centers of the export-import trade. Sijilmasa grew into a thriving market center. Koumbi Saleh, with between fifteen thousand and twenty thousand inhabitants, was probably the largest city in the western Sudan in the twelfth century. (By European standards, Koumbi Saleh was a metropolis; London and Paris achieved this size only in the late thirteenth century.) Between 1100 and 1400 these cities played a dynamic role in West Africa's commercial life and became centers of intellectual creativity.

The Spread of Islam in Africa

Perhaps the most influential consequence of the trans-Saharan trade was the introduction of Islam to West Africa. In the eighth century Arab invaders overran all of coastal North Africa. They introduced the Berbers living there to Islam, and gradually the Berbers became Muslims. As traders, these Berbers carried Islam to sub-Saharan West Africa. From the eleventh century onward militant Almoravids, a coalition of fundamentalist western Saharan Berbers, preached Islam to the rulers of Ghana, Mali, Songhai, and Kanem-Bornu. These rulers, admiring Muslim administrative techniques and wanting to protect their kingdoms from Muslim Berber attacks, converted to Islam. Some merchants also sought to preserve their elite mercantile status with the Berbers by adopting Islam. By the tenth century Muslim Berbers controlled the north-south trade routes to the savanna. By the eleventh century African rulers of Gao and Timbuktu had accepted Islam. The king of Ghana was also influenced by Islam. Muslims quickly became integral to West African government and society. Hence, from roughly 1000 to 1400, Islam in West Africa was a class-based religion with conversion inspired by political or economic motives. Rural people in the Sahel region and the savanna and forest peoples farther south, however, largely retained their traditional animism.

The Spread of Islam in Africa

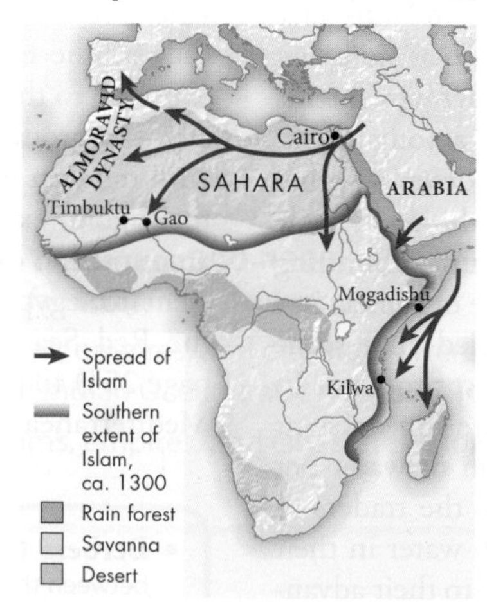

Conversion to Islam introduced West Africans to a rich and sophisticated culture. By the late eleventh century Muslims were guiding the ruler of Ghana in the operation of his administrative machinery. Ghana's king adopted the Muslim diwān, the agency for keeping financial records (see page 241). Because efficient government depends on keeping and preserving records, Islam's arrival in West Africa marked the advent of written documents there. Arab Muslims also taught Ghana's rulers how to manufacture bricks, and royal palaces and mosques began to be built of brick. African rulers corresponded with Arab and North African Muslim architects, theologians, and other intellectuals, who advised them on statecraft and religion. Islam accelerated the development of the West African empires of the ninth through fifteenth centuries.

After the Muslim conquest of Egypt in 642 (see page 239), Islam spread southward from Egypt up the Nile Valley and west to Darfur and Wadai. This Muslim penetration came not suddenly by military force but, as in the trans-Saharan trade routes in West Africa, gradually through commercial networks.

Muslim expansion from the Arabian peninsula across the Red Sea to the Horn of Africa, then southward along the coast of East Africa, represents a third direction of Islam's growth in Africa. From ports on the Red Sea and the Gulf of Aden, maritime trade carried the Prophet's teachings to East Africa and the Indian Ocean. Muslims founded the port city of **Mogadishu** between the eighth and tenth centuries, today Somalia's capital. In the twelfth century Mogadishu developed into a Muslim sultanate, a monarchy that employed a slave military corps against foreign and domestic enemies. Archaeological evidence, confirmed by Arabic sources, reveals a rapid Islamic expansion along Africa's east coast in the thirteenth century as far south as Kilwa, where Ibn Battuta visited a center for Islamic law in 1331.

African Kingdoms and Empires, ca. 800–1500

□ How were the East African city-states, Aksum, and Great Zimbabwe different from and similar to the kingdoms of the western Sudan?

All African societies shared one basic feature: a close relationship between political and social organization. Ethnic or blood ties bound clan members together. What scholars call **stateless societies** were culturally homogeneous ethnic societies, generally organized around kinship groups. The smallest ones numbered fewer than a hundred people and were nomadic hunting groups. Larger stateless, or decentralized, societies, such as the Tiv in modern central Nigeria, consisted of perhaps several thousand people who lived a settled and often agricultural and/or herding life. These societies lacked a central authority figure, such as a king, capital city, or military. A village or group of villages might recognize a chief who held very limited powers and whose position was not hereditary, but more commonly they were governed by local councils, whose members were either elders or persons of merit. Although stateless societies functioned successfully, their weakness lay in their inability to organize and defend themselves against attack by the powerful armies of neighboring kingdoms or by the European powers of the colonial era.

While stateless societies were relatively common in Africa, the period from about 800 to 1500 is best known as the age of Africa's great empires (see Map 10.2). This period witnessed the flowering of several powerful African states. In the western Sudan the large empires of Ghana, Mali, and Songhai developed, complete with sizable royal bureaucracies. On the east coast emerged thriving city-states based on sophisticated mercantile activities and, like the western Sudan, heavily influenced by Islam. In Ethiopia, in central East Africa, kings relied on their peoples' Christian faith to strengthen political authority. In southern Africa the empire of Great Zimbabwe, built on the gold trade with the east coast, flourished.

The Kingdom of Ghana, ca. 900–1100

So remarkable was the kingdom of **Ghana** during the age of Africa's great empires that Arab and North African visitors praised it as a model for other rulers. Even in modern times, ancient Ghana holds a central place in Africa's historical consciousness. When the Gold Coast colony gained its independence from British colonial rule in 1957, its new political leaders paid tribute to their heritage by naming their new country Ghana. Although modern Ghana lies far from the site of the old kingdom, the name was selected to signify the rebirth of ancient Ghana's illustrious past.

The Soninke people inhabited the nucleus of the territory that became the Ghanaian kingdom. They called their ruler *ghana*, or war chief. By the late eighth century Muslim traders and other foreigners applied the king's title to the region where the Soninke lived, the kingdom south of the Sahara. The Soninke themselves called their land Wagadou (WAH-guh-doo). Only the southern part of Wagadou received enough rainfall to be agriculturally productive, and it was here that the civilization of Ghana developed (see Map 10.2). Skillful farming and efficient irrigation systems led to abundant crop production, which eventually supported a population of as many as two hundred thousand.

- **Mogadishu** A Muslim port city in East Africa founded between the eighth and tenth centuries; today it is the capital of Somalia.
- **stateless societies** African societies bound together by ethnic or blood ties rather than by being political states.
- **Ghana** From the word for "ruler," the name of a large and influential African kingdom inhabited by the Soninke people.

The Soninke name for their king—war chief—aptly describes the king's major preoccupation in the tenth century. In 992 Ghana captured the Berber town of Awdaghost, strategically situated on the trans-Saharan trade route. Thereafter Ghana controlled the southern portion of a major caravan route. Before the year 1000 Ghana's rulers had extended their influence almost to the Atlantic coast and had captured a number of small kingdoms in the south and east. By the early eleventh century the Ghanaian king exercised sway over a territory approximately the size of Texas. No other power in the western Sudan could successfully challenge him.

Throughout this vast West African territory, all authority sprang from the king. Religious ceremonies and court rituals emphasized the king's sacredness and were intended to strengthen his authority. The king's position was hereditary in the matrilineal line—that is, the ruling king's heir was one of the king's sister's sons (presumably the eldest or fittest for battle). According to the eleventh-century Spanish Muslim geographer al-Bakri (1040?–1094), "This is their custom . . . the kingdom is inherited only by the son of the king's sister. He the king has no doubt that his successor is a son of his sister, while he is not certain that his son is in fact his own."[4]

A council of ministers assisted the king in the work of government, and from the ninth century on most of these ministers were Muslims. Detailed evidence about the early Ghanaian bureaucracy has not survived, but scholars suspect that separate agencies were responsible for taxation, royal property, foreigners, forests, and the army. The royal administration was well served by ideas, skills, and especially literacy brought from the North African and Arab Muslim worlds. The king and his people, however, clung to their ancestral religion and basic cultural institutions.

The Ghanaian king held court in the large and vibrant city of **Koumbi Saleh**, which al-Bakri actually describes as two towns—one in which the king and the royal court lived, and the other Muslim. Al-Bakri provides a valuable description of the Muslim part of the town in the eleventh century:

> The city of Ghana consists of two towns lying on a plain, one of which is inhabited by Muslims and is large, possessing twelve mosques—one of which is a congregational mosque for Friday prayer; each has its imam, its muezzin and paid reciters of the Quran. The town possesses a large number of jurisconsults and learned men.[5]

• **Koumbi Saleh** The city in which the king of Ghana held his court.

Either to protect themselves or to preserve their special identity, the Muslims of Koumbi Saleh lived separately from the African artisans and tradespeople. Ghana's Muslim community was large and prosperous, as indicated by the twelve mosques. Muslim religious leaders exercised civil authority over their fellow Muslims. The imam was the religious leader who conducted the ritual worship, especially the main prayer service on Fridays (see page 241). The muezzin led the prayer responses after the imam; he needed a strong voice so that those at a distance and the women in the harems, or enclosures, could hear (see page 252). The presence of religious leaders and other learned Muslims suggests that Koumbi Saleh was a city of vigorous intellectual activity.

Al-Bakri also described the royal court:

> The town inhabited by the king is six miles from the Muslim one and is called Al Ghana. . . . The residence of the king consists of a palace and a number of dome-shaped dwellings, all of them surrounded by a strong enclosure, like a city wall. In the town . . . is a mosque, where Muslims who come on diplomatic missions to the king pray.[6]
>
> The king adorns himself, as do the women here, with necklaces and bracelets; on their heads they wear caps decorated with gold, sewn on material of fine cotton stuffing. When he holds court in order to hear the people's complaints and to do justice, he sits in a pavilion around which stand ten horses wearing golden trappings; behind him ten pages stand, holding shields and swords decorated with gold; at his right are the sons of the chiefs of the country, splendidly dressed and with their hair sprinkled with gold. . . . When the king's coreligionists appear before him, they fall on their knees and toss dust on their heads—this is their way of greeting their sovereign. Muslims show respect by clapping their hands.[7]

Justice derived from the king, who heard cases at court or on his travels throughout his kingdom. As al-Bakri recounts:

> When a man is accused of denying a debt or of having shed blood or some other crime, a headman (village chief) takes a thin piece of wood, which is sour and bitter to taste, and pours upon it some water which he then gives to the defendant to drink. If the man vomits, his innocence is recognized and he is congratulated. If he does not vomit and the drink remains in his stomach, the accusation is accepted as justified.[8]

This appeal to the supernatural for judgment was similar to the justice by ordeal that prevailed among the Germanic peoples of western Europe at the same time (discussed in Chapter 14). Complicated cases were appealed to the king, who often relied on the advice of Muslim legal experts.

The king's elaborate court, the administrative machinery he built, and the extensive territories he governed were all expensive. To support the kingdom, the royal estates — some hereditary, others conquered in war — produced annual revenue, mostly in the form of foodstuffs for the royal household. The king also received tribute annually from subordinate chieftains. Customs duties on goods entering and leaving the country generated revenues as well. Salt was the largest import. Berber merchants paid a tax to the king on the cloth, metalwork, weapons, and other goods they brought into the country from North Africa; in return these traders received royal protection from bandits. African traders bringing gold into Ghana from the south also paid the customs duty.

Finally, the royal treasury held a monopoly on the export of gold. The gold industry was undoubtedly the king's largest source of income. Medieval Ghana's fame rested on gold. The ninth-century Persian geographer al-Ya-qubi wrote, "Its king is mighty, and in his lands are gold mines. Under his authority are various other kingdoms — and in all this region there is gold."[9]

The governing aristocracy — the king, his court, and Muslim administrators — occupied the highest rung on the Ghanaian social ladder. On the next rung stood the merchant class. Considerably below the merchants stood the farmers, cattle breeders, gold mine supervisors, and skilled craftsmen and weavers — what today might be called the middle class. Some merchants and miners must have enjoyed great wealth, but, as in all aristocratic societies, money alone did not grant prestige. High status was based on blood and royal service. On the social ladder's lowest rung were slaves, who worked in households, on farms, and in the mines. As in Asian and European societies of the time, slaves accounted for only a small percentage of the population.

Apart from these social classes stood the army. According to al-Bakri, "The king of Ghana can put 200,000 warriors in the field, more than 40,000 being armed with bow and arrow." Like most medieval estimates, this is probably a gross exaggeration. Ghana's king maintained at his palace a standing force of a thousand men, comparable to the bodyguards of the Roman emperors. These thoroughly disciplined, well-armed, totally loyal troops protected the king and the royal court. They lived in special compounds, enjoyed the king's favor, and sometimes acted as his personal ambassadors to subordinate rulers. In wartime this regular army was augmented by levies of soldiers from conquered peoples and by the use of slaves and free reserves. The force that the king could field was sizable, if not as substantial as al-Bakri estimated.

The reasons for ancient Ghana's decline are still a matter of much debate. By al-Bakri's time there were other increasingly powerful neighbors, such as the Mandinka, to challenge Ghana's influence in the region. The most commonly accepted theory for Ghana's rapid decline held, however, that the Berber Almoravid dynasty of North Africa invaded and conquered Ghana around 1100 and forced its rulers and people to convert to Islam. Some historians examining this issue have concluded that while Almoravid and Islamic pressures certainly disrupted the empire, weakening it enough for its incorporation into the rising Mali empire, there was no Almoravid military invasion and subsequent forced conversion to Islam.[10]

The Kingdom of Mali, ca. 1200–1450

Ghana and its capital of Koumbi Saleh were in decline between 1100 and 1200, and a cloud of obscurity hung over the western Sudan. The old empire split into several small kingdoms that feuded among themselves. One people, the Mandinka, from the kingdom of Kangaba on the upper Niger River, gradually asserted their dominance over these kingdoms. The Mandinka had long been part of the Ghanaian empire, and the Mandinka and Soninke belonged to the same language group. Kangaba formed the core of the new empire of Mali. Building on Ghanaian foundations, Mali developed into a better-organized and more powerful state than Ghana.

Mali owed its greatness to two fundamental assets. First, its strong agricultural and commercial base supported a large population and provided enormous wealth. Second, Mali had two rulers, Sundiata (soon-JAH-tuh) and Mansa Musa, who combined military success with exceptionally creative personalities.

The Expansion of Mali, ca. 1200–1450

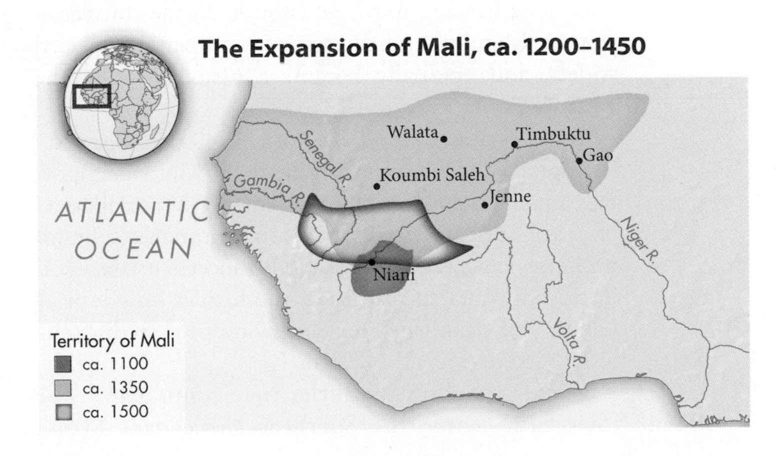

The Great Friday Mosque, Jenne The mosque at Jenne was built in the form of a parallelogram. Inside, nine long rows of adobe columns run along a north-south axis and support a flat roof of palm logs. A pointed arch links each column to the next in its row, forming nine east-west archways facing the *mihrab*, the niche in the wall of the mosque indicating the direction of Mecca, and from which the imam speaks. This mosque (rebuilt in 1907 based on the original thirteenth-century structure) testifies to the considerable wealth, geometrical knowledge, and manpower of Mali. (Gerard Degeorge/akg-images)

The earliest surviving evidence about the Mandinka, dating from the early eleventh century, indicates that they were extremely successful at agriculture. Consistently large harvests throughout the twelfth and thirteenth centuries meant a plentiful food supply, which encouraged steady population growth. Kangaba's geographical location also ideally positioned the Mandinka in the heart of the West African trade networks. Earlier, during the period of Ghanaian hegemony, the Mandinka had acted as middlemen in the gold and salt traffic flowing north and south. In the thirteenth century Mandinka traders formed companies, traveled widely, and gradually became a major force in the entire West African trade.

Mali's founder, Sundiata (r. ca. 1230–1255), set up his capital at Niani, transforming the city into an important financial and trading center. He then embarked on a policy of imperial expansion. Through a series of military victories, Sundiata and his successors absorbed into Mali other territories of the former kingdom of Ghana and established hegemony over the trading cities of Gao, Jenne, and Walata.

These expansionist policies were continued in the fourteenth century by Sundiata's descendant Mansa Musa (r. ca. 1312–1337), early Africa's most famous ruler. In the language of the Mandinka, *mansa* means "emperor." Mansa Musa fought many campaigns and curbed rebellions. His influence extended northward to several Berber cities in the Sahara, eastward to the trading cities of Timbuktu and Gao, and westward to the Atlantic Ocean. Throughout his territories, he maintained strict royal control over the flourishing trans-Saharan trade. Thus this empire, roughly twice the size of the Ghanaian kingdom and containing perhaps 8 million people, brought Mansa Musa fabulous wealth.

Mansa Musa built on the foundations of his predecessors. Malian society's stratified aristocratic structure perpetuated the pattern set in Ghana, as did the system of provincial administration and annual tribute. The emperor took responsibility for the territories that formed the heart of the empire and appointed governors to rule the outlying provinces and dependent kingdoms. But Mansa Musa made a significant innovation: in a practice strikingly similar to a system used in both China and France at the time, he appointed royal family members as provincial governors. He could count on their loyalty, and they received valuable experience in the work of government.

In another aspect of administration, Mansa Musa also differed from his predecessors. He became a devout Muslim. Although most of the Mandinka clung to their ancestral animism, Islamic practices and influences in Mali multiplied.

The most celebrated event of Mansa Musa's reign was his pilgrimage to Mecca in 1324–1325, during which he paid a state visit to the Egyptian sultan. Mansa Musa's entrance into Cairo was magnificent. Preceded by five hundred slaves, each carrying a six-pound staff of gold, he followed with a huge host of retainers, including one hundred elephants each bearing one hundred pounds of gold. The emperor lavished his wealth on the citizens of the Egyptian capital. Writing twelve years later, al-Omari, one of the sultan's officials, recounts:

> This man Mansa Musa spread upon Cairo the flood of his generosity: there was no person, officer of the court, or holder of any office of the Sultanate who did not receive a sum of gold from him. The people of Cairo earned incalculable sums from him, whether by buying and selling or by gifts. So much gold was current in Cairo that it ruined the value of money.[11]

For the first time, the Mediterranean world learned firsthand of Mali's wealth and power, and the kingdom began to be known as one of the world's great empires. Mali retained this international reputation into the fifteenth century. Musa's pilgrimage also had significant consequences within Mali. He gained some understanding of the Mediterranean countries and opened diplomatic relations with the Muslim rulers of Morocco and Egypt. His zeal for the Muslim faith and Islamic culture increased. Musa brought back from Arabia the distinguished architect al-Saheli, whom he commissioned to build new mosques in Timbuktu and other cities. These mosques served as centers for African conversion to Islam. Musa employed Muslim engineers to build in brick. He also encouraged Malian merchants and traders to wear the distinctive flowing robes and turbans of Muslim males.

Timbuktu began as a campsite for desert nomads, but under Mansa Musa it grew into a thriving entrepôt (trading center), attracting merchants and traders from North Africa and all parts of the Mediterranean world. They brought with them cosmopolitan attitudes and ideas. In the fifteenth century Timbuktu developed into a great center for scholarship and learning. Architects, astronomers, poets, lawyers, mathematicians, and theologians flocked there. One hundred fifty schools, for men only, were devoted to Qur'anic studies. The school of Islamic law enjoyed a distinction comparable to the prestige of the Cairo school (see page 255). The vigorous traffic in books that flourished in Timbuktu made them the most common items of trade. Timbuktu's tradition and reputation for African scholarship lasted until the eighteenth century.

Moreover, in the fourteenth and fifteenth centuries many Arab and North African Muslim intellectuals and traders married native African women. The necessity of living together harmoniously, the traditional awareness of diverse cultures, and Timbuktu's cosmopolitan atmosphere contributed to a rare degree of racial tolerance and understanding. After visiting the court of Mansa Musa's successor in 1352–1353, Ibn Battuta observed:

> [T]he Negroes possess some admirable qualities. They are seldom unjust, and have a greater abhorrence of injustice than any other people. Their sultan shows no mercy to anyone who is guilty of the least act of it. There is complete security in their country. Neither traveler nor inhabitant in it has anything to fear from robbers. . . . They do not confiscate the property of any white man who dies in their country, even if it be uncounted wealth. On the contrary, they give it into the charge of some trustworthy person among the whites.[12]

The third great West African empire, Songhai, succeeded Mali in the fourteenth century. It encompassed the old empires of Ghana and Mali and extended its territory farther north and east to become one of the largest African empires in history (see Map 10.2).

Ethiopia: The Christian Kingdom of Aksum

Just as the ancient West African empires were significantly affected by Islam and the Arab culture that accompanied it, the African kingdoms that arose in modern Sudan and Ethiopia in northeast Africa were heavily influenced by Egyptian culture, and they influenced it in return. This was particularly the case in ancient Nubia. Nubia's capital was at Meroë (see Map 10.2); thus the country is often referred to as the Nubian kingdom of Meroë.

As part of the Roman Empire, Egypt was subject to Hellenistic and Roman cultural forces, and it became an early center of Christianity. Nubia, however, was never part of the Roman Empire; its people clung to ancient Egyptian religious ideas. Christian missionaries traveled to the Upper Nile region and successfully converted the Nubian rulers around 600 C.E. By that time, there were three separate Nubian states, of

• **Timbuktu** Originally a campsite for desert nomads, it grew into a thriving city under Mansa Musa, king of Mali and Africa's most famous ruler.

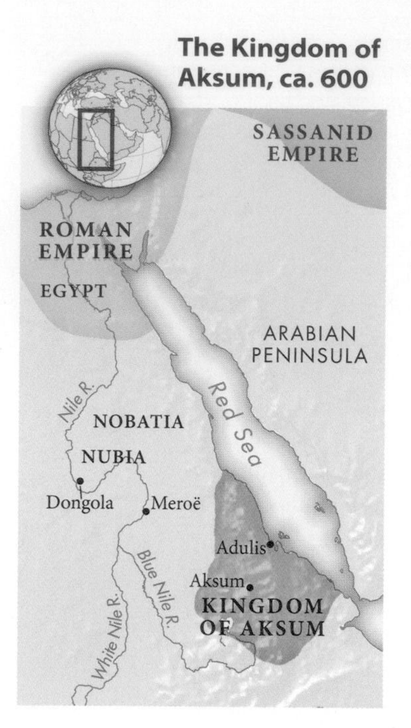

which the kingdom of Nobatia, centered at Dongola, was the strongest. The Christian rulers of Nobatia had close ties with the **Aksum** kingdom in Ethiopia, and through this relationship Egyptian culture spread to Ethiopia.

Two-thirds of Ethiopia consists of the Ethiopian highlands, the rugged plateau region of East Africa. The Great Rift Valley divides this territory into two massifs (mountain masses), of which the Ethiopian Plateau is the larger. Sloping away from each side of the Great Rift Valley are a series of mountains and valleys. Together with this mountainous environment, the three Middle Eastern religions—Judaism, Christianity, and Islam—have all influenced Ethiopian society.

By the first century C.E. the Aksum kingdom in northwestern Ethiopia was a sizable trading state. Merchants at Adulis, its main port on the Red Sea, sold ivory, gold, emeralds, rhinoceros horns, shells, and slaves to the Sudan, Arabia, Yemen, and various cities across the Indian Ocean in exchange for glass, ceramics, fabrics, sugar, oil, spices, and precious gems. Adulis contained temples, stone-built houses, and irrigated agriculture. Between the first and eighth centuries Aksum served as the capital of an empire extending over much of what is now northern Ethiopia. The empire's prosperity rested on trade. Aksum even independently minted specie (coins) modeled on the Roman *solidus*; at that time, only the Roman Empire, Persia, and some Indian states issued coins that circulated in Middle Eastern trade. It was the first and only sub-Saharan African state to have its own currency. After Aksum's decline, coins were not minted again in Africa until the Swahili city-state of Kilwa minted gold coins beginning perhaps as early as the eleventh century.

Islam's expansion into northern Ethiopia in the eighth century (see page 276) weakened Aksum's commercial prosperity. The Arabs first ousted the Greek Byzantine merchants who traded on the Dahlak Archipelago (in the southern Red Sea) and converted the islands' inhabitants. Then Muslims attacked and destroyed Adulis. Some Aksumites converted to Islam; many others found refuge in the rugged mountains north of the kingdom, where they were isolated from outside contacts. Thus began the insularity that characterized later Ethiopian society.

Tradition ascribes to Frumentius (ca. 300–380 C.E.), a Syrian Christian trader, the introduction of Coptic Christianity, an Orthodox form of Christianity that originated in Egypt, into Ethiopia. Kidnapped as a young boy en route from India to Tyre (in southern Lebanon), Frumentius was taken to Aksum, given his freedom, and appointed tutor to the future king, Ezana. Upon Ezana's accession to the throne, Frumentius went to Alexandria, Egypt, where he was consecrated the first bishop of Aksum around 328 C.E. He then returned to Ethiopia with some priests to spread Christianity. Shortly after members of the royal court accepted Christianity, it became the Ethiopian state religion. Ethiopia's future was to be inextricably linked to Christianity, a unique situation in sub-Saharan Africa.

Ethiopia's acceptance of Christianity led to the production of ecclesiastical documents and royal chronicles, making Ethiopia the first sub-Saharan African society that can be studied from written records. The Scriptures were translated into Ge'ez (gee-EHZ), an ancient language and script used in Ethiopia and Aksum. Pagan temples were dedicated to Christian saints, and, as in early medieval Ireland and in the Orthodox Church of the Byzantine world, monasteries were the Christian faith's main cultural institutions in Ethiopia. Monks preached and converted the people, who resorted to the monasteries in times of need. As the Ethiopian state expanded, vibrant monasteries provided inspiration for the establishment of convents for nuns, as in medieval Europe (see page 399).

Monastic records provide fascinating information about early Ethiopian society. Settlements were formed on the warm and moist plateau lands, not in the arid lowlands or the river valleys. Farmers used a scratch plow (unique in sub-Saharan Africa) to cultivate wheat and barley, and they regularly rotated these cereals. Plentiful rainfall seems to have helped produce abundant crops, which in turn led to population growth. Unlike in most of sub-Saharan Africa, both sexes probably married young. Because of ecclesiastical opposition to polygyny (the practice of having multiple wives), monogamy was the norm, other than for kings and the very rich. An abundance of land meant that young couples could establish independent households. Widely scattered farms, with the parish church as the central social unit, seem to have been the usual pattern of existence.

Above the broad class of peasant farmers stood warrior-nobles. Their wealth and status derived from their fighting skills, which kings rewarded with grants of estates and with the right to collect tribute from the

- **Aksum** A kingdom in northwestern Ethiopia that was a sizable trading state and the center of Christian culture.

Christianity and Islam in Ethiopia The prolonged contest between the two religions in Ethiopia was periodically taken to the battlefield. This drawing from the eighteenth century by an Ethiopian artist shows his countrymen (left) advancing victoriously and celebrates national military success. (© The British Library Board/The Image Works)

peasants. To acquire lands and to hold warriors' loyalty, Ethiopian kings pursued a policy of constant territorial expansion. (See "Individuals in Society: Amda Siyon," page 284.) Nobles maintained order in their regions, supplied kings with fighting men, and displayed their superior status by the size of their households and their generosity to the poor.

Sometime in the fourteenth century, six scribes in the Tigrayan highlands of Ethiopia combined oral tradition, Jewish and Islamic commentaries, apocryphal (noncanonical) Christian texts, and the writings of the early Christian Church fathers to produce the *Kebra Nagast* (The Glory of Kings). This history served the authors' goals: it became an Ethiopian national epic, glorifying a line of rulers descended from the Hebrew king Solomon (see page 53), arousing patriotic feelings, and linking Ethiopia's identity to the Judeo-Christian tradition. The book mostly deals with the origins of Emperor Menilek I of Ethiopia in the tenth century B.C.E.

The *Kebra Nagast* asserts that Queen Makeda of Ethiopia (called Sheba in the Jewish tradition) had little governmental experience when she came to the throne. So she sought the advice and wise counsel of King Solomon (r. 965–925 B.C.E.) in Jerusalem. Makeda learned Jewish statecraft, converted to Judaism, and expressed her gratitude to Solomon with rich gifts of spices, gems, and gold. Desiring something more precious, Solomon prepared a lavish banquet for his attractive pupil. Satiated with spicy food and rich wines, Makeda fell asleep. In the middle of the night Solomon tricked Makeda into allowing him into her bed. Their son, Menilek, was born some months later. When Menilek reached maturity, he visited Solomon in Jerusalem. There Solomon anointed him crown prince of Ethiopia and sent a retinue of young Jewish nobles to accompany him home as courtiers. Unable to face life without the Hebrews' Ark of the Covenant, the courtiers stole the cherished wooden chest, which the Hebrews believed contained the Ten Commandments. God apparently approved the theft, for he lifted the youths, pursued by Solomon's army, across the Red Sea and into Ethiopia. Thus, according to the *Kebra Nagast*, Menilek avenged his mother's shame, and God gave his legal covenant to Ethiopia, Israel's successor.[13] Although written around twenty-three hundred years after the events, the myths and legends contained in the *Kebra Nagast* effectively served the purpose of building nationalistic fervor.

Based on this lineage, from the tenth to the sixteenth centuries, and even in the Ethiopian constitution of 1955, Ethiopia's rulers claimed they belonged to the Solomonic line of succession. Thus the church and state in Ethiopia were inextricably linked.

Ethiopia's high mountains isolated the kingdom and hindered access from the outside, but through trade word gradually spread about this African kingdom's Christian devotion. Twelfth-century Crusaders returning from the Middle East told of a powerful Christian ruler, Prester John, whose lands lay behind Muslim lines and who was eager to help restore the Holy Land to Christian control. The story of Prester John sparked European imaginations and led to exploration aimed at finding his legendary kingdom, which

Viewpoints 10.2

Visiting Africa

• *Indirect trade contacts between China and Egypt began perhaps as early as 700 B.C.E. By the time of the Tang Dynasty (618–907 C.E.), there were several Chinese accounts of Africa's eastern coast acquired through direct contact.* You Yang Za Zu (A General Book of Knowledge), *written by Duan Chengshi (803–863? C.E.), contains a description of people living along the coast around modern Somalia ("the country of Po-pa-li"), which is excerpted here.*

A Portuguese mariner named Gomes Eannes de Azurara left the first account of the people and places along the West African coast. The selection here recounts the capture of the first slaves of the Atlantic slave trade along the West African coast in 1441 by two Portuguese ship captains, Antam Gonçalvez and Nuno Tristam.

Duan Chengshi

"The country of Po-pa-li is in the southwestern sea. (The people) do not eat any of the five grains but eat only meat. They often stick a needle into the veins of cattle and draw blood which they drink raw, mixed with milk. They wear no clothes except that they cover (the parts) below their loins with sheepskins. Their women are clean and of proper behaviour. The inhabitants themselves kidnap them, and if they sell them to foreign merchants, they fetch several times their price. The country produces only ivory and ambergris.

If Persian merchants wish to go into the country, they collect around them several thousand men and present them with strips of cloth. All whether old or young draw blood and swear an oath, and then only do they trade their products. From olden times on they were not subject to any foreign country. In fighting they use elephants' tusks and ribs and the horns of wild buffaloes as lances and they wear cuirasses and bow and arrows. They have twenty myriads of foot soldiers. The Arabs make frequent raids upon them."

Gomes Eannes de Azurara

"Thereupon [Nuno Tristam] caused Antam Gonçalvez to be called. . . . "You," said he, "my friend Antam Gonçalvez, are not ignorant of the will of the Infant* our Lord, and you know that . . . he hath toiled in vain in this part of the world, never being able to arrive at any certainty as to the people of this land, under what law or lordship they do live. And although you are carrying off these two captives, and by their means the Infant may come to know something about this folk, yet that doth not prevent what is still better, namely, for us to carry off many more; for, besides the knowledge which the Lord Infant will gain by their means, profit will also accrue to him by their service or ransom. Wherefore, it seemeth to me that we should do well to act after this manner. That is to say, in this night now following, you should choose ten of your men and I another ten of mine . . . and let us then go together and seek those whom you have found. . . ."

And so it chanced that in the night they came to where the natives lay scattered in two encampments. . . . And when our men had come nigh to them, they attacked them very lustily, shouting at the top of their voices, "Portugal" . . . the fright of which so abashed the enemy, that it threw them all into disorder. And so, all in confusion, they began to fly without any order or carefulness. Except indeed that the men made some show of defending themselves . . . , especially one of them who fought face to face with Nuno Tristam, defending himself till he received his death. And besides this one, . . . the others killed three and took ten prisoners, what of men, women and boys."

Sources: J. J. L. Duyvendak, *China's Discovery of Africa* (London: A. Probsthain, 1949), pp. 12–13; Gomes Eannes de Azurara, *The Chronicle of the Discovery and Conquest of Guinea*, vol. 1, trans. C. R. Beazley and E. Prestage (New York: Burt Franklin, 1963), pp. 46–48.

QUESTIONS FOR ANALYSIS

1. What does Duan Chengshi's account reveal about the inhabitants of Po-pa-li?
2. In general, how would you assess Duan Chengshi's opinion of the Africans?
3. What reasons do the Portuguese mariners give for enslaving the ten Africans?

*Portuguese term for any prince other than the eldest; here it refers to Prince Henry the Navigator (see page 465).

African goods satisfied the global aristocratic demand for luxury goods. In Arabia leopard skins were made into saddles, shells were made into combs, and ambergris was used in the manufacture of perfumes. Because African elephants' tusks were larger and more durable than those of Indian elephants, African ivory was in great demand in India for sword and dagger handles, carved decorative objects, and the ceremonial bangles used in Hindu marriage rituals. Wealthy Chinese also valued African ivory for use in sedan chair construction. (See "Viewpoints 10.2: Visiting Africa," at left.)

Copper Coin from Mogadishu, Twelfth Century Islamic proscriptions against representation of the human form prevented the use of rulers' portraits on coinage, unlike the practice of the Romans, Byzantines, and Sassanids. Instead Islamic coins since the Umayyad period were decorated exclusively with writing. Sultan Haran Ibn Suleiman of Kilwa on the East African coast minted this coin, a symbol of the region's Muslim culture and of its rich maritime trade.

In exchange for these natural products, the Swahili cities brought in, among many other items, incense, glassware, glass beads, and carpets from Arabia; textiles, spices, rice, and cotton from India; and grains, fine porcelain, silk, and jade from China. Swahili kings imposed enormous duties on imports, perhaps more than 80 percent of the value of the goods themselves. Even so, traders who came to Africa made fabulous profits.

Slaves were another export from the East African coast. Reports of East African slave trading began with the publication of the *Periplus*. The trade accelerated with the establishment of Muslim settlements in the eighth century and continued up through the arrival of the Portuguese in the late fifteenth century, which provided a market for African slaves in the New World (discussed in Chapter 15). In fact, the global slave market fueled the East African coastal slave trade until at least the beginning of the twentieth century.

As in West Africa, traders obtained slaves primarily through raids and kidnapping. As early as the tenth century Arabs from Oman enticed hungry children with dates. When the children accepted the sweet fruits, they were abducted and enslaved.

The Arabs called the northern Somalia coast *Ras Assir* (Cape of Slaves). From there, Arab traders transported slaves northward up the Red Sea to the markets of Arabia and Persia. Muslim dealers also shipped blacks from the Zanzibar region across the Indian Ocean to markets in India. Rulers of the Deccan Plateau in central India used large numbers of black slave soldiers in their military campaigns. Slaves also worked on the docks and dhows (typical Arab lateen-rigged ships) in the Muslim-controlled Indian Ocean and as domestic servants and concubines throughout South and East Asia.

As early as the tenth century sources mention persons with "lacquer-black bodies" in the possession of wealthy families in Song China.[15] In 1178 a Chinese official noted in a memorial to the emperor that Arab traders were shipping thousands of blacks from East Africa to the Chinese port of Guangzhou (Canton) by way of the Malay Archipelago. The Chinese employed these slaves as household servants, as musicians, and, because East Africans were often expert swimmers, as divers to caulk leaky ship seams below the waterline.

By the thirteenth century Africans living in many parts of South and East Asia had made significant economic and cultural contributions to their societies. It appears, however, that in Indian, Chinese, and East African markets, slaves were never as valuable a commodity as ivory. Thus the volume of the Eastern slave trade did not approach that of the trans-Saharan slave trade.[16]

Southern Africa and Great Zimbabwe

Southern Africa, bordered on the northwest by the Kalahari Desert and on the northeast by the Zambezi River (see Map 10.2), enjoys a mild and temperate climate. Desert conditions prevail along the Atlantic coast, which gets less than five inches of annual rainfall. Eastward toward the Indian Ocean rainfall increases, amounting to fifty to ninety inches a year in some places. Temperate grasslands characterize the interior highlands. Considerable variations in climate occur throughout much of southern Africa from year to year.

Southern Africa has enormous mineral resources: gold, copper, diamonds, platinum, and uranium. Preindustrial peoples mined some of these deposits in open excavations down several feet, but fuller exploitation required modern technology. (Today, gold-mining operations can penetrate two miles below the surface.)

Located at the southern extremity of the Afroeurasian landmass, southern Africa has a history that is very different from those of West Africa, the Nile Valley, and the East African coast. Unlike the rest of coastal Africa, southern Africa remained far removed

Ruins of Great Zimbabwe Considered the most impressive monument in the African interior south of the Ethiopian highlands, these ruins of Great Zimbabwe consist of two complexes of dry-stone buildings, some surrounded by a massive serpentine wall 32 feet high and 17 feet thick at its maximum. (Robert Harding World Imagery/Superstock)

from the outside world until the Portuguese arrived in the late fifteenth century—with one important exception. Bantu-speaking people reached southern Africa in the eighth century. They brought skills in ironworking and mixed farming (settled crop production plus cattle and sheep raising) and immunity to the kinds of diseases that later decimated the Amerindians of South America (discussed in Chapter 16).

The earliest residents of southern Africa were hunters and gatherers. In the first millennium C.E. new farming techniques from the north arrived. Lack of water and timber (both needed to produce the charcoal used in iron smelting) slowed the spread of iron technology and tools and thus of crop production in southwestern Africa. These advances reached the western coastal region by 1500. By that date, Khoisan-speakers were tending livestock in the arid western regions. The area teemed with wild game—elephants, buffalo, lions, hippopotamuses, leopards, zebras, and many varieties of antelope. To the east, descendants of Bantu-speaking immigrants grew sorghum, raised cattle and sheep, and fought with iron-headed spears. However, disease-bearing insects such as the tsetse fly, which causes sleeping sickness, attacked the cattle and sheep and retarded their domestication.

The nuclear family was the basic social unit among early southern African peoples, who practiced polygyny and traced descent in the male line. Several families formed bands numbering between twenty and eighty people. Such bands were not closed entities; people in neighboring territories identified with bands speaking the same language. As in most preindustrial societies, a division of labor existed whereby men hunted and women cared for children and raised edible plants. People lived in caves or in camps made of portable material, and they moved from one watering or hunting region to another as seasonal or environmental needs required.

In 1871 a German explorer came upon the ruined city of **Great Zimbabwe** southeast of what is now Masvingo in Zimbabwe. Archaeologists consider Great Zimbabwe the most impressive monument in Africa south of the Nile Valley and the Ethiopian highlands. The ruins consist of two vast complexes of dry-stone buildings, a fortress, and an elliptically shaped enclosure commonly called the Temple. Stone carvings, gold and copper ornaments, and Asian ceramics once decorated the buildings. The ruins extend over sixty acres and are encircled by a massive wall. The entire city was

• **Great Zimbabwe** A ruined southern African city discovered by a German explorer in 1871; it is considered the most impressive monument south of the Nile Valley and Ethiopian highlands.

built from local granite between the eleventh and fifteenth centuries without any outside influence.

These ruins tell a remarkable story. Great Zimbabwe was the political and religious capital of a vast empire. During the first millennium C.E. settled crop cultivation, cattle raising, and work in metal led to a steady buildup in population in the Zambezi-Limpopo region. The area also contained a rich gold-bearing belt. Gold ore lay near the surface; alluvial gold lay in the Zambezi River tributaries. In the tenth century the inhabitants collected the alluvial gold by panning and washing; after the year 1000 the gold was worked in open mines with iron picks. Traders shipped the gold eastward to Sofala (see Map 10.2). Great Zimbabwe's wealth and power rested on this gold trade.

Great Zimbabwe declined in the fifteenth century, perhaps because the area had become agriculturally exhausted and could no longer support the large population. Some people migrated northward and settled in the Mazoe River Valley, a tributary of the Zambezi. This region also contained gold, and the settlers built a new empire in the tradition of Great Zimbabwe. This empire's rulers were called Mwene Mutapa, and their power was also based on the gold trade down the Zambezi River to Indian Ocean ports. It was this gold that the Portuguese sought when they arrived on the East African coast in the late fifteenth century.

CHRONOLOGY

ca. 1000 B.C.E.–1500 C.E.	Bantu-speakers expand across central and southern Africa
ca. 600 C.E.	Christian missionaries convert Nubian rulers
639–642 C.E.	Islam introduced to Africa
642 C.E.	Muslim conquest of Egypt
650–1500 C.E.	Slave trade from sub-Saharan Africa to the Mediterranean
700–900 C.E.	Berbers develop caravan routes
ca. 900–1100 C.E.	Kingdom of Ghana; bananas and plantains arrive in Africa from Asia
ca. 1100–1400 C.E.	Great Zimbabwe is built, flourishes
ca. 1200–1450 C.E.	Kingdom of Mali
ca. 1312–1337 C.E.	Reign of Mansa Musa in Mali
1314–1344 C.E.	Reign of Amda Siyon in Ethiopia
1324–1325 C.E.	Mansa Musa's pilgrimage to Mecca

Chapter Summary

Africa is a huge continent with many different climatic zones and diverse geography. The African peoples are as varied as the topography. North African peoples were closely connected with the Middle Eastern and European civilizations of the Mediterranean basin. New crops introduced from Asia and the adoption of agriculture profoundly affected early societies across western and northeastern Africa as they transitioned from hunting and gathering in small bands to settled farming communities. Beginning in modern Cameroon and Nigeria, Bantu-speakers spread across central and southern Africa over a two-thousand-year period. Possessing iron tools and weapons, domesticated livestock, and a knowledge of agriculture, these Bantu-speakers assimilated, killed, or drove away the region's previous inhabitants.

Africans in the West African Sahel participated in the trans-Saharan trade, which affected West African society in three important ways: it stimulated gold mining; it increased the demand for West Africa's second-most important commodity, slaves; and it stimulated the development of large urban centers in West Africa.

Similarly, the Swahili peoples along the East African coast organized in city-states, such as Kilwa and Mogadishu, and traded with Arabia, the Persian Gulf, India, China, and the Malay Archipelago. They depended on Indian Ocean commercial networks, which they used to trade African products for luxury items from Arabia, Southeast Asia, and East Asia. Great Zimbabwe, in southern Africa's interior, traded gold to the coast for the Indian Ocean trade.

The Swahili city-states and the western Sudan kingdoms were both part of the Islamic world. Arabian merchants brought Islam with them as they settled along the East African coast, and Berber traders brought Islam to West Africa. Differing from its neighbors, Ethiopia formed a unique enclave of Christianity in the midst of Islamic societies. The Bantu-speaking peoples of Great Zimbabwe, and central and southern Africa generally, were neither Islamic nor Christian.

NOTES

1. T. Spear, "Bantu Migrations," in *Problems in African History: The Precolonial Centuries*, ed. R. O. Collins et al. (New York: Markus Weiner Publishing, 1994), p. 98.
2. J. S. Trimingham, *Islam in West Africa* (Oxford: Oxford University Press, 1959), pp. 6–9.
3. R. A. Austen, "The Trans-Saharan Slave Trade: A Tentative Census," in *The Uncommon Market: Essays in the Economic History of the Atlantic Slave Trade*, ed. H. A. Gemery and J. S. Hogendorn (New York: Academic Press, 1979), pp. 1–71, esp. p. 66.
4. Quoted in J. O. Hunwick, "Islam in West Africa, A.D. 1000–1800," in *A Thousand Years of West African History*, ed. J. F. Ade Ajayi and I. Espie (New York: Humanities Press, 1972), pp. 244–245.
5. Quoted in A. A. Boahen, "Kingdoms of West Africa, c. A.D. 500–1600," in *The Horizon History of Africa* (New York: American Heritage, 1971), p. 183.
6. Al-Bakri, *Kitab al-mughrib fdhikr bilad Ifriqiya wa'l-Maghrib (Description de l'Afrique Septentrionale)*, trans. De Shane (Paris: Adrien-Maisonneuve, 1965), pp. 328–329.
7. Quoted in R. Oliver and C. Oliver, eds., *Africa in the Days of Exploration* (Englewood Cliffs, N.J.: Prentice-Hall, 1965), p. 10.
8. Quoted in Boahen, "Kingdoms of West Africa," p. 184.
9. This quotation and the next appear in E. J. Murphy, *History of African Civilization* (New York: Delta, 1972), pp. 109, 111.
10. Pekka Masonen and Humphrey J. Fisher, "Not Quite Venus from the Waves: The Almoravid Conquest of Ghana in the Modern Historiography of Western Africa," *History in Africa* 23 (1996): 197–232.
11. Quoted in Murphy, *History of African Civilization*, p. 120.
12. Quoted in Oliver and Oliver, *Africa in the Days of Exploration*, p. 18.
13. See H. G. Marcus, *A History of Ethiopia*, updated ed. (Berkeley: University of California Press, 2002), pp. 17–20.
14. Ibn Battuta, *The Travels of Ibn Battuta, A.D. 1325–1354*, vol. 1, ed. H. A. R. Gibb (London: University Press, 1972), pp. 379–380.
15. Austen, "The Trans-Saharan Slave Trade," p. 65; J. H. Harris, *The African Presence in Asia* (Evanston, Ill.: Northwestern University Press, 1971), pp. 3–6, 27–30; P. Wheatley, "Analecta Sino-Africana Recensa," in Neville Chittick and Robert Rotberg, *East Africa and the Orient* (New York: Africana Publishing, 1975), p. 109.
16. I. Hrbek, ed., *General History of Africa*. Vol. 3: *Africa from the Seventh to the Eleventh Century* (Berkeley: University of California Press; New York: UNESCO, 1991), pp. 294–295, 346–347.

CONNECTIONS

Because our ancestors first evolved in Africa, Africa's archaeological record is rich with material artifacts, such as weapons, tools, ornaments, and eating utensils. But its written record is much less complete, and thus the nonmaterial dimensions of human society—human interaction in all its facets—is much more difficult to reconstruct. The only exception is in Egypt, where hieroglyphic writings give us a more complete picture of Egyptian society than of nearly any other ancient culture.

Not until the Phoenicians, Greeks, and Romans were there written accounts of the peoples of North and East Africa. These accounts document Africa's early connections and contributions to the vast trans-Saharan and Indian Ocean trading networks that stretched from Europe to China. This trade brought wealth to the kingdoms, empires, and city-states that developed alongside the routes. But the trade in ideas more profoundly connected the growing African states to the wider world, most notably through Islam, which had arrived by the seventh century, and Christianity, which developed a foothold in Ethiopia.

Prior to the late fifteenth century Europeans had little knowledge about African societies. All this would change during the European Age of Discovery. Chapter 16 traces the expansion of Portugal from a small, poor European nation to an overseas empire, as it established trading posts and gained control of the African gold trade. Portuguese expansion led to competition, spurring Spain and then England to strike out for gold of their own in the Americas. The acceleration of this conquest would forever shape the history of Africa and the Americas (discussed in Chapters 11 and 15) and intertwine them via the African slave trade that fueled the labor needs of the colonies in the Americas.

Review and Explore

Make It Stick

LearningCurve

Go online and use LearningCurve to retain what you've read.

Identify Key Terms

Identify and explain the significance of each item below.

Bantu (p. 271)
Sudan (p. 272)
Berbers (p. 275)
Mogadishu (p. 277)
stateless societies (p. 277)
Ghana (p. 277)
Koumbi Saleh (p. 278)
Timbuktu (p. 281)
Aksum (p. 282)
Swahili (p. 286)
Kilwa (p. 286)
Great Zimbabwe (p. 292)

Review the Main Ideas

Answer the focus questions from each section of the chapter.

1. How did Africa's geography shape its history and contribute to its diverse population? (p. 268)
2. How did agriculture affect life among the early societies in the western Sudan and among the Bantu-speaking societies of central and southern Africa? (p. 270)
3. What characterized trans-Saharan trade, and how did it affect West African society? (p. 273)
4. How were the East African city-states, Aksum, and Great Zimbabwe different from and similar to the kingdoms of the western Sudan? (p. 277)

Make Connections

Analyze the larger developments and continuities within and across chapters.

1. How did the geography and size of Africa affect African societies and their contact with the rest of the world?
2. What different cultures influenced the African people living along the continent's eastern coast?
3. How did Islam influence the different societies of West and East Africa?

LaunchPad

Online Document Project

Creating an Ethiopian National Identity

What role did religion play in the formation of Ethiopian identity?
Explore early Ethiopian chronicles, and then complete a quiz and writing assignment based on the evidence and details from this chapter.

See inside the front cover to learn more.

Suggested Reading

Allen, J. de Vere. *Swahili Origins*. 1993. A study of the problem of Swahili identity.

Austen, Ralph. *African Economic History*. 1987. Classic study of Africa's economic history.

Austen, Ralph. *Trans-Saharan Africa in World History*. 2010. Excellent new introduction to the Sahara region and the trans-Saharan trade that gave it life.

Beck, Roger B. *The History of South Africa*, 2d ed. 2014. Introduction to this large and important country.

Bouvill, E. W., and Robin Hallett. *The Golden Trade of the Moors: West African Kingdoms in the Fourteenth Century*. 1995. Classic description of the trans-Saharan trade.

Ehret, Christopher. *An African Classical Age: Eastern and Southern Africa in World History, 1000 B.C. to A.D. 400*. 2001. Solid introduction by a renowned African scholar.

Ehret, Christopher. *The Civilizations of Africa: A History to 1800*, 2d ed. 2013. The best study of pre-1800 African history.

Gilbert, Erik, and Jonathan Reynolds. *Africa in World History*. 2007. Groundbreaking study of Africa's place in world history.

Iliffe, John. *Africans: The History of a Continent*, 2d ed. 2007. Thoughtful introduction to African history.

Klieman, Kairn A. *The Pygmies Were Our Compass: Bantu and Batwa in the History of West Central Africa, Early Times to c. 1900 C.E.* 2003. A unique study of Bantu and forest people in precolonial African history.

Levtzion, Nehemia, and Randall L. Pouwels. *History of Islam in Africa*. 2000. Comprehensive survey of Islam's presence in Africa.

Marcus, H. G. *A History of Ethiopia*, updated ed. 2002. Standard introduction to Ethiopian history.

Mitchell, Peter. *African Connections: Archaeological Perspectives on Africa and the Wider World*. 2005. Places ancient Africa and its history in a global context.

Newman, J. L. *The Peopling of Africa: A Geographic Interpretation*. 1995. Explores population distribution and technological change up to the late nineteenth century.

Schmidt, Peter R. *Historical Archaeology in Africa: Representation, Social Memory, and Oral Traditions*. 2006. An excellent introduction to archaeology and the reconstruction of Africa's history.

The Americas

2500 B.C.E.–1500 C.E.

Moche Portrait Vessel
A Moche artist captured the commanding expression of a ruler in this ceramic vessel. The Moche were one of many cultures in Peru that developed technologies that were simultaneously useful and beautiful, including brightly colored cloth, hanging bridges made of fiber, and intricately fit stone walls. (Private Collection/Photo © Boltin Picture Library/The Bridgeman Art Library)

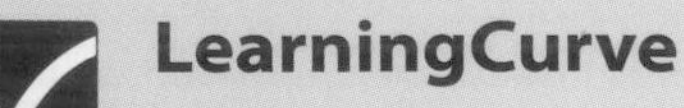

LearningCurve
After reading the chapter, go online and use LearningCurve to retain what you've read.

Chapter Preview

Societies of the Americas in a Global Context
Ancient Societies
The Incas
The Maya and Teotihuacan
The Aztecs
American Empires and the Encounter

When peoples of the Americas first came into sustained contact with peoples from Europe, Africa, and Asia at the turn of the sixteenth century, their encounters were uneven. Thousands of years of isolation from other world societies made peoples of the Americas vulnerable to diseases found elsewhere in the world. When indigenous peoples were first exposed to these diseases through contact with Europeans, the devastating effects of epidemics facilitated European domination and colonization. But this exchange also brought into global circulation the results of thousands of years of work by peoples of the Americas in plant domestication that changed diets worldwide, making corn, potatoes, and peppers into the daily staples of many societies.

The ancient domestication of these crops intensified agriculture across the Americas that sustained increasingly complex societies. At times these societies grew into vast empires built on trade, conquest, and tribute. Social stratification and specialization produced lands not just of kings but of priests, merchants, artisans, scientists, and engineers who achieved extraordinary feats.

In **Mesoamerica**—the region stretching from present-day Nicaragua to California—the dense urban centers of Maya, Teotihuacan, Toltec, and Mexica city-states and empires featured great monuments, temples, and complex urban planning. Roadways and canals extended trade networks that reached from South America to the Great Lakes region of North America. Sophisticated calendars guided systems of religious, scientific, medical, and agricultural knowledge.

These achievements were rivaled only in the Andes, the mountain range that extends from southernmost present-day Chile north to Colombia and Venezuela. Andean peoples adapted to the mountain range's stark vertical stratification of climate and ecosystems to produce agricultural abundance similar to that of Mesoamerica. The technological, agricultural, and engineering innovations of ancient Andean civilizations allowed people to make their difficult mountain terrain a home rather than a boundary.

Societies of the Americas in a Global Context

☐ How did ancient peoples of the Americas adapt to, and adapt, their environment?

Ancient societies of the Americas shared many characteristics that were common to other premodern societies around the world that stretched from the Pacific Rim to the Mediterranean. But many elements were also unique to the ancient peoples of the Americas, and we must consider these on their own terms. Since societies of the Americas developed in isolation, their history offers a counterpoint to premodern histories of other parts of the world. Like people everywhere, civilizations of the Americas interpreted the meaning of the world and their place in the cosmos. They organized societies stratified not just by gender, class, and ethnicity but also by professional roles and wealth, and they adapted to and reshaped their physical and natural world. But they did all this on their own, without outside influences and within a distinct environment.

If the differences between civilizations in the Americas and other world regions are remarkable, the similarities are even more so. By studying the peoples of the Americas before their encounters with other world societies, we gain a clearer view of universal aspects of the human experience.

Trade and Technology

The domestication of crops and animals created an abundance of food and livestock, which allowed people to take on new social roles and to develop specialized occupations. As cities emerged, they became hubs of a universal human activity: trade. These cities were home to priests who interpreted the nature of our world, as well as a nobility from which kings emerged, some of whom forged vast empires based on their ability to coordinate conquest, trade, tribute from conquered subjects, and systems of religious beliefs.

The differences in the development and application of three different kinds of technologies—the wheel, writing and communications systems, and calendars—capture this essential nature of human adaptability.

Before their encounters with other world peoples that began in 1492, societies in Mesoamerica and the Andes did not use wheeled transportation. Had they failed to invent one of the basic technologies used elsewhere in the world? No, they had not. As it happens, wheels were used in children's toys, just not for transportation. Tools emerged (or did not emerge) from specific needs. In Mesoamerica there were no large animals like horses or oxen to domesticate as beasts of burden, so there was no way to power wagons or chariots. In the Andes, domesticated llamas and alpacas served as pack animals and were a source of wool and meat. But in the most densely settled, cultivated, and developed areas, the terrain was too difficult for wheeled transportation. Instead Andean peoples developed extensive networks of roads that navigated steep changes in altitude, supported by elaborate suspension bridges made from woven vegetable fibers.

Peoples of the Americas also did not develop an alphabet or character-based writing systems, but this did not mean they did not communicate or record information. If we separate our understanding of the alphabetical reading you are doing right now from its functions—communicating and storing of information—we can appreciate the ways in which Andean and Mesoamerican civilizations accomplished both. Peoples of the Americas spoke thousands of languages (hundreds are still spoken today). Mesoamericans, beginning with the Olmecs (1500–400 B.C.E.), used pictographic glyphs similar to those of ancient Egyptian writing to record and communicate information. Later civilizations continued to adapt these systems. The Aztecs produced hieroglyphic books written on paper and deerskin.

The Andean innovation for recording information was particularly remarkable. The **khipu** (KEY-pooh) was an assemblage of colored and knotted strings. The differences in color, arrangement, and type of knot, as well as the knots' order and placement, served as a binary system akin to a contemporary computer database. As archaeologists and linguists struggle to decode khipus, they have discerned their role in recording demographic, economic, and political information that allowed imperial rulers and local leaders to understand and manage complex data.

Mesoamerican peoples used a sophisticated combination of calendars. These were based on a Calendar Round that combined a 365-day solar calendar with a 260-day calendar based on the numbers thirteen and twenty, which were sacred to peoples of Mesoamerica. Annual cycles were completed when twenty 13-day bundles converged with thirteen 20-day bundles. Together with the solar calendar, these formed a fifty-two-year cycle whose precision was unsurpassed in the premodern world. It also provided an incredibly intricate mechanism not only for following the solar and lunar years but also for connecting these to aspects of daily life and religion, helping users of the calendar to interpret their world.

- **Mesoamerica** The term used to designate the area of present-day Mexico and Central America.
- **khipu** An intricate system of knotted and colored strings used by early Andean cultures to store information such as census and tax records.

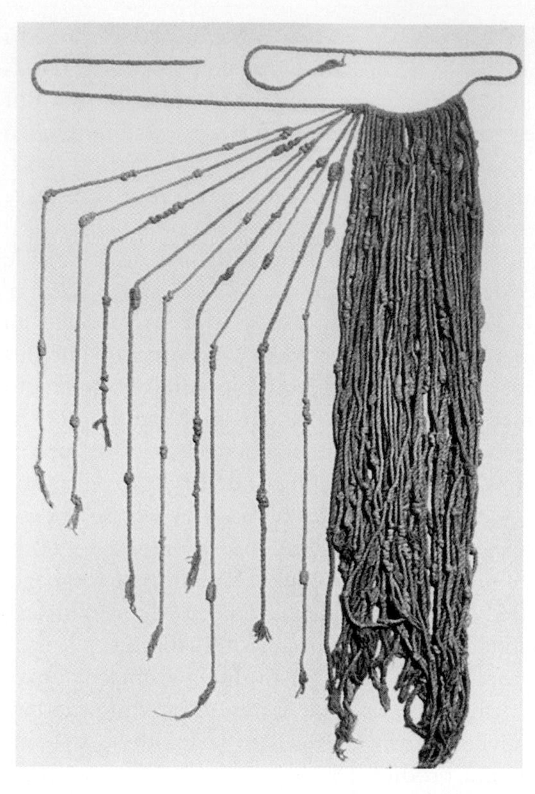

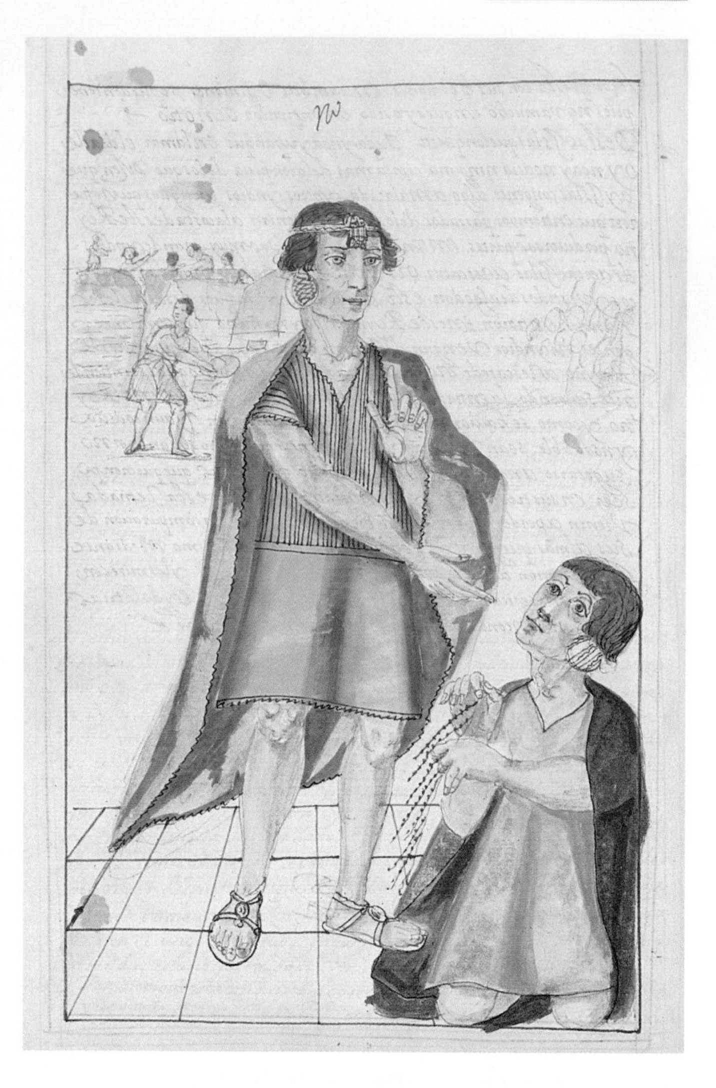

Inca Khipu Khipus like these (above) were used by communities and by Inca imperial officials to store and communicate data. The dyes, weaves, and knots made by their users recorded data much like contemporary binary computer storage, allowing users (right) to read information about populations, production, and tribute. (khipu: The Granger Collection, NYC — All rights reserved; illustration: from *Historia y Genealogia Real de los Reyes Incas del Peru, de sus hechos, constumbres, trajes y manera de Gobierno*, known as the *Codice Murua* [vellum], 16th century/ Private Collection/The Bridgeman Art Library)

Settlement and Environment

Ancient settlers in the Americas adapted to and adapted diverse environments ranging from the high plateau of the Andes and central plateau of Mesoamerica to the tropical rain forest and river systems of the Amazon and Caribbean, as well as the prairies of North and South America. But, given the isolation of these societies, where did the first peoples to settle the continent come from?

The first settlers migrated from Asia, though their timing and their route are debated. One possibility is that the first settlers migrated across the Bering Strait from what is now Russia to Alaska and gradually migrated southward sometime between 15,000 and 13,000 B.C.E. But archaeological excavations have identified much earlier settlements along the Andes in South America, perhaps dating to over 40,000 years ago, than they have for Mesoamerica or North America. These findings suggest that the original settlers in the Americas arrived instead (or also) as fishermen circulating the Pacific Ocean.

Like early settlers elsewhere in the world, populations of the Americas could be divided into three categories: nomadic peoples, semi-sedentary farming communities, and dense agricultural communities capable of sustaining cities. Urban settlement and empire formation centered around two major regions. The first area, Lake Titicaca, located at the present-day border between Peru and Bolivia, is the highest lake in the world (12,500 feet high) and the largest lake in South America (3,200 square miles). The second area was in the Valley of Mexico on the central plateau of Mesoamerica, where empires emerged from the cities around Lake Texcoco. Access to these large freshwater lakes allowed settlers to expand agriculture through irrigation, which in turn supported growing urban populations.

The earliest farming settlements emerged around 5000 B.C.E. These farming communities began the long process of domesticating and modifying plants, including maize (corn) and potatoes. Farmers also domesticated other crops native to the Americas such as peppers, beans, squash, and avocados.

Making Tortillas A mother teaches her daughter to roll tortillas on a metate. The dough at the right of the metate was masa made with maize and lime. The preparation process, known as nixtamalization, enriched the maize paste by adding calcium, potassium, and iron. (Page from the *Codex Mendoza*, Mexico, c. 1541–42 [pen and ink on paper], Bodleian Library, Oxford, UK/The Bridgeman Art Library)

The origins of maize in Mesoamerica are unclear, though it became a centerpiece of the Mesoamerican diet and spread across North and South America. Unlike other grains such as wheat and rice, the kernels of maize—which are the seeds as well as the part that is eaten for food—are wrapped in a husk, so the plant cannot propagate itself easily, meaning that farmers had to intervene to cultivate the crop. In addition, no direct ancestor of maize has been found. Biologists believe that Mesoamerican farmers identified a mutant form of a related grass called teosinte and gradually adapted it through selection and hybridization. Eaten together with beans, maize provided Mesoamerican peoples with a diet sufficient in protein despite the scarcity of meat. Mesoamericans processed kernels through **nixtamalization**, boiling the maize in a solution of water and mineral lime. The process broke down compounds in the kernels, increasing their nutritional value, while enriching the resulting *masa*, or paste, with dietary minerals including calcium, potassium, and iron.

The masa could then be cooked with beans, meat, or other ingredients to make tamales. It could also be rolled flat on a stone called a *metate* and baked into tortillas. Tortillas played roles similar to bread in wheat-producing cultures: they could be stored, they were light and easy to transport, and they were used as the basic building block of meals. Aztec armies of the fifteenth century could travel long distances because they carried tortillas for sustenance. Along their route, communities were obligated to provide tribute in tortillas. The rapid military expansion of the Aztec Empire was sustained in part by the versatility of the tortilla, which gave soldiers the ability to fight far from home.

Andean peoples cultivated another staple of the Americas, the potato. Potatoes first grew wild, but selective breeding produced many different varieties. For Andean peoples, potatoes became an integral part of a complex system of cultivation at varying altitudes. Communities created a system of "vertical archipelagos" through which they took advantage of the changes of climate along the steep escarpments of the Andes. Different crops could be cultivated at different altitudes, allowing communities to engage in intense and varied farming in what would otherwise have been inhospitable territory.

The settlement of communities, including what would become the largest cities, often took place at an altitude of nearly two miles (about 10,000 feet), in a temperate region at the boundary between ecological zones for growing maize and potatoes. The notable exception was the Lake Titicaca basin, at an elevation of 12,500 feet, where the abundance of fresh water tempered the climate and made irrigation possible. Communities raised multiple crops and engaged in year-round farming by working at different altitudes located within a day's journey from home. Some of these zones of cultivation were so distant—sometimes over a week's journey—that they were tended by

• **nixtamalization** Boiling maize in a solution of water and mineral lime to break down compounds in the kernels, increasing their nutritional value.

temporary or permanent colonies, called *mitmaq*, of the main settlement.

At higher elevations, members of these communities cultivated potatoes. Arid conditions across much of the altiplano, or high-plains plateau, meant that crops of potatoes could sometimes be planted only every few years. But the climate—dry with daily extremes of heat and cold—could be used to freeze-dry potatoes that could be stored indefinitely. Above the potato-growing zone, shepherds tended animals such as llamas and alpacas, which provided wool and dried meat, or *ch'arki* (the origin of the word *jerky*). They also served as pack animals that helped farmers bring in the crops from their high- and low-altitude plots. The animals' manure served as fertilizer for farming at lower altitudes.

At middle altitudes, communities used terraces edged by stone walls to extend cultivation along steep mountainsides to grow corn. In the lowlands, they cultivated the high-protein grain quinoa, as well as beans, peppers, and coca. Farmers chewed coca (the dried leaves of a plant native to the Andes from which cocaine is derived) to alleviate the symptoms of strenuous labor at extremely high altitudes. Coca also added nutrients such as calcium to the Andean diet and played an important role in religious rituals. In the lowlands communities also grew cotton, and in coastal areas they harvested fish and mussels. Fishermen built inflatable rafts made of sealskin.

MAP 11.1 The Olmecs, ca. 1500–300 B.C.E. Olmec civilization flourished in the coastal lowlands of southern Mexico along the Caribbean coast. Olmec patterns of settlement, culture, religion, organization, and trade are known almost solely through excavation of archaeological sites.

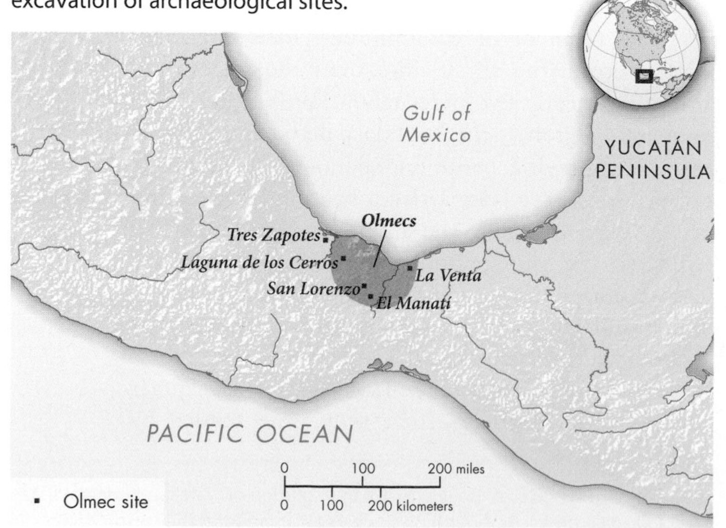

Ancient Societies

☐ What patterns established by early societies shaped civilization in Mesoamerica and the Andes?

Between 1500 and 1200 B.C.E. emerging civilizations in Mesoamerica and the Andes established lasting patterns of production, culture, and social organization that would long influence societies of the Americas. In Mesoamerica, Olmec civilization brought together practices of farming and trade, as well as religious and technological innovations that served future empires. The imprint of Olmec civilization spread across long networks of trade that would one day extend from Central America to the Mississippi Valley and the Great Lakes of North America. In the Andes, Chavín and Moche civilizations formed the early part of a long cycle of centralization and decentralization. This political and economic centralization helped spread technology, culture, and religion.

Olmec Agriculture, Technology, and Religion

The **Olmecs** were an early civilization that shaped the religion, trade practices, and technology of later civilizations in Mesoamerica. They flourished in the coastal lowlands of Mexico along a region stretching from Veracruz to the Yucatán from 1500 to 300 B.C.E. The Olmecs formed the first cities of Mesoamerica, and these cities served as centers of agriculture, trade, and religion (Map 11.1). Through long-distance trade, the Olmecs spread their culture and technology across Mesoamerica, establishing beliefs and practices that became common to the civilizations that followed.

The Olmecs settled and farmed along rivers in coastal lowlands, where they cultivated maize, squash, beans, and other plants and supplemented their diet with wild game and fish. But they lacked many other resources. In particular, they carried stone for many miles for the construction of temples and for carving massive monuments, many in the shape of heads. Across far-flung networks the Olmecs traded rubber, cacao (from which chocolate is made), pottery, clay figures, and jaguar pelts, as well as the services of artisans such as painters and sculptors, in exchange for obsidian, a volcanic glass that could be carved to a razor-sharp edge and used for making knives, tools, spear tips, and other weapons.

These ties between the Olmecs and other communities spread religious practices, creating a shared framework of beliefs among later civilizations. These practices included the construction of large pyramid temples, as well as acts that ranged from blood sacri-

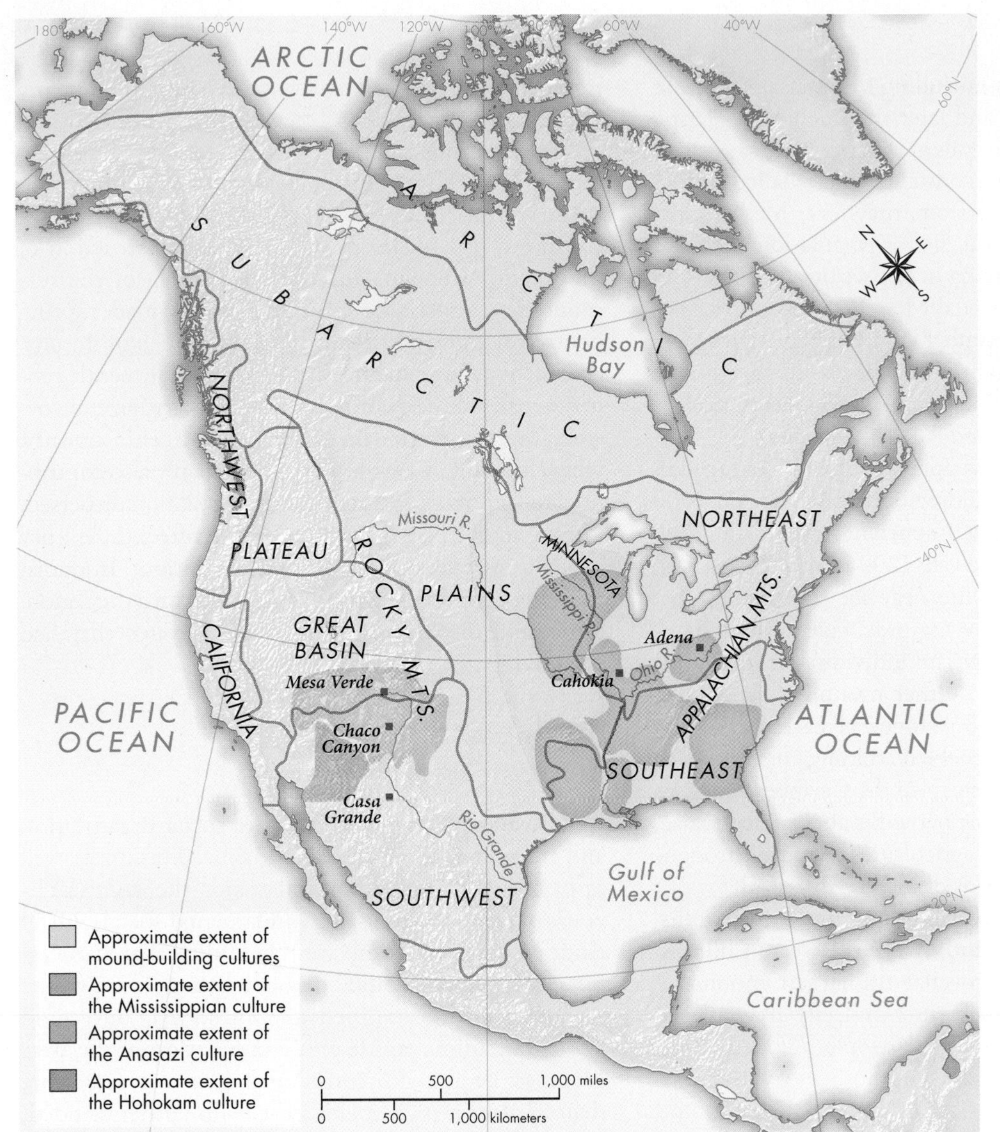

MAP 11.2 Major North American Agricultural Societies, ca. 600–1500 C.E. Many North American groups used agriculture to increase the available food supply and allow greater population density and the development of urban centers. This map shows three of these cultures: the Mississippian, Anasazi, and Hohokam.

fice, in which nobles ritually cut and bled themselves but did not die, to human sacrifice, in which the subject died. In addition to the manner of worship, archaeologists can trace the nature of the deities common in Mesoamerica. Olmec deities, like those of their successors, were combinations of gods and humans, included merged animal and human forms, and had both male and female identities. People practicing later religions based their gods on the fusion of human and spirit traits along the lines of the Olmec were-jaguar: a half-man, half-jaguar figure.

The Olmecs also used a Long Count solar calendar—a calendar based on a 365-day year. This calendar begins with the year 3114 B.C.E., though its origins and the significance of this date are unclear. Archaeologists presume that the existence of the Long Count calendar meant that the Calendar Round combining the 260-day and 365-day years already existed as well. All the later Mesoamerican civilizations used at least one of these calendars, and most used both of them.

Hohokam, Hopewell, and Mississippian Societies

Mesoamerican trading networks extended into southwestern North America, where by 300 B.C.E. the Hohokam people and other groups were using irrigation canals, dams, and terraces to enhance their farming of arid lands (Map 11.2). Like the Olmecs and other Mesoamerican peoples, the Hohokam built ceremonial platforms and played games with rubber balls that were traded over a long distance in return for turquoise and other precious stones. Along with trade goods came religious ideas, including the belief in local divinities who created, preserved, and destroyed. The Mesoamerican feathered serpent god became important to desert peoples. They planted desert crops such as agave, as well as cotton and maize that came from

• **Olmecs** The oldest of the early advanced Mesoamerican civilizations.

Mexico. Other groups, including the Anasazi (ah-nah-SAH-zee), the Yuma, and later the Pueblo and Hopi, also built settlements in this area using large sandstone blocks and masonry to construct thick-walled houses that offered protection from the heat. Mesa Verde, the largest Anasazi town, had a population of about twenty-five hundred living in houses built into and on cliff walls. Roads connected Mesa Verde to other Anasazi towns, allowing timber and other construction materials to be brought in more easily. Eventually drought, deforestation, and soil erosion led to decline in both the Hohokam and Anasazi cultures.

To the east, the Mississippian culture also engaged in monumental mound building beginning around 2000 B.C.E. One of the most important mound-building cultures was the Hopewell (200 B.C.E.–600 C.E.), named for a town in Ohio near the site of the most extensive mounds. Some mounds were burial chambers holding either a powerful individual or thousands of more average people. Other mounds formed animal or geometric figures. Hopewell earthworks also included canals that enabled trading networks to expand, bringing products from the Caribbean far into the interior. Those trading networks also carried maize, allowing more intensive agriculture to spread throughout the eastern woodlands of North America.

At Cahokia (kuh-HOE-kee-uh), near the confluence of the Mississippi and Missouri Rivers in Illinois, archaeologists have uncovered the largest mound of all, part of a ceremonial center and city that housed perhaps thirty-eight thousand people. Work on this complex of mounds, plazas, and houses—which covered 5½ square miles—began about 1050 C.E. and was completed about 1250 C.E. A fence of wooden posts surrounded the center of the complex. Several hundred rectangular mounds inside and outside the fence served as tombs and as the bases for temples and palaces. Within the fence, the largest mound rose in four stages to a height of one hundred feet and was nearly one thousand feet long. On its top stood a large building, used perhaps as a temple.

Cahokia engaged in long-distance trade reaching far across North America and became a highly stratified society. Mississippian mound builders relied on agriculture to support their complex cultures, and by the time Cahokia was built, maize agriculture had spread to the Atlantic coast. Particularly along riverbanks and the coastline, fields of maize, beans, and squash surrounded large, permanent villages containing many houses, all encompassed by walls made of earth and timber. Hunting and fishing provided animal protein, but the bulk of people's food came from farming.

At its peak in about 1150 Cahokia was the largest city north of Mesoamerica. However, construction of the interior wooden fence stripped much of the surrounding countryside of trees, which made spring floods worse and eventually destroyed much of the city. An earthquake at the beginning of the thirteenth century furthered the destruction, and the city never recovered. The worsening climate of the fourteenth century, which brought famine to Europe, probably also contributed to Cahokia's decline, and its population dispersed. Throughout Mississippian areas, the fifteenth century brought increased warfare and migration. Iroquois-speaking peoples in particular migrated into the region, sometimes displacing, through war, groups that had been living in these areas.

Kinship and Ancestors in the Andes

As in Mesoamerica, in the Andes social organization and religion shaped ideas of spiritual kinship as well as patterns of production and trade. The *ayllu* (EYE-you), or clan, served as the fundamental social unit of Andean society. Kinship was based on a shared ancestor, or *huaca*, who could be a once-living person whose remains were mummified and preserved, but could also be an animal spirit or a combination of the two. Members of an ayllu considered their huaca as more than a spirit: it owned lands the ayllu farmers tended, and the huaca served as the center of community obligations such as shared labor.

Ancestor worship provided the foundations of Andean religion and spirituality, served as the basis of authority, and guided food production. All members of the ayllu owed allegiance to *kuracas*, or clan leaders, who typically traced the most direct lineage to the ancestor, or huaca. This lineage made them both temporal and spiritual leaders of their ayllu: the kuraca was the living member of the community who had the most direct communion with the spirit world inhabited by the huaca. An Andean family's identity came from membership in an ayllu's ancestral kinship, and its subsistence came from participation in the broader community's shared farming across vertical climate zones. People often labored collectively and reciprocally. Within the ayllu, a reciprocal labor pool first tended to the fields of the huaca and the kuraca, then to the fields of widows and the infirm, and then to the other fields of the ayllu members.

Andean history unfolded in a cycle of centralization and decentralization. There were three great periods of

- **Moche** A Native American culture that thrived along Peru's northern coast between 100 and 800 C.E. The culture existed as a series of city-states and was distinguished by an extraordinarily rich and diverse pottery industry.
- **Inca** The name of the dynasty of rulers who built a large empire across the Andes that was at its peak around 1500.

centralization, which archaeologists call the Early, Middle, and Late Horizon. The Late Horizon, which included the Inca Empire, was the briefest, cut short by the Spanish conquest (see page 324). The first period, the Early Horizon (ca. 1200–200 B.C.E.), centered on the people of Chavín, upland from present-day Lima. The Chavín spread their religion along with technologies for the weaving and dyeing of wool and cotton. Weaving became the most widespread means of recording and representing information in the Andes.

After the end of the Early Horizon, regional states emerged, including **Moche** (MOH-cheh) civilization, which flourished along a 250-mile stretch of Peru's northern coast between 100 and 800 C.E. Rivers that flowed out of the Andes into the valleys allowed the Moche people to develop complex irrigation systems, with which they raised food crops and cotton. Each Moche valley contained a large ceremonial center with palaces and pyramids surrounded by settlements of up to ten thousand people. Their dazzling gold and silver artifacts, as well as elaborate headdresses, display a remarkable skill in metalwork. The Moche were also skilled potterymakers and weavers of cotton and other fibers. Their refined vessels, like the one shown at the beginning of this chapter, offer a rich look into their aesthetics and their world.

Politically, the Moche were organized into a series of small city-states rather than one unified state, and warfare was common among them. Beginning about 500 the Moche suffered several severe El Niños, changes in ocean current patterns in the Pacific that bring searing drought and flooding. They were not able to respond effectively to the devastation, and their urban population declined.

Pan-Andean cultures re-emerged during the Middle Horizon (500–1000 C.E.), centered to the south in Tiwanaku, near Lake Titicaca, and to the north at Wari, near present-day southern Peru. The city-state of Wari's dominion stretched from the altiplano north of Lake Titicaca to the Pacific coast, drawing on Moche cultural influences. Its reach between mountain and coastal regions led to extensive exchanges of goods and beliefs between ecologically different farming zones. The city-state of Tiwanaku extended its influence in the other direction, south of the lake. Both Wari and Tiwanaku practiced ancestor worship, and Tiwanaku religion centered on the figure of Viracocha, the god creator and father of humanity, who was identified with the sun and storms.

Storms and climate shifts were central to Andean people's worldview because changes in climate, particularly abrupt changes brought by El Niño, could devastate whole civilizations. El Niño disrupted Moche culture and contributed to the decline of Wari and Tiwanaku. The remains of elaborate projects designed to extend irrigation and reclaim land for farming along Lake Titicaca reveal the social and political impact of drought in already-arid Andean environments. As the Middle Horizon ended, the cities of Tiwanaku and Wari endured on a smaller scale, but between 1000 and 1200 C.E. they lost their regional influence. The eras between the Early, Middle, and Late Horizon, known as Intermediate Periods, were times of decentralization in which local cultures and practices re-emerged. It was out of these local developments that new centralizing empires would over time emerge.

The Incas

☐ What were the sources of strength and prosperity, and of problems, for the Incas?

Inca was the name of a ruling family that settled in the basin of Cuzco and formed the largest and last Andean empire. The empire, whose people we will call the Incas, was called Tawantinsuyu (TAH-want-een-soo-you), meaning "from the four parts, one," expressing the idea of a unified people stretching in all directions.

The Inca Model of Empire

In the Late Intermediate Period (1200–1470), the Pan-Andean influences of Wari and Tiwanaku waned. City-states around Lake Titicaca competed and fought with each other. The strongest ones to emerge again followed the division between the region north of the lake and toward the coast, and south of the lake and across the altiplano. To the north, the Chimu claimed the legacy of the Moche and Wari. To the south, the city of Cuzco became the hub of a growing kingdom under the hereditary control of the Inca (Map 11.3). *Inca* refers to the empire's ruler, while the empire was called Tawantinsuyu. According to their religious beliefs, the Inca rulers invented civilization. In reality, they inherited it from the civilizations of the Titicaca basin and the Chimu on the northern coast.

From the 1420s until 1438 Viracocha Inca emerged as the first Inca leader to attempt permanent conquest. Unlike the *sinchis* (SEEN-cheese), or kings, of earlier and rival city-states, Viracocha Inca fashioned himself an emperor and, in adopting the name Viracocha, connected himself to the god of creation. In 1438 rivals invaded Viracocha Inca's territories and he fled. His son, Pachacuti, remained in Cuzco and fended off the invaders. He crowned himself emperor and embarked on a campaign of conquest. Pachacuti Inca (r. 1438–1471) conquered the Chimu near the end of his reign, and he incorporated beliefs and practices from this northern civilization.

After conquering the Chimu, Pachacuti instituted practices that quickly expanded the empire across the Andes. He combined Andean ancestor worship with the Chimu system of a split inheritance, a combination that drove swift territorial expansion and transformed Tawantinsuyu into one of the largest empires in the world within less than fifty years. Under the system of ancestor worship, the Incas believed the dead emperor's spirit was still present, and they venerated him through his mummy. Split inheritance meant that the dead emperor retained all the lands he had conquered, commanded the loyalty of all his subjects, and continued to receive tribute. A *panaqa* (pan-AH-kah), a trust formed by his closest relatives, managed both the cult of his mummy and his temporal affairs. Chimu split inheritance became the political structure that determined the Inca emperor's authority.

When the ruler died, his corpse was preserved as a mummy in elaborate clothing and housed in a sacred and magnificent chamber. A sixteenth-century account of the death of Pachacuti Inca in 1471 described the practices for burying and honoring him:

> He was buried by putting his body in the earth in a large new clay urn, with him very well dressed. Pachacuti Inca [had] ordered that a golden image made to resemble him be placed on top of his tomb. And it was to be worshiped in place of him by the people who went there. . . . [He had] ordered those of his own lineage to bring this statue out for the feasts that were held in Cuzco. When they brought it out like this, they sang about the things that the Inca did in his life, both in the wars and in his city. Thus they served and revered him, changing its garments as he used to do, and serving it as he was served when he was alive.[1]

The panaqa of descendants of each dead ruler managed his lands and used his income to care for his mummy, maintain his cult, and support themselves, all at great expense. When a ruler died, one of his sons was named the new Inca emperor. He received the title, but not the lands and tribute—nor, for that matter, the

Mapping the Past

MAP 11.3 The Inca Empire, 1532 Andean peoples turned their stark mountain landscape to their advantage by settling and farming in vertical archipelagos. Settlements were located at temperate altitudes, while farming and herding took place at higher and lower altitudes.

ANALYZING THE MAP In what ways did Andean peoples turn their mountain landscape from an obstacle into a resource?

CONNECTIONS What types of geographic features did other peoples of the Americas, or peoples in other regions of the world, adapt to their advantage? How did adaptation to their geography shape those societies?

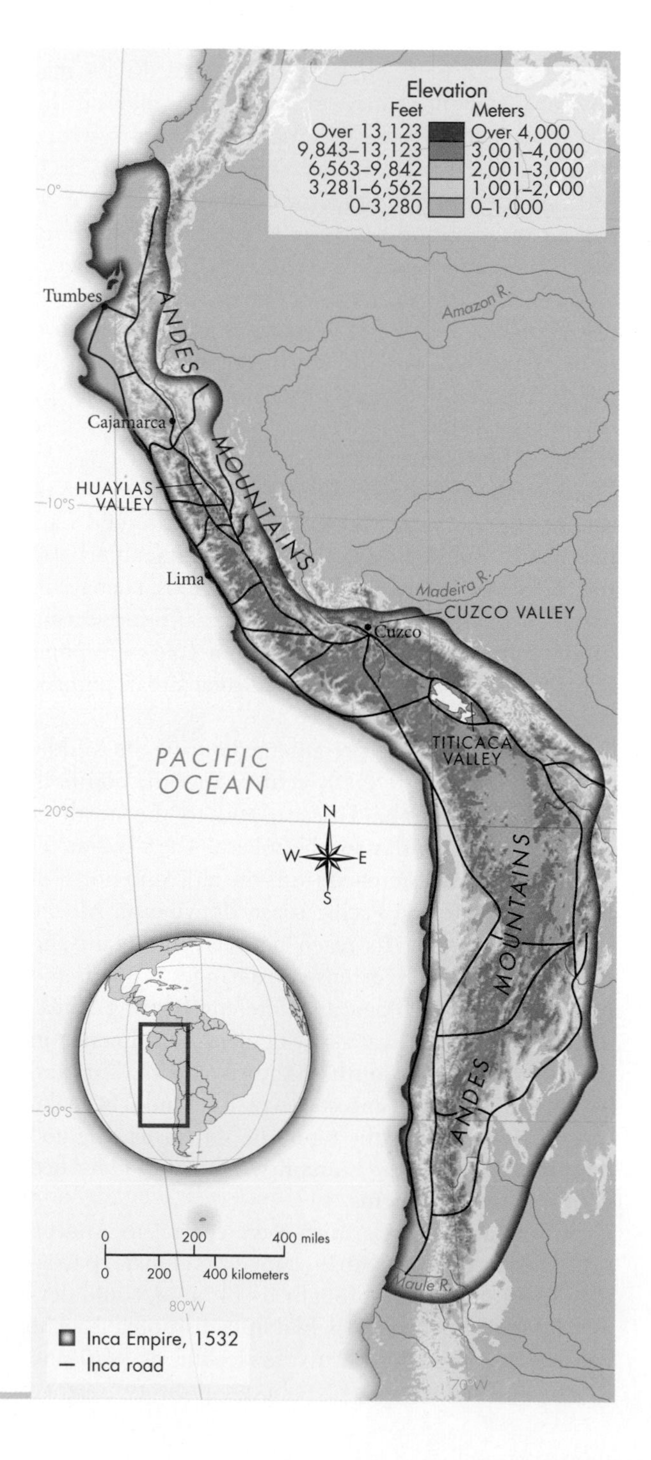

Machu Picchu The Inca ruins of Machu Picchu rise spectacularly above the steep valley of the Urubamba River. The site was built around 1450 as a royal estate and abandoned after the Spanish conquest. (Tony Camacho/Photo Researchers, Inc.)

direct allegiance of the nobility, bound as it was to the deceased ruler. The new emperor built his own power and wealth by conquering new lands.

Inca Imperial Expansion

The combination of ancestor worship and split inheritance provided the logic and impulse for expanding Inca power. The desire for conquest provided incentives for courageous (or ambitious) nobles: those who succeeded in battle and gained new territories for the state could expect to receive lands, additional wives, servants, herds of llamas, gold, silver, fine clothes, and other symbols of high status. Even common soldiers who distinguished themselves in battle could be rewarded with booty and raised to noble status. Under Pachacuti Inca and his successors, Inca domination was extended by warfare to the frontier of present-day Ecuador and Colombia in the north and to the Maule River in present-day Chile in the south, an area of about 350,000 square miles. Eighty provinces, scores of ethnic groups, and 16 million people came under Inca control.

The Incas pursued the integration of regions they conquered by imposing their language and their gods. Magnificent temples scattered throughout the expanding empire housed images of these gods. Priests led prayers and elaborate rituals, and during occasions such as terrible natural disasters or great military victories they sacrificed humans. The Incas forced conquered peoples to adopt **Quechua** (KEH-chuh-wuh), the official language of the empire, which extinguished many regional languages, although another major Andean language, Aymara, endured. Though Quechua did not exist in written form until the Spanish in Peru adopted it as a second official language, it is still spoken by millions in Peru and Bolivia, as well as in regions of Ecuador, Argentina, and Chile.

The pressure for growth strained the Inca Empire. Open lands became scarce, so the Incas tried to penetrate the tropical Amazon forest east of the Andes—an effort that led to repeated military disasters. Traditionally, the Incas waged war with highly trained armies drawn up in massed formation and fought pitched battles on level ground, often engaging in hand-to-hand combat. But in dense jungles the troops could not maneuver or maintain order against enemies, who used

- **Quechua** First deemed the official language of the Incas under Pachacuti, it is still spoken by most Peruvians today.

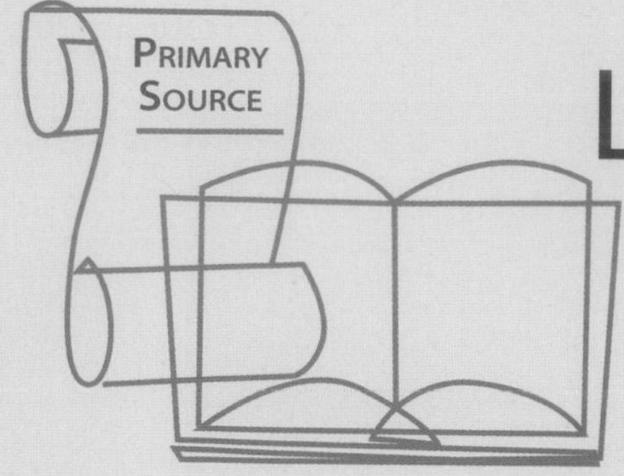

Listening to the Past

Felipe Guaman Poma de Ayala, *The First New Chronicle and Good Government*

Felipe Guaman Poma de Ayala (1550?–1616) came from a noble indigenous family in Peru. He spoke Quechua, Aymara, and Spanish and was baptized as a Christian. As an assistant to a Spanish friar and a Spanish judge, he saw firsthand the abuses of the Spanish authorities in what had been the Inca Empire. In the early seventeenth century he began writing and illustrating what became his masterpiece, a handwritten book of almost eight hundred pages of text and nearly four hundred line drawings addressed to the king of Spain that related the history of the Inca Empire and the realities of Spanish rule. He hoped to send the book to Spain, where it would convince the king to make reforms that would bring about the "good government" of the book's title. (The book apparently never reached the king, though it did make its way to Europe. It was discovered in the Danish Royal Library in Copenhagen in 1908.) In the following section, Guaman Poma sets out certain traditional age-group categories of Inca society, which he terms "paths," ten for men and ten for women.

"The first path was that of the brave men, the soldiers of war. They were thirty-three years of age (they entered this path as young as twenty-five, and left it at fifty). These brave men were held very much apart and distinguished in every manner possible. The Inca [the Inca ruler] selected some of these Indians to serve in his battles and wars. He selected some from among these brave Indians to settle as *mitmaqs* (foreigners) in other provinces, giving them more than enough land, both pasture and cropland, to multiply, and giving each of them a woman from the same land. He did this to keep his kingdom secure; they served as overseers. . . .

The Fifth Path was that of the *sayapayac* [those who stand upright]. These were the Indians of the watch, aged from eighteen to twenty years. They served as messenger boys between one pueblo and another, and to other nearby places in the valley. They also herded flocks, and accompanied the Indians of war and the great lords and captains. They also carried food. . . .

The Eighth Path was that of boys aged from five to nine years. These were the "boys who play" (*puellacoc wamracuna*). They served their mothers and fathers in whatever ways they could, and bore many whippings and thumpings; they also served by playing with the toddlers and by rocking and watching over the babies in cradles. . . .

The Tenth Path was that of those called *wawa quirawpi cac* (newborn babies at the breast, in cradles), from the age of one month. It is right for others to serve them; their mothers must necessarily serve them for no other person can give milk to these children. . . .

The First Path was that of the married women and widows called *auca camayocpa warmin* [the warriors' women], whose occupation is weaving fine cloth for the Inca, the other lords, the captains, and the soldiers. They were thirty-three years of age when they married; up until then, they remained virgins and maidens. . . . These wives of brave men were not free [from tribute obligations]. These women had the occupation of weaving fine *awasca* cloth and spinning yarn; they assisted the commons in their pueblos and provinces, and they assisted with everything their titled noble lords decreed. . . .

The Sixth Path was that of those called *coro tasqui-cunas, rotusca tasqui*, which means "young girls with short-cropped hair." They were from twelve to eighteen years of age and served their fathers, mothers, and grandmothers. They also began to

guerrilla tactics against them. Another source of stress came from revolts among subject peoples in conquered territories. Even the system of roads and message-carrying runners couldn't keep up with the administrative needs of the empire. The average runner could cover about 175 miles per day—a remarkable feat of physical endurance, especially at a high altitude—but the larger the empire became, the greater the distances to be covered grew. The round trip from the capital at Cuzco to Quito in Ecuador, for example, took from ten to twelve days, so an emperor might have to base urgent decisions on incomplete or out-of-date information. The empire was overextended.

Imperial Needs and Obligations

At its height, the Inca Empire extended over 2,600 miles. The challenges of sustaining an empire with that reach, not to mention one built so fast, required extraordinary resourcefulness. The Inca Empire met these demands by adapting aspects of local culture to meet imperial needs. For instance, the empire demanded that the ayllus, the local communities with shared ancestors, include imperial tribute in the rotation of labor and the distribution of harvested foods. (See "Listening to the Past: Felipe Guaman Poma de Ayala, *The First New Chronicle and Good Government*," above.)

serve the great ladies so that they could learn to spin yarn and weave delicate materials. They served as animal herders and workers in the fields, and in making *chica* [corn beer] for their fathers and mothers, and they assisted in other occupations insofar as they could, helping out . . . they were filled with obedience and respect, and were taught to cook, spin, and weave. Their hair was kept cropped until they reached the age of thirty, when they were married and given the dowry of their destitution and poverty.

The Seventh Path was that of the girls called flower pickers. . . . They picked flowers to dye wool for *cumpis*, cloth, and other things, and they picked the edible herbs mentioned above, which they dried out and stored in the warehouse to be eaten the following year. These girls were from nine to twelve years of age. . . .

The Ninth Path was that of the girls aged one and two, who were called *llucac warmi wawa* ("young girls who crawl"). They do nothing; instead, others serve them. Better said, they ought to be served by their mothers, who should be exempt [from tribute] because of the work of raising their children. Their mothers have to walk around carrying them, and never let go of their hands. ”

Source: Felipe Guaman Poma de Ayala, *The First New Chronicle and Good Government* (abridged), translated by David Frye (Cambridge, Mass.: Hackett Publishing Company, 2006).

Guaman Poma's line drawing shows a woman weaving fine cloth on a back-strap loom. (De Agostini Picture Library/The Bridgeman Art Library)

QUESTIONS FOR ANALYSIS

1. The "First Path" among both men and women is the one with the highest status. Judging by the way Guaman Poma describes these, what do the Incas especially value? How do his descriptions of other paths support your conclusions about this?
2. In what ways are the paths set out for boys and men different from those for girls and women? In what ways are they similar? What does this suggest about Inca society?
3. Guaman Poma wrote this about eighty years after the Spanish conquest of Peru. How do the date and the colonial setting affect your evaluation of this work as a source?

As each new Inca emperor conquered new lands and built his domain, he mobilized people and resources by drawing on local systems of labor and organization. Much as ayllus had developed satellite communities called mitmaq, populated by settlers from the ayllu in order to take advantage of remote farming areas, the emperor relocated families or even whole villages over long distances to consolidate territorial control or quell unrest. What had been a community practice became a tool of imperial expansion. The emperor sent mitmaq settlers, known as *mitmaquisuna*, far and wide, creating diverse ethnic enclaves. The emperor also consolidated the empire by regulating marriage, using maternal lines to build kinship among conquered peoples. Inca rulers and nobles married the daughters of elite families among the peoples they conquered. Very high-ranking Inca men sometimes had many wives, but marriage among commoners was generally monogamous.

The reciprocal labor carried out within ayllus expanded into a labor tax called the *mit'a* (MEE-tuh), which rotated among households in an ayllu throughout the year. Tribute paid in labor provided the means for building the infrastructure of empire. Rotations of laborers carried out impressive engineering feats, allowing the vast empire to extend over the most difficult and inhospitable terrain. An excellent system of roads—averaging three feet in width, some paved and others not—facilitated the transportation of armies and the rapid communication of royal orders by runners. Like Persian and Roman roads, these great feats of Inca engineering linked an empire. The government also made an ayllu responsible for maintaining state-owned granaries, which distributed grain in times of shortage and famine and supplied assistance in natural disasters.

On these roads Inca officials, tax collectors, and accountants traveled throughout the empire, using elaborate khipus to record financial and labor obligations, the output of fields, population levels, land transfers, and other numerical records. Khipus may also have been used to record narrative history, but this is speculation, as knowledge of how to read them died out after the Spanish conquest. Only around 650 khipus are known to survive today, because colonial Spaniards destroyed them, believing khipus might contain religious messages that would encourage people to resist Spanish authority.

Palace Doorway Lintel at Yaxchilan, Mexico
Lady Xoc, principal wife of King Shield-Jaguar, who holds a torch over her, pulls a thorn-lined rope through her tongue to sanctify with her blood the birth of a younger wife's child—reflecting the importance of blood sacrifice in Maya culture. The elaborate headdresses and clothes of the couple show their royal status. (© The Trustees of the British Museum/Art Resource, NY)

The Maya and Teotihuacan

☐ How did the Maya and Teotihuacan develop prosperous and stable societies in the classical era?

In Mesoamerica the classical period (300 C.E. to 900 C.E.) saw major advances in religion, art, architecture, and farming, akin to those of the classical civilizations of the Mediterranean (see Chapters 5 and 6). It saw the rise of many city-states, and although the **Maya** city-states, which peaked between 600 C.E. and 900 C.E., were the longest lasting, others were significant as well. The city of **Teotihuacan** in the Valley of Mexico emerged as a major center of trade (300–650 C.E.). It was followed by the postclassical Toltec Empire (900–1200 C.E.), which adapted the cultural, ritual, and aesthetic practices that influenced later empires like the Aztecs.

Maya Agriculture and Trade

The Maya inhabited the highlands of Guatemala and the Yucatán peninsula in present-day Mexico and Belize. Their physical setting shaped two features of Maya society. First, the abundance of high-quality limestone allowed them to build monumental architecture. Second, limestone formations created deep natural wells called *cenotes* (say-NOH-tehs), which became critical sources of water in an often-arid environment. Cenotes were essential to farming and also became important religious and spiritual sites. The staple crop of the Maya was maize, often raised in small remote plots called *milpas* in combination with other foodstuffs, including beans, squash, chili peppers, some root crops, and fruit trees. They farmed on raised narrow rectangular plots that they built above the seasonally flooded low-lying land bordering rivers.

The entire Maya region may have had as many as 14 million inhabitants. Sites like Uxmal, Uaxactún, Copán, Piedras Negras, Tikal, Palenque, and Chichén Itzá (Map 11.4) emerged as independent city-states, each ruled by a hereditary king. These cities produced

MAP 11.4 The Maya World, 300–900 C.E. The Maya built dozens of cities linked together in trading networks of roads and rivers. Only the largest of them are shown here.

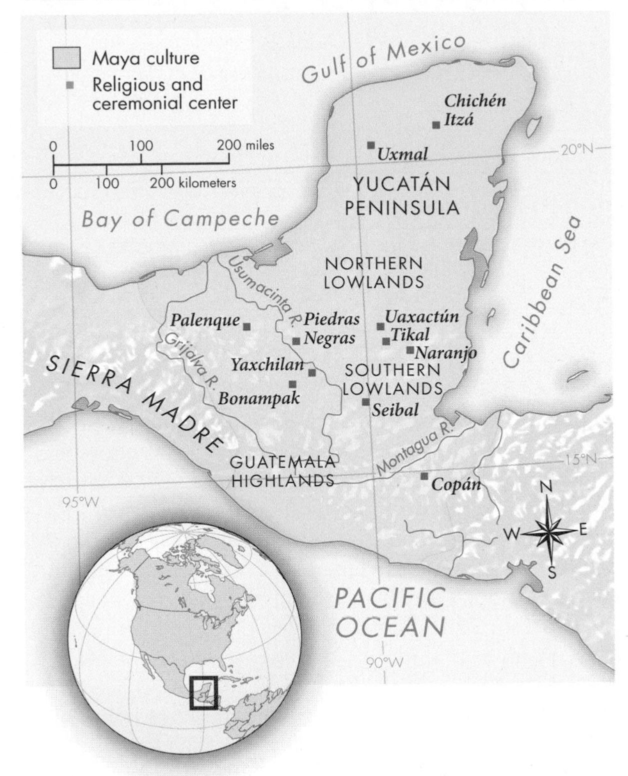

polychrome pottery and featured altars, engraved pillars, masonry temples, palaces for nobles, pyramids where nobles were buried, and courts for ball games. The largest site, Tikal, may have had forty thousand people and served as a religious and ceremonial center. A hereditary nobility owned land, waged war, traded, exercised political power, and directed religious rituals. Artisans and scribes made up the social level below. Other residents were farmers, laborers, and slaves, the latter including prisoners of war.

At Maya markets, jade, obsidian, beads of red spiny oyster shell, lengths of cloth, and cacao beans—all in high demand in the Mesoamerican world—served as media of exchange. The extensive trade among Maya communities, plus a common language, promoted unity among the peoples of the region. Merchants traded beyond Maya regions, particularly with the Zapotecs of Monte Albán, in the Valley of Oaxaca, and with the Teotihuacanos of the central valley of Mexico. Since this long-distance trade played an important part in international relations, the merchants conducting it were high nobles or even members of the royal family.

Maya Science and Religion

The Maya developed the most complex writing system in the Americas, a script with nearly a thousand glyphs. They recorded important events and observations in books made of bark paper and deerskin, on pottery, on stone pillars called steles, and on temples and other buildings. Archaeologists and anthropologists have demonstrated that the inscriptions are historical documents that record major events in the lives of Maya kings and nobles. As was common for elites everywhere, Maya leaders stressed the ancient ancestry of their families. "In the year 3114 B.C.E. my forefathers were present, during the Creation of the World," reads one stele in the city of Tikal, recording the lineage of the Maya lord Kan Boar.[2]

Learning about Maya religion through written records is difficult. In the sixteenth century Spanish religious authorities viewed Maya books as demonic and ordered them destroyed. Only a handful survived, offering a window into religious rituals and practices, as well as Maya astronomy. (See "Viewpoints 11.1: Creation in the *Popol Vuh* and in Okanogan Tradition," page 312.) From observation of the earth's movements around the sun, the Maya used a calendar of eighteen 20-day months and one 5-day month, for a total of 365 days, along with the 260-day calendar based on 20 weeks of 13 days. When these calendars coincided every fifty-two years, the Maya celebrated with feasting, ball-game competitions, and religious observance. These and other observances included blood sacrifice by kings to honor the gods.

Using a system of bars, where a single bar equals five (— = 5) and a single dot equals one (• = 1), the Maya devised a form of mathematics based on the vigesimal (20) rather than the decimal (10) system. More unusual was their use of the number zero, which allows for more complex calculations than are possible in number systems without it. The zero may have actually been discovered by the Olmecs, who used it in figuring their calendar, but the Maya used it mathematically as well. The Maya's proficiency with numbers made them masters of abstract knowledge—notably in astronomy and mathematics.

Between the eighth and tenth centuries the Maya abandoned their cultural and ceremonial centers. Archaeologists attribute their decline to a combination of agricultural failures due to drought, land exhaustion, overpopulation, disease, and constant wars fought for economic and political gain. These wars brought widespread destruction, which aggravated agricultural problems. Royalty also suffered from the decline in Maya

- **Maya** A highly developed Mesoamerican culture centered in the Yucatán peninsula of Mexico. The Maya created the most intricate writing system in the Western Hemisphere.
- **Teotihuacan** The monumental city-state that dominated trade in classical era Mesoamerica.

Viewpoints 11.1

Creation in the *Popul Vuh* and in Okanogan Tradition

• *Every people of the world appears to have had a creation account that describes the way the world and the people within it came to be. These are excerpts from the accounts of the Maya people, as recorded in the sixteenth century in the* Popul Vuh, *and of the Okanogan people of the Pacific Northwest, as recorded in the twentieth century from oral traditions.*

Popul Vuh

"Heart of Sky arrived here with Sovereign and Quetzal Serpent [three creator gods] in the darkness, in the night. . . . They thought and they pondered. They reached an accord, bringing together their words and their thoughts. . . . Then the earth was created by them. Merely their word brought about the creation of it. In order to create the earth, they said, "Earth," and immediately it was created. . . . Then were conceived the animals of the mountains, the guardians of the forest, and all that populate the mountains — the deer and the birds, the puma and the jaguar, the serpent and the rattlesnake. . . . This, then, is the beginning of the conception of humanity, when that which would become the flesh of mankind was sought. Then spoke they who are called She Who Has Borne Children and He Who Has Begotten Sons, the Framer and the Shaper [four other gods associated with creation], Sovereign and Quetzal Serpent: "The dawn approaches, and our work is not completed. A provider and a sustainer have yet to appear — a child of light, a son of light. Humanity has yet to appear to populate the face of the earth," they said. Thus they gathered together and joined their thoughts in the darkness, in the night. They searched and they sifted. Here they thought and they pondered. Their thoughts came forth bright and clear. They discovered and established that which would become the flesh of humanity. . . . Thus their frame and shape were given expression by our first Mother and our first Father. Their flesh was merely yellow ears of maize and white ears of maize. . . . And so there were four who were made, and mere food was their flesh. . . . Then their companions, their wives, also came to be. It was the gods who conceived them as well."

Okanogan Tradition

"The earth was once a human being: Old One made her out of a woman. "You will be the mother of all people," he said.

Earth is alive yet, but she has been changed. The soil is her flesh, the rocks are her bones, the wind is her breath, trees and grass are her hair. She lives spread out, and we live on her. When she moves, we have an earthquake.

After taking the woman and changing her to earth, Old One gathered some of her flesh and rolled it into balls, as people do with mud or clay. He made the first group of these balls into the ancients, the beings of the early world. . . .

Besides the ancients, real people and real animals lived on the earth at that time. Old One made the people out of the last balls of mud he took from the earth. He rolled them over and over, shaped them like Indians, and blew on them to bring them alive. They were so ignorant that they were the most helpless of all the creatures Old One had made.

Old One made people and animals into males and females so that they might breed and multiply. Thus all living things came from the earth. When we look around, we see part of our mother everywhere."

QUESTIONS FOR ANALYSIS

1. Who carries out the creation of the world and human beings in each of these accounts? How does the process of creation combine the spiritual and the material world?
2. How are humans created? What does this process suggest about the relations between humans and the rest of creation?

☐ Picturing the Past

Maya Calendar This Maya calendar (at right) from Yaxchilan, Mexico, bears a date equivalent to February 11, 526 C.E. The animals represent blocks of time, while the dots and profiles of gods mark numbers. The monkey (right column, second from top) signals a day date. The day is defined by the god's head in its hand, which means six, and the skull beneath the hand, which means ten: sixteen days. (Otis Imboden/National Geographic Creative)

ANALYZING THE IMAGE Calendars show not only dates but also the sense of time of the people who used them. What do the figures in this calendar show you about the Maya and their world?

CONNECTIONS How does the Maya system of numbers (near right) resemble other numerical systems with which you are familiar?

civilization: just as in good times kings attributed moral authority and prosperity to themselves, so in bad times, when military, economic, and social conditions deteriorated, their subjects saw the kings as the cause and turned against them.

Decline did not mean disappearance. The Maya ceased building monumental architecture around 900 C.E., which likely marked the end of the era of rule by powerful kings who could mobilize the labor required to build it. The Maya persisted in farming communities, a pattern of settlement that helped preserve their culture and language in the face of external pressures. They resisted invasions from warring Aztec armies by dispersing from their towns and villages and residing in their milpas during invasions. When Aztec armies entered the Yucatán, communities vanished, leaving Aztec armies with nothing to conquer. This tactic continued to serve the Maya under Spanish colonial rule. Though Spaniards claimed the Yucatán, the Maya continued to use the strategy that had served them so well in resisting the Aztecs. Many communities avoided Spanish domination for generations. The last independent Maya kingdom succumbed only in 1697, and resistance continued well into the nineteenth century.

Teotihuacan and the Toltecs

The most powerful city in classical Mesoamerica emerged at Teotihuacan, northwest of the lands of the Maya. By 100 C.E. it had a population of 60,000. At its height, between 300 and 600 C.E., its population reached as high as 250,000, making it one of the largest cities in the world at that time. The heart of Teotihuacan was a massive ceremonial center anchored by a colossal Pyramid of the Sun, 700 feet wide and 200 feet tall, and a Pyramid of the Moon. Connecting them was the Avenue of the Dead, 150 feet wide and 2 miles long, along which stood the homes of scores of priests and lords. The monuments of Teotihuacan were so massive that centuries later the Aztecs thought they had been built by giants. A cave under the Pyramid of the Sun suggests the ceremonial center's origins. Caves symbolized the womb from which the sun and moon were born. It is possible that, like other pilgrimage sites around the world that became important marketplaces, the cave served as both a ceremonial and trade center.[3]

The monuments of the ceremonial district of Teotihuacan were matched in grandeur by the city's markets, which extended its influence across Mesoamerica.

The Pyramid of the Sun at Teotihuacan Built in several stages beginning in about 100 C.E., the Pyramid of the Sun has sides measuring 700 feet long and 200 feet high. Originally it was covered with lime plaster decorated with brightly colored murals. Smaller pyramids surround it in what was the heart of the bustling city of Teotihuacan. (© age fotostock/SuperStock)

The city's trade empire lay in its control of a resource vital to Mesoamerican society and religion: obsidian, a glasslike volcanic rock that could be worked into objects with both material and spiritual uses. Obsidian knives were used for daily tasks and for important rituals such as the blood sacrifice practiced by the Maya. Teotihuacan merchants traded directly with Maya and Zapotec kings, whose local control of obsidian enhanced their power. Teotihuacan's power was unrivaled in its time, so it was able to extend its influence through trade networks, which included a colony in Kaminaljuyu, near present-day Guatemala City. This outpost in another obsidian-rich area allowed Teotihuacan to dominate the obsidian market.[4]

Religion followed trade. Teotihuacan was a religious and cultural center whose influence extended over large distances. One factor in the city's success was its ethnic diversity. Teotihuacan grew through the migration of outsiders along trade networks, and these groups built separate ethnic neighborhoods. Two gods that were particularly important to classical period civilizations were Tlaloc (Chac in Maya), the god of rain, and Quetzalcoatl, the plumed serpent. The worship of these deities became an enduring aspect of Mesoamerican religion that the Toltecs and the Aztecs embraced. In fact, after their defeat by the Spanish, Aztecs would invoke prophesies of Quetzalcoatl as foretelling the arrival of the Spaniard Hernán Cortés.[5]

Teotihuacan thrived because it controlled trade of the most valuable goods. This helped it grow, and in turn the trade networks it sustained helped other regions in Mesoamerica develop through intensified contact with other groups and the spread of technologies. Over time, improvements in other regions decreased Teotihuacan's comparative advantage, as its trading partners produced increasingly valuable goods, spurring competition. By 600 its influence had begun to decline, and in 650 the residents of the city seem to have burned its ceremonial center in what may have been a revolt against the city's leadership. The city had ceased to be a major trade center by 900 C.E.[6]

The Toltecs (900–1200 C.E.) filled the void created by Teotihuacan's decline. The Toltecs inaugurated a new era, the postclassical, which ended with the Spanish conquest of the Aztec Empire. The postclassical period saw fewer technological or artistic advances. Instead it was a time of intensified warfare in Mesoamerica and a time of rapid and bold imperial expansion through conquest. After the decline of Teotihuacan, whose rulers had considered the Toltecs barbarians and kept

The Toltecs, ca. 900–1200 C.E.

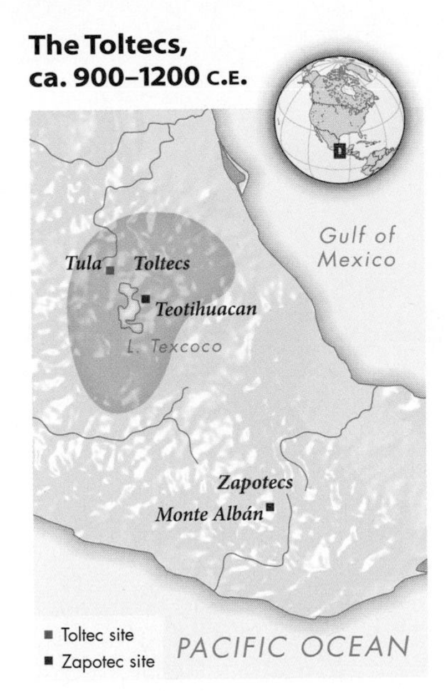

them out of the Valley of Mexico, the Toltecs entered and settled in Tula. The Toltecs' legend of their origins held that in 968 C.E. their people were led into the valley by a charismatic leader who fused himself to the plumed serpent god and called himself Topiltzin-Quetzalcoatl. In 987, amid infighting, Topiltzin-Quetzalcoatl and his followers were expelled from Tula. They marched south, where they conquered and settled in a Maya region.

The Toltec origin myth later merged with the mythology of the Aztecs, who fashioned themselves modern Toltecs, and in turn these myths were adapted in the sixteenth century in order to explain conquest by the Spanish. Through this long and distorted course, the legend went like this: Topiltzin-Quetzalcoatl and his followers marked their journey into exile by shooting arrows into saplings, forming crosslike images. Settled in the east, he sent word that he would return to take back his rightful throne in the Mesoamerican calendar year Ce Acatl. And by tradition, the god Quetzalcoatl's human manifestation was bearded and light skinned. Ce Acatl corresponded to the European year 1519, when Hernán Cortés marched into the Aztec capital Tenochtitlan (light skinned, bearded, and coming from the east bearing crosses). Perhaps the demise of the Aztec Empire at the hands of a vengeful god had been foretold by half a millennium.

The Toltecs built a military empire and gradually absorbed the culture, practices, and religion of their neighbors in the Valley of Mexico. Their empire waned amid war, drought, and famine over the eleventh and twelfth centuries. After the demise of the Toltec Empire, city-states in the Valley of Mexico competed with each other militarily and to cast themselves as the legitimate descendants and heirs of the Toltecs.

The Aztecs

☐ How did the Aztecs build on the achievements of earlier Mesoamerican cultures and develop new traditions to create their large empire?

According to their oral tradition, between 1300 and 1345 a group of **Nahuatl**-speaking people, the **Mexica**, migrated southward from what is now northern Mexico, settling on the shores and islands of Lake Texcoco in the central valley of Mexico (Map 11.5). They formed a vast and rapidly expanding empire centered around the twin cities of Tenochtitlan (tay-nawch-TEET-lahn) and Tlatelolco, which by 1500 were probably larger than any city in Europe except Istanbul. This was the Aztec Empire, a network of alliances and tributary states with the Mexica at its core. Examining the means by which they formed and expanded their empire, as well as the vulnerabilities of that empire, can help us build a rich understanding of Mesoamerican society.

The Mexica: From Vassals to Masters

In the early fourteenth century, the Mexica, a migrant, seminomadic group, arrived in the crowded and highly cultured Valley of Mexico. They found an environment that, since the collapse of the Toltec Empire in the twelfth century, had divided into small, fragile alliances that battled to claim the legacy of the Toltecs. At the moment of their arrival, control over much of the valley lay in the hands of the Tepanec Alliance. The Mexica negotiated the right to settle on a swampy island on Lake Texcoco in exchange for military service to the Tepanecs.

Residents of the city-states that ringed the lake looked down upon the Mexica. But the Mexica adopted the customs of their new region, organizing clan-based communities called *calpolli*, incorporating the deities of their new neighbors, and serving the Tepanecs. They gradually reclaimed land around their island to form two urban centers, Tenochtitlan and Tlatelolco. They adopted a farming technique used in parts of Lake Texcoco called *chinampa* (chee-NAHM-pah) agriculture. Though later chroniclers would frequently refer to chinampas as floating gardens, they were a means of land reclamation by which farmers built up reeds and mud along the margins of Lake Texcoco to gradually extend farming well into the lake.

- **Nahuatl** The language of both the Toltecs and the Aztecs.
- **Mexica** The dominant ethnic group of what is now Mexico, who created an empire based on war and religion that reached its height in the mid-1400s; in the nineteenth century the people became known as Aztecs.

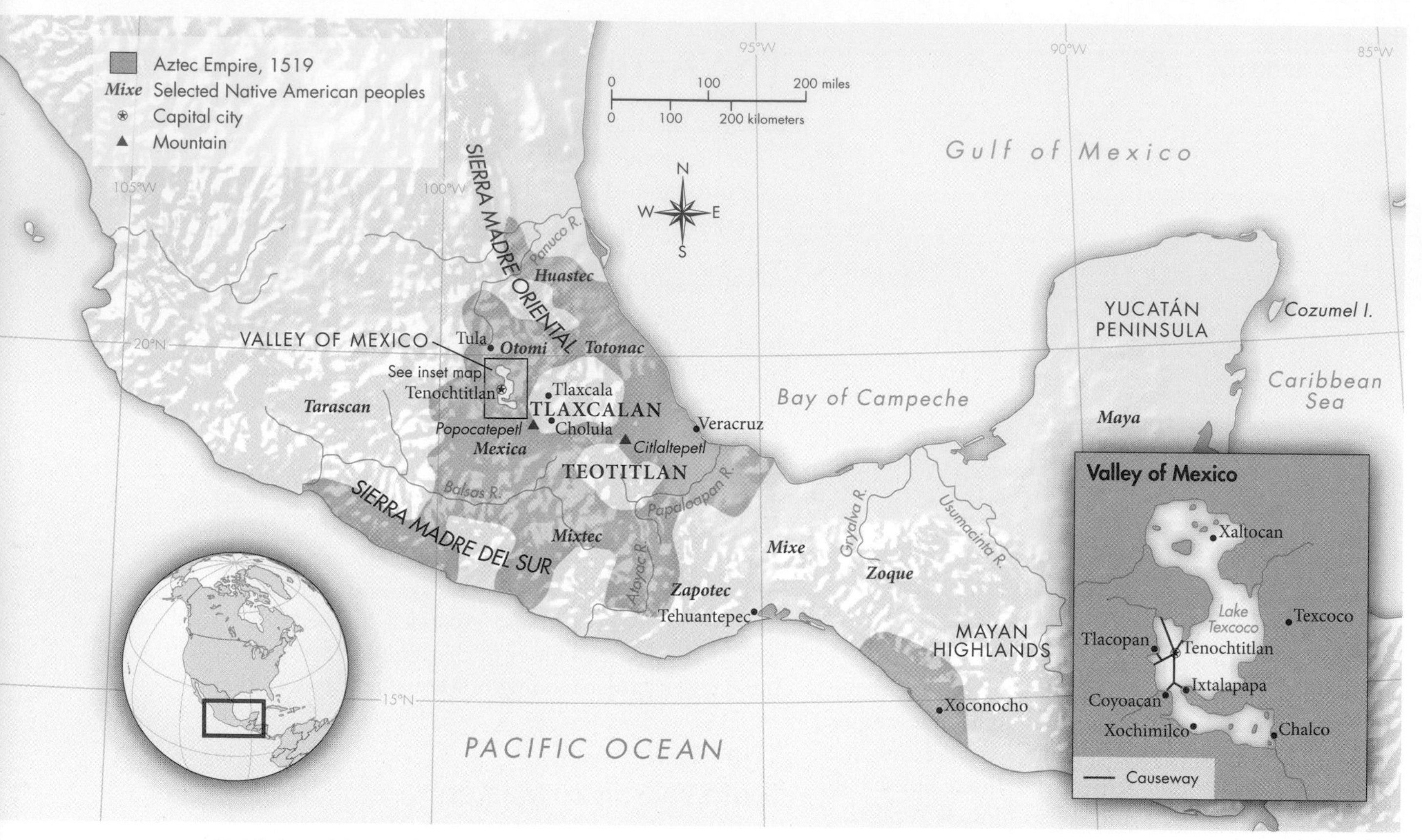

MAP 11.5 The Aztec (Mexica) Empire in 1519 The Mexica migrated into the central valley of what is now Mexico from the north, conquering other groups and establishing an empire, later called the Aztec Empire. The capital of the Aztec Empire was Tenochtitlan, built on islands in Lake Texcoco.

At its peak, the chinampa farming system formed vast areas of tidy rectangular plots divided by canals that allowed for canoe transportation of people and crops. When the Spanish entered **Tenochtitlan** (which they called Mexico City) in November 1519, they could not believe their eyes. The Aztec city, built in 1325, impressed them greatly. Bernal Díaz del Castillo, one of Cortés's companions, reported:

> When we saw all those cities and villages built in the water, and other great towns on dry land, and that straight and level causeway leading to Mexico, we were astounded. These great towns and cues (temples) and buildings rising from the water, all made of stone, seemed like an enchanted vision. . . . Indeed, some of our soldiers asked whether it was not all a dream.[7]

Over time, the Mexica improved their standing in the Valley of Mexico by asking a powerful neighboring city-state to name a prince considered to be of noble Toltec descent to rule them, forming a dynasty that would become the most powerful in Mesoamerica. The new ruler, or *tlatoani* (tlah-toh-annie), Acamapichtli (ah-camp-itch-lee), brought the Mexica higher social rank and the ability to form alliances. While the naming of a new ruler of noble origins initially made the Mexica into closer allies of their neighbors, it gave them their own noble dynasty of rulers who gradually made the Mexica more militarily powerful and more competitive with neighboring states, which they would eventually dominate.

By the end of Acamapichtli's reign (1372–1391), the Mexica had fully adapted to their new environment and had adopted the highly stratified social organization that would encourage the ambitions of their own warrior class. Under the rule of Acamapichtli's successors Huitzilihuitl (r. 1391–1417) and Chimalpopoca (r. 1417–1427), the Mexica remained subordinate to the Tepanec Alliance. But in 1427 a dispute over the succession of the Tepanec king created an opportunity for the Mexica.

Anthropologist Ross Hassig described the manner in which Mexica ruler Itzcoatl (r. 1427–1440) turned the dispute to his advantage: "Itzcoatl sent his nephew,

- **Tenochtitlan** A large and prosperous Aztec city that was built starting in 1325. The Spanish admired it when they entered in 1519.

Chinampa Farming This illustration shows farmers in the Aztec Empire building chinampa farming plots by reclaiming land from Lake Texcoco. Farmers created the plots by packing them with vegetation and mud from the lake, supporting their boundaries by planting willow trees. Chinampas allowed for intensive farming in a region that had limited rainfall, and the canals between them permitted easy transportation. (© Gianni Dagli Orti/Corbis)

Tlacaelel, to Azcapotzalco [the Tepanec capital], where he asked first if peace was possible. On learning it was not, he smeared pitch on the king and feathered his head, as was done with the dead, and gave him a shield, sword, and gilded arrows — the insignia of the sovereign — and thus declared war." In 1428, the Mexica formed a coalition with other cities in the Valley of Mexico, besieged the Tepanec capital for nearly three months, and then defeated it. A powerful new coalition had emerged: the Triple Alliance, with the Mexica as its most powerful partner. The Aztec Empire was born.[8]

To consolidate the new political order, Tlatoani Itzcoatl, guided by his nephew Tlacaelel, burned his predecessors' books and drafted a new history. Tlacaelel advised his tlatoani: "It is not necessary for all the common people to know of the writings: government will be defamed, and this will only spread sorcery in the lands; for they contained many falsehoods."[9]

The new history placed the warrior cult and its religious pantheon at the center of Mexica history, making the god of war, Huitzilopochtli, the patron deity of the empire. Huitzilopochtli, "Hummingbird of the South," was a god unique to the Mexica who, according to the new official origin stories of the Mexica people, had ordered them to march south until they found an island where he gave them the sign of an eagle eating a serpent, which appeared to them in Tenochtitlan. (See "Individuals in Society: Tlacaelel," page 318.)

Under the new imperial order, government offices combined military, religious, and political functions. Eventually, tlatoanis formalized these functions into distinct noble and common classes. This gave soldiers opportunities for social advancement. After securing five sacrificial victims in battle, a commoner soldier entered the lower nobility, which freed him from paying tribute. He could show his new status by publicly wearing feathers and flowers. The Valley of Mexico had sustained itself through chinampa agriculture, but as the empire grew, crops provided as tribute from distant

Individuals in Society

Tlacaelel

THE HUMMINGBIRD GOD HUITZILOPOCHTLI WAS originally a somewhat ordinary god of war and of young men, but in the fifteenth century he was elevated in status among the Mexica. He became increasingly associated with the sun and gradually became the most important Mexica deity. This change appears to have been primarily the work of Tlacaelel, the very long-lived chief adviser to the emperors Itzcoatl (r. 1427–1440), Moctezuma I (r. 1440–1469), and Axayacatl (r. 1469–1481). Tlacaelel first gained influence during wars in the 1420s in which the Mexica defeated the rival Tepanecs, after which he established new systems of dividing military spoils and enemy lands. At the same time, he advised the emperor that new histories were needed in which the destiny of the Mexica people was made clearer. Tlacaelel ordered the destruction of older historical texts, and under his direction the new chronicles connected Mexica fate directly to Huitzilopochtli. Mexica writing was primarily pictographic, drawn and then read by specially trained scribes who used written records as an aid to oral presentation, especially for legal issues, historical chronicles, religious and devotional poetry, and astronomical calculations.

Tlacaelel emphasized human sacrifice as one of the Aztecs' religious duties. (From the *Codex Magliabechiano* [vellum]/Biblioteca Nazionale Centrale, Florence, Italy/The Bridgeman Art Library)

According to these new texts, the Mexica had been guided to Lake Texcoco by Huitzilopochtli; there they saw an eagle perched on a cactus, which a prophecy foretold would mark the site of their new city. Huitzilopochtli kept the world alive by bringing the sun's warmth, but to do this he required the Mexica, who increasingly saw themselves as the "people of the sun," to provide a steady offering of human blood.

The worship of Huitzilopochtli became linked to cosmic forces as well as daily survival. In Nahua tradition, the universe was understood to exist in a series of five suns, or five cosmic ages. Four ages had already passed, and their suns had been destroyed; the fifth sun, the age in which the Mexica were now living, would also be destroyed unless the Mexica fortified the sun with the energy found in blood. Warfare thus brought new territory under Mexica control and provided sacrificial victims to nourish the sun-god. With these ideas, Tlacaelel created what Miguel León-Portilla, a leading contemporary scholar of Nahua religion and philosophy, has termed a "mystico-militaristic" conception of Aztec destiny.

Human sacrifice was practiced in many cultures of Mesoamerica, including the Olmec and the Maya as well as the Mexica, before the changes introduced by Tlacaelel, but historians believe the number of victims increased dramatically during the last period of Mexica rule. A huge pyramid-shaped temple in the center of Tenochtitlan, dedicated to Huitzilopochtli and the god of rain Tlaloc, was renovated and expanded many times, the last in 1487. To dedicate each expansion, priests sacrificed war captives. Similar ceremonies were held regularly throughout the year on days dedicated to Huitzilopochtli and were attended by many observers, including representatives from neighboring states as well as masses of Mexica. According to many accounts, victims were placed on a stone slab, and their hearts were cut out with an obsidian knife; the officiating priest then held the heart up as an offering to the sun. Sacrifices were also made to other gods at temples elsewhere in Tenochtitlan, and perhaps in other cities controlled by the Mexica.

Estimates of the number of people sacrificed to Huitzilopochtli and other Mexica gods vary enormously and are impossible to verify. Both Mexica and later Spanish accounts clearly exaggerated the numbers, but most historians today assume that between several hundred and several thousand people were killed each year.

Sources: Miguel León-Portilla, *Pre-Columbian Literatures of Mexico* (Norman: University of Oklahoma Press, 1969); Inga Clendinnen, *Aztecs: An Interpretation* (Cambridge: Cambridge University Press, 1991).

QUESTIONS FOR ANALYSIS

1. How did the worship of Huitzilopochtli contribute to Aztec expansion? To hostility toward the Aztecs?
2. Why might Tlacaelel have believed it was important to destroy older texts as he created this new Aztec mythology?

conquered peoples increasingly fed the valley's rapidly growing population. The Mexica sustained themselves through military conquest, imposing their rule over a vast part of modern Mexico.

Life in the Aztec Empire

The Aztecs wrote many pictographic books recounting their history, geography, and religious practices. They also preserved records of their legal disputes, which amounted to vast files. The Spanish conquerors subsequently destroyed much of this material, but surviving documents offer a rich picture of the Mexica people at the time of the Spanish invasion.

Few sharp social distinctions existed among the Aztecs during their early migrations, but by the early sixteenth century Aztec society had changed. A stratified social structure had emerged, and the warrior aristocracy exercised great authority. Men who had distinguished themselves in war occupied the highest military and social positions in the state. Generals, judges, and governors of provinces were appointed by the emperor from among his servants who had earned reputations as war heroes. These great lords, or *tecuhtli* (teh-COOT-lee), dressed luxuriously and lived in palaces. Acting as provincial governors, they exercised full political, judicial, and military authority on the emperor's behalf. In their territories they maintained order, settled disputes, and judged legal cases; oversaw the cultivation of land; and made sure that tribute was paid.

Beneath the great nobility of military leaders and imperial officials was the class of warriors. Theoretically, every free man could be a warrior, and parents dedicated their male children to war, burying a male child's umbilical cord with arrows and a shield on the day of his birth. In actuality, the sons of nobles were more likely to become warriors because of their fathers' positions and influence in the state. At the age of six, boys entered a school that trained them for war. They were taught to fight with a *ma-cana*, a paddle-shaped wooden club edged with bits of obsidian, and learned to live on little food and sleep and to accept pain without complaint. At about age eighteen, a warrior fought his first campaign. If he captured a prisoner for ritual sacrifice, he acquired the title *iyac*, or warrior. If in later campaigns he succeeded in killing or capturing four of the enemy, he became a *tequiua*—one who shared in the booty and was thus a member of the nobility. If a young man failed in several campaigns to capture the required four prisoners, he became a *macehualli* (plural *macehualtin*), a commoner.

The macehualtin were the ordinary citizens—the backbone of Aztec society and the vast majority of the population. The word *macehualli* means "worker" and implies boorish speech and vulgar behavior. Members of this class performed agricultural, military, and domestic services and carried heavy public burdens not required of noble warriors. Government officials assigned them to work on the temples, roads, and bridges. Unlike nobles, priests, orphans, and slaves, macehualtin paid taxes. Macehualtin in the capital, however, possessed certain rights: they held their plots of land for life, and they received a small share of the tribute paid by the provinces to the emperor.

Beneath the macehualtin were the *tlalmaitl*, the landless workers or serfs who provided agricultural labor, paid rents in kind, and were bound to the soil—they could not move off the land. In many ways the tlalmaitl resembled the serfs of western Europe, but unlike serfs they performed military service when called on to do so. Slaves were the lowest social class. Most were prisoners captured in war or kidnapped from enemy tribes. People convicted of crimes could be sentenced to slavery, and people in serious debt sometimes voluntarily sold themselves. Female slaves often became their masters' concubines. Mexica slaves differed fundamentally from European ones, for they could possess goods; save money; buy land, houses, and even slaves for their own service; and purchase their freedom. If a male slave married a free woman, their offspring were free. Most slaves eventually gained their freedom.

Women of all social classes operated within the domestic sphere. As the little hands of the newborn male were closed around a tiny bow and arrow indicating his warrior destiny, so the infant female's hands were wrapped around miniature weaving instruments and a small broom: weaving was a sacred and exclusively female art, and the broom signaled a female's responsibility for the household shrines and for keeping the home swept and free of contamination. Save for the few women vowed to the service of the temple, marriage and the household were a woman's fate, and marriage represented social maturity for both sexes. Pregnancy became the occasion for family and neighborhood feasts, and a successful birth launched celebrations lasting from ten to twenty days.

The Limits of the Aztec Empire

Mesoamerican empires like that of the Aztecs were not like modern nation-states that consolidate control of the territory within their borders. Instead the Aztec Empire was a syndicate in which the Mexica, their allies, and their subordinates thrived on trade and tribute backed by the threat of force.

When a city succumbed, its captive warriors were marched to Tenochtitlan to be sacrificed. The defeated city was obligated to provide tribute to be distributed within the empire, including corn and other foods, flowers, feathers, gold, and hides. But conquest stopped

Huitzilopochtli This painting of the hummingbird god of war carrying a shield in one hand and a serpent-headed knife in the other was made by Aztec priests in a book written on bark paper about the time of the Spanish conquest. He is shown descending from a step-pyramid, perhaps a reference to the great pyramid in the center of Tenochtitlan, where he was worshipped. (© Foundation for the Advancement of Mesoamerican Studies, Inc., www.famsi.org)

short of assimilation. Rulers and nobles remained in place. Subjects were not required to adopt Mexica gods. Some children of nobles would be sent to Tenochtitlan for their education and were encouraged to intermarry with the nobles of other states within the empire, but otherwise local communities and their leaders remained intact.

The death of a ruler is always a time of uncertainty, and this was especially true in Mesoamerica under the Aztec Empire. For peoples of the Valley of Mexico and beyond, this meant war was sure to arrive. The council of high nobles who served the deceased ruler chose the new tlatoani, who was often the commander of the army. Once the new tlatoani was named, he would embark on a military campaign in order to answer the questions his succession raised: Would he bring sacrificial victims to the gods and thus ensure prosperity and fertility during his reign? Could he preserve and strengthen the alliances that composed the empire? Could he keep rivals at bay?

A success in the tlatoani's inaugural military campaign provided new tribute-paying subjects, produced a long train of sacrificial victims captured in battle, maintained the stability of the empire's alliances, warned off potential foes, and kept conquered areas in subordination. After the successful campaign, the new tlatoani invited the rulers of allied, subject, and enemy city-states alike to his coronation ceremony—a pageant of gifts, feasts, and bloody sacrifice that proclaimed Tenochtitlan's might.

But success was not always possible, as the troubled rule of Tizoc (r. 1481–1486) demonstrated. His wars sometimes resulted in a greater number of casualties among his own forces than of sacrificial victims for his altars. Five years after he was crowned, he was poisoned by his own subjects. His successor, Ahuitzotl (r. 1486–1502), faced the challenge of reinvigorating the empire through renewed displays of strength. He had little margin for failure. To symbolize the restoration of Tenochtitlan's power, he waged wars of conquest that defied precedence in their scale, culminating in two coronation ceremonies, the second of which incorporated sacrificing over eighty thousand captive warriors.

Blood sacrifice was not new to the Aztecs. For centuries Mesoamerican peoples had honored their gods this way. For instance, the cult honoring Xipe Totec, the god of spring renewal, involved two emblematic sacrifices. Priests wore the skin of a sacrificial victim to symbolize the shedding of leaves and new growth, and they greeted the arrival of spring by binding a human sacrifice to a post and shooting his body full of arrows with slits carved along their shafts. Blood channeled off the arrows and dripped to the ground, symbolizing the spring rains.

The Aztecs elevated the warrior cult as the central observance. They were the chosen people, who faced a bleak struggle to stave off the apocalypse. The Mexica believed the earth had been destroyed and re-created four times. The end of creation loomed after their age, the fifth sun. Since this apocalypse might be forestalled through divine intervention, their sacrifice could show that humans were worthy of divine intervention. If ancient deities had given their lives to save the sun, how could mortals refuse to do the same? Their service to the gods culminated on the altar of the temple to Huitzilopochtli, where priests cut into the chests of warriors with their obsidian knives to pull out their beating hearts and raise them in sacrifice to the sun.

Such sacrifice evoked the power of Aztec rulers, but the ceremony observing the end of each fifty-two-year bundle better reflected the Mexica worldview. Had humans sacrificed enough for the gods to intercede and ensure the sun would rise again? In preparation for the end, families broke their earthenware vessels, cleansed their homes, and extinguished all fires. As the new day came, priests made a fire on the chest of a living, powerful captive warrior. Noble warriors lit torches from this new fire and relayed the flame of creation into each hearth in the empire. For the next fifty-two years, all would know the fire in their hearth, like the rising of the sun itself, was the fruit of a sacred warrior sacrifice.

The need for sacrifice, as well as the glorification of the warriors who provided it through battle, was a powerful rationale for the expansion of the Aztec Empire. The role of the Aztecs' sacrifice-based religious system is the subject of scholarly debate: Did the religious system guide imperial expansion? Or did imperial expansion guide the religious system? These views are by no means incompatible: for the Aztecs, the peoples who came under their rule, and the peoples who resisted them, the twin goals of empire building and service to the gods were inseparable.

American Empires and the Encounter

- What did the European encounter mean for peoples of the major American empires?

By 1500 the Incas and Aztecs strained under the burdens of managing the largest empires the Americas had seen. Both faced the challenges of consolidating their gains, bearing the costs of empire and of the swelling nobility, and waging war in increasingly distant and difficult conditions.

The Fall of the Aztecs

In 1502 Moctezuma II, the last Mexica to rule before the arrival of the Spaniards, was named tlatoani. His reign presents a paradox. On one hand, we know the most about it because it was narrated in detail both by Spanish chroniclers and by indigenous informants (the defeated Mexica continued to create books narrating their history for decades after the conquest). On the other hand, we interpret this information knowing that between 1519 and 1521 the Aztec Empire fell to the Spanish conquistador Hernán Cortés, and our tendency is to analyze Moctezuma II's reign with the knowledge that six hundred foreigners could topple the most powerful empire ever seen in Mesoamerica. Was the Aztecs' loss the result of an empire in crisis? Was it a technological failure? A political failure? A mismatch between a more advanced and a less advanced civilization?

Moctezuma inherited a strained empire. His predecessors had expanded the empire's reach from the Caribbean coast to the Pacific. At the margins of the empire the Aztecs encountered peoples who were semi-nomadic or who, like the Maya, abandoned their cities to resist conquest. An empire that had expanded rapidly through conquest found itself with little room to grow.

Aztec leaders had sought targets for conquest that were easy to overpower or were strategic for trade, or that possessed resources or produced goods that made for valuable tribute. This created an empire riddled with independent enclaves that had resisted conquest. The most powerful of these was Tlaxcala, at the edge of the Valley of Mexico. In addition, even those areas nominally under Aztec rule retained local leadership and saw themselves as subjected peoples, not as Aztecs. An Aztec army en route to conquer new lands frequently had to reconquer cities along its path.

Finally, the costs of expanding and sustaining the empire had become onerous. Generations of social mobility through distinction in combat had produced a bloated nobility both exempt from and sustained by tribute. Tenochtitlan became dependent on tributary maize in order to feed itself. Materially, the lack of new peoples to conquer meant the empire had little promise of increased prosperity. Spiritually, the dwindling flow of sacrificial victims meant the Mexica might be losing the great cosmic struggle to keep creation from ending.

Faced with these challenges, Moctezuma II reformed the empire. His predecessors had formalized social stratification and defined both the classes of nobility and the means by which to ascend into them. Moctezuma reduced the privileges (and thus the costs to the empire) of the lesser nobility and narrowed the pathways of social mobility. The austerity he imposed in the imperial capital caused unrest. He also pressed the consolidation of territory by seeking to conquer the autonomous enclaves left by his predecessors. As Moctezuma targeted these enclaves, their ability to resist sapped their resources and strained their morale without

Viewpoints 11.2

Inca and Spanish Views on Religion, Authority, and Tribute

• *In 1532 Inca emperor Atahualpa traveled to Cajamarca to meet with the band of Spaniards led by Francisco Pizarro. At the meeting, Pizarro's men captured Atahualpa. Before the capture, a remarkable exchange took place. The priest accompanying Pizarro, Friar Vicente de Valverde, read to Atahualpa, through a translator, a document prepared in Spain in 1513 called the* Requerimiento. *The document presented core Christian teachings about Jesus Christ and explained the establishment of the Roman Church, led by the pope, who granted Spanish emperor Charles V the right to conquer and Christianize the Americas. Conquistadors were legally obligated to read the* Requerimiento *in front of witnesses before waging a war of conquest. A portion of the friar's reading and Atahualpa's response are related here by Garcilaso de la Vega, the son of an Andean woman and a Spanish soldier, who published a history of the Inca Empire and the Spanish conquest in 1609.*

Friar Vicente de Valverde Presents the *Requerimiento*

" It is proper that you should know, most famous and most powerful king, that it is necessary that Your Highness and all your subjects should not only learn the true Catholic faith but that you should hear and believe the following. . . .

Therefore the holy pope of Rome . . . has conceded the conquest of these parts to Charles V, . . . the most powerful king of Spain and monarch of all the earth. . . . The great emperor Charles V has chosen as his lieutenant and ambassador Don Francisco Pizarro, who is now here, . . . so that Your Highness and all your realms will become tributaries; that is to say, you will pay tribute to the emperor, and will become his vassal and deliver your kingdom wholly into his hands, renouncing the administration of it, as other kings and lords have done. . . . If you seek obstinately to resist, you may rest assured that God will suffer that you and all your Indians shall be destroyed by our arms, even as Pharaoh of old and all his host perished in the Red Sea. "

The Inca Atahualpa Responds

" I will be no man's tributary. I am greater than any prince upon the earth. Your emperor may be a great prince; I do not doubt it, when I see that he has sent his subjects so far across the waters; and I am willing to hold him as a brother. As for the pope of whom you speak, he must be crazy to talk of giving away countries that do not belong to him. For my faith, I will not change it. Your own God, as you say, was put to death by the very men he created. But mine . . . [pointing to the sun] still lives in the heavens, and looks down upon his children. . . .

You threaten us with war and death . . . and say that I must renounce my kingdom and become the tributary of another, either willingly or by force. Whence I deduce one of two things: either your prince and you are tyrants who are destroying the world, depriving others of their realms, slaying and robbing those who have done you no harm and owe you nothing, or you are ministers of God, whom we call Pachacámac, who has chosen you to punish and destroy us. . . . [If so,] you should therefore act like divine messengers and ministers and put a stop to the slayings and lootings and acts of cruelty. . . .

You have mentioned five great men I should know. The first is God three and one, or four, whom you call the creator of the universe: he is perchance the same as our Pachacámac and Viracocha. The second is he whom you say is the father of all other men on whom they have all heaped their sins. The third you call Jesus Christ, the only one who did not lay his sins on the first man, but he was killed. The fourth you call pope. The fifth is Charles, whom you call the most powerful and monarch of the universe and supreme above the rest, without regard for the other four. If this Charles is prince and lord of the whole world, why should he need the pope to give him a new grant and concession to make war on me and usurp these kingdoms? If he has to ask the pope's permission, is not the pope a greater lord than he, and more powerful, and prince of all the world? Also, I am surprised that you say that I must pay tribute to Charles and not to the others, for you give no reason for paying the tribute, and I have certainly no obligation whatever to pay it. If there were any right or reason for paying tribute, it seems to me that it should go to the God you say created everyone and the man you say was the father of all men and to Jesus Christ . . . and finally it should go to the pope who can grant my kingdoms and my person to others. But if you say I owe these nothing, I owe even less to Charles, who was never lord of these regions and has never set eyes on them. . . .

I wish also to know about the good man called Jesus Christ who never cast his sins on the other and who you say died — if he died of a sickness or at the hands of his enemies; and if he was included among the gods before his death or after it. I also desire to know [if] you regard these five you have mentioned to me as gods, since you honor them so. For in this case, you have more gods than we, who adore only Pachacámac as the Supreme God and the Sun as the lower god, and the Moon as the Sun's wife and sister. ”

Sources: Excerpts "It is proper that you should know" and "You threaten us with war" from Garcilaso de la Vega, *Royal Commentaries of the Incas, and General History of Peru*, translated by H. V. Livermore (Austin: University of Texas Press, 1989). Used by permission of the University of Texas Press; excerpt "I will be no man's tributary" from William Prescott, *History of the Conquest of Peru*, vol. 1. 1892 [1847], p. 370.

QUESTIONS FOR ANALYSIS

1. According to Atahualpa, what is the source of his authority? What is the source of the Spaniards' authority?
2. Why does Atahualpa believe that the Spaniards have more gods than the Incas?
3. How does Atahualpa perceive the Spaniards and their intentions?

producing a corresponding reward for the empire in sacrifice or tribute.

Would Moctezuma have been able to consolidate these reforms and help the empire make the transition from expansion to stable maturity? Or was he a modern version of Tizoc, whose failures led to his assassination and a successor who responded to his predecessor's weakness with a surge of human sacrifice? The Aztec Empire had no real military or political rivals. As a result, the empire was well poised to continue despite its limitations, but it was also vulnerable to disruption upon the arrival of Europeans.

By the time he reached the gates of Tenochtitlan in 1519, Hernán Cortés had forged alliances with foes of the Aztec Empire, particularly Tlaxcala, which had so ably resisted conquest. The Tlaxcalans saw in the foreigners an opportunity that could aid their struggle against the Mexica and formed an alliance with the Spanish. Cortés's band of six hundred Spaniards arrived in Tenochtitlan accompanied by tens of thousands of Tlaxcalan soldiers. In Tlaxcala the defeat of Tenochtitlan would be seen as the Tlaxcalans' victory, not that of the handful of Spaniards.

Mexica accounts from after the Spanish conquest are filled with prophecies that foretold the conquest of Tenochtitlan and the fall of the Aztec Empire. One of the most evocative was the myth of the return of Quetzalcoatl. Surely Moctezuma could not resist a man he believed to be a powerful god descended from the Toltecs. Whatever he made of the strangers, he received them as guests, probably because he sought to understand the nature of this encounter and its significance for his empire. Perhaps Moctezuma hesitated, losing the opportunity to act against them. Perhaps he concluded that he had no chance of defeating them, since at that moment most of the men he could count on in battle were tending to their crops and the capital had been so riddled with division and resentment of his reforms that he was powerless to act.

Either way, Cortés and his men managed the encounter skillfully and succeeded in taking Moctezuma prisoner. When the residents of Tenochtitlan rose up to expel the Spaniards, Moctezuma was killed, either at the hands of the Spaniards or by his own subjects, depending on the account. Though the Spaniards were cast out of the city, they left an unwelcome guest, smallpox. The first epidemic of the disease swept through the city in 1520, killing Moctezuma's successor, Cuitlahuac, within a matter of months. Cuauhtemoc, the last tlatoani of the Mexica, was named that same year.

The Aztec Empire and the Mexica people were not defeated by technology, cultural superiority, or a belief that the Europeans were gods. Instead the Mexica suffered a political defeat: they fell because of ruptures in

Past and Present Meet in Mexico City Construction for the Pino Suárez metro station unearthed the Aztec ceremonial altar of Ehecatl, the Aztec god of wind. (David Hiser/National Geographic/SuperStock)

their leadership due to the death of Moctezuma and his successor, as well as the willingness of allies and enemies alike to join with the Spaniards against them when they perceived an opportunity.

Through the lens of history, the destruction of the Aztec Empire seems sudden and swift, but Tenochtitlan resisted for two years, surrendering only in 1521. During this time the Spaniards and Tlaxcalans brokered alliances across the Valley of Mexico and beyond, leaving the Mexica virtually alone in their fight. In this sense, the end of the Aztec Empire looked a lot like its beginning: people who had obeyed the Mexica now took advantage of the opportunity to defeat them, just as the Mexica had done with the Tepanec Alliance. Even so, abandoned by their allies, the besieged Mexica fought on through famine and disease, defending their city street by street until they were finally vanquished.

The Fall of the Incas

In 1525 Huayna Capac Inca, the grandson of Pachacuti Inca, became ill while carrying out a military campaign in present-day Ecuador, at the northern frontier of the empire. Campaigns of conquest always take place at frontiers (even if these frontiers are between enclaves within an empire, as was the case for the Aztecs). But in this case, because of split inheritance, Huayna Capac's entire dominion would have to be created by expanding outward beyond the frontiers of his father's empire. His illness was plague, introduced by Europeans waging wars of conquest in Mesoamerica, and it would kill him. But as he waged war, he also received news of the foreigners in the north and anticipated that they would come southward. From his deathbed, he urged his successor to make peace with them.

But peace did not follow Huayna Capac's death. Instead civil war erupted between two of his sons over succession to the throne. Huascar claimed it as the firstborn. His half-brother Atahualpa, Huayna Capac's favorite and an experienced military commander who had accompanied him in his Ecuadorean campaign, claimed it as well. Atahualpa asserted that Huayna Capac's dying wish was that Atahualpa succeed him. The brothers fought for seven years, turning the empire's armies against each other. In 1532 Atahualpa vanquished and imprisoned his brother and consolidated his rule in Cuzco. That same year a group of Spaniards led by Francisco Pizarro landed on the Peruvian coast, pursuing rumors of a city of gold in the mountains.

Atahualpa agreed through emissaries to meet the Spaniards at the city of Cajamarca in northern Peru. In a demonstration of his imperial authority, he entered Cajamarca carried on a golden litter, accompanied by four military squadrons of eight thousand men each. Other members of the nobility followed, carried on their own litters. Their procession was preceded by a multitude of servants who cleared the ground, removing all stones, pebbles, and even bits of straw. Atahualpa met the Spanish intending not to fight a battle, but to understand them and hear them out. The meeting between Atahualpa and Pizarro reflected two deeply different worldviews. (See "Viewpoints 11.2: Inca and Spanish Views on Religion, Authority, and Tribute," page 322.)

In the scuffle that ensued at the meeting, the Spaniards took Atahualpa prisoner, and they eventually executed him. The Spaniards named a new indigenous leader, Manco Capac, whom they hoped to control. But Manco Capac turned against the Spaniards. He, and later his son Tupac Amaru, led resistance against the Spaniards until 1567. Each time the Inca forces besieged a Spanish-controlled city or town, however, their proximity to the Spaniards exposed them to European diseases. They were more successful in smaller-scale attacks, which delayed and limited Spanish colonization, but did not undo it.

CHRONOLOGY

ca. 40,000–13,000 B.C.E.	Initial human migration to the Americas
ca. 5000 B.C.E.	Intensification of agriculture
ca. 2000 B.C.E.	Earliest mound building in North America
ca. 1500–300 B.C.E.	Olmec culture
ca. 1200 B.C.E.	Emergence of Chavín culture in the Andes
ca. 100–800 C.E.	Moche culture
ca. 300–650 C.E.	Peak of Teotihuacan's influence
ca. 600–900 C.E.	Peak of Maya culture
ca. 1050–1250 C.E.	Construction of mounds at Cahokia
ca. 1325 C.E.	Construction of Aztec city of Tenochtitlan begins
ca. 1428–1521 C.E.	Aztec Empire dominates Mesoamerica
ca. 1438–1532 C.E.	Inca Empire dominates the Andes

Chapter Summary

The Inca and Aztec Empires that encountered Spanish conquerors were short-lived products of the cycle of centralization and decentralization that had characterized the Andes and Mesoamerica for thousands of years. In this sense, there was nothing new in the toppling of these empires. The empires preceding those of the Incas and Aztecs had been undone when their own people turned against them, when climate changes disrupted them, or when they faced outside competition. What was new in the sixteenth century was that this outside competition came from Europeans.

The civilizations of the Andes and Mesoamerica from which the Incas and Aztecs emerged had remarkable similarities with and differences from other ancient and premodern civilizations in other regions of the world. Without being influenced by developments in Africa, Asia, or Europe, indigenous societies of the Americas developed extensive networks of trade. In Mesoamerica and the Andes, the domestication of crops led to the kind of bountiful production that allowed for diversification of labor among farmers, priests, nobles, merchants, and artisans. In these environments, cycles of centralization occurred in which powerful city-states emerged and embarked on campaigns of conquest, bringing vast regions under their political, religious, and cultural influence.

But civilizations of the Americas developed in unique ways as well. This was particularly true in the Andes, where peoples developed specialized patterns of farming in vertical archipelagos in their inhospitable mountain environment. Similarly, though Andean peoples did not develop writing, they instead developed the khipu into a sophisticated system of recording and communicating information.

Ultimately, the history of the peoples of the Americas was defined by their diverse experiences as they coped with varied climates, ecology, and geography. Chinampa agriculture in the Valley of Mexico and raised-bed farming practiced by the Maya are examples. And peoples' experiences of adapting to their environments, and of transforming those environments to meet their needs, shaped the ways they understood their world. These experiences led them to produce precise calendars, highly detailed readings of the stars, and an elaborate architecture of religious beliefs through which they interpreted their relationships to their world and their place in the cosmos.

NOTES

1. *Narrative of the Incas by Juan de Betanzos*, trans. and ed. Roland Hamilton and Dana Buchanan from the Palma de Mallorca manuscript, p. 138.
2. "Maya Writing," Authentic Maya, http://www.authenticmaya.com/maya_writing.htm.
3. Michael Coe, *Mexico from the Olmecs to the Aztecs*, 5th ed. (New York: Thames and Hudson, 2002), p. 107.
4. Ross Hassig, *War and Society in Ancient Mesoamerica* (Berkeley: University of California Press, 1992), p. 56.
5. Ibid., p. 49.
6. Ibid., pp. 81, 85.
7. Bernal Díaz, *The Conquest of New Spain*, trans. J. M. Cohen (New York: Penguin Books, 1978), p. 214.
8. Ross Hassig, *Aztec Warfare* (Norman: University of Oklahoma Press, 1988), p. 143.
9. Miguel León-Portilla, "Mexico to 1519," in *Cambridge History of Latin America*, ed. Leslie Bethell, vol. 1 (Cambridge: Cambridge University Press, 1984), p. 14.

CONNECTIONS

Though we often think of history unfolding along differences between peoples (Spaniards versus Aztecs, for instance), a more common division is often evident: rural versus urban experiences. The disruption of American societies and cultures after the encounter with Europeans occurred in both rural and urban areas, but there were deep differences in the effects of colonization upon urban and rural peoples of the Americas.

The early sixteenth century marked the end of independent empires of the Americas and the gradual integration of American peoples into global empires seated in Europe. Spaniards were the most motivated and had their greatest success when they encountered dense, organized urban areas. Here they displaced existing overlords as the recipients of tribute in goods and labor. The Spanish were less interested in sparsely settled areas that did not have well-established systems of trade and tribute and were harder to subdue. As a result, European conquest was a surprisingly drawn-out process. Peoples of the Americas resisted conquest until well into the nineteenth century.

The incidental companion of conquest—disease—was also uneven in its effects. Over the course of the sixteenth century, epidemic diseases decimated the population of the Americas, which fell from 50 million to just 5 million. But epidemics of diseases that are spread through human contact, such as measles and smallpox, are primarily urban phenomena: these diseases emerged as ancient cities grew large enough that the diseases could spread quickly among dense populations. As a result, the impact of the diseases brought by Europeans was the most severe and the most destructive in the cities of the Americas.

Since cities faced the brunt of both disease and wars of conquest, the disruptions caused by the encounter were disproportionally felt there. Whole systems of knowledge, sets of artisanal skills, political cultures, and religious thought resided in cities. As epidemics erupted, as besieging armies tore down buildings stone by stone, and as survivors dispersed, many of the most remarkable aspects of American civilizations were lost. Rural peoples and cultures were much more resilient. It was in rural areas that languages, foodways, farming practices, and approaches to healing—indeed whole worldviews—endured and evolved. This process occurred either in isolation from or in dialogue with European cultures, but local practices in rural regions were not obliterated, as they were in major cities. In the end, the European encounter destroyed the urban cultures and systems of knowledge in the Americas.

Review and Explore

Make It Stick

LearningCurve

Go online and use LearningCurve to retain what you've read.

Identify Key Terms

Identify and explain the significance of each item below.

Mesoamerica (p. 298)
khipu (p. 299)
nixtamalization (p. 301)
Olmecs (p. 302)
Moche (p. 305)
Inca (p. 305)
Quechua (p. 307)
Maya (p. 310)
Teotihuacan (p. 310)
Nahuatl (p. 315)
Mexica (p. 315)
Tenochtitlan (p. 316)

Review the Main Ideas

Answer the focus questions from each section of the chapter.

1. How did ancient peoples of the Americas adapt to, and adapt, their environment? (p. 299)
2. What patterns established by early societies shaped civilization in Mesoamerica and the Andes? (p. 302)
3. What were the sources of strength and prosperity, and of problems, for the Incas? (p. 305)
4. How did the Maya and Teotihuacan develop prosperous and stable societies in the classical era? (p. 310)
5. How did the Aztecs build on the achievements of earlier Mesoamerican cultures and develop new traditions to create their large empire? (p. 315)
6. What did the European encounter mean for peoples of the major American empires? (p. 321)

Make Connections

Analyze the larger developments and continuities within and across chapters.

1. Why didn't societies of the Americas adopt the wheel for transportation, as peoples of other world regions did?
2. How does the connection between religion and imperial expansion among the Aztecs and Incas resemble the role of religion in other societies?
3. Much of what we know of ancient societies of the Americas is based on archaeological data rather than written sources. How does the reliance on archaeological data shape our understanding of history? What does it help us understand? What is hard for us to interpret from it?

LaunchPad
Online Document Project

The Making and Remaking of Aztec History

Why did Tlacaelel believe the Aztec Empire needed a new history?
Read documents that examine Aztec history and culture, and then complete a quiz and writing assignment based on the evidence and details from this chapter.

See inside the front cover to learn more.

Suggested Reading

Carassco, David, and Scott Sessions. *Daily Life of the Aztecs: People of the Sun and Earth.* 2008. An overview of Aztec culture designed for general readers.

Clendinnen, Inga. *Aztecs: An Interpretation.* 1992. Pays particular attention to the role that rituals and human sacrifice played in Aztec culture.

Coe, Michael D. *The Maya.* 2011. A new edition of a classic survey that incorporates the most recent scholarship.

Coe, Michael D. *Mexico: From the Olmecs to the Aztecs.* 2013. A rich examination of Mesoamerican peoples with the exception of the Maya.

Conrad, G. W., and A. A. Demarest. *Religion and Empire: The Dynamics of Aztec and Inca Expansionism.* 1993. Compares the two largest American empires.

Freidel, David. *A Forest of Kings: The Untold Story of the Ancient Maya.* 1990. A splendidly illustrated work providing expert treatment of the Maya world.

Hassig, Ross. *Mexico and the Spanish Conquest.* 2006. A study of indigenous participation in the conquest by a leading historical anthropologist.

Kehoe, Alice Beck. *America Before the European Invasion.* 2002. An excellent survey of North America before the coming of the Europeans, by an eminent anthropologist.

León-Portilla, Miguel. *The Aztec Image of Self and Society: An Introduction to Nahua Culture.* 1992. A rich appreciation of Aztec religious ritual and symbolism.

Mann, Charles C. *1491: New Revelations of the Americas Before Columbus.* 2006. A thoroughly researched overview of all the newest scholarship, written for a general audience.

Mumford, Jeremy Ravi. *Vertical Empire: The General Resettlement of Indians in the Colonial Andes.* 2012. A study of Andean mountain life between Inca and Spanish rule.

Ramirez, Susan. *To Feed and Be Fed: The Cosmological Bases of Authority and Identity in the Andes.* 2008. Examines the relationships between ancestors, the spiritual world, and the physical world that shaped Andean societies.

Restall, Matthew, and Amara Solari. *2012 and the End of the World: The Western Roots of the Maya Apocalypse.* 2011. Reflects on popular interpretations of the Maya calendar and cosmology.

Cultural Exchange in Central and Southern Asia

300–1400

12

Mongol Woman
Women played influential roles among the Mongols. The Mongol woman portrayed in this painting is Chabi, wife of Khubilai Khan. Like other Mongols, she maintained Mongol dress even though she spent much of her time in China. (The Granger Collection, NYC —)

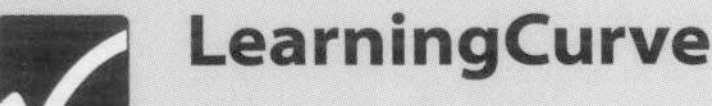

LearningCurve
After reading the chapter, go online and use LearningCurve to retain what you've read.

Chapter Preview

The large expanse of Asia treated in this chapter underwent profound changes during the centuries examined here. The north saw the rise of nomadic pastoral societies, first the Turks, then more spectacularly the Mongols. The nomads' mastery of the horse and mounted warfare gave them a military advantage that agricultural societies could rarely match. From the fifth century on, groups of Turks appeared along the fringes of the settled societies of Eurasia, from China and Korea to India and Persia. Often Turks were recruited as auxiliary soldiers; sometimes they gained the upper hand. By the tenth century many were converting to Islam (see Chapter 9).

Much more dramatic was the rise of the Mongols under the charismatic leadership of Chinggis Khan in the late twelfth and early thirteenth centuries. A military genius with a relatively small army, Chinggis subdued one society after another from Byzantium to the Pacific. For a century Mongol hegemony fostered unprecedented East-West trade and contact. More Europeans made their way east than ever before, and Chinese inventions such as printing and the compass made their way west.

Over the course of several centuries, Arab and Turkish armies brought Islam to India, but the Mongols never gained power there. In the Indian subcontinent during these centuries, regional cultures flourished. Although Buddhism declined, Hinduism continued to flourish. India continued to be the center of a very active seaborne trade, and this trade helped carry Indian ideas and practices to Southeast Asia. Buddhism was adopted in much of Southeast Asia, along with other ideas and techniques from India. The maritime trade in spices and other goods brought increased contact with the outside world to all but the most isolated of islands in the Pacific.

Central Asian Nomads

☐ What aspects of nomadic life gave the nomads of Central Asia military advantages over nearby settled civilizations?

One experience Rome, Persia, India, and China all shared was conflict with **nomads** who came from the very broad region referred to as Central Asia. This region was dominated by the **steppe**, arid grasslands that stretched from modern Hungary, through southern Russia and across Central Asia (today's Tajikistan, Turkmenistan, Kazakhstan, Kyrgyzstan, and Uzbekistan) and adjacent parts of China, to Mongolia and parts of present northeast China. Initially small in number, the nomadic peoples of this region used their military superiority to conquer first other nomads, then the nearby settled societies. In the process they created settled empires of their own that drew on the cultures they absorbed.

Nomadic Society

Easily crossed by horses but too dry for crop agriculture, the grasslands could support only a thin population of nomadic herders who lived off their sheep, goats, camels, horses, or other animals. Following the seasons, they would break camp at least twice a year and move their animals to new pastures, going north in the spring and south in the fall.

In their search for water and good pastures, nomadic groups often came into conflict with other nomadic groups pursuing the same resources, which the two would then fight over, as there was normally no higher political authority able to settle disputes. Groups on the losing end, especially if they were small, faced the threat of extermination or slavery, which prompted them to make alliances with other groups or move far away. Groups on the winning end of intertribal conflicts could exact tribute from those they defeated, sometimes so much that they could devote themselves entirely to war, leaving the work of tending herds to their slaves and vassals.

To get the products of nearby agricultural societies, especially grain, woven textiles, iron, tea, and wood, nomadic herders would trade their own products, such as horses and furs. When trade was difficult, they would turn to raiding to seize what they needed. Much of the time nomadic herders raided other nomads, but nearby agricultural settlements were common targets as well. The nomads' skill as horsemen and archers made it difficult for farmers and townsmen to defend against them. It was largely to defend against the raids of the Xiongnu nomads, for example, that the Chinese built the Great Wall.

Manichaean Priests Many religions spread through Central Asia before it became predominantly Muslim after 1300. This fragment of a tenth- to twelfth-century illustrated document, found at the Silk Road city of Turfan, is written in the Uighur language and depicts Manichaean priests. (Archives Charmet/The Bridgeman Art Library)

Political organization among nomadic herders was generally very simple. Clans—members of an extended family—had chiefs, as did tribes (coalitions of clans). Leadership within a group was based on military prowess and was often settled by fighting. Occasionally a charismatic leader would emerge who was able to extend alliances to form confederations of tribes. From the point of view of the settled societies, which have left most of the records about these nomadic groups, large confederations were much more of a threat, since they could plan coordinated attacks on cities and

- **nomads** Groups of people who move from place to place in search of food, water, and pasture for their animals, usually following the seasons.
- **steppe** Grasslands that are too dry for crops but support pasturing animals; they are common across much of the center of Eurasia.

towns. Large confederations rarely lasted more than a century or so, however, and when they broke up, tribes again spent much of their time fighting with each other, relieving some of the pressure on their settled neighbors.

The three most wide-ranging and successful confederations were those of the Xiongnu—Huns, as they were known in the West—who emerged in the third century B.C.E. in the area near China; the Turks, who had their origins in the same area in the fourth and fifth centuries C.E.; and the Mongols, who did not become important until the late twelfth century. In all three cases, the entire steppe region was eventually swept up in the movement of peoples and armies.

The Turks

The Turks were the first of the Inner Asian peoples to have left a written record in their own language; the earliest Turkish documents date from the eighth century. Turkic languages may have already been spoken in dispersed areas of the Eurasian steppe when the Turks first appeared; today these languages are spoken by the Uighurs in western China; the Uzbeks, Kazakhs, Kyrghiz (KIHR-guhz), and Turkmens of Central Asia; and the Turks of modern Turkey. The original religion of the Turks was shamanistic and involved worship of Heaven, making it similar to the religions of many other groups in the steppe region.

In 552 a group called Turks who specialized in metalworking rebelled against their overlords, the Rouruan, whose empire dominated the region from the eastern Silk Road cities of Central Asia through Mongolia. The Turks quickly supplanted the Rouruan as overlords of the Silk Road in the east. When the first Turkish khagan (ruler) died a few years later, the Turkish empire was divided between his younger brother, who took the western part (modern Central Asia), and his son, who took the eastern part (modern Mongolia). Sogdians—who were influential merchants along the Silk Road—convinced the Turks to send a delegation to both the Persian (see Chapter 9) and the Byzantine courts (see Chapter 8). Repeated diplomatic overtures in both directions did not prevent hostilities, however, and in 576 the Western Turks captured the Byzantine city of Bosporus in the Crimea.

The Eastern Turks frequently raided China and just as often fought among themselves. The Chinese history of the Sui Dynasty, written in the seventh century, records that "the Turks prefer to destroy each other rather than to live side-by-side. They have a thousand, nay ten thousand clans who are hostile to and kill one another. They mourn their dead with much grief and swear vengeance."[1] In the early seventh century the empire of the Eastern Turks ran up against the growing military might of the Tang Dynasty in China and soon broke apart.

In the eighth century a Turkic people called the Uighurs (Wee-gurs) formed a new empire based in Mongolia that survived about a century. It had close ties to Tang China, providing military aid but also extracting large payments in silk. During this period many Uighurs adopted religions then current along the Silk Road, notably Buddhism, Nestorian Christianity, and Manichaeism. In the ninth century this Uighur empire was destroyed by another Turkic people from north of Mongolia called the Kyrghiz. Some Uighurs fled to what is now western China. Setting up their capital city in Kucha, the Uighurs created a remarkably stable and prosperous kingdom that lasted four centuries (ca. 850–1250). Because of the dry climate of the region, many buildings, wall paintings, and manuscripts written in a variety of languages have been preserved from this era. They reveal a complex urban civilization in which Buddhism, Manichaeism, and Christianity existed side by side, practiced by Turks as well as by Tokharians, Sogdians, and other Iranian peoples.

Farther west in Central Asia other groups of Turks, such as the Karakhanids, Ghaznavids, and Seljuks, rose to prominence. Often local Muslim forces would try to capture them, employ them as slave soldiers, and convert them. By the mid- to late tenth century many were serving in the armies of the Abbasid caliphate. Also in the tenth century Central Asian Turks began converting to Islam (which protected them from being abducted as slaves). Then they took to raiding unconverted Turks.

In the mid-eleventh century Turks had gained the upper hand in the caliphate, and the caliphs became little more than figureheads. From there Turkish power was extended into Syria, Palestine, and Asia Minor. (Asia Minor is now called Turkey because Turks migrated there by the thousands over several centuries.) In 1071 Seljuk Turks inflicted a devastating defeat on the Byzantine army in eastern Anatolia (see page 246). Other Turkish confederations established themselves in Afghanistan and extended their control into north India (see page 349).

In India, Persia, and Anatolia the formidable military skills of nomadic Turkish warriors made it possible for them to become overlords of settled societies. Just as the Uighurs developed a hybrid urban culture along the eastern end of the Silk Road, adopting many elements from the mercantile Sogdians, the Turks of Central and West Asia created an Islamic culture that drew from both Turkish and Iranian sources. Often Persian was used as the administrative language of the states they formed. Nevertheless, despite the presence of Turkish overlords all along the southern fringe of the steppe, no one group of Turks was able to unite them all into a single political unit. That feat had to wait for the next major power on the steppe, the Mongols.

Gold Belt Plaques Like earlier nomads, the Mongols favored art with animal designs, such as these two gold belt plaques, which depict deer under trees or flowers. Belts and horses were often exchanged to seal or commemorate an alliance. (Nasser D. Khalili Collection of Islamic Art, © Nour Foundation. Courtesy of the Khalili Family Trust)

The Mongols

In the twelfth century ambitious Mongols did not aspire to match the Turks or other groups that had migrated west, but rather wanted to be successors to the Khitans and Jurchens, nomadic groups that had stayed in the east and mastered ways to extract resources from China, the largest and richest country in the region. The Khitans and Jurchens had formed hybrid nomadic-urban states, with northern sections where tribesmen continued to live in the traditional way and southern sections politically controlled by the non-Chinese rulers but settled largely by taxpaying Chinese. The Khitans and Jurchens had scripts created to record their languages and adopted many Chinese governing practices. They built cities in pastoral areas that served as trading centers and places to enjoy their newly acquired wealth. In both the Khitan and Jurchen cases, their elite became culturally dual, adept in Chinese ways as well as in their own traditions.

The Mongols lived north of these hybrid nomadic-settled societies and maintained their traditional ways. Chinese, Persian, and European observers have all left descriptions of the daily life of the Mongols, which they found strikingly different from their own. They lived in tents called **yurts** rather than in houses. The yurts, about twelve to fifteen feet in diameter, were constructed of light wooden frames covered by layers of wool felt, greased to make them waterproof. Yurts were round, since this shape held up better against the strong winds that blew across the treeless grasslands. The floor of a yurt was covered first with dried grass or straw, then with felt, skins, or rugs. In the center, directly under the smoke hole, was the hearth. The master's bed was on the north. Goat horns attached to the frame of the yurt were used as hooks to hang joints of meat, cooking utensils, bows, quivers of arrows, and the like. A group of families traveling together would set up their yurts in a circle open to the south and draw up their wagons in a circle around the yurts for protection.

The Mongol diet consisted mostly of animal products. The most common meat was mutton, supplemented with wild game. When grain or vegetables could be obtained through trade, they were added to the diet. Wood was scarce, so dried animal dung or grasses fueled the cook fires.

The Mongols milked sheep, goats, cows, and horses and made cheese and fermented alcoholic drinks from the milk. A European visitor to Mongolia in the 1250s described how they milked mares, a practice unfamiliar to Europeans:

> They fasten a long line to two posts standing firmly in the ground, and to the line they tie the young colts of the mares which they mean to milk. Then come the mothers who stand by their foals, and allow themselves to be milked. And if any of them be too unruly, then one takes her colt and puts it under her, letting it suck a while, and presently taking it away again, and the milker takes its place.[2]

He also described how they made the alcoholic drink koumiss from the milk, a drink that "goes down very pleasantly, intoxicating weak brains."[3]

Because of the intense cold of the winter, the Mongols made much use of furs and skins for clothing. Both men and women usually wore silk trousers and tunics (the silk obtained from China). Over these they wore robes of fur, for the very coldest times in two layers—an inner layer with the hair on the inside and an outer layer with the hair on the outside. Hats were of felt or fur, boots of felt or leather. Men wore leather belts to which their bows and quivers could be attached.

- **yurts** Tents in which the pastoral nomads lived; they could be quickly dismantled and loaded onto animals or carts.

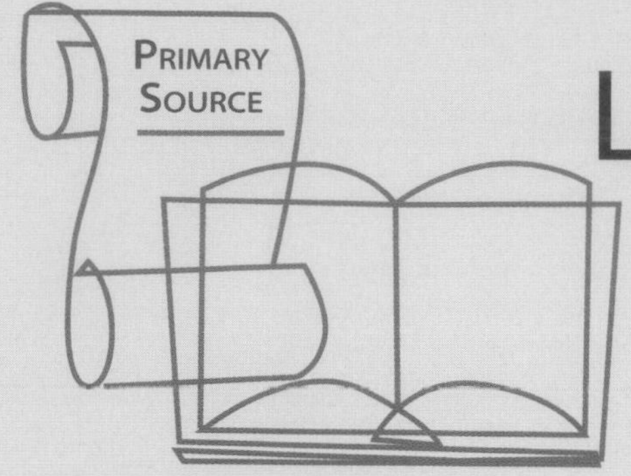

Listening to the Past

The Abduction of Women in *The Secret History of the Mongols*

Within a few decades of Chinggis Khan's death, oral traditions concerning his rise were written down in the Mongolian language in The Secret History of the Mongols. *The account begins with the cycles of revenge among the tribes in Mongolia, many of which began when women were abducted for wives. The following passages relate how Temujin's (Chinggis Khan's) father, Yesugei, seized Hogelun, Temujin's future mother, from a passing Merkid tribesman; how twenty years later three Merkids in return seized women from Temujin; and how Temujin got revenge.*

"That year Yesugei the Brave was out hunting with his falcon on the Onan. Yeke Chiledu, a nobleman of the Merkid tribe, had gone to the Olkhunugud people to find himself a wife, and he was returning to the Merkid with the girl he'd found when he passed Yesugei hunting by the river. When he saw them riding along Yesugei leaned forward on his horse. He saw it was a beautiful girl. Quickly he rode back to his tent and just as quick returned with his two brothers, Nekun Taisi and Daritai Odchigin. When Chiledu saw the three Mongols coming he whipped his dun-colored horse and rode off around a nearby hill with the three men behind him. He cut back around the far side of the hill and rode to Lady Hogelun, the girl he'd just married, who stood waiting for him at the front of their cart. "Did you see the look on the faces of those three men?" she asked him. "From their faces it looks like they mean to kill you. As long as you've got your life there'll always be girls for you to choose from. There'll always be women to ride in your cart. As long as you've got your life you'll be able to find some girl to marry. When you find her, just name her Hogelun for me, but go now and save your own life!" Then she pulled off her shirt and held it out to him, saying: "And take this to remember me, to remember my scent." Chiledu reached out from his saddle and took the shirt in his hands. With the three Mongols close behind him he struck his dun-colored horse with his whip and took off down the Onan River at full speed.

The three Mongols chased him across seven hills before turning around and returning to Hogelun's cart. Then Yesugei the Brave grasped the reins of the cart, his elder brother Nekun Taisi rode in front to guide them, and the younger brother Daritai Odchigin rode along by the wheels. As they rode her back toward their camp, Hogelun began to cry, . . . and she cried till she stirred up the waters of the Onan River, till she shook the trees in the forest and the grass in the valleys. But as the party approached their camp Daritai, riding beside her, warned her to stop: "This fellow who held you in his arms, he's already ridden over the mountains. This man who's lost you, he's crossed many rivers by now. You can call out his name, but he can't see you now even if he looks back. If you tried to find him now you won't even find his tracks. So be still now," he told her. Then Yesugei took Lady Hogelun to his tent as his wife. . . .

[Some twenty years later] one morning just before dawn Old Woman Khogaghchin, Mother Hogelun's servant, woke with a start, crying: "Mother! Mother! Get up! The ground is shaking, I hear it rumble. The Tayichigud must be riding back to attack us. Get up!"

Mother Hogelun jumped from her bed, saying: "Quick, wake my sons!" They woke Temujin and the others and all ran for the horses. Temujin, Mother Hogelun, and Khasar each took a horse. Khachigun, Temuge Odchigin, and Belgutei each took a horse. Bogorchu took one horse and Jelme another. Mother Hogelun lifted the baby Temulun onto her saddle. They saddled the last horse as a lead and there was no horse left for [Temujin's wife] Lady Borte. . . .

Old Woman Khogaghchin, who'd been left in the camp, said: "I'll hide Lady Borte." She made her get into a black covered cart. Then she harnessed the cart to a speckled ox. Whipping the ox, she drove the cart away from the camp down the Tungelig. As the first light of day hit them, soldiers rode up and told them to stop. "Who are you?" they asked her, and Old Woman Khogaghchin answered: "I'm a servant of Temujin's. I've just come from shearing his sheep. I'm on my way back to my own tent to make felt from the wool." Then they asked her: "Is Temujin at his tent? How far is it from here?" Old Woman Khogaghchin said: "As for the tent, it's not far. As for Temujin, I couldn't see whether he was there or not. I was just shearing his sheep out back." The soldiers rode off toward the camp, and Old Woman Khogaghchin whipped the ox. But as the cart moved faster its axletree

Women of high rank wore elaborate headdresses decorated with feathers.

Mongol women had to work very hard and had to be able to care for the animals when the men were away hunting or fighting. They normally drove the carts and set up and dismantled the yurts. They also milked the sheep, goats, and cows and made the butter and cheese. In addition, they made the felt, prepared the skins, and sewed the clothes. Because water was scarce, clothes were not washed with water, nor were dishes. Women, like men, had to be expert riders, and many also learned to shoot. They participated actively in family decisions, especially as wives and mothers. In *The Secret History of the Mongols*, a work written in Mongolian in

snapped. "Now we'll have to run for the woods on foot," she thought, but before she could start the soldiers returned. They'd made [Temujin's half brother] Belgutei's mother their captive, and had her slung over one of their horses with her feet swinging down. They rode up to the old woman shouting: "What have you got in that cart!" "I'm just carrying wool," Khogaghchin replied, but an old soldier turned to the younger ones and said, "Get off your horses and see what's in there." When they opened the door of the cart they found Borte inside. Pulling her out, they forced Borte and Khogaghchin to ride on their horses, then they all set out after Temujin. . . .

The men who pursued Temujin were the chiefs of the three Merkid clans, Toghtoga, Dayin Usun, and Khagatai Darmala. These three had come to get their revenge, saying: "Long ago Mother Hogelun was stolen from our brother, Chiledu." When they couldn't catch Temujin they said to each other: "We've got our revenge. We've taken their wives from them," and they rode down from Mount Burkhan Khaldun back to their homes. . . .

Having finished his prayer Temujin rose and rode off with Khasar and Belgutei. They rode to [his father's sworn brother] Toghoril Ong Khan of the Kereyid camped in the Black Forest on the Tula River. Temujin spoke to Ong Khan, saying: "I was attacked by surprise by the three Merkid chiefs. They've stolen my wife from me. We've come to you now to say, 'Let my father the Khan save my wife and return her.'" . . .

[Temujin and his allies] moved their forces from Botoghan Bogorjin to the Kilgho River where they built rafts to cross over to the Bugura Steppe, into [the Merkid] Chief Toghtoga's land. They came down on him as if through the smoke-hole of his tent, beating down the frame of his tent and leaving it flat, capturing and killing his wives and his sons. They struck at his door-frame where his guardian spirit lived and broke it to pieces. They completely destroyed all his people until in their place there was nothing but emptiness. . . .

As the Merkid people tried to flee from our army running down the Selenge with what they could gather in the darkness, as our soldiers rode out of the night capturing and killing the Merkid, Temujin rode through the retreating camp shouting out: "Borte! Borte!"

Lady Borte was among the Merkid who ran in the darkness and when she heard his voice, when she recognized Temujin's voice, Borte leaped from her cart. Lady Borte and Old Woman Khogaghchin saw Temujin charge through the crowd and they ran to him, finally seizing the reins of his horse. All about them was moonlight. As Temujin looked down to see who had stopped him he recognized Lady Borte. In a moment he was down from his horse and they were in each other's arms, embracing. ”

Source: Paul Kahn, trans., *The Secret History of the Mongols: The Origin of Chinghis Khan*. Copyright © 1984. Reprinted with permission of Paul Kahn.

Chinggis and his wife Borte are seated together at a feast in this fourteenth-century Persian illustration. (Bibliothèque Nationale, Paris, France/The Bridgeman Art Library)

QUESTIONS FOR ANALYSIS

1. What do you learn from these stories about the Mongol way of life?
2. "Marriage by capture" has been practiced in many parts of the world. Can you infer from these stories why such a system would persist? What was the impact of such practices on kinship relations?
3. Can you recognize traces of the oral origins of these stories?

about 1240, the mother and wife of the Mongol leader Chinggis Khan frequently make impassioned speeches on the importance of family loyalty. (See "Listening to the Past: The Abduction of Women in *The Secret History of the Mongols*," above.)

Mongol men kept as busy as the women. They made the carts and wagons and the frames for the yurts. They also made harnesses for the horses and oxen, leather saddles, and the equipment needed for hunting and war, such as bows and arrows. Men also had charge of the horses, and they milked the mares. Young horses were allowed to run wild until it was time to break them in. Catching them took great skill in the use of a long springy pole with a noose at the end. One specialist among the nomads was the blacksmith, who made stirrups, knives, and other metal tools.

Kinship underlay most social relationships among the Mongols. Normally each family occupied a yurt, and groups of families camping together were usually related along the male line (brothers, uncles, nephews, and so on). More distant patrilineal relatives were recognized as members of the same clan and could call on each other for aid. People from the same clan could not marry each other, so men had to get wives from other clans. When a woman's husband died, she would be inherited by another male in the family, such as her husband's brother or his son by another woman. Tribes were groups of clans, often distantly related. Both clans and tribes had chiefs who would make decisions on where to graze and when to retaliate against another tribe that had stolen animals or people. Women were sometimes abducted for brides. When tribes stole men from each other, they normally made them into slaves, and slaves were forced to do much of the heavy work. They would not necessarily remain slaves their entire lives, however, as their original tribes might be able to recapture them or make exchanges for them, or their masters might free them.

Even though population was sparse in the regions where the Mongols lived, conflict over resources was endemic, and each camp had to be on the alert for attacks. Defending against attacks and retaliating against raids was as much a part of the Mongols' daily life as caring for their herds and trading with nearby settlements.

Mongol children learned to ride at a young age, first on goats. The horses they later rode were short and stocky, almost like ponies, but nimble and able to endure long journeys and bitter cold. Even in the winter the horses survived by grazing, foraging beneath the snow. The prime weapon boys had to learn to use was the compound bow, which had a pull of about 160 pounds and a range of more than 200 yards; it was well suited for using on horseback, giving Mongol soldiers an advantage in battle. Other commonly used weapons were small battle-axes and lances fitted with hooks to pull enemies off their saddles.

Hunting was a common form of military training among the Mongols. Each year tribes would organize one big hunt; mounted hunters would form a vast ring perhaps ten or more miles in circumference, then gradually shrink it down, trapping all the animals before killing them. On military campaigns a Mongol soldier had to be able to ride for days without stopping to cook food; he ate from a supply of dried milk curd and cured meat, which could be supplemented by blood let from the neck of his horse. When time permitted, the soldiers would pause to hunt, adding dogs, wolves, foxes, mice, and rats to their food.

As with the Turks and other steppe nomads, religious practices centered around the shaman, a religious expert believed to be able to communicate with the gods. The high god of the Mongols was Heaven/Sky, but they recognized many other gods as well. Some groups of Mongols, especially those closer to settled communities, converted to Buddhism, Nestorian Christianity, or Manichaeism.

Chinggis Khan and the Mongol Empire

- How did Chinggis Khan and his successors conquer much of Eurasia, and how did the Mongol conquests change the regions affected?

In the mid-twelfth century the Mongols were just one of many peoples in the eastern grasslands, neither particularly numerous nor especially advanced. Why then did the Mongols suddenly emerge as an overpowering force on the historical stage? One explanation is ecological. A drop in the mean annual temperature created a subsistence crisis. As pastures shrank, the Mongols and other nomads had to look beyond the steppe to get more of their food from the agricultural world. A second reason for their sudden rise was the appearance of a single individual, the brilliant but utterly ruthless Temujin (ca. 1162–1227), later and more commonly called Chinggis Khan (sometimes spelled Genghis or Ghengis).

Chinggis Khan

What we know of Temujin's early career was recorded in *The Secret History of the Mongols*, written within a few decades of his death. In Temujin's youth, his father had built a modest tribal following. When Temujin's father was poisoned by a rival, his followers, not ready to follow a boy of twelve, drifted away, leaving Temujin and his mother and brothers in a vulnerable position. Temujin slowly collected followers. In 1182 Temujin was captured and carried in a cage to a rival's camp. After a daring midnight escape, he led his followers to join a stronger chieftain whom his father had once aided. With the chieftain's help, Temujin began avenging the insults he had received.

Temujin proved to be a natural leader, and as he subdued the Tartars, Kereyids, Naimans, Merkids, and other Mongol and Turkish tribes, he built up an army of loyal followers. He mastered the art of winning allies through displays of personal courage in battle and gen-

- **Chinggis Khan** The title given to the Mongol ruler Temujin in 1206; it means Great Ruler.

The Tent of Chinggis Khan In this fourteenth-century Persian illustration from Rashid al-Din's *History of the World*, two guards stand outside while Chinggis is in his tent. (From a book by Rashid al-Din [1247–1318] [vellum], Persian School [14th century]/Bibliothèque Nationale, Paris, France/The Bridgeman Art Library)

erosity to his followers. To those who opposed him, he could be merciless. He once asserted that nothing gave more pleasure than massacring one's enemies, seizing their horses and cattle, and ravishing their women. Sometimes Temujin would kill all the men in a defeated tribe to prevent later vendettas. At other times he would take them on as soldiers in his own armies. Courage impressed him. One of his leading generals, Jebe, first attracted his attention when he held his ground against overwhelming opposition and shot Temujin's horse out from under him. Another prominent general, Mukhali, became Temujin's personal slave at age twenty-seven after his tribe was defeated by Temujin in 1197. Within a few years he was leading a corps of a thousand men from his own former tribe.

In 1206, at a great gathering of tribal leaders, Temujin was proclaimed **Chinggis Khan**, or Great Ruler. Chinggis decreed that Mongol, until then an unwritten language, be written down in the script used by the Uighur Turks. With this script a record was made of the Mongol laws and customs, ranging from the rules for the annual hunt to punishments of death for robbery and adultery. Another measure adopted at this assembly was a postal relay system to send messages rapidly by mounted courier, suggesting that Chinggis already had ambitions to rule a vast empire.

With the tribes of Mongolia united, the energies previously devoted to infighting and vendettas were redirected to exacting tribute from the settled populations nearby, starting with the Jurchen (Jin) state that extended into north China (see Map 13.2, page 370). Because of his early experiences with intertribal feuding, Chinggis mistrusted traditional tribal loyalties, and as he fashioned a new army, he gave it a new, nontribal decimal structure (based on units of ten). He conscripted soldiers from all the tribes and assigned them to units that were composed of members from different tribes. He selected commanders for each unit whom he could remove at will, although he allowed commanders to pass their posts on to their sons.

After Chinggis subjugated a city, he would send envoys to cities farther out to demand submission and threaten destruction. Those who opened their city gates and submitted without fighting could join the Mongols, but those who resisted faced the prospect of mass slaughter. He despised city dwellers and would sometimes use them as living shields in the next battle. After the Mongol armies swept across north China in 1212–1213, ninety-odd cities lay in rubble. Beijing, captured in 1215, burned for more than a month. Not surprisingly many governors of cities and rulers of small states hastened to offer submission.

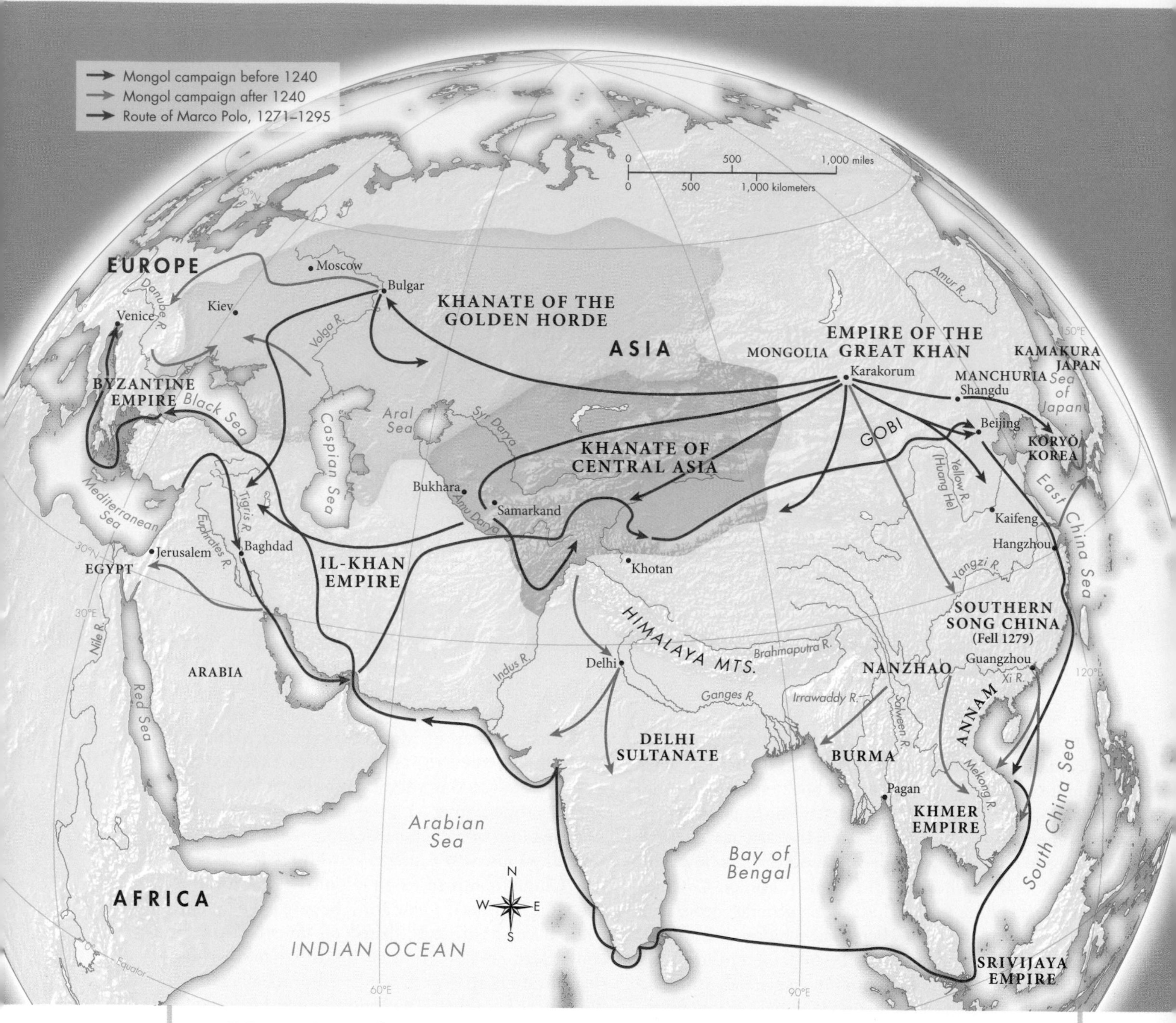

Mapping the Past

MAP 12.1 The Mongol Empire The creation of the vast Mongol Empire facilitated communication across Eurasia and led to both the spread of deadly plagues and the transfer of technical and scientific knowledge. After the death of Chinggis Khan in 1227, the empire was divided into four khanates ruled by different lines of his successors. In the 1270s the Mongols conquered southern China, but most of their subsequent campaigns did not lead to further territorial gains.

ANALYZING THE MAP Trace the campaigns of the Mongols. Which ones led to acquisition of territory, and which ones did not?

CONNECTIONS Would the division of the Mongol Empire into separate khanates have made these areas easier for the Mongols to rule? What drawbacks might it have had from the Mongols' point of view?

Chinggis preferred conquest to administration and did not stay in north China to set up an administrative structure. He left that to subordinates and turned his attention westward, to Central Asia and Persia, then dominated by different groups of Turks. In 1218 Chinggis proposed to the Khwarizm shah of Persia that he accept Mongol overlordship and establish trade relations. The shah, to show his determination to resist, ordered the envoy and the merchants who had accompanied him killed. The next year Chinggis led an army of one hundred thousand soldiers west to retaliate. Mongol forces destroyed the shah's army and sacked one Persian city after another, demolishing buildings and massacring hundreds of thousands of people.

After returning from Central Asia, Chinggis died in 1227 during the siege of a city in northwest China. Before he died, he instructed his sons not to fall out among themselves but instead to divide the spoils.

Chinggis's Successors

Although Mongol leaders traditionally had had to win their positions, after Chinggis died the empire was divided into four states called **khanates**, with one of the lines of his descendants taking charge of each (Map 12.1). Chinggis's third son, Ögödei, assumed the title of khan, and he directed the next round of invasions.

In 1237 representatives of all four lines led 150,000 Mongol, Turkish, and Persian troops into Europe. During the next five years, they gained control of Moscow and Kievan Russia and looted cities in Poland and Hungary. They were poised to attack deeper into Europe when they learned of the death of Ögödei in 1241. To participate in the election of a new khan, the army returned to the Mongols' new capital city, Karakorum.

Once Ögödei's son was certified as his successor, the Mongols turned their attention to Persia and the Middle East. In 1256 a Mongol army took northwest Iran, then pushed on to the Abbasid capital of Baghdad. When it fell in 1258, the last Abbasid caliph was murdered, and the population was put to the sword. The Mongol onslaught was successfully resisted, however, by both the Delhi sultanate (see page 349) and the Mamluk rulers in Egypt (see page 246).

Under Chinggis's grandson Khubilai Khan (r. 1260–1294), the Mongols completed their conquest of China. South China had never been captured by non-Chinese, in large part because horses were of no strategic advantage in a land of rivers and canals. Proceeding deliberately, the Mongols first surrounded the Song empire in central and south China (discussed in Chapter 13) by taking its westernmost province in 1252, as well as Korea to its east in 1258; destroying the Nanzhao kingdom in modern Yunnan in 1254; and then continuing south and taking Annam (northern Vietnam) in 1257. A surrendered Song commander advised the Mongols to build a navy to attack the great Song cities located on rivers. During the five-year siege of a central Chinese river port, both sides used thousands of boats and tens of thousands of troops. The Mongols employed experts in naval and siege warfare from all over their empire—Chinese, Korean, Jurchen, Uighur, and Persian. Catapults designed by Muslim engineers launched a barrage of rocks weighing up to a hundred pounds each. During their advance toward the Chinese capital of Hangzhou, the Mongols ordered the total slaughter of the people of the major city of Changzhou, and in 1276 the Chinese empress dowager surrendered in hopes of sparing the people of the capital a similar fate.

Having overrun China and Korea, Khubilai turned his eyes toward Japan. In 1274 a force of 30,000 soldiers and support personnel sailed from Korea to Japan. In 1281 a combined Mongol and Chinese fleet of about 150,000 made a second attempt to conquer Japan. On both occasions the Mongols managed to land but were beaten back by Japanese samurai armies. Each time fierce storms destroyed the Mongol fleets. The Japanese claimed that they had been saved by the *kamikaze*, the "divine wind" (which later lent its name to the thousands of Japanese aviators who crashed their airplanes into American warships during World War II). Twelve years later, in 1293, Khubilai tried sending a fleet to the islands of Southeast Asia, including Java, but it met with no more success than the fleets sent to Japan.

Why were the Mongols so successful against so many different types of enemies? Even though their population was tiny compared to the populations of the large agricultural societies they conquered, their tactics, their weapons, and their organization all gave them advantages. Like other nomads before them, they were superb horsemen and excellent archers. Their horses were extremely nimble, able to change direction quickly, thus allowing the Mongols to maneuver easily and ride through infantry forces armed with swords, lances, and javelins. Usually only other nomadic armies, like the Turks, could stand up well against the Mongols. (See "Viewpoints 12.1: Chinese and European Accounts About the Mongol Army," page 340.)

The Mongols were also open to trying new military technologies. To attack walled cities, they learned how to use catapults and other engines of war. At first they employed Chinese catapults, but when they learned that those used by the Turks in Afghanistan were more powerful, they adopted the better model. The Mongols also used exploding arrows and gunpowder projectiles developed by the Chinese.

• **khanates** The states ruled by a khan; the four units into which Chinggis divided the Mongol Empire.

Viewpoints 12.1

Chinese and European Accounts About the Mongol Army

• *The Mongols received little attention from historians until they were united under Chinggis and began their military conquests. The following documents offer different perspectives on the Mongol army. The first, one of the earliest surviving accounts, was written about 1220 by a Chinese historian, Li Xinchuan, living in south China under the Song Dynasty. He would have learned of the Mongols secondhand, as the Song had diplomatic relations with Jin, which was then under attack by the Mongols. He reported how the Tartars—referring to the Mongols—gained control of north China in 1213–1214. The second excerpt refers to the time that the state of Song in south China sustained its first major attack by the Mongols in 1236, when Mongol armies entered the western province of Sichuan and destroyed major cities like Chengdu. A man who survived the slaughter, Zhu Sisun, later reported what he went through. Marco Polo, encountering the Mongols a half century later, after most of their conquests through Eurasia were complete, had a different view of the warriors.*

Li Xinchuan

“In the spring of 1213 [the Tartars] attacked Yanjing [modern Beijing] and that fall Yunji [the Jin emperor] was killed. Chinggis left Samohe in charge of Yanjing and incorporated the 46 divisions of the surrendered [Jin] armies of Yang Boyu and Liu Bolin into the great Tartar armies, which were divided into three divisions to conquer the prefectural cities of [the circuits of] River North, River East, and Mountains East. . . . At this time the troops of the various circuits of north China pulled back to defend the region west of the mountains, but there were not enough troops, so commoners were drafted as soldiers and put on the tops of the city walls to defend them. The Tartars drove their family members to attack them, and fathers and sons or brothers often got close enough to recognize and call out to each other. Because of this, [the drafted soldiers] were not firmly resolved, and all of the cities surrendered as soon as the fighting began. From the twelfth month of 1213 to the first month of 1214, more than ninety prefectures fell. Every place the armies passed through was devastated. For several thousand *li*, throughout River East, River North, and Mountains East, the people were slaughtered. Gold and silk, boys and girls, oxen and sheep, horses and other animals were all "rolled up" and taken away. Houses were burnt down and defensive walls smashed.”

Zhu Sisun

“Here is how the people of Sichuan went to their deaths: groups of fifty people were clustered together, and the Mongols impaled them all with swords and piled up the corpses. At sunset, those who did not appear dead were again stabbed. Sisun lay at the bottom of a pile of corpses, and by chance the evening stabbing did not reach him. The blood of the corpses above him dripped steadily into his mouth. Halfway through the night Sisun began to revive, and crawling into the woods he made his escape.”

Marco Polo

“They are brave in battle, almost to desperation, setting little value upon their lives, and exposing themselves without hesitation to all manner of danger. Their disposition is cruel. They are capable of supporting every kind of privation, and when there is a necessity for it, can live for a month on the milk of their mares, and upon such wild animals as they may chance to catch. The men are habituated to remain on horseback during two days and two nights, without dismounting, sleeping in that situation whilst their horses graze. No people on earth can surpass them in fortitude under difficulties, nor show greater patience under wants of every kind.”

Sources: Li Xinchuan, *Jianyan yilai chaoye zaji* (Beijing: Zhonghua shuju, 2000), pp. 847–851, trans. Patricia Ebrey; Paul J. Smith, "Family, *Landsmann*, and Status-Group Affinity in Refugee Mobility Strategies: The Mongol Invasions and the Diaspora of Sichuanese Elites, 1230–1330," *Harvard Journal of Asiatic Studies* 52.2 (1992): 671–672, slightly modified; *The Travels of Marco Polo, the Venetian*, ed. Manuel Komroff (New York: Boni and Liveright, 1926), p. 93.

QUESTIONS FOR ANALYSIS

1. How would you explain the differences in what these writers chose to mention?
2. If you were writing a history of the Mongols, would you consider these sources as equally valid evidence, or do you find some more reliable than others? Does anything in the accounts seem exaggerated? How can you judge?

The Mongols made good use of intelligence and tried to exploit internal divisions in the countries they attacked. Thus in north China they appealed to the Khitans, who had been defeated by the Jurchens a century earlier, to join them in attacking the Jurchens. In Syria they exploited the resentment of Christians against their Muslim rulers.

The Mongols as Rulers

The success of the Mongols in ruling vast territories was due in large part to their willingness to incorporate other ethnic groups into their armies and governments. Whatever their original country or religion, those who served the Mongols loyally were rewarded. Uighurs, Tibetans, Persians, Chinese, and Russians came to hold powerful positions in the Mongol governments. Chinese helped breach the walls of Baghdad in the 1250s, and Muslims operated the catapults that helped reduce Chinese cities in the 1270s.

Since, in Mongol eyes, the purpose of fighting was to gain riches, the Mongols would regularly loot the settlements they conquered, taking whatever they wanted, including the residents. Land would be granted to military commanders, nobles, and army units to be governed and exploited as the recipients wished. Those working the land would be given to them as serfs. The Mongols built a capital city called Karakorum in modern Mongolia, and to bring it up to the level of the cities they conquered, they transported skilled workers from those cities. For instance, after Bukhara and Samarkand were captured in 1219–1220, some thirty thousand artisans were enslaved and transported to Mongolia. Sometimes these slaves gradually improved their status. A French goldsmith from Budapest named Guillaume Boucher was captured by the Mongols in 1242 and taken to Karakorum, where he gradually won favor and was put in charge of fifty workers to make gold and silver vessels for the Mongol court.

The traditional nomad disdain for farmers led some commanders to suggest turning north China into a gigantic pasture after it was conquered. In time, though, the Mongols came to realize that simply appropriating the wealth and human resources of the settled lands was not as good as extracting regular revenue from them. A Chinese-educated Khitan who had been working for the Jurchens in China explained to the Mongols that collecting taxes from farmers would be highly profitable: they could extract a revenue of 500,000 ounces of silver, 80,000 bolts of silk, and more than 20,000 tons of grain from the region by taxing it. The Mongols gave this a try, but soon political rivals convinced the khan that he would gain even more by letting Central Asian Muslim merchants bid against each other for licenses to collect taxes any way they could, a system called **tax-farming**. Ordinary Chinese found this method of tax collecting much more oppressive than traditional Chinese methods, since there was little to keep the tax collectors from seizing everything they could.

MONGOL CONQUESTS

1206	Temujin made Chinggis Khan
1215	Fall of Beijing (Jurchens)
1219–1220	Fall of Bukhara and Samarkand in Central Asia
1227	Death of Chinggis
1237–1241	Raids into eastern Europe
1257	Conquest of Annam (northern Vietnam)
1258	Conquest of Abbasid capital of Baghdad; conquest of Korea
1260	Khubilai succeeds to khanship
1274	First attempt at invading Japan
1276	Surrender of Song Dynasty (China)
1281	Second attempt at invading Japan
1293	Mongol fleet unsuccessful in invasion of Java
mid-14th century	Decline of Mongol power

By the second half of the thirteenth century there was no longer a genuine pan-Asian Mongol Empire. Much of Asia was in the hands of Mongol successor states, but these were generally hostile to each other. Khubilai was often at war with the khanate of Central Asia, then held by his cousin Khaidu, and he had little contact with the khanate of the Golden Horde in south Russia. The Mongols adapted their methods of government to the existing traditions of each place they ruled, and the regions went their separate ways.

In China the Mongols resisted assimilation and purposely avoided many Chinese practices. The rulers conducted their business in the Mongol language and spent their summers in Mongolia. Khubilai discouraged Mongols from marrying Chinese and took only Mongol women into the palace. Some Mongol princes preferred to live in yurts erected on the palace grounds rather than in the grand palaces constructed at Beijing. Chinese were treated as legally inferior not only to the Mongols but also to all other non-Chinese. In cases of assault the discrepancy was huge, as a Mongol who murdered a Chinese could get off with a fine, but a Chinese who hit a Mongol to defend himself would face severe penalties.

- **tax-farming** Assigning the collection of taxes to whoever bids the most for the privilege.

In Central Asia, Persia, and Russia the Mongols tended to merge with the Turkish groups already there and, like them, converted to Islam. Russia in the thirteenth century was not a strongly centralized state, and the Mongols allowed Russian princes and lords to continue to rule their territories as long as they turned over adequate tribute (thus adding to the burden on peasants). The city of Moscow became the center of Mongol tribute collection and grew in importance. In the Middle East the Mongol Il-khans (as they were known in Persia) were more active as rulers, again continuing the traditions of the caliphate. In Mongolia itself, however, Mongol traditions were maintained.

Mongol control in each of the khanates lasted about a century. In the mid-fourteenth century the Mongol dynasty in China deteriorated into civil war, and in the 1360s the Mongols withdrew back to Mongolia. There was a similar loss of Mongol power in Persia and Central Asia. Only on the south Russian steppe did the Golden Horde maintain its hold for another century.

As Mongol rule in Central Asia declined, a new conqueror emerged, Timur, also known as Tamerlane (Timur the Lame). Not a nomad but a highly civilized Turkish noble, Timur in the 1360s struck out from his base in Samarkand into Persia, north India (see page 349), southern Russia, and beyond. His armies used the terror tactics that the Mongols had perfected, massacring the citizens of cities that resisted. In the decades after his death in 1405, however, Timur's empire went into decline.

East-West Communication During the Mongol Era

☐ How did the Mongol conquests facilitate the spread of ideas, religions, inventions, and diseases?

The Mongol governments did more than any earlier political entities to encourage the movement of people and goods across Eurasia. With these vast movements came cultural accommodation as the Mongols, their conquered subjects, and their trading partners learned from one another. This cultural exchange involved both physical goods and the sharing of ideas, including the introduction of new religious beliefs and the adoption of new ways to organize and rule the Mongol Empire. It also facilitated the spread of the plague and the unwilling movement of enslaved captives.

The Movement of Peoples

The Mongols had never looked down on merchants the way the elites of many traditional states did, and they welcomed the arrival of merchants from distant lands. Even when different groups of Mongols were fighting among themselves, they usually allowed caravans to pass without harassing them.

The Mongol practice of transporting skilled people from the lands they conquered also brought people into contact with each other in new ways. Besides those forced to move, the Mongols recruited administrators from all over. Especially prominent were the Uighur Turks of Chinese Central Asia, whose familiarity with Chinese civilization and fluency in Turkish were extremely valuable in facilitating communication. Literate Uighurs staffed much of the Mongol administration.

One of those who served the Mongols was Rashid al-Din (ca. 1247–1318). A Jew from Persia and the son of an apothecary, Rashid al-Din converted to Islam at the age of thirty and entered the service of the Mongol Il-khan of Persia as a physician. He rose in government service, traveled widely, and eventually became prime minister. Rashid al-Din became friends with the ambassador from China, and together they arranged for translations of Chinese works on medicine, agronomy, and statecraft. Aware of the great differences between cultures, he believed that the Mongols should try to rule in accord with the moral principles of the majority in each land. On that basis he convinced the Mongol khan of Persia to convert to Islam. Rashid al-Din undertook to explain the great variety of cultures by writing a world history more comprehensive than any previously written. (See "Viewpoints 12.2: Circulating Paper Money," at right.)

The Mongols were remarkably open to religious experts from all the lands they encountered. More Europeans made their way as far as Mongolia and China in the Mongol period than ever before. Popes and kings sent envoys to the Mongol court in the hope of enlisting the Mongols on their side in their long-standing conflict with Muslim forces over the Holy Land. European visitors were also interested in finding Christians who had been cut off from the West by the spread of Islam, and in fact there were considerable numbers of Nestorian Christians in Central Asia. In 1245 Pope Innocent IV wrote two letters to the "King and people of the Tartars" asking him to become a Christian and cease attacks against Europe. They were delivered to a Mongol general in Armenia. The next year another envoy, Giovanni di Pian de Carpine, reached the Volga River and the camp of Batu, the khan of the Golden Horde. Batu sent him on to the new Great Khan in Karakorum with two Mongol guides, riding so fast that they had to change horses five to seven times a day. Their full journey of more than three thousand miles took a remarkably short five and a half months. Carpine spent four months at the Great Khan's court but never succeeded in convincing the khan to embrace Christianity or drop his demand

Viewpoints 12.2

Circulating Paper Money

• *In China the Mongols maintained the established practice of circulating paper money (see page 378), which amazed visitors from other parts of Eurasia. The three texts below give different perspectives on the use of paper money. The first is a legal ruling issued in 1291 by the Mongols in China, the second is Marco Polo's description of the practice as he witnessed it in the 1290s, and the third is Rashid al-Din's account of the failed attempt to introduce the practice in Mongol-ruled Persia in 1294.*

The Yuan Code of 1291

"At any Treasury for Note Circulation, when a person comes to exchange worn-out notes for new notes, the responsible official shall oversee the counting of the notes in the presence of the owner. If none of the notes are patched or counterfeited, the official shall apply the stamp "Exchanged" to them and place them in the treasury and hand over new notes to the owner. The supervising authorities shall send inspectors to make frequent inspections. Any violator of these provisions shall be investigated and punished."

Marco Polo

"The coinage of this paper money is authenticated with as much form and ceremony as if it were actually pure gold or silver; for to each note a number of officers, specially appointed, not only subscribe their names, but affix their seals also. . . . When thus coined in large quantities, this paper currency is circulated in every part of the Great Khan's dominions; nor dares any person, at the peril of his life, refuse to accept it in payment. All his subjects receive it without hesitation, because, wherever their business may call them, they can dispose of it again in the purchase of merchandise they may require; such as pearls, jewels, gold, or silver. With it, in short, every article may be procured. . . .

When any person happens to be possessed of paper money which from long use has become damaged, they carry it to the mint, where, upon the payment of only three per cent, they receive fresh notes in exchange. Should any be desirous of procuring gold or silver for the purpose of manufacture, such as of drinking-cups, girdles, or other articles wrought of these metals, they in like manner apply to the mint, and for their paper obtain the bullion they require."

Rashid al-Din

"On Friday [July 27, 1294], Akbuka, Togachar, Sadr al-Din, and Tamachi-Inak went to Tabriz to launch the paper money [*chao*]. They arrived there on [August 13], promulgated the decree, and prepared a great quantity of paper money. On Saturday [September 12, 1294], in the city of Tabriz, they put the paper money into circulation. The decree laid down that any person who refused to accept it would be summarily executed. For one week, in fear of the sword, they accepted it, but they gave very little in return. Most of the people of Tabriz perforce chose to leave, taking the textiles and foodstuffs from the bazaars with them, so that nothing was available, and people who wanted to eat fruit went secretly to the orchards. The city, which had been so populous, was completely emptied of people. Vagabonds and ruffians looted whatever they found in the streets. Caravans ceased to go there. . . .

Sadr al-Din, affected by the words [of a dervish], and with the assent of the retainers after this ruination, obtained a decree authorizing the sale of foodstuffs for gold. Because of this people became bold and transacted business openly in gold, and the absent returned to the city, and within a short time it was flourishing again. In the end, the attempt to introduce paper money did not succeed."

Sources: *Dayuan tongzhi tiaoge* (Taipei: Huasheng shuju, 1980), 14.1b–2a, trans. Patricia Ebrey; Manuel Komroff, ed., *The Travels of Marco Polo* (New York: Boni and Liveright, 1926), pp. 159–161; Bernard Lewis, ed. and trans., *Islam from the Prophet Muhammad to the Capture of Constantinople*. Vol. 2: *Religion and Society* (New York: Oxford University Press, 1987), 292w from p. 192, slightly modified.

QUESTIONS FOR ANALYSIS

1. What do you learn about the processes of cultural borrowing from these sources?
2. What features of paper money most impressed Marco Polo?
3. What made it difficult to introduce paper money in Tabriz?

that the pope appear in person to tender his submission to the khan. When Carpine returned home, he wrote a report that urged preparation for a renewed Mongol attack on Europe. The Mongols had to be resisted "because of the harsh, indeed intolerable, and hitherto unheard-of slavery seen with our own eyes, to which they reduce all peoples who have submitted to them."[4]

A few years later, in 1253, Flemish friar William of Rubruck set out with the permission of King Louis IX of France as a missionary to convert the Mongols. He too made his way to Karakorum, where he found many Europeans. At Easter, Hungarians, Russians, Georgians, Armenians, and Alans all took communion in a Nestorian church.

The most famous European visitor to the Mongol lands was the Venetian Marco Polo (ca. 1254–1324). In his famous *Travels*, Marco Polo described all the places he visited or learned about during his seventeen years away from home. He reported being warmly received by Khubilai, who impressed him enormously. He was also awed by the wealth and splendor of Chinese cities and spread the notion of Asia as a land of riches. In Marco Polo's lifetime some skeptics did not believe his tale, and even today some scholars speculate that he may have learned about China from Persian merchants he met in the Middle East without actually going to China. But Mongol scholars staunchly defend Marco Polo, even though they admit that he stretched the truth to make himself look good in several places.

The Spread of Disease, Goods, and Ideas

The rapid transfer of people and goods across Central Asia spread more than ideas and inventions. It also spread diseases, the most deadly of which was the plague known in Europe as the Black Death, which scholars identify today as the bubonic plague. In the early fourteenth century, transmitted by rats and fleas, the plague began to spread from Central Asia into West Asia, the Mediterranean, and western Europe. When the Mongols were assaulting the city of Kaffa in the Crimea in 1346, they were infected by the plague and had to withdraw. In retaliation, they purposely spread the disease to their enemy by catapulting the bodies of victims into the city of Kaffa. Soon the disease was carried from port to port throughout the Mediterranean by ship. The confusion of the mid-fourteenth century that led to the loss of Mongol power in China, Iran, and Central Asia undoubtedly owes something to the effect of the spread of the plague and other diseases. (For more on the Black Death, see Chapter 14.)

Traditionally, the historians of each of the countries conquered by the Mongols portrayed them as a scourge. Russian historians, for instance, saw this as a period of bondage that set Russia back and cut it off from western Europe. Among contemporary Western historians, it is now more common to celebrate the genius of the Mongol military machine and treat the spread of ideas and inventions as an obvious good, probably because we see global communication as a good in our own world. There is no reason to assume, however, that people benefited equally from the improved communications and the new political institutions of the Mongol era. Merchants involved in long-distance trade prospered, but those enslaved and transported hundreds or thousands of miles from home would have seen themselves not as the beneficiaries of opportunities to encounter cultures different from their own but rather as the most pitiable of victims.

The places that were ruled by Mongol governments for a century or more—China, Central Asia, Persia, and Russia—do not seem to have advanced at a more

Planting Trees The illustrations in early copies of Marco Polo's book show the elements that Europeans found most interesting. This page illustrates Khubilai's order that trees be planted along the main roads. (Illumination from *Le Livre des Merveilles du Monde* [Travels of Marco Polo], by the Paris studio of the Boucicaut Master, c. 1412/Bibliothèque Nationale, Paris/akg-images)

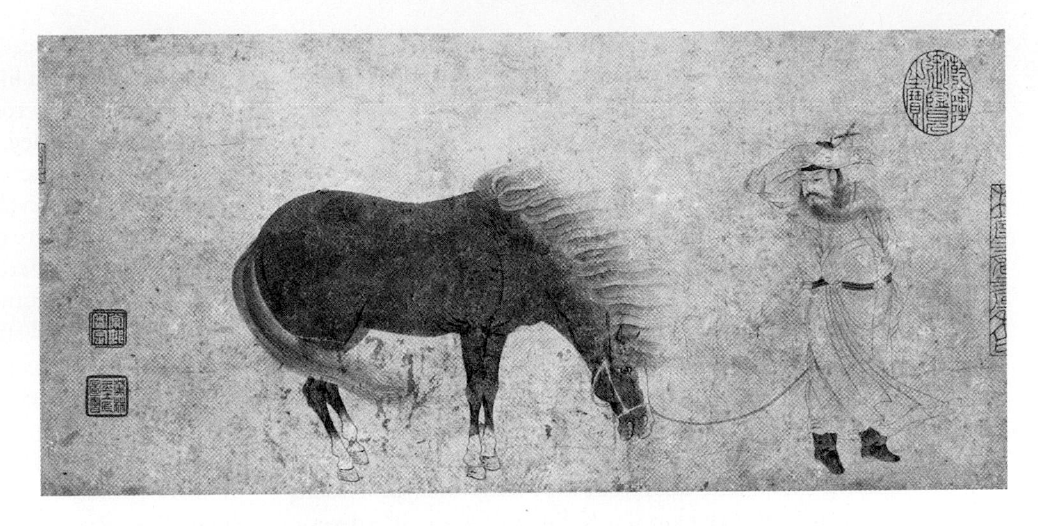

Horse and Groom Zhao Mengfu (1254–1322), the artist of this painting and a member of the Song imperial family, took up service under the Mongol emperor Khubilai. The Mongol rulers, great horsemen themselves, would likely have appreciated this depiction of a horse buffeted by the wind. (*Horse and Groom in Winter* [ink on paper], Chao Meng-Fu, or Zhao Mengfu [1254–1322], National Palace Museum, Taipei, Taiwan/The Bridgeman Art Library)

rapid rate during that century than they did in earlier centuries, either economically or culturally. By Chinese standards, Mongol imposition of hereditary status distinctions was a step backward from a much more mobile and open society, and placing Persians, Arabs, or Tibetans over Chinese did not arouse interest in foreign cultures. Many more styles of foreign music, clothing, art, and furnishings were integrated into Chinese civilization in Tang times than in Mongol times.

In terms of the spread of technological and scientific ideas, Europe seems to have been by far the main beneficiary of increased communication, largely because in 1200 it lagged farther behind than the other areas. Chinese inventions such as printing, gunpowder, and the compass spread westward. Persian and Indian expertise in astronomy and mathematics also spread. In terms of the spread of religions, Islam probably gained the most. It came to dominate in Chinese Central Asia, which had previously been Buddhist.

India, Islam, and the Development of Regional Cultures, 300–1400

☐ What was the result of India's encounters with Turks, Mongols, and Islam?

South Asia, although far from the heartland of the steppe, still felt the impact of the arrival of the Turks in Central Asia. Over the course of many centuries, horsemen from both the east and the west (Scythians, Huns, Turks, and Mongols) all sent armies south to raid or invade north India. After the Mauryan Empire broke apart in 185 B.C.E. (see page 84), India was politically divided into small kingdoms for several centuries. Only the Guptas in the fourth century would emerge to unite much of north India, though their rule was cut short by the invasion of the Huns in about 450. A few centuries later, India was profoundly shaped by Turkish nomads from Central Asia who brought their culture and, most important, Islam to India. Despite these events, the lives of most Indians remained unchanged, with the majority of the people living in villages in a society defined by caste.

The Gupta Empire, ca. 320–480

In the early fourth century a state emerged in the Ganges plain that was able to bring large parts of north India under its control. The rulers of this Indian empire, the Guptas, consciously modeled their rule after that of the Mauryan Empire, and the founder took the name of the founder of that dynasty, Chandragupta. Although the Guptas never controlled as much territory as the Mauryans had, they united north India and received tribute from states in Nepal and the Indus Valley, thus giving large parts of India a period of peace and political unity.

The Gupta Empire, ca. 320–480

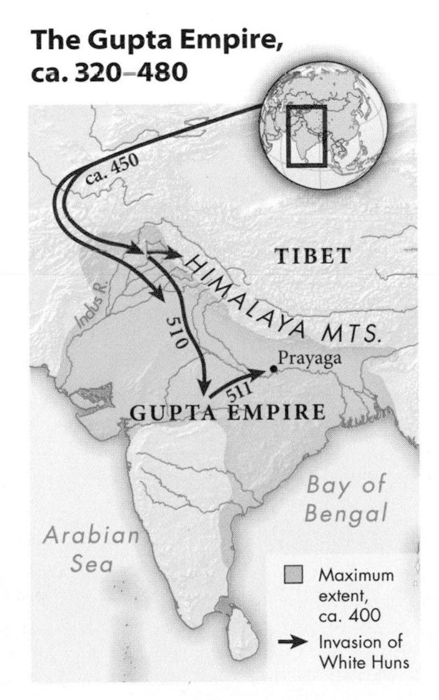

The Guptas' administrative system was not as centralized as that of the Mauryans. In the central regions they drew their revenue from a tax on agriculture of one-quarter of the harvest and maintained monopolies on key products such as metals and salt (reminiscent of Chinese practice). They also exacted labor service for the construction and upkeep of roads, wells, and irrigation systems. More distant areas were assigned to governors who were allowed considerable leeway, and governorships often became hereditary. Areas still farther away were encouraged to become vassal states, able to participate in the splendor of the capital and royal court in subordinate roles and to engage in profitable trade, but did not have to provide much revenue.

The Gupta kings were patrons of the arts. Poets composed epics for the courts of the Gupta kings, and other writers experimented with prose romances and popular tales. India's greatest poet, Kalidasa (ca. 380–450), like Shakespeare, wrote poems as well as plays in verse. His most highly esteemed play, *Shakuntala*, concerns a daughter of a hermit who enthralls a king who is out hunting. The king sets up house with her, then returns to his court and, owing to a curse, forgets her. Only much later does he acknowledge their child as his true heir. Equally loved is Kalidasa's one-hundred-verse poem "The Cloud Messenger" about a demigod who asks a passing cloud to carry a message to his wife, from whom he has long been separated. At one point he instructs the cloud to tell her: "I see your body in the sinuous creeper, your gaze in the startled eyes of deer, your cheek in the moon, your hair in the plumage of peacocks, and in the tiny ripples of the river I see your sidelong glances, but alas, my dearest, nowhere do I see your whole likeness."[5]

In mathematics, too, the Gupta period could boast of impressive intellectual achievements. The so-called Arabic numerals are actually of Indian origin. Indian mathematicians developed the place-value notation system, with separate columns for ones, tens, and hundreds, as well as a zero sign to indicate the absence of units in a given column. This system greatly facilitated calculation and had spread as far as Europe by the seventh century.

The Gupta rulers were Hindus, but they tolerated all faiths. Buddhist pilgrims from other areas of Asia reported that Buddhist monasteries with hundreds or even thousands of monks and nuns flourished in the cities. The success of Buddhism did not hinder Hinduism with its many gods, which remained popular among ordinary people.

The great crisis of the Gupta Empire was the invasion of the Huns in about 450. Mustering his full might, the Gupta ruler Skandagupta (r. ca. 455–467) threw back the invaders, but they had dealt the dynasty a fatal blow.

Wall Painting at Ajanta Many of the best surviving examples of Gupta period painting are found at the twenty-nine Buddhist cave temples at Ajanta in central India. The walls of these caves were decorated in the fifth and sixth centuries with scenes from the former lives of the Buddha. This scene shows members of different castes. (SEF/Art Resource, NY)

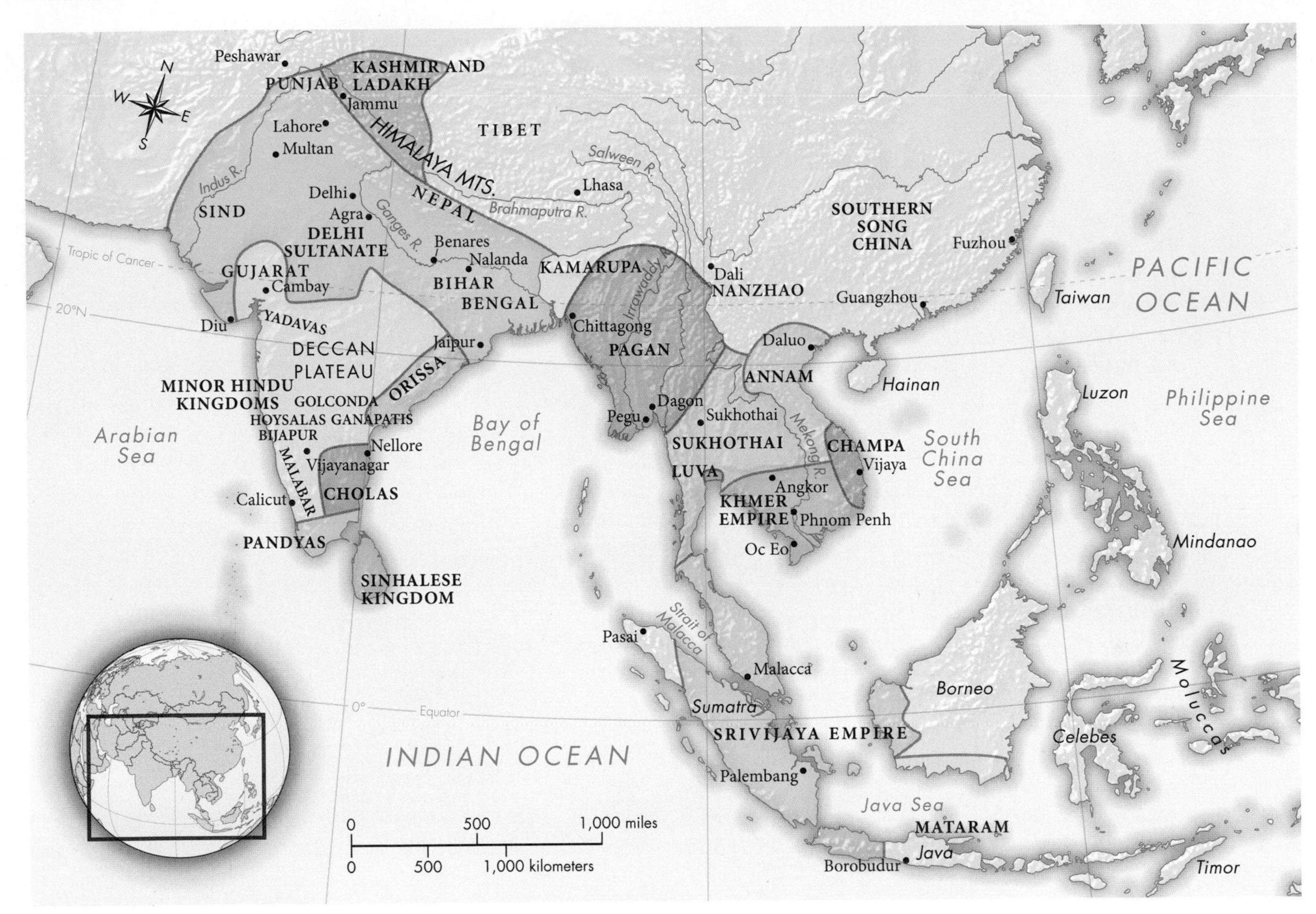

MAP 12.2 South and Southeast Asia in the Thirteenth Century The extensive coastlines of South and Southeast Asia and the predictable monsoon winds aided seafaring in this region. Note the Strait of Malacca, through which most east-west sea trade passed.

India's Medieval Age and the First Encounter with Islam

After the decline of the Gupta Empire, India once again broke into separate kingdoms that were frequently at war with each other. Most of the dynasties of India's medieval age (ca. 500–1400) were short-lived, but a balance of power was maintained between the major regions of India, with none gaining enough of an advantage to conquer the others. Particularly notable are the Cholas, who dominated the southern tip of the peninsula, Sri Lanka, and much of the eastern Indian Ocean to the twelfth century (Map 12.2).

Political division fostered the development of regional cultures. Literature came to be written in India's regional languages, among them Marathi, Bengali, and Assamese. Commerce continued as before, and the coasts of India remained important in the sea trade of the Indian Ocean.

The first encounters with Islam occurred in this period. In 711, after pirates had plundered a richly laden Arab ship near the mouth of the Indus, the Umayyad governor of Iraq sent a force with six thousand horses and six thousand camels to seize the Sind area in western India (modern Pakistan). The western part of India remained part of the caliphate for centuries, but Islam did not spread much beyond this foothold. During the ninth and tenth centuries Turks from Central Asia moved into the region of today's northeastern Iran and western Afghanistan, then known as Khurasan. Converts to Islam, they first served as military forces for the caliphate in Baghdad, but as its authority weakened (see pages 339, 341), they made themselves rulers of an effectively independent Khurasan and frequently sent raiding parties into north India. Beginning in 997 Mahmud of Ghazni (r. 997–1030) led seventeen annual forays into India from his base in modern Afghanistan. His goal was plunder to finance his wars against other Turkish rulers in Central Asia. Toward this end, he systematically looted Indian palaces and temples, viewing religious statues as infidels' idols. Eventually the Arab conquerors of the Sind

Kandariyâ Mahâdeva Hindu Temple Built around 1050 by a local king in central India, this is one of the best-preserved Hindu temples from the medieval period. The main spire rises 100 feet, and the sides are decorated with more than six hundred stone statues. (Yvan Travert/akg-images)

fell to the Turks. By 1030 the Indus Valley, the Punjab, and the rest of northwest India were in the grip of the Turks.

The new rulers encouraged the spread of Islam, but the Indian caste system (see page 69) made it difficult to convert higher-caste Indians. Al-Biruni (d. 1048), a Persian scholar who spent much of his later life at the court of Mahmud and learned Sanskrit, wrote of the obstacles to Hindu-Muslim communication. The most basic barrier was language, but the religious gulf was also fundamental:

> They totally differ from us in religion, as we believe in nothing in which they believe, and vice versa. On the whole, there is very little disputing about theological topics among them; at the utmost they fight with words, but they will never stake their soul or body or property on religious controversy. . . . They call foreigners impure and forbid having any connection with them, be it by intermarriage or any kind of relationship, or by sitting, eating, and drinking with them, because thereby, they think, they would be polluted.[6]

• **protected people** The Muslim classification used for Hindus, Christians, and Jews; they were allowed to follow their religions but had to pay a special tax.

After the initial period of raids and destruction of temples, the Muslim Turks came to an accommodation with the Hindus, who were classed as a **protected people**, like the Christians and Jews, and allowed to follow their religion. They had to pay a special tax but did not have to perform military service. Local chiefs and rajas were often allowed to remain in control of their domains as long as they paid tribute. Most Indians looked on the Muslim conquerors as a new ruling caste, capable of governing and taxing them but otherwise peripheral to their lives. The myriad castes largely governed themselves, isolating the newcomers.

Nevertheless, over the course of several centuries Islam gained a strong hold on north India, especially in the Indus Valley (modern Pakistan) and in Bengal at the mouth of the Ganges River (modern Bangladesh). Moreover, the sultanate seems to have had a positive effect on the economy. Much of the wealth confiscated from temples was put to more productive use, and India's first truly large cities emerged. The Turks also were eager to employ skilled workers, giving new opportunities to low-caste manual and artisan labor.

The Muslim rulers were much more hostile to Buddhism than to Hinduism, seeing Buddhism as a competitive proselytizing religion. In 1193 a Turkish raiding party destroyed the great Buddhist university at Nalanda in Bihar. Buddhist monks were killed or forced to flee to Buddhist centers in Southeast Asia, Nepal, and Tibet. Buddhism, which had thrived for so long in peaceful and friendly competition with Hinduism, subsequently went into decline in its native land.

Hinduism, however, remained as strong as ever. South India was largely unaffected by these invasions, and traditional Hindu culture flourished there under native kings ruling small kingdoms. (See "Individuals in Society: Bhaskara the Teacher," page 350.) Devotional cults and mystical movements flourished. This was a great age of religious art and architecture in India. Extraordinary temples covered with elaborate bas-relief were built in many areas. Sexual passion and the union of men and women were frequently depicted, symbolically representing passion for and union with the temple god.

The Delhi Sultanate

In the twelfth century a new line of Turkish rulers arose in Afghanistan, led by Muhammad of Ghur (d. 1206). Muhammad captured Delhi and extended his control nearly throughout north India. When he fell to an assassin in 1206, one of his generals, the former slave Qutb-ud-din, seized the reins of power and established a government at Delhi, separate from the government in Afghanistan. This sultanate of Delhi lasted for three centuries, even though dynasties changed several times.

The North African Muslim world traveler Ibn Battuta (see "Individuals in Society: Ibn Battuta," page 256) served for several years as a judge at the court of one of the Delhi sultans. He praised the sultan for his insistence on the observance of ritual prayers and many acts of generosity to those in need, but he also considered the sultan overly violent. Here is just one of many examples he offered of how quick the sultan was to execute:

> During the years of the famine, the Sultan had given orders to dig wells outside the capital, and have grain crops sown in those parts. He provided the cultivators with the seed, as well as with all that was necessary for cultivation in the way of money and supplies, and required them to cultivate these crops for the [royal] grain-store. When the jurist 'Afif al-Din heard of this, he said, "This crop will not produce what is hoped for." Some informer told the Sultan what he had said, so the Sultan jailed him, and said to him, "What reason have you to meddle with the government's business?" Some time later he released him, and as 'Afif al-Din went to his house he was met on the way by two friends of his, also jurists, who said to him, "Praise be to God for your release," to which our jurist replied, "Praise be to God who has delivered us from the evildoers." They then separated, but they had not reached their houses before this was reported to the Sultan, and he commanded all three to be fetched and brought before him. "Take out this fellow," he said, referring to 'Afif al-Din, "and cut off his head baldrickwise," that is, the head is cut off along with an arm and part of the chest, "and behead the other two." They said to him, "He deserves punishment, to be sure, for what he said, but in our case for what crime are you killing us?" He replied, "You heard what he said and did not disavow it, so you as good as agreed with it." So they were all put to death, God Most High have mercy on them.[7]

A major accomplishment of the Delhi sultanate was holding off the Mongols. Chinggis Khan and his troops entered the Indus Valley in 1221 in pursuit of the shah of Khurasan. The sultan wisely kept out of the way, and when Chinggis Khan left some troops in the area, the sultan made no attempt to challenge them. Two generations later, in 1299, a Mongol khan launched a campaign into India with two hundred thousand men, but the sultan of the time was able to defeat them. Two years later the Mongols returned and camped at Delhi for two months, but they eventually left without taking the sultan's fort. Another Mongol raid in 1306–1307 also was successfully repulsed.

Although the Turks by this time were highly cosmopolitan and no longer nomadic, they had retained their martial skills and understanding of steppe warfare. They were expert horsemen, and horses thrived in northwest India. The south and east of India, however, like the south of China, were less hospitable to raising horses. In India's case, though, the climate of the south and east was well suited to elephants, which had been used as weapons of war in India since early times. Rulers in the northwest imported elephants from more tropical regions. The Delhi sultanate is said to have had as many as one thousand war elephants at its height.

During the fourteenth century, however, the Delhi sultanate was in decline and proved unable to ward off the armies of Timur (see page 342), who took Delhi in 1398. Timur's chronicler reported that when the troops drew up for battle outside Delhi, the sultanate had 10,000 horsemen, 20,000 foot soldiers, and 120 war elephants. Though alarmed at the sight of the elephants, Timur's men dug trenches to trap them and shot at their drivers. The sultan fled, leaving the city to surrender. Timur took as booty all the elephants, loading them with treasures seized from the city. Ruy Gonzalez de Clavijo, an ambassador from the king of Castile (now part of Spain), who arrived in Samarkand in 1403, was greatly impressed by these well-trained elephants. "When all the elephants together charged abreast, it seemed as though the solid earth itself shook at their onrush," he observed, noting that he thought each elephant was worth a thousand foot soldiers in battle.[8]

Individuals in Society

Bhaskara the Teacher

IN INDIA, AS IN MANY OTHER SOCIETIES, ASTRONOMY AND mathematics were closely linked, and many of the most important mathematicians served their rulers as astronomers. Bhaskara (1114–ca. 1185) was such an astronomer-mathematician. For generations his Brahmin family had been astronomers at the Ujjain astronomical observatory in north-central India, and his father had written a popular book on astrology.

Bhaskara was a highly erudite man. A disciple wrote that he had thoroughly mastered eight books on grammar, six on medicine, six on philosophy, five on mathematics, and the four Vedas. Bhaskara eventually wrote six books on mathematics and mathematical astronomy. They deal with solutions to simple and quadratic equations and show his knowledge of trigonometry, including the sine table and relationships between different trigonometric functions, and even some of the basic elements of calculus. Earlier Indian mathematicians had explored the use of zero and negative numbers. Bhaskara developed these ideas further, in particular improving on the understanding of division by zero.

A court poet who centuries later translated Bhaskara's book titled *The Beautiful* explained its title by saying Bhaskara wrote it for his daughter named Beautiful (Lilavati) as consolation when his divination of the best time for her to marry went awry. Whether Bhaskara did or did not write this book for his daughter, many of the problems he provides in it have a certain charm:

> On an expedition to seize his enemy's elephants, a king marched two yojanas the first day. Say, intelligent calculator, with what increasing rate of daily march did he proceed, since he reached his foe's city, a distance of eighty yojanas, in a week?*
>
> Out of a heap of pure lotus flower, a third part, a fifth, and a sixth were offered respectively to the gods Siva, Vishnu, and the Sun; and a quarter was presented to Bhavani. The remaining six lotuses were given to the venerable preceptor. Tell quickly the whole number of lotus.†
>
> If eight best variegated silk scarfs, measuring three cubits in breadth and eight in length, cost a hundred nishkas, say quickly, merchant, if thou understand trade, what a like scarf, three and a half cubits long and half a cubit wide will cost.‡

In the conclusion to *The Beautiful*, Bhaskara wrote:

> Joy and happiness is indeed ever increasing in this world for those who have *The Beautiful* clasped to their throats, decorated as the members are with neat reduction of fractions, multiplication, and involution, pure and perfect as are the solutions, and tasteful as is the speech which is exemplified.

Bhaskara had a long career. His first book on mathematical astronomy, written in 1150 when he was thirty-six, used mathematics to calculate solar and lunar eclipses or planetary conjunctions. Thirty-three years later he was still writing on the subject, this time providing simpler ways to solve problems encountered before. Bhaskara wrote his books in Sanskrit, already a literary language rather than a vernacular language, but even in his own day some of them were translated into other Indian languages.

The observatory where Bhaskara worked in Ujjain today stands in ruins. (Dinodia Photo Library)

Within a couple of decades of his death, a local ruler endowed an educational institution to study Bhaskara's works, beginning with his work on mathematical astronomy. In the text he had inscribed at the site, the ruler gave the names of Bhaskara's ancestors for six generations, as well as of his son and grandson, who had continued in his profession.

QUESTIONS FOR ANALYSIS

1. What might have been the advantages of making occupations like astronomer hereditary in India?
2. How does Bhaskara link joy and happiness to mathematical concepts?

*Quotations from Haran Chandra Banerji, *Colebrooke's Translation of the Lilavati*, 2d ed. (Calcutta: The Book Co., 1927), pp. 80–81, 30, 51, 200. The answer is that each day he must travel 22/7 yojanas farther than the day before.

†The answer is 120.

‡The answer, from the formula $x = (1 \times 7 \times 1 \times 100) / (8 \times 3 \times 8 \times 2 \times 2)$, is given in currencies smaller than the nishka: 14 drammas, 9 panas, 1 kakini, and $6\frac{2}{3}$ cowry shells. (20 cowry shells = 1 kakini, 4 kakini = 1 pana, 16 panas = 1 dramma, and 16 drammas = 1 nishka.)

LaunchPad
Online Document Project

What ideas and beliefs were central to Indian culture? Read a Persian account of medieval India, and then complete a quiz and writing assignment based on the evidence and details from this chapter.

See inside the front cover to learn more.

Men at Work This stone frieze from the Buddhist stupa in Sanchi depicts Indian men doing a variety of everyday jobs. Although the stone was carved to convey religious ideas, we can use it as a source for such details of daily life as the sort of clothing men wore while working and how they carried loads. (Dinodia Photo Library)

Timur's invasion left a weakened sultanate. The Delhi sultanate endured under different rulers until 1526, when it was conquered by the Mughals, a Muslim dynasty that would rule over most of northern India from the sixteenth into the nineteenth century.

Life in Medieval India

Local institutions played a much larger role in the lives of people in medieval India than did the state. Craft guilds oversaw conditions of work and trade, local councils handled law and order at the town or village level, and local castes gave members a sense of belonging and identity.

Like peasant societies elsewhere, including in China, Japan, and Southeast Asia, agricultural life in India ordinarily meant village life. The average farmer worked a small plot of land outside the village. All the family members pooled their resources—human, animal, and material—under the direction of the head of the family. These joint efforts strengthened family solidarity.

The agricultural year began with spring plowing. The traditional plow, drawn by two oxen wearing yokes and collars, had an iron-tipped share and a handle with which the farmer guided it. Rice, the most important grain, was sown at the beginning of the long rainy season. Beans, lentils, and peas were the farmer's friends, for they grew during the cold season and were harvested in the spring, when fresh food was scarce. Cereal crops such as wheat, barley, and millet provided carbohydrates and other nutrients. Some families cultivated vegetables, spices, fruit trees, and flowers in their gardens. Sugarcane was another important crop.

Farmers also raised livestock. Most highly valued were cattle, which were raised for plowing and milk, hides, and horns, but Hindus did not slaughter them for meat. Like the Islamic and Jewish prohibition on the consumption of pork, the eating of beef was forbidden among Hindus.

Local craftsmen and tradesmen were frequently organized into guilds, with guild heads and guild rules. The textile industries were particularly well developed. Silk (which had entered India from China), linen, wool, and cotton fabrics were produced in large quantities and traded throughout India and beyond. The cutting and polishing of precious stones was another industry associated closely with foreign trade.

Global Trade

Spices

Spices were a major reason from ancient times on for both Europeans and Chinese to trade with South and Southeast Asia. Pepper, nutmeg, cloves, cinnamon, and other spices were in high demand not only because they could be used to flavor food but also because they were thought to have positive pharmacological properties. Unlike other highly desired products of India and farther east — such as sugar, cotton, rice, and silk — no way was found to produce the spices close to where they were in demand. Because of the location where these spices were produced, this trade was from earliest times largely a maritime trade conducted through a series of middlemen. The spices were transported from where they were grown to nearby ports, and from there to major entrepôts, where merchants would take them in many different directions.

Two types of pepper grew in India and Southeast Asia. Black pepper is identical to our familiar peppercorns. "Long pepper," from a related plant, was hotter. The Mediterranean world imported its pepper from India; China imported it from Southeast Asia. After the discovery of the New World, the importation of long pepper declined, as the chili pepper found in Mexico was at least as spicy and grew well in Europe and China.

By Greek and Roman times trade in pepper was substantial. According to the Greek geographer Strabo (64 B.C.E.–24 C.E.), 120 ships a year made the trip to India to acquire pepper, the round trip taking a year because sailors had to wait for the monsoon winds to shift direction. Pliny in about 77 C.E. complained that the Roman Empire wasted 50 million sesterces per year on long pepper and white and black pepper combined.

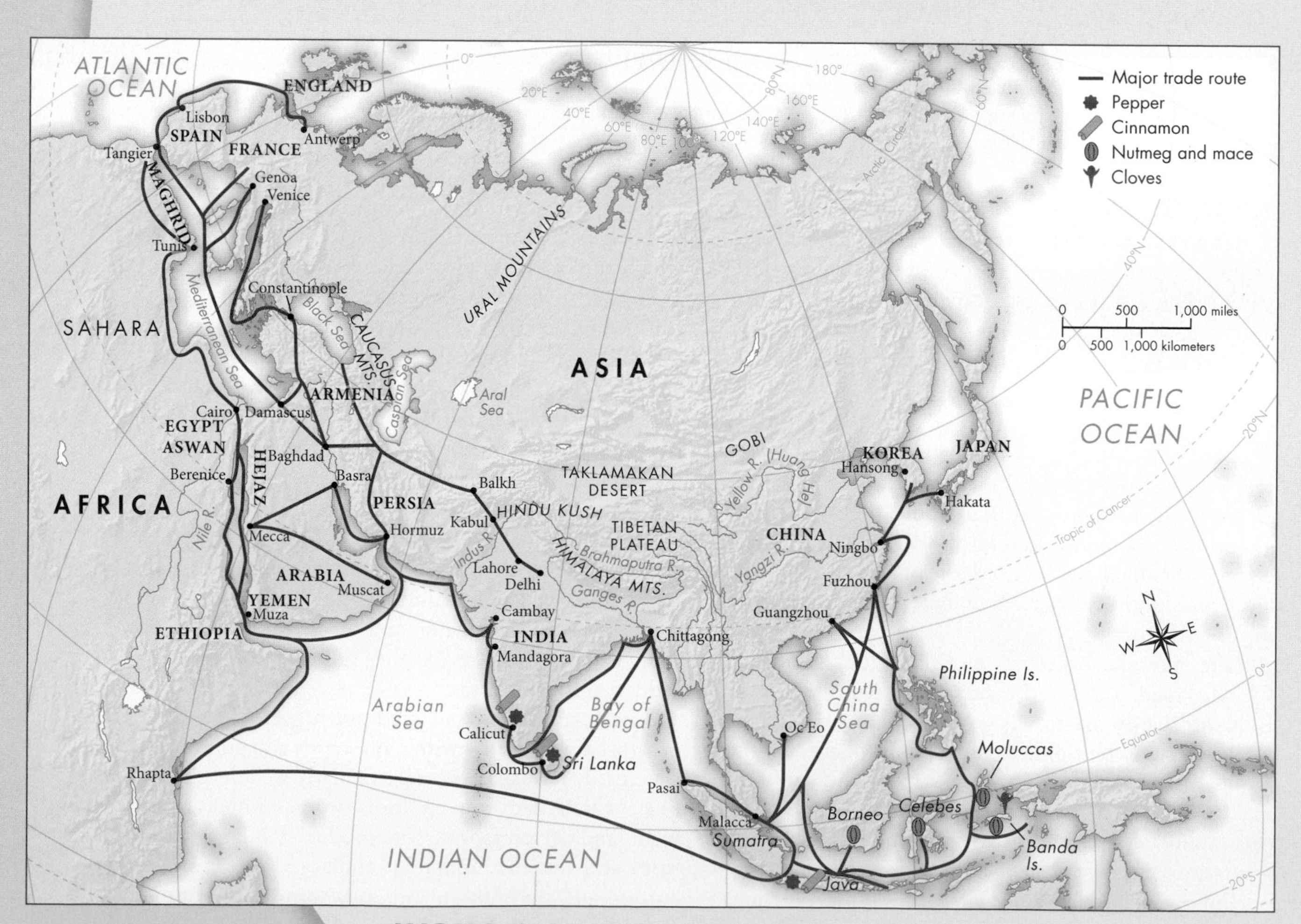

MAP 12.3 The Spice Trade, ca. 100 B.C.E.–1500 C.E.

Cloves and nutmeg entered the repertoire of spices somewhat later than pepper. They are interesting because they could be grown in only a handful of small islands in the eastern part of the Indonesian archipelago. Merchants in China, India, Arab lands, and Europe got them through intermediaries and did not know where they were grown. An Arab source from about 1000 C.E. reported that cloves came from an island near India that had a Valley of Cloves, and that they were acquired by a silent barter. The sailors would lay the items they were willing to trade out on the beach, and the next morning they would find cloves in their place.

The demand for these spices in time encouraged Chinese, Indian, and Arab seamen to make the trip to the Strait of Malacca or east Java. Malay seamen in small craft such as outrigger canoes would bring the spices the thousand or more miles to the major ports where foreign merchants would purchase them. This trade was important to the prosperity of the Srivijayan kingdom. The trade was so profitable, however, that it also attracted pirates.

In the Mongol era, travelers like Marco Polo, Ibn Battuta, and Odoric of Pordenone (in modern Italy) reported on the cultivation and marketing of spices in the various places they visited. Ibn Battuta described pepper plants as vines planted to grow up coconut palms. He also reported seeing the trunks of cinnamon trees floated down rivers in India. Odoric reported that pepper was picked like grapes from groves so huge it would take eighteen days to walk around them. Marco Polo referred to the 7,459 islands in the China Sea that local mariners could navigate and that produced a great variety of spices as well as aromatic wood. He also reported that spices, including pepper, nutmeg, and cloves, could be acquired at the great island of Java, perhaps not understanding that they had often been shipped from the innumerable small islands to Java.

Gaining direct access to the spices of the East was one of the motivations behind Christopher Columbus's voyages. Not long after, Portuguese sailors did reach India by sailing around Africa, and soon the Dutch were competing with them for control of the spice trade and setting up rival trading posts. Pepper was soon successfully planted in other tropical places, including Brazil. India, however, has remained the largest exporter of spices to this day.

In the cities shops were open to the street; families lived on the floors above. The busiest tradesmen dealt in milk and cheese, oil, spices, and perfumes. Equally prominent but disreputable were tavern keepers. Indian taverns were haunts of criminals and con artists, and in the worst of them fighting was as common as drinking. In addition to these tradesmen and merchants, a host of peddlers shuffled through towns and villages selling everything from needles to freshly cut flowers.

The Chinese Buddhist pilgrim Faxian (FAH-shehn), during his six years in Gupta India, described it as a peaceful land where people could move about freely without needing passports and where the upper castes were vegetarians. He was the first to make explicit reference to "untouchables," remarking that they hovered around the margins of Indian society, carrying gongs to warn upper-caste people of their polluting presence.

During the first millennium C.E., the caste system reached its mature form. Within the broad division into the four varnas (strata) of Brahmin, Kshatriya, Vaishya, and Shudra (see page 69), the population was subdivided into numerous castes, or **jati**. Each caste had a proper occupation. In addition, its members married only within the caste and ate only with other members. Members of high-status castes feared pollution from contact with lower-caste individuals and had to undertake rituals of purification to remove the taint.

Eventually Indian society comprised perhaps as many as three thousand castes. Each caste had its own governing body, which enforced the rules of the caste. Those incapable of living up to the rules were expelled, becoming outcastes. These unfortunates lived hard lives, performing tasks that others considered unclean or lowly.

Villages were often walled, as in north China and the Middle East. The streets were unpaved, and the rainy season turned them into a muddy soup. Cattle and sheep roamed as freely as people. Some families kept pets, such as cats or parrots. Half-wild mongooses served as effective protection against snakes. The pond outside the village was its main source of water and also a spawning ground for fish, birds, and mosquitoes. Women drawing water frequently encountered water buffalo wallowing in the shallows. After the farmers returned from the fields in the evening, the village gates were closed until morning.

The life of the well-to-do is described in the *Kamasutra* (Book on the Art of Love). Comfortable surroundings provided a place for men to enjoy poetry, painting, and music in the company of like-minded friends. Courtesans well trained in entertaining men added to the pleasures of wealthy men. A man who had more than one wife was advised not to let one wife

• **jati** The thousands of Indian castes.

speak ill of the other and to try to keep all of them happy by taking them to gardens, giving them presents, telling them secrets, and loving them well.

For all members of Indian society regardless of caste, marriage and family were the focus of life. As in China, the family was under the authority of the eldest male, who might take several wives, and ideally sons stayed home with their parents after they married. The family affirmed its solidarity by the religious ritual of honoring its dead ancestors—a ritual that linked the living and the dead, much like ancestor worship in China (see pages 92–94). People commonly lived in extended families: grandparents, uncles and aunts, cousins, and nieces and nephews all lived together in the same house or compound.

Children were viewed as a great source of happiness. The poet Kalidasa described children as the greatest joy of their father's life:

> With their teeth half-shown in causeless laughter,
> and their efforts at talking so sweetly uncertain,
> when children ask to sit on his lap
> a man is blessed, even by the dirt on their bodies.[9]

Children in poor households worked as soon as they were able. Children in wealthier households faced the age-old irritations of learning reading, writing, and arithmetic. Less attention was paid to daughters than to sons, though in more prosperous families they were often literate. Because girls who had lost their virginity could seldom hope to find good husbands and thus would become financial burdens and social disgraces to their families, daughters were customarily married as children, with consummation delayed until they reached puberty.

A wife was expected to have no life apart from her husband. A widow was expected to lead the hard life of the ascetic: sleeping on the ground; eating only one simple meal a day, without meat, wine, salt, or honey; wearing plain, undyed clothes without jewelry; and shaving her head. She was viewed as inauspicious to everyone but her children, and she did not attend family festivals. Among high-caste Hindus, a widow would be praised for throwing herself on her husband's funeral pyre. Buddhist sects objected to this practice, called **sati**, but some Hindu religious authorities declared that by self-immolation a widow could expunge both her own and her husband's sins, so that both would enjoy eternal bliss in Heaven.

Within the home the position of a wife depended on her own intelligence and strength of character. Wives were supposed to be humble, cheerful, and diligent, even toward worthless husbands. As in other patriarchal societies, however, occasionally a woman ruled the household. For women who did not want to accept the strictures of married life, the main way out was to join a Buddhist or Jain religious community (see pages 190–191).

- **sati** A practice whereby a high-caste Hindu woman would throw herself on her husband's funeral pyre.

Southeast Asia, the Pacific Islands, and the Growth of Maritime Trade

☐ How did states develop along the maritime trade routes of Southeast Asia and beyond?

Much as Roman culture spread to northern Europe and Chinese culture spread to Korea, Japan, and Vietnam, in the first millennium C.E. Indian learning, technology, and material culture spread to the mainland and islands of Southeast Asia. The spread of Indian culture was facilitated by the growth of maritime trade, but this interchange did not occur uniformly, and by 1400 there were still isolated societies in this region, most notably in the Pacific Islands east of Indonesia.

Southeast Asia is a tropical region that is more like India than China, with temperatures hovering around 80°F and rain falling dependably throughout the year. The topography of mainland Southeast Asia is marked by north-south mountain ranges separated by river valleys. It was easy for people to migrate south along these rivers but harder for them to cross the heavily forested mountains that divided the region into areas that had limited contact with each other. The indigenous population was originally mostly Malay, but migrations over the centuries brought many other peoples, including speakers of Austro-Asiatic (such as Vietnamese and Cambodian), Austronesian (such as Malay and Polynesian), and Sino-Tibetan-Burmese (such as Burmese and possibly Thai) languages, some of whom moved to the islands offshore and farther into the Pacific Ocean.

State Formation and Indian Influences

Southeast Asia was long a crossroads. Traders from China, India, Africa, and Europe either passed through the region when traveling from the Indian to the Pacific Ocean, or came for its resources, notably spices. (See "Global Trade: Spices," page 352.)

The northern part of modern Vietnam was under Chinese political control off and on from the second century B.C.E. to the tenth century C.E. (see pages 196–197), but Indian influence was of much greater significance for the rest of Southeast Asia. The first state to appear in historical records, called Funan by Chi-

Picturing the Past

Bayan Relief, Angkor Among the many relief sculptures at the temples of Angkor are depictions of royal processions, armies at war, trade, cooking, cockfighting, and other scenes of everyday life. In the relief shown here, the boats and fish convey something of the significance of the sea to life in Southeast Asia. (Hervé Champollion/akg-images)

ANALYZING THE IMAGE Find the boat. What do the people on it seem to be doing? What fish and animals do you see in the picture? Can you find the alligator eating a fish?

CONNECTIONS Why would a ruler devote so many resources to decorating the walls of a temple? Why include scenes like this one?

nese visitors, had its capital in southern Vietnam. In the first to sixth centuries C.E. Funan extended its control over much of Indochina and the Malay Peninsula. Merchants from northwest India would offload their goods and carry them across the narrowest part of the Malay Peninsula. The ports of Funan offered food and lodging to the merchants as they waited for the winds to shift to continue their voyages. Brahmin priests and Buddhist monks from India settled along with the traders, serving the Indian population and attracting local converts. Rulers often invited Indian priests and monks to serve under them, using them as foreign experts knowledgeable about law, government, architecture, and other fields.

Sixth-century Chinese sources report that the Funan king lived in a multistory palace and the common people lived in houses built on piles with roofs of bamboo leaves. The king rode around on an elephant, but narrow boats measuring up to ninety feet long were a more important means of transportation. The people enjoyed both cockfighting and pig fighting. Instead of drawing water from wells, as the Chinese did, they made pools, from which dozens of nearby families would draw water.

After the decline of Funan, maritime trade continued to grow, and petty kingdoms appeared in many places. Indian traders frequently established small settlements, generally located on the coast. Contact with

Angkor Wat Temple The Khmers built several stone temple complexes at Angkor. This aerial view catches something of the scale of the largest of these complexes, Angkor Wat. (© Roy Garner/Alamy)

the local populations led to intermarriage and the creation of hybrid cultures. Local rulers often adopted Indian customs and values, embraced Hinduism and Buddhism, and learned **Sanskrit**, India's classical literary language. Sanskrit gave different peoples a common mode of written expression, much as Chinese did in East Asia and Latin did in Europe.

When Indian traders, migrants, and adventurers entered mainland Southeast Asia, they encountered both long-settled peoples and migrants moving southward from the frontiers of China. As in other extensive migrations, the newcomers fought one another as often as they fought the native populations. In 939 the north Vietnamese became independent of China and extended their power southward along the coast of present-day Vietnam. The Thais had long lived in what is today southwest China and north Myanmar. In the eighth century the Thai tribes united in a confederacy and expanded northward against Tang China. Like China, however, the Thai confederacy fell to the Mongols in 1253. Still farther west another tribal people, the Burmese, migrated to the area of modern Myanmar in the eighth century. They also established a state, which they ruled from their capital, Pagan, and came into contact with India and Sri Lanka.

The most important mainland state was the Khmer (kuh-MAIR) Empire of Cambodia (802–1432), which controlled the heart of the region. The Khmers were indigenous to the area. Their empire eventually extended south to the sea and the northeast Malay Peninsula. Indian influence was pervasive; the impressive temple complex at Angkor Wat built in the early twelfth century was dedicated to the Hindu god Vishnu. Social organization, however, was modeled not on the Indian caste system but on indigenous traditions of social hierarchy. A large part of the population was of slave status, many descended from non-Khmer mountain tribes defeated by the Khmers. Generally successful in a long series of wars with the Vietnamese, the Khmers reached the peak of their power in 1219 and then gradually declined.

- **Sanskrit** India's classical literary language.
- **Srivijaya** A maritime empire that held the Strait of Malacca and the waters around Sumatra, Borneo, and Java.

The Srivijayan Maritime Trade Empire

Far different from these land-based states was the maritime empire of **Srivijaya**, based on the island of Sumatra in modern Indonesia. From the sixth century on, it held the important Strait of Malacca, through which most of the sea traffic between China and India passed. This state, held together as much by alliances as by direct rule, was in many ways like the Gupta state of the same period in India, securing its prominence and binding its vassals and allies through its splendor and the promise of riches through trade.

Much as the Korean and Japanese rulers adapted Chinese models (see pages 197–198), the Srivijayan rulers drew on Indian traditions to justify their rule and organize their state. The Sanskrit writing system was used for government documents, and Indians were often employed as priests, scribes, and administrators. Using Sanskrit overcame the barriers raised by the many different native languages of the region. Indian mythology took hold, as did Indian architecture and sculpture. Kings and their courts, the first to embrace Indian culture, consciously spread it to their subjects. The Chinese Buddhist monk Yixing (d. 727) stopped at Srivijaya for six months in 671 on his way to India and for four years on his return journey. He found a thousand monks there, some of whom helped him translate Sanskrit texts.

After several centuries of prosperity, Srivijaya suffered a stunning blow in 1025. The Chola state in south India launched a large naval raid and captured the Srivijayan king and capital. Unable to hold their gains, the Indians retreated, but the Srivijayan Empire never regained its vigor.

During the era of the Srivijayan kingdom, other kingdoms flourished as well in island Southeast Asia. Borobudur, the magnificent Buddhist temple complex, was begun under patronage of Javan rulers around 780. This stone monument depicts the ten tiers of Buddhist cosmology. When pilgrims made the three-mile-long winding ascent, they passed numerous sculpted reliefs depicting the journey from ignorance to enlightenment.

Buddhism became progressively more dominant in Southeast Asia after 800. Mahayana Buddhism became important in Srivijaya and Vietnam, but Theravada Buddhism, closer to the original Buddhism of early India, became the dominant form in the rest of mainland Southeast Asia. Buddhist missionaries from India and Sri Lanka played a prominent role in these developments. Local converts continued the process by making pilgrimages to India and Sri Lanka to worship and to observe Indian life for themselves.

The Spread of Indian Culture in Comparative Perspective

The social, cultural, and political systems developed in India, China, and Rome all had enormous impact on neighboring peoples whose cultures were originally not as technologically advanced. Some of the mechanisms for cultural spread were similar in all three cases, but differences were important as well.

In the case of Rome and both Han and Tang China, strong states directly ruled outlying regions, bringing their civilizations with them. India's states, even its largest empires, such as the Mauryan and Gupta, did not have comparable bureaucratic reach. Outlying areas tended to be in the hands of local lords who had consented to recognize the overlordship of the stronger state. Moreover, most of the time India was politically divided.

The expansion of Indian culture into Southeast Asia thus came not from conquest and the extension of direct political control but from the extension of trading networks, with missionaries following along. This made it closer to the way Japan adopted features of Chinese culture, often through the intermediary of Korea. In both cases, the cultural exchange was largely voluntary, as the Japanese or Southeast Asians sought to adopt more up-to-date technologies (such as writing) or were persuaded of the truth of religious ideas they learned from foreigners.

The Settlement of the Pacific Islands

Through most of Eurasia, societies became progressively less isolated over time. But in 1400 there still remained many isolated societies, especially in the Islands east of modern Indonesia. As discussed in Chapter 1, *Homo sapiens* began settling the western Pacific Islands very early, reaching Australia by 50,000 years ago and New Guinea by 35,000 years ago. The process did not stop there, however. The ancient Austronesians (speakers of Austronesian languages) were skilled mariners who used double-canoes and brought pottery, the root vegetable taro, pigs, and chickens to numerous islands of the Pacific in subsequent centuries, generally following the coasts. Their descendants, the Polynesians, learned how to sail into the open ocean with only the stars, currents, wind patterns, paths of birds, and perhaps paths of whales and dolphins to help them navigate. They reached Tahiti and the Marquesas Islands in the central Pacific by about 200 C.E. Undoubtedly, seafarers were sometimes blown off their intended course, but communities would not have developed unless the original groups had included women as well as men, so probably in many cases they were looking for new places to live.

After reaching the central Pacific, Polynesians continued to fan out, in some cases traveling a thousand or more miles away. They reached the Hawaiian Islands in about 300 C.E., Easter Island in perhaps 1000, and New Zealand not until about 1000–1300. There even were groups who sailed west, eventually settling in Madagascar between 200 and 500.

In the more remote islands, such as Hawai'i, Easter Island, and New Zealand, the societies that developed were limited by the small range of domesticated plants and animals that the settlers brought with them and those that were indigenous to the place. Easter Island is perhaps the most extreme case. Only 15 miles wide at its widest point (only 63 square miles in total area), it is 1,300 miles from the nearest inhabited island (Pitcairn) and 2,240 miles from the coast of South America. At some point there was communication with South America, as sweet potatoes originally from there made their way to Easter Island. The community that developed on the island raised chickens and cultivated sweet potatoes, taro, and sugarcane. The inhabitants also engaged in deep-sea fishing, catching dolphins and tuna. Their tools were made of stone, wood, or bone. The population is thought to have reached about fifteen thousand at Easter Island's most prosperous period, which began about 1200 C.E. It was then that its people devoted remarkable efforts to fashioning and erecting the large stone statues that still dot the island.

What led the residents of such a small island to erect more than eight hundred statues, most weighing around ten tons and standing twenty to seventy feet tall? When the first Europeans arrived in 1722, no stat-

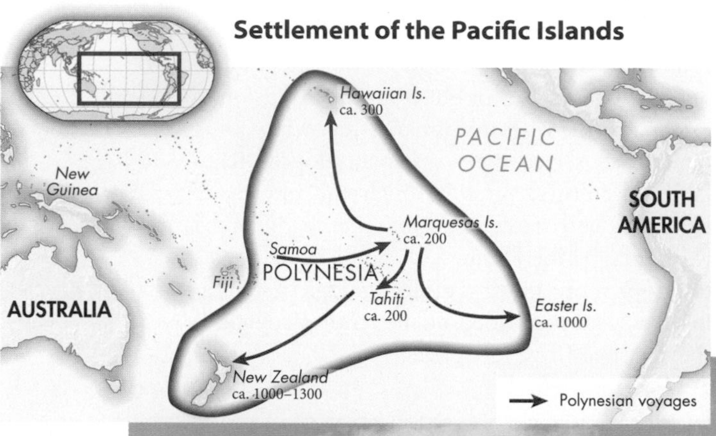

Easter Island Statues Archaeologists have excavated and restored many of Easter Island's huge statues, which display remarkable stylistic consistency, with the heads disproportionately large and the legs not visible. (Jean-Pierre De Mann/Robert Harding World Imagery)

ues had been erected for several generations, and the local residents explained them as representing ancestors. One common theory is that they were central to the islanders' religion and that rival clans competed with each other to erect the most impressive statues. The effort they had to expend to carve them with stone tools, move them to the chosen site, and erect them would have been formidable.

After its heyday, Easter Island suffered severe environmental stress with the decline of its forests. Whether the rats that came with the original settlers ate too many of the trees' seeds or the islanders cut down too many of the trees to transport the stone statues, the impact of deforestation was severe. The islanders could not make boats to fish in the ocean, and bird colonies shrank as nesting areas decreased, also reducing the food supply. Scholars still disagree on how much weight to give the many different elements that contributed to the decline in the prosperity of Easter Island from the age when the statues were erected.

Certainly, early settlers of an island could have a drastic impact on its ecology. When Polynesians first reached New Zealand, they found large birds up to ten feet tall. They hunted them so eagerly that within a century the birds had all but disappeared. Hunting seals and sea lions also led to their rapid depletion. But the islands of New Zealand were much larger than Easter Island, and in time the Maori (the indigenous people of New Zealand) found more sustainable ways to feed themselves, depending more and more on agriculture.

CHRONOLOGY

ca. 320–480	Gupta Empire in India
ca. 380–450	Life of India's greatest poet, Kalidasa
ca. 450	Huns invade northern India
ca. 500	Srivijaya gains control of Strait of Malacca
ca. 500–1400	India's medieval age; caste system reaches its mature form
552	Turks rebel against Rouruan and rise to power in Central Asia
ca. 780	Borobudur temple complex begun in Srivijaya
802–1432	Khmer Empire of Cambodia
ca. 850–1250	Kingdom of the Uighurs
1030	Turks control north India
ca. 1100–1200	Buddhism declines in India
ca. 1200–1300	Easter Island society's most prosperous period
1206	Temujin proclaimed Chinggis Khan; Mongol language recorded; Delhi sultanate established
ca. 1240	*The Secret History of the Mongols*
1276	Mongol conquest of Song China
ca. 1300	Plague begins to spread throughout Mongol Empire
1398	Timur takes control of the Delhi sultanate

Chapter Summary

The pastoral societies that stretched across Eurasia had the great military advantage of being able to raise horses in large numbers and support themselves from their flocks of sheep, goats, and other animals. Nomadic pastoralists generally were organized on the basis of clans and tribes that selected chiefs for their military talent. Much of the time these tribes fought with each other, but several times in history leaders formed larger confederations capable of coordinated attacks on cities and towns.

From the fifth to the twelfth centuries the most successful nomadic groups on the Eurasian steppes were Turks who gained ascendancy in many of the societies from the Middle East to northern India. In the early thirteenth century, through his charismatic leadership and military genius, the Mongol leader Chinggis Khan conquered much of Eurasia. Those who submitted without fighting could become vassals, but those who resisted faced the prospect of mass slaughter or enslavement.

After Chinggis's death, the empire was divided into four khanates ruled by four of Chinggis's descendants. For a century the Mongol Empire fostered unprecedented East-West contact. The Mongols encouraged trade and often moved craftsmen and other specialists from one place to another. They were tolerant of other religions. As more Europeans made their way east, Chinese inventions such as printing and the compass made their way west. Europe especially benefited from the spread of technical and scientific ideas. Diseases also spread, including the Black Death, carried by fleas and rats that found their way into the goods of merchants and other travelers.

India was invaded by the Mongols but not conquered. After the fall of the Gupta Empire in about 480, India was for the next millennium ruled by small kingdoms, which allowed regional cultures to flourish. For several centuries Muslim Turks ruled north India from Delhi. Over time Islam gained adherents throughout South Asia. Hinduism continued to flourish, but Buddhism declined.

Throughout the medieval period India continued to be the center of active seaborne trade, and this trade helped carry Indian ideas and practices to Southeast Asia. Local rulers used experts from India to establish strong states, such as the Khmer kingdom and the Srivijayan kingdom. Buddhism became the dominant religion throughout the region, though Hinduism also played an important role. The Pacific islands east of Indonesia remained isolated culturally for centuries.

NOTES

1. Trans. in Denis Sinor, "The Establishment and Dissolution of the Türk Empire," in *The Cambridge History of Early Inner Asia*, ed. Denis Sinor (Cambridge: Cambridge University Press, 1990), p. 307.
2. Manuel Komroff, ed., *Contemporaries of Marco Polo* (New York: Dorset Press, 1989), p. 65.
3. Ibid.
4. Cited in John Larner, *Marco Polo and the Discovery of the World* (New Haven, Conn.: Yale University Press, 1999), p. 22.
5. Quoted in A. L. Basham, *The Wonder That Was India*, 2d ed. (New York: Grove Press, 1959), p. 420. Copyright © Picador, A. L. Basham. Reprinted by permission of Pan Macmillan, London.
6. Edward C. Sachau, *Alberuni's India*, vol. 1 (London: Kegan Paul, 1910), pp. 19–20, slightly modified.
7. H. A. R. Gibb, *The Travels of Ibn Battuta* (Cambridge: Cambridge University Press for the Hakluyt Society, 1971), pp. 700–701. Reprinted by permission of David Higham Associates on behalf of the Hakluyt Society.
8. Guy le Strang, trans., *Clavijo, Embassy to Tamerlane, 1403–1406* (London: Routledge, 1928), pp. 265–266.
9. Quoted in Basham, *The Wonder That Was India*, p. 161. Copyright © Picador, A. L. Basham. Reprinted by permission of Pan Macmillan, London.

CONNECTIONS

The societies of Eurasia became progressively more connected to each other during the centuries discussed in this chapter. One element promoting connection was the military superiority of the nomadic warriors of the steppe: first the Turks, then the Mongols, who conquered many of the settled civilizations near them. Invading Turks brought Islam to India. Connection between societies also came from maritime trade across the Indian Ocean and East Asia. Maritime trade was a key element in the spread of Indian culture to both the mainland and insular Southeast Asia. Other elements connecting these societies included Sanskrit as a language of administration and missionaries who brought both Hinduism and Buddhism far beyond their homelands. Some societies did remain isolated, probably none more than the remote islands of the Pacific, such as Hawai'i, Easter Island, and New Zealand.

East Asia was a key element in both the empires created by nomadic horsemen and the South Asian maritime trading networks. As discussed in Chapter 13, before East Asia had to cope with the rise of the Mongols, it experienced one of its most prosperous periods, during which China, Korea, and Japan became more distinct culturally. China's economy boomed during the Song Dynasty, and the scholar-official class, defined through the civil service examination, came more and more to dominate culture. In Korea and Japan, by contrast, aristocrats and military men gained ascendancy. Although China, Korea, and Japan all drew on both Confucian and Buddhist teachings, they ended up with elites as distinct as the Chinese scholar-official, the Korean aristocrat, and the Japanese samurai.

Review and Explore

Make It Stick

LearningCurve
Go online and use LearningCurve to retain what you've read.

Identify Key Terms

Identify and explain the significance of each item below.

nomads (p. 331)
steppe (p. 331)
yurts (p. 333)
Chinggis Khan (p. 337)
khanates (p. 339)
tax-farming (p. 341)
protected people (p. 348)
jati (p. 353)
sati (p. 354)
Sanskrit (p. 356)
Srivijaya (p. 357)

Review the Main Ideas

Answer the focus questions from each section of the chapter.

1. What aspects of nomadic life gave the nomads of Central Asia military advantages over nearby settled civilizations? (p. 331)
2. How did Chinggis Khan and his successors conquer much of Eurasia, and how did the Mongol conquests change the regions affected? (p. 336)
3. How did the Mongol conquests facilitate the spread of ideas, religions, inventions, and diseases? (p. 342)
4. What was the result of India's encounters with Turks, Mongols, and Islam? (p. 345)
5. How did states develop along the maritime trade routes of Southeast Asia and beyond? (p. 354)

Make Connections

Analyze the larger developments and continuities within and across chapters.

1. How do the states established by Arabs in the seventh and eighth centuries compare to those established by Turks in the tenth and eleventh centuries?
2. What similarities and differences are there in the military feats of Alexander the Great and Chinggis Khan?
3. How does the slow spread of Buddhism and Indian culture to Southeast Asia compare to the slow spread of Christianity and Roman culture in Europe?

astoundingly. With advances in metallurgy, iron production reached around 125,000 tons per year in 1078, a sixfold increase over the output in 800. At first charcoal was used in the production process, leading to deforestation of parts of north China. By the end of the eleventh century, however, bituminous coke had largely taken the place of charcoal. Much of the iron was put to military purposes. Mass-production methods were used to make iron armor in small, medium, and large sizes. High-quality steel for swords was made through high-temperature metallurgy. Huge bellows, often driven by water wheels, were used to superheat the molten ore. The needs of the army also brought Chinese engineers to experiment with the use of gunpowder. In the twelfth-century wars against the Jurchens (see page 333), those defending a besieged city used gunpowder to propel projectiles at the enemy.

Economic expansion fueled the growth of cities. Dozens of cities had 50,000 or more residents, and quite a few had more than 100,000, very large populations compared to other places in the world at the time. China's two successive capitals, Kaifeng (kigh-fuhng) and Hangzhou (hahng-joh), each had an estimated 1 million residents. Marco Polo described Hangzhou as the finest and most splendid city in the world. He reported that it had ten marketplaces, each half a mile long, where 40,000 to 50,000 people would shop on any given day. There were also bathhouses; permanent shops selling items such as spices, drugs, and pearls; and innumerable courtesans, whom Marco Polo described as "adorned in much finery, highly perfumed, occupying well-furnished houses, and attended by many female domestics."[2]

The medieval economic revolution shifted the economic center of China south to the Yangzi River drainage area. This area had many advantages over the north China plain. Rice, which grew in the south, provides more calories per unit of land and therefore allows denser settlement. The milder temperatures often allowed two crops to be grown on the same plot of land, first a summer crop of rice and then a winter crop of wheat or vegetables. The abundance of rivers and streams facilitated shipping, which reduced the cost of transportation and thus made regional specialization economically more feasible. In the first half of the Song Dynasty, the capital was still at Kaifeng in the north, close to the Grand Canal (see page 191), which linked the capital to the rich south.

The economic revolution of Song times cannot be attributed to intellectual change, as Confucian scholars did not reinterpret the classics to defend the morality of commerce. But neither did scholar-officials take a unified stand against economic development. As officials they had to work to produce revenue to cover government expenses such as defense, and this was much easier to do when commerce was thriving.

Ordinary people benefited from the Song economic revolution in many ways. There were more opportunities for the sons of farmers to leave agriculture and find work in cities. Those who stayed in agriculture had a better chance of improving their situations by taking up sideline production of wine, charcoal, paper,

Transplanting Rice To get the maximum yield per plot and to make it possible to grow two crops in the same field, Chinese farmers grew rice seedlings in a seedbed and then, when a field was free, transplanted the seedlings into the flooded field. Because the Song government wanted to promote up-to-date agricultural technology, in the twelfth century it commissioned a set of twelve illustrations of the steps to be followed. This painting comes from a later version of those illustrations. (*Tilling Rice*, Yuan Dynasty [ink and colour on paper], Qi, Cheng [13th century] [attr. to]/ Freer Gallery of Art, Smithsonian Institution, Washington, D.C., U.S.A./The Bridgeman Art Library)

or textiles. Energetic farmers who grew cash crops such as sugar, tea, mulberry leaves (for silk), and cotton (recently introduced from India) could grow rich. Greater interregional trade led to the availability of more goods at the rural markets held every five or ten days.

Of course, not everyone grew rich. Poor farmers who fell into debt had to sell their land, and if they still owed money they could be forced to sell their daughters as maids, concubines, or prostitutes. The prosperity of the cities created a huge demand for women to serve the rich in these ways, and Song sources mention that criminals would kidnap girls and women to sell in distant cities at huge profits.

China During the Song and Yuan Dynasties, 960–1368

☐ How did the civil service examinations and the scholar-official class shape Chinese society and culture, and what impact did the Mongol conquest have on them?

In the tenth century Tang China broke up into separate contending states, some of which had non-Chinese rulers. The two states that proved to be long lasting were the Song, which came to control almost all of China proper south of the Great Wall, and the Liao, whose ruling house was Khitan and which held the territory of modern Beijing and areas north (Map 13.2). Although the Song Dynasty had a much larger population, the Liao was militarily the stronger of the two. In the early twelfth century the Liao state was defeated by the Jurchens, another non-Chinese people, who founded the Jin Dynasty and went on to conquer most of north China, leaving Song to control only the south. After a century the Jurchens' Jin Dynasty was defeated by the Mongols, who extended their Yuan Dynasty to control all of China by 1276.

The Song Dynasty

The founder of the Song Dynasty, Taizu (r. 960–976), was a general whose troops elevated him to emperor (somewhat reminiscent of Roman practice). Taizu worked to make sure that such an act could not happen in the future by placing the armies under central government control. To curb the power of his generals, he retired or rotated them and assigned civil officials to supervise them. In time these civil bureaucrats came to dominate every aspect of Song government and society. The civil service examination system established during the Sui Dynasty (see page 191) was greatly expanded to provide the dynasty with a constant flow of men trained in the Confucian classics.

Curbing the generals' power ended warlordism but did not solve the military problem of defending against the nomadic Khitans' Liao Dynasty to the north. After several attempts to push the Liao back beyond the Great Wall, the Song concluded a peace treaty with them. The Song agreed to make huge annual payments of gold and silk to the Khitans, in a sense paying them not to invade. Even so, the Song rulers had to maintain a standing army of more than a million men. By the middle of the eleventh century military expenses consumed half the government's revenues. Song had the industrial base to produce swords, armor, and arrowheads in huge quantities, but had difficulty maintaining enough horses and well-trained horsemen. Even though China was the economic powerhouse of the region, with by far the largest population, the horse was a major weapon of war in this period, and it was not easy to convert wealth to military advantage.

In the early twelfth century the military situation rapidly worsened when the Khitan state was destroyed by another tribal confederation led by the Jurchens. Although the Song allied with the Jurchens, the Jurchens quickly realized how easy it would be to defeat the Song. When they marched into the Song capital in 1126, they captured the emperor and former emperor and took them and the entire court into captivity. Song forces rallied around one of the emperor's sons who had escaped capture, and this prince re-established a Song court in the south at Hangzhou (see Map 13.2). This Southern Song Dynasty controlled only about two-thirds of the former Song territories, but the social, cultural, and intellectual life there remained vibrant until the Song fell to the Mongols in 1279.

The Scholar-Officials and Neo-Confucianism

The Song period saw the full flowering of one of the most distinctive features of Chinese civilization, the **scholar-official class** certified through highly competitive civil service examinations. This elite was both broader and better educated than the elites of earlier periods in Chinese history. Once the **examination system** was fully developed, aristocratic habits and prejudices largely disappeared. Ancestry did not matter as

- **scholar-official class** Chinese educated elite that included both scholars and officials. The officials had usually gained office by passing the highly competitive civil service examination. Scholars without office had often studied for the examinations but failed repeatedly.
- **examination system** A system of selecting officials based on competitive written examinations.

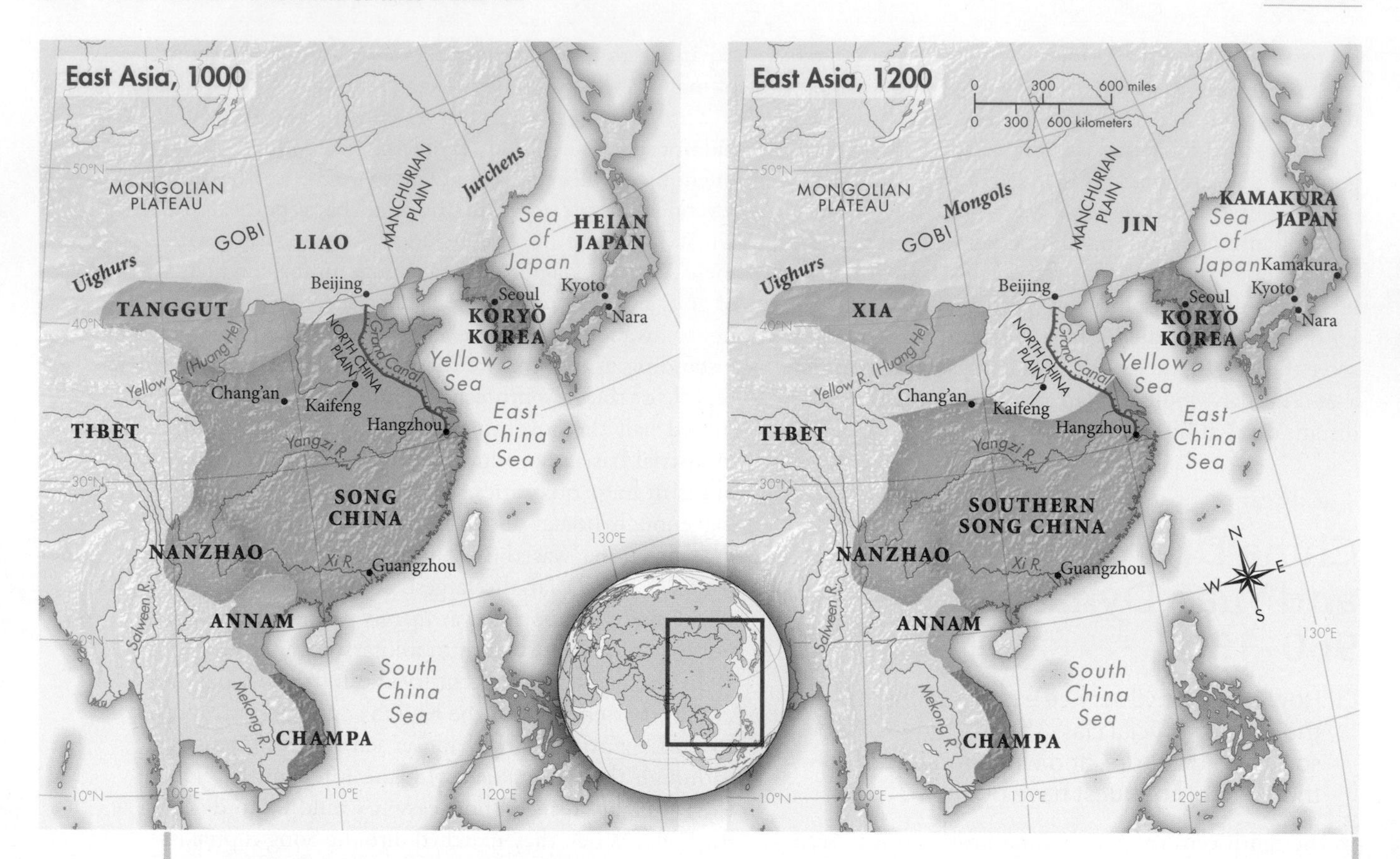

Mapping the Past

MAP 13.2 East Asia in 1000 and 1200 The Song empire did not extend as far as its predecessor, the Tang, and faced powerful rivals to the north — the Liao Dynasty of the Khitans and the Xia Dynasty of the Tanguts. Koryŏ Korea maintained regular contact with Song China, but Japan, by the late Heian period, was no longer deeply involved with the mainland. By 1200 military families dominated both Korea and Japan, but the borders were little changed. On the mainland the Liao Dynasty had been overthrown by the Jurchens' Jin Dynasty, which also seized the northern third of the Song empire. Because the Song relocated its capital to Hangzhou in the south, this period is called the Southern Song period.

ANALYZING THE MAP What were the countries of East Asia in 1000? What were the major differences in 1200?

CONNECTIONS What connections do you see between the length of their northern borders and the histories of China, Korea, and Japan?

much when office depended more on study habits than on connections.

The examination system came to carry such prestige that the number of scholars entering each competition escalated rapidly, from fewer than 30,000 early in the eleventh century, to nearly 80,000 by the end of that century, to about 400,000 by the dynasty's end. To prepare for the examinations, men had to memorize the classics in order to be able to recognize even the most obscure passages. They also had to master specific forms of composition, including poetry, and be ready to discuss policy issues, citing appropriate historical examples. Those who became officials this way had usually tried the exams several times and were on average a little over thirty years of age when they succeeded. Because the competition was so fierce, the great majority of those who devoted years to preparing for the exams never became officials.

The invention of printing should be given some credit for the trend toward a better-educated elite. Tang craftsmen developed the art of carving words and pictures into wooden blocks, inking the blocks, and pressing paper onto them. Each block held an entire page of text. Such whole-page blocks were used for printing as early as the middle of the ninth century, and in the eleventh century **movable type** (one piece of type for each character) was invented, but it was rarely used because whole-block printing was cheaper. In China,

☐ Picturing the Past

On a Mountain Path in Spring With spare, sketchy strokes, the court painter Ma Yuan (ca. 1190–1225) depicts a scholar on an outing accompanied by his boy servant carrying a lute. The scholar gazes into the mist, his eyes attracted by a bird in flight. The poetic couplet was inscribed by Emperor Ningzong (r. 1194–1124), at whose court Ma Yuan served. It reads: "Brushed by his sleeves, wild flowers dance in the wind. / Fleeing from him, hidden birds cut short their songs." (National Palace Museum, Taipei, Taiwan/photo © AISA/The Everett Collection)

ANALYZING THE IMAGE Find the key elements in this picture: the scholar, the servant boy, the bird, the willow tree. Are these elements skillfully conveyed? Are there other elements in the painting that you find hard to read?

CONNECTIONS What do you think is the reason for writing a poetic couplet on this painting? Does it enhance the experience of viewing the painting or detract from it?

as in Europe a couple of centuries later, the introduction of printing dramatically lowered the price of books, thus aiding the spread of literacy.

Among the upper class the availability of cheaper books enabled scholars to amass their own libraries. Song publishers printed the classics of Chinese literature in huge editions to satisfy scholarly appetites. Works on philosophy, science, and medicine were also avidly consumed, as were Buddhist texts. Han and Tang poetry and historical works became the models for Song writers. One popular literary innovation was the encyclopedia, which first appeared in the Song period, at least five centuries before the publication of the first European encyclopedia.

The life of the educated man involved more than study for the civil service examinations and service in office. Many took to refined pursuits such as collecting antiques or old books and practicing the arts—especially poetry writing, calligraphy, and painting. (See "Viewpoints 13.1: Painters of Uncanny Skill in China and Rome," page 372.) For many individuals these cultural interests overshadowed any philosophical, political, or economic concerns; others found in them occasional outlets for creative activity and aesthetic pleasure. In the Song period, the engagement of

• **movable type** A system of printing in which one piece of type is used for each unique character.

Viewpoints 13.1

Painters of Uncanny Skill in China and Rome

• *Chinese art critics often expressed astonishment at the ability of exceptional painters to evoke an emotional reaction in viewers. A good example is the account of the eighth-century painter Wu Daozi, written by a ninth-century critic, Zhu Jingxuan, in his* Famous Painters of the Tang Dynasty. *It can be compared to remarks on painters by the Roman man of letters Pliny the Elder (23–79 C.E.).*

Zhu Jingxuan on the Painter Wu Daozi

"A poor orphan, Wu Daozi was so talented by nature that even before he was twenty he had mastered all the subtleties of painting. When he was in Luoyang, the emperor heard of his fame and summoned him to court. . . .

The General Pei Min sent a gift of gold and silk to Wu Daozi and asked him to paint the walls of the Paradise Buddhist monastery. Wu Daozi returned the gold and silk with a note saying, "I have long heard of General Pei. If he would do a sword dance for me, that would be reward enough, and the sight of such vigor will inspire my brush." So the general, even though in mourning, did the sword dance for Wu Daozi, and when the dance was finished Wu made his brush fly with such strength that the painting was done in no time, as though some god was helping him. Wu Daozi also did the laying on of the colors himself. One can still see the painting in the western corridor of the temple. . . .

During the Tianbao period (742–755), the emperor Xuanzong suddenly longed for the Jialing River on the road to Sichuan. So he allowed Wu Daozi the use of post horses and ordered him to go there and make sketches of the scenery. On his return, in response to the emperor's query, Wu said, "I have not brought back a single sketch, but everything is recorded in my mind." He was commanded to depict it on the walls of Great Accord Hall. He painted a landscape of more than 300 *li*, finishing it all in a single day. . . . He also painted five dragons in the Inner Hall whose scales seemed to move. Whenever it was about to rain, mist would emanate from them. . . .

Early in the Yuanhe period (806–820), while I was taking the civil service examinations and living in Dragon Rising Buddhist Temple, an elderly official, more than eighty years old, told me that when Master Wu was about to paint the halo of a god on the central gate of Xingshan Buddhist monastery, residents of the city, old and young, gathered around to watch, standing as deep as a hedge. He raised his brush then swirled it around with the force of a whirlwind, apparently with divine help. I also heard from an old monk of Scenic Clouds Monastery that when Master Wu painted a Hell scene at the temple, butchers and fishmongers who saw it became so frightened by it that they decided to change their profession and turn to doing good works."

Pliny on the Painters Arellius and Lepidus

"Not long before the time of the god Augustus, Arellius had earned distinction at Rome, save for the sacrilege by which he notoriously degraded his art. Always desirous of flattering some woman or other with whom he chanced to be in love, he painted goddesses in the person of his mistresses, of whom his paintings are a mere catalogue. The painter Famulus also lived not long ago; he was grave and severe in his person, while his painting was rich and vivid. He painted an Athena whose eyes are turned to the spectator from whatever side he may be looking. . . .

While on the subject of painting I must not omit the well-known story of Lepidus. Once during his triumvirate he had been escorted by the magistrates of a certain town to a lodging in the middle of a wood, and on the next morning complained with threats that the singing of the birds prevented him from sleeping. They painted a snake on an immense strip of parchment and stretched it all round the grove. We are told that by this means they terrified the birds into silence and that this has ever since been a recognized device for quieting them."

Sources: Zhu Jingxuan, *Tangchao minghua lu*, in *Tang Wudai hualun* (Changsha: Hunan Meishu Chubanshe, 1997), pp. 83–85, trans. Patricia Ebrey; *The Elder Pliny's Chapters on the History of Art*, trans. K. Jex-Blake (London: Macmillan, 1896), pp. 149–150.

QUESTIONS FOR ANALYSIS

1. What assumptions, if any, did the Chinese and Roman authors share about artistic creativity?
2. In what ways did painters gain fame in these two societies?

the elite with the arts led to extraordinary achievement in calligraphy and painting, especially landscape painting. A large share of the social life of upper-class men was centered on these refined pastimes, as they gathered to compose or criticize poetry, to view each other's art treasures, and to patronize young talents.

The new scholar-official elite produced some extraordinary men able to hold high court offices while pursuing diverse intellectual interests. (See "Individuals in Society: Shen Gua," page 375.) Ouyang Xiu spared time in his busy official career to write love songs, histories, and the first analytical catalogue of rubbings of ancient stone and bronze inscriptions. Sima Guang, besides serving as chancellor, wrote a narrative history of China from the Warring States Period (403–221 B.C.E.) to the founding of the Song Dynasty. Su Shi wrote more than twenty-seven hundred poems and eight hundred letters while active in opposition politics. He was also an esteemed painter, calligrapher, and theorist of the arts. Su Song, another high official, constructed an eighty-foot-tall mechanical clock. He adapted the water-powered clock invented in the Tang period by adding a chain-driven mechanism. The clock told not only the time of day but also the day of the month, the phase of the moon, and the position of certain stars and planets in the sky. As in Renaissance Europe a couple of centuries later (discussed in Chapter 15), gifted men made advances in a wide range of fields.

These highly educated men accepted the Confucian responsibility to aid the ruler in the governing of the country. Factional disputes often made government service stressful, especially during the period when the emperor supported the New Policies of the reformer Wang Anshi, which many leading men opposed.

Besides politics, scholars also debated issues in ethics and metaphysics. For several centuries Buddhism had been more vital than Confucianism. Beginning in the late Tang period, Confucian teachers began claiming that the teachings of the Confucian sages contained all the wisdom one needed and that a true Confucian would reject Buddhist teachings. During the eleventh century many Confucian teachers urged students to set their sights not on exam success but on the higher goals of attaining the wisdom of the sages. Metaphysical theories about the workings of the cosmos in terms of *li* (principle) and *qi* (vital energy) were developed in response to the challenge of the sophisticated metaphysics of Buddhism.

Neo-Confucianism, as this movement is generally termed, was more fully developed in the twelfth century by the immensely learned Zhu Xi (joo shee) (1130–1200). Besides serving in office, he wrote, compiled, or edited almost a hundred books; corresponded with dozens of other scholars; and still regularly taught groups of disciples, many of whom stayed with him for years at a time. Although he was treated as a political threat during his lifetime, within decades of his death his writings came to be considered orthodox, and in subsequent centuries candidates for the examinations had to be familiar with his commentaries on the classics.

Women's Lives in Song Times

Thanks to the spread of printing, more books survive from the Song period than from earlier periods, giving us more glimpses of women's lives. Stories, documents, and legal cases show us widows who ran inns, maids who were sent out by their mistresses to do errands, midwives who delivered babies, pious women who spent their days chanting Buddhist sutras, nuns who called on such women to explain Buddhist doctrine, girls who learned to read with their brothers, farmers' daughters who made money by weaving mats, childless widows who accused their nephews of stealing their property, wives who were jealous of the concubines their husbands brought home, and women who used part of their own large dowries to help their husbands' sisters marry well.

Families who could afford it usually tried to keep their wives and daughters within the walls of the house, rather than let them work in the fields or in shops or inns. At home there was plenty for them to do. Not only was there the work of tending children and preparing meals, but spinning, weaving, and sewing were considered women's work as well and took a great deal of time. Families that raised silkworms also needed women to do much of the work of coddling the worms and getting them to spin their cocoons. Within the home women generally had considerable say and took an active interest in issues such as the selection of marriage partners for their children.

Women tended to marry between the ages of sixteen and twenty. Their husbands were, on average, a couple of years older than they were. Marriages were arranged by their parents, who would have either called on a professional matchmaker (most often an older woman) or turned to a friend or relative for suggestions. Before a wedding took place, written agreements were exchanged, listing the prospective bride's and groom's birth dates, parents, and grandparents; the gifts that would be exchanged; and the dowry the bride would bring. The goal was to match families of approximately equal status, but a young man who had just passed the civil service exams would be considered a good prospect even if his family had little wealth.

A few days before the wedding, the bride's family sent her dowry to the groom's family, which at a mini-

• **Neo-Confucianism** The revival of Confucian thinking that began in the eleventh century, characterized by the goal of attaining the wisdom of the sages, not exam success.

mum contained boxes full of clothes and bedding. In better-off families, the dowry also included items of substantial value, such as gold jewelry or deeds to land. On the day of the wedding, the groom and some of his friends and relatives went to the bride's home to get her. She would be elaborately dressed and would tearfully bid farewell to everyone in her family. She was carried to her new home in a fancy sedan chair to the sound of music, alerting everyone on the street that a wedding was taking place. Meanwhile, the groom's family's friends and relatives had gathered at his home, ready to greet the bridal party. The bride would kneel and bow to her new parents-in-law and later also to the tablets with the names of her husband's ancestors. A classical ritual still practiced was for the new couple to drink wine from the same cup. A ritual that had become popular in Song times was to attach a string to the bride and groom, literally tying them together. Later they were shown to their new bedroom, where the bride's dowry had already been placed, and people tossed beans or rice on the bed, symbolizing the desired fertility. After teasing them, the guests left them alone and went out to the courtyard for a wedding feast.

The young bride's first priority was to try to win over her mother-in-law, since everyone knew that mothers-in-law were hard to please. One way to do this was to quickly bear a son for the family. Within the patrilineal system, a woman fully secured her position in the family by becoming the mother of one of the men. Every community had older women skilled in midwifery who were called to help when a woman went into labor. If the family was well-to-do, arrangements might be made for a wet nurse to help her take care of the newborn.

Women frequently had four, five, or six children, but likely one or more would die in infancy. If a son reached adulthood and married before the woman herself was widowed, she would be considered fortunate, for she would have always had an adult man who could take care of business for her — first her husband, then her grown son. But in the days when infectious diseases took many people in their twenties and thirties, it was not uncommon for a woman to be widowed while in her twenties, when her children were still very young.

A woman with a healthy and prosperous husband faced another challenge in middle age: her husband could bring home a **concubine** (and more than one if he could afford them). Moralists insisted that it was wrong for a wife to be jealous of her husband's concubines, but contemporary documents suggest that jealousy was very common. Wives outranked concubines and could give them orders in the house, but a concubine had her own ways of getting back through her hold on the husband. The children born to a concubine were considered just as much children of the family as the wife's children, and if the wife had had only daughters and the concubine had a son, the wife would find herself dependent on the concubine's son in her old age.

As a woman's children grew up, she would start thinking of suitable marriage partners. Many women liked the idea of bringing other women from their families of birth — perhaps a brother's daughter — to be their daughters-in-law. No matter who was selected, a woman's life became easier once she had a daughter-in-law to do the cooking and cleaning. Many found more time for religious devotions at this stage of their lives. Their sons, still living with them, could be expected to look after them and do their best to make their late years comfortable.

Neo-Confucianism is sometimes blamed for a decline in the status of women in Song times, largely because one of the best known of the Neo-Confucian teachers, Cheng Yi, once told a follower that it would be better for a widow to die of starvation

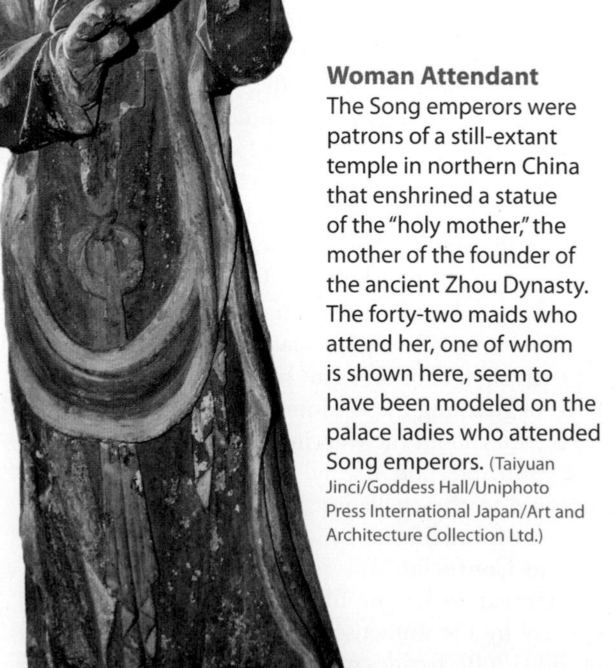

Woman Attendant
The Song emperors were patrons of a still-extant temple in northern China that enshrined a statue of the "holy mother," the mother of the founder of the ancient Zhou Dynasty. The forty-two maids who attend her, one of whom is shown here, seem to have been modeled on the palace ladies who attended Song emperors. (Taiyuan Jinci/Goddess Hall/Uniphoto Press International Japan/Art and Architecture Collection Ltd.)

• **concubine** A woman contracted to a man as a secondary spouse; although subordinate to the wife, her sons were considered legitimate heirs.

Individuals in Society

Shen Gua

IN THE ELEVENTH CENTURY IT WAS NOT RARE FOR CHINESE men of letters to have broad interests, but few could compare to Shen Gua (1031–1095), a man who tried his hand at everything from mathematics, geography, economics, engineering, medicine, divination, and archaeology to military strategy and diplomacy.

Shen Gua's father was an official, and Shen Gua often accompanied him on his assignments, which built up his knowledge of geography. In 1063 he passed the civil service examinations, and in 1066 he received a post in the capital. He eventually held high astronomical, ritual, and financial posts and became involved in waterworks and the construction of defense walls. He was sent as an envoy to the Khitans in 1075 to try to settle a boundary dispute. When a military campaign that he advised failed in 1082, he was demoted and later retired to write.

It is from his book of miscellaneous notes that we know the breadth of his interests. In one note Shen describes how, on assignment to inspect the frontier, he made a relief map of wood and glue-soaked sawdust to show the mountains, roads, rivers, and passes. The emperor was so impressed when he saw it that he ordered all the border prefectures to make relief maps. Elsewhere Shen describes the use of petroleum and explains how to make movable type from clay. Shen Gua often applied a mathematical approach to issues that his contemporaries did not think of in those terms. He once computed the total number of possible situations on a Go board, and another time he calculated the longest possible military campaign given the limits of human carriers, who had to carry their own food as well as food for the soldiers.

Shen Gua is especially known for his scientific explanations. He explained the deflection of the compass from due south. He identified petrified bamboo and from its existence argued that the region where it was found must have been much warmer and more humid in ancient times. He argued against the theory that tides are caused by the rising and setting of the sun, demonstrating that they correlate with the cycles of the moon. He proposed switching from a lunar calendar to a solar one of 365 days, saying that even though his contemporaries would reject his idea, "surely in the future some will adopt my idea." To convince his readers that the sun and the moon were spherical, not flat, he suggested that they cover a ball with fine powder on one side and then look at it obliquely. The powder was the part of the moon illuminated by the sun, and as the viewer looked at it obliquely, the white part would be crescent shaped, like a waxing moon. Shen Gua, however, did not realize that the sun and moon had entirely different orbits, and he explained why they did not collide by positing that both were composed of *qi* (vital energy) and had form but not substance.

Shen Gua also wrote on medicine and criticized his contemporaries for paying more attention to old treatises than to clinical experience. Yet he, too, was sometimes stronger on theory than on observation. In one note he argued that longevity pills could be made from cinnabar. He reasoned that if cinnabar could be transformed in one direction, it ought to be susceptible to transformation in the opposite direction as well. Therefore, since melted cinnabar causes death, solid cinnabar should prevent death.

Shen Gua played Go with white and black markers on a grid-like board like this one. (Courtesy of Library of Congress, LC-USZC4-8471/8472)

QUESTIONS FOR ANALYSIS

1. How did Shen Gua's travels add to his curiosity about the material world?
2. In what ways could Shen Gua have used his scientific interests in his work as a government official?
3. How does Shen Gua's understanding of the natural world compare to that of the early Greeks? (See pages 128–131.)

LaunchPad Online Document Project

What cultural pursuits interested the scholar-official class? View images from the Song period, and then complete a quiz and writing assignment based on the evidence and details from this chapter.

See inside the front cover to learn more.

Viewpoints 13.2

Zhu Xi and Yuan Cai on Family Management

• *The Confucian tradition put considerable emphasis on the ethics and rituals that should govern family life. Filial piety was considered a central virtue in Confucius's* Analects, *and an early Confucian text, the* Greater Learning, *argued that a man who wanted to serve the ruler or bring peace to the realm had to first manage his own family. These Confucian precepts were honored not only in China but also in Korea and Japan.*

What could one do to bring harmony to his family? Zhu Xi, one of the leading Neo-Confucian philosophers of his day, placed emphasis on ritual. His discussion of the importance of setting up an ancestral shrine is the first item in his influential book Family Rituals. *Other parts of this book detail the steps to be taken in funerals, weddings, coming-of-age ceremonies, and ancestral rites. His contemporary Yuan Cai (ca. 1140–ca. 1190) was a local government official whose views about how to attain family harmony seem to have come from his personal experience rather than the study of Confucian texts. Yuan Cai's* Precepts for Social Life *also gives advice on arranging marriages, managing servants, and avoiding bankruptcy. These two books, while written in Chinese, circulated in Korea and Japan as well as China, with Zhu Xi's* Family Rituals *becoming especially important in Korea.*

Zhu Xi on the Offering Hall

"When a man of virtue builds a house his first task is always to set up an offering hall to the east of the main room of his house. For this hall four altars to hold the spirit tablets of the ancestors are made; collateral relatives who died without descendants may have associated offerings made to them there according to their generational seniority. Sacrificial fields should be established and sacrificial utensils prepared. Once the hall is completed, early each morning the master enters the outer gate to pay a visit. All comings and goings are reported there. On New Year's Day, the solstices, and each new and full moon, visits are made. On the customary festivals, seasonal foods are offered, and when an event occurs, reports are made. Should there be flood, fire, robbers, or bandits, the offering hall is the first thing to be saved. The spirit tablets, inherited manuscripts, and then the sacrificial utensils should be moved; only afterward may the family's valuables be taken. As one generation succeeds another, the spirit tablets are reinscribed and moved to their new places."

Yuan Cai on Forbearance

"People say that lasting harmony in families begins with the ability to forbear. But knowing how to forbear without knowing how to live with forbearing can lead to a great many errors. Some seem to think that forbearance means to repress anger; that is, when someone offends you, you repress your feelings and do not reveal them. If this happens only once or twice it would be all right. But if it happens repeatedly the anger will come bursting forth like an irrepressible flood.

A better method is to dissipate anger as the occasion arises instead of hiding it in your chest. Do this by saying to yourself, "He wasn't thinking," "He doesn't know any better," "He made a mistake," "He is narrow in his outlook," "How much harm can this really do?" If you keep the anger from entering your heart, then even if someone offends you ten times a day, neither your speech nor your behavior will be affected. You will then see the magnitude of the benefits of forbearance."

Yuan Cai on Dislike Among Relatives

"Dislike among blood relatives may start from a very minor incident but end up ingrained. It is just that once two people take a dislike to each other they become irascible, and neither is willing to be the first to cool off. When they are in each other's company day in and day out, they cannot help but irritate each other. If, having reached this state, one of them would be willing to take the initiative in cooling off and would talk to the other, then the other would reciprocate, and the situation would return to normal. This point is worth deep consideration."

Sources: Patricia Buckley Ebrey, trans., *Chu Hsi's* Family Rituals*: A Twelfth-Century Chinese Manual for the Performance of Cappings, Weddings, Funerals, and Ancestral Rites* (Princeton, N.J.: Princeton University Press, 1991), p. 5. © 1991 Princeton University Press. Reprinted by permission of Princeton University Press; Patricia Buckley Ebrey, trans., *Family and Property in Sung China: Yuan Ts'ai's* Precepts for Social Life (Princeton, N.J.: Princeton University Press, 1984), pp. 186–187. © 1984 Princeton University Press. Reprinted by permission of Princeton University Press.

QUESTIONS FOR ANALYSIS

1. Would attention to the details of ancestral rites of the sort Zhu Xi outlines help avoid the sorts of problems among relatives that Yuan Cai discusses, or could it make them worse?
2. The ideal Chinese family was one that did not divide during the parents' lifetimes, so that adult brothers and their families all lived together with their elderly parents. What can you infer about problems connected to such large, complex families from these two authors?

than to lose her virtue by remarrying. In later centuries this saying was often quoted to justify pressuring widows, even very young ones, to stay with their husbands' families and not remarry. In Song times, however, widows frequently remarried. (See "Viewpoints 13.2: Zhu Xi and Yuan Cai on Family Management," at left.)

It is true that **foot binding** began during the Song Dynasty, but it was not recommended by Neo-Confucian teachers; rather it was associated with the pleasure quarters and with women's efforts to beautify themselves. Mothers bound the feet of girls aged five to eight with long strips of cloth to keep them from growing and to bend the four smaller toes under to make the foot narrow and arched. The hope was that the girl would be judged more beautiful. Foot binding spread gradually during Song times but was probably still largely an elite practice. In later centuries it became extremely common in north and central China, eventually spreading to all classes. Women with bound feet were less mobile than women with natural feet, but only those who could afford servants bound their feet so tightly that walking was difficult.

Blue-and-White Jars of the Yuan Period Chinese ceramics had long been in demand outside of China, and an innovation of the Mongol period — decorating white porcelain with underglaze designs in blue — proved especially popular. Persia imported large quantities of Chinese blue-and-white ceramics, and Korean, Japanese, and Vietnamese potters took up versions of the style themselves. (© The Trustees of the British Museum/Art Resource, NY)

China Under Mongol Rule

As discussed in Chapter 12, the Mongols conquered China in stages, gaining much of north China by 1215 and all of it by 1234, but not taking the south till the 1270s. The north suffered the most devastation. The non-Chinese rulers in the north, the Jin Dynasty of the Jurchen — with 150,000 cavalry, mostly Jurchen, and more than 300,000 Chinese infantrymen — thought they had the strongest army known to history. Yet Mongol tactics frustrated them. The Mongols would take a city, plunder it, and then withdraw, letting the Jin take it back and deal with the resulting food shortages and destruction. Under these circumstances, Jurchen power rapidly collapsed.

Not until Khubilai was Great Khan was the Song Dynasty defeated and south China brought under the control of the Mongols' Yuan Dynasty. Non-Chinese rulers had gained control of north China several times in Chinese history, but none of them had been able to secure control of the region south of the Yangzi River, which required a navy. By the 1260s Khubilai had put Chinese shipbuilders to work building a fleet, crucial to his victory over the Song (see page 339).

Life in China under the Mongols was much like life in China under earlier alien rulers. Once order was restored, people did their best to get on with their lives. Some were deprived of their land, business, or freedom and suffered real hardship. Yet people still spoke Chinese, followed Chinese customary practices in dividing their family property, made offerings at local temples, and celebrated the new year and other customary festivals. Teachers still taught students the classics, scholars continued to write books, and books continued to be printed.

The Mongols, like other foreign rulers before them, did not see anything particularly desirable in the social mobility of Chinese society. Preferring stability, they assigned people hereditary occupations such as farmer, Confucian scholar, physician, astrologer, soldier, artisan, salt producer, miner, and Buddhist monk; the occupations came with obligations to the state. Besides these occupational categories, the Mongols classified the population into four grades, with the Mongols occupying the top grade. Next came various non-Chinese, such as the Uighurs and Persians. Below them were Chinese former subjects of the Jurchen, called the Han. At the bottom were the former subjects of the Song, called southerners.

The reason for codifying ethnic differences this way was to preserve the Mongols' privileges as conquerors. Chinese were not allowed to take Mongol names, and great efforts were made to keep them from passing as

• **foot binding** The practice of binding the feet of girls with long strips of cloth to keep them from growing large.

Mongols or marrying Mongols. To keep Chinese from rebelling, they were forbidden to own weapons or congregate in public. Khubilai even prohibited Chinese from dealing in bamboo because it could be used to make bows and arrows.

As the Mongols captured Chinese territory, they recruited Chinese into their armies and government. Although some refused to serve the Mongols, others argued that the Chinese would fare better if Chinese were the administrators and could shield Chinese society from the most brutal effects of Mongol rule. A few Confucian scholars devoted themselves to the task of patiently teaching Mongol rulers the principles of Confucian government.

Nevertheless, government service, which had long been central to the identity and income of the educated elite in China, was not as widely available under the Mongols. The Mongols reinstituted the civil service examinations in 1315, but filled only about 2 percent of the positions in the bureaucracy through them and reserved half of those places for Mongols.

The scholar-official elite without government employment turned to alternative ways to support themselves. Those who did not have land to live off of found work as physicians, fortune-tellers, children's teachers, Daoist priests, publishers, booksellers, or playwrights. Many took leadership roles at the local level, such as founding academies for Confucian learning or promoting local charitable ventures. Through such activities, scholars without government offices could assert the importance of civil over military values and see themselves as trustees of the Confucian tradition.

Since the Mongols wanted to extract wealth from China, they had every incentive to develop the economy. They encouraged trade both within China and beyond its borders and tried to keep paper money in circulation. (See "Viewpoints 12.2: Circulating Paper Money," page 343.) They repaired the Grand Canal, which had been ruined during their initial conquest of north China. Chinese industries with strong foreign markets, such as porcelain, thrived. Nevertheless, the economic expansion of late Tang and Song times did not continue under the alien rule of the Jurchens and Mongols. The economy of north China, with its strong iron industry, contracted under the Jurchens, and the destruction of cities was extensive during the first five decades of Mongol rule of the north.

The Mongols' Yuan Dynasty began a rapid decline in the 1330s as disease, rebellions, and poor leadership led to disorder throughout the country. When a Chinese strongman succeeded in consolidating the south, the Mongol rulers retreated to Mongolia before he could take Beijing. By 1368 the Yuan Dynasty had given way to a new Chinese-led dynasty: the Ming.

Korea Under the Koryŏ Dynasty, 935–1392

☐ How did Korean society and culture develop in an age when its northern neighbors were Khitans, Jurchens, and Mongols?

During the Silla period, Korea was strongly tied to Tang China and avidly copied China's model (see page 198). This changed along with much else in North Asia between 800 and 1400. In this period Korea lived more in the shadows of the powerful states of the Khitans, Jurchens, and Mongols than of the Chinese.

The Silla Dynasty began to decline after the king was killed in a revolt in 780. For the next 155 years the kings were selected from several collateral lines, and the majority of them met violent deaths. Rebellions and coups d'état followed one after the other, as different groups of nobles placed their candidates on the throne and killed as many of their opponents as they could. As conditions deteriorated, serfs absconded in large numbers, and independent merchants and seamen of humble origins came to dominate the three-way trade between China, Korea, and Japan.

The dynasty that emerged from this confusion was called Koryŏ (KAW-ree-oh) (935–1392). (The English word *Korea* derives from the name of this dynasty.) During this time Korea developed more independently of the China model than it had in Silla times, just as contemporary Japan was doing (see the next section). This was not because the Chinese model was rejected; the Koryŏ capital was laid out on the Chinese model, and the government was closely patterned on the Tang system. But despite Chinese influence, Korean society remained deeply aristocratic.

The Koryŏ Dynasty, 935–1392

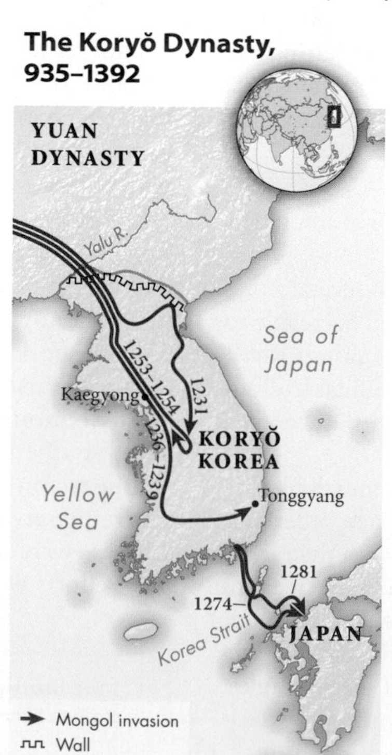

The founder of the dynasty, Wang Kon (877–943), was a man of relatively obscure maritime background, and he needed the support of the old aristocracy to maintain control. His successors introduced civil service examinations on the Chinese model, as well as examinations for Buddhist clergy, but because the aristocrats were the best educated and the government schools admitted only the sons of aristocrats, this system served primarily to solidify their control. Politics was largely the competition among aristocratic clans for influence at court and marriage of their daughters to the royal princes. Like the Heian aristocrats in Japan (see pages 381–384), the Koryŏ aristocrats wanted to stay in the capital and only reluctantly accepted posts in the provinces.

At the other end of the social scale, the number of people in the serf-slave stratum seems to have increased. This lowborn stratum included not only privately held slaves but also large numbers of government slaves as well as government workers in mines, porcelain factories, and other government industries. Sometimes entire villages or groups of villages were considered lowborn. There were occasional slave revolts, and some freed slaves did rise in status, but prejudice against anyone with slave ancestors was so strong that the law provided that "only if there is no evidence of lowborn status for eight generations in one's official household registration may one receive a position in the government."[3] In China and Japan, by contrast, slavery was a much more minor element in the social landscape.

The commercial economy declined in Korea during this period, showing that it was not closely linked to China's then-booming economy. Except for the capital, there were no cities of commercial importance, and in the countryside the use of money declined. One industry that did flourish was ceramics. Connoisseurs have long appreciated the elegance of the pale green Koryŏ celadon pottery, decorated with designs executed in inlaid white or gray clay.

Buddhism remained strong throughout Korea, and monasteries became major centers of art and learning. As in Song China and Kamakura Japan, Chan (Zen) and Tiantai (Tendai) were the leading Buddhist teachings (see pages 194, 384). The founder of the Koryŏ Dynasty attributed the dynasty's success to the Buddha's protection, and he and his successors were ardent patrons of the church. The entire Buddhist canon was printed in the eleventh century and again in the thirteenth. (The 81,258 individual woodblocks used to print it still survive in a Korean Buddhist monastery.) As in medieval Europe, aristocrats who entered the church occupied the major abbacies. Monasteries played the same roles as they did in China and Japan, such as engaging in money-lending and charitable works. As in Japan (but not China), some monasteries accumulated military power.

Not all cultural advances were connected to monasteries or Buddhism. The most important literary work

Wooden Blocks for Printing The Heainsa Buddhist Temple in Korea has preserved the more than eighty thousand woodblocks used to print the huge Buddhist canon in the thirteenth century. The monk shown here is replacing a block. All the blocks are carved on both sides and stabilized by wooden frames that have kept them from warping. (© OUR PLACE THE WORLD HERITAGE COLLECTION, www.ourplaceworldheritage.com)

of the Koryŏ period is *The History of the Three Kingdoms*, compiled in 1145 in Chinese. Modeled on Chinese histories, it is the best source of information on early Korean history.

The Koryŏ Dynasty was preserved in name long after the ruling family had lost most of its power. In 1170 the palace guards massacred the civil officials at court and placed a new king on the throne. The coup leaders scrapped the privileges that had kept the aristocrats in power and appointed themselves to the top posts. After incessant infighting among the generals and a series of coups, in 1196 the general Ch'oe Ch'ung-hon took control. Ch'oe had a private army of about three thousand warrior-retainers and an even larger number of slaves. The domination of Korea by the Ch'oe family was much like the contemporaneous situation in Japan, where warrior bands were seizing power. Moreover, because the Ch'oes were content to dominate the government while leaving the Koryŏ king on the throne, they had much in common with the Japanese shoguns, who followed a similar strategy.

Although Korea adopted many ideas from China, it could not so easily adopt the Chinese assumption that it was the largest, most powerful, and most advanced society in the world. Korea, from early times, recognized China as being in many ways senior to it, but when strong non-Chinese states emerged to its north in Manchuria, Korea was ready to accommodate them as well. Koryŏ's first neighbor to the north was the Khitan state of Liao, which in 1010 invaded and sacked the capital. To avoid destruction, Koryŏ acceded to vassal status, but Liao invaded again in 1018. This time Koryŏ was able to repel the nomadic Khitans. Afterward a defensive wall was built across the Korean peninsula south of the Yalu River. When the Jurchens and their Jin Dynasty supplanted the Khitans' Liao Dynasty, Koryŏ agreed to send them tribute as well.

As mentioned in Chapter 12, Korea was conquered by the Mongols, and the figurehead Koryŏ kings were moved to Beijing, where they married Mongol princesses, their descendants becoming more Mongol than Korean. This was a time of hardship for the Korean people. In the year 1254 alone, the Mongols enslaved two hundred thousand Koreans and took them away. Ordinary people in Korea suffered grievously when their land was used as a launching pad for the huge Mongol invasions of Japan: nine hundred ships and the provisions for the soldiers on them had to be procured from the Korean countryside. In this period Korea also suffered from frequent attacks by Japanese pirates, somewhat like the depredations of the Vikings in Europe a little earlier (see page 393). The Mongol overlords did little to provide protection, and the harried coastal people had little choice but to retreat inland.

When Mongol rule in China fell apart in the mid-fourteenth century, it declined in Korea as well. Chinese rebels opposing the Mongols entered Korea and even briefly captured the capital in 1361. When the Ming Dynasty was established in China in 1368, the Koryŏ court was unsure how to respond. In 1388 a general, Yi Song-gye, was sent to oppose a Ming army at the northwest frontier. When he saw the strength of the Ming, he concluded that making an alliance was more sensible than fighting, and he led his troops back to the capital, where in 1392 he usurped the throne, founding the Chosŏn Dynasty.

Japan's Heian Period, 794–1185

☐ How did the Heian form of government contribute to the cultural flowering of Japan in this period?

As described in Chapter 7, during the seventh and eighth centuries the Japanese ruling house pursued a vigorous policy of adopting useful ideas, techniques, and policies from the more advanced civilization of China. The rulers built a splendid capital along Chinese lines in Nara and fostered the growth of Buddhism. Monasteries grew so powerful in Nara, however, that in less than a century the court decided to move away from them and encourage other sects of Buddhism.

The new capital was built about twenty-five miles away at Heian (HAY-ahn; modern Kyoto). Like Nara, Heian was modeled on the Tang capital of Chang'an (although neither of the Japanese capitals had walls, a major feature of Chinese cities). For the first century at Heian the government continued to follow Chinese models, but it turned away from them with the decline of the Tang Dynasty in the late ninth century. The last official embassy to China made the trip in 894. During the Heian period (794–1185), Japan witnessed a literary and cultural flowering under the rule of the Fujiwara family.

Fujiwara Rule

Only the first two Heian emperors were much involved in governing. By 860 political management had been taken over by a series of regents from the Fujiwara family, who supplied most of the empresses in this period. The emperors continued to be honored, even venerated, because of their presumed divine descent, but the Fujiwaras ruled. Fujiwara dominance represented the privatization of political power and a return to clan politics. Political history thus took a very different course in Japan than in China, where, when a dynasty

The Tale of Genji In this scene from a twelfth-century painting illustrating *The Tale of Genji*, Genji has his inkstone and brushes ready to respond to the letter he is reading. (Tokugawa Reimeikai Foundation, Tokyo, Japan/Photo © AISA/The Bridgeman Art Library)

weakened, military strongmen would compete to depose the emperor and found their own dynasties. In Japan for the next thousand years, political contenders sought to manipulate the emperors rather than supplant them.

The Fujiwaras reached the apogee of their glory under Fujiwara Michinaga (r. 995–1027). Like many aristocrats of the period, he was learned in Buddhism, music, poetry, and Chinese literature and history. He dominated the court for more than thirty years as the father of four empresses, the uncle of two emperors, and the grandfather of three emperors. He acquired great landholdings and built fine palaces for himself and his family. After ensuring that his sons could continue to rule, he retired to a Buddhist monastery, all the while continuing to maintain control.

By the end of the eleventh century several emperors who did not have Fujiwara mothers had found a device to counter Fujiwara control: they abdicated but continued to exercise power by controlling their young sons on the throne. This system of rule has been called **cloistered government** because the retired emperors took Buddhist orders, while maintaining control of the government from behind the scenes. Thus for a time the imperial house was a contender for political power along with other aristocratic groups.

Aristocratic Culture

A brilliant aristocratic culture developed in the Heian period. In the capital at Heian, nobles, palace ladies, and imperial family members lived a highly refined and leisured life. In their society, niceties of birth, rank, and breeding counted for everything. From their diaries we know of the pains aristocratic women took in their dress, selecting the color combinations of the kimonos they wore, layer upon layer. The elegance of one's calligraphy and the allusions in one's poems were matters of intense concern to both men and women at court. Courtiers did not like to leave the capital, and some like the court lady Sei Shonagon shuddered at the sight of ordinary working people. In her *Pillow Book*, she wrote of encountering a group of commoners on a pilgrimage: "They looked like so many basketworms as they crowded together in their hideous clothes, leaving hardly an inch of space between themselves and me. I really felt like pushing them all over sideways."[4] (See "Listening to the Past: *The Pillow Book* of Sei Shonagon," page 382.)

In this period a new script was developed for writing Japanese phonetically. Each symbol was based on a simplified Chinese character and represented one of the syllables used in Japanese (such as *ka*, *ki*, *ku*, *ke*, *ko*). Although "serious" essays, histories, and government documents continued to be written in Chinese, less formal works such as poetry and memoirs were written in Japanese. Mastering the new writing system took much less time than mastering writing in Chinese

- **cloistered government** A system in which an emperor retired to a Buddhist monastery but continued to exercise power by controlling his young son on the throne.

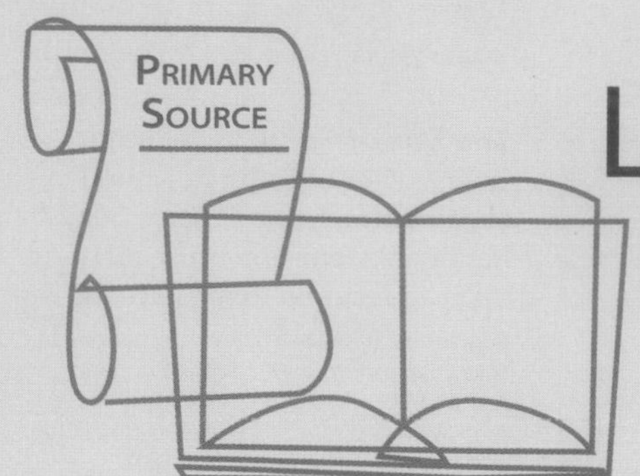

Listening to the Past

The Pillow Book of Sei Shonagon

Beginning in the late tenth century Japan produced a series of great women writers. At the time women were much freer than men to write in vernacular Japanese, giving them a large advantage. Lady Murasaki, author of the novel The Tale of Genji, *is the most famous of the women writers of the period, but her contemporary Sei Shonagon is equally noteworthy. Sei Shonagon served as a lady in waiting to Empress Sadako during the last decade of the tenth century (990–1000). Her only known work is* The Pillow Book, *a collection of notes, character sketches, anecdotes, descriptions of nature, and eccentric lists such as boring things, awkward things, hateful things, and things that have lost their power.*

The Pillow Book *portrays the lovemaking/marriage system among the aristocracy more or less as it is depicted in* The Tale of Genji. *Marriages were arranged for family interests, and a man could have more than one wife. Wives and their children commonly stayed in their own homes, where their husbands and fathers would visit them. But once a man had an heir by his wife, there was nothing to prevent him from establishing relations with other women. Some relationships were long-term, but many were brief, and men often had several lovers at the same time. Some women became known for their amorous conquests, others as abandoned women whose husbands ignored them. The following passage from* The Pillow Book *looks on this lovemaking system with amused detachment.*

" It is so stiflingly hot in the Seventh Month that even at night one keeps all the doors and lattices open. At such times it is delightful to wake up when the moon is shining and to look outside. I enjoy it even when there is no moon. But to wake up at dawn and see a pale sliver of a moon in the sky — well, I need hardly say how perfect that is.

I like to see a bright new straw mat that has just been spread out on a well-polished floor. The best place for one's three-foot curtain of state is in the front of the room near the veranda. It is pointless to put it in the rear of the room, as it is most unlikely that anyone will peer in from that direction.

It is dawn and a woman is lying in bed after her lover has taken his leave. She is covered up to her head with a light mauve robe that has a lining of dark violet; the colour of both the outside and the lining is fresh and glossy. The woman, who appears to be asleep, wears an unlined orange robe and a dark crimson skirt of stiff silk whose cords hang loosely by her side, as if they have been left untied. Her thick tresses tumble over each other in cascades, and one can imagine how long her hair must be when it falls freely down her back.

Nearby another woman's lover is making his way home in the misty dawn. He is wearing loose violet trousers, an orange hunting costume, so lightly coloured that one can hardly tell whether it has been dyed or not, a white robe of still silk, and a scarlet robe of glossy, beaten silk. His clothes, which are damp from the mist, hang loosely about him. From the dishevelment of his side locks one can tell how negligently he must have tucked his hair into the black lacquered headdress when he got up. He wants to return and write his next-morning letter before the dew on the morning glories has had time to vanish; but the path seems endless, and to divert himself he hums "the sprouts in the flax fields."

As he walks along, he passes a house with an open lattice. He is on his way to report for official duty, but cannot help stopping to lift up the blind and peep into the room. It amuses him to think that a man has probably been spending the night here and has only recently got up to leave, just as happened to himself. Perhaps that man too had felt the charm of the dew.

Looking around the room, he notices near the woman's pillow an open fan with a magnolia frame and purple paper; and at the foot of her curtain of state he sees some narrow strips of

and aided the spread of literacy, especially among women in court society.

In the Heian period, women played important roles at all levels of society. Women educated in the arts and letters could advance at court as attendants to the ruler's empress and other consorts. Women could inherit property from their parents, and they would compete with their brothers for shares of the family property. In political life, marrying a daughter to an emperor or shogun (see page 384) was one of the best ways to gain power, and women often became major players in power struggles.

The literary masterpiece of this period is ***The Tale of Genji***, written in Japanese by Lady Murasaki over several years (ca. 1000–1010). This long narrative depicts a cast of characters enmeshed in court life, with close

• ***The Tale of Genji*** A Japanese literary masterpiece about court life written by Lady Murasaki.

During the Heian period, noblewomen were fashion conscious. Wearing numerous layers of clothing gave women the opportunity to choose different designs and colors for their robes. The layers also kept them warm in drafty homes. (© INTERFOTO/Alamy)

Michinoku paper and also some other paper of a faded colour, either orange-red or maple.

The woman senses that someone is watching her and, looking up from under her bedclothes, sees a gentleman leaning against the wall by the threshold, a smile on his face. She can tell at once that he is the sort of man with whom she need feel no reserve. All the same, she does not want to enter into any familiar relations with him, and she is annoyed that he should have seen her asleep.

"Well, well, Madam," says the man, leaning forward so that the upper part of his body comes behind her curtains, "what a long nap you're having after your morning adieu! You really are a lie-abed!"

"You call me that, Sir," she replied, "only because you're annoyed at having had to get up before the dew had time to settle."

Their conversation may be commonplace, yet I find there is something delightful about the scene.

Now the gentleman leans further forward and, using his own fan, tries to get hold of the fan by the woman's pillow. Fearing his closeness, she moves further back into her curtain enclosure, her heart pounding. The gentleman picks up the magnolia fan and, while examining it, says in a slightly bitter tone, "How standoffish you are!"

But now it is growing light; there is a sound of people's voices, and it looks as if the sun will soon be up. Only a short while ago this same man was hurrying home to write his next-morning letter before the mists had time to clear. Alas, how easily his intentions have been forgotten!

While all this is afoot, the woman's original lover has been busy with his own next-morning letter, and now, quite unexpectedly, the messenger arrives at her house. The letter is attached to a spray of bush-clover, still damp with dew, and the paper gives off a delicious aroma of incense. Because of the new visitor, however, the woman's servants cannot deliver it to her.

Finally it becomes unseemly for the gentleman to stay any longer. As he goes, he is amused to think that a similar scene may be taking place in the house he left earlier that morning. ”

Source: *The Pillow Book of Sei Shonagon*, edited and translated by Ivan Morris, pp. 60–62.

QUESTIONS FOR ANALYSIS

1. What sorts of images does Sei Shonagon evoke to convey an impression of a scene?
2. What can you learn from this passage about the material culture of Japan in this period?
3. Why do you think Sei Shonagon was highly esteemed as a writer?

attention to dialogue and personality. Murasaki also wrote a diary that is similarly revealing of aristocratic culture. In one passage she tells of an occasion when word got out that she had read the Chinese classics:

> Worried what people would think if they heard such rumors, I pretended to be unable to read even the inscriptions on the screens. Then Her Majesty asked me to read to her here and there from the collected works of [the Tang Chinese poet] Bo Juyi, and, because she evinced a desire to know much more about such things, we carefully chose a time when other women would not be present and, amateur that I was, I read with her the two books of Bo Juyi's New Ballads in secret; we started the summer before last.[5]

Despite the reluctance of Murasaki and the lady she served to let others know of their learning, there were, in fact, quite a few women writers in this period. The wife of a high-ranking court official wrote a poetic memoir of her unhappy twenty-year marriage to him and his rare visits. A woman wrote both an autobiography that related her father's efforts to find favor at court and a love story of a hero who travels to China. Another woman even wrote a history that concludes with a triumphal biography of Fujiwara Michinaga.

Buddhism remained very strong throughout the Heian period. A mission sent to China in 804 included two monks in search of new texts. One of the monks, Saichō, spent time at the monasteries on Mount Tiantai and brought back the Buddhist teachings associated with that mountain (called Tendai in Japanese). Tendai's basic message is that all living beings share the Buddha nature and can be brought to salvation. Tendai practices include strict monastic discipline, prayer, textual study, and meditation. Once back in Japan, Saichō established a monastery on Mount Hiei outside Kyoto, which grew to be one of the most important monasteries in Japan. By the twelfth century this monastery and its many branch temples had vast lands and a powerful army of monk-soldiers to protect its interests. Whenever the monastery felt that its interests were at risk, it sent the monk-soldiers into the capital to parade its sacred symbols in an attempt to intimidate the civil authorities.

Kūkai, the other monk on the 804 mission to China, came back with texts from another school of Buddhism — Shingon, "True Word," a form of **Esoteric Buddhism**. Esoteric Buddhism is based on the idea that teachings containing the secrets of enlightenment had been secretly transmitted from the Buddha. People can gain access to these mysteries through initiation into the mandalas (cosmic diagrams), mudras (gestures), and mantras (verbal formulas). On his return to Japan, Kūkai attracted many followers and was allowed to establish a monastery at Mount Kōya, south of Osaka. The popularity of Esoteric Buddhism was a great stimulus to Buddhist art.

- **Esoteric Buddhism** A sect of Buddhism that maintains that the secrets of enlightenment have been secretly transmitted from the Buddha and can be accessed through initiation into the mandalas, mudras, and mantras.
- **shogun** The Japanese general-in-chief, whose headquarters was the shogunate.
- **Bushido** Literally, the "way of the warrior"; the code of conduct by which samurai were expected to live.

The Samurai and the Kamakura Shogunate, 1185–1333

☐ What were the causes and consequences of military rule in Japan?

The gradual rise of a warrior elite over the course of the Heian period finally brought an end to the domination of the Fujiwaras and other Heian aristocratic families. In 1156 civil war broke out between the Taira and Minamoto warrior clans based in western and eastern Japan, respectively. Both clans relied on skilled warriors, later called samurai, who were rapidly becoming a new social class. A samurai and his lord had a double bond: in return for the samurai's loyalty and service, the lord granted him land or income. From 1159 to 1181 a Taira named Kiyomori dominated the court, taking the position of prime minister and marrying his daughter to the emperor. His relatives became governors of more than thirty provinces, managed some five hundred tax-exempt estates, and amassed a fortune in the trade with Song China and Koryŏ Korea. Still, the Minamoto clan managed to defeat the Taira, and the Minamoto leader, Yoritomo, became **shogun**, or general-in-chief. With him began the Kamakura Shogunate (1185–1333). This period is often referred to as Japan's feudal period because it was dominated by a military class whose members were tied to their superiors by bonds of loyalty and supported by landed estates rather than salaries.

Military Rule

The similarities between military rule in Japan and feudalism in medieval Europe during roughly the same period have fascinated scholars, as have the very significant differences. In Europe feudalism emerged out of the fusion of Germanic and Roman social institutions and flowered under the impact of Muslim and Viking invasions. In Japan military rule evolved from a combination of the native warrior tradition and Confucian ethical principles of duty to superiors.

The emergence of the samurai was made possible by the development of private landholding. The government land allotment system, copied from Tang China, began breaking down in the eighth century (much as it did in China). By the ninth century local lords had begun escaping imperial taxes and control by commending (formally giving) their land to tax-exempt entities such as monasteries, the imperial family, and high-ranking officials. The local lord then received his land back as a tenant and paid his protector a small rent. The monastery or privileged individual received a

The Shogun Minamoto Yoritomo in Court Dress
This wooden sculpture, 27.8 inches tall, was made about a half century after Yoritomo's death for use in a shrine dedicated to his memory. The bold shapes convey Yoritomo's dignity and power. (*Yoritomo [Minamotono-Yoritomo]*, wood with colored painting and quartz eyes, Kamakura Period, 1300/ National Museum, Tokyo, Japan/akg-images)

steady income from the land, and the local lord escaped imperial taxes and control. By the end of the thirteenth century most land seems to have been taken off the tax rolls this way. Each plot of land could thus have several people with rights to shares of its produce, ranging from the cultivator, to a local lord, to an estate manager working for him, to a regional strongman, to a noble or temple in the capital. Unlike peasants in medieval Europe, where similar practices of commendation occurred, those working the land in Japan never became serfs. Moreover, Japanese lords rarely lived on the lands they had rights in, unlike English or French lords who lived on their manors.

Samurai resembled European knights in several ways. Both were armed with expensive weapons, and both fought on horseback. Just as the knight was supposed to live according to the chivalric code, so Japanese samurai were expected to live according to **Bushido** (or "way of the warrior"), a code that stressed military honor, courage, stoic acceptance of hardship, and, above all, loyalty. Physical hardship was accepted as routine, and soft living was despised as weak and unworthy. Disloyalty brought social disgrace, which the samurai could avoid only through *seppuku*, ritual suicide by slashing his belly.

The Kamakura Shogunate derives its name from Kamakura, a city near modern Tokyo that was the seat of the Minamoto clan. The founder, Yoritomo, ruled the country much the way he ran his own estates, appointing his retainers to newly created offices. To cope with the emergence of hard-to-tax estates, he put military land stewards in charge of seeing to the estates' proper operation. To bring order to the lawless countryside, he appointed military governors to oversee the military and enforce the law in the provinces. They supervised the conduct of the land stewards in peacetime and commanded the provincial samurai in war.

Yoritomo's wife, Masako, protected the interests of her own family, the Hōjōs, especially after Yoritomo died. She went so far as to force her first son to abdicate when he showed signs of preferring the family of his wife to the family of his mother. She later helped her brother take power away from her father. Thus the process of reducing power holders to figureheads went one step further in 1219 when the Hōjō family reduced the shogun to a figurehead. The Hōjō

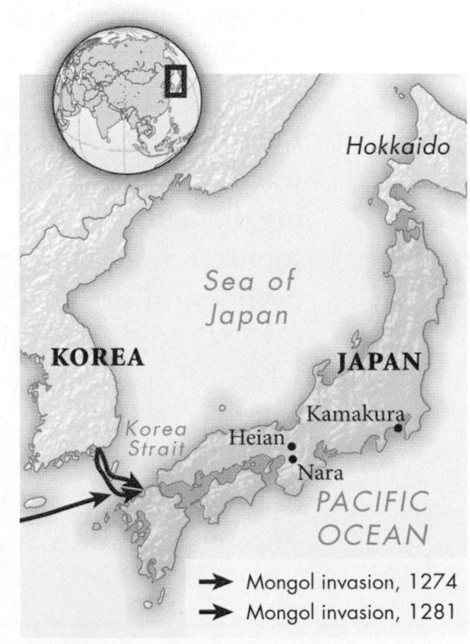

Kamakura Shogunate, 1185–1333

family held the reins of power for more than a century until 1333.

The Mongols' two massive seaborne invasions in 1274 and 1281 (see page 339) were a huge shock to the shogunate. The Kamakura government was hard-pressed to gather adequate resources for its defense. Temples were squeezed, farmers were taken away from their fields to build walls, and warriors were promised generous rewards in return for their service. Although the Hōjō regents, with the help of a "divine wind" (kamikaze), repelled the Mongols, they were unable to reward their vassals in the traditional way because little booty was found among the wreckage of the Mongol fleets. Discontent grew among the samurai, and by the fourteenth century the entire political system was breaking down. Both the imperial and the shogunate families were fighting among themselves. As land grants were divided, samurai became impoverished and took to plunder and piracy, or shifted their loyalty to local officials who could offer them a better living.

The factional disputes among Japan's leading families remained explosive until 1331, when the emperor Go-Daigo tried to recapture real power. His attempt sparked an uprising by the great families, local lords, samurai, and even Buddhist monasteries, which had thousands of samurai retainers. Go-Daigo destroyed the Kamakura Shogunate in 1333 but soon lost the loyalty of his followers. By 1338 one of his most important military supporters, Ashikaga Takauji, had turned on him and established the Ashikaga Shogunate, which lasted until 1573. Takauji's victory was also a victory for the samurai, who took over civil authority throughout Japan.

Cultural Trends

The cultural distance between the elites and the commoners narrowed a little during the Kamakura period. Buddhism was spread to ordinary Japanese by energetic preachers. Honen (1133–1212) propagated the Pure Land teaching, preaching that paradise could be reached through simple faith in the Buddha and repeating the name of the Buddha Amitabha. Neither philosophical understanding of Buddhist scriptures nor devotion to rituals was essential. His follower Shinran (1173–1263) taught that monks should not shut themselves off in monasteries but should marry and have children. A different path was promoted by Nichiren (1222–1282), a fiery and intolerant preacher who proclaimed that to be saved people had only to invoke sincerely the Lotus Sutra, one of the most important of the Buddhist sutras. These lay versions of Buddhism found a receptive audience among ordinary people in the countryside.

It was also during the Kamakura period that **Zen** came to flourish in Japan. Zen teachings originated in Tang China, where they were known as Chan (see page 195). Rejecting the authority of the sutras, Zen teachers claimed the superiority of mind-to-mind transmission of Buddhist truth. When Japanese monks went to China in the twelfth century looking for ways to revitalize Japanese Buddhism, they were impressed by the rigorous monastic life of the Chan/Zen monasteries. One school of Zen held that enlightenment could be achieved suddenly through insight into one's own true nature. This school taught rigorous meditation and the use of kōan riddles to unseat logic and free the mind for enlightenment. This teaching found eager patrons among the samurai, who were attracted to its discipline and strong master-disciple bonds.

Buddhism remained central to the visual arts. Many temples in Japan still house fine sculptures done in this period. In painting, narrative hand scrolls brought to life the miracles that faith could bring and the torments of Hell awaiting unbelievers. All forms of literature were depicted in these scrolls, including *The Tale of Genji*, war stories, and humorous anecdotes.

During the Kamakura period, war tales continued the tradition of long narrative prose works. *The Tale of the Heike* tells the story of the fall of the Taira family and the rise of the Minamoto clan. The tale reached a large and mostly illiterate audience because blind minstrels would chant sections to the accompaniment of a lute. The story is suffused with the Buddhist idea of the transience of life and the illusory nature of glory. Yet it also celebrates strength, courage, loyalty, and pride. The Minamoto warriors from the east are portrayed as the toughest. In one scene one of them dismisses his own prowess with the bow, claiming that other warriors from his region could pierce three sets of armor with their arrows. He then brags about the martial spirit of warriors from the east: "They are bold horsemen who never fall, nor do they let their horses stumble on the roughest road. When they fight they do not care if even their parents or children are killed; they ride over their bodies and continue the battle."[6] In this they stood in contrast to the warriors of the west, who in good Confucian fashion would retire from battle to mourn their parents.

After stagnating in the Heian period, agricultural productivity began to improve in the Kamakura period, and the population grew, reaching perhaps 8.2 million by 1333. Much like farmers in contemporary Song China, Japanese farmers adopted new strains of rice, often double-cropped in warmer regions, made increased use of fertilizers, and improved irrigation for paddy rice. Besides farming, ordinary people made their liv-

• **Zen** A school of Buddhism that emphasized meditation and truths that could not be conveyed in words.

ings as artisans, traders, fishermen, and entertainers. Although trade in human beings was banned, those who fell into debt might sell themselves or their children, and professional slave traders kidnapped women and children. A vague category of outcastes occupied the fringes of society, in a manner reminiscent of India. Buddhist strictures against killing and Shinto ideas of pollution probably account for the exclusion of butchers, leatherworkers, morticians, and lepers, but other groups, such as bamboo whisk makers, were also traditionally excluded for no obvious reason.

CHRONOLOGY

794–1185	Heian period in Japan
804	Two Japanese Buddhist monks, Saichō and Kūkai, travel to China
935–1392	Koryŏ Dynasty in Korea
960–1279	Song Dynasty in China; emergence of scholar-official class; invention of movable type
995–1027	Fujiwara Michinaga dominant at Heian court
ca. 1000–1010	*The Tale of Genji*
1119	First reported use of compass
1120s	First government-issued paper money introduced by Song
1126	Song loss of north China to the Jurchens; Song capital relocated to Hangzhou
1130–1200	Zhu Xi, Neo-Confucian philosopher
1185–1333	Kamakura Shogunate in Japan; Zen Buddhism flourishes
1234–1368	Mongols' Yuan Dynasty in China
ca. 1275–1292	Marco Polo travels in China

Chapter Summary

The countries of East Asia—China, Japan, and Korea—all underwent major changes in the six centuries from 800 to 1400. In China the loosening of the central government's control of the economy stimulated trade and economic growth. Between 800 and 1100 China's population doubled to 100 million, reflecting in part the spread of wet-field rice cultivation, especially in the south. The economic center of China shifted from the north China plain to the south, the milder region drained by the Yangzi River.

In the Song period, the booming economy and the invention of printing allowed for expansion of the scholar-official class, which came to dominate government and society. Men who aspired to this life spent a decade or more studying for the highly competitive civil service examinations. Many educated men pursued interests in literature, antiquities, philosophy, and art. Repeatedly, the Song government chose to pay tribute to its militarily powerful neighbors—first the Khitans, then the Jurchens, then the Mongols—to keep the peace. Eventually, however, Song fell to the Mongols. The Mongols instituted hereditary occupations, ending much of the social mobility that characterized the Song Dynasty.

During the Koryŏ Dynasty, Korea evolved more independently of China than it had previously, in part because it had to placate powerful non-Chinese neighbors. The commercial economy declined, and an increasing portion of the population was unfree, working as slaves for aristocrats or the government. Military strongmen dominated the government, but their armies were no match for the much larger empires to their north. The period of Mongol domination was particularly difficult.

In Heian Japan, a tiny aristocracy dominated government and society. A series of regents, most of them from the Fujiwara family and fathers-in-law of the emperors, controlled political life. The aristocratic court society put great emphasis on taste and refinement. Women were influential at the court and wrote much of the best literature of the period. The Heian aristocrats had little interest in life in the provinces, which gradually came under the control of military clans.

After a civil war between the two leading military clans, a military government, called the shogunate, was established. The Kamakura Shogunate was dominated by a military class of samurais, who were bound to their lord by loyalty and service in return for land and income. Emperors had little power. Two invasions by the Mongols caused major crises in military control. Although both times the invaders were repelled, defense costs were high. During this period culture was less centered around the capital, and Buddhism spread to ordinary people.

NOTES

1. *The Travels of Marco Polo, the Venetian*, ed. Manuel Komroff (New York: Boni and Liveright, 1926), p. 227.
2. Ibid., p. 235.
3. Peter H. Lee, ed., *Sourcebook of Korean Civilization* (New York: Columbia University Press, 1993), p. 327.
4. *The Pillow Book of Sei Shonagon*, edited and translated by Ivan Morris, p. 258. © Ivan Morris 1967. Copyright © 1991 Columbia University Press. Reprinted by permission of Columbia University Press and Oxford University Press.
5. Quoted in M. Collcott, M. Jansen, and I. Kumakura, *Cultural Atlas of Japan* (New York: Facts on File, 1988), p. 82, slightly modified.
6. Ibid., p. 101.

CONNECTIONS

East Asia faced many internal and external challenges between 800 and 1400, and the ways societies responded to them shaped their subsequent histories. In China the first four centuries of this period saw economic growth, urbanization, the spread of printing, and the expansion of the educated class. In Korea and Japan aristocratic dominance and military rule were more typical of the era. All three areas, but especially China and Korea, faced an unprecedented challenge from the Mongols, with Japan less vulnerable because it did not share a land border. The challenges of the period did not hinder creativity in the literary and visual arts; among the greatest achievements of this era are the women's writings of Heian Japan, such as *The Tale of Genji*, and landscape painting of both Song and Yuan China.

Europe during these six centuries, the subject of the next chapter, also faced invasions from outside; in its case, the pagan Vikings were especially dreaded. Europe had a social structure more like that of Korea and Japan than of China, with less centralization and a more dominant place in society for military men. The centralized church in Europe, however, was unlike anything known in East Asian history. These centuries in Europe saw a major expansion of Christendom, especially to Scandinavia and eastern Europe, through both conversion and migration. Although there were scares that the Mongols would penetrate deeper into Europe, the greatest challenge in Europe was the Black Death and the huge loss of life that it caused.

Review and Explore

Make It Stick

LearningCurve
Go online and use LearningCurve to retain what you've read.

Identify Key Terms

Identify and explain the significance of each item below.

dynastic cycle (p. 365)
compass (p. 367)
scholar-official class (p. 369)
examination system (p. 369)
movable type (p. 370)
Neo-Confucianism (p. 373)
concubine (p. 374)
foot binding (p. 377)
cloistered government (p. 381)
The Tale of Genji (p. 382)
Esoteric Buddhism (p. 384)
shogun (p. 384)
Bushido (p. 385)
Zen (p. 386)

Review the Main Ideas

Answer the focus questions from each section of the chapter.

1. What made possible the expansion of the Chinese economy, and what were the outcomes of this economic growth? (p. 365)
2. How did the civil service examinations and the scholar-official class shape Chinese society and culture, and what impact did the Mongol conquest have on them? (p. 369)
3. How did Korean society and culture develop in an age when its northern neighbors were Khitans, Jurchens, and Mongols? (p. 378)
4. How did the Heian form of government contribute to the cultural flowering of Japan in this period? (p. 380)
5. What were the causes and consequences of military rule in Japan? (p. 384)

Make Connections

Analyze the larger developments and continuities within and across chapters.

1. What elements in women's lives in Song China were common in other parts of the world as well? What elements were more distinctive?
2. How did the impact of Mongol rule on China compare to its impact on Muslim lands?
3. How did being an island country affect Japan's history? What other island countries make good comparisons?
4. Did the countries of East Asia have more in common at the end of the Mongol period than they did in the seventh or eighth century (discussed in Chapter 7)?

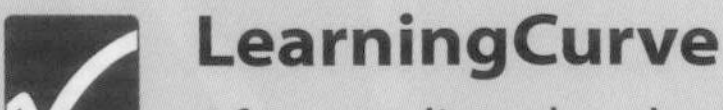

LearningCurve
After reading the chapter, go online and use LearningCurve to retain what you've read.

Chapter Preview

Political Developments
The Christian Church
The Crusades
The Life of the People
Learning and Culture
Crises of the Later Middle Ages

By the fifteenth century scholars in the growing cities of northern Italy had begun to think that they were living in a new era, one in which the glories of ancient Greece and Rome were being reborn. What separated their time from classical antiquity, in their opinion, was a long period of darkness and barbarism, to which a seventeenth-century professor gave the name "Middle Ages." In this conceptualization, the history of Europe was divided into three periods — ancient, medieval, and modern — an organization that is still in use today. Later, the history of other parts of the world was sometimes fit into this three-period schema as well, with discussions of the "classical" period in Maya history, of "medieval" India and China, and of "modern" everywhere.

Today historians often question whether labels of past time periods for one culture work on a global scale, and some scholars are uncertain about whether "Middle Ages" is a just term even for European history. They assert that the Middle Ages was not simply a period of stagnation between two high points but rather a time of enormous intellectual energy and creative vitality. While agrarian life continued to dominate Europe, political structures that would influence later European history began to form, and Christianity continued to spread. People at the time did not know that they were living in an era that would later be labeled "middle" or sometimes even "dark," and we can wonder whether they would have shared this negative view of their own times.

Political Developments

☐ How did medieval rulers restore order and centralize political power?

Later scholars dated the beginning of the Middle Ages to the fifth century, the time of the fall of the Roman Empire in the West. However, the growth of Germanic kingdoms such as those of the Merovingians and the Carolingians (see Chapter 8) is generally viewed as the beginning of "medieval" politics in Europe, and that is why we begin this chapter with the ninth century. In 800 Charlemagne, the most powerful of the Carolingians, was crowned Holy Roman emperor. After his death his empire was divided among his grandsons, and their kingdoms were weakened by nobles vying for power. In addition, beginning around 800 western Europe was invaded by several different groups. Local nobles were the strongest power, and common people turned to them for protection. By the eleventh century, however, rulers in some parts of Europe had reasserted authority and were slowly building centralized states.

Invasions and Migrations

From the moors of Scotland to the mountains of Sicily, there arose in the ninth century the prayer "Save us, O God, from the violence of the Northmen." The feared Northmen were pagan Germanic peoples from Norway, Sweden, and Denmark who came to be known as Vikings. They began to make overseas expeditions, which they themselves called *vikings*, and the word came to be used for people who went on such voyages as well.

Viking assaults began around 800, and by the mid-tenth century the Vikings had brought large sections of continental Europe and Britain under their sway. In the east they sailed the rivers of Russia as far as the Black Sea. In the west they established permanent settlements in Iceland and short-lived ones in Greenland and Newfoundland in Canada (Map 14.1).

The Vikings were superb seamen with advanced methods of boatbuilding. Propelled either by oars or by sails, deckless, and about sixty-five feet long, a Viking ship could carry between forty and sixty men—enough to harass an isolated monastery or village. Against these ships navigated by experienced and fearless sailors, the Carolingian Empire, with no navy, was helpless. At first the Vikings attacked and sailed off laden with booty. Later, on returning, they settled down and colonized the areas they had conquered, often marrying local women and adopting the local languages and some of the customs.

Along with the Vikings, groups of central European steppe peoples known as Magyars (MAG-yahrz) also raided villages in the late ninth century, taking plunder and captives and forcing leaders to pay tribute in an effort to prevent further destruction. Moving westward, small bands of Magyars on horseback reached far into Europe. They subdued northern Italy, compelled Bavaria and Saxony to pay tribute, and penetrated into the Rhineland and Burgundy. Western Europeans thought of them as returning Huns, so the Magyars came to be known as Hungarians. They settled in the area that is now Hungary, became Christian, and in the eleventh century allied with the papacy.

From North Africa, the Muslims also began new encroachments in the ninth century. They already ruled most of Spain and now conquered Sicily, driving northward into central Italy and the south coast of France.

From the perspective of those living in what had been Charlemagne's empire, Viking, Magyar, and Muslim attacks contributed to increasing disorder and violence. Italian, French, and English sources often describe this period as one of terror and chaos. People in other parts of Europe might have had a different opinion. In Muslim Spain and Sicily scholars worked in thriving cities, and new crops such as cotton and sugar enhanced ordinary people's lives. In eastern Europe states such as Moravia and Hungary became strong kingdoms. A Viking point of view might be the most positive, for by 1100 descendants of the Vikings not only ruled their homelands in Norway, Sweden, and Denmark but also ruled northern France (a province known as Normandy, or land of the Northmen), England, Sicily, Iceland, and Russia, with an outpost in Greenland and occasional voyages to North America.

"Feudalism" and Manorialism

The large-scale division of Charlemagne's empire into three parts in the ninth century led to a decentralization of power at the local level. Civil wars weakened the power and prestige of kings, who could do little about regional violence. Likewise, the invasions of the ninth century, especially those of the Vikings, weakened royal authority. The Frankish kings were unable to halt the invaders, and the local aristocracy had to assume responsibility for defense. Thus, in the ninth and tenth centuries, aristocratic families increased their authority in their local territories, and distant and weak kings could not interfere. Common people turned for protection to the strongest power, the local nobles.

The most powerful nobles were those who gained warriors' allegiance, often symbolized in an oath-swearing ceremony of homage and fealty that grew out of earlier Germanic oaths of loyalty. In this ceremony a warrior (knight) swore his loyalty as a **vassal**—from a Celtic term meaning "servant"—to the more powerful individual, who became his lord. In return for the vassal's loyalty, aid, and military assistance, the lord promised him protection and material support. This support might be a place in the lord's household but was more likely land of the vassal's own, called a **fief** (*feudum* in Latin). The fief, which might contain forests, churches, and towns, technically still belonged to the lord, and the vassal had only the use of it. Peasants living on a fief produced the food and other goods necessary to maintain the knight. Most legal scholars and historians have identified these personal ties of loyalty cemented by grants of land rather than allegiance to an abstract state as a political and social system they term **feudalism**. In the last several decades, however, increasing numbers of medieval historians have found the

- **vassal** A knight who has sworn loyalty to a particular lord.
- **fief** A portion of land, the use of which was given by a lord to a vassal in exchange for the latter's oath of loyalty.
- **feudalism** A medieval European political system that defines the military obligations and relations between a lord and his vassals and involves the granting of fiefs.

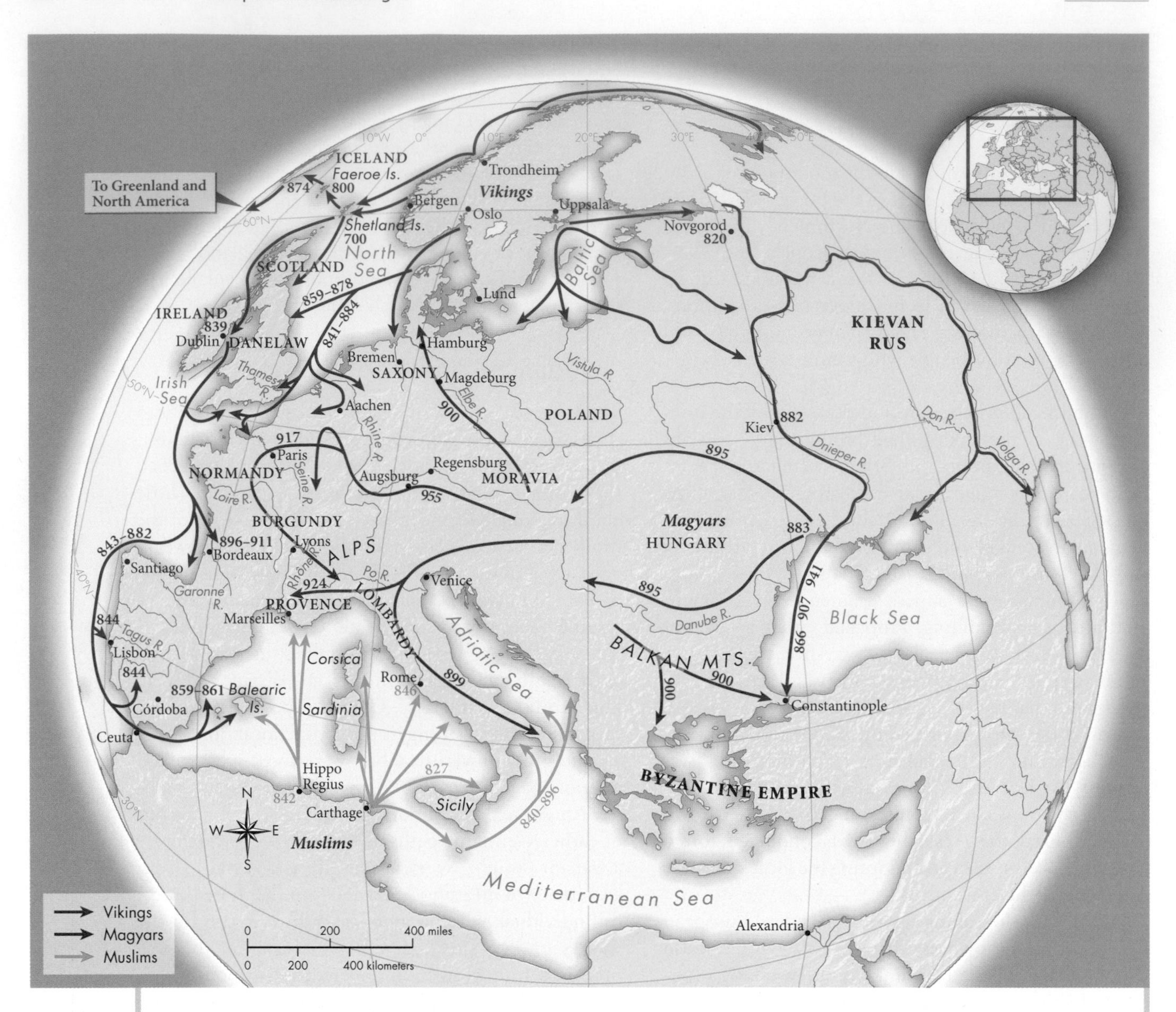

Mapping the Past

MAP 14.1 Invasions and Migrations of the Ninth and Tenth Centuries This map shows the Viking, Magyar, and Muslim invasions and migrations in the ninth and tenth centuries. Compare it with Map 8.2 (page 221) on the barbarian migrations of late antiquity to answer the following questions.

ANALYZING THE MAP What similarities do you see in the patterns of migration in these two periods? What significant differences?

CONNECTIONS How did the Vikings' expertise in shipbuilding and sailing make their migrations different from those of earlier Germanic tribes? How did this set them apart from the Magyar and Muslim invaders of the ninth century?

idea of "feudalism" problematic, because the word was a later invention and the system was so varied and changed over time. They still point to the personal relationship between lords and vassals as the key way political authority was organized and note that the church also received and granted land.

The economic power of the warrior class rested on landed estates, which were worked by peasants under a system of **manorialism**. Free farmers surrendered themselves and their land to the lord's jurisdiction in exchange for protection. The land was given back to them to farm, but they were tied to the land by various payments and services. Most significantly, a peasant lost his or her freedom and became a **serf**, part of the lord's permanent labor force. Unlike slaves, serfs were personally free, but they were bound to the land and unable to leave it without the lord's permission.

By the year 800 perhaps 60 percent of the population of western Europe had been reduced to serfdom. Over the next several centuries unstable conditions and insecurity further increased the need for protection, so that by around 1000 the majority of western Europeans were serfs. While serfs ranged from the highly prosperous to the desperately poor, all had lost their freedom. In eastern Europe the transition was slower but longer lasting. Western European peasants began to escape from serfdom in the later Middle Ages, at the very point that serfs were more firmly tied to the land in eastern Europe, especially in eastern Germany, Poland, and Russia.

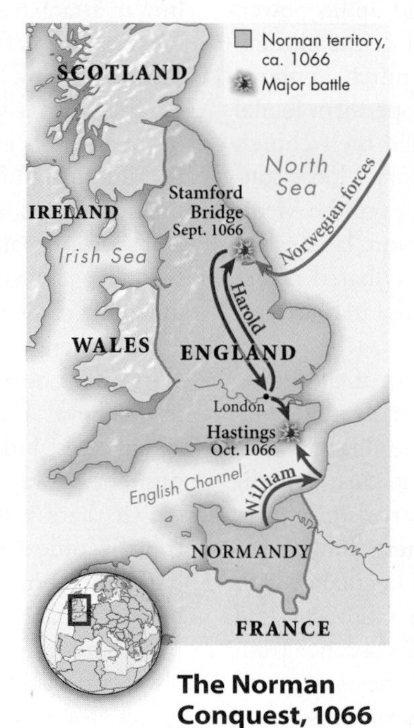

The Norman Conquest, 1066

The Restoration of Order

The eleventh century witnessed the beginnings of political stability in western Europe. Foreign invasions gradually declined, and in some parts of Europe lords in control of large territories built up their power even further, becoming kings over growing and slowly centralizing states. In a process similar to that occurring at the same time in the West African kingdom of Ghana (see pages 277–279), rulers expanded their territories and extended their authority by developing larger bureaucracies, armies, judicial systems, and other institutions to maintain control, as well as taxation systems to pay for them. These new institutions and practices laid the foundations for modern national states. Political developments in England, France, and Germany provide good examples of the beginnings of the national state in the central Middle Ages.

Throughout the ninth century the Vikings made a concerted effort to conquer and rule all of Anglo-Saxon England, and in the early eleventh century they succeeded. The Viking Canute (r. 1016–1035) made England the center of his empire, while promoting a policy of assimilation and reconciliation between Anglo-Saxons and Vikings. At the same time, England was divided into local shires, or counties, each under the jurisdiction of a sheriff appointed by the king. When Canute's heir Edward died childless, there were three claimants to the throne. One of these, Duke William of Normandy, crossed the Channel and won the English throne by defeating and killing his Anglo-Saxon rival, Harold II, at the Battle of Hastings in 1066. Later dubbed "the Conqueror," William (r. 1066–1087) limited the power of the nobles and church officials and built a unified monarchy. He retained the Anglo-Saxon institution of sheriff, but named Normans to the posts.

In 1085 William decided to conduct a systematic survey of the entire country to determine how much wealth there was and who had it. This process was described by a contemporary chronicler:

> He sent his men over all England into every shire and had them find out . . . what or how much everybody had who was occupying land in England, in land or cattle, and how much money it was worth. So very narrowly did he have it investigated, that there was no single . . . yard of land, nor indeed . . . one ox nor one cow nor one pig was there left out, and not put down in his record: and all these records were brought to him afterwards.[1]

The resulting record, called the *Domesday Book* (DOOMZ-day) from the Anglo-Saxon word *doom*, meaning "judgment," provided William and his descendants with vital information for governing the country. Completed in 1086, the book still survives, and it is an invaluable source of social and economic information about medieval England.

In 1128 William's granddaughter Matilda married a powerful French noble, Geoffrey of Anjou. Their son, who became Henry II of England, inherited provinces in northwestern France from his father. When Henry married the great heiress Eleanor of Aquitaine in 1152, he claimed lordship over Aquitaine and other provinces in southwestern France as well. The histories of England and France were thus closely intertwined in the Middle Ages.

In the early twelfth century France consisted of a number of nearly independent provinces, each governed by its local ruler. The work of unifying and enlarging France began under Philip II (r. 1180–1223), also known as Philip Augustus. By the end of his reign Philip was effectively master of northern France, and by 1300

- **manorialism** The economic system that governed rural life in medieval Europe, in which the landed estates of a lord were worked by the peasants under the lord's jurisdiction in exchange for his protection.
- **serf** A peasant who lost his or her freedom and became permanently bound to the landed estate of a lord.

most of the provinces of modern France had been added to the royal domain through diplomacy, marriage, war, and inheritance.

In central Europe the German king Otto I (r. 936–973) defeated many other lords to build up his power, based on an alliance with and control of the church. Otto asserted the right to control church appointments, and bishops and abbots had to perform feudal homage for the lands that accompanied their church positions. Under Otto I and his successors, a loose confederation stretching from the North Sea to the Mediterranean developed. In this confederation, later called the Holy Roman Empire, the emperor shared power with princes, dukes, counts, city officials, archbishops, and bishops.

Frederick Barbarossa (r. 1152–1190) of the house of Hohenstaufen tried valiantly to make the Holy Roman Empire a united state. He made alliances with the high nobles and even compelled the great churchmen to become his vassals. When he tried to enforce his authority over the cities of northern Italy, however, they formed a league against him in alliance with the pope, and infantrymen from the cities defeated Frederick's mounted knights. Frederick's absence from the German part of his empire allowed the princes and other rulers of independent provinces to consolidate their power there as well, and Germany did not become a unified state.

Law and Justice

Throughout Europe in the twelfth and thirteenth centuries, the law was a hodgepodge of customs, feudal rights, and provincial practices. Rulers wanted to blend these elements into a uniform system of rules acceptable and applicable to all their peoples, though their success in doing so varied.

The French king Louis IX (r. 1226–1270) was famous for his concern for justice. Each French province, even after being made part of the kingdom of France, retained its unique laws and procedures. But Louis IX created a royal judicial system, establishing the Parlement of Paris, a kind of supreme court that heard appeals from lower courts.

Under Henry II (r. 1154–1189), England developed and extended a common law — a law common to and accepted by the entire country, unique in medieval Europe. Henry's son John (r. 1199–1216), however, met with serious disappointment after taking the throne. He lost the French province of Normandy to Philip Augustus in 1204 and spent the rest of his reign trying to win it back. Saddled with heavy debt from his father and his brother Richard (r. 1189–1199), John tried to squeeze more money from nobles and town dwellers, creating an atmosphere of resentment. When John's military campaign failed in 1214, it was clear that the French lands that had once belonged to the English king were lost for good. A rebellion begun by northern barons grew, and in 1215 the barons forced him to attach his seal to the Magna Carta — the "Great Charter," which became the cornerstone of English justice and law.

The Magna Carta was simply meant to assert traditional rights enjoyed by certain groups, but in time it came to signify the broader principle that everyone, including the king and the government, must obey the law. Because later generations referred to the Magna Carta as a written statement of English liberties, it gradually came to have an almost sacred importance.

Statements of legal principles such as the Magna Carta were not how most people experienced the law in medieval Europe. Instead they were involved in actual cases. Judges determined guilt or innocence in a number of ways. In some cases, particularly those in which there was little clear evidence, they ordered a trial by ordeal, in which the accused might be tied hand and foot and dropped in a lake or river. People believed that water was a pure substance and would reject anything foul or unclean, although God could always affect the outcome. Thus a person who sank was considered innocent, while a person who floated was found guilty. Trials by ordeal were relatively rare, and courts increasingly favored more rational procedures, in which judges heard testimony, sought witnesses, and read written evidence if it was available. Violent crimes were often punished by public execution. Hanging was the most common method of execution, although nobles might be beheaded because hanging was seen as demeaning. Executioners were feared figures, but they were also well-paid public officials and were a necessary part of the legal structure.

The Christian Church

☐ How did the Christian Church enhance its power and create new institutions and religious practices?

Kings and emperors were not the only rulers consolidating their power in the eleventh and twelfth centuries; the papacy did as well, although the popes' efforts were sometimes challenged by medieval kings and emperors. Despite such challenges, monasteries continued to be important places for learning and devotion, and new religious orders were founded. Christianity expanded into Europe's northern and eastern regions, and Christian rulers expanded their holdings in Muslim Spain.

Córdoba Mosque and Cathedral The huge arches of the Great Mosque at Córdoba dwarf the cathedral built in its center after the city was conquered by Christian armies in 1236. During the reconquista (see page 401), Christian kings often transformed mosques into churches, often by simply adding Christian elements such as crosses and altars to existing structures. (© dbimages/Alamy)

Papal Reforms

During the ninth and tenth centuries the church came under the control of kings and feudal lords, who chose priests, bishops, abbots, and other church officials in their territories, granting them fiefs that provided an income and expecting loyalty and service in return. Church offices were sometimes sold outright — a practice called *simony*. Although the Roman Church encouraged clerical celibacy, many priests were married or living with women. Wealthy Roman families chose popes from among their members; thus popes paid more attention to their families' political fortunes or their own pleasures than to the church's institutional or spiritual health. Not surprisingly, clergy at all levels who had bought their positions or had been granted them for political reasons provided little spiritual guidance and were rarely models of high moral standards.

Serious efforts to reform the church began in the eleventh century. A series of popes believed that secular or lay control over the church was largely responsible for the lack of moral leadership, so they proclaimed the church independent from secular rulers. The Lateran Council of 1059 decreed that the authority and power to elect the pope rested solely in the college of cardinals, a special group of priests from the major churches in and around Rome. The college retains that power today.

Pope Gregory VII (pontificate 1073–1085) vigorously championed reform and the expansion of papal power. He ordered all priests to give up their wives and children or face dismissal, invalidated the ordination of church officials who had purchased their offices, and placed nuns under firmer control of male authorities. He believed that the pope, as the successor of Saint Peter, was the vicar of God on earth and that papal orders were the orders of God. He emphasized the political authority of the papacy, ordering that any church official selected or appointed by a layperson should be deposed, and any layperson, including rulers, who appointed a church official should be excommunicated — cut off from the sacraments and the Christian community.

European rulers immediately protested this restriction of their power, and the strongest reaction came from Henry IV, the ruler of Germany who later became

Individuals in Society

Hildegard of Bingen

THE TENTH CHILD OF A LESSER NOBLE FAMILY, HILDEGARD (1098–1179) was turned over to the care of an abbey in the Rhineland when she was eight years old. There she learned Latin and received a good education. She spent most of her life in various women's religious communities, two of which she founded herself. When she was a child, she began having mystical visions, often of light in the sky, but told few people about them. In middle age, however, her visions became more dramatic: "And it came to pass . . . when I was 42 years and 7 months old, that the heavens were opened and a blinding light of exceptional brilliance flowed through my entire brain. And so it kindled my whole heart and breast like a flame, not burning but warming . . . and suddenly I understood of the meaning of expositions of the books."* She wanted the church to approve of her visions and wrote first to Saint Bernard of Clairvaux, who answered her briefly and dismissively, and then to Pope Eugenius, who encouraged her to write them down. Her first work was *Scivias* (Know the Ways of the Lord), a record of her mystical visions that incorporates extensive theological learning.

Obviously possessed of leadership and administrative talents, Hildegard left her abbey in 1147 to found the convent of Rupertsberg near Bingen. There she produced *Physica* (On the Physical Elements) and *Causa et Curae* (Causes and Cures), scientific works on the curative properties of natural elements; poems; a religious play; and several more works of mysticism. She carried on a huge correspondence with scholars, prelates, and ordinary people. When she was over fifty, she left her community to preach to audiences of clergy and laity, and she was the only woman of her time whose opinions on religious matters were considered authoritative by the church.

Hildegard's visions have been explored by theologians and also by neurologists, who judge that they may have originated in migraine headaches, as she reports many of the same phenomena that migraine sufferers do: auras of light around objects, areas of blindness, feelings of intense doubt and intense euphoria. The interpretations that she develops come from her theological insight and learning, however, not from her illness. That same insight also emerges in her music, which is what she is best known for today. Eighty of her compositions survive — a huge number for a medieval composer — most of them written to be sung by the nuns in her convent, so they have strong lines for female voices. Many of her songs and chants have been recorded recently by various artists and are available on compact disk, as downloads, and on several Web sites.

Inspired by heavenly fire, Hildegard begins to dictate her visions to her scribe. The original of this elaborately illustrated copy of *Scivias* disappeared from Hildegard's convent during World War II, but fortunately a facsimile had already been made. (Private Collection/The Bridgeman Art Library)

QUESTIONS FOR ANALYSIS

1. Why do you think Hildegard might have kept her visions secret at first? Why do you think she eventually sought church approval for them?
2. In what ways were Hildegard's accomplishments extraordinary given women's general status in the Middle Ages?

*From *Scivias*, trans. Mother Columba Hart and Jane Bishop, *The Classics of Western Spirituality* (New York/Mahwah: Paulist Press, 1990).

LaunchPad
Online Document Project

Why was Hildegard of Bingen considered a worthy instrument for the transmission of God's word? Read excerpts from Hildegard's correspondence, and then complete a quiz and writing assignment based on the evidence and details from this chapter.

See inside the front cover to learn more.

the Holy Roman emperor. Henry continued to appoint officials, and Gregory responded by excommunicating bishops who supported Henry and threatening to depose him. In January 1077 Henry arrived at the pope's residence in Canossa in northern Italy and, according to a letter later sent by Gregory to his German allies, stood outside in the snow for three days seeking forgiveness. Gregory readmitted the emperor into the Christian community. Although Henry bowed before the pope, he actually won a victory, maintaining authority over his subjects and in 1084 being crowned emperor. This victory was temporary, however, for high nobles within the empire took advantage of further conflicts with the pope to enhance their position, siding with the church to gain power. They subordinated lesser nobles, expanded restrictions on peasants, and prevented later emperors such as Frederick Barbarossa from unifying the empire.

Monastic Life

Although they were in theory cut off from the world (see page 216), monasteries and convents were deeply affected by issues of money, rank, and power. By the eighth century monasteries and convents dotted the European landscape, and during the ninth and tenth centuries they were often the target of Viking attacks or raids by local looters seeking valuable objects. Some religious communities fled and dispersed, while others fell under the control and domination of local feudal lords. Powerful laymen appointed themselves or their relatives as abbots, took the lands and goods of monasteries, and spent monastic revenues.

Medieval monasteries also provided noble boys with education and opportunities for ecclesiastical careers. Although a few men who rose in the ranks of church officials were of humble origins, most were from high-status families. Social class also defined the kinds of religious life open to women. Kings and nobles usually established convents for their female relatives and other elite women, and the position of abbess, or head of a convent, became the most powerful position a woman could hold in medieval society. (See "Individuals in Society: Hildegard of Bingen," at left.) People of lower social standing did live and work in monasteries, but as lay brothers and sisters who performed manual labor, not religious duties.

Routines within individual monasteries varied widely from house to house and from region to region. In every monastery, however, daily life centered on the liturgy or Divine Office, psalms, and other prayers, which monks and nuns said seven times a day and once during the night. Praying was looked on as a vital service, as crucial as the labor of peasants and the military might of nobles. Prayers were said for peace, rain, good harvests, the civil authorities, the monks' and nuns' families, and their benefactors. Monastic patrons in turn lavished gifts on the monasteries, which often became very wealthy, controlling large tracts of land and the peasants who farmed them.

The combination of lay control and wealth created problems for monasteries as monks and nuns concentrated on worldly issues and spiritual observance and intellectual activity declined. To counteract this problem, new religious orders, such as the Cistercians (sihs-TUHR-shuhnz), founded in 1098, established their houses in isolated areas, rejected the traditional feudal sources of income (such as the possession of mills and serfs), and lived very simply. Their innovative methods of farming, sheep raising, and cloth production brought financial success, however, and by the late twelfth century economic prosperity and political power had begun to compromise the original Cistercian ideals.

In the thirteenth century the growth of cities provided a new challenge for the church. Many urban people thought that the church did not meet their spiritual needs. They turned instead to heresies — that is, to versions of Christianity outside of those approved by the papacy, many of which called on the church to give up its wealth and power. Combating **heresy** became a principal task of new religious orders, most prominently the Dominicans and Franciscans, who preached and ministered to city dwellers; the Dominicans also staffed the papal Inquisition, a special court designed to root out heresy.

Popular Religion

Apart from the land, the weather, and local legal and social conditions, religion had the greatest impact on the daily lives of ordinary people in medieval Europe. Religious practices varied widely from country to country and even from province to province. But everywhere, religion permeated everyday life.

For Christians, the village church was the center of community life — social, political, and economic as well as religious — with the parish priest in charge of a host of activities. People gathered at the church for services on Sundays and holy days, breaking the painful routine of work. The feasts that accompanied baptisms, weddings, funerals, and other celebrations were commonly held in the churchyard. In everyday life people engaged in rituals and used language heavy with religious symbolism. Before planting began on local lands, the village priest customarily went out and sprinkled the fields with water, symbolizing renewal

• **heresy** An opinion, belief, or action counter to doctrines that church leaders defined as correct; heretics could be punished by the church.

and life. Everyone participated in village processions to honor the saints and ask their protection. The entire calendar was designed with reference to Christmas, Easter, and Pentecost, events in the life of Jesus and his disciples.

The Christian calendar was also filled with saints' days. Saints were individuals who had lived particularly holy lives and were honored locally or more widely for their connection with the divine. Veneration of the saints had been an important tool of Christian conversion since late antiquity (see Chapter 8), and the cult of the saints was a central feature of popular culture in the Middle Ages. People believed that the saints possessed supernatural powers that enabled them to perform miracles, and each saint became the special property of the locality in which his or her relics—remains or possessions—rested. In return for the saint's healing powers and support, peasants would offer prayers, loyalty, and gifts. The Virgin Mary, Christ's mother, became the most important saint, with churches built in her honor and special hymns, prayers, and ceremonies created.

Most people in medieval Europe were Christian, but there were small Jewish communities scattered through many parts of Europe, as well as Muslims in the Iberian Peninsula, Sicily, other Mediterranean islands, and southeastern Europe. Increasing suspicion and hostility marked relations among believers in different religions throughout the Middle Ages, but there were also important similarities in the ways that European Christians, Jews, and Muslims understood and experienced their faiths. In all three traditions, every major life transition was marked by a ceremony that involved religious officials or spiritual elements. In all three faiths, death was marked by religious rituals, and the living had obligations to the dead, including prayers and special mourning periods.

The Expansion of Christianity

The eleventh and twelfth centuries saw not only reforms in monasticism and the papacy but also an expansion of Christianity into Scandinavia, the Baltic lands, eastern Europe, and Spain that had profound cultural consequences. The expansion was accomplished through wars, the establishment of new bishoprics, and the vast migration of Christian colonists into non-Christian territories. As it occurred, more and more Europeans began to think of themselves as belonging to a realm of Christianity that was political as well as religious, a realm they called Christendom.

Christian influences entered Scandinavia and the Baltic lands primarily through the creation of dioceses (church districts headed by bishops). This took place in Denmark and Norway in the tenth and eleventh centuries, and then in Sweden and Finland. In all of these areas, Christian missionaries preached, baptized, and built churches. Royal power advanced institutional Christianity, and traditional Norse religions practiced by the Vikings were outlawed. In eastern Europe the German emperor Otto I (see page 396) planted a string of dioceses along his northern and eastern frontiers, hoping to pacify the newly conquered Slavs in eastern Europe. German nobles built castles and ruthlessly crushed revolts by Slavic peoples.

The church also moved into central Europe, first into Bohemia in the tenth century and from there into Poland and Hungary in the eleventh century. In the twelfth and thirteenth centuries thousands of settlers poured into eastern Europe from the west. These new immigrants, German in descent, name, language, and

Statue of Saint Anne, the Virgin Mary, and the Christ Child Nearly every church had at least one image of the Virgin Mary, the most important figure of Christian devotion in medieval Europe. In this thirteenth-century wooden sculpture, she is shown holding the infant Jesus, and is herself sitting on the lap of her mother, Anne. Statues such as this reinforced people's sense that the heavenly family was much like theirs, with grandparents who sometimes played important roles. (Museo Nazionale del Bargello, Florence, Italy/Scala/Art Resource, NY)

law, settled in Silesia, Mecklenburg, Bohemia, Poland, Hungary, and Transylvania, where they established towns.

The Iberian Peninsula was another area of Christian expansion. In about 950 Caliph Abd al-Rahman III (912–961) of the Umayyad Dynasty of Córdoba ruled most of the peninsula. Christian Spain consisted of the small kingdoms of Castile, León, Catalonia, Aragon, Navarre, and Portugal. In the eleventh century divisions and civil wars in the caliphate of Córdoba allowed Christian armies to conquer an increasingly large part of the Iberian Peninsula. By 1248 Christians held all of the peninsula save for the small state of Granada in the south. As the Christians advanced, they changed the face of Spanish cities, transforming mosques into cathedrals.

Fourteenth-century clerical writers would call the movement to expel the Muslims the **reconquista** (ray-kon-KEES-tah; reconquest)—a sacred and patriotic crusade to wrest the country from "alien" Muslim hands. This religious idea became part of Spanish political culture and of the national psychology. Rulers of the Christian kingdoms of Spain increasingly passed legislation discriminating against Muslims and Jews living under Christian rule, and they attempted to exclude anyone from the nobility who could not prove "purity of blood"—that is, that they had no Muslim or Jewish ancestors. As a consequence of the reconquista, the Spanish and Portuguese also learned how to administer vast tracts of newly acquired territory. In the sixteenth century they used their claims about the rightful dominance of Christianity to justify their colonization of new territories in Mexico, Brazil, Peru, Angola, and the Philippines and relied on their experiences at home to provide models of how to govern.

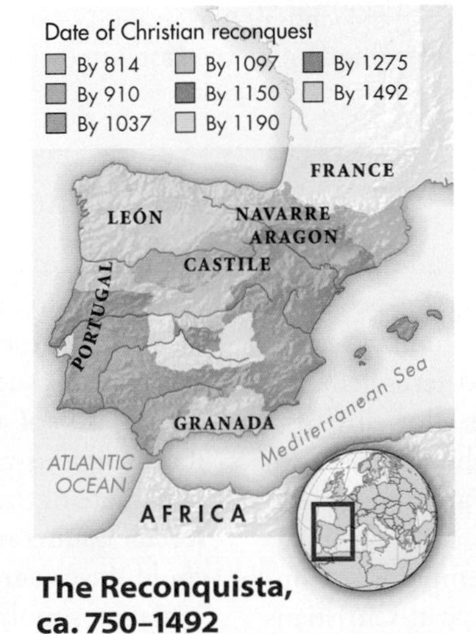

The Reconquista, ca. 750–1492

Spain was not the only place in Europe where "blood" became a way of understanding differences among people and a basis for discriminatory laws. When Germans moved into eastern Europe and English forces took over much of Ireland, they increasingly barred local people from access to legal courts and denied them positions in monasteries or craft guilds. They banned intermarriage between ethnic groups in an attempt to maintain ethnic purity, even though everyone was Christian. As Europeans later came into contact with people from Africa and Asia, and particularly as they developed colonial empires there, these notions of blood also became a way of conceptualizing racial categories.

The Crusades

☐ What were the causes, course, and consequences of the Crusades?

The expansion of Christianity in the Middle Ages was not limited to Europe but extended to the eastern Mediterranean in what were later termed the **Crusades**. Occurring in the late eleventh and early twelfth centuries, the Crusades were wars sponsored by the papacy to recover the holy city of Jerusalem from the Muslims. The word *crusade* was not actually used at the time and did not appear in English until the late sixteenth century. It means literally "taking the cross," a vow to spread Christianity symbolized by the cross that soldiers sewed on their garments. Although people of all ages and classes participated in the Crusades, so many knights did that crusading became a distinctive feature of the upper-class lifestyle. In an aristocratic military society, men coveted reputations as Crusaders; the Christian knight who had been to Jerusalem enjoyed great prestige.

Background and Motives

In the eleventh century the papacy had strong reasons for wanting to launch an expedition against Muslims in the East. If the pope could muster a large army against the enemies of Christianity, his claim to be the leader of Christian society in the West would be strengthened. Moreover, in 1054 a serious theological disagreement had split the Greek Church of Byzantium and the Roman Church of the West. The pope believed that a crusade would lead to strong Roman influence in Greek territories and eventually the reunion of the two churches.

Popes and other church officials gained support for war in defense of Christianity by promising spiritual benefits to those who joined a campaign or died fighting. Church leaders said that these people would be forgiven for their sins without having to do penance, that is, without having to confess to a priest and carry

- **reconquista** A fourteenth-century term used to describe the long Christian crusade to wrest Spain back from the Muslims; clerics believed it was a sacred and patriotic mission.
- **Crusades** Holy wars sponsored by the papacy for the recovery of the Holy Land from the Muslims.

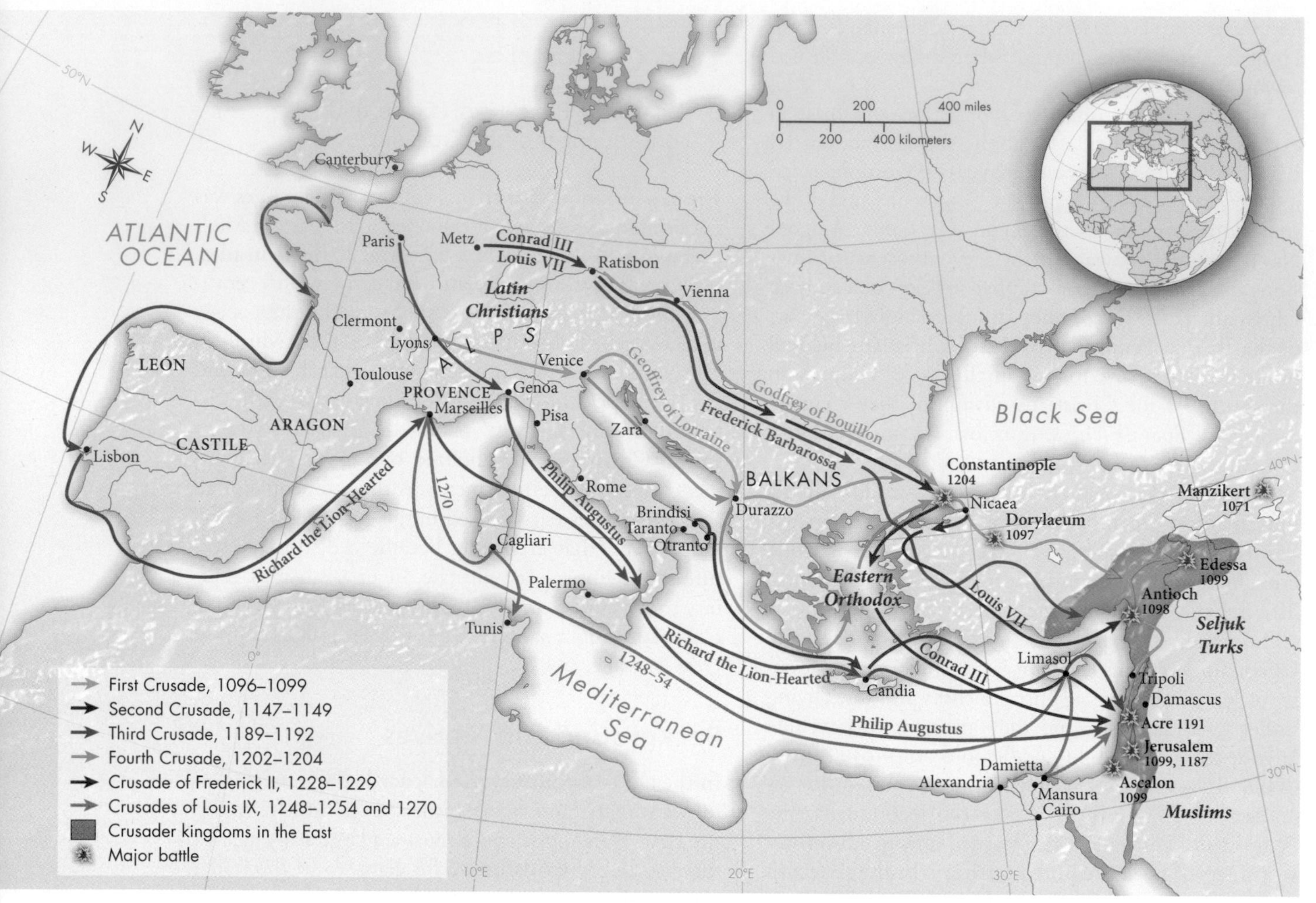

MAP 14.2 The Crusades, 1096–1270 The Crusaders took many different sea and land routes on their way to Jerusalem, often crossing the lands of the Byzantine Empire, which led to conflict with Eastern Christians. The Crusader kingdoms in the East lasted only briefly.

out some action to make up for the sins. Preachers communicated these ideas widely and told stories about warrior-saints who slew hundreds of enemies.

Religious zeal led increasing numbers of people to go on pilgrimages to holy places, including Jerusalem. The Arab Muslims who had ruled Jerusalem and the surrounding territory for centuries allowed Christian pilgrims to travel freely, but in the late eleventh century the Seljuk Turks took over Palestine, defeating both Arab and Byzantine armies, and pilgrimage became more difficult. The Byzantine emperor at Constantinople appealed to western European Christians for support. The emperor's appeal fit well with papal aims, and in 1095 Pope Urban II called for a great Christian holy war against the infidels — a term Christians and Muslims both used to describe the other. Urban urged Christian knights who had been fighting one another to direct their energies against those he claimed were the true enemies of God, the Muslims.

The Course of the Crusades

Thousands of people of all classes responded to Urban's call, streaming southward and then toward Jerusalem in what became known as the First Crusade. The First Crusade was successful, mostly because of the dynamic enthusiasm of the participants, who had little more than religious zeal. They knew little of the geography or climate of the Middle East, and although there were several counts with military experience, the Crusaders could never agree on a leader. Adding to these disadvantages, supply lines were never set up, starvation and disease wracked the army, and the Turks slaughtered hundreds of noncombatants. Nevertheless, the army pressed on, besieging and taking several cities, including Antioch. (See "Viewpoints 14.1: Christian and Muslim Views of the Fall of Antioch," at right.) After a monthlong siege, the Crusaders took Jerusalem in July 1099 (Map 14.2). Fulcher of Chartres, a chaplain on

Viewpoints 14.1

Christian and Muslim Views of the Fall of Antioch

• *Christian and Muslim accounts of the Crusades differ in their basic perspectives—were they a holy war or an invasion?—and sometimes also in their details, which can be revealing. In June 1098 the Crusaders captured the city of Antioch after a siege of more than seven months. They were assisted in this by an Armenian Christian convert to Islam named Firouz, an armor maker and official in the government of Yaghi-Siyan, the Seljuk Turkish ruler of Antioch. The* Gesta Francorum *[The Deeds of the Franks], written by an anonymous Crusader who was an eyewitness, provides a Christian view of this event, and the history of Ibn al-Athir (1160–1223) provides a Muslim view.*

Gesta Francorum

"There was a certain Emir [ruler] of the race of the Turks, whose name was Pirus [i.e., Firouz], who took up the greatest friendship with Bohemund [a Norman leader of the Crusades]. By an interchange of messengers Bohemund often pressed this man to receive him within the city in a most friendly fashion, and, after promising Christianity to him most freely, he sent word that he would make him rich with much honor. Pirus yielded to these words and promises, saying, "I guard three towers, and I freely promise them to him, and at whatever hour he wishes I will receive him within them." . . . All the night they [the Crusaders] rode and marched until dawn, and then began to approach the towers which that person (Pirus) was watchfully guarding. Bohemund straightaway dismounted and gave orders to the rest, saying, "Go with secure mind and happy accord, and climb by ladder into Antioch which, if it please God, we shall have in our power immediately." . . . Now the men began to climb up there in wondrous fashion. Then they reached the top and ran in haste to the other towers. Those whom they found there they straightaway sentenced to death; they even killed a brother of Pirus. . . . [Then] all ran to [a certain gate], and, having broken it open, we entered through it. . . . But Cassianus [Yaghi-Siyan], their lord, fearing the race of the Franks greatly, took flight with the many others who were with him. . . . They killed the Turks and Saracens whom they found there. . . . All the squares of the city were already everywhere full of the corpses of the dead, so that no one could endure it there for the excessive stench. No one could go along a street of the city except over the bodies of the dead."

Ibn al-Athir

"After the siege had been going on for a long time the Franks made a deal with . . . a cuirass [breastplate] maker called Ruzbih [Firouz] whom they bribed with a fortune in money and lands. He worked in the tower that stood over the riverbed, where the river flowed out of the city into the valley. The Franks sealed their pact with the cuirass-maker, God damn him! and made their way to the water-gate. They opened it and entered the city. Another gang of them climbed the tower with ropes. At dawn, when more than 500 of them were in the city and the defenders were worn out after the night watch, they sounded their trumpets. . . . Panic seized Yaghi-Siyan and he opened the city gates and fled in terror, with an escort of thirty pages. His army commander arrived, but when he discovered on enquiry that Yaghi-Siyan had fled, he made his escape by another gate. This was of great help to the Franks, for if he had stood firm for an hour, they would have been wiped out. They entered the city by the gates and sacked it, slaughtering all the Muslims they found there."

Sources: Edward Peters, ed., *The First Crusade: The Chronicle of Fulcher of Chartres and Other Source Materials* (Philadelphia: University of Pennsylvania Press, 1971), pp. 163–166. Copyright © 1971 by the University of Pennsylvania Press. Reprinted by permission of the University of Pennsylvania Press; *Arab Historians of the Crusades*, selected and translated from the Arabic sources by Francesco Gabrieli. Translated from the Italian by E. J. Costello. © 1969 by Routledge & Kegan Paul Ltd. Reproduced by permission of Taylor & Francis Books UK and The University of California Press.

QUESTIONS FOR ANALYSIS

1. Why did Firouz agree to help the Crusaders, according to the two accounts? Why do you think they differ in this regard?
2. Do either of the two accounts recognize that many people in Antioch, including Firouz and his brother, were Christian? Do you think the Crusaders recognized this?
3. What other similarities and differences do you see in the two accounts?

the First Crusade, described the scene:

> Amid the sound of trumpets and with everything in an uproar they attacked boldly, shouting "God help us!" . . . They ran with the greatest exultation as fast as they could into the city and joined their companions in pursuing and slaying their wicked enemies without cessation. . . . If you had been there your feet would have been stained to the ankles in the blood of the slain. What shall I say? None of them were left alive. Neither women nor children were spared.[2]

With Jerusalem taken, some Crusaders regarded their mission as accomplished and set off for home, but the appearance of more Muslim troops convinced other Crusaders that they needed to stay. Slowly institutions were set up to rule local territories and the Muslim population. Four small "Crusader states"— Jerusalem, Edessa, Tripoli, and Antioch—were established, and castles and fortified towns were built in these states to defend against Muslim reconquest. Reinforcements arrived in the form of pilgrims and fighters from Europe, so that there was constant coming and going by land and more often by sea after the Crusaders conquered port cities. Most Crusaders were men, but some women came along as well, assisting in the besieging of towns and castles by providing water to fighting men or foraging for food, working as washerwomen, and providing sexual services.

Between 1096 and 1270 the crusading ideal was expressed in eight papally approved expeditions, though none after the First Crusade accomplished very much. The Muslim states in the Middle East were politically fragmented when the Crusaders first came, and it took them about a century to reorganize. They did so dramatically under Saladin (Salah al-Din), who unified Egypt and Syria. In 1187 the Muslims retook Jerusalem, but the Christians held onto port towns, and Saladin allowed pilgrims safe passage to Jerusalem. From that point on, the Crusader states were more important economically than politically or religiously, giving Italian and French merchants direct access to Eastern products such as perfumes and silk.

After the Muslims retook Jerusalem, the crusading movement faced other setbacks. During the Fourth Crusade (1202–1204), Crusaders stopped in Constantinople, and when they were not welcomed, they sacked the city and grabbed thousands of relics, which were later sold in Europe. The Byzantine Empire splintered into three parts and soon consisted of little more than the city of Constantinople. Moreover, the assault of one Christian people on another—when one of the goals of the Crusades was reunion of the Greek and Latin Churches—made the split between the churches permanent and discredited the entire crusading movement in the eyes of many Christians.

In the late thirteenth century Turkish armies, after gradually conquering all other Muslim rulers, turned against the Crusader states. In 1291 the Christians' last stronghold, the port of Acre, fell in a battle that was just as bloody as the first battle for Jerusalem two centuries earlier. Knights then needed a new battlefield for military actions, which some found in Spain, where the rulers of Aragon and Castile continued fighting Muslims until 1492.

Consequences of the Crusades

The Crusades testified to the religious enthusiasm of the High Middle Ages and the influence of the papacy, gave kings and the pope opportunities to expand their bureaucracies, and provided an outlet for nobles' dreams of glory. The Crusades also introduced some Europeans to Eastern luxury goods, but their immediate cultural impact on the West remains debatable. By the late eleventh century there were already strong economic and intellectual ties with the East; however, the Crusades were a boon to Italian merchants, who profited from outfitting military expeditions as well as from the opening of new trade routes and the establishment of trading communities in the Crusader states.

Despite these advantages, the Crusades had some seriously negative sociopolitical consequences. For one thing, they proved to be a disaster for Jewish-Christian relations. Inspired by the ideology of holy war, Christian armies on their way to Jerusalem on the First Crusade joined with local mobs to attack Jewish families and communities, sometimes burning people alive in the synagogue or Jewish section of town. Later Crusades brought similar violence, enhanced by accusations that Jews engaged in the ritual murder of Christians to use their blood in religious rites.

Legal restrictions on Jews gradually increased throughout Europe. Jews were forbidden to have Christian servants or employees, to hold public office, to appear in public on Christian holy days, or to enter Christian parts of town without a badge marking them as Jews. They were prohibited from engaging in any trade with Christians except money-lending and were banished from England and France.

The Crusades also left an inheritance of deep bitterness in Christian-Muslim relations. Each side dehumanized the other, viewing those who followed the other religion as unbelievers. Whereas Europeans perceived the Crusades as sacred religious movements, Muslims saw them as expansionist and imperialistic. The ideal of a sacred mission to conquer or convert Muslim peoples entered Europeans' consciousness and became a continuing goal. When in 1492 Christopher

Columbus sailed west, he used the language of the Crusades in his diaries, and he hoped to establish a Christian base in India from which a new crusade against Islam could be launched (see page 467).

The Life of the People

☐ How did the lives of common people, nobles, and townspeople differ, and what new commercial developments increased wealth?

In the late ninth century medieval intellectuals described Christian society as composed of those who pray (the monks), those who fight (the nobles), and those who work (the peasants). This image of society became popular in the Middle Ages, especially among people who were worried about the changes they saw around them. They asserted that the three categories of citizens had been established by God and that every person had been assigned a fixed place in the social order.

This three-category model does not fully describe medieval society—there were degrees of wealth and status within each group. Also, the model does not take townspeople and the emerging commercial classes into consideration, and it completely excludes those who were not Christian, such as Jews, Muslims, and pagans. Furthermore, those who used the model, generally bishops and other church officials, ignored the fact that each of these groups was made up of both women and men; they spoke only of warriors, monks, and farmers. Despite—or perhaps because of—these limitations, the model of the three categories was a powerful mental construct. Therefore, we can use it to organize our investigation of life in the Middle Ages, broadening it to include groups and issues that medieval authors did not. (See page 399 for a discussion of the life of monks and nuns—"those who pray.")

The Life and Work of Peasants

The men and women who worked the land in medieval Europe made up probably more than 90 percent of the population, as they did in China, India, and other parts of the world where agriculture predominated. The evolution of localized systems of authority into more centralized states had relatively little impact on the daily lives of these peasants except when it involved warfare. While only nobles fought, their battles often destroyed the houses, barns, and fields of ordinary people, who might also be killed either directly or as a result of the famine and disease that often accompanied war. Villagers might seek protection in the local castle during times of war, but typically they worked and lived without paying much attention to political developments within castle walls.

Agricultural Work In this scene from a German manuscript written about 1190, men and women of different ages are sowing seeds and harvesting grain. All residents of a village, including children, engaged in agricultural tasks. (Rheinisches Landesmuseum, Bonn, Germany/Giraudon/The Bridgeman Art Library)

At the same time, since villagers did not perform what were considered "noble" deeds, the aristocratic monks and clerics who wrote the records that serve as historical sources did not spend time or precious writing materials on them. So it is more difficult to find information on the majority of Europeans who were peasants than on the small group at the top of society.

Medieval theologians lumped everyone who worked the land into the category of "those who work," but in fact there were many levels of peasants, ranging from slaves to free and sometimes very rich farmers. Most peasants were serfs, required to stay in the village and perform labor on the lord's land. The number of workdays varied, but serfs usually worked three days a week except in the planting or harvest seasons, when the number of days increased. Serfs were also often obliged to pay fees on common occurrences, such as marriage or inheritance of property. A free person had to do none of these things.

Serfdom was a hereditary condition. A person born a serf was likely to die a serf, though many serfs did secure their freedom, and the economic revival that began in the eleventh century (see pages 407–410) allowed some to buy their freedom. Further opportunities for increased personal freedom came when lords organized groups of villagers to migrate to sparsely settled frontier areas or to cut down forests or fill in swamps so that there was more land available for farming. Those who took on this extra work often gained a reduction in traditional manorial obligations and an improvement of their social and legal conditions.

In the Middle Ages most European peasants, free and unfree, lived in family groups in small villages that were part of a manor, the estate of a lord (see page 393). The manor was the basic unit of medieval rural organization and the center of rural life. Within the manors of western and central Europe, villages were made up of small houses for individual families, a church, and perhaps the large house of the lord. Peasant households consisted of one married couple, their children (including stepchildren), and perhaps one or two other relatives, such as a grandparent or unmarried aunt. In southern and eastern Europe, extended families were more likely to live in the same household or very near

Baking Bread In this fourteenth-century French manuscript, women bake bread in a large oven, using a long wooden paddle to insert the loaves, just as modern pizza bakers do. Medieval families cooked in pots and on spits over fires in their own homes, but rarely had ovens because of the danger of fire. Instead they bought their bread, just as they did beer or ale, another staple of the medieval diet. (The Granger Collection, New York —)

one another. Between one-third and one-half of children died before age five, though many people lived into their sixties.

The arable land of the manor was divided between the lord and the peasantry, with the lord's portion known as the demesne (dih-MAYN) or home farm. A peasant family's land was not usually one particular field but a scattering of strips across many fields, some of which would be planted in grain, some in other crops, and some left unworked to allow the soil to rejuvenate. That way if one field yielded little, strips in a different field might be more bountiful.

The peasants' work was typically divided according to gender. Men and boys were responsible for clearing new land, plowing, and caring for large animals; women and girls were responsible for the care of small animals, spinning, and food preparation. Both sexes harvested and planted, though often there were gender-specific tasks within each of these major undertakings. Women and men worked in the vineyards and in the harvest and preparation of crops needed by the textile industry—flax and plants used for dyeing cloth. Beginning in the eleventh century water mills and windmills aided in some tasks, especially grinding grain, and an increasing use of horses rather than oxen speeded up plowing.

The mainstay of the diet for peasants everywhere—and for all other classes—was bread. Peasants also ate vegetables; animals were too valuable to be used for food on a regular basis, but weaker animals were often slaughtered in the fall so that they did not need to be fed through the winter, and their meat was preserved with salt and eaten on great feast days such as Christmas and Easter. Ale was the universal drink of common people, and it provided needed calories and some relief from the difficult and monotonous labor that filled people's lives.

The Life and Work of Nobles

The nobility, though a small fraction of the total population, influenced all aspects of medieval culture. Despite political, scientific, and industrial revolutions, nobles continued to hold real political and social power in Europe into the nineteenth century.

In the early Middle Ages noble status was limited to a very few families, but in the eleventh century knights in service to kings began to claim such status because it gave them special legal privileges. Nobles generally paid few taxes, and they had power over the people living on their lands. They maintained order, resolved disputes, and protected their dependents from attacks. They appointed officials who oversaw agricultural production. The liberty and privileges of the noble were inheritable, perpetuated by blood and not by wealth alone.

The nobles' primary obligation was warfare, just as it was for nobles among the Mexica (see pages 315–319) and the samurai in Japan (see page 384). Nobles were also obliged to attend the lord's court on important occasions when the lord wanted to put on great displays, such as on religious holidays or the wedding of a son or daughter.

Originally, most knights focused solely on military skills, but around 1200 a different ideal of knighthood emerged, usually termed **chivalry**. Chivalry was a code of conduct in which fighting to defend the Christian faith and protecting one's countrymen was declared to have a sacred purpose. Other qualities gradually became part of chivalry: bravery, generosity, honor, graciousness, mercy, and eventually gallantry toward women, which came to be called "courtly love." (See "Listening to the Past: Courtly Love Poetry," page 408.) The chivalric ideal—and it was an ideal, not a standard pattern of behavior—created a new standard of masculinity for nobles, in which loyalty and honor remained the most important qualities, but graceful dancing and intelligent conversation were not considered unmanly.

Noblewomen played a large and important role in the functioning of the estate. They were responsible for managing the household's "inner economy"—cooking, brewing, spinning, weaving, and caring for yard animals. When the lord was away for long periods, his wife became the sole manager of the family properties. Often the responsibilities of the estate fell permanently to her if she became a widow.

Towns, Cities, and the Growth of Commercial Interests

Most people continued to live in villages in the Middle Ages, but the rise of towns and the growth of a new business and commercial class were central to Europe's recovery after the disorders of the tenth century. Several factors contributed to this growth: a rise in population; increased agricultural output, which provided an adequate food supply for new town dwellers; and enough peace and political stability to allow merchants to transport and sell goods.

Towns in Europe were generally enclosed by walls as were towns in China, India, and the Middle East. (The terms *burgher* and *bourgeois* derive from the Old English and Old German words *burg*, *burgh*, *borg*, and *borough* for "a walled or fortified place.") Most towns were first established as trading centers, with a marketplace in the middle, and they were likely to have a mint for coining money and a court for settling disputes. In each town, many people inhabited a small, cramped area. As population increased, towns rebuilt their walls,

• **chivalry** A code of conduct that was supposed to govern the behavior of a knight.

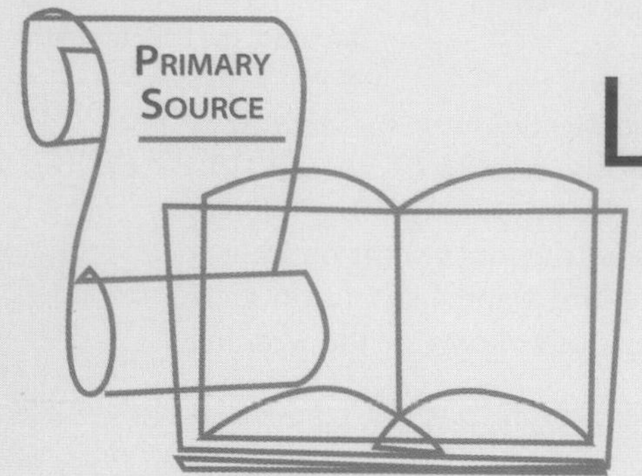

Listening to the Past

Courtly Love Poetry

Whether female or male, troubadour poets celebrated fin'amor, *a Provençal word for the pure or perfect love a knight was supposed to feel for his lady, which has in English come to be called "courtly love." In courtly love poetry, the writer praises his or her love object, idealizing the beloved and promising loyalty and great deeds. Most of these songs are written by, or from the perspective of, a male lover who is socially beneath his female beloved; her higher status makes her unattainable, so the lover's devotion can remain chaste and pure, rewarded by her handkerchief, or perhaps a kiss, but nothing more.*

Scholars generally agree that poetry praising pure and perfect love originated in the Muslim culture of the Iberian Peninsula, where heterosexual romantic love had long been the subject of poems and songs. Spanish Muslim poets sang at the courts of Christian nobles, and Provençal poets picked up their romantic themes. Other aspects of courtly love are hotly debated. Was it simply a literary convention, or did it shape actual behavior? Did it celebrate adultery, or was true courtly love pure (and unrequited)? How should we interpret medieval physicians' reports of people (mostly young men) becoming gravely ill from "lovesickness"? Were there actually "courts of love" in which women judged lovers based on a system of rules? Did courtly love lead to greater respect for women or toward greater misogyny, as desire for a beloved so often ended in frustration?

It is very difficult to know whether courtly love literature influenced the treatment of real women to any great extent, but it did introduce a new ideal of heterosexual romance into Western literature. Courtly love ideals still shape romantic conventions, and often appear in movies, songs, and novels that explore love between people of different social groups.

The following poem was written by Arnaut Daniel, a thirteenth-century troubadour praised by poets from Dante in the thirteenth century to Ezra Pound in the twentieth. Not much is known about him, but his surviving songs capture courtly love conventions perfectly.

I only know the grief that comes to me,
to my love-ridden heart, out of over-loving,
since my will is so firm and whole
that it never parted or grew distant from her
whom I craved at first sight, and afterwards:
and now, in her absence, I tell her burning words;
then, when I see her, I don't know, so much I have to, what to say.

To the sight of other women I am blind, deaf to hearing them
since her only I see, and hear and heed,
and in that I am surely not a false slanderer,
since heart desires her more than mouth may say;
wherever I may roam through fields and valleys, plains and mountains
I shan't find in a single person all those qualities
which God wanted to select and place in her.

I have been in many a good court,
but here by her I find much more to praise:
measure and wit and other good virtues,
beauty and youth, worthy deeds and fair disport;
so well kindness taught and instructed her
that it has rooted every ill manner out of her:
I don't think she lacks anything good.

No joy would be brief or short
coming from her whom I endear to guess [my intentions],
otherwise she won't know them from me,
if my heart cannot reveal itself without words,
since even the Rhone [River], when rain swells it,
has no such rush that my heart doesn't stir
a stronger one, weary of love, when I behold her.

Joy and merriment from another woman seems false and ill to me,
since no worthy one can compare with her,
and her company is above the others'.
Ah me, if I don't have her, alas, so badly she has taken me!
But this grief is amusement, laughter and joy,
since in thinking of her, of her am I gluttonous and greedy:
ah me, God, could I ever enjoy her otherwise!

And never, I swear, I have liked game or ball so much,
or anything has given my heart so much joy
as did the one thing that no false slanderer
made public, which is a treasure for me only.
Do I tell too much? Not I, unless she is displeased:
beautiful one, by God, speech and voice
I'd lose ere I say something to annoy you.

And I pray my song does not displease you
since, if you like the music and lyrics,
little cares Arnaut whether the unpleasant ones like them as well.

Desire for his beloved has so tormented the poet in this thirteenth-century manuscript that his cheeks are flushed and he has become literally bedridden with lovesickness. (Heinrich Von Morungen [ca. 1150–1222], German poet. *Codex Manesse* [ca. 1300]/Photo © Tarker/The Bridgeman Art Library)

Far fewer poems by female trobairitz have survived than by male troubadours, but those that have survived express strong physical and emotional feelings. The following song was written in the twelfth century by the Countess of Dia. She was purportedly the wife of a Provençal nobleman, though biographies of both troubadours and trobairitz were often made up to fit the conventions of courtly love, so we don't know for sure. The words to at least four of her songs have survived, one of them with the melody, which is very rare.

I've suffered great distress
From a knight whom I once owned.
Now, for all time, be it known:
I loved him — yes, to excess. His jilting I've
 regretted,
Yet his love I never really returned. Now for my
 sin I can only burn:
Dressed, or in my bed.

O if I had that knight to caress
Naked all night in my arms,
He'd be ravished by the charm
Of using, for cushion, my breast. His love I more
 deeply prize
Than Floris did Blancheor's
Take that love, my core, My sense, my life, my
 eyes!

Lovely lover, gracious, kind,
When will I overcome your fight?
O if I could lie with you one night!
Feel those loving lips on mine! Listen, one thing sets me afire:
Here in my husband's place I want you,
If you'll just keep your promise true: Give me everything I desire.

Sources: First poem used by permission of Leonardo Malcovati, editor and translator of *Prosody in England and Elsewhere: A Comparative Approach* (London: Gival Press, 2006) and online at http://www.trobar.org/troubadours/arnaut_daniel/arnaut_daniel_17.php; three verses from lyrics by the Countess of Dia, often called Beatritz, the Sappho of the Rhone, in *Lyrics of the Middle Ages: An Anthology*, edited and translated by James J. Wilhelm. Reproduced with permission of GARLAND PUBLISHING, INCORPORATED, in the format Republish in a book via Copyright Clearance Center.

QUESTIONS FOR ANALYSIS

1. Both of these songs focus on a beloved who does not return the lover's affection. What similarities and differences do you see in them?
2. How does courtly love reinforce other aspects of medieval society? What aspects of medieval society does it contradict?
3. Can you find examples from current popular music that parallel the sentiments expressed in these two songs?

expanding the living space to accommodate growing numbers. Residents bargained with lords to make the town politically independent, which gave them the right to hold legal courts, select leaders, and set taxes.

Townspeople also tried to acquire liberties, above all personal freedom, for themselves. It gradually developed that an individual who lived in a town for a year and a day, and was accepted by the townspeople, was free of servile obligations and status. Thus serfs who fled their manors for towns and were able to find work and avoid recapture became free of personal labor obligations. In this way the growth of towns contributed to a slow decline of serfdom in western Europe, although the complete elimination of serfdom took centuries.

Merchants constituted the most powerful group in most towns, and they were often organized into merchant guilds, which prohibited nonmembers from trading, pooled members' risks, monopolized city offices, and controlled the economy of the town. Towns became centers of production as well, and artisans in particular trades formed their own **craft guilds**, including guilds of butchers, weavers, blacksmiths, bakers, silversmiths, and so on. Members of the craft guilds determined the quality, quantity, and price of the goods produced and the number of apprentices and journeymen affiliated with the guild. Formal membership in guilds was generally limited to men, but women often worked in guild shops without official membership.

Artisans generally made and sold products in their own homes, with production taking place on the ground floor. A window or door opened from the main workroom directly onto the street, and passersby could look in and see the goods being produced. The family lived above the business on the second or third floor. As the business and the family expanded, additional stories were added.

Most medieval towns and cities developed with little planning or attention to sanitation. Horses and oxen, the chief means of transportation and power, dropped tons of dung on the streets every year. It was universal practice in the early towns to dump household waste, both animal and human, into the road in front of one's house. The stench must have been abominable, as officials of the king noted in their order to the citizens of one English town in 1298:

> The air is so corrupted and infected by the pigsties situated in the king's highways and in the lanes of that town and by the swine feeding and frequently wandering about . . . and by dung and dunghills and many other foul things placed in the streets and lanes, that great repugnance overtakes the king's ministers staying in that town and . . . the advantage of more wholesome air is impeded. . . . [So] the king, being unwilling longer to tolerate such great and unbearable defects there, orders . . . the pigsties, aforesaid streets and lanes to be cleansed from all dung.[3]

Despite such unpleasant aspects of urban life, people wanted to get into medieval towns because they represented opportunities for economic advancement, social mobility, and improvement in legal status.

The Expansion of Trade and the Commercial Revolution

The growth of towns went hand in hand with a revival of trade as artisans and craftsmen manufactured goods for local and foreign consumption. As in the city-states of East Africa (see pages 285–291), most trade centered in towns and was controlled by merchants. They began to pool their money to finance trading expeditions, sharing the profits and also sharing the risks. If disaster struck the ship or caravan, an investor's loss was limited to the amount of that individual's investment, a legal concept termed "limited liability" that is essential to the modern capitalist economy.

Italian cities, especially Venice, led the West in trade in general and completely dominated trade with Asia and North Africa. Venetian ships carried salt from the Venetian lagoon; pepper and other spices from North Africa; and slaves, silk, and purple textiles from the East to northern and western Europe. Wealthy European consumers had greater access to foreign luxuries than they had earlier, and their tastes became more sophisticated. Merchants from Florence and Milan were also important traders, and they developed new methods of accounting and record keeping that facilitated the movement of goods and money. The towns of Bruges, Ghent, and Ypres in Flanders were leaders in long-distance trade and built up a vast industry in the manufacture of cloth, aided by ready access to wool from England, just across the Channel. The availability of raw wool also encouraged the development of cloth manufacture within England itself, and commercial families in manufacturing towns grew fabulously rich.

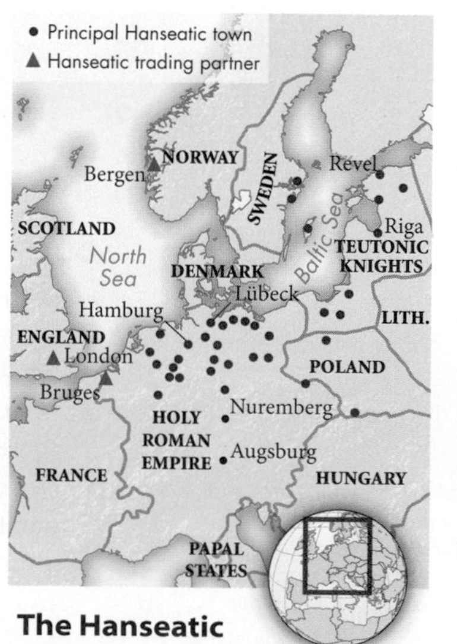

The Hanseatic League, 1300–1400

In much of northern Europe, the Hanseatic League (known as the Hansa for short), a mercantile association of towns formed to achieve mutual security and exclusive trading rights, controlled trade. During the thirteenth century perhaps two hundred cities from Holland to Poland joined the league. The ships of the Hansa cities carried furs, wax, copper, fish, grain, timber, and wine. These goods were exchanged for other products, mainly cloth and salt, from western cities. At cities such as Bruges and London, Hanseatic merchants secured special concessions exempting them from all tolls and allowing them to trade at local fairs. Hanseatic merchants also established foreign trading centers, which they called "factories," because the commercial agents within them were called "factors." (Later the word *factory* would be applied to centers of production as well.)

These developments added up to what historians of Europe have called the **commercial revolution**, a direct parallel to the economic revolution going on in Song Dynasty China at the same time (see pages 369–373). In giving the transformation this name, historians point not only to an increase in the sheer volume of trade and in the complexity and sophistication of business procedures but also to the new attitude toward business and making money. Some even detect a "capitalist spirit" in which making a profit was regarded as a good thing in itself.

The commercial revolution created a great deal of new wealth, which did not escape the attention of kings and other rulers. Wealth could be taxed, and through taxation kings could create strong and centralized states. Through the activities of merchants, Europeans again saw products from Africa and Asia in city marketplaces, as they had in Roman times. The commercial revolution also provided the opportunity for thousands of serfs in western Europe to improve their social position. There were also strong continuities: many people continued to live hand to mouth on low wages; most towns remained small; and the nobility and churchmen continued to determine the preponderant social attitudes, values, and patterns of thought and behavior.

Learning and Culture

☐ What were the primary educational and cultural developments in medieval Europe?

The towns that became centers of trade and production in the High Middle Ages also developed into cultural and intellectual centers. Trade brought in new ideas as well as merchandise, and in many cities a new type of educational institution—the university—emerged, meeting the needs of the new bureaucratic states and the church for educated administrators. As universities emerged, so did other cultural advancements, such as new forms of architecture and literature.

Universities and Scholasticism

Since the time of the Carolingian Empire, monasteries and cathedral schools had offered the only formal instruction available. Monasteries, geared to religious concerns, were located in rural environments. In contrast, schools attached to cathedrals and run by the bishop and his clergy were frequently situated in bustling cities, where people of many backgrounds stimulated the growth and exchange of ideas. In the eleventh century in Bologna and other Italian cities, wealthy businessmen established municipal schools; in the twelfth century municipal schools in Italy and cathedral schools in France developed into much larger universities, a transformation parallel to the opening of madrasas in Muslim cities (see page 255).

The growth of the University of Bologna coincided with a revival of interest in Roman law. The study of Roman law as embodied in Justinian's *Code* (see page 210) had never completely died out in the West, but in the eleventh century the discovery of a complete manuscript of the code in a library in northern Italy led scholars to study and teach Roman law intently. They applied it to practical situations, such as cases of inheritance and landownership.

At the Italian city of Salerno, interest in medicine had persisted for centuries. Greek and Muslim physicians there had studied the use of herbs as cures and had experimented with surgery. The twelfth century ushered in a new interest in Greek medical texts and in the work of Arab and Greek doctors. Ideas from this medical literature spread throughout Europe from Salerno and became the basis of training for physicians at other medieval universities. University training gave physicians high social status and allowed them to charge high fees, although their diagnoses and treatments were based on classical theories, not on interactions with patients.

Although medicine and law were important academic disciplines in the Middle Ages, theology was "the queen of sciences," so termed because it involved the study of God, who was said to make all knowledge possible. Paris became the place to study theology, and in the first decades of the twelfth century students from all over Europe crowded into the cathedral school of Notre Dame in that city.

- **craft guilds** Associations of artisans organized to regulate the quality, quantity, and price of the goods produced as well as the number of affiliated apprentices and journeymen.
- **commercial revolution** The transformation of the economic structure of Europe, beginning in the eleventh century, from a rural, manorial society to a more complex mercantile society.

University professors (a term first used in the fourteenth century) were known as "schoolmen" or **Scholastics**. They developed a method of thinking, reasoning, and writing in which questions were raised and authorities cited on both sides of a question. The goal of the Scholastic method was to arrive at definitive answers and to provide a rational explanation for what was believed on faith.

One of the most famous Scholastics was Peter Abelard (1079–1142). Fascinated by logic, which he believed could be used to solve most problems, Abelard used a method of systematic doubting in his writing and teaching. As he put it, "By doubting we come to questioning, and by questioning we perceive the truth." Abelard was censured by a church council, but he was highly popular with students.

Thirteenth-century Scholastics devoted an enormous amount of time to collecting and organizing knowledge on all topics. These collections were published as summae (SOO-may), or reference books. There were summae on law, philosophy, vegetation, animal life, and theology. Thomas Aquinas (1225–1274), a professor at the University of Paris, produced the most famous collection, the *Summa Theologica*, which deals with a vast number of theological questions.

In northern Europe—at Paris and later at Oxford and Cambridge in England—university faculties grouped themselves according to academic disciplines, or schools: law, medicine, arts, and theology. Students lived in privately endowed residential colleges and were considered to be lower-level members of the clergy, so that any student accused of a crime was tried in church, rather than in city, courts. This clerical status, along with widely held ideas about women's lesser intellectual capabilities, meant that university education was restricted to men.

At all universities the standard method of teaching was the lecture—that is, a reading. With this method the professor read a passage from the Bible, Justinian's *Code*, or one of Aristotle's treatises. He then explained and interpreted the passage. Students wrote down everything. Because books had to be copied by hand, they were extremely expensive, and few students could afford them. Examinations were given after three, four, or five years of study, when the student applied for a degree. Examinations were oral and very difficult. If the candidate passed, he was awarded the first, or bachelor's, degree. Further study, about as long, arduous, and expensive as it is today, enabled the graduate to try for the master's and doctor's degrees. Degrees were technically licenses to teach. Most students, however, did not become teachers. They staffed the expanding royal and papal administrations.

- **Scholastics** Medieval professors who developed a method of thinking, reasoning, and writing in which questions were raised and authorities cited on both sides of a question.
- **Gothic** The term for the architectural and artistic style that prevailed in Europe from the mid-twelfth to the sixteenth century.
- **vernacular literature** Literature written in the everyday language of a region rather than Latin; this included French, German, Italian, and English.

Cathedrals and a New Architectural Style

As we have seen, religious devotion was expressed through daily rituals, holiday ceremonies, and the creation of new institutions such as universities and religious orders. People also wanted permanent visible representations of their piety, and both church and city leaders wanted physical symbols of their wealth and power. These aims found their outlet in the building of tens of thousands of churches, chapels, abbeys, and, most spectacularly, cathedrals. A cathedral is the church of a bishop and the administrative headquarters of a diocese. The word comes from the Greek word *kathedra*, meaning "seat," because the bishop's throne, a symbol of the office, is located in the cathedral.

In the tenth and eleventh centuries cathedrals were built in a style that resembled ancient Roman architecture, with massive walls, rounded stone arches, and small windows—features later labeled Romanesque. In the twelfth century a new style spread out from central France. It was dubbed **Gothic** by later Renaissance architects who thought that only the uncouth Goths could have invented such a disunified style. The basic features of Gothic architecture—pointed arches, high ceilings, and exterior supports called flying buttresses that carried much of the weight of the roof—allowed unprecedented interior light. Stained-glass windows were cut into the stone, so that the interior, one French abbot exclaimed, "would shine with the wonderful and uninterrupted light of most sacred windows, pervading the interior beauty."[4] Between 1180 and 1270 in France alone, eighty cathedrals, about five hundred abbey churches, and tens of thousands of parish churches were constructed in this new style. They are testimony to the deep religious faith and piety of medieval people and also to the civic pride of urban residents, for towns competed with one another to build the largest and most splendid cathedral. In addition to marriages, baptisms, and funerals, there were scores of feast days on which the entire town gathered in the cathedral.

Cathedrals served secular as well as religious purposes. Local guilds met in the cathedrals to arrange business deals, and municipal officials held political meetings there. Pilgrims slept there, lovers courted there, and traveling actors staged plays there. Through its statuary, paintings, and stained-glass windows, the cathedral was designed to teach the people the doc-

Notre Dame Cathedral, Paris, begun 1163 This view offers a fine example of the twin towers (left), the spire, the great rose window over the south portal (center), and the flying buttresses that support the walls and the vaults. Like hundreds of other churches in medieval Europe, it was dedicated to the Virgin Mary. With a spire rising more than 300 feet, Notre Dame was the tallest building in Europe at the time of its construction. (David R. Frazier/Photo Researchers, Inc.)

trines of Christian faith through visual images, though these also often showed scenes from the lives of the artisans and merchants who paid for them.

Vernacular Literature and Drama

Latin was the language used in university education, scholarly writing, and works of literature. By the High Middle Ages, however, no one spoke Latin as his or her first language. The barbarian invasions, the mixture of peoples, and the usual changes in language that occurred over time resulted in a variety of local dialects that blended words and linguistic forms in various ways. As kings increased the size of their holdings, they often ruled people who spoke many different dialects.

In the High Middle Ages, some authors departed from tradition and began to write in their local dialect, that is, in the everyday language of their region, which linguistic historians call the vernacular. This new **vernacular literature** gradually transformed some local dialects into literary languages, such as French, German, Italian, and English, while other local dialects, such as Breton and Bavarian, remained (and remain to this day) means of oral communication.

Stories and songs in the vernacular were composed and performed at the courts of nobles and rulers. In southern Europe, especially in Provence in southern France, poets who called themselves troubadours wrote and sang lyric verses celebrating love, desire, beauty, and gallantry. Troubadours included a few women, with their poetry often chiding knights who did not live up to the ideal. (See "Listening to the Past: Courtly Love Poetry," page 408.) The songs of the troubadours were widely imitated in Italy, England, and Germany, so they spurred the development of vernacular literature there as well. Drama, derived from the church's liturgy, emerged as a distinct art form. Amateurs and later professional actors performed plays based on biblical themes and on the lives of the saints; these dramas were presented in the towns, first in churches and then at the marketplace. By combining comical farce based on ordinary life with serious religious scenes, plays gave ordinary people an opportunity to identify with religious figures and think about their faith.

Beginning in the fourteenth century a variety of evidence attests to the increasing literacy of laypeople. Wills and inventories reveal that many people, not just nobles, possessed books — mainly devotional texts, but also romances, manuals on manners and etiquette, histories, and sometimes legal and philosophical texts. The spread of literacy represents a response to the needs of an increasingly complex society.

Crises of the Later Middle Ages

☐ Why have the later Middle Ages been seen as a time of calamity and crisis?

During the later Middle Ages, the last book of the New Testament, the book of Revelation, inspired thousands of sermons and hundreds of religious tracts. Revelation deals with visions of the end of the world, with disease, war, famine, and death—often called the "Four Horsemen of the Apocalypse"—triumphing everywhere. It is no wonder that this part of the Bible was so popular. Between 1300 and 1450 Europeans experienced a frightful series of shocks: climate change, economic decline, plague, war, social upheaval, and increased crime and violence. Death and preoccupation with death made the fourteenth century one of the most wrenching periods of history in Europe.

The Great Famine and the Black Death

In the first half of the fourteenth century Europe experienced a series of climate changes, especially the beginning of a period of colder and wetter weather that historical geographers label the "little ice age." Its effects were dramatic and disastrous. Population had steadily increased in the twelfth and thirteenth centuries, but with colder weather, poor harvests led to scarcity and starvation. The costs of grain, livestock, and dairy products rose sharply. Almost all of northern Europe suffered a terrible famine between 1315 and 1322, with dire social consequences: peasants were forced to sell or mortgage their lands for money to buy food, and the number of vagabonds, or homeless people, greatly increased, as did petty crime. An undernourished population was ripe for the Grim Reaper, who appeared in 1347 in the form of a virulent new disease, later called the **Black Death** (Map 14.3). The symp-

MAP 14.3 The Course of the Black Death in Fourteenth-Century Europe The plague followed trade routes as it spread into and across Europe. A few cities that took strict quarantine measures were spared.

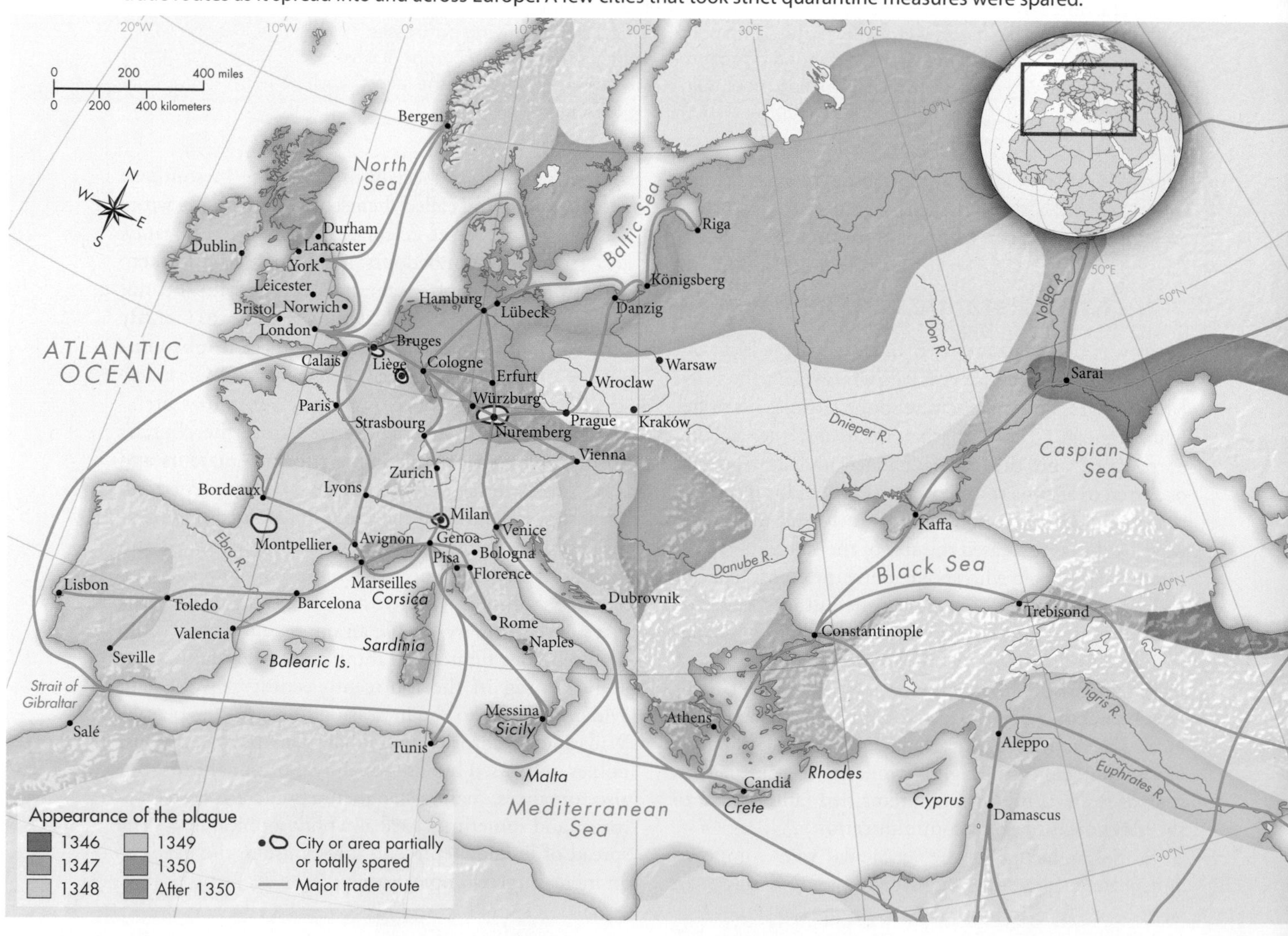

Procession of Flagellants In this manuscript illumination from 1349, shirtless flagellants, men and women who whipped and scourged themselves as penance for their and society's sins, walk through the Flemish city of Tournai, which had just been struck by the plague. Many people believed that the Black Death was God's punishment for humanity's wickedness. (The Flagellants at Doornik in 1349, copy of a miniature from the *Chronicle of Aegidius Li Muisis*/Private Collection/The Bridgeman Art Library)

toms of this disease were first described in 1331 in southwestern China, then part of the Mongol Empire (see page 333). From there it spread across Central Asia by way of Mongol armies and merchant caravans, arriving in the ports of the Black Sea by the 1340s. In October 1347 Genoese ships traveling from the Crimea in southern Russia brought the plague to Messina, from which it spread across Sicily and into Italy. From Italy it traveled in all directions.

Most historians and almost all microbiologists identify the disease that spread in the fourteenth century as the bubonic plague, caused by the bacillus *Yersinia pestis*. The disease normally afflicts rats. Fleas living on the infected rats drink their blood and pass the bacteria that cause the plague on to the next rat they bite. Usually the disease is limited to rats and other rodents, but at certain points in history the fleas have jumped from their rodent hosts to humans and other animals. The fourteenth-century disease showed some differences from later outbreaks of bubonic plague; there are no reports of massive rat die-offs, and the disease was often transmitted directly from one person to another through coughing and sneezing. These differences have led a few historians to ask whether the fourteenth-century outbreak was some disease other than the bubonic plague—perhaps something like the Ebola virus. Debates about the nature of the disease fuel continued study of medical aspects of the plague, with scientists using innovative techniques such as studying the tooth pulp of bodies in medieval cemeteries to see if it contains DNA from plague-causing agents.

Whatever it was, the disease had dreadful effects on the body. The classic symptom was a growth the size of a nut or an apple in the armpit, in the groin, or on the neck. This was the boil, or *bubo*, that gave the disease its name and caused agonizing pain. If the bubo was lanced and the pus thoroughly drained, the victim had a chance of recovery. The secondary stage was the appearance of black spots or blotches caused by bleeding under the skin. Finally, the victim began to cough violently and spit blood. This stage, indicating the presence of millions of bacilli in the bloodstream, signaled the end, and death followed in two or three days. Physicians could sometimes ease the pain but had no cure.

Most people believed that the Black Death was caused by poisons or by "corrupted air" that carried the disease from place to place. They sought to keep poisons from entering the body by smelling or ingesting

- **Black Death** The plague that first struck Europe in 1347, killing perhaps one-third of the population.

strong-smelling herbs, and they tried to remove the poisons through bloodletting. They also prayed and did penance. Anxiety and fears about the plague caused people to look for scapegoats, and they found them in the Jews, who they believed had poisoned the wells of Christian communities and thereby infected the drinking water. This charge led to the murder of thousands of Jews across Europe.

Because population figures for the period before the arrival of the plague do not exist for most countries and cities, only educated guesses can be made about mortality rates. Of a total English population of perhaps 4.2 million, probably 1.4 million died of the Black Death in its several visits. In Italy densely populated cities endured incredible losses. Florence lost between one-half and two-thirds of its population when the plague visited in 1348. The disease recurred intermittently in the 1360s and 1370s and reappeared many times, as late as the early 1700s in Europe. (It still continues to infect rodent and human populations sporadically today.)

In the short term the economic effects of the plague were severe because the death of many peasants disrupted food production. But in the long term the dramatic decline in population eased pressure on the land, and wages and per capita wealth rose for those who survived. The psychological consequences of the plague were profound. (See "Viewpoints 14.2: Italian and English Views of the Plague," at right.) Some people sought release in wild living, while others turned to the severest forms of asceticism and frenzied religious fervor.

The Hundred Years' War

While the plague ravaged populations in Asia, North Africa, and Europe, a long international war in western Europe added further death and destruction. England and France had engaged in sporadic military hostilities from the time of the Norman Conquest in 1066 (see page 395), and in the middle of the fourteenth century these became more intense. From 1337 to 1453 the two countries intermittently fought one another in what was the longest war in European history, ultimately dubbed the Hundred Years' War, though it actually lasted 116 years.

The Hundred Years' War had a number of causes. Both England and France claimed the duchy of Aquitaine in southwestern France, and the English king Edward III argued that, as the grandson of an earlier French king, he should have rightfully inherited the French throne. Nobles in provinces on the borders of France who were worried about the growing power of the French king supported Edward, as did wealthy wool merchants and clothmakers in Flanders who depended on English wool. The governments of both England and France promised wealth and glory to those who fought, and each country portrayed the other as evil.

The war, fought almost entirely in France, consisted mainly of a series of random sieges and raids. During the war's early stages, England was successful, primarily through the use of longbows fired by well-trained foot soldiers against mounted knights and, after 1375, by early cannons. By 1419 the English had advanced to the walls of Paris. But the French cause was not lost. Though England scored the initial victories, France won the war.

The ultimate French success rests heavily on the actions of Joan, an obscure French peasant girl whose vision and military leadership revived French fortunes and led to victory. (Over the centuries, she acquired the name "of Arc"—*d'Arc* in French—based on her father's name; she never used this name for herself, but called herself "the maiden"—*la Pucelle* in French.) Born in 1412 to well-to-do peasants, Joan grew up in a pious household. During adolescence she began to hear voices, which she later said belonged to Saint Michael, Saint Catherine, and Saint Margaret. In 1428 these voices told her that the dauphin of France—Charles VII, who was uncrowned as king because of the English occupation—had to be crowned and the English expelled from France. Joan went to the French court disguised as a male for safety and secured the support of the dauphin to travel, dressed as a knight, with the French army to the besieged city of Orléans.

At Orléans, Joan inspired and led French attacks, and the English retreated. As a result of her successes, Charles made Joan co-commander of the entire army, and she led it to a string of military victories in the summer of 1429; many cities surrendered without a fight. Two months after the victory at Orléans, Charles VII was crowned king at Reims.

Joan and the French army continued their fight against the English. In 1430 England's allies, the Burgundians, captured Joan and sold her to the English, and the French did not intervene. The English wanted Joan eliminated for obvious political reasons, but the primary charge against her was heresy, and the trial was conducted by church authorities. She was interrogated about the angelic voices and about why she wore men's clothing. She apparently answered skillfully, but in 1431 the court condemned her as a heretic, and she was burned at the stake in the marketplace at Rouen. (A new trial in 1456 cleared her of all charges, and in 1920 she was canonized as a saint.) Joan continues to be a symbol of deep religious piety to some, of conservative nationalism to others, and of gender-bending cross-dressing to others. Beneath the pious and popu-

Viewpoints 14.2

Italian and English Views of the Plague

• *Eyewitness commentators on the plague include the Italian writer Giovanni Boccaccio (1313–1375), who portrayed the course of the disease in Florence in the preface to his book of tales,* The Decameron, *and the English monastic chronicler Henry Knighton (d. 1396), who described the effects of the plague on English towns and villages in his four-volume chronicle of English history.*

Giovanni Boccaccio

" Against this pestilence no human wisdom or foresight was of any avail. . . . Men and women in great numbers abandoned their city, their houses, their farms, their relatives, and their possessions and sought other places, going at least as far away as the Florentine countryside — as if the wrath of God could not pursue them with this pestilence wherever they went but would only strike those it found within the walls of the city! . . . Almost no one cared for his neighbor, and relatives hardly ever visited one another — they stayed far apart. This disaster had struck such fear into the hearts of men and women that brother abandoned brother, uncle abandoned nephew, sister left brother, and very often wife abandoned husband, and — even worse, almost unbelievable — fathers and mothers neglected to tend and care for their children as if they were not their own. . . . So many corpses would arrive in front of a church every day and at every hour that the amount of holy ground for burials was certainly insufficient for the ancient custom of giving each body its individual place; when all the graves were full, huge trenches were dug in all the cemeteries of the churches and into them the new arrivals were dumped by the hundreds; and they were packed in there with dirt, one on top of another, like a ship's cargo, until the trench was filled. . . . Oh how many great palaces, beautiful homes and noble dwellings, once filled with families, gentlemen, and ladies, were now emptied, down to the last servant! "

Henry Knighton

" Then that most grievous pestilence penetrated the coastal regions [of England] by way of Southampton, and came to Bristol, and people died as if the whole strength of the city were seized by sudden death. For there were few who lay in their beds more than three days or two and half days; then that savage death snatched them about the second day. In Leicester, in the little parish of St. Leonard, more than three hundred and eighty died; in the parish of Holy Cross, more than four hundred. . . . And so in each parish, they died in great numbers. . . . At the same time, there was so great a lack of priests everywhere that many churches had no divine services. . . . One could hardly hire a chaplain to minister to the church for less than ten marks, whereas before the pestilence, when there were plenty of priests, one could hire a chaplain for five or four marks. . . . Meanwhile, the king ordered that in every county of the kingdom, reapers and other labourers should not receive more than they were accustomed to receive, under the penalty provided in the statute, and he renewed the statute at this time. The labourers, however, were so arrogant and hostile that they did not heed the king's command, but if anyone wished to hire them, he had to pay them what they wanted, and either lose his fruits and crops or satisfy the arrogant and greedy desire of the labourers as they wished. . . . Similarly, those who received day-work from their tenants throughout the year, as is usual from serfs, had to release them and to remit such service. They either had to excuse them entirely or had to fix them in a laxer manner at a small rent, lest very great and irreparable damage be done to the buildings and the land everywhere remain uncultivated. "

Sources: Giovanni Boccaccio, *The Decameron*, trans. Mark Musa and Peter Bondanella (New York: W. W. Norton, 1982), pp. 7, 9, 12. Henry Knighton, *Chronicon Henrici Knighton*, in James Bruce Ross and Mary Martin McLaughlin, eds., *The Portable Medieval Reader* (New York: Viking, 1949), pp. 218, 220, 222.

QUESTIONS FOR ANALYSIS

1. How did the residents of Florence respond to the plague, as described by Boccaccio?
2. What were some of the effects of the plague in England, as described by Knighton?
3. How might the fact that Boccaccio was writing in an urban setting and Knighton was writing from a rural monastery that owned a large amount of land have shaped their perspectives?

Picturing the Past

Siege of the Castle of Mortagne near Bordeaux This miniature of a battle in the Hundred Years' War shows the French besieging an English-held castle. Medieval warfare usually consisted of small skirmishes and attacks on castles. (from *The Coronation of Richard II to 1387* by Jean de Batard Wavrin/© British Library Board. All Rights Reserved./The Bridgeman Art Library)

ANALYZING THE IMAGE What types of weapons are the attackers and defenders using? How have the attackers on the left enhanced their position?

CONNECTIONS This painting shows a battle that occurred in 1377, but it was painted about a hundred years later and shows the military technology available at the time it was painted, not at the time of the actual siege. Which of the weapons represent newer forms of military technology? What impact would you expect them to have on warfare?

lar legends is a teenage girl who saved the French monarchy, which was the embodiment of France. The French army continued its victories without her, and demands for an end to the war increased among the English, who were growing tired of the mounting loss of life and the flow of money into a seemingly bottomless pit. Slowly the French reconquered Normandy and finally ejected the English from Aquitaine. At the war's end in 1453, only the town of Calais remained in English hands.

The long war had a profound impact on the two countries. In England and France the war promoted nationalism — the feeling of unity and identity that binds together a people. It led to technological experimentation, especially with gunpowder weaponry, whose firepower made the protective walls of stone castles obsolete. However, such weaponry also made warfare increasingly expensive. The war also stimulated the development of the English Parliament. Between 1250 and 1450 representative assemblies from several classes of society flourished in many European countries, but only the English Parliament became a powerful national body. Edward III's constant need for money to pay for the war compelled him to summon it many times, and its representatives slowly built up their powers.

Challenges to the Church

In times of crisis or disaster people of all faiths have sought the consolation of religion, but in the fourteenth century the official Christian Church offered little solace. While local clergy eased the suffering of many, a dispute over who was the legitimate pope weakened the church as an institution. In 1309 pressure by the French monarchy led the pope to move his permanent residence to Avignon in southern France, the location of the papal summer palace. This marked the start of seven successive papacies in Avignon. Not surprising, all these popes were French—a matter of controversy among church followers outside France. Also, the popes largely concentrated on bureaucratic and financial matters to the exclusion of spiritual objectives.

In 1376 one of the French popes returned to Rome, and when he died there several years later Roman citizens demanded an Italian pope who would remain in Rome. The cardinals elected Urban VI, but his tactless, arrogant, and bullheaded manner caused them to regret their decision. The cardinals slipped away from Rome and declared Urban's election invalid because it had come about under threats from the Roman mob. They elected a French cardinal who took the name Clement VII (pontificate 1378–1394) and set himself up at Avignon in opposition to Urban. There were thus two popes, a situation that was later termed the Great Schism.

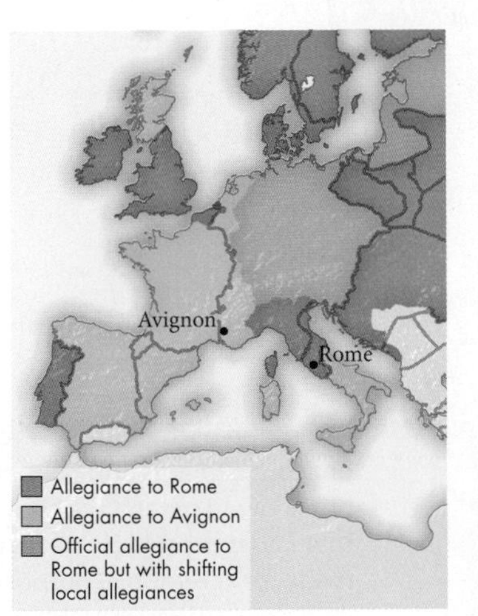

The Great Schism, 1378–1417

The powers of Europe aligned themselves with Urban or Clement along strictly political lines. France recognized the Frenchman, Clement; England, France's historic enemy, recognized Urban. The rest of Europe lined up behind one or the other. In all European countries the common people—hard-pressed by inflation, wars, and plague—were thoroughly confused about which pope was legitimate. In the end the schism weakened the religious faith of many Christians and brought church leadership into serious disrepute.

A first attempt to heal the schism led to the installation of a third pope and a threefold split, but finally a church council meeting at Constance (1414–1418) successfully deposed the three schismatic popes and elected a new leader, who took the name Martin V (pontificate 1417–1431). The schism was over, but those who had hoped that the council would also reform problems in the church were disappointed. In the later fifteenth century the papacy concentrated on building up its wealth and political power in Italy rather than on the concerns of the whole church. As a result, many people decided that they would need to rely on their own prayers and pious actions rather than on the institutional church for their salvation.

Peasant and Urban Revolts

The difficult conditions of the fourteenth and fifteenth centuries spurred a wave of peasant and urban revolts across Europe. In 1358, when French taxation for the Hundred Years' War fell heavily on the poor, the frustrations of the French peasantry exploded in a massive uprising called the Jacquerie (zhah-kuh-REE), after a supposedly happy agricultural laborer, Jacques Bonhomme (Good Fellow). Adding to the anger over taxes was the toll taken by the plague and by the famine that had struck some areas. Crowds swept through the countryside, slashing the throats of nobles, burning their castles, raping their wives and daughters, and killing or maiming their horses and cattle. Artisans, small merchants, and parish priests joined the peasants, and residents of both urban and rural areas committed terrible destruction. For several weeks the nobles were on the defensive, until the upper class united to repress the revolt with merciless ferocity. Thousands of the "Jacques," innocent as well as guilty, were cut down.

Taxes and other grievances also led to the 1381 English Peasants' Revolt, involving tens of thousands of people. The Black Death had dramatically reduced the supply of labor, and peasants had demanded higher wages and fewer manorial obligations. Parliament countered with a law freezing wages and binding workers to their manors. Although the law was difficult to enforce, it contributed to an atmosphere of discontent, which was further enhanced by popular preachers who proclaimed that great disparities between rich and poor went against Christ's teachings. Moreover, decades of aristocratic violence, much of it perpetrated against the weak peasantry, had bred hostility and bitterness.

In 1380 Parliament imposed a poll tax on all citizens to fund the Hundred Years' War, requiring rich and poor to pay the same amount and ordering sheriffs to collect it. This tax imposed a greater burden on the poor than on wealthier citizens, and it sparked revolt. Beginning with assaults on the tax collectors, the uprising in England followed much the same course as had the Jacquerie in France. Castles and manors were sacked; manorial records were destroyed; nobles were murdered. Urban discontent merged with rural violence. Apprentices and journeymen, frustrated because the highest positions in the guilds were closed to them, rioted.

The boy-king Richard II (r. 1377–1399) met the leaders of the revolt, agreed to charters ensuring the peasants' freedom, tricked them with false promises, and then proceeded to crush the uprising with terrible ferocity. The nobility tried to use this defeat to restore the labor obligations of serfdom, but they were not successful, and the conversion to money rents continued. In Flanders, France, and England peasant revolts often blended with conflicts involving workers in cities. Unrest also occurred in Italian, Spanish, and German cities. In Florence in 1378 the *ciompi*, or poor propertyless wool workers, revolted and briefly shared government of the city with wealthier artisans and merchants. Rebellions and uprisings everywhere revealed deep peasant and worker frustration with the socioeconomic conditions of the time.

Suit of Armor This fifteenth-century suit of Italian armor protected its wearer, but its weight made movement difficult. Both English and French mounted knights wore full armor at the beginning of the Hundred Years' War, but by the end they wore only breastplates and helmets, which protected their vital organs but allowed greater mobility. This suit has been so well preserved that it was most likely never used in battle; it may have been made for ceremonial purposes. (Armor, Italy, ca. 1400 and later. Steel, brass, textile. Bashford Dean Memorial Collection. Gift of Helen Fahnestock, in memory of her father, Harris C. Fahnestock, 1929 [29.154.3]/The Metropolitan Museum of Art, New York, NY, USA/Image copyright © The Metropolitan Museum of Art/Image source: Art Resource, NY)

Chapter Summary

Invasions by Vikings, Magyars, and Muslims, along with civil wars, created instability in the ninth and tenth centuries. Local nobles became the strongest powers against external threats, establishing a form of decentralized government later known as feudalism. By the twelfth century rulers in some parts of Europe had reasserted authority and were beginning to develop new institutions of government and legal codes that enabled them to assert power over lesser lords and the general population. The papacy also consolidated its power, though these moves were sometimes challenged by kings and emperors. Monasteries continued to be important places for learning and devotion, and new religious orders were founded. A papal call to retake the holy city of Jerusalem led to the Crusades, nearly two centuries of warfare between Christians and Muslims. Many of the effects of the Crusades were disastrous, including attacks on Jewish communities and more uniformly hostile Christian-Muslim relations.

The vast majority of medieval Europeans were peasants who lived in small villages and worked their own and their lord's land. Most Europeans were Christian, and the village church was generally the center of community life. Nobles were a tiny fraction of the total population, but they exerted great power over all aspects of life. Medieval towns and cities grew initially as trading centers and then became centers of production.

Towns also developed into cultural and intellectual centers, as trade brought in new ideas as well as merchandise. Universities offered courses of study based on classical models, and townspeople built churches and cathedrals as symbols of their Christian faith and their civic pride. New types of vernacular literature arose in which poems, songs, and stories were written down in local dialects.

In the fourteenth century a worsening climate brought poor harvests, which contributed to an international economic depression and fostered disease. The Black Death caused enormous population losses and social, psychological, and economic consequences. Additional difficulties included the Hundred Years' War, a schism among rival popes that weakened the Western Christian Church, and peasant and worker frustrations that exploded into uprisings.

CHRONOLOGY

722–1492	Reconquista, the Christian reconquest of Spain from Muslims
ca. 800–950	Viking, Magyar, and Muslim attacks on Europe
1066–1087	Reign of William the Conqueror
1086	*Domesday Book*
1095–1270	Crusades
1180–1270	Height of construction of cathedrals in France
1215	Magna Carta
1225–1274	Life of Saint Thomas Aquinas, author of *Summa Theologica*
1309–1376	Papacy in Avignon
1315–1322	Famine in northern Europe
ca. 1337–1453	Hundred Years' War
1347	Black Death arrives in Europe
1358	Jacquerie peasant uprising in France
1378–1417	Great Schism
1381	English Peasants' Revolt
1429	Joan of Arc leads French troops to victory at Orléans

NOTES

1. D. C. Douglas and G. E. Greenaway, eds., *English Historical Documents*, vol. 2 (London: Eyre & Spottiswoode, 1961), p. 853.
2. Fulcher of Chartres, *A History of the Expedition to Jerusalem, 1095–1127*, trans. Frances Rita Ryan, ed. Harold S. Fink (Knoxville: University of Tennessee Press, 1969), pp. 121–123.
3. H. Rothwell, ed., *English Historical Documents*, vol. 3 (London: Eyre & Spottiswoode, 1975), p. 854.
4. Erwin Panofsky, trans. and ed., *Abbot Suger on the Abbey Church of St.-Denis and Its Art Treasures* (Princeton, N.J.: Princeton University Press, 1946), p. 101.

CONNECTIONS

Medieval Europe continues to fascinate us today. We go to medieval banquets, fairs, and even weddings; visit castle-themed hotels and amusement parks; watch movies about knights and their conquests; play video games in which we become warriors, trolls, or sorcerers; and read stories with themes of great quests, some set in the Middle Ages and some set in places that just seem medieval, with humble but brave villagers, beautiful ladies, powerful wizards, and gorgeous warriors on horseback. From all these amusements the Middle Ages emerges as a strange and wonderful time, when people's emotions were more powerful, challenges more dangerous, and friendships more lasting than in the safe, shallow, fast-paced modern world. Characters from other parts of the world often heighten the exoticism: a Muslim soldier joins the fight against a common enemy, a Persian princess rescues the hero and his sidekick, a Buddhist monk teaches martial arts techniques. These characters from outside Europe are fictional, but they also represent aspects of reality, because medieval Europe was not isolated, and political and social structures similar to those in Europe developed elsewhere.

In reality few of us would probably want to live in the real Middle Ages, when most people worked in the fields all day, a banquet meant a piece of tough old rooster instead of the usual meal of pea soup and black bread, and even wealthy lords lived in damp and drafty castles. We do not really want to return to a time when one-third to one-half of all children died before age five and alcohol was the only real pain reliever. But the contemporary appeal of the Middle Ages is an interesting phenomenon, particularly because it stands in such sharp contrast to the attitude of educated Europeans who lived in the centuries immediately afterward. They were the ones who dubbed the period "middle" and viewed the soaring cathedrals as dreadfully "Gothic." They saw their own era as the one to be celebrated, and the Middle Ages as best forgotten.

Review and Explore

Make It Stick

LearningCurve

Go online and use LearningCurve to retain what you've read.

Identify Key Terms

Identify and explain the significance of each item below.

vassal (p. 393)
fief (p. 393)
feudalism (p. 393)
manorialism (p. 394)
serf (p. 395)
heresy (p. 399)
reconquista (p. 401)
Crusades (p. 401)
chivalry (p. 407)
craft guilds (p. 410)
commercial revolution (p. 411)
Scholastics (p. 412)
Gothic (p. 412)
vernacular literature (p. 413)
Black Death (p. 414)

Review the Main Ideas

Answer the focus questions from each section of the chapter.

1. How did medieval rulers restore order and centralize political power? (p. 392)
2. How did the Christian Church enhance its power and create new institutions and religious practices? (p. 396)
3. What were the causes, course, and consequences of the Crusades? (p. 401)
4. How did the lives of common people, nobles, and townspeople differ, and what new commercial developments increased wealth? (p. 405)
5. What were the primary educational and cultural developments in medieval Europe? (p. 411)
6. Why have the later Middle Ages been seen as a time of calamity and crisis? (p. 414)

Make Connections

Analyze the larger developments and continuities within and across chapters.

1. What similarities and differences do you see between the institutions and laws established by medieval European rulers and those of the Roman (Chapter 6), Byzantine (Chapter 8), and Chinese (Chapter 13) emperors?
2. What factors over the centuries enabled the Christian Church (Chapters 6, 8) to become the most powerful and wealthy institution in Europe, and what problems did this create?
3. How would you compare the role of trade in economic development in the Islamic world (Chapter 9), Africa (Chapter 10), Southeast Asia (Chapter 12), China (Chapter 13), and Europe in the period from 800 to 1400?

LaunchPad
Online Document Project

Hildegard of Bingen

Why was Hildegard of Bingen considered a worthy instrument for the transmission of God's word?

Read excerpts from Hildegard's correspondence, and then complete a quiz and writing assignment based on the evidence and details from this chapter.

See inside the front cover to learn more.

Suggested Reading

Allmand, Christopher. *The Hundred Years War: England and France at War, ca. 1300–1450*, rev. ed. 2005. Designed for students; examines the war from political, military, social, and economic perspectives and compares the way England and France reacted to the conflict.

Bartlett, Robert. *The Making of Europe: Conquest, Colonization and Cultural Change, 950–1350*. 1993. A broad survey of many of the developments traced in this chapter.

Bennett, Judith M. *A Medieval Life: Cecelia Penifader of Brigstock, c. 1297–1344*. 1998. An excellent brief introduction to all aspects of medieval village life from the perspective of one woman; designed for students.

Brooke, Rosalind, and Christopher Brooke. *Popular Religion in the Middle Ages*. 1984. A readable synthesis of material on the beliefs and practices of ordinary Christians.

Epstein, Steven A. *An Economic and Social History of Later Medieval Europe, 1000–1500*. 2009. Examines the most important themes in European social and economic history, with a wide geographic sweep.

Glick, Leonard B. *Abraham's Heirs: Jews and Christians in Medieval Europe*. 1999. Provides information on many aspects of Jewish life and Jewish-Christian relations.

Herlihy, David. *The Black Death and the Transformation of the West*, 2d ed. 1997. A fine treatment of the causes and cultural consequences of the disease that remains the best starting point for study of the great epidemic.

Janin, Hunt. *The University in Medieval Life, 1179–1499*. 2008. An overview of medieval universities designed for general readers.

Kaeuper, Richard W. *Chivalry and Violence in Medieval Europe*. 2006. Examines the role chivalry played in promoting violent disorder.

Madden, Thomas. *The New Concise History of the Crusades*. 2005. A highly readable brief survey by the pre-eminent American scholar of the Crusades.

Sawyer, Peter, ed. *The Oxford Illustrated History of the Vikings*. 1997. A sound account of the Vikings by an international team of scholars.

Shahar, Shulamit. *The Fourth Estate: A History of Women in the Middle Ages*, 2d ed. 2003. Analyzes attitudes toward women and provides information on the lives of a variety of women, including nuns, peasants, noblewomen, and townswomen.

Shinners, John. *Medieval Popular Religion, 1000–1500*, 2d ed. 2006. An excellent collection of a wide variety of sources that provide evidence about the beliefs and practices of ordinary Christians.

Spufford, Peter. *Power and Profit: The Merchant in Medieval Europe*. 2003. A comprehensive history of medieval commerce, designed for general readers; includes many illustrations.

Tuchman, Barbara. *A Distant Mirror: The Calamitous Fourteenth Century*. 1978. A vivid description of this tumultuous time written for a general audience.

Europe in the Renaissance and Reformation

1350–1600

15

Portrait of Baldassare Castiglione

The author and courtier Baldassare Castiglione directs his calm gaze toward the viewer in this portrait by the renowned Italian Renaissance artist Raphael. Individual portraits like this one expressed the ideals of the Renaissance: elegance, balance, proportion, and self-awareness. (© Samuel Courtauld Trust, The Courtauld Gallery, London, UK/The Bridgeman Art Library)

LearningCurve
After reading the chapter, go online and use LearningCurve to retain what you've read.

Chapter Preview

While disease, famine, and war marked the fourteenth century in much of Europe, the era also witnessed the beginnings of remarkable changes in many aspects of intellectual and cultural life. First in Italy and then elsewhere, artists and writers thought that they were living in a new golden age, later termed the Renaissance, French for "rebirth." The word *renaissance* was used initially to describe art that seemed to recapture, or perhaps even surpass, the glories of the classical past and then came to be used for many aspects of life of the period. The new attitude diffused slowly out of Italy, with the result that the Renaissance "happened" at different times in different parts of Europe. It shaped the lives of Europe's educated elites, although families, kin networks, religious beliefs, and the rhythms of the agricultural year still remained important.

Religious reformers carried out even more dramatic changes. Calls for reform of the Christian Church began very early in its history and continued throughout the Middle Ages. In the sixteenth century these calls gained wide acceptance, due not only to religious issues and problems within the church but also to political and social factors. In a movement termed the Protestant Reformation, Western Christianity broke into many divisions, a situation that continues today. The Renaissance and the Reformation were very different types of movements, but both looked back to a time they regarded as purer and better than their own, and both offered opportunities for strong individuals to shape their world in unexpected ways. Both have also been seen as key elements in the creation of the "modern" world.

Renaissance Culture

☐ What were the major cultural developments of the Renaissance?

The **Renaissance** was characterized by self-conscious awareness among fourteenth- and fifteenth-century Italians, particularly scholars and writers known as humanists, that they were living in a new era. Their ideas influenced education and were spread through the new technology of the printing press. Interest in the classical past and in the individual also shaped Renaissance art in terms of style and subject matter. Also important to Renaissance art were the wealthy patrons who helped fund it.

Wealth and Power in Renaissance Italy

Economic growth laid the material basis for the Italian Renaissance and its cultural achievements. Ambitious merchants gained political power to match their economic power and then used their money to buy luxuries and hire talent in a **patronage** system. Through this system, cities, groups, and individuals commissioned writers and artists to produce specific works. Thus economics, politics, and culture were interconnected.

The Renaissance began in the northern Italian city of Florence, which possessed enormous wealth. From their position as tax collectors for the papacy, Florentine mercantile families began to dominate European banking on both sides of the Alps, setting up offices in major European and North African cities. The profits from loans, investments, and money exchanges allowed banking families to control the city's politics and culture. Although Florence was officially a republic, starting in 1434 the great Medici (MEH-duh-chee) banking family held power almost continually for centuries. They supported an academy for scholars and a host of painters, sculptors, poets, and architects. (See "Individuals in Society: Cosimo and Lorenzo de' Medici," page 428.)

In other Italian cities as well, wealthy merchants and bankers built magnificent palaces and required that all political business be done there. They became patrons of the arts, hiring not only architects to design and build these palaces but also artists to fill them with paintings and sculptures, and musicians and composers to fill them with music. Attractions like these appealed to the rich, social-climbing residents of Venice, Florence, Genoa, and Rome, who came to see life more as an opportunity for enjoyment than as a painful pilgrimage to Heaven.

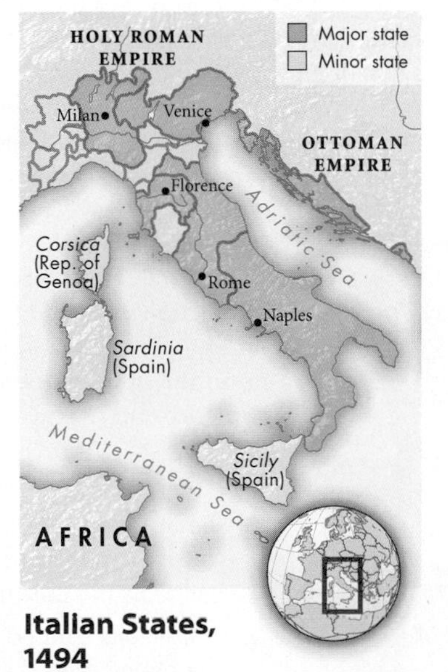

Italian States, 1494

This cultural flowering took place amid political turmoil. In the fifteenth century five powers dominated the Italian peninsula: Venice, Milan, Florence, the Papal States, and the kingdom of Naples. These powers competed furiously for territory and ruthlessly tried to extend their authority over smaller city-states. While the states of northern Europe were moving toward centralization and consolidation, Italian politics resembled a jungle where the powerful dominated the weak.

In one significant respect, however, the Italian city-states anticipated future relations among competing European states after 1500. Whenever one Italian state appeared to gain a predominant position within the peninsula, other states combined to establish a balance of power against the major threat. In the formation of these alliances, Renaissance Italians invented the machinery of modern diplomacy: permanent embassies with resident ambassadors in capitals where political relations and commercial ties needed continual monitoring.

Although the resident ambassador was one of the great political achievements of the Italian Renaissance, diplomacy did not prevent invasions of Italy. These began in 1494 as Italy became the focus of international ambitions and the battleground of foreign armies, and Italian cities suffered severely from continual warfare for decades. Thus the failure of the city-states to form some type of federal system — or at least to establish a common foreign policy — led to centuries of subjugation by outside invaders. Italy was not to achieve unification until 1870.

The Rise of Humanism

The Renaissance was a self-conscious intellectual movement. The realization that something new and unique was happening first came to writers in the fourteenth century, especially to the Italian poet and humanist Francesco Petrarch (frahn-CHEH-skoh PEH-trahrk) (1304–1374). For Petrarch, the barbarian migrations (see pages 220–224) had caused a sharp cultural break with the glories of Rome and inaugurated what he called the "dark ages." Along with many of his contemporaries, Petrarch sought to reconnect with the classical past, and he believed that such efforts were bringing on a new golden age of intellectual achievement.

Petrarch and other poets, writers, and artists showed a deep interest both in the physical remains of the Roman Empire and in classical Latin texts. The study of Latin classics became known as the *studia humanitates*, usually translated as "liberal studies" or the "liberal arts." People who advocated it were known as *humanists*, and their program was known as **humanism**. Like all programs of study, humanism contained an implicit philosophy: that human nature and achievements, evident in the classics, were worthy of contemplation. Humanists did not reject religion; instead they sought to synthesize

- **Renaissance** A French word meaning "rebirth," used to describe a cultural movement that began in fourteenth-century Italy and looked back to the classical past.
- **patronage** Financial support of writers and artists by cities, groups, and individuals, often to produce specific works or works in specific styles.
- **humanism** A program of study designed by Italians that emphasized the critical study of Latin and Greek literature with the goal of understanding human nature.

Individuals in Society

Cosimo and Lorenzo de' Medici

THE RENAISSANCE IS OFTEN DESCRIBED AS A TIME OF growing individualism, a development evidenced in the era's many personal portraits and individual biographies. But a person's family also remained important, even for those at the very top of society. The Medici of Florence were one of Europe's wealthiest families and used their money to influence politics and culture. The Medici got their start in banking in the late fourteenth century, with smart bets on what would happen politically in turbulent Italy and the adoption of the best new business practices. By the early fifteenth century the Medici bank had branches in Rome, Pisa, London, and other important European cities, and it served as the pope's primary banker.

Cosimo (1389–1464) and his grandson Lorenzo (1449–1492) were the most influential Medici. Not content with great wealth, Cosimo operated behind the scenes to gain control of the Florentine political system, although he held no office and officially the city remained a republic. Worries about his growing power led the Florentine city council to exile him, but he took his money and his business with him and was soon asked to return.

Cosimo supported artists and thinkers, sponsoring what became known as the Platonic Academy, an informal group of Florence's cultural elite named in honor of Plato's famous academy in ancient Athens. Here Marsilio Ficino and other humanists translated Plato's works into Latin, making Greek learning available to a much wider European audience. Cosimo collected books and manuscripts from all over Europe, assembling an impressive library within the equally impressive Medici palace that he built in the heart of Florence.

Like his grandfather, Lorenzo was the head of the Medici bank and the de facto ruler of Florence. He, too, survived an attempt to oust him, this one led by the rival Pazzi family. The Pazzi went beyond simply trying to exile the Medici, and instead tried to murder them: Lorenzo was wounded and his brother Giuliano was killed. Medici revenge was swift and many Pazzi were executed, which led the pope — who sided with the Pazzi — to back an invasion of Florence. Lorenzo ended the conflict through personal diplomacy, and the constitution of Florence was modified to favor the Medici.

Botticelli's *Adoration of the Magi* shows many members of the Medici family and their circle, including the artist himself at the far right. (De Agostini Picture Library/akg-images)

Lorenzo came to be known during his lifetime — with no irony — as "Lorenzo the Magnificent," primarily for his support for learning and the arts. As they had in Cosimo's day, a group of poets, philosophers, and artists spent much of their time at the Medici palace, where Lorenzo patronized writing in Italian as well as humanist scholarship in Latin and Greek. Lorenzo himself wrote love lyrics, sonnets, pastorals, odes, and carnival songs, many of them meditations on nature or on the fleetingness of human life. The group included the humanists Ficino and Pico della Mirandola and the artists Michelangelo, Leonardo da Vinci, and Botticelli, all of them influenced by Platonic concepts of beauty and love. Botticelli's *Adoration of the Magi*, painted while he was at the Medici court, shows Cosimo (who was dead by the time the picture was painted) kneeling in front of the Virgin Mary as one of the three kings giving gifts to the infant Jesus, while a black-haired Lorenzo stands with other important Florentines on the right.

As Lorenzo reached his forties, many of the Medici bank branches collapsed because of bad loans, and his diplomacy was not successful in maintaining a peaceful balance of power. Like many others in Florence, Lorenzo came under the spell of the charismatic preacher Savonarola, who preached that God would punish Italy for its vice and corruption. Lorenzo died before the prediction appeared to come true when the French invaded Italy in 1494. The Medici were again ousted, but just as before, they returned, and later became the official and hereditary rulers of Florence and its environs as the Grand Dukes of Tuscany.

QUESTIONS FOR ANALYSIS

1. Renaissance people were fascinated by the quality of virtù, the ability to shape the world around one according to one's will. How did Cosimo and Lorenzo exhibit virtù?
2. The Medici created a model for very wealthy people of how to obtain political and cultural influence. Can you think of more recent examples of those who followed this model?

LaunchPad
Online Document Project

What role did patrons play in shaping Renaissance artistic and intellectual life? Examine paintings and letters by Renaissance artists, and complete a quiz and writing assignment based on the evidence and details from this chapter.

See inside the front cover to learn more.

Christian and classical teachings, pointing out the harmony between them.

Families, religious brotherhoods, workers' organizations, and other groups continued to have meaning in people's lives, but humanists and other Renaissance thinkers increasingly viewed these groups as springboards to far greater individual achievement. They were especially interested in individuals who had risen above their background to become brilliant, powerful, or unique. Such individuals had the admirable quality of *virtù* (vir-TOO), which is not virtue in the sense of moral goodness, but the ability to shape the world around them according to their will. Humanists thought that their recommended course of study in the classics would provide essential skills for future diplomats, lawyers, military leaders, businessmen, and politicians, as well as for writers and artists. Just as Confucian officials did in Song China, they also taught that taking an active role in the world and working for the common good should be the aim of all educated individuals.

Humanists put their educational ideas into practice. They opened schools and academies in Italian cities and courts in which pupils began with Latin grammar and rhetoric, went on to study Roman history and political philosophy, and then learned Greek in order to study Greek literature and philosophy. These classics, humanists taught, would provide models of how to write clearly, argue effectively, and speak persuasively. Gradually humanist education became the basis for intermediate and advanced education for well-to-do urban boys and men.

Humanists disagreed about education for women. Many saw the value of exposing women to classical models of moral behavior and reasoning, but they also wondered whether a program of study that emphasized eloquence and action was proper for women, whose sphere was generally understood to be private and domestic. Humanists never established schools for girls, though through tutors or programs of self-study a few women did become educated in the classics. (See "Viewpoints 15.1: Lauro Quirini and Cassandra Fedele: Women and Humanist Learning," page 430.)

Humanists looked to the classical past for political as well as literary models. The best-known political theorist of this era was Niccolò Machiavelli (1469–1527), who worked as an official for the city of Florence until he was ousted in a power struggle. He spent the rest of his life writing, and his most famous work is the short political treatise *The Prince* (1513). Using the examples of classical and contemporary rulers, *The Prince* argues that the function of a ruler (or a government) is to preserve order and security. The inability to do so would lead to disorder, which might end in civil war or conquest by an outsider, situations clearly not conducive to any people's well-being. To preserve the state, a ruler should use whatever means necessary—brutality, lying, manipulation—but he should not do anything that would make the populace turn against him. Stealing or cruel actions done for a ruler's own pleasure would lead to resentment and destroy the popular support needed for a strong, stable realm. "It is much safer for the prince to be feared than loved," Machiavelli advised, "but he ought to avoid making himself hated."[1]

The Prince is often seen as the first modern guide to politics in the West, though Machiavelli was denounced for writing it, and people later came to use the word *Machiavellian* to mean cunning and ruthless. Machiavelli put a new spin on the Renaissance search for perfection, arguing that ideals needed to be measured in the cold light of the real world.

Christian Humanism

In the last quarter of the fifteenth century students from the Low Countries, France, Germany, and England flocked to Italy, absorbed the "new learning" of humanism, and carried it back to their own countries. Northern humanists shared the Italians' ideas about the wisdom of ancient texts and felt even more strongly that the best elements of classical and Christian cultures should be combined. These **Christian humanists**, as they were later called, saw humanist learning as a way to bring about reform of the church and to deepen people's spiritual lives.

The Englishman Thomas More (1478–1535) began life as a lawyer, studied the classics, and entered government service. He became best known for his controversial dialogue *Utopia* (1516), a word More invented from the Greek words for "nowhere." *Utopia* describes a community on an island somewhere beyond Europe where all children receive a good humanist education and adults divide their days between manual labor or business pursuits and intellectual activities. The problems that plagued More's fellow citizens, such as poverty and hunger, are solved by a beneficent government. Inequality and greed are prevented because profits from business and property are held in common, not privately. Furthermore, there is religious tolerance, and order and reason prevail. Because Utopian institutions are perfect, however, dissent and disagreement are not acceptable.

More's purposes in writing *Utopia* have been hotly debated. Some view it as a revolutionary critique of More's own hierarchical and violent society, some as a call for an even firmer hierarchy, and others as part of the humanist tradition of satire. It was widely read by learned Europeans in the Latin in which More wrote

- **Christian humanists** Humanists from northern Europe who thought that the best elements of classical and Christian cultures should be combined and saw humanist learning as a way to bring about reform of the church and deepen people's spiritual lives.

Viewpoints 15.1

Lauro Quirini and Cassandra Fedele: Women and Humanist Learning

• *Italian humanists promoted the value of their new style of education, and several women from the bustling cities of northern Italy obtained humanist education, writing letters, dialogues, and orations. Some male humanists criticized women who publicly shared their ideas, but others celebrated them. The Venetian humanist and nobleman Lauro Quirini (ca. 1420–ca. 1475) wrote to one of these, the learned Isotta Nogarola (1418–1466), praising her accomplishments and advising her on a plan of study. The second document is an excerpt from an oration that the Venetian Cassandra Fedele (1465–1558) gave in Latin at the University of Padua in honor of her (male) cousin's graduation. Fedele applied advice such as Quirini's to her own studies and became the best-known female scholar of her time.*

Letter from Lauro Quirini to Isotta Nogarola, ca. 1450

"This letter asks of you nothing else than that you pursue in the most splendid way, until death, that same course of right living that you have followed since childhood. . . . Rightful therefore, should you also, famous Isotta, receive the highest praises, since you have, if I may so speak, overcome your own nature. For that true virtue that is proper to men you have pursued with remarkable zeal — not the mediocre virtue that many men seek, but that which would befit a man of the most flawless and perfect wisdom. . . . Therefore dissatisfied with the lesser studies, you have applied your noble mind to those highest disciplines, in which there is need for keenness of intelligence and mind. For you are engaged in the art of dialectic, which shows the way to learning the truth. After you have also digested this part of philosophy, which is concerned with human matters, equipped with your nobility of the soul you should also set out for that ample and vast other part [divine matters]. . . . Here you should begin especially with those disciplines that we call by the Greek term mathematics. . . . You should also make use of those studies, moreover, that you have splendidly embraced from your youth, and especially history, for history is as it were the teacher of life."

Cassandra Fedele, In Praise of Letters, ca. 1485

"I shall speak very briefly on the study of the liberal arts, which for humans is useful and honorable, pleasurable and enlightening since everyone, not only philosophers but also the most ignorant man, knows and admits that it is by reason that man is separated from beasts. For what is it that so greatly helps both the learned and the ignorant? What so enlarges and enlightens men's minds the way that an education in and knowledge of literature and the liberal arts do? . . . But erudite men who are filled with the knowledge of divine and human things turn all their thoughts and considerations toward reason as though toward a target, and free their minds from all pain, though plagued by many anxieties. . . .

But enough on the utility of literature since it produces not only an outcome that is rich, precious, and sublime, but also provides one with advantages that are extremely pleasurable, fruitful, and lasting — benefits that I myself have enjoyed. And when I meditate on the idea of marching forth in life with the lowly and execrable weapons of the little woman — the needle and the distaff [the rod onto which yarn is wound after spinning] — even if the study of literature offers women no rewards or honors, I believe women must nonetheless pursue and embrace such studies alone for the pleasure and enjoyment they contain."

Sources: Isotta Nogarola, *Complete Writings, Letterbook, Dialogue on Adam and Eve, Orations*, ed. and trans. Margaret L. King and Diana Robin, pp. 108–113. Reproduced with permission of University of Chicago Press in the format Republish in a book via Copyright Clearance Center; Cassandra Fedele, *Letters and Orations*, ed. and trans. Diana Robin, pp. 159–162. Reproduced with permission of University of Chicago Press in the format Republish in a book via Copyright Clearance Center.

QUESTIONS FOR ANALYSIS

1. What do Quirini and Fedele view as the best course and purposes of study? How are these different, or similar, for men and women?
2. Quirini is male and Fedele female. Does the gender of the authors shape their ideas about the appropriateness of humanist learning for women? If so, how?

it, and later in vernacular translations, and its title quickly became the standard word for any idealized imaginary society.

Better known by contemporaries than Thomas More was the Dutch humanist Desiderius Erasmus (1466?–1536) of Rotterdam. His fame rested largely on his exceptional knowledge of Greek and the Bible. Erasmus's long list of publications includes *The Education of a Christian Prince* (1504), a book combining idealistic and practical suggestions for the formation of a ruler's character through the careful study of Plutarch, Aristotle, Cicero, and Plato; *The Praise of Folly* (1509), a witty satire poking fun at social, political, and especially religious institutions; and, most important, a critical edition of the Greek New Testament (1516). For Erasmus, education was the key to moral and intellectual improvement, and true Christianity was an inner attitude of the spirit, not a set of outward actions.

Printing and Its Social Impact

The fourteenth-century humanist Petrarch and the sixteenth-century humanist Erasmus had many similar ideas, but the immediate impact of their ideas was very different because of one thing: the printing press with movable metal type. While Petrarch's works spread slowly from person to person by hand copying, Erasmus's works spread quickly through printing, in which hundreds or thousands of identical copies could be made in a short time.

While printing with movable type was invented in China (see page 370), movable *metal* type was actually developed in the thirteenth century in Korea, though it was tightly controlled by the monarchy and did not have the broad impact there that printing did in Europe. Printing with movable metal type developed in Germany in the middle of the fifteenth century as a combination of existing technologies. Several metalsmiths, most prominently Johann Gutenberg (ca. 1400–1468), transformed the metal stamps used to mark signs on jewelry into type that could be covered with ink and used to mark symbols onto a page. This type could be rearranged for every page and so used over and over. Historians have speculated whether German printers somehow learned of the Korean invention, but there is no evidence that they did. The printing revolution was also enabled by the ready availability of paper, which was made using techniques that had originated in China and spread from Muslim Spain to the rest of Europe.

The effects of the invention of movable-type printing were not felt overnight. Nevertheless, within a half century of the publication of Gutenberg's Bible of 1456, movable type had brought about radical changes. Historians estimate that somewhere between 8 million and 20 million books were printed in Europe between 1456 and 1500, many more than the total number of books that had been produced in the West during the many millennia between the invention of writing and 1456.

Printing transformed both the private and the public lives of Europeans. In the public realm, government and church leaders both used and worried about printing. They printed laws, declarations of war, battle accounts, and propaganda, but they also attempted to censor or ban books and authors whose ideas they thought were wrong. These efforts were rarely effective.

In the private realm, printing enabled people to read identical books so that they could more easily discuss the ideas that the books contained. Although most of the earliest books and pamphlets dealt with religious subjects, printers produced anything that would sell: professional reference sets, historical romances, biographies, poetry, prose fiction, and how-to manuals for the general public. Illustrations increased a book's sales, so printers published both history and pornography full of woodcuts and engravings. Additionally, single-page broadsides and fly sheets allowed public events and "wonders" such as comets and two-headed calves to be experienced vicariously. Since books and other printed materials were read aloud to illiterate listeners, print bridged the gap between the written and oral cultures.

Because many laypeople could not read Latin, printers put out works in vernacular languages, fostering standardization in these languages. Works in these languages were also performed onstage, for plays of all types were popular everywhere. Traveling companies of actors performed before royal courts and in town squares, and in larger cities public theaters offered bawdy comedies and bloody tragedies. In London the works of William Shakespeare (1564–1616) were especially popular. (See "Viewpoints 16.2: Two Views of 'Natural Man,'" page 484.)

Art and the Artist

No feature of the Renaissance evokes greater admiration than its artistic masterpieces. In Renaissance Italy wealthy merchants, bankers, popes, and princes spent vast sums to commission art as a means of glorifying themselves and their families. Patrons varied in their level of involvement as a work progressed; some simply ordered a specific subject or scene, while others oversaw the work of the artist or architect very closely, suggesting themes and styles and demanding changes while the work was in progress.

As a result of patronage, certain artists gained great public acclaim and adulation, leading many historians to view the Renaissance as the beginning of the concept of the artist as genius. In the Middle Ages, people believed that only God created, albeit through individuals, and artistic originality was not particularly valued. By contrast, Renaissance artists and humanists came to think that a work of art was the deliberate creation of a unique personality, of an individual who transcended traditions, rules, and theories.

In terms of artistic themes, religious topics, such as the Annunciation of the Virgin Mary and the Nativity, remained popular among both patrons and artists, but frequently the patron had himself and his family portrayed in the scene. As the fifteenth century advanced and humanist ideas spread more widely, classical themes and motifs, such as the lives and loves of pagan gods and goddesses, figured increasingly in painting and sculpture, with the facial features of the gods sometimes modeled on those of living people. Classical styles also influenced architecture, as architects designed build-

Michelangelo's *David* (1501–1504) and the *Last Judgment* (detail, 1537–1541) Like all Renaissance artists, Michelangelo worked largely on commissions from patrons. Officials of the city of Florence contracted the young sculptor to produce a statue of the Old Testament hero David (left) to be displayed in the city's main square. Michelangelo portrayed David anticipating his fight against the giant Goliath, and the statue came to symbolize the republic of Florence standing up to its larger and more powerful enemies. More than thirty years later, Michelangelo was commissioned by the pope to paint a scene of the Last Judgment on the altar wall of the Sistine Chapel, where he had earlier spent four years covering the ceiling with magnificent frescoes. The massive work shows a powerful Christ standing in judgment, with souls ascending into Heaven while others are dragged by demons into Hell (above). The *David* captures ideals of human perfection and has come to be an iconic symbol of Renaissance artistic brilliance, while the dramatic and violent *Last Judgment* conveys both terror and divine power. (sculpture: Galleria dell'Accademia, Florence, Italy/Ken Welsh/The Bridgeman Art Library; painting: Vatican Museum and Galleries, Vatican City/Alinari/The Bridgeman Art Library)

ings that featured carefully proportioned arches and domes modeled on the structures of ancient Rome.

The individual portrait emerged as a distinct genre in Renaissance art. Rather than reflecting a spiritual ideal, as medieval painting and sculpture tended to do, Renaissance portraits showed human ideals, often portrayed in a more realistic style. The Florentine sculptor Donatello (1386–1466) revived the classical figure, with its balance and self-awareness. Leonardo da Vinci (1452–1519) was particularly adept at portraying female grace and beauty in his paintings of upper-class urban women and biblical figures such as the Virgin Mary. Another Florentine artist, Raphael Sanzio (1483–1520), painted hundreds of portraits and devotional images in his relatively short life, becoming the most sought-after artist in Europe (see page 425).

In the late fifteenth century the center of Renaissance art shifted from Florence to Rome, where wealthy cardinals and popes wanted visual expression of the church's and their own families' power and piety. To meet this demand, Michelangelo Buonarroti (1475–1564) went to Rome from Florence in about 1500 and began the series of statues, paintings, and architectural projects from which he gained an international reputation. For example, he produced sculptures of Moses and of the Virgin Mary holding Jesus after his crucifixion (the Pietà), he redesigned the Capitoline Hill in central Rome, and most famously, between 1508 and 1512, he painted religiously themed frescoes on the ceiling and altar wall of the Sistine Chapel. Pope Julius II, who commissioned Michelangelo for the Sistine Chapel project, demanded that the artist work as fast as he could and frequently visited him to offer suggestions and criticism. Michelangelo complained in person and by letter about the pope's meddling, but his fame did not match the power of the pope, and he kept working.

Donatello, *Gattamelata*, 1450 The Florentine sculptor Donatello's bronze statue of the powerful military captain nicknamed Gattamelata (Honey-Cat) mounted on his horse was erected in the public square of Padua. The first bronze equestrian statue made since Roman times, the larger-than-life-size work seems to capture in metal the shrewd and determined type of ruler Machiavelli described in *The Prince*. (Scala/Art Resource, NY)

Though they might show individual genius, Renaissance artists were still expected to be schooled in proper artistic techniques and stylistic conventions, for the notion that artistic genius could show up in the work of the untrained did not emerge until the twentieth century. Therefore, in both Italy and northern Europe most aspiring artists were educated in the workshops of older artists. By the later sixteenth century formal academies were also established to train artists. Like universities, artistic workshops and academies were male-only settings in which students of different ages came together to learn and to create bonds of friendship, influence, patronage, and sometimes intimacy. Several women did become well known as painters during the Renaissance, but they were trained by their artist fathers and often quit painting when they married.

Women were not alone in being excluded from the institutions of Renaissance culture. Though a few talented artists such as Leonardo and Michelangelo emerged from artisanal backgrounds, most scholars and artists came from families with at least some money. The audience for artists' work was also exclusive, limited mostly to educated and prosperous citizens. Although common people in large cities might have occasionally seen plays such as those of Shakespeare, most people lived in villages with no access to formal schooling or to the work of prominent artists. In general a small, highly educated minority of literary humanists and artists created the culture of and for a social elite. In this way the Renaissance maintained, and even enhanced, a gulf between the learned minority and the uneducated multitude that has survived for many centuries.

***The Chess Game*, 1555** In this oil painting, the Italian artist Sofonisba Anguissola (1532–1625) shows her three younger sisters playing chess, a game that was growing in popularity in the sixteenth century. Each sister looks at the one immediately older than herself, with the girl on the left looking out at her sister, the artist. Anguissola's father, a minor nobleman, recognized his daughter's talent and arranged for her to study with several painters. She became a court painter at the Spanish royal court, where she painted many portraits. Returning to Italy, she continued to be active, painting her last portrait when she was over eighty. (Museum Narodowe, Poznan, Poland/ The Bridgeman Art Library)

Social Hierarchies

☐ What were the key social hierarchies in Renaissance Europe, and how did these hierarchies shape people's lives?

The division between the educated and uneducated was one of many social hierarchies evident in the Renaissance. Other hierarchies were built on those of the Middle Ages, but also developed new features that contributed to modern social hierarchies, such as those of race, class, and gender.

Race and Slavery

Renaissance people did not use the word *race* the way we do, but often used *race*, *people*, and *nation* interchangeably for ethnic, national, and religious groups—for example, the French race, the Irish people, the Jewish nation. They did make distinctions based on skin color that were in keeping with later conceptualizations of race, but these distinctions were interwoven with other characteristics when people thought about human differences.

Ever since the time of the Roman Republic, a few black Africans had lived in western Europe. They had come, along with white slaves, as the spoils of war. After the collapse of the Roman Empire and throughout the Middle Ages, Muslim and Christian merchants continued to import black slaves, and long tradition sanctioned the practice of slavery. The black population was especially concentrated in the cities of the Iberian Peninsula, where African slaves sometimes gained their freedom and intermingled with the local population. By the mid-sixteenth century blacks, slave and free, constituted roughly 3 percent of the Portuguese population, and because of intermarriage cities such as Lisbon had significant numbers of people of mixed African and European descent.

In Renaissance Portugal, Spain, and Italy, African slaves supplemented the labor force in virtually all occupations—as servants, agricultural laborers, craftsmen, and seamen on ships. Slaves also formed the primary workforce on the sugar plantations set up by Europeans on the Atlantic islands in the late fifteenth century (see page 477). European aristocrats sometimes had themselves painted with their black servants to indicate their wealth or, in the case of noblewomen, to highlight their fair skin.

Until their voyages down the African coast in the late fifteenth century, Europeans had little concrete knowledge of Africans and their cultures. They perceived Africa as a remote place, the home of strange people isolated by heresy and Islam from superior European civilization. Africans' contact, even as slaves, with Christian Europeans would only "improve" the blacks, they believed. The expanding slave trade reinforced negative preconceptions about the inferiority of black Africans.

- **debate about women** A discussion, which began in the later years of the fourteenth century, that attempted to answer fundamental questions about gender and to define the role of women in society.

Wealth and the Nobility

The word *class*—as in working class, middle class, upper class—was not used in the Renaissance to describe social division, but by the thirteenth century, and even more so by the fifteenth, the idea of a hierarchy based on wealth was emerging. This was particularly true in cities, where wealthy merchants oversaw vast trading empires, held positions of political power, and lived in splendor rivaling that enjoyed by the richest nobles. (See "Individuals in Society: Cosimo and Lorenzo de' Medici," page 428.)

The development of a hierarchy of wealth did not mean an end to the prominence of nobles, however, and even poorer nobles still had higher status than wealthy commoners. Thus wealthy Italian merchants enthusiastically bought noble titles and country villas in the fifteenth century, and wealthy English and Spanish merchants eagerly married their daughters and sons into often-impoverished noble families. The nobility maintained its status in most parts of Europe not by maintaining rigid boundaries, but by taking in and integrating the new social elite of wealth.

Gender Roles

Renaissance people would not have understood the word *gender* to refer to categories of people, but they would have easily grasped the concept. Toward the end of the fourteenth century learned men (and a few women) began what was termed the **debate about women** (*querelle des femmes*), an argument about women's character and nature that would last for centuries. Misogynist critiques of women from both clerical and secular authors denounced females as devious, domineering, and demanding. In response, several authors compiled long lists of famous and praiseworthy women exemplary for their loyalty, bravery, and morality. Some writers, including a few women who had gained a humanist education, were interested not only in defending women but also in exploring the reasons behind women's secondary status—that is, why the great philosophers, statesmen, and poets had generally been men. In this they were anticipating more recent discussions about the "social construction of gender" by six hundred years.

□ Picturing the Past

***Laura de Dianti*, 1523** The Venetian artist Titian portrays a young Italian woman with a gorgeous blue dress and an elaborate pearl and feather headdress accompanied by a young black page with a gold earring. Slaves from Africa and the Ottoman Empire were common in wealthy Venetian households. (Photographer: Human Bios International AG, CH-8280, Kreuzlingen, www.humanbios.com)

ANALYZING THE IMAGE How does the artist convey the message that this woman comes from a wealthy family? How does he use the skin color of the slave to highlight the woman's fair skin, which was one of the Renaissance ideals of female beauty?

CONNECTIONS Household slaves worked at various tasks, but they were also symbols of the exotic. What other elements does Titian include in the painting to represent foreign places and the wealth brought to Venice by overseas trade? What does this painting suggest about Venetian attitudes toward slaves, who were part of that trade?

Beginning in the sixteenth century the debate about women also became a debate about female rulers, because in Spain, England, France, and Scotland women served as advisers to child-kings or ruled in their own right. There were no successful rebellions against female rulers simply because they were women, but in part this was because female rulers, especially Queen Elizabeth I of England, emphasized qualities regarded as masculine—physical bravery, stamina, wisdom, duty—whenever they appeared in public.

The dominant notion of the "true" man was that of the married head of household, so men whose class and age would have normally conferred political power but who remained unmarried were sometimes excluded from ruling positions. Actual marriage patterns in Europe left many women unmarried until late in life, but this did not lead to greater equality. Women who worked for wages, as was typical, earned about half to two-thirds of what men did even for the same work. Regulations for German vineyard workers in the early sixteenth century, for example, specified:

> Men who work in the vineyards, doing work that is skilled, are to be paid 16 pence per day; in addition, they are to receive soup and wine in the morning, at midday beer, vegetables and meat, and in the evening soup, vegetables and wine. Young boys are to be paid 10 pence per day. Women who work as haymakers are to be given 6 pence a day. If the employer wants to have them doing other work, he may make an agreement with them to pay them 7 or 8 pence. He may also give them soup and vegetables to eat in the morning—but no wine—milk and bread at midday, but nothing in the evening.[2]

Of all the ways in which Renaissance society was hierarchically arranged—by class, age, level of education, rank, race, occupation—gender was regarded as the most "natural" distinction and therefore the most important one to defend.

Italian City Scene In this detail from a fresco, the Italian painter Lorenzo Lotto captures the mixing of social groups in a Renaissance Italian city. The crowd of men in the left foreground includes wealthy merchants in elaborate hats and colorful coats. Two mercenary soldiers (carrying a sword and a pike) wear short doublets and tight hose stylishly slit to reveal colored undergarments, while boys play with toy weapons at their feet. Clothing like that of the soldiers, which emphasized the masculine form, was frequently criticized for its expense and its "indecency." At the right, women sell vegetables and bread, which would have been a common sight at any city marketplace. (Scala/Art Resource, NY)

Politics and the State in the Renaissance, ca. 1450–1521

☐ How did the nation-states of western Europe evolve in this period?

The High Middle Ages had witnessed the origins of many of the basic institutions of the modern state. Sheriffs, inquests, juries, circuit judges, professional bureaucracies, and representative assemblies all trace their origins to the twelfth and thirteenth centuries. The linchpin for the development of states, however, was strong monarchy. Beginning in the fifteenth century rulers used aggressive methods to build up their governments. They began the work of reducing violence, curbing unruly nobles, and establishing domestic order. As they built and maintained power, they emphasized royal majesty and royal sovereignty and insisted on the respect and loyalty of all subjects.

France

The Black Death and the Hundred Years' War left France drastically depopulated, commercially ruined, and agriculturally weak (see page 416). Nonetheless, the ruler whom Joan of Arc had seen crowned at Reims, Charles VII (r. 1422–1461), revived the monarchy and France. He reorganized the royal council, giving increased influence to middle-class men, and strengthened royal finances through taxes on certain products and on land. These taxes remained the Crown's chief sources of income until the Revolution of 1789. By establishing regular companies of cavalry and archers—recruited, paid, and inspected by the state—Charles created the first permanent royal army anywhere in Europe.

Two further developments strengthened the French monarchy. The marriage of Louis XII (r. 1498–1515) and Anne of Brittany added the large western duchy of Brittany to the state. Louis XII's successor, Francis I (r. 1515–1547), and Pope Leo X reached a mutually satisfactory agreement about church and state powers in 1516 that gave French kings the power to control the appointment and thus the policies of church officials in the kingdom.

England

English society suffered severely in the fourteenth and fifteenth centuries. Population, decimated by the Black Death, continued to decline. Between 1455 and 1471 adherents of the ducal houses of York and Lancaster waged civil wars over control of the English throne, commonly called the Wars of the Roses because the symbol of the Yorkists was a white rose and that of the Lancastrians a red one. The chronic disorder hurt trade, agriculture, and domestic industry, and the authority of the monarchy sank lower than it had been in centuries.

The Yorkist Edward IV (r. 1461–1483) succeeded in defeating the Lancastrian forces and after 1471 began to reconstruct the monarchy and consolidate royal power. Henry VII (r. 1485–1509) of the Welsh house of Tudor worked to restore royal prestige, to crush the power of the nobility, and to establish order and law at the local level. Because the government halted the long period of anarchy, it won the key support of the merchant and agricultural upper middle class. Early in his reign Henry VII summoned several meetings of Parliament, primarily to confirm laws, but the center of royal authority was the royal council, which governed at the national level. There Henry VII revealed his distrust of the nobility: very few great lords were among the king's closest advisers, who instead were lesser landowners and lawyers. They were, in a sense, middle class. The royal council handled any business the king put before it—executive, legislative, and judicial.

Secretive, cautious, and thrifty, Henry VII rebuilt the monarchy. He encouraged the cloth industry and built up the English merchant marine. He crushed an invasion from Ireland, secured peace with Scotland through the marriage of his daughter Margaret to the Scottish king, and enhanced English prestige through the marriage of his eldest son, Arthur, to Catherine of Aragon, the daughter of Ferdinand and Isabella of Spain. (Several years after Arthur's death, Catherine would become the wife of his younger brother and the next king of England, Henry VIII; see page 446.) When Henry VII died in 1509, he left a country at peace both domestically and internationally, a substantially augmented treasury, and the dignity and role of the Crown much enhanced.

Spain

While England and France laid the foundations of unified nation-states during the Renaissance, Spain remained a conglomerate of independent kingdoms. Even the wedding in 1469 of the dynamic and aggressive Isabella of Castile and the crafty and persistent Ferdinand of Aragon did not bring about administrative unity. Isabella and Ferdinand were, however, able to exert their authority in ways similar to the rulers of France and England. They curbed aristocratic power by excluding aristocrats and great territorial magnates from the royal council, and instead appointed only men of middle-class background. The council and various government boards recruited men trained in Roman law, which exalted the power of the Crown. They also secured from the Spanish pope Alexander VI the right to appoint bishops in Spain and in the Hispanic territories in America, enabling them to establish the equivalent of a national church. In 1492 their armies conquered Granada, the last territory held by Arabs in southern Spain.

Ferdinand and Isabella's rule also marked the start of greater persecution of the Jews. In the Middle Ages, the kings of France and England had expelled the Jews from their kingdoms, and many had sought refuge in Spain. During the long centuries of the reconquista (see page 401), Christian kings in Spain had renewed Jewish rights and privileges; in fact, Jewish industry, intelligence, and money had supported royal power. But while Christians of all classes borrowed from Jewish moneylenders and while all who could afford them sought Jewish physicians, a strong undercurrent of resentment of Jewish influence and wealth festered.

In the fourteenth century anti-Semitism in Spain was aggravated by fiery anti-Jewish preaching, by economic dislocation, and by the search for a scapegoat during the Black Death. Anti-Semitic pogroms, violent massacres and riots directed against Jews, swept the towns of Spain, and perhaps 40 percent of the Jewish population was killed or forced to convert. Those who converted were called *conversos* (kuhn-VEHR-sohz) or New Christians. Conversos were often well educated and held prominent positions in government, the church, medicine, law, and business.

Such successes bred resentment. Aristocrats resented their financial dependence on conversos, the poor hated the converso tax collectors, and churchmen doubted the sincerity of their conversions. Queen Isabella shared

MAP 15.1 The Global Empire of Charles V, ca. 1556 Charles V exercised theoretical jurisdiction over more European territory than anyone since Charlemagne. He also claimed authority over large parts of North and South America, although actual Spanish control was weak in much of this area.

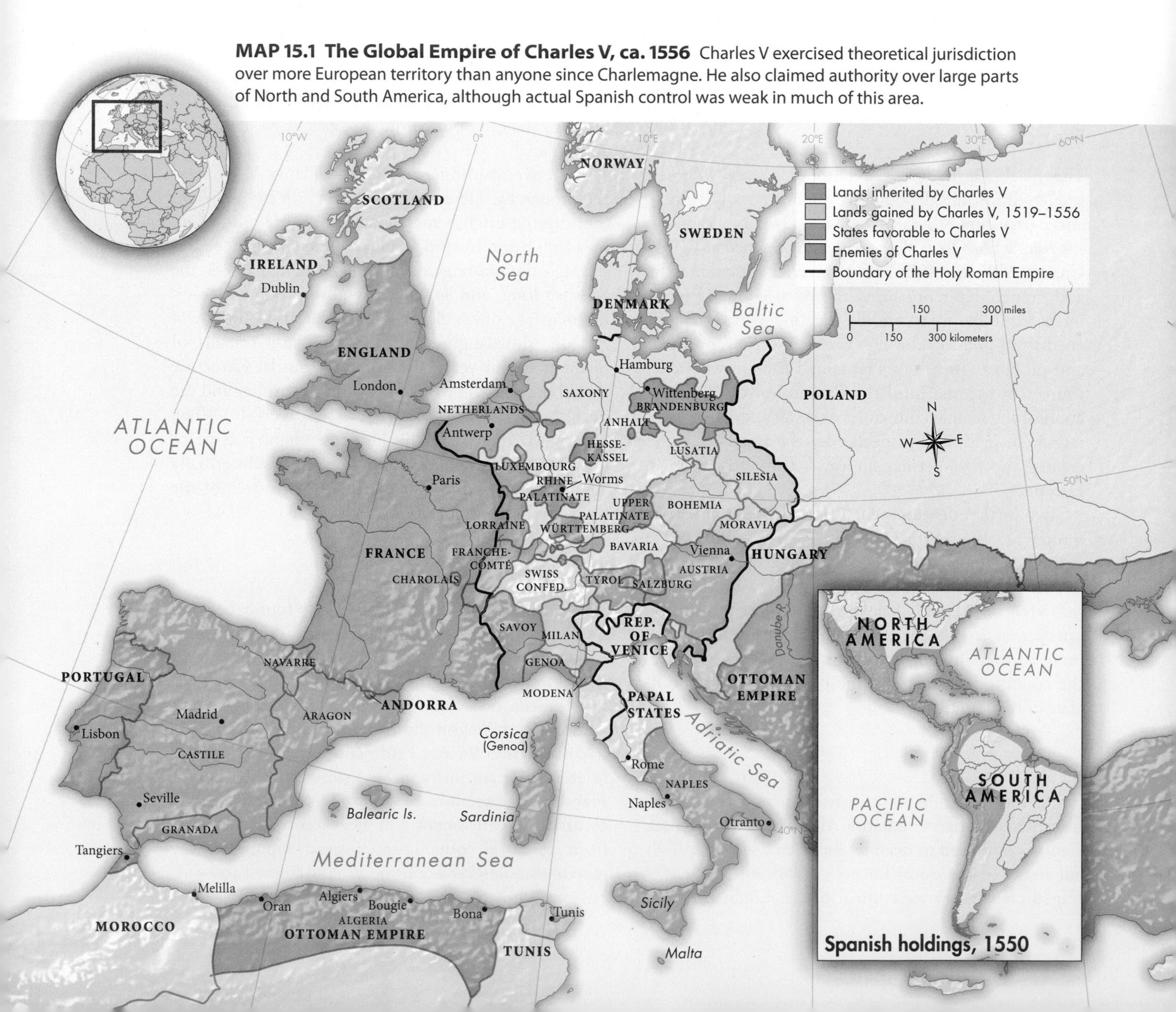

these suspicions, and she and Ferdinand received permission from Pope Sixtus IV to establish an Inquisition to "search out and punish converts from Judaism who had transgressed against Christianity by secretly adhering to Jewish beliefs and performing rites of the Jews."[3] Investigations and trials began immediately, with officials of the Inquisition looking for conversos who showed any sign of incomplete conversion, such as not eating pork.

Recent scholarship has carefully analyzed documents of the Inquisition. Most conversos identified themselves as sincere Christians; many came from families that had received baptism generations before. In response, officials of the Inquisition developed a new type of anti-Semitism. A person's status as a Jew, they argued, could not be changed by religious conversion, but was in the person's blood and was heritable, so Jews could never be true Christians. Under what were known as "purity of blood" laws, having "pure Christian blood" became a requirement for noble status. Ideas about Jews developed in Spain became important components in European concepts of race, and discussions of "Jewish blood" later expanded into discriminatory definitions of the "Jewish race."

In 1492, shortly after the conquest of Granada, Isabella and Ferdinand issued an edict expelling all practicing Jews from Spain. Of the community of perhaps 200,000 Jews, 150,000 fled. Absolute religious orthodoxy and "purity of blood" served as the theoretical foundation of the Spanish national state.

The Habsburgs

War and diplomacy were important ways that states increased their power in sixteenth-century Europe, but so was marriage. Because almost all of Europe was ruled by hereditary dynasties — the Papal States and a few cities being the exceptions — claiming and holding resources involved shrewd marital strategies, for it was far cheaper to gain land by inheritance than by war.

The benefits of an advantageous marriage stretched across generations, as can be seen most dramatically with the Habsburgs. The Holy Roman emperor Frederick III, a Habsburg who was the ruler of most of Austria, acquired only a small amount of territory — but a great deal of money — with his marriage to Princess Eleanore of Portugal in 1452. He arranged for his son Maximilian to marry Europe's most prominent heiress, Mary of Burgundy, in 1477; she inherited the Netherlands, Luxembourg, and the county of Burgundy in what is now eastern France. Through this union with the rich and powerful duchy of Burgundy, the Austrian house of Habsburg, already the strongest ruling family in the empire, became an international power. The marriage of Maximilian and Mary angered the French, who considered Burgundy French territory, and it inaugurated centuries of conflict between the Habsburgs and the kings of France. Within the empire, German principalities that resented Austria's pre-eminence began to see that they shared interests with France.

Maximilian learned the lesson of marital politics well, marrying his son and daughter to the children of Ferdinand and Isabella, the rulers of Spain, much of southern Italy, and eventually the Spanish New World empire. His grandson Charles V (1500–1558) fell heir to a vast and incredibly diverse collection of states and peoples, each governed in a different manner and held together only by the person of the emperor (Map 15.1). Charles was convinced that it was his duty to maintain the political and religious unity of Western Christendom. This conviction would be challenged far more than Charles ever anticipated.

The Protestant Reformation

☐ What were the central ideas of Protestant reformers, and why were they appealing to various groups across Europe?

Calls for reform in the church came from many quarters in early-sixteenth-century Europe — from educated laypeople such as Christian humanists and urban residents, from villagers and artisans, and from church officials themselves. This dissatisfaction helps explain why the ideas of Martin Luther, an obscure professor from a new and not very prestigious German university, found a ready audience. Within a decade of his first publishing his ideas (using the new technology of the printing press), much of central Europe and Scandinavia had broken with the Catholic Church in a movement that came to be known as the **Protestant Reformation**. In addition, even more radical concepts of the Christian message were being developed and linked to calls for social change.

Criticism of the Church

Sixteenth-century Europeans were deeply pious. Despite — or perhaps because of — the depth of their piety, many people were also highly critical of the Roman Catholic Church and its clergy. Papal conflicts with rulers and the Great Schism (see page 419) badly damaged the prestige of church leaders. Papal tax collection methods were also attacked, and some criticized the papacy itself as an institution. Court records, written descriptions of bishops' visitations of parishes,

- **Protestant Reformation** A religious reform movement that began in the early sixteenth century that split the Western Christian Church.

and even popular songs and printed images show widespread anticlericalism, or opposition to the clergy.

In the early sixteenth century, critics of the church concentrated their attacks on clerical immorality, ignorance, and absenteeism. Charges of immorality were aimed at a number of priests who were drunkards, neglected the rule of celibacy, gambled, or indulged in fancy dress. Charges of ignorance applied to barely literate priests who delivered poor-quality sermons and who were obviously ignorant of the Latin words of the Mass.

In regard to absenteeism, many clerics, especially higher ecclesiastics, held several benefices (offices) simultaneously—a practice termed pluralism. However, they seldom visited the communities served by the benefices, let alone performed the spiritual responsibilities those offices entailed. Instead, they collected revenues from all the benefices assigned to them and hired a poor priest to fulfill their spiritual duties, paying him just a fraction of the income.

There was also local resentment of clerical privileges and immunities. Priests, monks, and nuns were exempt from civic responsibilities, such as defending the city and paying taxes. Yet religious orders frequently held large amounts of urban property, in some cities as much as one-third. City governments were increasingly determined to integrate the clergy into civic life. This brought city leaders into opposition with bishops and the papacy, which for centuries had stressed the independence of the church from lay control and the distinction between members of the clergy and laypeople.

Martin Luther

By itself, widespread criticism of the church did not lead to the dramatic changes of the sixteenth century. Those resulted from the personal religious struggle of a German university professor, Martin Luther (1483–1546). Luther's father wanted him to be a lawyer, but a sense of religious calling led him to join the Augustinian friars, an order whose members often preached to, taught, and assisted the poor. Luther was ordained a priest in 1507 and after additional study earned a doctorate of theology. From 1512 until his death in 1546 he served as professor of the Scriptures at the new University of Wittenberg.

- **indulgence** A papal statement granting remission of a priest-imposed penalty for sin. (No one knew what penalty God would impose after death.)
- **Diet of Worms** An assembly of representatives from the territories of the Holy Roman Empire convened by Charles V in the German city of Worms in 1521. It was here that Martin Luther refused to recant his writings.
- **Protestant** Originally meaning "a follower of Luther," this term came to be generally applied to all non-Catholic western European Christians.

Martin Luther was a very conscientious friar, but his scrupulous observance of the religious routine, frequent confessions, and fasting gave him only temporary relief from anxieties about sin and his ability to meet God's demands. Through his study of Saint Paul's letters in the New Testament, he gradually arrived at a new understanding of Christian doctrine. His understanding is often summarized as "faith alone, grace alone, scripture alone." He believed that salvation and justification (righteousness in God's eyes) come through faith, and that faith is a free gift of God, not the result of human effort. God's word is revealed only in biblical scripture, not in the traditions of the church.

At the same time that Luther was engaged in scholarly reflections and professorial lecturing, Pope Leo X authorized a special Saint Peter's indulgence to finance his building plans in Rome. An **indulgence** was a document, signed by the pope or another church official, that substituted for penance. The archbishop who controlled the area in which Wittenberg was located, Albert of Mainz, also promoted the sale of indulgences, in his case to pay off a debt he had incurred to be named bishop of several additional territories. Albert's sales campaign, run by a Dominican friar who mounted an advertising blitz, promised that the purchase of indulgences would bring full forgiveness for one's own sins or buy release from purgatory for a loved one. One of the slogans—"As soon as coin in coffer rings, the soul from purgatory springs"—brought phenomenal success.

Luther was severely troubled that many people believed that they had no further need for repentance once they had purchased indulgences. He wrote a letter to Archbishop Albert on the subject and enclosed in Latin his "Ninety-five Theses on the Power of Indulgences." His argument was that indulgences undermined the seriousness of the sacrament of penance and competed with the preaching of the Gospel. After Luther's death, biographies reported that the theses were also posted on the door of the church at Wittenberg Castle on October 31, 1517. Such an act would have been very strange—they were in Latin and written for those learned in theology, not for normal churchgoers—but it has become a standard part of Luther lore. In any case, Luther intended the theses for academic debate, but by December 1517 they had been translated into German and were being read throughout central Europe. Luther was ordered to go to Rome, but he was able to avoid this because the ruler of the territory in which he lived protected him. The pope nonetheless ordered him to recant many of his ideas, and Luther publicly burned the letter containing the papal order. In this highly charged atmosphere, the twenty-one-year-old emperor Charles V summoned Luther to appear before the **Diet of Worms**, an assembly of representatives from the territories of

Ego
Confessor et pniarius Monasterij et Capelle bte Marie virginis diuinitus consecrate loci heremitarum Cōstan. dyoc. deputatus pniibus recognosco discretum
dictum locum et Capellā visitasse mihiqz sua pctā in forma ecclesie confessum et auctoritate a sede aplica mihi in hac parte cōcessa iniūcta pnia salutari absolutum. In quorum fide pntes litteras tradidi sigilloqz in huiusmodi litteris cōsueto signaui. Anno M.cccc.xvi

Selling Indulgences A German single-page pamphlet shows a monk offering an indulgence, with the official seals of the pope attached, as people run to put their money in the box in exchange for his promise of heavenly bliss, symbolized by the dove above his head. Indulgences were sold widely in Germany, and they were the first Catholic practice that Luther criticized openly. This pamphlet also attacks the sale of indulgences, calling it devilish and deceitful, a point of view expressed in the woodcut by the peddler's riding on a donkey, an animal that had long been used as a symbol of ignorance. Indulgences were often printed as fill-in-the-blank forms. This one, purchased in 1521, has space for the indulgence seller's name at the top, the buyer's name in the middle, and the date at the bottom. (woodcut: akg-images; indulgence: Visual Connection Archive)

the Holy Roman Empire meeting in the city of Worms in 1521. Luther refused to give in to demands that he take back his ideas:

> Unless I am convinced by the evidence of Scripture or by plain reason—for I do not accept the authority of the Pope or the councils alone, since it is established that they have often erred and contradicted themselves—I am bound by the Scriptures I have cited and my conscience is captive to the Word of God. I cannot and will not recant anything, for it is neither safe nor right to go against conscience.[4]

Protestant Thought and Its Appeal

As he developed his ideas, Luther gathered followers, who came to be called Protestants. The word **Protestant** derives from a "protest" drawn up by a small group of reforming German princes in 1529. At first *Protestant* meant "a follower of Luther," but as many other reformers appeared, it became a general term for all non-Catholic western European Christians.

Catholics and Protestants disagreed on many issues. First, how is a person to be saved? Catholic teaching held that salvation is achieved by both faith and good works. Protestants held that salvation comes by faith alone, irrespective of good works or the sacraments. God, not people, initiates salvation. (See "Listening to the Past: Martin Luther, *On Christian Liberty*," page 442.) Second, where does religious authority reside? Christian doctrine had long maintained that authority rests both in the Bible and in the traditional teaching of the church. For Protestants, however, authority rests in the Bible alone, and for a doctrine or issue to be valid, it has to have a scriptural basis. Third, what is the church? Protestants held that the church is a spiritual priesthood of all believers, an invisible fellowship not fixed in any place or person, which differed markedly from the Roman Catholic practice of looking to a clerical, hierarchical institution headed by the pope in Rome. Fourth, what is the highest form of Christian life? The medieval church had stressed the superiority of the monastic and religious life over the secular. Protestants disagreed and argued that every person should serve God in his or her individual calling.

Pulpits and printing presses spread the Protestant message all over Germany, and by the middle of the sixteenth century people of all social classes had rejected

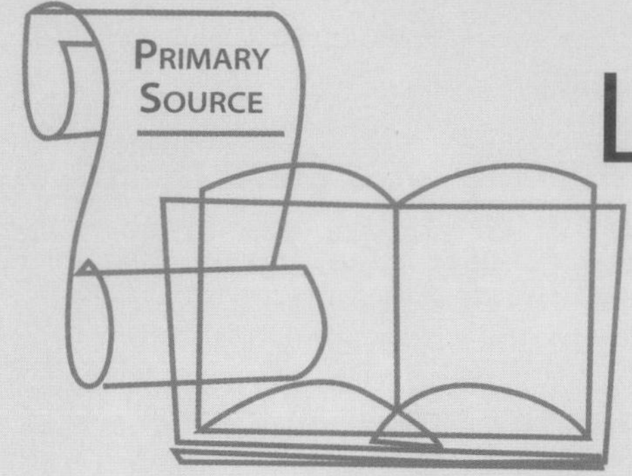

Listening to the Past

Martin Luther, *On Christian Liberty*

The idea of liberty or freedom has played a powerful role in the history of human society and culture, but the meaning and understanding of liberty have undergone continual change and interpretation. In the Roman world, where slavery was a basic institution, liberty meant the condition of being a free man, independent of obligations to a master. In the Middle Ages, possessing liberty meant having special privileges or rights that other persons or institutions did not have. A lord or a monastery, for example, might speak of his or its liberties, and citizens in London were said to possess the "freedom of the city," which allowed them to practice trades and own property without interference.

The idea of liberty also has a religious dimension, and the reformer Martin Luther formulated a classic interpretation of liberty in his treatise On Christian Liberty *(sometimes translated as* On the Freedom of a Christian*), arguably his finest piece. Written in Latin for the pope but translated immediately into German and published widely, it contains the main themes of Luther's theology: the importance of faith, the relationship of Christian faith and good works, the dual nature of human beings, and the fundamental importance of scripture. Luther writes that Christians were freed from sin and death through Christ, not by their own actions.*

" A Christian man is the most free lord of all, and subject to none; a Christian man is the most dutiful servant of all, and subject to everyone. Although these statements appear contradictory, yet, when they are found to agree together, they will do excellently for my purpose. They are both the statements of Paul himself, who says, "Though I be free from all men, yet have I made myself a servant unto all" (I Corinthians 9:19), and "Owe no man anything but to love one another" (Romans 13:8). Now love is by its own nature dutiful and obedient to the beloved object. Thus even Christ, though Lord of all things, was yet made of a woman; made under the law; at once free and a servant; at once in the form of God and in the form of a servant.

Let us examine the subject on a deeper and less simple principle. Man is composed of a twofold nature, a spiritual and a bodily. As regards the spiritual nature, which they name the soul, he is called the spiritual, inward, new man; as regards the bodily nature, which they name the flesh, he is called the fleshly, outward, old man. The Apostle speaks of this: "Though our outward man perish, yet the inward man is renewed day by day" (II Corinthians 4:16). The result of this diversity is that in the Scriptures opposing statements are made concerning the same man, the fact being that in the same man these two men are opposed to one another; the flesh lusting against the spirit, and the spirit against the flesh (Galatians 5:17).

We first approach the subject of the inward man, that we may see by what means a man becomes justified, free, and a true Christian; that is, a spiritual, new, and inward man. It is certain that absolutely none among outward things, under whatever name they may be reckoned, has any influence in producing Christian righteousness or liberty, nor, on the other hand, unrighteousness or slavery. This can be shown by an easy argument. What can it profit to the soul that the body should be in good condition, free, and full of life, that it should eat, drink, and act according to its pleasure, when even the most impious slaves of every kind of vice are prosperous in these matters? Again, what harm can ill health, bondage, hunger, thirst, or any other outward evil, do to the soul, when even the most pious of men, and the freest in the purity of their conscience, are harassed by these things? Neither of these states of things has to do with the liberty or the slavery of the soul.

And so it will profit nothing that the body should be adorned with sacred vestment, or dwell in holy places, or be occupied in sacred offices, or pray, fast, and abstain from certain meats, or do whatever works can be done through the body and in the body. Something widely different will be necessary for the justification and liberty of the soul, since the things I have spoken of can be done by an impious person, and only hypocrites are produced by devotion to these things. On the other hand, it will not at all injure the soul that the body should be clothed in profane raiment, should dwell in profane places, should eat and drink in the ordinary fashion, should not pray aloud, and should

Catholic teachings and become Protestant. What was the immense appeal of Luther's religious ideas and those of other Protestants?

Educated people and humanists were attracted by Luther's ideas. He advocated a simpler personal religion based on faith, a return to the spirit of the early church, the centrality of the Scriptures in the liturgy and in Christian life, and the abolition of elaborate ceremonies—precisely the reforms the Christian humanists had been calling for. His insistence that everyone should read and reflect on the Scriptures attracted the literate middle classes, including many priests and monks who became clergy in the new Protestant churches. Luther's ideas also appealed to townspeople who envied the church's wealth and resented paying for it. After cities became Protestant, the city council taxed the clergy and placed them under the jurisdiction of civil courts.

For effective preaching, especially to the uneducated, Luther urged the minister "to keep it simple for the simple." (*Martin Luther's Sermon*, detail from a triptych, Lucas Cranach the Elder, 1547 [oil on panel]/ Church of St. Marien, Wittenberg, Germany/Giraudon/The Bridgeman Art Library)

leave undone all the things above mentioned, which may be done by hypocrites. . . .

One thing, and one alone, is necessary for life, justification, and Christian liberty; and that is the most Holy Word of God, the Gospel of Christ, as He says, "I am the resurrection and the life; he that believeth in me shall not die eternally" (John 9:25), and also, "If the Son shall make you free, ye shall be free indeed" (John 8:36), and "Man shall not live by bread alone, but by every word that proceedeth out of the mouth of God" (Matthew 4:4).

Let us therefore hold it for certain and firmly established that the soul can do without everything except the Word of God, without which none at all of its wants is provided for. But, having the Word, it is rich and wants for nothing, since that is the Word of life, of truth, of light, of peace, of justification, of salvation, of joy, of liberty, of wisdom, of virtue, of grace, of glory, and of every good thing. . . .

But you will ask, "What is this Word, and by what means is it to be used, since there are so many words of God?" I answer, "The Apostle Paul (Romans 1) explains what it is, namely the Gospel of God, concerning His Son, incarnate, suffering, risen, and glorified through the Spirit, the Sanctifier." To preach Christ is to feed the soul, to justify it, to set it free, and to save it, if it believes the preaching. For faith alone, and the efficacious use of the Word of God, bring salvation. "If thou shalt confess with thy mouth the Lord Jesus, and shalt believe in thine heart that God hath raised Him from the dead, thou shalt be saved" (Romans 9:9); . . . and "The just shall live by faith" (Romans 1:17). . . .

But this faith cannot consist of all with works; that is, if you imagine that you can be justified by those works, whatever they are, along with it. . . . Therefore, when you begin to believe, you learn at the same time that all that is in you is utterly guilty, sinful, and damnable, according to that saying, "All have sinned, and come short of the glory of God" (Romans 3:23). . . . When you have learned this, you will know that Christ is necessary for you, since He has suffered and risen again for you, that, believing on Him, you might by this faith become another man, all your sins being remitted, and you being justified by the merits of another, namely Christ alone. . . .

And since it [faith] alone justifies, it is evident that by no outward work or labour can the inward man be at all justified, made free, and saved; and that no works whatever have any relation to him. . . . Therefore the first care of every Christian ought to be to lay aside all reliance on works, and strengthen his faith alone more and more, and by it grow in knowledge, not of works, but of Christ Jesus, who has suffered and risen again for him, as Peter teaches (I Peter 5). ”

Source: *Luther's Primary Works*, ed. H. Wace and C. A. Buchheim (London: Holder and Stoughton, 1896). Reprinted in *The Portable Renaissance Reader*, ed. James Bruce Ross and Mary Martin McLaughlin (New York: Penguin Books, 1981), pp. 721–726.

QUESTIONS FOR ANALYSIS

1. What did Luther mean by liberty?
2. Why, for Luther, was scripture basic to Christian life?

Scholars in many disciplines have attributed Luther's fame and success to the invention of the printing press, which rapidly reproduced and made known his ideas. Many printed works included woodcuts and other illustrations, so that even those who could not read could grasp the main ideas. Hymns were also important means of conveying central points of doctrine, as was Luther's translation of the New Testament into German in 1523.

Luther worked closely with political authorities, viewing them as fully justified in reforming the church in their territories. He instructed all Christians to obey their secular rulers, whom he saw as divinely ordained to maintain order. Individuals may have been convinced of the truth of Protestant teachings by hearing sermons, listening to hymns, or reading pamphlets, but a territory became Protestant when its ruler, whether a noble or a city council, brought in a reformer or two to re-educate the territory's clergy, sponsored public sermons, and confiscated church property. This happened in many of the states of the empire during the 1520s and then moved beyond the empire to Denmark-Norway and Sweden.

The Radical Reformation and the German Peasants' War

In the sixteenth century the practice of religion remained a public matter. The ruler determined the official form of religious practice in his (or occasionally her) jurisdiction. Almost everyone believed that the presence of a faith different from that of the majority represented a political threat to the security of the state. Few believed in religious liberty; people with different ideas had to convert or leave.

Some individuals and groups rejected the idea that church and state needed to be united, however, and they sought to create a voluntary community of believers as they understood it to have existed in New Testament times. In terms of theology and spiritual practices, these individuals and groups varied widely, though they are generally termed "radicals" for their insistence on a more extensive break with prevailing ideas. Some adopted the custom of baptizing adult believers — for which they were given the title of "Anabaptists" or rebaptizers by their enemies — while others saw all outward sacraments or rituals as misguided. Some groups attempted communal ownership of property, living very simply and rejecting anything they thought unbiblical. Some reacted harshly to members who deviated from the group's accepted practices, but others argued for complete religious tolerance and individualism.

Religious radicals were met with fanatical hatred and bitter persecution, including banishment and execution. Both Protestant and Catholic authorities felt threatened by the social, political, and economic implications of radicals' religious ideas and by their rejection of a state church, which the authorities saw as key to maintaining order. Their community spirit and heroism in the face of martyrdom, however, contributed to the survival of radical ideas. Later, the Quakers, with their pacifism; the Baptists, with their emphasis on inner spiritual light; the Congregationalists, with their democratic church organization; and, in 1787, the authors of the U.S. Constitution, with their opposition to the "establishment of religion" (state churches), would all trace the origins of their beliefs, in part, to the radicals of the sixteenth century.

Another group to challenge state authorities was the peasantry. In the early sixteenth century the economic condition of peasants varied from place to place but was generally worse than it had been in the fifteenth century and was deteriorating. Peasants demanded limitations on the new taxes and labor obligations their noble landlords were imposing. They believed that their demands conformed to the Scriptures and cited Luther as a theologian who could prove that they did.

Wanting to prevent rebellion, Luther initially sided with the peasants, blasting the lords for robbing their subjects. But when rebellion broke out, the peasants who expected Luther's support were soon disillusioned. Freedom for Luther meant independence from the authority of the Roman Church, not opposition to legally established secular powers. Firmly convinced that rebellion would hasten the end of civilized society, he wrote the tract *Against the Murderous, Thieving Hordes of the Peasants*, which said, in part, "Let everyone who can smite, slay, and stab [the peasants], secretly and openly, remembering that nothing can be more poisonous, hurtful or devilish than a rebel."[5] The nobility ferociously crushed the revolt, which became known as the German Peasants' War of 1525. That year, historians estimate, more than seventy-five thousand peasants were killed.

The Peasants' War greatly strengthened the authority of lay rulers. Because Luther turned against the peasants who revolted, the Reformation lost much of its popular appeal after 1525, though peasants and urban rebels sometimes found a place for their social and religious ideas in radical groups. Peasants' economic conditions did moderately improve, however. For example, in many parts of Germany enclosed fields, meadows, and forests were returned to common use instead of being controlled by noble landlords.

Marriage and Women's Roles

Luther and other Protestants believed that a priest's or nun's vows of celibacy went against human nature and God's commandments. Luther married a former nun, Katharina von Bora (1499–1532), who quickly had several children. Most other Protestant reformers also married, and their wives had to create a new and respectable role for themselves — pastor's wife — to overcome being viewed as simply a new type of priest's concubine. They were living demonstrations of their husband's convictions about the superiority of marriage to celibacy, and they were expected to be models of wifely obedience and Christian charity.

Catholics viewed marriage as a sacramental union that, if validly entered into, could not be dissolved. Protestants saw marriage as a contract in which each partner promised the other support, companionship, and the sharing of mutual goods. They believed that spouses who did not comfort or support one another endangered their own souls and the surrounding community; therefore, most Protestants came to allow divorce. Divorce remained rare, however, because marriage was such an important social and economic institution.

Protestants did not break with medieval scholastic theologians in their view that, within marriage, women were to be subject to men. Women were advised to be cheerful rather than grudging in their obedience, for in doing so they demonstrated their willingness to follow God's plan. Men were urged to treat their wives kindly and considerately, but also to enforce their authority, through physical coercion if necessary. Both continental and English marriage manuals use the metaphor of breaking a horse for teaching a wife obedience, though laws did set limits on the husband's power to control his wife. A few women took the Protestant idea about the priesthood of all believers to heart and wrote religious pamphlets and hymns, but no sixteenth-century Protestants officially allowed women to hold positions of religious authority. Monarchs such as Elizabeth I of England and female territorial rulers of the states of the Holy Roman Empire did determine religious policies, however.

Because the Reformation generally brought the closing of monasteries and convents, marriage became virtually the only occupation for upper-class Protestant women. Recognizing this, women in some convents fought the Reformation or argued that they could still be pious Protestants within convent walls. Most nuns left, however, and we do not know what happened to them. The Protestant emphasis on marriage made unmarried women (and men) suspect, for they did not belong to the type of household regarded as the cornerstone of a proper, godly society.

The Reformation and German Politics

Criticism of the church was widespread in Europe in the early sixteenth century, and calls for reform came from many areas. Yet such movements could be more easily squelched by the strong central governments of Spain, France, and England. The Holy Roman Empire, in contrast, included hundreds of largely independent states in which the emperor had far less authority than did the monarchs of western Europe. Thus local rulers of the many states in the empire continued to exercise great power.

Luther's ideas appealed to local rulers within the empire for a variety of reasons. Though Germany was not a nation, people did have an understanding of being German because of their language and traditions. Luther frequently used the phrase "we Germans" in his attacks on the papacy, and his appeal to national feeling influenced many rulers. Also, while some German rulers were sincerely attracted to Lutheran ideas, material considerations swayed many others to embrace the new faith. The rejection of Roman Catholicism and the adoption of Protestantism would mean the legal confiscation of lush farmlands, rich monasteries, and wealthy shrines owned by monasteries, bishops, and other officials. Thus many political authorities in the empire used the religious issue to extend their financial and political power and to enhance their independence from the emperor.

The Habsburg Charles V, elected as emperor in 1521, was a vigorous defender of Catholicism, so it is

Martin Luther and Katharina von Bora Lucas Cranach the Elder painted this double marriage portrait to celebrate Luther's wedding in 1525 to Katharina von Bora, a former nun. The artist was one of the witnesses at the wedding and, in fact, had presented Luther's marriage proposal to Katharina. The couple quickly became a model of the ideal marriage, and many churches wanted their portraits. More than sixty similar paintings, with slight variations, were produced by Cranach's workshop and hung in churches and wealthy homes. (Painting by Lucas Cranach the Elder [1472–1553], oil on wood/Galleria degli Uffizi, Florence, Italy/akg-images)

not surprising that the Reformation led to religious wars. Protestant territories in the empire formed military alliances, and the emperor could not oppose them effectively given other military engagements. In southeastern Europe Habsburg troops were already fighting the Ottoman Turks, who were expanding their holdings at just the point that the Reformation began. Habsburg soldiers were also engaged in a series of wars with the Valois (VAL-wah) kings of France. The cornerstone of French foreign policy in the sixteenth and seventeenth centuries was the desire to keep the German states divided. Thus Europe witnessed the paradox of the Catholic king of France supporting Lutheran princes in their challenge to his fellow Catholic, Charles V. The Habsburg-Valois wars advanced the cause of Protestantism and promoted the political fragmentation of the German Empire.

Finally, in 1555, Charles agreed to the Peace of Augsburg, which officially recognized Lutheranism and ended religious war in Germany for many decades. Under this treaty, the political authority in each territory of the Holy Roman Empire was permitted to decide whether the territory would be Catholic or Lutheran. Most of northern and central Germany became Lutheran, while southern Germany was divided between Lutheran and Catholic. His hope of uniting his empire under a single church dashed, Charles V abdicated in 1556, transferring power over his Spanish and Netherlandish holdings to his son Philip II and his imperial power to his brother Ferdinand.

England's Shift Toward Protestantism

States within the Holy Roman Empire and the kingdom of Denmark-Norway were the earliest territories to accept the Protestant Reformation, but by the later 1520s religious change had also come to England, France, and eastern Europe. In all these areas, a second generation of reformers, most prominently John Calvin (see below), built on earlier ideas to develop their own theology and plans for institutional change.

As on the continent, the Reformation in England had economic and political as well as religious causes. The impetus for England's break with Rome was the desire of King Henry VIII (r. 1509–1547) for a new wife. When the personal matter of his need to divorce his first wife became enmeshed with political issues, a complete break with Rome resulted.

In 1527, after eighteen years of marriage, Henry's wife Catherine of Aragon had failed to produce a male child, and Henry had also fallen in love with a court lady in waiting, Anne Boleyn. So Henry petitioned Pope Clement VII for an annulment of his marriage to Catherine. When the pope procrastinated in granting the annulment, Henry decided to remove the English Church from papal authority. In this way, he was able to get the annulment and marry Anne.

Henry used Parliament to legalize the Reformation in England and to make himself the supreme head of the Church of England. Some opposed the king and were beheaded, among them Thomas More, the king's chancellor and author of *Utopia* (see page 429). Anne had a daughter, Elizabeth, but failed to produce a son, so Henry VIII charged her with adulterous incest and in 1536 had her beheaded. His third wife, Jane Seymour, gave Henry the desired son, Edward, but she died a few days after childbirth. Henry went on to three more wives.

Between 1535 and 1539, influenced by his chief minister, Thomas Cromwell, Henry decided to dissolve the English monasteries primarily because he wanted their wealth. Hundreds of former church properties were sold to the middle and upper classes, strengthening the upper classes and tying them to the Tudor dynasty, to which Henry belonged. How did everyday people react to Henry's break from the Catholic Church? Recent scholarship points out that people rarely "converted" from Catholicism to Protestantism overnight. Instead they responded to the local consequences of the shift from Catholicism—for example, the closing of a monastery, the ending of Masses for the dead—with a combination of resistance, acceptance, and collaboration.

Loyalty to the Catholic Church remained particularly strong in Ireland. Ireland had been claimed by English kings since the twelfth century, but in reality the English had firm control of only the area around Dublin known as the Pale. In 1536, on orders from London, the Irish Parliament, which represented only the English landlords and the people of the Pale, approved the English laws severing the church from Rome. The (English) ruling class adopted the new reformed faith, but most of the Irish people remained Roman Catholic. Irish armed opposition to the Reformation led to harsh repression by the English, thus adding religious antagonism to the ethnic hostility that had been a feature of English policy toward Ireland for centuries.

In the short reign of Henry's sickly son Edward VI (r. 1547–1553), strongly Protestant ideas exerted a significant influence on the religious life of the country. The equally brief reign of Mary Tudor (r. 1553–1558), the devoutly Catholic daughter of Catherine of Aragon, witnessed a sharp move back to Catholicism, and many Protestants fled to the continent. Mary's death raised to the throne her half sister Elizabeth (r. 1558–1603) and inaugurated the beginning of religious stability.

Elizabeth had been raised a Protestant, but at the start of her reign sharp differences existed in England. On the one hand, Catholics wanted a Roman Catholic ruler. On the other hand, a vocal number of returning

Viewpoints 15.2

Wang Yangming and John Calvin Encourage Proper Behavior

• *Protestant reformers in Europe had clear ideas about virtuous behavior and how to encourage it, and the same was true of Neo-Confucian scholar-officials in China (see page 369). The reformer John Calvin designed ordinances for the city of Geneva that regulated public and family life, while in China the official and military leader Wang Yangming (1472–1529) called for "community compacts," agreements between community members in which all pledged to act in a moral fashion.*

Wang Yangming, Community Compact for Southern Ganzhou, 1520s

"Nothing can be done to change what has already gone by, but something can still be done in the future. Therefore a community compact is now specially prepared to unite and harmonize all of you.

From now on, all of you who enter into this compact should be filial to your parents and respectful to your elders, teach your children, live in harmony with your fellow villagers, help one another when there is death in the family and assist one another in times of difficulty, encourage one another to do good and warn one another not to do evil, stop litigations and rivalry, cultivate faithfulness and promote harmony, and be sure to be good citizens so that together you may establish the custom of humanity and kindness. . . .

Elect from the compact membership an elderly and virtuous person respected by all to be the compact chief and two persons to be assistant chiefs [and other officials]. . . . Have three record books. One of these is to record the names of compact members and their daily movements and activities, and is to be in the charge of the compact executives. Of the remaining record books, one is for the purpose of displaying good deeds and the other for the purpose of reporting evil deeds. . . . To display good deeds, the language used must be clear and decisive, but in reporting mistakes, the language must be indirect and gentle."

John Calvin, Ecclesiastical Ordinances for the City of Geneva, 1541

"[The office of the elders appointed to the Consistory] is to keep watch over the lives of everyone, to admonish in love those whom they see in error and leading disorderly lives. Whenever necessary they shall make a report concerning these to the ministers who will be designated to make brotherly corrections. . . .

If the church deems it wise, it will be well to choose two from the Little Council, four from the Council of Two Hundred, honest men of good demeanor, without reproach and free from all suspicion, above all fearing God and possessed of good and spiritual judgment. It will be well to elect them from every part of the city so as to be able to maintain supervision over all. . . .

If there shall be anyone who lays down opinions contrary to received doctrine, he is to be summoned. If he recants, he is to be dismissed without prejudice. If he is stubborn, he is to be admonished from time to time until it shall be evident that he deserves greater severity. . . .

If anyone is negligent in attending worship so that a noticeable offense is evident for the communion of the faithful, or if anyone shows himself contemptuous of ecclesiastical discipline, he is to be admonished. . . .

For the correction of faults, it is necessary to proceed after the ordinance of our Lord. That is, vices are to be dealt with secretly and no one is to be brought before the church for accusation if the fault is neither public nor scandalous, unless he has been found rebellious in the matter. . . .

Let all these measures be moderate; let there not be such a degree of rigor that anyone should be cast down, for all corrections are but medicinal, to bring back sinners to the Lord."

QUESTIONS FOR ANALYSIS

1. What types of actions do Wang and Calvin encourage and discourage?
2. What similarities and differences do you see in the institutions and procedures Wang and Calvin established to enforce proper conduct?
3. How do these documents reflect Confucian and Protestant Christian values and ideals?

exiles wanted all Catholic elements in the Church of England eliminated. Members of the latter group, because they wanted to "purify" the church, were called "Puritans." Shrewdly, Elizabeth chose a middle course between Catholic and Puritan extremes. She referred to herself as the "supreme governor of the Church of England," which allowed Catholics to remain loyal to her without denying the pope. She required her subjects to attend church or risk a fine but did not interfere with their privately held beliefs. The Anglican Church, as the Church of England was called, moved in a moderately Protestant direction.

Calvinism and Its Moral Standards

In 1509, while Luther was preparing for a doctorate at Wittenberg, John Calvin (1509–1564) was born in Noyon in northwestern France. As a young man he studied law, but in 1533 he experienced a religious crisis, as a result of which he converted from Catholicism to Protestantism. Calvin believed that God had specifically selected him to reform the church. Accordingly, he accepted an invitation to assist in the reformation of the city of Geneva. There, beginning in 1541, Calvin worked assiduously to establish a Christian society ruled by God through civil magistrates and reformed ministers. Geneva thereby became the model of a Christian community for sixteenth-century Protestant reformers.

To understand Calvin's Geneva, it is necessary to understand Calvin's ideas. These he embodied in *The Institutes of the Christian Religion*, first published in 1536 and modified several times afterward. The cornerstone of Calvin's theology was his belief in the absolute sovereignty and omnipotence of God and the total weakness of humanity. Before the infinite power of God, he asserted, men and women are as insignificant as grains of sand.

Calvin did not ascribe free will to human beings, because that would detract from the sovereignty of God. According to his beliefs, men and women could not actively work to achieve salvation; rather, God decided at the beginning of time who would be saved and who damned. This viewpoint constitutes the theological principle called **predestination**. Many people consider the doctrine of predestination, which dates back to Saint Augustine and Saint Paul, to be a pessimistic view of the nature of God. But "this terrible decree," as even Calvin called it, did not lead to pessimism or fatalism. Instead, although Calvinists believed that one's own actions could do nothing to change one's fate, many came to believe that hard work, thrift, and moral conduct could serve as signs that one was among the "elect" chosen for salvation. Any occupation or profession could be a God-given "calling" and should be carried out with diligence and dedication.

Calvin transformed Geneva into a community based on his religious principles. The most powerful organization in the city became the Consistory, a group of laymen and pastors charged with investigating and disciplining deviations from proper doctrine and conduct. (See "Viewpoints 15.2: Wang Yangming and John Calvin Encourage Proper Behavior," page 447.)

Religious refugees from France, England, Spain, Scotland, and Italy visited Calvin's Geneva, which became the model of a Christian community for many. Subsequently, the Reformed Church of Calvin served as the model for the Presbyterian Church in Scotland, the Huguenot (HYOO-guh-naht) Church in France, and the Puritan Churches in England and New England. Calvinism became the compelling force in international Protestantism, first in Europe and then in many Dutch and English colonies around the world.

• **predestination** Calvin's teaching that, by God's decree, some persons are guided to salvation and others to damnation; that God has called people not according to their works but according to his purpose and grace.

The Catholic Reformation

□ How did the Catholic Church respond to the new religious situation?

Between 1517 and 1547 Protestantism made remarkable advances. Nevertheless, the Roman Catholic Church made a significant comeback. After about 1540 no new large areas of Europe, other than the Netherlands, accepted Protestant beliefs (Map 15.2). Many historians see the developments within the Catholic Church after the Protestant Reformation as two interrelated movements, one a drive for internal reform linked to earlier reform efforts, and the other a Counter-Reformation that opposed Protestants intellectually, politically, militarily, and institutionally. In both movements, papal reforms and new religious orders were important agents.

Papal Reforms and the Council of Trent

Renaissance popes and advisers were not blind to the need for church reforms, but they resisted calls for a general council representing the entire church, fearing loss of power, revenue, and prestige. This changed beginning with Pope Paul III (pontificate 1534–1549), under whom the papal court became the center of the reform movement rather than its chief opponent.

In 1542 Pope Paul III established the Supreme Sacred Congregation of the Roman and Universal Inquisition, often called the Holy Office, with jurisdiction over the Roman Inquisition, a powerful instrument of the Catholic Reformation. The Inquisition was a committee of six cardinals with judicial authority over all Catholics and the power to arrest, imprison, and execute. Within the Papal States, the Inquisition effectively destroyed heresy (and some heretics).

Pope Paul III also called a general council, which met intermittently from 1545 to 1563 at Trent, an imperial city close to Italy. It was called not only to reform the church but also to secure reconciliation with the Protestants. Lutherans and Calvinists were invited to participate, but their insistence that the Scriptures be the sole basis for discussion made reconciliation impossible.

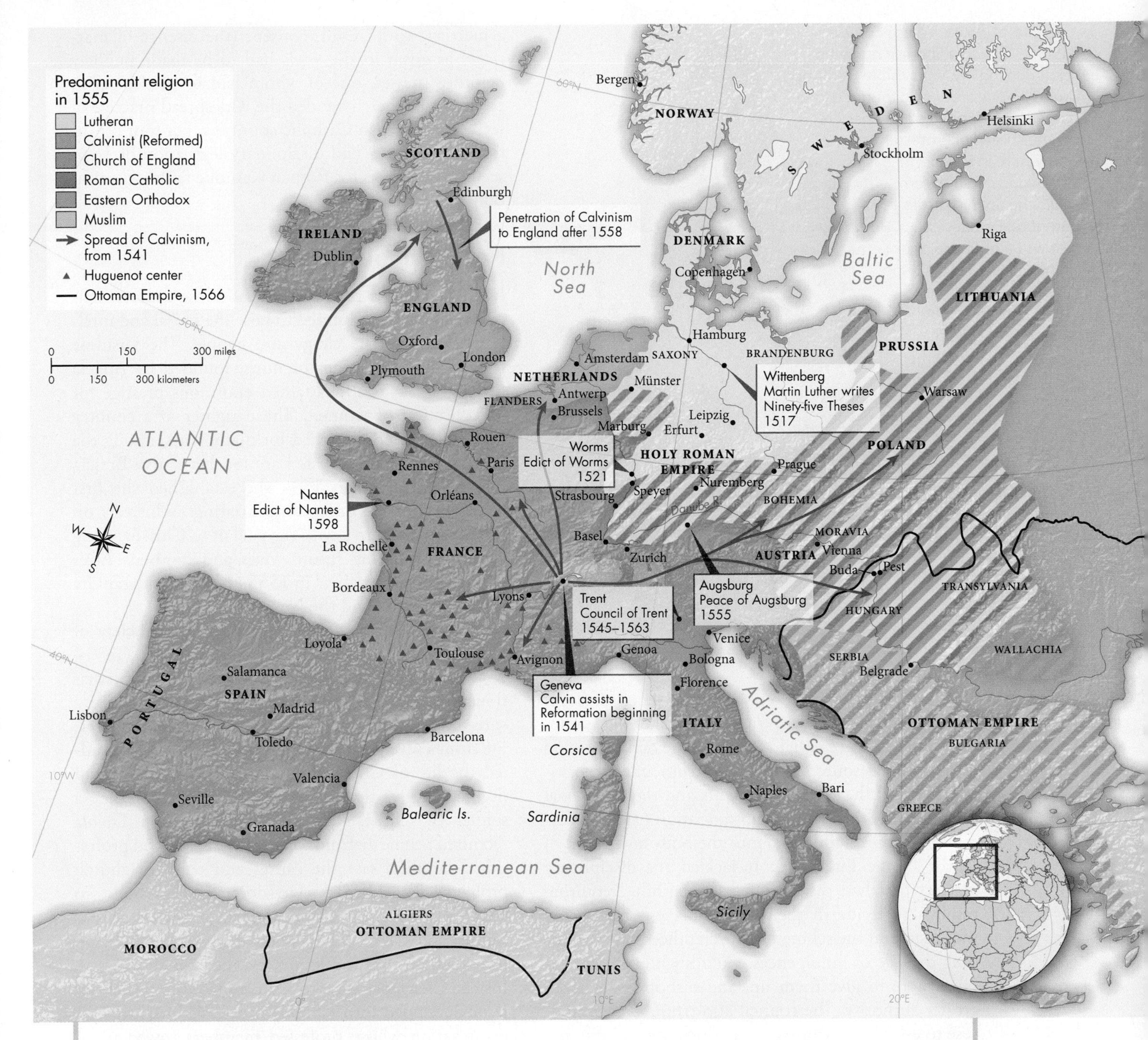

Mapping the Past

MAP 15.2 Religious Divisions in Europe, ca. 1555 The Reformation shattered the religious unity of Western Christendom. The situation was even more complicated than a map of this scale can show. Many cities within the Holy Roman Empire, for example, accepted a different faith than did the surrounding countryside; Augsburg, Basel, and Strasbourg were all Protestant, though surrounded by territory ruled by Catholic nobles.

ANALYZING THE MAP Which countries in Europe were the most religiously diverse? Which were the least diverse?

CONNECTIONS Where was the first arena of religious conflict in Europe, and why did it develop there and not elsewhere? What nonreligious factors contributed to the religious divisions that developed in sixteenth-century Europe, and to what degree can they explain these divisions?

Teresa of Ávila Teresa of Ávila (1515–1582) was a Spanish nun who experienced mystical visions, reformed her religious order, and founded new convents, seeing them as answers to the spread of Protestantism elsewhere in Europe. In this wood carving from 1625, the Spanish artist Gregorio Fernandez shows Saint Teresa book in hand, actively teaching. The influence of her ideas and actions led the pope to give Teresa the title "Doctor of the Church" in 1970, the first woman to be so honored. (Gregorio Fernandez [1576–1636], *Saint Teresa of Ávila*, 1625. Polychromatic Baroque carving on wood, Valladolid, Spain. National Museum of Sculpture/ © P. Rotger/Iberfoto/The Image Works)

Nonetheless, the decrees of the Council of Trent laid a solid basis for the spiritual renewal of the Catholic Church. It gave equal validity to the Scriptures and to tradition as sources of religious truth and authority. It reaffirmed the seven sacraments and the traditional Catholic teaching on transubstantiation (the transformation of bread and wine into the body and blood of Christ in the Eucharist). It tackled the disciplinary matters that had disillusioned the faithful, requiring bishops to reside in their own dioceses, suppressing pluralism and the selling of church offices, and forbidding the sale of indulgences. Clerics who kept concubines were to give them up, and bishops were given greater authority. The council also required every diocese to establish a seminary for educating and training clergy. Seminary professors were to determine whether candidates for ordination had vocations, genuine callings to the priesthood. This was a novel idea, since from the time of the early church, parents had determined their sons' (and daughters') religious careers. Finally, great emphasis was placed on preaching to and instructing the laity, especially the uneducated. One decision had especially important social consequences for laypeople. The Council of Trent stipulated that for a marriage to be valid, consent (the essence of marriage) as given in the vows had to be made publicly before witnesses, one of whom had to be the parish priest. Trent thereby ended the widespread practice of secret marriages in Catholic countries. For four centuries the doctrinal and disciplinary legislation of Trent served as the basis for Roman Catholic faith, organization, and practice.

New Religious Orders

Just as seminaries provided education, so did new religious orders, which aimed to raise the moral and intellectual level of the clergy and people. The Ursuline (UHR-suh-luhn) order of nuns, founded by Angela Merici (1474–1540), attained enormous prestige for its education of women. The daughter of a country gentleman, Merici worked for many years among the poor, sick, and uneducated around her native Brescia in northern Italy. In 1535 she established the first women's religious order concentrating exclusively on teaching young girls, with the goal of re-Christianizing society by training future wives and mothers. After receiving papal approval in 1565, the Ursulines rapidly spread to France and the New World.

Another important new order was the Society of Jesus, or **Jesuits**. Founded by Ignatius Loyola (1491–1556) in 1540, this order played a powerful international role in strengthening Catholicism in Europe and spreading the faith around the world. While recuperating from a severe battle wound in his legs, Loyola studied the life of Christ and other religious books and decided to give up his military career and become a soldier of Christ. The first Jesuits, whom Loyola recruited primarily from wealthy merchant and professional families, saw the causes and cures of church problems as related not to doctrinal issues but to people's spiritual condition. Reform of the church, as Luther and Calvin understood that term, played no role in the future the Jesuits planned for themselves. Instead their goal was "to help souls." The Society of Jesus developed into a highly centralized, tightly knit organization whose professed members vowed to go anywhere the pope said they were needed. They established schools that adopted the modern humanist curricula and methods and that educated the sons of the nobility as well as the poor. The Jesuits attracted many recruits and achieved phenomenal success for the papacy and the reformed Catholic Church, carrying Christianity to much of South and Central America, India, and Japan before 1550 and to Brazil, North America, and the Congo in the seventeenth century. Within Europe the Jesuits brought almost all of southern Germany and much of eastern Europe back to Catholicism. Also, as confessors and spiritual directors to kings, Jesuits exerted great political influence.

- **Jesuits** Members of the Society of Jesus, founded by Ignatius Loyola and approved by the papacy in 1540, whose goal was the spread of the Roman Catholic faith through humanistic schools and missionary activity.

Religious Violence

☐ What were the causes and consequences of religious violence, including riots, wars, and witch-hunts?

In 1559 France and Spain signed the Treaty of Cateau-Cambrésis, which ended the long conflict known as the Habsburg-Valois wars. However, over the next century religious differences led to riots, civil wars, and international conflicts. Especially in France and the Netherlands, Protestants and Catholics opposed one another through preaching, teaching, and violence, for each side regarded the other as a poison in the community that would provoke the wrath of God. Catholics and Protestants alike feared people of other faiths, whom they often saw as agents of Satan. Even more, they feared those explicitly identified with Satan: people believed to be witches. This era saw the most virulent witch persecutions in European history, as both Protestants and Catholics tried to make their cities and states more godly.

French Religious Wars

The costs of the Habsburg-Valois wars, waged intermittently through the first half of the sixteenth century, forced the French to increase taxes and borrow heavily. King Francis I's treaty with the pope (see page 437) gave the French crown a rich supplement of money and offices and also a vested financial interest in Catholicism. Significant numbers of French people, however, were attracted to the "reformed religion," as Calvinism was called. Calvinism drew converts from among reform-minded members of the Catholic clergy, the industrious middle classes, and artisan groups. Additionally, some French nobles became Calvinist, either because of religious conviction or because this allowed them to oppose the monarchy. By the middle of the sixteenth century perhaps one-tenth of the French population had become **Huguenots**, the name given to French Calvinists.

Both Calvinists and Catholics believed that the others' books, services, and ministers polluted the community. Preachers communicated these ideas in sermons, triggering violence at the baptisms, marriages, and funerals of the other faith. Armed clashes between Catholic royalist nobles and Calvinist antimonarchical nobles occurred in many parts of France.

Calvinist teachings called the power of sacred images into question, and mobs in many cities destroyed statues, stained-glass windows, and paintings. Though it was often inspired by fiery Protestant sermons, this iconoclasm is an example of men and women carrying out the Reformation themselves, rethinking the church's system of meaning. Catholic mobs responded by defending the sacred images, and crowds on both sides killed their opponents, often in gruesome ways.

A savage Catholic attack on Calvinists in Paris on August 24, 1572—Saint Bartholomew's Day—followed the usual pattern. The occasion was the marriage of the king's sister Margaret of Valois to the Protestant Henry of Navarre, which was intended to help reconcile Catholics and Huguenots. Instead Huguenot wedding guests in Paris were massacred, and other Protestants were slaughtered by mobs. Violence spread to the provinces, where thousands were killed. The Saint Bartholomew's Day massacre led to a civil war that dragged on for fifteen years. As a result, agriculture in many areas was destroyed, commercial life declined severely, and starvation and death haunted the land.

What ultimately saved France was a small group of moderates of both faiths called **politiques** (POH-lee-teeks) who believed that only the restoration of a strong monarchy could reverse the trend toward collapse. The politiques also favored officially recognizing the Huguenots. The death of the French queen Catherine de' Medici, followed by the assassination of her son King Henry III, paved the way for the accession of Henry of Navarre (the unfortunate bridegroom of the Saint Bartholomew's Day massacre), a politique who became Henry IV (r. 1589–1610).

Henry's willingness to sacrifice religious principles to political necessity saved France. He converted to Catholicism but also, in 1598, issued the Edict of Nantes (nahnt), which granted liberty of conscience (freedom of thought) and liberty of public worship to Huguenots in 150 fortified towns. By helping restore internal peace in France, the reign of Henry IV and the Edict of Nantes paved the way for French kings to claim absolute power in the seventeenth century.

Civil Wars in the Netherlands

In the Netherlands a movement for church reform developed into a struggle for Dutch independence. The Catholic emperor Charles V had inherited the seventeen provinces that compose present-day Belgium and the Netherlands (see page 439). In the Netherlands, as elsewhere, corruption in the Roman Catholic Church and the critical spirit of the Renaissance provoked pressure for reform, and Lutheran ideas took root. Charles V had grown up in the Netherlands, however, and he was able to limit the impact of the new ideas. Charles V abdicated in 1556 and transferred power over the Netherlands to his son Philip II, who had grown up in Spain. Although Philip, like his father,

- **Huguenots** French Calvinists.
- **politiques** Catholic and Protestant moderates who sought to end the religious violence in France by restoring a strong monarchy and granting official recognition to the Huguenots.

Chapter Summary

The Renaissance was characterized by self-conscious awareness among educated Europeans, particularly scholars and writers known as humanists, that they were living in a new era. Central to humanists were interest in the Latin classics, belief in individual potential, education for a career of public service, and, in northern Europe, the reform of church and society. Their ideas spread as a result of the development of the printing press with movable metal type, which revolutionized communication. Interest in the classical past and in the individual shaped Renaissance art in terms of style and subject matter, and patrons provided the money needed for an outpouring of painting, sculpture, and architecture. Social hierarchies in the Renaissance developed new features that contributed to the modern social hierarchies of race, class, and gender. In politics, feudal monarchies gradually evolved into nation-states, as rulers used war, diplomacy, new forms of taxation, centralized institutions, and strategic marital alliances to build up their power.

Many individuals and groups had long called for reforms in the Catholic Church, providing a ready audience in the early sixteenth century for the ideas of Martin Luther, a German priest and university professor. Luther and other reformers, called Protestants, developed a new understanding of Christian doctrine that emphasized faith and grace; Protestant ideas spread rapidly through preaching, hymns, and the printing press; and soon western Europe was split religiously. Local situations influenced religious patterns. In England the king's need for a church-approved divorce triggered the break with Rome, while in France and eastern Europe the ideas of John Calvin gained wide acceptance, especially among middle-class people and nobles. The Roman Catholic Church responded slowly to the Protestant challenge, but by the middle of the sixteenth century it had begun a process of internal reform along with opposing Protestants intellectually, politically, militarily, and institutionally. This reinvigorated Catholic Church would carry Christian ideas around the world, while in Europe religious differences led to riots, witch persecutions, civil wars, and international conflicts.

NOTES

1. Niccolò Machiavelli, *The Prince*, trans. Leo Paul S. de Alvarez (Prospect Heights, Ill.: Waveland Press, 1980), p. 101.
2. Stuttgart, Württembergische Hauptstaatsarchiv, General-reskripta, A38, Bü. 2, 1550, trans. Merry Wiesner-Hanks.
3. Quoted in Benzion Netanyahu, *The Origins of the Inquisition in Fifteenth Century Spain* (New York: Random House, 1995), p. 921.
4. Quoted in E. H. Harbison, *The Age of Reformation* (Ithaca, N.Y.: Cornell University Press, 1963), p. 52.
5. Quoted ibid., p. 284.

CONNECTIONS

The Renaissance and the Reformation are often seen as key to the creation of the modern world. The radical changes of these times contained many elements of continuity, however. Artists, humanists, and religious reformers looked back to the classical era and early Christianity for inspiration, viewing those times as better and purer than their own. Political leaders played important roles in cultural and religious developments, just as they had for centuries in Europe and other parts of the world.

The events of the Renaissance and Reformation were thus linked with earlier developments, and they were also closely connected with another important element in the modern world: European exploration and colonization (discussed in Chapter 16). Renaissance monarchs paid for expeditions' ships, crews, and supplies, expecting a large share of any profits gained and increasingly viewing overseas territory as essential to a strong state. Only a week after Martin Luther stood in front of Charles V at the Diet of Worms declaring his independence in matters of religion, Ferdinand Magellan, a Portuguese sea captain using Spanish ships, was killed by indigenous people in a group of islands off the coast of Southeast Asia. Charles V had provided the backing for Magellan's voyage, the first to circumnavigate the globe. Magellan viewed one of the purposes of his trip as the spread of Christianity, and later in the sixteenth century institutions created as part of the Catholic Reformation, including the Jesuit order and the Inquisition, would operate in European colonies overseas as well as in Europe itself. The islands where Magellan was killed were later named the Philippines, in honor of Charles's son Philip, who sent the ill-fated Spanish Armada against England. The desire for fame, wealth, and power that was central to the Renaissance, and the religious zeal central to the Reformation, were thus key to the European voyages and to colonial ventures as well.

Review and Explore

Make It Stick

LearningCurve
Go online and use LearningCurve to retain what you've read.

Identify Key Terms

Identify and explain the significance of each item below.

Renaissance (p. 426)
patronage (p. 427)
humanism (p. 427)
Christian humanists (p. 429)
debate about women (p. 435)
Protestant Reformation (p. 439)
indulgence (p. 440)
Diet of Worms (p. 440)
Protestant (p. 441)
predestination (p. 448)
Jesuits (p. 450)
Huguenots (p. 451)
politiques (p. 451)
witch-hunts (p. 452)

Review the Main Ideas

Answer the focus questions from each section of the chapter.

1. What were the major cultural developments of the Renaissance? (p. 426)
2. What were the key social hierarchies in Renaissance Europe, and how did these hierarchies shape people's lives? (p. 434)
3. How did the nation-states of western Europe evolve in this period? (p. 437)
4. What were the central ideas of Protestant reformers, and why were they appealing to various groups across Europe? (p. 439)
5. How did the Catholic Church respond to the new religious situation? (p. 448)
6. What were the causes and consequences of religious violence, including riots, wars, and witch-hunts? (p. 451)

Make Connections

Analyze the larger developments and continuities within and across chapters.

1. The word *Renaissance*, invented to describe the cultural flowering in Italy that began in the fifteenth century, has often been used for other periods of advance in learning and the arts, such as the "Carolingian Renaissance" that you read about in Chapter 8. Can you think of other, more recent "Renaissances" or ways the term is used today?
2. The "debate about women" was not simply a European phenomenon, as educated men (and occasionally a few educated women) in many cultures discussed women's nature and character. How would you compare ideas about women in classical Islamic society (Chapter 9), Song China (Chapter 13), Heian Japan (Chapter 13), Renaissance Italy, and Protestant Germany? How were these ideas reflected (or not reflected) in women's actual lives?
3. Martin Luther is always on every list of the one hundred most influential people of all time. Should he be? Why or why not? Who else from this chapter should be on such a list, and why?

LaunchPad
Online Document Project

Cosimo and Lorenzo de' Medici

What role did patrons play in shaping Renaissance artistic and intellectual life?

Examine paintings and letters by Renaissance artists, and then complete a quiz and writing assignment based on the evidence and details from this chapter.

See inside the front cover to learn more.

Suggested Reading

Bethencourt, Francisco. *The Inquisition: A Global History, 1478–1834.* 2009. A comprehensive study that examines the Inquisition in Spain, Portugal, Italy, and the Iberian empires overseas.

Cameron, Euan. *The European Reformation*, 2d ed. 2012. A thorough analysis of the Protestant and Catholic Reformations throughout Europe.

Earle, T. F., and K. J. P. Lowe, eds. *Black Africans in Renaissance Europe*. 2005. Includes essays discussing many aspects of ideas about race and the experience of Africans in Europe.

Ertman, Thomas. *The Birth of Leviathan: Building States and Regimes in Medieval and Early Modern Europe*. 1997. A good introduction to the creation of nation-states.

Hendrix, Scott. *Luther*. 2009. A brief introduction to his thought; part of the Abingdon Pillars of Theology series.

Hsia, R. Po-Chia. *The World of Catholic Renewal, 1540–1770*, 2d ed. 2005. Situates the Catholic Reformation in a global context and examines colonial Catholicism.

Johnson, Geraldine. *Renaissance Art: A Very Short Introduction*. 2005. Excellent brief survey that includes male and female artists and sets the art in its cultural and historical context.

Levack, Brian. *The Witch-Hunt in Early Modern Europe*, 3d ed. 2007. A good introduction to the vast literature on witchcraft, with helpful bibliographies.

Man, John. *Gutenberg Revolution: The Story of a Genius and an Invention That Changed the World*. 2002. Presents a rather idealized view of Gutenberg but has good discussions of his milieu and excellent illustrations.

Matheson, Peter, ed. *Reformation Christianity.* 2004. This volume in the People's History of Christianity series explores social issues and popular religion.

Nauert, Charles. *Humanism and the Culture of Renaissance Europe*, 2d ed. 2006. A thorough introduction to humanism throughout Europe.

Waley, Daniel, and Trevor Dean. *The Italian City-Republics*, 4th ed. 2010. Analyzes the rise of independent city-states in northern Italy, including discussion of the artistic and social lives of their inhabitants.

Wiesner-Hanks, Merry E. *Women and Gender in Early Modern Europe*, 3d ed. 2008. Discusses all aspects of women's lives as well as ideas about gender.

The Acceleration of Global Contact

1450–1600

16

Nezahualpilli

At the time of the arrival of Europeans, Nezahualpilli was ruler of the city-state of Texcoco, the second most important city in the Aztec Empire after Tenochtitlan. (Nezahualpilli, portrait from *Codex Ixtlilxochitl*, 1582, pigment on European paper/Bibliothèque Nationale, Paris, France/De Agostini Picture Library/akg-images)

hundreds of ships and tens of thousands of men (see page 639). In one voyage alone, Zheng sailed more than 12,000 miles, compared to Columbus's 2,400 miles on his first voyage some sixty years later.[2] Although the ships brought back many wonders, such as giraffes and zebras, the purpose of the voyages was primarily diplomatic, to enhance China's prestige and seek tribute-paying alliances. The high expense of the voyages in a period of renewed Mongol encroachment led to the abandonment of the maritime expeditions after the deaths of Zheng He and the emperor.

China's decision to forego large-scale exploration was a decisive turning point in world history, one that left an opening for European states to expand their role in Asian trade. Nonetheless, Zheng He's voyages left a legacy of increased Chinese trading in the South China Sea and Indian Ocean. Following Zheng He's voyages, tens of thousands of Chinese emigrated to the Philippines, where they acquired commercial dominance of the island of Luzon by 1600.

Another center of Indian Ocean trade was India, the crucial link between the Persian Gulf and the Southeast Asian and East Asian trade networks. The subcontinent had ancient links with its neighbors to the northwest: trade between South Asia and Mesopotamia dates back to the origins of human civilization. Trade among ports bordering the Indian Ocean was revived in the Middle Ages by Arab merchants who circumnavigated India on their way to trade in the South China Sea. The need for stopovers led to the establishment of trading posts at Gujarat and on the Malabar coast, where the cities of Calicut and Quilon became thriving commercial centers.

The inhabitants of India's Coromandel coast traditionally looked to Southeast Asia, where they had ancient trading and cultural ties. Hinduism and Buddhism arrived in Southeast Asia from India during the Middle Ages, and a brisk trade between Southeast Asian and Coromandel port cities persisted from that time until the arrival of the Portuguese in the sixteenth century. India itself was an important contributor of goods to the world trading system. Most of the world's pepper was grown in India, and Indian cotton and silk textiles, mainly from the Gujarat region, were also highly prized.

Peoples and Cultures of the Indian Ocean

Indian Ocean trade connected peoples from the Malay Peninsula (the southern extremity of the Asian continent), India, China, and East Africa, among whom there was an enormous variety of languages, cultures, and religions. In spite of this diversity, certain sociocultural similarities linked these peoples, especially in Southeast Asia.

For example, by the fifteenth century inhabitants of what we call Indonesia, Malaysia, the Philippines, and the many islands in between all spoke languages of the Austronesian family, reflecting continuing interactions

The Port of Calicut in India The port of Calicut, located on the west coast of India, was a center of the Indian Ocean spice trade during the Middle Ages. Vasco da Gama arrived in Calicut in 1498 and obtained permission to trade there, leading to hostilities between the Portuguese and the Arab traders who had previously dominated the port. (Private Collection/The Stapleton Collection/The Bridgeman Art Library)

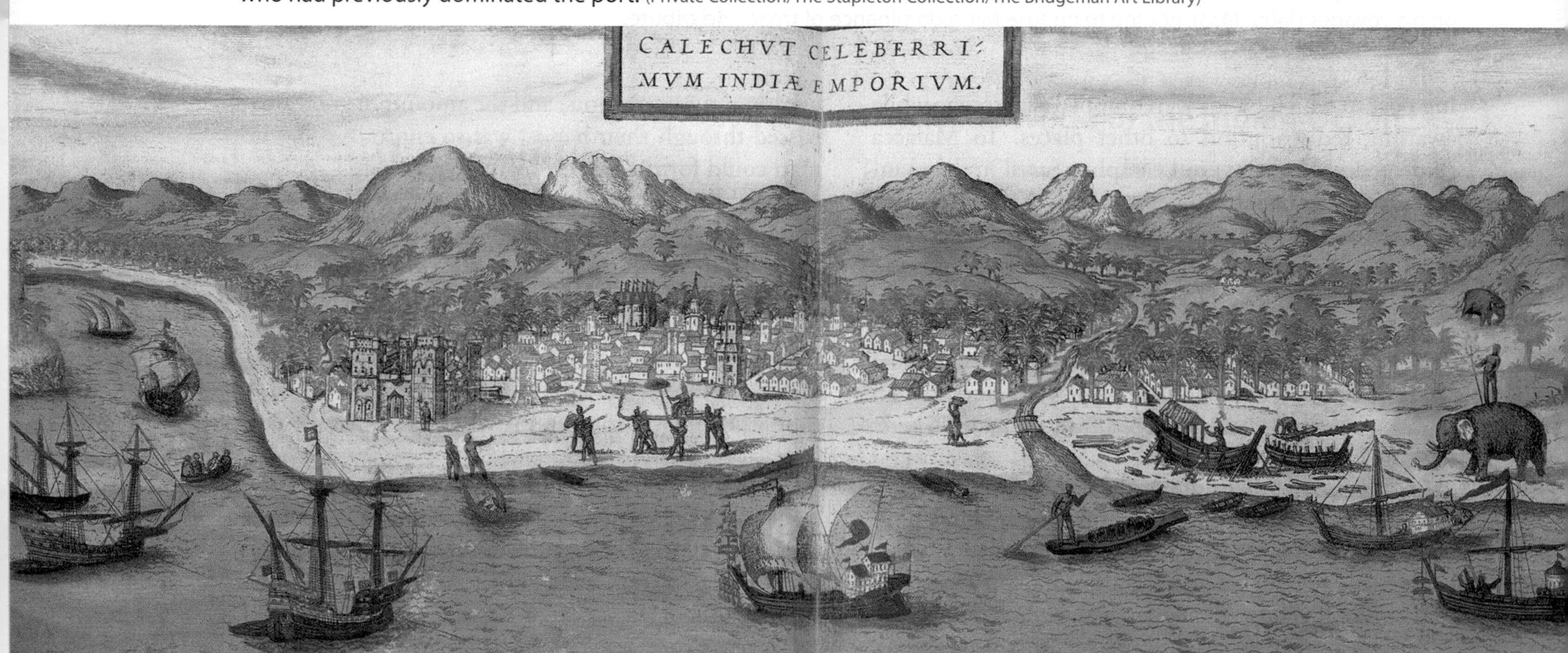

among them. A common environment led to a diet based on rice, fish, palms, and palm wine. Rice, harvested by women, is probably indigenous to the region, and it formed the staple of the diet. The seas provided many varieties of fish, crabs, and shrimp, and fishing served as the chief male occupation, well ahead of agriculture. Also, sugarcane grew in profusion, and it was chewed as a confectionery and used as a sweetener.[3]

In comparison to India, China, or even Europe after the Black Death, Southeast Asia was sparsely populated. People were concentrated in port cities and in areas of intense rice cultivation. Another difference between Southeast Asia and India, China, and Europe was the higher status of women — their primary role in planting and harvesting rice gave them authority and economic power. At marriage, which typically occurred around age twenty, the groom paid the bride (or sometimes her family) a sum of money called **bride wealth**, which remained under her control. This practice was in sharp contrast to the Chinese, Indian, and European dowry, which came under the husband's control. Property was administered jointly, in contrast to the Chinese principle and Indian practice that wives had no say in the disposal of family property. All children, regardless of gender, inherited equally, and when Islam arrived in the region, the rule requiring sons to receive double the inheritance of daughters was never implemented.

Respect for women carried over to the commercial sphere. Women participated in business as partners and independent entrepreneurs, even undertaking long sea voyages to accompany their wares. When Portuguese and Dutch men settled in the region and married local women, their wives continued to play important roles in trade and commerce.

In contrast to most parts of the world other than Africa, Southeast Asian peoples had an accepting attitude toward premarital sexual activity and placed no premium on virginity at marriage. Divorce carried no social stigma and was easily attainable if a pair proved incompatible. Either the woman or the man could initiate a divorce, and common property and children were divided.

Trade with Africa and the Middle East

On the east coast of Africa, Swahili-speaking city-states engaged in the Indian Ocean trade, exchanging ivory, rhinoceros horn, tortoise shells, copra (dried coconut), and slaves for textiles, spices, cowrie shells, porcelain, and other goods. The most important cities were Mogadishu, Mombasa, and Kilwa, which had converted to Islam by the eleventh century. Peopled by confident and urbane merchants, the cities were known for their prosperity and culture.

Mansa Musa This detail from the Catalan Atlas of 1375, a world map created for the Catalan king, depicts a king of Mali, Mansa Musa, who was legendary for his wealth in gold. European desires for direct access to the trade in sub-Saharan gold helped inspire Portuguese exploration of the west coast of Africa in the fifteenth century. (Detail from the *Catalan Atlas*, 1375 [vellum], by Abraham Cresques (1325–1387)/Bibliothèque Nationale, Paris, France/The Bridgeman Art Library)

West Africa also played an important role in world trade. In the fifteenth century most of the gold that reached Europe came from the Sudan region in West Africa and, in particular, from the kingdom of Mali near present-day Ghana. Transported across the Sahara by Arab and African traders on camels, the gold was sold in the ports of North Africa. Other trading routes led to the Egyptian cities of Alexandria and Cairo, where the Venetians held commercial privileges.

Inland nations that sat astride the north-south caravan routes grew wealthy from this trade. In the mid-thirteenth century the kingdom of Mali emerged as an important player on the overland trade route. In later centuries, however, the diversion of gold away from the trans-Sahara routes would weaken the inland states of Africa politically and economically.

• **bride wealth** In early modern Southeast Asia, a sum of money the groom paid the bride or her family at the time of marriage. This practice contrasted with the dowry in China, India, and Europe, which the husband controlled.

Gold was one important object of trade; slaves were another. Slavery was practiced in Africa, as it was virtually everywhere else in the world, long before the arrival of Europeans. Arab and African merchants took West African slaves to the Mediterranean to be sold in European, Egyptian, and Middle Eastern markets and also brought eastern Europeans to West Africa as slaves. In addition, Indian and Arab merchants traded slaves in the coastal regions of East Africa.

The Middle East served as an intermediary for trade between Europe, Africa, and Asia and was also an important supplier of goods for foreign exchange, especially silk and cotton. Two great rival empires, the Persian Safavids and the Turkish Ottomans, dominated the region, competing for control over western trade routes to the East. By the mid-sixteenth century the Ottomans had established control over eastern Mediterranean sea routes to trading centers in Syria, Palestine, Egypt, and the rest of North Africa. Their power also extended into Europe as far west as Vienna.

Genoese and Venetian Middlemen

Compared to the riches and vibrancy of the East, Europe constituted a minor outpost in the world trading system, for European craftsmen produced few products to rival those of Asia. However, Europeans desired luxury goods from the East, and in the late Middle Ages such trade was controlled by the Italian city-states of Venice and Genoa. Venice had opened the gateway to Asian trade in 1304, when it established formal relations with the sultan of Mamluk Egypt and started operations in Cairo. In exchange for European products like Spanish and English wool, German metal goods, and Flemish textiles, the Venetians obtained luxury items like spices, silks, and carpets from middlemen in the eastern Mediterranean and Asia Minor. Because Eastern demand for European goods was low, Venetians funded their purchases through shipping and trade in firearms and slaves.

Venice's ancient trading rival was Genoa. By the time the Crusades ended around 1270, Genoa dominated the northern route to Asia through the Black Sea. From then until the fourteenth century, the Genoese expanded their trade routes as far as Persia and the Far East. In 1291 they sponsored a failed expedition into the Atlantic in search of India. This voyage reveals the early origins of Genoese interest in Atlantic exploration.

In the fifteenth century, with Venice claiming victory in the spice trade, the Genoese shifted focus from trade to finance and from the Black Sea to the western Mediterranean. Located on the northwestern coast of Italy, Genoa had always been active in the western Mediterranean, trading with North African ports, southern France, Spain, and even England and Flanders through the Strait of Gibraltar. When Spanish and Portuguese voyages began to explore the western Atlantic (see page 467), Genoese merchants, navigators, and financiers provided their skills and capital to the Iberian monarchs.

A major element of Italian trade was slavery. Merchants purchased slaves, many of whom were fellow Christians, in the Balkans of southeastern Europe. After the loss of the Black Sea trade routes—and thus the source of slaves—to the Ottomans, the Genoese sought new supplies of slaves in the West, eventually seizing or buying and selling the Guanches (indigenous peoples from the Canary Islands), Muslim prisoners and Jewish refugees from Spain, and, by the early 1500s, both black and Berber Africans. With the growth of Spanish colonies in the New World, Genoese and Venetian merchants became important players in the Atlantic slave trade.

Italian experience in colonial administration, slaving, and international trade served as a model for the Iberian states as they pushed European expansion to new heights. Mariners, merchants, and financiers from Venice and Genoa—most notably Christopher Columbus—played crucial roles in bringing the fruits of this experience to the Iberian Peninsula and to the New World.

The European Voyages of Discovery

☐ Why and how did Europeans undertake ambitious voyages of expansion?

Europe was by no means isolated before the voyages of exploration and its "discovery" of the New World. But because Europeans did not produce many products desired by Eastern elites, they were modest players in the Indian Ocean trading world. As Europe recovered after the Black Death, new European players entered the scene with novel technology, eager to spread Christianity and to undo Italian and Ottoman domination of trade with the East. A century after the plague, Iberian explorers began the overseas voyages that helped create the modern world, with immense consequences for their own continent and the rest of the planet.

Causes of European Expansion

European expansion had multiple causes. The first was economic. By the middle of the fifteenth century Europe was experiencing a revival of population and economic activity after the lows of the Black Death. This revival created renewed demand for luxuries, especially spices, from the East. The fall of Constantinople and the subsequent Ottoman control of trade routes created obstacles to fulfilling these demands. European merchants and rulers eager for the profits of trade thus needed to find new sources of precious metal to exchange with the Ottomans or trade routes that bypassed the Ottomans.

Why were spices so desirable? Introduced into western Europe by the Crusaders in the twelfth century, pepper, nutmeg, ginger, mace, cinnamon, and cloves added flavor and variety to the monotonous European diet. Not only did spices serve as flavorings for food, but they were also used in anointing oil and as incense for religious rituals, and as perfumes, medicines, and dyes in daily life. Apart from their utility, the expense and exotic origins of spices meant that they were a high-status good, which European elites could use to demonstrate their social standing.

Religious fervor and the crusading spirit were another important catalyst for expansion. Just seven months separated Isabella and Ferdinand's conquest of the emirate of Granada, the last remaining Muslim state on the Iberian Peninsula, and Columbus's departure across the Atlantic. Overseas exploration thus transferred the militaristic religious fervor of the reconquista (reconquest) to new non-Christian territories. As they conquered indigenous empires, Iberians brought the attitudes and administrative practices developed during the reconquista to the Americas. Conquistadors fully expected to be rewarded with land, titles, and power over conquered peoples, just as the leaders of the reconquista had been.

A third motivation was the dynamic spirit of the Renaissance. Like other men of the Renaissance era, explorers sought to win glory for their amazing exploits and demonstrated a genuine interest in learning more about unknown waters. Scholars have frequently described the European discoveries as an outcome of Renaissance curiosity about the physical universe. The detailed journals kept by European voyagers attest to their fascination with the new peoples and places they visited.

Individual explorers often manifested all of these desires at once. Columbus, a devout Christian, aimed to discover new territories where Christianity could be spread while seeking a direct trade route to Asia. The motives of Portuguese explorer Bartholomew Diaz were, in his own words, "to serve God and His Majesty, to give light to those who were in darkness and to grow rich as all men desire to do." When the Portuguese explorer Vasco da Gama reached the port of Calicut, India, in 1498 and a native asked what he wanted, he replied, "Christians and spices."[4] The bluntest of the Spanish **conquistadors** (kahn-KEES-tuh-dawrz), or conquerors, Hernán Cortés, announced as he prepared to conquer Mexico, "I have come to win gold, not to plow the fields like a peasant."[5]

Ordinary seamen joined these voyages to escape poverty at home, to continue a family trade, or to win a few crumbs of the great riches of empire. Common sailors were ill-paid, and life at sea meant danger, unbearable stench, hunger, and overcrowding. For months at a time, 100 to 120 people lived and worked in a space of 1,600 to 2,000 square feet.

The people who stayed at home had a powerful impact on the voyages of discovery. Merchants provided the capital for many early voyages and had a strong say in their course. To gain authorization and financial support for their expeditions, they sought official sponsorship from the Crown. Competition among European monarchs for the prestige and profit of overseas exploration thus constituted another crucial factor in encouraging the steady stream of expeditions that began in the late fifteenth century.

The small number of Europeans who could read provided a rapt audience for tales of fantastic places and unknown peoples. Cosmography, natural history, and geography aroused enormous interest among educated people in the fifteenth and sixteenth centuries. One of the most popular books of the time was the fourteenth-century text *The Travels of Sir John Mandeville*, which purported to be a firsthand account of the author's travels in the Middle East, India, and China. Although we now know they were fictional, these fantastic tales of cannibals, one-eyed giants, men with the heads of dogs, and other marvels were believed for centuries. Columbus took a copy of Mandeville and the equally popular and more reliable *The Travels of Marco Polo* on his voyage in 1492.

Technology and the Rise of Exploration

Technological developments in shipbuilding, navigation, and weaponry enabled European expansion. Since ancient times, most seagoing vessels had been narrow, open boats called galleys, propelled by slaves or convicts manning the oars. Though well suited to the placid waters of the Mediterranean, galleys could not withstand the rougher conditions in the Atlantic. The need for sturdier craft, as well as population losses caused by the Black Death, forced the development of a new style of ship that would not require much manpower. Over the course of the fifteenth century the Portuguese developed the **caravel**, a small, light, three-mast sailing ship with triangular lateen sails. The caravel was much

- **conquistador** Spanish for "conqueror"; a Spanish soldier-explorer, such as Hernán Cortés or Francisco Pizarro, who sought to conquer the New World for the Spanish crown.
- **caravel** A small, maneuverable, three-mast sailing ship developed by the Portuguese in the fifteenth century that gave the Portuguese a distinct advantage in exploration and trade.

more maneuverable than the galley. When fitted with cannon, it could dominate larger vessels.

This period also saw great strides in cartography and navigational aids. Around 1410 Arab scholars reintroduced Europeans to **Ptolemy's *Geography***. Written in the second century, the work synthesized the geographical knowledge of the classical world. It represented a major improvement over medieval cartography, showing the world as round and introducing the idea of latitude and longitude to plot a ship's position accurately. It also contained significant errors. Unaware of the Americas, Ptolemy showed the world as much smaller than it is, so that Asia appeared not very far to the west of Europe. Both the assets and the flaws of Ptolemy's work shaped the geographical knowledge that explorers like Christopher Columbus brought to their voyages.

The magnetic compass made it possible for sailors to determine their direction and position at sea. The astrolabe, an instrument invented by the ancient Greeks and perfected by Muslim navigators, was used to determine the altitude of the sun and other celestial bodies. It permitted mariners to plot their latitude, that is, their precise position north or south of the equator.

Like the astrolabe, much of the new technology that Europeans used on their voyages was borrowed from the East. Gunpowder, the compass, and the sternpost rudder were Chinese inventions. Advances in cartography also drew on the rich tradition of Judeo-Arabic mathematical and astronomical learning in Iberia. In exploring new territories, European sailors thus called on techniques and knowledge developed over centuries in China, the Muslim world, and trading centers along the Indian Ocean.

The Portuguese in Africa and Asia

For centuries Portugal was a small and poor nation on the margins of European life whose principal activities were fishing and subsistence farming. It would have been hard for a medieval European to predict Portugal's phenomenal success overseas after 1450. Yet Portugal had a long history of seafaring and navigation. Blocked from access to western Europe by Spain, the Portuguese turned to the Atlantic, whose waters they knew better than did other Europeans. Nature favored the Portuguese: winds blowing along their coast offered passage to Africa, its Atlantic islands, and, ultimately, Brazil. Once they had mastered the secret to sailing against the wind to return to Europe (by sailing farther west to catch winds from the southwest), they were ideally poised to lead Atlantic exploration.

The Portuguese Fleet Embarked for the Indies This image shows a Portuguese trading fleet in the late fifteenth century bound for the riches of the Indies. Between 1500 and 1635 over nine hundred ships sailed from Portugal to ports on the Indian Ocean in annual fleets composed of five to ten ships. Portuguese sailors used astrolabes, such as the one pictured here, to accurately plot their position. (fleet: British Museum/HarperCollins Publishers/The Art Archive at Art Resource, NY; astrolabe: © The Trustees of the British Museum/Art Resource, NY)

Pepper Harvest To break the monotony of their bland diet, Europeans had a passion for pepper, which — along with cinnamon, cloves, nutmeg, and ginger — was the main object of the Asian trade. We can appreciate the fifteenth-century expression "as dear as pepper": one kilo of pepper cost 2 grams of silver at the place of production in the East Indies and from 1 to 10 grams of silver in Alexandria, Egypt; 14 to 18 grams in Venice; and 20 to 30 grams at the markets of northern Europe. Here natives fill vats, and the dealer tastes a peppercorn for pungency. (Bibliothèque Nationale, Paris, France/Archives Charmet/The Bridgeman Art Library)

In the early phases of Portuguese exploration, Prince Henry (1394–1460), a dynamic younger son of the king, played a leading role. A nineteenth-century scholar dubbed Henry "the Navigator" because of his support for the study of geography and navigation and for the annual expeditions he sponsored down the western coast of Africa. Although he never personally participated in voyages of exploration, Henry's involvement ensured that Portugal did not abandon the effort despite early disappointments.

Portugal's conquest of Ceuta, an Arab city in northern Morocco, in 1415 marked the beginning of European overseas expansion. In the 1420s, under Henry's direction, the Portuguese began to settle the Atlantic islands of Madeira (ca. 1420) and the Azores (1427). In 1443 they founded their first African commercial settlement at Arguin in North Africa. By the time of Henry's death in 1460, his support for exploration was vindicated — in Portuguese eyes — by thriving sugar plantations on the Atlantic islands, the first arrival of enslaved Africans in Portugal (see page 477), and new access to African gold.

The Portuguese next established fortified trading posts, called factories, on the gold-rich Guinea coast and penetrated into the African continent all the way to Timbuktu (Map 16.2). By 1500 Portugal controlled the flow of African gold to Europe. In contrast to the Spanish conquest of the Americas (see page 471), the Portuguese did not establish large settlements in West Africa or seek to control the political or cultural lives of those with whom they traded. Instead they sought easier and faster profits by inserting themselves into pre-existing trading systems. For the first century of their relations, African rulers were equal partners with the Portuguese, protected by their experienced armies and European vulnerability to tropical diseases.

In 1487 Bartholomew Diaz (ca. 1451–1500) rounded the Cape of Good Hope at the southern tip of Africa (Map 16.2), but storms and a threatened mutiny forced him to turn back. A decade later Vasco da Gama (ca. 1469–1524) succeeded in rounding the Cape while commanding a fleet in search of a sea route to India. With the help of an Indian guide, da Gama reached the port of Calicut in India. He returned to Lisbon with spices and samples of Indian cloth, having proved the possibility of lucrative trade with the East via the

- **Ptolemy's *Geography*** A second-century-C.E. work that synthesized the classical knowledge of geography and introduced the concepts of longitude and latitude. Reintroduced to Europeans in 1410 by Arab scholars, its ideas allowed cartographers to create more accurate maps.

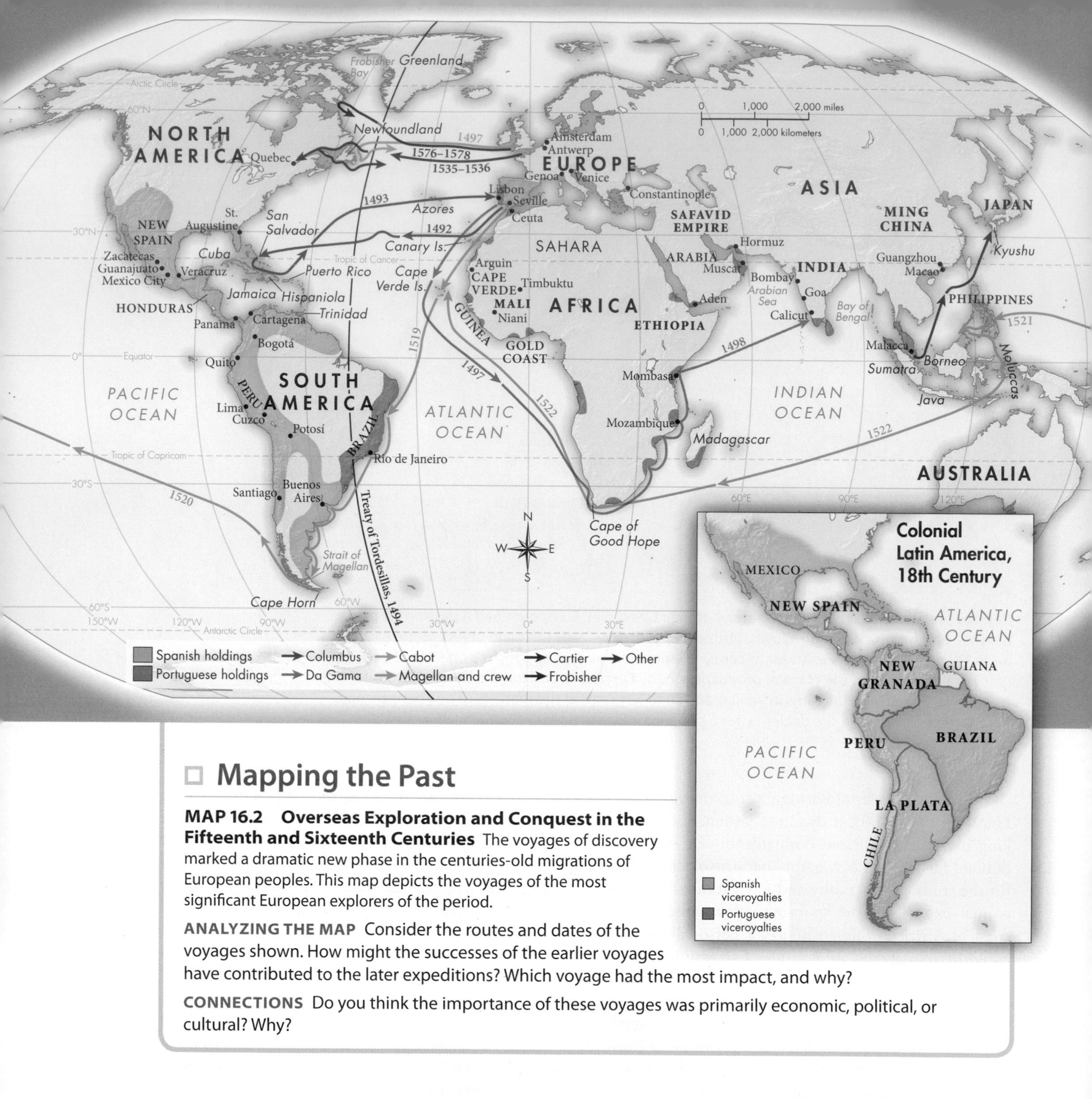

Mapping the Past

MAP 16.2 Overseas Exploration and Conquest in the Fifteenth and Sixteenth Centuries The voyages of discovery marked a dramatic new phase in the centuries-old migrations of European peoples. This map depicts the voyages of the most significant European explorers of the period.

ANALYZING THE MAP Consider the routes and dates of the voyages shown. How might the successes of the earlier voyages have contributed to the later expeditions? Which voyage had the most impact, and why?

CONNECTIONS Do you think the importance of these voyages was primarily economic, political, or cultural? Why?

Cape route. Thereafter, a Portuguese convoy set out for passage around the Cape every March.

Lisbon became the entrance port for Asian goods into Europe, but this was not accomplished without a fight. Muslim-controlled port city-states had long controlled the rich trade of the Indian Ocean, and they did not surrender it willingly. From 1500 to 1515 the Portuguese used a combination of bombardment and diplomatic treaties to establish trading factories at Goa, Malacca, Calicut, and Hormuz, thereby laying the foundation for a Portuguese trading empire in the sixteenth and seventeenth centuries. The acquisition of port cities and their trade routes brought riches to Portugal, but, as in Africa, the Portuguese had limited impact on the lives and religious faith of peoples beyond Portuguese coastal holdings. Moreover, Portuguese ability to enforce a monopoly on trading in the Indian Ocean was always limited by the sheer distances involved and the stiff resistance of Indian, Ottoman, and other rivals.

Inspired by the Portuguese, the Spanish had also begun the quest for empire. Theirs was to be a second, entirely different, mode of colonization leading to large-scale settlement and the forced assimilation of huge indigenous populations.

Spain's Voyages to the Americas

Christopher Columbus was not the first navigator to explore the Atlantic. In the ninth century Vikings established short-lived settlements in Newfoundland, and it is probable that others made the voyage, either on purpose or accidentally, carried by westward currents off the coast of Africa. In Africa, Mansa Musa, emperor of Mali, reportedly came to the throne after the previous king failed to return from a naval expedition he led to explore the Atlantic Ocean. A document by a scholar of the time, al-Umari, quoted Mansa Musa's description of his predecessor as a man who "did not believe that the ocean was impossible to cross. He wished to reach the other side and was passionately interested in doing so."[6] Portugal's achievements in Atlantic navigation made the moment right for Christopher Columbus to attempt to find a westward route across the Atlantic to Asia in the late fifteenth century.

Christopher Columbus, a native of Genoa, was an experienced seaman and navigator. He had worked as a mapmaker in Lisbon and had spent time on Madeira. He was familiar with such fifteenth-century Portuguese navigational aids as *portolans*—written descriptions of the courses along which ships sailed—and the use of the compass as a nautical instrument. Columbus asserted in his journal: "I have spent twenty-three years at sea and have not left it for any length of time worth mentioning, and I have seen every thing from east to west [meaning he had been to England] and I have been to Guinea [North and West Africa]."[7]

Columbus was also a deeply religious man. He had witnessed the Spanish conquest of Granada and shared fully in the religious fervor surrounding that event. Like the Spanish rulers and most Europeans of his age, Columbus understood Christianity as a missionary religion that should be carried to all places of the earth. He thus viewed himself as a divine agent: "God made me the messenger of the new heaven and the new earth of which he spoke in the Apocalypse of St. John . . . and he showed me the post where to find it."[8]

Rejected for funding by the Portuguese in 1483 and by Ferdinand and Isabella in 1486, Columbus finally won the support of the Spanish monarchy in 1492. Buoyed by the success of the reconquista and eager to earn profits from trade, the Spanish crown agreed to make him viceroy over any territory he might discover and to give him one-tenth of the material rewards of the journey.

Columbus and his small fleet left Spain on August 3, 1492. Columbus dreamed of reaching the court of the Mongol emperor, the Great Khan, not realizing that the Ming Dynasty had overthrown the Mongols in 1368. Based on Ptolemy's *Geography* and other texts, he expected to pass the islands of Japan and then land on the east coast of China.

After a brief stop in the Canary Islands, he landed on an island in the Bahamas on October 12, which he christened San Salvador and claimed on behalf of the Spanish crown. In a letter he wrote to Ferdinand and Isabella on his return to Spain, Columbus described the natives as handsome, peaceful, and primitive. Believing he was somewhere off the east coast of Japan, in what he considered the Indies, he called them "Indians," a name that was later applied to all inhabitants of the Americas. Columbus concluded that they would make good slaves and could quickly be converted to Christianity. (See "Listening to the Past: Columbus Describes His First Voyage," page 468.)

Columbus's First Voyage to the New World, 1492–1493

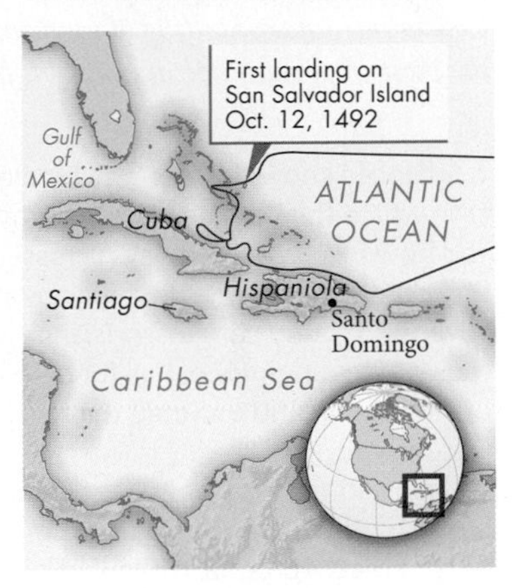

Scholars have identified the inhabitants of the islands as the Taino (TIGH-noh) people, speakers of the Arawak language, who inhabited Hispaniola (modern-day Haiti and the Dominican Republic) and other islands in the Caribbean. From San Salvador, Columbus sailed southwest, landing on Cuba on October 28. Deciding that he must be on the mainland of China near the coastal city of Quinsay (now Hangzhou), he sent a small embassy inland with letters from Ferdinand and Isabella and instructions to locate the grand city. Although they found no large settlement or any evidence of a great kingdom, the sight of Taino people wearing gold ornaments on Hispaniola suggested that gold was available in the region. In January, confident that its source would soon be found, he headed back to Spain to report on his discovery.

On his second voyage, Columbus took control of the island of Hispaniola and enslaved its indigenous peoples. On this and subsequent voyages, he brought with him settlers for the new Spanish territories, along with agricultural seed and livestock. Columbus himself, however, had little interest in or capacity for governing. Arriving in Hispaniola on his third voyage, he found revolt had broken out against his brother, whom Columbus had left behind to govern the colony. An investigatory expedition sent by the Spanish crown arrested Columbus and his brother for failing to maintain order. Columbus returned to Spain in disgrace and a royal governor assumed control of the colony.

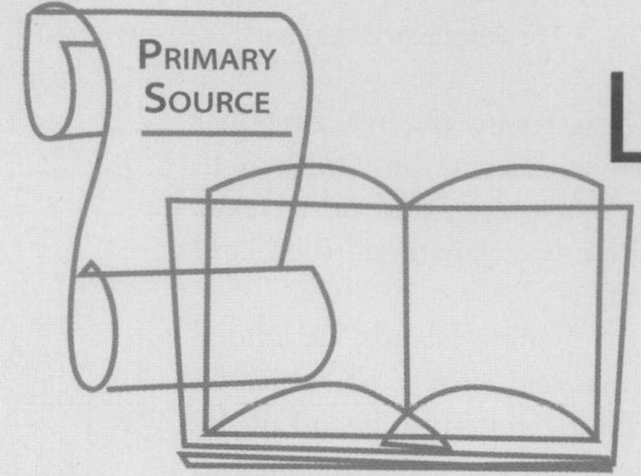

Listening to the Past

Columbus Describes His First Voyage

On his return voyage to Spain in February 1493, Christopher Columbus composed a letter intended for wide circulation and had copies of it sent ahead to Isabella, Ferdinand, and others when his ship docked at Lisbon. Because the letter sums up Columbus's understanding of his achievements, it is considered the most important document of his first voyage.

"Since I know that you will be pleased at the great success with which the Lord has crowned my voyage, I write to inform you how in thirty-three days I crossed from the Canary Islands to the Indies, with the fleet which our most illustrious sovereigns gave me. I found very many islands with large populations and took possession of them all for their Highnesses; this I did by proclamation and unfurled the royal standard. No opposition was offered.

I named the first island that I found "San Salvador," in honour of our Lord and Saviour who has granted me this miracle. . . . When I reached Cuba, I followed its north coast westwards, and found it so extensive that I thought this must be the mainland, the province of Cathay.* . . . From there I saw another island eighteen leagues eastwards which I then named "Hispaniola."† . . .

Hispaniola is a wonder. The mountains and hills, the plains and meadow lands are both fertile and beautiful. They are most suitable for planting crops and for raising cattle of all kinds, and there are good sites for building towns and villages. The harbours are incredibly fine and there are many great rivers with broad channels and the majority contain gold.‡ The trees, fruits and plants are very different from those of Cuba. In Hispaniola there are many spices and large mines of gold and other metals.§ . . .

The inhabitants of this island, and all the rest that I discovered or heard of, go naked, as their mothers bore them, men and women alike. A few of the women, however, cover a single place with a leaf of a plant or piece of cotton which they weave for the purpose. They have no iron or steel or arms and are not capable of using them, not because they are not strong and well built but because they are amazingly timid. All the weapons they have are canes cut at seeding time, at the end of which they fix a sharpened stick, but they have not the courage to make use of these, for very often when I have sent two or three men to a village to have conversation with them a great number of them have come out. But as soon as they saw my men all fled immediately, a father not even waiting for his son. And this is not because we have harmed any of them; on the contrary, wherever I have gone and been able to have conversation with them, I have given them some of the various things I had, a cloth and other articles, and received nothing in exchange. But they have still remained incurably timid. True, when they have been reassured and lost their fear, they are so ingenuous and so liberal with all their possessions that no one who has not seen them would believe it. If one asks for anything they have they never say no. On the contrary, they offer a share to anyone with demonstrations of heartfelt affection, and they are immediately content with any small thing, valuable or valueless, that is given them. I forbade the men to give them bits of broken crockery, fragments of glass or tags of laces, though if they could get them they fancied them the finest jewels in the world.

I hoped to win them to the love and service of their Highnesses and of the whole Spanish nation and to persuade them to collect and give us of the things which they possessed in abundance and which we needed. They have no religion and are not idolaters; but all believe that power and goodness dwell in the sky and they are firmly convinced that I have come from the sky with these ships and people. In this belief they gave me a good reception everywhere, once they had overcome their fear; and this is not because they are stupid — far from it, they are men of great intelligence, for they navigate all those seas, and give a marvellously good account of everything — but because they have never before seen men clothed or ships like these. . . .

Columbus was very much a man of his times. To the end of his life in 1506, he believed that he had found small islands off the coast of Asia. He never realized the scope of his achievement: that he had found a vast continent unknown to Europeans, except for a fleeting Viking presence centuries earlier. He could not know that the lands he discovered would become a crucial new arena for international trade and colonization, with grave consequences for native peoples.

Spain "Discovers" the Pacific

The Florentine navigator Amerigo Vespucci (veh-SPOO-chee) (1454–1512) realized what Columbus had not. Writing about his discoveries on the coast of modern-day Venezuela, Vespucci stated: "Those new regions which we found and explored with the fleet . . . we may rightly call a New World." This letter, titled *Mundus Novus* (The New World), was the first docu-

In all these islands the men are seemingly content with one woman, but their chief or king is allowed more than twenty. The women appear to work more than the men and I have not been able to find out if they have private property. As far as I could see whatever a man had was shared among all the rest and this particularly applies to food. . . . In another island, which I am told is larger than Hispaniola, the people have no hair. Here there is a vast quantity of gold, and from here and the other islands I bring Indians as evidence.

In conclusion, to speak only of the results of this very hasty voyage, their Highnesses can see that I will give them as much gold as they require, if they will render me some very slight assistance; also I will give them all the spices and cotton they want. . . . I will also bring them as much aloes as they ask and as many slaves, who will be taken from the idolaters. I believe also that I have found rhubarb and cinnamon and there will be countless other things in addition. . . .

So all Christendom will be delighted that our Redeemer has given victory to our most illustrious King and Queen and their renowned kingdoms, in this great matter. They should hold great celebrations and render solemn thanks to the Holy Trinity with many solemn prayers, for the great triumph which they will have, by the conversion of so many peoples to our holy faith and for the temporal benefits which will follow, for not only Spain, but all Christendom will receive encouragement and profit.

This is a brief account of the facts.

Written in the caravel off the Canary Islands.**

15 February 1493

At your orders
THE ADMIRAL ”

Source: J. M. Cohen, ed. and trans., *The Four Voyages of Christopher Columbus* (Penguin Classics, 1958), pp. 115–123. Copyright © J. M. Cohen, 1969, London. Reproduced by permission of Penguin Books Ltd.

***Christopher Columbus*, by Ridolfo Ghirlandio. Friend of Raphael and teacher of Michelangelo, Ghirlandio (1483–1561) enjoyed distinction as a portrait painter, and so we can assume that this is a good likeness of the older Columbus.**
(Museo Navale di Pegli, Genoa, Italy/Scala/Art Resource, NY)

QUESTIONS FOR ANALYSIS

1. How did Columbus explain the success of his voyage?
2. What was Columbus's view of the Native Americans he met?
3. Evaluate Columbus's statements that the Caribbean islands possessed gold, cotton, and spices.
4. Why did Columbus cling to the idea that he had reached Asia?

*Cathay is the old name for China. In the logbook and later in this letter Columbus accepts the natives' story that Cuba is an island that they can circumnavigate in something more than twenty-one days, yet he insists here and during the second voyage that it is in fact part of the Asiatic mainland.

†Hispaniola is the second-largest island of the West Indies; Haiti occupies the western third of the island, the Dominican Republic the rest.

‡This did not prove to be true.

§These statements are also inaccurate.

**Actually, Columbus was off Santa Maria in the Azores.

ment to describe America as a continent separate from Asia. In recognition of Amerigo's bold claim, the continent was named for him.

To settle competing claims to the Atlantic discoveries, Spain and Portugal turned to Pope Alexander VI. The resulting **Treaty of Tordesillas** (tawr-duh-SEE-yuhs) in 1494 gave Spain everything to the west of an imaginary line drawn down the Atlantic and Portugal everything to the east. This arbitrary division worked in Portugal's favor when in 1500 an expedition led by Pedro Álvares Cabral landed on the coast of Brazil, which Cabral claimed as Portuguese territory.

The search for profits determined the direction of Spanish exploration and expansion in South America.

- **Treaty of Tordesillas** The 1494 agreement giving Spain everything west of an imaginary line drawn down the Atlantic and giving Portugal everything to the east.

Because its profits from Hispaniola and other Caribbean islands were insignificant compared to Portugal's enormous riches from the Asian spice trade, Spain renewed the search for a western passage to Asia. In 1519 Charles V of Spain commissioned Ferdinand Magellan (1480–1521) to find a direct sea route to the spices of the Moluccas, islands off the southeast coast of Asia. Magellan sailed southwest across the Atlantic to Brazil, and after a long search along the coast he located the treacherous strait off the southern tip of South America that now bears his name (see Map 16.2). After passing through the strait, his fleet sailed north up the west coast of South America and then headed west into the Pacific toward the Malay Archipelago. (Some of these islands were conquered in the 1560s and were named the Philippines for Philip II of Spain.)

Terrible storms, disease, starvation, and violence haunted the expedition. Sailors on two of Magellan's five ships attempted mutiny on the South American coast; one ship was lost, and another ship deserted and returned to Spain before even traversing the strait. Magellan himself was killed in a skirmish in the Malay Archipelago. At this point, the expedition had enough survivors to man only two ships, and one of them was captured by the Portuguese. Finally, in 1522, one ship with only eighteen men returned to Spain, having traveled from the east by way of the Indian Ocean, the Cape of Good Hope, and the Atlantic. The voyage—the first to circumnavigate the globe—had taken close to three years.

Despite the losses, this voyage revolutionized Europeans' understanding of the world by demonstrating the vastness of the Pacific. The earth was clearly much larger than Ptolemy's map had shown. Magellan's expedition also forced Spain's rulers to rethink their plans for overseas commerce and territorial expansion. Although the voyage made a small profit in spices, the westward passage to the Indies was too long and dangerous for commercial purposes. Thus Spain soon abandoned the attempt to oust Portugal from the Eastern spice trade and concentrated on exploiting its New World territories.

Early Exploration by Northern European Powers

Spain's northern European rivals also set sail across the Atlantic during the early days of exploration, searching for a northwest passage to the Indies. In 1497 John

Juan Vespucci's World Map, 1526 As chief pilot to the Spanish crown, Juan Vespucci oversaw constant revisions to royal maps necessitated by ongoing voyages of discovery and exploration. This map shows the progress of Spanish knowledge of the New World some thirty years after Columbus. (The Granger Collection, NYC—All rights reserved.)

Cabot (ca. 1450–1499), a Genoese merchant living in London, landed on Newfoundland. The next year he returned and explored the New England coast. These forays proved futile, and at that time the English established no permanent colonies in the territories they explored.

News of the riches of Mexico and Peru later inspired the English to renew their efforts, this time in the extreme north. Between 1576 and 1578 Martin Frobisher (ca. 1535–1594) made three voyages in and around the Canadian bay that now bears his name. Frobisher brought a quantity of ore back to England with him in hopes that it contained precious metals, but it proved to be worthless.

Early French exploration of the Atlantic was equally frustrating. Between 1534 and 1541 Frenchman Jacques Cartier (1491–1557) made several voyages and explored the St. Lawrence region of Canada, searching for a passage to the wealth of Asia. When this hope proved vain, the French turned to a new source of profit within Canada itself: trade in beavers and other furs. As had the Portuguese in Asia, French traders bartered with local peoples whom they largely treated as autonomous and equal partners. French fishermen also competed with the Spanish and English for the teeming schools of cod they found in the Atlantic waters around Newfoundland.

Conquest and Settlement

☐ What was the impact of Iberian conquest and settlement on the peoples and ecologies of the Americas?

Before Columbus's arrival, the Americas were inhabited by thousands of groups of indigenous peoples with distinct languages and cultures. These groups ranged from hunter-gatherer tribes organized into tribal confederations to settled agriculturalists to large-scale empires connecting bustling cities and towns. The best estimate is that the peoples of the Americas numbered between 35 and 50 million in 1492. Their lives were radically altered by the arrival of Europeans.

The growing European presence in the New World transformed its land and its peoples forever. Violence, forced labor, and disease wrought devastating losses, while surviving peoples encountered new political, social, and economic organizations imposed by Europeans. Although the exchange of goods and people between Europe and the New World brought diseases to the Americas, it also gave both the New and Old Worlds new crops that eventually altered consumption patterns across the globe.

Spanish Conquest of the Aztec and Inca Empires

In the first two decades after Columbus's arrival in the New World, the Spanish colonized Hispaniola, Cuba, Puerto Rico, and other Caribbean islands. Based on rumors of a wealthy mainland civilization, the Spanish governor in Cuba sponsored expeditions to the Yucatán coast of the Gulf of Mexico, including one in 1519 under the command of the conquistador Hernán Cortés (1485–1547). Alarmed by Cortés's brash ambition, the governor decided to withdraw his support, but Cortés quickly set sail before being removed from command. Accompanied by eleven ships, 450 men, sixteen horses, and ten cannon, Cortés landed on the Mexican coast on April 21, 1519. His camp soon received visits by delegations of unarmed Aztec leaders bearing gifts and news of their great emperor.

The **Aztec Empire**, also known as the Mexica Empire, comprised the Mexica people and the peoples they had conquered, and it had grown rapidly in size and power in the early fifteenth century. At the time of the Spanish arrival, the empire was ruled by Moctezuma II (r. 1502–1520), from his capital at Tenochtitlan (tay-nawch-teet-LAHN), now Mexico City. The Aztecs were a sophisticated civilization with an advanced understanding of mathematics, astronomy, and engineering and with oral poetry and historical traditions. As in European nations at the time, a hereditary nobility dominated the army, the priesthood, and the state bureaucracy and reaped the gains from the agricultural labor of the common people.

Within weeks of his arrival, Cortés acquired translators who provided vital information on the empire and its weaknesses. (See "Individuals in Society: Doña Marina / Malintzin," page 472.) To legitimize his authority, Cortés founded the settlement of Veracruz and had himself named its military commander. He then burned his ships to prevent any disloyal or frightened followers from returning to Cuba.

Through his interpreters, Cortés learned of strong local resentment against the Aztec Empire. The Aztec state practiced warfare against neighboring peoples to secure captives for religious sacrifices and laborers for agricultural and building projects. Once conquered, subject tribes paid continual tribute to the empire through their local chiefs. Realizing that he could exploit dissensions within the empire to his own advantage, Cortés forged an alliance with Tlaxcala (tlah-SKAH-lah), a subject kingdom of the Aztecs. In October a

• **Aztec Empire** Also known as the Mexica Empire, a large and complex Native American civilization in modern Mexico and Central America that possessed advanced mathematical, astronomical, and engineering technology.

Individuals in Society

Doña Marina / Malintzin

IN APRIL 1519 HERNÁN CORTÉS AND HIS FOLLOWERS received a number of gifts from the Tabasco people after he defeated them, including a group of twenty female captives. Among them was a young woman the Spanish baptized as Marina, which became Malin in the Nahuatl (NAH-wha-tuhl) language spoken in the Aztec Empire. Her high status and importance were recognized with the honorific title of *doña* in Spanish and the suffix *-tzin* in Nahuatl. Bernal Díaz del Castillo, who accompanied Cortés and wrote the most important contemporary history of the Aztec Empire and its conquest, claimed that Doña Marina (or Malintzin) was the daughter of a leader of a Nahuatl-speaking tribe. According to his account, the family sold Marina to Maya slave traders as a child to protect the inheritance rights of her stepbrother.

Marina possessed unique skills that immediately caught the attention of Cortés. Fluent both in Nahuatl and Yucatec Maya (spoken by a Spanish priest accompanying Cortés), she offered a way for him to communicate with the peoples he encountered. She quickly learned Spanish as well and came to play a vital role as an interpreter and diplomatic guide. Indigenous pictures and writings created after the conquest depict Malintzin as a constant presence beside Cortés as he negotiated with and fought and killed Amerindians. The earliest known images show her interpreting for Cortés as he meets with the Tlaxcalan lord Xicotencatl, forging the alliance that would prove vital to Spanish victory against the Aztecs. Malintzin also appears prominently in the images of the *Florentine Codex*, an illustrated history of the Aztec Empire and its conquest created near the end of the sixteenth century by indigenous artists working under the direction of Friar Bernardino de Sahagún. All the images depict her as a well-dressed woman standing at the center of interactions between the Spanish and Amerindians.

Malintzin bore Cortés a son, Don Martín Cortés, in 1522 and accompanied him on expeditions to Honduras between 1524 and 1526. It is impossible to know the true nature of their personal relationship. Cortés was married to a Spanish woman in Cuba at the time, and Malintzin was a slave, in no position to refuse any demands he made of her. Cortés recognized their child and provided financial support for his upbringing. Malintzin later married one of Cortés's Spanish followers, Juan Jaramillo, with whom she had a daughter. It is unknown when and how she died.

Doña Marina translating for Hernán Cortés. (The Granger Collection, NYC — All rights reserved)

Bernal Díaz gave Malintzin high praise. In his history, written decades after the fact, he described her as beautiful and intelligent, revered by native tribesmen, and devotedly loyal to the Spanish. He stated repeatedly that it would have been impossible for them to succeed without her help. Cortés mentioned Malintzin only twice in his letters to Spanish king Charles V. He acknowledged her usefulness as his interpreter but described her only as "an Indian woman of this land," giving no hint of their personal relationship. No writings from Malintzin herself exist.

Malintzin is commonly known in Mexico and Latin America as La Malinche, a Spanish rendering of her Nahuatl name. She remains a compelling and controversial figure. Popular opinion has often condemned La Malinche as a traitor to her people, whose betrayal enabled the Spanish conquest and centuries of subjugation of indigenous peoples. Other voices have defended her as an enslaved woman who had no choice but to serve her masters. As the mother of a *mestizo* (mixed-race) child, she has also been seen as a founder of the mixed-race population that dominates modern Mexico. She will always be a reminder of the complex interactions between indigenous peoples and Spanish conquistadors that led to the conquest and the new culture born from it.

QUESTIONS FOR ANALYSIS

1. Why was the role of interpreter so important in Cortés's conquest of the Aztec Empire? Why did Malintzin become such a central figure in interactions between Cortés and the Amerindians?
2. What options were open to Malintzin in following her path? If she intentionally chose to aid the Spanish, what motivations might she have had?

LaunchPad
Online Document Project

How did Spanish and Amerindian artists depict Malintzin? Examine Spanish and Amerindian representations of Malintzin's role in the conquest, and then complete a quiz and writing assignment based on the evidence and details from this chapter.

See inside the front cover to learn more.

combined Spanish-Tlaxcalan force occupied the Aztec city of Cholula, second largest in the empire, and massacred thousands of inhabitants. Strengthened by this display of ruthless power, Cortés formed alliances with other native kingdoms. In November 1519, with a few hundred Spanish men and some six thousand indigenous warriors, he marched on Tenochtitlan.

Historians have long debated Moctezuma's response to the arrival of the Spanish. Unlike other native leaders, he refrained from attacking the Spaniards but instead welcomed Cortés and his men into Tenochtitlan. Moctezuma was apparently deeply impressed by Spanish victories and believed the Spanish were invincible. Sources written after the conquest claimed that the emperor believed Cortés was an embodiment of the god Quetzalcoatl, whose return was promised in Aztec myth.

While it is impossible to verify those claims, it is clear that Moctezuma's weak and hesitant response was disastrous. When Cortés—with incredible boldness—took Moctezuma hostage, the emperor's influence crumbled. During the ensuing attacks and counterattacks, Moctezuma was killed. The Spaniards and their allies escaped from the city suffering heavy losses. Cortés quickly began gathering forces and making new alliances against the Aztecs. In May 1521 he led a second assault on Tenochtitlan, leading an army of approximately one thousand Spanish and seventy-five thousand native warriors.[9]

Inca Women Milking Cows This illustration of Inca women milking cows is from a collection of illustrations by a Spanish bishop that offers a valuable view of life in Peru in the 1780s. (From *Codex Trujillo*, Bishop Baltasar Jaime Martínez Compañón, Palacio Real, Madrid, Spain/Photo: Albers Foundation/Art Resource, NY)

The Spanish victory in late summer 1521 was hard-won and was greatly aided by the effects of smallpox, which had devastated the besieged population of the city. After establishing a new capital in the ruins of Tenochtitlan, Cortés and other conquistadors began the systematic conquest of Mexico.

Invasion of Tenochtitlan, 1519–1521

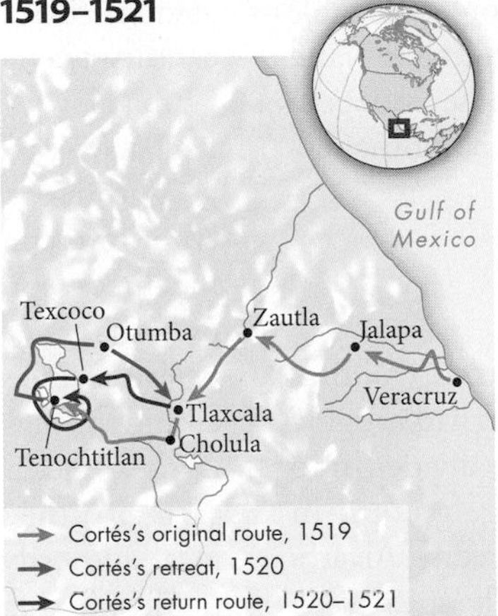

More remarkable than the defeat of the Aztec Empire was the fall of the remote **Inca Empire** in Peru. Living in a settlement perched more than 9,800 feet above sea level, the Incas were isolated from the Mesoamerican civilization of the Aztecs. Nonetheless, they too had created a vast empire in the fifteenth century that rivaled those of the Europeans in population and complexity. The Incas' strength lay largely in their bureaucratic efficiency. They divided their empire into four major regions containing eighty provinces and twice as many districts. Officials at each level used the extensive network of roads to transmit information and orders back and forth through the empire. While the Aztecs used a system of glyphs for writing, the Incas had devised a complex system of colored and knotted cords, called khipus, for administrative bookkeeping. The empire also benefited from the use of llamas as pack animals (by contrast, no beasts of burden existed in Mesoamerica).

By the time of the Spanish invasion, however, the Inca Empire had been weakened by a civil war over succession and an epidemic of disease, possibly smallpox, spread through trade with groups in contact with Europeans. The Spanish conquistador Francisco Pizarro (ca. 1475–1541) landed on the northern coast of Peru on May 13, 1532, the very day the Inca leader Atahualpa (ah-tuh-WAHL-puh) won control of the empire after five years of fighting his brother for the throne. As Pizarro advanced across the Andes toward Cuzco, the capital of the Inca Empire, Atahualpa was also heading there for his coronation.

Like Moctezuma in Mexico, Atahualpa was aware of the Spaniards' movements. He sent envoys to greet the Spanish and invited them to meet him in the provincial town of Cajamarca. Motivated by curiosity

• **Inca Empire** The vast and sophisticated Peruvian empire centered at the capital city of Cuzco that was at its peak in the fifteenth century.

about the Spanish, he intended to meet with them to learn more about them and their intentions. Instead the Spaniards ambushed and captured him, extorted an enormous ransom in gold, and then executed him on trumped-up charges in 1533. The Spanish then marched on to Cuzco, profiting, as with the Aztecs, from internal conflicts and forming alliances with local peoples. When Cuzco fell in 1533, the Spanish plundered immense riches in gold and silver.

How was it possible for several hundred Spanish conquistadors to defeat powerful empires commanding large armies, vast wealth, and millions of inhabitants? Historians seeking answers to this question have emphasized a combination of factors: the boldness and audacity of conquistadors like Cortés and Pizarro; the military superiority endowed by Spanish firepower and horses; the fervent belief in a righteous Christian God imparted by the reconquista; division within the Aztec and Inca Empires that produced native allies for the Spanish; and, of course, the devastating impact of contagious diseases among the indigenous population. Ironically, the well-organized, urban-based Aztec and Inca Empires were more vulnerable to wholesale takeover than more decentralized and fragmented groups like the Maya, whose independence was not wholly crushed until the end of the seventeenth century.

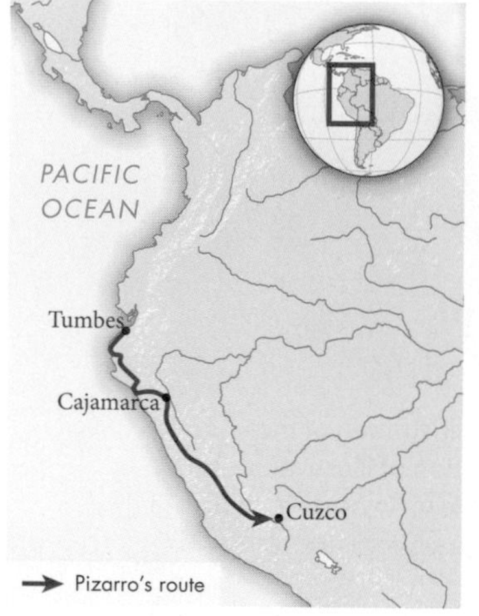

The Conquest of Peru, 1532–1533

Portuguese Brazil

Unlike Mesoamerica or the Andes, the territory of Brazil contained no urban empires but instead had roughly 2.5 million nomadic and settled people divided into small tribes and many different language groups. In 1500 the Portuguese crown named Pedro Álvares Cabral commander of a fleet headed for the spice trade of the Indies. En route, the fleet sailed far to the west, accidentally landing on the coast of Brazil, which Cabral claimed for Portugal under the terms of the Treaty of Tordesillas. The Portuguese soon undertook a profitable trade with local people in brazilwood, a source of red dye.

In the 1520s Portuguese settlers brought sugarcane production to Brazil. They initially used enslaved indigenous laborers on sugar plantations, but the rapid decline in the indigenous population soon led to the use of forcibly transported Africans. In Brazil the Portuguese thus created a new form of colonization in the Americas: large plantations worked by enslaved people. This model of slave-worked sugar plantations would spread throughout the Caribbean in the seventeenth century.

Colonial Administration

By the end of the sixteenth century the Spanish and Portuguese had successfully overcome most indigenous groups and expanded their territory throughout modern-day Mexico, the southwestern United States, and Central and South America. In Mesoamerica and the Andes, the Spanish had taken over the cities and tribute systems of the Aztecs and the Incas, basing their control on the prior existence of well-established polities with organized tribute systems.

While early conquest and settlement were conducted largely by private initiatives (authorized and sponsored by the state), the Spanish and Portuguese governments soon assumed more direct control. In 1503 the Spanish granted the port of Seville a monopoly over all traffic to the New World and established the House of Trade, or *Casa de Contratación*, to oversee economic matters. In 1523 Spain created the Royal and Supreme Council of the Indies, with authority over all colonial affairs subject to approval by the king. Spanish territories themselves were divided initially into two **viceroyalties**, or administrative divisions: New Spain, created in 1535, with its capital at Mexico City; and Peru, created in 1542, with its capital at Lima. In the eighteenth century two additional viceroyalties were added: New Granada, with Bogotá as its administrative center; and La Plata, with Buenos Aires as its capital (see Map 16.2).

Within each territory, the viceroy, or imperial governor, exercised broad military and civil authority as the direct representative of Spain. The viceroy presided over the *audiencia* (ow-dee-EHN-see-ah), a board of twelve to fifteen judges that served as his advisory council and the highest judicial body. As in Spain, settlement in the Americas was centered on cities and towns. In each city, the municipal council, or *cabildo*, exercised local authority. Women were denied participation in public life, a familiar pattern from both Spain and precolonial indigenous societies.

In Portugal, the India House in Lisbon functioned much like the Spanish House of Trade, and royal representatives oversaw its possessions in West Africa and Asia, as did governors in Spanish America. To secure the vast expanse of Brazil, however, the Portuguese implemented a distinctive system of rule, called **captaincies**, in the 1530s. These were hereditary grants of land given to nobles and loyal officials who bore the costs of settling and administering their territories. Over time, the Crown secured greater power over the captaincies, appointing royal governors to act as administrators. The captaincy of Bahia was the site of the capital, Salvador, home to the governor general and other royal officials.

Throughout the Americas, the Catholic Church played an integral role in Iberian rule. Churches and cathedrals were consecrated, often on precolonial sacred sites, and bishoprics were established. The papacy allowed Portuguese and Spanish officials greater control over the church than was the case at home, allowing them to appoint clerics and collect tithes. This control helped colonial powers use the church as an instrument to indoctrinate indigenous people in European ways of life (see page 479).

Indigenous Population Loss and Economic Exploitation

From the time of Christopher Columbus in Hispaniola, the conquerors of the New World made use of the **encomienda system** to profit from the peoples and territories they encountered. This system was a legacy of the methods used to reward military leaders in the time of the reconquista, when victorious officers received feudal privileges over conquered areas in return for their service. First in the Caribbean and then on the mainland, conquistadors granted their followers the right to employ groups of Native Americans as laborers and to demand tribute payments from them in exchange for providing food, shelter, and instruction in the Christian faith. Commonly, an individual conquistador was assigned a tribal chieftain along with all the people belonging to his kin group. This system was first used in Hispaniola to work goldfields and then in Mexico for agricultural labor and, when silver was discovered in the 1540s, for silver mining.

A 1512 Spanish law authorizing the use of the encomienda called for indigenous people to be treated fairly, but in practice the system led to terrible abuses, including overwork, beatings, and sexual violence. Spanish missionaries publicized these abuses, leading to debates in Spain about the nature and proper treatment of indigenous people (see page 481). King Charles V responded to such complaints in 1542 with the New Laws, which set limits on the authority of encomienda holders, including their ability to transmit their privileges to heirs.

The New Laws provoked a revolt among elites in Peru and were little enforced throughout Spanish territories. Nonetheless, the Crown gradually gained control over encomiendas in central areas of the empire and required indigenous people to pay tributes in cash, rather than in labor. To respond to a shortage of indigenous workers, royal officials established a new government-run system of forced labor, called *repartimiento* in New Spain and *mita* in Peru. Administrators assigned a certain percentage of the inhabitants of native communities to labor for a set period each year in public works, mining, agriculture, and other tasks. Laborers received modest wages, which they could use to fulfill tribute obligations. In the seventeenth century, as land became a more important source of wealth than labor, elite settlers purchased *haciendas*, enormous tracts of farmland worked by dependent indigenous laborers and slaves.

Spanish systems for exploiting the labor of indigenous peoples were both a cause of and a response to the disastrous decline in the numbers of such peoples that began soon after the arrival of Europeans. Some indigenous people died as a direct result of the violence of conquest and the disruption of agriculture and trade caused by warfare. The most important cause of death, however, was infectious disease. Having little or no resistance to diseases brought from the Old World, the inhabitants of the New World fell victim to smallpox, typhus, influenza, and other illnesses. Overwork and exhaustion reduced indigenous people's ability to survive infectious disease. Moreover, labor obligations diverted local people from tending to their own crops, leading to malnutrition, starvation, and low fertility rates. Labor obligations also separated nursing mothers from their babies, resulting in high infant mortality rates.

The pattern of devastating disease and population loss established in the Spanish colonies was repeated everywhere Europeans settled. Overall, population declined by as much as 90 percent or more but with important regional variations. In general, densely populated urban centers were worse hit than rural areas, and tropical, low-lying regions suffered more than cooler, higher-altitude ones. Some scholars have claimed that losses may have been overreported, since many indigenous people fled their communities — or listed themselves as mixed race (and thus immune from forced labor) — to escape Spanish exploitation. By the mid-seventeenth century the worst losses had occurred and a slight recovery began.

Colonial administrators responded to native population decline by forcibly combining dwindling indigenous communities into new settlements and imposing the rigors of the encomienda and the repartimiento.

- **viceroyalties** The name for the four administrative units of Spanish possessions in the Americas: New Spain, Peru, New Granada, and La Plata.
- **captaincies** A system established by the Portuguese in Brazil in the 1530s, whereby hereditary grants of land were given to nobles and loyal officials who bore the costs of settling and administering their territories.
- **encomienda system** A system whereby the Spanish crown granted the conquerors the right to forcibly employ groups of Indians; it was a disguised form of slavery.

By the end of the sixteenth century the search for fresh sources of labor had given birth to the new tragedy of the Atlantic slave trade (see page 603).

Patterns of Settlement

The century after the discovery of silver in 1545 marked the high point of Iberian immigration to the Americas. Although the first migrants were men—conquistadors, priests, and colonial officials—soon whole families began to cross the Atlantic, and the European population began to increase through natural reproduction. By 1600 American-born Europeans, called *Creoles*, outnumbered immigrants. By 1650 European-born and Creole Spaniards numbered approximately 200,000 in Mexico and 350,000 in the remaining colonies. Portuguese immigration to Brazil was relatively slow, and Portuguese-born settlers continued to dominate the colony.

Iberian settlement was predominantly urban in nature. Spaniards settled into the cities and towns of the former Aztec and Inca Empires as the native population dwindled through death and flight. They also established new cities, such as Santo Domingo on Hispaniola and Vera Cruz in Mexico. Settlers were quick to establish urban institutions familiar to them from home: city squares, churches, schools, and universities.

Despite the growing number of Europeans and the rapid decline of the native population, Europeans remained a small minority of the total inhabitants of the Americas. Cortés and his followers had taken native women as concubines and, less frequently, as wives. This pattern was repeated with the arrival of more Iberians, leading to a substantial population of mixed Iberian and Indian descent known as *mestizos* (meh-STEE-zohz). The large-scale arrival of enslaved Africans, starting in Brazil in the mid-sixteenth century, added new ethnic and racial dimensions to the population (see pages 603–611).

The Era of Global Contact

☐ How was the era of global contact shaped by new commodities, commercial empires, and forced migrations?

The centuries-old Afroeurasian trade world was forever changed by the European voyages of discovery and their aftermath. For the first time, a truly global economy emerged in the sixteenth and seventeenth centuries, and it forged new links among far-flung peoples, cultures, and societies. The ancient civilizations of Europe, Africa, the Americas, and Asia confronted each other in new and rapidly evolving ways. Those confrontations often led to conquest, forced migration, and brutal exploitation, but they also contributed to cultural exchange and renewal.

The Columbian Exchange

The travel of people and goods between the Old and New Worlds led to an exchange of animals, plants, and diseases, a complex process known as the **Columbian exchange**. As we have seen, the introduction of new diseases to the Americas had devastating consequences. But other results of the exchange brought benefits not only to the Europeans but also to native peoples.

European immigrants wanted to eat foods familiar to them, so they searched the Americas for climatic zones favorable to crops grown in their homelands. Everywhere they settled, the Spanish and Portuguese brought and raised wheat with labor provided by the encomienda system. Grapes and olives brought over from Spain did well in parts of Peru and Chile. Perhaps the most significant introduction to the diet of Native Americans came via the meat and milk of the livestock that the early conquistadors brought with them, including cattle, sheep, and goats. The horse enabled both the Spanish conquerors and native populations to travel faster and farther and to transport heavy loads more easily.

In turn, Europeans returned home with many food crops that became central elements of their diet. Crops originating in the Americas included tomatoes, squash, pumpkins, peppers, and many varieties of beans, as well as tobacco. One of the most important of such crops was maize (corn). Because maize gives a high yield per unit of land, has a short growing season, and thrives in climates too dry for rice and too wet for wheat, it proved an especially important crop for the Old World. By the late seventeenth century, maize had become a staple in Spain, Portugal, southern France, and Italy, and in the eighteenth century it became one of the chief foods of southeastern Europe and southern China.

Even more valuable was the nutritious white potato, which slowly spread from west to east—to Ireland, England, and France in the seventeenth century, and to Germany, Poland, Hungary, and Russia in the eighteenth, contributing everywhere to a rise in population. Ironically, the white potato reached New England from old England in the early eighteenth century. The Portuguese quickly began exporting chili peppers from Brazil to Africa, India, and Southeast Asia along the trade routes they dominated. Chili peppers arrived in continental North America when plantation owners began to plant them as a food source for enslaved Africans, for whom they were a dietary staple.

The initial reaction to these crops was sometimes fear and hostility. Adoption of the tomato and the

A New World Sugar Refinery in Brazil Sugar was the most important and most profitable plantation crop in the New World. This image shows the processing and refinement of sugar on a Brazilian plantation. Sugarcane was grown, harvested, and processed by African slaves who labored under brutal and ruthless conditions to generate enormous profits for plantation owners. (Bibliothèque Nationale, Paris, France/Giraudon/The Bridgeman Art Library)

potato, for example, was long hampered by the belief that they were unfit for human consumption and potentially poisonous. Both plants belong to the deadly nightshade family, and both contain poison in their leaves and stems. Consequently, it took time and persuasion for these plants to win over tradition-minded European peasants, who used potatoes mostly as livestock feed. During the eighteenth-century Enlightenment, scientists and doctors played an important role in popularizing the nutritional benefits of the potato.

While the exchange of foods was a great benefit to cultures across the world, the introduction of European pathogens to the New World had a disastrous impact on the native population. The wave of catastrophic epidemic disease that swept the Western Hemisphere after 1492 can be seen as an extension of the swath of devastation wreaked by the Black Death in the 1300s, first on Asia and then on Europe. The world after Columbus was thus unified by disease as well as by trade and colonization.

Sugar and Early Transatlantic Slavery

Two crucial and interrelated elements of the Columbian exchange were the transatlantic trade in sugar and slaves. Throughout the Middle Ages, slavery was deeply entrenched in the Mediterranean, but it was not based on race; many slaves were European in origin. How, then, did black African slavery enter the European picture and take root in South and then North America? In 1453 the Ottoman capture of Constantinople halted the flow of European slaves from the eastern Mediterranean. Additionally, the successes of the Christian reconquest of the Iberian Peninsula drastically diminished the supply of Muslim captives. Cut off from its traditional sources of slaves, Mediterranean Europe turned to sub-Saharan Africa, which had a long history of slave trading.

As Portuguese explorers began their voyages along the western coast of Africa, one of the first commodities they sought was slaves. In 1444 the first ship returned to Lisbon with a cargo of enslaved Africans. While the first slaves were simply seized by small raiding parties, Portuguese merchants soon found that it was easier and more profitable to trade with African leaders, who were accustomed to dealing in enslaved people captured through warfare with neighboring powers. In 1483 the Portuguese established an alliance with the kingdom of Kongo. The royal family eventually converted to Christianity, and Portuguese merchants intermarried with Kongolese women, creating a permanent Afro-Portuguese community. From 1490 to 1530 Portuguese traders brought between three hundred and two thousand enslaved Africans to Lisbon each year. There they performed most of the manual labor and constituted 10 percent of the city's population.

In this stage of European expansion, the history of slavery became intertwined with the history of sugar. Originally sugar was an expensive luxury, but population increases and greater prosperity in the fifteenth century led to increasing demand. The establishment of sugar plantations on the Canary and Madeira Islands in the fifteenth century testifies to this demand.

• **Columbian exchange** The exchange of animals, plants, and diseases between the Old and the New Worlds.

Sugar was a particularly difficult crop to produce for profit. Seed-stems were planted by hand, thousands to the acre. When mature, the cane had to be harvested and processed rapidly to avoid spoiling. Moreover, sugarcane has a virtually constant growing season, meaning that there was no fallow period when workers could recuperate. The invention of roller mills to crush the cane more efficiently meant that yields could be significantly augmented, but only if a sufficient labor force was found to supply the mills. Europeans solved the labor problem by forcing first native islanders and then transported Africans to perform the backbreaking work.

The transatlantic slave trade that would ultimately result in the forced transport of over 12 million individuals began in 1518, when Spanish king Charles V authorized traders to bring enslaved Africans to New World colonies. The Portuguese brought the first slaves to Brazil around 1550; by 1600 four thousand were being imported annually. After its founding in 1621, the Dutch West India Company transported thousands of Africans to Brazil and the Caribbean, mostly to work on sugar plantations. In the late seventeenth century, with the chartering of the Royal African Company, the English began to bring slaves to Barbados and other English colonies in the Caribbean and mainland North America.

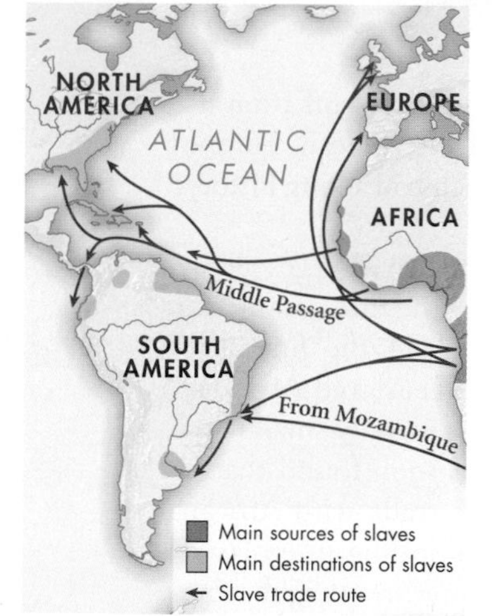

The Transatlantic Slave Trade

Before 1700, when slavers decided it was better business to improve conditions, some 20 percent of slaves died on the voyage from Africa to the Americas.[10] The most common cause of death was dysentery induced by poor-quality food and water, lack of sanitation, and intense crowding. (To increase profits, slave traders packed several hundred captives on each ship.) Men were often kept in irons during the passage, while women and girls were subject to sexual abuse by sailors. On sugar plantations, death rates among enslaved people from illness and exhaustion were extremely high, leading to a constant stream of new human shipments from Africa. Driven by rising demands for sugar, cotton, tobacco, and other plantation crops, the tragic transatlantic slave trade reached its height in the eighteenth century.

The Birth of the Global Economy

With Europeans' discovery of the Americas and their exploration of the Pacific, the entire world was linked for the first time in history by seaborne trade. The opening of that trade brought into being three successive commercial empires: the Portuguese, the Spanish, and the Dutch.

The Portuguese were the first worldwide traders. In the sixteenth century they controlled the sea route to India (Map 16.3). From their fortified bases at Goa on the Arabian Sea and at Malacca on the Malay Peninsula, ships carried goods to the Portuguese settlement at Macao, founded in 1557, in the South China Sea. From Macao Portuguese ships loaded with Chinese silks and porcelains sailed to the Japanese port of Nagasaki and to the Philippine port of Manila, where Chinese goods were exchanged for Spanish silver from New Spain. Throughout Asia the Portuguese traded in slaves. They also exported horses from Mesopotamia and copper from Arabia to India; from India they exported hawks and peacocks for the Chinese and Japanese markets. Back to Portugal they brought Asian spices that had been purchased with textiles produced in India and with gold and ivory from East Africa. They also shipped back sugar from their colony in Brazil, produced by African slaves whom they had transported across the Atlantic.

Becoming an imperial power a few decades later than the Portuguese, the Spanish were determined to claim their place in world trade. This was greatly facilitated by the discovery of immense riches in silver, first at Potosí in modern-day Bolivia and later in Mexico. Silver poured into Europe through the Spanish port of Seville, contributing to steep inflation across Europe. Demand for silver also created a need for slaves to work in the mines. (See "Global Trade: Silver," page 482.)

The Spanish Empire in the New World was basically land based, but across the Pacific the Spaniards built a seaborne empire centered at Manila in the Philippines. The city of Manila served as the transpacific bridge between Spanish America and China. In Manila Spanish traders used silver from American mines to purchase Chinese silk for European markets. The European demand for silk was so huge that in 1597, for example, 12 million pesos of silver, almost the total value of the transatlantic trade, moved from Acapulco in New Spain to Manila (see Map 16.4). After 1640, however, the Spanish silk trade declined in the face of stiff competition from Dutch imports.

In the seventeenth century the Dutch challenged the Spanish and Portuguese Empires. The Dutch East India Company was founded in 1602 with the stated intention of capturing the spice trade from the Portuguese. Drawing on their commercial wealth and long experience in European trade, by the end of the century the Dutch emerged as the most powerful worldwide seaborne trading power (see Chapter 19).

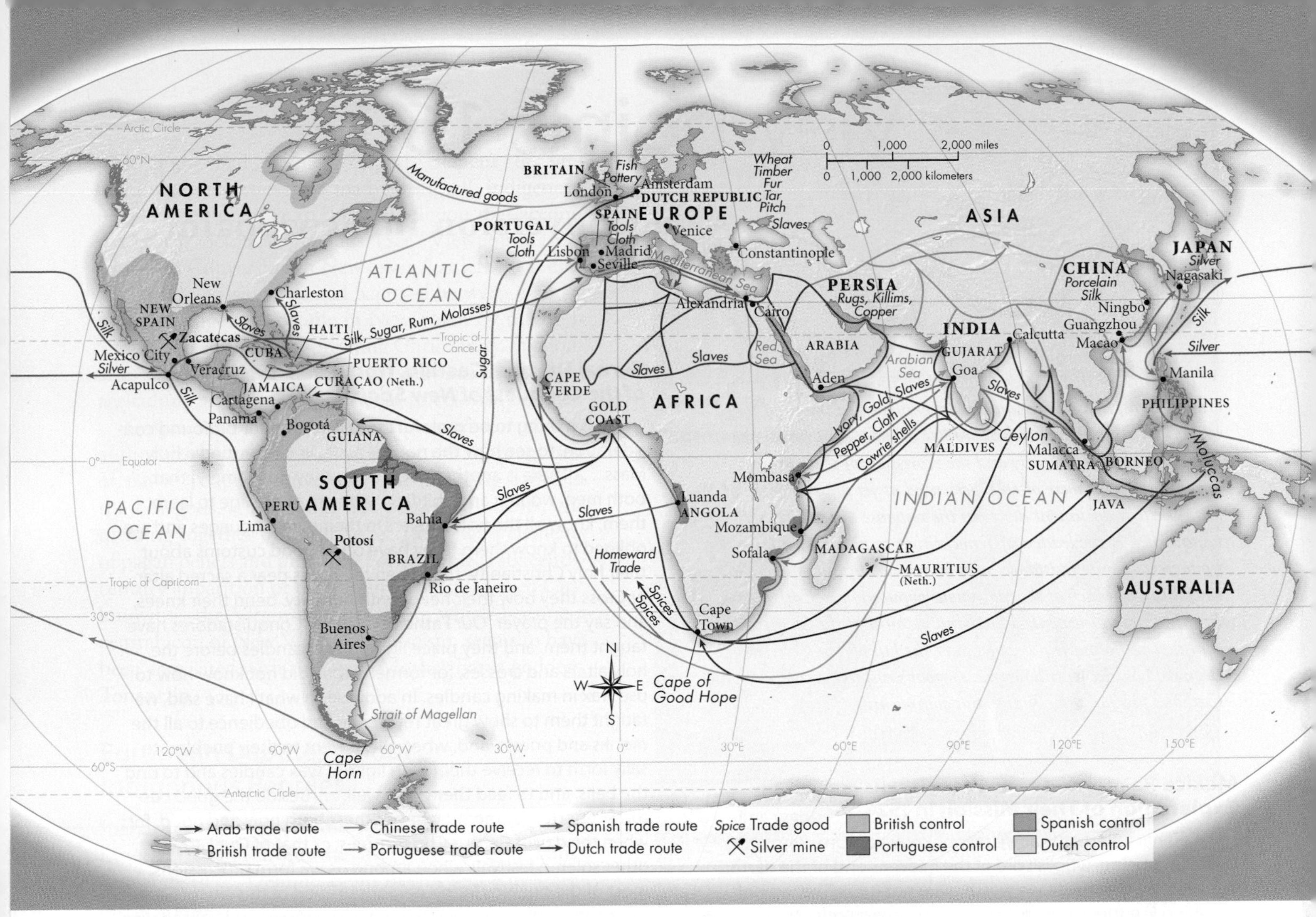

MAP 16.3 Seaborne Trading Empires in the Sixteenth and Seventeenth Centuries
By the mid-seventeenth century trade linked all parts of the world except for Australia. Notice that trade in slaves was not confined to the Atlantic but involved almost all parts of the world.

Changing Attitudes and Beliefs

☐ How did new encounters shape cultural attitudes and beliefs in Europe and the New World?

The age of overseas expansion heightened Europeans' contacts with the rest of the world. These contacts gave birth to new ideas about the inherent superiority or inferiority of different races, in part to justify European participation in the slave trade. Religion became another means of cultural contact, as European missionaries aimed to spread Christianity in both the New World and East Asia, with mixed results. While Christianity was embraced in parts of the New World, it was met largely with suspicion in China and Japan. However, the East-West contacts led to exchanges of influential cultural and scientific ideas.

Religious Conversion

Converting indigenous people to Christianity was one of the most important justifications for European expansion. Jesuit missionaries were active in Japan and China in the sixteenth and seventeenth centuries, until authorities banned their teachings (see page 644). The first missionaries to the New World accompanied Columbus on his second voyage, and more than 2,500 Franciscans, Dominicans, Jesuits, and other friars crossed the Atlantic in the following century. Later French explorers were also accompanied by missionaries who preached to the Native American tribes who traded with the French.

Catholic friars were among the first Europeans to seek an understanding of native cultures and languages as part of their effort to render Christianity comprehensible to indigenous people. In Mexico they not only learned the Nahuatl language, but also taught it to non-Nahuatl-speaking groups to create a shared language for Christian teaching. They were also the most vociferous opponents of abuses committed by Spanish settlers.

Global Trade

Silver in vast quantities was discovered in 1545 by the Spanish, at an altitude of fifteen thousand feet, at Potosí in unsettled territory conquered from the Inca Empire. A half century later, 160,000 people lived in Potosí, making its population comparable to that of the city of London. In the second half of the sixteenth century the mine (in present-day Bolivia) yielded perhaps 60 percent of all the silver mined in the world. From Potosí and the mines at Zacatecas and Guanajuato in Mexico, huge quantities of precious metals poured forth.

Mining became the most important industry in the colonies. The Spanish crown claimed the quinto, one-fifth of all precious metals mined in South America, and gold and silver yielded the Spanish monarchy 25 percent of its total income. One scholar has estimated that 260 tons of silver arrived in Europe each year by 1600.* Seville was the official port of entry for all Spanish silver, although a lively smuggling trade existed.

The real mover of world trade was not Europe, however, but China, which in this period had a population approaching 100 million. By 1450 the collapse of its paper currency had led the Ming government to shift to a silver-based currency. Instead of rice, the traditional form of payment, all Chinese now had to pay their taxes in silver. The result was an insatiable demand for the world's production of silver.

Japan was China's original source, and the Japanese continued to ship large quantities of silver ore until the depletion of its mines near the end of the seventeenth century. The discovery of silver in the New World provided a vast and welcome new supply for the Chinese market. In 1571 the Spanish founded a port city at Manila in the Philippines to serve as a bridge point for bringing silver to Asia. Throughout the seventeenth century Spanish galleons annually carried 2 million pesos (or more than fifty tons) of silver from Acapulco to Manila, where Chinese

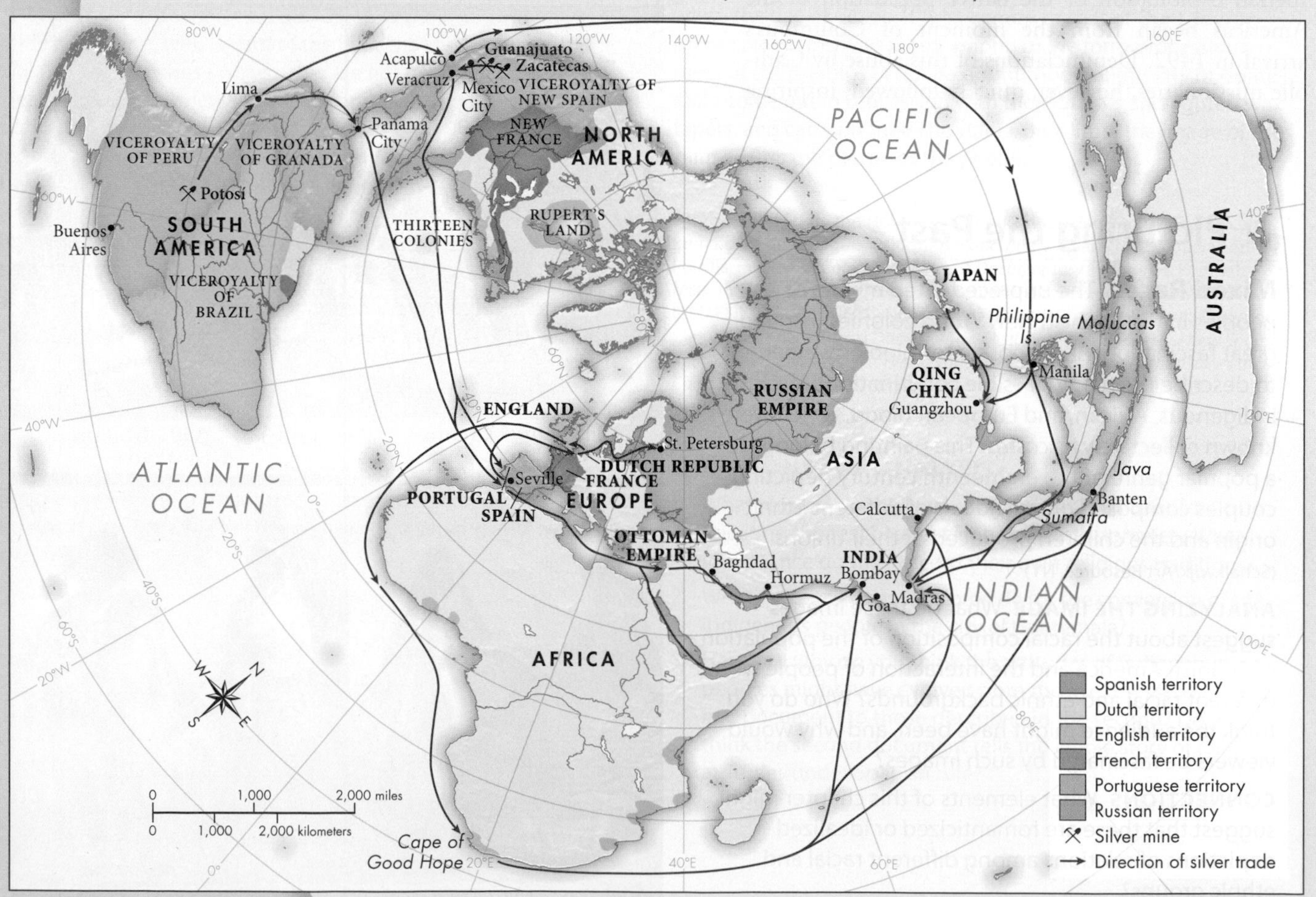

MAP 16.4 The Global Silver Trade

merchants carried it on to China. Even more silver reached China through exchange with European merchants who purchased Chinese goods using silver shipped across the Atlantic. European trade routes to China passed through the Baltic, the Mediterranean, and the Ottoman Empire, as well as around the Cape of Good Hope in Africa. Historians estimate that ultimately the majority of the world's silver in this period ended up in China.

In exchange for silver, the Chinese traded high-quality finished goods desired by elites across the world, including fine silks, porcelain, and spices. To ensure continued demand for their products, Chinese merchants adapted them to Western tastes.

Silver had a mixed impact on the regions involved. Spain's immense profits from silver paid for the tremendous expansion of its empire and for the large armies that defended it. However, the easy flow of money also dampened economic innovation. It exacerbated the rising inflation Spain was already experiencing in the mid-sixteenth century. When the profitability of the silver mines diminished in the 1640s, Spain's power was fundamentally undercut.

China experienced similarly mixed effects. On the one hand, the need for finished goods to trade for silver led to the rise of a merchant class and a new specialization of regional production. On the other hand, inflation resulting from the influx of silver weakened the finances of the Ming Dynasty. As the purchasing power of silver declined in China, so did the value of silver taxes. The ensuing fiscal crisis helped bring down the Ming and led to the rise of the Qing in 1644. Ironically, the two states that benefited the most from silver — Ming China and Spain — also experienced political decline as a result of their reliance on it.

The consequences were most tragic elsewhere. In New Spain millions of indigenous laborers suffered brutal conditions and death in the silver mines. Demand for new labor for the mines contributed to the intensification of the African slave trade.

Silver ore mined at Potosí thus built the first global trade system in history. Previously, a long-standing Afroeurasian trading world had involved merchants and consumers from the three Old World continents. Once Spain opened a trade route across the Pacific through Manila, all continents except Australia and Antarctica were linked.

Silver remained a crucial element in world trade through the nineteenth century. When Mexico won independence from Spain in 1821, it began to mint its own silver dollar, which became the most prized coin in trade in East Asia. By the beginning of the twentieth century, when the rest of the world had adopted gold as the standard of currency, only China and Mexico remained on the silver standard, testimony to the central role this metal had played in their histories.

*Artur Attman, *American Bullion in the European World Trade, 1600–1800* (Goteborg, 1986).

vociferous debates in both Europe and the colonies about the nature of indigenous peoples and how they should be treated. Bartolomé de Las Casas (1474–1566), a Dominican friar and former encomienda holder, was one of the earliest and most outspoken critics of the brutal treatment inflicted on indigenous peoples. He wrote:

> To these quiet Lambs . . . came the Spaniards like most c(r)uel Tygres, Wolves and Lions, enrag'd with a sharp and tedious hunger; for these forty years past, minding nothing else but the slaughter of these unfortunate wretches, whom with divers kinds of torments neither seen nor heard of before, they have so cruelly and inhumanely butchered, that of three millions of people which Hispaniola itself did contain, there are left remaining alive scarce three hundred persons.[12]

Mounting criticism in Spain led King Charles V to assemble a group of churchmen and lawyers to debate the issue in 1550 in the city of Valladolid. One side of the **Valladolid debate**, led by Juan Ginés de Sepúlveda, argued that conquest and forcible conversion were both necessary and justified to save indigenous people from the horrors of human sacrifice, cannibalism, and idolatry. He described them as barbarians who belonged to a category of inferior beings identified by the ancient Greek philosopher Aristotle as naturally destined for slavery. To counter these arguments, Las Casas and his supporters depicted indigenous people as rational and innocent children, who deserved protection and tutelage from more advanced civilizations. Both sides claimed victory in the debate, but it had little effect on the situation in the Americas.

Elsewhere in Europe, audiences also debated these questions. (See "Viewpoints 16.2: Two Views of 'Natural Man,'" page 484.) Eagerly reading denunciations of Spanish abuses by critics like Las Casas, they derived the **Black Legend** of Spanish colonialism, the notion that the Spanish were uniquely brutal and cruel in their conquest and settlement of the Americas. This legend helped other European powers overlook their own record of colonial violence and exploitation.

New Ideas About Race

At the beginning of the transatlantic slave trade, most Europeans would have thought of Africans, if they thought of them at all, as savages in their social customs

- **Valladolid debate** A debate organized by Spanish king Charles V in 1550 in the city of Valladolid that pitted defenders of Spanish conquest and forcible conversion against critics of these practices.
- **Black Legend** The notion that the Spanish were uniquely brutal and cruel in their conquest and settlement of the Americas, an idea propagated by rival European powers.

Primary Sources

Viewpoints 16.2

Two Views of "Natural Man"

• *European encounters with the New World produced contentious debates over the nature of native peoples and how to treat them. In contrast to prevailing views of the time, French jurist Michel de Montaigne rejected the notion that there is one universally correct way of life. In his essay "On Cannibals," he argued that indigenous cultures seemed barbaric only because they were unfamiliar and that their natural simplicity was superior to the artifice of European civilization. In his play* The Tempest, *William Shakespeare refuted Montaigne's trust in nature with his harsh portrait of Caliban (a play on the word* cannibal*). Caliban is the primitive and violent inhabitant of a Caribbean island, who has been enslaved by the sorcerer Prospero for the attempted rape of Prospero's daughter Miranda.*

Montaigne on Natural Virtue

"I find that there is nothing barbarous and savage in this nation [Brazil], by anything that I can gather, excepting, that everyone gives the title of barbarism to everything that is not in use in his own country: as indeed we have no other level of truth and reason, than the example and idea of the opinions and customs of the place wherein we live; there is always the perfect religion, there the perfect government, and the most exact and accomplished usage of all things. They are savages at the same rate that we say fruits are wild, which nature produces of herself and by her own ordinary progress; whereas in truth, we ought rather to call those wild whose natures we have changed by our artifice and diverted from the common order. In those, the genuine, most useful, and natural virtues and properties are vigorous and sprightly, which we have helped to degenerate in these, by accommodating them to the pleasure of our own corrupted palate. . . .

These nations then seem to me to be . . . not much remote from their original simplicity. The laws of nature . . . govern them still. . . . It is a nation wherein there is no manner of traffic, no knowledge of letters, no science of numbers, no name of magistrate nor political superiority; no use of service, riches or poverty, no contracts, no successions, no dividends, no properties, no employments, but those of leisure, no respect of kindred, but common, no clothing, no agriculture, no metal, no use of corn or wine; and where so much as the very words that signify lying, treachery, dissimulation, avarice, envy, detraction and pardon were never heard of."

William Shakespeare, *The Tempest*

CALIBAN: This island's mine, by Sycorax my mother,
Which thou takest from me. When thou camest first,
Thou strokedst me and madest much of me, wouldst give me
Water with berries in't, and teach me how
To name the bigger light, and how the less,
That burn by day and night: and then I loved thee
And show'd thee all the qualities o' the isle,
The fresh springs, brine-pits, barren place and fertile:
Cursed be I that did so! All the charms
Of Sycorax, toads, beetles, bats, light on you!
For I am all the subjects that you have,
Which first was mine own king: and here you sty me
In this hard rock, whiles you do keep from me
The rest o' the island.

PROSPERO: Thou most lying slave,
Whom stripes may move, not kindness! I have used thee,
Filth as thou art, with human care, and lodged thee
In mine own cell, till thou didst seek to violate
The honour of my child.

CALIBAN: O ho, O ho! would't had been done!
Thou didst prevent me; I had peopled else
This isle with Calibans.

PROSPERO: Abhorred slave,
Which any print of goodness wilt not take,
Being capable of all ill! I pitied thee,
Took pains to make thee speak, taught thee each hour
One thing or other: when thou didst not, savage,
Know thine own meaning, but wouldst gabble like
A thing most brutish, I endow'd thy purposes
With words that made them known. But thy vile race,
Though thou didst learn, had that in't which good natures
Could not abide to be with; therefore wast thou
Deservedly confined into this rock,
Who hadst deserved more than a prison.

CALIBAN: You taught me language; and my profit on't
Is, I know how to curse. The red plague rid you
For learning me your language!

Sources: *The Essays of Michel Seigneur de Montaigne*, trans. C. Cotton (London: Alex Murray & Son, 1870), pp. 133–134; William Shakespeare, *The Tempest* (New York: The Macmillan Company, 1915), pp. 25–27.

QUESTIONS FOR ANALYSIS

1. What evidence does Montaigne provide for his claim that the Brazilians were closer to nature than Europeans? Why does he judge their society to be in some ways superior to that of Europeans?
2. In Shakespeare's play, what advantages does Prospero believe he has given to Caliban, and how does Caliban react to his claims?
3. What contrasting view of "natural man" emerges from these two passages? What evidence do they provide for Europeans' reaction to the peoples encountered in the New World?

and religious practices. They grouped Africans into the despised categories of pagan heathens or Muslim infidels. As Europeans turned to Africa for new sources of slaves, they drew on beliefs about Africans' primitiveness and barbarity to defend slavery and even argue, like Sepúlveda with regard to indigenous Americans, that enslavement benefited Africans by bringing civilization and Christianity to heathen peoples. In 1444 an observer defended the enslavement of the first Africans by Portuguese explorers as necessary "because they lived like beasts, without any of the customs of rational creatures, since they did not even know what were bread and wine, nor garments of cloth, nor life in the shelter of a house; and worse still was their ignorance, which deprived them of knowledge of good, and permitted them only a life of brutish idleness."[13]

Over time, the institution of slavery fostered a new level of racial inequality. Africans gradually became seen as utterly distinct from and wholly inferior to Europeans. In a transition from rather vague assumptions about Africans' non-Christian religious beliefs and general lack of civilization, Europeans developed increasingly rigid ideas of racial superiority and inferiority to safeguard the growing profits gained from plantation slavery. Black skin became equated with slavery itself as Europeans at home and in the colonies convinced themselves that blacks were destined by God to serve them as slaves in perpetuity.

Support for this belief went back to the Greek philosopher Aristotle's argument that some people are naturally destined for slavery and to biblical associations between darkness and sin. A more explicit justification was found in the story of Noah's curse upon the descendants of his disobedient son Ham to be the "servant[s] of servants." Biblical genealogies listing Ham's sons as those who peopled North Africa and Kush (which includes parts of modern Egypt and Sudan) were interpreted to mean that all inhabitants of those regions bore Noah's curse. From the sixteenth century onward, many defenders of slavery cited this story as justification.

After 1700 the emergence of new methods of observing and describing nature led to the use of science to define race. Although previously the term referred to a nation or an ethnic group, henceforth "race" would be used to describe supposedly biologically distinct groups of people whose physical differences produced differences in culture, character, and intelligence. Biblical justifications for inequality thereby gave way to allegedly scientific ones (see page 740).

CHRONOLOGY

1271–1295	Marco Polo travels to China
1443	Portuguese establish first African trading post at Arguin
1492	Columbus lands on San Salvador
1494	Treaty of Tordesillas ratified
1518	Atlantic slave trade begins
1519–1522	Magellan's expedition circumnavigates the world
1521	Cortés conquers Aztec Empire
1533	Pizarro conquers Inca Empire
1571	Spanish establish port of Manila in the Philippines
1602	Dutch East India Company founded

Chapter Summary

Prior to Columbus's voyages, well-developed trade routes linked the peoples and products of Africa, Asia, and Europe. Overall, Europe played a minor role in the Afroeurasian trade world because it did not produce many products desired by Eastern elites. Nevertheless, Europeans — especially Venetian and Genoese merchants — sought to tap into the goods and wealth of Afroeurasian commerce. As the economy and population recovered from the Black Death, Europeans began to seek more direct and profitable access to the Afroeurasian trade world. Technological developments such as the invention of the caravel and the magnetic compass enabled men like Christopher Columbus and Ferdinand Magellan to undertake ever more ambitious voyages.

In the aftermath of their conquest of the Aztec and Inca Empires, the Spanish established new forms of governance to dominate native peoples and exploit their labor, including the encomienda system. The arrival of Europeans brought enormous population losses to native communities, primarily through the spread of infectious diseases. Disease was one element of the Columbian exchange, a complex transfer of germs, plants, and animals between the Old and New Worlds. Over time, the Columbian exchange brought new crops to both the New and Old Worlds — crops that eventually altered consumption patterns internationally. These exchanges contributed to the creation of the first truly global economy. Tragically, a major component of global trade was the transatlantic slave trade, in which Europeans transported, under horrific conditions, Africans to labor in the sugar plantations and silver mines of the New World. European nations vied for supremacy in global trade, with early Portuguese success in India and Asia being challenged first by the Spanish and then by the Dutch, who took control of trade with the East in the mid-seventeenth century.

Increased contact with the outside world led Europeans to develop new ideas about cultural and racial differences. Debates occurred in Spain and its colonies over the nature of the indigenous peoples of the Americas and how they should be treated. Europeans had long held negative attitudes about Africans; as the slave trade grew, they began to express more rigid notions of racial inequality and to claim that Africans were inherently suited for slavery. Most Europeans, with some important exceptions, shared such views. Religion became another means of cultural contact, as European missionaries aimed to spread Christianity in the New World.

NOTES

1. Marco Polo, *The Book of Ser Marco Polo, the Venetian: Concerning the Kingdoms and Marvels of the East*, vol. 2, trans. and ed. Colonel Sir Henry Yule (London: John Murray, 1903), pp. 185–186.
2. Thomas Benjamin, *The Atlantic World: Europeans, Africans, Indians and Their Shared History, 1400–1900* (Cambridge: Cambridge University Press, 2009), p. 56.
3. A. Reid, *Southeast Asia in the Age of Commerce, 1450–1680*. Vol. 1: *The Land Under the Winds* (New Haven, Conn.: Yale University Press, 1988), pp. 3–20.
4. Quoted in C. M. Cipolla, *Guns, Sails, and Empires: Technological Innovation and the Early Phases of European Expansion, 1400–1700* (New York: Minerva Press, 1965), p. 132.
5. Quoted in F. H. Littell, *The Macmillan Atlas: History of Christianity* (New York: Macmillan, 1976), p. 75.
6. Quoted in J. Devisse, "Africa in Inter-Continental Relations," in *General History of Africa*. Vol. 4: *Africa from the Twelfth to the Sixteenth Century*, ed. D. T. Niane (Berkeley, Calif.: Heinemann Educational Books, 1984), p. 664.
7. Quoted in F. Maddison, "Tradition and Innovation: Columbus' First Voyage and Portuguese Navigation in the Fifteenth Century," in *Circa 1492: Art in the Age of Exploration*, ed. J. A. Levenson (Washington, D.C.: National Gallery of Art, 1991), p. 69.
8. Quoted in R. L. Kagan, "The Spain of Ferdinand and Isabella," in *Circa 1492: Art in the Age of Exploration*, ed. J. A. Levenson (Washington, D.C.: National Gallery of Art, 1991), p. 60.
9. Benjamin, *The Atlantic World*, p. 141.
10. Herbert S. Klein, "Profits and the Causes of Mortality," in *The Atlantic Slave Trade*, ed. David Northrup (Lexington, Mass.: D. C. Heath, 1994), p. 116.
11. David Carrasco, *The Oxford Encyclopedia of Mesoamerican Cultures* (Oxford: Oxford University Press, 2001), p. 208.
12. Quoted in C. Gibson, ed., *The Black Legend: Anti-Spanish Attitudes in the Old World and the New* (New York: Knopf, 1971), pp. 74–75.
13. Quoted in James H. Sweet, "The Iberian Roots of American Racist Thought," *The William and Mary Quarterly*, Third Series, 54 (January 1997): 155.

CONNECTIONS

Just three years separated Martin Luther's attack on the Catholic Church in 1517 and Ferdinand Magellan's discovery of the Pacific Ocean in 1520. Within a few short years western Europeans' religious unity and notions of terrestrial geography were shattered. Old medieval certainties about Heaven and earth collapsed. In the ensuing decades Europeans struggled to come to terms with religious differences among Protestants and Catholics at home and with the multitudes of new peoples and places they encountered abroad. While some Europeans were fascinated and inspired by this new diversity, too often the result was suffering and violence. Europeans endured decades of religious civil war, and indigenous peoples overseas underwent massive population losses as a result of European warfare, disease, and exploitation. Tragically, both Catholic and Protestant religious leaders condoned the trade in slaves that ultimately brought suffering and death to millions of Africans.

Even as the voyages of discovery contributed to the fragmentation of European culture, they also played a role in state centralization and consolidation in the longer term. Henceforth, competition to gain overseas colonies became an integral part of European politics. While Spain's enormous profits from conquest ultimately led to a weakening of its power, over time the Netherlands, England, and France used profits from colonial trade to help build modernized, centralized states.

Two crucial consequences emerged from this era of expansion. The first was the creation of enduring contacts among five of the seven continents of the globe—Europe, Asia, Africa, North America, and South America. From the sixteenth century onward, the peoples of the world were increasingly entwined in divergent forms of economic, social, and cultural exchange. The second was the growth of European power. Europeans controlled the Americas and gradually assumed control over existing trade networks in Asia and Africa. Although China remained the world's most powerful economy until at least 1800, the era of European dominance was born.

Review and Explore

Make It Stick

LearningCurve

Go online and use LearningCurve to retain what you've read.

Identify Key Terms

Identify and explain the significance of each item below.

bride wealth (p. 461)
conquistador (p. 463)
caravel (p. 463)
Ptolemy's *Geography* (p. 464)
Treaty of Tordesillas (p. 469)
Aztec Empire (p. 471)
Inca Empire (p. 473)
viceroyalties (p. 474)
captaincies (p. 474)
encomienda system (p. 475)
Columbian exchange (p. 476)
Valladolid debate (p. 483)
Black Legend (p. 483)

Review the Main Ideas

Answer the focus questions from each section of the chapter.

1. What was the Afroeurasian trade world like prior to the era of European exploration? (p. 458)
2. Why and how did Europeans undertake ambitious voyages of expansion? (p. 462)
3. What was the impact of Iberian conquest and settlement on the peoples and ecologies of the Americas? (p. 471)
4. How was the era of global contact shaped by new commodities, commercial empires, and forced migrations? (p. 476)
5. How did new encounters shape cultural attitudes and beliefs in Europe and the New World? (p. 479)

Make Connections

Analyze the larger developments and continuities within and across chapters.

1. What range of attitudes toward new and unknown peoples did you encounter in this chapter? How do you explain similarities and differences in attitudes toward such peoples?
2. To what extent did the European voyages of expansion and conquest inaugurate an era of global history? Did this era represent the birth of "globalization"? Why or why not?
3. How did European motivations for expansion compare to those of the Roman Empire, the Arab world under Islam, or the Mongols in Central Asia?

LaunchPad
Online Document Project

Interpreting Conquest

How did Spanish and Amerindian artists depict Malintzin?
Examine Spanish and Amerindian representations of Malintzin's role in the conquest, and then complete a quiz and writing assignment based on the evidence and details from this chapter.

See inside the front cover to learn more.

Suggested Reading

Crosby, Alfred W. *The Columbian Exchange: Biological and Cultural Consequences of 1492*, 30th anniversary ed. 2003. An innovative and highly influential account of the environmental impact of Columbus's voyages.

Elliot, J. H. *Empires of the Atlantic World: Britain and Spain in America, 1492–1830*. 2006. A masterful account of the differences and similarities between the British and Spanish Empires in the Americas.

Fernández-Armesto, Felip. *Columbus*. 1992. An excellent biography of Christopher Columbus.

Mann, Charles C. *1491: New Revelations on the Americas Before Columbus*, 2d ed. 2011. A highly readable account of the peoples and societies of the Americas before the arrival of Europeans.

Menard, Russell. *Sweet Negotiations: Sugar, Slavery, and Plantation Agriculture in Early Barbados*. 2006. Explores the intertwined history of sugar plantations and slavery in seventeenth-century Barbados.

Northrup, David, ed. *The Atlantic Slave Trade*. 1994. Collected essays by leading scholars on many different aspects of the slave trade.

Parker, Charles H. *Global Interactions in the Early Modern Age, 1400–1800*. 2010. An examination of the rise of global connections in the early modern period, which situates the European experience in relation to the world's other empires and peoples.

Pérez-Mallaína, Pablo E. *Spain's Men of the Sea: Daily Life on the Indies Fleet in the Sixteenth Century*. 1998. A description of the recruitment, daily life, and career paths of ordinary sailors and officers in the Spanish fleet.

Pomeranz, Kenneth, and Steven Topik. *The World That Trade Created: Society, Culture, and the World Economy, 1400 to the Present*. 1999. Explores the creation of a world market through the rich and vivid stories of merchants, miners, slaves, and farmers.

Restall, Matthew. *Seven Myths of Spanish Conquest*. 2003. A re-examination of common ideas about why and how the Spanish conquered native civilizations in the New World.

Schmidt, Benjamin. *Innocence Abroad: The Dutch Imagination and the New World, 1570–1670*. 2001. Examines changing Dutch attitudes toward the New World, from criticism of the cruelty of the Spanish conquest to eagerness for their own overseas empire.

Index

A Note About the Index: Names of individuals appear in boldface. Letters in parentheses after page numbers refer to the following:

(b) boxed features
(i) illustrations, including photographs and artifacts
(f) figures, including charts and graphs
(m) maps

Timeline A History of World Societies: An Overview

	Africa	The Americas
10,000 B.C.E.	*Homo sapiens* evolve, ca. 250,000 years ago Farming begins in Nile River Valley, ca. 9000 Domestication of cattle; plow agriculture, ca. 7000 Unification of Egypt, 3100–2660	Possible migration into Americas begins, ca. 20,000–30,000 Farming begins, ca. 8000 Maize domesticated in Mexico, ca. 3000
2500 B.C.E.	Egypt's Old Kingdom, 2660–2180 Egypt's Middle Kingdom, 2080–1640 Hyksos migrate into Egypt, 1640–1570	First cities in Peru; earliest mound building in North America, ca. 2500 Textiles become important part of Peruvian culture, ca. 2500 Farmers in southwestern North America grow maize, ca. 2000
1500 B.C.E.	Egypt's New Kingdom, ca. 1550–1070 Ironworking spreads throughout Africa, ca. 1500 B.C.E.–300 C.E. Akhenaten institutes monotheistic worship of Aton, ca. 1360	Olmec civilization in Mexico, ca. 1500–300 Earliest cities in the Andes built by Chavin people, ca. 1200
1000 B.C.E.	Political fragmentation of Egypt; rise of small kingdoms, ca. 1100–653 Bantu migrations across central and southern Africa, ca. 1000 B.C.E.–1500 C.E. Persians conquer Egypt, 525	Olmec center at San Lorenzo destroyed; power passes to La Venta, ca. 900
500 B.C.E.	Ptolemy conquers Egypt, 323	
250 B.C.E.	Scipio Africanus defeats Hannibal at Zama, 202 Meroë becomes iron-smelting center, ca. 100	Hopewell culture flourishes in North America, ca. 200 B.C.E.–600 C.E.

Asia and Oceania	Europe	Middle East
Farming begins in Yellow River Valley, ca. 9000 Domestication of cattle; plow agriculture begins, ca. 7000	Farming spreads to Greece, ca. 6500 Smelting of copper in Balkans, ca. 5500 Farming spreads to Britain, ca. 4000	Farming begins; domestication of goats and sheep in the Fertile Crescent, ca. 9000 Invention of pottery wheel in Mesopotamia, ca. 5000 First writing in Sumeria; city-states emerge, ca. 3500
Harappan civilization, ca. 2800–1800	Minoan culture emerges, ca. 2000 Arrival of Greeks in peninsular Greece; founding of Mycenaean kingdom, ca. 1650	Smelting of iron begins in Mesopotamia, ca. 2500 Akkadian empire, ca. 2331–2200 Hammurabi's law code, ca. 1790
Shang Dynasty; first writing in China, ca. 1500–1050 Vedic Age: Aryans dominate in North India; caste system develops; the *Rigveda*, ca. 1500–500	Mycenaeans conquer Minoan Crete, ca. 1450 Greek Dark Age; evolution of the polis, ca. 1100–800	Hittites expand empire in Mesopotamia, ca. 1600 Moses leads Hebrews out of Egypt, ca. 1300–1200 United Hebrew kingdom, ca. 1020–930
Early Zhou Dynasty, ca. 1050–400 *Upanishads*, foundation of Hinduism, 750–500 Life of Confucius, 551–479 Persians conquer parts of India, 513 Founding of Buddhism and Jainism, ca. 500	Fall of Minoan and Mycenaean cultures, ca. 1000 Rise of Sparta and Athens, 800–500 Roman Republic founded, 509	Assyrian Empire, ca. 800–612 Spread of Zoroastrianism, ca. 600–500 Babylonian captivity of Hebrews, 587–538 Cyrus the Great founds Persian Empire, 550
Warring States period; golden age of Chinese philosophy, 403–221 Brahmanic religion develops into Hinduism, ca. 400 B.C.E.–200 C.E. Zhuangzi and development of Daoism, 369–268 Alexander the Great invades India, 326 Seleucus establishes Seleucid Empire, 323 Mauryan Empire, ca. 322–185 Reign of Ashoka; Buddhism spreads in central Asia, 269–232	Flowering of Greek art and philosophy, 500–400 Persian wars, 499–479 Peloponnesian War, 431–404 Roman expansion, 390–146 Conquests of Alexander the Great, 336–323 Punic Wars; destruction of Carthage, 264–146	Persian Empire falls to Alexander the Great, 330 Alexander the Great dies in Babylon, 323
Qin Dynasty unifies China; construction of Great Wall, 221–206 Han Dynasty, 206 B.C.E.–220 C.E. Han government controls Silk Road across central Asia, 114 Chinese armies conquer Nam Viet, 111 *Bhagavad Gita*, ca. 100 B.C.E.–100 C.E.	Late Roman republic, 133–27 Julius Caesar killed, 44 Octavian seizes power, rules imperial Rome as Augustus, 27 B.C.E.–14 C.E.	

	Africa	The Americas
1 C.E.	Expansion of Bantu-speaking peoples into eastern and southern Africa, ca. 100	Moche civilization flourishes in Peru, ca. 100–800
200 C.E.	Aksum (Ethiopia) controls Red Sea trade, ca. 250	
300	Christianity comes to Ethiopia from Egypt, 328 Aksum accepts Christianity, ca. 350	Hohokam use irrigation to enhance farming in southwestern North America, ca. 300 Classical era in Mesoamerican and North America; Maya and other groups develop large advanced states, 300–900 Peak of Teotihuacan civilization in Mexico, ca. 450
500	Political and commercial ascendancy of Aksum, ca. 500–700 Christian missionaries convert Nubian rulers, ca. 600 Muslim conquest of Egypt; Islam introduced to Africa, 642 Height of African Mediterranean slave trade, ca. 650–1500	Peak of Maya civilization, ca. 600–900
700	Expansion of Islam into Ethiopia weakens state, 700–800 Berbers control trans-Saharan trade, ca. 700–900 Islam spreads across Sahara, 800–900 Kingdom of Ghana, ca. 900–1300	Teotihuacan destroyed, 750 Period of crop failure, disease, and war in Mesoamerica; collapse of Maya civilization, 800–1000 Toltec hegemony, ca. 980–1000
1000	Islam penetrates sub-Saharan Africa, ca. 1000–1100 Great Zimbabwe built, flourishes, ca. 1100–1400	Inca civilization in South America, ca. 1000–1500 Peak of Cahokia culture in North America, ca. 1150 Toltec state collapses, 1174
1200	Kingdom of Mali, ca. 1200–1450 Mongols conquer Baghdad; fall of Abbasid Dynasty, 1258	Cahokia's decline begins after earthquake, ca. 1200

Asia and Oceania	Europe	Middle East
Shakas and Kushans invade eastern Parthia and India, ca. 1–100 Maritime trade between Chinese and Roman ports begins, ca. 100 Roman attacks on Parthian empire, ca. 100–200 Chinese invent paper, 105	Roman Empire at greatest extent, 117	Life of Jesus, ca. 3 B.C.E.–29 C.E.
Buddhism gains popularity in China, Japan, and Korea, ca. 200–600 Age of Division in China, 220–589 Fall of the Parthian empire; rise of the Sassanid, ca. 226	Life of Diocletian: reforms Roman Empire; divides into western and eastern halves, 284–305	Sassanid dynasty in Persia, 226–651
Three Kingdoms Period in Korea, 313–668 China divides into northern and southern regimes, 316 Gupta Empire unites northern India, ca. 320–480 Huns invade India, ca. 450	Life of Constantine: legalizes Christianity; founds Constantinople, 306–337 Christianity official state religion of Roman Empire, 380 Germanic raids on western Europe, 400s Clovis rules Gauls, ca. 481–511	
Sui Dynasty restores order in China, 581–618 Prince Shōtoku introduces Chinese-style government in Japan, 604 Tang Dynasty in China; cultural flowering, 618–907 Korea unified, 668	Reign of Justinian; *Code* and *Digest*, 527–565 *Rule* of Saint Benedict, 529	Life of Muhammad, 570–632 Publication of the Qur'an, 651 Umayyad Dynasty; expansion of Islam, 661–750
Creation of Japan's first capital at Nara, 710 Islam reaches India, 713 Heian era in Japan, 794–1185 Khmer Empire of Cambodia founded, 802 Koryŏ Dynasty in Korea, 935–1392 North Vietnam gains independence from China, 939 Song Dynasty in China; invention of movable type, 960–1279	Muslims defeat Visigothic kingdom in Spain, 711 Christian reconquest of Spain from Muslims, 722–1492 Carolingians defeat Muslims at Poitiers, 732 Viking, Magyar invasions, ca. 800–950 Treaty of Verdun divides Carolingian Empire, 843	Abbasid caliphate; Islamic capital moved to Baghdad, 750–1258 Height of Muslim learning and creativity, ca. 800–1300
Construction of Angkor Wat, ca. 1100–1150 Muslim conquests lead to decline of Buddhism in India, ca. 1100–1200 China divided into Song and Jin empires, 1127 Kamakura Shogunate in Japan, 1185–1333	Latin, Greek churches split, 1054 Norman Conquest of England, 1066 Crusades, 1095–1270 Growth of trade and towns, ca. 1100–1400	Seljuk Turks take Baghdad, 1055
Easter Island's most prosperous period, ca. 1200–1300 Turkish sultanate at Dehli, 1206–1526 Peak of Khmer Empire, 1219 Mongol's Yuan Dynasty in China, 1234–1368 Mongols invade Japan, 1274, 1281 Marco Polo travels in China, ca. 1275–1292 Mongol conquest of Song China, 1276	Magna Carta, 1215 Life of Thomas Aquinas; *Summa Theologica*, 1225–1274 Mongol raids into eastern Europe; Mongols gain control of Kieven Russia, 1237–1241	Mongols conquer Baghdad, 1238 Ottoman Empire, 1299–1922

	Africa	The Americas
1300	Height of Swahili city-states in East Africa, ca. 1300–1500 Mansa Musa rules Mali, ca. 1312–1337 Ibn Battuta's travels, 1325–1354	Construction of Aztec city Tenochtitlan begins, ca. 1325
1400	Songhai Empire, ca. 1464–1591 Arrival of Portuguese in Benin, 1485 Da Gama reaches East Africa; Swahili coast enters period of economic decline, 1498	Height of Inca Empire, 1438–1532 Reign of Montezuma I; height of Aztec culture, 1440–1467 Inca city of Machu Picchu built, 1450 Columbus reaches Americas, 1492
1500	Portugal dominates East Africa, ca. 1500–1600 Era of transatlantic slave trade, ca. 1500–1900 Muslim occupation of Christian Ethiopia, 1531–1543 Height of Kanem-Bornu, 1571–1603	Portuguese reach Brazil, 1500 Atlantic slave trade begins, 1518 Cortés arrives in Mexico, 1519 Aztec Empire falls, 1521 Pizarro conquers Inca Empire, 1533 First English colony in North America founded at Roanoke, 1585
1600	Dutch West India Company founded; starts to bring slave coast of West Africa under its control, 1621 Jesuit missionaries expelled from Ethiopia, 1633 Dutch East India Company settles Cape Town, 1652 Importation of slaves into Cape Colony begins, 1658	British settle Jamestown, 1607 Champlain founds first permanent French settlement at Quebec, 1608 Caribbean islands colonized by French, English, Dutch, 1612–1697 English seize New Amsterdam from Dutch, 1664
1700	Major famine in West Africa, 1738–1756	Silver production quadruples in Mexico and Peru, ca. 1700–1800 Colonial dependence on Spanish goods, ca. 1700–1800
1750	Peak of transatlantic slave trade, 1780–1820 Olaudah Equiano publishes autobiography, 1789 British seize Cape Town, 1795 Napoleon's army invades Egypt, 1798	Seven Years' War, 1756–1763 Quebec Act, 1774 American Revolution, 1775–1783 Comunero revolution in New Granada, 1781 Haitian Revolution, 1791–1804

Asia and Oceania	Europe	Middle East
Ashikaga Shogunate, 1336–1573 Mongols defeated in China, 1368 Ming Dynasty in China, 1368–1644 Timur conquers the Delhi sultanate, 1398	Hundred Years' War, ca. 1337–1453 Black Death arrives in Europe, 1347 Great Schism, 1378–1417	
Maritime trade and piracy connects East Asia and Southeast Asia with Europe, ca. 1400–1800 Zheng He's maritime expeditions to India, Middle East, Africa, 1405–1433 Reign of Sultan Mehmed II, 1451–1481	Development of movable type in Germany, ca. 1450 Italian Renaissance, ca. 1450–1521 Age of Discovery, ca. 1450–1650 Ottomans capture Constantinople; end of Byzantine Empire, 1453 Unification of Spain; Jews expelled, 1492	Ottoman Empire conquers Byzantine Empire under rule of Sultan Mehmet II, 1451–1481
Increased availability of books in China, 1500–1600 Barbur defeats Delhi sultanate; founds Mughal Empire, 1526 Japan unified under Toyotomi Hideyoshi, 1537–1598 First Christian missionaries land in Japan, 1549 Akbar expands Mughal Empire, 1556–1605 Spain founds port city of Manila in the Philippines, 1571	Michelangelo paints Sistine Chapel, 1508–1512 Luther's Ninety-five Theses, 1517 English Reformation begins, 1527 Scientific revolution, ca. 1540–1690 Council of Trent, 1545–1563 Peace of Augsburg ends religious wars in Germany, 1555 Netherlands declares independence from Spain, 1581	Safavid Empire in Persia, 1501–1722 Peak of Ottoman power; cultural flowering under Suleiman, 1520–1566 Battle of Lepanto, 1571 Height of Safavid Empire under Shah Abbas, 1587–1629
Tokogawa Shogunate in Japan, 1603–1867 Japan closes its borders, 1639 Manchus establish Qing Dynasty in China, 1644–1911 Dutch expel Portuguese in East Indies; gain control of spice trade, ca. 1660 French arrive in India, ca. 1670	Thirty Years' War, 1619–1648 Growth of absolutism in Austria and Prussia, 1620–1740 English civil war, 1642–1649 Habsburgs expel Ottomans from Hungary, 1683–1718 Revocation of Edict of Nantes, 1685 Glorious Revolution in England, 1688–1689 The Enlightenment, ca. 1690–1789	Shah Abbas captures much of Armenia from the Ottomans, 1603
Height of Edo urban culture in Japan, ca. 1700 Christian missionary work forbidden in China, 1715 Persian invaders loot Delhi, 1739 French and British fight for control of India, 1740–1763	Growth of book publishing, ca. 1700–1789 War of the Spanish Succession, 1701–1713 Peace of Utrecht, 1713	Afghans seize Isfahan from Persians, 1722
Treaty of Paris gives French colonies in India to Britain, 1763 Cook claims land in Australia for Britain, 1770 East India Act, 1784 First British convict-settlers arrive in Australia, 1788	Watt produces first steam engine, 1769 Industrial Revolution in Great Britain, ca. 1780–1850 French Revolution, 1789–1799 Romantic movement in literature and the arts, ca. 1790s–1890s National Convention declares France a republic, 1792	Ottoman ruler Selim III introduces reforms, 1761–1808

	Africa	The Americas
1800	Muhammad Ali modernizes Egypt, 1805–1848 Slavery abolished in British Empire, 1807	Latin American wars of independence, 1806–1825 Brazil wins independence, 1822 Political instability in most Latin American countries, 1825–1870 U.S.-Mexican War, 1846–1848
1850	Suez Canal opens, 1869 Western and central Sudan unite under Islam, 1880 European "scramble for Africa"; decline of slave trade, 1880–1900 Battle of Omdurman, 1898 South African War, 1899–1902	U.S. Civil War, 1861–1865 Dominion of Canada formed, 1867 Latin American neocolonialism, ca. 1870–1929 Diaz controls Mexico, 1876–1911 Immigration from Europe and Asia to the Americas, 1880–1914 Spanish-American War, 1898
1900	Union of South Africa formed, 1910 Native Land Act in South Africa, 1913 Du Bois organizes first Pan-African congress, 1919	Mexican Revolution, 1910 Panama Canal opens, 1914 Mexico adopts constitution, 1917
1920	Cultural nationalism in Africa, 1920s Gold Coast farmers organize cocoa holdups, 1930–1931	U.S. consumer revolution, 1920s Stock market crash in U.S.; Great Depression begins, 1929 Revolutions in six South American countries, 1930 Flowering of Mexican culture, 1930s New Deal begins in United States, 1933
1940	Decolonization in Africa, 1946–1964 Apartheid system in South Africa, 1948–1991	"Mexican miracle," 1940s–1970s Surprise attack by Japan on Pearl Harbor, 1941 United Nations established, 1945
1950	Egypt declared a republic; Nasser named premier, 1954 French-British Suez invasion, 1956 Morocco, Tunisia, Sudan, and Ghana gain independence, 1956–1957 France offers commonwealth status to its territories; only Guinea chooses independence, 1958 Belgian Congo gains independence; violence follows, 1959	Cuban revolution, 1953–1959 Military rule ends in Venezuela, 1958 Castro takes power in Cuba, 1959

Asia and Oceania	Europe	Middle East
British found Singapore, 1819 Java War, 1825–1830 Opium War, 1839–1842 Treaty of Nanjing; Manchus surrender Hong Kong to British, 1842	Napoleonic Europe, 1804–1814 Congress of Vienna, 1814–1815 European economic penetration of non-Western countries, ca. 1816–1880 Greece wins independence, 1830 Revolutions in France, Austria, and Prussia, 1848	Ottoman Empire launches Tanzimat reforms, 1839
Taiping Rebellion, 1851–1864 Perry opens Japan to trade; Japan begins to industrialize, 1853 Great Mutiny/Revolt in India, 1857 Meiji Restoration in Japan, 1867 Indian National Congress, 1885 French acquire Indochina, 1893 Sino-Japanese War, 1894–1895 U.S. gains Philippines, 1898	Unification of Italy, 1859–1870 Freeing of Russian serfs, 1861 Unification of Germany, 1866–1871 Massive industrialization surge in Russia, 1890–1900	Crimean War, 1853–1856 Ottoman state declares partial bankruptcy; European creditors take over, 1875
Boxer Rebellion in China, 1900 Commonwealth of Australia, 1901 Russo-Japanese War, 1904–1905 Muslim League formed, 1906 Korea becomes province of Japan, 1910 Chinese revolution; fall of Qing Dynasty, 1911 Chinese republic, 1912–1949 Amritsar Massacre in India, 1919	Revolution in Russia, 1905 World War I, 1914–1918 Bolshevik Revolution and civil war in Russia, 1917–1922 Treaty of Versailles, 1919	Young Turks seize power in Ottoman Empire, 1908 Turkish massacre of Armenians, 1915–1917 Sykes-Picot Agreement divides Ottoman Empire, 1916 Balfour Declaration establishes Jewish homeland in Palestine, 1917
Gandhi launches nonviolent campaign against British rule in India, 1920 Jiang Jieshi unites China, 1928 Japan invades China, 1931 Mao Zedong's Long March, 1934 Sino-Japanese War, 1937–1945 Japan conquers Southeast Asia, 1939–1942	Mussolini seizes power in Italy, 1922 Stalin takes power in U.S.S.R., 1927 Great Depression, 1929–1933 Hitler gains power in Germany, 1933 Civil war in Spain, 1936–1939 World War II, 1939–1945	Large numbers of European Jews immigrate to Palestine, 1920s–1930s Turkish republic recognized; Kemal begins to modernize and secularize, 1923 Reza Shah leads Iran, 1925–1941 Iraq gains independence, 1932
Japan announces "Asia for Asians"; signs alliance with Germany and Italy, 1940 United States drops atomic bombs on Hiroshima and Nagasaki, 1945 Chinese civil war; Communists win, 1945–1949 Philippines gain independence, 1946 Independence and separation of India and Pakistan, 1947	Marshall Plan, 1947 NATO formed, 1949 Soviet Union and Communist China sign 30-year alliance, 1949	Arabs and Jews at war in Palestine; Israel created, 1948
Japan begins long period of rapid economic growth, 1950 Korean War, 1950–1953 Vietnamese nationalists defeat French; Vietnam divided, 1954 Mao announces Great Leap Forward in China, 1958	Death of Stalin, 1953 Warsaw Pact, 1955 Revolution in Hungary, 1956 Common Market formed, 1957	Turkey joins NATO, 1953 Suez crisis, 1956

	Africa	The Americas
1960	Mali and Nigeria gain independence, 1960 Biafra declares independence from Nigeria, 1967	U.S. Alliance for Progress promotes development and reform in Latin America, 1961 Cuban missile crisis, 1962 U.S. Civil Rights Act; United States starts Vietnam War, 1964 Military dictatorship in Brazil, 1964–1985 Military takeovers lead to brutal dictatorships in Argentina, 1966, 1976
1970	Growth of Islamic fundamentalism, 1970s to present	U.S. Watergate scandal, 1972 Nixon visits China; reconciliation between U.S. and China, 1972 Military coup in Chile, 1973 Revolution in Nicaragua, 1979
1980	Blacks win long civil war with white settlers in Zimbabwe, 1980 AIDS epidemic, 1980s to present South African government opens talks with African National Congress, 1989	Democratic wave gains momentum throughout Latin America, 1980s Nationalization of Mexico's banking system, 1982 Argentina restores civilian rule, 1983 Brazilians elect first civilian government in twenty years, 1985
1990	Nelson Mandela freed in South Africa, 1990 Rwandan genocide, 1994 Second Congo War, 1998 to present	Canada, Mexico, and United States form free-trade area (NAFTA), 1994 Haiti establishes democratic government, 1994 Socialist "Bolivarian revolution" in Venezuela, 1999
2000	Civil war and genocide in Darfur, 2003 to present Mugabe increases violence against opponents after losing Zimbabwean election, 2008	Terrorist attack on United States, 2001 Economic, social, and political crisis in Argentina, 2002 Formation of the Union of South American Nations, 2008 Raúl Castro succeeds his ailing brother Fidel as president of Cuba, 2008
2010	Populist uprisings and protests break out in Tunisia, Egypt, and elsewhere in North Africa, 2010–2011 South Sudan becomes an independent nation, 2011 Nelson Mandela dies, 2013	Catastrophic earthquake in Haiti, 2010 U.S. withdraws combat troops from Iraq, 2010 U.S. begins troop drawdown in Afghanistan, 2011 Jorge Mario Bergoglio from Argentina elected as Pope Francis, 2013

Asia and Oceania	Europe	Middle East
Sino-Soviet split becomes apparent, 1960 Vietnam War, 1964–1975 Great Proletarian Cultural Revolution launched in China, 1965	Building of Berlin Wall, 1961 Student revolution in France, 1968 Soviet invasion of Czechoslovakia, 1968	OPEC founded, 1960 Arab-Israeli Six-Day War, 1967
Bangladesh breaks away from Pakistan, 1971 Communist victory in Vietnam War, 1975 China pursues modernization, 1976 to present	Helsinki Accord on human rights, 1975 Soviet invasion of Afghanistan, 1979	Revival of Islamic fundamentalism, 1970s to present Arab-Israeli Yom Kippur War, 1973 OPEC oil embargo, 1973 Civil war in Lebanon, 1975–1990 Islamic revolution in Iran, 1979 Camp David Accords, 1979
Japanese foreign investment surge, 1980–1992 Sikh nationalism in India, 1984 to present China crushes democracy movement, 1989	Soviet reform under Gorbachev, 1985–1991 Communism falls in eastern Europe, 1989–1990	Iran-Iraq War, 1980–1988 Palestinians start the intifada, 1987
Collapse of Japanese stock market, 1990–1992 Economic growth and political repression in China, 1990 to present Congress Party in India embraces Western capitalist reforms, 1991 Kyoto Protocol on global warming, 1997 Hong Kong returns to Chinese rule, 1997	Conservative economic policies, 1990s End of Soviet Union, 1991 Civil war in Yugoslavia, 1991–2001 Maastricht Treaty creates single currency, 1992 Creation of European Union, 1993	Persian Gulf War, 1990–1991 Israel and Palestinians sign peace agreement, 1993 Assassination of Israeli prime minster Yitzak Rabin, 1995
China joins World Trade Organization, 2001 India and Pakistan come close to all-out war, 2001 North Korea withdraws from 1970 Nuclear Non-Proliferation Treaty, 2003 Tsunami in Southeast Asia, 2004 Terrorist attack in Mumbai, India, 2008	Resurgence of Russian economy under Putin, 2000–2008 Euro note enters circulation, 2002 Madrid train bombing, 2004 London subway and bus bombing, 2005	Israel begins construction of West Bank barrier, 2003 Wars in Iraq and Afghanistan, 2003 to present Hamas establishes Palestinian Authority government, 2007
Massive earthquake in Japan, 2011 Al-Qaeda leader Osama bin Laden killed in Pakistan, 2011 Typhoon Haiyan kills thousands in the Philippines, 2013	European financial crisis intensifies, 2010 France legalizes same-sex marriage, 2013 Russia annexes Crimea region in Ukraine, 2014	Populist uprisings and protests across the Middle East, 2010–2011 Civil war in Syria begins; refugee crisis intensifies, 2011 Egyptian President Mohamed Morsi ousted following protests, 2013